A Treasury of War British and American Poems of the World War 1914-1919

George Herbert Clarke

Alpha Editions

This Edition Published in 2020

ISBN: 9789354219825

Design and Setting By
Alpha Editions
www.alphaedis.com
Email – info@alphaedis.com

AMERICAN COLLEGE
OF SURGEONS

NINTH YEAR BOOK
1922/23

40 EAST ERIE STREET
CHICAGO

CONTENTS

v

FELLOWSHIP PLEDGE

RECOGNIZING that the American College of Surgeons seeks to develop, exemplify, and enforce the highest traditions of our calling, I hereby pledge myself, as a condition of Fellowship in the College, to live in strict accordance with all its principles, declarations, and regulations. ✻ ✻ In particular, I pledge myself to pursue the practice of surgery with thorough self-restraint and to place the welfare of my patients above all else; to advance constantly in knowledge by the study of surgical literature, the instruction of eminent teachers, interchange of opinion among associates, and attendance on the important societies and clinics; to regard scrupulously the interests of my professional brothers and seek their counsel when in doubt of my own judgment; to render willing help to my colleagues and to give freely my services to the needy. ✻ ✻ Moreover, I pledge myself, so far as I am able, to avoid the sins of selfishness; to shun unwarranted publicity, dishonest money-seeking, and commercialism as disgraceful to our profession; to refuse utterly all secret money trades with consultants and practitioners; to teach the patient his financial duty to the physician and to urge the practitioner to obtain his reward from the patient openly; to make my fees commensurate with the service rendered and with the patient's rights; and to avoid discrediting my associates by taking unwarranted compensation. ✻ ✻ Finally, I pledge myself to co-operate in advancing and extending, by every lawful means within my power, the influence of the American College of Surgeons.

ix

OFFICERS

1913-1916

JOHN M. T. FINNEY, Baltimore
President

JOHN G. BOWMAN, Chicago
Director

WALTER W. CHIPMAN, Montreal
First Vice-President

RUDOLPH MATAS, New Orleans
Second Vice-President

FRANKLIN H. MARTIN, Chicago
Secretary General

ALBERT J. OCHSNER, Chicago
Treasurer

1916-1917

GEORGE W. CRILE, Cleveland
President

JOHN G. BOWMAN, Chicago
Director

RUDOLPH MATAS, New Orleans
First Vice-President

ROBERT G. LeCONTE, Philadelphia
Second Vice-President

FRANKLIN H. MARTIN, Chicago
Secretary General

ALBERT J. OCHSNER, Chicago
Treasurer

1917-1919

WILLIAM J. MAYO, Rochester
President

JOHN G. BOWMAN, Chicago
Director

RUDOLPH MATAS, New Orleans
First Vice-President

CHARLES E. KAHLKE, Chicago
Second Vice-President

FRANKLIN H. MARTIN, Chicago
Secretary General

ALBERT J. OCHSNER, Chicago
Treasurer

1919-1920

GEORGE E. ARMSTRONG, Montreal
President

JOHN G. BOWMAN, Chicago
Director

RUDOLPH MATAS, New Orleans
First Vice-President

HORACE PACKARD, Boston
Second Vice-President

FRANKLIN H. MARTIN, Chicago
Secretary General

ALBERT J. OCHSNER, Chicago
Treasurer

1920-1921

JOHN B. DEAVER, Philadelphia
President

JOHN G. BOWMAN, Chicago
Director

HARVEY G. MUDD, St. Louis
First Vice-President

CHARLES E. SAWYER, Marion
Second Vice-President

FRANKLIN H. MARTIN, Chicago
Secretary General

ALBERT J. OCHSNER, Chicago
Treasurer

BOARD OF REGENTS

xiii

FOUNDERS OF THE COLLEGE

ROBERT ABBE	New York	DOUGAL BISSELL	New York
AMOS W. ABBOTT	Minneapolis	VILRAY P. BLAIR	St. Louis
LOUIS ABRAMSON	Shreveport	JOSEPH A. BLAKE	New York
FRANK C. AINLEY	Los Angeles	JOHN BAPST BLAKE	Boston
ELIOT ALDEN	Los Angeles	R. J. BLANCHARD	Winnipeg
CARROLL W. ALLEN	New Orleans	A. L. BLESH	Oklahoma City
LYMAN ALLEN	Burlington	JOSEPH C. BLOODGOOD	Baltimore
EDGAR ALLIN	Edmonton	RUPERT BLUE	Washington
NATHANIEL ALLISON	St. Louis	*J. A. BODINE	New York
E. WYLLYS ANDREWS	Chicago	ARTHUR H. BOGART	Brooklyn
FRANK T. ANDREWS	Chicago	JOHN BION BOGART	Brooklyn
E. W. ARCHIBALD	Montreal	HERMANN J. BOLDT	New York
GEORGE E. ARMSTRONG	Montreal	WILLIAM CLINE BORDEN	Washington
*ALFRED B. ATHERTON	Fredericton	*LEWIS C. BOSHER	Richmond
CHARLES S. BACON	Chicago	JOHN T. BOTTOMLEY	Boston
WILLIAM S. BAER	Baltimore	R. E. BOUCHER	Vancouver
ALVIN W. BAIRD	Portland	J. WESLEY BOVÉE	Washington
FRANKLIN G. BALCH	Boston	FRANK BOYD	Paducah
RALPH E. BALCH	Kalamazoo	GEOFFREY BOYD	Toronto
L. GRANT BALDWIN	Brooklyn	E. G. BRACKETT	Boston
SAMUEL C. BALDWIN	Salt Lake City	B. J. BRANDSON	Winnipeg
J. M. BALDY	Philadelphia	GEORGE E. BREWER	New York
MAX BALLIN	Detroit	GEORGE W.W. BREWSTER	Boston
EDWARD A. BALLOCH	Washington	WILLIAM B. BRINSMADE	Brooklyn
*JOHN HENRY BARBAT	San Francisco	CLARK D. BROOKS	Detroit
ARCHIBALD H. BARKLEY	Lexington	LEROY BROUN	New York
WALTER L. BARLOW	Westmont	*DANIEL J. BROWN	Springfield
WALTER S. BARNES	Chicago	*JOHN YOUNG BROWN	St. Louis
DAVID BARROW	Lexington	REXWALD BROWN	Santa Barbara
WILLARD BARTLETT	St. Louis	TRUMAN W. BROPHY	Chicago
A. T. BAZIN	Westmont	HERBERT A. BRUCE	Toronto
CARL BECK	Chicago	WILLIAM E. BRUNER	Cleveland
*E. H. BECKMAN	Rochester	C. DEWITT BRYANT	Omaha
*SIMON C. BEEDE	David City	*JOSEPH D. BRYANT	New York
BERTRAM M. BERNHEIM	Baltimore	JOHN J. BUCHANAN	Pittsburgh
FREDERIC A. BESLEY	Chicago	COLEMAN G. BUFORD	Chicago
ARTHUR DEAN BEVAN	Chicago	FRANK E. BUNTS	Cleveland
GEORGE A. BINGHAM	Toronto	H. C. BURGESS	Montreal
J. F. BINNIE	Kansas City	*JAMES BURRY	Chicago
H. S. BIRKETT	Montreal	JAMES C. BURT	Pittsburgh
W. H. BISHOP	New York	HENRY T. BYFORD	Chicago

*Deceased

W. J. FRICK	Kansas City
HOMER GAGE	Worcester
W. E. GALLIE	Toronto
H. P. H. GALLOWAY	Winnipeg
A. E. GARROW	Montreal
OTTO C. GAUB	Pittsburgh
GEORGE GELLHORN	St. Louis
ARPAD G. GERSTER	New York
HERMAN B. GESSNER	New Orleans
CHARLES L. GIBSON	New York
HAROLD GIFFORD	Omaha
THOMAS L. GILMER	Chicago
JOEL E. GOLDTHWAIT	Boston
GEORGE S. GORDON	Vancouver
DAVID W. GRAHAM	Chicago
W. W. GRANT	Denver
WILLIAM P. GRAVES	Boston
J. D. GRIFFITH	Kansas City
LEGRAND GUERRY	Columbia
J. A. GUNN	Winnipeg
*GEORGE W. GUTHRIE	Wilkes-Barre
W. D. HAGGARD	Nashville
FRANCIS R. HAGNER	Washington
RUFUS BARTLETT HALL	Cincinnati
J. HALPENNY	Winnipeg
ALBERT E. HALSTEAD	Chicago
C. A. HAMANN	Cleveland
LUTHER H. HAMILTON	Portland
OLIVER D. HAMLIN	Oakland
GRANVILLE S. HANES	Louisville
*F. B. HARRINGTON	Boston
M. L. HARRIS	Chicago
ARCHIBALD C. HARRISON	Baltimore
WILLIAM M. HARSHA	Chicago
JOHN A. HARTWELL	New York
GEORGE L. HAYS	Pittsburgh
EDWARD B. HECKEL	Pittsburgh
ALFRED J. HELTON	Yakima
GEORGE A. HENDON	Louisville
W. B. HENDRY	Toronto
A. E. HERTZLER	Kansas City
HERBERT W. HEWITT	Detroit
HOWARD HILL	Kansas City
D. A. HINGSTON	Montreal
LOUIS J. HIRSCHMAN	Detroit
B. C. HIRST	Philadelphia
JUNIUS C. HOAG	Chicago
GERRY R. HOLDEN	Jacksonville
WILLIAM B. HOLDEN	Portland
J. SHELTON HORSLEY	Richmond
GEORGE M. HORTON	Seattle
L. W. HOTCHKISS	New York
HENRY W. HOWARD	Los Angeles
WALTER CLARKE HOWE	Boston
JOSHUA C. HUBBARD	Boston
RALEIGH R. HUGGINS	Pittsburgh
JOHN MASON HUNDLEY	Baltimore
T. W. HUNTINGTON	San Francisco
FRANK LEMOYNE HUPP	Wheeling
J. W. HUTCHINSON	Montreal
R. J. HUTCHINSON	Grand Rapids
JAMES A. HUTCHISON	Montreal
J. M. INGERSOLL	Cleveland
CHEVALIER JACKSON	Pittsburgh
JABEZ N. JACKSON	Kansas City
JOHN D. JACKSON	Danville
WILLIAM R. JACKSON	Mobile
JOHN EDWARD JENNINGS	Brooklyn
F. W. JOHNSON	Boston
*JOSEPH TABER JOHNSON	Washington
PEER P. JOHNSON	Beverly
*GEORGE BEN JOHNSTON	Richmond
AUGUST F. JONAS	Omaha
DANIEL FISKE JONES	Boston
WILLIAM WARNER JONES	Toronto
E. S. JUDD	Rochester
CHARLES E. KAHLKE	Chicago
MAURICE KAHN	Leadville
FREDERIC KAMMERER	New York
ALLEN B. KANAVEL	Chicago
JOHN W. KEEFE	Providence
C. B. KEENAN	Montreal
HOWARD A. KELLY	Baltimore
E. L. KEYES, JR.	New York
FREDERICK C. KIDNER	Detroit
FREDERICK A. KIEHLE	Portland
EDMUND E. KING	Toronto
J. H. KING	Cranbrook
DANIEL LAFERTÉ	Detroit
FRANK H. LAHEY	Boston
ADRIAN V. S. LAMBERT	New York
ARTHUR AYER LAW	Minneapolis
ALBERT I. LAWBAUGH	Calumet
ROBERT G. LECONTE	Philadelphia
J. E. LEHMANN	Winnipeg
SOUTHGATE LEIGH	Norfolk
GEORGE A. LELAND	Boston
CHARLES G. LEVISON	San Francisco

Bransford Lewis	St. Louis	L. L. McArthur	Chicago
Dean Lewis	Chicago	J. A. McCollum	Toronto
Ernest S. Lewis	New Orleans	Arthur T. McCormack	Bowling Green
Howard Lilienthal	New York	John C. McCoy	Paterson
*Lawrence W. Littig	Davenport	Edward B. McDaniel	Portland
H. M. Little	Montreal	John R. McDill	Milwaukee
*J. Warren Little	Minneapolis	*Theodore A. McGraw	Detroit
Samuel Lloyd	New York	Stuart McGuire	Richmond
Andrew S. Lobinger	Los Angeles	Robert E. McKechnie	Vancouver
F. A. L. Lockhart	Montreal	J. E. McKenty	Winnipeg
Charles D. Lockwood	Pasadena	Walter McKeown	Toronto
James E. Logan	Kansas City	James F. McKernon	New York
John Wesley Long	Greensboro	Lewis S. McMurtry	Louisville
*Howard W. Longyear	Detroit	F. X. McPhillips	Vancouver
John Prentiss Lord	Omaha	*Floyd Wilcox McRae	Atlanta
Robert W. Lovett	Boston	Frederick Menge	Chicago
William E. Lower	Cleveland	E. W. Meredith	Pittsburgh
Henry B. Luhn	Spokane	William F. Metcalf	Detroit
Fred B. Lund	Boston	Frank H. Mewburn	Calgary
William C. Lusk	New York	Willy Meyer	New York
*Frank J. Lutz	St. Louis	C. Jeff Miller	New Orleans
C. J. Lynch	Yakima	G. Brown Miller	Washington
Frank W. Lynch	Chicago	Harold A. Miller	Pittsburgh
*John S. Mabon	Pittsburgh	Robert T. Miller, Jr.	Pittsburgh
James W. Macfarlane	Pittsburgh	Albert R. Mitchell	Lincoln
Granville MacGowan	Los Angeles	A. S. Monro	Vancouver
*K. A. J. MacKenzie	Portland	E. E. Montgomery	Philadelphia
*Harry G. Mackid	Calgary	E. C. Moore	Los Angeles
Archibald MacLaren	St. Paul	*James E. Moore	Minneapolis
Murray MacLaren	St. John	M. L. Moore	Los Angeles
N. J. Maclean	Winnipeg	Andrew S. Moorhead	Toronto
*Ernest P. Magruder	Washington	John F. Moran	Washington
W. J. O. Malloch	Toronto	William H. Morley	Detroit
Arthur T. Mann	Minneapolis	Robert T. Morris	New York
*Matthew D. Mann	Buffalo	Lewis B. Morton	Los Angeles
Walter P. Manton	Detroit	Harvey G. Mudd	St. Louis
J. G. R. Manwaring	Flint	Edward W. Mulligan	Rochester
*James W. Markoe	New York	*James G. Mumford	Clifton Springs
Frederick W. Marlow	Toronto	Fred T. Murphy	St. Louis
E. Denegre Martin	New Orleans	*John B. Murphy	Chicago
Edward Martin	Philadelphia	Francis W. Murray	New York
*Frank Martin	Baltimore	James M. Neff	Spokane
Franklin H. Martin	Chicago	Thomas R. Neilson	Philadelphia
James Monroe Mason	Birmingham	Henry P. Newman	San Diego
William M. Mastin	Mobile	Edward Hall Nichols	Boston
Rudolph Matas	New Orleans	Herbert S. Nichols	Portland
John W. Maury	Memphis	George Henry Noble	Atlanta
Charles H. Mayo	Rochester	A. J. Ochsner	Chicago
William J. Mayo	Rochester	John Chadwick Oliver	Cincinnati

J. H. OLIVER	Indianapolis	JOHN D. RUSHMORE	Brooklyn
ROBERT B. OSGOOD	Boston	WILLIAM W. RUSSELL	Baltimore
HORACE PACKARD	Boston	C. E. RUTH	Des Moines
CHARLES E. PADDOCK	Chicago	E. S. RYERSON	Toronto
OMAR B. PANCOAST	Baltimore	EDWIN W. RYERSON	Chicago
FREDERICK W. PARHAM	New Orleans	HAROLD P. SALTER	Norfolk
*ROSWELL PARK	Buffalo	BACON SAUNDERS	Fort Worth
WALTER R. PARKER	Detroit	*B. R. SCHENCK	Detroit
ROLLAND PARMETER	Detroit	LOUIS E. SCHMIDT	Chicago
CHARLES H. PECK	New York	WILLIAM E. SCHROEDER	Chicago
J. R. PENNINGTON	Chicago	ARNOLD SCHWYZER	St. Paul
J. F. PERCY	Galesburg	GUSTAV SCHWYZER	Minneapolis
JOHN W. PERKINS	Kansas City	WALLACE A. SCOTT	Toronto
GUY S. PETERKIN	Seattle	CHARLES L. SCUDDER	Boston
REUBEN PETERSON	Ann Arbor	M. G. SEELIG	St. Louis
NORVAL H. PIERCE	Chicago	RALPH H. SEELYE	Springfield
S. C. PLUMMER	Chicago	AURELIUS RIVES SHANDS	Washington
JOHN OSBORN POLAK	Brooklyn	C. W. SHARPLES	Seattle
CHARLES A. PORTER	Boston	NORMAN S. SHENSTONE	Toronto
JOHN L. PORTER	Chicago	HENRY HOWARD SHERK	Pasadena
MILES F. PORTER	Fort Wayne	*HARRY M. SHERMAN	San Francisco
WILLIAM C. POSEY	Philadelphia	J. GARLAND SHERRILL	Louisville
WALTER B. POWER	Redlands	WALTER A. SHERWOOD	Brooklyn
CHARLES A. POWERS	Denver	ARTHUR M. SHIPLEY	Baltimore
A. PRIMROSE	Toronto	HAROLD SIDEBOTHAM	Santa Barbara
S. W. PROWSE	Winnipeg	DAVID SILVER	Pittsburgh
E. P. QUAIN	Bismarck	G. SILVERTHORN	Toronto
*JOSEPH RANSOHOFF	Cincinnati	CHANNING C. SIMMONS	Boston
*J. MORRISON RAY	Louisville	FRANK F. SIMPSON	Pittsburgh
ALFRED RAYMOND	Seattle	R. M. SIMPSON	Winnipeg
CHARLES A. L. REED	Cincinnati	JOHN DEVINNE SINGLEY	Pittsburgh
*RICHARD A. REEVE	Toronto	ROLAND E. SKEEL	Cleveland
L. H. REICHELDERFER	Washington	WILLIAM H. SKENE	Portland
EDWARD REYNOLDS	Boston	*OLIVER COTTON SMITH	Hartford
J. J. RICHARDSON	Washington	REA SMITH	Los Angeles
W. W. RICHARDSON	Los Angeles	RICHARD R. SMITH	Grand Rapids
H. M. RICHTER	Chicago	W. HARVEY SMITH	Winnipeg
BENJAMIN M. RICKETTS	Cincinnati	G. B. SOMERS	San Francisco
HAROLD E. RIDEWOOD	Victoria	ERNEST A. SOMMER	Portland
H. W. RIGGS	Vancouver	RAYMOND SPEAR	Washington
HUNTER ROBB	Cleveland	THOMAS BRAY SPENCE	Brooklyn
FREDERICK W. ROBBINS	Detroit	J. BENTLEY SQUIER	New York
J. A. ROBERTS	Toronto	MYLES STANDISH	Boston
JOHN B. ROBERTS	Philadelphia	CLARENCE L. STARR	Toronto
ERNEST F. ROBINSON	Kansas City	F. N. G. STARR	Toronto
JOHN T. ROGERS	St. Paul	ALBERT L. STAVELY	Washington
JOHN L. ROTHROCK	St. Paul	D. A. K. STEELE	Chicago
HUBERT A. ROYSTER	Raleigh	CHARLES W. STEWART	Newport
JACQUES C. RUSHMORE	Brooklyn	GEORGE D. STEWART	New York

WILLIAM STICKNEY	Rutland
STANLEY STILLMAN	San Francisco
*LEWIS A. STIMSON	New York
CHARLES F. STOKES	Washington
ISAAC S. STONE	Washington
JAMES S STONE	Boston
W. E. STUDDIFORD	New York
MILTON C. STURGIS	Seattle
JOHN E. SUMMERS	Omaha
H. B. SWEETSER	Minneapolis
PARKER SYMS	New York
*DUDLEY TAIT	San Francisco
FREDERICK J. TAUSSIG	St. Louis
HOWARD C. TAYLOR	New York
WALLACE IRVING TERRY	San Francisco
JAMES EDWIN THOMPSON	Galveston
JOHN A. THOMPSON	Cincinnati
JOHN J. THOMPSON	Kansas City
*GEORGE H. TORNEY	Washington
HARRY N. TORREY	Detroit
HUGH HENRY TROUT	Roanoke
PHILEMON E. TRUESDALE	Fall River
WALTER TRUSLOW	Brooklyn
ERNEST F. TUCKER	Portland
HERMAN TUHOLSKE	St. Louis
PAUL Y. TUPPER	St Louis
RAYMOND C. TURCK	Jacksonville
W. G. TURNER	Montreal
EDGAR A. VANDER VEER	Albany
*W. B. VANLENNEP	Philadelphia
C. VAN ZWALUWENBURG	Riverside
GEORGE TULLY VAUGHAN	Washington
EDMOND M. VON EBERTS	Montreal
W. F. B. WAKEFIELD	San Francisco
FRANK B. WALKER	Detroit
GEORGE WALKER	Baltimore
JOHN B. WALKER	New York
*THOMAS DYSON WALKER	St. John
GEORGE G. WARD, JR.	New York
WILBUR WARD	New York
JOHN R. WATHEN	Louisville
THOMAS J. WATKINS	Chicago
STEPHEN H. WATTS	University
J. CLARENCE WEBSTER	Chicago
ALANSON WEEKS	San Francisco
JOHN R. WELLINGTON	Washington
*BROOKS HUGHES WELLS	New York
*X. O. WERDER	Pittsburgh
RICHARD W. WESTBROOK	Brooklyn
HORACE G. WETHERILL	Denver
CHARLES S. WHITE	Washington
WILLIAM H. WILDER	Chicago
ESPY MILO WILLIAMS	Paterson
HADLEY WILLIAMS	London
J. WHITRIDGE WILLIAMS	Baltimore
A. MURAT WILLIS	Richmond
PARK REED WILLIS	Seattle
WILLIAM H. WILMER	Washington
H. AUGUSTUS WILSON	Philadelphia
RANDOLPH WINSLOW	Baltimore
DAVID J. G. WISHART	Toronto
JOHN WISHART	London
O. O. WITHERBEE	Los Angeles
T. CASEY WITHERSPOON	Butte
JOHN MURPHY WITHROW	Cincinnati
FRANK C. WITTER	Petoskey
CASEY A. WOOD	Chicago
JAMES CRAVEN WOOD	Cleveland
GEORGE WOOLSEY	New York
ARTHUR WRIGHT	Toronto
JOHN LAWRENCE YATES	Milwaukee
HUGH HAMPTON YOUNG	Baltimore
E. GUSTAV ZINKE	Cincinnati

GENERAL STATEMENT

ORGANIZATION OF THE COLLEGE

THE American College of Surgeons is a society of surgeons of North and South America which aims to include within its Fellowship all who are of worthy character and who possess a practical knowledge of the science and art of surgery. The College is fundamentally concerned with matters of character and of training, with the betterment of hospitals and of teaching facilities in medical schools and hospitals, with laws which relate to medical practice and privilege, and with an unselfish protection of the public from incompetent medical service.

The College was organized on May 5, 1913, in Washington, D. C., when four hundred and fifty prominent surgeons came together at the invitation of an Organization Committee which had been appointed by the Clinical Congress of Surgeons of North America at its meeting in November, 1912. This Committee consisted of Edward Martin of Philadelphia, Emmet Rixford of San Francisco, John B. Murphy of Chicago, Rudolph Matas of New Orleans, Albert J. Ochsner of Chicago, Charles H. Mayo of Rochester, Frederic J. Cotton of Boston, George Emerson Brewer of New York, John M. T. Finney of Baltimore, Walter W. Chipman of Montreal, George W. Crile of Cleveland, and Franklin H. Martin of Chicago. By-laws, rules, and regulations were adopted, and the Board of Regents, the Board of Governors, and officers of the College were elected. Details of these matters are published in the Year Book and in bulletins of the College.

THE ENDOWMENT FUND

In order to provide funds for the organization of the College, an initial fee of fifty dollars from each Fellow was voted at the

I

first meeting. Realizing that the income to be derived in this manner was temporary and inadequate, and desiring to place the College on a sound financial basis, the Fellows voted in June, 1914, to raise an Endowment Fund of one million dollars. This plan provided that the Endowment should be invested in perpetuity and only the income used for the budget of the College.

It developed later that the educational work of the College called for expenditures beyond the income provided by the interest of the Endowment, and the Fellows of the College, at the annual meeting held in Philadelphia in 1916, voted that those who had not subscribed to the fund should be assessed by annual dues of twenty-five dollars each. The full resolution provided:

1. That the initial Fellowship fee of the College is $100, payable upon notification of election to Fellowship. The initial Fellowship fee of candidates whose applications were filed at the executive offices of the College before November 1, 1914, is $50.

2. That annual dues of the College are provided as follows:

    1. That the annual dues of the Fellows of the College be $25, payable January 1.

    2. That all Fellows who have subscribed $500 to the Endowment Fund of the College be exempt from annual dues.

    3. That the total amount required of any Fellow in annual dues or other fees shall not exceed $500.

    4. That the Board of Regents cancel the indebtedness of any Fellow of the College, without publicity, to whom, in its judgment, such dues are a hardship.

    5. That no Fellow of the College be asked to contribute any fee whatever to the College either after sixty-five years of age or after he has retired from the active practice of surgery.

More than half a million dollars has already been raised for the Endowment, and the Regents desire to bring the fund up to one million dollars as rapidly as possible. A Fellow may become a life member of the College at any time by subscribing five hundred dollars to the permanent Endowment Fund. Subscription cards, similar to the illustrated form, may be obtained from the Director General of the College.

In case of death all unpaid balances are cancelled.

ENDOWMENT FUND

I hereby subscribe Five Hundred Dollars ($500) to the Endowment Fund of the American College of Surgeons, the amount to be paid in installments as follows:

Date	Amount	Date	Amount	Date	Amount
	$		$		$
	$		$		$

I further agree to pay interest on unpaid balances of this pledge at the rate of 5 per cent per annum.

Signed..

Date..

THE CLINICAL CONGRESS OF THE AMERICAN COLLEGE OF SURGEONS

By the joint action of a committee appointed by the Clinical Congress of Surgeons of North America and of the Regents of the College, the Clinical Congress of Surgeons became, on October 25, 1917, the Clinical Congress of the American College of Surgeons. The following resolution effected the merger of these two organizations:

WHEREAS, the past presidents of the Clinical Congress of Surgeons were, on October 26, 1916, in Philadelphia, appointed as a Committee with power to act, to confer with the American College of Surgeons with a view to closer affiliation between these two organizations; and

WHEREAS, the Regents of the College, in accordance with Section VI, Article 3 of the By-Laws of the College, constitute a governing board with power to act with regard to the proposed affiliation. Now, therefore,

BE IT RESOLVED, that it is the unanimous decision of the Committee of the Clinical Congress of Surgeons of North America, as above stated, and of the Regents of the American College of Surgeons in joint session, first, that for the welfare of the two organizations the management and the control of the Clinical Congress of Surgeons shall be vested hereafter in the American College of Surgeons; second, that hereafter the Clinical Congress of Surgeons shall be known as the Clinical Congress of the American College of Surgeons with its invited guests.

The past presidents of the Clinical Congress of Surgeons are Dr. Albert J. Ochsner of Chicago, Dr. Edward Martin of Philadelphia, Dr. George E. Brewer of New York, Dr. John B. Murphy of Chicago, Dr. Charles H. Mayo of Rochester, Dr. Fred B. Lund of Boston, Dr. John G. Clark of Philadelphia, and Dr. William J. Mayo of Rochester.

REQUIREMENTS FOR FELLOWSHIP

Immediately after the organization of the College the Board of Regents authorized the appointing of Committees on Credentials. These Committees consist of the Central Committee which reports its recommendations for Fellowship directly to the Regents, and of State and Provincial Committees which report to the Central Committee.

In a separate bulletin the requirements for admission are published in detail. Briefly stated, these requirements are as follows:

1. The candidate shall be a graduate in medicine, licensed to practice medicine in his respective state or province, or accepted as a medical officer in the service of his country.

2. To be eligible for Fellowship without technical examination the candidate shall be a graduate of a medical school approved by the American College of Surgeons. If the candidate's school of graduation is not accredited by the American College of Surgeons, he may be required to pass a technical examination in one subject or all subjects of the medical curriculum.

3. The candidate shall give evidence that he has served at least one year as interne in a creditable hospital and two years as surgical assistant, or he shall give evidence of apprenticeship of equivalent value. Five to eight years after graduation in medicine, devoted to special training and to practice, are normally the time-requirement for eligibility to Fellowship. Due importance is attached to laboratory and research work.

4. The moral and ethical fitness of the candidate shall be determined by reports of surgeons whose names are submitted by the candidate himself, and by such other reports and data as the Credentials Committee and the administration of the College may obtain.

5. The professional activity of the candidate shall be restricted to the study, diagnosis, and operative work in general surgery or in special fields of surgery, such as eye, ear, nose, and throat, genito-urinary, orthopedics, and gynecology and obstetrics, as follows: First, if the candidate resides in a city of less than fifty thousand inhabitants, at least fifty per cent of his professional activity shall be restricted to practice of general surgery or to practice within special fields of surgery as stated. Second, in cities of over fifty thousand inhabitants, at least eighty per cent of the professional activity of the candidate shall be restricted to practice of general surgery or to practice within special fields of surgery. In other words, the College desires to admit to its Fellowship only those who are primarily specialists in surgery, and the minimum proportion of specialization which is acceptable may vary according to the size of the city in which the candidate resides.

6. The candidate shall make formal application for Fellowship. Blank forms for this purpose may be had from the Director General of the College upon request.

7. In making application for Fellowship the candidate shall sign a declaration which reads as follows:

"Upon my honor as a gentleman, I hereby declare that I will not practice the division of fees, either directly or indirectly, in any manner whatsoever."

In the meaning of this declaration the signer agrees that in order to obviate any semblance of division of fees, he will as a general principle of practice not collect fees for others referring patients to him; nor permit other doctors to collect fees for him; nor make joint fees with physicians or surgeons referring patients to him for operation or consultation.

8. As evidence of his qualifications in the technique of surgery, the candidate is requested to submit in complete detail the case records of fifty consecutive major operations which he has performed himself.

9. In addition to the complete case records of fifty consecutive major operations, the candidate is asked to submit in brief abstract a report of at least fifty other major operations in which he has acted as assistant or which he has performed himself.

10. Surgeons widely recognized by the profession as progressive leaders and exponents of finished technique may, by a unanimous vote of the Board of Regents, be admitted to Fellowship on recommendation of the Committee on Examinations.

11. The Regents of the College reserve the right to alter, as they may think proper, the regulations respecting admission of Fellows to the College.

PROCEDURE OF THE AMERICAN COLLEGE OF SURGEONS IN CONSIDERING CANDIDATES FOR FELLOWSHIP

The American College of Surgeons pursues a definite routine program in receiving and considering applications for Fellowship in the College. Before a final decision is reached an applicant's papers must necessarily pass through several stages. In outline, these are as follows:

1. Any legalized practitioner in medicine in North and South America may apply for Fellowship, and an application blank will be forwarded by the College upon receipt of a request.

2. The formal application which is required of all candidates for Fellowship supplies the following information: Date and place of birth; preliminary education; medical schools attended as an under-graduate and as a graduate; hospitals in which interneship or residentship was served; period of assistantship and with whom; present hospital connections; medical teaching positions; specialty and period of specialization; percentage of professional activity devoted to surgery or one of the surgical specialties; research conducted; medical society affiliations; and a list of personal contributions to medical literature. The candidate is also required to furnish five references, and to sign a pledge against the practice of the division of fees.

3. Upon receipt of the formal application, the College endeavors to verify the statements recorded therein. Each individual given as a reference is communicated with and is asked to fill out a comprehensive questionnaire that will furnish definite statements about the candidate's surgical judgment and ability, and confidential information about his moral and ethical standing. A questionnaire is also sent to Fellows of the College who live in the vicinity of the candidate.

4. When the data received from this preliminary survey are complete the candidate's application is then presented to the Credentials Committee of his state or province for recommendation. The state or provincial Committee, acting as a preliminary court, makes its recommendation upon the evidence as presented together with such facts concerning the candidate as may be in the possession of the individual members of the Committee because of personal acquaintance.

5. In favorably considering a candidate for Fellowship, the State Committee on Credentials suggests the following procedure: a. If the candidate is under forty years of age he be required to submit case histories; b. If the candidate is over forty-five years of age, he be admitted without having to submit the case histories; c. If the candidate is between forty and forty-five years of age, he be or be not required to submit the case histories, as may be determined by the Central Committee on Credentials. Candidates

required to submit case histories are notified of the requirements for Fellowship on that basis.

6. According to a resolution adopted by the Board of Regents on October 28, 1921, all applicants for Fellowship in the American College of Surgeons whose applications shall bear a date later than January 1, 1923, will be required to furnish the Committee on Examinations fifty complete case-records of major surgical operations. Applicants over forty years of age may have the histories of these operations prepared by assistants.

7. When case-records are received from a candidate they are referred to the Committee on History Reviews. This Committee is comprised of a group of competent surgeons who volunteer to serve in the capacity of examiners, and who spend many hours in the execution of their task. After each set of records has been carefully reviewed by the Committee, a summary of the findings with the recommendation signed by the examiner is attached to the records for the guidance of the Central Committee on Credentials.

8. All accumulated evidence that has come into the executive offices is finally brought before the Central Committee on Credentials. This Committee, as the higher court, peruses in detail the records of each candidate, sifts all the evidence on file in regard to his qualifications, and makes its recommendation.

9. One of three recommendations is made by the Central Committee: Acceptance, rejection, or postponement. An application may be postponed to enable the executive offices to secure further evidence of the candidate's fitness or unfitness for Fellowship; to afford the candidate an opportunity to correct or elaborate his records, which may have been lacking in some particulars; or to give the candidate an opportunity to prove that he is doing a sufficient amount of surgery to entitle him to Fellowship.

10. The central office endeavors to give every candidate for Fellowship such information as will aid him in completing his records. If his case-records are lacking in any essential which in the judgment of the Committee can be corrected, he is notified

of the fact and an opportunity is given him to supply the omissions. Throughout its dealings with the candidate the central office endeavors to simplify the routine as much as possible, and to aid each applicant for membership in his task of furnishing satisfactory evidence of his qualifications.

11. Occasionally complaints are filed in the central office against what is considered unnecessary "red tape" in determining a candidate's qualifications for Fellowship. It is absolutely necessary that the uniform regulations formulated for the admission of candidates by the executive offices after several years of experience should be disinterestedly observed. Even though the candidate may appear most worthy to the officials of the College, short-cut methods cannot be employed without subjecting the Committee to severe criticism and lessening the judicial standing of the College.

12. The central office for obvious reasons must decline to furnish information about a candidate's application to other than the candidate himself.

13. Any candidate who is rejected, or whose candidature is delayed, may make a direct appeal to the Board of Regents for information.

14. The State and Provincial Committees on Credentials of the College are elected by the Fellows in the respective states and provinces, one-half of the membership being retired at each yearly election. The Central Committee on Credentials is appointed by the Board of Regents, and is changed from year to year.

PAN-AMERICAN PROGRESS

In the Spring of 1920, Dr. W. J. Mayo, ex-President, and the Director General of the College visited Panama, Peru, Chile, Argentina, and Uruguay in behalf of the American College of Surgeons. The 1921 Year Book of the College contains an outline of the affiliation between the surgeons of South and North America which resulted from this trip.

The Director General again journeyed to South America in the Spring of 1921, on this occasion accompanied by Dr. Thomas J. Watkins of Chicago, a Governor of the College. In addition to the countries which were visited the previous year the itinerary included the United States of Brazil, and was supplemented by a visit to the Republics of Ecuador and Bolivia by Dr. Francis P. Corrigan of Cleveland, Ohio, as official representative of the College.

The medical profession of South America was found to be both ready and willing to affiliate with the American College of Surgeons, and the representatives of the College received a most cordial reception at the hands of their southern confreres. Thirty-five South American surgeons were admitted to Fellowship at the 1920 Convocation in Montreal; at the 1921 Convocation held in Philadelphia, Fellowships were conferred upon fifty-four candidates, five of these being from Argentina, three from Bolivia, twenty-three from Brazil, ten from Chile, four from Ecuador, one from Peru, and eight from Uruguay.

A number of leading South American surgeons were recommended by the Board of Regents for Honorary Fellowship of the College, and four of them received this degree at the Philadelphia Convocation. Because of the ruling established by the Board of Regents that Honorary Fellowships shall not be conferred *in absentia*, several distinguished South American surgeons who were selected for this honor will receive the honorary degree at a future Convocation.

Committees on Credentials have been appointed in each of the seven countries in which there are Fellows of the College, and a number of applications for Fellowship from surgeons in these countries are now on file and under consideration for future membership.

It is contemplated that the Latin American countries with which we do not have an affiliation at the present time shall be visited at as early a date as possible in order that the College may be truly Pan-American in its scope.

In our work of extending Fellowship to South American surgeons we have had the most hearty cooperation of the South

SOUTH AND EAST EXPOSURE

LOWER ENTRANCE HALL

THE NEW HOME OF THE COLLEGE

American diplomatic representatives in Washington, of the Pan-American Union, and of our own Department of State. Four surgeons were sent to the Philadelphia Convocation as official representatives of their respective countries.

THE NEW HOME OF THE COLLEGE

On May 1, 1920, the administrative offices of the American College of Surgeons were transferred to the permanent location at 40 East Erie Street, Chicago.

The new home of the College, which is a commodious and handsome structure with adjoining land suitable for future extension, was purchased and presented to the College by public-spirited lay citizens of Chicago and a group of Fellows of the College residing in that city. The home, besides furnishing an adequate business office for the College, will provide a dignified and suitable meeting place for local and visiting surgeons. This property, coming to the College as an absolute gift, becomes a valuable asset, and its central location in the heart of Chicago makes it an ideal permanent home for the institution.

The adjoining pages contain a reproduction of the bronze tablet which adorns the building and which records the names of those who contributed to its purchase, and also two cuts which very imperfectly illustrate the building with its surroundings. This property is within a few blocks of the center of the business loop of Chicago, and in a location that is not only ideal for the home of our institution but one in which the land value will rapidly increase.

The Fellows of the American College of Surgeons are invited to inspect the new home and to make it their headquarters when visiting Chicago.

THE COLLEGE LIBRARY

In accordance with the action of the Board of Regents last June, the assembling of a large reference library is one of the very vital tasks before the Fellows of the College at the present time.

A library built up by the Fellows of the College, for the Fellows of the College and the future members of the surgical profession of America, is bound to become a most complete and valuable collection of surgical literature. It cannot fail to grow rapidly. Such a library, to be representative of the best in American surgery, must contain the works of each and every member of the College. The Board has asked that each Fellow contribute autographed copies of books and reprints of articles written by him. In addition, it has requested him to send in a list of the books and journals, bound and unbound, which he is willing to donate or loan to the College from his private collection. The Board has also laid stress upon the collection of old works of historical interest.

Every effort is being made to obtain the cooperation of the medical publishers, other medical libraries, and the general medical profession throughout the country. Eighty medical journals and year books have already placed the College Library upon their complimentary mailing lists. Soon special funds and endowments will be forthcoming, it is hoped, for the purchase of various groups of books and for the completion of the journal files.

Already the requests have brought a sufficiently hearty response to overflow the available shelf space and to make the College feel the need of the new building, a portion of which will be especially devoted to a research library, with seminar rooms for intensive study, reading rooms, and suitable stack space.

Let the College set as its goal for the coming year the accumulation of a working reference library, which will be of immediate service to each Fellow.

THE DEPARTMENT OF LITERARY RESEARCH

The Department of Literary Research will bring such a library within the reach of all the Fellows. Every effort will be made to meet the needs both of the surgeon in the large centers who is too busy to spend hours in a library and has no editorial department in his clinic, and of the pioneer surgeon in the outlying districts. For the latter, there will be special files of clippings, abstracts, and unbound journals, which may be loaned upon request. No pains will be spared in getting to him quickly the data needed on a difficult case or for the preparation of a paper. The Department will do for the Fellows, wherever they may be located, what the editorial or publication department of a large clinic does for the staff of that clinic. It will assist Fellows in the preparation and publication of their scientific books, papers, or lectures. It will prepare special bibliographies, collect material, and make abstracts and translations on any given surgical subject. There will be trained persons on the staff for the various types of editorial work, and with the growth of the Department there will be specialized workers who can be sent out to assist in the preparation of surgical monographs. Later this Department, like the publication department of a clinic, will assist commissions composed of Fellows in the making of surveys, analyses, and statistical studies, based on various branches of the work of the Fellows. With the establishment of the Library in the near future, it is hoped that the Department will be able, through an endowment, to render a reasonable amount of service to each Fellow as a part of his yearly membership privileges. The need for such service is obvious. Only the largest clinics have editorial staffs. The high cost of literary assistance given by individuals in libraries or by any of the existing bureaus makes it absolutely prohibitive to the average surgeon.

The Department in the meantime is giving these various types of literary assistance to Fellows at a minimum cost, sufficient only to cover the actual expense of the individual piece of work. That the Fellows are glad to have such work done under the supervision of the College is evidenced by the number and variety of requests which have already been received. During the development of the College Library, the Department has the use of the already existing medical libraries in Chicago. The Department is making every effort to give the greatest service to the greatest number and eventually, through an endowment, to bring the service within the reach of all.

THE GREAT MACE PRESENTED TO THE AMERICAN COLLEGE OF SURGEONS BY THE CONSULTING SURGEONS OF THE BRITISH ARMIES

This Mace has been designed so as to tell in a symbolic way of the close union between British and American surgery, and of the ties which unite Great Britain to Canada and to the United States of America. It retains the traditional shape and proportions of the Civic Mace of the seventeenth century, and is of hand-wrought chiselled and repoussé silver gilt. It was made by Omar Ramsden, who embodied in his design some suggestions of the donors.

THE DEDICATORY INSCRIPTION engraved on the plate under the Crown sets forth that the Mace is a gift "From the Consulting Surgeons of the British Armies to the American College of Surgeons, in memory of mutual work and good-fellowship in the Great War, 1914-1918."

THE CROWN SHAPED FINIAL is formed of six rich scroll buttresses upholding the "Sacred Flame of Science" issuing from a mortar of antique pattern, the model of which was recently found on the field of battle near Salonika. These buttresses spring from a cresting composed of alternating Maple leaves and American Eagles interwined with the Serpents of Esculapius, while the position usually occupied by a band of jewels in a monarchical crown is filled with the words "The American College of Surgeons."

THE BODY OR HEAD is divided into six panels by the Winged Caduceus, being an ornamental rendering of the badge of the United States Army Medical Corps. The panels set forth the following "Achievements at Arms" in delicate and finely detailed repoussé work:

1. The full Blazon of the United States of America.
2. The Dominion of Canada.
3. The Royal College of Surgeons of England.
4. The Badge of the Royal Army Medical Corps.
5. The Shields of Arms of John Hunter and Lord Lister.
6. A Cartouche bearing the words "Philip Syng Physick 1768-1837, Father of American Surgery."

THE GREAT MACE

The lower portion of the Head is decorated with a symbolic band of water indicating the ocean which both unites and separates America and the Mother Country. The latter is symbolized by the British Lion Brackets of highly chiselled work which support the head and terminate the upper part of the staff. The talons of the lion's feet grip the hammered decoration of the upper knop, which consists of a design of American and Canadian Maple seed-pods and heart-shaped spaces. This hammered work is protected by boldly projecting, solid, jewel-like bosses of chiselled work.

THE STAFF is decorated with a free design of the national floral emblems of the United Kingdom — the Rose, the Thistle, the Shamrock, and the Leek. Intertwined among these are a number of ribbon scrolls, each one of which bears the name of one of the donors.

THE FOOT bears, as decoration, the root form from which the above spring and a series of six small shields which may be used for possible future arms of inscriptions. The extreme bottom knop is fluted with leaves of *Isatlis tinctoria*.

The various parts are held together, in the traditional manner, by a rod of British Oak cut from a tree grown at Wytham, Berks. The extreme length is 3 feet 11⅛ inches, and the weight of silver is 140 ounces troy.

CONSULTING SURGEONS OF THE BRITISH ARMIES WHO GAVE THE GREAT MACE TO THE AMERICAN COLLEGE OF SURGEONS.

Sir Charles A. Ballance, K.C.M.G., C.B., M.V.O.
Sir Hamilton Ballance, K.B.E., O.B.
Sir Gilbert Barling, Bart., C.B.
Seymour Barling, C.M.G.
Sir Anthony Bowlby, K.C.B., K.C.M.G., K.C.V.O., D.S.M. (U. S. A.)
Dr. Herbert A. Bruce
Frederic Burghard, C.B.
H. Burrows, C.B.E.
A. Carless, C.B.E.

Sir A. Chance, C.B.E.
Charles C. Choyce, C.M.G., C.B.E.
Sir Kennedy Dalziel
R. Davies-Colley, C.M.G.
T. P. Dunhill, C.M.G.
J. M. Elder, C.M.G.
Sir Crisp English, K.C.M.G.
H. A. Fairbank, D.S.O.
C. H. S. Frankau, C.B.E., D.S.O.
Forbes Fraser, C.B.E.
Sir Peter Freyer, K.C.B.
A. Fullerton, C.B., C.M.G.
George Gask, C.M.G., D.S.O.
Sir Henry Gray, K.B.E., C.B.
Sir Robert Jones, K.B.E., C.B., D.S.M. (U.S.A.)
R. E. Kelly, C.B.
Sir Arbuthnot Lane, Bart., C.B.
Sir William Lister, K.C.M.G.
V. Warren Low, C.B.
Sir George Makins, G.C.M.G., C.B.
Sir Arthur Mayo-Robson, K.B.E., C.B., C.V.O.
A. B. Mitchell, O.B.E.
Sir Berkeley Moynihan, K.C.M.G., C.B.
Sir Thomas Myles, C.B.
T. H. Openshaw, C.B., C.M.G.
Colonel A. Pilcher, C.B., D.S.O.
Owen Richards, C.M.G., D.S.O.
Sir Hugh Rigby, K.C.V.O.
Percy Sargent, C.B., D.S.O.
James Sherren, C.B.E.
Thomas Sinclair, C.B.
Maynard Smith, C.B.
Sir Harold Stiles, K.B.E.
James Swain, C.B., C.B.E.
Sir Charters Symonds, K.B.E., C.B.
Sir William Taylor, K.B.E.
Sir John Lynn-Thomas, K.B.E., C.B.

Alexis Thomson, C.M.G.

Sir William Thorburn, K.B.E., C.B.

A. H. Tubby, C.B., C.M.G.

H. Wade, C.M.G., D.S.O.

Sir Cuthbert Wallace, K.C.M.G., C.B.

Sir Charles Gordon Watson, K.B.E., C.M.G.

A. Webb-Johnson, C.B.E., D.S.O.

Sir W. de C. Wheeler

RARE GIFT PRESENTED TO THE AMERICAN COLLEGE OF SURGEONS BY THE ROYAL COLLEGE OF SURGEONS IN IRELAND

A gift of priceless paleontological value was made to the American College of Surgeons by Sir William Taylor, K.B.E., F.R.C.S., and by Sir Robert Hy Woods, M.Ch. (Hon.), Past President R.C.S.I., both of Dublin, in the name of the Royal College of Surgeons in Ireland. It consisted of the antlers of the extinct Megaceros Hibernicus, popularly known as the Irish Elk, which was found in a bed of marl underlying the peat bog of Bally Batagh.

Below is a copy of the inscribed plate which accompanied the gift.

HEAD OF EXTINCT IRISH DEER
(MEGACEROS HIBERNICUS)

PRESENTED TO THE

AMERICAN COLLEGE OF SURGEONS

BY THE

ROYAL COLLEGE OF SURGEONS IN IRELAND

OCTOBER, 1921

Although there are other specimens in existence, this particular specimen is unusual, both by virtue of its perfect condition and of its great size.   It weighs more than 70 pounds and has a spread of over 5 feet.

It was found in 1876, by Mr. W. Williams, a naturalist and geologist, and formed the subject of an article by him in the Geological Magazine, August, 1881.

This gift will make a unique and valuable addition to the present collection of heads and antlers already in the College home.

CONVOCATIONS

The first Convocation of the College was held in Chicago on November 12, 1913.   The Fellowship address was delivered by Sir Rickman Godlee, Bart., K.C.V.O., LL.D., F.R.C.S., President of the Royal College of Surgeons of England.   Fellowships were conferred upon 1,059 candidates.   At this time Sir Rickman presented to the College the following greetings from the Royal College of Surgeons:

"We, the Council of the Royal College of Surgeons of England, have heard with much interest of the approaching inauguration of the American College of Surgeons.   We hereby convey to it our hearty good wishes, and express the hope that it may have a successful career and fill a position beneficial alike to the Profession and to the Community.

"We cannot forget the important advances in the Science and Art of Surgery achieved by many distinguished Surgeons in the Continent of America during the past, and are proud to have enrolled upon our list of Honorary Fellows the names of some of the most active workers in these fields at the present day.

"In accepting the invitation for our President to take part in the opening Ceremony, we desire to show how we appreciate the intention of the American College to strengthen the bonds that already unite the Medical Profession amongst English-speaking peoples.   It is a sentiment which always meets with a cordial response in this country, and it is one which this College will endeavor to support by all the means in its power.

"In witness whereof we have caused the Common Seal of the College to be hereunto affixed this 9th day of October, 1913.

President RICKMAN J. GODLEE

Vice-Presidents {G. H. MAKINS
FREDERIC EVE."

The second Convocation was held in Philadelphia on June 22, 1914. Fellowships were conferred upon 1,065 candidates. The Fellowship address was delivered by Dr. James G. Mumford of Clifton Springs, New York.

The third Convocation was held in Washington, D. C., on the evening of November 16, 1914. Fellowships were conferred upon 646 candidates. The Fellowship address was delivered by Dr. Edward H. Bradford, Dean of Harvard Medical School.

The fourth Convocation was held in Boston on October 29, 1915. Fellowships were conferred upon 484 candidates. The Fellowship address was delivered by President E. J. James of the University of Illinois.

The fifth Convocation was held in Philadelphia on October 27, 1916. The Fellowship address was delivered by President John H. Findley of the University of the State of New York, and Fellowships were conferred upon 228 candidates.

The sixth Convocation was held in Chicago on October 26, 1917. Fellowships were conferred upon 313 candidates, 37 of these being in the regular service of the United States Army and 25 in the regular service of the United States Navy. The occasion was a great military gathering, hundreds of medical officers being present on leave. The Fellowship address, entitled "What is the War About," was delivered by Sir Berkeley Moynihan, K.C.M.G., F.R.C.S., Colonel in the Royal Army Medical Corps.

The seventh Convocation of the College was scheduled to be held in New York on the evening of October 25, 1918. On October 12, because of the prevalence of influenza throughout Canada and the United States, the Regents considered it imperative to cancel the meeting.

In the meantime the surgeons from England, France, and Italy who had accepted the invitation of the College to take part in the Clinical Congress program had sailed for New York. These surgeons were Sir Thomas Myles, C.B., F.R.C.S., Dublin, Ireland, Honorary Surgeon to His Majesty King George, Consulting Surgeon, Irish Command, Member Board of Consultants, British War Office, and Senior Surgeon, Richmond Hospital, Dublin; Lieutenant Colonel Raffaele Bastianelli, F.R.C.S., Italian Army Medical Corps, Rome, Italy, Associate Professor of Clinical Surgery, Royal University, and Surgeon-in-Chief, First Pavillion, Hospital Policlinico Umberto I; Major Pierre Duval, French Army Medical Corps, Paris, France, Consulting Surgeon to Seventh Army, Honorary Professor, Faculty of Medicine, Paris, and Surgeon to hospitals of Paris; Colonel George Ernest Gask, C.M.G., D.S.O., F.R.C.S., London, England, Consulting Surgeon, British Expeditionary Forces, Joint Lecturer on Surgery, St. Bartholomew's Hospital, University of London, and Surgeon in Charge of Out-Patients, St. Bartholomew's Hospital; Major George Grey Turner, F.R.C.S., Royal Army Medical Corps, Newcastle-on-Tyne, England, Lecturer on Surgery, University of Durham, and Honorary Assistant Surgeon, Royal Infirmary, Newcastle-on-Tyne; and Major Adrien L. P. Piollet and Major Henri Béclerc, both of the French Army Medical Corps. Lieutenant Colonel George E. Brewer of New York, at the time in service in France, came with these guests as the official representative of the Medical Corps with the American Expeditionary Forces.

In order that the value of the messages which these surgeons brought from the allied lines at the front might not be lost as a result of the cancelled meeting, the College arranged visits to as many of the surgical centers in this country as possible. These visits included Washington, where the foreign guests were greeted by President Woodrow Wilson; Camp Greenleaf, Georgia, where approximately 1,500 doctors were in training; Minneapolis, Rochester, Chicago, Pittsburgh, Philadelphia, and New York.

The seventh Convocation was held in New York on October 24, 1919, when 325 candidates from the preceding year were formally admitted to Fellowship together with 213 new candidates. The Fellowship address was delivered by Sir Anthony Bowlby,

K.C.B., K.C.M.G., K.C.V.O., F.R.C.S., of London, Senior Vice-President of the Royal College of Surgeons of England.

The eighth Convocation was held in Montreal on October 15, 1920, this being the first Convocation to be held in the Dominion of Canada. Fellowships were conferred upon 691 candidates, 497 of these being from the United States, 156 from Canada, 35 from South America, and 3 from China. The Fellowship address was delivered by Sir William Taylor, of Dublin, Ireland.

At the Presidential Meeting of the Clinical Congress, held on the evening of October 11, 1920, the first John B. Murphy Oration on Surgery was delivered by Sir Berkeley Moynihan, K.C.M.G., C.B., of Leeds, England. At the same meeting the Great Mace described on page 14, was presented to the American College of Surgeons by the Consulting Surgeons of the British Armies in the World War.

The ninth Convocation of the College was held in Philadelphia on October 28, 1921. Fellowships were conferred upon 724 candidates, 646 of these being from the United States and possessions, 18 from Canada, 54 from South America, 3 from China, 1 from Korea, 1 from Syria, and 1 from Bahrein Islands.

The Fellowship address was delivered by Sir Harold J. Stiles, K.B.E., Edinburgh, Scotland. Honorary Fellowships were conferred upon Sir Harold J. Stiles, K.B.E., Edinburgh; Sir Robert Hy Woods, M.Ch. (Hon.), Past President, R.C.S.I., Dublin; Professor Hans Christian Jacobaeus, M.D., Stockholm; Professor Jean Frederic de Quervain, M.D., Berne; Jan Schoemaker, M.D., The Hague; Miguel H. Alcivar, M.D., Guayaquil, Ecuador; Guillermo Gastañeta, M.D., Lima, Peru; Joaô Alves de Lima, M.D., Sao Paulo, Brazil; José de Mendonca, M.D., Rio de Janeiro, Brazil; and Surgeon General Edward Rhodes Stitt, United States Navy, Washington, D. C.

An interesting feature of the Convocation was the ceremony incident to the conferring of Honorary Fellowships in the Royal College of Surgeons in Ireland upon eight distinguished American surgeons, the details of which are recorded on pages 22 to 28.

The second Doctor John B. Murphy Oration on Surgery* was delivered by Dr. William J. Mayo of Rochester, Minnesota, at the Presidential Meeting of the Clinical Congress, held on the evening of October 24, 1921.

CONFERRING OF HONORARY FELLOWSHIPS IN THE ROYAL COLLEGE OF SURGEONS IN IRELAND

The ceremony of conferring Honorary Fellowships in the Royal College of Surgeons in Ireland upon eight eminent American Surgeons was an occasion of deep interest to all Fellows of the College who were present at the ninth Convocation.

The delegation from the Irish College consisted of Sir Robert Hy Woods, M.Ch. (Hon.), Past President, R.C.S.I., and Sir William Taylor, K.B.E., C.B., also a Past President, R.C.S.I. These distinguished guests of the American College were introduced by Dr. Harvey Cushing of Boston, who said:

"On March 2, 1784, a College of Surgeons came into the world, as was quite fitting in a Maternity Hospital. This was none other that the famous Dublin Rotunda founded long before by Surgeon Bartholomew Moss, but the event of which I speak took place not in a ward but in the Board Room and by Royal proclamation.

"To the country of Jonathan Swift, of Oliver Goldsmith, and of Edmund Burke the world owes a great debt. But in medicine no less than in literature and public affairs have Irishmen stood high in the English-speaking world. The medical history of ancient Erin reaches back to times prehistoric, when Druids were priests and physicians. She had in Thomas Molyneux in the 17th century a figure likened to the English Sydenham, and the following years have produced Irishmen whose names are permanently enrolled among the leaders of our profession.

"Irish doctors have not always stayed in Ireland for their life's work, but the names of some of those who did we may recall in association with their great contributions. John Cheyne and

*Published in full in the official Journal, *Surgery, Gynecology, and Obstetrics*, November, 1921, Vol. XXXIII, page 463.

Hydrocephalus, Abraham Colles and Colles' Law, Robert Adams and Heart-Block, Corrigan and Aortic Insufficiency,— but above all there stand out two figures, Robert Graves and William Stokes, to whom students the world over flocked for inspiration at their rounds in the old Meath Hospital, where they so long served as friends and colleagues.

"Surgery, physic, and midwifery were not so differentiated in their day as in ours, and so it is that such a one as Abraham Colles, twice President of the College and its Professor of Anatomy and Surgery, is no less famed for the law he established before the spirochete was discovered than for the description of the fracture with which his name is coupled on the lips of every medical student the world over.

"Another of the band of Irish surgeons who made Dublin famous in Colles' day was Sir Philip Crompton, four times President of the College between the years 1811 and 1856 and one of the founders of that unique organization, the Zoological Society of Dublin. Members of the medical profession have indeed always been prominent in the highly cultivated and select social circle for which Dublin, like Edinburgh, has been so celebrated.

"In the winter of 1917-18, the Base Hospital to which I was attached had as its neighbor in Wimereux a hospital set up on the site where, one hundred years before, Napoleon had gathered his legions for an invasion of England. This was No. 83 Dublin General Hospital, the Chief Surgeon and organizer of which was Colonel Sir William Taylor, then President of the Irish College; and we learned to love and respect him and the members of his Unit, not only for their personal qualities but for the stand they had taken in regard to the war. At that time, in May of 1918, there had been something over one thousand persons holding degrees of the Irish College who had been in uniform; thirty-five of them had been killed in action or had died in service; thirty-six had received the Military Cross; forty-five the Distinguished Service Order; and one hundred seventy-three had been 'mentioned in despatches.' I may give a single instance of what it may mean for an Irish doctor to be mentioned in despatches.

" 'Captain Henry James Burke, R.A.M.C., for conspicuous gallantry on November 8, 1915, near Turco Farm. A sergeant in the front line had his leg crushed by the blowing in of a dug-out, and Captain Burke found immediate amputation necessary. In order to save time he crawled across the open to get his instruments, while the enemy turned a machine gun on him. In spite of their fire he returned the same way, and coolly performed the operation in the trench while the enemy were shelling it heavily.'

"Irishmen do not do things according to precedent. Chary of its honorary degrees, the Irish College, though it has been known to give its honors *in absentia*, has never before, so far as I am aware, sent delegates to another country to confer them. But these delegates should feel at home in a land to which, since the establishment of the colonies, the Irish have come in such shoals that now the largest ward of Dublin is in South Boston, and the County Mayo in the minds of many is identified with Rochester, Minnesota.

"Favored indeed may our own American College regard itself by the acts of friendship displayed, first by the Royal College of Surgeons of England in sending its President, Sir Rickman John Godlee, to our inaugural, and by the gift from members of their College (representing the Consulting Surgeons of the Armies of Britain) of the beautiful mace before us which will always figure in our future ceremonies. Now come representatives from the still older Irish College to bestow their honors on a few of our Fellows as a mark of their good will to us all.

"It is my privilege, gentlemen, to introduce to you Sir William Taylor and Sir Robert Hy Woods, of the Royal College of Surgeons in Ireland."

Sir William Taylor presented the United States surgeons for Honorary Fellowship in the Royal College of Surgeons in Ireland as follows:

"It is an unspeakable delight to me to be here amongst you again, and I shall long cherish the honor which has fallen to me to come here on this occasion.

"I now beg to propose that the President of the American

College of Surgeons do leave the Chair temporarily, and that Sir Robert Woods, Acting President of the Royal College of Surgeons in Ireland, do take the Chair.

"Mr. President: It is only right and proper that nations which have a common inheritance in language, institutions, customs, and sympathies, and which are actuated by the same high ideals of love of liberty and of justice, should do honor to each other, and I do not believe there is a place on the habitable surface of the globe so appropriate for such a function as that in which we are now engaged, as this City of Philadelphia.

"If I remember my Greek aright, Philadelphia is derived from two Greek words, φιλος and ἀδελφος, which translated freely mean 'Brotherly Love.'

"The responsibility of my duty is great, but yet greater is the happiness that it has fallen to my lot, in these days of political and sectarian disputes in our country, to be able to speak of the unanimous and genuine pleasure that the intention on the part of our College of conferring these Honorary Fellowships created throughout the length and breadth of the land.

"We trust that the honors now about to be conferred by us as the representatives of the Royal College of Surgeons in Ireland may be taken, not only as an appreciation on the part of the College of the distinguished services rendered by each of the recipients to the great advance in the science and art of surgery, and of the very exalted position they individually occupy in the profession, but, as a further evidence of our desire to perpetuate that friendship which was established between the members of the profession of your great nation and ours in the recent war.

"Established in the year 1784 by Royal Charter, with two main objects in view, namely, the improvement of medical education and the providing of a sufficient number of properly qualified surgeons for His Majesty's Navy and Army, the Royal College of Surgeons in Ireland has steadfastly endeavored to fulfill those two functions for which it was established, and I think it will be readily admitted that it has done so with commendable success.

"From time to time during the one hundred and thirty-seven

and one half years of its existence, the President, Vice-President, and Council of the College have exercised the right given them by the Royal Charter, of conferring the highest honor, namely, the Honorary Fellowship of the College, upon men of great distinction and eminence in the profession and, on three occasions, upon men of eminence and distinction, not members of the profession, who did honor to the profession and helped to advance the cause of surgical science to some considerable extent.

"In conferring such honors, no doubt the College did honor to itself.

"That the College has by no means been lavish in the distribution of its honors is evidenced by the fact that in the one hundred and thirty-seven and one-half years of its existence we find only sixty-nine names on its Honorary Roll. These names include such men of eminence and distinction as John Hunter, Percival Pott, Abernathy, Sir Astley Cooper, Sir Benjamin Brodie, Sir John Erichsen, Helmholtz, Lord Lister, Pasteur, Sir James Paget, and John Shaw Billings, all of whom have passed away.

"There are but thirteen Honorary Fellows now alive, of whom one is not a member of the profession, namely, His Royal Highness the Duke of Connaught, K.G., who, when be became Colonel-in-Chief of the Royal Army Medical Corps, was elected an Honorary Fellow. There are, therefore, only twelve members of the medical profession who now possess the honor. Of these, three were directors of the Army Medical Service who did magnificent work for the profession in their department.

"That leaves nine members of the surgical profession throughout the world who possess our Honorary Fellowship. Of these, two belong to the great American continent — Harvey Cushing, of Harvard, and Professor Cameron, of Toronto. We are now about to add eight more distinguished names to our roll, thus making twenty-one Honorary Fellows, of whom nine will be citizens of the United States.

"In calling upon the distinguished surgeons whom we are to honor to come forward, I may say that I owe a deep debt of gratitude to the ancient Phœnicians and Greeks, who, when questions of precedence arose, which might lead to unpleasantness or diplomatic troubles, settled such questions by the use of the alphabet.

"I propose, therefore, to follow their wise example, and call up those whom we are to honor, alphabetically: George E. Brewer, New York; George W. Crile, Cleveland; John M. T. Finney, Baltimore; Richard H. Harte, Philadelphia; William Williams Keen, Philadelphia; Charles H. Mayo, Rochester; William J. Mayo, Rochester, and Albert J. Ochsner, Chicago.

"These are all men who have never ceased to be students. They have always been learning while teaching, thus, providing by their example that best of all teaching — the teaching how to learn — and showing by their enthusiasm the intense pleasure they derive from their search after truth.

"We respect them for their work, we rejoice in their success, and we now honor them for their work. Men who have served their day and race as these men have all done require no further eulogy from me to commend them to you.

"I pray you, therefore, Mr. President, confer upon them all the highest honor of the Royal College of Surgeons in Ireland."

The Honorary degrees were conferred by Sir Robert Hy Woods, acting for the President of the Irish College, Sir Edward H. Taylor, B.Ch., B.A.O., who, because of illness, was unable to come to America.

The closing remarks of the ceremony were delivered by Dr. William Williams Keen of Philadelphia, who is universally acknowledged dean of surgery. In thanking the delegation from the Royal College of Surgeons in Ireland, Dr. Keen said:

"Twenty-one years ago, when the Royal College of Surgeons of England conferred the first Honorary Fellowships upon American surgeons, it was my privilege to respond for the Americans. I then said that, though your beloved Queen 'was not monarch of our persons, she was surely queen of our hearts.'

"Since that declaration a new and deeper tie has bound us more closely than ever, and forever, to you. Two million American troops, even though so late, when you had borne the burden and heat of the conflict for three years, joined you as 'trustees for civilization' (with two million more training at home and pining to join them), and helped to give the *coup de grace* to the German Army of Desolation. Thousands of our own boys lie beside your own dear ones in Flanders Fields, and in the sacred soil of France. Never can we forget this tie of blood brotherhood. 'A future breach in our peaceful and friendly relations,' as President Harding well declared but a few days ago, 'is unthinkable.'

"And now in Philadelphia, instead of in Dublin, an unexampled generous exception in your whole history since your charter was granted in 1784, you gentlemen, by order of the Royal College of Surgeons in Ireland, have conferred upon us the highest medical honor which you could bestow.

"As spokesman for my colleagues, I offer to you our sincere and heartfelt thanks, and request that you will convey this message to the College you so well represent."

ACADEMIC ROBE

The gown adopted by the Board of Regents to be worn by the Fellows at the Convocations of the College consists of a body of navy blue mohair faced with scarlet velvet. The mortar-board cap is of the same blue material, with a scarlet tassel.

STATE AND PROVINCIAL CLINICAL MEETINGS

During the past year state clinical meetings were held in a majority of the states in this country and in two of the provinces of Canada. The purpose of these meetings, as stated by the Board of Regents, was to promote a closer unity of the Fellows within the individual states and provinces, to elevate the standards of the College, and to bring the ideals of the College, information regarding scientific medicine, and the benefits of hospital standardization before the public.

Thirty-eight of these meetings have been held, thirty-six in the United States and two in the Dominion of Canada. The plan of these two day sessions included clinics by the Fellows of the College and their staffs on the mornings of the two days; a scientific meeting, where papers relating to surgery were read; a hospital conference, where the standardization of hospitals was discussed; and a public meeting in which visiting speakers explained the aims of the College, discussed various phases of preventive medicine, and made clear the advantages of standardized hospitals.

Four thousand medical men including approximately eighty per cent of the Fellowship of the College attended some one of these meetings; more than three thousand hospital superintendents, trustees, and nurses were present at the hospital meetings; and over fifty thousand laymen heard the speakers in the evening. Besides this more than fifty thousand additional laymen were reached by addresses given before Chambers of Commerce, Rotary Clubs, Parent Teachers' Associations, and other organizations interested in civic betterment.

After one year of these meetings the following results are already apparent: A feeling of state consciousness has arisen among the Fellows. Gathering for the first time in state meetings they have become conscious of the power they can wield as a group

29

to advance scientific medicine within their own commonwealths. These meetings afforded individual Fellows an opportunity to show their work as clinicians and identified them in the eyes of the public as members of the American College of Surgeons.

The local medical profession in each city was invited to attend the afternoon and evening sessions and many of them have now a new conception of the ideals and purposes of the College.

The hospital conferences held in twenty-seven states gave a new impetus to the work in this field. Local hospital superintendents appeared on these programs and told of the results obtained by hospital standardization. The Minimum Standard was explained, the work of the hospital visitor was made clear, and community needs for hospital betterment were discussed.

The public health mass meetings held in thirty-six states and two provinces of Canada constituted the foundation for a new movement in the education of the laity. The universal enthusiastic cooperation of the press, of all societies interested in civic betterment, and, in many cases, of municipal and state offices, attested to the widespread desire of the public to receive authentic information regarding better health. This message was carried to over one hundred thousand people during the year and through articles in the press reached between six and eight million readers. In many cases either the governor of the state or a United States senator presided at these meetings and welcomed the visiting surgeons to the state. The Director General of the College, Franklin H. Martin, M.D., and Director of Hospital Activities, Judge Harold M. Stephens, attended these meetings in addition to other officials from the central office. Reverend C. B. Moulinier, S.J., President of the Catholic Hospital Association, and Malcolm T. MacEachern, M.D., First Vice-President of the American Hospital Association, were also in attendance. The list below gives the localities and dates of the meetings held and the names of the Fellows who spoke at the public meetings.

ALABAMA (Jointly with Georgia and Florida)

Meeting held at Birmingham, January 14-15, 1921.
Visiting Speakers: John Osborn Polak, M.D., Joseph Colt
Bloodgood, M.D.
Executive Committee:
    Chairman — Cunningham Wilson, Birmingham
    Secretary —Wyatt Heflin, Birmingham
    Counselors—Lewis Coleman Morris, Birmingham
            Charles A. Thigpen, Montgomery
            William Thomas Henderson, Mobile

ARIZONA

Meeting held at Phoenix, November 15, 1920.
Visiting Speakers: Frederic A. Besley, M.D., John G. Bowman.
Executive Committee:
    Chairman—Winfred Wylie, Phoenix
    Secretary—William A. Holt, Globe
    Counselor—Roderick D. Kennedy, Globe

ARKANSAS

Meeting held at Little Rock, February 18-19, 1921.
Visiting Speakers: William R. Cubbins, M.D., C. Jeff Miller, M.D.
Executive Committee:
    Chairman—St. Cloud Cooper, Fort Smith
    Secretary—W. R. Brooksher, Fort Smith

CALIFORNIA

Meeting held at San Francisco, November 18-19, 1920.
Visiting Speakers: Chester H. Rowell, Frederic A. Besley,
M.D., John G. Bowman.
Executive Committee:
    Chairman —Stanley Stillman, San Francisco
    Secretary —Lewis B. Morton, Los Angeles
    Counselors—H. A. L. Ryfkogel, San Francisco
            Granville MacGowan, Los Angeles
            D. C. Strong, San Bernardino
            H. H. Sherk, Pasadena
            Rexwald Brown, Santa Barbara

COLORADO

Meeting held at Denver, November 26-27, 1920.
Visiting Speakers: Frederic A. Besley, M.D., John G. Bowman.
Executive Committee:
  Chairman—Edward Jackson, Denver
  Secretary—Oscar M. Shere, Denver
  Counselor—Peter O. Hanford, Colorado Springs

CONNECTICUT (Jointly with New England States)

Meeting held at Springfield, May 13-14, 1921.
Visiting Speakers listed under Massachusetts.
Executive Committee:
  Chairman—D. C. Brown, Danbury
  Secretary—Seldom B. Overlock, Pomfret

DISTRICT OF COLUMBIA

Meeting held at Washington, May 11, 1921.
  Visiting Speakers: John B. Deaver, M.D., Brigadier General
Charles E. Sawyer.
Executive Committee:
  Chairman—Harry H. Kerr, Washington
  Secretary—William G. Irving, Washington
  Counselor—Virgil B. Jackson, Washington

FLORIDA (Jointly with Alabama and Georgia)

Meeting held at Birmingham, Alabama, January 14-15, 1921.
Visiting Speakers listed under Alabama.
Executive Committee:
  Chairman—Gerry R. Holden, Jacksonville
  Secretary—W. S. Manning, Jacksonville
  Counselor—John S. Helms, Tampa

GEORGIA (Jointly with Alabama and Florida)

Meeting held at Birmingham, Alabama, January 14-15, 1921.
Visiting Speakers listed under Alabama.
Executive Committee:
  Chairman—William S. Goldsmith, Atlanta
  Secretary—Edgar G. Ballenger, Atlanta
  Counselor—Agnew H. Hilsman, Albany

IDAHO

Meeting held at Boise, September 6-7, 1920.
Visiting Speakers: William D. Haggard, M.D., John G. Bowman.
Executive Committee:
    Chairman—E. E. Maxey, Boise
    Secretary—William F. Howard, Pocatello
    Counselor—Clifford M. Cline, Idaho Falls

ILLINOIS

Meeting held at Peoria, December 16-17-18, 1921.
Visiting Speakers: John B. Deaver, M.D., Frederic A. Besley, M.D., John G. Bowman.
Executive Committee:
    Chairman—Charles H. Brobst, Peoria
    Secretary—Frederic A. Besley, Chicago
    Counselors—Clarence W. East, Springfield
                   Edmond B. Montgomery, Quincy
                   Jonathan L. Wiggins, East St. Louis

INDIANA

Meeting held at Indianapolis, April 28-29, 1921.
Visiting Speakers: William D. Haggard, M.D., Carl A. Hamann, M.D., Joseph C. Bloodgood, M.D.
Executive Committee:
    Chairman—James Y. Welborn, Evansville
    Secretary—Eldridge M. Shanklin, Hammond
    Counselor—Albert E. Bulson, Fort Wayne

IOWA

Meeting held at Des Moines, February 28-March 1, 1921.
Visiting Speakers: J. N. Jackson, M.D., John B. Deaver, M.D.
Executive Committee:
    Chairman—W. W. Pearson, Des Moines
    Secretary—J. C. Rockafellow, Des Moines
    Counselor—Donald Macrae, Jr., Council Bluffs

KANSAS

Meeting held at Wichita, March 7-8, 1921.
Visiting Speakers: Jabez M. Jackson, M.D., Allen B. Kanavel, M.D.
Executive Committee:
    Chairman—Robert B. Stewart, Topeka
    Secretary—William Merrill Mills, Topeka
    Counselor—Howard L. Snyder, Winfield

KENTUCKY

Meeting held at Louisville, March 25-26, 1921.
Visiting Speakers: George W. Crile, M.D., Carl B. Davis, M.D.
Executive Committee:
  Chairman—David Barrow, Lexington
  Secretary—Charles A. Vance, Lexington
  Counselor—Joseph A. Stucky, Lexington

LOUISIANA

Meeting held at New Orleans, January 10, 1921.
Visiting Speaker: Thomas Stephen Cullen, M.D.
Executive Committee:
  Chairman—C. Jeff Miller, New Orleans
  Secretary—Lucian H. Landry, New Orleans
  Counselor—John Luther Wilson, Alexandria

MAINE (Jointly with New England States)

Meeting held at Springfield, Massachusetts, May 13-14, 1921.
Visiting Speakers listed under Massachusetts.
Executive Committee:
  Chairman—Owen Smith, Portland
  Counselor—Eugene B. Sanger, Bangor

MARYLAND

Meeting held at Baltimore and Washington, D. C., May 11, 1921.
Visiting Speakers listed under District of Columbia.
Executive Committee:
  Chairman—J. M. Hundley, Baltimore
  Secretary—Charles Bagley, Jr., Baltimore
  Counselor—A. H. Hawkins, Cumberland

MASSACHUSETTS (Jointly with New England States)

Meeting held at Springfield, May 13-14, 1921.
Visiting Speakers: Charles H. Peck, M.D., John Osborn Polak, M.D.
Executive Committee:
  Chairman —Homer Gage, Worcester
  Counselors—H. G. Stetson, Greenfield
           P. E. Truesdale, Fall River

MICHIGAN

Meeting held at Detroit, April 28-29, 1921.
Visiting Speakers: Allen B. Kanavel, M.D., Harry E. Mock, M.D.
Executive Committee:
    Chairman—F. C. Warnshuis, Grand Rapids
    Secretary—Ray C. Stone, Battle Creek
    Counselors—Walter R. Parker, Detroit
              J. G. R. Manwaring, Flint
              C. E. Boys, Kalamazoo

MINNESOTA

Executive Committee:
    Chairman—Thomas McDavitt, St. Paul
    Secretary—Arthur T. Mann, Minneapolis
    Counselor—Charles H. Mayo, Rochester

MISSISSIPPI (Jointly with Louisiana)

Meeting held at New Orleans, Louisiana, January 10, 1921.
Visiting Speakers listed under Louisiana.
Executive Committee:
    Chairman—Walter W. Crawford, Hattiesburg
    Secretary—James P. Wall, Jackson
    Counselor—John W. D. Dicks, Natchez

MISSOURI

Meeting held at St. Louis, March 10-11, 1921.
Visiting Speaker: George W. Crile, M.D.
Executive Committee:
    Chairman—John F. Binnie, Kansas City
    Secretary—John G. Hayden, Kansas City
    Counselor—Daniel Morton, St. Joseph

MONTANA

Meeting held at Butte, September 3-4, 1921.
Visiting Speakers: William D. Haggard, M.D., John G. Bowman.
Executive Committee:
    Chairman—Fred F. Attix, Lewiston
    Secretary—James H. Irwin, Great Falls
    Counselor—Rudolph Horsky, Helena

NEBRASKA

Meeting held at Omaha, March 3-4, 1921.
Visiting Speaker: Francis Carter Wood, M.D.
Executive Committee:
    Chairman—A. R. Mitchell, Lincoln
    Secretary—Stanley Welch, Lincoln
    Counselor—F. A. Long, Madison

NEW HAMPSHIRE (Jointly with New England States)

Meeting held at Springfield, Massachusetts, May 13-14, 1921.
Visiting Speakers listed under Massachusetts.
Executive Committee:
    Chairman—John M. Gile, Hanover
    Secretary—Frank E. Kittredge, Nashua

NEW JERSEY

Meeting held at Newark, April 11-12, 1921.
Visiting Speakers: Robert L. Dickinson, M.D., Howard C. Taylor, M.D.
Executive Committee:
    Chairman—Edward J. Ill, Newark
    Secretary—Carl E. Sutphen, Newark
    Counselor—James S. Brown, Montclair

NEW YORK

Meeting held at Buffalo, December 2-3, 1920.
Visiting Speakers: John Osborn Polak, M.D., John B. Deaver, M.D., John G. Bowman.
Executive Committee:
    Chairman —Russell S. Fowler, Brooklyn
    Secretary —Frederick T. Van Buren, Jr., New York City
    Counselors—Marshall Clinton, Buffalo
              Edwin Stanton, Schenectady
              John Osborn Polak, Brooklyn

NORTH CAROLINA

Meeting held at Charlotte, January 20-21, 1921.
Visiting Speakers: John G. Clark, M.D., W. S. Rankin, M.D., John Osborn Polak, M.D., J. M. T. Finney, M.D., John B. Deaver, M.D.
Executive Committee:
    Chairman—Jacob F. Highsmith, Fayetteville
    Secretary—J. Wesley Long, Greensboro
    Counselor—Hubert A. Royster, Raleigh

NORTH DAKOTA

Meeting held at Bismarck, June 24-25, 1921.
Visiting Speakers: Jabez N. Jackson, M.D., Richard R. Smith, M.D., A. T. Mann, M.D.

Executive Committee:
Chairman—Murdock MacGregor, Fargo
Secretary—Paul H. Burton, Fargo
Counselor—Robert D. Campbell, Grand Forks

OHIO

Meeting held at Cleveland, April 1-2, 1921.
Visiting Speakers: Willard Bartlett, M.D., Hugh Cabot, M.D.

Executive Committee:
Chairman—Charles S. Hamilton, Columbus
Secretary—J. Edward Pirrung, Cincinnati
Counselor—Walter H. Snyder, Toledo

OKLAHOMA

Meeting held at Oklahoma City, February 21-22, 1921.
Visiting Speakers: Jabez N. Jackson, M.D., C. Jeff Miller, M.D.

Executive Committee:
Chairman—William D. Berry, Muskogee
Vice-Chairman—Fred Yohn Cronk, Tulsa
Secretary—John S. Hartford, Oklahoma City
Counselor—Dolph D. McHenry, Oklahoma City

OREGON

Meeting held at Portland, August 29-30, 1921.
Visiting Speakers: Allen B. Kanavel, M.D., John Osborn Polak, M.D.

Executive Committee:
Chairman—Ernest F. Tucker, Portland
Secretary—Joseph A. Pettit, Portland
Counselor—W. B. Holden, Portland

PENNSYLVANIA

Meeting held at Pittsburgh, October 7-8-9, 1920.
Visiting Speakers: Charles Davison, M.D., Emil Beck, M.D., Frank L. Hupp, M.D., John G. Bowman.

Executive Committee:
Chairman—William L. Estes, Bethlehem
Secretary —Astley P. C. Ashhurst, Philadelphia
Counselor—J. J. Buchanan, Pittsburgh

RHODE ISLAND (Jointly with New England States)

Meeting held at Springfield, Massachusetts, May 13-14, 1921.
Visiting Speakers listed under Massachusetts.
Executive Committee:
 Chairman—Roland Hammond, Providence
 Secretary—George W. Gardner, Providence
 Counselor—Edgar B. Smith, Providence

SOUTH CAROLINA

Meeting held at Charleston, January 17-18, 1921.
Visiting Speakers: John Osborn Polak, M.D., John G. Clark,
M.D., Joseph Colt Bloodgood, M.D.
Executive Committee:
 Chairman —Charles W. Kollock, Charleston
 Secretary —Archibald E. Baker, Charleston
 Counselors—Charles A. Mobley, Orangeburg
      W. W. Fennell, Rock Hill
      Julius H. Taylor, Columbia
      Leland O. Mauldin, Greenville
      Frank M. McLeod, Florence

SOUTH DAKOTA

Meeting held at Aberdeen, June 27-28, 1921.
Visiting Speakers: Richard R. Smith, M.D., Jabez N. Jackson,
M.D., A. T. Mann, M.D.
Executive Committee:
 Chairman—Gilbert G. Cottam, Sioux Falls
 Secretary—Frederick A. Spafford, Flandreau
 Counselor—Frank Israel Putnam, Sioux Falls

TENNESSEE

Meeting held at Nashville, March 21-22, 1921.
Visiting Speaker: V. P. Blair, M.D.
Executive Committee:
 Chairman—W. A. Bryan, Nashville
 Secretary —William D. Haggard, Nashville
 Counselor—John M. Maury, Memphis

TEXAS

Meeting held at Dallas, January 7-8, 1921.
Visiting Speaker: Thomas Stephen Cullen, M.D.
Executive Committee:
 Chairman—Bacon Saunders, Fort Worth
 Secretary —Francis M. Hicks, San Antonio
 Counselor—W. Booth Russ, San Antonio

UTAH

Meeting held at Salt Lake City, November 22-23, 1920.
Visiting Speakers: Frederic A. Besley, M.D., John G. Bowman.
Executive Committee:
    Chairman—Frederick Stauffer, Salt Lake City
    Secretary—Robert R. Hampton, Salt Lake City
    Counselor—John F. Critchlow, Salt Lake City

VERMONT (Jointly with New England States)

Meeting held at Springfield, Massachusetts, May 13-14, 1921.
Visiting Speakers listed under Massachusetts.
Executive Committee:
    Chairman—John B. Wheeler, Burlington
    Secretary—William W. Townsend, Burlington
    Counselor—John M. Allen, St. Johnsbury

VIRGINIA

Meeting held at Richmond, April 14-15, 1921.
Visiting Speakers: Dean Lewis, M.D., Carl A. Hamann, M.D.
Executive Committee:
    Chairman—Lomax Gwathmey, Norfolk
    Secretary—J. L. Rawls, Norfolk
    Counselor—S. S. Gale, Roanoke

WASHINGTON

Meeting held at Spokane, August 25-26, 1921.
Visiting Speakers: John Osborn Polak, M.D., Joseph A. Pettit,
M.D., Ernest F. Tucker, M.D.
Executive Committee:
    Chairman—John B. McNerthney, Tacoma
    Secretary—Horace J. Whitacre, Tacoma
    Counselor—John Hunt, Seattle

WEST VIRGINIA

Meeting held at Wheeling, April 18-19, 1921.
Visiting Speakers: William E. Lower, M.D., Howard C.
Taylor, M.D.
Executive Committee:
    Chairman—J. Ross Hunter, Huntington
    Secretary—Thomas W. Moore, Huntington
    Counselor—J. Schwinn, Wheeling

WISCONSIN

Executive Committee:
  Chairman—G. E. Seaman, Milwaukee·
  Secretary—Philip F. Rogers, Milwaukee
  Counselors—F. Gregory Connell, Oshkosh
        Karl Doege, Marshfield
        John M. Dodd, Ashland

CANADA

ALBERTA

Meeting held at Calgary, August 16-19, 1921.
Visiting Speaker: John Osborn Polak, M.D.
Executive Committee:
  Chairman—F. W. Gershaw, Medicine Hat
  Secretary—A. R. Munroe, Edmonton
  Counselor—W. E. Graham, Calgary

BRITISH COLUMBIA

Meeting held at Vancouver, August 22-27, 1921.
Visiting Speaker: John Osborn Polak, M.D.
Executive Committee:
  Chairman—W. B. Burnett, Vancouver
  Secretary—A. B. Schinbein, Vancouver
  Counselor—J. J. Mason, Vancouver

MANITOBA

Executive Committee:
  Chairman—John A. Gunn, Winnipeg
  Secretary—Robert D. Fletcher, Winnipeg
  Counselor—James McKenty, Winnipeg

NEW BRUNSWICK

Executive Committee:
  Chairman—Murray MacLaren, St. John
  Secretary—George Clowes Van Wart, Fredericton
  Counselor—William Donald Rankin, Woodstock

NOVA SCOTIA

Executive Committee:
  Chairman—H. K. MacDonald, Halifax
  Secretary—Philip Weatherbe, Halifax
  Counselor—John George McDougall, Halifax

ONTARIO

Executive Committee:
    Chairman—B. P. Watson, Toronto
    Secretary—Frederick Bruce Mowbray, Hamilton
    Counselor—Edward R. Secord, Brantford

QUEBEC

Executive Committee:
    Chairman—George E. Armstrong, Montreal
    Secretary—Campbell B. Keenan, Montreal
    Counselor—Eugene Saint-Jacques, Montreal

SASKATCHEWAN

Executive Committee:
    Chairman—Andrew Croll, Saskatoon
    Secretary—George R. Peterson, Saskatoon
    Counselor—Frederick A. F. Corbett, Regina

Members of the State Executive Committees who brought these meetings to a successful issue are of the opinion that uniting the states and provinces into small groups will increase the efficiency of the meetings for the coming year. An annual meeting in each state takes too great an expenditure of time on the part of the Fellows, especially in states where there is but one city capable of accommodating the gathering. For this reason it has been determined to unite the states in small groups to effect larger and better sessions, and to lighten the burden of time and labor required for individual state meetings. This arrangement will in no way impair the individuality of the various existing state organizations. It is simply a grouping of states for better meetings. The Executive Committee of the state holding the group meeting will be responsible for its management. A representative from the central office will visit each meeting place in advance and assist the local committee. The clinical program will be arranged by the local committee; the Hospital Standardization meeting and the public meeting will be arranged for by the central office. Attendance at these meetings should comprise Fellows of the College and invited guests, the latter to include candidates approved for Fellowship in the College by the respective State

Credentials Committees, but who may not have completed their case records. At the discretion of Executive Committees, the local medical profession may be invited to the afternoon and evening sessions.

The legitimate routine expenses of the group meetings shall be cared for by the central body through an appropriation of a sum not to exceed $3.00 for each contributing Fellow of the College within the group.

In the conduct of the group meetings it is the purpose to adhere as closely as possible to the plans which have been universally approved by surgeons who have attended the National Clinical Congresses held in large cities of the United States and Canada during the past ten years.

The following grouping of states has been made for meetings during the year 1922:

Wisconsin, Minnesota, North Dakota, Montana
Missouri, Kansas
Nebraska, Iowa, South Dakota
California, Arizona, Nevada
Texas, New Mexico, Oklahoma
Alabama, Mississippi, Louisiana, Arkansas
Kentucky, Tennessee
Florida, Georgia
North Carolina, South Carolina
Virginia, Washington, D. C., Maryland, West Virginia
Pennsylvania, Delaware
New York, New Jersey
Ontario
Quebec
New England States
Nova Scotia, New Brunswick, Newfoundland, Prince
    Edward Island
Manitoba
Saskatchewan, Alberta
British Columbia, Idaho, Washington, Oregon
Utah, Wyoming, Colorado
Ohio, Michigan
Illinois, Indiana

HOSPITAL STANDARDIZATION

The following is a report on the standardization of hospitals for the year 1921. Since the inception of this movement in 1915, and after the minimum standard was evolved from the combined experience of surgeons, internists, and hospital executives, it has met with increasing recognition, until today seventy-four per cent of the hundred bed hospitals in the United States and Canada have adopted it.

Surely, the time for debate has passed. It is beside the mark to argue the wisdom of a movement which has enlisted the cooperation of three-fourths of hospital America. Any advance in medicine must begin — and end — with the welfare of the patient. He must be at once the actuating impulse and the final beneficiary. Just so surely as the patient is benefited, so also will be the doctor and the hospital. And, precisely, because the minimum standard was evolved to bring every group in the hospital together to work for the patient, it has created an organization which has resulted in better work for the individual surgeon, internist, hospital superintendent, and nurse.

The minimum standard embodies the basic principles of scientific research. Research begins with securing facts, compiling facts, analyzing facts. This done, Research draws tentative conclusions gained from analysis of the facts. These conclusions, if supported by sufficient evidence and corroborated by practice, become known as scientific truths.

This standard consists of a working arrangement by which these same principles of research are applied daily in the hospital for the benefit of the patient. Accurate, adequate case records, modern laboratory equipment manned by skilled technicians — what are these but provisions to marshal the facts before the physician for examination? The monthly clinical staff meeting — what is this but an opportunity to test out the data which the

43

records and laboratories have furnished? Insistence on competent and ethical practitioners — what is this but a guarantee that the interpreters of the facts regarding each patient are skilled medical men, on whose judgment the public has every right to rely? The working formula for this program is the minimum standard which follows:

THE MINIMUM STANDARD

1. That physicians and surgeons privileged to practice in the hospital be organized as a definite group or staff. Such organization has nothing to do with the question as to whether the hospital is "open" or "closed," nor need it affect the various existing types of staff organization. The word *staff* is here defined as the group of doctors who practice in the hospital inclusive of all groups such as the "regular staff," the "visiting staff," and the "associate staff."

2. That membership upon the staff be restricted to physicians and surgeons who are (a) competent in their respective fields and (b) worthy in character and in matters of professional ethics; that in this latter connection the practice of the division of fees, under any guise whatever, be prohibited.

3. That the staff initiate and, with the approval of the governing board of the hospital, adopt rules, regulations, and policies governing the professional work of the hospital; that these rules, regulations, and policies specifically provide:

a. That staff meetings be held at least once each month. (In large hospitals, the departments may choose to meet separately.)

b. That the staff review and analyze at regular intervals the clinical experience of the staff in the various departments of the hospital, such as medicine, surgery, and obstetrics; the clinical records of patients, free and pay, to be the basis for such review and analyses.

4. That accurate and complete case records be written for all patients and filed in an accessible manner in the hospital, a

complete case record being one, except in an emergency, which includes the personal history; the physical examination, with clinical, pathological, and X-ray findings when indicated; the working diagnosis; the treatment, medical and surgical; the medical progress; the condition on discharge with final diagnosis; and, in case of death, the autopsy findings when available.

5. That clinical laboratory facilities be available for the study, diagnosis, and treatment of patients, these facilities to include at least chemical, bacteriological, serological, histological, radiographic, and fluoroscopic service in charge of trained technicians.

The minimum standard is, in essence, an arrangement by which the hospital can insure its patients the best care known to the science of medicine. We have shown how it provides an application of the principles of scientific research to the care of the patient — the same principles which the individual doctor or surgeon uses for arriving at a diagnosis. And because medical men the country over were quick to see not only the practical but the scientific basis underlying the minimum standard, they have given it, in increasing numbers, their unqualified support.

It is easy to devise a system of rules which — on paper — is perfect. It is quite another matter to evolve a standard of such simplicity that it stands the test of actual conditions in hospital work. Whether the minimum standard is eminently practicable in the every day administration of hospitals is best answered by the following report:

THE ACCEPTANCE OF THE PROGRAM

In 1918, of the general hospitals of one hundred or more beds in the United States and Canada, eighty-nine met the standard. In 1919, one hundred and ninety-eight fulfilled the requirements; in 1920, four hundred and seven, or fifty-seven per cent, met the standard; and this year five hundred and seventy-three or seventy-five per cent of the seven hundred and sixty-one general hospitals are on the "approved" list.

Further, what has been the experience of other organizations interested in hospital betterment? Manifestly, their reaction toward the program furnishes another reliable index as to its applicability. A decided impetus has been given to hospital standardization by the acceptance and endorsement of the minimum standard by such influential and powerful organizations as the American Hospital Association, the Canadian Medical Association, the Catholic Hospital Association, the Conference Board of Hospitals and Homes of the Methodist Church, the Medical and Surgical Section of the American Railway Association, the Methodist Hospital Association, the Protestant Hospital Association, and numerous state, provincial, and local organizations.

What do hospital superintendents of experience think of the minimum standard after they have seen it in actual operation for a period of years? Quick to recognize its advantages, their endorsements have been numerous. The following quotation from Mr. Frank Chapman, Director of the Mt. Sinai Hospital, Cleveland, serves as a representative example:

"Certainly, the establishment of a laboratory for purposes of check is just as essential in handling human life, as in handling inert commodities. Certainly the recording of a performance is just as essential in a hospital as are the production records of any manufacturing plant. It is undebatable that the only exact way of improving our future performance is on a basis of study of our actual performance in the past, and certainly the basis of that study must be as exact as it is humanly possible to make it. Therefore, the establishment of a practice of routine complete case histories is, without a doubt, sound. The desirability, and in fact necessity, of a laboratory is equally undebatable. The necessity for regular staff meetings at which can be discussed, in an impersonal and unbiased way, the performance of that staff, cannot help but be productive of great good to the performance of the whole. Is it not these things and these things alone that the College is asking for in its minimum standard?

"These procedures do not require large expenditures of money, but they do require a very material increase in expenditure of energy and endeavor, and require bringing to the problem of hospital administration an ideal of scientific medical practice that, if followed, cannot help but bring the hospital performance of the country as a whole to a higher plane than has ever been attained in the past."

As another instance, the following opinion from Dr. Louis H. Burlingham, superintendent of the Barnes Hospital, St. Louis, is presented:

"To reduce the whole problem to its simplest terms, I believe it a self-evident fact that any hospital superintendent would prefer to be connected with a hospital where every patient is guaranteed the best possible care. There is no question that the minimum standard as set forth by the American College of Surgeons contributes markedly toward this end. Therefore, if he has any criticism it can only be that the standard does not perhaps go quite far enough."

Hospital staff members have been similarly responsive, as is evidenced by this viewpoint from a surgeon, Dr. Irvin Abell, of Louisville, Kentucky:

"Now that the ideals of hospital standardization have been demonstrated to be advisable and attainable and are in process of consummation, the advantages both to the physician and patient are so potent one marvels that the recognition of their need has been so tardy.

"Standardization does not imply commercialism; this would be as objectionable in the medical profession as in the profession of the ministry. But it does imply that all patients, rich and poor, receiving treatment in recognized hospitals will be assured of competent and efficient service fully meeting the requirements and standards which knowledge, experience, and humanitarianism demand as the unequivocal right of the sick at the hands of those to whom their health and well-being are entrusted.

"It applies the great moral force of man's duty to man, which by its appeal to reason as well as to the heart leads the hospital authorities and the doctors practicing in such institutions so to realize the modern addenda to medical and surgical knowledge and so to correlate the work of hospital management with the work of doctors, nurses, and technicians, that the patient is assured of proper and competent treatment in so far as it is humanly possible to secure it."

Hospital boards of trustees are taking an increasing interest in the professional work of the hospital. They are beginning to study the medical as well as the financial audits of the hospital's activities each month. As a result, they are obtaining a keener appreciation of the need for adequate case-records and laboratory facilities. An example of the reaction of boards of trustees to the College program is furnished by the following quotation from Dr. M. G. Seelig, of St. Louis:

"The relationship between the standardization program and the layman is a most interesting one. In most communities the word hospital signifies brick and mortar containers for sick people. It means this not merely to the community at large, but only too frequently to the members of boards of directors themselves. Quite unexpectedly these boards of directors found themselves face to face with an agency which, to use the words of Mr. Bowman, was selling the idea of hospital efficiency. As far as my own experience goes, I can certify to the facts that the idea was sold to them and that they value their purchase. My own board realizes, as never before, what records mean, they are awake to the importance of all varieties of hospital interdepartmental cooperation and they have gone through the period of school boy suspense waiting to see how they would be graded.

"What does this mean? It means a beginning of educating the layman to understand and appreciate the real functions of a hospital. Such understanding and appreciation carries with it the corollary that laymen will be better able to appreciate and estimate the services of the medical staff. The rendering of adequate medical service begins to take form in the lay mind as a very concrete idea.

"To sum up then, in just a word, the program of standardization, as I interpret, has resulted in the first place in stimulating surgery to higher and better efforts. It has done this by a subtle strengthening of esprit de corps, and by setting the great body of surgeons to work doing their own housecleaning on an adequately comprehensive scale. In the second place it has resulted in starting the education of groups of laymen, scattered throughout our country. Education is highly infectious, and one may safely hope that knowledge will spread until the layman will gain an intelligent appreciation of hospital ideals."

THE METHOD AND SCOPE OF THE WORK

The hospital surveys of the College are conducted through a trained corps of hospital visitors, all of whom are graduates in medicine. Their purpose is to explain the minimum standard, to interpret its application to each hospital, and to offer constructive criticism and helpful suggestions to remedy any existent short-comings. Upon these detailed personal surveys, the College is dependent for an accurate estimate of each hospital's status relative to the minimum standard.

An important adjunct to the work of the hospital surveyors has been the emphasis placed on hospital standardization at the state and provincial sectional meetings of the College. At these meetings conferences are held which are devoted to a discussion of pertinent hospital problems by those intimately connected with hospitals. In addition, the community interest is stimulated at public meetings where the benefits of hospital standardization are portrayed.

In 1920, the general hospitals of one hundred or more beds in the United States and Canada were visited. A complete report of the survey of 1920 is contained in bulletin No. 1, Vol. V, issued by the College in January, 1921. This year particular attention has been directed toward those hospitals which in 1920 either were not included in the list, or which were listed with an asterisk. Hospitals which were fully approved in 1920 were not as a routine visited this year, although in all probability visits to these institutions will be resumed in the future.

In addition, seven hundred and four general hospitals of fifty to one hundred beds were visited during the past two years; three hundred and six in 1920 and three hundred and ninety-eight in 1921. As there are approximately eight hundred and fifty-four of these smaller hospitals in the United States and Canada, one hundred and fifty remain to be visited. Of these seven hundred and four visited during 1920 and 1921, one hundred and seventy-six, or twenty-five per cent of the total number, met the standard. The individual listing of this group of institutions will appear next year.

THE PROGRAM FOR THE FUTURE

Consequently, the survey of 1922 will be extended to include all general hospitals of fifty or more beds in the United States and Canada. Of these institutions already visited, many showed a working knowledge of the minimum standard and evinced an active desire to cooperate. The percentage of these—meeting the standard at their first visit — compares favorably with the percentage of hundred bed hospitals which were approved on their first inspection. If proof were needed of the universal application of the minimum standard, the acceptance by the smaller hospitals would furnish it. Stressing only broad fundamentals, the minimum standard molds itself to meet specific needs, nowhere impeding initiative or fettering judgment. Rightly conceived and carried out, it makes the hospital the proved guardian of the community health, rendering scientific service to all.

LIST OF APPROVED HOSPITALS
CAPACITY OF 100 BEDS AND OVER

The following list contains the names of those general hospitals of one hundred or more beds, in the United States and Canada, which meet the minimum standard. In this list a certain number of the institutions are designated with an asterisk. This group includes those hospitals which, when visited, had adopted the fundamental principles of the minimum standard, but which at that time had not had sufficient opportunity to develop all of them to a degree meriting the fullest approval. The hospitals listed without an asterisk, having instituted these measures at an earlier date, had received the benefits of a longer experience in the workings of the program and consequently a broader conception of its application.

UNITED STATES

ALABAMA

Employees Hospital, T. C. I. & R. R. Co., Birmingham
*Hillman Hospital, Birmingham
Mobile City Hospital, Mobile
South Highlands Infirmary, Birmingham

ARKANSAS

*Logan H. Roots Memorial Hospital, Little Rock
St. Louis Southwestern Hospital, Texarkana
St. Vincent's Hospital, Little Rock

CALIFORNIA

Alameda County Hospital, San Leandro
Children's Hospital, San Francisco
*Franklin Hospital, San Francisco
*French Hospital, San Francisco
*Hospital of the Good Samaritan, Los Angeles
Lane Hospital, San Francisco
Los Angeles County Hospital, Los Angeles
Mary's Help Hospital, San Francisco
Mt. Zion Hospital, San Francisco
*O'Connor Sanitarium, San Jose
Pasadena Hospital, Pasadena
*Providence Hospital, Oakland
St. Francis' Hospital, San Francisco
St. Joseph's Hospital, San Francisco
St. Joseph's Sanitarium, San Diego
*St. Luke's Hospital, San Francisco
St. Mary's Hospital, San Francisco
St. Vincent's Hospital, Los Angeles
San Diego County Hospital, San Diego
San Francisco Hospital, San Francisco
*San Joaquin County Hospital, French Camp
Santa Barbara Cottage Hospital, Santa Barbara
Santa Clara County Hospital, San Jose
Santa Fe Coast Lines Hospital, Los Angeles
Southern Pacific Hospital, San Francisco
*Stanford Hospital, San Francisco
University of California Hospital, San Francisco
White Memorial Hospital, Los Angeles

COLORADO

*Denver City and County Hospital, Denver
Glockner Sanatorium and Hospital, Colorado Springs
*Mercy Hospital, Denver
Minnequa Hospital, Pueblo
*St. Anthony's Hospital, Denver
*St. Francis' Hospital, Colorado Springs
*St. Mary's Hospital, Pueblo

CONNECTICUT

Bridgeport Hospital, Bridgeport
Grace Hospital, New Haven
Greenwich General Hospital, Greenwich
Hartford Hospital, Hartford
Lawrence and Memorial Associated Hospitals, New London
New Haven Hospital, New Haven
St. Francis' Hospital, Hartford
St. Mary's Hospital, Waterbury
St. Vincent's Hospital, Bridgeport
*Stamford Hospital, Stamford
Waterbury Hospital, Waterbury

DELAWARE

Delaware Hospital, Wilmington

DISTRICT OF COLUMBIA

Central Dispensary and Emergency Hospital, Washington
Children's Hospital, Washington
Columbia Hospital for Women, Washington
Freedman's Hospital, Washington
Garfield Memorial Hospital, Washington
George Washington University Hospital, Washington
Georgetown University Hospital, Washington
Providence Hospital, Washington
*Washington Sanitarium, Washington

GEORGIA

Georgia Baptist Hospital, Atlanta
Grady Memorial Hospital, Atlanta
University Hospital, Augusta

IDAHO

St. Alphonsus Hospital, Boise

ILLINOIS

Alexian Brothers' Hospital, Chicago
*American Hospital, Chicago
Augustana Hospital, Chicago
Chicago Lying-In Hospital, Chicago
Children's Memorial Hospital, Chicago
Columbus Hospital, Chicago
Cook County Hospital, Chicago
Evanston Hospital, Evanston
*Frances E. Willard Hospital, Chicago
Grant Hospital, Chicago
Hahnemann Hospital, Chicago
*Hospital of St. Anthony de Padua, Chicago
Illinois Central Hospital, Chicago
*Illinois Charitable Eye and Ear Infirmary, Chicago
*John C. Proctor Hospital, Peoria
Mercy Hospital, Chicago
Michael Reese Hospital, Chicago
Presbyterian Hospital, Chicago
Rockford Hospital, Rockford
St. Anne's Hospital, Chicago
St. Bernard's Hospital, Chicago
*St. Elizabeth's Hospital, Chicago
*St. Elizabeth's Hospital, Danville
St. Francis' Hospital, Blue Island
*St. Francis' Hospital, Evanston
*St. Francis' Hospital, Peoria
St. Joseph's Hospital, Chicago
St. Luke's Hospital, Chicago
*St. Mary's Hospital, Cairo
*St. Mary's Hospital, East St. Louis
St. Mary's Hospital, La Salle
St. Mary of Nazareth Hospital, Chicago
*St. Vincent's Hospital, Belleville
South Shore Hospital, Chicago
Swedish Covenant Hospital, Chicago
Wesley Memorial Hospital, Chicago

INDIANA

Indianapolis City Hospital, Indianapolis
Methodist Episcopal Hospital, Indianapolis
Robert W. Long Hospital, Indianapolis
St. Anthony's Hospital, Terre Haute
St. Elizabeth's Hospital, LaFayette

54   *American College of Surgeons*

INDIANA — Continued

St. Joseph's Hospital, Fort Wayne
St. Margaret's Hospital, Hammond
St. Mary's Hospital, Evansville
St. Mary's Mercy Hospital, Gary
St. Vincent's Hospital, Indianapolis

IOWA

Finley Hospital, Dubuque
Iowa Lutheran Hospital, Des Moines
*Iowa Methodist Hospital, Des Moines
Jennie Edmundson Hospital, Council Bluffs
Mercy Hospital, Council Bluffs
Mercy Hospital, Davenport
*Mercy Hospital, Des Moines
St. Francis' Hospital, Waterloo
St. Joseph's Mercy Hospital, Dubuque
St. Joseph's Mercy Hospital, Sioux City
St. Vincent's Hospital, Sioux City
University Hospital, Iowa City

KANSAS

*Bethany Methodist Hospital, Kansas City
St. Francis' Hospital, Wichita
St. Margaret's Hospital, Kansas City

KENTUCKY

Good Samaritan Hospital, Lexington
Louisville City Hospital, Louisville
Norton Memorial Infirmary, Louisville
St. Anthony's Hospital, Louisville
*St. Elizabeth's Hospital, Covington
Sts. Mary and Elizabeth Hospital, Louisville
St. Joseph's Hospital, Lexington
St. Joseph's Infirmary, Louisville

LOUISIANA

Charity Hospital, New Orleans
*Hotel Dieu, New Orleans
St. Francis' Hospital, Monroe
T. E. Schumpert Memorial Hospital, Shreveport
Touro Infirmary, New Orleans

MAINE

Eastern Maine General Hospital, Bangor
*St. Mary's General Hospital, Lewiston

MARYLAND

Bay View City Hospital, Baltimore
Church Home and Infirmary, Baltimore
*Franklin Square Hospital, Baltimore
Hebrew Hospital and Asylum, Baltimore
Hospital for Women of Maryland, Baltimore
Johns Hopkins Hospital, Baltimore
Maryland General Hospital, Baltimore
Mercy Hospital, Baltimore
Morrow Hospital, Baltimore
St. Agnes' Hospital, Baltimore
St. Joseph's Hospital, Baltimore
Union Memorial Hospital, Baltimore
University Hospital, Baltimore

MASSACHUSETTS

Boston City Hospital, Boston
Brockton Hospital, Brockton
*Burbank Hospital, Fitchburg
Cambridge City Hospital, Cambridge
Carney Hospital, Boston
Children's Hospital, Boston
City Hospital, Fall River
*Cooley-Dickinson Hospital, Northampton
Holyoke City Hospital, Holyoke
Lawrence General Hospital, Lawrence
Long Island Hospital, Boston
Lowell Corporation Hospital, Lowell
Lowell General Hospital, Lowell
Lynn Hospital, Lynn
Massachusetts Charitable Eye and Ear Infirmary, Boston
Massachusetts General Hospital, Boston
Massachusetts Homeopathic Hospital, Boston
Memorial Hospital, Worcester
Mercy Hospital, Springfield
New England Hospital for Women and Children, Boston
Newton Hospital, Newton Lower Falls
Peter Bent Brigham Hospital, Boston
Providence Hospital, Holyoke
St. Elizabeth's Hospital, Boston
St. John's Hospital, Lowell

MASSACHUSETTS — Continued
*St. Luke's Hospital, New Bedford
St. Vincent's Hospital, Worcester
Salem Hospital, Salem
Springfield Hospital, Springfield
Union Hospital, Fall River
Worcester City Hospital, Worcester

MICHIGAN

Battle Creek Sanitarium, Battle Creek
Blodgett Memorial Hospital, Grand Rapids
Butterworth Hospital, Grand Rapids
Children's Free Hospital, Detroit
Detroit Receiving Hospital, Detroit
Grace Hospital, Detroit
Harper Hospital, Detroit
Hackley Hospital, Muskegon
Henry Ford Hospital, Detroit
Highland Park General Hospital, Highland Park
House of Providence, Detroit
St. Joseph's Hospital, Ann Arbor
St. Mary's Hospital, Grand Rapids
St. Mary's Hospital, Detroit
University Hospital, Ann Arbor
University of Michigan Homeopathic Hospital, Ann Arbor
Woman's Hospital and Infants' Home, Detroit

MINNESOTA

Bethesda Hospital, St. Paul
City and County Hospital, St. Paul
Colonial Hospital, Rochester
Deaconess Hospital, Minneapolis
*Eitel Hospital, Minneapolis
*Fairview Hospital, Minneapolis
Minneapolis General Hospital, Minneapolis
Mounds Park Sanitarium, St. Paul
St. Joseph's Hospital, St. Paul
*St. Luke's Hospital, St. Paul
St. Mary's Hospital, Duluth
St. Mary's Hospital, Minneapolis
St. Mary's Hospital, Rochester
*St. Paul Hospital, St. Paul
*Swedish Hospital, Minneapolis
University of Minnesota Hospital, Minneapolis
Worrell Hospital, Rochester

MISSISSIPPI
Matty Hersee Hospital, Meridian

MISSOURI
Alexian Brothers' Hospital, St. Louis
Barnes Hospital, St. Louis
Children's Hospital, Kansas City
*Christian Church Hospital, Kansas City
*Evangelical Deaconess Home and Hospital, St. Louis
Jewish Hospital, St. Louis
Kansas City General Hospital, Kansas City
Lutheran Hospital, St. Louis
*Mullanphy Hospital, St. Louis
Research Hospital, Kansas City
St. Anthony's Hospital, St. Louis
St. John's Hospital, St. Louis
St. Joseph's Hospital, Kansas City
St. Louis Children's Hospital, St. Louis
St. Louis City Hospital, St. Louis
St. Luke's Hospital, St. Louis
St. Mary's Hospital, Kansas City
St. Mary's Infirmary, St. Louis

MONTANA
Columbus Hospital, Great Falls
Montana Deaconess Hospital, Great Falls
Murray Hospital, Butte
St. James' Hospital, Butte
St. Patrick's Hospital, Missoula

NEBRASKA
*Nebraska Methodist Hospital, Omaha
*Nebraska Orthopedic Hospital and Home, Lincoln
St. Elizabeth's Hospital, Lincoln
St. Francis' Hospital, Grand Island
St. Joseph's Hospital, Omaha
*St. Mary's Hospital, Columbus
University of Nebraska Hospital, Omaha

NEW HAMPSHIRE
St. Joseph's Hospital, Nashua

NEW JERSEY

*Alexian Brothers' Hospital, Elizabeth
Atlantic City Hospital, Atlantic City
Bayonne Hospital and Dispensary, Bayonne
Christ Hospital, Jersey City
Cooper Hospital, Camden
Elizabeth General Hospital, Elizabeth
Hackensack Hospital, Hackensack
Jersey City Hospital, Jersey City
Mercer Hospital, Trenton
Monmouth Memorial Hospital, Long Branch
Morristown Memorial Hospital, Morristown
Mountainside Hospital, Montclair
Muhlenberg Hospital, Plainfield
Newark Beth Israel Hospital, Newark
Newark City Hospital, Newark
Newark Memorial Hospital, Newark
Orange Memorial Hospital, Orange
Passaic General Hospital, Passaic
Paterson General Hospital, Paterson
St. Elizabeth's Hospital, Elizabeth
St. Francis' Hospital, Trenton
*St. Joseph's Hospital, Paterson
*St. Mary's Hospital, Hoboken
*St. Michael's Hospital, Newark

NEW YORK

Albany Hospital, Albany
Bellevue Hospital, New York
Beth Israel Hospital, New York
Beth Moses Hospital, Brooklyn
*Binghamton City Hospital, Binghamton
Broad Street Hospital, New York
Brooklyn Hospital, Brooklyn
Brownsville and East New York Hospital, Brooklyn
Buffalo City Hospital, Buffalo
Buffalo General Hospital, Buffalo
*Buffalo Homeopathic Hospital, Buffalo
*Buffalo Hospital of Sisters of Charity, Buffalo
*Bushwick Hospital, Brooklyn
Carson C. Peck Memorial Hospital, Brooklyn
*Children's Hospital, Buffalo
Clifton Springs Sanitarium, Clifton Springs
Community Hospital, New York

NEW YORK — Continued

Coney Island Hospital, Brooklyn
*Crouse-Irving Hospital, Syracuse
Cumberland Street Hospital, Brooklyn
Ellis Hospital, Schenectady
*Flower Hospital, New York
Flushing Hospital and Dispensary, Flushing
Fordham Hospital, New York
French Benevolent Hospital, New York
*Good Shepherd Hospital, Syracuse
Gouverneur Hospital, New York
Greenpoint Hospital, Brooklyn
Hahnemann Hospital, New York
Harlem Hospital, New York
Highland Hospital of Rochester, Rochester
Holy Family Hospital, Brooklyn
Homeopathic Hospital, Albany
Jewish Hospital, Brooklyn
Kings County Hospital, Brooklyn
Lebanon Hospital, New York
*Lenox Hill Hospital, New York
Lincoln Hospital, New York
Long Island College Hospital, Brooklyn
*Manhattan Eye and Ear Hospital, New York
Memorial Hospital, New York
Methodist Episcopal Hospital, Brooklyn
Metropolitan Hospital, New York
Misericordia Hospital, New York
Mount St. Mary's Hospital, Niagara Falls
Mount Sinai Hospital, New York
*Mount Vernon Hospital, Mount Vernon
New York City Hospital, Blackwell's Island, New York
*New York Eye and Ear Infirmary, New York
*New York Foundling Home, New York
New York Hospital, New York
New York Infirmary for Women and Children, New York
New York Nursery and Children's Hospital, New York
New York Orthopedic Hospital, New York
New York Post-Graduate Hospital, New York
New York Hospital for Ruptured and Crippled, New York
New York Skin and Cancer Hospital, New York
*New York State Hospital for Crippled Children, West Haver-
straw
*Niagara Falls Memorial Hospital, Niagara Falls

NEW YORK — Continued

Norwegian Lutheran Deaconess Hospital, Brooklyn
*Oneida County Hospital, Rome
Presbyterian Hospital, New York
Rochester General Hospital, Rochester
Rochester Homeopathic Hospital, Rochester
Roosevelt Hospital, New York
St. Catherine's Hospital, Brooklyn
St. Francis' Hospital, New York
St. John's Brooklyn Hospital, Brooklyn
St. John's Hospital, Long Island
St. John's Riverside Hospital, Yonkers
*St. Joseph's Hospital, Syracuse
St. Luke's Hospital, New York
St. Mark's Hospital, New York
St. Mary's Free Hospital for Children, New York
St. Mary's Hospital, Brooklyn
*St. Mary's Hospital, Rochester
*St. Peter's Hospital, Albany
*St. Peter's Hospital, Brooklyn
St. Vincent's Hospital, New York
Samaritan Hospital, Troy
Sloane Hospital for Women, New York
Staten Island Hospital, Tompkinsville
Syracuse Memorial Hospital, Syracuse
Troy Hospital, Troy
Woman's Hospital, New York
Wyckoff Heights Hospital, Brooklyn
*Yonkers Homeopathic Hospital, Yonkers

NORTH CAROLINA

*Watts Hospital, West Durham

NORTH DAKOTA

Bismarck Evangelical Deaconess Hospital, Bismarck
*Grand Forks Deaconess Hospital, Grand Forks
St. Alexius' Hospital, Bismarck
St. John's Hospital, Fargo
St. Luke's Hospital, Fargo

OHIO

*Aultman Hospital, Canton
Bethesda Hospital, Cincinnati
Christ Hospital, Cincinnati

OHIO — Continued

Cincinnati General Hospital, Cincinnati
City Hospital of Akron, Akron
Cleveland City Hospital, Cleveland
Good Samaritan Hospital, Cincinnati
Good Samaritan Hospital, Zanesville
Grant Hospital, Columbus
Hawkes Hospital of Mount Carmel, Columbus
Jewish Hospital, Cincinnati
Lakeside Hospital, Cleveland
Miami Valley Hospital, Dayton
*Mercy Hospital, Hamilton
Mount Sinai Hospital, Cleveland
*Peoples Hospital, Akron
*Protestant Hospital Association, Columbus
St. Alexis' Hospital, Cleveland
St. Elizabeth's Hospital, Youngstown
St. Francis' Hospital, Columbus
St. John's Hospital, Cleveland
*St. Luke's Hospital, Cleveland
St. Mary's Hospital, Cincinnati
St. Rita's Hospital, Lima
St. Vincent's Hospital, Cleveland
St. Vincent's Hospital, Toledo
Springfield City Hospital, Springfield
Toledo Hospital, Toledo
*Youngstown Hospital, Youngstown

OKLAHOMA

St. Anthony's Hospital, Oklahoma
State University Hospital, Oklahoma

OREGON

Emanuel Hospital, Portland
*Good Samaritan Hospital, Portland
St. Vincent's Hospital, Portland

PENNSYLVANIA

Allegheny General Hospital, Pittsburgh
Allentown Hospital, Allentown
Altoona Hospital, Altoona
Braddock General Hospital, Braddock
Chester County Hospital, West Chester
Chester Hospital, Chester

PENNSYLVANIA — Continued

Children's Homeopathic Hospital, Philadelphia
Clearfield Hospital, Clearfield
Columbia Hospital, Pittsburgh
Conemaugh Valley Memorial Hospital, Johnstown
Easton Hospital, Easton
Elizabeth Steel Magee Hospital, Pittsburgh
Frankford Hospital, Philadelphia
George F. Geisinger Hospital, Danville
Germantown Dispensary and Hospital, Philadelphia
Hahnemann Medical College Hospital, Philadelphia
*Hamot Hospital, Erie
Harrisburg Hospital, Harrisburg
Homeopathic Medical and Surgical Hospital, Pittsburgh
Hospital of the Protestant Episcopal Church, Philadelphia
Hospital of the University of Pennsylvania, Philadelphia
Hospital of the Women's Medical College, Philadelphia
Jefferson Medical College Hospital, Philadelphia
Jewish Hospital, Philadelphia
Lancaster General Hospital, Lancaster
Lankenau Hospital, Philadelphia
*Medical, Surgical, and Maternity Hospital of the Women's
    Homeopathic Association, Philadelphia
Medico-Chirurgical Hospital, Philadelphia
*Memorial Hospital, Philadelphia
Mercy Hospital, Johnstown
Mercy Hospital, Pittsburgh
Mercy Hospital, Wilkes-Barre
Methodist Episcopal Hospital, Philadelphia
Misericordia Hospital, Philadelphia
Moses Taylor Hospital, Scranton
Passavant Hospital, Pittsburgh
Pennsylvania Hospital, Philadelphia
Philadelphia General Hospital, Philadelphia
Philadelphia Polyclinic Hospital, Philadelphia
Pittsburgh Hospital, Pittsburgh
Pottsville Hospital, Pottsville
Presbyterian Hospital, Philadelphia
Presbyterian Hospital, Pittsburgh
Reading Hospital, Reading
Robert Packer Hospital, Sayre
Sacred Heart Hospital, Allentown
St. Agnes' Hospital, Philadelphia
St. Francis' Hospital, Pittsburgh

PENNSYLVANIA — Continued

*St. John's General Hospital, Pittsburgh
*St. Joseph's Hospital, Lancaster
St. Joseph's Hospital, Philadelphia
St. Joseph's Hospital, Pittsburgh
St. Luke's Hospital, South Bethlehem
St. Margaret's Hospital, Pittsburgh
St. Mary's Hospital, Philadelphia
St. Vincent's Hospital, Erie
Samaritan Hospital, Philadelphia
South Side Hospital, Pittsburgh
*State Hospital for Injured Persons, Ashland
State Hospital of the Middle Coal Fields, Hazelton
*State Hospital of the Northern Anthracite Coal Regions,
    Scranton
*Western Pennsylvania Hospital, Pittsburgh
Wilkes-Barre City Hospital, Wilkes-Barre
Wills Hospital, Philadelphia
Woman's Hospital, Philadelphia
York Hospital and Dispensary, York

RHODE ISLAND

Rhode Island Hospital, Providence
St. Joseph's Hospital, Providence

SOUTH CAROLINA

Chick Springs Sanitarium, Chick Springs
Florence Infirmary, Florence
Roper Hospital, Charleston

SOUTH DAKOTA

McKennan Hospital, Sioux Falls
*St. Luke's Hospital, Aberdeen

TENNESSEE

Baptist Memorial Hospital, Memphis
Erlanger Hospital, Chattanooga
Memphis General Hospital, Memphis
*Nashville City Hospital, Nashville
St. Joseph's Hospital, Memphis
St. Thomas' Hospital, Nashville

TEXAS

Baptist Sanitarium and Hospital, Houston
Baylor Hospital, Dallas
John Sealy Hospital, Galveston
*Parkland Hospital, Dallas
Providence Hospital, Waco
Robert B. Green Memorial Hospital, San Antonio
St. Joseph's Infirmary, Fort Worth
St. Joseph's Infirmary, Houston
St. Mary's Infirmary, Galveston
St. Paul's Sanitarium, Dallas
Santa Rosa Infirmary, San Antonio
Temple Sanitarium, Temple

UTAH

*Doctor W. H. Groves Latter Day Saints Hospital, Salt Lake
  City
Holy Cross Hospital, Salt Lake City
St. Mark's Hospital, Salt Lake City

VERMONT

Mary Fletcher Hospital, Burlington

VIRGINIA

Hospital Division of the Medical College of Virginia, Richmond
Norfolk Protestant Hospital, Norfolk
St. Vincent's Hospital, Norfolk
University of Virginia Hospital, Charlottesville
Virginia Hospital, Richmond

WASHINGTON

Children's Orthopedic Hospital, Seattle
Columbus Sanitarium, Seattle
*Northern Pacific Hospital, Tacoma
Providence Hospital, Seattle
Sacred Heart Hospital, Spokane
St. Elizabeth's Hospital, North Yakima
St. Joseph's Hospital, Tacoma
St. Luke's Hospital, Spokane
Seattle City Hospital, Seattle
Seattle General Hospital, Seattle
Swedish Hospital, Seattle
Tacoma General Hospital, Tacoma

WEST VIRGINIA

*Charleston General Hospital, Charleston
Kessler-Hatfield Hospital, Huntington
Ohio Valley General Hospital, Wheeling
St. Mary's Hospital, Clarksburg
Sheltering Arms Hospital, Hansford
*Wheeling Hospital, Wheeling

WISCONSIN

LaCrosse Lutheran Hospital, LaCrosse
Luther Hospital, Eau Claire
Madison General Hospital, Madison
Milwaukee County Hospital, Milwaukee
Milwaukee Hospital, Milwaukee
Mount Sinai Hospital, Milwaukee
Sacred Heart Hospital, Eau Claire
St. Agnes' Hospital, Fond du Lac
St. Francis' Hospital, LaCrosse
St. Joseph's Hospital, Marshfield
St. Joseph's Hospital, Milwaukee
St. Mary's Hospital, Green Bay
*St. Mary's Hospital, Superior
Trinity Hospital, Milwaukee

CANADA

ALBERTA

General Hospital, Calgary
*General Hospital, Edmonton
General Hospital, Medicine Hat
Holy Cross Hospital, Calgary
*Royal Alexandra Hospital, Edmonton

BRITISH COLUMBIA

Provincial Royal Jubilee Hospital, Victoria
Royal Columbia Hospital, New Westminster
Royal Inland Hospital, Kamloops
St. Joseph's Hospital, Victoria
St. Paul's Hospital, Vancouver
Vancouver General Hospital, Vancouver

MANITOBA

Children's Hospital, Winnipeg
General Hospital, Winnipeg
Misericordia Hospital, Winnipeg
St. Boniface Hospital, St. Boniface

NEW BRUNSWICK

General Hospital, St. John

NOVA SCOTIA

St. Joseph's Hospital, Glace Bay
Victoria General Hospital, Halifax

ONTARIO

*General Hospital, Hamilton
General Hospital, Kingston
Grace Hospital, Toronto
Hospital for Sick Children, Toronto
Hotel Dieu, Kingston
St. Michael's Hospital, Toronto
*Toronto General Hospital, Toronto
Victoria General Hospital, London

QUEBEC

Children's Memorial Hospital, Montreal
Hotel Dieu, Montreal
Jeffrey Hale Hospital, Quebec
Montreal General Hospital, Montreal
Notre Dame Hospital, Montreal
Royal Victoria Hospital, Montreal
*Western Hospital, Montreal

SASKATCHEWAN

City Hospital, Saskatoon
Grey Nun's Hospital, Regina
Regina General Hospital, Regina
St. Paul's Hospital, Saskatoon

THE BY-LAWS

I. NAME. The name of the corporation shall be the American College of Surgeons.

II. OBJECT. The object of the College shall be to elevate the standard of surgery, to establish a standard of competency and of character for practictioners of surgery, to provide a method of granting Fellowships in the organization, and to educate the public and the profession to understand that the practice of surgery calls for special training and that the surgeon elected to Fellowship in this College has had such training and is properly qualified to practice surgery.

III. THE COLLEGE. 1. The College shall consist of all members of the corporation. Such members are to be designated as Fellows. The College shall vest the general management of the corporation in a Board of Governors. The Board of Governors shall, in turn, vest the details of the management in a board of trustees to be known as the Board of Regents.

2. The College shall hold an annual meeting on the day and at the place selected for the annual meeting of the Board of Governors.

IV. BOARD OF GOVERNORS. 1. The original Board of Governors shall consist of the surgeons invited by the Organization Committee to serve as Founders of the College, who have qualified as Fellows. The members of this first Board of Governors shall also be known as the Founders of the American College of Surgeons.

2. The original Board of Governors shall be divided by lot into three classes to serve one, two, and three years, respectively. At the annual meeting in 1914, and at the annual meeting in each year thereafter, the Fellows of the College shall elect (in a manner to be determined by the Board of Regents) fifty surgeons from among the Fellows of the College to membership on the Board of Governors, each to serve for a term of three years; thirty of these members

are to be elected from a list of nominations, consisting of three members, each nominated by the following sixteen surgical associations and societies of North America, including one each from the United States Army and from the United States Navy:

1. American Surgical Association.
2. Surgical Section of the American Medical Association.
3. Section on Obstetrics, Gynecology, and Abdominal Surgery of the American Medical Association.
4. General Surgical Division of the Clinical Congress of the American College of Surgeons.
5. Division of Surgical Specialties of the Clinical Congress of the American College of Surgeons.
6. American Gynecological Society.
7. Southern Surgical Association.
8. Western Surgical Association.
9. Section on Surgery of the Canadian Medical Association.
10. American Association of Obstetricians and Gynecologists.
11. American Orthopedic Association.
12. American Association of Genito-Urinary Surgeons.
13. American Laryngological Association.
14. American Ophthalmological Society.
15. American Otological Society.
16. American Institute of Homeopathy.

Twenty members shall be elected at large to represent surgeons of North America not affiliated with the above societies or associations. In case of failure of any of the above-named organizations to make its quota of nominations, or in case of duplication of nominees, the Board of Regents shall nominate members from among the Fellows at large for the vacancies so caused in the list of nominees. The Board of Regents shall in the same manner fill all vacancies in the current membership of the Board of Governors due to death, resignation, or other causes.

3. The Board of Governors shall at its first meeting elect from among its own membership fifteen who shall be members of the Board of Regents; this group shall be divided into three classes of five members each, whose terms of office shall expire in one, two,

and three years, respectively. As the term of service in each class expires, their successors shall be elected, each for a term of three years, by the Board of Governors in a manner to be determined by the Board of Regents. Not more than four of each class shall be selected from one country. In event of death or resignation of any member of the Board of Regents, his successor shall be elected at the next regular or special meeting of the Board of Governors, but the Board of Regents may appoint a member of the Board of Governors to serve as Regent until this election takes place.

4. The Board of Governors shall meet in executive session annually for the transaction of business, which business shall include the election of members of the Board of Regents and other routine business which may be brought before it by the corporation or the Board of Regents. Such meetings shall be called by the Director General, at the direction of the Board of Regents. Special meetings of the Board of Governors may be called by the Director General at any other time at the request of the Board of Regents. Members of the Board of Governors shall be expected to attend other formal meetings and convocations called by the Board of Regents for the purpose of conferring Fellowships and for the transaction of other business.

5. Fifty members of the Board of Governors shall constitute a quorum for the transaction of business.

V. OFFICERS. 1. The officers of the College shall be a President of the College, a First Vice-President, a Second Vice-President, a Director General, and a Treasurer.

2. The President, the First Vice-President, and the Second Vice-President shall be elected each for a term of one year or until his successor is elected by the Fellows of the College at their annual meeting. The Director General and the Treasurer shall be appointed by the Board of Regents. The Treasurer shall be appointed for a term of one year or until his successor is elected; the Director General shall hold office during the pleasure of the Board.

3. The President of the College shall preside at all regular

and special meetings of the College and of the Board of Governors, and at all Convocations for the conferring of Fellowships.

4. The First Vice-President shall preside at all meetings of the College in the absence of the President, and in the event of the death or resignation of the President shall assume the duties of that officer.

5. The Second Vice-President shall preside at all meetings of the College in the absence of the President and of the First Vice-President, and in the event of the death or resignation of these two officers shall assume the duties of the President.

6. The Director General shall be the chief executive officer of the College. Under the direction of the Board of Regents he shall have supervision of all activities and business affairs of the College, including the direction of the general executive office; he shall audit all expenditure and disbursement of funds of the College; he shall have charge of the Convocations and of the Clinical Congress of the College; he shall mail to the proper addresses all notices of all regular and special meetings of the College; he shall issue at stated intervals the Year Book of the College; he shall attend all meetings of the Board of Regents.

7. The Treasurer shall receive all funds of the College and disburse the same on checks, signed by him and countersigned by the Director General. He shall make a report in writing to the Board of Regents at each meeting of that Board of the moneys received and expended, and shall furnish a detailed statement of the financial condition of the College at each annual meeting of the Board of Regents. The Treasurer shall furnish a bond to the Board of Regents for the faithful performance of his trust.

VI. BOARD OF REGENTS. 1. The Board of Regents shall consist of sixteen members, fifteen of whom shall be elected from among the Fellows by the Board of Governors in a manner to be determined by the Board of Regents. One member shall be elected by the Fellows of the College at their annual meeting as hereinafter provided, the Fellow thus elected to membership in the Board of Regents to be President of the College.

2. The Chairman of the Board of Regents shall be elected from among the members of the Board of Regents for a term of one year and shall preside at all meetings of the Board. In the event of his death or resignation, the office shall be filled by election at the next meeting of the Board.

3. The Director General of the corporation shall be the Secretary of the Board of Regents.

4. The duties of the Board of Regents shall be those ordinarily performed by a governing board, namely: To transact all detail business devolving upon the Board of Governors in carrying out the object of the organization; to regulate and to conserve the property interests of the College; to adopt rules and regulations for the admission of Fellows; to fix initial fees and annual dues of Fellowship; to create, appoint, and direct all standing committees; to elect Fellows to the College; to call all meetings of the corporation not already provided for; to arrange Convocations or other meetings for the conferring of Fellowships; to transact all business not otherwise provided for that may pertain to the organization.

5. Nine members of the Board of Regents shall constitute a quorum for the transaction of business.

6. Regular meetings of the Board of Regents shall occur once in twelve months at the call of the Director General. Special meetings may be convened at any time by the Director General, or on a request to him made in writing and signed by thirty members of the Board of Governors, or by nine members of the Board of Regents.

VII. EXECUTIVE COMMITTEE. 1. There shall be an Executive Committee, consisting, first, of the President of the College, of the Director General, and of the Treasurer; and second, of four other Regents elected by the Board of Regents to serve for one year and who shall be eligible for re-election.

2. During the intervals between the meetings of the Boards, the Executive Committee shall exercise all the powers of the Board of Regents in the management and direction of the business and the conduct of the affairs of the corporation, except that it shall not

have power to elect Fellows, or to regulate initial fees or annual dues of Fellowship. It shall keep a record of its proceedings and report the same to the Board of Regents at the next succeeding meeting for its approval. Whenever any vacancy shall occur in the Executive Committee, or in any office of the corporation, by death, resignation, or otherwise, which is not already provided for, it shall be filled by appointment by the Executive Committee for the remainder of the current corporate year. It may hold its meetings at such place or places as it may from time to time determine. A majority of the Executive Committee shall constitute a quorum for the transaction of business.

VIII. FELLOWS. 1. The Fellows of the College shall be graduates in medicine who are licensed to practice medicine in their respective states and provinces, or medical officers of the federal services who have made an application for Fellowship (such application being endorsed by three Fellows of the College, one of whom shall be a member of the Board of Governors), who meet the qualification requirements that shall from time to time be established by the Board of Regents, and who shall be elected to Fellowship by the Board of Regents on recommendation of the Committee on Credentials, and who shall have signed the roll.

2. Each individual elected to Fellowship in the College shall be designated as a Fellow of the American College of Surgeons and shall be authorized and encouraged to use the letters F.A.C.S. after his name on professional cards, in professional directories, and in articles published in surgical literature.

IX. PUBLICATIONS. The Board of Regents shall issue each year a directory containing the names and addresses of the Fellows of the American College of Surgeons arranged by states, provinces, and colonies.

X. Any Fellow of the College may be expelled for conduct which, in the opinion of the Board of Regents, is derogatory to the dignity of the College or inconsistent with its purposes. Such expulsion must be voted by a majority vote of the whole Board of Regents at any meeting, at which meeting the Fellow against whom charges are made shall be invited to be present, and may appear or may be represented, in a manner to be determined by the Board of Regents.

XI. These by-laws may be amended by a majority vote of those present at any regular or special meeting of the Board of Governors, or at a meeting called for the purpose on request made in writing by a hundred members of the Corporation, provided that such proposed amendments are included in the call of the meeting at which such action is contemplated.

XII. The College shall hold an annual session of about one week in length at such place and time as may be determined by the Board of Regents which may include:

1. The Clinical Congress of the American College of Surgeons consisting of (a) scientific and literary papers concerning or relating to the art and science of surgery; (b) surgical and diagnostic clinics.

2. Annual meeting of the Fellows of the College, as provided by Article III, Section 2.

3. Annual meeting of the Board of Governors of the College, as provided in Article IV, Section 4.

4. Convocation of the College at which occasion candidates for Fellowship may be admitted to Fellowship in the College.

INCORPORATION

STATE OF ILLINOIS

Department of State

CORNELIUS J. DOYLE, Secretary of State

To All to Whom these Presents Shall Come, Greeting:

WHEREAS, a CERTIFICATE, duly signed and acknowledged, has been filed in the Office of the Secretary of State, on the 25th day of November, A. D. 1921, for the organization of the

AMERICAN COLLEGE OF SURGEONS

under and in accordance with the provisions of "AN ACT CONCERNING CORPORATIONS" approved April 18, 1872, and in force July 1, 1872, and all acts amendatory thereof, a copy of which certificate is hereto attached; Now Therefore, I, CORNELIUS J. DOYLE, Secretary of State, of the State of Illinois, by virtue of the powers and duties vested in me by law, do hereby certify that the said

AMERICAN COLLEGE OF SURGEONS

is a legally organized Corporation under the laws of this State.

IN TESTIMONY WHEREOF, I hereto set my hand and cause to be affixed the great Seal of State. Done at the City of Springfield this 25th day of November, A. D. 1912, and of the Independence of the United States the one hundred and thirty-seventh.

[SEAL]   (Signed) C. J. DOYLE, Secretary of State.

HONORARY FELLOWS

CHICAGO, NOVEMBER 13, 1913

SIR RICKMAN JOHN GODLEE . . . . London
WILLIAM STEWART HALSTEAD . . . . Baltimore
WILLIAM WILLIAMS KEEN . . . . Philadelphia
JOHN COLLINS WARREN . . . . Boston
ROBERT F. WEIR . . . . New York

PHILADELPHIA, JUNE 22, 1914

*THOMAS ADDIS EMMET . . . . New York
FRANCIS J. SHEPHERD . . . . Montreal
EDMOND SOUCHON . . . . New Orleans

WASHINGTON, NOVEMBER 16, 1914

*DUDLEY P. ALLEN . . . . Cleveland
*WILLIAM C. GORGAS . . . . Washington
LEWIS STEPHEN PILCHER . . . . Brooklyn
SIR THOMAS GEORGE RODDICK . . . . Montreal
*J. WILLIAM WHITE . . . . Philadelphia

BOSTON, OCTOBER 29, 1915

*DAVID WILLIAM CHEEVER . . . . Boston
SIR WILFRED THOMASON GRENFELL . . . . Labrador
STEPHEN SMITH . . . . New York
*LOUIS McLANE TIFFANY . . . . Baltimore

PHILADELPHIA, OCTOBER 27, 1916

ERNEST SIDNEY LEWIS . . . . New Orleans

CHICAGO, OCTOBER 26, 1917

RUPERT BLUE . . . . Washington
WILLIAM C. BRAISTED . . . . Washington
CHARLES U. DERCLE . . . . Paris
SIR THOMAS HERBERT JOHN GOODWIN . . . . London
SIR BERKELEY MOYNIHAN . . . . Leeds

*Deceased

NEW YORK, NOVEMBER 6, 1918

RAFFAELE BASTIANELLI	Rome
PIERRE DUVAL	Paris
GEORGE ERNEST GASK	London
MERRITTE W. IRELAND	Washington
SIR THOMAS MYLES	Dublin
GEORGE GREY TURNER	Newcastle-on-Tyne

NEW YORK, OCTOBER 24, 1919

SIR ANTHONY ALFRED BOWLBY	London
IRVING HEWARD CAMERON	Toronto
SIR ROBERT JONES	Liverpool
THEODORE TUFFIER	Paris

MONTREAL, OCTOBER 15, 1920

ALBERT CARLESS	London
JOHN C. FOTHERINGHAM	Toronto
WILLIAM GARDNER	Montreal
GUY CARLETON JONES	Ottawa
JOHN STEWART	Halifax
SIR WILLIAM TAYLOR	Dublin

PHILADELPHIA, OCTOBER 28, 1921

MIGUEL H. ALCIVAR	Guayaquil
JOAÔ ALVES DE LIMA	Sao Paulo
JEAN F. DE QUERVAIN	Berne
GUILLERMO GASTAÑETA	Lima
H. C. JACOBAEUS	Stockholm
JOSE DE MENDONCA	Rio de Janeiro
JAN SCHOEMAKER	The Hague
SIR HAROLD J. STILES	Edinburgh
EDWARD RHODES STITT	Washington
SIR ROBERT WOODS	Dublin

FELLOWS OF THE COLLEGE

LISTED BY STATES, PROVINCES, AND CITIES
WITH SPECIALTIES INDICATED

UNITED STATES OF AMERICA

ALABAMA

ANDALUSIA

Louis Edward Broughton, 50 East Three Notch Street . *Surgery*

BESSEMER

R. W. Waldrop, 306 Realty Building . . . . . . *Surgery*

BIRMINGHAM

Samuel R. Benedict, Empire Building . . . . . . *Surgery*

Kosciusko W. Constantine, Empire Building . . *Ophthalmology*

J. D. S. Davis, 2029 Avenue G . . . . *Surgery*

W. Earle Drennen, 519 American Trust Building . . *Surgery*

William G. Harrison, 903 Empire Building *Rhinol., Oto-Laryngology*

Howell T. Heflin, 407 Empire Building . . *Surgery, Obstetrics*

Wyatt Heflin, 3216 Cliff Road . . . . *Surgery*

Edgar Poe Hogan, 412 Empire Building . . . . . *Surgery*

Walter Clinton Jones, St. Vincent's Hospital . . . . *Surgery*

William Mudd Jordan, 910 Empire Building . . . . *Surgery*

Samuel L. Ledbetter, Jr., 516 Empire Building . . . *Surgery*

Joseph Leland, 603 First National Bank Building . . *Surgery*

Thomas V. Magruder, Jefferson County Bank Building . *Surgery*

James Monroe Mason, Jefferson County Bank Building . *Surgery*

Lewis Coleman Morris, 1203 Empire Building . . . *Surgery*

Lloyd Noland, Employes' Hospital . . . . . . *Surgery*

Mack Rogers, 2118 Avenue H . . . . *Surgery*

Edmund Winchester Rucker, Jr., Woodward Building
Rhinol., Oto-Laryngology

Walter Francis Scott, 1301 Empire Building . . . . *Urology*

Courtney W. Shropshire, 327 First National Bank
Building . . . . *Urology*

77

ALABAMA — Continued
BIRMINGHAM — Continued

E. P. Solomon, 4 Fairview Avenue	*Surgery*
Dyer Findley Talley, 1808 7th Avenue, North . . .	*Surgery*
Charles Whelan, 438 First National Bank Building . .	*Surgery*
William Hinton Wilder, Woodward Building	*Surgery*
Cunningham Wilson, Jefferson County Bank Building .	*Surgery*

CHICKASAW

Thomas I. Conwell	*Surgery*

DOTHAN

Alfred Smith Frasier, Young Building	*Surgery*
Earle F. Moody, Young Building	*Surgery*

GREENVILLE

Andrew Lee Stabler, 103 West Commerce Street . .	*Surgery*

MOBILE

Paul Jerome Moeris Acker, 153 Government Street . .	*Surgery*
Herbert Phalon Cole, 901 Van Antwerp Building . .	*Surgery*
William Thomas Henderson, 259 St. Francis Street . .	*Surgery*
William R. Jackson, 164 St. Michael Street	*Surgery*
William McDowell Mastin, Conti and Joachim Streets .	*Surgery*
Alfred Edward Maumenee, 209 Van Antwerp Building	
Ophth., Rhinol., Oto-Laryngology	
Jesse Ullman Reaves, 305 Van Antwerp Building . .	*Urology*
John Osgood Rush, 706 Van Antwerp Building . . .	*Urology*
Gilman Joseph Winthrop, Van Antwerp Building . .	*Surgery*

MONTGOMERY

J. Norment Baker, Bell Building	*Surgery*
John H. Blue, Bell Building	*Surgery*
L. L. Hill, 422 South Perry Street	*Surgery*
Robert Sommerville Hill, 21 South Perry Street . . .	*Surgery*
Paul Stearns Mertins, 1115 Bell Building	
Ophth., Rhinol., Oto-Laryngology	
Henry Stanford Persons, 21 South Perry Street	
Ophth., Rhinol., Oto-Laryngology	
Charles A. Thigpen, First National Bank Building *Ophthalmology*	

OPELIKA

Jesse G. Palmer, 709 Avenue A	*Surgery*

PRATTVILLE

Malcolm Daniel Smith	*Surgery*

ALABAMA — Continued

SELMA

Francis Goodwin DuBose, 400 Lauderdale Street . . *Surgery*
John Neilson Furniss, 100 Church Street . . . . . *Surgery*
William Wade Harper, 201 Broad Street . . . . . *Surgery*
James Kenan, 120 Broad Street . . . . *Surgery*
Samuel Kirkpatrick, Parish Building . . *Ophth., Oto-Laryngology*

WAVERLY

Leckinski Ware Spratling . . . . *Surgery*

ARIZONA

BISBEE

George A. Bridge . . . . *Surgery*
William M. Randolph, Medigovich Building . . . . *Surgery*

DOUGLAS

Edward William Adamson . . . . *Surgery*
Harry S. McGee, 745 9th Street . . . . *Surgery*
Frederick T. Wright, 636 10th Street . . . . . . *Surgery*

GLOBE

Clarence Gunter, Amster Building . . . . *Surgery*
William A. Holt, 167 Mesquite Street . . . . . . *Surgery*
Roderick D. Kennedy . . . . *Orthopedic Surgery*

HAYDEN

Fitz Randolph Winslow, Hayden Hospital . . . . *Surgery*

MIAMI

John Elmer Bacon . . . . *Surgery*

MORENCI

Turner B. Smith . . . . *Surgery*

PHOENIX

Ancil Martin, 207 Goodrich Building . . . . *Ophth., Otology*
John J. McLoone, 611 Heard Building
Ophth., Rhinol., Oto-Laryngology
E. Payne Palmer, 305 Goodrich Building . . . . . *Surgery*
William A. Schwartz, 207 Goodrich Building
Ophth., Oto-Laryngology
Willard Wallace Smith, 805 North 4th Avenue . . . *Surgery*
William O. Sweek, 404 Heard Building . . . . . *Surgery*
Alexander Mackenzie Tuthill, 416 Goodrich Building . *Surgery*
Winfred Wylie . . . . *Surgery*

ARIZONA — Continued

PRESCOTT

 Charles R. K. Swetnam . . . . . *Rhinol., Oto-Laryngology*
 Clarence Edgar Yount, 214 South Mt. Vernon Street . *Surgery*

TUCSON

 Joel I. Butler, 123 South Stone Avenue . *Genito-Urinary Surgery*
 Meade Clyne, 123 South Stone Avenue . . . . *Surgery*
 George E. Dodge, 108 North Stone Avenue . . . *Surgery*

ARKANSAS

BATESVILLE

 R. C. Dorr . . . . *Surgery*

BENTONVILLE

 Charles Hastings Cargile, 212 West 12th Street . . . *Surgery*

CONWAY

 George Snider Brown, Front Street . . . . . *Surgery*

DERMOTT

 Edward E. Barlow, 101 Iowa Street . . . . . *Surgery*

FAYETTEVILLE

 Edward F. Ellis, 104 North College Avenue . . . *Surgery*
 Andrew S. Gregg, First National Bank Building . . . *Surgery*

FORT SMITH

 W. R. Brooksher, First National Bank Building . . . *Surgery*
 St. Cloud Cooper, 604 First National Bank Building . *Surgery*
 James A. Foltz, Merchants National Bank Building . *Surgery*
 Herbert Moulton, Merchants National Bank Building
           Ophth., Oto-Laryngology
 Jefferson D. Southard, 101 North 6th Street . . . *Surgery*

HOT SPRINGS

 Howard Paxton Collings, Dugan-Stuart Building
           Genito-Urinary Surgery
 William V. Laws, Dugan-Stuart Building . . . . *Surgery*
 John F. Rowland, Thompson Building . . . . *Surgery*
 Zuber Nathaniel Short, Dugan-Stuart Building
        Ophth., Rhinol., Oto-Laryngology
 Albert Henry Tribble, 340 Central Avenue . . . *Surgery*

JONESBORO

 Homer A. Stroud, 506 Main Street . . . . . *Surgery*

ARKANSAS — Continued

LITTLE ROCK

Rupert Mitchum Blakely, 426 Exchange Bank Building *Surgery*
Robert Caldwell, Exchange Bank Building
Ophth., Rhinol., Oto-Laryngology
Dewell Gann, Jr., 315 Boyle Building . . . . . . *Surgery*
Mahlon D. Ogden, 900 Scott Street . . . . . . *Surgery*
James I. Scarborough, 900 Scott Street . . . . . *Surgery*
Wells Ferrin Smith, Donaghey Building . . . . . *Surgery*
William A. Snodgrass, Donaghey Building . . . . *Surgery*
Frank Vinsonhaler, Urquhart Building
Ophth., Rhinol., Oto-Laryngology
A. Watkins, 513 Donaghey Building . . . . . . *Surgery*

PARIS

John James Smith . . . . *Surgery*

PINE BLUFF

J. S. Jenkins, 508 Citizens Bank Building . . *Orthopedic Surgery*
Arthur Clifford Jordan, 122½ Main Street . . . . *Surgery*
J. William Scales, 204½ Main Street
Ophth., Rhinol., Oto-Laryngology

PRAIRIE GROVE

Will Hugh Mock, Neal Street . . . . *Surgery*

ROGERS

Charles Forrest Perkins . . . . *Surgery*

TEXARKANA

Archibald Eastwood Chace, 1404 Dudley Avenue . . *Surgery*
John Richard Dale, 6th and Beech Streets . . . . *Surgery*
Theron Earle Fuller, Texarkana National Bank Building
Ophth., Rhinol., Oto-Laryngology
Thomas F. Kittrell, 308 State National Bank Building . *Surgery*
Robert Howell T. Mann, State National Bank Building
Ophth., Rhinol., Oto-Laryngology
H. H. Smiley, State Bank Building . . . . . . *Surgery*

CALIFORNIA

ANAHEIM

A. H. Galvin, 117 North Claudina Street . . *Orthopedic Surgery*

BAKERSFIELD

Frank Joseph Gundry, Hopkins Building . . . . . *Surgery*

CALIFORNIA — Continued

BANNING

    John C. King, Livingston Avenue . . . . *Surgery*

BERKELEY

    Vard H. Hulen, Berkeley Bank Building . . . *Ophthalmology*
    Robert T. Legge, University of California Infirmary . *Surgery*
    John Sayre Marshall, 2521 Durant Avenue . . . *Oral Surgery*

BURBANK

    Elmer H. Thompson, 102½ East San Fernando Road . *Surgery*

CHICO

    Edward E. Baumeister . . . . *Surgery*

CORONADO

    Paul Wegeforth, Bank of Coronado Building . . . . *Surgery*

EUREKA

    Charles Clifford Falk, First National Bank Building . *Surgery*

FRESNO

    Allen Bonner McConnell, Griffith-McKenzie Building . *Surgery*
    John H. Pettis, Mattei Building . . . . *Surgery*

GILROY

    Jonas Clark . . . . *Surgery*

HOLLISTER

    Leonard Charles Hull, 343 5th Street . . . . . . *Surgery*

LOS ANGELES

    F. C. Ainley, 1117 Brockman Building . *Gynecology, Obstetrics*
    Eliot Alden, 6422 Hollywood Boulevard . . . . . *Surgery*
    Milton A. Barndt, 511 Consolidated Realty Building
                                  Ophth., Rhinol., Oto-Laryngology
    John Mackenzie Brown, Brockman Building . . *Oto-Laryngology*
    De Witt C. Bryant, 716 Broadway Central Building
                                  Ophth., Oto-Laryngology
    Ernest Albert Bryant, 520 Los Angeles Railway Building *Surgery*
    William Patrick Burke, 502 Merritt Building . . . *Surgery*
    Guy Cochran, 596 Pacific Electric Building . . . . *Surgery*
    Titian Coffey, 326 Marsh-Strong Building . . . . *Obstetrics*
    A. Bennett Cooke, 1019 Hollingsworth Building . . . *Surgery*
    Robert V. Day, 621 Baker-Detwiler Building . . . *Urology*
    Frank E. Detling, 756 South Broadway
                                  Ophth., Rhinol., Oto-Laryngology

CALIFORNIA — Continued

Los ANGELES — Continued

Edward Thomas Dillon, St. Vincent's Hospital . . . *Surgery*

Philip Schuyler Doane, 424 Consolidated Realty Building
Gynecology

William Henry Dudley, 512 Brockman Building
Ophth., Rhinol., Oto-Laryngology

John Dunlop, 803 Pacific Mutual Building . *Orthopedic Surgery*

Willoughby G. Dye, 502 Merritt Building . . . . *Surgery*

William A. Edwards, Security Building . . . . *Surgery*

H. Bert. Ellis, 1219 Marsh-Strong Building . *Ophth., Laryngology*

Carl Fisher, Pacific Mutual Building . . . . *Ophthalmology*

E. W. Fleming, 806 Pacific Mutual Building
Rhinol., Oto-Laryngology

John Knox Gailey, 823 North Kenmore Avenue . . . *Retired*

Edgar E. Gelder, 319 Merritt Building . . . . *Gynecology*

R. Watson Graham, 801 Pacific Mutual Building *Ophthalmology*

Walter O. Henry, 917 Baker-Detwiler Building . . . *Surgery*

Henry W. Howard, Charles C. Chapman Building . . *Surgery*

Walter Leslie Huggins, 916 Pacific Mutual Building . *Surgery*

Maurice Kahn, 1111 Brockman Building . . . . . *Surgery*

L. P. Kaull, 1023 Pacific Mutual Building . . . *Surgery*

Arthur L. Kelsey, 1005 Brockman Building
Ophth., Rhinol., Oto-Laryngology

Hugo Albert Kiefer, 406 Brockman Building
Ophth., Rhinol., Oto-Laryngology

William H. Kiger, 711 Pacific Mutual Building . . *Proctology*

Cyrus A. Kirkley, 432 South Serrano Avenue . . *Gynecology*

Carl Kurtz, 609 H. W. Hellman Building . . . . . *Surgery*

Edmond M. Lazard, 547 South Kingsley Drive *Gynecology, Obstetrics*

Eugene Richards Lewis, 1920 Orange Street
Ophth., Rhinol., Oto-Laryngology

Andrew Stewart Lobingier, 710 Merritt Building . . *Surgery*

Theodore C. Lyster, 1920 Orange Street . *Ophth., Oto-Laryngology*

Granville MacGowan, Brack Shops Building . . . . *Urology*

Wilbur W. MacKenzie, Hollingsworth Building . . . *Surgery*

Archibald L. Macleish, 1104 Brockman Building . *Ophthalmology*

Leon Wallace Mansur, 1109 Brockman Building . *Ophthalmology*

Harry N. Mayo, 408 Hibernian Building . . . . . *Surgery*

William Taylor McArthur, 2025 Western Avenue . . *Surgery*

CALIFORNIA — Continued

Los Angeles — Continued

G. W. McCoy, Security Building *Ophth., Rhinol., Oto-Laryngology*
Thomas McHugh, 510 Van Nuys Building . . . . *Surgery*
Robert Phillips McReynolds, 307 Coulter Building . . *Surgery*
Frank W. Miller, 811 Pacific Mutual Building . *Ophthalmology*
Lloyd Mills, 927 Citizens National Bank Building *Ophthalmology*
E. C. Moore, 1005 Merchants National Bank Building . *Surgery*
M. L. Moore, 1007 Merchants National Bank Building
Gynecology, Obstetrics
Lewis Burrows Morton, St. Vincent's Hospital . . . *Surgery*
Harold Struan Muckleston, 912 Van Nuys Building
Oto-Laryngology
Charles Eaton Phillips, 706 Pacific Mutual Building . *Surgery*
Carl W. Rand, 1034 Pacific Mutual Building . . . *Surgery*
William W. Richardson, 311 Brockman Building . . *Surgery*
Frederick W. Rinkenberger, Merchants National Bank
Building . . . . *Surgery*
Turner F. Roberts, 924 Pacific Mutual Building
Ophth., Rhinol., Oto-Laryngology
Leon Joseph Roth, 927 Pacific Mutual Building
Genito-Urinary Surgery
Hans Ernst Walter Schiffbauer, Title Insurance Building *Surgery*
James Harvey Seymour, 502 Brockman Building . . *Surgery*
Henry Newton Shaw, 901 Pacific Mutual Building . *Gynecology*
Francis Eppes Shine, 1120 Brockman Building . . . *Surgery*
Roland E. Skeel, Title Insurance Building . . . . *Surgery*
Josiah Morris Slemons, 819 Pacific Mutual Building
Gynecology, Obstetrics
Rea Smith, 22 Chester Place . . . . *Surgery*
Paul F. Straub, 1900 North Vermont Avenue . . . *Surgery*
Charles T. Sturgeon, 710 Merritt Building . . . . *Surgery*
George Thomason, 317 Hollingsworth Building . . . *Surgery*
Clarence Gaines Toland, 1027 Pacific Mutual Building . *Surgery*
Adolph Tyroler, 337 Kerckhoff Building . . . . . *Surgery*
Jean J. A. Van Kaathoven, 628 Van Nuys Building . . *Surgery*
W. E. Waddell, 927 Citizens National Bank Building
Rhinol., Oto-Laryngology
Ralph Williams, Charles C. Chapman Building . . . *Urology*
William LeMoyne Wills, International Bank Building . *Surgery*

CALIFORNIA — Continued

LOS ANGELES — Continued

Orville O. Witherbee, Pacific Mutual Building . . . *Surgery*
Charles W. Yerxa, 520 Los Angeles Railway Building . *Surgery*
Charles E. Zerfing, 400 Pantages Building . . . . *Surgery*

MCCLOUD

Joseph Marshall Flint . . . . *Surgery*

MODESTO

Earl Roby McPheeters, Evans Hospital . . . . . *Surgery*

OAKLAND

Clark L. Abbott, Central Bank Building . . . . . *Surgery*
Lemuel Payson Adams, Federal Realty Building . . *Surgery*
Samuel H. Buteau, 1307 Broadway . . . . . . *Surgery*
Thomas J. Clark, Oakland Bank of Savings Building
Genito-Urinary Surgery
Daniel Crosby, 20th and Webster Streets . . . . . *Surgery*
Dennis D. Crowley, Central Bank Building . . . . *Surgery*
Clarence A. DePuy, 532 15th Street . . *Gynecology, Obstetrics*
Charles Alfred Dukes, Central Bank Building . . *Gynecology*
Mark Lewis Emerson, 1307 Broadway . . . . . *Surgery*
E. N. Ewer, Federal Realty Building . *Gynecology, Obstetrics*
John Radford Fearn, First National Bank Building . . *Surgery*
William L. Friedman, 1706 Broadway . . . *Ophthalmology*
John de Lafayette Grissim, Dalziel Building . . . . *Surgery*
David Hadden, Oakland Bank of Savings Building . *Gynecology*
Oliver D. Hamlin, Federal Realty Building . . . . *Surgery*
George G. Reinle, 532 15th Street . . . . *Urology*
Robert Thompson Stratton, 441 Fairmount Avenue . . *Surgery*
Hayward G. Thomas, Dalziel Building
Ophth., Rhinol., Oto-Laryngology

ONTARIO

Geoffrey Joseph Fleming, 612 North Euclid Avenue . *Urology*

OXNARD

William Reinhardt Livingston, 426 B Street . *Surgery, Obstetrics*

PALO ALTO

Harry B. Reynolds, Fraser Building . . . . . . *Surgery*

PASADENA

John H. Breyer, 414 Chamber of Commerce Building . *Surgery*
William D. Dilworth, 1220 South Pasadena Avenue
Ophth., Rhinol., Oto-Laryngology

CALIFORNIA — Continued

PASADENA — Continued

H. M. Griffith, 515 Citizens Savings Bank Building
Rhinol., Oto-Laryngology
Charles D. Lockwood, 295 Markham Place . . . . *Surgery*
Fitch C. E. Mattison, Chamber of Commerce Building . *Surgery*
Samuel Jones Mattison, 712 Citizens Savings Bank Building
Surgery, Obstetrics
J. R. Reed, 203 Citizens Bank Building . . . *Ophthalmology*
William Humes Roberts, 461 East Colorado Street
Ophth., Rhinol., Oto-Laryngology
Charles H. Rodi, 990 Atchison Street . . . . *Surgery*
Henry Howard Sherk, 268 South Orange Grove Avenue . *Surgery*

POMONA

B. A. McBurney, Palm Villa Ranch . . . . . *Surgery*
Joseph K. Swindt, Investment Building . . . . . *Surgery*

REDLANDS

Ernest O. J. Eytinge, 118 Cajon Street . . . . *Surgery*
Carlos Grout Hilliard, 126 Cajon Street . . . . *Surgery*
Walter B. Power, 233 Cajon Street. . . . . . . *Surgery*

RIVERSIDE

Bon. O. Adams, 306 Loring Building . . . . . *Surgery*
Cornelius Van Zwaluwenburg, 1111 Main Street . . . *Surgery*

SACRAMENTO

William Ellery Briggs, 1027 10th Street
Ophth., Rhinol., Oto-Laryngology
Andrew Mitchell Henderson, 824 J Street . . . . *Surgery*
Carl William Wahrer, Physicians Building . . . . *Surgery*

SAN BERNARDINO

Henry William Mills, Chamber of Commerce Building . *Surgery*
Philip M. Savage, 499 E Street . . . . *Surgery*
D. C. Strong, 425 4th Street . . . . *Surgery*

SAN DIEGO

Thomas O. Burger, 1200 First National Bank Building. *Surgery*
Vernon Greene Clark, 415 Elm Street. . . . . . *Surgery*
J. F. Grant, 423 First National Bank Building . *Ophthalmology*
H. P. Newman, American National Bank Building . *Gynecology*
B. J. O'Neill, Jr., First National Bank Building . . . *Surgery*

CALIFORNIA — Continued

SAN DIEGO — Continued

Thomas F. Wier, 708 Timkin Building . . . . . *Obstetrics*
Peleg Benson Wing, 1000 Watts Building . . . *Ophthalmology*

SAN FRANCISCO

Thomas Edward Bailly, 870 Market Street . . . . *Surgery*
Gilbert M. Barrett, 516 Sutter Street . . . . . . *Surgery*
Henry Alexander Brown, 275 Post Street . . . *Ophthalmology*
Harold Brunn, 350 Post Street . . . . *Surgery*
Guido E. Caglieri, 21 Columbus Avenue . . . . *Surgery*
Paul S. Campiche, 560 Sutter Street . . . . . *Surgery*
Frank B. Carpenter, 715 Howard Building . . . . *Surgery*
Walter B. Coffey, Medical Building . . . . . . *Surgery*
Asa W. Collins, 126 Post Street . . . . *Surgery*
F. J. S. Conlan, 135 Stockton Street . . *Ophth., Oto-Laryngology*
Alfred Lawrence Draper, Shreve Building . . . . . *Surgery*
Frederick Fehleisen. 400 Clayton Street . . . . . *Surgery*
Arthur L. Fisher, Medical Building . . . *Orthopedic Surgery*
Walter Scott Franklin, Butler Building . . . *Ophthalmology*
Philip Kingsnorth Gilman, 350 Post Street . . . . *Surgery*
Harrington B. Graham, Shreve Building *Rhinol., Oto-Laryngology*
Joseph Underwood Hall, 133 Geary Street . . . . *Surgery*
Frank Hinman, 516 Sutter Street . . . . *Urology*
L. H. Hoffman, 177 Post Street . . . . . . *Gynecology*
Louis Philippe Howe, 200 Bush Street . . . . . *Surgery*
Thomas Waterman Huntington, Mills Building . . . *Surgery*
Solomon Hyman, 135 Stockton Street . . . . . . *Surgery*
S. Nicholas Jacobs, 209 Post Street . . . . . . *Surgery*
August J. Lartigau, 391 Sutter Street . . . . . . *Surgery*
Charles Gabriel Levison, 870 Market Street . . . . *Surgery*
Frank W. Lynch, University of California Hospital
Gynecology, Obstetrics
William Crawford Mackintosh, 1095 Market Street . . *Surgery*
George Jewett McChesney, 1202 Flood Building *Orthopedic Surgery*
Henry Meyer, 240 Stockton Street . . . *Genito-Urinary Surgery*
Martin Molony, 1054 Sutter Street . . . . . . *Urology*
Fermin Ralph Orella, 323 Geary Street . . . . *Gynecology*
Kaspar Pischel, 135 Stockton Street *Ophth., Rhinol., Oto-Laryngology*
Theodore C. Rethers, 650 Phelan Building . . . . *Surgery*
Emmet Rixford, 1795 California Street . . . . . *Surgery*

CALIFORNIA — Continued

SAN FRANCISCO — Continued

Russell Colquhoun Ryan, 362 Flood Building . . . *Surgery*
Henry Anthon Lewis Ryfkogel, 516 Sutter Street . . *Surgery*
George Burbank Somers, 2662 Vallejo Street . . . *Gynecology*
Burt Smith Stevens, Medical Building . . . . *Surgery*
William E. Stevens, 210 Post Street . . *Genito-Urinary Surgery*
Stanley Stillman, Lane Hospital . . . . . . *Surgery*
Chester James Teass, Medical Building . . . *Gynecology*
Wallace Irving Terry, 240 Stockton Street . . . . *Surgery*
Isaac Walton Thorne, 516 Sutter Street . . . . . *Surgery*
Richard Frank Tomlinson, 1286 Flood Building . . *Surgery*
William Francis B. Wakefield, 1065 Sutter Street
Gynecology, Obstetrics
James Thomas Watkins, Medical Building . *Orthopedic Surgery*
Alanson Weeks, 350 Post Street . . . . . . *Surgery*
Cullen F. Welty, 210 Post Street . . *Rhinol., Oto-Laryngology*
Emma K. Willits, 408 Stockton Street . . . . . *Surgery*
Walter H. Winterberg, 516 Sutter Street . . . . *Surgery*
Alfred Jacob Zobel, 210 Post Street . . . . . . *Proctology*

SAN JOSE

David A. Beattie, 210 South 1st Street . . . . *Surgery*
Charles Walter Delaney, 1555 The Alameda . . . *Surgery*
Doxey R. Wilson, Santa Clara County Hospital . . . *Surgery*

SAN LUIS OBISPO

William Miller Stover, 1130 Garden Street . . . . *Surgery*

SAN MATEO

Walter C. Chidester, Red Cross Hospital . . . . . *Surgery*

SANTA ANA

Jesse Manning Burlew, Spurgeon Building . . . . *Surgery*

SANTA BARBARA

Joseph Alfred Andrews, 1229 State Street . *Ophth., Oto-Laryngology*
Elmer Jefferson Bissell, Mission Canyon . . . *Ophthalmology*
Rexwald Brown, Santa Barbara Clinic . . . . *Surgery*
Theodore L. Chase . . . . *Retired*
Benjamin F. Cunningham . . . . *Surgery*
Lucius W. Hotchkiss, San Marcos Building . . . *Surgery*
George W. Jean, San Marcos Building . . . *Ophthalmology*

CALIFORNIA — Continued

SANTA BARBARA — Continued

Samuel Robinson, San Marcos Building . . . . . *Surgery*
Harold Sidebotham, San Marcos Building . . . . *Surgery*
George S. Wells, San Marcos Building . *Rhinol., Oto-Laryngology*

SANTA CRUZ

Percy Todd Phillips, Hihn Building . . . . . . *Surgery*

SANTA MARIA

Moses Thorner, North Vine Street . . . . . . *Surgery*

SANTA ROSA

Joseph Hughes Shaw, 213 Exchange Place . . . . *Surgery*

SIERRA MADRE

Norman H. Goodenow, 71 Baldwin Avenue . *Ophth., Laryngology*

SONORA

Elisha Tolman Gould, 631 Washington Street . . . *Surgery*

STOCKTON

Robert R. Hammond, 435 Park Street, West . . . . *Surgery*
Charles Rees Harry, F. and M. Bank Building . . . *Surgery*

WHITTIER

Benjamin Franklin Miller, 101½ East Philadelphia Avenue
Ophth., Rhinol., Oto-Laryngology
Horace P. Wilson, Whittier National Bank Building . *Surgery*

WOODLAND

Fred R. Fairchild, 754 College Street . . . . . . *Surgery*

YORBA LINDA

Lester Keller . . . . *Retired*

COLORADO

BOULDER

Walter W. Reed, Physicians Building . . *Gynecology, Obstetrics*

COLORADO SPRINGS

Frank L. Dennis, Ferguson Building . . . . *Oto-Laryngology*
Peter Oliver Hanford, 720 North Nevada Avenue . . *Surgery*
John B. Hartwell, Burns Building . . . . . . *Surgery*
Alexander C. Magruder, Ferguson Building . . *Ophthalmology*
David Porter Mayhew, 218 Burns Building . . . . *Surgery*
L. H. McKinnie, 316 Ferguson Building . . . . . *Surgery*
William Valentine Mullin, 301 Ferguson Building *Oto-Laryngology*
Beverley Tucker, 301 Ferguson Building . . . . . *Surgery*

COLORADO — Continued

DENVER

Melville Black, 424 Metropolitan Building   .   .   *Ophthalmology*
T. Mitchell Burns, 640 Metropolitan Building *Obstetrics, Gynecology*
Thomas Edward Carmody, 806 Metropolitan Building
                                   Rhinol., Oto-Laryngology
Foster H. Cary, Metropolitan Building   .   *Gynecology, Obstetrics*
Haskell Cohen, 302 Metropolitan Building   .   .   .   .   *Surgery*
David H. Coover, 412 Metropolitan Building   .   *Ophthalmology*
William H. Crisp, 530 Metropolitan Building .   .   *Ophthalmology*
John B. Davis, 660 Metropolitan Building   .   .   .   .   *Urology*
Edward F. Dean, 100 Metropolitan Building .   .   .   .   *Surgery*
John McEwen Foster, 708 Metropolitan Building
                           Ophth., Rhinol., Oto-Laryngology
O. S. Fowler, 530 Metropolitan Building .   .   .   .   *Surgery*
Robert T. Frank, 511 Majestic Building   .   .   .   *Gynecology*
Leonard Freeman, 424 Metropolitan Building   .   .   *Surgery*
Thomas J. Gallaher, 605 California Building .   .   *Oto-Laryngology*
Eugene C. Gehrung, 4177 King Street .   .   .   .   .   *Retired*
William W. Grant, Mack Building .   .   .   .   .   .   *Surgery*
Casper Frank Hegner, Metropolitan Building   .   .   *Surgery*
C. B. Ingraham, Jr., Metropolitan Building   .   .   .   *Surgery*
Edward Jackson, 318 Majestic Building   .   .   *Ophthalmology*
Walter A. Jayne, 535 Majestic Building   .   .   .   *Gynecology*
Samuel Fosdick Jones, 516 Majestic Building .   *Orthopedic Surgery*
Robert Levy, 406 Metropolitan Building .   .   .   *Oto-Laryngology*
Lorenzo B. Lockard, 920 Metropolitan Building .   *Oto-Laryngology*
Charles Baldwin Lyman, Metropolitan Building .   .   .   *Surgery*
Oliver Lyons, 266 Metropolitan Building .   .   .   .   .   *Urology*
Francis H. McNaught, 742 Metropolitan Building   .   .   *Surgery*
George B. Packard, 1344 Franklin Street .   .   *Orthopedic Surgery*
Cuthbert Powell, 2261 Albion Street   .   .   *Gynecology, Obstetrics*
Charles Andrews Powers, University Club   .   .   .   *Surgery*
John F. Roe, Metropolitan Building   .   .   .   .   .   *Surgery*
Edmund James A. Rogers, 222 West Colfax Avenue   .   *Surgery*
Frank E. Rogers, Majestic Building   .   .   .   .   .   *Surgery*
Matt R. Root, 312 Majestic Building .   .   .   .   .   *Surgery*
William Alexander Sedwick, 764 Metropolitan Building
                                           Ophthalmology
Oscar Maurice Shere, 610 Metropolitan Building   .   .   *Surgery*

COLORADO — Continued

DENVER — Continued

W. M. Spitzer, Metropolitan Building . . *Genito-Urinary Surgery*
Hiram R. Stilwill, 820 Metropolitan Building . *Ophthalmology*
David A. Strickler, 612 Empire Building
Ophth., Rhinol., Oto-Laryngology
Chauncey E. Tennant, Empire Building . . . . . *Surgery*
Horace G. Wetherill, 1127 Race Street . . . . . *Surgery*
Henry W. Wilcox, 302 Majestic Building . . *Orthopedic Surgery*

ENGLEWOOD

Alden D. Catterson, 3533 South Broadway . . . . *Surgery*

FORT COLLINS

William A. Kickland, 210 Colorado Building . . . . *Surgery*

GRAND JUNCTION

Heman Rowlee Bull, 407 North 7th Street . . . . *Surgery*
Knud Hanson, Canon Block . . . . *Surgery*

PUEBLO

William T. H. Baker, 217 West Orman Avenue . . . *Surgery*
John A. Black, 103 West Pitkin Avenue . . . . . *Surgery*
Richard Warren Corwin, Minnequa Hospital . . . . *Surgery*
Crum Epler, 650 Thatcher Building . . . . . *Surgery*
James Jay Pattee, 511 Thatcher Building . . . *Ophth., Otology*
William Senger, Minnequa Hospital . . . . . *Surgery*
Thomas A. Stoddard, Thatcher Block . . . . . *Surgery*

TRINIDAD

John R. Espey, 335 East Main Street . . . . . *Surgery*

CONNECTICUT

BRIDGEPORT

Charles C. Godfrey, 340 State Street . . . . . *Surgery*
J. Murray Johnson, 276 West Avenue . . . . . *Gynecology*
Henry Shillingford Miles, 881 Lafayette Street . *Ophthalmology*
John F. Shea, 1254 East Main Street . . . . . *Surgery*
Herbert E. Smyth, 476 John Street . *Rhinol., Oto-Laryngology*
Frank William Stevens, 829 Myrtle Avenue . . . *Gynecology*
John W. Wright, 810 Myrtle Avenue . . . . . *Surgery*

DANBURY

David Chester Brown, 330 Main Street . . . . . *Surgery*
Harris F. Brownlee, 342 Main Street . . . . . *Surgery*

CONNECTICUT — Continued

DANIELSON

George McClellan Burroughs, 5 Broad Street . *Ophthalmology*

GREENWICH

Fritz C. Hyde, Maple Avenue . . . . *Surgery*

HARTFORD

George Newton Bell, 44 High Street . . . . . . *Surgery*
John B. Boucher, 25 Charter Oak Avenue . . . . *Surgery*
Thomas W. Chester, 50 Farmington Avenue *Gynecology, Obstetrics*
Donald Brett Cragin, 179 Allyn Street . . . . . *Surgery*
John Wellington Felty, 902 Main Street . . . . . *Surgery*
Michael H. Gill, 36 Pearl Street *Ophth., Rhinol., Oto-Laryngology*
Thomas N. Hepburn, 179 Allyn Street . . . . . *Surgery*
H. Gildersleeve Jarvis, 179 Allyn Street . . . . *Surgery*
Edward Rutledge Lampson, 175 North Beacon Street . *Surgery*
Wilbert E. McClellan, 179 Allyn Street
Ophth., Rhinol., Oto-Laryngology
John Butler McCook, 396 Main Street . . . . . *Surgery*
Alfred M. Rowley, 179 Allyn Street . . . . . . *Surgery*
E. Terry Smith, 36 Pearl Street . . . . . *Ophth., Otology*
Paul Plummer Swett, 179 Allyn Street . . *Orthopedic Surgery*
Charles Ezra Taft, 50 Farmington Avenue . . . . *Surgery*
Ernest Alden Wells, 580 Asylum Street . . . . . *Surgery*
Thacher W. Worthen, 179 Allyn Street . . . . . *Surgery*

MERIDEN

Edward Wier Smith, 34 West Main Street . . . . *Surgery*

MIDDLETOWN

John E. Loveland, 93 Broad Street . . . . . . *Surgery*

NEW HAVEN

Arthur N. Alling, 257 Church Street . . . . *Ophthalmology*
A. Nowell Creadick, Yale University . . *Gynecology, Obstetrics*
Willis Hanford Crowe, 59 College Street . . . . *Surgery*
William Core Duffy, New Haven Hospital . . . . *Surgery*
Willis E. Hartshorn, 67 Trumbull Street . . . . *Surgery*
Samuel C. Harvey, New Haven Hospital . . . . . *Surgery*
Gabriel J. Jackowitz, 347 Orange Street . . . . *Surgery*
Arthur Henry Morse, 71 College Street . *Gynecology, Obstetrics*
Francis H. Reilly, 230 Church Street . . . . . . *Surgery*
Thomas Hubbard Russell, 57 Trumbull Street . . . *Surgery*

CONNECTICUT — Continued

NEW HAVEN — Continued

F. N. Sperry, 59 College Street . . . *Rhinol., Oto-Laryngology*
Herbert Thoms, 59 College Street . . . . . . *Surgery*
William Francis Verdi, 27 Elm Street . . . . . *Surgery*
E. Reed Whittemore, 19 Whitney Avenue . . . . *Surgery*

NEW LONDON

Thomas Adams Woodruff, Plant Building . . *Ophthalmology*

NORWALK

William Joseph Tracey, 23 West Avenue . . . . . *Surgery*

POMFRET

Seldom Burden Overlock . . . . *Surgery*

STAMFORD

George R. R. Hertzberg, 40 South Street . . . . *Surgery*

WATERBURY

Henry Gray Anderson, 39 Leavenworth Street . . *Gynecology*
Charles H. Brown, 57 North Main Street . . . . *Gynecology*
Augustin Averill Crane, 300 West Main Street . . . *Surgery*
John Sinclair Dye, Lilley Building . . . . . . *Surgery*
Carl Eugene Munger, 81 North Main Street . . *Oto-Laryngology*
Nelson Asa Pomeroy, 76 Center Street . . . . . *Surgery*
George Milton Smith, 76 Center Street . . . . . *Surgery*

DELAWARE

WILMINGTON

William E. Bird, 1022 Dupont Building . . . . . *Surgery*
James A. Draper, 1015 Washington Street . . . . *Surgery*
Joshua A. Ellegood, Equitable Building
Ophth., Rhinol., Oto-Laryngology
William Oscar La Motte, Industrial Trust Building
Ophth., Rhinol., Oto-Laryngology
John Palmer, Jr., 1900 Delaware Avenue . . . . . *Surgery*
William H. Speer, 805 West Street . . . . . *Surgery*
Harold L. Springer, 1013 Washington Street . . . *Surgery*

DISTRICT OF COLUMBIA

WASHINGTON

William H. Arthur, 2130 Le Roy Place . . . . . *Retired*
Edward A. Balloch, 2000 16th Street, N. W. . . . . *Surgery*

DISTRICT OF COLUMBIA — Continued

WASHINGTON — Continued

Daniel Le Ray Borden, 815 Connecticut Avenue	. . *Surgery*
William Cline Borden, 2306 Tracy Place	*Surgery*
J. Wesley Bovée, 815 Connecticut Avenue . . .	*Gynecology*
W. S. Bowen, The Farragut	*Obstetrics*
Joseph H. Bryan, 818 17th Street, N. W. . . .	*Oto-Laryngology*
W. P. Carr, 1801 K Street, N. W.	*Surgery*

Virginius Dabney, 1633 Connecticut Avenue
Rhinol., Oto-Laryngology
William Thornwall Davis, 927 Farragut Square . *Ophthalmology*
William Gage Erving, 1621 Connecticut Avenue *Orthopedic Surgery*
Thomas M. Foley, 1334 19th Street . . . *Orthopedic Surgery*
H. A. Fowler, 1621 Connecticut Avenue *Genito-Urinary Surgery*
Homer Gifford Fuller, 204 The Farragut *Genito-Urinary Surgery*
Louis Storrow Greene, 1624 I Street, N. W. . . *Ophthalmology*
Francis Randall Hagner, The Farragut *Genito-Urinary Surgery*
Charles M. Hammett, 1330 I Street, N. W. . . *Ophthalmology*
A. Barnes Hooe, 1220 16th Street, N. W. . . . . *Gynecology*
Edmund J. Horgan, Stoneleigh Court . . . . . . *Surgery*
Howard Hume, 1830 Jefferson Place, N. W. . . . . *Surgery*
Virgil B. Jackson, 1801 K Street, N. W. . . . . . *Surgery*
Howard Francis Kane, Stoneleigh Court . . . . . *Obstetrics*
J. Thomas Kelley, Jr., 1312 15th Street, N. W. . . *Gynecology*
Harry Hyland Kerr, 1742 N Street, N. W. . . . . *Surgery*
Arthur H. Kimball, The Farragut . . . . . *Ophthalmology*
Robert Scott Lamb, Stoneleigh Court . . . . *Ophthalmology*
Huron W. Lawson, 1706 Rhode Island Avenue
Gynecology, Obstetrics
Louis C. Lehr, 1737 H Street, N. W. . . *Genito-Urinary Surgery*
Francis B. Loring, 1420 K Street, N. W. . . . *Ophth., Otology*
Thomas L. Macdonald, 1501 Massachusetts Avenue,
N. W. . . . . *Gynecology*
William B. Marbury, 1403 21st Street, N. W. . . . *Surgery*
William Beverley Mason, 1738 M Street, N. W.
Rhinol., Oto-Laryngology
Oscar A. M. McKimmie, 1330 Massachusetts Avenue,
N. W. . . . . *Rhinol., Oto-Laryngology*
G. Brown Miller, 1730 K Street, N. W. . *Gynecology, Obstetrics*
James Farnandis Mitchell, 1344 19th Street, N. W. . . *Surgery*

DISTRICT OF COLUMBIA — Continued

WASHINGTON — Continued

John F. Moran, 2426 Pennsylvania Avenue . . . . . *Obstetrics*

William S. Newell, 1029 Vermont Avenue . . *Ophthalmology*

Eugene G. Northington . . . . *Surgery*

William O. Owen, 2719 Ontario Road, N. W. . . . *Surgery*

Edward Mason Parker, 1726 M Street, N. W. . . . *Surgery*

Daniel Webster Prentiss, 1213 M Street, N. W. . . . *Surgery*

Robert C. Ransdell, The St. Nicholas . . . . . . *Surgery*

Luther Halsey Reichelderfer, 1721 Connecticut Avenue *Surgery*

Charles W. Richardson, 1317 Connecticut Avenue
Rhinol., Oto-Laryngology

James Julius Richardson, 1509 16th Street, N. W. *Oto-Laryngology*

John Lewis Riggles, Stoneleigh Court . . *Gynecology, Obstetrics*

Charles E. Sawyer, Army and Navy Building . . . *Surgery*

Edward Grant Seibert, 1545 I Street, N. W.
Ophth., Oto-Laryngology

Aurelius Rives Shands, 901 16th Street, N. W.
Orthopedic Surgery

Daniel Kerfoot Shute, 1727 De Sales Street . . *Ophthalmology*

A. Camp Stanley, The Farragut . . . . *Surgery*

A. L. Stavely, 1744 M Street, N. W. . . *Gynecology, Obstetrics*

Isaac Scott Stone, 1618 Rhode Island Avenue . . *Gynecology*

Robert Y. Sullivan, Stoneleigh Court . . *Gynecology, Obstetrics*

George Tully Vaughan, 1718 I Street, N. W. . . . . *Surgery*

Reginald R. Walker, The Rochambeau *Rhinol., Oto-Laryngology*

Walter Duvall Webb, Stoneleigh Court . . . . . *Surgery*

John R. Wellington, 1723 Connecticut Avenue . . . *Surgery*

Walter A. Wells, The Rochambeau . . . . *Oto-Laryngology*

Charles Stanley White, 911 16th Street, N. W. . . . *Surgery*

William Holland Wilmer, 1610 I Street, N. W. . *Ophthalmology*

MEDICAL CORPS, UNITED STATES ARMY

Arthur M. Alden

Percy M. Ashburn

Bailey K. Ashford

Mahlon Ashford

Frank Cole Baker

William B. Banister

Joseph E. Bastion

DISTRICT OF COLUMBIA — Continued

MEDICAL CORPS, UNITED STATES ARMY — Continued

Henry Beeuwkes
James L. Bevans
Henry P. Birmingham
William N. Bispham
Edgar Allan Bocock
Albert S. Bowen
Thomas S. Bratton
Roger Brooke
Orville Graham Brown
Earl H. Bruns
Carroll Deforest Buck
Daniel P. Card
Weston P. Chamberlain
Albert Patton Clark
Jere B. Clayton
Jacob M. Coffin
C. Clark Collins
Clarence H. Connor
Charles F. Craig
Samuel S. Creighton
Robert M. Culler
Carl R. Darnall
Elmer A. Dean
Matthew A. DeLaney
Wallace DeWitt
Douglas F. Duval
William R. Eastman
Benjamin Jones Edger, Jr.
George M. Edwards
George Macy Ekwurzel
Powell Conrad Fauntleroy
Peter Conover Field
James D. Fife
Henry C. Fisher
Joseph Herbert Ford
Charles L. Foster
Ernest R. Gentry
Harry L. Gilchrist

DISTRICT OF COLUMBIA — Continued

MEDICAL CORPS, UNITED STATES ARMY — Continued

James D. Glennan
Ralph Harvard Goldthwaite
George H. R. Gosman
Henry S. Greenleaf
Junius Claiborne Gregory
Jay W. Grissinger
Paul S. Halloran
John W. Hanner
Haywood S. Hansell
W. Lee Hart
Frederick M. Hartsock
Louis Thales Hess
Deane C. Howard
Paul C. Hutton
Merritte W. Ireland
Howard H. Johnson
Harold W. Jones
Percy L. Jones
George F. Juenemann
Jefferson R. Kean
Frank Royer Keefer
William L. Keller
James M. Kennedy
Edgar King
Albert G. Love
Charles Lynch
William J. Lyster
Clarence J. Manly
Charles F. Mason
Walter D. McCaw
Champe C. McCulloch
Raymond F. Metcalfe
Reuben B. Miller
William Henry Moncrief
Samuel J. Morris
Charles F. Morse
Edward Lyman Munson
Henry J. Nichols

DISTRICT OF COLUMBIA — Continued

MEDICAL CORPS, UNITED STATES ARMY — Continued

Robert E. Noble
Leartus J. Owen
Robert Urie Patterson
George P. Peed
Elbert E. Persons
James M. Phalen
Hiram A. Phillips
Robert Hamilton Pierson
Henry C. Pillsbury
Henry F. Pipes
Francis Herbert Poole
Ralph S. Porter
Will L. Pyles
Guy Logan Qualls
Mathew A. Reasoner
Charles R. Reynolds
Frederick P. Reynolds
Thomas L. Rhoads
Ernest L. Ruffner
Edward R. Schreiner
Henry A. Shaw
John L. Shepard
M. A. W. Shockley
J. Ralph Shook
Joseph Franklin Siler
George A. Skinner
Lloyd Llewellyn Smith
Alexander N. Stark
William H. Thearle
Albert E. Truby
Arnold Dwight Tuttle
Alfred P. Upshur
James Wallace Van Dusen
Edward B. Vedder
Sanford H. Wadhams
Frank W. Weed
Arthur Maunder Whaley
Charles Willcox

DISTRICT OF COLUMBIA — Continued

MEDICAL CORPS, UNITED STATES ARMY— Continued
   Allie Walter Williams
   Llewellyn P. Williamson
   Francis A. Winter
   Edwin Philip Wolfe

MEDICAL CORPS, UNITED STATES NAVY
   Frederick G. Abeken
   William A. Angwin
   Frederick Asser Asserson
   Robert A. Bachmann
   William H. Bell
   Frederick Leslie Benton
   Norman S. Betts
   Louis W. Bishop
   Edward Maurice Blackwell
   Norman Jerome Blackwood
   Edward S. Bogert
   Joel T. Boone
   William Clarence Braisted
   John M. Brister
   Charles S. Butler
   Dudley N. Carpenter
   David C. Cather
   William Chambers
   Addison B. Clifford
   Alfred Lee Clifton
   George F. Cottle
   Holton C. Curl
   John B. Dennis
   Paul T. Dessez
   Charles M. De Valin
   Benjamin H. Dorsey
   Arthur White Dunbar
   William E. Eaton
   Middleton Stuart Elliott, Jr.
   Ammen Farenholt
   Wrey G. Farwell
   Archibald Magill Fauntleroy

DISTRICT OF COLUMBIA — Continued

MEDICAL CORPS, UNITED STATES NAVY — Continued

James Gaven Field
Charles Norman Fiske
George F. Freeman
Francis M. Furlong
Harry Alfred Garrison
Will Melville Garton
James Duncan Gatewood
James Edward Gill
Cary T. Grayson
Charles Courtney Grieve
Eugene J. Grow
Gordon Dyer Hale
George S. Hathaway
Reynolds Hayden
James Plummer Haynes
Robert Graham Heiner
Harry R. Hermesch
Montgomery E. Higgins
Richmond Cranston Holcomb
Robert Eustis Hoyt
Earle P. Huff
John Hooe Iden
Lucius W. Johnson
John Brooks Kaufman
Herbert Lester Kelley
John T. Kennedy
Robert Morris Kennedy
Charles Poor Kindleberger
Frank X. Koltes
Harry Hamilton Lane
Howard F. Lawrence
Robert Emmet Ledbetter
James F. Leys
Rudolph I. Longabaugh
Charles H. T. Lowndes
John D. Manchester
Henry A. May
Albert M. D. McCormick

DISTRICT OF COLUMBIA — Continued

MEDICAL CORPS, UNITED STATES NAVY — Continued

Frank Edward McCullough
W. Neil McDonell
Ralph W. McDowell
Allen Donald McLean
Norman T. McLean
Owen J. Mink
James M. Minter
Joseph J. Mundell
Curtis B. Munger
Joseph A. Murphy
John Land Neilson
Henry Edward Odell
Karl Ohnesorg
Edward Henry Herbert Old
John Joseph O'Malley
Charles Malden Oman
Joseph Royal Phelps
George Pickrell
Frank Lester Pleadwell
Ralph Walter Plummer
Frederick E. Porter
James Chambers Pryor
Edward U. Reed
Theodore W. Richards
Charles Edward Riggs
Ausey H. Robnett
Samuel S. Rodman
Perceval Sherer Rossiter
Lawrence Maurice Schmidt
Frank E. Sellers
Luther Sheldon, Jr.
Herbert O. Shiffert
Charles Gordon Smith
George Tucker Smith
Harold W. Smith
Edward H. Sparkman, Jr.
Raymond Spear
Paul R. Stalnaker

DISTRICT OF COLUMBIA — Continued

MEDICAL CORPS, UNITED STATES NAVY — Continued

Edward Rhodes Stitt
Howard Francis Strine
Montgomery A. Stuart
James Spottiswoode Taylor
Edgar Thompson
Joseph P. Traynor
George Barnett Trible
Eugene A. Vickery
Richard Ambrose Warner
Ulys Robert Webb
Francis W. F. Wieber
Condie K. Winn
Edgar Lyons Woods
James S. Woodward
William J. Zalesky

UNITED STATES PUBLIC HEALTH SERVICE

Hiram W. Austin
Rupert Blue
Hugh S. Cumming
Robert Daniel Maddox
John Rich McDill
William Colby Rucker
Ferdinand Shoemaker

FLORIDA

DAYTONA

Dean Tyler Smith, 121 Bay Street . . . . *Surgery*

JACKSONVILLE

Norman M. Heggie, Buckman Building   *Ophth., Oto-Laryngology*
Gerry R. Holden, 513 Laura Street . . . . . *Gynecology*
W. S. Manning, 513 Laura Street . . *Ophth., Oto-Laryngology*
Carey Pegram Rogers, 1433 Riverside Avenue . . . *Surgery*
Edmund H. Teeter, 305 Duval Building . . . . . *Surgery*
Raymond Custer Turck, 1535 Riverside Avenue . . . *Surgery*

MIAMI

Charles Frederick Sayles, 145 East Flagler Street . . *Surgery*

FLORIDA — Continued

ORLANDO

R. R. Kime, 301 North Orange Avenue . . . . . *Surgery*

Milne Barker Swift . . . . *Retired*

ST. PETERSBURG

Mary Almira Smith, 101 Fifth Avenue, North . . . *Retired*

TAMPA

John S. Helms, 812 Citizens Bank Building . . . . *Surgery*

GEORGIA

ALBANY

James Miller Barnett, 208 Pine Street . . . . . *Surgery*

Agnew Hodge Hilsman, Broad and Washington Streets *Surgery*

ATHENS

Ralph Montgomery Goss, 297 Hancock Avenue . . . *Surgery*

ATLANTA

Augustus Milton Anderson, Connally Building
. *Rhinol., Oto-Laryngology*

Edgar Garrison Ballenger, 805 Healey Building . . . *Urology*

Stephen T. Barnett, 20 East Linden Avenue *Gynecology, Obstetrics*

Rudolph A. Bartholomew, 746 Peachtree Street
Obstetrics, Gynecology

Marion T. Benson, 504 Atlanta National Bank Building
Gynecology, Obstetrics

Frank Kells Boland, 436 Peachtree Street . . . . *Surgery*

F. Phinizy Calhoun, 833 Candler Building . . *Ophth., Otology*

James LeRoy Campbell, 325 Candler Building . . . *Surgery*

William E. Campbell, Atlanta National Bank Building
Ophth., Rhinol., Oto-Laryngology

William L. Champion, Grant Building . . *Genito-Urinary Surgery*

Walter Andrew Crowe, 1501 Hurt Building . . . *Gynecology*

Edward Campbell Davis, 25 East Linden Avenue . *Gynecology*

John F. Denton, Doctors' Building . . . . . *Gynecology*

Charles Edward Dowman, 78 Forrest Avenue . . . *Surgery*

William Simpson Elkin, 1029 Candler Building . . . *Surgery*

James N. Ellis, 1205 Fourth National Bank Building . *Surgery*

Walter B. Emery, 429 Candler Building . *Genito-Urinary Surgery*

William S. Goldsmith, 404 Healey Building . . . . *Surgery*

Lewis Sage Hardin, 812 Hurt Building . . . . . *Surgery*

GEORGIA — Continued

ATLANTA — Continued

Emmett D. Highsmith, 445 Trust Company of Georgia
Building . . . . *Surgery*
F. G. Hodgson, 746 Peachtree Street . . . *Orthopedic Surgery*
Walter Richard Holmes, Jr., 436 Peachtree Street . . *Surgery*
George Pope Huguley, 54 Forrest Avenue . . . . *Surgery*
Edward Groves Jones, 714 Hurt Building . . . . . *Surgery*
Hugh M. Lokey, 413 Candler Building
Ophth., Rhinol., Oto-Laryngology
William C. Lyle, Candler Building . . *Ophth., Oto-Laryngology*
Oscar H. Matthews, Flatiron Building . *Gynecology, Obstetrics*
James R. McCord, 373 Courtland Street . *Obstetrics, Gynecology*
Hal Curtis Miller, 720 Hurt Building . . . . . . *Surgery*
William Perrin Nicolson, Healey Building . . . . *Surgery*
George Henry Noble, 980 Peachtree Street . . . *Gynecology*
Weldon E. Person, Candler Building . . . . . . *Surgery*
R. B. Ridley, Jr., Atlanta National Bank Building
Ophth., Rhinol., Oto-Laryngology
Dunbar Roy, Grand Opera House Building . . *Ophth., Otology*
William A. Selman, 604 Candler Building . . . . . *Surgery*
William F. Shallenberger, 820 Hurt Building *Gynecology, Obstetrics*
A. W. Stirling, Atlanta Trust Company Building
Ophth., Rhinol., Oto-Laryngology
Willis Foreman Westmoreland, 53 Forrest Avenue . . *Surgery*

AUGUSTA

Joseph Akerman, 1496 Harper Street . . . . . . *Obstetrics*
Guy Talmadge Bernard, 204 13th Street . . . . . *Surgery*
Charles Williams Crane, 1106 Lamar Building . . . *Surgery*
William Henry Doughty, Jr., 822 Greene Street . . . *Surgery*
William Henry Goodrich, 508 Lamar Building . . . *Surgery*
William C. Kellogg, Lamar Building
Ophth., Rhinol., Oto-Laryngology
Henry Middleton Michel, 638 Greene Street . *Orthopedic Surgery*
Theodore Eugene Oertel, Lamar Building
Ophth., Rhinol., Oto-Laryngology
Robert Lewis Rhodes, 1103 Lamar Building . . . . *Surgery*
George Albert Traylor, Lamar Building . . . . . *Surgery*
Thomas R. Wright, 402 9th Street . . . . *Surgery*

GEORGIA — Continued

GAINESVILLE

James Henry Downey, 13 Sycamore Street . . . . *Surgery*

MACON

Charles Cotton Harrold, 550 Orange Street . . . . *Surgery*
Kingman P. Moore, Bibb Realty Building   *Gynecology, Obstetrics*
Olin H. Weaver, 722 Spring Street . . . . *Surgery*

ROME

Ross Parker Cox . . . . . *Ophth., Rhinol., Oto-Laryngology*
Robert Maxwell Harbin, 100 3rd Avenue . . . . . *Surgery*
William Pickens Harbin, 100 3rd Avenue . . . . . *Surgery*
George Barker Smith   . . . *Ophth., Rhinol., Oto-Laryngology*

SAVANNAH

Jabez Jones, De Renne Apartments . . . . . . *Surgery*
Henry Hager Martin, 247 Bull Street .   *Ophth., Oto-Laryngology*
Walter A. Norton, 105 Oglethorpe Avenue, East . . *Surgery*
Thomas Pinckney Waring, De Renne Apartments . . *Surgery*
George Reeves White, 2 Liberty Street, East . . . . *Surgery*

THOMASVILLE

Arthur D. H. Little, 203 Masonic Building . . . . *Surgery*
Charles Hansell Watt, 403 Masonic Building . . . . *Surgery*

VALDOSTA

Alexander G. Little, 134½ North Patterson Street . . *Surgery*

IDAHO

BOISE

Franz H. Brandt, Overland Building . *Rhinol., Oto-Laryngology*
E. E. Maxey, Idaho Building . . . *Ophth., Oto-Laryngology*
Lucien P. McCalla, Boise City Bank Building . . . *Surgery*
Robert L. Nourse, Idaho Building *Ophth., Rhinol., Oto-Laryngology*
Joseph R. Numbers, 212 Idaho Building . . . . . *Surgery*
Fred A. Pittenger, 407 Overland Building . . . . . *Surgery*
John S. Springer, 208 Idaho Building . . . . . . *Surgery*
James L. S. Stewart, 410 Overland Building . . . . *Surgery*
John M. Taylor, Empire Building . . . . *Surgery*

IDAHO FALLS

Clifford M. Cline, Farmers and Merchants Bank Building *Surgery*

IDAHO — Continued

LEWISTON

    Charles Whiting Shaff, 212 5th Street . . . . *Surgery*

MOSCOW

    Warner H. Carithers, 1st and Jackson Streets . . . *Surgery*

POCATELLO

    William Forrest Howard, 303 Carlson Building . . . *Surgery*
    Thomas Francis Mullen, Kane Building . . . . . *Surgery*
    Abram Mark Newton, 300 Kane Building . . . . *Surgery*
    Edward Newman Roberts, 407 Kane Building . . . *Surgery*
    William A. Wright, 300 Kane Building . . . . . *Surgery*

WALLACE

    Charles Rothelles Mowery, 6th and Cedar Streets . . *Surgery*

ILLINOIS

BELLEVILLE

    Grover C. Otrich, Commercial Building   *Rhinol., Oto-Laryngology*
    Charles H. Starkel, 11 South Church Street . . . . *Surgery*

BLOOMINGTON

    Thomas Wilbur Bath . . . . *Surgery*
    Ernest Mammen, 308 Griesheim Building . . . . . *Surgery*
    Robert Avery Noble, 1406 East Washington Street . . *Surgery*
    Joseph Whitefield Smith, 1122 East Grove Street
                      Ophth., Rhinol., Oto-Laryngology

BUSHNELL

    George S. Duntley, 408 East Main Street
                      Ophth., Rhinol., Oto-Laryngology

CAIRO

    Flint Bondurant, Cairo National Bank Building . . . *Surgery*
    William Franklin Grinstead, 808 Commercial Avenue . *Surgery*

CANTON

    James Edmund Coleman, 24 North Main Street . . . *Surgery*

CARBONDALE

    Henry C. Mitchell, 202 West Main Street . . . . *Surgery*

CHAMPAIGN

    James Hugh Finch, 308 Illinois Building . . . . . *Surgery*
    William L. Gray . . . . *Surgery*
    Thomas J. McKinney, 300 First National Bank Building *Surgery*

ILLINOIS — Continued

CHICAGO

Charles Adams, 920 North Michigan Avenue . . . . *Retired*
Frank Allport, 7 West Madison Street . . . *Ophth., Otology*
George C. Amerson, 31 North State Street . . . . *Surgery*
E. Wyllys Andrews, 1235 Astor Street . . . . . *Surgery*
Frank T. Andrews, 448 Barry Avenue . . . . *Gynecology*
Cecil V. Bachellé, 30 North Michigan Avenue . . *Gynecology*
Charles S. Bacon, 2156 Sedgwick Street . *Obstetrics, Gynecology*
Joseph Louis Baer, 104 South Michigan Avenue
Obstetrics, Gynecology
E. Stillman Bailey, 22 East Washington Street . . *Gynecology*
Walter S. Barnes, 29 East Madison Street . . . . *Surgery*
Channing W. Barrett, 25 East Washington Street . *Gynecology*
W. L. Baum, 30 North Michigan Avenue . *Genito-Urinary Surgery*
Carl Beck, 601 Deming Place . . . . *Surgery*
Emil G. Beck, 2632 Lake View Avenue . . . . . *Surgery*
Joseph C. Beck, 108 North State Street . . . *Oto-Laryngology*
William T. Belfield, 32 North State Street *Genito-Urinary Surgery*
Joseph Z. Bergeron, 104 South Michigan Avenue
Rhinol., Oto-Laryngology
Frederic A. Besley, 104 South Michigan Avenue . . . *Surgery*
Ralph Boerne Bettman, 5 South Wabash Avenue . . *Surgery*
Arthur Dean Bevan, 122 South Michigan Avenue . . *Surgery*
John W. Birk, 4654 Sheridan Road . . *Gynecology, Obstetrics*
Arthur D. Black, 122 South Michigan Avenue . . *Oral Surgery*
Wallace Blanchard, 15 East Washington Street *Orthopedic Surgery*
Carl F. Bookwalter, 104 South Michigan Avenue
Rhinol., Oto-Laryngology
Jesse Franklin Boone, 818 East 47th Street
Ophth., Rhinol., Oto-Laryngology
George William Boot, 25 East Washington Street
Rhinol., Oto-Laryngology
William Edson Boynton, 110 North Wabash Avenue
Ophth., Oto-Laryngology
Frank Brawley, 30 North Michigan Avenue
Ophth., Rhinol., Otology
Lewis Wine Bremerman, 1919 Prairie Avenue . . . *Urology*
Truman W. Brophy, 81 East Madison Street . . *Oral Surgery*
Edward J. Brougham, 163 West Chicago Avenue . . *Surgery*

ILLINOIS — Continued

CHICAGO — Continued

Edward M. Brown, 25 East Washington Street . . . *Surgery*
Coleman Graves Buford, 122 South Michigan Avenue . *Surgery*
George N. Bussey, 1810 Wilson Avenue . . *Surgery, Obstetrics*
Clark A. Buswell, 1952 Irving Park Boulevard . . . *Surgery*
Henry Turman Byford, 122 South Michigan Avenue *Gynecology*
Frank Byrnes, 3203 North Clark Street . . . . . *Surgery*
James Tweedie Campbell, 30 North Michigan Avenue
Rhinol., Oto-Laryngology
Frank Cary, 2536 Prairie Avenue . . . . *Obstetrics*
French S. Cary, 30 North Michigan Avenue . . . . *Urology*
John Algernon Cavanaugh, 7 West Madison Street
Rhinol., Oto-Laryngology
Howard Roy Chislett, 4721 Greenwood Avenue . . . *Surgery*
Charles C. Clark, 765 Oakwood Boulevard . . . . *Surgery*
Peter S. Clark, 818 East 47th Street . . . . . . *Surgery*
Clinton C. Collier, 25 East Washington Street
Ophth., Rhinol., Oto-Laryngology
Sylvan Coombs, Surf Apartments . . . . *Surgery*
Budd C. Corbus, 30 North Michigan Avenue
Genito-Urinary Surgery
Edward L. Cornell, 122 South Michigan Avenue
Obstetrics, Gynecology
John Stanley Coulter, 5 North Wabash Avenue . . . *Surgery*
William R. Cubbins, 29 East Madison Street . . . . *Surgery*
Carey Culbertson, 30 North Michigan Avenue *Gynecology, Obstetrics*
Ralph Clinton Cupler, 5222 Blackstone Avenue . . . *Surgery*
Arthur H. Curtis, 104 South Michigan Avenue . . *Gynecology*
George Luther Davenport, 31 North State Street . . *Surgery*
Frank Elmer David, 25 East Washington Street . . *Proctology*
Ray H. Davies, 30 North Michigan Avenue . . . . *Surgery*
Carl B. Davis, 122 South Michigan Avenue . . . . *Surgery*
George G. Davis, 122 South Michigan Avenue . . . *Surgery*
Thomas Archibald Davis, 2344 Jackson Boulevard . . *Surgery*
Charles Davison, 30 North Michigan Avenue . . . *Surgery*
Joseph B. DeLee, 5028 Ellis Avenue . . *Obstetrics, Gynecology*
John C. Delprat, 25 East Washington Street . . . . *Surgery*
Edmund J. Doering, 81 East Madison Street . *Obstetrics, Surgery*
W. A. Newman Dorland, 7 West Madison Street
Obstetrics, Gynecology

ILLINOIS — Continued

CHICAGO — Continued

Guy Grigsby Dowdall, 135 East 11th Place . . . . . *Surgery*
Emilius Clark Dudley, 242 East Walton Place . . *Gynecology*
Frederick G. Dyas, 25 East Washington Street . . . *Surgery*
Daniel Nathan Eisendrath, 4840 Woodlawn Avenue . *Surgery*
Joseph S. Eisenstaedt, 25 East Washington Street . . *Urology*
P. J. H. Farrell, 25 East Washington Street
　　　　　　　　　　Ophth., Rhinol., Oto-Laryngology
Leon Feingold, 714 Grace Street . . . . *Surgery*
C. Gurnee Fellows, 30 North Michigan Avenue
　　　　　　　　　　Ophth., Rhinol., Oto-Laryngology
Ephraim Kirkpatrick Findlay, 30 North Michigan
　Avenue . . . . *Ophthalmology*
Egon Walter Fischmann, 30 North Michigan Avenue
　　　　　　　　　　Gynecology, Obstetrics
William A. Fisher, 31 North State Street
　　　　　　　　　　Ophth., Rhinol., Oto-Laryngology
David Fiske, 25 East Washington Street
　　　　　　　　　　Ophth., Rhinol., Oto-Laryngology
George F. Fiske, 25 East Washington Street . . *Ophth., Otology*
Gilbert Fitz-Patrick, 122 South Michigan Avenue . . *Obstetrics*
R. E. Flannery, 3117 Logan Boulevard . . . . . *Surgery*
Edson B. Fowler, 7 West Madison Street . . . . . *Surgery*
Ira Frank, 104 South Michigan Avenue . . . *Oto-Laryngology*
Jacob Frank, 25 East Washington Street . . . . . *Surgery*
Lester E. Frankenthal, 4825 Woodlawn Avenue
　　　　　　　　　　Gynecology, Obstetrics
Emanuel Friend, 5 North Wabash Avenue . . . . *Surgery*
H. B. Frost, 30 North Michigan Avenue . *Genito-Urinary Surgery*
William Fuller, 25 East Washington Street . . . . *Surgery*
William E. Gamble, 30 North Michigan Avenue . *Ophthalmology*
Edwin J. Gardiner, 15 East Washington Street . *Ophth., Otology*
Edward Francis Garrahgan, 25 East Washington Street
　　　　　　　　　　Ophth., Rhinol., Oto-Laryngology
Edgar J. George, 110 North Wabash Avenue . . *Ophthalmology*
Thomas L. Gilmer, 122 South Michigan Avenue . . *Oral Surgery*
John Ferdinand Golden, 104 South Michigan Avenue . *Surgery*
Albert Goldspohn, 2120 Cleveland Avenue . . . . *Surgery*
Mark T. Goldstine, 25 East Washington Street . . *Gynecology*

ILLINOIS — Continued

CHICAGO — Continued

Archie James Graham, 6250 South Halsted Street . . *Surgery*
David Wilson Graham, 7 West Madison Street . . . *Surgery*
John Alfred Graham, 30 North Michigan Avenue . . *Surgery*
George Willard Green, 4654 Sheridan Road . . . *Surgery*
Louis A. Greensfelder, 31 North State Street . . . *Surgery*
Paul Gronnerud, 25 East Washington Street . . . *Surgery*
Wallace F. Grosvenor, 4700 Sheridan Road . *Gynecology, Obstetrics*
Garrett J. Hagens, 7207 South Halsted Street

Gynecology, Obstetrics

Albert E. Halstead, 30 North Michigan Avenue . . . *Surgery*
Walter C. Hammond, 737 Sheridan Road . *Obstetrics, Gynecology*
T. Melville Hardie, 30 North Michigan Avenue . *Oto-Laryngology*
John Ross Harger, 25 East Washington Street . . . *Surgery*
Malcolm LaSalle Harris, 25 East Washington Street . *Surgery*
William McIntire Harsha, 30 North Michigan Avenue . *Surgery*
William Thomas Harsha, 30 North Michigan Avenue . *Surgery*
Andrew Magee Harvey, 836 South Michigan Avenue . *Surgery*
James Alexander Harvey, 25 East Washington Street . *Surgery*
Burton Haseltine, 122 South Michigan Avenue

Ophth., Oto-Laryngology

Austin A. Hayden, 25 East Washington Street

Ophth., Rhinol., Oto-Laryngology

Noble Sproat Heaney, 104 South Michigan Avenue

Gynecology, Obstetrics

Robert H. Herbst, 32 North State Street . *Genito-Urinary Surgery*
William Hessert, 547 Fullerton Parkway . . . . *Surgery*
William F. Hewitt, 122 South Michigan Avenue

Obstetrics, Gynecology

David S. Hillis, 104 South Michigan Avenue . . . *Obstetrics*
Junius C. Hoag, 1725 East 53rd Street . . . . *Obstetrics*
Rudolph W. Holmes, 414 Arlington Place . *Gynecology, Obstetrics*
Clarence W. Hopkins, 322 North Wells Street . . *Surgery*
Edward DeM. Howland, 30 North Michigan Avenue . *Surgery*
Lawrence Lee Iseman, 30 North Michigan Avenue . . *Surgery*
Harry Jackson, 104 South Michigan Avenue . . . *Surgery*
Charles M. Jacobs, 31 North State Street . . *Orthopedic Surgery*
Charles E. Kahlke, 25 East Washington Street . . . *Surgery*
Allen B. Kanavel, 30 North Michigan Avenue . . . *Surgery*

ILLINOIS — Continued

CHICAGO — Continued

Elmer L. Kenyon, 104 South Michigan Avenue
Rhinol., Oto-Laryngology
Norman Kerr, 25 East Washington Street . . . . *Surgery*
A. Belcham Keyes, 122 South Michigan Avenue . . . *Surgery*
John Joseph Killeen, 104 South Michigan Avenue
Rhinol., Oto-Laryngology
Irvin S. Koll, 31 North State Street . . *Genito-Urinary Surgery*
Oscar H. Kraft, 25 East Washington Street . . *Ophthalmology*
Herman L. Kretschmer, 122 South Michigan Avenue
Genito-Urinary Surgery
Philip H. Kreuscher, 30 North Michigan Avenue . . *Surgery*
Wladyslaw A. Kuflewski, 1366 North Robey Street . . *Surgery*
V. D. Lespinasse, 7 West Madison Street . *Genito-Urinary Surgery*
Dean Lewis, 122 South Michigan Avenue . . . . *Surgery*
A. Lewy, 110 North Wabash Avenue . *Rhinol., Oto-Laryngology*
Effie L. Lobdell, Marshall Field Building . *Obstetrics, Gynecology*
William H. G. Logan, 29 East Madison Street . . *Oral Surgery*
J. B. Loring, 25 East Washington Street . *Ophth., Oto-Laryngology*
Benjamin F. Lounsbury, 2449 Washington Boulevard . *Surgery*
Burton Wilson Mack, 4159 West North Avenue . . . *Surgery*
Otis Hardy Maclay, 5436 Hyde Park Boulevard
Rhinol., Oto-Laryngology
Paul B. Magnuson, 30 North Michigan Avenue . . . *Surgery*
George W. Mahoney, 30 North Michigan Avenue *Ophthalmology*
Goeke Henry Mammen, 2706 North Rockwell Street . *Surgery*
George Paull Marquis, 30 North Michigan Avenue *Oto-Laryngology*
Franklin H. Martin, 30 North Michigan Avenue . *Gynecology*
Lewis Linn McArthur, 4724 Drexel Boulevard . . . *Surgery*
George M. McBean, 22 East Washington Street . *Ophth., Otology*
Mary Gilruth McEwen, 25 East Washington Street . *Gynecology*
Edwin McGinnis, 104 South Michigan Avenue
Rhinol., Oto-Laryngology
John D. McGowan, 72 West Adams Street . . . . *Surgery*
James J. McGuinn, 5850 Kenmore Avenue . . . . *Surgery*
Charles Morgan McKenna, 25 East Washington Street
Genito-Urinary Surgery
Hugh McKenna, 104 South Michigan Avenue . . . *Surgery*
Golder Lewis McWhorter, 122 South Michigan Avenue . *Surgery*

ILLINOIS — Continued

CHICAGO — Continued

John J. Meany, 30 North Michigan Avenue . . . . *Surgery*
Frederick Menge, 25 East Washington Street
Rhinol., Oto-Laryngology
Harry Edgar Mock, 122 South Michigan Avenue . . *Surgery*
James John Monahan, 25 East Washington Street . . *Surgery*
David Monash, 4735 South Michigan Avenue
Gynecology, Obstetrics
Frank D. Moore, 30 North Michigan Avenue . . . *Surgery*
Frederick Brown Moorehead, 122 South Michigan
Avenue . . . . *Oral Surgery*
Edward Louis Moorhead, 31 North State Street . . . *Surgery*
Paul F. Morf, 746 Fullerton Avenue . . . . . . *Surgery*
G. Morgenthau, 1116 East 46th Street . . . *Oto-Laryngology*
Frank Roy Morton, 25 East Washington Street . . . *Surgery*
George Mueller, 209 South State Street . . . . . *Surgery*
G. Henry Mundt, 25 East Washington Street
Ophth., Oto-Laryngology
Alfred Nicholas Murray, 4654 Sheridan Road
Ophth., Rhinol., Oto-Laryngology
Oscar E. Nadeau, 2106 Sedgwick Street . . . . . *Surgery*
James M. Neff, 30 North Michigan Avenue . . . . *Surgery*
Edward Powers Norcross, 30 North Michigan Avenue
Rhinol., Oto-Laryngology
Albert John Ochsner, 2106 Sedgwick Street . . . . *Surgery*
Edward H. Ochsner, 2155 Cleveland Avenue . . . . *Surgery*
Rudolph J. E. Oden, 5412 North Clark Street . . . *Surgery*
Oscar Ofner, 635 Center Street . . . . *Surgery*
Paul Oliver, 104 South Michigan Avenue . . . . . *Surgery*
A. Augustus O'Neill, 4607 Champlain Avenue . . . *Surgery*
Daniel A. Orth, 209 South State Street . . . . . *Surgery*
John E. Owens, 2127 Prairie Avenue . . . . . . *Surgery*
Charles E. Paddock, 104 South Michigan Avenue . . *Obstetrics*
Charles H. Parkes, 1910 Lincoln Avenue . . . . . *Surgery*
Edward Patera, 1809 Loomis Street . . . . . . *Surgery*
John Rawson Pennington, 31 North State Street . . *Surgery*
Nelson Mortimer Percy, 2106 Sedgwick Street . . . *Surgery*
John P. Pfeifer, 1572 Milwaukee Avenue . . . . . *Surgery*
Dallas B. Phemister, 122 South Michigan Avenue . . *Surgery*

ILLINOIS — Continued

CHICAGO — Continued

Charles Herbert Phifer, 30 North Michigan Avenue . .   *Surgery*
Frank E. Pierce, 5114 Harper Avenue . . . . .   *Surgery*
Norval H. Pierce, 22 East Washington Street   . *Oto-Laryngology*
Samuel C. Plummer, 4539 Oakenwald Avenue   . . .   *Surgery*
Darwin Brayton Pond, 4363 Lincoln Avenue   . . .   *Surgery*
John Lincoln Porter, 7 West Madison Street .   *Orthopedic Surgery*
George Washington Post, Jr., 4158 West Lake Street   .   *Surgery*
Herbert A. Potts, 31 North State Street   . . . .   *Oral Surgery*
Edward N. Redden, 17 South Crawford Avenue .   . .   *Surgery*
Charles B. Reed, 31 North State Street   . . . .   *Obstetrics*
H. M. Richter, Wesley Memorial Hospital   . . . .   *Surgery*
John Ridlon, 7 West Madison Street   . . .   *Orthopedic Surgery*
Oscar Theodore Roberg, 2749 West Foster Avenue .   .   *Surgery*
Charles Moore Robertson, 30 North Michigan Avenue
                                        Oto-Laryngology
Cassius Clay Rogers, 25 East Washington Street   . .   *Surgery*
Lawrence Ryan, 32 North State Street   . . . . .   *Surgery*
E. W. Ryerson, 122 South Michigan Avenue .   *Orthopedic Surgery*
Lena Kellogg Sadler, 533 Diversey Parkway .   . .   *Gynecology*
William S. Sadler, 533 Diversey Parkway .   . . . .   *Surgery*
Charles Frye Sanborn, Municipal Tuberculosis
    Sanitarium . . . . " . .   *Surgery*
Ernst Saurenhaus, 59 Bellevue Place   . .   *Gynecology, Obstetrics*
Charles F. Sawyer, 2526 Calumet Avenue   . . . .   *Surgery*
Heliodor Schiller, 29 East Madison Street   . . .   *Gynecology*
Louis E. Schmidt, 60 Bellevue Place   . . . . . .   *Urology*
Henry Schmitz, 25 East Washington Street   . . .   *Gynecology*
A. John Schoenberg, 747 Fullerton Avenue   . . .   *Gynecology*
William E. Schroeder, Wesley Memorial Hospital   . .   *Surgery*
Mathias J. Seifert, 30 North Michigan Avenue   . . .   *Surgery*
William N. Senn, 25 East Washington Street .   . . .   *Urology*
George E. Shambaugh, 122 South Michigan Avenue
                                        Oto-Laryngology
Ludwig S. Simon, 4743 Forrestville Avenue   . . . .   *Obstetrics*
Robert Sonnenschein, 29 East Madison Street   . *Oto-Laryngology*
Alva Sowers, 30 North Michigan Avenue
                        Ophth., Rhinol., Oto-Laryngology
Kellogg Speed, 122 South Michigan Avenue . . . .   *Surgery*

ILLINOIS — Continued

CHICAGO — Continued

William Marion Stearns, 22 East Washington Street
Rhinol., Oto-Laryngology
Daniel Atkinson King Steele, 2920 Indiana Avenue . . *Surgery*
Charles Frederick Stotz, 1954 Milwaukee Avenue
Genito-Urinary Surgery
David C. Straus, 30 North Michigan Avenue . . . *Surgery*
Jerome F. Strauss, 104 South Michigan Avenue
Rhinol., Oto-Laryngology
Julia C. Strawn, 22 East Washington Street . . . *Gynecology*
Richard H. Street, 25 East Washington Street
Rhinol., Oto-Laryngology
Thomas J. Sullivan, 4709 South Michigan Avenue . . *Surgery*
Carl Gustaf Swenson, 440 Fullerton Parkway . . . *Surgery*
William J. Swift, 220 South State Street . . . . . *Surgery*
George de Tarnowsky, 30 North Michigan Avenue . . *Surgery*
Henry Bascom Thomas, 30 North Michigan Avenue
Orthopedic Surgery
George F. Thompson, 4100 West Madison Street . . *Surgery*
LeRoy Thompson, 30 North Michigan Avenue
Ophth., Rhinol., Oto-Laryngology
William McIlwain Thompson, 25 East Washington Street . *Surgery*
Richard J. Tivnen, 800 Monroe Building
Ophth., Rhinol., Oto-Laryngology
Roger Throop Vaughan, 30 North Michigan Avenue . *Surgery*
Oren J. Waters, 3 West Delaware Place . . . . . *Surgery*
Thomas J. Watkins, 104 South Michigan Avenue . *Gynecology*
Axel Werelius, 6725 Constance Avenue . . . . . *Surgery*
Cassius D. Wescott, 22 East Washington Street . *Ophthalmology*
Edward William White, 7 West Madison Street
Genito-Urinary Surgery
William H. Wilder, 122 South Michigan Avenue . *Ophthalmology*
Daniel Hale Williams, 3129 Indiana Avenue . . . . *Surgery*
Thomas J. Williams, 30 North Michigan Avenue
Ophth., Rhinol., Oto-Laryngology
J. Gordon Wilson, 104 South Michigan Avenue . *Oto-Laryngology*
John A. Wolfer, 30 North Michigan Avenue . . . . *Surgery*
Casey Albert Wood, 7 West Madison Street . . . . *Retired*

ILLINOIS — Continued

CHICAGO — Continued

Herbert Boothe Woodard, 25 East Washington Street
                                        Rhinol., Oto-Laryngology
Wesley John Woolston, 25 East Washington Street . *Gynecology*
Charles Ira Wynekoop, 4931 Sheridan Road . . . . *Surgery*
Gilbert H. Wynekoop, 4500 Sheridan Road . . . . *Surgery*
Thaddeus Zigmund Xelowski, 30 North Michigan
    Avenue . . . . *Surgery*
Rachelle S. Yarros, 800 South Halsted Street
                                        Gynecology, Obstetrics
Charles Benjamin Younger, 25 East Washington Street
                                        Rhinol., Oto-Laryngology
Joseph Zabokrtsky, 31 North State Street   . . . . *Surgery*
Frederick Carl Zapffe, 25 East Washington Street . . *Surgery*
A. G. Zimmerman, 30 North Michigan Avenue . . . *Surgery*

DANVILLE

Henri S. Babcock, 419 Temple Building . . . . . *Surgery*
Francis William Barton, 402 First National Bank
    Building . . . . *Surgery*
Raymond L. Hatfield, 508 First National Bank Building . *Surgery*
Frank M. Mason, 501 Temple Building . . . . . *Surgery*
A. Merrill Miller, 1222 Vermilion Street . . . . . *Surgery*
Hiram Earl Ross, 1008 First National Bank Building . *Surgery*

DIXON

Edmund Burt Owens, 123 East 1st Street   . . . . *Surgery*
Edward Allen Sickels, 123 East 1st Street   . . . . *Surgery*

EAST ST. LOUIS

Albert Baptiste McQuillan, Cahokia Building   . . . *Surgery*
Jonathan Leaming Wiggins, 11½ North Main Street . *Surgery*
Charles F. W. Wilhelmj, Murphy Building . . . . *Surgery*

ELGIN

Fred H. Langhorst, 6 Spring Street . . . . . . *Surgery*
O. L. Pelton, 102 North Spring Street . . . . . . *Surgery*
O. L. Pelton, Jr., 102 North Spring Street . . . . *Surgery*
Frederick C. Schurmeier, 820 Spring Street . . . . *Surgery*
John R. Tobin, 165 Milwaukee Street . . . . . . *Surgery*

ILLINOIS — Continued

EVANSTON

    Dwight Freeman Clark, 800 Davis Street . . . . . *Surgery*

    William C. Danforth, 1620 Hinman Avenue *Gynecology, Obstetrics*

    Oscar Dodd, 1604 Chicago Avenue . . . . *Ophth., Otology*

    Ernest Jason Ford, 2009 Harrison Street . . . . . *Surgery*

    William Ross Parkes, 800 Davis Street . . . . . *Surgery*

    Charles Joseph Swan, 1818 Hinman Avenue . *Ophth., Laryngology*

    Will Walter, 1414 Chicago Avenue . . . *Ophth., Oto-Laryngology*

FAIRBURY

    James Hartzell Langstaff . . . . *Surgery*

FREEPORT

    Charles Lorton Best, 3½ East Stephenson Street . . *Surgery*

    John Sheldon Clark, State Bank Building

                      Ophth., Rhinol., Oto-Laryngology

    William Leonard Karcher, 1½ West Stephenson Street . *Surgery*

    William Buckley Peck, 86 Stephenson Street . . . . *Surgery*

    William J. Rideout, State Bank Building

                      Ophth., Rhinol., Oto-Laryngology

    Karl F. Snyder, State Bank Building . . . . . . *Surgery*

GALESBURG

    Edward C. G. Franing, 306 East Main Street . . . *Surgery*

    Ralph Charles Matheny, 306 East Main Street

                      Ophth., Oto-Laryngology

    Edwin N. Nash, 411 Bank of Galesburg Building . . *Obstetrics*

    James Fulton Percy, 147 South Cherry Street . . . *Surgery*

GENEVA

    Raymond G. Scott, 216 3rd Street . . . . *Surgery*

HIGHLAND PARK

    Alfred E. Bradley, 295 Prospect Avenue . . . . . *Surgery*

JACKSONVILLE

    Albyn L. Adams, 323 West State Street *Ophth., Oto-Laryngology*

    Carl E. Black, 200 Ayers Bank Building . . . . . *Surgery*

    John Whitlock Hairgrove, 339 East State Street . . *Surgery*

    Frank A. Norris, 409 Ayers Bank Building . . . . *Surgery*

JOLIET

    Raymond Samuel Brown, 511 Barber Building

                      Ophth., Rhinol., Oto-Laryngology

    Thomas H. Wagner, 315 Jefferson Street . . . . . *Surgery*

ILLINOIS — Continued

KANKAKEE

Eugene Cohn, Kankakee State Hospital . . . . . *Surgery*

LA SALLE

Edmund W. Weis, 151 5th Street . . . . *Surgery*

MACOMB

Joseph Barnes Bacon . . . . *Surgery*

MATTOON

Charles Bernard Voigt, 1702 Broadway
Ophth., Rhinol., Oto-Laryngology

MOLINE

Frank Jesse Otis, 512 Reliance Building . . . . . *Surgery*

MONMOUTH

Edward L. Mitchell, 122 West 2nd Avenue . . . . *Surgery*
A. G. Patton, 122 West 1st Avenue . . . . . . *Surgery*

MURPHYSBORO

Charles Otto Molz, 1103 Chestnut Street . . . . . *Surgery*

OAK PARK

E. E. Henderson, 644 Linden Avenue . . . . . *Surgery*
Thomas Ira Motter, 127 North Oak Park Avenue . . *Surgery*
Harry John Stewart, 801 South Boulevard . . . . *Surgery*

PAXTON

Samuel M. Wylie, 308 West Center Street . . . . *Surgery*

PEORIA

Jay Harvey Bacon, 804 Peoria Life Building . . . . *Surgery*
Charles H. Brobst, Central National Bank Building
Ophth., Rhinol., Oto-Laryngology
Clifford U. Collins, 427 Jefferson Building . . . . *Surgery*
R. A. Hanna, Lehmann Building . . . . *Surgery*
Charles Derastus Thomas, 464 Moss Avenue
Ophth., Rhinol., Oto-Laryngology

PERU

Benjamin J. Nauman, Masonic Temple Building . . *Surgery*

QUINCY

John A. Koch, 804 Broadway . . . . *Surgery*
Edmund B. Montgomery, 132 North 8th Street . . . *Surgery*
O. Frank Shulian, 312 Illinois State Bank Building . . *Surgery*
Walter Stevenson . . . . *Ophth., Rhinol., Oto-Laryngology*
William Warren Williams, 1250 Main Street . . . . *Surgery*

ILLINOIS — Continued

ROCHELLE

A. W. Chandler . . . . *Surgery*

ROCKFORD

Sanford Robinson Catlin, Stewart Building . . . . *Surgery*
Thomas H. Culhane, 305 Stewart Building . . . . *Surgery*
William H. Fitch, 849 Main Street, North . . . . *Surgery*
William Rudisel Fringer, William Brown Building *Ophthalmology*
John A. Green, William Brown Building . . . . . *Surgery*
T. Arthur Johnson, 503 7th Street . . . . *Surgery*
Darwin Mills Keith, 420 Main Street, North
Rhinol., Oto-Laryngology

ROCK ISLAND

George Loughead Eyster, 413 Safety Building . . . *Surgery*
Joseph Ralston Hollowbush, 509 Central Trust Building *Surgery*

SPRINGFIELD

Clarence W. East, St. John's Hospital . . *Orthopedic Surgery*
G. N. Kreider, 522 East Capitol Avenue . . . . . *Surgery*
Charles Lanphier Patton, 407 South 7th Street . . . *Surgery*

SPRING VALLEY

J. Herbert Franklin, 409 East Erie Street . . . . . *Surgery*

STERLING

Frank Wilson Brodrick, Lawrence Building . . . . *Surgery*

URBANA

James S. Mason, 129 West Elm Street . . . . . *Surgery*

WAUKEGAN

John C. Foley, County and Washington Streets . . . *Surgery*

WOODSTOCK

William Hyde West, State Bank Building . . . . *Surgery*
Emil Windmueller, Clinic Building . . . *Surgery, Obstetrics*

INDIANA

ANDERSON

Maynard Alvernise Austin, 359 Union Building . . . *Surgery*
George A. Whitledge, 453 Union Building
Ophth., Rhinol., Oto-Laryngology

BLOOMINGTON

George Frank Holland, 514 North College Avenue
Gynecology, Obstetrics

INDIANA — Continued

BLUFFTON

    Luzerne H. Cook, 429 West Market Street . . . . *Surgery*

    Fred A. Metts . . . . *Surgery*

BROOKVILLE

    John Albert Thompson . . . . *Retired*

COLUMBUS

    Alfred P. Roope . . . . *Surgery*

CRAWFORDSVILLE

    Paul J. Barcus, Ben Hur Building . . . . . . *Surgery*

EAST CHICAGO

    Alexander G. Schlieker, 721 Chicago Avenue . . . . *Surgery*

EVANSVILLE

    Louis D. Brose, 501 Upper 1st Street

                        Ophth., Rhinol., Oto-Laryngology

    William R. Davidson, 712 South 4th Street . . . . *Surgery*

    William S. Ehrich, Citizens Bank Building *Genito-Urinary Surgery*

    William Hill Field, 424 Upper 1st Street

                        Ophth., Rhinol., Oto-Laryngology

    Benjamin L. W. Floyd, 517 Chandler Avenue

                        Ophth., Rhinol., Oto-Laryngology

    A. M. Hayden, 22 Walnut Street . . . . *Surgery*

    Bleeker Knapp, Cleveland Building . *Ophth., Rhinol., Otology*

    William E. McCool, Walker Hospital . . . . . . *Surgery*

    J. W. Phares, 22 Walnut Street . . . . *Surgery*

    Marcus Ravdin, Citizens Bank Building *Ophth., Oto-Laryngology*

    Paul Charles Rietz, American Trust Building . . . *Surgery*

    Edwin Walker, 5 Cherry Street . . . . *Surgery*

    James Y. Welborn, 712 South 4th Street . . . . . *Surgery*

FORT WAYNE

    Charles E. Barnett, 301 Medical Arts Building

                        Genito-Urinary Surgery

    Henry Otto Bruggeman . . . . *Surgery*

    Albert Eugene Bulson, Jr., 406 West Berry Street

                        Ophth., Oto-Laryngology

    Miles Fuller Porter, 2326 Fairfield Avenue . . . . *Surgery*

    Maurice I. Rosenthal, 336 West Berry Street . . . *Surgery*

    Ben Perley Weaver, Carroll Building . . . . . . *Surgery*

INDIANA — Continued

GARY

Theodore B. Templin, 583 Broadway . . . . . *Surgery*

HAMMOND

Eldridge M. Shanklin, 575 Hohman Street
Ophth., Rhinol., Oto-Laryngology

INDIANA HARBOR

Clifford C. Robinson, 3410 Michigan Avenue . . . *Surgery*

INDIANAPOLIS

John F. Barnhill, Pennway Building . *Rhinol., Oto-Laryngology*
Harry Kraylor Bonn, 201 Pennway Building . . . . *Surgery*
Edmund D. Clark, Hume-Mansur Building . . . . *Surgery*
William Franklin Clevenger, 403 Hume-Mansur Building
Rhinol., Oto-Laryngology
Joseph Rilus Eastman, 331 North Delaware Street . . *Surgery*
Bernhard Erdman, 224 North Meridian Street
Genito-Urinary Surgery
Charles E. Ferguson, 412 East 17th Street . . . . *Obstetrics*
William Province Garshwiler, 716 Indiana Pythian
Building . . . . *Genito-Urinary Surgery*
Willis D. Gatch, 1440 Central Avenue . . . . . *Surgery*
Alois Bachman Graham, 30 Willoughby Building . *Proctology*
Murray Nathan Hadley, 608 Hume-Mansur Building . *Surgery*
Homer G. Hamer, 723 Hume-Mansur Building
Genito-Urinary Surgery
Thomas C. Hood, 1008 Hume-Mansur Building . *Ophthalmology*
Gustavus Brown Jackson, 603 Hume-Mansur Building
Gynecology, Obstetrics
Alfred S. Jaeger, 430 Bankers Trust Building *Gynecology, Obstetrics*
Norman E. Jobes, 305 Traction Terminal Building . . *Surgery*
Bernays Kennedy, 50 Willoughby Building . . . *Gynecology*
Daniel W. Layman, 608 Hume-Mansur Building
Rhinol., Oto-Laryngology
Carleton B. McCulloch, 1135 State Life Building . . *Surgery*
Harvey A. Moore . . . . *Surgery*
Frank A. Morrison, Willoughby Building . . . *Ophthalmology*
John Ray Newcomb, 411 Hume-Mansur Building *Ophthalmology*
John Holliday Oliver, 510 Hume-Mansur Building . . *Surgery*
Everett Ervin Padgett, 423 Hume-Mansur Building . . *Surgery*

INDIANA — Continued

INDIANAPOLIS — Continued

LaFayette Page, 603 Hume-Mansur Building
Rhinol., Oto-Laryngology

Hugo O. Pantzer, 601 Hume-Mansur Building . . *Gynecology*

O. G. Pfaff, 333 Bankers Trust Building . . . . . *Surgery*

David Ross, 416 Board of Trade Building . . . . *Surgery*

Orange Scott Runnels, 522 North Illinois Street . . . *Surgery*

John W. Sluss, 227 Newton Claypool Building . . . *Surgery*

William S. Tomlin, 520 Hume-Mansur Building
Rhinol., Oto-Laryngology

Ernest de W. Wales, 1236 North Pennsylvania Street
Oto-Laryngology

Homer H. Wheeler, Hume-Mansur Building . . . . *Surgery*

William Niles Wishard, 723 Hume-Mansur Building
Genito-Urinary Surgery

JASPER

John Paul Salb, 6th Street . . . . *Surgery*

LAFAYETTE

Arett C. Arnett, 716 LaFayette Life Building . . . *Surgery*

Frank S. Crockett, 601 LaFayette Life Building
Genito-Urinary Surgery

Edward Clement Davidson, 114 North 7th Street . . *Surgery*

George Frederick Keiper, 14 North 6th Street
Ophth., Rhinol., Oto-Laryngology

Charles B. Kern, 610 Columbia Street . . *Surgery, Obstetrics*

Guy Percival Levering, 616 Columbia Street . . . . *Surgery*

Edward Barnard Ruschli, 510 LaFayette Life Building *Surgery*

Frank B. Thompson, 417 Ferry Street . . . . . *Surgery*

George K. Throckmorton, 110 North 7th Street . . . *Surgery*

Richard B. Wetherill, 525 Columbia Street . . . *Gynecology*

LAPORTE

Bo Carr Bowell, 806 Maple Avenue . . . . . . *Surgery*

Harvey H. Martin, 806 Maple Avenue . . . . . *Surgery*

LEBANON

William H. Williams, 117 South East Street . . . . *Surgery*

MUNCIE

George Rex Andrews . . . . *Surgery*

Charles M. Mix, 109 Western Reserve Life Building . *Surgery*

INDIANA — Continued

PERU
> Edward Harvey Griswold, Telephone Building   .   .   .   *Surgery*

PLYMOUTH
> S. C. Loring, Richard Block   .   .   .   .   *Surgery*

RICHMOND
> Charles Marvel, 127 North 10th Street   .   .   .   .   .   *Surgery*

ROCHESTER
> Howard O. Shafer   .   .   .   .   *Surgery*

SOUTH BEND
> Walter H. Baker, 122 North Lafayette Boulevard   .   .   *Surgery*
> J. B. Berteling, 228 West Colfax Avenue   .   .   .   .   .   *Surgery*
> Harry Boyd-Snee, 716 J. M. S. Building   .   .   .   *Oto-Laryngology*
> Stanley A. Clark, 314 J. M. S. Building   .   .   .   .   .   *Surgery*
> Walter A. Hager, North Lafayette Street
>   *Ophth., Rhinol., Oto-Laryngology*
> Edwin J. Lent, 122 South Lafayette Street
>   *Ophth., Rhinol., Oto-Laryngology*
> Charles Stoltz, 311 West Jefferson Boulevard   .   .   .   *Surgery*
> Charles C. Terry, 122 North Lafayette Street   .   .   .   *Surgery*

SULLIVAN
> Garland Dix Scott, Sherman Building   .   .   .   .   .   *Surgery*

TERRE HAUTE
> Malachi R. Combs, 418 Tribune Building   .   .   .   .   .   *Surgery*
> Byron Merle Hutchings, 304 McKeen Building   .   .   *Gynecology*
> Frank Hubert Jett, 221 South 6th Street   .   .   .   .   .   *Surgery*
> Spencer M. Rice, 106 Rose Dispensary Building .   .   .   *Surgery*
> Frederick W. Shaley, Swope Block   .   .   .   .   .   .   *Surgery*
> Jonathan P. Worrell, 20 South 7th Street .   .   .   *Ophth., Otology*

VINCENNES
> Vance A. Funk, La Plante Building   .   .   .   .   .   .   *Surgery*

WARSAW
> Angus C. McDonald, 212 South Indiana Street   .   .   .   *Surgery*

IOWA

ALBIA
> H. C. Eschbach, 116 West Benton Avenue   .   .   .   .   *Surgery*

ANAMOSA
> Aram G. Hejinian, 216 Main Street   .   .   .   .   .   .   *Surgery*

IOWA — Continued

BOONE

Albert B. Deering, 809 8th Street . . . . *Surgery*
Edward M. Myers, 703 8th Street . . . . *Surgery*

BURLINGTON

Charles P. Frantz, Iowa State Bank Building
                              Ophth., Rhinol., Oto-Laryngology
F. M. Tombaugh, Iowa State Bank Building . . . *Surgery*

CARROLL

Louis Greenlee Patty, 126 East 5th Avenue . . . . *Surgery*

CEDAR FALLS

William L. Hearst, 903 Main Street . . . . . . *Surgery*

CEDAR RAPIDS

Frederick William Bailey, 309 Security Building
                                        Ophth., Oto-Laryngology

CENTERVILLE

Charles Stephen James, Clinic Building . . . . . *Surgery*

CHARLES CITY

Julius Niemack, 105 Main Street . . . . *Surgery*

CLARINDA

Thomas Edwin Powers, 19th and State Streets . . . *Surgery*

CLINTON

D. S. Fairchild, 845 6th Avenue . . . . *Surgery*
David Sturgess Fairchild, Jr., Wilson Building . . . *Surgery*
Elmer P. Weih, 605 Wilson Building
                              Ophth., Rhinol., Oto-Laryngology

COUNCIL BLUFFS

Frank Wilson Dean, 401 City National Bank Building
                                        Ophth., Oto-Laryngology
Louis L. Henninger, 401 City National Bank Building
                                        Rhinol., Oto-Laryngology
Donald Macrae, Jr., City National Bank Building . . *Surgery*

CRESCO

George Kessel, 212 6th Avenue, East . . . . . . *Surgery*
George Alfred Plummer, 215 East 6th Avenue . . . *Surgery*

DAVENPORT

William Larned Allen, 216 West 3rd Street . . . . *Surgery*
Peter Alfred Bendixen, 406 Lane Building . . . . *Surgery*
George Edward Decker, Central Office Building . . . *Surgery*

IOWA — Continued

DAVENPORT — Continued

Albert William Elmer, 810 East Locust Street
Ophth., Rhinol., Oto-Laryngology

J. T. Haller, 205 Security Building . . . . . . *Surgery*

Gordon F. Harkness, 509 New Putnam Building
Ophth., Rhinol., Oto-Laryngology

John Vincent Littig, 211 Central Office Building
Ophth., Rhinol., Oto-Laryngology

Henry E. Matthey, Kahl Building . . . . *Surgery*

DES MOINES

Wilbur S. Conkling, 407 Bankers Trust Building . . *Surgery*

Oliver James Fay, 1213 Bankers Trust Building . . . *Surgery*

Joseph J. Flannery, 916 Equitable Building . . . . *Surgery*

Edward John Harnagel, 913 Bankers Trust Building . *Surgery*

Charles E. Holloway, 427 Iowa Building . . . . . *Surgery*

Ellis Gregg Linn, Fleming Building *Ophth., Rhinol., Oto-Laryngology*

Wilton McCarthy, Fleming Building . . . . . . *Surgery*

Ralph H. Parker, 1101 Fleming Building
Ophth., Rhinol., Oto-Laryngology

W. W. Pearson, Bankers Trust Building
Ophth., Rhinol., Oto-Laryngology

J. C. Rockafellow, 1205 Bankers Trust Building . . . *Surgery*

Charles Edward Ruth, 415 Iowa Building . . . . *Surgery*

John Charles Ryan, 811 Hippee Building . . . . . *Surgery*

Francis E. V. Shore, Citizens National Bank Building
Ophth., Rhinol., Oto-Laryngology

Alva Porter Stoner, Iowa Building . . . . *Surgery*

Charles M. Werts, 217 Bankers Trust Building
Ophth., Rhinol., Oto-Laryngology

DUBUQUE

H. B. Gratiot, 256 10th Street . *Ophth., Rhinol., Oto-Laryngology*

John C. Hancock, 209 Bank and Insurance Building . *Surgery*

Ray R. Harris, 1270 Main Street . . . . *Surgery*

Bernard A. Michel, 257 10th Street . . . . . . *Surgery*

Harry Caldwell Parker . . . . *Retired*

Alanson M. Pond, 1098 Locust Street . . . . . . *Surgery*

FAIRFIELD

James Frederic Clarke, 500 South Main Street . . . *Surgery*

IOWA — Continued

FORT DODGE

W. W. Bowen, 630 Snell Building . . . . *Surgery*

Robert Evans, 630 Snell Building . . . . *Surgery*

INDEPENDENCE

Fred F. Agnew, 2nd Street and 2nd Avenue, S. W.

Ophth., Rhinol., Oto-Laryngology

IOWA CITY

William F. Boiler, 426 South Dodge Street . . *Ophthalmology*

Lee Wallace Dean, 12½ South Clinton Street . *Oto-Laryngology*

Charles Joseph Rowan, North Dubuque Road . . . *Surgery*

Arthur Steindler, State University Hospital . *Orthopedic Surgery*

KEOKUK

Robert M. Lapsley, 625 Blondeau Street *Ophth., Oto-Laryngology*

LADORA

Jasper L. Augustine . . . . *Surgery*

LEON

Bert L. Eiker . . . . *Surgery*

MASON CITY

Thomas A. Burke, 524 M. B. A. Building . . . . *Surgery*

George Melville Crabb, 102 North Washington Avenue . *Surgery*

Channing E. Dakin, 502 M. B. A. Building . . . . *Surgery*

William J. Egloff, 21½ East State Street . . . . . *Surgery*

MUSCATINE

Frederick Henry Little, 108 West 5th Street . . . . *Surgery*

Arthur John Weaver, 107 West 2nd Street . . . . *Surgery*

NEW HAMPTON

Nicholas Schilling . . . . *Surgery*

OTTUMWA

Murdoch Bannister, Hofmann Building . . . . . *Surgery*

David C. Brockman, Ennis Building . . . . . . *Surgery*

D. E. Graham, First National Bank Building

Ophth., Rhinol., Oto-Laryngology

John Francis Herrick, Hofmann Building . . . . . *Surgery*

Burdette Dudley LaForce, Hofmann Building . *Ophthalmology*

Smith Augustus Spilman, Hofmann Building . . . *Surgery*

Charles B. Taylor, Ennis Building . . *Rhinol., Oto-Laryngology*

SIGOURNEY

Clarence L. Heald, Sigourney Hospital . . . . . *Surgery*

IOWA — Continued

SIOUX CITY

William Joseph Bussey, 517 Frances Building
Ophth., Rhinol., Oto-Laryngology

Frederick E. Franchère, 4th and Nebraska Streets
Ophth., Rhinol., Oto-Laryngology

Ernest Albert Jenkinson, 533 Frances Building . . . *Surgery*

William Jepson, United Bank Building . . . . . *Surgery*

Charles T. Maxwell, 109 Sioux National Bank Building . *Surgery*

A. J. McLaughlin, 210 Davidson Building   *Genito-Urinary Surgery*

Philip Benedict McLaughlin, 310 Davidson Building . *Surgery*

Jesse B. Naftzger, 401 Davidson Building
Ophth., Rhinol., Oto-Laryngology

Frederick H. Roost, 515 Trimble Building
Ophth., Rhinol., Oto-Laryngology

Robert Q. Rowse, 107 Sioux National Bank Building . *Surgery*

Prince E. Sawyer, 306 F. L. and T. Building . . . . *Surgery*

John Nelson Warren, 536 Davidson Building . . . *Surgery*

WATERLOO

Edward T. Alford, Black Building . . . . *Surgery*

William H. Bickley, 2625 West 4th Street . . . . *Surgery*

Ben Chester Everall, Marsh-Place Building . . . . *Surgery*

Frank T. Hartman, 623 Mulberry Street . . . . . *Surgery*

T. U. McManus, Black Building   *Ophth., Rhinol., Oto-Laryngology*

Edwin Raymond Shannon, Black Hawk Bank Building . *Surgery*

W. B. Small, Black Building . *Ophth., Rhinol., Oto-Laryngology*

WAVERLY

Lester C. Kern, 122½ East Bremer Avenue . . . . *Surgery*

William A. Rohlf, 123 South East Water Street . . . *Surgery*

WEBSTER CITY

Guy T. McCauliff, 644½ 2nd Street . . . . . . *Surgery*

KANSAS

COFFEYVILLE

Charles Samuel Campbell, 114 West 9th Street . . . *Surgery*

Fred W. Duncan, 818 Maple Street . . . . . . *Surgery*

DODGE CITY

Winfield Otis Thompson, 1401 Central Avenue . . . *Surgery*

KANSAS — Continued

ELDORADO

Frenn L. Preston, 220 West Central Avenue . . . . *Surgery*

GREAT BEND

Elmer E. Morrison, 1223 Main Street . . . . . . *Surgery*

Marion F. Russell, 1305 Main Street . . . . . . *Surgery*

HUTCHINSON

Clarence Walter Hall, Gage-Hall Clinic . . . . . *Surgery*

Robert Young Jones, 403 First National Bank Building *Surgery*

Horace G. Welsh, First National Bank Building . . . *Surgery*

KANSAS CITY

Louie Frank Barney, Wahlenmaier Building . . . . *Surgery*

George Morris Gray, 800 Minnesota Avenue . . . . *Surgery*

John Franklin Hassig, 800 Minnesota Avenue . . . *Surgery*

Richard C. Lowman, 218 Portsmouth Building . . . *Surgery*

Lot Dalbert Mabie, 800 Minnesota Avenue . . . . *Surgery*

James Whittier May, 800 Minnesota Avenue . . *Ophthalmology*

Clifford C. Nesselrode, 800 Minnesota Avenue . . . *Surgery*

LEAVENWORTH

Charles James McGee, Woolfe Building . . . . *Gynecology*

ROSEDALE

Mervin T. Sudler, University of Kansas . . . . . *Surgery*

SABETHA

Samuel Murdock, Jr., 1015 Main Street . . . . . *Surgery*

SALINA

John De Witt Riddell, 148 South Santa Fe Avenue . . *Surgery*

TOPEKA

William Merrill Mills, 616 Mills Building . . . . . *Surgery*

Robert B. Stewart, 627 Mills Building . . . . . *Surgery*

WICHITA

David Walker Basham, 802 Schweiter Building . . . *Surgery*

Charles E. Bowers, Beacon Building . . . . . . *Surgery*

John D. Clark, 910 Schweiter Building . . . . . *Obstetrics*

Jacob G. Dorsey, 201 North Main Street . . . *Ophthalmology*

Edwin Delta Ebright, 919 Beacon Building . *Orthopedic Surgery*

John Lillie Evans, 729 Beacon Building . . . . . *Surgery*

J. F. Gsell, 911 Beacon Building *Ophth., Rhinol., Oto-Laryngology*

KANSAS — Continued

WICHITA — Continued

Harry W. Horn, 910 Schweiter Building . . . . . *Surgery*
D. I. Maggard, Beacon Building   *Ophth., Rhinol., Oto-Laryngology*
Ernest M. Seydell, 201 North Main Street
Rhinol., Oto-Laryngology

WINFIELD

Ralph W. James, First National Bank Building . . *Gynecology*
Howard L. Snyder, 402 First National Bank Building . *Surgery*
Francis M. Wilmer, First National Bank Building
Ophth., Rhinol., Oto-Laryngology

KENTUCKY

BOWLING GREEN

John Henry Blackburn, 1119 State Street . . . . *Surgery*
J. O. Carson, 442½ Main Street   *Ophth., Rhinol., Oto-Laryngology*

COVINGTON

Robert Walter Bledsoe, 1005 Madison Avenue
Ophth., Rhinol., Oto-Laryngology
John R. Murnan, 11th and Scott Streets . . . . . *Surgery*

DANVILLE

John Rice Cowan, 336 Main Street . . . . . . *Surgery*
John D. Jackson, Main Street . . . . *Surgery*

HENDERSON

Archibald Dixon, 330 North Green Street . . . . *Surgery*

LEBANON

Robert Caldwell McChord . . . . *Surgery*

LEXINGTON

Archibald Henry Barkley, 138 North Upper Street . . *Surgery*
David Barrow, 190 North Upper Street . . . . . *Surgery*
D. Woolfolk Barrow, 190 North Upper Street . . . *Surgery*
Scott Dudley Breckinridge, Security Trust Company
Building . . . . *Gynecology, Obstetrics*
Waller O. Bullock, 190 North Upper Street . . . . *Surgery*
Samuel B. Marks, 164 Market Street . . . . . . *Surgery*
William Nelson Offutt, 230 North Broadway
Ophth., Rhinol., Oto-Laryngology
Orrin LeRoy Smith, Security Trust Company Building
Ophthalmology

KENTUCKY — Continued

LEXINGTON — Continued

J. A. Stucky, 2nd and Upper Streets . *Ophth., Oto-Laryngology*
Charles A. Vance, 310 Security Trust Company Building *Surgery*
Benjamin F. Van Meter, Jr., 183 North Upper Street . *Surgery*

LOUISVILLE

Irvin Abell, Francis Building . . . . *Surgery*
Bernard Asman, Francis Building . . . . . . *Surgery*
Oscar E. Bloch, 316 West Broadway . . . . . *Surgery*
I. N. Bloom, 222 Francis Building . . *Genito-Urinary Surgery*
Herbert Bronner, 222 Francis Building . *Genito-Urinary Surgery*
George S. Coon, 440 Francis Building . . . . . *Surgery*
S. G. Dabney, 911 Starks Building
          Ophth., Rhinol., Oto-Laryngology
Ellis Duncan, 705 Starks Building . . . . . . *Surgery*
Charles Farmer, 1110 Francis Building . . . . *Surgery*
Challon G. Forsee, 501 Francis Building . . . . *Surgery*
Frank Thomas Fort, 472 Francis Building . . . . *Surgery*
Louis Frank, 400 Francis Building . . . . . . *Surgery*
L. Wallace Frank, 400 Francis Building . . . . *Surgery*
Guy P. Grigsby, 612 Francis Building . . . . . *Surgery*
Granville S. Hanes, Francis Building . . . . . *Surgery*
George A. Hendon, Francis Building . . . . . . *Surgery*
Charles W. Hibbitt, Francis Building . . . . . *Gynecology*
Lee Kahn, Francis Building . . . . *Surgery*
George C. Leachman, 615 Francis Building . . . . *Surgery*
Isaac A. Lederman, Francis Building
          Ophth., Rhinol., Oto-Laryngology
Arthur Thomas McCormack, State Board of Health . *Surgery*
Stephen C. McCoy, 300 Francis Building . . . . . *Surgery*
Lewis Samuel McMurtry, 542 Francis Building . . . *Surgery*
William Barnett Owen, Francis Building . . *Orthopedic Surgery*
Adolph O. Pfingst, Francis Building . . . . *Ophthalmology*
Robert T. Pirtle, 400 Francis Building . . . *Orthopedic Surgery*
John Williamson Price, Jr., 705 Starks Building . . . *Surgery*
Harry N. Ritter, 515 Francis Building
          Ophth., Rhinol., Oto-Laryngology
David Yandell Roberts, 501 Francis Building . . . *Surgery*
August Schachner, 844 4th Avenue . . . . . . *Surgery*
J. Garland Sherrill, 308 Masonic Building . . . . *Surgery*

KENTUCKY — Continued

LOUISVILLE — Continued

John R. Wathen, 350 Francis Building . . . . . . *Surgery*
James Tolbert Windell, 715 West Jefferson Street . . *Urology*
Joseph J. Wynn, 456 Francis Building
Ophth., Rhinol., Oto-Laryngology
Benjamin F. Zimmerman, Francis Building . . . . *Surgery*

MAYSVILLE

Jackson B. Taulbee, State National Bank Building . . *Surgery*

OWENSBORO

Daniel M. Griffith, 207 West 4th Street
Ophth., Rhinol., Oto-Laryngology
Otway Watkins Rash, 213 West 4th Street . . . . *Surgery*

PADUCAH

Frank Boyd, 4th Street and Broadway . . . . . *Surgery*
Henry Gilbert Reynolds, City National Bank Building
Ophth., Laryngology
Philip H. Stewart, 4th Street and Broadway . . . . *Surgery*

LOUISIANA

ALEXANDRIA

Richard Oliver Simmons, Guaranty Bank and Trust
Building . . . . *Surgery*
George M. G. Stafford, Guaranty Bank and Trust
Building . . . . *Surgery*
John Luther Wilson, 4th and Jackson Streets . . . *Surgery*

BATON ROUGE

John Allen Caruthers, New Reymond Building
Ophth., Rhinol., Oto-Laryngology
Robert Christie Kemp, 211 Reymond Building . . . *Surgery*

LAKE CHARLES

John Greene Martin, 825 South Division Street . . . *Surgery*

MONROE

Jesse L. Adams, 201 De Siard Street . . . . . . *Surgery*
James Q. Graves, 201½ De Siard Street . . . . . *Surgery*

NEW ORLEANS

Carroll W. Allen, 43 Audubon Boulevard . . . . . *Surgery*
Jacob Barnett, Medical Building . . . *Gynecology, Obstetrics*

LOUISIANA — Continued

NEW ORLEANS — Continued

James Madison Batchelor, 2010 State Street . . . . *Surgery*
Jefferson Davis Bloom, 5718 St. Charles Avenue . . *Surgery*
Henry Nathan Blum, Maison Blanche Building . *Ophthalmology*
Charles N. Chavigny, 5515 Hurst Street . *Gynecology, Obstetrics*
Samuel M. D. Clark, 108 Baronne Street . *Gynecology, Obstetrics*
Henry S. Cocram, 108 Baronne Street . . . . *Gynecology*
Isidore Cohn, Maison Blanche Building . . . . . *Surgery*
C. Grenes Cole, 1503 Pine Street . . . . *Surgery*
John Fleming Dicks, 3529 Prytania Street *Gynecology, Obstetrics*
Theodore J. Dimitry, 3601 Prytania Street . . *Ophthalmology*
Marcus Feingold, 4206 St. Charles Avenue . . *Ophthalmology*
E. D. Fenner, 1915 St. Charles Avenue . . *Orthopedic Surgery*
Maurice Joseph Gelpi, 3601 Prytania Street . . . . *Surgery*
Hermann Bertram Gessner, 119 Audubon Boulevard . *Surgery*
Edward S. Hatch, 3439 Prytania Street . . *Orthopedic Surgery*
Joseph Hume, 724 Baronne Street . . . *Genito-Urinary Surgery*
Alfred Jacoby, 412 Medical Building . . . . . . *Surgery*
Otto Joachim, 1630 Robert Street . . *Rhinol., Oto-Laryngology*
P. Jorda Kahle, 636 Common Street . . *Genito-Urinary Surgery*
Alfred C. King, 305 Vallette Street . . . . . . *Surgery*
Edward Lacy King, 124 Baronne Street . *Obstetrics, Gynecology*
Charles J. Landfried, 5907 Garfield Street *Rhinol., Oto-Laryngology*
Lucian Hyppolite Landry, 2122 Peters Avenue . . . *Surgery*
John P. Leake, Canal and Dauphine Streets
Rhinol., Oto-Laryngology
Ernest S. Lewis, 1625 Louisiana Avenue . *Gynecology, Obstetrics*
Robert C. Lynch, 634 Maison Blanche Building
Rhinol., Oto-Laryngology
Urban Maes, 1671 Octavia Street . . . . *Surgery*
Edmund Denegre Martin, 3513 Prytania Street . . . *Surgery*
Rudolph Matas, 2255 St. Charles Avenue . . . . *Surgery*
Paul Avery McIlhenny, 3513 Prytania Street *Orthopedic Surgery*
C. Jeff Miller, 124 Baronne Street . . . *Gynecology, Obstetrics*
Abraham Nelken, 126 Baronne Street . . . . . . *Urology*
Jacob Warren Newman, 3523 Prytania Street . . . *Obstetrics*
John Frederick Oechsner, 621 Macheca Building . . *Surgery*
J. T. O'Ferrall, 3439 St. Charles Avenue . . *Orthopedic Surgery*
James P. O'Kelley, Macheca Building . *Rhinol., Oto-Laryngology*

LOUISIANA — Continued

NEW ORLEANS — Continued

Frederick William Parham, 3513 Prytania Street . . *Surgery*
W. T. Patton, 1116 Maison Blanche Building
Rhinol., Oto-Laryngology
William D. Phillips, 1201 Maison Blanche Building
Gynecology, Obstetrics
Peter Blaise Salatich, 3202 St. Charles Avenue . . *Gynecology*
Thomas Benton Sellers, 108 Baronne Street   *Obstetrics, Gynecology*
Victor Conway Smith, 2311 Magazine Street . . *Ophthalmology*
John Smyth, 724 Baronne Street . . . . *Surgery*
Marion Sims Souchon, Whitney Central Bank Building   *Surgery*
Russell Edward Stone, Interstate Bank Building . . *Surgery*
Paul T. Talbot, Maison Blanche Building . . . . *Surgery*
H. W. E. Walther, Macheca Building . . . . . . *Urology*
Arthur I. Weil, 717 Maison Blanche Building Annex
Rhinol., Oto-Laryngology

PATTERSON

Lewis B. Crawford . . . . *Surgery*

SHREVEPORT

Louis Abramson, 722 Cotton Street . . . . . . *Surgery*
Alfred Penn Crain, 914 Oneonta Street . . . . . *Surgery*
Rawley Martin Penick, 1109 Sheridan Avenue . . . *Surgery*
Thomas Ragan, Hutchinson Building . . . . . . *Surgery*
John Lytle Scales, 907 Commercial Bank Building
Ophth., Rhinol., Oto-Laryngology
James Clinton Willis, 843 South Highlands . . . . *Surgery*

MAINE

AUBURN

John Sturgis, 137 Court Street . . . . *Surgery*

BANGOR

Herbert T. Clough, 209 State Street . . . . *Ophth., Otology*
William C. Peters, 45 State Street . . . . *Orthopedic Surgery*
Daniel A. Robinson, 142 Hammond Street . . . . *Surgery*
Eugene Boutelle Sanger, 42 Broadway . . . . . *Surgery*

MAINE — Continued

BAR HARBOR

Ralph Waldo Wakefield, 16 High Street . . . . . *Surgery*

BOOTHBAY HARBOR

George A. Gregory, 2 Commercial Street . . . . . *Surgery*

CALAIS

Walter N. Miner, 9 Calais Avenue . . . . *Surgery*

HOULTON

Frank H. Jackson, Masonic Building . . . . . . *Surgery*

LEWISTON

William L. Haskell, 111 Pine Street . . . . . *Surgery*
William Henry Hawkins, 149 Pine Street . . . . . *Surgery*

PORTLAND

Edville Gerhardt Abbott, 156 Free Street . . *Orthopedic Surgery*
Sylvester Judd Beach, 776 Congress Street . . *Ophthalmology*
William H. Bradford, 208 State Street . . . . . *Surgery*
Henry Herbert Brock, 687 Congress Street . . . . *Surgery*
William Lewis Cousins, 231 Woodford Street . . . . *Surgery*
Erastus Eugene Holt, 723 Congress Street . . *Ophth., Otology*
Charles M. Leighton, 14 Deering Street . . . . . *Surgery*
Alfred Mitchell, Jr., 657 Congress Street *Genito-Urinary Surgery*
W. Bean Moulton, 690 Congress Street . . . . . *Surgery*
Harold Ashton Pingree, 131 State Street . . *Orthopedic Surgery*
Carl M. Robinson, Longfellow Square . . . . . . *Surgery*
Richard D. Small, 7 Deering Street . . . *Surgery, Obstetrics*
Owen Smith, 690 Congress Street . . *Rhinol., Oto-Laryngology*
James Alfred Spalding, 627 Congress Street . . *Ophth., Otology*
John F. Thompson, 211 State Street . . . . . *Gynecology*
Philip P. Thompson, 203 State Street . . . . . . *Surgery*
Herbert Francis Twitchell, 10 Pine Street . . . . *Surgery*

PRESQUE ISLE

Lindley Dobson, 163 Main Street . . . . *Surgery*

ROCKLAND

Walter M. Spear, 135 Camden Street . . . . . . *Surgery*

WATERVILLE

Edward Hammond Risley, 27 College Avenue . . . *Surgery*
Frederick C. Thayer, 214 Main Street . . . . . *Surgery*

MARYLAND

BALTIMORE

Howard Elmer Ashbury, 810 St. Paul Street . . . . *Surgery*
William S. Baer, 4 East Madison Street . . *Orthopedic Surgery*
Charles Bagley, Jr., Latrobe Apartments . . . . . *Surgery*
Robert Parke Bay, 1800 North Charles Street . . . *Surgery*
John McFarland Bergland, 4 West Biddle Street . . *Obstetrics*
Bertram M. Bernheim, 2313 Eutaw Place . . . . *Surgery*
Charles French Blake, 20 East Preston Street . . *Proctology*
Herbert C. Blake, 1014 West Lafayette Avenue . . . *Surgery*
Joseph Colt Bloodgood, 904 North Charles Street . . *Surgery*
James Bordley, Jr., 330 North Charles Street . *Ophthalmology*
Charles Emil Brack, 500 East 20th Street . . . . *Obstetrics*
Hugh Brent, 16 East Chase Street . . . . . . *Gynecology*
Curtis F. Burnam, 1418 Eutaw Place . . . . . . *Surgery*
James J. Carroll, 405 North Charles Street
                        Ophth., Rhinol., Oto-Laryngology
DeWitt Bellinger Casler, 13 West Chase Street . . *Gynecology*
Clyde Alvin Clapp, 513 North Charles Street . *Ophthalmology*
Lee Cohen, 1820 Eutaw Place . *Ophth., Rhinol., Oto-Laryngology*
Sydney M. Cone, 2326 Eutaw Place . . . *Orthopedic Surgery*
Albertus Cotton, 1303 Maryland Avenue . . *Orthopedic Surgery*
Samuel J. Crowe, 4332 North Charles Street
                            Rhinol., Oto-Laryngology
Thomas Stephen Cullen, 20 East Eager Street . . *Gynecology*
Hoagland Cook Davis, 405 North Charles Street
                        Ophth., Rhinol., Oto-Laryngology
John Staige Davis, The Severn Apartments . . . . *Surgery*
S. Griffith Davis, Jr., 1230 Light Street . . . . . *Surgery*
George W. Dobbin, 58 West Biddle Street   *Gynecology, Obstetrics*
J. W. Downey, Jr., 529 North Charles Street . . *Ophth., Otology*
Samuel T. Earle, Jr., 1431 Linden Avenue . . . *Proctology*
Page Edmunds, 605 Park Avenue . . *Genito-Urinary Surgery*
Roades Fayerweather, 529 North Charles Street *Orthopedic Surgery*
John Miller Turpin Finney, 1300 Eutaw Place . . . *Surgery*
William A. Fisher, Jr., 715 Park Avenue . . . . . *Surgery*
H. K. Fleck, 924 North Charles Street . . . *Ophth., Otology*
George Alexander Fleming, 1018 Madison Avenue *Ophth., Otology*
Richard Holden Follis, 3 East Read Street . . . . *Surgery*
Harry Friedenwald, 1029 Madison Avenue . . *Ophth., Otology*

MARYLAND — Continued

BALTIMORE — Continued

William Sisson Gardner, 6 West Preston Street . . *Gynecology*
John T. Geraghty, 330 North Charles Street . . . . *Urology*
Leo John Goldbach, 322 North Charles Street . *Ophth., Otology*
Albert E. Goldstein, 330 North Charles Street . . . *Urology*
Archibald C. Harrison, 31 East North Avenue . ` . . *Surgery*
E. H. Hayward, 23 West Franklin Street . . . . . *Surgery*
Arthur Hebb, 330 North Charles Street . . . . *Proctology*
Joseph William Holland, 1624 Linden Avenue . . . *Surgery*
Harry L. Homer, 1011 North Charles Street . . . . *Surgery*
John Mason Hundley, 1009 Cathedral Street . . . *Gynecology*
Guy LeRoy Hunner, 2305 St. Paul Street . . . . *Gynecology*
Elizabeth Hurdon, 31 West Preston Street . . . *Gynecology*
Amos F. Hutchins, 1010 North Charles Street . . . *Surgery*
Elliott H. Hutchins, 1010 North Charles Street . . . *Surgery*
Frank Leslie Jennings, 1800 North Charles Street . . *Surgery*
Howard A. Kelly, 1418 Eutaw Place . . . . . . *Surgery*
Francis J. Kirby, 110 East North Avenue . . . . . *Surgery*
M. Lazenby, 18 West Franklin Street . . *Gynecology, Obstetrics*
Robert M. Lewis, 1418 Eutaw Place . . . . . . *Surgery*
Sylvan H. Likes, 1134 Linden Avenue . . . . . . *Urology*
G. Milton Linthicum 817 Park Avenue . . *Proctology, Surgery*
James C. Lumpkin, 818 Park Avenue . . . . . . *Surgery*
Frank S. Lynn, 41 West Preston Street . . . . . *Surgery*
Charles Walter Maxson, 827 North Charles Street . . *Surgery*
Alexius McGlannan, 115 West Franklin Street . . . *Surgery*
Samuel K. Merrick, 824 Park Avenue . . *Rhinol., Laryngology*
G. W. Mitchell, 11 East Chase Street . *Rhinol., Oto-Laryngology*
Leonard E. Neale, 822 Park Avenue . . *Gynecology, Obstetrics*
William Neill, Jr., 1418 Eutaw Place . . . . . *Gynecology*
Grover C. Ney, 2401 Linden Avenue . . . . . . *Surgery*
F. K. Nichols, 904 North Charles Street . *Gynecology, Obstetrics*
Emil Novak, 26 East Preston Street . . . . . *Gynecology*
Omar B. Pancoast, 1111 North Charles Street . . . *Surgery*
William B. Perry, 1 West Biddle Street . . . . *Gynecology*
Harry Elmer Peterman, 518 North Charles Street
Ophth., Rhinol., Oto-Laryngology
Walter Brewster Platt, 802 Cathedral Street . . . . *Surgery*
J. C. Pound, 904 North Charles Street . *Rhinol., Laryngology*

136   *American College of Surgeons*

MARYLAND — Continued

<small>BALTIMORE</small> — Continued

J. Dawson Reeder, 30 East Preston Street   . . .   *Proctology*
A. J. N. Reik, 1102 North Charles Street   *Rhinol., Oto-Laryngology*
Henry O. Reik, 300 East 30th Street   . . . .   *Ophth., Otology*
William Whitall Requardt, 805 Park Avenue . . . . *Surgery*
Edward H. Richardson, 1200 North Charles Street .   *Gynecology*
Lewis J. Rosenthal, 1622 Linden Avenue . . . . *Proctology*
M. S. Rosenthal, 1222 Madison Avenue . *Genito-Urinary Surgery*
James M. H. Rowland, 1204 Madison Avenue   . . . *Obstetrics*
William Wood Russell, 1208 Eutaw Place   . . . *Gynecology*
Anton G. Rytina, Professional Building . *Genito-Urinary Surgery*
Abraham Samuels, 1928 Eutaw Place . . . . . *Gynecology*
Frank D. Sanger, 525 North Charles Street   *Rhinol., Laryngology*
Otto Schaefer, 1105 Madison Avenue . . . *Ophth., Otology*
J. K. B. E. Seegar, 904 North Charles Street *Gynecology, Obstetrics*
Arthur M. Shipley, 1827 Eutaw Place . . . . . *Surgery*
George A. Stewart, 904 North Charles Street   . . *Surgery*
Harvey Brinton Stone, 18 West Franklin Street .   . *Surgery*
William Tarun, 605 Park Avenue . . . . . *Ophth., Otology*
R. Tunstall Taylor, 1102 North Charles Street *Orthopedic Surgery*
Gideon Timberlake, 816 St. Paul Street   *Genito-Urinary Surgery*
Alfred Ullman, 1712 Eutaw Place . . . . . . *Surgery*
A. J. Underhill, 1800 North Charles Street *Genito-Urinary Surgery*
Cecil Woods Vest, 700 Park Avenue . . . . *Gynecology*
George Walker, 1 East Center Street . *Genito-Urinary Surgery*
J. Whitridge Williams, 107 East Chase Street *Obstetrics, Gynecology*
J. R. Winslow, Latrobe Apartments . *Rhinol., Oto-Laryngology*
Nathan Winslow, 1900 Mt. Royal Terrace   . . . *Surgery*
Randolph Winslow, 1900 Mt. Royal Terrace .   . . *Surgery*
Walter Dent Wise, 1800 North Charles Street   . . *Surgery*
William B. Wolf, 113 West Franklin Street *Genito-Urinary Surgery*
Hiram Woods, 842 Park Avenue . . . . . *Ophth., Otology*
Thomas Chew Worthington, 1102 North Charles Street
                              Rhinol., Laryngology
  Hugh H. Young, Johns Hopkins Hospital *Genito-Urinary Surgery*

<small>CAMBRIDGE</small>

Brice W. Goldsborough, 8 High Street   . . . . *Surgery*

<small>CUMBERLAND</small>

Edwin B. Claybrook, Riverside Building .   . . . *Surgery*

MARYLAND — Continued

CUMBERLAND — Continued
Arthur Hanson Hawkins, Center Street . . . . . *Surgery*
George Oliver Sharrett, 45 Bedford Street
Ophth., Rhinol., Oto-Laryngology

EASTON
Charles F. Davidson, 126 Goldsborough Street . . . *Surgery*

ELKTON
Henry Arthur Mitchell, East Main Street . . . . *Surgery*

FREDERICK
T. B. Johnson, 7 East Church Street . . . . . . *Surgery*

HAGERSTOWN
O. H. Williams Ragan, 155 West Washington Street . *Surgery*
Peregrine Wroth, Jr., 131 West Washington Street . . *Surgery*

PRINCESS ANNE
George Wallace Jarman . . . . *Gynecology*

MASSACHUSETTS

BEVERLY
Peer P. Johnson, 163 Cabot Street . . . . *Surgery*

BOSTON
John D. Adams, 45 Bay State Road . . . *Orthopedic Surgery*
Harold Virgil Andrews, 1083 Boylston Street *Obstetrics, Gynecology*
Harold W. Baker, 49 Gloucester Street . . . . . *Surgery*
Franklin Greene Balch, 279 Clarendon Street . . . *Surgery*
J. D. Barney, 99 Commonwealth Avenue . *Genito-Urinary Surgery*
Howard P. Bellows, 220 Clarendon Street . . . . *Otology*
Horace Binney, 403 Beacon Street . . . . *Surgery*
John Bapst Blake, 657 Boylston Street . . . . . *Surgery*
George D. Bliss, 508 Washington Street . . . . *Obstetrics*
Charles R. C. Borden, 520 Commonwealth Avenue
Rhinol., Oto-Laryngology
John Taylor Bottomley, 165 Beacon Street . . . . *Surgery*
Herbert Drummond Boyd, 687 Boylston Street . . . *Surgery*
Elliott Gray Brackett, 166 Newbury Street . *Orthopedic Surgery*
Edward H. Bradford, 133 Newbury Street . . . . *Surgery*
Austin Brant, 483 Beacon Street . . . . *Surgery, Obstetrics*
John George Breslin, 514 Commonwealth Avenue . . *Surgery*

MASSACHUSETTS — Continued

BOSTON — Continued

George W. W. Brewster, 213 Beacon Street   .   .   . *Surgery*
J. Emmons Briggs, 477 Beacon Street .   .   .   .   .   . *Surgery*
Edith M. Brooks, 483 Beacon Street   .   .   *Gynecology, Obstetrics*
Lloyd T. Brown, 372 Marlborough Street .   .   *Orthopedic Surgery*
Alice G. Bryant, 502 Beacon Street   .   *Rhinol., Oto-Laryngology*
Charles W. Bush, 202 Huntington Avenue   *Rhinol., Laryngology*
Thomas E. Chandler, 19 Bay State Road .   .   .   .   . *Surgery*
Henry Melville Chase, 520 Commonwealth Avenue .   . *Surgery*
David Cheever, 193 Marlborough Street   .   .   .   .   . *Surgery*
W. E. Chenery, 377 Commonwealth Avenue

Rhinol., Oto-Laryngology
Frederick E. Cheney, 64 Commonwealth Avenue   *Ophthalmology*
Arthur L. Chute, 352 Marlborough Street *Genito-Urinary Surgery*
Joseph Payson Clark, 71 Marlborough Street   .   . *Laryngology*
Howard M. Clute, 638 Beacon Street .   .   .   .   .   . *Surgery*
Farrar Cobb, 419 Boylston Street .   .   .   . *Surgery*
Robert C. Cochrane, 86 Bay State Road .   .   .   .   . *Surgery*
Ernest Amory Codman, 227 Beacon Street   .   .   .   . *Surgery*
Frederick W. Colburn, 510 Commonwealth Avenue .   .   *Otology*
William M. Conant, 486 Commonwealth Avenue   .   . *Surgery*
Algernon Coolidge, 613 Beacon Street .   .   *Rhinol., Laryngology*
Frederic J. Cotton, 520 Commonwealth Avenue .   .   . *Surgery*
William P. Coues, 31 Massachusetts Avenue .   .   .   . *Surgery*
Le Roi Goddard Crandon, 366 Commonwealth Avenue .   *Surgery*
Clarence Crane, 520 Beacon Street   .   .   .   .   .   . *Surgery*
Eugene A. Crockett, 298 Marlborough Street   .   *Oto-Laryngology*
Arthur Hallam Crosbie, 520 Commonwealth Avenue

Genito-Urinary Surgery
John White Cummin, 9 Massachusetts Avenue   .   .   . *Surgery*
John Henry Cunningham, 46 Gloucester Street   .   .   . *Surgery*
Harvey Cushing, Peter Bent Brigham Hospital   .   .   . *Surgery*
Hayward W. Cushing, 70 Commonwealth Avenue   .   .   *Retired*
Elliott Carr Cutler, Peter Bent Brigham Hospital   .   . *Surgery*
Francis H. Davenport, 390 Commonwealth Avenue .   *Gynecology*
Lincoln Davis, 217 Beacon Street .   .   .   . *Surgery*
Hilbert Francis Day, 45 Bay State Road .   .   *Surgery, Obstetrics*
Robert L. DeNormandie, 355 Marlborough Street

Obstetrics, Gynecology

MASSACHUSETTS — Continued

BOSTON — Continued

George S. Derby, 23 Bay State Road . . . . *Ophthalmology*
Dana Warren Drury, 483 Beacon Street *Rhinol., Oto-Laryngology*
Florence W. Duckering, 520 Beacon Street . . . . *Surgery*
George H. Earl, 1138 Boylston Street . . . . . . *Obstetrics*
Albert Ehrenfried, 21 Bay State Road . . . . . *Surgery*
Francis Patten Emerson, 520 Commonwealth Avenue
Rhinol., Oto-Laryngology
Nathaniel W. Emerson, 118 Forest Hills Street . . . *Surgery*
William Edward Faulkner, 290 Marlborough Street . . *Surgery*
Calvin B. Faunce, Jr., 320 Commonwealth Avenue *Oto-Laryngology*
Henry J. FitzSimmons, 520 Beacon Street . *Orthopedic Surgery*
Archibald McKay Fraser, 270 Commonwealth Avenue . *Surgery*
Somers Fraser, 514 Commonwealth Avenue . . . . *Surgery*
Leo Victor Friedman, 425 Marlborough Street . . . *Obstetrics*
Joel E. Goldthwait, 372 Marlborough Street . *Orthopedic Surgery*
Joseph Lincoln Goodale, 258 Beacon Street . . . *Laryngology*
W. P. Graves, 244 Marlborough Street . . . . *Gynecology*
Charles M. Green, 78 Marlborough Street . *Gynecology, Obstetrics*
Daniel Crosby Greene, 23 Bay State Road . . . *Laryngology*
Robert Battey Greenough, 8 Marlborough Street . . *Surgery*
Allen Greenwood, 101 Newbury Street . . . *Ophthalmology*
Frederick W. Halsey, 272 Newbury Street . . . *Gynecology*
Charles Henry Hare, 483 Beacon Street . *Gynecology, Obstetrics*
Clifford Dawes Harvey, 510 Commonwealth Avenue . *Surgery*
James J. Hepburn, 56 Bay State Road . . . . . *Surgery*
T. Chittenden Hill, 31 Bay State Road . . . . *Proctology*
Albert Winslow Horr, 419 Boylston Street . . *Ophthalmology*
Alonzo Gale Howard, 636 Beacon Street . . *Orthopedic Surgery*
Charles Tilden Howard, 510 Commonwealth Avenue . *Surgery*
Walter Clarke Howe, 303 Beacon Street . . . . . *Surgery*
Joshua C. Hubbard, 86 Bay State Road . . . . . *Surgery*
Edward Daniel Hurley, 419 Boylston Street . . *Ophthalmology*
John J. Hurley, 194 Bay State Road . *Rhinol., Oto-Laryngology*
Henry T. Hutchins, 520 Commonwealth Avenue . *Gynecology*
Harry James Inglis, 43 Bay State Road *Rhinol., Oto-Laryngology*
Frederick L. Jack, 215 Beacon Street . *Rhinol., Oto-Laryngology*
Frederick William Johnson, 167 Newbury Street . *Gynecology*
Daniel Fiske Jones, 195 Beacon Street . . . . . *Surgery*

MASSACHUSETTS — Continued

BOSTON — Continued

George Francis Keenan, 207 Bay State Road   . . .   *Surgery*
Charles Joseph Kickham, 536 Commonwealth Avenue
                                              Gynecology, Obstetrics
Arthur Ronald Kimpton, 66 Bay State Road   . . .   *Surgery*
William F. Knowles, 520 Commonwealth Avenue
                                              Rhinol., Oto-Laryngology
James Krauss, 419 Boylston Street   . .   *Genito-Urinary Surgery*
William Edwards Ladd, 326 Dartmouth Street   . . .   *Surgery*
Frank H. Lahey, 638 Beacon Street   . . . . .   *Surgery*
Walter B. Lancaster, 520 Commonwealth Avenue   *Ophthalmology*
John W. Lane, 520 Beacon Street   . . . .   *Surgery*
Harry Jason Lee, 535 Beacon Street   . . . . . .   *Surgery*
George A. Leland, 354 Commonwealth Avenue   .   *Oto-Laryngology*
John Mason Little, 374 Marlborough Street   . . . .   *Surgery*
Halsey Beach Loder, 520 Commonwealth Avenue   . .   *Surgery*
Howard Augustus Lothrop, 101 Beacon Street   . . .   *Surgery*
Robert W. Lovett, 234 Marlborough Street   .   *Orthopedic Surgery*
Fred Bates Lund, 529 Beacon Street   . . . . .   *Surgery*
Daniel Francis Mahoney, 520 Commonwealth Avenue   .   *Surgery*
Henry Orlando Marcy, 180 Commonwealth Avenue .   .   *Surgery*
Nathaniel R. Mason, 483 Beacon Street   .   *Gynecology, Obstetrics*
George Elisha May, 353 Commonwealth Avenue   . .   *Surgery*
Charles Galloupe Mixter, 180 Marlborough Street   . .   *Surgery*
Samuel Jason Mixter, 180 Marlborough Street   . . .   *Surgery*
William Jason Mixter, 180 Marlborough Street   . . .   *Surgery*
George H. Monks, 51 Commonwealth Avenue   . . .   *Surgery*
Howard Moore, 520 Beacon Street   . . .   *Orthopedic Surgery*
George W. Morse, 375 Commonwealth Avenue   . . .   *Surgery*
Harris Peyton Mosher, 828 Beacon Street   . .   *Oto-Laryngology*
Franklin S. Newell, 443 Beacon Street   .   *Gynecology, Obstetrics*
Edward Hall Nichols, 294 Marlborough Street   . . .   *Surgery*
Richard F. O'Neil, 374 Marlborough Street   *Genito-Urinary Surgery*
Robert B. Osgood, 372 Marlborough Street   .   *Orthopedic Surgery*
Horace Packard, 470 Commonwealth Avenue   . . .   *Surgery*
Alonzo Kingman Paine, 80 Bay State Road   *Gynecology, Obstetrics*
Charles Fairbank Painter, 520 Commonwealth Avenue
                                              Orthopedic Surgery
Sarah Ellen Palmer, 483 Beacon Street   . . . .   *Gynecology*

MASSACHUSETTS — Continued

BOSTON — Continued

Luther G. Paul, 321 Beacon Street . . . . . . *Surgery*

Frank A. Pemberton, 311 Beacon Street . . . . *Gynecology*

L. E. Phaneuf, 514 Commonwealth Avenue   *Gynecology, Obstetrics*

Charles Allen Porter, 116 Beacon Street . . . . . *Surgery*

George H. Powers, Jr., 298 Marlborough Street
Rhinol., Oto-Laryngology

Alex. Quackenboss, 143 Newbury Street . . . *Ophthalmology*

William Carter Quinby, Peter Bent Brigham Hospital . *Surgery*

Edward Reynolds, 321 Dartmouth Street . . . . *Gynecology*

George B. Rice, 293 Commonwealth Avenue
Rhinol., Oto-Laryngology

Anna Gove Richardson, 22 Evans Way . . . . *Gynecology*

Edward Peirson Richardson, 224 Beacon Street . . . *Surgery*

Mark Homer Rogers, 483 Beacon Street . . *Orthopedic Surgery*

Luther Colby Rood, 419 Boylston Street . . . *Ophthalmology*

Stephen Rushmore, 520 Commonwealth Avenue
Gynecology, Obstetrics

Jane D. Kelly Sabine, 348 Marlborough Street
Gynecology, Orthopedic Surgery

David Daniel Scannell, 366 Commonwealth Avenue . . *Surgery*

Charles Locke Scudder, 144 Commonwealth Avenue . *Surgery*

Channing C. Simmons, 317 Marlborough Street . . . *Surgery*

Conrad Smith, 510 Commonwealth Avenue   *Rhinol., Laryngology*

Edwin Wallace Smith, 510 Commonwealth Avenue . . *Obstetrics*

George G. Smith, 352 Marlborough Street *Genito-Urinary Surgery*

George Rinaldo Southwick, 433 Marlborough Street . *Surgery*

Robert Soutter, 133 Newbury Street . . . *Orthopedic Surgery*

Myles Standish, 51 Hereford Street . . . . *Ophthalmology*

Henry Burt Stevens, 520 Commonwealth Avenue   *Ophthalmology*

Horace Paine Stevens, 520 Commonwealth Avenue . . *Surgery*

James S. Stone, 286 Marlborough Street . . . . . *Surgery*

Howard Townsend Swain, 226 Commonwealth Avenue . *Obstetrics*

Benjamin Tenney, 308 Marlborough Street *Genito-Urinary Surgery*

Augustus Thorndike, 496 Commonwealth Avenue . . *Retired*

Louisa Paine Tingley, 9 Massachusetts Avenue . *Ophthalmology*

George L. Tobey, Jr., 416 Marlborough Street . *Oto-Laryngology*

James R. Torbert, 252 Marlborough Street . *Gynecology, Obstetrics*

Frederick Herman Verhoeff, 101 Newbury Street . *Ophthalmology*

MASSACHUSETTS — Continued

Boston — Continued

Agnes C. Vietor, Trinity Court . . . . *Surgery*
Beth Vincent, 295 Beacon Street . . . . *Surgery*
Richard G. Wadsworth, 520 Commonwealth Avenue
Gynecology, Obstetrics
David Harold Walker, 390 Commonwealth Avenue
Rhinol., Oto-Laryngology
Irving James Walker, 520 Commonwealth Avenue . . *Surgery*
David Washburn Wells, Hotel Westminster . . *Ophthalmology*
William F. Wesselhoeft, 483 Beacon Street . . . . *Surgery*
Wyman Whittemore, 199 Beacon Street . . . . . *Surgery*
Ralph Cleaves Wiggin, 483 Beacon Street . . . . *Surgery*
DeWitt Gilbert Wilcox, 496 Commonwealth Avenue . *Surgery*
Hugh Williams, 301 Beacon Street . . . . *Surgery*
John Thomas Williams, 483 Beacon Street *Gynecology, Obstetrics*
Ernest B. Young, 434 Marlborough Street *Gynecology, Obstetrics*

Brockton

Michael Francis Barrett, 231 Main Street . . . . *Surgery*
Samuel Warren Goddard, 15 Ellsworth Avenue . . . *Surgery*
George A. Moore, 167 Newbury Street . . . . . *Surgery*

Brookline

William A. Brooks, 227 Summit Avenue . . . . . *Surgery*
John Homans, 33 Leicester Street . . . . *Surgery*

Cambridge

Augustus William Dudley, 1740 Massachusetts Avenue *Surgery*
Edmund Horace Stevens, 1911 Massachusetts Avenue . *Surgery*
William K. S. Thomas, 1718 Massachusetts Avenue . *Surgery*

Charlestown

Edward Marwick Plummer, 5 Adams Street . . *Oto-Laryngology*

Clinton

Charles Roger Abbott, 70 Walnut Street . . . . . *Surgery*
Walter Prentice Bowers, 264 Chestnut Street . . . *Surgery*
Gilman Leeds Chase, 185 Chestnut Street . . . . *Surgery*
James Joseph Goodwin, 202 Church Street . . . . *Surgery*
Edward Hart Mackay, 92 Walnut Street . . . . . *Surgery*

Duxbury

Robert T. Miller . . . . *Surgery*

MASSACHUSETTS — Continued

FALL RIVER

George Willard Blood, 151 Rock Street . . . . . *Surgery*
Augustus W. Buck, 252 Pine Street . . . . . . *Surgery*
Ralph W. French, 151 Rock Street . . . . . . *Surgery*
Ralph W. Jackson, 251 Cherry Street . . . . *Proctology*
George L. Richards, 124 Franklin Street *Rhinol., Oto-Laryngology*
Delano R. Ryder, 151 Rock Street . . . . . *Oto-Laryngology*
Philemon Edwards Truesdale, 151 Rock Street . . . *Surgery*

FRAMINGHAM

Leon Webster Jessaman, 182 Concord Street
Ophth., Rhinol., Laryngology

GREENFIELD

Halbert Greenleaf Stetson, 39 Federal Street . . . . *Surgery*

HAVERHILL

William Cogswell, 51 North Avenue . . . . . . *Surgery*
Charles Edwin Durant, 105 Emerson Street . . . . *Surgery*

HOLYOKE

Edward John Hussey, 1093 Dwight Street
Ophth., Rhinol., Oto-Laryngology
Stephen Andrew Mahoney, 630 Dwight Street . . . *Surgery*

LAWRENCE

Frank A. Conlon, Bay State Building . . . . *Ophth., Otology*
Fred D. McAllister, 301 Essex Street . . . . . . *Surgery*
William Howe Merrill, Bay State Building . . *Ophth., Otology*

LOWELL

Marshall L. Alling, 627 Wyman's Exchange . . . . *Surgery*
James Arthur Gage, 18 Shattuck Street . . . . . *Surgery*
Archibald Robert Gardner, 18 Shattuck Street . . . *Surgery*
George A. Leahey, 128 Merrimack Street *Ophth., Rhinol., Otology*
G. Forrest Martin, 45 Harvard Street . . . . . . *Surgery*

LYNN

George Henry Gray, 11 Lynn Shore Drive . . . . *Surgery*
William Francis O'Reilly, 44 South Common Street
Ophth., Rhinol., Oto-Laryngology
Joseph Gurney Pinkham, 64 Nahant Street . . . *Gynecology*

MALDEN

Charles Edwin Prior, 1 Mountain Avenue . . . . *Surgery*

MASSACHUSETTS — Continued

NEW BEDFORD

Horatio Cushing Allen, 11 8th Street . . . . . . *Surgery*
E. Edwin Foster . . . . *Retired*
Daniel Paul O'Brien, 330 Union Street . . . . . *Surgery*
Henry D. Prescott, 26 Grove Street . . . . . . *Retired*
Edwin P. Seaver, Jr., 271 Union Street   *Rhinol., Oto-Laryngology*

NEWTON

Henry Orlando Marcy, Jr., 140 Sargent Street . . . *Surgery*

NORTH ADAMS

Martin Millard Brown, 117 Main Street . . . . . *Surgery*
Frank Dalmon Stafford, 56 Summer Street . . . . *Surgery*
George H. Thompson, 18 Ashland Street . . . *Ophth., Otology*

NORTHAMPTON

Herbert Brainerd Perry, 55 New South Street . . . *Surgery*

PALMER

Harry Cleveland Cheney, 18 Thorndike Street . . . *Surgery*
George Andrew Moore, Post Office Block   *Ophth., Oto-Laryngology*

PITTSFIELD

Nathan Finkelstein, 184 North Street . . . . . . *Surgery*

QUINCY

Francis R. Burke, 1200 Hancock Street . . . . . *Surgery*
Nathaniel Stevens Hunting, 1136 Hancock Street . . *Surgery*
Daniel B. Reardon, 1186 Hancock Street . . . . . *Surgery*
Walter Leslie Sargent, 1155 Hancock Street . . . . *Surgery*
George M. Sheahan, 12 School Street . . . . . . *Surgery*

ROXBURY

George Arthur Webster, 53A Dale Street . . . . . *Otology*

SALEM

Martin Thomas Field, 23 Winter Street . . . . . *Surgery*
Thomas Kittredge, 13 Chestnut Street . . . . . *Surgery*
Hardy Phippen, 84 Washington Square . . . . . *Surgery*
Walter Gray Phippen, 31 Chestnut Street . . . . *Surgery*

SOUTH DARTMOUTH

Francis S. Watson . . . . *Retired*

MASSACHUSETTS — Continued

SPRINGFIELD

John Mathews Birnie, 6 Chestnut Street . . . . . . *Surgery*

Harry Francis Byrnes, 67 Chestnut Street
Ophth., Rhinol., Oto-Laryngology

Dudley Carleton, 137½ State Street . . . . . . *Surgery*

John Hosea Carmichael, 41 Maple Street . . . . . *Surgery*

Charles Ratchford Chapman, 174 State Street
Ophth., Rhinol., Oto-Laryngology

M. W. Conrow, 31 Maple Street   *Ophth., Rhinol., Oto-Laryngology*

William Goodell, 6 Chestnut Street   . *Rhinol., Oto-Laryngology*

Frederick Eugene Hopkins, 25 Harrison Avenue . *Oto-Laryngology*

Robert Ferry Hovey, 5 Oak Street . . . . . . *Surgery*

Charles Francis Lynch, 387 Main Street . . . . . *Surgery*

Edward J. Mahoney, 4 Mattoon Street . . . . . *Surgery*

Ralph Beverley Ober, 76 Maple Street . . . . . *Surgery*

Allen Galpin Rice, 33 School Street . . . . . . *Surgery*

Ralph H. Seelye, 73 Chestnut Street . . . . . . *Surgery*

Erdix Tenney Smith, 480 Belmont Avenue . . . . *Surgery*

Frederick Benoni Sweet, 81 Chestnut Street . . . . *Surgery*

Winford O. Wilder, 175 State Street . . . . . . *Urology*

VINEYARD HAVEN

Garry de N. Hough . . . . *Surgery*

WALTHAM

Richard Collins, 837 Main Street . . . . . . *Surgery*

Henry Austin Wood, 751 Main Street . . . . . *Surgery*

WESTFIELD

James Billings Atwater, 82 Broad Street . . . . . *Surgery*

Miles Dudley Chisholm, 106 Elm Street . . . . . *Surgery*

Frederick T. Clark, 29 Parks Block   *Ophth., Rhinol., Oto-Laryngology*

George H. Janes, 57 Court Street . . . . *Surgery*

Edward S. Smith, 15 Noble Avenue . . . . . . *Surgery*

WINCHENDON

John Goodrich Henry, 33 Pleasant Street . . . . *Surgery*

WINCHESTER

Hunter Robb, 55 Bacon Street . . . . *Gynecology*

WOLLASTON

Elmon R. Johnson, 389 Newport Avenue .   *Rhinol., Laryngology*

MASSACHUSETTS — Continued

WORCESTER

Benjamin Harrison Alton, 72 Pearl Street . . . . *Surgery*
James Arthur Barnes, Slater Building . . . . . *Surgery*
William Irving Clark, Jr., 53 West Street . . . . . *Surgery*
Kendall Emerson, 56 William Street . . . *Orthopedic Surgery*
Michael F. Fallon, Slater Building . . . . . . *Surgery*
Edgar Alexander Fisher, 25 Elm Street . . . . . *Surgery*
Homer Gage, 72 Pearl Street . . . . *Surgery*
Albert Colby Getchell, 6 Linden Street . *Rhinol., Laryngology*
David Harrower, 13 Elm Street . . . . . *Ophth., Otology*
George Hillard Hill, 15 High Street . . . . . . *Surgery*
Ernest Leroi Hunt, 120 Lovell Street . . . . . . *Surgery*
William F. Lynch, 390 Main Street . . . . . . *Surgery*
Arthur White Marsh, 690 Main Street . . . . . *Surgery*
Winthrop D. Mitchell, "Stone House," Olean Street . *Retired*
O. Draper Phelps, 452 Main Street . . *Genito-Urinary Surgery*
William Henry Rose, 13 Elm Street . . . . . . *Surgery*
Walter Clark Seelye, 390 Main Street . . . . . . *Surgery*
Edward Henry Trowbridge, 28 Pleasant Street . . *Gynecology*
John Kelso Warren, 78 Pleasant Street . . . . . *Surgery*
Royal Phillips Watkins, 17 West Street . . . . . *Surgery*
Charles Douglas Wheeler, 18 Chestnut Street . . . *Surgery*
Lemuel Fox Woodward, 52 Pearl Street . . . . . *Surgery*

YARMOUTHPORT

Gorham Bacon . . . . *Retired*

MICHIGAN

ALBION

George Clinton Hafford, 400½ South Superior Street . *Surgery*

ALLEGAN

Arthur Letchford Robinson, Marshall Street . . . . *Surgery*

ANN ARBOR

Hugh McDowell Beebe, 317 South State Street . . . *Surgery*
Hugh Cabot, University Hospital . . . . *Surgery*
R. B. Canfield, 330 South State Street *Rhinol., Oto-Laryngology*
Howard H. Cummings, 202 Nickels Arcade *Gynecology, Obstetrics*
Cyrenus G. Darling, 722 Forest Avenue . . . . . *Surgery*
Ira D. Loree, 122 North Thayer Street . *Genito-Urinary Surgery*

MICHIGAN — Continued

ANN ARBOR — Continued

Dean Wentworth Myers, 317 South State Street
Ophth., Rhinol., Oto-Laryngology
Max Minor Peet, University Hospital . . . . . . *Surgery*
Reuben Peterson, 1416 Hill Street . . . *Gynecology, Obstetrics*
George Slocum, 311 South State Street . . . *Ophthalmology*
C. L. Washburne, 225 East Liberty Street . . . . *Surgery*

BATTLE CREEK

James Thomas Case, 124 Manchester Street . . . . *Surgery*
B. N. Colver, 182 Manchester Street . *Rhinol., Oto-Laryngology*
Rowland Hill Harris, 41 North Washington Avenue . . *Surgery*
John Harvey Kellogg, 202 Manchester Street . . . *Surgery*
Harry Butler Knapp, Battle Creek Sanitarium . *Orthopedic Surgery*
Archibald E. MacGregor, Post Tavern . . . . . *Surgery*
Clarence Mavel Mercer, 41 North Washington Avenue . *Surgery*
Ray Clinton Stone, 618 Post Building . . . . . . *Surgery*
Rollin Curtis Winslow, 612 Post Building . . . . . *Surgery*

BIG RAPIDS

William T. Dodge, 115 South State Street . . . . *Surgery*

CALUMET

George M. Rees, 1215 Calumet Avenue . . . . . *Surgery*

DETROIT

Norman McLeod Allen, 2407 Woodward Avenue . . *Surgery*
E. Amberg, David Whitney Building . *Rhinol., Oto-Laryngology*
Bruce Anderson, 804 Forest Avenue, West . . . *Gynecology*
Joseph H. Andries, 1633 David Whitney Building . . *Surgery*
Raymond Carl Andries, 1737 David Whitney Building . *Surgery*
Max Ballin, 2407 Woodward Avenue . . . . . . *Surgery*
Robert Beattie, 1229 David Whitney Building
Ophth., Rhinol., Oto-Laryngology
John N. Bell, 1149 David Whitney Building *Gynecology, Obstetrics*
Neil I. Bentley, 1161 David Whitney Building
Ophth., Rhinol., Oto-Laryngology
Edward J. Bernstein, 507 Fine Arts Building
Ophth., Rhinol., Oto-Laryngology
Alexander W. Blain, 2201 Jefferson Avenue, East . . *Surgery*
W. E. Blodgett, Kresge Medical Building . . *Orthopedic Surgery*
James Henry Boulter, 1601 David Whitney Building . *Surgery*

MICHIGAN — Continued

DETROIT — Continued

Clark D. Brooks, David Whitney Building . . . . *Surgery*
Don M. Campbell, 1613 David Whitney Building
Ophth., Rhinol., Oto-Laryngology
William J. Cassidy, 1787 David Whitney Building . . *Surgery*
Ray Connor, 503 Washington Arcade . . . . *Ophth., Otology*
Ernest Keys Cullen, 1053 David Whitney Building . *Gynecology*
Mortimer Edwin Danforth, Concord and Lafayette
Streets, East . . . . *Surgery*
Leo Dretzka, 1002 David Whitney Building . . . . *Surgery*
G. E. Frothingham, 3790 Woodward Avenue . . *Ophth., Otology*
Robert W. Gillman, 61 Peterboro Street . . . *Ophth., Otology*
John E. Gleason, 1061 David Whitney Building
Ophth., Rhinol., Oto-Laryngology
Andrew R. Hackett, 2035 West Jefferson Avenue . . *Surgery*
Walter L. Hackett, 712 David Whitney Building
Gynecology, Obstetrics
William A. Hackett, 708 David Whitney Building . . *Surgery*
Hugh A. Hagerty, 1201 David Whitney Building . . *Surgery*
Herbert W. Hewitt, 1131 David Whitney Building . . *Surgery*
Preston M. Hickey, 62 Adams Avenue, West . . . . *Surgery*
Louis J. Hirschman, Kresge Medical Building . . *Proctology*
Edwin Cornue Hoff, 1101 David Whitney Building . . *Surgery*
Willard Hunter Hutchings, 2951 Jefferson Avenue, East . *Surgery*
C. Hollister Judd, David Whitney Building *Gynecology, Obstetrics*
George Kamperman, 1807 David Whitney Building
Gynecology, Obstetrics
William Edward Keane, 101 Fort Street, West . . . *Urology*
Frank A. Kelly, 1429 David Whitney Building . . . *Surgery*
F. C. Kidner, 1337 David Whitney Building . *Orthopedic Surgery*
Stephen Herrick Knight, 69 East Willis Avenue . . . *Surgery*
Charles F. Kuhn, 90 Warren Avenue, East . . . . *Surgery*
Alfred D. LaFerté, 1551 David Whitney Building
Orthopedic Surgery
Daniel LaFerté, David Whitney Building . . *Orthopedic Surgery*
D. A. MacLachlan, David Whitney Building
Ophth., Rhinol., Oto-Laryngology
James A. MacMillan, 938 David Whitney Building . . *Surgery*
Walter Manton, 62 Adams Avenue, West . *Obstetrics, Gynecology*

MICHIGAN — Continued

DETROIT — Continued

W. P. Manton, 62 Adams Avenue, West . *Gynecology, Obstetrics*
J. D. Matthews, 948 David Whitney Building . . . *Surgery*
Archibald D. McAlpine, 512 Washington Arcade . . *Surgery*
Carl C. McClelland, 1857 David Whitney Building
                 Ophth., Rhinol., Oto-Laryngology
Roy Donaldson McClure, Henry Ford Hospital . . . *Surgery*
Angus McLean, David Whitney Building . . . . . *Surgery*
Richard E. Mercer, David Whitney Building *Rhinol., Laryngology*
William F. Metcalf, 1905 West Grand Boulevard . . *Surgery*
Fred Towsley Murphy, Penobscot Building . . . . *Surgery*
Charles H. Oakman, David Whitney Building . . *Oral Surgery*
Edward J. O'Brien, 2560 Woodward Avenue . . . . *Surgery*
Anna Odell, 74 Adams Avenue, West . *Ophth., Oto-Laryngology*
George H. Palmerlee, 410 Washington Arcade . . . *Surgery*
Edward J. Panzner, Breitmeyer Building . . . . . *Surgery*
Walter Robert Parker, David Whitney Building . *Ophthalmology*
Rolland Parmeter, 76 Adams Avenue, West . *Surgery, Obstetrics*
Grover Cleveland Penberthy, David Whitney Building . *Surgery*
Harry Ward Plaggemeyer, 1701 David Whitney Building *Urology*
Harry Prewitt Poston, 1337 David Whitney Building . *Surgery*
George E. Potter, 6509 Woodward Avenue . . . . *Surgery*
Wilson Randolph, 405 West Fort Street
                 Ophth., Rhinol., Oto-Laryngology
W. A. Repp, 1002 David Whitney Building *Gynecology, Obstetrics*
James Milton Robb, 641 David Whitney Building
                 Ophth., Rhinol., Oto-Laryngology
Frederick W. Robbins, 1212 Kresge Medical Building . *Urology*
Hermon H. Sanderson, David Whitney Building . *Ophth., Otology*
Ward F. Seeley, David Whitney Building *Obstetrics, Gynecology*
William J. Seymour, 2506 Park Boulevard . . . . *Surgery*
Harold Koch Shawan, 1701 David Whitney Building . *Surgery*
Burt Russell Shurly, 62 Adams Avenue, West . *Oto-Laryngology*
Eugene Smith, 32 Adams Avenue, West . . . *Ophth., Otology*
William Albert Spitzley, 62 Adams Avenue, West . . *Surgery*
Claude Maurice Stafford, 801 Smith Building . . *Gynecology*
Alexander M. Stirling, 1515 David Whitney Building . *Surgery*
Glenn Wiley Stockwell, 408 Washington Arcade . . . *Surgery*
Frank Burr Tibbals, 1212 Kresge Medical Building . . *Surgery*

MICHIGAN — Continued

H. N. Torrey, 1033 David Whitney Building . . . . *Surgery*
J. Walter Vaughan, 987 Jefferson Avenue, East . . . *Surgery*
George Matthew Waldeck, 1001 David Whitney Building
Ophth., Rhinol., Oto-Laryngology
Frank B. Walker, 1320 David Whitney Building . . *Surgery*
Walter E. Welz, 608 Mt. Elliott Avenue . *Obstetrics, Gynecology*
Harold Wilson, David Whitney Building *Ophth., Oto-Laryngology*
Frank C. Witter, David Whitney Building *Gynecology, Obstetrics*
H. Wellington Yates, 1229 David Whitney Building *Gynecology*

DOWAGIAC

George W. Green, 501 Main Street . . . . . . *Surgery*

ESCANABA

Arthur Samuel Kitchen, 1229 Hartnett Avenue . . . *Surgery*

FLINT

W. G. Bird, 510 F. P. Smith Building . *Ophth., Oto-Laryngology*
Joshua George Ross Manwaring, Dryden Building . . *Surgery*
Herbert Elmer Randall, 302 Smith Building . . . . *Surgery*
David L. Treat, 221 East 3rd Street . . . . . . *Surgery*

GOODRICH

Amos S. Wheelock . . . . *Surgery*

GRAND RAPIDS

Corda E. Beeman, 311 Widdicomb Building
Ophth., Rhinol., Oto-Laryngology
Alexander M. Campbell, Metz Building . . *Surgery, Obstetrics*
John Dearborn Hastie, 122 East Fulton Street . . . *Surgery*
Robert James Hutchinson, 100 Weston Street, S. E . . *Surgery*
Ansel B. Smith, 324 Metz Building . . . . . . *Surgery*
Ferris Smith, 407 Metz Building . . *Rhinol., Oto-Laryngology*
Richard R. Smith, Metz Building . . . . . . *Surgery*
Pius L. Thompson, 307 Metz Building . . . . . *Surgery*
R. T. Urquhart, Ashton Building *Ophth., Rhinol., Oto-Laryngology*
Henry J. Van den Berg, Metz Building . . . . . *Surgery*
William Henry Veenboer, Metz Building . . *Surgery, Obstetrics*
Frederick Cook Warnshuis, Powers Theater Building . *Surgery*
Rowland F. Webb, 406 Ashton Building . . . . *Gynecology*
D. Emmett Welsh, Powers Theater Building
Ophth., Rhinol., Oto-Laryngology

MICHIGAN — Continued

GREENVILLE

    Albert J. Bower, 227 South Lafayette Street . . . . *Surgery*

HANCOCK

    Arthur F. Fischer, Quincy Mine . . . . *Surgery*

    Joseph E. Scallon, First National Bank Building . . *Surgery*

HASTINGS

    Arthur W. Woodburne, 304 South Jefferson Street . . *Surgery*

HILLSDALE

    Burt Francis Green, First National Bank Building . . *Surgery*

    Walter Hulme Sawyer, 12 Manning Street . . . . *Surgery*

HOLLAND

    William G. Winter, 14 West 8th Street . *Gynecology, Obstetrics*

HOUGHTON

    Neil Sutherland MacDonald, 100 Hubbell Avenue . . *Surgery*

    James Gibbons Turner, 60 Sheldon Street . . . . *Surgery*

IRON MOUNTAIN

    William J. Anderson . . . . *Surgery*

    Joseph A. Crowell, 301 East Ludington Street . . . *Surgery*

IRON RIVER

    Edward M. Libby, Iron River Hospital . . . . . *Surgery*

ISHPEMING

    Vivian H. Vandeventer, 403 North Main Street . . . *Surgery*

JACKSON

    Walter Lloyd Finton, 410 South Jackson Street . . . *Surgery*

    Delbert Edgar Robinson, 410 South Jackson Street . . *Surgery*

    George A. Seybold, 604 Peoples National Bank Building *Surgery*

KALAMAZOO

    Ralph E. Balch, 115 West Lovell Street . . . . . *Surgery*

    Charles E. Boys, 1008 Hanselman Building . . . . *Surgery*

    Clarke B. Fulkerson, 308 Kalamazoo National Bank

        Building . . . . *Ophth., Oto-Laryngology*

    Edward P. Wilbur, Kalamazoo National Bank Building

            Ophth., Rhinol., Oto-Laryngology

MICHIGAN — Continued

LAKE LINDEN

Simon Levin　.　.　.　.　.　.　.　.　.　.　.　.　*Surgery*

LANSING

Earl Ingram Carr, 300 West Ottawa Street　.　.　.　.　*Surgery*

Berten M. Davey, 221 North Capitol Avenue　.　.　.　*Surgery*

William E. McNamara, 300 West Ottawa Street .　.　.　*Surgery*

LAURIUM

Albert I. Lawbaugh, 117 Willow Avenue .　.　.　.　.　*Surgery*

MANISTEE

Lewis Stanton Ramsdell, 57 Poplar Street　.　.　.　.　*Surgery*

MARQUETTE

Alfred W. Hornbogen, Savings Bank Building　.　.　.　*Surgery*

Harry J. Hornbogen, 212 East Michigan Street

Ophth., Rhinol., Oto-Laryngology

MOHAWK

George A. Conrad　.　.　.　.　.　.　.　.　.　.　.　*Surgery*

MUSKEGON

Charles J. Bloom, Landreth Block .　.　.　.　.　.　.　*Surgery*

Robert I. Busard, First Street and Webster Avenue .　.　*Surgery*

Frank Webster Garber, 159 Jefferson Street　.　.　.　.　*Surgery*

George L. LeFevre, Union National Bank Building .　.　*Surgery*

Albertus B. Poppen, Union National Bank Building　*Gynecology*

OWOSSO

Arthur M. Hume, 224 North Ball Street .　.　.　.　.　*Surgery*

PAINESDALE

William Kerr West　.　.　.　.　.　.　.　.　.　.　.　*Surgery*

PONTIAC

William Horace Morley .　.　.　.　.　.　.　.　.　.　*Obstetrics*

PORT HURON

James Arthur Attridge, 516 Water Street .　.　.　.　.　*Surgery*

Alexander J. MacKenzie, 504 Meisel Building　.　.　.　*Surgery*

SAGINAW

James D. Bruce, 333 South Jefferson Avenue .　.　.　.　*Surgery*

Matthew Kollig, 704 Holland Avenue .　.　.　.　.　.　*Surgery*

Bert Bessac Rowe, 315 South Jefferson Avenue　.　.　.　*Surgery*

C. H. Sample, 309 South Washington Avenue　.　.　.　*Surgery*

Walter L. Slack, 308 Eddy Building

Ophth., Rhinol., Oto-Laryngology

MICHIGAN — Continued

ST. JOHNS
Athur O. Hart, 200 East Walker Street . . . . . *Surgery*

ST. JOSEPH
Theron G. Yeomans, St. Joseph Sanitarium . . . . *Surgery*

TRENTON
Claudius Bligh Kinyon . . . . *Surgery*

MINNESOTA

BEMIDJI
Rowland Thomas Stratton Gilmore, 905 Lake Boulevard *Surgery*

BRAINERD
Walter Courtney, 19 Bluff Avenue . . . . *Retired*
John A. Evert . . . . *Surgery*
John A. Thabes, 417 Holly Street . . . . *Surgery*

CALEDONIA
William E. Browning . . . . *Surgery*

CROOKSTON
Halvor Holte, 220 South Broadway . . . . . . *Surgery*

DETROIT
Leonard Case Weeks, 827 Washington Avenue . . . *Surgery*

DULUTH
William Richardson Bagley, 510 Fidelity Building . . *Surgery*
Alexander J. Braden, 400 Lyceum Building . . . . *Surgery*
Theodore Leete Chapman, 700 Fidelity Building . . *Surgery*
Arthur Nelson Collins, Lyceum Building . . . . . *Surgery*
W. A. Coventry, 600 Fidelity Building . *Gynecology, Obstetrics*
John J. Eklund, 7 East Superior Street . . . . . *Surgery*
Veader N. Leonard, 25 10th Avenue, East . . . *Gynecology*
Clarence E. Lum, 304 Providence Building
Ophth., Rhinol., Oto-Laryngology
William Henry Magie, 401 Sellwood Building . . . *Surgery*
T. H. Shastid, 400 Lyceum Building . . . . *Ophthalmology*
John Arthur Winter, 600 Fidelity Building
Ophth., Rhinol., Oto-Laryngology

ELY
Owen W. Parker . . . . *Surgery*

MINNESOTA — Continued

EVELETH

    Charles W. More, 605 Grant Avenue . . . . . . *Surgery*

GRACEVILLE

    Clifford I. Oliver . . . . *Surgery*

HIBBING

    Bertram S. Adams, 812 3rd Avenue . . . . . . *Surgery*

LITCHFIELD

    Karl A. Danielson . . . . *Surgery*
    John J. Donovan, 606 Armstrong Avenue . . . . . *Surgery*
    Archibald W. Robertson, Robertson Building . . . *Surgery*

MANKATO

    John W. Andrews, National Citizens Bank Building . *Surgery*
    John S. Holbrook, 301 South Front Street . . . . *Surgery*
    Carl J. Holman, 201 National Citizens Bank Building . *Surgery*
    John Henry James, National Citizens Bank Building
                 Ophth., Rhinol., Oto-Laryngology
    Aaron Franklin Schmitt, 645 South 4th Street . . . *Surgery*
    Alphonse Edward John Sohmer, 307 South Front Street *Surgery*

MINNEAPOLIS

    Amos W. Abbott, 1717 1st Avenue, South . . . . *Surgery*
    Fred L. Adair, 730 La Salle Building . . *Gynecology, Obstetrics*
    Stephen H. Baxter, Physicians and Surgeons Building . *Surgery*
    Alfred N. Bessesen, 301 Donaldson Building . . . . *Surgery*
    Fred Macon Bogan, 108 East 24th Street . . . . . *Surgery*
    A. E. Booth, 1132 Metropolitan Bank Building . . . *Surgery*
    Hermann A. H. Bouman, 403 Physicians and Surgeons
      Building . . . . *Surgery*
    Arthur F. Bratrud, 302 Physicians and Surgeons Building *Surgery*
    Paul F. Brown, 1101 Metropolitan Bank Building . . *Surgery*
    Kenneth Bulkley, 420 Syndicate Building . . . . *Surgery*
    Chester M. Carlaw, Physicians and Surgeons Building . *Surgery*
    Howard S. Clark, 607 La Salle Building *Ophth., Oto-Laryngology*
    William H. Condit, 1009 Nicollet Avenue . *Gynecology, Obstetrics*
    J. Frank Corbett, 808 Physicians and Surgeons Building . *Surgery*
    John G. Ericson, 603 Syndicate Building
                 Ophth., Rhinol., Oto-Laryngology
    Robert Emmett Farr, 2433 Bryant Avenue, South . . *Surgery*
    Emil S. Geist, 704 Besse Building . . . . *Orthopedic Surgery*

MINNESOTA — Continued

MINNEAPOLIS — Continued

Eugene K. Green, 808 Physicians and Surgeons Building   *Surgery*
Earle Russell Hare, 730 La Salle Building   . . . . *Surgery*
Knut Hoegh, 131 West 36th Street, South   . . . . *Surgery*
Conrad Jacobson, 225 Millard Hall   . . . . . *Surgery*
August E. Johnson, 905 Metropolitan Bank Building   . *Surgery*
James A. Johnson, 1009 Nicollet Avenue . . . . *Surgery*
Hannibal H. Kimball, 602 Nicollet Avenue   . . . *Surgery*
Laura Arlene Lane, 3201 Clinton Avenue
                      Ophth., Rhinol., Oto-Laryngology
Arthur Ayer Law, 420 Syndicate Building   . . . *Surgery*
Henry H. Leavitt, 700 Donaldson Building
                      Ophth., Rhinol., Oto-Laryngology
Joseph D. Lewis, 516 La Salle Building
                      Ophth., Rhinol., Oto-Laryngology
Jennings Crawford Litzenberg, 1009 Nicollet Avenue
                      Gynecology, Obstetrics
Matthew John Lynch, 710 Physicians and Surgeons Building
                      Surgery
John Silliman Macnie, 503 Donaldson Building
                      Ophth., Rhinol., Oto-Laryngology
Clarence O. Maland, 730 LaSalle Building   *Obstetrics, Gynecology*
Arthur T. Mann, 910 Donaldson Building   . . . *Surgery*
J. Matthews, Metropolitan Bank Building   *Rhinol., Laryngology*
Howard McIlvain Morton, Metropolitan Bank Building
                      Ophthalmology
W. R. Murray, 1009 Nicollet Avenue . . *Ophth., Oto-Laryngology*
H. Newhart, 910 Donaldson Building . . *Ophth., Oto-Laryngology*
C. F. Nootnagel, 600 Physicians and Surgeons Building   *Surgery*
Frederick A. M. Olson, 420 Syndicate Building . . . *Surgery*
O. A. Olson, 1117 Metropolitan Bank Building . . . *Surgery*
Oscar Owre, 707 Masonic Temple . . . . . . *Urology*
E. H. Parker, 730 La Salle Building   . . *Rhinol., Laryngology*
Frederick Harold Poppe, 730 La Salle Building . . *Surgery*
John A. Pratt, 919 Metropolitan Bank Building
                      Ophth., Rhinol., Oto-Laryngology
Charles Anthony Reed, 1009 Nicollet Avenue . *Orthopedic Surgery*
John H. Rishmiller, 1101 Metropolitan Bank Building .   *Surgery*
William E. Rochford, 527 Syndicate Building   . . . *Surgery*

MINNESOTA — Continued

MINNEAPOLIS — Continued

Samuel C. Schmitt, 705 Physicians and Surgeons Building *Surgery*
Gustav Schwyzer, 410 Donaldson Building . . . . *Surgery*
Jalmar Hendrik Simons, 609 La Salle Building
Gynecology, Obstetrics
Arthur Edward Smith, Donaldson Building
Ophth., Rhinol., Oto-Laryngology
Frederic J. Souba, 600 Physicians and Surgeons Building *Surgery*
C. N. Spratt, 900 Nicollet Avenue . . *Ophth., Oto-Laryngology*
Arthur C. Strachauer, 1009 Nicollet Avenue . . . . *Surgery*
Eugene S. Strout, Donaldson Building . *Ophth., Oto-Laryngology*
George Elmer Strout, 900 Donaldson Building
Ophth., Oto-Laryngology
Henry C. Stuhr, 900 Donaldson Building . . . . . *Surgery*
Horatio B. Sweetser, Physicians and Surgeons Building . *Surgery*
James A. Watson, Physicians and Surgeons Building
Ophth., Oto-Laryngology
Roscoe Clayton Webb, 300 La Salle Building . . . *Surgery*
Charles Galen Weston, 803 Physicians and Surgeons
Building . . . . *Gynecology, Obstetrics*
Archa Edward Wilcox, 920 Nicollet Avenue . . . '. *Surgery*
Douglas F. Wood, 610 Donaldson Building
Ophth., Rhinol., Oto-Laryngology
F. R. Wright, 707 Donaldson Building . *Genito-Urinary Surgery*
Herbert M. N. Wynne, 300 La Salle Building *Gynecology, Urology*
Otto William Yoerg, 527 Syndicate Building . . . . *Surgery*

NEW ULM
O. C. Strickler . . . . *Surgery*

ORTONVILLE
Charles Bolsta . . . . *Surgery*

OWATONNA
John H. Adair, 322 East Vine Street . . . . . . *Surgery*
Christian P. Nelson . . . . *Surgery*

PRINCETON
Henry C. Cooney . . . . *Surgery*

ROCHESTER
Alfred Washington Adson, Mayo Clinic . . . . . *Surgery*
Rudolph George Andres, Mayo Clinic . . . . . . *Surgery*

MINNESOTA — Continued

ROCHESTER — Continued

Donald C. Balfour, 427 South Glencoe Street . . . *Surgery*
Roy Alexander Barlow, Mayo Clinic . *Rhinol., Oto-Laryngology*
William Lemuel Benedict, 102 2nd Street, S. W. . *Ophthalmology*
Walter Meredith Boothby, Mayo Clinic . . . . . *Surgery*
Stuart W. Harrington, Mayo Clinic . . . . . . *Surgery*
Carl Arthur Hedblom, Mayo Clinic . . . . . . *Surgery*
Melvin S. Henderson, 428 4th Street, S. W. . *Orthopedic Surgery*
Verne Carlton Hunt, Mayo Clinic . . . . *Surgery*
Edward Starr Judd, 705 2nd Street, S.W. . . . . . *Surgery*
Harold I. Lillie, Mayo Clinic . . . *Rhinol., Oto-Laryngology*
Ambrose L. Lockwood, Mayo Clinic . . . . . . *Surgery*
James Carruthers Masson, Mayo Clinic . . . . . *Surgery*
Charles Horace Mayo, Mayowood . . . . *Surgery*
William J. Mayo, 701 College Hill . . . . *Surgery*
Henry W. Meyerding, 525 9th Avenue, S.W. . *Orthopedic Surgery*
Gordon B. New, Mayo Clinic . . . *Laryngology, Oral Surgery*
John de Jarnette Pemberton, Mayo Clinic . . . . *Surgery*
Fred Rankin, Mayo Clinic . . . . *Surgery*
Walter E. Sistrunk, 806 4th Street, S.W. . . . . . *Surgery*
George Ellsworth Sutton, Mayo Clinic . . . . . *Surgery*

ST. CLOUD

Warren Loring Beebe, 5th Avenue and St. Germain
Street . . . . *Surgery*

ST. PAUL

Henry E. Binger, 1027 Lowry Building *Ophth., Oto-Laryngology*
Frank E. Burch, 754 Linwood Place . . . . *Ophthalmology*
William C. Carroll, Lowry Building . . . . . . *Surgery*
Carl C. Chatterton, Moore Building . . . *Orthopedic Surgery*
Alexander R. Colvin, Lowry Building . . . . . . *Surgery*
Louis Eugene Daugherty, 914 Lowry Building . . . *Surgery*
Warren A. Dennis, Hamm Building . . . . . . *Surgery*
George Arthur Earl, 1210 Lowry Building . . . . *Surgery*
Robert Earl, Lowry Building . . . . *Surgery*
George Arthur Geist, 133 West 7th Street . . . . *Surgery*
Eric O. Giere, 319 Hamm Building . . . . . . *Surgery*
Albert C. Heath, 339 Lowry Building . *Rhinol., Oto-Laryngology*
Oscar W. Holcomb, 942 Lowry Building . . . . . *Surgery*

MINNESOTA — Continued

ST. PAUL — Continued

Arthur W. Ide, 1515 Charles Street . . . . . . *Surgery*
Elmer M. Jones, 1014 Lowry Building . . . . . *Surgery*
Carl L. Larsen, 1027 Lowry Building . . . . . . *Surgery*
William Lerche, Lowry Building . . . . *Surgery*
William W. Lewis, 836 Lowry Building
                              Ophth., Rhinol., Oto-Laryngology
Archibald MacLaren, 914 Lowry Building . . . . *Surgery*
Thomas McDavitt, Lowry Building . . . . *Ophth., Otology*
Harry Parks Ritchie, 914 Lowry Building . . . . *Surgery*
John T. Rogers, Hamm Building . . . . *Surgery*
John L. Rothrock, Hamm Building . . *Gynecology, Obstetrics*
Frederick C. Schuldt, 1137 Lowry Building . . . . *Surgery*
Arnold Schwyzer, 123 West 7th Street . . . . . *Surgery*
John L. Shellman, Hamm Building . *Ophth., Oto-Laryngology*
Anton Shimonek, 642 Lowry Building . . . . . *Surgery*
John C. Staley, 1235 Lowry Building . . . . . . *Surgery*
Harry Bernard Zimmermann, Hamm Building . . . *Surgery*

TRACY

Harper M. Workman, Partridge Block . . . . . *Surgery*

VIRGINIA

Charles B. Lenont, Lenont Hospital . . . . . . *Surgery*
Edward H. McIntyre . . . . *Surgery*

WARREN

Theodor Bratrud, Warren Hospital . . . . . . *Surgery*
Orville N. Meland, Warren Hospital . . . . . *Surgery*

WILLMAR

Berton J. Branton, Willmar Clinic . . . . . . *Surgery*
Peter C. Davison . . . . . *Ophth., Rhinol., Oto-Laryngology*

MISSISSIPPI

COLUMBUS

Walter Russell McKinley, 618 Main Street . . . . *Surgery*

GREENVILLE

Hugh Agnew Gamble, 505 Washington Avenue . . . *Surgery*

HATTIESBURG

Walter W. Crawford, South Mississippi Infirmary . . *Surgery*
Theophilus Erskine Ross, 416 Bay Street . . . . . *Surgery*

MISSISSIPPI — Continued

JACKSON
Wallace L. Britt, Century Building . *Genito-Urinary Surgery*
W. B. Dobson, Century Building . . *Ophth., Oto-Laryngology*
Samuel Hoskins McLean, Century Building . . . . *Surgery*
Harley R. Shands, Century Building . . . . . *Surgery*
James Percy Wall, Jackson Sanatorium . . . . . *Surgery*

MERIDIAN
Samuel Henry Hairston, Miazza-Woods Building . . *Surgery*
Robert Lee Turner, 1421 20th Avenue . . . . . *Surgery*

NATCHEZ
Charles T. Chamberlain, 313 Franklin Street . . . . *Surgery*
John W. D. Dicks, 207 Linton Avenue . . . . . *Surgery*
Richard Dunckley Sessions, 305 Franklin Street . . . *Surgery*

VICKSBURG
Benson Blake Martin, 1918 Washington Street . . . *Surgery*

WINONA
John Woodson Barksdale, 106 Railroad Avenue . . . *Surgery*

YAZOO CITY
John Darrington, Yazoo and Madison Streets . . . *Surgery*

MISSOURI

CAPE GIRARDEAU
John D. Porterfield, Jr., 6 North Spanish Street . . . *Surgery*

CARROLLTON
Richard Franklin Cook, 5 East Benton Street . . . *Surgery*

COLUMBIA
Dudley Steele Conley, Guitar Building . . . . . *Surgery*
Frank G. Nifong, 12 South 9th Street . . . . . *Surgery*
Guy Lincoln Noyes, 311 Hitt Street . . . . *Ophth., Otology*
Carl Miller Sneed, 909 Elm Street . . . . . *Ophth., Otology*

EDINA
H. J. Jurgens . . . . *Surgery*

JEFFERSON CITY
William Alfred Clark, 406 Central Trust Building . . *Surgery*

JOPLIN
Robert L. Neff, Frisco Building . . . . *Surgery*

MISSOURI — Continued

KANSAS CITY

John Fairbairn Binnie, 917 Rialto Building . . . . *Surgery*
Edward Giles Blair, 404 Bryant Building . . . . . *Surgery*
T. S. Blakesley, 638 Lathrop Building
                    Ophth., Rhinol., Oto-Laryngology
Jonathan E. Burns, 403 Waldheim Building . . . . *Urology*
Clarence S. Capell, 1135 Rialto Building . . . . . *Urology*
Robert James Curdy, Rialto Building . . . . *Ophthalmology*
Frank M. Denslow, 715 Bryant Building *Genito-Urinary Surgery*
Frank D. Dickson, 403 Waldheim Building . *Orthopedic Surgery*
Hal Foster, 402 Altman Building . . *Rhinol., Oto-Laryngology*
William Davis Foster, 4125 Warwick Boulevard . . . *Surgery*
Clarence B. Francisco, 416 Argyle Building . *Orthopedic Surgery*
J. M. Frankenburger, Rialto Building . . . . . . *Surgery*
William J. Frick, 924 Rialto Building . . . . . . *Surgery*
Jefferson D. Griffith, 1225 Rialto Building . *Orthopedic Surgery*
D. C. Guffey, 909 Waldheim Building . . *Gynecology, Obstetrics*
C. Lester Hall, 2720 Troost Avenue . . . . . *Gynecology*
Edward P. Hall, 124 West 33rd Street
                    Ophth., Rhinol., Oto-Laryngology
M. A. Hanna, Lathrop Building . . . *Obstetrics, Gynecology*
Nathan O. Harrelson, 638 Lathrop Building . . . . *Surgery*
John Gardner Hayden, 1222 Rialto Building . . . . *Surgery*
James P. Henderson, 3615 Wabash Avenue . . . . *Urology*
Arthur E. Hertzler, 1316 Rialto Building . . . . . *Surgery*
Ellery M. Hetherington, 738 Lathrop Building . . . *Surgery*
Howard Hill, 1334 Rialto Building . . . . *Surgery*
Robert D. Irland, 924 Rialto Building . . . . . *Surgery*
Jabez North Jackson, 425 Argyle Building . . . . *Surgery*
Kerwin Weidman Kinard, 3520 Main Street . . . . *Surgery*
Harold Phillip Kuhn, Rialto Building . . . . . . *Surgery*
Joseph Stanly Lichtenberg, Rialto Building . . *Ophthalmology*
J. E. Logan, 1208 Wyandotte Street . *Rhinol., Oto-Laryngology*
Ernest G. Mark, 1010 Rialto Building . *Genito-Urinary Surgery*
Andrew W. McAlester, Jr., 625 Bryant Building . *Ophthalmology*
F. M. McCallum, 721 Lathrop Building *Genito-Urinary Surgery*
Reginald H. Meade, 817 Rialto Building . . . . . *Surgery*
James C. Minor, 511 Commerce Building . . . . *Proctology*
George Clark Mosher, 1100 Grand Avenue *Obstetrics, Gynecology*

MISSOURI — Continued

KANSAS CITY — Continued

Thomas G. Orr, 822 Rialto Building . . . . . . *Surgery*
Michael J. Owens, Rialto Building . . . . . . *Surgery*
Joseph M. Patterson, 518 Bryant Building
         Ophth., Rhinol., Oto-Laryngology
Herman Elwyn Pearse, 1305 Rialto Building . . . . *Surgery*
John W. Perkins, 1005 Campbell Street . . . . . *Surgery*
Matthew W. Pickard, Union Station Hospital . . . *Surgery*
Bert A. Poorman, 1010 Rialto Building . . . . . *Surgery*
W. T. Reynolds, 520 Chambers Building . . . . . *Surgery*
Caleb A. Ritter, 702 Bryant Building . . *Obstetrics, Gynecology*
Sam E. Roberts, 906 Waldheim Building *Rhinol., Oto-Laryngology*
J. Archie Robertson, 501 Gate City National Bank
 Building . . . . *Surgery*
Ernest F. Robinson, 603 Bryant Building . . . . *Surgery*
Leon Rosenwald, 326 Argyle Building . . *Genito-Urinary Surgery*
Robert McE. Schauffler, 416 Argyle Building *Orthopedic Surgery*
Joseph W. Sherer, 1232 Rialto Building
         Ophth., Rhinol., Oto-Laryngology
Frank R. Teachenor, 425 Argyle Building . . . . *Surgery*
H. E. Thomason, 1020 Rialto Building *Rhinol., Oto-Laryngology*
John H. Thompson, 406 Bryant Building . . . *Ophthalmology*
H. G. Tureman, 1100 Rialto Building . *Rhinol., Oto-Laryngology*
Elmer D. Twyman, 416 Argyle Building . . . . . *Surgery*
Charles E. Wilson, 924 Rialto Building . . . . . *Surgery*

MEXICO

Josiah G. Moore, 721 East Love Street . . . . . *Surgery*

MONETT

William M. West, 213 4th Street . . . . *Surgery*

SEDALIA

Wilson Jones Ferguson, I. O. O. F. Building . . . . *Surgery*
E. F. Yancey, 803 West Broadway . . . . . . *Surgery*

SPRINGFIELD

Roche W. Hogeboom, 704 Woodruff Building . . . *Surgery*
William Rienhoff, 564 St. Louis Street . . . . . *Surgery*

ST. JOSEPH

Joseph J. Bansbach, 825 Frederick Avenue *Genito-Urinary Surgery*
John Monohan Doyle, Corby-Forsee Building . . . *Surgery*

MISSOURI — Continued

St. Joseph — Continued

Jacob Geiger, 619 Francis Street . . . . *Surgery*

William H. Minton, Bartlett Trust Company Building
Ophth., Rhinol., Oto-Laryngology

Daniel Morton, King Hill Building . . . *Surgery, Proctology*

Floyd H. Spencer, Physicians and Surgeons Building . *Surgery*

St. Louis

F. H. Albrecht, 3657 Delmar Boulevard . . *Orthopedic Surgery*

Robert DuBose Alexander, University Club Building . *Surgery*

Nathaniel Allison, Humboldt Building . . *Orthopedic Surgery*

Robert Fleming Amyx, 1943 North 11th Street . . . *Surgery*

Millard Fillmore Arbuckle, University Club Building
Rhinol., Oto-Laryngology

Fred Warren Bailey, 611 Metropolitan Building . . . *Surgery*

Leo Bartels, 650 Century Building . . *Genito-Urinary Surgery*

Willard Bartlett, 410 Metropolitan Building . . . . *Surgery*

Vilray Papin Blair, Metropolitan Building . . . . *Surgery*

W. M. C. Bryan, 910 University Club Building
Rhinol., Oto-Laryngology

Cyrus Edgar Burford, Arcade Building *Genito-Urinary Surgery*

Robert Burns, Jr., Lister Building . . . . . . *Surgery*

George W. Cale, Jr., Wall Building . . . . . *Surgery*

James Alexander Campbell, Equitable Building
Ophth., Rhinol., Oto-Laryngology

Norman Bruce Carson, 4379 Westminster Place . . . *Surgery*

John R. Caulk, University Club Building *Genito-Urinary Surgery*

J. W. Charles, 505 Humboldt Building . . . *Ophthalmology*

Malvern Bryan Clopton, 405 Humboldt Building . . *Surgery*

William Thomas Coughlin, University Club Building . *Surgery*

Hanley C. Creveling, Frisco Building . . . . *Oto-Laryngology*

H. S. Crossen, Metropolitan Building . . *Gynecology, Obstetrics*

John McH. Dean, Metropolitan Building . . . . . *Surgery*

Edward Lee Dorsett, 505 University Club Building
Gynecology, Obstetrics

William Joseph Doyle, City Dairies Building . . . . *Surgery*

Hugo Ehrenfest, Metropolitan Building . *Gynecology, Obstetrics*

O. H. Elbrecht, 423 Metropolitan Building . . . . *Surgery*

Arthur E. Ewing, 520 Metropolitan Building . . *Ophthalmology*

Arthur O. Fisher, 608 Humboldt Building . . . . *Surgery*

MISSOURI — Continued

St. Louis — Continued

Robert Monroe Funkhouser, 4354 Olive Street . . . *Surgery*
George Gellhorn, Metropolitan Building . *Gynecology, Obstetrics*
Frank A. Glasgow, University Club Building . . . *Gynecology*
William P. Glennon, 4500 Olive Street . . . . *Surgery*
Max A. Goldstein, 3858 Westminster Place
Rhinol., Oto-Laryngology
Evarts Ambrose Graham, Washington University Medical
School . . . . *Surgery*
John Green, Jr., 626 Metropolitan Building . . *Ophthalmology*
Louis K. Guggenheim, 1000 Carleton Building
Rhinol., Oto-Laryngology
Horace E. Happel, Wall Building . . . . . . *Surgery*
Frank L. Henderson, 501 Humboldt Building . *Ophthalmology*
Edward H. Higbee, 417 Metropolitan Building . *Ophthalmology*
Roland Hill, 4500 Olive Street . . . . *Surgery*
Philip Hoffman, 3657 Delmar Boulevard . . *Orthopedic Surgery*
Alexander E. Horwitz, University Club Building *Orthopedic Surgery*
Charles E. Hyndman, Humboldt Building . . . . *Surgery*
John Ellis Jennings, 807 Carleton Building
Ophth., Rhinol., Oto-Laryngology
Ernst Jonas, Lister Building . . . . *Surgery*
Walter M. Jones, 5800 Arsenal Street . . . . *Surgery*
William Kerwin, 4500 Olive Street . . *Gynecology, Obstetrics*
Walter C. G. Kirchner, 229 Metropolitan Building . . *Surgery*
Marion L. Klinefelter, Wall Building . . . *Orthopedic Surgery*
William Elston Leighton, 305 Lister Building . . . *Surgery*
Bransford Lewis, 550 Century Building *Genito-Urinary Surgery*
Hanau W. Loeb, 537 North Grand Avenue . . *Oto-Laryngology*
Virgil Loeb, 537 North Grand Avenue . . . . *Oral Surgery*
William H. Luedde, 311 Metropolitan Building . *Ophthalmology*
Hartwell Nelles Lyon, Humboldt Building . . . . *Surgery*
John W. Marchildon, University Club Building
Genito-Urinary Surgery
L. Clifford McAmis, 501 Humboldt Building . . . . *Surgery*
William A. McCandless, 5056 Westminster Place . . *Surgery*
Harvey S. McKay, University Club Building . . . *Surgery*
Mary Hancock McLean, 4339 Delmar Boulevard . . *Retired*
Harry M. Moore, Wall Building . . . . . . *Surgery*

MISSOURI — Continued

St. Louis — Continued

Neil S. Moore, 316 Frisco Building . . . . . . *Urology*
John Campbell Morfit, University Club Building . . *Surgery*
Harvey Gilmer Mudd, 408 Humboldt Building . . . *Surgery*
Max W. Myer, University Club Building . . . . . *Surgery*
Quitman U. Newell, 411 Wall Building . *Gynecology, Obstetrics*
Clarence M. Nicholson, Lister Building . . . . . *Surgery*
Archer O'Reilly, 3534 Washington Avenue . *Orthopedic Surgery*
Scott E. Parsons, Wall Building . . . . *Surgery*
Christian F. Pfingsten, 508 North Grand Avenue
                            Rhinol., Oto-Laryngology
Lawrence T. Post, 520 Metropolitan Building . *Ophthalmology*
Martin H. Post, Jr., 520 Metropolitan Building . *Ophthalmology*
Louis Rassieur, 318 University Club Building . . . *Surgery*
Francis Reder, University Club Building . . . . . *Surgery*
W. M. Robertson, Humboldt Building . *Genito-Urinary Surgery*
Ernest Sachs, 97 Arundel Place . . . . *Surgery*
W. E. Sauer, 537 North Grand Avenue . . . *Oto-Laryngology*
Henry Joseph Scherck, Century Building . *Genito-Urinary Surgery*
Robert Ernst Schlueter, 514 Metropolitan Building . . *Surgery*
Henry Schwarz, 440 North Newstead Avenue *Gynecology, Obstetrics*
Major G. Seelig, University Club Building . . . . *Surgery*
E. T. Senseney, 308 Lister Building . *Rhinol., Oto-Laryngology*
William Ewing Shahan, 520 Metropolitan Building *Ophthalmology*
John B. Shapleigh, Humboldt Building . . . . . *Otology*
Norvelle Wallace Sharpe, 3520 Lucas Avenue . . . *Surgery*
William A. Shoemaker, 1006 Carleton Building . *Ophthalmology*
Cleveland H. Shutt, Metropolitan Building . . . . *Surgery*
Frederick C. Simon, Arcade Building . *Rhinol., Oto-Laryngology*
Greenfield Sluder, 3542 Washington Avenue *Rhinol., Laryngology*
Carroll Smith, 306 Humboldt Building . . . . . *Surgery*
Selden Spencer, University Club Building . . *Oto-Laryngology*
Percy H. Swahlen, 5301 Page Avenue . . *Gynecology, Obstetrics*
Frank Joseph Tainter, 816 University Club Building . *Surgery*
Hudson Talbott, 426 Metropolitan Building . . . . *Surgery*
F. J. Taussig, 4506 Maryland Avenue . . *Gynecology, Obstetrics*
Herman Tuholske, 453 North Taylor Avenue . . . *Surgery*
Paul Yoer Tupper, Wall Building . . . . *Surgery*
Paul F. Vasterling, 1600 California Avenue . . . . *Surgery*

MISSOURI — Continued

Sᴛ. Louis — Continued

W. H. Vogt, 330 Metropolitan Building . *Gynecology, Obstetrics*
William S. Wiatt, 4506 Lewis Place . . . . . . *Surgery*
Meyer Wiener, 900 Carleton Building . . . . *Ophthalmology*
Leo A. Will, 434 University Club Building . . . . *Surgery*
Reinhard E. Wobus, 713 Metropolitan Building *Surgery,Obstetrics*
Frederick Eno Woodruff, Metropolitan Building . *Ophthalmology*
Ross Arlington Woolsey, 4960 Laclede Avenue . . . *Surgery*
Henry McClure Young, 622 University Club Building . *Urology*
Willis Brock Young, 516 Metropolitan Building . . . *Surgery*
Oliver B. Zeinert, 618 University Club Building . . . *Surgery*

MONTANA

Aɴᴀᴄᴏɴᴅᴀ

Alfred J. Willits, 523 Hickory Street . . . . . . *Surgery*

Bɪʟʟɪɴɢs

Henry Edward Armstrong, Stapleton Building . . . *Surgery*
Arthur J. Movius, Hart-Albin Building . . . . . *Surgery*
Edward W. Thuerer, 227 Hart-Albin Building . . . *Surgery*
Charles F. Watkins, 217 Montana Power Building . . *Surgery*
James I. Wernham, 227 Hart-Albin Building . *Surgery, Obstetrics*

Bᴜᴛᴛᴇ

John Alexander Donovan, 507 Phoenix Building
Ophth., Rhinol., Oto-Laryngology
I. D. Freund, 518 North Emmett Street . . . . . *Surgery*
Alfred Karsted, 209 Metals Bank Building . . . . *Surgery*
Herbert D. Kistler, Murray Hospital . . . . . . *Surgery*
Edward F. Maginn, 403 Lewisohn Building . . . . *Surgery*
Ashley W. Morse, 507 Phoenix Building
Ophth., Rhinol., Oto-Laryngology
Thomas J. Murray, 401 West Granite Street . . . . *Surgery*
Michael James Scott, 313 Daly Bank Building . . . *Surgery*
John R. E. Sievers, 75 Owsley Block . . . . . . *Surgery*
Thomas Casey Witherspoon, Quartz and Alaska Streets *Surgery*

Fᴏʀsʏᴛʜ

Malcolm Eadie Smith, Bank of Commerce Building . *Surgery*

Gʟᴇɴᴅɪᴠᴇ

Robert H. Beach, Northern Pacific Hospital . . . . *Surgery*

MONTANA — Continued

GREAT FALLS

Clifton C. Albright, 313 Ford Building
Ophth., Rhinol., Oto-Laryngology
James H. Irwin, Ford Building . . . . *Surgery*
Albert Forrest Longeway, 505 3rd Avenue, North . . *Surgery*
Enoch Marvin Porter, Conrad Bank Building . . . *Surgery*
LeRoy Southmayd, Ford Building . . . . *Surgery*

HELENA

Ben C. Brooke, Brooke and Lanstrum Building . . . *Surgery*
Rudolph Horsky, 326 Fuller Avenue . . . . . . *Surgery*

KALISPELL

Hugh E. Houston, Buffalo Block . . . . *Surgery*

LEWISTOWN

Fred Franklin Attix, Attix Clinic Building . . . . *Surgery*
Joseph T. Brice, Brice Hospital Building . . *Surgery, Obstetrics*
Frank C. Davis, 618 West Main Street
Ophth., Rhinol., Oto-Laryngology

LIVINGSTON

Robert D. Alton, First State Bank Building
Ophth., Rhinol., Oto-Laryngology
Byron L. Pampel . . . . *Gynecology, Obstetrics*

MILES CITY

William Henry Buskirk, 413 Main Street . . . . . *Surgery*
John H. Garberson, 413 Main Street . . . . . . *Surgery*

MISSOULA

George Michael Jennings, 220 North 2nd Street . . . *Surgery*
Harry Clay Smith, Higgins Block . . . . *Surgery*

ROUNDUP

Creswell Tayleur Pigot . . . . *Surgery*

SIDNEY

Houston Haddon Parsons, First National Bank Building *Surgery*

TOWNSEND

Charles Wolff Smith . . . . *Surgery*

NEBRASKA

AURORA

Donald B. Steenburg, 1018 12th Street . . . . . *Surgery*

BEATRICE

Harry M. Hepperlen, 114 South 6th Street . . . . *Surgery*

COLUMBUS

Christian Alexander Allenburger, Columbus State Bank
  Building . . . . *Surgery*
Charles H. Campbell, Columbus State Bank Building
  Ophth., Rhinol., Oto-Laryngology
Frank H. Morrow, 2512 13th Street . . . . . . *Surgery*

FAIRBURY

Albert Lynch, 612 5th Street . . . . *Surgery*

FREMONT

George James Haslam, 215 East 5th Street . . . . *Surgery*

HASTINGS

Oscar Herman Hahn, 212½ Hastings Avenue . . . *Surgery*
Samuel R. Hopkins, First National Bank Building . . *Surgery*

LINCOLN

Wesley L. Curtis, 612 Security Mutual Building
  Ophth., Rhinol., Oto-Laryngology
Clarence Emerson, Security Mutual Life Building . . *Surgery*
Everett B. Finney, 802 Security Mutual Life Building . *Surgery*
David Clark Hilton, 305 Richards Block . . . . . *Surgery*
Karl Siegfried J. Hohlen, 1010 Terminal Building . . *Surgery*
Frank Bradbury Hollenbeck, 206 Richards Block . . *Surgery*
Artemas I. McKinnon, 503 Security Mutual Life Building *Surgery*
Albert Roscoe Mitchell, Bankers Life Building . . . *Surgery*
H. Winnett Orr, 1010 Terminal Building . . *Orthopedic Surgery*
Henry Peter Wekesser, Orpheum Theatre Building . . *Surgery*
J. Stanley Welch, 514 First National Bank Building . *Surgery*

MADISON

Francis A. Long . . . . *Surgery*

NORFOLK

Stuart Avery Campbell, 0433 Norfolk Avenue . . . *Surgery*
Peter Harold Salter, 409 Norfolk Avenue . . . . . *Surgery*

NORTH PLATTE

George B. Dent, 620 West 4th Street . . . . . . *Surgery*

NEBRASKA — Continued

OMAHA

John Monro Banister, 400 Brandeis Theatre Building
Ophth., Rhinol., Oto-Laryngology
Alfred Jerome Brown, 402 City National Bank Building　*Surgery*
Louis B. Bushman, 631 City National Bank Building
Ophth., Rhinol., Oto-Laryngology
Karl Connell, Presbyterian Hospital . . . . . . *Surgery*
Byron B. Davis, 1502 South 32nd Avenue . . . . *Surgery*
Delmer L. Davis, 670 Brandeis Theatre Building . . *Surgery*
Edwin G. Davis, 670 Brandeis Theatre Building . . . *Urology*
Palmer Findley, Brandeis Theatre Building　*Gynecology, Obstetrics*
Dellizon A. Foote, 788 Brandeis Theatre Building . . *Surgery*
Harold Gifford, 702 Brandeis Building . . . *Ophth., Otology*
Herschel P. Hamilton, 617 City National Bank Building　*Surgery*
Charles A. Hull, 1200 First National Bank Building . *Surgery*
August Frederic Jonas, 512 McCague Building . . . *Surgery*
Charles R. Kennedy, McCague Building . *Genito-Urinary Surgery*
Henry Bassett Lemere, 400 Brandeis Theatre Building
Ophth., Rhinol., Oto-Laryngology
J. P. Lord, 830 City National Bank Building . *Orthopedic Surgery*
Charles McMartin, 828 City National Bank Building . *Urology*
Charles C. Morison, Brandeis Theatre Building . . *Surgery*
John Rudolph Nilsson, 426 World Herald Building . . *Surgery*
Frank S. Owen, 648 Brandeis Building,
Ophth., Rhinol., Oto-Laryngology
James M. Patton, 702 Brandeis Building . . . *Ophthalmology*
Daniel T. Quigley, 727 City National Bank Building . *Surgery*
Charles O. Rich, 432 Brandeis Theatre Building . . . *Surgery*
Clyde Augustus Roeder, 834 Brandeis Theatre Building　*Surgery*
George F. Simanek, 1262 South 13th Street . . . . *Surgery*
Arthur Charles Stokes, 4724 Davenport Street . . *Surgery*
John E. Summers, 618 Brandeis Theatre Building . . *Surgery*
Herbert C. Sumney, 1011 W. O. W. Building . . . *Urology*
Elmer J. Updegraff, 512 McCague Building . . . . *Surgery*
Chester H. Waters, 500 Brandeis Theatre Building . . *Surgery*
William P. Wherry, 703 Brandeis Theatre Building *Ophth., Otology*
W. Eugene Wolcott, 830 City National Bank Building
Orthopedic Surgery

SUPERIOR

Charles Gilbert McMahon, 448 Central Avenue . . . *Surgery*

NEBRASKA—Continued

TEKAMAH
Henry A. Johnson . . . . *Surgery*
Isaiah Lukens . . . . *Surgery*

NEVADA

CARSON CITY
Donald Maclean, 314 Nevada Street . . . . . . *Surgery*
EAST ELY
Ralph A. Bowdle, Steptoe Valley Hospital . . . . *Surgery*
RENO
George McKenzie, Thoma-Bigelow Building . . . . *Surgery*

NEW HAMPSHIRE

CLAREMONT
Emery Moore Fitch, 19 Pleasant Street . . . . . *Surgery*
CONCORD
Chancey Adams, 11 South Main Street . . . . . *Surgery*
Henry H. Amsden, 4 North State Street *Rhinol., Oto-Laryngology*
Robert John Graves, 4 North State Street . . . . *Surgery*
James Walker Jameson, 5 South State Street . . . . *Surgery*
Carleton Ray Metcalf, 4 North State Street . *Orthopedic Surgery*
Loren A. Sanders, 23 West Street . . . . *Surgery*
FRANKLIN
James Brown Woodman, 336 Central Street . . . . *Surgery*
HANOVER
Percy Bartlett, 8 Parkway . . . . *Surgery*
John Martin Gile, 3 Maynard Street . . . . . . *Surgery*
KEENE
Ira Joslin Prouty, 81 Court Street . . . . *Surgery*
LACONIA
Clifton S. Abbott, 8 Academy Street . . . . . . *Surgery*
Alpha H. Harriman, 440 Main Street . . . . . . *Surgery*
LITTLETON
Arthur T. Downing, 13 Main Street . . . . . . *Surgery*
MANCHESTER
Walter T. Crosby, 814 Elm Street . . . . *Surgery*
Emdon Fritz, 913 Elm Street . *Ophth., Rhinol., Oto-Laryngology*

NEW HAMPSHIRE — Continued

MANCHESTER — Continued

John Hiram Gleason, Merchants Bank Building . . . *Surgery*
John Franklin Holmes, 951 Elm Street . . . . . *Surgery*
William H. A. Lyons, 788 Elm Street . . . *Surgery, Obstetrics*
John C. O'Connor, 1037 Elm Street . . . . . . *Surgery*
David W. Parker, 967 Elm Street . . . . *Surgery*
Arthur F. Wheat, 944 Elm Street . . . . *Surgery*
George Clarence Wilkins, 402 Beacon Building . . . *Surgery*

NASHUA

Ella Blaylock Atherton, 148 Main Street . . . . *Gynecology*
Charles Everett Congdon, 77 Main Street . . . . *Surgery*
Sam Starrett Dearborn, 3 Abbot Street . . . . . *Surgery*
James Thornton Greeley, 115 Main Street . . . . *Surgery*
Frank E. Kittredge, Masonic Temple . *Rhinol., Oto-Laryngology*
Benjamin G. Moran, 174 Main Street . . . . . . *Surgery*
Charles Francis Nutter, 16 Amherst Street . . *Ophthalmology*
Augustus W. Shea, 266 Main Street . . . . . . *Surgery*
Herbert L. Smith, Goodrich Block . . . . *Surgery*
Alonzo S. Wallace, 198 Main Street . . . . . . *Surgery*

PLYMOUTH

Ernest Lorne Bell, 174 Main Street . . . . . . *Surgery*

PORTSMOUTH

John J. Berry . . . . *Surgery*
Arthur Cowton Heffenger, 53 Austin Street . . . . *Surgery*
Herbert Leonel Taylor, 160 Middle Street . . . . *Surgery*

NEW JERSEY

ATLANTIC CITY

Walt Ponder Conaway, 1723 Pacific Avenue . . . . *Surgery*
William Edgar Darnall, 1704 Pacific Avenue . . . . *Surgery*
R. Johnson Held, 3531 Pacific Avenue . . . *Oto-Laryngology*

BAYONNE

William Wallace Brooke, 915 Avenue C . . . . *Gynecology*
Lucius Francis Donohoe, 33 Dodge Street . . . . *Surgery*
George H. Sexsmith, 719 Avenue C . . . . . . *Surgery*
Ernst Thum, 819 Avenue C . . *Ophth., Rhinol., Oto-Laryngology*

CAMDEN

Paul Mulford Mecray, 405 Cooper Street . . . . . *Surgery*

NEW JERSEY — Continued

EAST ORANGE

  William Boardman Graves, 426 Main Street . . . . *Surgery*

ELIZABETH

  James S. Green, 463 North Broad Street . . . . . *Surgery*

  Edgar Boileau Grier, 400 Westminster Avenue . . . *Surgery*

  Stephen T. Quinn, 83 Broad Street . . . . . . *Surgery*

  John Philip Reilly, 215 Elizabeth Avenue . . . . . *Surgery*

  Charles Henry Schlichter, 556 North Broad Street

                                                 Ophth., Oto-Laryngology

  Milton A. Shangle, 34 Prince Street . . . . . . *Surgery*

  N. L. Wilson, 410 Westminster Avenue   *Ophth., Oto-Laryngology*

JERSEY CITY

  Henry J. Bogardus, 427 Bergen Avenue . . *Orthopedic Surgery*

  Frank Bortone, 809 Montgomery Street . . . . . *Surgery*

  T. R. Chambers, 15 Exchange Place . *Ophth., Oto-Laryngology*

  Gordon Kimball Dickinson, 280 Montgomery Street . *Surgery*

  William Freile, 108 Palisade Avenue . . . . . . *Surgery*

  Wallace Pyle, 15 Exchange Place   *Ophth., Rhinol., Oto-Laryngology*

  Henry Spence, 2540 Hudson Boulevard . . . . . *Surgery*

  Stanley R. Woodruff, 16 Enos Place . *Genito-Urinary Surgery*

MONTCLAIR

  James Spencer Brown, 43 South Fullerton Avenue . . *Surgery*

  William Schauffler Dodd, 81 South Mountain Avenue . *Surgery*

  James T. Hanan, 11 The Crescent . . . . *Surgery*

  Victor Bayard Seidler, 16 Plymouth Street . . . . *Surgery*

MORRISTOWN

  Francis H. Glazebrook, 171 South Street . . . . . *Surgery*

  Clifford Mills, 36 Maple Avenue . . . . *Surgery, Obstetrics*

  Edward Blair Sutphen, 174 South Street

                                       Ophth., Rhinol., Oto-Laryngology

NEWARK

  Linus Worthington Bagg, 712 Clinton Avenue . . . *Surgery*

  Edward Hill Baldwin, 85 Clinton Avenue

                                       Ophth., Rhinol., Oto-Laryngology

  Hugh F. Cook, 2 Lombardy Street . . . . *Surgery*

  Theodore W. Corwin, 671 Broad Street   *Rhinol., Oto-Laryngology*

  Max Danzis, 608 High Street . . . . *Surgery*

  Richard Hagen Dieffenbach, 570 Mt. Prospect Avenue . *Surgery*

NEW JERSEY — Continued

NEWARK — Continued

Widmer E. Doremus, 32 Fulton Street . . . . . *Surgery*
W. P. Eagleton, 15 Lombardy Street . . . . *Ophth., Otology*
William Gauch, 177 Elwood Avenue . . . . . *Gynecology*
John F. Hagerty, 30 Wallace Place . . . . . . *Surgery*
Albert Scott Harden, 540 Warren Street . *Gynecology, Obstetrics*
Francis Reynolds Haussling, 661 High Street . . . . *Surgery*
Edward M. Z. Hawkes, 84 Washington Street . . . *Surgery*
Charles Ludwig Ill, 188 Clinton Avenue . . . . *Gynecology*
Edward J. Ill, 1002 Broad Street . . . . . . *Gynecology*
William D. Miningham, 11 Astor Street . . . . . *Surgery*
John Bennett Morrison, 97 Halsey Street . . . . . *Surgery*
Albert B. Nash, 10 South 13th Street . . . . . . *Surgery*
Dennis F. O'Connor, 671 Broad Street . . . *Ophthalmology*
Henry Boylon Orton, 671 Broad Street   *Rhinol., Oto-Laryngology*
Clarence Rutherford O'Crowley, Ordway Building . . *Urology*
George A. Rogers, 1 Wallace Street . . *Gynecology, Obstetrics*
Samuel E. Robertson, 21 Walnut Street . . . . . *Surgery*
Elbert S. Sherman, 671 Broad Street . . . . *Ophthalmology*
Robert E. Soule, 671 Broad Street . . . . *Orthopedic Surgery*
Edward W. Sprague, 65 Washington Street . . . . *Surgery*
Edward Staehlin, 15 Lincoln Park . . . . *Surgery*
Carlyle Edgar Sutphen, Jr., 31 Roseville Avenue . . *Surgery*
Theron Y. Sutphen, 1038 Broad Street . . . *Ophth., Otology*
Sidney A. Twinch, 24 Fulton Street . . . *Orthopedic Surgery*

ORANGE

John Hammond Bradshaw, 27 High Street . . . . *Surgery*
Frank Caulkins Bunn, 30 Hillyer Street . . . . . *Surgery*
Linn Emerson, Metropolitan Building . . . . *Ophth., Otology*
Thomas William Harvey, 59 Main Street . . . . . *Surgery*

PASSAIC

Harry C. Reynolds, Passaic Avenue . . . . . . *Surgery*
Edward P. Whelan, Lawyers Building . . . . . *Surgery*

PATERSON

Thomas A. Dingman, 330 Broadway . . . . . *Surgery*
Philander A. Harris, 26 Church Street . . . . *Gynecology*
Walter B. Johnson, 170 Broadway . . *Ophth., Oto-Laryngology*
Charles Joseph Kane, 349 Grand Street . . . . . *Surgery*

NEW JERSEY — Continued

PATERSON — Continued

Bryan C. Magennis, 170 Hamilton Avenue . . . . *Surgery*
J. C. McCoy, 292 Broadway . . . . *Surgery*
William Neer, 245 Broadway . . . . *Surgery*

PLAINFIELD

B. van D. Hedges, 703 Watchung Avenue . . . . *Surgery*
Ellis W. Hedges, 703 Watchung Avenue . . . . . *Surgery*

RED BANK

Edwin Field, 74 West Front Street . . . . . . *Surgery*
Biddle H. Garrison, 23 Monmouth Street . . . . . *Surgery*

SOUTH ORANGE

Mefford Runyon, 110 Irvington Avenue . . . . . *Surgery*

SUMMIT

Harry Hallowell Bowles, 36 Woodland Avenue . . . *Surgery*
William Henry Lawrence, 129 Summit Avenue . . . *Surgery*

TRENTON

Alvan W. Atkinson, 423 East State Street *Gynecology, Obstetrics*
Martin W. Reddan, 126 West State Street . . . . *Surgery*
George N. J. Sommer, 120 West State Street . . . *Surgery*

NEW MEXICO

ALBUQUERQUE

Percy Gillette Cornish . . . . *Surgery*
George Stuart McLandress . . . . *Surgery*

CARLSBAD

William F. Glasier . . . . *Surgery*

SANTA RITA

Frank N. Carrier . . . . *Surgery*

TYRONE

Lucien Luttrell Miner, Parker Hospital . . . . . *Surgery*

NEW YORK

ALBANY

Arthur J. Bedell, 344 State Street . . . . . . *Ophth., Otology*
George E. Beilby, 247 State Street . . . . . . *Surgery*
Joseph Lewi Bendell, 178 State Street . . . . . *Surgery*
John McWilliams Berry, 35 Elk Street . . . . . *Surgery*

NEW YORK — Continued

ALBANY — Continued

J. B. Congdon, 140 Washington Avenue . . . . . . *Surgery*
Joseph Lewi Donhauser, 252 State Street . . . . . *Surgery*
J. Ivimey Dowling, 116 Washington Avenue
                          Ophth., Rhinol., Oto-Laryngology
Arthur Wells Elting, 119 Washington Avenue . . *Surgery*
Charles William Louis Hacker, 352 Hudson Avenue . . *Surgery*
Christian Gottlieb Hacker, 107 Washington Avenue . . *Surgery*
Eugene E. Hinman, 146 Washington Avenue
                               Rhinol., Oto-Laryngology
Brayton Eugene Kinne, 40 Eagle Street . . . . . *Surgery*
John A. Sampson, 180 Washington Avenue . . . *Gynecology*
Alvah H. Traver, 27 Eagle Street . . . . . . *Surgery*
Albert Vander Veer, 28 Eagle Street . . . . . *Retired*
Edgar A. Vander Veer, 28 Eagle Street . . . . . *Surgery*
James N. Vander Veer, 28 Eagle Street   *Genito-Urinary Surgery*
Arthur Burton Van Loon, 198 State Street . . . . *Surgery*

AMSTERDAM

James B. Conant, 13 Grove Street . . . . *Surgery*
Lew Henri Finch, 188 Market Street . . . . . . *Surgery*

AUBURN

Ledra Heazlit, 149 Genesee Street . . . . *Surgery*
Frederick A. Lewis, 16 William Street
                          Ophth., Rhinol., Oto-Laryngology

BATAVIA

William David Johnson, 5 Jackson Street . . . . *Surgery*

BATH

Douglass H. Smith, 5 Liberty Street . . . . . . *Surgery*
Henry John Wynkoop, 7 East Steuben Street . . . *Surgery*

BEDFORD

George P. Coopernail . . . . *Surgery*

BINGHAMTON

William A. Behan, 91 Front Street . . . . . . *Surgery*
Arthur Smith Chittenden, 106 Oak Street . . . . *Surgery*
Frank M. Dyer, 51 Main Street . . . . *Surgery*
William H. Hobbs, 103 Main Street . . . . . . *Surgery*
George H. Jenkins, 139 Main Street . . . . . . *Surgery*
Joseph J. Kane, 123 Front Street . . . . *Surgery*

NEW YORK — Continued

BINGHAMTON — Continued
Frederick Mason Miller, 143 Court Street . . . . *Surgery*
Silas D. Molyneux, 29 Main Street . . . . . *Surgery*

BRONXVILLE
Brock McGeorge Dear, 21 Bolton Gardens *Gynecology, Obstetrics*

BROOKLYN
Herbert Coleman Allen, 171 Lefferts Place *Gynecology, Obstetrics*
Robert B. Anderson, 872 Park Place . . . . . . *Urology*
James H. Andrew, 163 Hancock Street . . . *Ophthalmology*
Hubert Arrowsmith, 170 Clinton Street . . . *Oto-Laryngology*
Fred DeForest Bailey, 260 Hancock Street . . *Ophthalmology*
L. Grant Baldwin, 20 Schermerhorn Street . . . *Gynecology*
Calvin F. Barber, 57 South Oxford Street . . . . *Surgery*
Robert F. Barber, 1140 Dean Street . . . . . *Surgery*
John Leopold Bauer, 984 Bushwick Parkway . . . . *Surgery*
Harold Kennedy Bell, 857 President Street . . . *Surgery*
Hector W. Benoit, 520 Nostrand Avenue . . . . . *Surgery*
Eliot Bishop, 46 Gates Avenue . . . . *Gynecology, Obstetrics*
Silas Canady Blaisdell, 331 Jefferson Avenue . . . . *Surgery*
Dominic G. Bodkin, 897 Lafayette Avenue . . . . *Surgery*
Martin Laurence Bodkin, 290 Clinton Avenue . . *Proctology*
Arthur H. Bogart, 27 7th Avenue . . . . . . *Surgery*
John Bion Bogart, 463 Clinton Avenue . . . . . *Surgery*
William C. Braislin, 425 Clinton Avenue . . . . . *Otology*
Thomas M. Brennan, 39 8th Avenue . . . . . . *Surgery*
William Barrett Brinsmade, 172 Clinton Street . . . *Surgery*
William Francis Campbell, 394 Clinton Avenue . . . *Surgery*
William H. Cary, 36 Pierrepont Street . *Gynecology, Obstetrics*
C. S. Cochrane, 400 Vanderbilt Avenue . *Genito-Urinary Surgery*
C. N. Cox, 257 Jefferson Avenue . . *Rhinol., Oto-Laryngology*
Claude G. Crane, 121 St. James Place . *Rhinol., Oto-Laryngology*
Henry W. Dangler, 455 Classon Avenue . . . . *Surgery*
George Edward Deely, 132 Montague Street
Ophth., Rhinol., Oto-Laryngology
H. Beeckman Delatour, 73 8th Avenue . . . . . *Surgery*
James Maurice Downey, 381 Clinton Street . . . *Surgery*
Francis B. Doyle, 145 6th Avenue . . . *Obstetrics, Gynecology*
Warren L. Duffield, 119 Berkeley Place . . . . . *Surgery*
Roger Durham, 322 Park Place . . . . . . *Surgery*

NEW YORK — Continued

BROOKLYN — Continued

William C. Durrin, 1215 Dean Street . . . . . *Gynecology*
Edward D. Ferris, 418 50th Street . . . . . . *Surgery*
Mathias Figueira, 14 Stuyvesant Avenue . . . . *Surgery*
Edwin H. Fiske, 152 Lafayette Avenue . . . . *Surgery*
Royale Hamilton Fowler, 280 Jefferson Avenue . . *Surgery*
Russell Story Fowler, 301 DeKalb Avenue . . . . *Surgery*
Homer E. Fraser, 20 South Portland Avenue
                                    Genito-Urinary Surgery
Thomas R. French, 150 Joralemon Street . . . . *Laryngology*
Gordon Gibson, 176 State Street . . . *Gynecology, Obstetrics*
Charles P. Gildersleeve, 18 Schermerhorn Street . . . *Surgery*
James P. Glynn, 474 9th Street . . . . . . *Gynecology*
Emil Goetsch, 2 Sidney Place . . . . *Surgery*
Charles Howard Goodrich, 280 Park Place . *Surgery, Obstetrics*
Charles Albert Gordon, 847 Putnam Avenue *Gynecology, Obstetrics*
Onslow Allen Gordon, 71 Halsey Street . . . . . *Surgery*
Onslow Allen Gordon, Jr., 71 Halsey Street . . . . *Surgery*
Henry Flack Graham, 474 1st Street . . . . . . *Surgery*
J. F. Griffin, 397 Stuyvesant Avenue . . *Genito-Urinary Surgery*
James Cole Hancock, 135 Cambridge Place . . *Ophthalmology*
Burton Harris, 475 Greene Avenue . . *Genito-Urinary Surgery*
William L. Heeve, 138 Hancock Street . . . . . *Surgery*
John Horni, 447 Nostrand Avenue . . . . *Surgery*
A. C. Howe, 40 South Oxford Street . *Rhinol., Oto-Laryngology*
O. Paul Humpstone, 327 Washington Avenue *Gynecology, Obstetrics*
Clarence Reginald Hyde, 242 Henry Street . . . *Gynecology*
James Warren Ingalls, 328 Stuyvesant Avenue . *Ophthalmology*
P. Chalmers Jameson, 139 Montague Street . . *Ophthalmology*
Frank D. Jennings, 1083 Bushwick Avenue . . . . *Surgery*
John Edward Jennings, 23 South Portland Avenue . . *Surgery*
William Averill Jewett, 380 Vanderbilt Avenue
                                    Gynecology, Obstetrics
Albert M. Judd, 375 Grand Avenue . . *Gynecology, Obstetrics*
James Charles Kennedy, 762 Willoughby Avenue . . *Surgery*
John Richard Kevin, 252 Gates Avenue . . . . . *Surgery*
Howard T. Langworthy, 480 Franklin Avenue . . . *Surgery*
John Linder, 1780 St. John's Place . . . . *Surgery*
William Linder, 889 St. Mark's Avenue . . . . . *Surgery*

NEW YORK — Continued

BROOKLYN — Continued

William Edward Lippold, 221 St. Nicholas Avenue . . *Surgery*
Ralph Irving Lloyd, 450 9th Street . . . . *Ophth., Otology*
John Hathaway Long, 110 Gates Avenue . . . . . *Surgery*
John Cowell MacEvitt, 407 Clinton Street . . . *Gynecology*
H. B. Matthews, 643 St. Mark's Avenue . *Gynecology, Obstetrics*
Earl H. Mayne, 139 Bay 17th Street . . . . . *Gynecology*
Edward James McEntee, 196 Hancock Street . . . *Surgery*
Sylvester J. McNamara, 369 Union Street *Gynecology, Obstetrics*
Frederick R. Meeks, 100 Hancock Street . . . . . *Surgery*
Henry Mateland Mills, 902 President Street *Gynecology, Obstetrics*
Edward J. Morris, 282 Sterling Place . . *Gynecology, Obstetrics*
Robert J. Morrison, 1173 Dean Street . . . . . . *Surgery*
Henry H. Morton, 32 Schermerhorn Street . . . . *Urology*
Joseph Paul Murphy, 653 St. Mark's Avenue . . *Surgery*
Frederic Chauncey Paffard, 89 Remsen Street . . . *Surgery*
Stanley Wilson Pallister, 222 Jefferson Avenue . . . *Surgery*
William Vincent Pascual, 690 St. Marks Avenue . . . *Surgery*
William Pfeiffer, 368 McDonough Street . *Gynecology, Obstetrics*
John Osborn Polak, 20 Livingston Street . *Gynecology, Obstetrics*
R. H. Pomeroy, 93 Remsen Street . . . *Gynecology, Obstetrics*
William Pohlman Pool, 166 Clinton Street . . . *Gynecology*
Henry R. Price, 146 Remsen Street . . . . *Ophthalmology*
Alexander Rae, 117 Henry Street . . . . *Surgery*
John Francis Ranken, 852 Park Place . . . . . . *Surgery*
William Henry Rankin, 151 Hancock Street . . . . *Surgery*
Nathaniel Philip Rathbun, 67 Hanson Place . . . . *Urology*
John Sturdivant Read, 174 Clinton Street . . . . *Urology*
Michael Thomas Reynolds, 191 Arlington Avenue . . *Surgery*
Victor A. Robertson, 51 8th Avenue . . . . . . *Surgery*
Nathaniel Robinson, 89 Halsey Street . . . . . . *Surgery*
Russel Murray Rome, 246 Clermont Avenue . . . . *Surgery*
Jaques C. Rushmore, 477 Washington Avenue *Orthopedic Surgery*
John D. Rushmore, 129 Montague Street . . . . . *Surgery*
George Frank Sammis, 98 Brooklyn Avenue . . . . *Surgery*
John M. Scannell, 364 Jefferson Avenue . . . . . *Surgery*
John Hubley Schall, 119 St. Mark's Avenue . . . . *Surgery*
Herbert Dana Schenck, 75 Halsey Street . . . *Ophth., Otology*
Leo S. Schwartz, 849 Park Place . . *Gynecology, Obstetrics*

NEW YORK — Continued

BROOKLYN — Continued

Charles E. Scofield, 880 Park Place   .   *Rhinol., Oto-Laryngology*
Marcus Fowler Searle, 34 Plaza Street   .   *Gynecology, Obstetrics*
Walter Aikman Sherwood, 145 Gates Avenue   .   .   .   *Surgery*
William Sidney Smith, 370 Washington Avenue
                                                    Gynecology, Obstetrics
Thomas Bray Spence, 541 3rd Street   .   .   .   .   .   *Surgery*
John Daniel Sullivan, 74 McDonough Street .   .   .   .   *Surgery*
Ernest K. Tanner, 1205 Dean Street   .   .   .   .   .   *Surgery*
Joseph F. Todd, 402 Sterling Place   .   .   .   .   .   *Gynecology*
Walter Truslow, 67 Hanson Place .   .   .   .   *Orthopedic Surgery*
Roy Upham, 300 McDonough Street   .   .   .   .   .   *Surgery*
Theodore Luther Vosseler, 390A Monroe Street   .   .   .   *Surgery*
Henry A. Wade, 495 Greene Avenue   .   .   *Gynecology, Obstetrics*
Robert Forrester Walmsley, 468 Washington Avenue   .   *Surgery*
James Peter Warbasse, 384 Washington Avenue .   .   .   *Surgery*
Alton G. Warner, 19 Schermerhorn Street   .   *Ophth., Otology*
J. S. Waterman, 676 St. Mark's Avenue   .   *Rhinol., Laryngology*
Thurston Scott Welton, 842 Union Street .   *Gynecology, Obstetrics*
Richard Ward Westbrook, 1145 Dean Street .   .   .   .   *Surgery*
Alfred Winfield White, 88 McDonough Street *Gynecology, Obstetrics*
Jarvis S. Wight, 30 Schermerhorn Street   .   .   .   .   .   *Surgery*
Robert Lowell Wood, 129 Hancock Street   .   .   .   .   *Obstetrics*
V. L. Zimmerman, 839 Carroll Street   .   .   *Gynecology, Obstetrics*

BUFFALO

Henry Adsit, 37 Allen Street   .   .   .   *Genito-Urinary Surgery*
Arthur G. Bennett, 26 Allen Street   .   .   .   .   *Ophthalmology*
Charles R. Borzilleri, 298 Niagara Street .   .   .   .   .   *Surgery*
C. M. Brown, 510 Delaware Avenue   .   *Rhinol., Oto-Laryngology*
John L. Butsch, Buffalo Clinic .   .   .   .   *Surgery*
Francis J. Carr, 345 Eagle Street   .   .   .   .   .   .   *Surgery*
James Henry Carr, 345 Eagle Street   .   .   .   .   .   .   *Surgery*
Alfred Hull Clark, 153 Delaware Avenue .   .   .   .   *Gynecology*
Marshall Clinton, 556 Franklin Street .   .   .   .   .   .   *Surgery*
Chester C. Cott, 1001 Main Street .   .   *Rhinol., Oto-Laryngology*
H. W. Cowper, 543 Franklin Street   .   .   .   .   *Ophthalmology*
George Read Critchlow, 647 Lafayette Avenue   .   .   .   *Surgery*
John F. Fairbairn, 503 Delaware Avenue *Rhinol., Oto-Laryngology*
E. A. Forsyth, 471 Virginia Street   .   .   *Rhinol., Oto-Laryngology*

NEW YORK — Continued

BUFFALO — Continued

Lee Masten Francis, 636 Delaware Avenue . . *Ophthalmology*
James A. Gardner, 500 Electric Building . . . . . *Urology*
Francis C. Goldsborough, 515 Franklin Street
Gynecology, Obstetrics
Herman E. Hayd, 493 Delaware Avenue . . . . . *Surgery*
Lawrence Hendee, 346 Elmwood Avenue . . . . . *Surgery*
Ray Henry Johnson, 449 Franklin Street . . . . . *Surgery*
James Edward King, 1248 Main Street . . . . *Gynecology*
Prescott Le Breton, 125 Allen Street . . . *Orthopedic Surgery*
F. Park Lewis, 454 Franklin Street . . . . *Ophthalmology*
James Hoyt Lewis, 135 Linwood Avenue . . . . . *Surgery*
Earl Perkins Lothrop, 153 Delaware Avenue . . . . *Surgery*
James A. MacLeod, 448 Delaware Avenue . . . . *Surgery*
William Henry Marcy, 32 West Utica Street . . . . *Surgery*
Edgar R. McGuire, 622 Delaware Avenue . . . . *Surgery*
Francis W. McGuire, 470 Franklin Street . . . . . *Surgery*
Descum Clayton McKenney, 1250 Main Street
Gynecology, Proctology
Edward John Meyer, 1312 Main Street . . . . . *Surgery*
George T. Moseley, 202 Delaware Avenue . . . . *Surgery*
Alfred H. Noehren, 1196 Main Street . . . . . *Surgery*
Frederick J. Parmenter, 616 Potomac Avenue *Surgery, Urology*
William Linton Phillips, 469 Franklin Street . . *Ophthalmology*
Harry Blaine Pinkerton, 597 Elmwood Avenue . . . *Surgery*
William Ward Plummer, 523 Franklin Street . *Orthopedic Surgery*
Irving White Potter, 420 Franklin Street . . . . *Obstetrics*
William Scott Renner, 341 Linwood Avenue . . *Oto-Laryngology*
Herriot C. Rooth, 350 Ashland Avenue . . . . . *Surgery*
Bernard F. Schreiner, 231 Humboldt Parkway . . . *Surgery*
Elmer G. Starr, 523 Delaware Avenue . . . . *Ophthalmology*
Harry R. Trick, 522 West Ferry Street . . . . . *Surgery*
Harry M. Weed, 196 Linwood Avenue . . *Ophth., Rhinology*
Thew Wright, 575 Delaware Avenue . . . . . . *Surgery*

COHOES

James Henry Mitchell, 268 Remsen Street . . . . *Surgery*

COOPERSTOWN

Bennett W. Dewar, 59 Chestnut Street . . . . . *Surgery*

NEW YORK — Continued

CORNING

Harry Edwin Battin, 116 East First Street . . . . *Surgery*
Harry H. Hubbell, 103 Pine Street . . . . *Surgery*
Edward Hyatt Hutton, 134 East First Street . . . *Surgery*

CORTLAND

R. P. Higgins, 20 Court Street . . . *Ophth., Oto-Laryngology*

CROTON-ON-HUDSON

William H. Galland . . . . *Surgery*

DUNKIRK

Walter Hall Vosburg, Masonic Temple . . . . . *Surgery*
John A. Weidman, 20 East 4th Street . . . . . *Surgery*

ELMIRA

Arthur Woodward Booth, 222 West Church Street . . *Surgery*
Ross George Loop, 359 Main Street . . . . . *Surgery*

FLUSHING

Archer W. Jagger, 410 Amity Street . . . . . *Surgery*

GENEVA

Homer James Knickerbocker, 196 Genesee Street . . *Surgery*
Claude Carl Lytle, 7 Schnirel Building . . . . *Surgery*
John Arthur Spengler, 73 Seneca Street . . . *Ophthalmology*

GLENS FALLS

Davis Baker, Insurance Company Building . . . . *Surgery*
Thomas Hart Cunningham, Glens Falls Insurance
Building . . . . *Surgery*

HASTINGS-ON-HUDSON

Francis Romeyn Lyman, 600 Broadway . . . . . *Surgery*

HUDSON

John L. Edwards, 12 South Fifth Street . . . . *Surgery*
Sherwood V. Whitbeck, 431 Warren Street . . . *Surgery*

ITHACA

Edward L. Bull, 124 East State Street
Ophth., Rhinol., Oto-Laryngology
John S. Kirkendall, 317 North Aurora Street . . *Ophth., Otology*
Martin B. Tinker, 101 South Aurora Street . . . . *Surgery*

JAMAICA

George Kissam Meynen, 43 Clinton Avenue . . . . *Surgery*

NEW YORK — Continued

JAMESTOWN

George W. Cottis, 310 Wellman Building . . . . . *Surgery*
Charles E. Goodell, 63 Allen Street . . . . . . *Surgery*
Milton J. Johnson, 213 Main Street . . . . . . *Surgery*

JOHNSON CITY

Charles Sumner Wilson, 301 Main Street ' . . . . . *Surgery*

KINGSTON

George F. Chandler, 11 East Chestnut Street . . . *Surgery*
Ervin E. Norwood, 21 Franklin Street . . . . . *Surgery*
Frederick Snyder, 44 Clinton Avenue . . . . . . *Surgery*
Alexander A. Stern, 22 East Strand . . . . . . *Surgery*

LAWRENCE

Leonard S. Rau, Central Avenue . . . *Gynecology, Obstetrics*

MOHEGAN LAKE

Harold Thomas Royce . . . . *Gynecology*

MT. VERNON

John J. Thomson, 3 Park Avenue *Ophth., Rhinol., Oto-Laryngology*

NEWBURGH

John Taylor Howell, 205 Grand Street . . . . . *Surgery*
Edward Cameron Thompson, 139 Grand Street . . . *Surgery*
Charles E. Townsend, 231 Liberty Street . . . . . *Surgery*

NEW ROCHELLE

Matthias Lanckton Foster, 106 Centre Avenue . *Ophthalmology*
George Augustus Peck, 189 Centre Avenue . . . . *Surgery*

NEW YORK

Robert Abbe, 13 West 50th Street . . . . *Surgery*
Joseph H. Abraham, 130 West 58th Street *Rhinol., Oto-Laryngology*
Fred H. Albee, 40 East 41st Street . . . *Orthopedic Surgery*
Lawrence Dade Alexander, Jr., 130 West 59th Street
Rhinol., Oto-Laryngology
Ellice M. Alger, 40 East 41st Street . . . . *Ophthalmology*
Harry Aranow, 355 East 149th Street . . *Gynecology, Obstetrics*
John Aspell, 34 West 76th Street . . . . . . *Gynecology*
Hugh Auchincloss, 800 Park Avenue . . . . . . *Surgery*
Horace Ernest Ayers, 9 West 67th Street . . . . *Surgery*
Clinton L. Bagg, 56 West 52nd Street . . . . . *Surgery*
Harold C. Bailey, 22 East 68th Street . . *Gynecology, Obstetrics*
Frederic Wolcott Bancroft, 100 East 66th Street . . . *Surgery*

New York — Continued

Clarence G. Bandler, 8 East 48th Street . *Genito-Urinary Surgery*
S. W. Bandler, 134 West 87th Street . . *Gynecology, Obstetrics*
William Howard Barber, 616 Madison Avenue . . . *Surgery*
George Barrie, 15 East 48th Street . . . . *Surgery*
Benjamin S. Barringer, 134 East 76th Street . . . . *Urology*
Emily D. Barringer, 134 East 76th Street . . . . *Gynecology*
David Nye Barrows, 130 East 56th Street *Gynecology, Obstetrics*
Edwin Beer, 11 East 48th Street . . . . *Surgery*
George Huston Bell, 40 East 41st Street . . . *Ophthalmology*
Abraham J. Beller, 1155 Park Avenue . . . . . . *Surgery*
T. Passmore Berens, 25 Park Avenue . . . *Oto-Laryngology*
Warren Stone Bickham, 440 Riverside Drive . . . . *Surgery*
Robert S. Bickley, 339 West 57th Street . . . . . *Surgery*
Frederic Bierhoff, 155 West 58th Street . . . . . *Urology*
Anson Holden Bingham, 2345 Broadway . . *Orthopedic Surgery*
W. H. Bishop, 667 Madison Avenue . . . . . . *Surgery*
Dougal Bissell, 219 West 79th Street . . . . . *Gynecology*
Joseph A. Blake, 216 East 53rd Street . . . . . *Surgery*
Joseph L. Boehm, 540 Park Avenue . *Genito-Urinary Surgery*
Hermann J. Boldt, 616 Madison Avenue . . . . *Gynecology*
Milton Ralph Bookman, 473 East 141st Street . . . *Surgery*
Samuel W. Boorstein, 529 Courtlandt Avenue *Orthopedic Surgery*
Wesley C. Bowers, 27 West 49th Street *Rhinol., Oto-Laryngology*
Charles Cumberson Boyle, 40 East 41st Street . *Ophth., Otology*
Alfred Braun, 31 East 72nd Street . . *Rhinol., Oto-Laryngology*
Robert Emery Brennan, 1 West 64th Street . . . . *Surgery*
Edward Christopher Brenner, 20 West 50th Street . . *Surgery*
Joseph Brettauer, 1063 Madison Avenue . . . . *Gynecology*
George Emerson Brewer, 19 East 65th Street . . . *Surgery*
Walter M. Brickner, 151 Central Park, West . . . . *Surgery*
William R. Broughton, 341 Madison Avenue . . *Ophthalmology*
LeRoy Broun, 148 West 77th Street . . . . . *Gynecology*
W. Sohier Bryant, 107 East 39th Street *Rhinol., Oto-Laryngology*
Leo Buerger, 1000 Park Avenue . . . . *Surgery*
Henry G. Bugbee, 40 East 41st Street . . . . . *Urology*
Edward Arthur Bullard, 47 East 57th Street . . . *Gynecology*
Carl Goodwin Burdick, 126 East 37th Street . . . *Surgery*
Samuel B. Burk, 969 Madison Avenue . . . . . *Surgery*

NEW YORK — Continued

William E. Caldwell, 58 West 55th Street .   *Obstetrics, Gynecology*
Peter A. Callan, 452 5th Avenue .   .   .   .   .   *Ophthalmology*
Sprague Carleton, 75 West 50th Street   . *Genito-Urinary Surgery*
Alexis Carrel, Rockefeller Institute   .   .   .   .   .   *Surgery*
W. W. Carter, 2 West 67th Street .   . *Rhinol., Oto-Laryngology*
Michele G. Caturani, 136 East 79th Street   .   .   .   *Gynecology*
P. F. Chambers, 18 East 94th Street .   .   .   .   *Gynecology*
Marie L. Chard, 616 Madison Avenue .   .   .   .   *Gynecology*
Herbert Clifton Chase, 45 East 62nd Street   .   .   .   .   *Surgery*
Thomas H. Cherry, 47 West 50th Street   . *Gynecology, Obstetrics*
Charles H. Chetwood, 25 Park Avenue   .   .   .   .   *Urology*
John W. Churchman, 65 Central Park, West .   .   .   *Surgery*
Arthur H. Cilley, 120 East 34th Street   .   . *Orthopedic Surgery*
John Herbert Claiborne, 9 East 46th Street   .   . *Ophthalmology*
J. Bayard Clark, 114 East 54th Street .   . *Genito-Urinary Surgery*
James B. Clemens, 10 East 71st Street   .   .   .   .   *Retired*
Clement Cleveland, 925 Park Avenue .   .   .   .   *Gynecology*
Cornelius G. Coakley, 53 West 56th Street   . *Oto-Laryngology*
Henry Clarke Coe, 45 East 62nd Street   .   .   .   *Gynecology*
Lewis A. Coffin, 114 East 54th Street   . *Rhinol., Oto-Laryngology*
Ira Cohen, 178 East 70th Street   .   .   .   .   .   .   *Surgery*
Martin Cohen, 1 West 85th Street .   .   .   .   .   *Ophthalmology*
William Bradley Coley, 340 Park Avenue .   .   .   .   *Surgery*
Howard Dennis Collins, 630 Park Avenue   .   .   .   .   *Surgery*
John F. Connors, 616 Madison Avenue   .   .   .   .   *Surgery*
Royal Samuel Copeland, 58 Central Park, West
                              Ophth., Rhinol., Oto-Laryngology
William Cowen, 35 East 60th Street   . *Ophth., Oto-Laryngology*
Henry C. Cowles, 97 Central Park, West . *Gynecology, Obstetrics*
Gerard H. Cox, 137 East 54th Street .   .   .   . *Oto-Laryngology*
Walter C. Cramp, 369 West End Avenue .   .   .   .   *Surgery*
Walter Gray Crump, 837 Madison Avenue   .   .   .   *Surgery*
W. L. Culbert, 16 East 54th Street   . *Rhinol., Oto-Laryngology*
Walter T. Dannreuther, 2020 Broadway .   .   .   *Gynecology*
William Darrach, 128 East 60th Street   .   .   .   .   *Surgery*
Asa Barnes Davis, 42 East 35th Street   . *Gynecology, Obstetrics*
William Burton DeGarmo, 616 Madison Avenue   .   . *Surgery*
D. Bryson Delavan, 40 East 41st Street   . *Rhinol., Laryngology*

NEW YORK — Continued

New York — Continued

Edward Bradford Dench, 15 East 53rd Street	*Otology*
Paolo De Vecchi, 43 5th Avenue	*Surgery*
Robert L. Dickinson, 13 East 65th Street	*Gynecology, Obstetrics*
Franklin A. Dorman, 133 East 57th Street	*Gynecology, Obstetrics*
Daniel S. Dougherty, 111 West 85th Street	*Oto-Laryngology*
John Douglas, 568 Park Avenue	*Surgery*
Charles N. Dowd, 138 West 58th Street	*Surgery*
William Augustus Downes, 424 Park Avenue	*Surgery*
John William Draper, 9 East 40th Street	*Surgery*
Arthur Baldwin Duel, 27 East 57th Street	*Otology*
Kirby Dwight, 1045 Madison Avenue	*Surgery*
J. Clifton Edgar, 28 West 56th Street	*Obstetrics, Gynecology*
Carl Eggers, 850 Park Avenue	*Surgery*
George Robert Elliott, 40 East 41st Street	*Orthopedic Surgery*
Charles A. Elsberg, 64 East 58th Street	*Surgery*
Seward Erdman, 134 East 64th Street	*Surgery*
John F. Erdmann, 60 West 52nd Street	*Surgery*
Ernest Fahnestock, 417 Park Avenue	*Surgery*
Charles Everett Farr, 568 Park Avenue	*Surgery*
Lilian K. P. Farrar, The Hendrik Hudson	*Gynecology, Obstetrics*
Hermann Fischer, 73 East 80th Street	*Surgery*
Arthur Lyman Fisk, 41 West 50th Street	*Surgery*
Fred J. C. Fitzgerald, 47 East 57th Street	*Ophth., Oto-Laryngology*
Edward A. Flemming, 213 113th Street	*Obstetrics, Gynecology*
Austin Flint, 52 East 54th Street	*Gynecology, Obstetrics*
Joseph Henry Fobes, 1 West 68th Street	*Surgery*
Henry Hall Forbes, 40 East 41st Street	*Rhinol., Oto-Laryngology*
William Miller Ford, 52 East 54th Street	*Gynecology*
Eben Foskett, 106 Central Park, West	*Gynecology*
Harold A. Foster, 204 West 55th Street	*Rhinol., Oto-Laryngology*
Edmund Prince Fowler, 114 East 54th Street	
	Rhinol., Oto-Laryngology
Henry W. Frauenthal, 160 West 59th Street	*Orthopedic Surgery*
Percy Fridenberg, 38 West 59th Street	*Ophthalmology*
Isidore Friesner, 814 Lexington Avenue	*Rhinol., Oto-Laryngology*
Claude Augustine Frink, 464 West 144th Street	*Surgery*
Eugene Fuller, 530 5th Avenue	*Genito-Urinary Surgery*
Henry D. Furniss, 54 East 48th Street	*Gynecology, Urology*

NEW YORK — Continued

NEW YORK — Continued

Vincent Gaudiani, 145 East 49th Street . . . . . *Surgery*
Julien A. Géhrung, 783 5th Avenue   *Ophth., Rhinol-Laryngology*
Samuel H. Geist, 300 Central Park, West .   *Gynecology, Obstetrics*
Arpad G. Gerster, 34 East 75th Street . . . . . *Surgery*
John C. A. Gerster, 18 East 78th Street . . . . . *Surgery*
William Travis Gibb, 42 West 75th Street . . . *Gynecology*
Virgil P. Gibney, 16 Park Avenue . . . . *Orthopedic Surgery*
Charles Langdon Gibson, 72 East 54th Street . . . *Surgery*
W. Whitehead Gilfillan, 31 West 50th Street . . *Ophthalmology*
J. Riddle Goffe, 123 East 53rd Street . . . . . *Gynecology*
David D. Goldstein, 126 East 61st Street . . . . . *Surgery*
Nathan Goodfriend, 44 West 77th Street . . . *Ophthalmology*
Charles Goodman, 969 Madison Avenue . . . . . *Surgery*
Donald Gordon, 27 East 62nd Street . . . . . *Surgery*
Hermann Grad, 40 East 41st Street . . . . . *Gynecology*
John Prescott Grant, 11 East 48th Street . . . . . *Surgery*
Charles Perley Gray, 60 West 58th Street   *Gynecology, Obstetrics*
Nathan W. Green, 152 West 57th Street . . . . . *Surgery*
Robert Holmes Greene, 78 East 56th Street . . . . *Surgery*
J. Henry Güntzer, 40 East 41st Street
                          Ophth., Rhinol., Oto-Laryngology
Edward S. Gushee, 519 West End Avenue   *Gynecology, Obstetrics*
DeWayne Hallett, 274 West 86th Street . . . *Ophthalmology*
George Ray Hare, 107 East 39th Street . . . *Ophthalmology*
James A. Harrar, 100 East 66th Street . . . . . *Obstetrics*
Gove S. Harrington, 328 Convent Avenue . . . . *Surgery*
Thomas Jefferson Harris, 104 East 40th Street . *Oto-Laryngology*
Isaac Hartshorne, 30 West 59th Street
                          Ophth., Rhinol., Oto-Laryngology
John A. Hartwell, 27 East 63rd Street . . . . . . *Surgery*
William Henry Haskin, 40 East 41st Street . . *Oto-Laryngology*
Forbes Hawkes, 124 East 65th Street . . . . . *Surgery*
Irving Samuel Haynes, 107 West 85th Street . . . *Surgery*
Harold M. Hays, 2178 Broadway . . . . . *Oto-Laryngology*
William P. Healy, 525 Park Avenue . . . . . *Gynecology*
Charles H. Helfrich, 542 5th Avenue . . . . *Ophthalmology*
Alfred M. Hellman, 2 West 86th Street . *Gynecology, Obstetrics*
William Tod Helmuth, 616 Madison Avenue . . . . *Surgery*

NEW YORK — Continued

W. P. Herrick, 61 East 73rd Street . . *Genito-Urinary Surgery*
Llewellyn E. Hetrick, 30 West 48th Street . . *Oto-Laryngology*
Charles Gordon Heyd, 46 West 52nd Street . . . . *Surgery*
James Morley Hitzrot, 126 East 37th Street . . . . *Surgery*
Joseph P. Hoguet, 55 East 53rd Street . . . . . *Surgery*
F. C. Holden, 13 East 65th Street . . . *Gynecology, Obstetrics*
William Francis Honan, 24 East 48th Street . . . . *Surgery*
Ransom Spafard Hooker, 175 East 71st Street . . . *Surgery*
John Horn, 72 East 92nd Street . . *Rhinol., Oto-Laryngology*
Lester M. Hubby, 27 West 68th Street *Rhinol., Oto-Laryngology*
Edward Taylor Hull, 304 West 78th Street *Gynecology, Obstetrics*
Lee M. Hurd, 39 East 50th Street . . . . . *Oto-Laryngology*
Abraham Hyman, 144 East 36th Street . *Genito-Urinary Surgery*
Howard S. Jeck, 109 East 34th Street . . . . . . *Urology*
C. F. Jellinghaus, 572 Park Avenue . . *Gynecology, Obstetrics*
Richard Jordan, 165 West 58th Street . *Rhinol., Oto-Laryngology*
L. Miller Kahn, 29 East 93rd Street . . . . . . *Surgery*
Moses S. Kakels, 35 East 61st Street . . . . . . *Surgery*
Frederic Kammerer, Lenox Hill Hospital . . . . . *Surgery*
Arthur Matthew Kane, 32 West 48th Street . . . . *Surgery*
L. R. Kaufman, 150 West 80th Street . . *Genito-Urinary Surgery*
Frederick C. Keller, 41 West 71st Street . . . . . *Surgery*
Edward Leland Kellogg, 48 West 51st Street . . . . *Surgery*
Edwin Welles Kellogg, 616 Madison Avenue . . . . *Surgery*
James H. Kenyon, 57 West 58th Street . . . . . *Surgery*
Philip D. Kerrison, 58 West 56th Street . . . . . *Otology*
Ben Witt Key, 180 West 59th Street . . . . *Ophthalmology*
Edward L. Keyes, Jr., 109 East 34th Street . . . . *Urology*
Harold Brown Keyes, 128 East 60th Street . . . . *Surgery*
Otto G. T. Kiliani . . . . *Surgery*
Samuel Kleinberg, 1 West 85th Street . . . *Orthopedic Surgery*
W. H. W. Knipe, 59 West 54th Street . . *Gynecology, Obstetrics*
Samuel J. Kopetzky, 51 West 73rd Street *Rhinol., Oto-Laryngology*
George W. Kosmak, 23 East 93rd Street . *Gynecology, Obstetrics*
Louis Julius Ladin, 1289 Madison Avenue . . . *Gynecology*
Adrian Van Sinderen Lambert, 168 East 71st Street . *Surgery*
Walter Eyre Lambert, 112 East 35th Street . . *Ophthalmology*
Philip Leach, 358 Fifth Avenue . . . . *Retired*

NEW YORK — Continued

NEW YORK — Continued

Moses D. Lederman, 58 East 75th Street   *Rhinol., Oto-Laryngology*
Burton James Lee, 128 East 73rd Street . . . . . *Surgery*
John Crego Lester, 616 Madison Avenue . . . *Ophthalmology*
Robert Lewis, 48 West 40th Street . . *Rhinol., Oto-Laryngology*
Richard Lewisohn, 1155 Park Avenue . . . . . . *Surgery*
Howard Lilienthal, 52 East 82nd Street . . . . . *Surgery*
Howard E. Lindeman, 102 West 75th Street *Gynecology, Obstetrics*
Samuel Lloyd, 50 East 42nd Street . . . . . . *Surgery*
R. W. Lobenstine, 162 East 71st Street . *Gynecology, Obstetrics*
Leon S. Loizeaux, 68 East 86th Street . . *Gynecology, Obstetrics*
Oswald Swinney Lowsley, 853 7th Avenue . . . . *Urology*
William Henry Luckett, 18 West 87th Street . . . . *Surgery*
William Chittenden Lusk, 47 East 34th Street . . . *Surgery*
George W. Lutton, 51 East 78th Street . . . . . *Surgery*
Henry Hamilton Moore Lyle, 117 East 56th Street . . *Surgery*
Jerome M. Lynch, 205 East 61st Street . . . . . *Surgery*
Constantine J. MacGuire, 120 East 60th Street . . . *Surgery*
John Edmund MacKenty, 43 West 54th Street . *Oto-Laryngology*
Duncan Macpherson, 114 East 54th Street *Rhinol., Oto-Laryngology*
George Hooper Mallett, 244 West 73rd Street . . . *Surgery*
Walton Martin, 230 East 49th Street . . . . . . *Surgery*
Francis Stuart Mathews, 62 West 50th Street . . . *Surgery*
Charles Henry May, 698 Madison Avenue . . *Ophthalmology*
Jacob L. Maybaum, 1 West 70th Street . . . *Oto-Laryngology*
George Birmingham McAuliffe, 26 West 87th Street
  Ophth., Rhinol., Oto-Laryngology
Joseph F. McCarthy, 40 East 41st Street . *Genito-Urinary Surgery*
Lefferts A. McClelland, 2 Rector Street   *Rhinol., Oto-Laryngology*
John McCoy, 157 West 73rd Street . *Rhinol., Oto-Laryngology*
Samuel McCullagh, 17 East 38th Street   *Rhinol., Oto-Laryngology*
George W. McDowell, 40 East 41st Street . . *Ophth., Otology*
John F. McGrath, 119 East 30th Street . . . . *Gynecology*
John J. McGrath, 109 West 74th Street . . . . . *Surgery*
James Francis McKernon, 62 West 52nd Street . . . *Otology*
William Clark McKnight, 200 West 58th Street
  Ophth., Rhinol., Oto-Laryngology
Walter H. McNeill, Jr., 34 East 40th Street . . . . *Urology*
Ross McPherson, 125 East 39th Street . *Gynecology, Obstetrics*

NEW YORK — Continued

NEW YORK — Continued

Clarence A. McWilliams, 19 East 65th Street   . . .   *Surgery*
Harold D. Meeker, 47 East 57th Street   .   .   .   .   *Surgery*
Edward L. Meierhof, 1140 Madison Avenue

Ophth., Oto-Laryngology

Thomas D. Merrigan, 553 West 167th Street   . . .   *Surgery*
Leo B. Meyer, 2178 Broadway . . . .   *Surgery*
Willy Meyer, 700 Madison Avenue   . . . . .   *Surgery*
Seth Minot Milliken, 951 Madison Avenue   . . .   *Surgery*
John Joseph Moorhead, 115 East 64th Street   . . .   *Surgery*
Thomas Henry Morgan, 222 West 71st Street   . .   *Gynecology*
Robert Tuttle Morris, 616 Madison Avenue . . . .   *Surgery*
Albert S. Morrow, 114 East 54th Street   . . . .   *Surgery*
Alexis V. Moschcowitz, 925 Madison Avenue   . . .   *Surgery*
Edwin S. Munson, 8 West 49th Street   . . .   *Ophthalmology*
Frank W. Murray, 32 West 39th Street   . . . .   *Surgery*
Philip William Nathan, 110 East 78th Street   *Orthopedic Surgery*
Alexander Nicoll, 17 West 73rd Street . . . . .   *Surgery*
John Joseph Nutt, 853 7th Avenue   . . .   *Orthopedic Surgery*
Frank R. Oastler, 170 West 59th Street   .   *Gynecology, Obstetrics*
Charles Ogilvy, 40 East 41st Street   . . .   *Orthopedic Surgery*
Seymour Oppenheimer, 45 East 60th Street

Rhinol., Oto-Laryngology

Alfred T. Osgood, 40 East 41st Street .   . *Genito-Urinary Surgery*
John Randolph Page, 127 East 62nd Street   . . . .   *Otology*
Angenette Parry, 154 East 37th Street   .   *Gynecology, Obstetrics*
Sanders M. Payne, 542 5th Avenue   .   *Ophth., Oto-Laryngology*
Charles H. Peck, 30 West 50th Street . . . . . .   *Surgery*
James Pedersen, 40 East 41st Street   . . . . .   *Urology*
Victor Cox Pedersen, 45 West 9th Street . . . . .   *Urology*
Dunlap Pearce Penhallow, 23 West 43rd Street   . . .   *Surgery*
Charles E. Perkins, 114 East 54th Street   *Rhinol., Oto-Laryngology*
Edward Wadsworth Peterson, 525 Park Avenue . . .   *Surgery*
Wendell C. Phillips, 40 West 47th Street   *Rhinol., Oto-Laryngology*
Edward W. Pinkham, 40 East 41st Street   *Gynecology, Obstetrics*
Eugene Hillhouse Pool, 107 East 60th Street . . . .   *Surgery*
Charles R. L. Putnam, 24 East 70th Street   . . . .   *Surgery*
Edward H. Quinn, 108 West 71st Street   . . . .   *Surgery*
John Broadfoot Rae, 247 West 70th Street   . . . .   *Otology*

NEW YORK — Continued

NEW YORK — Continued

Edwin George Ramsdell, 25 East 64th Street . . . . *Surgery*
R. M. Rawls, 350 West 88th Street . . *Gynecology, Obstetrics*
Robert Grigg Reese, 50 West 52nd Street . . . *Ophthalmology*
Martin Rehling, 209 East 61st Street . . . . . . *Surgery*
Philip Rice, Sherman Square Hotel . . . . . . *Otology*
Frederic G. Ritchie, 314 West 106th Street . . *Ophthalmology*
George W. Roberts, 175 West 58th Street . . . . *Surgery*
Meyer R. Robinson, 950 Park Avenue . *Gynecology, Obstetrics*
John Rogers, 177 East 71st Street . . . . . . *Surgery*
Max S. Rohde, Lexington Hospital . . . . . *Urology*
Abraham J. Rongy, 345 West 88th Street . *Gynecology, Obstetrics*
Henry Roth, 409 East 140th Street . . . . . *Surgery*
Isidor C. Rubin, 261 Central Park, West . *Gynecology, Obstetrics*
Frederick Fuller Russell, 61 Broadway . . . . *Surgery*
James I. Russell, 37 East 61st Street . . . . . *Surgery*
Henry B. Safford, 47 West 94th Street . *Gynecology, Obstetrics*
Lucius A. Salisbury, 71 East 77th Street . . . . . *Surgery*
Truman L. Saunders, 121 East 61st Street *Rhinol., Oto-Laryngology*
Carlo Savini, 43 West 11th Street . . . . . . *Surgery*
Reginald Hall Sayre, 14 West 48th Street . . *Orthopedic Surgery*
Winfield Scott Schley, 24 West 45th Street . . . . *Surgery*
Herman Bernard Schoenberg, 490 West End Avenue . *Surgery*
Gustav Seeligmann, 33 East 72nd Street . *Gynecology, Obstetrics*
Isadore Seff, 252 West 85th Street . . . . . . *Surgery*
Albert Eugene Sellenings, 132 East 36th Street . . *Surgery*
George H. Semken, 16 West 85th Street . . . . *Surgery*
Newton M. Shaffer, 31 East 49th Street . . *Orthopedic Surgery*
John Rowlands Shannon, 17 East 38th Street. . *Ophthalmology*
J. Eastman Sheehan, 24 East 48th Street . . . . *Surgery*
George Andrew Shepard, 204 West 55th Street . *Ophth., Otology*
Milton A. Shlenker, Hotel Marie Antoinette *Gynecology, Obstetrics*
Walter Mandeville Silleck, 445 Park Avenue . . . . *Surgery*
Henry Mann Silver, 276 Madison Avenue . . . . *Surgery*
C. H. Smith, 616 Madison Avenue . . *Rhinol., Oto-Laryngology*
Frederick W. Smith, 40 East 41st Street . . . . . *Urology*
Harmon Smith, 44 West 49th Street . . . . *Oto-Laryngology*
Homer Erastus Smith, 276 Madison Avenue . . *Ophthalmology*
Morris K. Smith, 117 East 56th Street . . . . . *Surgery*

NEW YORK — Continued

NEW YORK — Continued

Thomas Allison Smith, 57 West 75th Street . . . . *Surgery*
Francis W. Sovak, 44 East 72nd Street . . . . *Gynecology*
Harry Van Ness Spaulding, 14 East 58th Street . . . *Surgery*
Samuel Spiegel, 1239 Madison Avenue . . . . . *Surgery*
J. Bentley Squier, 8 East 68th Street . . . . . . *Urology*
G. E. Steel, 256 West 79th Street . . *Rhinol., Oto-Laryngology*
Arthur Stein, 48 East 74th Street . . . *Gynecology, Obstetrics*
Franklin M. Stephens, 19 West 54th Street
                              Rhinol., Oto-Laryngology
DeWitt Stetten, 115 West 87th Street . . . . . . *Surgery*
Alexander Raymond Stevens, 40 East 41st Street . . *Urology*
D. H. Stewart, 128 West 86th Street . . *Gynecology, Obstetrics*
George David Stewart, 417 Park Avenue . . . . . *Surgery*
Ralph Alexander Stewart, 616 Madison Avenue . . . *Surgery*
Alfred Stillman, II, 35 East 39th Street . . . . . *Surgery*
Fordyce B. St. John, Presbyterian Hospital . . . . *Surgery*
Charles Francis Stokes, 6 West 77th Street . . . . *Surgery*
William E. Studdiford, 124 East 36th Street
                              Gynecology, Obstetrics
Arnold Sturmdorf, 51 West 74th Street . . . . . *Surgery*
Raymond Peter Sullivan, 270 Park Avenue . . . . *Surgery*
Fred B. Sutherland, 40 East 41st Street . . . *Ophth., Otology*
Samuel Swift, 55 East 61st Street . . . *Gynecology, Obstetrics*
Parker Syms, 361 Park Avenue . . . . *Surgery*
Alfred Simpson Taylor, 115 West 55th Street . . . *Surgery*
Henry Ling Taylor, 125 West 58th Street . . *Orthopedic Surgery*
Howard Canning Taylor, 32 West 50th Street . . *Gynecology*
Ira Brewster Terry, Jr., 129 East 92nd Street *Gynecology, Obstetrics*
Gustav J. E. Tieck, 40 East 41st Street *Rhinol., Oto-Laryngology*
Benjamin Trowbridge Tilton, 772 Madison Avenue . . *Surgery*
Franz Torek, 1021 Madison Avenue . . . . . . *Surgery*
Edward D. Truesdell, 136 West 58th Street . . . . *Surgery*
Edward Emory Tull, 40 East 41st Street . . . . *Gynecology*
Percy R. Turnure, 131 East 66th Street . . . . . *Surgery*
Henry Hawkins Tyson, 11 East 48th Street . . *Ophthalmology*
Frederick T. Van Beuren, Jr., 812 Park Avenue . . . *Surgery*
Royal C. Van Etten, 117 East 56th Street *Obstetrics, Gynecology*
John Colin Vaughan, 156 East 79th Street . . . . *Surgery*

NEW YORK — Continued

John A. Vietor, 8 East 66th Street . . . . . . *Surgery*
Wesley Grove Vincent, 498 West End Avenue . . . *Surgery*
Hiram N. Vineberg, 751 Madison Avenue *Gynecology, Obstetrics*
John Elmer Virden, 529 Courtlandt Avenue . . *Ophthalmology*
Antonie P. Voislawsky, 33 East 68th Street . . *Oto-Laryngology*
James Ditmars Voorhees, 106 East 60th Street . . . *Obstetrics*
Robert P. Wadhams, 11 East 48th Street . . . . . *Surgery*
Alice E. Wakefield, 154 East 37th Street . . . *Ophth., Otology*
Ralph Waldo, 54 West 71st Street . . . . . . *Gynecology*
John B. Walker, 51 East 50th Street . . . . . . *Surgery*
Charlton Wallace, 11 East 48th Street . . *Orthopedic Surgery*
Simon J. Walsh, 134 West 86th Street . . . . . *Surgery*
George Gray Ward, Jr., 48 East 52nd Street *Gynecology, Obstetrics*
Ralph Francis Ward, 895 West End Avenue . . . . *Surgery*
Wilbur Ward, 24 West 50th Street . . . *Gynecology, Obstetrics*
Martin W. Ware, 27 East 81st Street . . . . . . *Surgery*
George William Warren, 117 East 62nd Street
                                    Genito-Urinary Surgery
James Watt, 50 West 55th Street . . . . *Surgery*
John Elmer Weeks, 46 East 57th Street . . . *Ophthalmology*
Max A. Werner, 215 West 34th Street. . . . . . *Surgery*
James Nephew West, 71 West 49th Street . . . *Gynecology*
Brainerd Hunt Whitbeck, 50 East 61st Street *Orthopedic Surgery*
William C. White, 962 Lexington Avenue . . . . . *Surgery*
Frederick Whiting, 19 West 47th Street . . . . . *Otology*
Armitage Whitman, 283 Lexington Avenue . *Orthopedic Surgery*
Royal Whitman, 283 Lexington Avenue . . *Orthopedic Surgery*
Joseph Wiener, 41 East 78th Street . . . . . . *Surgery*
Solomon Wiener, 67 West 89th Street . . *Gynecology, Obstetrics*
Abraham O. Wilensky, 1200 Madison Avenue . . . *Surgery*
Percy Herbert Williams, 429 Park Avenue . . . *Gynecology*
Edward E. Woodland, 73 East 80th Street
                            Ophth., Rhinol., Oto-Laryngology
George Woolsey, 117 East 36th Street . . . : . . *Surgery*
Arthur M. Wright, 417 Park Avenue . . . . . . *Surgery*
Frank Clark Yeomans, 171 West 71st Street . . . . *Surgery*
Joseph G. Yocum, 44 West 44th Street . . . . . . *Surgery*
John Van Doren Young, 16 East 74th Street *Gynecology, Obstetrics*

NEW YORK — Continued

NIAGARA FALLS

    Thomas J. McBlain, 206 Elderfield Building . . . . *Surgery*

    Norman W. Price, 445 3rd Street *Ophth., Rhinol., Oto-Laryngology*

    Albert M. Rooker, 225 Gluck Building   *Rhinol., Oto-Laryngology*

OGDENSBURG

    Grant C. Madill, 92 Caroline Street . . . . . . *Surgery*

OLEAN

    James Ross Allen, 129 Hamilton Street . . . . . *Surgery*

    Jacob E. K. Morris, 119 Laurens Street . . . . . *Surgery*

ONEIDA

    Eugene H. Carpenter, 31 Broad Street . . . . . *Surgery*

ONEONTA

    Arthur Ward Cutler, 28 Watkins Avenue . . . . . *Surgery*

OSSINING

    Charles Clark Sweet, 13 Maple Place . . . . . . *Surgery*

OSWEGO

    Arthur W. Irwin, 116 West 3rd Street . . . . . . *Surgery*

    James Kirk Stockwell, 113 East 3rd Street . . . . *Surgery*

OYSTER BAY

    Richard Derby . . . . *Surgery*

PARKSTON

    Oscar LeSeure . . . . *Retired*

PLATTSBURG

    Lyman G. Barton, 47 Broad Street . . . . . . *Surgery*

    Robert Stevenson Macdonald, 12 Brinckerhoff Street . *Surgery*

PORT CHESTER

    John Franklyn White, 156 North Main Street . . . *Surgery*

PORT JERVIS

    Charles Nathan Skinner, Hubbard Building . . . . *Surgery*

POUGHKEEPSIE

    Robert Wesley Andrews, 235 Mill Street . . . . . *Surgery*

    John Henry Dingman, 258 Mill Street . . . . . *Surgery*

    James Taylor Harrington, 100 South Hamilton Street . *Surgery*

    Albert Rowcliffe Moffit, Vassar Brothers' Hospital . . *Surgery*

    John Wilson Poucher, 339 Mill Street . . . . . . *Surgery*

    James Edgar Sadlier, 295 Mill Street . . . . . . *Surgery*

NEW YORK — Continued

ROCHESTER

Willis Elliott Bowen, 827 East Main Street . . . . . *Surgery*

William Mortimer Brown, 1776 East Avenue
Gynecology, Obstetrics

George Gregory Carroll, 614 Main Street, West
Ophth., Rhinol., Oto-Laryngology

G. Kirby Collier, 525 Lake Avenue . . . . . . *Surgery*

William Insco Dean, 33 Chestnut Street . . . . . *Surgery*

Ralph R. Fitch, 366 East Avenue . . . . *Orthopedic Surgery*

Charles W. Hennington, 633 Park Avenue . . . . . *Surgery*

Loron Whitney Howk, 774 Main Street, West . . . *Surgery*

Owen Elon Jones, 267 University Avenue . . . . . *Surgery*

Nathan Davis McDowell, 275 Alexander Street
Rhinol.,Oto-Laryngology

Joseph Warren McGill, 284 Alexander Street . . . . *Surgery*

Edward Wright Mulligan, 400 Cutler Building . . . *Surgery*

William W. Percy, 12 West Avenue . . . . . . *Surgery*

Edgar W. Phillips, 758 Monroe Avenue . . . . . *Surgery*

Howard L. Prince, 366 East Avenue . . . . . . *Surgery*

Albert C. Snell, 53 Fitzhugh Street, South . . *Ophthalmology*

Audley Durand Stewart, 400 Cutler Building . . . *Surgery*

William Douglas Ward, 20 Grove Place . . . . *Gynecology*

Edward Tubbs Wentworth, 35 Chestnut Street *Orthopedic Surgery*

Henry Timothy Williams, 274 Alexander Street . . . *Surgery*

Frederick William Zimmer, 45 Monroe Avenue . . . *Surgery*

SARATOGA SPRINGS

George Foster Comstock, 540 Broadway . . . . . *Surgery*

Douglas Calhoun Moriarta, 511 Broadway . . . . *Surgery*

Frederic J. Resseguie, 509 North Broadway . . . . *Surgery*

George Scott Towne, 150 Phila Street . . . . . *Gynecology*

SCHENECTADY

William L. Fodder, 5 Jay Street . . . . *Surgery*

Dayton L. Kathan, 411 Union Street . . . . . . *Surgery*

Dudley R. Kathan, 621 Union Street . . . . . . *Surgery*

Charles Goul McMullen, 613 State Street . . . . . *Surgery*

Edwin MacDonald Stanton, 511 State Street . . . . *Surgery*

SENECA FALLS

Frederick W. Lester, 15 Cayuga Street . . . . . *Surgery*

NEW YORK — Continued

STATEN ISLAND

Henry T. Goodwin, 360 Van Duzer Street . . . . *Surgery*
Charles Edward Pearson, 55 Central Avenue . . . . *Surgery*
Frank R. Sedgley, Fox Hills . . . . *Surgery*

SYRACUSE

Arthur Bacon Breese, 434 James Street . . . . *Gynecology*
George Birney Broad, 608 East Genesee Street . . . *Surgery*
C. E. Coon, 405 East Fayette Street . . . *Orthopedic Surgery*
Frederick Flaherty, 831 University Building . . . . *Surgery*
Thomas H. Halsted, Syracuse Clinic . . . . *Oto-Laryngology*
James Herbert Irish, University Building . . . . . *Surgery*
G. G. Lewis, 600 University Building . . *Ophth., Oto-Laryngology*
Michael Milton Lucid, University Building . . . . *Surgery*
Frank William Marlow, 200 Highland Street . . *Ophthalmology*
Percival K. Menzies, 405 Fayette Park . . . . . *Surgery*
Aaron B. Miller, 102 Erie Street . . . . . . *Gynecology*
George M. Price, 114 Physicians Building . . . . *Surgery*
Edward Seguin Van Duyn, University Building . . . *Surgery*

TRENTON FALLS

James H. Glass . . . . *Surgery*

TROY

Edward Waterbury Becker, 6 St. Paul Place *Rhinol., Laryngology*
Burton S. Booth, 60 2nd Street . . . *Rhinol., Oto-Laryngology*
Melville Day Dickinson, 1937 Fifth Avenue . . . *Gynecology*
John Bruce Harvie, 41 2nd Street . . . . . . *Surgery*
David Walker Houston, 18 2nd Street . . . . . *Surgery*
Emmott Howd, 1825 7th Avenue . . . . . . *Surgery*
James P. Marsh, 1828 5th Avenue . . . . . . *Surgery*
Frank M. Sulzman, 1831 5th Avenue. *Ophth., Rhinol., Oto-Laryngology*

UTICA

Charles H. Baldwin, 282 Genesee Street . . *Orthopedic Surgery*
Louis W. Dean, 40 Gardner Building
                        Ophth., Rhinol., Oto-Laryngology
Fred J. Douglas, 285 Genesee Street . . . . . *Surgery*
Thomas H. Farrell, 250 Genesee Street . *Ophth., Oto-Laryngology*
James E. Gage, 250 Genesee Street *Ophth., Rhinol., Oto-Laryngology*
Arthur Rogers Grant, 321 Genesee Street . . . . *Surgery*
Louie Ward Locke, 288 Genesee Street . . . . *Surgery*
Sands C. Maxson, Mayo Building . . . . . . *Surgery*

NEW YORK — Continued

WAPPINGERS FALLS
  Robert Huntington Breed, Andrews Place . . . . *Surgery*

WARSAW
  William Ross Thomson . . . . *Surgery*

WARWICK
  Morris R. Bradner, 82 Main Street . . . . . . *Surgery*

WATERTOWN
  Frederic R. Calkins, 4 Cleveland Building . . . . *Surgery*
  Gilbert David Gregor, 255 Ten Eyck Street . . . . *Surgery*
  J. F. McCaw, Sherman Building *Ophth., Rhinol., Oto-Laryngology*

WEST NEW BRIGHTON
  William Bryan, 91 Bard Avenue . . . . *Surgery*

WHITE PLAINS
  John Fielding Black, 247 Main Street . . . . . . *Surgery*

YONKERS
  Samuel Emmet Getty, 84 Ashburton Avenue . . . . *Surgery*
  George Parker Holden, 122 McLean Avenue . *Surgery, Obstetrics*
  Henry Moffat, 139 Park Avenue . . . . *Surgery*
  George S. Mooney, 153 Warburton Avenue . . . . *Surgery*
  Godfrey Frederic Shimonek, 131 Alta Avenue . . . *Surgery*
  Angelo John Smith, 207 Park Avenue
                        Ophth., Rhinol., Oto-Laryngology

NORTH CAROLINA

ASHEVILLE
  Henry H. Briggs, 73 Haywood Street . *Ophth., Oto-Laryngology*
  Marshall Hall Fletcher, 199 Haywood Street . . . . *Surgery*
  Joseph B. Greene, Haywood Building . *Rhinol., Oto-Laryngology*
  Franklin Webb Griffith, Medical Building . . . . *Surgery*
  Arthur T. Pritchard, Citizens Building . . . . . *Surgery*

CHARLOTTE
  Addison G. Brenizer, Charlotte Sanatorium . . . . *Surgery*
  A. J. Crowell, 711 Independence Building *Genito-Urinary Surgery*
  Robert Lardner Gibbon, 705 South Tryon Street . . *Surgery*
  Richard Hall Johnston . . . *Ophth., Rhinol., Oto-Laryngology*
  James Pleasant Matheson, 511 Independence Building
                        Oto-Laryngology
  Oren Moore, 2 Medical Building . . . *Gynecology, Obstetrics*

NORTH CAROLINA — Continued

CHARLOTTE — Continued

Robert W. Petrie, 812 Independence Building
Ophth., Rhinol., Oto-Laryngology
George William Pressly, 1508 Elizabeth Avenue . . . *Surgery*
Charles Moore Strong, Medical Building . . . . *Gynecology*
Albert M. Whisnant, Independence Building
Ophth., Rhinol., Oto-Laryngology

CONCORD

Paul R. Macfadyen, 148 North Union Street . . . . *Surgery*

DURHAM

Numa Duncan Bitting . . . . *Surgery*
Lyle Steele Booker, First National Bank Building . . *Surgery*
Foy Roberson, First National Bank Building . . . . *Surgery*

FAYETTEVILLE

Jacob Franklin Highsmith, 304 Green Street . . . . *Surgery*
Marwin Le Roy Smoot, 203 Burgess Avenue
Ophth., Rhinol., Oto-Laryngology

FRANKLIN

Samuel Harley Lyle . . . . *Gynecology*

GASTONIA

Lucius Newton Glenn, 402 Realty Building . . . . *Surgery*

GREENSBORO

C. W. Banner, Banner Building   *Ophth., Rhinol., Oto-Laryngology*
Walter F. Cole . . . . *Orthopedic Surgery*
Parran Jarboe, 113 Dixie Building . . . . . . *Surgery*
John Wesley Long, 338 North Elm Street . . . . *Surgery*
James W. Tankersley, 306 Dixie Building . . . . . *Surgery*
John A. Williams, 123 Smith Street . . . . . *Surgery*

HICKORY

Jacob H. Shuford, 1416 12th Street . . . . . *Surgery*

HIGH POINT

David A. Stanton, 108 North Main Street . . . . *Surgery*

KINSTON

Albert D. Parrott, 107 West Gordon Street . . . . *Surgery*
James Marion Parrott . . . *Ophth., Rhinol., Oto-Laryngology*

LINCOLNTON

Lester A. Crowell, South Aspin Street . . . . . . *Surgery*

NORTH CAROLINA — Continued

LUMBERTON

Neill A. Thompson, 4th and Walnut Streets . . . . *Surgery*

NEWBERN

Richard N. Duffy, 130 Craven Street . . . . . . *Surgery*

RALEIGH

Claude Oliver Abernethy, 706 Citizens National Bank
Building . . . . *Genito-Urinary Surgery*
Kemp Plummer Battle, Citizens Bank Building
Ophth., Rhinol., Oto-Laryngology
Hubert Ashley Royster, 423 Fayetteville Street . . . *Surgery*

ROCKY MOUNT

Edmund S. Boice, Park View Hospital . . . . . *Surgery*
Byrd C. Willis, 404 Falls Road . . . . *Surgery*

RUTHERFORDTON

Montgomery Herman Biggs . . . . *Surgery*
Henry Norris . . . . *Surgery*

SALISBURY

James Ernest Stokes, 303 North Fullerton Street . *Gynecology*

SANFORD

J. P. Monroe . . . . *Surgery*

STATESVILLE

Henry F. Long, 834 North Center Street . . . . . *Surgery*

TARBORO

Julian M. Baker, 503 Main Street . . . . *Surgery*
Samuel Newbern Harrell, 424 Main Street . . . . *Surgery*

WASHINGTON

David Thomas Tayloe, Main Street . . . . . . *Surgery*

WILMINGTON

Thomas Meares Green, 11 Masonic Temple . . . . *Surgery*
J. Gerald Murphy, Murchison Bank Building
Ophth., Rhinol., Oto-Laryngology
James Farish Robertson, Jr., Masonic Temple Building *Surgery*
Robert Barnard Slocum, Murchison Bank Building . . *Surgery*

WILSON

Elijah Thomas Dickinson, 219 East Nash Street . . . *Surgery*
B. S. Herring, Corner Green and Spring Streets . . . *Surgery*

NORTH CAROLINA — Continued

WILSON — Continued

Richard H. Johnston, Fidelity Building
Ophth., Rhinol., Oto-Laryngology

Charles A. Woodard, Green and Spring Streets' . . .   *Surgery*

WINSTON-SALEM

Thomas W. Davis, 210 O'Hanlon Building
Ophth., Rhinol., Oto-Laryngology

Everett A. Lockett, O'Hanlon Building . . . . .   *Surgery*

Arthur de Talma Valk, Wachovia Bank Building . .   *Surgery*

NORTH DAKOTA

BISMARCK

Victor J. LaRose, City National Bank Building . . .   *Urology*

Eric P. Quain, City National Bank Building . . . .   *Surgery*

N. Oliver Ramstad, City National Bank Building . .   *Surgery*

Martin William Roan, First National Bank Building .   *Surgery*

Lloyd Albert Schipfer, City National Bank Building
Ophth., Rhinol., Oto-Laryngology

BOTTINEAU

George Alexander Durnin . . . .   *Surgery*

DEVILS LAKE

William F. Sihler, 301 4th Street . . . .   *Surgery*

DICKINSON

Jesse William Bowen, 221 7th Avenue, West . . . .   *Surgery*

Aloysius P. Nachtwey, Merchants Bank Building .   *Gynecology*

Victor H. Stickney, 101 Sims Street . . . . . .   *Surgery*

FARGO

James Prentiss Aylen, Edwards Building . . . . .   *Surgery*

Frederick H. Bailey . . . .   *Ophth., Rhinol., Oto-Laryngology*

Paul H. Burton, 51 Broadway . . . .   *Surgery*

Cyrus N. Callander, 620 Front Street . . .   *Orthopedic Surgery*

George A. Carpenter, 18 Broadway . . . . . .   *Proctology*

Murdock MacGregor, 1120 5th Avenue, South . . .   *Surgery*

John H. Rindlaub, De Lendrecie Block
Ophth., Rhinol., Oto-Laryngology

Martin P. Rindlaub, Jr., 500 De Lendrecie Block
Ophth., Rhinol., Oto-Laryngology

NORTH DAKOTA — Continued

FARGO—Continued

Nils L. Tronnes, Fargo Clinic . . . . *Surgery*
Ralph E. Weible, De Lendrecie Block . . . . . . *Surgery*

GRAFTON

John Edgar Countryman . . . . *Surgery*
Joseph Calvert Suter . . . . *Surgery*

GRAND FORKS

Robert D. Campbell, 2½ South 3rd Street . . . . *Surgery*
Henry Herbert Healy, Northwestern National Bank
   Building . . . . *Surgery*
Henry W. F. Law, Northwestern National Bank Building *Surgery*
Henry Mason Wheeler, 2½ South 3rd Street . . . *Surgery*
George McCullough Williamson . . . *Obstetrics, Gynecology*
Henry G. Woutat, Northwestern National Bank Building
                                        Genito-Urinary Surgery

JAMESTOWN

William A. Gerrish, Clinic Building . . . . . . *Surgery*

MANDAN

Bernard S. Nickerson, Greengard Block . . . . . *Surgery*

MINOT

A. J. McCannel, 44 South Main Street . *Gynecology, Obstetrics*
Archibald D. McCannel, 125 Main Street
                              Ophth., Rhinol., Oto-Laryngology

VALLEY CITY

Alexander W. Macdonald, 310 Fifth Avenue . . . . *Surgery*
Edgar Allen Pray, Pray Block . . . . *Surgery*

OHIO

AKRON

Walter A. Hoyt, 428 Ohio Building . . . . . . *Surgery*
Roy H. McKay, 321 Second National Bank Building . *Surgery*
Carl Rossow Steinke, 608 Metropolitan Building . . *Surgery*
John H. Weber, 330 Akron Savings and Loan Building . *Surgery*

ALLIANCE

Perry Firestone King, 317 East Market Street . . . *Surgery*

ASHLAND

Wilson M. McClellan, Orange Street . . . . . *Gynecology*

OHIO — Continued

ASHTABULA
Clarence E. Case, Park and Center Streets . . . . *Surgery*

BELLEFONTAINE
Robert H. Butler, 128 West Columbus Avenue
Ophth., Rhinol., Oto-Laryngology

BELLEVUE
F. Marion Kent, 128½ East Main Street . . . . . *Surgery*

BRIDGEPORT
James Owen Howells, Lincoln Avenue . . . . . *Surgery*

CANTON
Austin C. Brant, 116 Cleveland Avenue, N. W. . . . *Surgery*
John Pierce DeWitt, 122 Shorb Avenue, N. W. . . . *Surgery*
Harry M. Schuffell, 205 15th Street, N. W. . . . . *Surgery*
Alonzo Byron Walker, 815 4th Street, N. W.. . . . *Surgery*

CINCINNATI
J. Hadley Caldwell, 323 Broadway . . . . . . *Surgery*
John Alexander Caldwell, 628 Elm Street . . . . . *Surgery*
Archibald Irwin Carson, 46 East McMillan Street . . *Surgery*
Robert Barker Cofield, 19 West 7th Street . *Orthopedic Surgery*
Alfred Peters Cole . . . . *Genito-Urinary Surgery*
Carleton Graves Crisler, Groton Building . . . . . *Surgery*
Frank Bradley Cross, Livingston Building . . *Ophthalmology*
William McDowell Doughty, 628 Elm Street . . . *Surgery*
Frank Edgar Fee, 22 West 7th Street . . . . . . *Surgery*
Howard P. Fishbach, 1201 Traction Building . . . *Gynecology*
Thomas V. Fitzpatrick, 19 West 7th Street . . *Oto-Laryngology*
Albert Henry Freiberg, 7th and Race Streets . *Orthopedic Surgery*
William Gillespie, 670 June Street . . . . *Obstetrics*
Walter Richard Griess, 19 West 7th Street . . . . *Surgery*
W. D. Haines, 1606 Freeman Avenue . . . . . . *Surgery*
Joseph Arda Hall, 628 Elm Street . . . . *Surgery*
Rufus Bartlett Hall, 628 Elm Street . . . . . . *Surgery*
R. C. Heflebower, 22 West 7th Street . . . . *Ophth., Otology*
Carl R. Hiller, 19 West 7th Street . . . . *Surgery*
Harry Hayes Hines, 21 Groton Building . . . . . *Surgery*
Gustav A. Hinnen, 4 West 7th Street . . *Ophth., Rhinol., Otology*
Samuel Iglauer, 7th and Race Streets . *Rhinol., Oto-Laryngology*
Louis J. Krouse, 75 Groton Building . . . . . *Proctology*

OHIO — Continued

CINCINNATI — Continued

Frederick W. Lamb, 209 Provident Bank Building
Ophth., Rhinol., Oto-Laryngology
Charles Andrew Langdale, Union Central Life Building . *Surgery*
Inez Lapsley, 628 Elm Street . . . . *Surgery*
Gordon F. McKim, Union Central Life Building
Genito-Urinary Surgery
John D. Miller, 204 West 8th Street . . . . . *Gynecology*
William Mithoefer, 19 West 7th Street . . . *Oto-Laryngology*
John Wesley Murphy, Union Central Life Building
Ophth., Rhinol., Oto-Laryngology
John Chadwick Oliver, 628 Elm Street . . . . . *Surgery*
Henry Page, Cincinnati General Hospital . . . . *Surgery*
Dudley White Palmer, 707 Race Street . . . . . *Surgery*
Frank Douglas Phinney, 22 West 7th Street
Ophth., Rhinol., Oto-Laryngology
J. Edward Pirrung, 1218 Walnut Street . . . . . *Surgery*
J. Louis Ransohoff, Livingston Building . . . . . *Surgery*
Augustus Ravogli, 5 Garfield Place . . . . . . *Urology*
Charles A. L. Reed, 5 West 8th Street . . . . *Gynecology*
Goodrich Barbour Rhodes, 4th and Sycamore Streets . *Surgery*
Benjamin Merrill Ricketts, 4th Avenue and Broadway . *Surgery*
Robert Sattler, Groton Building . . . . . *Ophthalmology*
W. Edwards Schenck, 19 West 7th Street *Ophth., Oto-Laryngology*
E. O. Smith, 19 West 7th Street . . . *Genito-Urinary Surgery*
Charles Thaddeus Souther, Groton Building . . . . *Surgery*
Sigmar Stark, 11½ East 8th Street . . . . . *Gynecology*
Edgar C. Steinharter, 7th and Vine Streets . . . *Gynecology*
Thomas Milton Stewart, 901 Union Trust Building
Ophth., Rhinol., Oto-Laryngology
Frank U. Swing, Groton Building *Ophth., Rhinol., Oto-Laryngology*
Magnus Alfred Tate, 19 West 7th Street . *Gynecology, Obstetrics*
Allen B. Thrasher, 7th and Race Streets . . . . *Laryngology*
Derrick T. Vail, 24 East 8th Street . . . . *Ophthalmology*
Edward Wood Walker, 214 West 7th Street . . . . *Surgery*
Charles E. Walton, 8th and John Streets . . . . *Gynecology*
H. H. Wiggers, 410 Mercantile Library Building . . *Gynecology*
John Henry Wilms, 12 West 7th Street . . . . . *Surgery*
John Murphy Withrow, 22 West 7th Street . . . *Gynecology*

OHIO — Continued

CINCINNATI — Continued

E. Gustav Zinke, 4 West 7th Street . . *Gynecology, Obstetrics*
Stanley Gustav Zinke, 4 West 7th Street . . . . . *Surgery*

CLEVELAND

Henry A. Becker, 629 Guardian Building . . . . . *Surgery*
Hamilton Fisk Biggar, 1110 Euclid Avenue . . . . *Retired*
Arthur Holbrook Bill, 503 Osborn Building . . . *Obstetrics*
Russell H. Birge, 2417 Prospect Avenue . . . . . *Surgery*
M. Emmett Blahd, 301 Anisfield Building . . . . *Surgery*
Charles A. Bowers, 10553 Euclid Avenue . . . . . *Surgery*
Charles Edwin Briggs, 207 Osborn Building . . . . *Surgery*
William Evans Bruner, Guardian Building . . *Ophthalmology*
J. L. Bubis, 1725 East 82nd Street . . . *Obstetrics, Gynecology*
Frank E. Bunts, Clinic Building . . . . *Surgery*
W. B. Chamberlin, Osborn Building . *Rhinol., Oto-Laryngology*
James E. Cogan, Rose Building *Ophth., Rhinol., Oto-Laryngology*
Francis Patrick Corrigan, 1110 Euclid Avenue . . . *Surgery*
Ernest Harper Cox, 407 Osborn Building . . . . . *Surgery*
George W. Crile, Clinic Building . . . . *Surgery*
Franklin E. Cutler, Schofield Building . *Rhinol., Oto-Laryngology*
John Dickenson, 1021 Prospect Avenue . . . . . *Surgery*
G. Bourne Farnsworth, 1021 Prospect Avenue . . . *Obstetrics*
G. E. Follansbee, 614 Guardian Building . . . . . *Surgery*
Herbert Loring Frost, 1005 Rose Building . . . . *Surgery*
William D. Fullerton, 465 Rose Building . *Gynecology, Obstetrics*
Frank J. Gallagher, Schofield Building . . . . . *Surgery*
John V. Gallagher, 11448 Euclid Avenue . . . . . *Surgery*
C. Lee Graber, 15701 Detroit Avenue . . . . . . *Surgery*
Allen Graham, 939 East 152nd Street . . . . . . *Surgery*
Charles A. Hall, 1021 Prospect Avenue . . . . . *Surgery*
Carl A. Hamann, 416 Osborn Building . . . . . *Surgery*
Benjamin I. Harrison, Cleveland Clinic . . . . . *Surgery*
Frederick C. Herrick, 465 Rose Building . . . . . *Surgery*
Adolph Ernest Ibershoff, 2366 Stillman Road
                    Ophth., Rhinol., Oto-Laryngology
John M. Ingersoll, 1021 Prospect Avenue *Rhinol., Oto-Laryngology*
Nathaniel M. Jones, 815 Guardian Building . . . . *Surgery*
Samuel Walter Kelley, 2255 East 55th Street . . *Surgery*
Benjamin Bruce Kimmel, 206 Penn Square Building . *Surgery*

OHIO — Continued

CLEVELAND — Continued

Secord H. Large, 536 Rose Building . *Rhinol., Oto-Laryngology*
Edward Lauder, 1020 Huron Road . . . . *Ophthalmology*
Carl H. Lenhart, 2417 Prospect Avenue . . . . . *Surgery*
John N. Lenker, 314 Osborn Building . *Rhinol., Oto-Laryngology*
Francis George Leonard, 9300 Kinsman Road . . . *Surgery*
George H. Lewis, 2073 East 9th Street . . . . . *Surgery*
William E. Lower, Clinic Building . . . . *Surgery*
Myron Metzenbaum, Rose Building . *Rhinol., Oto-Laryngology*
Theodore Miller, 1836 Euclid Avenue . . . . . . *Obstetrics*
Edward P. Monaghan, 10308 Euclid Avenue . . . . *Surgery*
Gordon Niles Morrill, 1021 Prospect Avenue . *Orthopedic Surgery*
Edward P. Neary, Savoy Theatre Building . . . . *Surgery*
Frank Oakley, 432 Anisfield Building . . . . . . *Urology*
Edward Peterka, 5026 Broadway . . . . . . *Surgery*
William H. Phillips, 1018 Rose Building
Ophth., Rhinol., Oto-Laryngology
Lawrence A. Pomeroy, 2073 East 9th Street . . . . *Surgery*
George H. Quay, Sr., Rose Building . *Rhinol., Oto-Laryngology*
Carl H. Rust, Rose Building . . . *Rhinol., Oto-Laryngology*
Edwin G. Rust, 1158 Hanna Building . . . . *Ophthalmology*
Henry L. Sanford, 1110 Euclid Avenue . *Genito-Urinary Surgery*
Henry A. Schlink, 10208 Euclid Avenue . . . . . *Surgery*
N. Stone Scott, 10111 Euclid Avenue . . . . . *Gynecology*
Thomas Pollock Shupe, 93rd Street and Euclid Avenue
Genito-Urinary Surgery
Arthur J. Skeel, 1834 East 65th Street . . . . . *Obstetrics*
Harry Gordon Sloan, Clinic Building . . . . . . *Surgery*
Albert F. Spurney, 403 Osborn Building . . . . *Gynecology*
Anton B. Spurney, 403 Osborn Building . . . . . *Surgery*
Morris D. Stepp, 2403 Payne Avenue . . . . . . *Surgery*
Walter G. Stern, 821 Schofield Building . . *Orthopedic Surgery*
Jacob Edward Tuckerman, 733 Osborn Building . . . *Surgery*
Warner H. Tuckerman, 733 Osborn Building
Rhinol., Oto-Laryngology
William C. Tuckerman, 733 Osborn Building . . *Ophthalmology*
George Dwight Upson, 841 Hanna Building . . . . *Surgery*
Justin M. Waugh, Clinic Building . . *Rhinol., Oto-Laryngology*
Oliver A. Weber, 1021 Prospect Avenue . . . . . *Surgery*

OHIO — Continued

CLEVELAND — Continued

William Hawksley Weir, 1021 Prospect Avenue . . *Gynecology*
James Craven Wood, 816 Rose Building . . . . *Gynecology*

COLUMBUS

Hugh A. Baldwin, 347 East State Street . *Genito-Urinary Surgery*
James Fairchild Baldwin, 115 South Grant Avenue . . *Surgery*
H. G. Beatty, 327 East State Street . *Rhinol., Oto-Laryngology*
Leslie Lawson Bigelow, 185 East State Street . . . *Surgery*
Evan Coleman Brock, Hawkes Hospital of Mt. Carmel . *Surgery*
John Edwin Brown, 370 East Town Street *Ophth., Oto-Laryngology*
Claude A. Burrett, 1948 Iuka Avenue . . . . . . *Surgery*
André Crotti, 151 East Broad Street . . . . . . *Surgery*
William C. Davis, 350 East State Street
		Ophth., Rhinol., Oto-Laryngology
Verne Adams Dodd, 394 East Town Street . . . . *Surgery*
Robert Blee Drury, 283 East State Street . . . . *Surgery*
Uriah K. Essington, 289 East State Street . . . . *Surgery*
Judson A. Ferree, 232 East 16th Avenue
		Ophth., Rhinol., Oto-Laryngology
Fred Fletcher, 283 East State Street . . . . . . *Surgery*
Edgar Martin Freese, 322 East State Street . . . *Surgery*
Sylvester Jacob Goodman, 121 South 6th Street . . *Gynecology*
Charles Sumner Hamilton, 188 East State Street . . *Surgery*
William Drake Hamilton, East Broad Street and Columbia
	Avenue . . . . *Surgery*
Arthur M. Hauer, 327 East State Street
		Ophth., Rhinol., Oto-Laryngology
Conrade Alleyne Howell, 206 East State Street . . . *Surgery*
Carl DaCosta Hoy, McKinley Hospital . . . . . *Surgery*
W. A. Humphrey, 1674 North High Street . . . *Gynecology*
Florus Fremont Lawrence, 664 North Park Street . . *Surgery*
Charles S. Means, 137 East State Street
		Ophth., Rhinol., Oto-Laryngology
Joseph Price, 1452 South High Street . . . . . . *Surgery*
George C. Schaeffer, 246 East State Street
		Ophth., Rhinol., Oto-Laryngology
Cassius M. Shepard, 347 East State Street . *Orthopedic Surgery*
Alexander M. Steinfeld, 129 South Grant Avenue
		Orthopedic Surgery

OHIO — Continued

COLUMBUS — Continued

Gustavus A. Sulzer, 200 East State Street . . *Ophthalmology*
Wells Teachnor, 187 East State Street . . . . *Proctology*
Andrew Timberman, 525 Citizens Bank Building
Ophth., Rhinol., Oto-Laryngology
Frank Warner, 10 West Goodale Street . . . . . *Surgery*
Starling S. Wilcox, 340 East State Street . *Genito-Urinary Surgery*
Albertus C. Wolfe, 350 East State Street *Rhinol., Oto-Laryngology*

DAYTON

Elmer R. Arn, 1120 Fidelity Medical Building . . . *Surgery*
Frederick S. Baron, 740 Fidelity Medical Building
Ophth., Oto-Laryngology
L. G. Bowers, 1120 Fidelity Medical Building . . . *Surgery*
Howard Victor Dutrow, 1040 Fidelity Building
Ophth., Rhinol., Oto-Laryngology
George B. Evans, 17 South Wilkinson Street . *Urology, Proctology*
William A. Ewing, 810 Fidelity Medical Building . . *Surgery*
Curtiss Ginn, Reibold Building . . . . . . *Surgery*
George Goodhue, 133 North Perry Street . . . . . *Surgery*
Harry B. Harris, 1110 Fidelity Medical Building
Ophth., Rhinol., Oto-Laryngology
James A. Mattison, National Military Home Hospital . *Surgery*
John W. Millette, 58 Cambridge Avenue
Ophth., Rhinol., Oto-Laryngology

DOVER

Daniel W. Shumaker, 200 West 3rd Street . . . . *Surgery*

EAST LIVERPOOL

Wilbert A. Hobbs, 125 West 5th Street . . . . . *Surgery*

ELYRIA

George Gill, 800 Lorain County Bank Building
Ophth., Rhinol., Oto-Laryngology

FINDLAY

J. C. Tritch, American National Bank Building . . *Gynecology*

GALLIPOLIS

Charles E. Holzer, 1st Avenue and Cedar Street . . . *Surgery*

GREENFIELD

Robert J. Jones, 433 West Jefferson Street . . . . *Surgery*

OHIO — Continued

HAMILTON
    Francis M. Fitton, 144 North 3rd Street . . . . . *Surgery*
    Louis Henry Frechtling, 129 North 2nd Street . . . *Surgery*
    Mark Millikin, 311 South 2nd Street . . . . . . *Surgery*

HILLSBORO
    John Charles Larkin, 130 East Main Street . . . . *Surgery*

IRONTON
    Dan Feurt Gray, 321 South 5th Street . . . . . *Surgery*

KENTON
    Austin S. McKitrick, 115 North Detroit Street . . . *Surgery*

LIMA
    William Roush, 499 North Jameson Avenue . . . . *Surgery*

LORAIN
    W. E. Wheatley, 424 Broadway . . . . *Surgery*

MANSFIELD
    Charles Gailey Brown, 190 Park Avenue, West . . . *Surgery*
    Jerry M. Garber, 48 Park Avenue, West
                                Ophth., Rhinol., Oto-Laryngology
    John Hammel Nichols, 58 Park Avenue, West . . . *Surgery*
    John Lewis Stevens, 59 North Mulberry Street . . . *Surgery*

MARIETTA
    Arthur Howard Smith, 3rd and Putnam Streets . . . *Surgery*

MARION
    Auguste Rhu, 187 West Center Street . . . . . . *Surgery*

MASSILLON
    Logan B. Zintsmaster, 212 McClymonds Building . . *Surgery*

PORT CLINTON
    Henry Jacob Pool, 125 East 3rd Street . . . . . *Surgery*

PORTSMOUTH
    Daniel Albert Berndt, 1304 Gallia Avenue . . . . *Surgery*
    James William Fitch, 1021 9th Street . . . . . . *Surgery*
    Stephen S. Halderman, 826 Gay Street . . . . . *Surgery*
    Joseph S. Rardin, Gallia Avenue and Waller Street . . *Surgery*
    Harry A. Schirrman, 805 Chillicothe Street . . . . *Surgery*

SALEM
    Henry Klar Yaggi, Main Street and Broadway . . . *Surgery*

OHIO — Continued

SANDUSKY

Chester B. Bliss, 409 Columbus Avenue   *Ophth., Oto-Laryngology*

Charles Graefe, 631 Wayne Street.   .   .   .   .   .   .   *Surgery*

SIDNEY

Henry E. Beebe, 124 North Ohio Avenue .   .   .   .   *Surgery*

SPRINGFIELD

Charles L. Minor, 726 Fairbanks Building   .   .   *Ophth., Otology*

Robert C. Rind, Bushnell Building   .   .   .   .   .   *Surgery*

ST. MARYS

Harry S. Noble, 317 West Spring Street   .   .   .   .   *Surgery*

TIFFIN

Edwards H. Porter, 85 Madison Street

                Ophth., Rhinol., Oto-Laryngology

TOLEDO

William W. Alderdyce, 513 Madison Avenue

                Ophth., Rhinol., Oto-Laryngology

F. W. Alter, 314 Colton Building   *Ophth., Rhinol., Oto-Laryngology*

Pern J. Bidwell, Schmidt Building .   .   .   .   .   .   *Surgery*

George Bertram Booth, 506 Adams Street   .   .   .   *Surgery*

Walter William Brand, 316 Colton Building .   .   *Obstetrics*

Lyman A. Brewer, 115 Nasby Building   .   .   .   *Surgery*

Burt George Chollett, 421 Michigan Street   .   *Orthopedic Surgery*

Thomas M. Crinnion, 635 Oak Street .   .   .   .   .   *Surgery*

Ira O. Denman, Ohio Building   .   *Ophth., Rhinol., Oto-Laryngology*

William Gordon Dice, 240 Michigan Street   .   .   .   *Obstetrics*

Fred Melvin Douglass, 421 Michigan Street .   .   .   *Surgery*

William H. Fisher, 416 Colton Building   .   .   .   .   *Surgery*

Sidney Dix Foster, Colton Building   .   .   .   .   *Surgery*

John P. Gardiner, Colton Building .   .   .   .   .   *Obstetrics*

William J. Gillette, 1613 Jefferson Street .   .   *.   .   *Surgery*

C. M. Harpster, Wedgewood Building .   .   *Surgery, Urology*

Homer H. Heath, 656 Spitzer Building   .   .   .   .   *Surgery*

Frank Jacobi, 416 Colton Building .   .   .   *Ophth., Rhinology*

John G. Keller, 326 Ohio Building .   .   *Genito-Urinary Surgery*

Otto Landman, 230 Michigan Street   .   .   .   *Ophthalmology*

Charles Lukens, 218 Michigan Street .   .   *Ophth., Rhinol., Otology*

Charles W. Moots, 225 Michigan Street   .   .   .   *Gynecology*

Clarence D. Selby, 659 Spitzer Building   .   .   .   *Surgery*

OHIO — Continued

TOLEDO — Continued

Lewis F. Smead, 227 Michigan Street . . . . . . *Surgery*
Walter H. Snyder, 211 Ontario Street. *Ophth., Rhinol., Oto-Laryngology*
George Metzger Todd, 216 Colton Building . . . . *Surgery*
Robert S. Walker, 503 Nicholas Building . *Genito-Urinary Surgery*

WARREN

Delbert E. Hoover, 27 Monroe Street . . . . . . *Surgery*
Orville Titus Manley, Second National Bank Building . *Surgery*

WOOSTER

Harry J. Stoll, 229 North Market Street . . . . . *Surgery*

XENIA

Benjamin Rush McClellan, 7 East 2nd Street . . . *Surgery*

YOUNGSTOWN

Carlos Charles Booth, 232 North Phelps Street . . . *Surgery*
Warren Deweese Coy, 608 Market Street . . . . . *Surgery*
Robert D. Gibson, 310 Wick Avenue
Ophth., Rhinol., Oto-Laryngology
Sol. M. Hartzell, Dollar Savings and Trust Company
Building . . . . . . *Ophth., Rhinol., Oto-Laryngology*
Charles D. Hauser, 138 West Rayen Avenue . . . . *Surgery*
Maurice P. Jones, 419 Home Savings and Loan Building *Surgery*
William Eugene Ranz, Federal Building . . . . . *Surgery*
James A. Sherbondy, 415 Bryson Street . . . . . *Surgery*
Walter B. Turner, 300 North Phelps Street . . . . *Surgery*
John Lewis Washburn, 611 Home Savings and Loan
Building . . . . . . *Ophth., Rhinol., Oto-Laryngology*
Raymond E. Whelan, 201 Dollar Savings and Trust
Company Building . . . . *Surgery*

ZANESVILLE

Edmund C. Brush, 601 Market Street . . . . . *Surgery*
Henry Thomas Sutton, 38 South 6th Street . . . . *Surgery*

OKLAHOMA

ARDMORE

Walter Hardy, 212 1st Avenue, S. W. . . . . . . *Surgery*

CLINTON

Victor Maurice Gore, 520 Terrace Avenue . . . . *Surgery*
McLain Rogers . . . . *Surgery*

OKLAHOMA — Continued

EL RENO

Thomas Maze Aderhold, 405 South Williams Street . . *Surgery*

LAWTON

David A. Myers . . . . *Surgery*

MUSKOGEE

William D. Berry, Barnes Building . . . . . . *Surgery*

Francis Bartow Fite, 103½ North 2nd Street . . . *Surgery*

OKLAHOMA

Abraham L. Blesh, 308 Patterson Building . . . . *Surgery*

L. Haynes Buxton, 203 American National Bank
Building . . . . *Ophth., Oto-Laryngology*

Fred Herbert Clark, 308 Continental Building . . . *Surgery*

Edward Francis Davis, 343 American National Bank
Building . . . . . *Ophth., Rhinol., Oto-Laryngology*

William E. Dicken, 518 First National Bank Building . *Surgery*

W. Eugene Dixon, 706 State National Bank Building
Ophth., Rhinol., Oto-Laryngology

Edmund Sheppard Ferguson, 609 State National
Bank Building . . . . . *Ophth., Rhinol., Oto-Laryngology*

William Alonzo Fowler, 534 Liberty National Bank
Building . . . . *Obstetrics*

John S. Hartford, 411 First National Bank Building *Gynecology*

Robert M. Howard, 502 State National Bank Building . *Surgery*

William J. Jolly, Liberty National Bank Building . . *Surgery*

John Frederick Kuhn, 619 First National Bank
Building . . . . *Surgery*

LeRoy Long, Colcord Building . . . . *Surgery*

Dolph D. McHenry, Colcord Building
Ophth., Rhinol., Oto-Laryngology

Horace Reed, 611 First National Bank Building . . . *Surgery*

John William Riley, 119 West 5th Street . . . . . *Surgery*

Millington Smith, 318 Colcord Building . . . . . *Surgery*

H. C. Todd, 507 Colcord Building *Ophth., Rhinol., Oto-Laryngology*

William J. Wallace, 3 Shops Building . . . . . . *Urology*

Curt Otto von Wedel, Jr., American National Bank
Building . . . . *Surgery*

OKMULGEE

Virgil Berry, 5th and Okmulgee Streets . . . . . *Retired*

OKLAHOMA — Continued

SHAWNEE

Frank Leroy Carson, 14 East 9th Street . . . . . . *Surgery*

TULSA

Fred S. Clinton, New World Building . . . . . . *Surgery*
W. Albert Cook, 506 Palace Building . . . . *Ophthalmology*
Fred Yohn Cronk, 302 Daniel Building . . . . . *Surgery*
George Robert Osborn, 302 R. T. Daniel Building
Obstetrics, Gynecology
A. W. Roth, 303 Palace Building   *Ophth., Rhinol., Oto-Laryngology*
Ralph Vernon Smith, 502 Daniel Building . . . . *Surgery*

OREGON

ASHLAND

Francis Gustavus Swedenburg, 299 Main Street   *Surgery, Obstetrics*

ASTORIA

Jacob A. Fulton, 309 Astoria Savings Bank Building . *Surgery*

EUGENE

Floyd M. Day, Brown Building . . . . *Surgery*

MARSHFIELD

George E. Dix . . . . *Surgery*

MEDFORD

E. Barton Pickel, Main Street and Central Avenue . . *Surgery*

OREGON CITY

Hugh Stevens Mount, Weinhard Building
Ophth., Rhinol., Oto-Laryngology

PENDLETON

Frank E. Boyden, Smith-Crawford Building . . . . *Surgery*

PORTLAND

George Ainslie, Oregonian Building
Ophth., Rhinol., Oto-Laryngology
O. Miller Babbitt, 1001 Journal Building
Ophth., Rhinol., Oto-Laryngology
Augustus B. Bailey, 1008 Selling Building
Ophth., Rhinol., Oto-Laryngology
Alvin W. Baird, Medical Building . . . . . . *Surgery*
William Lee Bishop, 415 Stevens Building . . . . *Surgery*
Charles Delos Bodine, 285 Fargo Street . . . . . *Surgery*

OREGON — Continued

PORTLAND — Continued

Gustave E. Bruère, Journal Building
Ophth., Rhinol., Oto-Laryngology
Albert Hadley Cantril, 285 Fargo Street . . . . . *Surgery*
Robert C. Coffey, 789 Glisan Street . . . . . . *Surgery*
John Nicholas Coghlan, Selling Building
Ophth., Rhinol., Oto-Laryngology
E. DeWitt Connell, Selling Building
Ophth., Rhinol., Oto-Laryngology
John Forest Dickson, Selling Building
Ophth., Rhinol., Oto-Laryngology
Robert Hale Ellis, 1011 Corbett Building . *Gynecology, Obstetrics*
J. Earl Else, 709 Stevens Building . . . . . . *Surgery*
Marshall K. Hall, Corbett Building . . . . . *Surgery*
L. H. Hamilton, Journal Building . . . . . . *Surgery*
William B. Holden, 1002 Stevens Building . . . . *Surgery*
Henry Clarke Jefferds, 902 Stevens Building . . . . *Surgery*
Arthur Henry Johnson, 310 Medical Building . . . *Surgery*
Wilson Johnston, Stevens Building *Ophth., Rhinol., Oto-Laryngology*
Frederick A. Kiehle, Corbett Building . *Ophth., Oto-Laryngology*
F. B. Kistner, 909 Stevens Building . *Rhinol., Oto-Laryngology*
A. E. Mackay, 711 Oregonian Building . *Genito-Urinary Surgery*
Albert L. Mathieu, Selling Building . . . . *Ophthalmology*
Joseph L. McCool, 909 Stevens Building . . . *Ophthalmology*
Edward Bruce McDaniel, 923 Electric Building . . . *Surgery*
Chester C. Moore, 409 Medical Building . . . . . *Surgery*
Karl P. Moran, 1002 Stevens Building . *Genito-Urinary Surgery*
Herbert Strong Nichols, 802 Corbett Building . . . *Surgery*
George Norman Pease, 806 Stevens Building . . . *Surgery*
Joseph A. Pettit, Selling Building . . . . . . *Surgery*
Alpha Eugene Rockey, 508 Stevens Building . . . . *Surgery*
Eugene Watson Rockey, 508 Stevens Building . . . *Surgery*
Paul Rockey, 508 Stevens Building . . . . . . *Surgery*
Stuart Harris Sheldon, 1111 Selling Building *Surgery, Obstetrics*
William Henry Skene, Stevens Building . . . . . *Surgery*
Andrew C. Smith, 409 Medical Building . . . . . *Surgery*
Charles J. Smith, 707 Broadway Building . . . . *Gynecology*
Ernst A. Sommer, 908 Electric Building . . . . . *Surgery*
Ernest Fanning Tucker, Medical Building . . . . *Surgery*

OREGON — Continued

PORTLAND — Continued

George S. Whiteside, Journal Building .   .   *Genito-Urinary Surgery*

Sherman E. Wright, 822 Corbett Building

Ophth., Rhinol., Oto-Laryngology

SALEM

W. H. Byrd, State and High Streets .   .   .   .   .   .   *Surgery*

Willis Bent Morse, 406 State Street   .   .   .   .   .   .   *Surgery*

Charles H. Robertson, 406 State Street .   .   .   .   *Gynecology*

WILSONVILLE

Peter H. Jobse .   .   .   .   *Retired*

PENNSYLVANIA

ALLENTOWN

Edward W. Feldhoff, 1224 Turner Street .   .   .   .   .   *Surgery*

W. A. Hausman, Jr., 1116 Hamilton Street .   .   .   .   *Surgery*

Henry Dowling Jordan, 544 North 6th Street   .   .   .   *Surgery*

Charles D. Schaeffer, 28 North 8th Street .   .   .   .   *Surgery*

Robert L. Schaeffer, 30 North 8th Street .   .   .   .   .   *Surgery*

ALTOONA

Joseph Dysart Findley, 1121 13th Avenue   .   .   .   .   *Surgery*

ASHLAND

J. C. Biddle, State Hospital .   .   .   .   *Surgery*

BEAVER

Jefferson H. Wilson, 647 3rd Street   .   .   .   .   .   *Surgery*

BEAVER FALLS

Theodore Parker Simpson, 614 13th Street   .   .   .   .   *Surgery*

BELLEFONTE

Melvin Locke .   .   .   .   *Surgery*

BETHLEHEM

William Lawrence Estes, 805 Delaware Avenue .   .   .   *Surgery*

William L. Estes, Jr., 805 Delaware Avenue .   .   .   .   *Surgery*

William Pomp Walker, 3rd and Cherokee Streets   .   .   *Surgery*

BLOOMSBURG

John W. Bruner, 346 Market Street   .   .   .   .   .   .   *Surgery*

BRADFORD

George E. Benninghoff, 31 West Corydon Street .   .   .   *Surgery*

PENNSYLVANIA — Continued

BUTLER

L. Leo Doane, 558 3rd Street . *Ophth., Rhinol., Oto-Laryngology*
Robert Bruce Greer, 371 North Main Street . . . . *Surgery*

CARLISLE

Robert McMurran Shepler, 49 West Pomfret Street . . *Surgery*

CHESTER

Harry Marshall Armitage, 400 East 13th Street . . . *Surgery*
Richard C. Casselberry, 700 Madison Street . . . . *Surgery*

CLEARFIELD

John Weaver Gordon, 206 Locust Street . *Gynecology, Obstetrics*
Lever Flegal Stewart, 108 North 2nd Street . . . . *Surgery*
Samuel James Waterworth, 102 South 2nd Street . . *Surgery*

CONNELLSVILLE

William J. Bailey, First National Bank Building
Ophth., Oto-Laryngology

DANVILLE

Harold Leighton Foss, Geisinger Memorial Hospital . *Surgery*

DEVON

John Montgomery Baldy . . . . *Gynecology*

DUBOIS

Spencer Michael Free, 101 South Jared Street . . . *Surgery*
John Charles Sullivan, 10 South Main Street . . . . *Surgery*

EAST DOWNINGTOWN

Edward Kerr, 139 East Lancaster Avenue . . . . *Surgery*

EASTON

Henry Daniel Michler, 134 North 3rd Street . . . . *Surgery*
Thomas C. Zulick, 226 Ferry Street . . . . . . *Surgery*

EBENSBURG

Daniel S. Rice . . . . *Surgery*

ERIE

John J. Bell, 661 West 8th Street . . . . *Surgery*
Guy Cluxton Boughton, 810 Peach Street . . . . . *Surgery*
David Nichols Dennis, 221 West 9th Street . . *Ophthalmology*
Harrison A. Dunn, 230 West 8th Street . . . . . *Surgery*
Elmer Hess, 501 Commerce Building . . . . . *Urology*
Augustus Henry Roth, 629 Myrtle Street . . . . . *Surgery*
George W. Schlindwein, 138 West 9th Street
Ophth., Rhinol., Oto-Laryngology

PENNSYLVANIA — Continued

ERIE — Continued

Charles Gunnison Strickland, 153 West 7th Street
Gynecology, Obstetrics
Frank A. Walsh, 128 East 7th Street . . . . . . *Surgery*

GREENSBURG

Thomas Porter Cole, 218 South Pennsylvania Avenue . *Surgery*
John Walker Fairing, 204 Tribune Building
Ophth., Rhinol., Oto-Laryngology

GREENVILLE

Clarence W. McElhaney, 7 Penn Street . . . . . *Surgery*

HARRISBURG

John F. Culp, 240 North 3rd Street . *Rhinol., Oto-Laryngology*
H. Hershey Farnsler, 1438 Market Street
Ophth., Rhinol., Oto-Laryngology
George B. Kunkel, 118 Locust Street . . . . . . *Surgery*
J. W. Park, 32 North 2nd Street *Ophth., Rhinol., Oto-Laryngology*
Charles Stough Rebuck, 412 North 3rd Street
Ophth., Rhinol., Oto-Laryngology
Harvey F. Smith, 130 State Street . . . . *Surgery*

HAZLETON

Walter Lathrop, State Hospital of Middle Coal Field . *Surgery*

HUNTINGDON

Howard C. Frontz, 5th and Mifflin Streets . . . . *Surgery*

JOHNSTOWN

Charles Edmund Hannan, 531 Locust Street . . . . *Surgery*
James Jefferson, 415 Locust Street . . . . *Surgery*
John Bodine Lowman, 116 Market Street . . . . . *Surgery*
George Irving Naylor, 136 Park Place . . . . . . *Surgery*

KANE

Evan O'Neill Kane, 230 Clay Street . . . . . . *Surgery*

LANCASTER

Frank Alleman, 420 West Chestnut Street . . . . *Surgery*
Theodore Burton Appel, 305 North Duke Street . . . *Surgery*
John Light Atlee, 37 East Orange Street . . . . . *Surgery*
Newton Emerson Bitzer, 236 West Chestnut Street . . *Surgery*
C. R. Farmer, 573 West Lemoh Street . . *Surgery, Obstetrics*

LEWISTOWN

John Russell Wightman Hunter, 22 North Main Street . *Surgery*

PENNSYLVANIA — Continued

MEDIA

Charles H. Schoff, 7 West Washington Street   *Surgery, Obstetrics*

OIL CITY

James B. Siggins, 218 Sycamore Street . . . . . . *Surgery*

PATTON

John A. Murray, McGee Avenue . . . . *Surgery*

PHILADELPHIA

Lewis H. Adler, Jr., 1610 Arch Street . . . . . *Proctology*

Emory Graham Alexander, 1701 Spruce Street . . . *Surgery*

George James Alexander, 1831 Chestnut Street
                          Rhinol., Oto-Laryngology

Brooke M. Anspach, 1827 Spruce Street . *Gynecology, Obstetrics*

John Chew Applegate, 3540 North Broad Street . . . *Obstetrics*

Leon Thomas Ashcraft, 2103 Chestnut Street . . . *Urology*

Astley Paston Cooper Ashhurst, 1629 Spruce Street . . *Surgery*

William E. Ashton, 2011 Walnut Street . . . . . *Surgery*

J. A. Babbitt, 1901 Chestnut Street . *Rhinol., Oto-Laryngology*

W. Wayne Babcock, 2033 Walnut Street . . . . . *Surgery*

James Harvey Baldwin, 1426 Pine Street . . . . . *Surgery*

Kate W. Baldwin, 1117 Spruce Street . . . . . . *Surgery*

Moses Behrend, 1427 North Broad Street . . . . *Surgery*

C. Albert Bigler, Jr., 2009 Chestnut Street . . . . *Surgery*

P. Brooke Bland, 1621 Spruce Street . . . . . *Gynecology*

Frank Benton Block, 2035 Chestnut Street . . . . *Surgery*

John A. Boger, 2213 North Broad Street . . . . . *Surgery*

Charles W. Bonney, 1117 Spruce Street . . . . . *Surgery*

John O. Bower, 2033 Walnut Street . . . . . . *Surgery*

George M. Boyd, 1909 Spruce Street . . *Gynecology, Obstetrics*

John Alfred Brooke, 264 South 16th Street . *Orthopedic Surgery*

Henry P. Brown, Jr., 1822 Pine Street . . . . . *Surgery*

Mary Buchanan, 2106 Chestnut Street . . . *Ophthalmology*

Stillwell Corson Burns, 1925 Spring Garden Street . . *Surgery*

Margaret F. Butler, 1831 Chestnut Street *Rhinol., Oto-Laryngology*

Ralph Butler, 1926 Chestnut Street . *Rhinol., Oto-Laryngology*

Harry Stober Carmany, 366 Green Lane . . . . . *Surgery*

John Goodrich Clark, 2017 Walnut Street . . . *Gynecology*

Joseph V. F. Clay, 2102 Chestnut Street
                     Ophth., Rhinol., Oto-Laryngology

George M. Coates, 1811 Spruce Street . *Rhinol., Oto-Laryngology*

PHILADELPHIA — Continued

Lida Stewart Cogill, 1831 Chestnut Street . . . . *Obstetrics*
William D. Culin, 820 North 41st Street . . . . *Gynecology*
John Chalmers Da Costa, 2045 Walnut Street . . . *Surgery*
Arthur J. Davidson, 200 South 12th Street . *Orthopedic Surgery*
Edward P. Davis, 250 South 21st Street . *Gynecology, Obstetrics*
J. L. Davis, 135 South 18th Street . . *Rhinol., Oto-Laryngology*
Warren B. Davis, 135 South 18th Street *Rhinol., Oto-Laryngology*
Harry C. Deaver, 1701 Spruce Street . . . . . . *Surgery*
John B. Deaver, 1634 Walnut Street . . . . . . *Surgery*
George Morris Dorrance, 2025 Walnut Street . . . *Surgery*
H. A. Duncan, 2615 West Somerset Street *Obstetrics, Gynecology*
Eldridge Lyon Eliason, 330 South 16th Street . . . *Surgery*
John Dean Elliott, 1421 Spruce Street . . . . . *Surgery*
Walter G. Elmer, 1801 Pine Street . . . *Orthopedic Surgery*
Theodore A. Erck, 251 South 13th Street . . . . *Gynecology*
Ella B. Everitt, 1807 Spruce Street . . . . . *Gynecology*
Thomas Hanover Fenton, 1319 Spruce Street . *Ophthalmology*
John M. Fisher, 222 South 15th Street . *Obstetrics, Gynecology*
Marie K. Formad, Medical Arts Building . . . . . *Surgery*
Collin Foulkrod, 3910 Chestnut Street . . *Gynecology, Obstetrics*
L. Webster Fox, 303 South 17th Street . . . *Ophthalmology*
Clarence Payne Franklin, 1527 Spruce Street . . *Ophthalmology*
Melvin M. Franklin, 6124 Greene Street . . . . . *Surgery*
Charles Harrison Frazier, 1724 Spruce Street . . . . *Surgery*
John Harper Girvin, 2120 Walnut Street . . . . *Gynecology*
Ellis E. W. Given, 2714 Columbia Avenue . . . . *Surgery*
Herbert Maskell Goddard, 1531 Spruce Street
                                    Rhinol., Oto-Laryngology
Harold G. Goldberg, 1925 Chestnut Street . . *Ophthalmology*
A. Wiese Hammer, 218 South 15th Street . . . . *Surgery*
Frank C. Hammond, 3311 North Broad Street
                                    Gynecology, Obstetrics
Richard H. Harte, 1503 Spruce Street . . . . . . *Surgery*
C. H. Harvey, Corner 63rd and Jefferson Streets . . *Surgery*
Addinell Hewson, 2120 Spruce Street . . . . . . *Surgery*
Barton Cooke Hirst, 1821 Spruce Street . *Gynecology, Obstetrics*
Francois L. Hughes, 1524 Chestnut Street . . . *Gynecology*
William C. Hunsicker, 1625 Race Street . *Genito-Urinary Surgery*

PENNSYLVANIA — Continued

PHILADELPHIA — Continued

Robert Henry Ivy, 1503 Medical Arts Building . . . *Surgery*
Chevalier Jackson, 128 South 10th Street . . . . *Bronchoscopy*
D. Bushrod James, Medical Arts Building . . . *Gynecology*
John E. James, Jr., 118 South 19th Street *Obstetrics, Gynecology*
John F. X. Jones, 103 South 21st Street . . . . . *Surgery*
John Howard Jopson, 1824 Pine Street . . . . . *Surgery*
Joseph C. Keeler, Medical Arts Building . . . *Oto-Laryngology*
Floyd Elwood Keene, Medical Arts Building . . . *Gynecology*
James A. Kelly, 1815 Spruce Street . . . . . . *Surgery*
James W. Kennedy, 241 North 18th Street . . . *Gynecology*
Frederick Krauss, 1703 Chestnut Street
Ophth., Rhinol., Oto-Laryngology
Wilmer Krusen, 127 North 20th Street . . . . *Gynecology*
Nathaniel F. Lane, 1925 Chestnut Street . . . . *Gynecology*
Ernst Laplace, 1828 South Rittenhouse Square . . . *Surgery*
Robert Grier LeConte, 2000 Spruce Street . . . . *Surgery*
Walter Estell Lee, 905 Pine Street . . . . *Surgery*
Herbert P. Leopold, 2104 Chestnut Street . . . . *Surgery*
Fielding O. Lewis, 259 South 17th Street . . . *Oto-Laryngology*
Sarah H. Lockrey, 1701 Chestnut Street . . . . *Gynecology*
Hiram R. Loux, Medical Arts Building . *Genito-Urinary Surgery*
Catharine Macfarlane, 308 Medical Arts Building
Gynecology, Obstetrics
George W. Mackenzie, 1831 Chestnut Street
Ophth., Rhinol., Oto-Laryngology
William H. Mackinney, 1701 Chestnut Street
Genito-Urinary Surgery
Frederick Hurst Maier, 2019 Walnut Street . . . *Gynecology*
George Morley Marshall, 1819 Spruce Street
Rhinol., Oto-Laryngology
Linnaeus E. Marter, 1631 Race Street
Ophth., Rhinol., Oto-Laryngology
Edward Martin, 135 South 18th Street . . . . . *Surgery*
John A. McGlinn, 113 South 20th Street . *Gynecology, Obstetrics*
Warren C. Mercer, 24 South 21st Street . *Gynecology, Obstetrics*
E. E. Montgomery, 1426 Spruce Street . . . . *Gynecology*
George P. Müller, 1930 Spruce Street . . . . . . *Surgery*
Louis Henry Mutschler, 1625 Spruce Street . . . . *Surgery*

PENNSYLVANIA — Continued

PHILADELPHIA — Continued

Charles Francis Nassau, 1710 Locust Street . . . . *Surgery*
Thomas R. Neilson, 1937 Chestnut Street . . . . *Surgery*
Charles C. Norris, 22nd and Chestnut Streets *Gynecology, Obstetrics*
Herbert L. Northrop, 601 Medical Arts Building . . *Surgery*
G. J. Palen, 2102 Chestnut Street . . *Ophth., Oto-Laryngology*
Benjamin Dores Parish, 2039 Chestnut Street
　　　　　　　　　　　　　Rhinol., Oto-Laryngology
William E. Parke, 1739 North 17th Street *Gynecology, Obstetrics*
Elizabeth L. Peck, 4113 Walnut Street . *Gynecology, Obstetrics*
Charles Bingham Penrose, 1720 Spruce Street . . *Gynecology*
Luther C. Peter, 1529 Spruce Street . . . . *Ophthalmology*
Damon Beckett Pfeiffer, 2028 Pine Street . . . . *Surgery*
Edmund B. Piper, 1936 Spruce Street . . *Obstetrics, Gynecology*
Paul J. Pontius, 1831 Chestnut Street . . . . *Ophthalmology*
William Campbell Posey, 2049 Chestnut Street . *Ophthalmology*
Caroline M. Purnell, 132 South 18th Street . . . *Gynecology*
Alexander Randall, 1306 Medical Arts Building . . . *Urology*
John B. Roberts, 313 South 17th Street . . . . . *Surgery*
John Stewart Rodman, 1310 Medical Arts Building . . *Surgery*
Desiderio Roman, 1904 South Rittenhouse Square . . *Surgery*
George G. Ross, 1721 Spruce Street . . . . . *Surgery*
Theodore B. Schneideman, 1831 Chestnut Street *Ophthalmology*
Edward Armin Schumann, 124 South 18th Street
　　　　　　　　　　　　　Gynecology, Obstetrics
George E. de Schweinitz, 1705 Walnut Street . *Ophthalmology*
Peter N. K. Schwenk, 1417 North Broad Street . *Ophthalmology*
Oscar Seeley, 2009 Chestnut Street . *Rhinol., Oto-Laryngology*
Isaac Gray Shallcross, 112 South 20th Street
　　　　　　　　　　Ophth., Rhinol., Oto-Laryngology
George Erety Shoemaker, 1906 Chestnut Street . . *Gynecology*
William T. Shoemaker, 109 South 20th Street . *Ophthalmology*
E. Hollingsworth Siter, 1520 Locust Street *Genito-Urinary Surgery*
Penn-Gaskell Skillern, Jr., 1523 Locust Street . . . *Surgery*
Ross Hall Skillern, 1928 Chestnut Street . . . . *Laryngology*
Fred W. Smith, Medical Arts Building
　　　　　　　　　　Ophth., Rhinol., Oto-Laryngology
S. MacCuen Smith, 1429 Spruce Street . . . *Oto-Laryngology*
John Speese, 2032 Locust Street . . . . . . *Surgery*

PENNSYLVANIA — Continued

PHILADELPHIA — Continued

Nathan P. Stauffer, 1819 Walnut Street . *Rhinol., Oto-Laryngology*

William A. Steel, 3300 North Broad Street . . . . *Surgery*

Deacon Steinmetz, 1425 Spruce Street . . . . . *Surgery*

George Clymer Stout, 1611 Walnut Street . . *Oto-Laryngology*

Joshua Edwin Sweet, 301 St. Mark's Square . . . . *Surgery*

B. A. Thomas, 116 South 19th Street . . *Genito-Urinary Surgery*

Thomas Turner Thomas, 1905 Chestnut Street . . . *Surgery*

Stephen E. Tracy, 1527 Spruce Street . . *Gynecology, Obstetrics*

Gustave A. Van Lennep, 2104 Chestnut Street . . . *Surgery*

Eugene Larue Vansant, 1929 Chestnut Street
Rhinol., Oto-Laryngology

Harry Sands Weaver, 1433 Spruce Street
Ophth., Rhinol., Oto-Laryngology

A. B. Webster, 4821 Baltimore Avenue . . . . . *Surgery*

Alfred C. Wood, 2035 Walnut Street . . . . . *Surgery*

James Kelly Young, 222 South 16th Street . *Orthopedic Surgery*

S. Lewis Ziegler, 1625 Walnut Street . . . . *Ophthalmology*

PHILIPSBURG

William Baird Henderson, 724 Presqueisle Street . . *Surgery*

Charles Edward McGirk, 17 North Front Street . . *Gynecology*

PITTSBURGH

Charles Howard Aufhammer, 5004 Jenkins Arcade
Building . . . . *Surgery*

William M. Beach, 901 Bessemer Building . . . *Proctology*

Richard Joseph Behan, Jenkins Arcade Building . . . *Surgery*

Newman Hall Bennett, 1912 Carson Street . . . . *Surgery*

William W. Blair, 604 Diamond Bank Building . *Ophthalmology*

John J. Buchanan, 1409 North Highland Avenue . . *Surgery*

James C. Burt, Westinghouse Building . *Genito-Urinary Surgery*

William MacFarlane Campbell, 7133 Jenkins Arcade
Building . . . . *Surgery*

Thomas B. Carroll, Jenkins Arcade Building *Gynecology, Obstetrics*

Waid Edwin Carson, 7095 Jenkins Arcade Building *Ophthalmology*

Bender Z. Cashman, 226 South Evaline Street . . . *Surgery*

Sidney A. Chalfant, 7048 Jenkins Arcade Building . *Gynecology*

Glendon E. Curry, Westinghouse Building . . *Ophthalmology*

Nelson P. Davis, 1405 5th Avenue . . . . . . *Surgery*

Ewing W. Day, Westinghouse Building . . . *Oto-Laryngology*

PENNSYLVANIA — Continued

PITTSBURGH — Continued

Harry Ryerson Decker, Jenkins Arcade Building . . *Surgery*
Breese Morse Dickinson, 637 Union Arcade Building
Rhinol., Oto-Laryngology
Holland Hunter Donaldson, Union Arcade Building . *Surgery*
N. Arthur Fischer, 623 Union Arcade Building . *Oto-Laryngology*
Curtis Smiley Foster, 308 Diamond Bank Building . *Gynecology*
Otto C. Gaub, Westinghouse Building . . . . *Surgery*
John Perry Griffith, 4715 5th Avenue . . . . . *Surgery*
Elwood B. Haworth, 145 North Craig Street . . . *Surgery*
George L. Hays, Mercy Hospital . . . . . . *Surgery*
Edward B. Heckel, 719 Jenkins Arcade Building *Ophthalmology*
Raleigh R. Huggins, 1018 Westinghouse Building . *Gynecology*
Charles W. Jennings, 315 Highland Building . . *Ophthalmology*
S. Victor King, Bellefield Dwellings . . . . . *Surgery*
Lyndon H. Landon, 5074 Jenkins Arcade Building . . *Surgery*
William S. Langfitt, St. John's Hospital . . . . *Surgery*
James W. Macfarlane, Westinghouse Building . . . *Surgery*
James C. Markel, 1005 Westinghouse Building . *Ophthalmology*
W. Marshall, 604 Diamond Bank Building *Rhinol., Oto-Laryngology*
Albert R. Matheny, 1105 East End Trust Building . . *Surgery*
J. H. McCready, Empire Building . . *Rhinol., Oto-Laryngology*
Stewart LeRoy McCurdy, 8103 Jenkins Arcade Building
Orthopedic and Oral Surgery
William B. McKenna, Pittsburgh Hospital . . . . *Surgery*
Curtis Campbell Mechling, Jenkins Arcade Building *Proctology*
Evan William Meredith, 5004 Jenkins Arcade Building . *Surgery*
Harold A. Miller, Pittsburgh Life Building . . . . *Obstetrics*
John Davidson Milligan . . . . *Surgery*
Robert Milligan, Sandusky Street and Park Way, N. S.
Oto-Laryngology
Ellis S. Montgomery, 725 Jenkins Arcade Building . *Gynecology*
George Boulton Moreland, 810 Westinghouse Building . *Surgery*
Frederic S. Morris, 810 Westinghouse Building . . . *Surgery*
Ellen J. Patterson, 1018 Westinghouse Building
Rhinol., Oto-Laryngology
C. C. Sandels, Westinghouse Building . *Rhinol., Oto-Laryngology*
Kay I. Sanes, 519 Jenkins Building . . . . . *Gynecology*
William O'Neill Sherman, 434 5th Avenue . . . . *Surgery*

PENNSYLVANIA — Continued

PITTSBURGH — Continued

David Silver, Jenkins Arcade Building . . *Orthopedic Surgery*
Frank Farrow Simpson, Jenkins Arcade Building . *Gynecology*
John D. Singley, 812 North Highland Avenue . . . *Surgery*
Stanley Smith, 613 Jenkins Arcade Building . . *Ophthalmology*
Acheson Stewart, 637 Union Arcade Building . . . *Surgery*
William Alvah Stewart, 918 Westinghouse Building . . *Surgery*
Edward Stieren, Union Arcade Building . . . *Ophthalmology*
G. W. Stimson, Jenkins Arcade Building *Rhinol., Oto-Laryngology*
Lorenzo W. Swope, Park Building . . . . . . *Surgery*
Paul Titus, 1015 Highland Building . . . . . *Obstetrics*
Frank Lester Todd, 130 Bellefield Avenue . *Surgery, Obstetrics*
J. O. Wallace, 7034 Jenkins Arcade Building . *Orthopedic Surgery*
Edith Waldie Way . . . . *Retired*
Edgar Stanley Weimer, 1220 Highland Building . *Ophthalmology*
Edward A. Weiss, 714 Jenkins Arcade Building . . *Gynecology*
Edward A. Weisser, 806 May Building . . . *Ophthalmology*
Charles E. Ziegler, 4716 Bayard Street . *Gynecology, Obstetrics*

POTTSVILLE

G. R. S. Corson, 20 North Centre Street . *Ophth., Oto-Laryngology*

READING

Oscar E. Fox, 232 North 5th Street . . . . . . *Surgery*
John W. Kauffman, 814 North 11th Street *Gynecology, Obstetrics*
George W. Kehl, 313 North 5th Street . . . . . *Surgery*

SAYRE

Donald Guthrie, Robert Packer Hospital . . . . . *Surgery*
George William Hawk, Robert Packer Hospital . . . *Surgery*
Nelson S. Weinberger . . . . *Ophth., Otology*

SCRANTON

John B. Corser, 345 Wyoming Avenue
Ophth., Rhinol., Oto-Laryngology
Gilbert D. Murray, 528 Madison Avenue
Ophth., Rhinol., Oto-Laryngology
Charles B. Noecker, 213 Connell Building . . . . *Surgery*
John Lyman Peck, 524 Vine Street . . . . . . *Surgery*
Jonathan Mayhew Wainwright, 912 Clay Avenue . . *Surgery*
Horace Bacon Ware, Scranton Life Building
Ophth., Rhinol., Oto-Laryngology
Robert V. White, Brooks Building . . . . . . *Surgery*

PENNSYLVANIA — Continued

SHARON
Clifford C. Marshall, 233 East State Street . . . . *Surgery*

WASHINGTON
William J. L. McCullough, Slater Building . . . . *Surgery*
Albert E. Thompson, 625 Washington Trust Building . *Surgery*

WEST CHESTER
J. Oscar Dicks, 28 South High Street . . . . *Surgery*

WILKES-BARRE
Ernest U. Buckman, 70 South Franklin Street
Ophth., Rhinol., Oto-Laryngology
Herbert B. Gibby, 96 South Franklin Street . . . . *Surgery*
Granville T. Matlack, 33 West Northampton Street . *Surgery*
Samuel P. Mengel, 181 South Franklin Street . . . *Surgery*
Walter Scott Stewart, 98 South Franklin Street . . . *Surgery*
L. H. Taylor, 83 South Franklin Street   *Ophth., Oto-Laryngology*

WILKINSBURG
John W. Dixon, 820 Wood Street . . . . *Surgery*

WILLIAMSPORT
Harry J. Donaldson, 106 East 4th Street . . . . . *Surgery*
Albert Frederick Hardt, 414 Pine Street . . . . . *Surgery*
John A. Klump, 331 Elmira Street . . . . *Surgery*
Howard M. Ritter, First National Bank Building
Ophth., Oto-Laryngology

YORK
Edmund W. Meisenhelder, 1253 West Market Street . *Surgery*

RHODE ISLAND

EAST PROVIDENCE
John Bernard McKenna, 47 Taunton Avenue . . . *Surgery*

NEWPORT
Charles W. Stewart, 2 Kay Street . . . . *Surgery*

PROVIDENCE
George Rice Barden, 270 Elmwood Avenue . . . . *Surgery*
Henry J. C. Corrigan, 242 Broadway . . . . . . *Urology*
Fred A. Coughlin, 224 Thayer Street . . . . . . *Surgery*
William Bryant Cutts, 370 Broad Street . . . . . *Surgery*
Murray S. Danforth, 124 Waterman Street . *Orthopedic Surgery*

RHODE ISLAND — Continued

PROVIDENCE — Continued

Vance Lee Fitzgerald, 223 Thayer Street . . . . . *Proctology*
William Francis Flanagan, 379 Benefit Street . . . *Surgery*
George Warren Gardner, 44 Orchard Avenue . . . . *Surgery*
Roland Hammond, 219 Waterman Street . . *Orthopedic Surgery*
Norman Darrell Harvey, 112 Waterman Street
                           Ophth., Rhinol., Oto-Laryngology
Henry Joseph Hoye, 221 Thayer Street . . . . . *Surgery*
Frederic V. Hussey, 171 Angell Street . . . . . . *Surgery*
Arthur Thoms Jones, 131 Waterman Street . . . . *Surgery*
John William Keefe, 262 Blackstone Boulevard . . . *Surgery*
P. H. Keefe, 262 Benefit Street . *Ophth., Rhinol., Oto-Laryngology*
Lucius C. Kingman, 130 Slater Avenue . . . . . *Surgery*
William H. Magill, 221 Thayer Street . . . . . *Gynecology*
George Arnold Matteson, 454 Angell Street . . . . *Surgery*
Frank E. McEvoy, 224 Thayer Street . . . . . . *Surgery*
Andrew Joseph McLaughlin, 677 Broad Street . . *Gynecology*
William C. McLaughlin, 600 Broad Street *Ophth., Oto-Laryngology*
Walter Lee Munro, 62 North Main Street . . . . *Surgery*
Frank Edwin Peckham, 249 Thayer Street . *Orthopedic Surgery*
Herman C. Pitts, 124 Waterman Street . . . . *Gynecology*
Lewis B. Porter, 117 Waterman Street
                           Ophth., Rhinol., Oto-Laryngology
Edgar B. Smith, 76 Waterman Street . . . . . . *Surgery*
Henry Allen Whitmarsh, 167 Angell Street . . . . *Surgery*

WOONSOCKET

John James Baxter, 92 Main Street . . . . . . *Surgery*

SOUTH CAROLINA

CHARLESTON

Charles P. Aimar, 4 Vanderhorst Street . . . . . *Surgery*
Archibald E. Baker, 10 Meeting Street . . . . . *Surgery*
Ernest Cornish Baynard, 86½ Wentworth Street . . *Urology*
A. Johnston Buist, 279 Meeting Street . . . . . *Surgery*
Robert Spann Cathcart, 75 Hasell Street . . . . . *Surgery*
Charles Wilson Kollock, 86 Wentworth Street
                           Ophth., Rhinol., Oto-Laryngology

SOUTH CAROLINA — Continued

CHARLESTON — Continued
  Edward Frost Parker, 70 Hasell Street
                          Ophth., Rhinol., Oto-Laryngology
  J. Sumter Rhame, 81 Wentworth Street . . . . . *Surgery*
  Julius C. Sosnowski, 126 Meeting Street . . . . . *Surgery*

CHESTER
  Chauncey M. Rakestraw, Pryor Hospital . . . . . *Surgery*

COLUMBIA
  George Henry Bunch, 1404 Laurel Street . . . . . *Surgery*
  LeGrand Guerry, 1831 Pendleton Street . . . . . *Surgery*
  Julius Heyward Taylor, 1403 Hampton Street . . . *Surgery*
  Ephraim Mikell Whaley, 1430 Blanding Street
                          Ophth., Rhinol., Oto-Laryngology

FLORENCE
  Frank Hilton McLeod, 1 West Cheves Street . . . *Surgery*

GREENVILLE
  Ernest W. Carpenter, Professional Building
                          Ophth., Rhinol., Oto-Laryngology
  James Walker Curry, 328 North Main Street . . . *Surgery*
  Curran Bertram Earle, Wallace Building . . . . . *Surgery*
  James Wilkinson Jervey, Jervey-Jordan Building
                          Ophth., Rhinol., Oto-Laryngology
  Leland Osgood Mauldin, 502 Petigru Street
                          Ophth., Rhinol., Oto-Laryngology
  Thaddeus Benjamin Reeves, 324 North Main Street . *Surgery*
  George T. Tyler, Jr., 711 East North Street . . . . *Surgery*

ORANGEBURG
  Charles Arden Mobley, 25 West Glover Street . . . *Surgery*

SPARTANBURG
  Hugh R. Black, 509 Allen and Law Building . . . . *Surgery*
  Benjamin B. Steedly, Steedly's Private Hospital . . . *Surgery*

ROCK HILL
  W. W. Fennell . . . . *Surgery*
  William B. Ward, Fennell Infirmary . . . . . . *Surgery*

SOUTH DAKOTA

ABERDEEN

John Francis Adams, 114 South Main Street . . . . *Surgery*

R. D. Alway, 423 South Lincoln Street
Ophth., Rhinol., Oto-Laryngology

William Davidson Farrell, Wells Block . . *Surgery, Obstetrics*

Hiram Irving King . . . . *Surgery*

Charles Edward McCauley, Citizens Bank Building . . *Surgery*

Robert L. Murdy, 1021 South Washington Street . . *Surgery*

Jesse D. Whiteside, 416 Citizens Bank Building . . . *Surgery*

BROOKINGS

Burtis T. Green, Bradbury Building . . . . . . *Surgery*

CHAMBERLAIN

Frederick Treon, Scotts Building . . . . *Surgery*

DEADWOOD

Alfred George Allen, Waite Building . . . . . . *Surgery*

Frank Stewart Howe, Black Hills Bank Building . . *Surgery*

Thomas W. Moffitt, Martin and Mason Block . . . *Surgery*

DELL RAPIDS

Martin Melvin Grove . . . . *Surgery*

FLANDREAU

Frederick Angier Spafford . . . . *Surgery*

HOT SPRINGS

Charles William Hargens, River View Boulevard . . *Surgery*

HURON

Lorenzo Nelson Grosvenor, 378 Dakota Avenue
Ophth., Rhinol., Oto-Laryngology

John C. Shirley, Masonic Temple Building . . . . *Surgery*

LEAD

Francis Edgar Clough, 214 Prospect Avenue . . . . *Surgery*

John W. Freeman, 514 West Main Street . . . . *Surgery*

Arthur S. Jackson, 8 Main Street . . . . *Surgery*

MADISON

Daniel Sparks Baughman, 100 Egan Avenue, South . . *Surgery*

MITCHELL

Byron A. Bobb, 723 West 4th Avenue . . . . . *Surgery*

Edward William Jones, 214 Mitchell Realty Building . *Surgery*

SOUTH DAKOTA — Continued

MOBRIDGE

Granville Howard Twining . . . . *Surgery*

PIERRE

Theodore F. Riggs . . . . *Surgery*

RAPID CITY

George I. Kheiralla . . . . *Surgery*

Frederick Walter Minty, 609 Main Street . . . . *Surgery*

Joseph M. Walsh . . . . *Ophth., Rhinol., Oto-Laryngology*

SIOUX FALLS

Gilbert G. Cottam, 800 Sioux Falls National Bank
Building . . . . *Surgery*

Leslie Grant Hill, 14th Street and Main Avenue
Ophth., Oto-Laryngology

Edwin Lucien Perkins, 301 South Minnesota Avenue
Obstetrics, Gynecology

Edmund D. Putnam, 300 East 21st Street
Ophth., Rhinol., Oto-Laryngology

Frank Israel Putnam, 104 East 20th Street
Ophth., Rhinol., Oto-Laryngology

Roy G. Stevens, Sioux Falls Clinic . . . . *Surgery*

WATERTOWN

Anders Einar Johnson, 317 2nd Street, S. W.
Ophth., Rhinol., Oto-Laryngology

YANKTON

Silas Matthew Hohf, Clinic Building . . . . . . *Surgery*

Frank Conger Smith, 307½ Walnut Street
Ophth., Rhinol., Oto-Laryngology

TENNESSEE

CHATTANOOGA

George Manning Ellis, 515 Volunteer Building . . . . *Surgery*

Hampton Lansden Fancher, James Building . . . . *Surgery*

John Bunyan Haskins, 605 Volunteer Building . . . *Surgery*

Edward Dunbar Newell, Newell and Newell Sanitarium *Surgery*

Edward T. Newell, 707 Walnut Street . . . . . *Surgery*

Raymond Wallace, Hamilton National Bank Building . *Surgery*

George Richard West, 626 Volunteer Building . . *Gynecology*

John S. B. Woolford, 602 Georgia Avenue . . . . *Surgery*

TENNESSEE — Continued

GREENEVILLE

Claude P. Fox, 125 Charles Street   . . . . . .   *Surgery*

JACKSON

Jere Lawrence Crook, 110 West Baltimore Street   . .   *Surgery*

Alexander Brown Dancy, First National Bank Building
Ophth., Oto-Laryngology

KNOXVILLE

Herbert Acuff, 425 West Clinch Avenue   . . . . .   *Surgery*

Victor D. Holloway, 609 Walnut Street   . . . . .   *Surgery*

Albert G. Kern, 607 Walnut Street   . . . . . .   *Surgery*

John H. Kincaid, 421 West Church Avenue
Ophth., Rhinol., Oto-Laryngology

S. R. Miller, 406 West Church Avenue   . . . . .   *Surgery*

MEMPHIS

John Chambers Ayers, 1601 Exchange Building
Obstetrics, Gynecology

William Thomas Black, 620 Exchange Building   . . .   *Surgery*

Julian Baker Blue, 1224 Exchange Building
Ophth., Rhinol., Oto-Laryngology

William Britt Burns, Porter Building . . . . . .   *Surgery*

W. C. Campbell, 869 Madison Avenue   . .   *Orthopedic Surgery*

Joseph A. Crisler, Exchange Building . . . . . .   *Surgery*

Edward C. Ellett, Exchange Building . . . .   *Ophthalmology*

Pope McG. Farrington, 1728 Exchange Building
Rhinol., Oto-Laryngology

Elmer Ellsworth Francis, 1701 Central Bank Building   .   *Surgery*

M. Goltman, Memphis Trust Building   . . . . .   *Surgery*

Frank Graham, 57 North Bellevue Avenue   . . .   *Gynecology*

Louis Wardlaw Haskell, Bank of Commerce Building   .   *Surgery*

David M. Henning, 624 Exchange Building . . . .   *Surgery*

Eugene Michel Holder, Bank of Commerce Building   .   *Surgery*

John L. Jelks, 805 Union and Planters Bank Building
Surgery, Proctology

Louis Levy, Bank of Commerce Building   *Rhinol., Oto-Laryngology*

A. C. Lewis, 1224 Exchange Building   .   *Ophth., Oto-Laryngology*

George R. Livermore, Exchange Building   *Genito-Urinary Surgery*

Battle Malone, Exchange Building   . . . . .   *Surgery*

Robin Ferguson Mason, 200 Bank of Commerce Building   *Surgery*

TENNESSEE — Continued

MEMPHIS — Continued

John M. Maury, 720 Bank of Commerce Building   .   *Gynecology*
Oswald Stuart McCown, Bank of Commerce Building   .   *Urology*
John L. McGehee, 1705 Central Bank Building   .   .   .   *Surgery*
Richmond McKinney, Bank of Commerce Building
                                   Rhinol., Oto-Laryngology
James L. Minor, Bank of Commerce Building   .   *Ophthalmology*
Edward Dana Mitchell, Bank of Commerce Building   .   *Surgery*
Moore Moore, Jr., Bank of Commerce Building   .   .   *Gynecology*
Robert L. Sanders, 702 Goodwyn Institute Building   .   *Surgery*
Raphael Eustace Semmes, 1250 Bank of Commerce
   Building   .   .   .   .   *Surgery*
W. Likely Simpson, 601 Exchange Building
                                   Rhinol., Oto-Laryngology
Frank David Smythe, Exchange Building   .   .   .   .   *Surgery*
James B. Stanford, Exchange Building   *Ophth., Oto-Laryngology*
W. W. Taylor, 1422 Exchange Building   .   *Gynecology, Obstetrics*
Percy W. Toombs, 319 South Dudley Street   *Gynecology, Obstetrics*
James Albert Vaughan, Exchange Building   .   .   .   .   *Surgery*

NASHVILLE

Richard Alexander Barr, 800 19th Avenue, South   .   .   *Surgery*
Perry Bromberg, 510 Jackson Building   .   *Genito-Urinary Surgery*
W. A. Bryan, Doctors Building   .   .   .   .   .   .   *Surgery*
Lucius Edward Burch, Doctors Building   .   .   .   .   *Surgery*
Robert Caldwell, 510 Jackson Building   .   .   .   .   *Surgery*
Eldred B. Cayce, 301 Hitchcock Building   *Ophth., Oto-Laryngology*
Charles N. Cowden, 347 Doctors Building   .   .   .   *Gynecology*
Marvin McTyeire Cullom, 208 Hitchcock Building
                                   Ophth., Oto-Laryngology
William Clarence Dixon, 216 Doctors Building   .   .   .   *Surgery*
Duncan Eve, Eve Building   .   .   .   .   *Surgery*
Duncan Eve, Jr., 7th Avenue and Church Street   .   .   *Surgery*
William O. Floyd, 706 Church Street   .   .   .   .   .   *Surgery*
Rufus E. Fort, 303 7th Avenue, North   .   .   .   .   *Surgery*
Joseph F. Gallagher, 306 Jackson Building   .   .   .   *Surgery*
William D. Haggard, 706 Church Street   .   .   .   .   *Surgery*
James W. Handly, 714 Independent Life Building
                                   Genito-Urinary Surgery

TENNESSEE — Continued

NASHVILLE — Continued

W. M. McCabe, Doctors Building . . . . *Surgery*
Thomas D. McKinney, 304 Doctors Building . . . *Surgery*
Thomas George Pollard, Doctors Building . . . . *Surgery*
Alpheus Leslie Sharber, 301 Jackson Building . . . *Surgery*
Stanley Ross Teachout, 212 Eve Building . . . . *Surgery*
Holland McTyeire Tigert, 142 7th Avenue, North . *Gynecology*
H. Wood, Independent Life Building . . . *Ophth., Laryngology*

TEXAS

AMARILLO

R. S. Killough, 203 Blackburn Building
Ophth., Rhinol., Oto-Laryngology
Abram F. Lumpkin, Smith Building . . . . . . *Surgery*
George T. Thomas, Smith Building . *Ophth., Oto-Laryngology*

AUSTIN

Morris H. Boerner, Scarbrough Building
Ophth., Rhinol., Oto-Laryngology
Joseph Gilbert, 320 Scarbrough Building . . . . . *Surgery*
Sam N. Key, 320 Littlefield Building
Ophth., Rhinol., Oto-Laryngology
John C. Thomas, 326 Littlefield Building . . . . . *Surgery*
Joe Sil Wooten, 107 East 10th Street . . . . . . *Surgery*

BELTON

Ambrose Burdett Crain, 112½ Central Avenue . . . *Surgery*

BROWNWOOD

Luke Pryor Allison, 204½ Center Avenue . . . . *Surgery*

CORSICANA

Isaac Newton Suttle, 216½ North Beaton Street . . *Surgery*

CUERO

John W. Burns . . . . *Surgery*
Guilford M. Duckworth, Buchel Building *Ophth., Oto-Laryngology*

DALLAS

Joseph W. Bourland, 525 Wilson Building . *Surgery, Obstetrics*
Eugene R. Carpenter, Southwestern Life Building . . *Otology*
Edward Henry Cary, Southwestern Life Building
Ophth., Rhinol., Oto-Laryngology

TEXAS — Continued

DALLAS — Continued

Wilson Thompson Davidson, 403 Municipal Building . *Surgery*
Henry B. Decherd, 3708 Rawlins Street
　　　　　　　　　　　Ophth., Rhinol., Oto-Laryngology
Harold Medoris Doolittle, 4105 Live Oak Street . . . *Surgery*
Elbert Dunlap, 304 Southwestern Life Building . . *Gynecology*
Charles Watts Flynn, 704 Wilson Building . . . . *Surgery*
Garfield McCoy Hackler, 303 Southwestern Life
　Building . . . . *Surgery*
Mark E. Lott, 414 Wilson Building . . . . . . *Surgery*
J. O. McReynolds, Dallas County State Bank
　Building . . . . *Ophth., Rhinol., Oto-Laryngology*
Samuel Edwin Milliken, Westminster Building . . . *Surgery*
Lee M. Nance, 305 Southwestern Life Building . . *Gynecology*
Edwin J. Reeves, 3614 Lemmon Avenue . . . . . *Retired*
Joseph A. Robertson, 918 Dallas County State Bank
　Building . . . . *Surgery*
Charles M. Rosser, 4002 Gaston Avenue . . . . . *Surgery*
Jesse Bedford Shelmire, Southwestern Life Building . . *Surgery*
William W. Shortal, Linz Building . . . . . . *Surgery*
Andrew B. Small, 4942 Live Oak Street . . . . . *Surgery*
John B. Smoot, 523 Wilson Building . . . . . . *Surgery*
Sam Webb, Jr., 3712 Alice Circle . . . . *Orthopedic Surgery*
Robert Sherod Yancey, 422 Wilson Building
　　　　　　　　　　　Ophth., Rhinol., Oto-Laryngology

DENTON

James M. Inge, Inge Building . . . . *Surgery*

ELECTRA

Ralph E. Weller . . . . *Surgery*

EL PASO

W. Launcelot Brown, 404 Roberts-Banner Building . . *Surgery*
Hugh W. Crouse, 504 Roberts-Banner Building . . . *Surgery*
Felix Perryman Miller, 514 Martin Building . . . . *Surgery*
Robert Lee Ramey, 509 Two Republics Building . . *Surgery*
Harry Hinkle Stark, 301 Roberts-Banner Building
　　　　　　　　　　　Ophth., Rhinol., Oto-Laryngology
James Vance, 314 Mills Building . . . . *Surgery*
Louis G. Witherspoon, 314 Roberts-Banner Building . *Surgery*

TEXAS — Continued

ENNIS

Jacob Edward Gilcreest, Baylor Street . . . . . *Gynecology*

FORT WORTH

Frank Cooke Beall, 703 Lamar Street . . . . . . *Surgery*

Frank Douglas Boyd, F. and M. National Bank
Building . . . . *Ophth., Rhinol., Oto-Laryngology*

Ira Carleton Chase, Texas State Bank Building . . . *Surgery*

Alden Coffey, Moore Building . . . . *Surgery*

William A. Duringer, 205 Fort Worth Club Building . *Surgery*

William C. Duringer, 205 Fort Worth Club Building . *Surgery*

Charles Houston Harris, 1028 5th Avenue . . . . *Surgery*

Clay Johnson, 6th and Lamar Streets . . . . . . *Surgery*

John H. McLean, Fort Worth Club Building . . . *Gynecology*

Bacon Saunders, 704 Flatiron Building . . . . . *Surgery*

Roy F. Saunders, 704 Flatiron Building . . . . . *Surgery*

William Robert Thompson, Fort Worth National Bank
Building . . . . *Ophth., Rhinol., Oto-Laryngology*

Samuel A. Woodward, 406 Flatiron Building . . . *Gynecology*

GALVESTON

William Gammon, Tremont Hotel . . . . *Surgery*

G. H. Lee, American National Insurance Building . *Gynecology*

Seth M. Morris, American National Insurance Building
Ophth., Otology

Albert Olin Singleton, American National Insurance
Building . . . . *Surgery*

James Edwin Thompson, 3224 Broadway . . . . . *Surgery*

GREENVILLE

Joseph Daniel Becton . . . . *Surgery*

HOUSTON

Charles Marion Aves, Humble Oil and Refining Company
Building . . . . *Surgery*

Frank L. Barnes, 1408 Rosalie Avenue . . . . . *Surgery*

Ernst William Bertner, 411 Carter Building . . . . *Surgery*

Belle Constant Eskridge, 902 Dallas Avenue . . . . *Surgery*

John H. Foster, Kress Medical Building *Rhinol., Oto-Laryngology*

Charles Campbell Green, 411 Carter Building . . . *Surgery*

H. C. Haden, 913 Union National Bank Building *Ophthalmology*

Gavin Hamilton, 610 Scanlan Building . . . . . *Surgery*

TEXAS — Continued

HOUSTON — Continued
Reuben Morgan Hargrove, Humble Building . . . . *Surgery*
James A. Hill, Scanlan Building . . . . *Surgery*
A. Philo Howard, Kress Medical Building . . . . *Surgery*
Harold L. D. Kirkham, 735 Kress Medical Building . *Surgery*
Robert White Knox, 6B Beaconsfield Apartments . . *Surgery*
J. Allen Kyle, 402 Carter Building . . . . . . *Surgery*
Sidney M. Lister, 402 Carter Building . . . . . *Surgery*
John Thomas Moore, 431 Kress Medical Building . . *Surgery*
Oscar L. Norsworthy, 3015 Main Street . . . . *Gynecology*
Ira E. Pritchett, 631 Kress Medical Building . . . *Surgery*
Wallace Ralston, Kress Medical Building . . . *Ophthalmology*
Judson Ludwell Taylor, Scanlan Building . . . . *Surgery*
W. Burton Thorning, Kress Medical Building . . . *Surgery*
Benjamin W. Turner, 705 Scanlan Building . *Genito-Urinary Surgery*

HUNTSVILLE
John William Thomason, 1207 Avenue J
Ophth., Rhinol., Oto-Laryngology

KERRVILLE
William Lee Secor . . . . *Surgery*

MARSHALL
Rogers Cocke, 106½ East Austin Street . . . . . *Surgery*

MIDLAND
John B. Thomas, Llano Building . . . . *Surgery*

PALESTINE
E. B. Parsons, International and Great Northern Railroad
Hospital . . . . *Surgery*

PARIS
Lorenzo P. McCuistion, 215 Bonham Street . . . . *Surgery*

SAN ANGELO
Jesse S. Hixson, Central National Bank Building . . *Surgery*

SAN ANTONIO
Theodore B. Askew, 319 Moore Building . . . *Oto-Laryngology*
James Hall Bell, 319 Moore Building . . . . *Ophthalmology*
Jules L. A. Braunnagel, 212 City Street . . . . . *Surgery*
John H. Burleson, Central Trust Building
Ophth., Rhinol., Oto-Laryngology

TEXAS — Continued

SAN ANTONIO — Continued

Samuel Preston Cunningham, 714 Gibbs Building . . *Surgery*
Adolph Herff, 312 Avenue C . . . . *Surgery*
Ferdinand Peter Herff, 707 Central Trust Building . . *Surgery*
Francis Marion Hicks, 203 Hicks Building . . . . *Surgery*
Harry McC. Johnson, 801 Central Trust Building
Genito-Urinary Surgery
Byron F. Kingsley, Hicks Building . . . . . . *Surgery*
Robert E. Moss, Hicks Building *Ophth., Rhinol., Oto-Laryngology*
Frank Paschal, Hicks Building . . . . *Surgery*
Witten Booth Russ, Central Trust Building . . . . *Surgery*
Charles Scott Venable, 801 Central Trust Building . . *Surgery*
Ferdinand C. Walsh, Moore Building . . *Genito-Urinary Surgery*
William M. Wolf, Central Trust Building . . . . *Surgery*

SHERMAN

E. J. Neathery, Merchants and Planters Bank Building *Surgery*

TEMPLE

George V. Brindley, Temple Sanitarium . . . . . *Surgery*
John S. McCelvey, Temple State Bank Building . . . *Surgery*
George Street McReynolds, Temple State Bank Building
Ophth., Rhinol., Oto-Laryngology
Lewis William Pollok, Temple State Bank Building . . *Surgery*
Arthur Carroll Scott, 6 West French Avenue . . . *Surgery*
Marcel Wesley Sherwood, 704 South 3rd Street . . . *Surgery*
James Madison Woodson, Monroe and 11th Streets
Ophth., Rhinol., Oto-Laryngology

TEXARKANA

Spencer Allen Collom, 621 State Street . . . . . *Surgery*
Preston Hunt . . . . *Surgery*

TYLER

Irvin Pope, 112 South Bois d'Arc Avenue
Ophth., Rhinol., Oto-Laryngology

WACO

Robert J. Alexander, 1003 Amicable Building . . . *Surgery*
Horace Taylor Aynesworth, 1307 Amicable Building
Ophth., Rhinol., Oto-Laryngology
Kenneth Hazen Aynesworth, 315 North 12th Street . *Surgery*
Charles Ernest Collins, Providence Sanitarium . . . *Surgery*

TEXAS — Continued

WACO — Continued

Herschel Frank Connally, 2223 Calcard Street . . . *Surgery*
William L. Crosthwait, 803 Amicable Building . . . *Surgery*
Howard R. Dudgeon, 2200 Gorman Street . . . . *Surgery*
James Wyatt Hale, 1520 Washington Street . . . . *Surgery*

YOAKUM

James D. Gray, Neumann Building . . . . . . *Surgery*

YORKTOWN

George Washington Allen, Jr., Main Street . . . . *Surgery*

UTAH

OGDEN

Robert S. Joyce, Eccles Building . . . . *Surgery*
Edward I. Rich, First National Bank Building . . . *Surgery*
Ezra C. Rich, 2650 Washington Avenue . . . . . *Surgery*

PROVO

J. W. Aird, 65 East 2nd South Street . . . . . . *Surgery*
Frederick W. Taylor, 147 South University Avenue . . *Surgery*

SALT LAKE CITY

Samuel C. Baldwin, 316 McCornick Building *Orthopedic Surgery*
Francis S. Bascom, 815 Boston Building . . . . . *Surgery*
Augustus C. Behle, 512 Judge Building . . . . . *Surgery*
John F. Critchlow, The Bransford . . . . *Surgery*
Robert R. Hampton, 806 Boston Building
Ophth., Rhinol., Oto-Laryngology
Andrew Jackson Hosmer, 162 13th East Street . . . *Surgery*
Edwin Manson Neher, 806 Boston Building . . *Ophthalmology*
Samuel H. Pinkerton, Desert News Building . . . . *Surgery*
Franklin H. Raley, Boston Building
Ophth., Rhinol., Oto-Laryngology
Ralph T. Richards, 1111 Walker Bank Building . . . *Surgery*
Emerson Frank Root, 430 Judge Building . . . . *Surgery*
Frederick Stauffer, 81 1st Avenue . . *Ophth., Oto-Laryngology*
Joseph E. Tyree, Walker Bank Building . . . . . *Surgery*

TOOELE

Joseph Allen Phipps, 63 Main Street . . . . . . *Surgery*

VERMONT

BELLOWS FALLS
William F. Hazelton, 97 Westminster Street . . . . . *Surgery*

BRATTLEBORO
George Riley Anderson, Brooks House . . . . . *Surgery*

BURLINGTON
Lyman Allen, 288 Main Street . . . . *Surgery*
Edmund T. Brown, 30 Church Street
Ophth., Rhinol., Oto-Laryngology
Patrick Eugene McSweeney, 37 Elmwood Avenue . . *Surgery*
Clifford A. Pease, 301 College Street . . . . . . *Surgery*
George Millar Sabin, 244 Main Street . . . . . . *Surgery*
Henry Crain Tinkham, 46 North Winooski Avenue . . *Surgery*
W. W. Townsend, Y. M. C. A. Building *Genito-Urinary Surgery*
M. C. Twitchell, 162 College Street . *Ophth., Oto-Laryngology*
John Brooks Wheeler, 210 Pearl Street . . . . . *Surgery*

MONTPELIER
Charles Porter Chandler, 43 State Street . . . . . *Surgery*

RUTLAND
George G. Marshall, Gryphon Building
Ophth., Rhinol., Oto-Laryngology
William Stickney, 37 North Main Street . . . . . *Surgery*

ST. ALBANS
Alan Davidson, 39 Bank Street . . . . *Surgery*

ST. JOHNSBURY
John Milton Allen, 24 Railroad Street . . . . . *Surgery*
C. A. Cramton, 29 Main Street *Ophth., Rhinol., Oto-Laryngology*
Charlotte Fairbanks, 24 Main Street . . . . . *Gynecology*
W. G. Ricker, 29 Main Street . *Ophth., Rhinol., Oto-Laryngology*
Edward Harlan Ross, 10 Church Street . . . . . *Surgery*

VIRGINIA

ABINGDON
James Coleman Motley . . . . *Surgery*

ALEXANDRIA
Martin Donohue Delaney, 131 North Washington Street *Surgery*
Samuel Broders Moore, 811 Prince Street . . *Surgery, Obstetrics*

VIRGINIA — Continued

CHARLOTTESVILLE

R. F. Compton, 103 East Market Street
Ophth., Rhinol., Oto-Laryngology

William H. Goodwin, University of Virginia . . . . *Surgery*

Halstead S. Hedges, 104 East Market Street . . *Ophth., Otology*

CLIFTON FORGE

Benjamin B. Wheeler, 63 Alleghany Street . . . . *Surgery*

HAMPTON

Harry Dresser Howe, 176 Victoria Avenue . . . . *Surgery*

LYNCHBURG

Don Preston Peters, 1315 Church Street . . . . . *Surgery*

NEWPORT NEWS

Joseph Thomas Buxton, The Marlborough . . . . *Surgery*

J. Kennedy Corss, 3214 West Avenue . . . . . . *Surgery*

Clarence Porter Jones, 3117 West Avenue
Ophth., Rhinol., Oto-Laryngology

NORFOLK

Charles J. Andrews, 512 Taylor Building . *Obstetrics, Gynecology*

Israel Brown, 631 Boissevain Avenue . . . . . . *Surgery*

Charles W. Doughtie, 512 Taylor Building . . . . *Surgery*

Wilson E. Driver, 225 Granby Street . *Ophth., Oto-Laryngology*

Edward Everard Feild, 512 Taylor Building . *Orthopedic Surgery*

Stanley H. Graves, 109 College Place . . . . . . *Surgery*

Lomax Gwathmey, 220 Freemason Street . . . . *Surgery*

Edward T. Hargrave, 311 Taylor Building . . . . *Surgery*

B. R. Kennon, Taylor Building *Ophth., Rhinol., Oto-Laryngology*

Everett A. Land, Taylor Building *Ophth., Rhinol., Oto-Laryngology*

Burnley Lankford, 246 Freemason Street, West . . . *Obstetrics*

Southgate Leigh, 109 College Place . . . . . . *Surgery*

Philip St. L. Moncure, Taylor Building . . . . . *Surgery*

H. L. Myers, Taylor Building . *Ophth., Rhinol., Oto-Laryngology*

Levi Old, Taylor Building . . . . *Surgery*

Robert Lee Payne, Tazewell Building . . . . . . *Surgery*

Julian Lamar Rawls, 142 Main Street . . . . . *Surgery*

Kirkland Ruffin, 1101 Graydon Avenue . . . . . *Surgery*

Edward C. S. Taliaferro, 618 New Monroe Building *Gynecology*

J. Warren White, 629 Monroe Building *Ophth., Oto-Laryngology*

VIRGINIA — Continued

PHOEBUS

G. K. Vanderslice, Mellen Street and Willard Avenue . *Surgery*

PORTSMOUTH

Charles Holdsworth Barlow, 600 Court Street *Surgery, Obstetrics*

Joseph D. Collins, 314 Court Street . . . . . . *Surgery*

RICHMOND

Greer Baughman, 26 North Laurel Street . . . . *Obstetrics*

Karl S. Blackwell, 501 Franklin Street
Ophth., Rhinol., Oto-Laryngology

Robert C. Bryan, 401 West Grace Street . . . . . *Surgery*

Claude C. Coleman, Professional Building . . . . *Surgery*

Roy Clyde Fravel, 1000 West Grace Street . . . . *Surgery*

Emmette Trible Gatewood, Professional Building
Rhinol., Oto-Laryngology

James William Henson, 405 Allen Avenue . . . . *Surgery*

John Shelton Horsley, 617 West Grace Street . . . *Surgery*

Frank S. Johns, 601 East Franklin Street . . . . *Surgery*

G. Paul LaRoque, 603 East Grace Street . . . . . *Surgery*

Henry Stuart MacLean, 401 West Grace Street . . . *Surgery*

Stuart McGuire, 513 East Grace Street . . . . . *Surgery*

William F. Mercer, 1006 West Franklin Street
Ophth., Rhinol., Oto-Laryngology

Stuart Michaux, Stuart Circle Hospital . . . . *Gynecology*

Clifton M. Miller, Stuart Circle Hospital . *Ophth., Oto-Laryngology*

William Tell Oppenheimer, 321 West Grace Street . . *Surgery*

W. Lowndes Peple, 1209 West Franklin Street . . . *Surgery*

Charles R. Robins, Stuart Circle Hospital . . . . *Surgery*

Achille Murat Willis, Professional Building . . . . *Surgery*

Robert Herbert Wright, 316 East Franklin Street
Ophth., Rhinol., Oto-Laryngology

ROANES

Henry D. Beyea . . . . *Retired*

ROANOKE

Sparrell S. Gale, Roanoke Street and Luck Avenue . . *Surgery*

John R. Garrett, Strickland Building . *Ophth., Oto-Laryngology*

Harry B. Stone, MacBain Building . *Ophth., Oto-Laryngology*

Hugh Henry Trout, 1303 Franklin Road . . . . . *Surgery*

William R. Whitman, Roanoke Street and Luck Avenue . *Surgery*

VIRGINIA — Continued

STAUNTON

Richard Phillips Bell, Professional Building . . . . *Surgery*
Marshall John Payne, 220 West Frederick Street . . *Surgery*

UNIVERSITY

George T. Harrison, University of Virginia *Gynecology, Obstetrics*
Stephen H. Watts, University of Virginia . . . . *Surgery*

WINCHESTER

Philip Williams Boyd, 4 South Main Street . . . . *Surgery*
Hunter H. McGuire, 105 North Braddock Street
Ophth., Oto-Laryngology

WASHINGTON

ABERDEEN

George E. Chamberlain, Electric Building . . . . *Surgery*

BELLINGHAM

Hays A. Compton, Fischer Building . . . . . . *Surgery*
W. D. Kirkpatrick, Bellingham National Bank Building *Surgery*
J. Reid Morrison . . . . *Surgery*
A. Macrae Smith, Bellingham National Bank Building . *Surgery*
Frank J. Van Kirk, Bellingham National Bank Building
Ophth., Rhinol., Oto-Laryngology

EVERETT

William Columbus Cox, 410 American Bank Building . *Surgery*
Henry Pope Howard, 410 American Bank Building . . *Surgery*
William F. West, American Bank Building . . . . *Surgery*

HOQUIAM

George Hurley, Medical Building . . . . *Surgery*

MT. VERNON

Rufus J. Cassel, First National Bank Building . . . *Surgery*
Harry Thornton D'Arc, Stevenson Building . . . . *Surgery*

OLYMPIA

John Wilson Mowell, Columbia Building . . . . . *Surgery*

SEATTLE

Frederick William Adams, Roosevelt Clinic
Ophth., Rhinol., Oto-Laryngology
Harry Eugene Allen, 505 Cobb Building . . . . . *Surgery*
Frederick Bentley, 404 Cobb Building . . . *Ophthalmology*

WASHINGTON — Continued

SEATTLE — Continued

Albert Irving Bouffleur, 1110 White Building   .   .   .   *Surgery*

Hubbard Thomas Buckner, 508 Cobb Building .   .   .   *Surgery*

Arthur Edwin Burns, 619 Cobb Building .   .   .   *Ophth., Otology*

Francis M. Carroll, Burke Building   .   .   *Gynecology, Obstetrics*

E. Frank Chase, 1007 Cobb Building .   *Rhinol., Oto-Laryngology*

Frederic Huntington Coerr, 759 Harvard Avenue, North   *Surgery*

Clinton T. Cooke, 817 Summit Avenue   .   .   .   *Ophthalmology*

Lewis R. Dawson, Northern Life Building   *Gynecology, Obstetrics*

J. Thomas Dowling, 1101 Terry Avenue
Ophth., Rhinol., Oto-Laryngology

Homer D. Dudley, 403 Cobb Building   .   .   .   .   .   *Surgery*

James Beaty Eagleson, 902 Boren Avenue   .   .   :   .   *Surgery*

Bruce Elmore, Roosevelt Clinic   .   .   .   .   .   .   *Surgery*

Fred J. Fassett, 1155 Empire Building   .   .   *Orthopedic Surgery*

Robert D. Forbes, 908 Cobb Building   .   .   .   .   .   *Surgery*

Charles Bickham Ford, 908 Boren Avenue   .   .   .   *Gynecology*

Charlton Edward Hagyard, 407 Lumber Exchange
Building   .   .   .   .   *Surgery*

Stuart V. R. Hooker, 455 Empire Building   .   .   .   *Surgery*

Frank Lappin Horsfall, Roosevelt Clinic .   .   .   .   .   *Surgery*

George Monroe Horton, 1106 Cobb Building .   .   .   *Surgery*

John Hunt, 919 Cobb Building .   .   .   .   *Surgery*

Nils A. Johanson, 411 Cobb Building .   .   .   .   .   *Surgery*

Everett O. Jones, 508 Cobb Building .   .   .   .   .   *Surgery*

Walter Kelton, Empire Building   .   .   .   .   .   .   *Surgery*

L. H. Klemptner, 310 Cobb Building .   *Rhinol., Oto-Laryngology*

O. F. Lamson, 705 Broadway .   .   .   .   *Surgery*

Adolph O. Loe, 211 Cobb Building   .   .   .   .   .   *Surgery*

John A. MacKinnon, Alaska Building .   *Ophth., Oto-Laryngology*

J. Tate Mason, 1220 Federal Avenue .   .   .   .   .   .   *Surgery*

Frank Theodore Maxson, 621 Lumber Exchange Building   *Surgery*

Mark Ward McKinney, 621 Lumber Exchange Building   *Surgery*

George N. McLoughlin, 1114 Boylston Avenue   .   .   .   *Surgery*

Saxe W. Mowers, 1011 Cobb Building   .   .   .   .   *Surgery*

Richard J. O'Shea, Cobb Building .   .   .   *Gynecology, Obstetrics*

Don H. Palmer, 619 Lumber Exchange Building .   .   .   *Surgery*

Ivan A. Parry, 964 Empire Building   .   .   .   .   .   *Surgery*

WASHINGTON — Continued

SEATTLE — Continued

Richard Wilbert Perry, 811 American Bank Building
Ophth., Rhinol., Oto-Laryngology

G. S. Peterkin, 1105 Cobb Building . . . . . . *Urology*

Hiram M. Read, 2009 31st Avenue, South . . . . *Surgery*

William C. Riddell, 317 Lumber Exchange Building
Obstetrics, Gynecology

Walter Karl Seelye, 806 American Bank Building
Ophth., Oto-Laryngology

William A. Shannon, Cobb Building . . . . . *Surgery*

Caspar Wistar Sharples, Burke Building . . . . *Surgery*

Harry A. Shaw, Arcade Building . . . . . . *Surgery*

William C. Speidel, 519 Cobb Building . . . . *Surgery*

Hamilton Stillson, Seaboard Building
Ophth., Rhinol., Oto-Laryngology

Milton G. Sturgis, 514 Harvard Avenue, North . . . *Surgery*

George W. Swift, 817 Summit Avenue . . . . *Ophthalmology*

Gordon G. Thompson, 505 Cobb Building . *Gynecology, Obstetrics*

Allison T. Wanamaker, 817 Summit Avenue
Rhinol., Oto-Laryngology

Fenton B. Whiting, 316 Cobb Building . . . . . *Surgery*

Park Weed Willis, 1256 Empire Building . . . . . *Surgery*

Sherald F. Wiltsie, Cobb Building . . . . . . *Surgery*

Harry V. Wurdemann, 709 Cobb Building
Ophth., Rhinol., Oto-Laryngology

E. Weldon Young, 816 Cobb Building . . . . . . *Surgery*

SPOKANE

Oliver T. Batcheller, 508 Old National Bank Building
Ophth., Rhinol., Oto-Laryngology

Stephen D. Brazeau, 318 Old National Bank Building
Ophth., Rhinol., Oto-Laryngology

Thomas L. Catterson, 2025 4th Avenue . . . . . *Surgery*

A. T. R. Cunningham, 501 Old National Bank Building *Surgery*

Charles McClure Doland, 303 Spokane and Eastern Trust
Building . . . . *Surgery*

Charles F. Eikenbary, 702 Paulsen Building . *Orthopedic Surgery*

William S. Frost, 807 Paulsen Building
Ophth., Rhinol., Oto-Laryngology

WASHINGTON — Continued

SPOKANE — Continued

Ronald A. Greene, 517 Old National Bank Building
Ophth., Rhinol., Oto-Laryngology

Scott Bruce Hopkins, 204 Fernwell Building
Ophth., Rhinol., Oto-Laryngology

Arthur C. Johnson, 818 Paulsen Building . . . . . *Surgery*

Samuel E. Lambert, 401 Old National Bank Building . *Surgery*

Henry B. Luhn, Spokane and Eastern Trust Building . *Surgery*

A. Aldridge Matthews, 721 Paulsen Building . . . . *Surgery*

Edward R. Northrop, 417 Paulsen Building . . . . *Surgery*

James Lee Rogers, 318 Old National Bank Building
Ophth., Oto-Laryngology

James Sutherland, 604 Old National Bank Building . . *Surgery*

C. A. Veasey, 404 Paulsen Building . . *Ophth.,Oto-Laryngology*

Herbert Edward Wheeler, Fernwell Building . . . . *Surgery*

TACOMA

H. S. Argue, 817 National Realty Building . *Urology, Surgery*

Ivan Petroff Balabanoff, 415 Fidelity Building
Ophth., Rhinol., Oto-Laryngology

William Gooderham Cameron, 1404 National Realty
Building . . . . *Ophth., Rhinol., Oto-Laryngology*

Edgar F. Dodds, Perkins Building . . . . *Surgery*

B. H. Foreman, Perkins Building . . . . *Surgery*

William N. Keller, National Realty Building . . . . *Surgery*

John B. McNerthney, 1009 Fidelity Building . . . . *Surgery*

Wilmot Deleo Read, Tacoma Clinic . . . . . . *Surgery*

Horace J. Whitacre, 704 St. Helens Avenue . . . . *Surgery*

Harry G. Willard, 1614 Puget Sound Bank Building . *Surgery*

James R. Yocom, Perkins Building . . . . . *Surgery*

WALLA WALLA

George Corbin Bryan, 217 Baker Building . . . . *Surgery*

John Cushman Lyman, 217 Baker Building . . . . *Surgery*

Frank Crawford Robinson, 401 Baker-Boyer Bank
Building . . . . *Surgery, Obstetrics*

Ellsworth E. Shaw, 713 Baker Building . . . . . *Surgery*

Bert Thomas, Drumheller Building . . . . . . *Surgery*

WENATCHEE

Russell T. Congdon . . . . *Surgery*

WASHINGTON — Continued

YAKIMA

Alfred Joseph Helton, 406 Masonic Temple . . . . *Surgery*
Cornelius J. Lynch, 216 Miller Building . . . . . *Surgery*
James Frederick Scott, 216 Miller Building . . . . *Surgery*
James R. Thompson, 322 Miller Building
                    Ophth., Rhinol., Oto-Laryngology
Edmund S West, 306 Miller Building . . . . . . *Surgery*

WEST VIRGINIA

BLUEFIELD

J. Francke Fox . . . . *Surgery*
Charles Matthew Scott, 53 Bland Street . . . . . *Surgery*
Charles Tiffany St. Clair, Bland and Ramsey Streets
                    Ophth., Rhinol., Oto-Laryngology
Wade Hampton St. Clair, 204 Ramsey Street . . . *Surgery*

BUCKHANNON

Lloyd H. Forman, 49 South Florida Street . . . . *Surgery*

CHARLESTON

John Egerton Cannaday, Kanawha Banking and Trust
  Building . . . . *Surgery*
Vincent T. Churchman, Professional Building
                    Ophth., Rhinol., Oto-Laryngology
Peter Allen Haley, 1582 Virginia Street
                    Ophth., Rhinol., Oto-Laryngology
Hugh G. Nicholson, 330 Professional Building . . . *Surgery*
G. C. Schoolfield, Morrison Building . . . . . . *Surgery*
Benjamin H. Swint, Coyle and Richardson Building . *Surgery*

CLARKSBURG

Chester R. Ogden, Main and 2nd Streets . . . . . *Surgery*

ELKINS

Arthur Parker Butt, 209 Randolph Avenue . . . . *Surgery*
William Wolfe Golden . . . . *Surgery*

HINTON

Oswald O. Cooper, 315 Temple Street . . . . . . *Surgery*

HUNTINGTON

Henry Drury Hatfield, 1550 5th Avenue . . . . . *Surgery*
J. Ross Hunter, 305 First National Bank Building . . *Surgery*

WEST VIRGINIA — Continued

HUNTINGTON — Continued

Thomas Waterman Moore, 204 First National Bank
Building . . . . *Ophth., Rhinol., Oto-Laryngology*
Robert J. Wilkinson, Chesapeake and Ohio Hospital . *Surgery*

KEYSER

C. S. Hoffman, 60 Davis Street . . . . *Surgery*

MARTINSBURG

Theodore Kensell Oates, 110 North Raleigh Street . . *Surgery*

MORGANTOWN

Irvin Hardy, Willy and Prospect Streets . . . . . *Surgery*

WELCH

Charles F. Hicks . . . . *Surgery*

WHEELING

Gregory Ackermann, 2319 Chapline Street . . . . *Surgery*
Joseph R. Caldwell, Wheeling Steel Corporation Building *Surgery*
Robert U. Drinkard, Wheeling Steel Corporation Building *Surgery*
Ivan Fawcett, Wheeling Steel Corporation Building
Ophth., Rhinol., Oto-Laryngology
William Stewart Fulton, 16th and Market Streets . . *Surgery*
Frank LeMoyne Hupp, 61 14th Street . . . . . *Surgery*
Robert Jeffrey Reed, 100 12th Street . . . . . . *Surgery*
Jacob Schwinn, 56 14th Street . . . . *Surgery*

WISCONSIN

APPLETON

Victor F. Marshall, 587 Appleton Street . . . . . *Surgery*
George Nathaniel Pratt, 801 College Avenue . . . . *Surgery*

ASHLAND

John M. Dodd, 619 West 3rd Street . . . . . . *Surgery*

BELOIT

William Judson Allen, 401 East Grand Avenue . . . *Surgery*

EAU CLAIRE

John Van Reed Lyman, Opera House Block . . . . *Surgery*
Hans Christian Ulrik Midelfart, 343 Gilbert Avenue . *Surgery*
J. Fletcher Robinson, Opera House Block . . . . . *Surgery*

WISCONSIN — Continued

FOND DU LAC

Stephen Edward Gavin, 38 South Main Street   . . .   *Surgery*
Charles W. Leonard, 72 South Main Street   . . . .   *Surgery*
Ernest Vernon Smith, 39 South Main Street .   . . .   *Surgery*
David James Twohig, 11 North Main Street .   . . .   *Surgery*
Frank S. Wiley, 39 South Main Street   . . . . .   *Surgery*

GREEN BAY

William H. Bartran, 109 East Walnut Street .   . . .   *Surgery*
Ralph Merle Carter, Bellin Building   . . . . . .   *Surgery*
William Edward Fairfield, 805 South Monroe Avenue   .   *Surgery*
William Webber Kelly, Bellin Building   . . . . .   *Surgery*

JANESVILLE

Thomas Walter Nuzum, 225 West Milwaukee Street   .   *Surgery*
William Henry Palmer, 407 Jackman Building   . . .   *Surgery*
John Frank Pember, 225 West Milwaukee Street   . .   *Surgery*
Frank W. Van Kirk, 225 Milton Avenue .   . . .   *Gynecology*

LA CROSSE

William E. Bannen, State Bank Building .   . .   *Surgery, Urology*
John A. L. Bradfield, State Bank Building
                                Ophth., Rhinol., Oto-Laryngology
Edward Evans, State Bank Building   . . . .   *Surgery*
Adolf Gundersen, 1509 King Street   . . . . . .   *Surgery*
Matthew A. McGarty, State Bank Building .   . . .   *Surgery*

MADISON

Samuel R. Boyce, 105 Monona Avenue
                                Ophth., Rhinol., Oto-Laryngology
James P. Dean, 29 East Main Street   . . . .   . .   *Surgery*
Joseph Dean, Jr., 29 East Main Street   . . . . .   *Surgery*
Corydon G. Dwight, 113 West Washington Avenue
                                        Ophth., Oto-Laryngology
Philip Reginald Fox, 21 North Pinckney Street   . . .   *Surgery*
Reginald Henry Jackson, 110 North Hamilton Street   .   *Surgery*
Thomas William Tormey, Gay Building   . . . . .   *Surgery*

MARINETTE

Maurice D. Bird, 520 Main Street .   . . .   *Surgery*

MARSHFIELD

Karl Doege, West 3rd Street and Central Avenue   . .   *Surgery*

WISCONSIN — Continued

MILWAUKEE

J. A. Bach, 409 Wells Building . *Ophth., Rhinol., Oto-Laryngology*
Nelson M. Black, Wells Building   *Ophth., Rhinol., Oto-Laryngology*
Max Bornstein, 79 Wisconsin Street . . . . . . *Surgery*
George N. Brazeau, 819 Majestic Building . . *Ophthalmology*
George Van Ingen Brown, 445 Milwaukee Street . *Oral Surgery*
Horace Manchester Brown, 311 Prospect Avenue . . *Surgery*
Vernon A. Chapman, Wells Building
Ophth., Rhinol., Oto-Laryngology
Ernest Copeland, 141 Wisconsin Street . *Gynecology, Obstetrics*
Carl H. Davis, 141 Wisconsin Street . . *Obstetrics, Gynecology*
Curtis A. Evans, 809 Wells Building . . . . . . *Surgery*
Matthew N. Federspiel, 695 Astor Street . . . . *Oral Surgery*
Filip A. Forsbeck, 121 Wisconsin Street . . . . . *Surgery*
Frederick J. Gaenslen, 141 Wisconsin Street . *Orthopedic Surgery*
Harry Greenberg, Caswell Block . . . . . . *Surgery*
William E. Grove, 1330 Wells Building
Ophth., Rhinol., Oto-Laryngology
Dennis J. Hayes, 1014 Majestic Building . *Genito-Urinary Surgery*
H. B. Hitz, 309 Goldsmith Building . *Rhinol., Oto-Laryngology*
Gustavus Ingomar Hogue, 410 Jefferson Street
Ophth., Rhinol., Oto-Laryngology
Arthur Tenney Holbrook, 612 Kenwood Boulevard . . *Surgery*
Hjorleifur T. Kristjanson, 611 Wells Building . . . *Surgery*
William F. Malone, 511 Caswell Block . . . . . *Surgery*
Bernard Francis McGrath, Marquette University . . *Surgery*
Francis B. McMahon, 120 Wisconsin Street . . . . *Surgery*
Alexander Montgomery, 211 Grand Avenue . . . . *Surgery*
Lewis G. Nolte, Senn's Block . . . . *Surgery*
Franz Pfister, 1404 Majestic Building . . . . *Oto-Laryngology*
Arthur J. Puls, 400 First National Bank Building . *Gynecology*
Edward W. Quick, 502 Wells Building . . . . . *Surgery*
Herman Reineking, 3024 Wells Street . . . . . . *Surgery*
Philip Fletcher Rogers, 307 Grand Avenue . . . . *Surgery*
Robert George Sayle, 710 Merchants and Manufacturers
Bank Building . . . . *Surgery*
G. E. Seaman, 141 Wisconsin Street . *Ophth., Oto-Laryngology*
Stanley Joseph Seeger, 809 Wells Building . . . . *Surgery*
Harry A. Sifton, 519 Astor Street . . . . *Surgery*

WISCONSIN — Continued

MILWAUKEE — Continued

Frederick Alexander Stratton, 611 Wells Building . . *Surgery*
William C. F. Witte, 1203 Majestic Building . . . . *Surgery*
John Lawrence Yates, 141 Wisconsin Street . . . . *Surgery*
Charles Zimmermann, 428 Jefferson Street
Ophth., Rhinol., Oto-Laryngology

OSHKOSH

Leighton Pine Allen, 19 Jefferson Avenue
Ophth., Rhinol., Oto-Laryngology
Burton Clark, 420 Algoma Street . . . . *Surgery*
Clarendon J. Combs, 19 Jefferson Avenue . . . . *Surgery*
F. Gregory Connell, 19 Jefferson Avenue . . . . . *Surgery*

PLATTEVILLE

Wilson Cunningham . . . . *Surgery*

PORTAGE

Byron C. Meacher, John Graham Building . . . . *Surgery*

RACINE

Erick von Buddenbrock, 301 6th Street . . . . . *Surgery*

SHEBOYGAN

Otto B. Bock, 925 North 8th Street . . . . . . *Surgery*
Arthur E. Genter, 1028 North 7th Street . . . . . *Surgery*

SPARTA

Lawrence H. Prince . . . . *Retired*

STEVENS POINT

Carl von Neupert, Jr., 412 Church Street . . . . . *Surgery*

SUPERIOR

William Edwin Ground, Board of Trade Building . . *Surgery*
Anders G. Hovde, Board of Trade Building
Ophth., Rhinol., Oto-Laryngology
Richard C. Smith, 407 Board of Trade Building . *Ophthalmology*

TWO RIVERS

Albert M. Farrell, 17th and Washington Streets . . . *Surgery*

WAUSAU

Richard W. Jones, 301 3rd Street . . . . . . *Surgery*
Joseph Franklin Smith, 605 3rd Street . . . . . *Surgery*
Lee M. Willard, 520 3rd Street . *Ophth., Rhinol., Oto-Laryngology*

WISCONSIN RAPIDS

Oscar N. Mortensen, Citizen's National Bank Building . *Surgery*

WYOMING

BASIN

 Chester Ellis Harris, Pioneer Building . . . . *Surgery*

 Herbert Taylor Harris, Pioneer Building . . . . . *Surgery*

CASPER

 Homer Riale Lathrop, 113 East 2nd Street . . . . *Surgery*

CHEYENNE

 Frederick Louis Beck, 408 Hynds Building

         Ophth., Rhinol., Oto-Laryngology

 George Leslie Strader, Hynds Building . *Ophth., Oto-Laryngology*

ROCK SPRINGS

 Oliver Chambers, First National Bank Building . . . *Surgery*

THERMOPOLIS

 Albert G. Hamilton, 5th Street and Broadway . . . *Surgery*

CANAL ZONE

ANCON

 Troy W. Earhart, Ancon Hospital . . . . *Surgery*

HAWAII

HONOLULU

 James Robert Judd, 163 Beretania Street . . . . . *Surgery*

 John Christopher O'Day, 45 Young Building . . . . *Surgery*

 Frank Lawrence Putnam, Young Hotel . . . . . *Surgery*

PHILIPPINE ISLANDS

MANILA

 Frank Wilburn Dudley, St. Paul's Hospital . . . . *Surgery*

 James Walker Smith, 25 Pinpin . . . . *Surgery*

PORTO RICO

CAGUAS

 Alexander Giol Texidor, 3 Muñoz Rivera Street . . . *Surgery*

SAN JUAN

 Jacinto Avilés, 23 State Street . . . . *Surgery*

 Walter Ashley Glines, 45 Allen Street . . . . . *Surgery*

DOMINION OF CANADA

ALBERTA

CALGARY

Reginald Burton Deane, Alexander Corner . *Orthopedic Surgery*
Harry Alexander Gibson, 216 6th Avenue, West . . . *Surgery*
William E. Graham, Herald Block . . . . . . *Surgery*
John Nisbet Gunn, 309 Herald Block
Ophth., Rhinol., Oto-Laryngology
William Hackney, Herald Block . *Ophth., Rhinol., Oto-Laryngology*
William A. Lincoln, 515 Herald Block   . . . . . *Surgery*
Ludwig Stewart Mackid, 220 6th Avenue, East . . . *Surgery*
Daniel Stewart Macnab, 209 Herald Block   . . . . *Surgery*
John Sinclair McEachern, 200 Maclean Block   . . . *Surgery*
Frank Hamilton Mewburn . . . . *Surgery*
John Daniel Milne, 205 Grain Exchange Building . . *Surgery*
Robert H. L. O'Callaghan, 410 Herald Building . . . *Surgery*
John E. Palmer, 501 Maclean Building   . . . . . *Urology*
James W. Richardson, 3 Royal Bank Chambers . . . *Surgery*

DRUMHELLER

Thomas Robert Ross   . . . . *Surgery*

EDMONTON

Edgar W. Allin, 502 McLeod Building   . . . . . *Surgery*
Norman George Allin, 502 McLeod Building
Ophth., Rhinol., Oto-Laryngology
Robert G. Brett, Government House . . . . . . *Surgery*
William N. Condell, 10039 105th Street
Ophth., Rhinol., Oto-Laryngology
Leighton C. Conn, 625 Tegler Block . . . . . . *Surgery*
Gordon C. Gray, 320 Tegler Block   . . . . . . *Surgery*
Evan Greene, 8231 106th Street   . . . . . . *Surgery*
John D. Harrison, 10033 106th Street . . . . . . *Surgery*
Howard H. Hepburn, Bank of Montreal Building . . *Surgery*
Malcolm Edward MacKay, 406 McLeod Building . . *Surgery*
Isaac Whitney T. McEachern, 318 Empire Building . *Surgery*
Alexander R. Munroe, 416 McLeod Building   . . . *Surgery*
Rodger F. Nicholls, 405 McLeod Building
Ophth., Rhinol., Oto-Laryngology
Robert B. Wells, 623 Tegler Block *Ophth., Rhinol., Oto-Laryngology*
Wilfred A. Wilson, 215 McLeod Building   . . . . *Surgery*

ALBERTA — Continued

LAMONT
  Albert E. Archer, King Street . . . . *Surgery*

LETHBRIDGE
  Edward L. Connor, 109 Sherlock Building . . . . *Urology*

MEDICINE HAT
  Frederick William Gershaw, 826 2nd Street . . . . *Surgery*
  Charles E. Smyth, 874 2nd Street . . . . *Surgery*

RED DEER
  Richard Parsons, 171 1st Street, S. E. . . . . . . *Surgery*

BRITISH COLUMBIA

CRANBROOK
  Frank William Green, Armstrong Avenue . . . . *Surgery*

CUMBERLAND
  George Kerr MacNaughton . . . . *Surgery*

FERNIE
  S. Bonnell, Walmsley Street . . . . *Surgery*
  Douglas Corsan, 20 Victoria Avenue . . . . . . *Surgery*
  Ernest Lloyd Garner, 165 Victoria Avenue   *Urology, Gynecology*

KAMLOOPS
  J. Stanley Burris . . . . *Surgery*

KELOWNA
  Gordon L. Campbell . . . . *Surgery*
  William John Knox . . . . *Surgery*

NEW WESTMINSTER
  Edwin J. Rothwell . . . . *Surgery*

NORTH VANCOUVER
  Ernest A. Martin, 84 Lonsdale Avenue . . . . . *Surgery*

PRINCE RUPERT
  Charles A. Eggert . . . . *Surgery*
  William T. Kergin, 320 2nd Avenue, West . . . . *Surgery*

REVELSTOKE
  William Henry Sutherland, McKenzie Avenue . . . *Surgery*

SUMMERLAND
  Frederick W. Andrew . . . . *Surgery*

BRITISH COLUMBIA — Continued

VANCOUVER

Robert B. Boucher, 414 Birks Building   . . *Ophth., Laryngology*
William B. Burnett, 718 Granville Street . . . .   *Gynecology*
I. Glen Campbell, 736 Granville Street   . . . *Ophth., Otology*
Benjamin H. Champion, 510 Hastings Street, West . .   *Surgery*
Robert Crosby, 736 Granville Street
  Ophth., Rhinol., Oto-Laryngology
Henry M. Cunningham, 106 Birks Building
  Ophth., Rhinol., Oto-Laryngology
G. C. Draeseke, 543 Granville Street .   *Ophth., Oto-Laryngology*
Edwin H. Funk, 718 Granville Street . . . . . .   *Surgery*
James Andrew Gillespie, 718 Granville Street . .   *Surgery*
George Sinclair Gordon, 127 Vancouver Block . . .   *Urology*
Henry B. Gourlay, 543 Granville Street . . . .   *Surgery*
Colin W. Graham, Birks Building *Ophth., Rhinol., Oto-Laryngology*
Robert H. Ker, Vancouver Club . . . . . .   *Surgery*
Theodore H. Lennie, 736 Granville Street . . . .   *Surgery*
Lachlan Macmillan, 538 Broadway, West   . . . .   *Surgery*
John J. Mason, 718 Granville Street . .   *Obstetrics, Gynecology*
Robert Edward McKechnie, 718 Granville Street . .   *Surgery*
William B. McKechnie, Vancouver General Hospital .   *Surgery*
William C. McKechnie, 751 Granville Street . . .   *Gynecology*
Francis Xavier McPhillips, 1101 Burrard Street . . .   *Surgery*
Alexander Stewart Monro, 736 Granville Street . . .   *Surgery*
Francis John Nicholson, 1826 Nelson Street . . . .   *Surgery*
Frank P. Patterson, Birks Building   . .   *Orthopedic Surgery*
Herbert W. Riggs, 470 Granville Street . . . .   *Surgery*
Austin Birrell Schinbein, 124 Vancouver Block . . .   *Surgery*
George E. Seldon, 736 Granville Street . . . .   *Surgery*
Henry Randolph Storrs, 1411 18th Avenue, East . .   *Surgery*
James Wolsely Thomson, 112 Vancouver Block . . .   *Surgery*
James L. Turnbull, 718 Granville Street . . . .   *Gynecology*

VICTORIA

W. H. K. Anderson, Military District No. 11 *Gynecology, Obstetrics*
William T. Barrett, Union Bank Building   . . . .   *Surgery*
Roderick L. Fraser, 1005 Douglas Street . . . . .   *Surgery*
George William Hall . . . .   *Surgery*
Edward Charles Hart, 643 Courtenay Street . . . .   *Surgery*
Angus W. Kenning . . . .   *Surgery*

BRITISH COLUMBIA — Continued

VICTORIA — Continued

James Horace King . . . . *Surgery*
Forrest Bertram Leeder . . . . *Surgery*
Harold Edward Ridewood, Belmont Block . . . . *Surgery*
Hermann M. Robertson, 1549 Clive Drive . . . . *Surgery*
James N. Taylor, 1186 Monterey Avenue . . . . . *Surgery*

MANITOBA

BRANDON

Wilfred A. Bigelow, Bigelow Clinic . . . . . . *Surgery*
John Sutherland Matheson, 317 5th Street . . . . *Surgery*

CARMAN

Harry Clarkson Cunningham, Villard Avenue . . . *Surgery*

WINNIPEG

Percy G. Bell, 12 Ellesmere Apartments, Carlton Street
Ophth., Rhinol., Oto-Laryngology
Thomas Herbert Bell, 703 Boyd Building . . . *Ophthalmology*
O. Bjornson, 701 Lindsay Building . . . . . . *Obstetrics*
R. J. Blanchard, 288 Broadway . . . . *Surgery*
B. J. Brandson, 701 Lindsey Building . . . . . *Surgery*
John E. Coulter, 604 Boyd Building . . . . . . *Obstetrics*
Gordon S. Fahrni, 507 Boyd Building . . . . . *Surgery*
George W. Fletcher, 901 Boyd Building
Ophth., Rhinol., Oto-Laryngology
R. D. Fletcher, 206 Somerset Building . *Genito-Urinary Surgery*
Herbert P. H. Galloway, 661 Broadway . . *Orthopedic Surgery*
William A. Gardner, 307 Boyd Building . . *Orthopedic Surgery*
Alexander Gibson, 661 Broadway . . . . *Orthopedic Surgery*
James W. Good, 226 Somerset Building . *Ophth., Oto-Laryngology*
James A. Gorrell, 702 Sterling Bank Block . . . . *Surgery*
John A. Gunn, 922 Somerset Building . . . . . *Surgery*
Jasper Halpenny, 702 Sterling Bank Building . . . *Surgery*
T. Glendenning Hamilton, 210 Somerset Block . . . *Surgery*
Gerhard Hiebert, 412 Boyd Building . . . . . *Surgery*
Julius Eduard Lehmann, 606 Boyd Building . . . . *Surgery*
Daniel Sayre MacKay, 36 Purcell Avenue . . . . *Surgery*
Neil John Maclean, 67 Middle Gate . . . . . . *Surgery*
Donald F. McIntyre, 811 Boyd Building . . . . . *Surgery*

MANITOBA — Continued

WINNIPEG — Continued

Norman K. McIvor, 601 Boyd Building . . . . . *Surgery*

F. D. McKenty, 802 Boyd Building . *Rhinol., Oto-Laryngology*

James McKenty, 410 Sterling Bank Building . . . *Surgery*

John D. McQueen, 811 Boyd Building . *Gynecology, Obstetrics*

Rosslyn B. Mitchell, 811 Boyd Building . . . . . *Obstetrics*

Angus A. Murray, 514 Boyd Building . . . *Orthopedic Surgery*

William W. Musgrove, 712 Boyd Building . . . . *Surgery*

William Robson Nichols, 83 Carlton Street . . . . *Surgery*

S. Willis Prowse, 801 Boyd Building . . . . *Oto-Laryngology*

James Pullar, 286 Kennedy Street . . . . . . *Gynecology*

Robert Mills Simpson, 702 Sterling Bank Building . *Gynecology*

W. Harvey Smith, 901 Boyd Building

Ophth., Rhinol., Oto-Laryngology

John Orchard Todd, 166 Hargrave Street . . . . . *Surgery*

Thomas Turnbull, 226 Somerset Block

Ophth., Rhinol., Oto-Laryngology

Oliver S. Waugh, 510 Boyd Building . . . . . . *Surgery*

NEW BRUNSWICK

CAMPBELLTON

Louis George Pinault . . . . *Surgery*

FREDERICTON

George Clowes Van Wart, 141 York Street . . . . *Surgery*

MONCTON

William A. Ferguson, 43 Alma Street . . . . . . *Surgery*

SHEDIAC

J. Clarence Webster . . . . *Retired*

ST. JOHN

George Arthur Beldon Addy, 95 Union Street . . . *Surgery*

Murray MacLaren, 75 Coburg Street . . . . . . *Surgery*

Walter Woodworth White, 71 Sydney Street . . . . *Surgery*

WOODSTOCK

William Donald Rankin, 280 Main Street . . . . . *Surgery*

NOVA SCOTIA

AMHERST
Arthur E. Mackintosh, 87 Church Street . . . . . . *Surgery*
Ross Millar, 28 Crescent Avenue . . . . *Surgery*

ANTIGONISH
John L. MacIsaac, Main Street . . . . *Surgery*
William F. MacKinnon . . . . *Surgery*

BRIDGEWATER
Wallace N. Rehfuss . . . . *Surgery*

GLACE BAY
Allister Calder . . . . *Surgery*
M. T. Sullivan . . . . *Surgery*

HALIFAX
Murdoch Chisholm, 303 Brunswick Street . . . . *Surgery*
Allan R. Cunningham, 260 Barrington Street
       Ophth., Rhinol., Oto-Laryngology
J. A. M. Hemmeon, 41 Spring Garden Road
         Rhinol., Oto-Laryngology
Edward V. Hogan, 109 College Street . . . . . . *Surgery*
Donald J. Macdonald, 168 South Street . . . . . *Surgery*
Henry Kirkwood MacDonald, 317 Barrington Street . *Surgery*
Samuel J. MacLennan, 197 South Park Street
       Ophth., Rhinol., Oto-Laryngology
John George McDougall, 95 Spring Garden Road . . *Surgery*
George Henry Murphy, 28 Carleton Street . . . . *Surgery*
Philip Weatherbe, 66 Queen Street . . . . *Surgery*

LAWRENCETOWN
Leander R. Morse . . . . *Surgery*

LUNENBURG
Arthur E. G. Forbes . . . . *Surgery*

NEW GLASGOW
John W. McKay . . . . *Surgery*

NORTH SYDNEY
John W. McLean . . . . *Surgery*

STELLARTON
Robert M. Benvie, South Main Street . . . . . *Surgery*

SYDNEY
Donald Angus Macleod, 363 Charlotte Street . . . *Surgery*
John James Roy, 308 George Street . . . . . . *Surgery*

254 American College of Surgeons

NOVA SCOTIA — Continued

TRURO

    John W. T. Patton . . . . *Ophth., Rhinol., Oto-Laryngology*

WINDSOR

    Owen B. Keddy, Stannus Street . . . . *Surgery*

YARMOUTH

    George W. T. Farish . . . . *Surgery*
    Charles A. Webster . . . . *Surgery*

ONTARIO

BRANTFORD

    Benjamin C. Bell, 143 Market Street
                         Ophth., Rhinol., Oto-Laryngology
    Edward Reginald Secord, 112 Market Street . . . . *Surgery*

CEDAR SPRINGS

    George Thomas McKeough, Erie Manor . . . . . *Surgery*

FORT WILLIAM

    Andrew T. Gillespie, 304½ Victoria Avenue . . . . *Surgery*
    George E. McCartney, Simpson Street . . . . . *Surgery*
    Crawford C. McCullough, 101 Dominion Bank Building
                         Ophth., Rhinol., Oto-Laryngology
    Cecil E. Spence, 104 Cuthbertson Block . . . . . *Surgery*

GUELPH

    Henry Howitt, 128 London Road . . . . *Surgery*
    Angus MacKinnon, 44 Suffolk Street . . . . . . *Surgery*
    Peter Stuart, 176 Woolwich Street . . . . . . *Surgery*

HAMILTON

    Oscar Anson Cannon, 576 Main Street, East *Obstetrics, Gynecology*
    Percy B. Macfarlane, 152 James Street, South
                         Ophth., Rhinol., Oto-Laryngology
    James Kenneth McGregor, Main Street . . . . . *Surgery*
    John Pettigrew Morton, 148 James Street, South
                         Ophth., Rhinol., Oto-Laryngology
    Frederick Bruce Mowbray, 681 Main Street, East . . *Surgery*

ONTARIO — Continued

HAMILTON—Continued

Harry M. Nicholson, 134 James Street, South
Rhinol., Oto-Laryngology
Ingersoll Olmsted, 215 James Street, South . . . . *Surgery*

KINGSTON

William Gardiner Anglin, 52 Earl Street . . . . . *Retired*
James C. Connell, 265 King Street, East
Ophth., Rhinol., Oto-Laryngology
David Edward Mundell, 228 Brock Street . . . . *Surgery*
Gordon W. Mylks, 79 William Street . . . . . *Gynecology*
John F. Sparks, 100 Wellington Street . . . . . *Surgery*
A. R. B. Williamson, King and William Streets . . . *Surgery*

LONDON

Emerson LeRoy Hodgins, 312 Oxford Street . . . . *Surgery*
George McNeill, 245 Queens Avenue . . . . . . *Surgery*
Harry Meek, 330 Queens Avenue . . . *Gynecology, Obstetrics*
Edwin Seaborn, 469 Clarence Street . . . . . . *Surgery*
Septimus Thompson, 464 Clarence Street
Ophth., Rhinol., Oto-Laryngology
William E. Waugh, 537 Talbot Street . . . . . . *Surgery*
Hadley Williams, Park Avenue . . . . . . *Surgery*
John C. Wilson, 260 Queens Avenue . . . . . . *Surgery*
John Wishart, 195 Dufferin Avenue . . . . . . *Surgery*

NIAGARA-ON-THE-LAKE

George Sterling Ryerson . . . . *Retired*

OTTAWA

John Dickson Courtenay, 189 Metcalfe Street . *Ophth., Otology*
Evans G. Davis, Daly Building . . . . . . *Surgery*
William Hutchinson, Jackson Building . *Genito-Urinary Surgery*
John Franklin Kidd, 221 O'Connor Street . . . . *Surgery*
Frederick W. McKinnon, 171 Metcalfe Street . . . *Surgery*
Herbert Bayne Moffatt, 278 O'Connor Street . . . *Surgery*
Adam Tozeland Shillington, 281 Gilmour Street . . . *Surgery*
David Wallace, 82 Park Avenue . . . . *Surgery*

PETERBOROUGH

Ernest V. Frederick, 300 Charlotte Street . . . . *Surgery*

ONTARIO — Continued

PORT ARTHUR

Herman R. H. Bryan, 1A Cumberland Street, South . *Surgery*

James A. Crozier, 215 Park Street . . . . *Surgery*

William S. Hunt, Molson's Bank Building

Ophth., Rhinol., Oto-Laryngology

SARNIA

Alexander N. Hayes, 137 Wellington Street . . . . *Surgery*

STRATFORD

Lorne Forbes Robertson, 55 Albert Street . . . . *Surgery*

TORONTO

Herbert W. Baker, 606 Spadina Avenue . . . . . *Surgery*

Henry Albert Beatty, 52 Howland Avenue . . . . *Surgery*

George Arthur Bingham, 68 Isabella Street . . . . *Surgery*

Geoffrey Boyd, 48 Bloor Street, East . . . . . *Oto-Laryngology*

Herbert Alexander Bruce, 64 Bloor Street, East . . . *Surgery*

Irving Heward Cameron, 307 Sherbourne Street . . . *Surgery*

Malcolm H. V. Cameron, 11 Prince Arthur Avenue . . *Surgery*

William A. Cerswell, 862 Dovercourt Road . . . . *Surgery*

Frederick A. Cleland, 131 Bloor Street, West . . *Gynecology*

Herbert E. Clutterbuck, 148 Grace Street . . . . *Surgery*

Robert Edward Gaby, 662 Bathurst Street . . . . *Surgery*

John G. Gallie, 143 College Street . . . *Gynecology, Obstetrics*

W. Edward Gallie, 143 College Street . . . . . . *Surgery*

Perry G. Goldsmith, 84 Carlton Street *Rhinol., Oto-Laryngology*

Roscoe R. Graham, 31 Oriole Road . . . . . . *Surgery*

Wilbur Howard Harris, 1276 King Street, West . . . *Surgery*

Arthur Clinton Hendrick, 20 Bloor Street, East . . *Gynecology*

William Belfry Hendry, 112 College Street *Obstetrics, Gynecology*

William Warner Jones, 41 Avenue Road . . . . . *Urology*

Dennis Jordan, 253 Danforth Avenue . . . . . . *Surgery*

Edmund Eleazar King, 61 Queen Street, East . . . *Surgery*

Walter Whitney Lailey, 43 Avenue Road . *Gynecology, Obstetrics*

Oliver R. Mabee, 419 Bloor Street, West . . . . . *Surgery*

Duncan Neil Maclennan, 126 Bloor Street, West

Ophth., Oto-Laryngology

Jane Sproule Manson, 250 Huron Street *Rhinol., Oto-Laryngology*

Frederick William Marlow, 417 Bloor Street, West . . *Surgery*

ONTARIO — Continued

TORONTO — Continued

John Alexander McCollum, 12 Avenue Road . . . . *Surgery*
J. H. McConnell, 1653 Dundas Street, West . . . . *Surgery*
Kennedy C. McIlwraith, 30 Prince Arthur Avenue . . *Obstetrics*
Walter McKeown, 140 Wellesley Crescent . . . . *Surgery*
David William McPherson, 556 Bathurst Street . . . *Surgery*
Andrew Samuel Moorhead, 146 Bloor Street, West . . *Surgery*
Robin Pearse, 206 Bloor Street, West . . . . . . *Urology*
Alfred Harshaw Perfect, 201 Annette Street . . . . *Surgery*
Newton Albert Powell, 167 College Street . . . . *Surgery*
Alexander Primrose, 100 College Street . . . . . *Surgery*
James A. Roberts, 38 Charles Street, East . . . . *Surgery*
David Edwin Robertson, 112 College Street . . . . *Surgery*
L. Bruce Robertson, 143 College Street . . . . . *Surgery*
Thomas Arnold Robinson, 147 Howard Park Avenue . *Surgery*
Gilbert Royce, 100 College Street . . *Rhinol., Oto-Laryngology*
E. Stanley Ryerson, 143 College Street . . . . . *Surgery*
Wallace Arthur Scott, 627 Sherbourne Street . . . *Surgery*
William A. Scott, 75 Bloor Street, East . *Gynecology, Obstetrics*
Norman Strahan Shenstone, 196 Bloor Street, West . . *Surgery*
Gideon Silverthorn, 34 North Sherbourne Street . . . *Surgery*
Clarence L. Starr, 224 Bloor Street, West . . . . . *Surgery*
Frederic Newton Gisborne Starr, 112 College Street . . *Surgery*
John Franklin Uren, 520 Church Street . . . . . *Surgery*
B. P. Watson, 100 College Street . . . *Gynecology, Obstetrics*
George E. Wilson, 205 Bloor Street, East . . . . . *Surgery*
D. J. Gibb Wishart, 47 Grosvenor Street . . . *Oto-Laryngology*
Arthur Wright, 329 Church Street . . . . *Surgery*

WALKERTON

Malcolm Stalker . . . . *Surgery, Obstetrics*

WOODSTOCK

William Tiffany Parke, 411 Dundas Street . . . . *Surgery*

PRINCE EDWARD ISLAND

CHARLOTTETOWN

Stephen Rice Jenkins, 57 Grafton Street . . . . . *Surgery*

SUMMERSIDE

Alexander MacNeill, Fitzroy Street . . . . . . *Surgery*

QUEBEC

MONTREAL

Edward William Archibald, 52 Westmount Boulevard . *Surgery*
George E. Armstrong, 320 Mountain Street . . . . *Surgery*
David H. Ballon, 255 Bishop Street . . . . *Oto-Laryngology*
Walter Linley Barlow, 4769 Sherbrooke Street, West . *Surgery*
W. A. G. Bauld, 710 St. Urbain Street . *Gynecology, Obstetrics*
Alfred Turner Bazin, 583 Dorchester Street, West . . *Surgery*
Herbert Stanley Birkett, 252 Mountain Street . *Oto-Laryngology*
Rodolphe Boulet, 145 Ste. Catherine Street, West
                                    Ophth., Rhinol., Oto-Laryngology
Benjamin G. Bourgeois, 332 Sherbrooke Street, East . *Surgery*
Harry C. Burgess, 118 Crescent Street . *Gynecology, Obstetrics*
Kenneth Cameron, 400 Mackay Street . . . . . *Surgery*
W. W. Chipman, 285 Mountain Street . *Gynecology, Obstetrics*
Robert Henry Craig, 510 Sherbrooke Street, West
                                              Rhinol., Oto-Laryngology
James William Duncan, 141 Crescent Street . . . . *Obstetrics*
Edmond Melchior Eberts, 219 Peel Street . . . . *Surgery*
John Munro Elder, 731 Sherbrooke Street, West . . . *Surgery*
Frank Richardson England, 126 Bishop Street . . . *Surgery*
George Fisk, 166 Drummond Street . . . . . . *Surgery*
Alexander Mackenzie Forbes, 615 University Street
                                                    Orthopedic Surgery
John R. Fraser, 670 Sherbrooke Street, West *Gynecology, Obstetrics*
Alexander Esslemont Garrow, 289 Mountain Street . . *Surgery*
Fraser Baillie Gurd, 115 Stanley Street . . . . . *Surgery*
L. de L. Harwood, 228 Sherbrooke Street, West . . *Gynecology*
Charles K. P. Henry, 4549 Sherbrooke Street, West . . *Surgery*
Donald A. Hingston, 460 Sherbrooke Street, West . . *Surgery*
James Alexander Hutchison, 354 Mackay Street . . . *Surgery*
John G. W. Johnson, 453 Sherbrooke Street, West . . *Surgery*
Campbell B. Keenan, 376 Mountain Street· . . . . *Surgery*
Edgar C. Levine, 271 Bishop Street . . . . . . *Surgery*
Herbert M. Little, 285 Stanley Street . . *Gynecology, Obstetrics*
Frederick A. L. Lockhart, 38 Bishop Street . . . *Gynecology*
David W. MacKenzie, 624 Sherbrooke Street, West . . *Urology*
John A. MacMillan, 129 Stanley Street . . . . *Ophthalmology*
Albert G. McAuley, 579 Dorchester Street, West *Ophthalmology*
Francis E. McKenty, 648 Union Avenue . . . . . *Surgery*

QUEBEC — Continued

MONTREAL — Continued

Laurie H. McKim, 4880 Sherbrooke Street, West . . *Surgery*
Oscar Felix Mercier, 394 Sherbrooke Street, East . . *Surgery*
John Appleton Nutter, Drummond Building . *Orthopedic Surgery*
Frank Stewart Patch, 33 Bishop Street . *Genito-Urinary Surgery*
William J. Patterson, 386 Sherbrooke Street, West
Orthopedic Surgery

Ralph E. Powell, 132 Crescent Street . . *Genito-Urinary Surgery*
Pierre Z. Rhéaume, 127 Sherbrooke Street, East . . . *Surgery*
James T. Rogers, 758 Sherbrooke Street, West . *Oto-Laryngology*
Eugene Saint-Jacques, 29 Sherbrooke Street, West . . *Surgery*
Joseph A. Saint-Pierre, 703 St. Hubert Street . . . *Surgery*
Francis A. C. Scrimger, 154 Metcalfe Street . . . . *Surgery*
Archibald Stewart, 414 McKay Street . . . . . . *Surgery*
John W. Stirling, 386 Sherbrooke Street, West . *Ophthalmology*
Frederick James Tees, 6 Bishop Street . . . . . *Surgery*
Frederick Thomas Tooke, 368 Mountain Street . *Ophthalmology*
William George Turner, 386 Sherbrooke Street, West
Orthopedic Surgery

Charles W. Vipond, 462 Sherbrooke Street, West . . *Surgery*
E. Hamilton White, 589 Dorchester Street, West
Rhinol., Oto-Laryngology
Edward Johnston Williams, 700 Dorchester Street, West *Surgery*
R. P. Wright, 637 Union Avenue . . *Rhinol., Oto-Laryngology*

QUEBEC

Adrian R. F. Hubbard, 14 Cook Street . . . . . *Surgery*
James Stevenson, 258 Grande Allée . . . . . . *Surgery*

SHERBROOKE

J. A. Darche, 92 King Street . *Ophth., Rhinol., Oto-Laryngology*
William A. Farwell, 45 Dufferin Avenue
Ophth., Rhinol., Oto-Laryngology
George William Lamb Hume, 24 Montreal Street . . *Surgery*
Gordon MacKenzie Hume, 11 Moore Street . . . . *Surgery*
Joseph O. Ledoux, 44 Brooks Street . . . . . . *Surgery*
William Warren Lynch, 17 Bank Street . . . . . *Surgery*

260 American College of Surgeons

SASKATCHEWAN

KERROBERT

John Quincy Adams Scroggy . . . . Surgery

MOOSE JAW

Vaughan E. Black, Scott Block . . . . Surgery
Thomas McCrae Leask, 202 Walter Scott Building . . Surgery

PRINCE ALBERT

Stanley Butler MacMillan, Central Avenue . . . . Surgery

REGINA

Edward B. Alport, 710 McCallum-Hill Building . . . Surgery
Frederick A. F. Corbett, 414 McCallum-Hill Building . Surgery
Hervey L. Jackes, 711 McCallum-Hill Building . . . Surgery
Hugh MacLean . . . . Gynecology, Obstetrics
William Alexander Thompson, Canada Life Building . Surgery

SASKATOON

Harold E. Alexander, 311 Canada Building . . . . Surgery
Andrew Croll, 304 Canada Building . . . . . . Surgery
Arthur Louis Lynch, 213 Canada Building . . . . Surgery
Ronald Hugh Macdonald, Canada Building . . . . Surgery
Hugh E. Munroe, 407 Canada Building . . . . . Surgery
George R. Peterson, 2nd Avenue . . . . Surgery

SWIFT CURRENT

Douglas William Graham, Swift Current Clinic . . . Surgery

ARGENTINA

BUENOS AIRES

Nicomedes Antelo, Quinta Massini, Liniers . . . . Surgery
Pedro Belou, La Plata 1059 . . . . Rhinol., Oto-Laryngology
Robert E. Halahan, Calle Suipacha 1156 . . . . . Surgery
Rodolfo E. Pasman, Yuncal 2136 . . . . Surgery
Pedro del Pino, Alsina 451 . . . . Surgery
Luis A. Tamini, Santa Fe 2294 . . . . Surgery
Marcelino H. Vegas, Florida 846 . . . . Surgery

BAHREIN ISLANDS
BAHREIN
Paul Wilberforce Harrison . . . . *Surgery*

BOLIVIA
LA PAZ
Renato A. Riverin, Avenida 15 de Julio . . . . . *Surgery*
Claudio Sanjines F., Casilla 409 . . . . *Surgery*
Felix Veintemillas, Casilla 96A . . . . *Surgery*

BRAZIL
RIO DE JANEIRO
Pedro Ernesto, Rua Riackuelo 161 . . *Gynecology, Obstetrics*
José Antônio de Abreu Fialho, Rua Carvalho de Sá 85 . *Surgery*
Joas Marinho de Azevedo, Rua da Quitanda 5
Rhinol., Oto-Laryngology
Octavio Oliveira Pinto, Rua da Carioca 33 . . . . *Surgery*
Jayme Poggi de Figueirêdo, Rua Marquez de Abrantes 192
Gynecology
Olympio A. Ribeiro da Fonseca, Rua Camerino 162
Obstetrics, Gynecology
Augusto P. Soares de Souza, Alice Street . . . . . *Surgery*
Fernando Vaz, Rua Assembléa 27 . . . . *Surgery*

SAO PAULO
Nicolan de Moraes Barros, Rua S. Bento 35 *Gynecology, Obstetrics*
Antonio Candido de Camargo, Rua Alvaros Centralo 35 *Surgery*
Sergio de Paiva Meira Filho, Alameda Eduardo Prado 8 *Surgery*
Henrique Lindenberg, Rua Stambé 16 . *Rhinol., Oto-Laryngology*
Antonio Vieira Marcondes, Avenida Angelica 114 . . *Obstetrics*
Benedicto Montenegro, Rua S. Bento 22 . . . . . *Surgery*
Luiz Felippe Baeta Neves, Rua S. Vicente de Paula 37
Genito-Urinary Surgery
Luiz de Rezende Puech, Rua S. Bento 41 . . *Orthopedic Surgery*

CAMPINAS
José Barbosa de Barros, Rua Campos Salles 51 . . . *Surgery*
BELLO HORIZONTE
Hugo Werneck, Avenida Tacantius 499 . *Gynecology, Obstetrics*

BRAZIL — Continued

PORTO ALEGRE

Alfen Bica de Medeiros, Andradas 309 . . . . . . *Surgery*

RIBEIRAO PRETO

Francisco Antonio Ponipeo de Camargo, Rua Barao do
    Amazonas 31 . . . . *Gynecology*

CHILE

CHUGUICAMATA

William F. Shaw . . . . *Surgery*

SANTIAGO

Jerman V. Basterrica, Riqueleme 47 . . . . *Surgery*
Carlos Charlin, Compania 2115 . . . . . . *Ophthalmology*
Caupolican Pardo Correa, Ejercito, N., 119 *Gynecology, Obstetrics*
Victor Korner, Santo Domingo 628 . . . . . *Gynecology*
Francisco Navarro Valenzuela, Casilla 1259 . . . . *Surgery*
Lucas Sierra, Dieciocho 552 . . . . *Surgery*
Luis Vargas, Casilla 2122 . . . . *Surgery*
Eugenio Diaz Lira, Agustiunas 1270 . . . . . *Surgery*
Alberta Zuinga, Avenida Espana 472 . . . . . *Gynecology*

VALPARAISO

Alberto Adriasola, Salvador Donosa 234 . *Genito-Urinary Surgery*
Federico Engelbach Campo, Calle Victoria 796 . . . *Surgery*
Rudecindo de la Fuente, San Ignacio 419 . . . *Gynecology*
Ernesto Iturrieta V., Casilla 72 . . . . *Surgery*
Gaston Lachaise, Pedro Martt 475 . . . . *Orthopedic Surgery*
Miguel Manriquez, Rua Brazil 272 . *Rhinol., Oto-Laryngology*
Guillermo E. Münnich, Casilla 1542 . . . . . . *Surgery*
Edwyn P. Reed, Blanco Encalada 979 . . . *Surgery, Obstetrics*
Silvano Sepulveda P., Plaza Anibal Pinto 371 . . . *Surgery*
Jean H. Thierry, Plaza Anibal Pinto 175
                    Ophth., Rhinol., Oto-Laryngology
Julio C. Zilleruelo, Plaza Pinto 371 . . . . . . *Surgery*

CHINA

CANTON

Charles Arthur Hayes, Canton Hospital
                    Ophth., Rhinol., Oto-Laryngology
Joseph Oscar Thomson, Canton Hospital . . . . . *Surgery*

CHINA — Continued

CANTON — Continued
Paul J. Todd, Kung Yee Hospital . . . . *Surgery*
James Mann Wright, Canton Hospital . *Obstetrics, Gynecology*

CHANGCHOW
Wallace Boyd Russell, Sr., Changchow General Hospital *Surgery*

CHANGSHA
J. R. Bromwell Branch, Hunan-Yale Hospital . . . *Surgery*

NANKING
Allen C. Hutcheson, University Hospital . . . . . *Surgery*

PEKING
William Brooks La Force, Tsing Hua College . . . *Surgery*

SHANGHAI
Josiah Calvin McCracken, 8 Darroch Road . . . . *Surgery*
John H. Snoke, St. Luke's Hospital . . . . . . *Surgery*

YENPING
Charles Garnet Trimble . . . . *Surgery*

ECUADOR

GUAYAQUIL
Juan B. Arzube Cordero, Malecón 2006 . *Gynecology, Obstetrics*

QUITO
Isidro Ayora, Sodiro 116 . . . . . *Gynecology, Obstetrics*
Ricardo Villavicencio Ponce . . . . *Surgery*

EGYPT

CAIRO
Robert Valentine Dolbey, Kasr el Aini Hospital . . . *Surgery*

ENGLAND

LONDON
Lyle John Cameron, 87 Wimpole Street . . . . . *Surgery*

FRANCE

PARIS

John A. James James, 79 Rue de Sèvres   *Rhinol., Oto-Laryngology*

INDIA

ALIGARH

John Fletcher Robinson . . . . *Surgery*

MIRAJ

William J. Wanless . . . . *Surgery*

JAMAICA

KINGSTON

George Vernon Lockett, 3 Bedford Avenue . . . . *Surgery*

KOREA

SEOUL

Alfred Irving Ludlow, Severance Union Medical College . *Surgery*

MEXICO

EMPALME

Seabron Jenning Fuller, Empalme Hospital . . . . *Surgery*

PERU

LIMA

Miguel C. Aljovin, Fano 855 . . . . *Surgery*
Belisario J. Sosa Artola, Calonge 390 . . . . . *Surgery*
Eduardo Bello, Compax de la Concepcion 358 . . *Gynecology*
Constantino J. Carvallo, Vera Cruz 239 . . . . . *Surgery*
Manuel Castañeda, Pacal 987 . . . . *Surgery*
Luis F. de la Puente, Maison de Santé . . . . . *Surgery*
Juvenal Denegri, Mogollon 289 . . . . . *Oto-Laryngology*
Enrique Febres y Odriozola, Avenida Colmena 590 . . *Surgery*
Francisco Graña, Belaochaga 577 . . . . *Surgery*
Cárlos Morales Macedo, Mogollon 265 . . . . . *Surgery*

PERU — Continued

LIMA — Continued

Juan J. Mostajo, Calle del Pacal 971	*Surgery*
Ricardo Palma, Divorciades 671	*Surgery*
R. Pazos Varela, Plateros de San Pedro 109	*Urology*
Cárlos Villarán, Alfonso Ugarte 409	*Surgery*

REPUBLIC OF PANAMA

PANAMA

Augusto S. Boyd, 16 9th Street	*Surgery*
Alfred B. Herrick, Hospital de Panama	*Surgery*
Raymond Wentworth Runyan, Hospital de Panama .	*Surgery*

SYRIA

BEIRUT

Edwin St. John Ward	*Surgery*

TURKEY

CONSTANTINOPLE

Alden R. Hoover, Constantinople College	*Surgery*

KONIA

Wilfred McIlvaine Post	*Surgery*

URUGUAY

MONTEVIDEO

Manuel Albo, Calle Soriano 1270	*Surgery*
Gerardo Arrizabalaga, Calle Paraguay 1526	*Surgery*
Miguel Becerro de Bengoa, Seriano 1019	*Gynecology*
Luis Bottaro, Calle Uruguay 1316	*Surgery*
Baldomero Cuenca y Lamas, Rincon 615	*Urology*
Horacio G. Lagos, Andes 1287	*Surgery*
Alfonso Lamas, Colonia 1072	*Surgery*
Luis Mondino, Uruguay 936	*Surgery*
Juan C. Munyo, Rio Negro 1324 . .	*Rhinol., Oto-Laryngology*

URUGUAY — Continued

MONTEVIDEO — Continued

Julio Nin y Silva, Rivera 2122	*Surgery*
Alejandro Nogueira, Convencion 1454	*Urology*
James Hipolite Oliver, Calle Cuareim 1580	*Surgery*
Juan Pou Orfila, Calle Colonia 1270	*Surgery*
Enrique Pouey, Calle Uruguay 1205	*Gynecology*
Manuel Quintela, Calle 8 de Octubre 184	*Surgery*
Augusto Turenne, Paraguay 1438 . . .	*Gynecology, Obstetrics*

WALES

CARDIFF

Stanley Alwyn Smith, 80 Cathedral Road　.　*Orthopedic Surgery*

FELLOWS OF THE COLLEGE

ABBE, ROBERT, A.B., M.D., 13 West Fiftieth Street, New York, New York. Columbia University, College of Physicians and Surgeons, 1874. Senior Attending Surgeon, St. Luke's Hospital; Consulting Surgeon, Roosevelt Hospital, Hospital for the Ruptured and Crippled, Babies' Hospital of the City of New York, and Woman's Hospital.

ABBOTT, AMOS W., M.D., 1717 First Avenue, South, Minneapolis, Minnesota. Columbia University, College of Physicians and Surgeons, 1869. Surgeon-in-Chief, Abbott Hospital.

ABBOTT, CHARLES ROGER, M.D., 70 Walnut Street, Clinton, Massachusetts. Dartmouth Medical School, 1911. Junior Surgeon and Rœntgenologist, Clinton Hospital.

ABBOTT, CLARK LORENZO, M.Sc., M.D., Central Bank Building, Oakland, California. Rush Medical College, 1900. Surgeon, Abbott Hospital.

ABBOTT, CLIFTON S., M.D., 8 Academy Street, Laconia, New Hampshire. Dartmouth Medical School, 1894. Surgeon, Laconia Hospital.

ABBOTT, EDVILLE GERHARDT, A.M., M.D., D.Sc., 156 Free Street, Portland, Maine. Bowdoin Medical School, 1898. Professor of Orthopedic Surgery, Bowdoin Medical School; Surgeon-in-Chief, Children's Hospital.

ABEKEN, FREDERICK G., M.D., Medical Corps, United States Navy, Washington, District of Columbia. Washington University Medical School, 1899. Commander, Medical Corps, United States Navy.

ABELL, IRVIN, A.M., M.D., Francis Building, Louisville, Kentucky. University of Louisville, Medical Department (Louisville Medical College), 1897. Professor of Surgery and Clinical Surgery, University of Louisville, Medical Department; Visiting Surgeon, Louisville City Hospital.

ABERNETHY, CLAUDE OLIVER, B.Sc., M.D., 706 Citizen's National Bank Building, Raleigh, North Carolina. University of North Carolina, 1906. Urologist, Rex and St. Agnes' Hospitals.

ABRAHAM, JOSEPH H., M.D., 130 West Fifty-eighth Street, New York, New York. University of Virginia, Department of Medicine, 1894. Professor of Laryngology and Rhinology, New York Polyclinic Medical School; Laryngologist and Rhinologist, New York Polyclinic Medical School and Hospital; Otologist, New York City Children's Hospitals and Schools, Randall's Island.

ABRAMSON, LOUIS, M.D., 722 Cotton Street, Shreveport, Louisiana. Tulane University of Louisiana School of Medicine, 1898. Surgeon in Charge, North Louisiana Sanitarium.

ACKER, PAUL JEROME MOERIS, A.M., M.D., 153 Government Street, Mobile, Alabama. University of Alabama School of Medicine (Medical College of Alabama), 1892. Surgeon, City Hospital; Consulting Surgeon, United States Public Health Service.

ACKERMANN, GREGORY, M.D., 2319 Chapline Street, Wheeling, West Virginia. University of Berne, 1879. President of Staff, Wheeling Hospital.

ACUFF, HERBERT, Phar.G., M.D., 425 West Clinch Avenue, Knoxville, Tennessee. University of Louisville, Medical Department, 1911. Visiting Gynecologist, Knoxville General Hospital; Attending Surgeon, Riverside Hospital.

ADAIR, FRED LYMAN, M.A., M.D., 730 La Salle Building, Minneapolis, Minnesota. Rush Medical College, 1901. Associate Professor of Obstetrics, University of Minnesota Medical School; Chief of Service, in Obstetrics and Gynecology, Minneapolis City Hospital; Obstetrician and Gynecologist, St. Andrew's, Deaconess', and Fairview Hospitals; Obstetrician and Chief of Staff, Swedish Hospital.

ADAIR, JOHN H., M.D., 322 East Vine Street, Owatonna, Minnesota. Rush Medical College, 1883. Attending Surgeon, Owatonna City Hospital, State School for Dependent and Neglected Children.

ADAMS, ALBYN LINCOLN, M.D., 323 West State Street, Jacksonville, Illinois. Columbia University, College of Physicians and Surgeons, 1889. Oculist and Aurist, Passavant Memorial Hospital, Norbury Sanatorium, Illinois School for the Blind, Chicago and Alton Railroad.

ADAMS, BERTRAM S., B.Sc., M.D., 812 Third Avenue, Hibbing, Minnesota. University of Minnesota Medical School, 1901. Surgeon-in-Chief, Adams Hospital.

ADAMS, BON. O., B.Sc., M.D., 306 Loring Building, Riverside, California. Medical College of Indiana, 1901.

ADAMS, CHANCEY, A.M., M.D., 11 South Main Street, Concord, New Hampshire. Bowdoin Medical School, 1891. Senior Surgeon, Margaret Pillsbury General Hospital.

ADAMS, CHARLES, M.D., 920 North Michigan Avenue, Chicago, Illinois. Hahnemann Medical College and Hospital, Chicago, 1872; Rush Medical College, 1898. Retired.

ADAMS, FREDERICK WILLIAM, M.D., C.M., Roosevelt Clinic, Seattle, Washington. Western University Medical School, 1906. Member of Staff, Nose and Throat Department, Seattle City and Children's Orthopedic Hopitals.

ADAMS, JESSE L., B.Sc., M.D., 201 De Siard Street, Monroe, Louisiana. Tulane University of Louisiana, School of Medicine, 1906.

ADAMS, JOHN D., M.D., 45 Bay State Road, Boston, Massachusetts. Harvard Medical School, 1902. Assistant in Orthopedic Surgery, Harvard University Graduate School of Medicine; Orthopedic Surgeon-in-Chief, Boston Dispensary and Hospital for Children, Mt. Sinai Hospital; Orthopedic Surgeon, Cooley Dickinson Hospital, Northampton, Beverly Hospital, Beverly, Jordan Hospital, Plymouth.

ADAMS, JOHN FRANCIS, M.D., 114 South Main Street, Aberdeen, South Dakota. Rush Medical College, 1906. Attending Surgeon, St. Luke's Hospital.

ADAMS, LEMUEL PAYSON, A.B., M.D., Federal Realty Building, Oakland, California. University of Vermont College of Medicine, 1899. Chief of Staff, Alameda County Hospital and Infirmary, San Leandro.

ADAMSON, EDWARD WILLIAM, M.D., Douglas, Arizona. University of Michigan Medical School, 1904.

ADDY, GEORGE ARTHUR BELDON, M.D., C.M., 95 Union Street, St. John, New Brunswick. Faculty of Medicine, McGill University, 1890. Surgeon, General Public Hospital.

ADERHOLD, THOMAS MAZE, M.Sc., M.D., 405 South Williams Street, El Reno, Oklahoma. Northwestern University Medical School, 1901. Surgeon, El Reno Sanitarium.

ADLER, LEWIS H., JR., M.D., 1610 Arch Street, Philadelphia, Pennsylvania. University of Pennsylvania School of Medicine, 1888. Professor of Diseases of the Rectum, Polyclinic Section, University of Pennsylvania Graduate School of Medicine; Consulting Surgeon, Charity Hospital.

ADRIASOLA, ALBERTO, M.D., Salvador Donoso 234, Valparaiso, Chile. Faculty of Medicine, University of Chile, 1888. Chief Surgeon, Naval Hospital.

ADSIT, HENRY, A.B., M.D., 37 Allen Street, Buffalo, New York. Johns Hopkins University Medical Department, 1906. Attending Genito-Urinary Surgeon, State Institute for the Study of Malignant Disease, Buffalo Hospital of the Sisters of Charity, Children's Hospital of Buffalo.

ADSON, ALFRED WASHINGTON, B.Sc., A.M., M.D., M.Sc., Mayo Clinic, Rochester, Minnesota. University of Pennsylvania, 1914. Neurological Surgeon, Mayo Clinic.

AGNEW, FRED F., M.D., Second Street and Second Avenue, Southwest, Independence, Iowa. Jefferson Medical College, 1902.

AIMAR, CHARLES PONS, M.D., 4 Vanderhorst Street, Charleston, South Carolina. Medical College of the State of South Carolina, 1894. Professor of General Surgery, Medical College of the State of South Carolina; Visiting Surgeon and In Charge of General Surgery Department, Roper Hospital.

AINLEY, FRANK C., B.Sc., M.D., 1117 Brockman Building, Los Angeles, California. Johns Hopkins University, Medical Department, 1906.

AINSLIE, GEORGE, M.D., Oregonian Building, Portland, Oregon. University of Oregon Medical School, 1896; Rush Medical College, 1897.

AIRD, J. W., M.D., 65 East Second South Street, Provo, Utah. University of California Medical School, 1893. Surgeon, Provo General Hospital, Denver and Rio Grande Railway.

AKERMAN, JOSEPH, A.B., M.D., 1496 Harper Street, Augusta, Georgia. Johns Hopkins University, Medical Department, 1900. Assistant Professor of Obstetrics, University of Georgia, Medical Department; Visiting Obstetrician, University Hospital.

ALBEE, FRED H., A.B., M.D., D.Sc., 40 East Forty-first Street, New York, New York. Harvard Medical School, 1903. Director and Professor of

Orthopedic Surgery, University of Vermont College of Medicine, New York
Post-Graduate Medical School; Visiting Orthopedic Surgeon, New York
Post-Graduate Medical School and Hospital, Hawthorne Hospital; Con-
sulting Orthopedic Surgeon, Lutheran Hospital, Sea View Hospital,
Castleton Corners, Staten Island Hospital, Tompkinsville, Waterbury
Hospital, Waterbury, Connecticut, Muhlenberg Hospital, Plainfield,
Newark Memorial Hospital, Newark, New Jersey State Hospital, Trenton,
Rahway Hospital, Rahway, All Souls' Hospital, Morristown, New Jersey,
Mary Fletcher Hospital, Burlington, Vermont; Consulting Surgeon
Pennsylvania Railway.

ALBO, MANUEL, B.Sc., M.D., Calle Soriano 1270, Montevideo, Uruguay.
Faculty of Medicine, University of Montevideo, 1910.

ALBRECHT, FRANKLIN H., M.D., 3657 Delmar Boulevard, St. Louis, Missouri.
Washington University Medical School, 1902. Instructor in Orthopedic
Surgery, St. Louis University School of Medicine; Orthopedic Surgeon,
Lutheran, Bethesda, Deaconess, St. Louis Mullanphy Hospitals, Jewish
Home for Chronic Invalids; Associate Orthopedic Surgeon, Jewish Hos-
pital; Visiting Orthopedic Surgeon, St. Louis City Hospital.

ALBRIGHT, CLIFTON C., M.D., 313 Ford Building, Great Falls, Montana.
University of Missouri, School of Medicine, 1905. Member of Staff,
Columbus Hospital.

ALCIVAR, MIGUEL H., M.D., Clemente Ballen 917, Guayaquil, Ecuador.
University of Guayaquil, 1894. Professor, University of Guayaquil;
Chief Surgeon, General Hospital.

ALDEN, ARTHUR MAXWELL, A.B., A.M., M.D., Medical Corps, United States
Army, Washington, District of Columbia. St. Louis University School of
Medicine, 1915. Clinical Instructor in Rhinology and Oto-Laryngology,
United States Army Medical School; Chief of Clinic, Rhinology and
Oto-Laryngology, Walter Reed General Hospital; Major, Medical Corps,
United States Army.

ALDEN, ELIOT, A.B., M.D., 6422 Hollywood Boulevard, Los Angeles, California.
Harvard Medical School, 1901.

ALDERDYCE, WILLIAM W., M.D., 513 Madison Avenue, Toledo, Ohio. Toledo
Medical College, 1900.

ALEXANDER, EMORY GRAHAM, M.D., 1701 Spruce Street, Philadelphia, Penn-
sylvania. Jefferson Medical College, 1904. Professor of Clinical Surgery,
Woman's Medical College of Pennsylvania; Surgeon, St. Christopher's
Hospital for Children, Children's Hospital of Mary J. Drexel Home,
Philadelphia Hospital for Contagious Diseases, Methodist Episcopal and
Woman's Medical College Hospitals; Assistant Surgeon, Kensington
Hospital for Women.

ALEXANDER, GEORGE JAMES, M.D., 1831 Chestnut Street, Philadelphia,
Pennsylvania. Hahnemann Medical College and Hospital, Philadelphia,
1905. Senior Assistant, Ear, Nose, and Throat Department, West Philadelphia General Homeopathic Hospital.

ALEXANDER, HAROLD EGBERT, M.B., 311 Canada Building, Saskatoon, Saskatchewan. University of Toronto, Faculty of Medicine, 1910. Attending Surgeon, St. Paul's and City Hospitals.

ALEXANDER, LAWRENCE DADE, JR., M.D., 130 West Fifty-ninth Street, New York, New York. University of Virginia, Department of Medicine, 1901; University and Bellevue Hospital Medical College, 1902. Assistant Attending Surgeon, New York Eye and Ear Infirmary.

ALEXANDER, ROBERT DuBOSE, A.B., M.D., University Club Building, St. Louis, Missouri. Washington University Medical School, 1905. Surgeon in Charge, Missouri Pacific Railway Hospital.

ALEXANDER, ROBERT J., M.D., 1003 Amicable Building, Waco, Texas. University of Tennessee College of Medicine (Memphis Hospital Medical College), 1891. Visiting Surgeon, Providence Sanitarium; Member of Surgical Staff, Central Texas Baptist Sanitarium.

ALFORD, EDWARD T., Phar.G., M.D., Black Building, Waterloo, Iowa. Rush Medical College, 1901. Attending Surgeon, Synodical Presbyterian and St. Francis Hospitals.

ALGER, ELLICE M., A.B., M.D., 40 East Forty-first Street, New York, New York. University of Vermont College of Medicine, 1893. Professor of Ophthalmology, New York Post-Graduate Medical School; Attending Ophthalmologist, New York Post-Graduate Hospital.

ALJOVIN, MIGUEL C., M.D., Fano 855, Lima, Peru. Faculty of Medicine, University of San Marcos, 1909.

ALLEMAN, FRANK, Phar.G., M.D., 420 West Chestnut Street, Lancaster, Pennsylvania. Jefferson Medical College, 1896. Staff and Visiting Surgeon, Lancaster General Hospital.

ALLEN, ALFRED GEORGE, M.D., C.M., Waite Building, Deadwood, South Dakota. Queen's University, Faculty of Medicine, 1887. Surgeon, St. Joseph's Hospital.

ALLEN, CARROLL W., M.D., 43 Audubon Boulevard, New Orleans, Louisiana. Tulane University of Louisiana School of Medicine, 1901. Professor of Clinical Surgery, Tulane University of Louisiana School of Medicine; Professor of Anesthesia, Lecturer and Clinical Instructor in Genito-Urinary and Rectal Diseases, New Orleans Polyclinic; Associate Surgeon, Touro Infirmary; Visiting Surgeon, Charity Hospital.

ALLEN, GEORGE WASHINGTON, JR., M.D., Main Street, Yorktown, Texas. University of Texas, Department of Medicine, 1900. Chief Surgeon, Allen Hospital.

ALLEN, HARRY EUGENE, B.Sc., M.D., 505 Cobb Building, Seattle, Washington. Rush Medical College, 1898. District Surgeon, Chicago, Milwaukee and St. Paul Railway.

ALLEN, HERBERT COLEMAN, M.D., 171 Lefferts Place, Brooklyn, New York. New York Homeopathic Medical College and Flower Hospital, 1896. Obstetrician, Carson C. Peck Memorial Hospital; Visiting Surgeon,

Graham Home for Old Ladies, Brooklyn Nursery and Infants' Hospital; Consulting Obstetrician, Community Hospital, New York.

ALLEN, HORATIO CUSHING, A.B., M.D., 11 Eighth Street, New Bedford, Massachusetts. Harvard Medical School, 1901. Surgeon, St. Luke's Hospital.

ALLEN, JAMES ROSS, M.D., C.M., 129 Hamilton Street, Olean, New York. Queen's University, Faculty of Medicine, 1894. Surgeon, Higgins Memo rial Hospital; Consulting Surgeon, Rocky Crest Sanatorium.

ALLEN, JOHN MILTON, M.D., 24 Railroad Street, St. Johnsbury, Vermont. University of Vermont College of Medicine, 1890; University and Bellevue Hospital Medical College (Bellevue Hospital Medical College), 1891. Attending Surgeon, Brightlook and St. Johnsbury Hospitals, St. Johnsbury, Cleasby Hospital, Orleans; Consulting Surgeon, Littleton Hospital, Littleton, New Hampshire; Surgeon, Boston and Maine Railroad.

ALLEN, LEIGHTON PINE, M.D., 19 Jefferson Avenue, Oshkosh, Wisconsin. University of Michigan Medical School, 1889. Surgeon, Eye and Ear Department, St. Mary's and Mercy Hospitals.

ALLEN, LYMAN, A.B., M.Sc., M.D., 288 Main Street, Burlington, Vermont. University of Vermont College of Medicine, 1896. Associate Professor of Surgery, University of Vermont College of Medicine; Surgeon, Fanny Allen Hospital; Assistant Surgeon, Mary Fletcher Hospital.

ALLEN, NORMAN McLEOD, M.D., 2407 Woodward Avenue, Detroit, Michigan. Detroit College of Medicine, 1910. Instructor in Surgery, Detroit College of Medicine; Junior Attending Surgeon, Harper Hospital.

ALLEN, WILLIAM JUDSON, M.D., 401 East Grand Avenue, Beloit, Wisconsin. Hahnemann Medical College and Hospital, Chicago, 1901.

ALLEN, WILLIAM LARNED, M.D., 216 West Third Street, Davenport, Iowa. State University of Iowa College of Medicine, 1881. President, and Member of Surgical Staff, St. Luke's Hospital; Surgeon, State Orphans' Home.

ALLENBURGER, CHRISTIAN ALEXANDER, M.D., Columbus State Bank Building, Columbus, Nebraska. Rush Medical College, 1895. Surgeon, St. Mary's Hospital.

ALLIN, EDGAR W., M.D., C.M., L.R.C.P. (Lond.), M.R.C.S. (Eng.), 502 McLeod Building, Edmonton, Alberta. University of Toronto, Faculty of Medicine (Trinity Medical College), 1902. Examiner in Surgery, Alberta Medical Council; Surgeon, City Hospitals.

ALLIN, NORMAN GEORGE, M.D., C.M., L.R.C.P. (Lond.), M.R.C.S. (Eng.), 502 McLeod Building, Edmonton, Alberta. University of Toronto, Faculty of Medicine (Trinity Medical College), 1904.

ALLING, ARTHUR N., A.B., M.D., 257 Church Street, New Haven, Connecticut. Columbia University, College of Physicians and Surgeons, 1891. Clinical

Professor of Ophthalmology, Yale University School of Medicine; Ophthalmologist-in-Chief, New Haven Hospital.

ALLING, MARSHALL LOUIS, B.Sc., M.D., 627 Wyman's Exchange, Lowell, Massachusetts. Dartmouth Medical School, 1909. Member, Senior Surgical Staff, Lowell Corporation Hospital; Member, Junior Surgical Staff, Lowell General Hospital.

ALLISON, LUKE PRYOR, M.D., 204½ Center Avenue, Brownwood, Texas. St. Louis University School of Medicine (Beaumont Hospital Medical College), 1893. Chief Surgeon, Brownwood Infirmary.

ALLISON, NATHANIEL, M.D., Humboldt Building, St. Louis, Missouri. Harvard Medical School, 1901. Dean, and Professor of Orthopedic Surgery, Washington University Medical School; Associate Surgeon, St. Louis Children's and Washington University Hospitals; Consulting Surgeon, St. Luke's and St. Louis Maternity Hospitals.

ALLPORT, FRANK, M.D., LL.D., 7 West Madison Street, Chicago, Illinois. Northwestern University Medical School (Chicago Medical College), 1876. Member of Staff, St. Luke's Hospital.

ALPORT, EDWARD BISHOP, M.B., 710 McCallum-Hill Building, Regina, Saskatchewan. University of Toronto, Faculty of Medicine, 1910. Member of Staff, Regina General and Grey Nun's Hospitals.

ALTER, FRANCIS WILLIAM, M.D., 314 Colton Building, Toledo, Ohio. University and Bellevue Hospital Medical College (Bellevue Hospital Medical College), 1896. Chief of Eye, Ear, Nose, and Throat Department, Mercy Hospital.

ALTON, BENJAMIN HARRISON, B.Sc., M.S., M.D., 72 Pearl Street, Worcester, Massachusetts. Harvard Medical School, 1914. Assistant Surgeon, Memorial Hospital; Surgeon and Gynecologist, Out-Patient Department, Memorial Hospital.

ALTON, ROBERT DAVIS, M.D., First State Bank Building, Livingston, Montana. Western Reserve University School of Medicine (University of Wooster, Medical Department), 1881.

ALVES DE LIMA, JOAÔ, B.Sc., M.D., 16 Rua S. Luis, Sao Paulo, Brazil. University of Paris, 1897. Professor of Clinical Surgery, University of Sao Paulo, Faculty of Medicine; Surgeon, Maternity Hospital; Chief of Surgical Services, Central Hospital, Santa Casa, Misericordia and Maternity Hospitals, Sao Paulo.

ALWAY, ROBERT DOUGLAS, M.B., M.D., 423 South Lincoln Street, Aberdeen, South Dakota. University of Toronto, Faculty of Medicine, 1893. Oculist, Lincoln Hospital; Member of Staff, Aberdeen Clinic.

AMBERG, EMIL, M.D., David Whitney Building, Detroit, Michigan. University of Heidelberg, 1894. Attending Surgeon, Ear, Nose, and Throat Department, United Jewish Charities' Dispensary; Consulting Otologist, Grace Hospital.

AMERSON, GEORGE C., M.A., M.D., 31 North State Street, Chicago, Illinois. Hahnemann Medical College and Hospital, Chicago, 1902; University of Illinois College of Physicians and Surgeons, 1904. Professor of Surgery, Loyola University School of Medicine and of Illinois Post-Graduate Medical School; Surgeon, Garfield Park Hospital; Attending Surgeon, West Side and Municipal Tuberculosis Hospitals.

AMSDEN, HENRY HUBBARD, Ch.B., M.D., 4 North State Street, Concord, New Hampshire. Boston University School of Medicine, 1896. Surgeon, Ear, Nose, and Throat Department, Margaret Pillsbury General Hospital.

AMYX, ROBERT FLEMING, M.D., 1943 North Eleventh Street, St. Louis, Missouri. St. Louis University School of Medicine (Marion-Sims College of Medicine), 1897. Surgeon, St. Louis Mullanphy Hospital.

ANDERSON, AUGUSTUS MILTON, M.D., Connally Building, Atlanta, Georgia. Emory University School of Medicine (Atlanta Medical College), 1895.

ANDERSON, BRUCE, M.D., 804 Forest Avenue, West, Detroit, Michigan. Detroit Homeopathic College, 1901. Attending Gynecologist, Grace Hospital, Grace Hospital Polyclinic.

ANDERSON, GEORGE RILEY, M.D., Brooks House, Brattleboro, Vermont. University of Vermont College of Medicine, 1898. Surgeon-in-Chief, Brattleboro Memorial Hospital.

ANDERSON, HENRY GRAY, M.D., 39 Leavenworth Street, Waterbury, Connecticut. Columbia University, College of Physicians and Surgeons, 1889. Gynecologist, Waterbury Hospital.

ANDERSON, ROBERT B., B.Sc., M.D., 872 Park Place, Brooklyn, New York. Cornell University Medical College, 1899. Urologist, St. Mary's Hospital; Associate Surgeon, St. John's Hospital.

ANDERSON, WILLIAM HAROLD KERR, A.B., M.B., Military District No. 11, Victoria, British Columbia. University of Toronto, Faculty of Medicine, 1897. Lieutenant Colonel, Royal Canadian Army Medical Corps.

ANDERSON, WILLIAM J., M.D., Iron Mountain, Michigan. Rush Medical College, 1903. Surgeon, Westerlin Hospital.

ANDRES, RUDOLPH GEORGE, M.D., Mayo Clinic, Rochester, Minnesota. Loyola University School of Medicine (Chicago College of Medicine and Surgery), 1905. Member of Staff, St. Mary's Hospital.

ANDREW, FREDERICK WILLIAM, M.D., C.M., Summerland, British Columbia. Faculty of Medicine, University of Manitoba (Manitoba Medical College), 1907. Surgeon, Summerland Hospital.

ANDREW, JAMES H., M.D., 163 Hancock Street, Brooklyn, New York. University and Bellevue Hospital Medical College (Bellevue Hospital Medical College), 1896. Ophthalmologist, Greenpoint Hospital; Associate Ophthalmologist, St. John's Hospital; Associate Surgeon, Eye Department, Brooklyn Eye and Ear Hospital; Consulting Ophthalmologist, Huntington Hospital, Huntington; Chief Ophthalmologist, Bushwick Hospital.

ANDREWS, CHARLES JAMES, M.D., 512 Taylor Building, Norfolk, Virginia. Medical College of Virginia, 1902. Surgeon, Department of Obstetrics, Norfolk Protestant and St. Vincent's Hospitals.

ANDREWS, E. WYLLYS, A.M., M.D., 1235 Astor Street, Chicago, Illinois. Northwestern University Medical School (Chicago Medical College), 1881. Head Professor of Surgery, Northwestern University Medical School; Surgeon-in-Chief, Cook County Hospital; Attending Surgeon, St. Luke's and Michael Reese Hospitals.

ANDREWS, FRANK T., M.D., 448 Barry Avenue, Chicago, Illinois. Northwestern University Medical School, 1884.

ANDREWS, GEORGE REX, M.D., Muncie, Indiana. Indiana University School of Medicine (Medical College of Indiana), 1897. Member, Surgical Staff, Home Hospital.

ANDREWS, HAROLD VIRGIL, M.D., 1083 Boylston Street, Boston, Massachusetts. Harvard Medical School, 1896.

ANDREWS, JOHN WESLEY, M.D., National Citizens Bank Building, Mankato, Minnesota. Rush Medical College, 1877; University and Bellevue Hospital Medical College (Bellevue Hospital Medical College), 1880. Surgeon, St. Joseph's and Immanuel Hospitals.

ANDREWS, JOSEPH ALFRED, M.D., 1229 State Street, Santa Barbara, California. Columbia University, College of Physicians and Surgeons, 1877. Consulting Ophthalmic and Aural Surgeon, New York City Hospital, New York.

ANDREWS, ROBERT WESLEY, M.D., 235 Mill Street, Poughkeepsie, New York. Albany Medical College, 1898. Surgeon, Samuel W. Bowne Memorial Hospital; Attending Surgeon, General Hospital; Consulting Surgeon, Hudson River State Hospital.

ANDRIES, JOSEPH H., M.D., 1633 David Whitney Building, Detroit, Michigan. Royal Frederick William University, Berlin, 1897. Associate Professor of Clinical Surgery, Detroit College of Medicine and Surgery; Attending Surgeon, St. Mary's Hospital.

ANDRIES, RAYMOND CARL, A.B., M.D., 1737 David Whitney Building, Detroit, Michigan. Detroit College of Medicine and Surgery, 1907. Assistant Professor of Anatomy and Clinical Assistant to Chair of Surgery, Detroit College of Medicine and Surgery; Associate Surgeon, Providence Hospital.

ANGLIN, WILLIAM GARDINER, M.D., C.M., M.R.C.S. (Eng.), 52 Earl Street, Kingston, Ontario. Queen's University, Faculty of Medicine, 1883. Emeritus Professor of Clinical Surgery, Queen's University, Faculty of Medicine; Surgeon, Kingston Penitentiary.

ANGWIN, WILLIAM A., M.Sc., M.D., Medical Corps, United States Navy, Washington, District of Columbia. College of Physicians and Surgeons, San Francisco, 1903. Commander, Medical Corps, United States Navy.

ANSPACH, BROOKE M., M.D., 1827 Spruce Street, Philadelphia, Pennsylvania. University of Pennsylvania School of Medicine, 1897. Professor of Gynecology, Jefferson Medical College; Gynecologist, Stetson Hospital; Attending Gynecologist, Bryn Mawr Hospital, Bryn Mawr, and Jefferson Hospital.

ANTELO, NICOMEDES, M.D., Quinta Massini, Liniers, Buenos Aires, Argentina. Faculty of Medicine, National University of Buenos Aires, 1892. Professor of War Surgery, Army Medical School; Chief of Surgical Service, Military Hospital of Buenos Aires.

APPEL, THEODORE BURTON, A.M., M.D., D.Sc., 305 North Duke Street, Lancaster, Pennsylvania. University of Pennsylvania School of Medicine, 1894. Member of Staff, Lancaster General Hospital.

APPLEGATE, JOHN CHEW, M.D., 3540 North Broad Street, Philadelphia, Pennsylvania. Jefferson Medical College, 1887. Professor of Obstetrics, Temple University, Department of Medicine; Obstetrician, Samaritan and Garretson Hospitals.

ARANOW, HARRY, M.D., 355 East One Hundred Forty-ninth Street, New York, New York. Cornell University Medical College, 1904. Adjunct Attending Gynecologist and Obstetrician, Lebanon Hospital.

ARBUCKLE, MILLARD FILLMORE, M.D., University Club Building, St. Louis, Missouri. Washington University Medical School, 1909. Instructor in Clinical Laryngology and Rhinology, Assistant in Clinical Otology, Washington University Medical School; Surgeon, Out-Patient Department and Chief of Laryngological Clinic, Washington University Dispensary; Assistant Laryngologist, Barnes and St. Louis Children's Hospitals.

ARCHER, ALBERT ERNEST, M.B., King Street, Lamont, Alberta. University of Toronto, Faculty of Medicine, 1902. Surgeon, Lamont Public Hospital.

ARCHIBALD, EDWARD WILLIAM, A.B., M.D., C.M., 52 Westmount Boulevard, Montreal, Quebec. Faculty of Medicine, McGill University, 1896. Assistant Professor of Clinical Surgery, Faculty of Medicine, McGill University; Surgeon, Royal Victoria Hospital; Consulting Surgeon, Children's Memorial Hospital.

ARGUE, HIRAM S., M.D., 817 National Realty Building, Tacoma, Washington. University of Minnesota Medical School, 1905.

ARMITAGE, HARRY MARSHALL, M.D., 400 East Thirteenth Street, Chester, Pennsylvania. University of Pennsylvania, 1908. Surgeon, Chester Hospital.

ARMSTRONG, GEORGE E., M.D., C.M., C.M.G., D.Sc., LL.D., 320 Mountain Street, Montreal, Quebec. Faculty of Medicine, McGill University, 1877. Professor of Surgery, Faculty of Medicine, McGill University; Chief Surgeon, Royal Victoria Hospital; Consulting Surgeon, Montreal General Hospital, Montreal, Protestant Hospital for Insane, Verdun.

ARMSTRONG, HENRY EDWARD, M.D., C.M., Stapleton Building, Billings, Montana. University of Toronto, Faculty of Medicine (Trinity Medical College), 1894.

ARN, ELMER RAYMOND, M.D., 1120 Fidelity Medical Building, Dayton, Ohio. University of Cincinnati College of Medicine, 1911. Junior Surgeon, Miami Valley Hospital.

ARNETT, ARETT CAMPBELL, M.D., 716 LaFayette Life Building, LaFayette, Indiana. Indiana University School of Medicine (School of Medicine of Purdue University), 1907. Member of Surgical Staff, St. Elizabeth's Hospital; Member of Gynecological Staff, Home Hospital.

ARRIZABALAGA, GERARDO, M.D., Calle Paraguay 1526, Montevideo, Uruguay. University of Paris, 1894.

ARROWSMITH, HUBERT, M.D., 170 Clinton Street, Brooklyn, New York. Long Island College Hospital, 1886. Laryngologist, Kings County and St. Peter's Hospitals, Brooklyn, St. Anthony's Hospital, Woodhaven; Consulting Laryngologist, Brooklyn State and Jewish Hospitals, Brooklyn, Huntington Hospital, Huntington.

ARTHUR, WILLIAM H., M.D., 2130 Le Roy Place, Washington, District of Columbia. University of Maryland School of Medicine, 1877. Colonel, Medical Corps, United States Army, retired.

ARZUBE, CORDERO JUAN B., M.D., Malecón 2006, Guayaquil, Ecuador. Faculty of Medicine, University of Guayaquil, 1904.

ASHBURN, PERCY M., M.D., Medical Corps, United States Army, Washington, District of Columbia. Jefferson Medical College, 1893. Colonel, Medical Corps, United States Army.

ASHBURY, HOWARD ELMER, Phar.G., M.D., 810 St. Paul Street, Baltimore, Maryland. University of Maryland School of Medicine, 1903. Roentgenologist, St. Joseph's Hospital.

ASHCRAFT, LEON THOMAS, A.M., M.D., 2103 Chestnut Street, Philadelphia, Pennsylvania. Hahnemann Medical College and Hospital, Philadelphia, 1890. Professor of Genito-Urinary Diseases, Hahnemann Medical College and Hospital; Attending Surgeon, Hahnemann Medical College and Hospital; Senior Genito-Urinary Surgeon, Women's Homeopathic Hospital, West Philadelphia General Homeopathic Hospital and Dispensary; Consulting Genito-Urinary Surgeon, Mercy and Women's Southern Homeopathic Hospitals, Philadelphia, Carlisle General Hospital, Carlisle, West Chester Homeopathic Hospital, West Chester, Pottstown Homeopathic Hospital, Pottstown, Homeopathic State Hospital for Insane, Allentown, Wyoming Valley Homeopathic Hospital, Wilkes-Barre, Pennsylvania, West Jersey Homeopathic Hospital, Camden, William McKinley Memorial Hospital, Trenton, New Jersey.

ASHFORD, BAILEY K., M.D., D.Sc., Medical Corps, United States Army, Washington, District of Columbia. Georgetown University School of Medicine, 1896. Colonel, Medical Corps, United States Army.

ASHFORD, MAHLON, M.D., Medical Corps, United States Army, Washington, District of Columbia. Georgetown University School of Medicine, 1904. Major, Medical Corps, United States Army.

ASHHURST, ASTLEY PASTON COOPER, A.B., M.D., 1629 Spruce Street, Philadelphia, Pennsylvania. University of Pennsylvania School of Medicine, 1900. Associate in Surgery, University of Pennsylvania School of Medicine; Surgeon, Episcopal Hospital, Philadelphia Orthopedic Hospital and Infirmary for Nervous Diseases.

ASHTON, WILLIAM E., M.D., LL.D., 2011 Walnut Street, Philadelphia, Pennsylvania. University of Pennsylvania School of Medicine, 1881; Jefferson Medical College, 1884. Professor of Gynecology, University of Pennsylvania School of Medicine.

ASKEW, THEODORE B., M.D., 319 Moore Building, San Antonio, Texas. St. Louis College of Physicians and Surgeons, 1895.

ASMAN, BERNARD, A.M., M.D., Francis Building, Louisville, Kentucky. University of Louisville, Medical Department (Kentucky School of Medicine), 1897. Professor of Proctology, University of Louisville, Medical Department; Visiting Surgeon, St. Joseph's Infirmary and Louisville City Hospital.

ASPELL, JOHN, A.M., M.D., 34 West Seventy-sixth Street, New York, New York. University and Bellevue Hospital Medical College (Bellevue Hospital Medical College), 1885. Visiting Gynecologist, St. Vincent's and New York Foundling Hospitals.

ASSERSON, FREDERICK ASSER, M.D., Medical Corps, United States Navy, Washington, District of Columbia. University of Virginia, Department of Medicine, 1899. Commander, Medical Corps, United States Navy.

ATHERTON, ELLA BLAYLOCK, M.D., C.M., 148 Main Street, Nashua, New Hampshire. Queens University, Faculty of Medicine, 1887. Member of Staff, St. Joseph's and Nashua Memorial Hospitals.

ATKINSON, ALVAN WILLIAMS, A.B., M.D., 423 East State Street, Trenton, New Jersey. Hahnemann Medical College and Hospital, Philadelphia, 1893. Chief of Department of Gynecology and Obstetrics, William McKinley Memorial Hospital.

ATLEE, JOHN LIGHT, A.B., M.D., D.Sc., 37 East Orange Street, Lancaster, Pennsylvania. University of Pennsylvania School of Medicine, 1900. Consulting Surgeon, Lancaster General Hospital.

ATTIX, FRED FRANKLIN, M.D., Attix Clinic Building, Lewistown, Montana. University of Pennsylvania School of Medicine, 1900. Visiting Surgeon, St. Joseph's Hospital; Surgeon, Attix Private Clinic Hospital; District Surgeon, Chicago, Milwaukee and St. Paul Railroad.

ATTRIDGE, JAMES ARTHUR, M.D., 516 Water Street, Port Huron, Michigan. Detroit College of Medicine and Surgery, 1897.

ATWATER, JAMES BILLINGS, A.B., M.D., 82 Broad Street, Westfield, Massachusetts. University and Bellevue Hospital Medical College (University of the City of New York, Medical Department), 1882. Chief of Staff, Noble Hospital; Visiting Surgeon, Shurtleff Home for Destitute Children; Surgeon, New York Central Railroad at Westfield.

AUCHINCLOSS, HUGH, A.B., M.D., 800 Park Avenue, New York, New York. Columbia University, College of Physicians and Surgeons, 1905. Associate

Professor of Surgery, Columbia University, College of Physicians and Surgeons; Visiting Surgeon, Presbyterian Hospital.

AUFHAMMER, CHARLES HOWARD, M.D., 5004 Jenkins Arcade Building, Pittsburgh, Pennsylvania. University of Pennsylvania School of Medicine, 1906. Surgeon, Children's Hospital; Junior Gynecologist, Allegheny General Hospital; Urologist, Columbia Hospital, Wilkinsburg.

AUGUSTINE, JASPER L., M.D., Ladora, Iowa. State University of Iowa College of Medicine, 1893.

AUSTIN, HIRAM W., M.D., 1831 Belmont Road, Washington, District of Columbia. University of Michigan Medical School, 1875. Senior Surgeon, United States Public Health Service.

AUSTIN, MAYNARD ALVERNISE, M.D., 359 Union Building, Anderson, Indiana. Rush Medical College, 1897. Surgeon, St. John's Hospital.

AVES, CHARLES MARION, M.D., Humble Oil and Refining Company Building, Houston, Texas. University of Texas, Medical Department, 1907. Medical Director and Chief Surgeon, Humble Oil and Refining and Humble Pipe Line Companies; Member of Surgical Staff, St. Joseph's Infirmary; Surgeon, Baytown Refinery Hospital.

AVILÉS, JACINTO, A.B., M.D., 23 State Street, San Juan, Porto Rico. Ohio State University College of Medicine (Ohio Medical University), 1904. Visiting Surgeon, Municipal Hospital.

AYERS, HORACE ERNEST, M.D., 9 West Sixty-seventh Street, New York, New York. New York Homeopathic Medical College and Flower Hospital, 1909; Fordham University School of Medicine, 1912. Attending Surgeon, Community Hospital.

AYERS, JOHN CHAMBERS, M.D., 1601 Exchange Building, Memphis, Tennessee. University of Tennessee, College of Medicine (Memphis Hospital Medical College), 1905. Visiting Obstetrician, Methodist Hospital.

AYLEN, JAMES PRENTISS, M.D., Edwards Building, Fargo, North Dakota. University and Bellevue Hospital Medical College (Bellevue Hospital Medical College), 1888. Attending Surgeon, St. John's and St. Luke's Hospitals; Consulting Surgeon, Northern Pacific Railway; Local Surgeon, Great Northern and Chicago, Milwaukee and St. Paul Railways.

AYNESWORTH, HORACE TAYLOR, M.D., 1307 Amicable Building, Waco, Texas. University of Texas, Medical Department, 1904. Member of Staff, Providence and Central Texas Baptist Sanitariums.

AYNESWORTH, KENNETH HAZEN, M.D., 315 North Twelfth Street, Waco, Texas. University of Texas, Medical Department, 1899.

AYORA, ISIDOR, M.D., Sodiro 116, Quito, Ecuador. University of Quito Faculty of Medicine, 1905. Professor of Gynecology and Obstetrics, Central University of Ecuador.

BABBITT, JAMES A., A.M., M.D., 1901 Chestnut Street, Philadelphia, Pennsylvania. University of Pennsylvania School of Medicine, 1898. Associate Professor of Oto-Laryngology, University of Pennsylvania Graduate School of Medicine; Instructor in Otology, University of Pennsylvania School of Medicine; Assistant Laryngologist and Aurist, Lankenau Hospital; Laryngologist and Aurist, Children's Hospital, Out-Patient Department; Laryngologist, Children's Hospital of the Mary J. Drexel Home; Consulting Laryngologist and Aurist, Misericordia Hospital.

BABBITT, O. MILLER, M.D., 1001 Journal Building, Portland, Oregon. University of Oregon Medical School, 1906.

BABCOCK, HENRI S., M.D., 419 Temple Building, Danville, Illinois. University of Michigan Medical School, 1891. Gynecologist, St. Elizabeth's Hospital; Member of Surgical Staff, Lake View Hospital.

BABCOCK, W. WAYNE, A.M., M.D., 2033 Walnut Street, Philadelphia, Pennsylvania. University of Maryland School of Medicine and College of Physicians and Surgeons (College of Physicians and Surgeons, Baltimore), 1893; University of Pennsylvania School of Medicine, 1895; Medico-Chirurgical College, Philadelphia, 1900. Professor of Surgery and Clinical Surgery, Temple University, Department of Medicine; Surgeon-in-Chief, Samaritan Hospital; Surgeon, Garretson Hospital, American Hospital for Diseases of the Stomach.

BACH, JAMES ANTHONY, M.D., 409 Wells Building, Milwaukee, Wisconsin. University of Michigan Medical School, 1884. President of Staff, St. Mary's Hospital; Ophthalmologist, Notre Dame Convent Infirmary, Milwaukee, and Milwaukee County Dispensary.

BACHELLÉ, CECIL V., M.Sc., M.D., 30 North Michigan Avenue, Chicago, Illinois. Rush Medical College, 1900. Associate Professor of Gynecology, Chicago Policlinic; Assistant Professor of Obstetrics, University of Illinois College of Medicine; Gynecologist, Henrotin Memorial, Chicago Policlinic and Hospital.

BACHMANN, ROBERT A., M.D., Medical Corps, United States Navy, Washington, District of Columbia. Rush Medical College, 1900. Commander, Medical Corps, United States Navy.

BACON, CHARLES SUMNER, Ph.B., M.D., 2156 Sedgwick Street, Chicago, Illinois. Northwestern University Medical School, 1884. Professor of Obstetrics and Head of Department of Obstetrics and Gynecology, University of Illinois College of Medicine; Professor of Obstetrics, Chicago Policlinic; Attending Obstetrician, Chicago Policlinic and Hospital, Henrotin Memorial, University, Evangelical Deaconess, and Grant Hospitals, Chicago Lying-in Hospital and Dispensary.

BACON, GORHAM, A.B., M.D., Yarmouthport, Massachusetts. University and Bellevue Hospital Medical College (Bellevue Hospital Medical College), 1878. Retired.

BACON, JAY HARVEY, B.Sc., M.D., 804 Peoria Life Building, Peoria, Illinois. Johns Hopkins University Medical Department, 1904. Visiting Surgeon, John C. Proctor Hospital; Visiting Orthopedic Surgeon, Home for the Friendless.

BACON, JOHN ELMER, M.D., Miami, Arizona. University of Pennsylvania School of Medicine, 1892. Surgeon-in-Chief, Miami Inspiration Hospital.

BACON, JOSEPH BARNES, M.D., Macomb, Illinois. Texas Medical College and Hospital, 1879; Northwestern University Medical School, 1881. Surgeon-in-Chief, Bacon Clinic.

BAER, JOSEPH LOUIS, M.Sc., M.D., 104 South Michigan Avenue, Chicago, Illinois. Rush Medical College, 1904. Assistant Professor, Department of Gynecology and Obstetrics, Rush Medical College; Associate Attending Gynecologist and Obstetrician, Michael Reese Hospital; Director, Department of Gynecology, West Side Free Dispensary.

BAER, WILLIAM STEVENSON, A.B., M.D., 4 East Madison Street, Baltimore, Maryland. Johns Hopkins University, Medical Department, 1898. Associate Professor of Orthopedic Surgery, Johns Hopkins University, Medical Department; Head of Orthopedic Department and Visiting Orthopedic Surgeon, Johns Hopkins Hospital; Director, Children's Hospital School; Orthopedic Surgeon, Hospital for Women of Maryland; Visiting Orthopedic Surgeon, Union Protestant and Church Home Infirmaries; Consulting Orthopedic Surgeon, Cambridge-Maryland Hospital, Cambridge.

BAGG, CLINTON L., M.D., 56 West Fifty-second Street, New York, New York. University and Bellevue Hospital Medical College (University of the City of New York, Medical Department), 1879. Senior Surgeon, Metropolitan Hospital; Consulting Surgeon, Hahnemann Hospital.

BAGG, LINUS WORTHINGTON, M.D., 712 Clinton Avenue, Newark, New Jersey. Syracuse University College of Medicine, 1906. Member of Staff, Presbyterian and St. James Hospitals.

BAGLEY, CHARLES, JR., A.B., M.D., Latrobe Apartments, Baltimore, Maryland. University of Maryland School of Medicine, 1904. Associate in Experimental Neurology, Johns Hopkins University, Medical Department; Visiting Surgeon, Hebrew Hospital and Asylum, Church Home and Infirmary, St. Agnes' Hospital, United States Public Health Service Hospital, Number 56, Ft. McHenry; Consulting Surgeon, Baltimore and Presbyterian Eye, Ear, and Throat Charity Hospitals, Baltimore, Annapolis Emergency Hospital, Annapolis.

BAGLEY, WILLIAM RICHARDSON, M.D., 510 Fidelity Building, Duluth, Minnesota. University of Michigan Medical School, 1898. Chief of Staff, St. Mary's Hospital; Visiting Surgeon, Morgan Park Hospital.

BAILEY, AUGUSTUS BRUCE, D.D.S., M.D., 1008 Selling Building, Portland, Oregon. University of Oregon, Medical Department (Willamette University, Medical Department), 1904. Eye, Ear, Nose, and Throat Surgeon, Good Samaritan Hospital.

BAILEY, E. STILLMAN, A.M., M.D., Ph.D., 22 East Washington Street, Chicago, Illinois. Hahnemann Medical College and Hospital, Chicago, 1878. Special Lecturer on Radium as applied to Gynecology, Hahnemann

Medical College and Hospital; Member of Staff, Department of Gynecology, Hahnemann Hospital.

BAILEY, FRED DEFOREST, M.D., 260 Hancock Street, Brooklyn, New York. University and Bellevue Hospital Medical College (New York University Medical College), 1882. Surgeon, Brooklyn Eye and Ear Hospital; Consulting Ophthalmologist, Eastern District Dispensary and Hospital, St. Catherine's Hospital; Attending Ophthalmologist, Industrial Home for the Blind, Baptist Home, Brooklyn, St. Mary's Hospital, Jamaica; Ophthalmic Surgeon, Long Island Railroad.

BAILEY, FREDERICK HARRIS, M.D., Fargo, North Dakota. University of Buffalo, Department of Medicine, 1893.

BAILEY, FRED WARREN, B.Sc., M.D., 611 Metropolitan Building, St. Louis, Missouri. St. Louis University School of Medicine (Marion-Sims-Beaumont Medical College), 1903. Associate Professor of Surgery, St. Louis University School of Medicine; Surgeon, St. John's Hospital; Visiting Surgeon, St. Louis City Hospital.

BAILEY, FREDERICK WILLIAM, M.Sc., M.D., 309 Security Building, Cedar Rapids, Iowa. State University of Iowa College of Medicine, 1905. Member of Staff, St. Luke's Hospital; Ophthalmic Surgeon, Chicago, Milwaukee and St. Paul Railroad.

BAILEY, HAROLD CAPRON, M.D., 22 East Sixty-eighth Street, New York, New York. Cornell University Medical College, 1903. Instructor in Obstetrics, Cornell University Medical College; Assistant Obstetrician, Manhattan Maternity and Dispensary; Assistant Visiting Obstetrician, Bellevue Hospital; Associate Gynecologist, Memorial Hospital.

BAILEY, WILLIAM J., M.D., First National Bank Building, Connellsville, Pennsylvania. University of Pennsylvania School of Medicine, 1895. Consulting Opthalmologist and Oto-Laryngologist, Cottage State Hospital.

BAILLY, THOMAS EDWARD, M.D., Ph.D., 870 Market Street, San Francisco, California. Cooper Medical College, 1892. Surgeon, Gynecologist, and Chief of Staff, St. Mary's Hospital.

BAIRD, ALVIN W., A.B., M.D., Medical Building, Portland, Oregon. Cornell University Medical College, 1905. Assistant Professor of Surgery, University of Oregon Medical School; Attending Surgeon, Multnomah County Hospital.

BAKER, ARCHIBALD E., M.D., 10 Meeting Street, Charleston, South Carolina. Medical College of the State of South Carolina, 1889. Clinical Professor of Gynecology and Abdominal Surgery, Medical College of the State of South Carolina; Visiting Surgeon, Roper Hospital; Surgeon in Charge, Baker Sanatorium.

BAKER, DAVIS, M.D., Insurance Company Building, Glens Falls, New York. Cornell University Medical College, 1909. Surgeon, Glens Falls Hospital.

BAKER, FRANK COLE, M.D., Medical Corps, United States Army, Washington, District of Columbia. Georgetown University School of Medicine, 1899. Lieutenant Colonel, Medical Corps, United States Army.

BAKER, HAROLD W., B.Sc., M.D., 49 Gloucester Street, Boston, Massachusetts. Harvard Medical School, 1906. Instructor in Gynecology, Harvard University Graduate School of Medicine; Surgeon, Out-Patient Department, Free Hospital for Women, Brookline.

BAKER, HERBERT WILLIAM, B.A., M.B., 606 Spadina Avenue, Toronto, Ontario. University of Toronto, Faculty of Medicine, 1909. Assistant in Clinical Surgery, University of Toronto, Faculty of Medicine; Assistant Surgeon, Out-Patient Department, Toronto General Hospital.

BAKER, J. NORMENT, A.B., M.D., Bell Building, Montgomery, Alabama. University of Virginia, Department of Medicine, 1898. Surgeon, Highland Park Sanatorium.

BAKER, JULIAN MEREDITH, B.Sc., M.D., 503 Main Street, Tarboro, North Carolina. University of Maryland School of Medicine, 1879. Surgeon, Edgecombe General Hospital.

BAKER, WALTER H., M.D., 122 North Lafayette Boulevard, South Bend, Indiana. Indiana Medical College, 1907. Surgeon, Epworth and St. Joseph's Hospitals.

BAKER, WILLIAM T. H., B.Sc., M.D., 217 West Orman Avenue, Pueblo, Colorado. Northwestern University Medical School, 1896. Surgeon, St. Mary's Hospital.

BALABANOFF, IVAN PETROFF, A.M., M.D., 415 Fidelity Building, Tacoma, Washington. University and Bellevue Hospital Medical College (University of the City of New York, Medical Department), 1887. Member of Staff, St. Joseph's Hospital.

BALCH, FRANKLIN GREENE, A.M., M.D., 279 Clarendon Street, Boston, Massachusetts. Harvard Medical School, 1892. Chief of East Surgical Service, Massachusetts General Hospital; Surgeon, Faulkner Hospital.

BALCH, RALPH E., M.D., 115 West Lovell Street, Kalamazoo, Michigan. Northwestern University Medical School, 1897. Consulting Surgeon, Kalamazoo State Hospital.

BALDWIN, CHARLES HUME, A.B., M.D., 282 Genesee Street, Utica, New York. Harvard Medical School, 1904. Orthopedic Surgeon, St. Elizabeth's and St. Luke's Hospitals, Utica City Dispensary.

BALDWIN, EDWARD HILL, M.D., 85 Clinton Avenue, Newark, New Jersey. New York Homeopathic Medical College and Flower Hospital, 1895. Surgeon, Homeopathic Hospital of Essex County; Consulting Surgeon, St. Mary's Hospital, Passaic.

BALDWIN, HUGH ALLEN, M.D., 347 East State Street, Columbus, Ohio. Jefferson Medical College, 1901. Instructor in Genito-Urinary Surgery, Ohio State University College of Medicine; Genito-Urinary Surgeon, Grant, St. Francis, and Children's Hospitals.

BALDWIN, JAMES FAIRCHILD, A.M., M.D., 115 South Grant Avenue, Columbus, Ohio. Jefferson Medical College, 1874. Chief Surgeon, Grant Hospital; Consulting Surgeon, Children's Hospital.

BALDWIN, JAMES HARVEY, A.B., M.D., 1426 Pine Street, Philadelphia, Pennsylvania. University of Pennsylvania School of Medicine, 1900. Surgeon, Methodist Episcopal Hospital.

BALDWIN, KATE W., M.D., 1117 Spruce Street, Philadelphia, Pennsylvania. Woman's Medical College of Pennsylvania, 1890. Senior Surgeon, Woman's Hospital.

BALDWIN, L. GRANT, M.D., 20 Schermerhorn Street, Brooklyn, New York. Long Island College Hospital, 1886. Gynecologist, St. Peter's Hospital; Consulting Gynecologist, St. Joseph's Hospital, Far Rockaway, Hospital of St. Giles the Cripple, Garden City; Consulting Surgeon, Huntington Hospital, Huntington.

BALDWIN, SAMUEL C., M.D., 316 McCornick Building, Salt Lake City, Utah. University of Louisville, Medical Department, 1884. Orthopedic Surgeon, Dr. W. H. Groves Latter-Day Saints' Hospital.

BALDY, JOHN MONTGOMERY, M.D., Devon, Pennsylvania. University of Pennsylvania School of Medicine, 1884.

BALFOUR, DONALD C., M.D., 427 South Glencoe Street, Rochester, Minnesota. University of Toronto, Faculty of Medicine, 1906. Associate Professor of Surgery, University of Minnesota Medical School; Surgeon, St. Mary's Hospital (Mayo Clinic).

BALLENGER, EDGAR GARRISON, M.D., 805 Healey Building, Atlanta, Georgia. University of Maryland School of Medicine, 1901. Associate Professor of Genito-Urinary Diseases, Emory University School of Medicine; Urologist, Grady and Wesley Memorial Hospitals; Genito-Urinary Surgeon, Davis-Fischer Sanatorium.

BALLIN, MAX, M.D., 2407 Woodward Avenue, Detroit, Michigan. University of Berlin, 1892. Clinical Professor of Surgery, Detroit College of Medicine and Surgery; Surgeon, Harper Hospital; Consulting Surgeon, Children's Free, St. Mary's and Woman's Hospitals.

BALLOCH, EDWARD A., A.M., M.D., 2000 Sixteenth Street, Northwest, Washington, District of Columbia. Howard University School of Medicine, 1879. Dean and Professor of Surgery, Howard University School of Medicine; Attending Surgeon, Freedmen's Hospital.

BALLON, DAVID H., B.A., C.M., M.D., 255 Bishop Street, Montreal, Quebec. Faculty of Medicine, McGill University, 1909. Assistant Demonstrator in Oto-Laryngology, Faculty of Medicine, McGill University; Associate in Oto-Laryngology, Royal Victoria Hospital; Oto-Laryngologist, Alexandra Hospital.

BANCROFT, FREDERIC WOLCOTT, A.B., M.D., 100 East Sixty-sixth Street, New York, New York. Johns Hopkins University, Medical Department, 1906. Instructor in Surgery, Columbia University, College of Physicians and Surgeons; Associate Attending Surgeon, New York Hospital.

BANDLER, CLARENCE GARFIELD, M.D., 8 East Forty-eighth Street, New York, New York. Columbia University, College of Physicians and Surgeons,

1904. Associate Professor of Urology, New York Post-Graduate Medical School; Associate in Urology, Columbia University, College of Physicians and Surgeons; Assistant Attending Urologist, Presbyterian Hospital; Consulting Surgeon, Home for Aged and Infirm, Yonkers, King's Park State Hospital, King's Park.

BANDLER, SAMUEL WYLLIS, A.B., M.D., 134 West Eighty-seventh Street, New York, New York. Columbia University, College of Physicians and Surgeons, 1894. Professor of Diseases of Women, New York Post-Graduate Medical School.

BANISTER, JOHN MONRO, A.B., M.D., 400 Brandeis Theatre Building, Omaha, Nebraska. University of Virginia, Department of Medicine, 1878. Assistant Professor, University of Nebraska College of Medicine; Member of Staff, Eye, Ear, Nose, and Throat Department, Wise Memorial Hospital; Colonel, Medical Corps, United States Army, retired.

BANISTER, WILLIAM B., M.D., Medical Corps, United States Army, Washington, District of Columbia. University of Louisville Medical Department (Central University of Kentucky), 1883. Colonel, Medical Corps, United States Army.

BANNEN, WILLIAM EDWARD, M.D., State Bank Building, La Crosse, Wisconsin. Northwestern University Medical School, 1908. Member of Advisory and Attending Staffs, St. Francis Hospital.

BANNER, CHARLES W., D.D.S., M.D., Banner Building, Greensboro, North Carolina. University of Maryland School of Medicine, 1899. Laryngologist and Ophthalmologist, St. Leo's Hospital.

BANNISTER, MURDOCH, B.Sc., M.D., Hofmann Building, Ottumwa, Iowa. University of Pennsylvania School of Medicine, 1894. Visiting Surgeon, Ottumwa Hospital.

BANSBACH, JOSEPH J., M.D., 825 Frederick Avenue, St. Joseph, Missouri. Ensworth Medical College, 1898. Surgeon, Missouri Methodist, Noyes, and St. Joseph's Hospitals; Genito-Urinary Surgeon, Welfare Board; Director of Venereal Disease Clinic.

BARBER, CALVIN F., M.D., 57 South Oxford Street, Brooklyn, New York. Columbia University, College of Physicians and Surgeons, 1882. Attending Surgeon, Kings County and Bradford Street Hospitals; Consulting Surgeon, Long Island State, Harbor, Samaritan, and Coney Island Hospitals, St. Christopher's Hospital for Babies.

BARBER, ROBERT FORREST, A.B., M.D., 1140 Dean Street, Brooklyn, New York. Long Island College Hospital, 1908. Associate Professor of Surgery, Long Island College Hospital; Chief Attending Surgeon, Polhemus Clinic.

BARBER, WILLIAM HOWARD, A.B., M.D., 616 Madison Avenue, New York, New York. Columbia University, College of Physicians and Surgeons, 1911. Lecturer on Surgery and Director of Laboratory of Experimental Surgery, University and Bellevue Hospital Medical College; Assistant Visiting Surgeon, Bellevue Hospital.

BARBOSO DE BARROS, JOSÉ, M.D., Rua Campos Salles 51, Campinas, Brazil. Faculty of Medicine, University of Rio de Janeiro, 1901. Director, Portuguese and Maternity Hospitals; Surgeon, Mercy Home.

BARCUS, PAUL J., M.D., Ben Hur Building, Crawfordsville, Indiana. University of Cincinnati College of Medicine (Medical College of Ohio), 1887.

BARDEN, GEORGE RICE, M.D., 270 Elmwood Avenue, Providence, Rhode Island. University and Bellevue Hospital Medical College (Bellevue Hospital Medical College), 1896. Surgeon, St. Joseph's Hospital, State Hospital for Mental Diseases.

BARKLEY, ARCHIBALD HENRY, A.B., M.D., C.M., 138 North Upper Street, Lexington, Kentucky. Columbia University, College of Physicians and Surgeons, 1896. Consulting Surgeon, Good Samaritan Hospital; Surgeon, St. Joseph's Hospital, Lexington, Kentucky State House of Reform, Greendale.

BARKSDALE, JOHN WOODSON, M.D., 106 Railroad Avenue, Winona, Mississippi. Birmingham Medical College, 1899. Surgeon, Winona Infirmary; Visiting Surgeon, Mississippi State Charity Hospital, Jackson.

BARLOW, CHARLES HOLDSWORTH, M.D., 600 Court Street, Portsmouth, Virginia. University of Virginia, Department of Medicine, 1900.

BARLOW, EDWARD E., M.D., 101 Iowa Street, Dermott, Arkansas. University of Tennessee College of Medicine (Memphis Hospital Medical College), 1902. Surgeon, Lake Village Infirmary, Lake Village.

BARLOW, ROY ALEXANDER, B.Sc., M.D., Mayo Clinic, Rochester, Minnesota. University of Michigan Medical School, 1914. Assistant Professor of Rhinology and Oto-Laryngology, University of Minnesota, Mayo Foundation; Associate Oto-Laryngologist, Division of Surgery, Mayo Clinic and Worrell Hospital.

BARLOW, WALTER LINLEY, A.B., M.D., C.M., 4769 Sherbrooke Street, West, Montreal, Quebec. Faculty of Medicine, McGill University, 1898. Assistant Surgeon, Montreal General Hospital.

BARNDT, MILTON A., M.D., 511 Consolidated Realty Building, Los Angeles, California. Hahnemann Medical College and Hospital, Chicago (Chicago Homeopathic Medical College), 1893.

BARNES, FRANK L., M.D., 1408 Rosalie Avenue, Houston, Texas. University of Maryland School of Medicine (College of Physicians and Surgeons, Baltimore), 1896. Visiting Surgeon, St. Joseph's Infirmary.

BARNES, JAMES ARTHUR, A.B., M.D., Slater Building, Worcester, Massachusetts. Harvard Medical School, 1900. Surgeon, St. Vincent Hospital.

BARNES, WALTER S., M.D., 29 East Madison Street, Chicago, Illinois. University of Buffalo, Department of Medicine, 1892. Assistant Professor of Gynecology, Northwestern University Medical School; Attending Gynecologist, Mercy Hospital.

BARNETT, CHARLES E., M.D., Medical Arts Building, Fort Wayne, Indiana. Indiana University School of Medicine, 1890.

BARNETT, JACOB, M.D., Medical Building, New Orleans, Louisiana. Tulane University of Louisiana School of Medicine, 1897. Professor of Gynecology, Loyola Post-Graduate School of Medicine; Gynecologist, Charity Hospital, Touro Infirmary.

BARNETT, JAMES MILLER, M.D., 208 Pine Street, Albany, Georgia. Emory University School of Medicine (College of Physicians and Surgeons, Atlanta), 1902. Surgeon, Phoebe Putney Memorial Hospital.

BARNETT, STEPHEN TRENT, A.B., M.D., 20 East Linden Avenue, Atlanta, Georgia. University of Virginia, Department of Medicine, 1896. Gynecologist and Surgeon, St. Joseph's Infirmary; Consulting Surgeon, MacVicar Hospital of Spelman Seminary; Gynecologist, Georgia Baptist Hospital.

BARNEY, J. DELLINGER, A.B., M.D., 99 Commonwealth Avenue, Boston, Massachusetts. Harvard Medical School, 1904. Instructor in Genito-Urinary Surgery, Harvard Medical School; Chief of Genito-Urinary Service, Massachusetts General Hospital.

BARNEY, LOUIE FRANK, M.D., Wahlenmaier Building, Kansas City, Kansas. University of Kansas School of Medicine (Kansas City Medical College), 1903. Associate Professor of Clinical Surgery, University of Kansas School of Medicine; Attending Surgeon, St. Margaret's Hospital.

BARNHILL, JOHN F., M.D., Pennway Building, Indianapolis, Indiana. Indiana University School of Medicine (Central College of Physicians and Surgeons), 1888. Professor of Otology, Rhinology and Laryngology, Indiana University School of Medicine; Member of Staff, Robert W. Long and Methodist Episcopal Hospitals.

BARON, FREDERICK STEWART, M.D., 740 Fidelity Medical Building, Dayton, Ohio. University and Bellevue Hospital Medical College, 1900. Ophthalmologist and Oto-Laryngologist, Dayton State Hospital; Oto-Laryngologist, Good Samaritan Hospital, Zanesville; Ophthalmologist, Bethesda Hospital, Zanesville; Oculist, Baltimore and Ohio Railroad.

BARR, RICHARD ALEXANDER, A.B., M.D., 800 Nineteenth Avenue, South, Nashville, Tennessee. Vanderbilt University, Medical Department, 1894. Professor of Surgery and Clinical Surgery, Vanderbilt University, Medical Department; Member of Staff, Nashville City and Vanderbilt University Hospitals, Barr Infirmary.

BARRETT, CHANNING W., M.D., 25 East Washington Street, Chicago, Illinois. Detroit College of Medicine and Surgery, 1895. Professor and Head of Department of Gynecology, University of Illinois College of Medicine; Professor of Gynecology, Chicago Policlinic; Head of Department of Gynecology and Attending Gynecologist, Cook County Hospital; Attending Gynecologist, Chicago Policlinic and Hospital, Henrotin Memorial, West Side, and Columbus Hospitals.

BARRETT, GILBERT MICHAEL, A.M., M.D., 516 Sutter Street, San Francisco, California. University and Bellevue Hospital Medical College (Bellevue Hospital Medical College), 1895. Associate Surgeon, St. Luke's Hospital;

288 *American College of Surgeons*

Chief Surgeon, Union Plant Hospital and Alameda Works Hospital of the Bethlehem Shipbuilding Corporation, Limited, General Electric and Pacific States Electric Companies.

BARRETT, MICHAEL FRANCIS, A.B., M.D., 231 Main Street, Brockton, Massachusetts. Harvard Medical School, 1901. Surgeon-in-Chief, Brockton Hospital.

BARRETT, WILLIAM THOMAS, M.D., Union Bank Building, Victoria, British Columbia. Faculty of Medicine, University of Manitoba (Manitoba Medical College), 1897. Gynecologist, St. Joseph's Hospital; Member of Visiting Staff, Royal Provincial Jubilee Hospital.

BARRIE, GEORGE, M.D., 15 East Forty-eighth Street, New York, New York. Georgetown University School of Medicine, 1892. Visiting Surgeon, Blythedale Home for Crippled Children, Hawthorne; Consulting Orthopedic Surgeon, Gouverneur Hospital.

BARRINGER, BENJAMIN S., B.Sc., M.D., 134 East Seventy-sixth Street, New York, New York. Cornell University Medical College, 1902. Instructor in Urology, Cornell University Medical College; Surgeon, Urological Department, Memorial Hospital; Assistant Surgeon, Urological Department, Bellevue Hospital; Consultant Urologist, Mary McClellan Hospital; Consultant Cystoscopist, French Hospital.

BARRINGER, EMILY DUNNING, B.Sc., M.D., 134 East Seventy-sixth Street, New York, New York. Cornell University Medical College, 1901. In Charge of Female Gonorrheal Wards, City Board of Health.

BARROS, NICOLAN DE MORAES, M.D., Rua S. Bento 35, Sao Paulo, Brazil. Faculty of Medicine, University of Rio de Janeiro, 1900. Professor of Gynecology, Faculty of Medicine, Sao Paulo; Surgeon and Director of Gynecological Clinic, Santa Casa Hospital.

BARROW, D. WOOLFOLK, M.D., 190 North Upper Street, Lexington, Kentucky. University of Michigan Medical School, 1908. Member of Surgical Staff, Good Samaritan and St. Joseph's Hospitals.

BARROW, DAVID, M.D., 190 North Upper Street, Lexington, Kentucky. Tulane University of Louisiana School of Medicine, 1880. Visiting and Consulting Surgeon, Good Samaritan and St. Joseph's Hospitals.

BARROWS, DAVID NYE, A.B., M.D., 130 East Fifty-sixth Street, New York, New York. Cornell University Medical College, 1912. Instructor in Gynecology, University and Bellevue Hospital Medical College; Clinical Instructor in Surgery, Department of Gynecology, and Chief of Gynecological Clinic, Cornell University Medical School; Adjunct Attending Gynecologist, Bellevue Hospital; Assistant Attending Surgeon, Manhattan Maternity Hospital; Attending Gynecologist and Obstetrician, Volunteer Hospital; Consulting Cystoscopist, New Rochelle Hospital.

BARTELS, LEO, M.D., 650 Century Building, St. Louis, Missouri. Washington University Medical School, 1906. Visiting Genito-Urinary Surgeon, St. Louis Sanitarium, City Infirmary; Associate Genito-Urinary Surgeon, St. John's Hospital.

BARTHOLOMEW, RUDOLPH A., A.B., M.D., 746 Peachtree Street, Atlanta, Georgia. University of Michigan Medical School, 1912. Associate Professor of Obstetrics and Clinical Gynecology, Emory University School of Medicine; Visiting Obstetrician and Gynecologist, Wesley Memorial and Georgia Baptist Memorial Hospitals; Assistant Visiting Gynecologist and Obstetrician, Grady Memorial Hospital.

BARTLETT, PERCY, A.B., M.D., 8 Parkway, Hanover, New Hampshire. Dartmouth Medical School, 1900. Professor of Surgery, Dartmouth Medical School; Surgeon, Mary Hitchcock Memorial Hospital.

BARTLETT, WILLARD, A.M., M.D., 410 Metropolitan Building, St. Louis, Missouri. St. Louis University School of Medicine (Marion-Sims Medical College), 1895. Associate in Surgery, Washington University Medical School; Surgeon, Missouri Baptist Sanitarium.

BARTON, FRANCIS WILLIAM, B.Sc., M.D., 402 First National Bank Building, Danville, Illinois. Columbia University College of Physicians and Surgeons, 1901. Member of Surgical Staff, St. Elizabeth's and Lake View Hospitals.

BARTON, LYMAN G., M.D., 47 Broad Street, Plattsburg, New York. University and Bellevue Hospital Medical College (Bellevue Hospital Medical College), 1891. Visiting Surgeon, Champlain Valley Hospital; Consulting Surgeon, St. Lawrence State Hospital, Ogdensburg.

BARTRAN, WILLIAM H., M.D., 109 East Walnut Street, Green Bay, Wisconsin. Northwestern University Medical School, 1899. Attending Surgeon, St. Vincent's Hospital.

BASCOM, FRANCIS S., M.D., 815 Boston Building, Salt Lake City, Utah. Rush Medical College, 1882. Medical Director and Member of Consulting Staff, St. Mark's Hospital.

BASHAM, DAVID WALKER, M.D., 802 Schweiter Building, Wichita, Kansas. University of Kansas School of Medicine (Kansas City Medical College), 1884; University and Bellevue Hospital Medical College (New York University Medical College), 1891. Member of Surgical Staff, St. Francis Hospital.

BASTERRICA, JERMAN VALENZUELA, M.D., Riqueleme 47, Santiago, Chile. Faculty of Medicine, University of Chile, 1882. Surgeon, Hospital of San Juan de Dios.

BASTIANELLI, RAFFAELE, M.D., F.R.C.S. (Eng.), Hon., 83 Via Delle Terme, Rome, Italy. University of Rome, 1887. Associate Professor of Clinical Surgery, Royal University; Surgeon-in-Chief, First Pavilion, Hospital Policlinico Umberto I; Lieutenant Colonel, Italian Army Medical Corps.

BASTION, JOSEPH E., M.D., Medical Corps, United States Army, Washington, District of Columbia. Georgetown University School of Medicine, 1906. Major, Medical Corps, United States Army.

BATCHELLER, OLIVER T., M.D., 508 Old National Bank Building, Spokane, Washington. University of Minnesota Medical School, 1899.

BATCHELOR, JAMES MADISON, B.Sc., M.D., 2010 State Street, New Orleans, Louisiana. Tulane University of Louisiana School of Medicine, 1895. President, and Professor of Surgery, Loyola Post-Graduate School of Medicine; Chief, First Surgical Division, Charity Hospital.

BATH, THOMAS WILBUR, M.D., Bloomington, Illinois. St. Louis College of Physicians and Surgeons, 1892. Consulting Surgeon, St. Joseph's Hospital.

BATTIN, HARRY EDWIN, M.D., 116 East First Street, Corning, New York. Albany Medical College, 1897. Attending Surgeon, Corning Hospital.

BATTLE, KEMP PLUMMER, A.B., M.D., Citizens Bank Building, Raleigh, North Carolina. University of Virginia, Department of Medicine, 1881; University and Bellevue Hospital Medical College (Bellevue Hospital Medical College), 1882. Visiting Surgeon, Rex and St. Agnes' Hospitals.

BAUER, JOHN LEOPOLD, A.B., M.D., 984 Bushwick Parkway, Brooklyn, New York. Syracuse University College of Medicine, 1904. Attending Surgeon, Wyckoff Heights Hospital; Consulting Surgeon, Brooklyn State Hospital.

BAUGHMAN, DANIEL SPARKS, B.Sc., M.D., 100 Egan Avenue, South, Madison, South Dakota. Loyola University School of Medicine (Chicago College of Physicians and Surgeons), 1911. Surgeon and Member of Staff, New Madison Hospital.

BAUGHMAN, GREER, M.D., 26 North Laurel Street, Richmond, Virginia. Medical College of Virginia, 1897. Professor of Obstetrics, Medical College of Virginia; Visiting Obstetrician, Memorial, Virginia, and Stuart Circle Hospitals.

BAULD, WILLIAM ALFRED GORDON, A.B., M.D., C.M., 710 St. Urbain Street, Montreal, Quebec. Faculty of Medicine, McGill University, 1911. Medical Superintendent, Montreal Maternity Hospital.

BAUM, WILLIAM LOUIS, M.D., 30 North Michigan Avenue, Chicago, Illinois. Jefferson Medical College, 1888. Professor of Skin and Venereal Diseases, Post-Graduate Medical School; Dermatologist, St. Luke's, Post-Graduate, and Evangelical Deaconess Hospitals.

BAUMEISTER, EDWARD EMERY, Phar.G., M.D., Chico, California. University of California Medical School, 1904.

BAXTER, JOHN JAMES, M.D., 92 Main Street, Woonsocket, Rhode Island. University and Bellevue Hospital Medical College (University of the City of New York, Medical Department), 1885. Senior Visiting Surgeon, Woonsocket Hospital.

BAXTER, STEPHEN HENRY, A.B., M.D., Physicians and Surgeons Building, Minneapolis, Minnesota. University of Minnesota Medical School, 1902. Associate Surgeon, Hill Crest Surgical Hospital.

BAY, ROBERT PARKE, M.D., 1800 North Charles Street, Baltimore, Maryland. University of Maryland School of Medicine, 1905. Professor of Oral Surgery, University of Maryland, Department of Dentistry; Attending Surgeon, Church Home and Infirmary, Hebrew Hospital and Asylum; Visiting Surgeon, Union Hospital, Elkton, Havre-de-Grace Hospital,

Havre-de-Grace; Chief Medical Examiner, State Industrial Accident Commission.

BAYNARD, ERNEST CORNISH, M.D., 86½ Wentworth Street, Charleston, South Carolina. Medical College of the State of South Carolina, 1909. Professor of Urology, Medical College of the State of South Carolina; Visiting Urologist and Genito-Urinary Surgeon, Roper Hospital.

BAZIN, ALFRED TURNER, M.D., C.M., 583 Dorchester Street, West, Montreal, Quebec. Faculty of Medicine, McGill University, 1894. Assistant Professor of Surgery, and Clinical Surgery, Faculty of Medicine, McGill University; Attending Surgeon, Montreal General Hospital.

BEACH, ROBERT H., A.B., M.D., Northern Pacific Hospital, Glendive, Montana. University of Michigan Medical School, 1906. Chief Surgeon, Yellowstone District, Northern Pacific Railway, Northern Pacific Beneficial Association.

BEACH, SYLVESTER JUDD, A.B., M.D., 776 Congress Street, Portland, Maine. Harvard Medical School, 1905. Attending Physician, Maine Eye and Ear Infirmary.

BEACH, WILLIAM M., A.M., M.D., 901 Bessemer Building, Pittsburgh, Pennsylvania. Jefferson Medical College, 1889.

BEALL, FRANK COOKE, B.Sc., M.D., 703 Lamar Street, Fort Worth, Texas. Johns Hopkins University, Medical Department, 1906. Surgeon in Charge, The Johnson-Beall Hospital.

BEATTIE, DAVID A., M.B., M.D., C.M., 210 South First Street, San Jose, California. University of Toronto, Faculty of Medicine, 1892.

BEATTIE, ROBERT, M.D., 1229 David Whitney Building, Detroit, Michigan. Detroit College of Medicine and Surgery, 1903. Member of Staff, Providence Hospital.

BEATTY, HENRY ALBERT, M.B., M.R.C.S. (Eng.), L.R.C.P. (Lond.), 52 Howland Avenue, Toronto, Ontario. University of Toronto, Faculty of Medicine, 1897. Surgeon, Toronto Western Hospital; Chief Surgeon and Medical Officer, Canadian Pacific Railway.

BEATTY, HUGH GIBSON, Phar.G., M.D., 327 East State Street, Columbus, Ohio. Ohio State University College of Medicine, 1910. Instructor in Rhinology and Oto-Laryngology, Ohio State University College of Medicine; Assistant Surgeon, St. Francis and Children's Hospitals; Consultant, Columbus State Hospital, Hawkes Hospital of Mt. Carmel.

BECERRO DE BENGOA, MIGUEL, M.D., Seriano 1019, Montevideo, Uruguay. Faculty of Medicine, University of Montevideo, 1912. Chief of Clinical Gynecology, Maciel and Vilardebo Hospitals.

BECK, CARL, M.D., 601 Deming Place, Chicago, Illinois. Royal Imperial University of Prague, 1889. Surgeon, North Chicago Hospital.

BECK, EMIL G., M.D., 2632 Lake View Avenue, Chicago, Illinois. University of Illinois College of Medicine. 1896. Surgeon, North Chicago Hospital.

BECK, FREDERICK LOUIS, M.D., 408 Hynds Building, Cheyenne, Wyoming. University of Nebraska College of Medicine, 1903. Member of Staff, Laramie County Memorial Hospital.

BECK, JOSEPH C., M.D., 108 North State Street, Chicago, Illinois. University of Illinois College of Medicine (College of Physicians and Surgeons, Chicago), 1895. Associate Professor of Oto-Laryngology, University of Illinois College of Medicine; Chief Oto-Laryngologist, North Chicago Hospital.

BECKER, EDWARD WATERBURY, M.D., 6 St. Paul Place, Troy, New York. Albany Medical College, 1897. Lecturer on Diseases of the Lungs, Albany Medical College; Rhinologist and Laryngologist, Samaritan Hospital, Church Home, Troy Orphan Asylum.

BECKER, HENRY A., M.D., 629 Guardian Building, Cleveland, Ohio. Western Reserve University School of Medicine, 1894. Assistant Professor of Surgery, Western Reserve University School of Medicine; Visiting Surgeon, Fairview Park Hospital; Associate Surgeon, Lakeside Hospital; Assistant Head of Surgical Department, Cleveland City Hospital.

BECTON, JOSEPH DANIEL, M.D., Greenville, Texas. University of Nashville, Medical Department, 1890.

BEDELL, ARTHUR J., M.D., 344 State Street, Albany, New York. Albany Medical College, 1901. Clinical Professor of Ophthalmology and Otology, Albany Medical College; Attending Ophthalmologist and Otologist, Albany Hospital, South End and Albany Hospital Dispensaries; Attending Oculist, Albany Orphan Asylum, Old Ladies' Home.

BEEBE, HENRY E., M.D., 124 North Ohio Avenue, Sidney, Ohio. Ohio State University College of Homeopathic Medicine (Cleveland Homeopathic Hospital College), 1873.

BEEBE, HUGH McDOWELL, M.D., 317 South State Street, Ann Arbor, Michigan. University of Michigan Homeopathic Medical School, 1907. Professor of Surgery and Clincal Surgery, University of Michigan Homeopathic Medical School; Surgeon, University of Michigan Homeopathic Hospital.

BEEBE, WARREN LORING, A.M., M.D., Fifth Avenue and St. Germain Street, St. Cloud, Minnesota. University of Cincinnati College of Medicine (Medical College of Ohio), 1873; University and Bellevue Hospital Medical College (Bellevue Hospital Medical College), 1876. Member of Staff, St. Raphael's Hospital.

BEEMAN, CORDA E., M.D., 311 Widdicomb Building, Grand Rapids, Michigan. Cleveland Homeopathic Medical College, 1903. Member of Staff, Blodgett Memorial Hospital.

BEER, EDWIN, A.B., M.D., 11 East Forty-eighth Street, New York, New York. Columbia University, College of Physicians and Surgeons, 1899. Attending Surgeon, Mt. Sinai and Bellevue Hospitals.

BEEUWKES, HENRY, A.B., M.D., Medical Corps, United States Army, Washington, District of Columbia. Johns Hopkins University Medical School,

1906. Medical Director, Relief Work in Russia, with American Relief Administration. Major, Medical Corps, United States Army.

BEHAN, RICHARD JOSEPH, M.D., Jenkins Arcade Building, Pittsburgh, Pennsylvania. University of Pittsburgh School of Medicine (Western Pennsylvania Medical College), 1902; University of Berlin, 1914. Surgeon, Pittsburgh Tuberculosis Hospital, St. Joseph's Hospital and Dispensary.

BEHAN, WILLIAM ALOYSIUS, M.D., 91 Front Street, Binghamton, New York. University and Bellevue Hospital Medical College, 1910. Member of Staff, Binghamton City Hospital.

BEHLE, AUGUSTUS C., M.D., 512 Judge Building, Salt Lake City, Utah. Rush Medical College, 1894. Surgeon, St. Mark's Hospital.

BEHREND, MOSES, A.M., M.D., 1427 North Broad Street, Philadelphia, Pennsylvania. University of Pennsylvania, 1899. Demonstrator of Anatomy, Jefferson Medical College; Surgeon, Jewish Hospital of Philadelphia, and Mt. Sinai Hospital; Consulting Surgeon, Jewish Maternity Hospital, Hebrew Orphans' Home.

BEILBY, GEORGE EVERETT, M.D., 247 State Street, Albany, New York. Albany Medical College (Union University, Medical Department), 1899. Clinical Professor of Surgery, Albany Medical College; Assistant Attending Surgeon, Albany Hospital.

BELFIELD, WILLIAM T., M.D., 32 North State Street, Chicago, Illinois. Rush Medical College, 1878. Professor of Genito-Urinary Surgery, Rush Medical College; Professor of Genito-Urinary Diseases, Chicago Policlinic; Genito-Urinary Surgeon, Chicago Policlinic and Hospital, Henrotin Memorial and Presbyterian Hospitals.

BELL, BENJAMIN C., A.B., M.B., 143 Market Street, Brantford, Ontario. University of Toronto, Faculty of Medicine, 1898. Ophthalmologist and Oto-Laryngologist, Brantford General Hospital, Brant Sanatorium, Ontario School for the Blind.

BELL, ERNEST LORNE, M.D., 174 Main Street, Plymouth, New Hampshire. Dartmouth Medical School, 1894. Member of Staff, Soldiers' and Sailors' Memorial and Emily Balch Cottage Hospitals.

BELL, GEORGE HUSTON, M.D., 40 East Forty-first Street, New York, New York. University of Virginia, Department of Medicine, 1897. Ophthalmic Surgeon, New York Eye and Ear Infirmary; Consulting Ophthalmologist, St. Andrew's Convalescent Hospital, New York Polyclinic Medical School and Hospital; Visiting Ophthalmic Surgeon, Marine Hospital, Staten Island.

BELL, GEORGE NEWTON, M.D., 44 High Street, Hartford, Connecticut. Yale University School of Medicine, 1892. Surgeon, Hartford Hospital; Consulting Surgeon, Hartford Isolation Hospital, Hartford, Litchfield County Hospital, Winsted, Home for Crippled Children, Newington, Memorial Hospital, South Manchester.

BELL, HAROLD KENNEDY, A.B., M.D., 857 President Street, Brooklyn, New York. Columbia University College of Physicians and Surgeons, 1910.

Assistant Surgeon, Methodist Episcopal, St. John's, and Kingston Avenue Hospitals.

BELL, JAMES HALL, M.D., 319 Moore Building, San Antonio, Texas. Jefferson Medical College, 1884.

BELL, JOHN J., M.D., 661 West Eighth Street, Erie, Pennsylvania. University of Maryland School of Medicine (College of Physicians and Surgeons, Baltimore), 1901. Surgeon, St. Vincent's Hospital.

BELL, JOHN NORVAL, Phar.G., M.D., 1149 David Whitney Building, Detroit, Michigan. Detroit College of Medicine and Surgery, 1892. Associate Professor of Obstetrics, Detroit College of Medicine and Surgery; Consulting Surgeon, Harper Hospital; Consulting Obstetrician, Booth Memorial and Woman's Hospitals; Attending Obstetrician, Providence Hospital.

BELL, PERCY GEORGE, B.A., M.D., 12 Ellesmere Apartments, Carlton Street, Winnipeg, Manitoba. Faculty of Medicine, University of Manitoba (Manitoba Medical College), 1909. Associate Ophthalmologist, Winnipeg General Hospital.

BELL, RICHARD PHILLIPS, A.B., M.D., Professional Building, Staunton, Virginia. University of Virginia, Department of Medicine, 1905. President of Staff, King's Daughters Hospital.

BELL, THOMAS HERBERT, M.D., C.M., M.R.C.S. (Eng.), L.R.C.P. (Lond.), 703 Boyd Building, Winnipeg, Manitoba. University of Toronto, Faculty of Medicine (Trinity Medical College), 1896. Associate Professor of Clinical Ophthalmology, Faculty of Medicine, University of Manitoba; Associate Ophthalmic Surgeon, Winnipeg General Hospital.

BELL, WILLIAM HEMPHILL, M.D., Medical Corps, United States Navy, Washington, District of Columbia. University of Pennsylvania School of Medicine, 1897. Captain, Medical Corps, United States Navy.

BELLER, ABRAHAM J., B.Sc., M.D., 1155 Park Avenue, New York, New York. Columbia University College of Physicians and Surgeons, 1910. Instructor in Operative Surgery, Cornell University Medical College; Associate Visiting Surgeon, Broad Street Hospital; Chief of Surgical Clinic, Mt. Sinai Hospital and Dispensary.

BELLO, EDUARDO, M.D., Compas de la Concepcion 358, Lima, Peru. Faculty of Medicine, University of San Marcos, 1895. Chief Surgeon, Santa Ana Hospital.

BELLOWS, HOWARD P., M.Sc., M.D., 220 Clarendon Street, Boston, Massachusetts. Boston University School of Medicine, 1877. Professor of Otology, Boston University School of Medicine; Consulting Aurist, Massachusetts Homeopathic Hospital, Boston, Westborough State Hospital, Westborough; Aurist, Newton Hospital, Newton.

BELOU, PEDRO, M.D., La Plata 1059, Buenos Aires, Argentina. University of Buenos Aires Faculty of Medicine, 1906. Director, University of Buenos Aires, Faculty of Medicine.

BENDELL, JOSEPH LEWI, A.B., M.D., 178 State Street, Albany, New York. Albany Medical College, 1907. Assistant Attending Surgeon, Homeopathic Hospital; Attending Surgeon, South End Dispensary; Attending Dispensary Surgeon, Albany Hospital.

BENDIXEN, PETER ALFRED, B.Sc., M.D., 406 Lane Building, Davenport, Iowa. Rush Medical College, 1905. Surgeon, St. Luke's and Mercy Hospitals; Chief Surgeon, Davenport, Rock Island and Northwestern Railroad.

BENEDICT, SAMUEL R., M.D., Empire Building, Birmingham, Alabama. Medical College of Virginia (University College of Medicine), 1908. Attending Gynecologist, Hillman Hospital; Chief Surgeon, Alabama Power Company.

BENEDICT, WILLIAM LEMUEL, M.D., 102 Second Street, Southwest, Rochester, Minnesota. University of Michigan Medical School, 1912. Associate Professor of Ophthalmology, University of Minnesota Medical School, Mayo Foundation; Head of Ophthalmic Section, Mayo Clinic.

BENNETT, ARTHUR G., M.D., 26 Allen Street, Buffalo, New York. University of Buffalo, Department of Medicine, 1891. Associate Professor of Ophthalmology, University of Buffalo, Department of Medicine; Ophthalmologist, Deaconess, Children's, and Buffalo City Hospitals, Church Home and Infirmary, Buffalo, Craig Colony for Epileptics, Sonyea; Consulting Ophthalmologist, J. N. Adam Memorial Hospital, Perrysburg.

BENNETT, NEWMAN HALL, A.B., M.D., 1912 Carson Street, Pittsburgh, Pennsylvania. University of Pittsburgh School of Medicine (Western Pennsylvania Medical College), 1906. Member of Surgical Staff, St. Joseph's Hospital.

BENNINGHOFF, GEORGE EDWARD, M.D., 31 West Corydon Street, Bradford, Pennsylvania. Western Reserve University School of Medicine (University of Wooster, Medical Department), 1879. Surgeon, Bradford Hospital.

BENOIT, HECTOR WRIGHT, M.D., C.M., 520 Nostrand Avenue, Brooklyn, New York. Faculty of Medicine, McGill University, 1909. Visiting Surgeon, St. Christopher's Hospital for Babies; Assistant Visiting Surgeon, Kings County and Bradford Street Hospitals; Associate Surgeon, Bushwick Hospital.

BENSON, MARION T., M.D., 504 Atlanta National Bank Building, Atlanta, Georgia. Emory University School of Medicine (Atlanta College of Physicians and Surgeons), 1900. Gynecologist, Grady Memorial Hospital; Consulting Gynecologist, Georgia Baptist Hospital; Gynecologist and Obstetrician, Davis-Fischer Sanatorium.

BENTLEY, FREDERICK, M.D., 404 Cobb Building, Seattle, Washington. Rush Medical College, 1901. Member of Staff, Children's Orthopedic Hospital.

BENTLEY, NEIL I., A.B., M.D., 1161 David Whitney Building, Detroit, Michigan. University of Michigan Homeopathic Medical School, 1906. Attending Ophthalmologist and Oto-Laryngologist, Grace Hospital and Polyclinic.

BENTON, FREDERICK LESLIE, B.Sc., M.D., Medical Corps, United States Navy, Washington, District of Columbia.   Columbia University, College of Physicians and Surgeons, 1896; University of Havana, 1906.   Commander, Medical Corps, United States Navy.

BENVIE, ROBERT MACLEAN, M.D., C.M., South Main Street, Stellarton, Nova Scotia.   Faculty of Medicine, McGill University, 1907.   Visiting Surgeon, Aberdeen Hospital.

BERENS, T. PASSMORE, M.D., 25 Park Avenue, New York, New York.   University of Pennsylvania School of Medicine, 1887.   Director and Surgeon, Manhattan Eye, Ear, and Throat Hospital; Consulting Otologist, St. Bartholomew's and New Rochelle Hospitals.

BERGERON, JOSEPH Z., A.M., M.D., 104 South Michigan Avenue, Chicago, Illinois.   Rush Medical College, 1889.   Oto-Laryngologist and Rhinologist, St. Joseph's Hospital.

BERGLAND, JOHN MCFARLAND, B.Sc., M.D., 4 West Biddle Street, Baltimore, Maryland.   Johns Hopkins University, Medical Department, 1904.   Associate in Obstetrics, University of Maryland School of Medicine and College of Physicians and Surgeons; Visiting Obstetrician, Church Home and Infirmary, Hospital for Women of Maryland, Hebrew Hospital and Asylum.

BERNARD, GUY TALMADGE, M.D., 204 Thirteenth Street, Augusta, Georgia.   University of Georgia, Medical Department, 1907.   Instructor in Surgery, University of Georgia, Medical Department; Associate Attending Surgeon, University and Wilhenford Hospitals.

BERNDT, DANIEL ALBERT, M.D., 1304 Gallia Avenue, Portsmouth, Ohio.   University of Maryland School of Medicine (College of Physicians and Surgeons, Baltimore), 1896.   Visiting Surgeon, Hempstead Hospital; Surgeon, Norfolk and Western Railway, Portsmouth Street Railway and Light Company.

BERNHEIM, BERTRAM M., A.B., M.D., 2313 Eutaw Place, Baltimore, Maryland.   Johns Hopkins University, Medical Department, 1905.   Instructor in Clinical Surgery, Johns Hopkins University, Medical Department; Visiting Surgeon, Hospital for Women of Maryland, Union Protestant Infirmary, Hebrew Hospital and Asylum, Church Home and Infirmary; Surgeon, Out-Patient Department, Johns Hopkins Hospital.

BERNSTEIN, EDWARD J., M.D., 507 Fine Arts Building, Detroit, Michigan.   University of Maryland School of Medicine, 1887.

BERRY, JOHN J., M.D., Portsmouth, New Hampshire.   University and Bellevue Hospital Medical College (University of the City of New York), 1879.   Surgeon, Portsmouth Hospital, Mark H. Wentworth Home, Boston and Maine Railroad, Portsmouth Electric Railway.

BERRY, JOHN McWILLIAMS, B.Sc., M.D., 35 Elk Street, Albany, New York.   Johns Hopkins University, Medical Department, 1901.   Clinical Professor of Orthopedics and Rœntgenology, Albany Medical College; Attending Orthopedist and Rœntgenologist, Albany Hospital; Orthopedist and Rœntgenologist, Child's Hospital; Consulting Orthopedist, Ellis Hospital, Schenectady.

BERRY, VIRGIL, M.D., Fifth and Okmulgee Streets, Okmulgee, Oklahoma. St. Louis University School of Medicine (Beaumont Hospital Medical College), 1895. Retired.

BERRY, WILLIAM D., M.D., Barnes Building, Muskogee, Oklahoma. University of Louisville, Medical Department (Kentucky School of Medicine), 1899. Surgeon, Oklahoma State Baptist, and Physicians and Surgeons Hospitals.

BERTELING, J. B., M.S., A.M., M.D., 228 West Colfax Avenue, South Bend, Indiana. University of Cincinnati College of Medicine (Miami Medical College), 1883. Surgeon, Epworth Hospital; Gynecologist, St. Joseph's Hospital.

BERTNER, ERNST WILLIAM, A.B., M.D., 411 Carter Building, Houston, Texas. University of Texas, Department of Medicine, 1911. Member of Surgical Staff, Municipal Hospital and Baptist Sanitarium.

BESLEY, FREDERIC A., M.D., 104 South Michigan Avenue, Chicago, Illinois. Northwestern University Medical School, 1894. Professor of Surgery, Northwestern University Medical School; Attending Surgeon, Mercy and Cook County Hospitals.

BESSESEN, ALFRED N., M.D., 301 Donaldson Building, Minneapolis, Minnesota. Rush Medical College, 1893. Member of Staff, Asbury Hospital.

BEST, CHARLES LORTON, A.B., M.Sc., M.D., 3½ East Stephenson Street, Freeport, Illinois. Rush Medical College, 1904. Surgeon, St. Francis and Freeport General Hospitals.

BETTMAN, RALPH BOERNE, A.B., M.D., 5 South Wabash Avenue, Chicago, Illinois. Johns Hopkins University Medical Department, 1914. Clinical Assistant in Surgery, Northwestern University Medical School; Adjunct Surgeon, Michael Reese Hospital.

BETTS, NORMAN S., M.D., Medical Corps, United States Navy, Washington, District of Columbia. Hahnemann Medical College and Hospital, Philadelphia, 1904. Lieutenant, Medical Corps, United States Navy.

BEVAN, ARTHUR DEAN, M.D., 122 South Michigan Avenue, Chicago, Illinois. Rush Medical College, 1883. Professor of Surgery and Head of Surgical Department, Rush Medical College; Head of Surgical Department and Attending Surgeon, Presbyterian Hospital.

BEVANS, JAMES L., M.D., Medical Corps, United States Army, Washington, District of Columbia. Northwestern University Medical School, 1893. Lieutenant Colonel, Medical Corps, United States Army.

BEYEA, HENRY D., M.D., Roanes, Virginia. University of Pennsylvania School of Medicine, 1891. Retired.

BICA DE MEDEIROS, ALFEN, M.D., Porto Alegre, Brazil. Faculty of Medicine, Surgery and Pharmacy, Bahia, 1903.

BICKHAM, WARREN STONE, Phar.M., M.D., 440 Riverside Drive, New York, New York. Tulane University of Louisiana School of Medicine, 1886; Columbia University, College of Physicians and Surgeons, 1887.

BICKLEY, ROBERT S., M.D., 339 West Fifty-seventh Street, New York, New York. New York Homeopathic College and Flower Hospital, 1907. Attending Surgeon, Auxiliary Staff, Metropolitan Hospital; Assisting Surgeon, Broad Street Hospital.

BICKLEY, WILLIAM H., M.D., 2625 West Fourth Street, Waterloo, Iowa. New York Homeopathic Medical College and Flower Hospital, 1900. Surgeon, Synodical Presbyterian and St. Francis Hospitals.

BIDDLE, J. C., M.D., State Hospital, Ashland, Pennsylvania. Jefferson Medical College, 1877. Surgeon-in-Chief, and Superintendent, State Hospital.

BIDWELL, PERN J., M.D., Schmidt Building, Toledo, Ohio. Ohio State University College of Medicine (Starling Medical College), 1904. Surgeon, St. Vincent's Hospital.

BIERHOFF, FREDERIC, M.D., 155 West Fifty-eighth Street, New York, New York. Columbia University, College of Physicians and Surgeons, 1889. Consulting Cystoscopist, Gouverneur Hospital; Genito-Urinary Surgeon, West Side Dispensary, Home for Aged and Infirm Hebrews.

BIGELOW, LESLIE LAWSON, A.B., M.D., 185 East State Street, Columbus, Ohio. Harvard Medical School, 1906. Assistant Professor of Surgery, Ohio State University College of Medicine; Surgeon and Chief of Staff, Children's Hospital; Surgeon, Grant and Protestant Hospitals.

BIGELOW, WILFRED A., M.D., Bigelow Clinic, Brandon, Manitoba. Faculty of Medicine, University of Manitoba (Manitoba Medical College), 1903. Member of Staff, Brandon General Hospital.

BIGGAR, HAMILTON FISK, A.M., M.D., LL.D., 1110 Euclid Avenue, Cleveland, Ohio. Western Homeopathic College, 1866. Retired.

BIGGS, MONTGOMERY HERMAN, M.D., Rutherfordton, North Carolina. University of Pennsylvania School of Medicine, 1897. Surgeon, Rutherford Hospital.

BIGLER, C. ALBERT, JR., M.D., 2009 Chestnut Street, Philadelphia, Pennsylvania. Hahnemann Medical College and Hospital, Philadelphia, 1902. Instructor of Surgery and Clinical Professor of Rectal Surgery, Hahnemann Medical College and Hospital; Surgeon, Hahnemann Hospital; Consulting Surgeon, West Chester Homeopathic Hospital, West Chester; Consulting Proctologist, Allentown State Hospital, Allentown.

BILL, ARTHUR HOLBROOK, A.M., M.D., 503 Osborn Building, Cleveland, Ohio. Western Reserve University School of Medicine, 1901. Associate Professor of Obstetrics and Head of the Department, Western Reserve University School of Medicine; Obstetrician-in-Chief, Cleveland Maternity Hospital; Visiting Obstetrician and Head of Obstetrical Department, Cleveland City Hospital; Director of Out-Patient Department, Maternity Hospital, Western Reserve University.

BINGER, HENRY E., M.D., 1027 Lowry Building, St. Paul, Minnesota. University of Minnesota Medical School, 1910. Ophthalmologist and Oto-Laryngologist, St. Luke's and Bethesda Hospitals, State Hospital for Crippled Children.

BINGHAM, ANSON HOLDEN, M.D., 2345 Broadway, New York, New York. New York Homeopathic Medical College and Flower Hospital, 1900. Professor of Orthopedic Surgery, New York Homeopathic Medical College and Flower Hospital; Orthopedic Surgeon, New York Homeopathic Medical College and Flower Hospital, Metropolitan and Community Hospitals, Laura Franklin Hospital for Children, New York, Yonkers Homeopathic Hospital and Maternity, Yonkers.

BINGHAM, GEORGE ARTHUR, M.B., M.D., C.M., 68 Isabella Street, Toronto, Ontario. University of Toronto, Faculty of Medicine, 1884. Associate Professor of Clinical Surgery and Clinical Anatomy, University of Toronto, Faculty of Medicine; Chief of Service and Surgeon, Toronto General Hospital.

BINNEY, HORACE, A.B., M.D., 403 Beacon Street, Boston, Massachusetts. Harvard Medical School, 1901. Visiting Surgeon, Boston City Hospital.

BINNIE, JOHN FAIRBAIRN, A.M., M.B., C.M., 917 Rialto Building, Kansas City, Missouri. University of Aberdeen, 1886. Surgeon, Research, Christian Church, and Kansas City General Hospitals.

BIRD, MAURICE DUANE, M.D., 520 Main Street, Marinette, Wisconsin. Rush Medical College, 1896. President, Marinette and Menominee Hospital Company; Surgeon, Chicago, Milwaukee and St. Paul Railway.

BIRD, WILLIAM EDWIN, JR., A.B., M.D., 1022 Dupont Building, Wilmington, Delaware. Johns Hopkins University, Medical Department, 1911. Surgeon, Physicians and Surgeons and State Tuberculosis Hospitals; Associate Orthopedic Surgeon, Delaware Hospital. Editor, *Delaware State Medical Journal.*

BIRD, WILLIAM GRANT, M.D., 510 F. P. Smith Building, Flint, Michigan. Detroit College of Medicine and Surgery, 1895.

BIRGE, RUSSELL H., A.B., M.D., 2417 Prospect Avenue, Cleveland, Ohio. Harvard Medical School, 1898. Instructor in Surgery, Western Reserve University School of Medicine; Assistant Visiting Surgeon, Lakeside Hospital; Visiting Surgeon, Huron Road Hospital.

BIRK, JOHN W., M.D., 4654 Sheridan Road, Chicago, Illinois. University of Illinois College of Medicine (College of Physicians and Surgeons, Chicago), 1901. Instructor in Obstetrics, University of Illinois College of Medicine; Assistant Professor of Obstetrics, Chicago Policlinic; Obstetrician, Lake View Hospital.

BIRKETT, HERBERT STANLEY, C.B., M.D., C.M., 252 Mountain Street, Montreal, Quebec. Faculty of Medicine, McGill University, 1886. Dean and Professor of Oto-Laryngology, Faculty of Medicine, McGill University; Oto-Laryngologist, Royal Victoria, Alexandra, and Montreal Foundling and Baby Hospitals, Mackay Institute for Protestant Deaf Mutes and the Blind.

BIRMINGHAM, HENRY P., M.D., Medical Corps, United States Army, Washington, District of Columbia. University of Michigan Medical School, 1876. Brigadier General, Medical Corps, United States Army.

BIRNIE, JOHN MATHEWS, A.B., M.D., 6 Chestnut Street, Springfield, Massachusetts. Harvard Medical School, 1906. Assistant Surgeon, Springfield Hospital; Surgeon, Ware Hospital, Ware; Visiting Surgeon, Monson State Hospital, Monson.

BISHOP, ELIOT, A.B., M.D., 46 Gates Avenue, Brooklyn, New York. Dartmouth Medical School, 1904. Assistant Gynecologist and Obstetrician, Brooklyn Hospital.

BISHOP, LOUIS W., A.B., M.D., Medical Corps, United States Navy, Washington, District of Columbia. Long Island College Hospital, 1896. Commander, Medical Corps, United States Navy.

BISHOP, W. H., M.D., 667 Madison Avenue, New York, New York. Hahnemann Medical College and Hospital, Philadelphia, 1889. Surgeon, Fifth Avenue Hospital, New York, United Hospital, Port Chester, New York, Ann May Memorial Hospital, Spring Lake, New Jersey.

BISHOP, WILLIAM LEE, M.D., 415 Stevens Building, Portland, Oregon. University of Pennsylvania School of Medicine, 1894.

BISPHAM, WILLIAM N., M.D., Medical Corps, United States Army, Washington, District of Columbia. University of Maryland School of Medicine, 1897. Lieutenant Colonel, Medical Corps, United States Army.

BISSELL, DOUGAL, B.Sc., M.D., 219 West Seventy-ninth Street, New York, New York. University of Maryland School of Medicine, 1888. Attending Surgeon, Woman's Hospital; Attending Gynecologist, Central Islip State Hospital, Central Islip.

BISSELL, ELMER JEFFERSON, M.D., Mission Canyon, Santa Barbara, California. University of Michigan Homeopathic Medical College, 1883. Consulting Ophthalmic Surgeon, Rochester Homeopathic Hospital, Rochester, New York.

BITTING, NUMA DUNCAN, Phar.G., M.D., Durham, North Carolina. Jefferson Medical College, 1907. Surgeon, Watts Hospital, West Durham.

BITZER, NEWTON EMERSON, M.D., 236 West Chestnut Street, Lancaster, Pennsylvania. University of Pennsylvania School of Medicine, 1898. Medical Director and Chief Surgeon, St. Joseph's Hospital; Surgeon, Lancaster County Hospital.

BJORNSON, O., M.D., C.M., 701 Lindsay Building, Winnipeg, Manitoba. Faculty of Medicine, University of Manitoba (Manitoba Medical College), 1897. Associate Professor of Obstetrics, Faculty of Medicine, University of Manitoba; Attending Obstetrician, Winnipeg General Hospital.

BLACK, ARTHUR DAVENPORT, A.M., D.Sc., D.D.S., M.D., 122 South Michigan Avenue, Chicago, Illinois. Northwestern University Medical School, 1901.

BLACK, CARL ELLSWORTH, B.Sc., A.M., M.D., 200 Ayers Bank Building, Jacksonville, Illinois. Northwestern University Medical School (Chicago Medical College), 1887. Surgeon, Passavant Memorial and Our Saviour's Hospitals, Chicago and Alton, Chicago, Burlington and Quincy, and Chicago, Peoria and St. Louis Railroads, Illinois Traction System.

BLACK, HUGH RATCHFORD, M.D., 509 Allen and Law Building, Spartanburg, South Carolina. University of Maryland School of Medicine, 1883. Surgeon-in-Chief, Spartanburg Hospital; Attending Surgeon, Provident Hospital; Consulting Surgeon, Wofford College; Surgeon, Southern, Charleston and Western Carolina Railways.

BLACK, JOHN A., M.D., 103 West Pitkin Avenue, Pueblo, Colorado. George Washington University Medical School (Columbian University, Medical Department), 1882. Surgeon, St. Mary Hospital.

BLACK, JOHN FIELDING, M.D., 247 Main Street, White Plains, New York. Columbia University, College of Physicians and Surgeons, 1900. Attending Surgeon, White Plains Hospital, White Plains, Westchester County Hospital, East View; Consulting Surgeon, Bloomingdale Hospital; Cystoscopist, White Plains Hospital, White Plains, Tarrytown Hospital, Tarrytown, Ossining Hospital, Ossining, United Hospital, Port Chester.

BLACK, MELVILLE, M.D., 424 Metropolitan Building, Denver, Colorado. University and Bellevue Hospital Medical College, 1889. Professor of Ophthalmology, University of Colorado School of Medicine; Ophthalmologist, St. Luke's and Children's Hospitals, Chicago, Burlington and Quincy Railroad; Consulting Oculist, Denver Orphans' Home, Church Home for Convalescents, Colorado and Southern Railroad.

BLACK, NELSON MILES, Phar.G., M.D., Wells Building, Milwaukee, Wisconsin. University of Pennsylvania School of Medicine, 1894. Ophthalmologist, Children's Free Hospital; Head of Department of Ophthalmology, Columbia Hospital; Ophthalmologist and Otologist, Milwaukee Infants' Home and Hospital; Head of Department Ophthalmology and Oto-Laryngology, Milwaukee County Hospital, Wauwatosa.

BLACK, VAUGHAN E., A.B., M.D., Scott Block, Moose Jaw, Saskatchewan. Faculty of Medicine, McGill University, 1910. Member of Surgical Staff, Moose Jaw General, and Providence Hospitals.

BLACK, WILLIAM THOMAS, M.D., 620 Exchange Building, Memphis, Tennessee. University of Tennessee College of Medicine (Memphis Hospital Medical College), 1898. Associate Professor of Gynecology, University of Tennessee College of Medicine; Visiting Gynecologist, Baptist Memorial and St. Joseph's Hospitals; Associate Visiting Gynecologist, Memphis General Hospital; President of Staff and Surgeon, Porter Home and Leath Orphanage.

BLACKBURN, JOHN HENRY, M.D., 1119 State Street, Bowling Green, Kentucky. Vanderbilt University, Medical Department, 1899. Surgeon, Blackburn Hospital.

BLACKWELL, EDWARD MAURICE, M.D., Medical Corps, United States Navy, Washington, District of Columbia. University of Maryland School of Medicine, 1890. Commander, Medical Corps, United States Navy.

BLACKWELL, KARL S., A.B., A.M., M.D., 501 East Franklin Street, Richmond, Virginia. Medical College of Virginia (University College of Medicine),

1906. Associate Professor, Eye, Ear, Nose, and Throat Department, Medical College of Virginia; Member of Staff, Memorial and City Hospitals.

BLACKWOOD, NORMAN JEROME, M.D., Medical Corps, United States Navy, Washington, District of Columbia. Jefferson Medical College, 1888. Captain, Medical Corps, United States Navy.

BLAHD, M. EMMETT, M.D., 301 Anisfield Building, Cleveland, Ohio. Western Reserve University School of Medicine, 1906. Associate Surgeon, Mt. Sinai Hospital.

BLAIN, ALEXANDER W., M.D., 2201 Jefferson Avenue, East, Detroit, Michigan. Detroit College of Medicine and Surgery, 1906. Associate Professor of Surgery, Detroit College of Medicine and Surgery; Senior Attending Surgeon, St. Mary's Hospital; Chief of Staff, Jefferson Clinic.

BLAIR. EDWARD GILES, A.B., M.D., 404 Bryant Building, Kansas City, Missouri. Columbia University, College of Physicians and Surgeons, 1889. Attending Surgeon, St. Joseph's Hospital; Consulting Surgeon, Bethany Methodist Hospital, Kansas City, Kansas.

BLAIR, VILRAY PAPIN, A.M., M.D., Metropolitan Building, St. Louis, Missouri. Washington University Medical School, 1893. Associate in Surgery, Washington University Medical School; Professor of Oral Surgery, Washington University, Dental Department; Visiting Surgeon, St. Luke's Hospital; Assistant Surgeon, Barnes and St. Louis Children's Hospitals.

BLAIR, WILLIAM W., M.D., 604 Diamond Bank Building, Pittsburgh, Pennsylvania. Hahnemann Medical College and Hospital, Philadelphia, 1889. Professor of Ophthalmology, University of Pittsburgh School of Medicine; Staff Surgeon, Eye and Ear, Tuberculosis League, and Elizabeth Steel Magee Hospitals.

BLAISDELL, SILAS CANADY, M.D., 331 Jefferson Avenue, Brooklyn, New York. University and Bellevue Hospital Medical College (New York University Medical College), 1882. Surgeon-in-Chief, Brooklyn Eastern District Dispensary and Hospital; Visiting Surgeon, Bushwick Hospital.

BLAKE, CHARLES FRENCH, A.M., M.D., 20 East Preston Street, Baltimore, Maryland. University of Maryland School of Medicine (College of Physicians and Surgeons, Baltimore), 1893. Professor of Proctology, University of Maryland School of Medicine and College of Physicians and Surgeons; Surgeon, South Baltimore General and Mercy Hospitals.

BLAKE, HERBERT C., M.D., 1014 West Lafayette Avenue, Baltimore, Maryland. University of Maryland School of Medicine (Baltimore Medical College), 1905. Associate Professor of Surgery, University of Maryland School of Medicine and College of Physicians and Surgeons; Associate in Surgery, Maryland General Hospital.

BLAKE, JOHN BAPST, A.M., M.D., 657 Boylston Street, Boston, Massachusetts. Harvard Medical School, 1891. Assistant Professor of Surgery, Harvard Medical School; Surgeon-in-Chief, Boston City Hospital; Consulting

Surgeon, Boston State Hospital, Boston, Reformatory for Women, South Framingham.

BLAKE, JOSEPH AUGUSTUS, Ph.B., A.M., M.D., 216 East Fifty-third Street, New York, New York. Columbia University, College of Physicians and Surgeons, 1889. Consulting Surgeon, St. Luke's, Roosevelt, and Lincoln Hospitals, Clinic for Reconstruction Hospital, New York, Tarrytown Hospital, Tarrytown.

BLAKELY, RUPERT MITCHUM, A.B., M.D., 426 Exchange Bank Building, Little Rock, Arkansas. Tulane University of Louisiana School of Medicine, 1911. Member of Surgical Staff, University of Arkansas, Medical Department, and St. Vincent's Infirmary.

BLAKESLEY, THEODORE S., M.D., 638 Lathrop Building, Kansas City, Missouri. Rush Medical College, 1902. Member of Staff, Swedish and Kansas City General Hospitals.

BLANCHARD, R. J., M.B., C.M., 288 Broadway, Winnipeg, Manitoba. University of Edinburgh, 1877. Member of Consulting Staff, Winnipeg General Hospital.

BLANCHARD, WALLACE, M.D., 15 East Washington Street, Chicago, Illinois. Northwestern University Medical School, 1869. Assistant Clinical Professor of Orthopedic Surgery, Rush Medical College; Orthopedic Surgeon, University Hospital, Hospital for Destitute Crippled Children, Chicago, Convalescent Home for Crippled Children, Prince Crossing.

BLAND, PASCAL BROOKE, M.D., 1621 Spruce Street, Philadelphia, Pennsylvania. Jefferson Medical College, 1901. Assistant Professor Gynecology, Jefferson Medical College; Gynecologist, St. Joseph's Hospital; Assistant Gynecologist, Jefferson Medical College Hospital.

BLEDSOE, ROBERT WALTER, M.D., 1005 Madison Avenue, Covington, Kentucky. University of Cincinnati College of Medicine (Miami Medical College), 1900. Chief of Staff, Eye, Ear, Nose, and Throat Department, St. Elizabeth's Hospital.

BLESH, ABRAHAM LINCOLN, M.D., 308 Patterson Building, Oklahoma, Oklahoma. Northwestern University Medical School, 1889. Associate Professor of Surgery, University of Oklahoma School of Medicine; Chief of Staff and Chief Surgeon, Wesley Hospital; Surgeon, University Hospital.

BLISS, CHESTER B., M.D., 409 Columbus Avenue, Sandusky, Ohio. University of Michigan Medical School, 1896.

BLISS, GEORGE D., M.D., 508 Washington Street, Boston, Massachusetts. Boston University School of Medicine, 1881. Consulting Obstetrician, Massachusetts Homeopathic Hospital.

BLOCH, OSCAR EDGEWORTH, A.M., M.D., 316 West Broadway, Louisville, Kentucky. University of Louisville, Medical Department, 1893. Surgeon, SS. Mary and Elizabeth, Jewish, and Louisville Public Hospitals; Consultant in Surgery, United States War Risk Bureau; Operating Surgeon, United States Marine Hospital, No. 11.

BLOCK, FRANK BENTON, A.B., M.D., 2035 Chestnut Street, Philadelphia, Pennsylvania. University of Pennsylvania School of Medicine, 1911. Instructor of Gynecology, University of Pennsylvania School of Medicine; Surgeon, Jewish Hospital and Gynecological Dispensary, Hospital of the University of Pennsylvania.

BLODGETT, WILLIAM E., A.B., M.D., Kresge Medical Building, Detroit, Michigan. Harvard Medical School, 1900. Associate Professor of Orthopedic Surgery, Detroit College of Medicine and Surgery; Attending Orthopedic Surgeon, Grace Hospital; Consulting Surgeon, Harper, and St. Mary's Hospitals.

BLOOD, GEORGE WILLARD, M.D., 151 Rock Street, Fall River, Massachusetts. Tufts College Medical School, 1908. Surgeon, Fall River City and St. Anne's Hospitals.

BLOODGOOD, JOSEPH COLT, B.Sc., M.D., 904 North Charles Street, Baltimore, Maryland. University of Pennsylvania School of Medicine, 1891. Associate Professor of Clinical Surgery, Johns Hopkins University, Medical Department; Associate Visiting Surgeon, Johns Hopkins Hospital; Chief Surgeon, St. Agnes' Hospital.

BLOOM, CHARLES J., A.B., M.D., Landreth Block, Muskegon, Michigan. University of Minnesota Medical School, 1908. Consulting Surgeon, Hackley Hospital.

BLOOM, I. N., A.B., M.D., 222 Francis Building, Louisville, Kentucky. Harvard Medical School, 1881. Professor of Syphilography and Dermatology, University of Louisville, Medical Department; Member of Staff, Louisville City, Jewish, and SS. Mary and Elizabeth Hospitals, Masonic Widows' and Orphans' Home; Consultant, Children's Free Hospital.

BLOOM, JEFFERSON DAVIS, M.D., 5718 St. Charles Avenue, New Orleans, Louisiana. Tulane University of Louisiana School of Medicine, 1886.

BLUE, JOHN H., B.Sc., M.D., Bell Building, Montgomery, Alabama. Columbia University, College of Physicians and Surgeons, 1901. Attending Surgeon, St. Margaret's Hospital.

BLUE, JULIAN BAKER, M.D., 1224 Exchange Building, Memphis, Tennessee. University of Louisville, Medical Department, 1907. Instructor in Ophthalmology, University of Tennessee College of Medicine; Ophthalmologist, Baptist Memorial and Memphis General Hospitals; Oto-Laryngologist, Tri-State Crippled Children's Hospital.

BLUE, RUPERT, M.D., D.Sc., D.P.H., United States Public Health Service, Washington, District of Columbia. University of Maryland School of Medicine, 1892. Assistant Surgeon General, United States Public Health Service.

BLUM, HENRY NATHAN, B.Sc., M.D., Maison Blanche Building, New Orleans, Louisiana. Tulane University of Louisiana School of Medicine, 1900. Instructor in Ophthalmology, Tulane University of Louisiana School of Medicine; Visiting Oculist, Charity Hospital; Senior Associate in Ophthalmology, Touro Infirmary.

BOBB, BYRON A., M.D., 723 West Fourth Avenue, Mitchell, South Dakota. Northwestern University Medical School, 1894. Surgeon, Methodist State and St. Joseph's Hospitals.

BOCK, OTTO BISMARCK, Phar.G., M.D., 925 North Eighth Street, Sheboygan, Wisconsin. Rush Medical College, 1894. Surgeon, St. Nicholas Hospital.

BOCOCK, EDGAR ALLAN, M.D., Medical Corps, United States Army, Washington, District of Columbia. Medical College of Virginia, 1915. Major, Medical Corps, United States Army.

BODINE, CHARLES DELOS, M.D., 285 Fargo Street, Portland, Oregon. Northwestern University Medical School, 1902. Member of Staff, Emanuel Hospital.

BODKIN, DOMINIC GEORGE, M.D., 897 Lafayette Avenue, Brooklyn, New York. Columbia University, College of Physicians and Surgeons, 1899. Attending Surgeon, St. Catherine's Hospital.

BODKIN, MARTIN LAURENCE, M.D., 290 Clinton Avenue, Brooklyn, New York. Columbia University, College of Physicians and Surgeons, 1894. Rectal Surgeon, St. Catherine's and Williamsburgh Hospitals; Consulting Rectal Surgeon, Zion Hospital.

BOEHM, JOSEPH LEOPOLD, Phar.G., M.D., 540 Park Avenue, New York, New York. Washington University Medical School, 1899.

BOERNER, MORRIS H., M.D., Scarbrough Building, Austin, Texas. University of Texas, Medical Department, 1909.

BOGAN, FRED MACON, M.D., 108 East Twenty-fourth Street, Minneapolis, Minnesota. George Washington University Medical School (Columbian University, Medical Department), 1893.

BOGARDUS, HENRY J., M.D., 427 Bergen Avenue, Jersey City, New Jersey. University and Bellevue Hospital Medical College (New York University Medical College), 1883.

BOGART, ARTHUR H., M.D., 27 Seventh Avenue, Brooklyn, New York. University and Bellevue Hospital Medical College (New York University Medical College), 1893. Senior Surgeon, Methodist Episcopal Hospital; Consulting Surgeon, Coney Island Hospital.

BOGART, JOHN BION, A.M., M.D., 463 Clinton Avenue, Brooklyn, New York. University and Bellevue Hospital Medical College (New York University Medical College), 1884. Consulting Surgeon, Kings County, Jewish, Methodist Episcopal Hospitals, and Brooklyn Home for Consumptives.

BOGER, JOHN A., A.M., M.D., 2213 North Broad Street, Philadelphia, Pennsylvania. University of Pennsylvania School of Medicine, 1889. Surgeon, St. Mary's Hospital; Senior Surgeon, Stetson Hospital.

BOGERT, EDWARD S., M.D., Medical Corps, United States Navy, Washington, District of Columbia. Columbia University, College of Physicians and Surgeons, 1889. Captain, Medical Corps, United States Navy.

BOICE, EDMUND SIMPSON, B.A., M.D., Park View Hospital, Rocky Mount, North Carolina. University of Pennsylvania School of Medicine, 1909. Surgeon, Park View Hospital.

BOILER, WILLIAM F., M.Sc., M.D., 426 South Dodge Street, Iowa City, Iowa. State University of Iowa College of Medicine, 1906. Professor of Ophthalmology, State University of Iowa College of Medicine; Ophthalmologist, State University and Mercy Hospitals.

BOLAND, FRANK KELLS, A.B., M.D., 436 Peachtree Street, Atlanta, Georgia. Emory University School of Medicine (Atlanta College of Physicians and Surgeons), 1900. Professor of Clinical Surgery, Emory University School of Medicine; Surgeon, Grady Memorial, Wesley Memorial, and Georgia Baptist Hospitals.

BOLDT, HERMANN J., M.D., 616 Madison Avenue, New York, New York. University and Bellevue Hospital Medical College (New York University Medical College), 1879. Emeritus Professor of Gynecology, New York Post-Graduate Medical School; Consulting Gynecologist, New York Post-Graduate Medical School and Hospital, Stuyvesant Polyclinic, St. Vincent's, Beth Israel, and Union Hospitals.

BOLSTA, CHARLES, M.D., Ortonville, Minnesota. Rush Medical College, 1895. Surgeon, Ortonville Evangelical Hospital.

BONDURANT, FLINT, B.Sc., M.D., Cairo National Bank Building, Cairo, Illinois. Northwestern University Medical School, 1909. Head of Surgical Staff, St. Mary's Hospital.

BONN, HARRY KRAYLOR, M.D., 201 Pennway Building, Indianapolis, Indiana. Indiana University School of Medicine, 1908. Assistant in Gynecology, Indiana University School of Medicine; Alternate in General Surgery, Indianapolis City Hospital.

BONNELL, SAUL, M.D., C.M., Walmsley Street, Fernie, British Columbia. Faculty of Medicine, McGill University, 1896. Surgeon, Fernie General Hospital.

BONNEY, CHARLES W., A.B., M.D., 1117 Spruce Street, Philadelphia, Pennsylvania. Jefferson Medical College, 1904. Associate in Topographic and Applied Anatomy, Jefferson Medical College.

BOOKER, LYLE STEELE, M.D., First National Bank Building, Durham, North Carolina. Medical College of Virginia, 1908. Surgeon, Watts Hospital, West Durham.

BOOKMAN, MILTON RALPH, M.D., 473 East One Hundred Forty-first Street, New York, New York. Columbia University, College of Physicians and Surgeons, 1906. Adjunct Attending Surgeon, Lebanon Hospital.

BOOKWALTER, CARL FERDINAND, B.Sc., M.D., 104 South Michigan Avenue, Chicago, Illinois. Johns Hopkins University, Medical Department, 1910. Associate in Otology, Northwestern University Medical School; Adjunct in Otology, Wesley Memorial Hospital.

BOONE, JESSE FRANKLIN, M.D., 818 East Forty-seventh Street, Chicago, Illinois. Hahnemann Medical College, Chicago, 1912. Adjunct Professor of Oto-Laryngology, Hahnemann Medical College; Member of Staff, Hahnemann Hospital.

BOONE, JOEL T., M.D., Medical Corps, United States Navy, Washington, District of Columbia. Hahnemann Medical College and Hospital of Philadelphia, 1913. Lieutenant Commander, Medical Corps, United States Navy.

BOORSTEIN, SAMUEL W., M.D., 529 Courtlandt Avenue, New York, New York. University and Bellevue Hospital Medical College, 1909. Assistant Visiting Surgeon and Chief of Orthopedics, Out-Patient Department, Fordham Hospital; Adjunct Visiting Orthopedic Surgeon, Montefiore Hospital; Neurological Orthopedic Surgeon, Central Neurological Hospital.

BOOT, GEORGE WILLIAM, M.D., 25 East Washington Street, Chicago, Illinois. Sioux City College of Medicine, 1893; University of Pennsylvania School of Medicine, 1898. Assistant Professor, Ear, Nose, and Throat Department, University of Illinois; Attending Ear, Nose, and Throat Surgeon, Cook County Hospital; President of Staff, St. Francis' Hospital, Evanston.

BOOTH, ALBERT EDWIN, M.D., 1132 Metropolitan Bank Building, Minneapolis, Minnesota. University of Minnesota Medical School (College of Homeopathic Medicine and Surgery), 1899.

BOOTH, ARTHUR WOODWARD, M.D., 222 West Church Street, Elmira, New York. University of Pennsylvania School of Medicine, 1894. Attending Surgeon, Arnot-Ogden Memorial Hospital; Consulting Surgeon, People's Hospital, Sayre, Pennsylvania.

BOOTH, BURTON SYLVANDER, M.D., 60 Second Street, Troy, New York. Albany Medical College, 1889. Consulting Laryngologist, Leonard Hospital.

BOOTH, CARLOS CHARLES, M.D., 232 North Phelps Street, Youngstown, Ohio. Western Reserve University School of Medicine, 1883. Consulting Surgeon, Youngstown Hospital; Chief Surgeon, Republic Iron and Steel Company; Local Surgeon, New York Central Lines, Pittsburgh and Lake Erie, and Lake Erie and Eastern Railroads.

BOOTH, GEORGE BERTRAM, Phar.G., M.D., 506 Adams Street, Toledo, Ohio. Toledo Medical College, 1907. Surgeon, Mercy Hospital.

BOOTHBY, WALTER MEREDITH, A.M., M.D., Mayo Clinic, Rochester, Minnesota. Harvard Medical School, 1906.

BORDEN, CHARLES R. C., M.D., 520 Commonwealth Avenue, Boston, Massachusetts. Bowdoin Medical School, 1896. Aural Surgeon, Boston City Hospital, Boston, Hospital for Contagious Diseases, Somerville, Board of Health Hospital, Brookline.

BORDEN, DANIEL LeRAY, B.Sc., M.A., M.D., 815 Connecticut Avenue, Washington, District of Columbia. George Washington University Medical School, 1912. Associate Professor of Surgery, George Washington University Medical School; Associate Surgeon, George Washington University Hospital; Assistant Surgeon, Children's Hospital.

BORDEN, WILLIAM CLINE, M.D., 2306 Tracy Place, Washington, District of Columbia. George Washington University Medical School (Columbian University, Medical Department), 1883. Dean and Professor of Surgery, George Washington University Medical School; Surgeon-in-Chief, George Washington University Hospital; Lieutenant Colonel, United States Army. Retired.

BORDLEY, JAMES, JR., M.D., 330 North Charles Street, Baltimore, Maryland. University of Maryland School of Medicine, 1896. Surgeon, St. Agnes' Hospital, Hebrew Hospital and Asylum, Church Home and Infirmary, Home for Incurables, Baltimore, Annapolis Emergency Hospital, Annapolis, Easton Emergency Hospital, Easton.

BORNSTEIN, MAX, M.D., 79 Wisconsin Street, Milwaukee, Wisconsin. Jefferson Medical College, 1908. Attending Surgeon, Johnston Emergency and Mt. Sinai Hospitals.

BORTONE, FRANK, M.D., 809 Montgomery Street, Jersey City, New Jersey. Columbia University College of Physicians and Surgeons, 1912. Associate Visiting Surgeon, Christ and Jersey City Hospitals; Attending Surgeon, Out-Patient Department, Christ Hospital.

BORZILLERI, CHARLES R., M.D., 298 Niagara Street, Buffalo, New York. University of Buffalo, Department of Medicine, 1895. Chief Surgeon, Buffalo Columbus Hospital; Consulting Surgeon, Buffalo City Hospital.

BOTTARO, LUIS, M.D., Calle Uruguay 1316, Montevideo, Uruguay. Faculty of Medicine University of Montevideo, 1891.

BOTTOMLEY, JOHN TAYLOR, A.B., M.D., LL.D., 165 Beacon Street, Boston, Massachusetts. Harvard Medical School, 1894. Lecturer on Surgery, Harvard University Graduate School of Medicine; Surgeon-in-Chief, Carney Hospital.

BOUCHER, JOHN B., M.D., 25 Charter Oak Avenue, Hartford, Connecticut. University of Maryland School of Medicine (College of Physicians and Surgeons, Baltimore), 1894. Surgeon, Wilson Private Hospital; Consulting Surgeon, St. Mary's Hospital, Waterbury, Middlesex Hospital, Middletown.

BOUCHER, ROBERT B., M.D., C.M., 414 Birks Building, Vancouver, British Columbia. Faculty of Medicine, McGill University, 1895. Ophthalmologist, Laryngologist, Otologist, and Rhinologist, Vancouver General Hospital.

BOUFFLEUR, ALBERT IRVING, B.Sc., M.D., 1110 White Building, Seattle, Washington. Rush Medical College, 1887. Chief Surgeon, Chicago, Milwaukee and St. Paul Railway.

BOUGHTON, GUY CLUXTON, M.D., 810 Peach Street, Erie, Pennsylvania. University of Vermont College of Medicine, 1900. Chief of Surgical Service, Hamot Hospital; Chief Surgeon, General Electric Company at Erie; Surgeon, Pittsburgh Steamship and Inter-Lake Steamship Companies.

BOULET, RODOLPHE, B.L., M.D., 145 Ste. Catherine Street, West, Montreal, Quebec. Faculty of Medicine, University of Montreal (Laval University,

Medical Department), 1890. Joint Professor of Ophthalmology, Rhinology, and Otology, Faculty of Medicine, University of Montreal; Director, Ophthalmic Institute.

BOULTER, JAMES HENRY, B.A., M.D., C.M., 1601 David Whitney Building, Detroit, Michigan. Faculty of Medicine, McGill University, 1903. Assistant Professor of Clinical Surgery, Detroit College of Medicine and Surgery; Associate Attending Surgeon, Grace Hospital; Consulting Surgeon, Detroit United Railway.

BOUMAN, HERMANN A. H., A.M., M.D., 403 Physicians and Surgeons Building, Minneapolis, Minnesota. University of Minnesota Medical School, 1897. Surgeon, Northwestern and St. Andrew's Hospitals.

BOURGEOIS, BENJAMIN GEORGE, A.B., M.D., 332 Sherbrooke Street, East, Montreal, Quebec. Faculty of Medicine, University of Montreal (Laval University Faculty of Medicine), 1902. Associate Professor of Clinical Surgery, University of Montreal; Surgeon, Notre Dame Hospital.

BOURLAND, JOSEPH WILBUR, A.B., M.D., 525 Wilson Building, Dallas, Texas. Columbia University, College of Physicians and Surgeons, 1895. Visiting Surgeon, Parkland Hospital; Visiting Obstetrician, Baylor and Parkland Hospitals.

BOVÉE, J. WESLEY, M.D., 815 Connecticut Avenue, Washington, District of Columbia. George Washington University Medical School (Columbian University, Medical Department), 1885. Professor of Gynecology, George Washington University Medical School; Chief Gynecologist, George Washington University Hospital; Gynecologist, Columbia Hospital for Women, Government Hospital for Insane.

BOWDLE, RALPH ALVIN, M.D., Steptoe Valley Hospital, East Ely, Nevada. University of Cincinnati College of Medicine (Medical College of Ohio), 1909. Chief Surgeon, Steptoe Valley Hospital.

BOWELL, BO CARR, A.B., M.D., 806 Maple Avenue, Laporte, Indiana. University of Illinois College of Medicine (College of Physicians and Surgeons, Chicago), 1895. Surgeon, Holy Family Hospital.

BOWEN, ALBERT S., M.D., Medical Corps, United States Army, Washington, District of Columbia. Northwestern University Medical School, 1903. Major, Medical Corps, United States Army.

BOWEN, JESSE WILLIAM, M.D., 221 Seventh Avenue, West, Dickinson, North Dakota. State University of Iowa College of Medicine, 1898. Chief of Surgical Staff, St. Joseph's Hospital.

BOWEN, W. W., M.D., 630 Snell Building, Fort Dodge, Iowa. State University of Iowa College of Medicine, 1895. Surgeon, St. Joseph's Mercy Hospital.

BOWEN, WILLIAM SINCLAIR, M.D., The Farragut, Washington, District of Columbia. University of Maryland School of Medicine, 1888. Clinical Professor of Obstetrics, George Washington University Medical School; Obstetrician, Columbia Hospital for Women, Garfield Memorial Hospital.

BOWEN, WILLIS ELLIOTT, M.D., 827 East Main Street, Rochester, New York. Cornell University Medical College, 1902. Member of Junior Surgical Staff, Rochester General Hospital; Director, Park Avenue Clinical Hospital.

BOWER, ALBERT J., A.B., M.D., 227 South Lafayette Street, Greenville, Michigan. University of Michigan Medical School, 1905.

BOWER, JOHN O., M.D., 2033 Walnut Street, Philadelphia, Pennsylvania. Medico-Chirurgical College, Philadelphia, 1909. Adjunct Professor of Surgery, Temple University, Department of Medicine; Assistant Surgeon, Samaritan Hospital, American Hospital for Diseases of the Stomach.

BOWERS, CHARLES ALBERT, B.Sc., M.D., A.M., 10553 Euclid Avenue, Cleveland, Ohio. Johns Hopkins University, Medical Department, 1912. Instructor in Surgery, Western Reserve University School of Medicine; Consulting Urologist, United States Marine Hospital; Associate Visiting Urologist, St. Vincent's Charity Hospital; Visiting Urologist and Associate Surgeon, St. Luke's Hospital.

BOWERS, CHARLES E., M.D., Beacon Building, Wichita, Kansas. Rush Medical College, 1883. Chief Surgeon, St. Francis Hospital.

BOWERS, L. G., M.D., 1120 Fidelity Medical Building, Dayton, Ohio. University of Louisville, Medical Department (Louisville Medical College), 1898.

BOWERS, WALTER PRENTICE, M.D., 264 Chestnut Street, Clinton, Massachusetts. Harvard Medical School, 1879. Consulting Surgeon, Clinton Hospital.

BOWERS, WESLEY CREVELING, A.B., M.D., 27 West Forty-ninth Street, New York, New York. Columbia University, College of Physicians and Surgeons, 1908. Assistant to Chair of Otology, University and Bellevue Hospital Medical College; Associate Attending Otological Surgeon, St. Luke's Hospital; Associate Attending Otologist, Rhinologist, and Laryngologist, Bellevue Hospital; Consulting Otologist, Rhinologist, and Laryngologist, Sevilla Home, New York, Mountainside Hospital, Montclair, New Jersey.

BOWLBY, SIR ANTHONY ALFRED, K.C.B., K.C.M.G., K.C.V.O., D.S.M. (U.S.A.), F.R.C.S. (Eng.), 25 Manchester Square, London, England. M.R.C.S. (Eng.) (St. Bartholomew's Hospital), 1879. Consulting Surgeon, St. Bartholomew's Hospital; President, Royal College of Surgeons of England; Surgeon in Ordinary to His Majesty the King.

BOWLES, HARRY HALLOWELL, M.D., 36 Woodland Avenue, Summit, New Jersey. Medical College of Virginia (University College of Medicine), 1909. Attending Surgeon, Overlook Hospital.

BOYCE, SAMUEL R., Ph.C., M.D., 105 Monona Avenue, Madison, Wisconsin. University of Michigan Medical School, 1899.

BOYD, AUGUSTO SAMUEL, M.D., 16 Ninth Street, Panama, Republic of Panama. Columbia University, College of Physicians and Surgeons, 1899. Chief Surgeon, Santo Tomas Hospital.

BOYD, FRANK, M.D., Fourth Street and Broadway, Paducah, Kentucky. Rush Medical College, 1889. Surgeon, Riverside Hospital; Assistant Surgeon, Illinois Central Hospital; Division Surgeon, Nashville, Chattanooga and St. Louis Railway; Chief Surgeon, Paducah Traction Company.

BOYD, FRANK DOUGLAS, M.D., F. and M. National Bank Building, Fort Worth, Texas. University of Louisville, Medical Department, 1890. Professor of Oto-Laryngology, Baylor University School of Medicine; Surgeon, Eye, Ear, Nose, and Throat Department, City Hospital; Member of Staff, St. Joseph's Infirmary.

BOYD, GEOFFREY, A.B., M.B., 48 Bloor Street, East, Toronto, Ontario. University of Toronto, Faculty of Medicine, 1891.

BOYD, GEORGE M., M.D., 1909 Spruce Street, Philadelphia, Pennsylvania. University of Pennsylvania School of Medicine, 1882. Professor of Obstetrics, University of Pennsylvania Graduate School of Medicine; Obstetrician and Gynecologist, Medico-Chirurgical and Philadelphia Lying-in Charity Hospitals.

BOYD-SNEE, HARRY, M.D., 716 J. M. S. Building, South Bend, Indiana. Rush Medical College, 1889. Oto-Laryngologist, St. Joseph's Hospital.

BOYD, HERBERT DRUMMOND, M.D., 687 Boylston Street, Boston, Massachusetts. Boston University School of Medicine, 1892. Surgeon, Out-Patient Department, and Assistant Surgeon, Massachusetts Homeopathic Hospital.

BOYD, PHILIP WILLIAMS, M.D., 4 South Main Street, Winchester, Virginia. Medical College of Virginia (University College of Medicine), 1898. Visiting Surgeon, Winchester Memorial Hospital.

BOYDEN, FRANK E., B.Sc., Phar.G., M.D., Smith-Crawford Building, Pendleton, Oregon. Northwestern University Medical School, 1905. Surgeon, St. Anthony's Hospital.

BOYLE, CHARLES CUMBERSON, M.D., 40 East Forty-first Street, New York, New York. New York Homeopathic Medical College and Flower Hospital, 1877. Clinical Lecturer on Eye and Ear, New York Homeopathic Medical College and Flower Hospital; Eye and Ear Surgeon, Metropolitan and New York Ophthalmic Hospitals.

BOYNTON, WILLIAM EDSON, M.D., 110 North Wabash Avenue, Chicago, Illinois. Hahnemann Medical College and Hospital, Chicago (Chicago Homeopathic Medical College), 1898. Professor of Diseases of the Eye, Hahnemann Medical College and Hospital; Attending Surgeon, Diseases of the Eye, Hahnemann and Auburn Park Hospitals.

BOYS, CHARLES E., B.Sc., M.D., 1008 Hanselman Building, Kalamazoo, Michigan. Northwestern University Medical School, 1903.

BRACK, CHARLES EMIL, Phar.G., M.D., 500 East Twentieth Street, Baltimore, Maryland. University of Maryland, School of Medicine (College of Physicians and Surgeons, Baltimore), 1895. Professor of Clinical Obstetrics, University of Maryland School of Medicine and College of Physicians and Surgeons; Visiting Obstetrician, Mercy Hospital; Member of Staff, Hospital for Women of Maryland, Church Home and Infirmary.

BRACKETT, ELLIOTT GRAY, M.D., 166 Newbury Street, Boston, Massachusetts. Harvard Medical School, 1886.

BRADEN, ALEXANDER J., M.D., 400 Lyceum Building, Duluth, Minnesota. University of Michigan Medical School, 1888.

BRADFIELD, JOHN A. L., M.D., State Bank Building, La Crosse, Wisconsin. University of Illinois College of Medicine (College of Physicians and Surgeons, Chicago), 1888. Attending Surgeon, St. Francis Hospital.

BRADFORD, EDWARD H., M.D., 133 Newbury Street, Boston, Massachusetts. Harvard Medical School, 1873. Emeritus Professor of Orthopedic Surgery, Harvard Medical School; Consulting Surgeon, Children's Hospital.

BRADFORD, WILLIAM H., A.M., M.D., 208 State Street, Portland, Maine. Bowdoin Medical School, 1891. Professor of Clinical Surgery, Bowdoin Medical School; Visiting Surgeon, Maine General Hospital; Consulting Surgeon, Children's Hospital, Maine Eye and Ear Infirmary, Portland, Webber Hospital, Biddeford.

BRADLEY, ALFRED E., M.D., 295 Prospect Avenue, Highland Park, Illinois. Jefferson Medical College, 1887. Colonel, Medical Corps, United States Army, retired.

BRADNER, MORRIS RENFREW, M.D., 82 Main Street, Warwick, New York. University of Pennsylvania School of Medicine, 1912. Surgeon, Warwick Hospital, Warwick, Alexander Lynn Hospital, Sussex; Consulting Surgeon, New York Telephone Company.

BRADSHAW, JOHN HAMMOND, M.D., 27 High Street, Orange, New Jersey. Columbia University, College of Physicians and Surgeons, 1884. Consulting Surgeon, Orange Memorial Hospital.

BRAISLIN, WILLIAM C., M.D., 425 Clinton Avenue, Brooklyn, New York. Columbia University, College of Physicians and Surgeons, 1890. Surgeon, Brooklyn Eye and Ear Hospital; Aural Surgeon, Caledonian Hospital, Sheltering Arms Nursery; Consulting Aural Surgeon, Brooklyn Training School and Home for Young Girls.

BRAISTED, WILLIAM CLARENCE, Ph.B., M.D., D.Sc., LL.D., F.R.C.S. (Edin.), Medical Corps, United States Navy, Washington, District of Columbia. Columbia University, College of Physicians and Surgeons, 1886. Surgeon General, United States Navy, retired.

BRANCH, J. R. BROMWELL, A.B., M.D., Hunan-Yale Hospital, Changsha, China. Johns Hopkins University, Medical Department, 1908. Professor of Surgery and Gynecology, Hunan-Yale College of Medicine; Surgeon and Gynecologist-in-Chief, Hunan-Yale and Red Cross Hospitals.

BRAND, WALTER WILLIAM, M.D., 316 Colton Building, Toledo, Ohio. Jefferson Medical College, 1894. Chief of Staff and Obstetrician, Maternity and Children's Hospital; Director of Obstetrics, St. Vincent's Hospital.

BRANDSON, B. J., A.B., M.D., C.M., 701 Lindsey Building, Winnipeg, Manitoba. Faculty of Medicine, University of Manitoba (Manitoba Medical College), 1900. Associate Professor of Clinical Surgery, Faculty of Medicine, University of Manitoba; Attending Surgeon, Winnipeg General Hospital; Consulting Surgeon, King George Hospital.

BRANDT, FRANZ H., M D., Overland Building, Boise, Idaho. Northwestern University Medical School, 1901. Ear, Nose, and Throat Surgeon, St. Luke's Hospital.

BRANT, AUSTIN, A.B., M.D., 483 Beacon Street, Boston, Massachusetts. Harvard Medical School, 1907. Obstetrician, Roxbury Hospital, Roxbury.

BRANT, AUSTIN C., M.D., 116 Cleveland Avenue, Northwest, Canton, Ohio. University and Bellevue Hospital Medical College, 1877.

BRANTON, BERTON J., M.D., Willmar Clinic, Willmar, Minnesota. University of Minnesota Medical School, 1905. Surgeon, Willmar Hospital.

BRATRUD, ARTHUR F., B.Sc., M.D., 302 Physicians and Surgeons Building, Minneapolis, Minnesota. University of Minnesota Medical School, 1912. Member of Staff, Deaconess Hospital.

BRATRUD, THEODOR, A.B., M.D., Warren Hospital, Warren, Minnesota. University of Minnesota Medical School, 1899. Consulting Surgeon, Warren and Kitson County Memorial Hospitals.

BRATTON, THOMAS S., M.D., Medical Corps, United States Army, Washington, District of Columbia. Medical College of the State of South Carolina, 1890. Colonel, Medical Corps, United States Army.

BRAUN, ALFRED, A.B., M.D., 31 East Seventy-second Street, New York, New York. Columbia University, College of Physicians and Surgeons, 1902. Adjunct Professor Laryngology, New York Polyclinic Medical School; Attending Laryngologist, New York Polyclinic Medical School and Hospital; Adjunct Otologist, Mt. Sinai Hospital.

BRAUNNAGEL, JULES L. A., M.D., 212 City Street, San Antonio, Texas. St. Louis College of Physicians and Surgeons, 1883. Surgeon and Vice-President of Attending Staff, Santa Rosa Infirmary; Consulting Surgeon, Robert B. Green Memorial Hospital.

BRAWLEY, FRANK, Phar.G., M.D., 30 North Michigan Avenue, Chicago, Illinois. University of Illinois College of Medicine, 1902. Oculist and Aurist, St. Luke's Hospital.

BRAZEAU, GEORGE N., M.D., 819 Majestic Building, Milwaukee, Wisconsin. Northwestern University Medical School, 1894.

BRAZEAU, STEPHEN D., M.D., 318 Old National Bank Building, Spokane, Washington. University of Michigan Medical School, 1904. Member of Staff, Sacred Heart Hospital.

BRECKINRIDGE, SCOTT DUDLEY, M.D., Security Trust Company Building, Lexington, Kentucky. Georgetown University School of Medicine, 1907. Gynecologist, St. Joseph's Hospital.

BREED, ROBERT HUNTINGTON, M.D., Andrews Place, Wappingers Falls, New York. Columbia University, College of Physicians and Surgeons, 1904. Surgeon, Matteawan State and Highland Hospitals, Beacon, St. Francis Hospital, Poughkeepsie; Consulting Surgeon, Hudson River State Hospital, Poughkeepsie.

BREESE, ARTHUR BACON, M.D., 434 James Street, Syracuse, New York. Columbia University, College of Physicians and Surgeons, 1881. Associate Professor of Clinical Gynecology, Syracuse University College of Medicine; Surgeon, Syracuse Hospital for Women and Children.

BREMERMAN, LEWIS WINE, A.M., M.D., 1919 Prairie Avenue, Chicago, Illinois. Jefferson Medical College, 1900. Chief Urologist, Bremerman Urological Hospital.

BRENIZER, ADDISON G., A.B., M.D., Charlotte Sanatorium, Charlotte, North Carolina. Johns Hopkins University Medical Department, 1907. Member of Staff, Presbyterian Hospital and Charlotte Sanatorium.

BRENNAN, ROBERT EMERY, M.D., 1 West Sixty-fourth Street, New York, New York. University of Louisville, Medical Department, 1900. Professor of Surgery, New York Polyclinic Medical School; Surgeon, New York Polyclinic Medical School and Hospital, St. John's Hospital, Long Island City, and Misericordia Hospital.

BRENNAN, THOMAS M., M.D., 39 Eighth Avenue, Brooklyn, New York. Long Island College Hospital, 1906. Associate Clinical Professor of Operative Surgery, Long Island College Hospital; Attending Surgeon, St. Peter's Hospital, Brooklyn, St. Anthony's Hospital, Woodhaven; Associate Surgeon, St. Mary's Hospital.

BRENNER, EDWARD CHRISTOPHER, A.B., M.D., 20 West Fiftieth Street, New York, New York. Columbia University, College of Physicians and Surgeons, 1908. Surgical Director, Workhouse, Penitentiary, and Classification Hospitals; Assistant Visiting Surgeon, Lincoln Hospital; Associate Surgeon, New York Post-Graduate Medical School and Hospital.

BRENT, HUGH, M.D., 16 East Chase Street, Baltimore, Maryland. University of Maryland School of Medicine, 1903. Associate Professor of Gynecology, University of Maryland School of Medicine and College of Physicians and Surgeons; Consulting Gynecologist, City Hospitals; Visiting Gynecologist, St. Joseph's and University Hospitals, Hospital for Women of Maryland, Hebrew Hospital and Asylum; Consulting Surgeon, Annapolis Emergency Hospital, Annapolis.

BRESLIN, JOHN GEORGE, A.B., M.D., 514 Commonwealth Avenue, Boston, Massachusetts. Harvard Medical School, 1911. Instructor in Surgery, Tufts College Medical School.

BRETT, ROBERT GEORGE, M.D., Government House, Edmonton, Alberta. Victoria University, Medical Department, 1874. Superintendent, Brett Hospital, Banff.

BRETTAUER, JOSEPH, M.D., 1063 Madison Avenue, New York, New York. University of Gratz, 1887. Attending Gynecologist, Mt. Sinai Hospital;

Consulting Gynecologist, New Jersey State Hospital, Greystone, New Jersey, United Hospital, Port Chester, New York.

BREWER, GEORGE EMERSON, A.M., M.D., LL.D., F.R.C.S. (I.) (Hon.), 19 East Sixty-fifth Street, New York, New York. Harvard Medical School, 1885. Emeritus Professor of Surgery, Columbia University, College of Physicians and Surgeons; Consulting Surgeon, Presbyterian, Roosevelt, St. Vincent's, Woman's, and City Hospitals, New York Ophthalmic and Aural Institute, Manhattan Eye and Ear Infirmary, House of the Holy Comforter, New York, Flushing Hospital, Flushing, New York, Perth Amboy City Hospital, Perth Amboy, Muhlenberg Hospital, Plainfield, New Jersey.

BREWER, LYMAN AUGUSTUS, M.D., 115 Nasby Building, Toledo, Ohio. University of Michigan Medical School, 1887. Chief of Staff, Mercy Hospital.

BREWSTER, GEORGE W. W., A.B., M.D., 213 Beacon Street, Boston, Massachusetts. Harvard Medical School, 1893. Associate in Surgery, Harvard University Graduate School of Medicine; Visiting Surgeon, Massachusetts General Hospital.

BREYER, JOHN H., A.B., M.D., 414 Chamber of Commerce Building, Pasadena, California. Rush Medical College, 1909. Member of Surgical Staff, Pasadena Dispensary.

BRICE, JOSEPH THEOBOLD, M.D., Brice Hospital Building, Lewistown, Montana. Emory University School of Medicine (Atlanta Medical College), 1891. Surgeon, The Brice Hospital.

BRICKNER, WALTER M., B.Sc., M.D., 151 Central Park, West, New York, New York. Columbia University, College of Physicians and Surgeons, 1896. Attending Surgeon, Broad Street Hospital; Associate Surgeon, Mt. Sinai Hospital. Editor-in-Chief, *American Journal of Surgery*.

BRIDGE, GEORGE ALEXANDER, A.B., M.D., Bisbee, Arizona. Columbia University, College of Physicians and Surgeons, 1902. Chief Surgeon, Local Hospital, Phelps-Dodge Corporation.

BRIGGS, CHARLES EDWIN, A.M., M.D., 207 Osborn Building, Cleveland, Ohio. Harvard Medical School, 1897. Associate Professor of Surgery, Western Reserve University School of Medicine; Associate Visiting Surgeon, Lakeside Hospital.

BRIGGS, HENRY HARRISON, A.M., M.D., 73 Haywood Street, Asheville, North Carolina. Yale University School of Medicine, 1897. Ophthalmologist and Oto-Laryngologist, Asheville Mission Hospital.

BRIGGS, J. EMMONS, M.D., 477 Beacon Street, Boston, Massachusetts. Boston University School of Medicine, 1890. Professor of Surgery, Boston University School of Medicine; Surgeon-in-Chief, Massachusetts Homeopathic Hospital; Consulting Surgeon, Wesson Memorial Hospital, Springfield, Whidden Memorial Hospital, Everett, Leonard Morse Hospital, Natick, Morton Hospital, Taunton.

BRIGGS, WILLIAM ELLERY, M.D., 1027 Tenth Street, Sacramento, California. Western Reserve University School of Medicine (University of Wooster,

Medical Department), 1877. Oculist, Otologist, and Laryngologist, Southern Pacific Railway.

BRINDLEY, GEORGE VALTER, M.D., Temple Sanitarium, Temple, Texas. University of Texas, Department of Medicine, 1911. Surgeon, Temple Sanitarium; Assistant Surgeon, Gulf, Colorado and Santa Fe Railway Hospital.

BRINSMADE, WILLIAM BARRETT, A.B., M.D., 172 Clinton Street, Brooklyn, New York. Columbia University, College of Physicians and Surgeons, 1892. Senior Surgeon, Brooklyn Hospital; Consulting Surgeon, St. John's Hospital, St. Christopher's Hospital for Babies.

BRISTER, JOHN M., M.D., Medical Corps, United States Navy, Washington, District of Columbia. Medico-Chirurgical College, Philadelphia, 1898. Captain, Medical Corps, United States Navy.

BRITT, WALLACE L., M.D., Century Building, Jackson, Mississippi. Emory University School of Medicine (Atlanta College of Physicians and Surgeons), 1902. Genito-Urinary Surgeon, Mississippi State Charity, and Baptist Hospitals, Jackson Infirmary and Sanitarium.

BROAD, GEORGE BIRNEY, M.D., 608 East Genesee Street, Syracuse, New York. Syracuse University College of Medicine, 1896. Professor of Gynecology, Syracuse University College of Medicine; Surgeon, Syracuse Memorial Hospital; Consulting Gynecologist, St. Joseph's Hospital, Syracuse Free Dispensary.

BROBST, CHARLES H., M.D., Central National Bank Building, Peoria, Illinois. Medico-Chirurgical College, Philadelphia, 1888. Lecturer on Physiological Optics, Bradley Polytechnic Institute; Eye, Ear, Nose, and Throat Surgeon, John C. Proctor Hospital; Ophthalmologist, John C. Proctor Endowment Home.

BROCK, EVAN COLEMAN, M.D., Hawkes Hospital of Mt. Carmel, Columbus, Ohio. Ohio State University College of Medicine (Starling Medical College), 1904. Assistant Surgeon, Hawkes Hospital of Mt. Carmel.

BROCK, HENRY HERBERT, A.B., M.D., 687 Congress Street, Portland, Maine. Bowdoin Medical College, 1890. Professor of Clinical Surgery, Bowdoin Medical College; Consulting Surgeon, Maine General and Children's Hospitals, United States Public Health and Marine Hospital Service, Portland, Waldo County General Hospital, Belfast, Webber Hospital, Biddeford.

BROCKMAN, DAVID C., A.M., M.D., Ennis Building, Ottumwa, Iowa. State University of Iowa College of Medicine, 1878. Consulting Surgeon, Ottumwa and St. Joseph's Hospitals.

BRODRICK, FRANK WILSON, M.D., Lawrence Building, Sterling, Illinois. University of Illinois College of Medicine (College of Physicians and Surgeons, Chicago), 1897. Surgeon, Sterling Public Hospital.

BROMBERG, PERRY, M.D., 510 Jackson Building, Nashville, Tennessee. University of Tennessee College of Medicine, 1895. Professor of Genito-Urinary Surgery, Vanderbilt University, Medical Department; Genito-Urinary Surgeon, Nashville City, Vanderbilt University, and St. Thomas Hospitals.

BRONNER, HERBERT, B.Sc., A.B., M.D., 222 Francis Building, Louisville, Kentucky. University of Louisville, Medical Department, 1902. Professor of Genito-Urinary Surgery, University of Louisville, Medical Department; Visiting Genito-Urinary Surgeon, Louisville City, Jewish, and Children's Free Hospitals.

BROOKE, BEN C., M.D., Brooke and Lanstrum Building, Helena, Montana. University and Bellevue Hospital Medical College (Bellevue Hospital Medical College), 1896. Surgeon, St. John's and St. Peter's Hospitals, Barnes-King Mining Company, Montana Power Company, Helena Light and Railway Company, Great Northern Railway Company; Consulting Surgeon, Northern Pacific Railway; Medical Director, Montana Life Insurance Company.

BROOKE, JOHN ALFRED, A.M., M.D., 264 South Sixteenth Street, Philadelphia, Pennsylvania. Hahnemann Medical College and Hospital, Philadelphia, 1896. Lecturer on Orthopedic Surgery, Hahnemann Medical College; Chief of Orthopedic Department, Hahnemann Hospital; Orthopedist, Children's Homeopathic, Women's Homeopathic, Women's Homeopathic Southern Hospitals, Philadelphia, West Jersey Hospital, Camden, New Jersey.

BROOKE, ROGER, M.D., Medical Corps, United States Army, Washington, District of Columbia. University of Maryland School of Medicine (Baltimore Medical College), 1900. Lieutenant Colonel, Medical Corps, United States Army.

BROOKE, WILLIAM WALLACE, M.D., 915 Avenue C, Bayonne, New Jersey. Columbia University College of Physicians and Surgeons (College of Physicians and Surgeons, New York), 1900. Visiting Surgeon and Gynecologist, Bayonne Hospital; Associate Surgeon, Greenville Hospital.

BROOKS, CLARK D., M.D., David Whitney Building, Detroit, Michigan. Detroit College of Medicine and Surgery, 1905. Associate Professor of Surgery, Detroit College of Medicine and Surgery; Associate Surgeon, Harper Hospital.

BROOKS, EDITH M., M.D., 483 Beacon Street, Boston, Massachusetts. Tufts College Medical School, 1902.

BROOKS, WILLIAM A., A.M., M.D., 227 Summit Avenue, Brookline, Massachusetts. Harvard Medical School, 1892. Vice-President, Brooks Hospital, Brookline.

BROOKSHER, W. R., M.D., First National Bank Building, Fort Smith, Arkansas. University of Louisville, Medical Department (Kentucky School of Medicine), 1891. Surgeon, Sparks Memorial Hospital.

BROPHY, TRUMAN W., D.D.S., M.D., D.Sc., LL.D., 81 East Madison Street, Chicago, Illinois. Rush Medical College, 1880. President, Chicago College of Dental Surgery; Oral Surgeon, Michael Reese and St. Joseph's Hospitals.

BROSE, LOUIS D., M.D., Ph.D., 501 Upper First Street, Evansville, Indiana. University of Pennsylvania School of Medicine, 1881.

BROUGHAM, EDWARD J., M.D., 163 West Chicago Avenue, Chicago, Illinois. Northwestern University Medical School (Chicago Medical College), 1887. Surgeon, Passavant Memorial Hospital.

BROUGHTON, LOUIS EDWARD, B.Sc., A.B., M.D., 50 East Three Notch Street, Andalusia, Alabama. Tulane University of Louisiana School of Medicine, 1893.

BROUGHTON, WILLIAM ROBERT, A.B., M.D., 341 Madison Avenue, New York, New York. Columbia University, College of Physicians and Surgeons, 1890. Consulting Ophthalmic Surgeon, Mountainside Hospital, Montclair, New Jersey; Ophthalmic Surgeon, Children's Home, Montclair, New Jersey.

BROUN, LeROY, B.Sc., M.D., 148 West Seventy-seventh Street, New York, New York. Vanderbilt University, Medical Department, 1887. Attending Surgeon, Woman's Hospital; Consulting Surgeon, Manhattan State Hospital.

BROWN, ALFRED JEROME, A.B., M.D., 402 City National Bank Building, Omaha, Nebraska. Columbia University, College of Physicians and Surgeons, 1903. Assistant Professor of Surgery, University of Nebraska College of Medicine; Member of Surgical Staff, Swedish Mission Hospital.

BROWN, CHARLES GAILEY, A.B., M.D., 190 Park Avenue, West, Mansfield, Ohio. Jefferson Medical College, 1901. Member of Staff, Mansfield General Hospital.

BROWN, CHARLES HENRY, Phar.G., M.D., 57 North Main Street, Waterbury, Connecticut. University and Bellevue Hospital Medical College (New York University Medical College), 1893. Gynecologist and Radiologist, Waterbury Hospital.

BROWN, CLAYTON MILO, M.D., 510 Delaware Avenue, Buffalo, New York. University of Buffalo, Department of Medicine, 1896. Professor of Rhino-Laryngology, University of Buffalo, Department of Medicine; Rhino-Laryngologist, Ernest Wende, Children's, City and Municipal Hospitals; Consulting Otologist, Homeopathic Hospital; Oto-Laryngologist, Buffalo General and Deaconess Hospitals.

BROWN, DAVID CHESTER, M.D., 330 Main Street, Danbury, Connecticut. Yale University School of Medicine, 1884. Surgeon, Danbury Hospital.

BROWN, EDMUND TOWLE, M.D., 30 Church Street, Burlington, Vermont. University of Vermont College of Medicine, 1897. Professor of Diseases of the Eye, Ear, Nose, and Throat, University of Vermont College of Medicine; Surgeon, Mary Fletcher Hospital.

BROWN, EDWARD M., M.D., 25 East Washington Street, Chicago, Illinois. Northwestern University Medical School, 1893. Professor of Surgery, Loyola University School of Medicine; Surgeon, West Side Hospital.

BROWN, GEORGE SNIDER, M.D., Front Street, Conway, Arkansas. University and Bellevue Hospital Medical College (University of the City of New York, Medical Department), 1877.

BROWN, GEORGE VAN INGEN, A.B., D.D.S., M.D., C.M., 445 Milwaukee Street, Milwaukee, Wisconsin. Marquette University School of Medicine (Milwaukee Medical College), 1895. Plastic and Oral Surgeon, Columbia, St. Mary's, and Milwaukee Children's Hospitals, Milwaukee County Hospital, Wauwatoso, and Milwaukee County Clinic; Plastic Surgeon, Wisconsin State University Hospital.

BROWN, HENRY ALEXANDER, M.D., 275 Post Street, San Francisco, California. Medico-Chirurgical College, Philadelphia, 1900. Oculist, Southern Pacific Company.

BROWN, HENRY P., JR., B.Sc., M.D., 1822 Pine Street, Philadelphia, Pennsylvania. University of Pennsylvania School of Medicine, 1912. Instructor in Surgery and Assistant Instructor in Surgical Pathology, University of Pennsylvania School of Medicine; Instructor in Surgery, University of Pennsylvania, Graduate School of Medicine; Assistant Surgeon, Pennsylvania, Presbyterian and Children's Hospitals.

BROWN, HORACE MANCHESTER, M.D., 311 Prospect Avenue, Milwaukee, Wisconsin. University and Bellevue Hospital Medical College (New York University Medical College), 1880. Surgeon, Columbia Hospital; Consulting Surgeon, Milwaukee Protestant Orphan Asylum, Chicago, Milwaukee and St. Paul Railroad.

BROWN, ISRAEL, Ph.B., M.D., 631 Boissevain Avenue, Norfolk, Virginia. Medical College of the State of South Carolina, 1894. Surgeon, St. Vincent's Hospital and Sanitarium.

BROWN, JAMES SPENCER, M.D., 43 South Fullerton Avenue, Montclair, New Jersey. Columbia University, College of Physicians and Surgeons, 1885. Surgeon-in-Chief, Mountainside Hospital; Consulting Surgeon, Children's Home, Montclair, Essex County Hospital, Cedar Grove, Essex County Hospital for Contagious Diseases, Belleville.

BROWN, JOHN EDWIN, B.Sc., A.M., D.Sc., M.D., 370 East Town Street, Columbus, Ohio. Medical College of Ohio, 1887. Professor of Oto-Laryngology and Head of Department of Ophthalmology and Oto-Laryngology, Ohio State University College of Medicine; Oto-Laryngologist, University Homeopathic, and St. Francis Hospitals; Member of Staff, Grant Hospital.

BROWN, JOHN MACKENZIE, M.D., Brockman Building, Los Angeles, California. Western University Medical School, 1899.

BROWN, LLOYD T., A.B., M.D., 372 Marlborough Street, Boston, Massachusetts. Harvard Medical School, 1907. Assistant Orthopedic Surgeon, Massachusetts General Hospital.

BROWN, MARTIN MILLARD, M.D., 117 Main Street, North Adams, Massachusetts. Rush Medical College, 1888. Attending Surgeon, North Adams Hospital.

BROWN, ORVILLE GRAHAM, M.D., Medical Corps, United States Army, Washington, District of Columbia. George Washington University Medical School, 1900. Lieutenant Colonel, Medical Corps, United States Army.

BROWN, PAUL FRANCIS, B.A., M.D., 1101 Metropolitan Bank Building, Minneapolis, Minnesota. University of Minnesota Medical School, 1905. Assistant Professor of Surgery, University of Minnesota Medical School; Surgeon, Minneapolis General Hospital and United States Public Health Service.

BROWN, RAYMOND SAMUEL, M.D., 511 Barber Building, Joliet, Illinois. Rush Medical College, 1905. Member of Staff, St. Joseph's Hospital.

BROWN, REXWALD, M.D., Santa Barbara Clinic, Santa Barbara, California. Northwestern University Medical School, 1903. Attending Surgeon, Santa Barbara Cottage Hospital.

BROWN, W. LAUNCELOT, M.D., 404 Roberts-Banner Building, El Paso, Texas. Rush Medical College, 1896. Member of Surgical Staff, Sisters Hospital; Chief Surgeon, El Paso and Southwestern Railroad.

BROWN, WILLIAM MORTIMER, M.D., 1776 East Avenue, Rochester, New York. University and Bellevue Hospital Medical College (University of the City of New York, Medical Department), 1889. Attending Obstetrician, Rochester General Hospital.

BROWNING, WILLIAM E., M.D., C.M., Caledonia, Minnesota. Faculty of Medicine, McGill University, 1899. Surgeon, Caledonia Hospital.

BROWNLEE, HARRIS FENTON, M.D., 342 Main Street, Danbury, Connecticut. Columbia University, College of Physicians and Surgeons, 1888. Surgeon, Danbury Hospital.

BRUCE, HERBERT ALEXANDER, M.D., L.R.C.P. (Lond.), F.R.C.S. (Eng.), 64 Bloor Street, East, Toronto, Ontario. University of Toronto, Faculty of Medicine, 1892. Associate Professor of Clinical Surgery, University of Toronto, Faculty of Medicine; Chief of Surgical Service, Toronto General Hospital.

BRUCE, JAMES DEACON, M.D., 333 South Jefferson Avenue, Saginaw, Michigan. Detroit College of Medicine and Surgery, 1896.

BRUÈRE, GUSTAVE ERNST, M.D., Journal Building, Portland, Oregon. Washington University Medical School, 1891. Chief of Staff, Eye and Ear Department, St. Vincent's Hospital.

BRUGGEMAN, HENRY OTTO, M.D., Fort Wayne, Indiana. Rush Medical College, 1903. Attending Surgeon, St. Joseph's Hospital.

BRUNER, JOHN W., M.D., 346 Market Street, Bloomsburg, Pennsylvania. Jefferson Medical College, 1890. Chief Surgeon, Bloomsburg Hospital, Bloomsburg; Visiting Surgeon, Berwick Hospital, Berwick.

BRUNER, WILLIAM EVANS, A.M., M.D., Guardian Building, Cleveland, Ohio. University of Pennsylvania School of Medicine, 1891. Professor of Ophthalmology, Western Reserve University School of Medicine; Visiting Ophthalmologist, Lakeside Hospital; Consulting Ophthalmologist, St. Vincent's Charity and Rainbow Hospitals.

BRUNN, HAROLD, M.D., 350 Post Street, San Francisco, California. University of Pennsylvania School of Medicine, 1895. Clinical Professor of Surgery,

University of California Medical School; Surgeon-in-Chief, San Francisco Hospital, University of California Service; Surgeon, Mt. Zion Hospital.

BRUNS, EARL H., Medical Corps, United States Army, Washington, District of Columbia. University of Cincinnati College of Medicine (Miami Medical College), 1903. Major, Medical Corps, United States Army.

BRUSH, EDMUND CONE, A.M., M.D., 601 Market Street, Zanesville, Ohio. Ohio State University College of Medicine (Starling Medical College), 1875.

BRYAN, GEORGE CORBIN, M.D., 217 Baker Building, Walla Walla, Washington. University of Maryland School of Medicine (Baltimore Medical College), 1896.

BRYAN, HERMAN R. H., M.B., 1A Cumberland Street, South, Port Arthur, Ontario. University of Toronto, Faculty of Medicine, 1904.

BRYAN, JOSEPH HAMMOND, M.D., 818 Seventeenth Street, Northwest, Washington, District of Columbia. University of Virginia, Department of Medicine, 1877; University and Bellevue Hospital Medical College (University of the City of New York, Medical Department), 1879. Attending Surgeon, Episcopal Eye, Ear, and Throat Hospital; Consulting Laryngologist, Garfield Memorial Hospital.

BRYAN, ROBERT C., M.D., 401 West Grace Street, Richmond, Virginia. Columbia University, College of Physicians and Surgeons, 1899. Professor of Genito-Urinary Surgery, Medical College of Virginia; Surgeon, Grace Hospital; Visiting Surgeon, Memorial Hospital; Visiting Genito-Urinary Surgeon, Virginia Hospital.

BRYAN, W. A., A.M., M.D., Doctors Building, Nashville, Tennessee. Vanderbilt University, Medical Department, 1899. Professor of Surgery and Clinical Surgery, Vanderbilt University, Medical Department; Professor of Oral Surgery, Vanderbilt University, Dental Department; Surgeon, Woman's, Nashville City, and Vanderbilt University Hospitals, Nashville, Watauga Sanitarium, Ridgetop.

BRYAN, W. M. C., A.B., M.Sc., M.D., 910 University Club Building, St. Louis, Missouri. Johns Hopkins University, Medical Department, 1902. Instructor in Clinical Laryngology and Rhinology, Washington University Medical School; Consulting Oto-Laryngologist, Alexian Brothers' and St. John's Hospitals; Laryngologist, Barnes Hospital; Surgeon, Laryngological Service, Out-Patient Department, Washington University Dispensary.

BRYAN, WILLIAM, M.D., 91 Bard Avenue, West New Brighton, New York. University and Bellevue Hospital Medical College (University of the City of New York, Medical Department), 1880. Visiting Surgeon, Staten Island Hospital, Tompkinsville; Consulting Surgeon, St. Vincent's Hospital, West New Brighton, Sea View Hospital, Castleton Corners.

BRYANT, ALICE GERTRUDE, A.B., M.D., 502 Beacon Street, Boston, Massachusetts. Woman's Medical College of the New York Infirmary for Women and Children, 1890.

BRYANT, DeWITT C., A.M., M.D., 716 Broadway Central Building, Los Angeles, California. Western Reserve University School of Medicine (University of Wooster, Medical Department), 1875.

BRYANT, ERNEST ALBERT, M.D., 520 Los Angeles Railway Building, Los Angeles, California. University of Pennsylvania School of Medicine, 1890. Surgeon, Crocker Street Hospital; Chief Surgeon, Los Angeles Railroad; Consulting Surgeon, Southern Pacific, Southern Pacific de Mexico, and Arizona and Eastern Railroads; Medical Director, California Edison Company.

BRYANT, W. SOHIER, A.M., M.D., 107 East Thirty-ninth Street, New York, New York. Harvard Medical School, 1888.

BUBIS, JACOB L., M.D., 1725 East Eighty-second Street, Cleveland, Ohio. Western Reserve University School of Medicine (Cleveland College of Physicians and Surgeons), 1907. Senior Assistant in Obstetrics, Junior Assistant in Gynecology, Mt. Sinai Hospital; Senior Assistant in Gynecology and Obstetrics, Out-Patient Department, Mt. Sinai Hospital.

BUCHANAN, JOHN J., A.M., M.D., Ph.D., 1409 North Highland Avenue, Pittsburgh, Pennsylvania. University of Pennsylvania School of Medicine, 1881. Surgeon, Mercy Hospital.

BUCHANAN, MARY, M.D., 2106 Chestnut Street, Philadelphia, Pennsylvania. Woman's Medical College of Pennsylvania, 1899. Professor of Ophthalmology, Woman's Medical College of Pennsylvania; Chief Ophthalmologist, Woman's College Hospital; Oculist, Woman's College Hospital and Woman's Hospital; Consultant in Ophthalmology, West Philadelphia Hospital for Women and Woman's Department, State Hospital for Insane, Norristown.

BUCK, AUGUSTUS W., A.B., M.D., 252 Pine Street, Fall River, Massachusetts. University of Pennsylvania School of Medicine, 1892. Surgeon, Union Hospital.

BUCK, CARROLL DEFOREST, M.D., Medical Corps, United States Army, Washington, District of Columbia. University of Minnesota Medical School, 1897. Lieutenant Colonel, Medical Corps, United States Army.

BUCKMAN, ERNEST U., M.D., 70 South Franklin Street, Wilkes-Barre, Pennsylvania. University of Pennsylvania School of Medicine, 1892.

BUCKNER, HUBBARD THOMAS, M.D., 508 Cobb Building, Seattle, Washington. Jefferson Medical College of Philadelphia, 1913.

BUDDENBROCK, ERICK VON, M.D., 301 Sixth Street, Racine, Wisconsin. University of Pennsylvania School of Medicine, 1905.

BUERGER, LEO, A.M., M.D., 1000 Park Avenue, New York, New York. Columbia University, College of Physicians and Surgeons, 1901. Professor of Urological Surgery, New York Polyclinic Medical School.

BUFORD, COLEMAN GRAVES, M.D., 122 South Michigan Avenue, Chicago, Illinois. Northwestern University Medical School, 1894. Associate Surgeon, St. Luke's Hospital.

BUGBEE, HENRY GREENWOOD, M.D., 40 East Forty-first Street, New York, New York. Columbia University, College of Physicians and Surgeons, 1903. Attending Urologist, St. Luke's, New York City and Lawrence Hospitals, Bronxville; Urologist, Woman's and Lying-in Hospitals; Consulting Urologist, Mountainside Hospital, Montclair, New Jersey, Muhlenberg Hospital, Plainfield, New Jersey, and Vassar Brothers' Hospital, Poughkeepsie.

BUIST, A. JOHNSTON, A.B., M.D., 279 Meeting Street, Charleston, South Carolina. Medical College of the State of South Carolina, 1896. Professor of Gynecology, Medical College of the State of South Carolina; Visiting Gynecologist, Roper Hospital.

BULKLEY, KENNETH, A.B., M.D., 420 Syndicate Building, Minneapolis, Minnesota. Columbia University College of Physicians and Surgeons, 1909.

BULL, EDWARD LEONARD, M.D., 124 East State Street, Ithaca, New York. Columbia University, College of Physicians and Surgeons, 1888.

BULL, HEMAN ROWLEE, B.Sc., M.D., 407 North Seventh Street, Grand Junction, Colorado. Jefferson Medical College, 1887. Surgeon, St. Mary's Hospital, Denver and Rio Grande Railroad.

BULLARD, EDWARD ARTHUR, M.D., 47 East Fifty-seventh Street, New York, New York. Dartmouth Medical School, 1906. Assistant Surgeon, Woman's Hospital.

BULLOCK, WALLER O., M.D., 190 North Upper Street, Lexington, Kentucky. University of Virginia, Department of Medicine, 1896. Consulting Surgeon, St. Joseph's Hospital, Lexington Clinic.

BULSON, ALBERT EUGENE, JR., B.Sc., M.D., 406 West Berry Street, Fort Wayne, Indiana. Rush Medical College, 1891. Professor of Ophthalmology, Indiana University School of Medicine; Eye, Ear, Nose, and Throat Surgeon, Hope Methodist and St. Joseph's Hospitals. Editor, *Journal of the Indiana State Medical Association.*

BUNCH, GEORGE HENRY, A.B., M.D., 1404 Laurel Street, Columbia, South Carolina. University of Michigan Medical School, 1903.

BUNN, FRANK CAULKINS, M.D., 30 Hillyer Street, Orange, New Jersey. New York Homeopathic Medical College and Flower Hospital, 1889. Attending Surgeon, Homeopathic Hospital of Essex County, Newark; Consulting Surgeon, St. Mary's Hospital, Passaic, Ann May Memorial Homeopathic Hospital, Spring Lake.

BUNTS, FRANK E., M.D., Clinic Building, Cleveland, Ohio. Western Reserve University School of Medicine, 1886. Professor of Principles of Surgery and Clinical Surgery, Western Reserve University School of Medicine; Visiting Surgeon, St. Vincent's Charity Hospital; Consulting Surgeon, Lutheran and Woman's Hospitals, St. Ann's Infant Asylum and Maternity Hospital.

BURCH, FRANK E., M.D., 754 Linwood Place, St. Paul, Minnesota. University of Minnesota Medical School, 1897. Associate Professor of Ophthalmology, University of Minnesota Medical School; Ophthalmologist and Otologist, Miller Hospital.

BURCH, LUCIUS EDWARD, M.D., Doctors Building, Nashville, Tennessee. Vanderbilt University, Medical Department, 1896. Dean of Faculty and Professor of Gynecology, Vanderbilt University, Medical Department; Surgeon, Vanderbilt University Hospital; Gynecologist, Nashville City and Woman's Hospitals; Surgeon-in-Chief, Tennessee Central and Nashville Interurban Railroads.

BURDICK, CARL GOODWIN, M.D., 126 East Thirty-seventh Street, New York, New York. Columbia University, College of Physicians and Surgeons, 1903. Clinical Professor of Surgery, University and Bellevue Hospital Medical College; Visiting Surgeon, in charge Children's Surgical Service, Bellevue Hospital; Attending Surgeon, Knickerbocker Hospital; Associate Surgeon, Hernia Department, Hospital for Ruptured and Crippled; Assistant Surgeon, St. Francis and Willard Parker Hospitals.

BURFORD, CYRUS EDGAR, Ph.B., M.D., Arcade Building, St. Louis, Missouri. St. Louis University School of Medicine (Marion-Sims-Beaumont Medical College), 1902. Professor of Genito-Urinary Surgery, St. Louis University School of Medicine; Genito-Urinary Surgeon, St. Luke's, Bethesda, and St. Louis Maternity Hospitals, Missouri Baptist Sanitarium; Visiting Genito-Urinary Surgeon, St. Louis City Hospital; Consulting Genito-Urinary Surgeon, Jewish Hospital.

BURGER, THOMAS OVERTON, M.D., 1200 First National Bank Building, San Diego, California. Vanderbilt University, Medical Department, 1900. Gynecologist, San Diego County General Hospital; Surgeon, St. Joseph's and Agnew Hospitals.

BURGESS, HARRY CLIFTON, M.D., C.M., 118 Crescent Street, Montreal, Quebec. Faculty of Medicine, McGill University, 1905. Lecturer on Obstetrics and Gynecology, Faculty of Medicine, McGill University; Assistant Gynecologist, Royal Victoria Hospital; Assistant Surgeon, Montreal Maternity Hospital.

BURK, SAMUEL B., M.D., 969 Madison Avenue, New York, New York. Cornell University Medical College, 1911. Instructor in Surgery, University and Bellevue Hospital Medical College; Surgeon, United States Naval Hospital.

BURKE, FRANCIS RAMON, A.B., M.D., 1200 Hancock Street, Quincy, Massachusetts. Harvard Medical School, 1903.

BURKE, THOMAS ALLEN, M.D., 524 M. B. A. Building, Mason City, Iowa. Loyola University School of Medicine (Chicago College of Medicine and Surgery), 1909. Member of Staff, St. Joseph's Mercy Hospital.

BURKE, WILLIAM PATRICK, M.D., 502 Merritt Building, Los Angeles, California. University of Illinois College of Medicine, 1894.

BURLESON, JOHN HILL, M.D., Central Trust Building, San Antonio, Texas. Washington University Medical School (Missouri Medical College), 1890. Surgeon in Charge, St. Luke's Clinic of Santa Rosa Infirmary; Division Oculist, Southern Pacific and Missouri, Kansas and Texas Railways.

BURLEW, JESSE MANNING, Ph.B., M.Sc., M.D., Spurgeon Building, Santa Ana, California. Rush Medical College, 1903.

BURNAM, CURTIS F., A.B., M.D., 1418 Eutaw Place, Baltimore, Maryland. Johns Hopkins University, Medical Department, 1900. Surgeon, Howard A. Kelly Hospital; Consulting Surgeon, Cambridge-Maryland Hospital, Cambridge.

BURNETT, WILLIAM BRENTON, B.A., M.D., C.M., 718 Granville Street, Vancouver, British Columbia. Faculty of Medicine, McGill University, 1899. Gynecologist and Obstetrician, Vancouver General Hospital.

BURNS, ARTHUR EDWIN, LL.B., M.D., 619 Cobb Building, Seattle, Washington. University and Bellevue Hospital Medical College (Bellevue Hospital Medical College), 1887.

BURNS, JOHN W., M.D., Cuero, Texas. Vanderbilt University, Medical Department, 1891. Surgeon, Burns Hospital.

BURNS, JONATHAN EDWARD, B.A., M.D., 403 Waldheim Building, Kansas City, Missouri. Johns Hopkins University, Medical Department, 1908. Urologist, St. Luke's Hospital.

BURNS, ROBERT, JR., M.D., Lister Building, St. Louis, Missouri. Washington University Medical School, 1901. Associate Surgeon, Bethesda Hospital.

BURNS, STILLWELL CORSON, M.D., 1925 Spring Garden Street, Philadelphia, Pennsylvania. Medico-Chirurgical College, Philadelphia, 1898. Surgeon, Polyclinic Section, Medico-Chirurgical Hospital of the University of Pennsylvania, Baldwin Locomotive Works.

BURNS, THOMAS MITCHELL, M.D., 640 Metropolitan Building, Denver, Colorado. University of Colorado School of Medicine (Gross Medical College), 1893. Emeritus Professor of Obstetrics, University of Colorado School of Medicine; Attending Obstetrician, Mercy Hospital; Consulting Obstetrician, County and St. Anthony's Hospitals, Florence Crittenton Home.

BURNS, WILLIAM BRITT, M.D., Porter Building, Memphis, Tennessee. University of Louisville Medical Department (Kentucky School of Medicine), 1892. Division Surgeon, Frisco Emergency Hospital; Surgeon, Memphis General Hospital, Louisville and Nashville and Missouri Pacific Railways.

BURRETT, CLAUDE A., Ph.B., M.D., 1948 Iuka Avenue, Columbus, Ohio. Ohio State University College of Homeopathic Medicine (Cleveland Homeopathic Medical College), 1905. Dean and Professor of Surgery, Ohio State University College of Homeopathic Medicine; Medical Director, University Hospital.

BURRIS, J. STANLEY, M.D., C.M., Kamloops, British Columbia. McGill University Faculty of Medicine, 1899. Honorary Surgeon, King Edward Sanitarium, Tranquille.

BURROUGHS, GEORGE MCCLELLAN, M.D., 5 Broad Street, Danielson, Connecticut. University of Maryland School of Medicine (Baltimore Medical College), 1900. Oculist, Day Kimball Hospital.

BURT, JAMES C., Ph.B., M.D., Westinghouse Building, Pittsburgh, Pennsylvania. Jefferson Medical College, 1902. Genito-Urinary Surgeon, Allegheny General and St. Francis Hospitals.

BURTON, PAUL H., M.D., 51 Broadway, Fargo, North Dakota. University of Minnesota Medical School (Hamline University, Medical Department), 1901. Chief Surgeon, Cass County Hospital; President of Staff, St. John's Hospital.

BUSARD, ROBERT I., M.D., First Street and Webster Avenue, Muskegon, Michigan. Northwestern University Medical School, 1910. Consultant, Surgical Staff, Hackley Hospital.

BUSH, CHARLES WILLIAM, Ch.B., M.D., 202 Huntington Avenue, Boston, Massachusetts. Boston University School of Medicine, 1899. Nose and Throat Surgeon, Massachusetts Homeopathic Hospital and Out-Patient Department.

BUSHMAN, LOUIS B., A.M., M.D., 631 City National Bank Building, Omaha, Nebraska. Creighton College of Medicine, 1903. Professor of Rhinology, Oto-Laryngology, Creighton College of Medicine; Oculist and Aurist, St. Joseph's and St. Catherine's Hospitals; Oculist, Douglas County Hospital.

BUSKIRK, WILLIAM HENRY, M.D., 413 Main Street, Miles City, Montana. University of Michigan Medical School, 1904. Attending Surgeon, Miles City Hospital.

BUSSEY, GEORGE NEWTON, Ph.B., M.D., 1810 Wilson Avenue, Chicago, Illinois. Rush Medical College, 1893. Surgeon and Obstetrician, Ravenswood Hospital.

BUSSEY, WILLIAM JOSEPH, M.D., 517 Frances Building, Sioux City, Iowa. Jefferson Medical College, 1901. Oculist and Aurist, St. Joseph's Mercy Hospital.

BUSWELL, CLARK A., M.D., 1952 Irving Park Boulevard, Chicago, Illinois. University of Illinois College of Medicine, 1900. Attending Surgeon, Ravenswood Hospital.

BUTEAU, SAMUEL HAWKINS, M.D., 1307 Broadway, Oakland, California. Cooper Medical College, 1889. Consulting Surgeon, Samuel Merritt Hospital.

BUTLER, CHARLES S., A.B., M.D., Medical Corps, United States Navy, Washington, District of Columbia. University of Virginia, Department of Medicine, 1897. Captain, Medical Corps, United States Navy.

BUTLER, JOEL IVES, Ph.B., M.D., 123 South Stone Avenue, Tucson, Arizona. Johns Hopkins University, Medical Department, 1901. Member of Staff, Arizona Hospital.

BUTLER, MARGARET F., M.D., 1831 Chestnut Street, Philadelphia, Pennsylvania. Woman's Medical College of Pennsylvania, 1894. Professor of Rhinology and Laryngology, Woman's Medical College of Pennsylvania; Rhinologist, Laryngologist, and Otologist, Woman's Hospital of Philadelphia, West Philadelphia Hospital for Women; Rhinologist and Laryngologist, Woman's Medical College Hospital.

BUTLER, RALPH, M.D., 1926 Chestnut Street, Philadelphia, Pennsylvania. University of Pennsylvania School of Medicine, 1900. Professor of Laryngology, University of Pennsylvania Graduate School of Medicine; Assistant Professor of Otology, University of Pennsylvania School of Medicine; Chief of Ear Dispensary, Hospital of the University of Pennsylvania; Laryngologist and Otologist, Lankenau Hospital.

BUTLER, ROBERT H., M.D., 128 West Columbus Avenue, Bellefontaine, Ohio. University of Cincinnati College of Medicine (Miami Medical College), 1906.

BUTSCH, JOHN LOUIS, M.Sc., M.D., Ph.D., Buffalo Clinic, Buffalo, New York. Johns Hopkins University, Medical Department, 1912. Surgeon, Buffalo Clinic.

BUTT, ARTHUR PARKER, M.D., 209 Randolph Avenue, Elkins, West Virginia. University of Maryland School of Medicine (College of Physicians and Surgeons, Baltimore), 1895. Surgeon-in-Chief, Allegheny Heights Hospital, Davis, City Hospital, Elkins.

BUXTON, JOSEPH THOMAS, M.D., The Marlborough, Newport News, Virginia. University of Pennsylvania School of Medicine, 1897. Surgeon in Charge, Elizabeth Buxton Hospital; Visiting Surgeon, Virginia School for Deaf, Dumb, and Blind.

BUXTON, L. HAYNES, M.D., LL.D., 203 American National Bank Building, Oklahoma, Oklahoma. University and Bellevue Hospital Medical College (New York University Medical College), 1883; University of Vermont College of Medicine, 1884; University of Vienna, 1907. Professor and Head of Department of Oto-Laryngology, University of Oklahoma School of Medicine; Chief of Staff, Ear, Nose, and Throat Department, State University and University Emergency Hospitals; Oculist and Aurist, Oklahoma State Baptist Orphans' Home.

BYFORD, HENRY TURMAN, M.D., 122 South Michigan Avenue, Chicago, Illinois. Northwestern University Medical School, 1873. Emeritus Professor of Gynecology, University of Illinois College of Medicine; Consulting Gynecologist, St. Luke's Hospital.

BYRD, W. H., M.D., State and High Streets, Salem, Oregon. University of Oregon Medical School (Willamette University, Medical Department), 1881.

BYRNES, FRANK, M.D., 3203 North Clark Street, Chicago, Illinois. Rush Medical College, 1894. Attending Surgeon, Columbus Hospital.

BYRNES, HARRY FRANCIS, M.D., 67 Chestnut Street, Springfield, Massachusetts. University of Maryland School of Medicine (Baltimore Medical College), 1904. Aurist and Oculist, Mercy Hospital.

CABOT, HUGH, A.B., M.D., C.M.G., University Hospital, Ann Arbor, Michigan. Harvard Medical School, 1898. Professor of Surgery, University of Michigan Medical School.

CAGLIERI, GUIDO E., B.Sc., M.D., M.R.C.S. (Eng.), L.R.C.P. (Lond.), 21 Columbus Avenue, San Francisco, California. University of California Medical School, 1892. Associate Surgeon, St. Mary's Hospital.

CALDER, ALLISTER, M.D., C.M., Glace Bay, Nova Scotia. Dalhousie University, Faculty of Medicine, 1909. Surgeon, St. Joseph's and Glace Bay General Hospitals.

CALDWELL, J. HADLEY, M.D., 323 Broadway, Cincinnati, Ohio. University of Cincinnati College of Medicine (Medical College of Ohio), 1906.

CALDWELL, JOHN ALEXANDER, B.Sc., M.D., 628 Elm Street, Cincinnati, Ohio. University of Cincinnati College of Medicine (Miami Medical College), 1902. Senior Instructor in Clinical Surgery, University of Cincinnati College of Medicine; Assistant Attending Surgeon, Cincinnati General Hospital.

CALDWELL, JOSEPH R., M.D., Wheeling Steel Corporation Building, Wheeling, West Virginia. Rush Medical College, 1896. Member of Surgical Staff, Wheeling and Ohio Valley General Hospitals.

CALDWELL, ROBERT, M.D., 510 Jackson Building, Nashville, Tennessee. University of Tennessee College of Medicine, 1903. Professor of Surgical Anatomy, Vanderbilt University, Medical Department.

CALDWELL, ROBERT, M.D., Exchange Bank Building, Little Rock, Arkansas. University of Louisville Medical Department (Hospital Medical College), 1901. Member of Staff, St. Vincent's Infirmary; Oculist and Aurist, Baptist Hospital.

CALDWELL, WILLIAM EDGAR, M.D., 58 West Fifty-fifth Street, New York, New York. University and Bellevue Hospital Medical College, 1904. Associate Professor of Obstetrics, Columbia University, College of Physicians and Surgeons; Associate Director, Sloane Hospital for Women; Attending Surgeon, New York Nursery and Child's Hospital.

CALE, GEORGE W., JR., M.D., Wall Building, St. Louis, Missouri. St. Louis College of Physicians and Surgeons, 1887. Surgeon, St. Luke's Hospital; Consulting Surgeon, St. John's Hospital.

CALHOUN, F. PHINIZY, A.B., M.D., 833 Candler Building, Atlanta, Georgia. Emory University School of Medicine (Atlanta Medical College), 1904. Professor of Ophthalmology, Emory University School of Medicine; Visiting Ophthalmologist and Aurist, Grady Memorial and Wesley Memorial Hospitals, St. Joseph's Infirmary.

CALKINS, FREDERIC RUSSELL, M.D., 4 Cleveland Building, Watertown, New York. Consulting Surgeon, St. Joachim's and Watertown City Hospitals.

CALLAN, PETER A., M.D., 452 Fifth Avenue, New York, New York. University and Bellevue Hospital Medical College (New York University Medical College), 1867. Ophthalmologist, Columbus and St. Vincent's Hospitals; Consulting Surgeon, New York Eye and Ear Infirmary; President Emeritus of Medical Board, St. Joseph's Hospital, Yonkers.

CALLANDER, CYRUS NEWTON, M.D., C.M., 620 Front Street, Fargo, North Dakota. University of Toronto, Faculty of Medicine (Trinity Medical College), 1897. Staff Surgeon, St. John's and St. Luke's Hospitals; Orthopedic Surgeon, Fargo Clinic.

CAMERON, IRVING HEWARD, M.B., LL.D., F.R.C.S. (Eng., Edin., I.), 307 Sherbourne Street, Toronto, Ontario. University of Toronto, Faculty of Medicine, 1874. Professor of Surgery and Clinical Surgery, University of Toronto, Faculty of Medicine; Surgeon, Toronto General and St. John's Hospitals.

CAMERON, KENNETH, B.A., M.D., C.M., C.M.G., 400 Mackay Street, Montreal, Quebec. Faculty of Medicine, McGill University, 1887. Member of Consulting Staff, Montreal General Hospital; Consulting Surgeon, Children's Memorial Hospital.

CAMERON, LYLE JOHN, M.D., M.R.S.C., F.R.C.S. (Eng.), L.R.C.P. (Lond.), 87 Wimpole Street, London, England. Faculty of Medicine, University of Manitoba (Manitoba Medical College), 1913. Gynecologist, Out-Patient's Department, Royal Waterloo Hospital.

CAMERON, MALCOLM HECTORSON VALENTINE, M.B., 11 Prince Arthur Avenue, Toronto, Ontario. University of Toronto, Faculty of Medicine, 1905. Demonstrator of Clinical Surgery, University of Toronto, Faculty of Medicine; Assistant Surgeon, St. Michael's Hospital.

CAMERON, WILLIAM GOODERHAM, M.D., 1404 National Realty Building, Tacoma, Washington. University of Pennsylvania School of Medicine, 1897. Ophthalmic Surgeon, Northern Pacific Railway; Oculist and Oto-Laryngologist, Northern Pacific Hospital.

CAMPBELL, ALEXANDER MACKENZIE, M.D., Metz Building, Grand Rapids, Michigan. Detroit College of Medicine and Surgery, 1896. Visiting Surgeon, Blodgett Memorial Hospital; Consulting Surgeon, Blodgett Home for Children; Visiting Obstetrician, Butterworth Hospital.

CAMPBELL, CHARLES H., M.D., Columbus State Bank Building, Columbus, Nebraska. State University of Iowa College of Medicine, 1898. Chief of Eye, Ear, Nose, and Throat Department, St. Mary's Hospital.

CAMPBELL, CHARLES SAMUEL, M.Sc., M.D., 114 West Ninth Street, Coffeyville, Kansas. Rush Medical College, 1902. Surgeon, South East Kansas Hospital.

CAMPBELL, DON M., M.D., L.R.S.C. (Edin.), 1613 David Whitney Building, Detroit, Michigan. Detroit College of Medicine and Surgery, 1885. Royal College of Physicians and Surgeons, 1886. Professor of Ophthalmology and Otology, and Head of Department of Ophthalmology, Detroit College of Medicine and Surgery; Ophthalmologist and Otologist, Harper Hospital.

CAMPBELL, GORDON LOTHIAN, M.D., C.M., Kelowna, British Columbia. Queen's University, Faculty of Medicine, 1910. Attending Surgeon, Kelowna General Hospital.

CAMPBELL, I. GLEN, M.D., C.M., 736 Granville Street, Vancouver, British Columbia. Faculty of Medicine, McGill University, 1897. Surgeon, Eye, Ear, Nose, and Throat Department, Vancouver General Hospital; Honorary Consulting Ophthalmic and Aural Surgeon, Children's Aid Society, Anti-Tuberculosis Society of British Columbia.

CAMPBELL, JAMES ALEXANDER, M.D., Equitable Building, St. Louis, Missouri. Homeopathic Medical College of Missouri, 1869. Oculist and Aurist, Girls' Industrial Home, Christian Brothers' College.

CAMPBELL, JAMES LEROY, M.D., 325 Candler Building, Atlanta, Georgia. Emory University School of Medicine (Atlanta Medical College), 1893. Professor Clinical Surgery, Emory University, School of Medicine; Visiting Surgeon, Wesley Memorial and Grady Memorial Hospitals.

CAMPBELL, JAMES TWEEDIE, M.B., M.D., M.R.C.S. (Eng.), 30 North Michigan Avenue, Chicago, Illinois. University of Toronto, Faculty of Medicine, 1889; University and Bellevue Hospital Medical College, 1889. Professor of Otology, Rhinology, and Laryngology, Post-Graduate Medical School; Laryngologist and Rhinologist, St. Luke's Hospital; Otologist, Rhinologist, and Laryngologist, Post-Graduate Hospital.

CAMPBELL, ROBERT D., A.B., M.D., C.M., 2½ South Third Street, Grand Forks, North Dakota. Faculty of Medicine, University of Manitoba (Manitoba Medical College), 1893. Special Lecturer, University of North Dakota School of Medicine; Attending Surgeon, St. Michael's and Grand Forks Deaconess Hospitals.

CAMPBELL, STUART AVERY, M.D., 0433 Norfolk Avenue, Norfolk, Nebraska. University of Nebraska College of Medicine (Omaha Medical College), 1898.

CAMPBELL, WILLIAM E., M.D., Atlanta National Bank Building, Atlanta, Georgia. University and Bellevue Hospital Medical College (University of the City of New York, Medical Department), 1888. Surgeon, Eye, Ear, Nose, and Throat Department, Georgian, Grady Memorial, and Georgia Baptist Hospitals, Hospital for Nervous Diseases, Scottish Rite Hospital for Crippled Children.

CAMPBELL, WILLIAM FRANCIS, A.B., M.D., 394 Clinton Avenue, Brooklyn, New York. Long Island College Hospital, 1892. Clinical Professor of Surgery, Long Island College Hospital; Surgeon-in-Chief, Trinity Hospital; Attending Surgeon, Long Island College Hospital; Consulting Surgeon, Methodist Episcopal, Swedish, and Coney Island Hospitals, Brooklyn, Jamaica Hospital, Jamaica.

CAMPBELL, WILLIAM MACFARLANE, M.D., 7133 Jenkins Arcade Building, Pittsburgh, Pennsylvania. University of Pennsylvania School of Medicine, 1899.

CAMPBELL, WILLIS C., M.D., 869 Madison Avenue, Memphis, Tennessee. University of Virginia, Department of Medicine, 1904. Professor of Orthopedic Surgery, University of Tennessee College of Medicine; Orthopedic Surgeon, Memphis General, Baptist Memorial, and St. Joseph's Hospitals,

Tri-State Hospital School for Crippled Children, Home for Incurables, Porter Home and Leath Orphanage.

CAMPICHE, PAUL SAMUEL, A.B., M.D., M.R.C.S. (Eng.), L.R.C.P. (Lond.), 560 Sutter Street, San Francisco, California. University of Lausanne, 1899.

CANDIDO DE CAMARGO, ANTONIO, M.D., Rua Alvares Centralo 35, Sao Paulo, Brazil. University of Geneva Medical School, 1889. Professor of Clinical Surgery, Sao Paulo Medical School; Member of Faculty, Paulista Institute; Chief of Surgical Clinic, Santa Casa Hospital.

CANFIELD, R. BISHOP, A.B., M.D., 330 South State Street, Ann Arbor, Michigan. University of Michigan Medical School, 1899. Professor of Oto-Laryngology, University of Michigan Medical School; Attending Oto-Laryngologist, University Hospital.

CANNADAY, JOHN EGERTON, M.D., Kanawha Banking and Trust Building, Charleston, West Virginia. Medical College of Virginia (University College of Medicine), 1901. Visiting Surgeon, Charleston General Hospital.

CANNON, OSCAR ANSON, M.B., 576 Main Street, East, Hamilton, Ontario. University of Toronto, Faculty of Medicine, 1907.

CANTRIL, ALBERT HADLEY, M.D., 285 Fargo Street, Portland, Oregon. Northwestern University Medical School, 1902. Member of Staff, Emanuel Hospital.

CAPELL, CLARENCE S., A.B., M.D., 1135 Rialto Building, Kansas City, Missouri. John A. Creighton Medical College, 1903. Urologist, St. Joseph's, St. Mary's and Kansas City Municipal Hospitals.

CARD, DANIEL P., M.D., Medical Corps, United States Army, Washington, District of Columbia. University and Bellevue Hospital Medical College, 1904. Major, Medical Corps, United States Army.

CARGILE, CHARLES HASTINGS, M.D., 212 West Twelfth Street, Bentonville, Arkansas. Jefferson Medical College, 1877.

CARITHERS, WARNER H., M.D., First and Jackson Streets, Moscow, Idaho. Rush Medical College, 1887. Surgeon, Inland Empire Hospital.

CARLAW, CHESTER M., M.D., C.M., Physicians and Surgeons Building, Minneapolis, Minnesota. Faculty of Medicine, McGill University, 1891. Surgeon, Northwestern and Minneapolis General Hospitals.

CARLESS, ALBERT, C.B.E., M.B., M.S., F.R.C.S. (Eng.), Thurlby House, Woodford Bridge, Essex, England. University of London, 1886. Emeritus Professor of Surgery and Consulting Surgeon, King's College Hospital; Medical Director, Dr. Barnardo Homes.

CARLETON, DUDLEY, M.D., 137½ State Street, Springfield, Massachusetts. Harvard Medical School, 1895. Orthopedic and Visiting Surgeon, Springfield Hospital.

CARLETON, SPRAGUE, A.M., M.D., 75 West Fiftieth Street, New York, New York. New York Homeopathic Medical College and Flower Hospital, 1906. Genito-Urinary Surgeon, Metropolitan Hospital; Consulting Genito-Urinary Surgeon, Yonkers Homeopathic Hospital and Maternity Hospital, Yonkers, Ann May Memorial Homeopathic Hospital, Spring Lake, New Jersey, Charlotte Hungerford Hospital, Torrington, Connecticut.

CARMANY, HARRY STOBER, M.D., 366 Green Lane, Philadelphia, Pennsylvania. University of Pennsylvania School of Medicine, 1893. Visiting Surgeon, Memorial Hospital; Associate Surgeon, Methodist Episcopal Hospital.

CARMICHAEL, JOHN HOSEA, M.D., 41 Maple Street, Springfield, Massachusetts. Albany Medical College, 1873. Surgeon-in-Chief, Wesson Memorial Hospital; Consulting Surgeon, Brattleboro Memorial Hospital, Brattleboro, Vermont, Gilbert Memorial Hospital, Ware, Massachusetts.

CARMODY, THOMAS EDWARD, M.D., D.D.Sc., D.D.S., 806 Metropolitan Building, Denver, Colorado. University of Colorado School of Medicine (Denver and Gross College of Medicine), 1903. Professor of Oral Surgery and Rhinology, University of Denver, Dental Department; Oral Surgeon, Children's Hospital; Laryngologist, Rhinologist, and Otologist, St. Luke's and Mercy Hospitals; Consulting Laryngologist, Rhinologist, and Otologist, Children's Hospital, Denver, Evangelical Lutheran Sanitarium, Wheatridge, Sanatorium of the Jewish Consumptives' Relief Society, Edgewater.

CARPENTER, DUDLEY N., M.D., Medical Corps, United States Navy, Washington, District of Columbia. Harvard Medical School, 1896. Captain, Medical Corps, United States Navy.

CARPENTER, ERNEST W., M.D., Professional Building, Greenville, South Carolina. Medical College of the State of South Carolina, 1895.

CARPENTER, EUGENE H., M.D., 31 Broad Street, Oneida, New York. University of Maryland School of Medicine (College of Physicians and Surgeons, Baltimore), 1894. Surgeon-in-Chief, Broad Street Hospital.

CARPENTER, EUGENE R., M.D., Southwestern Life Building, Dallas, Texas. Jefferson Medical College, 1898. Instructor, Baylor Medical College.

CARPENTER, FRANK BENTON, M.D., 715 Howard Building, San Francisco, California. Columbia University, College of Physicians and Surgeons, 1883. Lecturer on Gynecology, Leland Stanford Junior University School of Medicine; Visiting Gynecologist, City and County, St. Luke's, and San Francisco Hospitals.

CARPENTER, GEORGE A., M.D., 18 Broadway, Fargo, North Dakota. University of Minnesota Medical School, 1885. Member of Attending Staff, St. John's Hospital.

CARR, EARL INGRAM, M.D., 300 West Ottawa Street, Lansing, Michigan. University of Michigan Medical School, 1910. Surgeon, Edward W. Sparrow Hospital and Orthopedic Clinic of Lansing.

CARR, FRANCIS J., M.D., 345 Eagle Street, Buffalo, New York. University of Buffalo, Department of Medicine (Niagara University, Medical Department), 1894. Attending Surgeon, Emergency Hospital, Buffalo, St. Joseph's Hospital, Gardenville; Consulting Surgeon, Mercy Hospital, Buffalo, St. Mary's Hospital, Niagara Falls, J. N. Adam Memorial Hospital, Perrysburg, St. Francis' Asylums, Buffalo and Gardenville.

CARR, JAMES HENRY, M.D., 345 Eagle Street, Buffalo, New York. University of Buffalo, Department of Medicine, 1900. Surgical Instructor, University of Buffalo, Department of Medicine; Attending Surgeon, Emergency, Buffalo City Hospitals, and St. Francis Asylum.

CARR, W. P., M.D., 1801 K Street, Northwest, Washington, District of Columbia. George Washington University Medical School, 1888. Professor of Clinical Surgery, George Washington University Medical School; Consulting Surgeon, Central Dispensary and Emergency Hospital, Government Hospital for Insane.

CARREL, ALEXIS, M.D., D.Sc , Rockefeller Institute, New York, New York. University of Lyons, 1900. Member of Rockefeller Institute.

CARRIER, FRANK N., M.D., Santa Rita, New Mexico. Jefferson Medical College, 1893. Surgeon, Chino Copper Company Hospital.

CARROLL, FRANCIS M., M.D., Burke Building, Seattle, Washington. Cooper Medical College, 1896. Member of Staff, Providence Hospital; Chief of Staff of Gynecology and Obstetrics, City Hospital.

CARROLL, GEORGE GREGORY, M.D., 614 Main Street, West, Rochester, New York. Member of Staff, Park Avenue Hospital; Assistant to Staff, St. Mary's Hospital.

CARROLL, JAMES J., A.M., M.D., 405 North Charles Street, Baltimore, Maryland. University of Maryland School of Medicine, 1893. Oculist and Aurist, St. Joseph's Hospital.

CARROLL, THOMAS B., M.D., Jenkins Arcade Building, Pittsburgh, Pennsylvania. Jefferson Medical College, 1903. Gynecologist, Presbyterian Hospital, Pittsburgh; Obstetrician, Columbia Hospital, Wilkinsburg; Consulting Obstetrician, St. Francis Hospital, Pittsburgh.

CARROLL, WILLIAM C., B.Sc., M.D., Lowry Building, St. Paul, Minnesota. University of Minnesota Medical School, 1912. Attending Surgeon, St. Joseph's Hospital.

CARSON, ARCHIBALD IRWIN, B.Sc., M.D., 46 East McMillan Street, Cincinnati, Ohio. University of Cincinnati College of Medicine (Miami Medical College), 1889. Professor of Clinical Surgery, University of Cincinnati College of Medicine; Surgeon, Cincinnati General Hospital.

CARSON, FRANK LEROY, Phar.C., M.D., 14 East Ninth Street, Shawnee, Oklahoma. Tulane University of Louisiana School of Medicine, 1906. Attending Surgeon, Shawnee General Hospital.

CARSON, JAMES OLIVER, A.B., M.D., 442½ Main Street, Bowling Green, Kentucky. University of Louisville, Medical Department, 1878.

CARSON, NORMAN BRUCE, M.D., 4379 Westminster Place, St. Louis, Missouri. Washington University Medical School (St. Louis Medical College), 1868. Member of Staff, St. Louis Mullanphy Hospital.

CARSON, WAID EDWIN, A.M., M.D., 7095 Jenkins Arcade Building, Pittsburgh, Pennsylvania. Johns Hopkins University, Medical Department, 1907. Assistant Professor of Ophthalmology, University of Pittsburgh School of Medicine; Ophthalmologist, Western Pennsylvania Hospital; Surgeon, Eye and Ear Hospital.

CARTER, RALPH MERLE, A.B., M.D., Bellin Building, Green Bay, Wisconsin. Rush Medical College, 1908. Surgeon, St. Vincent's and Wisconsin Deaconess Hospitals.

CARTER, WILLIAM WESLEY, A.M., M.D., 2 West Sixty-seventh Street, New York, New York. University and Bellevue Hospital Medical College (New York University Medical College), 1895. Visiting Laryngologist and Otologist, Bellevue and Allied Hospitals (Gouverneur Hospital); Consulting Laryngologist and Otologist, South Side Hospital.

CARUTHERS, JOHN ALLEN, B.Sc., M.D., New Reymond Building, Baton Rouge, Louisiana. University of Texas, Department of Medicine, 1899. Consultant, Baton Rouge Sanitarium; Oculist, Standard Oil Company Hospital.

CARVALLO, CONSTANTINO J., M.D., Vera Cruz 239, Lima, Peru. Faculty of Medicine, University of San Marcos, 1913.

CARY, EDWARD HENRY, M.D., LL.D., Southwestern Life Building, Dallas, Texas. University and Bellevue Hospital Medical College, 1898. Head of the Department, Diseases of Eye, Ear, Nose, and Throat, Baylor University School of Medicine; Oculist and Aurist, Missouri, Kansas and Texas Railway, Southern Pacific Lines, Cotton Belt Route, Southern and Texas Traction Lines.

CARY, FOSTER HARRINGTON, M.D., Metropolitan Building, Denver, Colorado. Harvard Medical School, 1898. Instructor in Obstetrics and Clinical Instructor in Gynecology, University of Colorado School of Medicine; Chief of Obstetrical Out-Patient Department, University of Colorado School of Medicine; Obstetrician, Denver City and County, and Mercy Hospitals.

CARY, FRANK, M.D., 2536 Prairie Avenue, Chicago, Illinois. Rush Medical College, 1882. Obstetrician, St. Luke's Hospital.

CARY, FRENCH STROTHER, M.D., 30 North Michigan Avenue, Chicago, Illinois. University of Maryland School of Medicine (College of Physicians and Surgeons, Baltimore), 1906. Professor of Genito-Urinary Surgery, Post-Graduate Medical School; Attending Urologist, Englewood Hospital; Attending Genito-Urinary Surgeon, Post-Graduate Hospital.

CARY, WILLIAM HOLLENBACK, M.D., 36 Pierrepont Street, Brooklyn, New York. Syracuse University College of Medicine, 1905. Associate Attending Gynecologist and Obstetrician, Brooklyn Hospital.

CASE, CLARENCE E., M.D., Park and Center Streets, Ashtabula, Ohio. Western Reserve University School of Medicine, 1895. Visiting Surgeon, Ashtabula General Hospital.

CASE, JAMES THOMAS, M.D., 124 Manchester Street, Battle Creek, Michigan. University of Illinois College of Medicine (American Medical Missionary College), 1905. Professor of Rœntgenology, Northwestern University Medical School; Surgeon, Battle Creek Sanitarium.

CASHMAN, BENDER Z., A.B., M.D., 226 South Evaline Street, Pittsburgh, Pennsylvania. Johns Hopkins University, Medical Department, 1909. Assistant Professor in Gynecology, University of Pittsburgh School of Medicine; Gynecologist, St. Francis and Elizabeth Steel Magee Hospitals.

CASLER, DeWITT BELLINGER, A.B., M.D., 13 West Chase Street, Baltimore, Maryland. Johns Hopkins University, Medical Department, 1904. Instructor in Gynecology and Gynecological Pathology, Johns Hopkins University, Medical Department; Dispensary Gynecologist and Assistant Visiting Gynecologist, Johns Hopkins Hospital; Consulting Gynecologist, Hospital for Women of Maryland, Union Protestant Infirmary, Church Home and Infirmary, Baltimore, Springfield State Hospital for Insane, Sykesville.

CASSEL, RUFUS J., M.D., First National Bank Building, Mt. Vernon, Washington. University of Minnesota Medical School, 1901. Consulting Surgeon, Skagit County Hospital; Visiting Surgeon, Mt. Vernon General Hospital.

CASSELBERRY, RICHARD C., A.B., M.D., 700 Madison Street, Chester, Pennsylvania. Hahnemann Medical College and Hospital, Philadelphia, 1903. Chief Surgeon, J. Lewis Crozer Home for Incurables and Homeopathic Hospital; Surgeon, Baldwin Locomotive Works, Eddystone.

CASSIDY, WILLIAM JOSEPH, Phar.B., M.D., 1787 David Whitney Building, Detroit, Michigan. Detroit College of Medicine and Surgery, 1908. Clinical Assistant in Surgery, Detroit College of Medicine and Surgery; Attending Junior Surgeon, Harper Hospital.

CASTAÑEDA, MANUEL, M.D., Pacal 987, Lima, Peru. Faculty of Medicine, University of San Marcos, 1915. Chief Consulting Surgeon, Santa Ana Hospital.

CATHCART, ROBERT SPANN, M.D., 75 Hasell Street, Charleston, South Carolina. Medical College of the State of South Carolina, 1893. Professor of Abdominal Surgery, Medical College of the State of South Carolina; Surgeon-in-Chief, Roper Hospital.

CATHER, DAVID C., M.D., Medical Corps, United States Navy, Washington, District of Columbia. University of Pennsylvania School of Medicine, 1903. Commander, Medical Corps, United States Navy.

CATLIN, SANFORD ROBINSON, Ph.B., M.D., Stewart Building, Rockford, Illinois. Harvard Medical School, 1897. Surgeon, Rockford Hospital.

CATTERSON, ALDEN D., M.D., 3533 South Broadway, Englewood, Colorado. University of Pennsylvania Graduate School of Medicine (Medico-Chirurgical College of Philadelphia), 1899.

CATTERSON, THOMAS L., M.D., 2025 Fourth Avenue, Spokane, Washington. Detroit College of Medicine and Surgery, 1887.

CATURANI, MICHELE G., M.D., 136 East Seventy-ninth Street, New York, New York. University of Naples, 1899. Visiting Gynecologist, Italian Hospital.

CAULK, JOHN ROBERTS, A.M., M.D., University Club Building, St. Louis, Missouri. Johns Hopkins University, Medical Department, 1906. Associate in Genito-Urinary Surgery, Washington University Medical School; Chief of Genito-Urinary Clinic, Washington University Dispensary; Genito-Urinary Surgeon, St. Luke's Hospital; Assistant Surgeon, Barnes Hospital.

CAVANAUGH, JOHN ALGERNON, M.D., 7 West Madison Street, Chicago, Illinois. University of Illinois College of Medicine, 1904. Associate Professor of Otology and Laryngology, University of Illinois College of Medicine; Professor of Otology and Laryngology, Chicago Eye, Ear, Nose, and Throat College; Member of Staff, St. Anthony de Padua Hospital.

CAYCE, ELDRED B., M.D., 301 Hitchcock Building, Nashville, Tennessee. University of Nashville Medical Department, 1910. Member of Staff, Woman's Hospital.

CERSWELL, WILLIAM ALFRED, M.B., M.R.C.S. (Eng.), L.R.C.P. (Lond.), 862 Dovercourt Road, Toronto, Ontario. University of Toronto, Faculty of Medicine, 1901. Assistant Surgeon, Grace Hospital.

CHACE, ARCHIBALD EASTWOOD, A.B., M.D., 1404 Dudley Avenue, Texarkana, Arkansas. Cornell University Medical College, 1906. Chief Surgeon, Medical Department, St. Louis Southwestern Railway Lines, St. Louis Southwestern Hospital.

CHALFANT, SIDNEY A., B.Sc., M.D., 7048 Jenkins Arcade Building, Pittsburgh, Pennsylvania. University of Pennsylvania School of Medicine, 1901. Assistant Professor of Gynecology, University of Pittsburgh Medical Department; Gynecologist, Allegheny General, Elizabeth Steel Magee Hospitals, Pittsburgh, and Columbia Hospital, Wilkinsburg.

CHAMBERLAIN, CHARLES THOMSON, M.D., 313 Franklin Street, Natchez, Mississippi. Tulane University of Louisiana School of Medicine, 1902. Visiting Surgeon, Natchez Hospital and Sanatorium.

CHAMBERLAIN, GEORGE ELLSWORTH, M.D., Electric Building, Aberdeen, Washington. University of Illinois College of Medicine (College of Physicians and Surgeons, Chicago), 1893. President, Aberdeen General Hospital.

CHAMBERLAIN, WESTON PERCIVAL, A.B., M.D., Medical Corps, United States Army, Washington, District of Columbia. Harvard Medical School, 1897. Colonel, Medical Corps, United States Army.

CHAMBERLIN, WILLIAM BRICKER, A.B., M.D., Osborn Building, Cleveland, Ohio. Western Reserve University School of Medicine, 1900. Associate in Diseases of Ear, Nose, and Throat, Western Reserve University School of Medicine; Assistant Visiting Otologist, Rhinologist and Laryngologist, Lakeside Hospital; Surgeon in Charge, Department of Ear, Nose, and Throat, Lakeside Hospital, Western Reserve University Dispensary.

CHAMBERS, P. F., A.B., M.D., 18 East Ninety-fourth Street, New York, New York. University and Bellevue Hospital Medical College (Bellevue Hospital Medical College), 1876. Professor of Clinical Gynecology, Columbia University, College of Physicians and Surgeons; Surgeon, Woman's Hospital; Consulting Surgeon, French Hospital.

CHAMBERS, OLIVER, M.D., First National Bank˙ Building, Rock Springs, Wyoming. University of Nebraska College of Medicine, 1903. Surgeon, Wyoming General Hospital.

CHAMBERS, TALBOT R., B.Sc., M.D., 15 Exchange Place, Jersey City, New Jersey. Columbia University, College of Physicians and Surgeons, 1878. Consultant, Eye, Ear, Nose, and Throat Department, Orange Memorial Hospital, Orange, City Hospital, Jersey City, North Hudson Hospital, Weehawken; Surgeon in Charge, Eye, Ear, Nose, and Throat Department, Christ Hospital.

CHAMBERS, WILLIAM, M.D., Medical Corps, United States Navy, Washington, District of Columbia. Jefferson Medical College, 1907. Lieutenant Commander, Medical Corps, United States Navy.

CHAMPION, BENJAMIN HIRAM, M.D., C.M., 510 Hastings Street, West, Vancouver, British Columbia. Faculty of Medicine, McGill University, 1910. Associate Surgeon, Vancouver General Hospital.

CHAMPION, WILLIAM L., M.D., Grant Building, Atlanta, Georgia. University of Maryland School of Medicine (College of Physicians and Surgeons, Baltimore), 1891. Genito-Urinary Surgeon, Wesley Memorial Hospital, Scottish Rite Hospital for Crippled Children, and St. Joseph's Infirmary.

CHANDLER, A. W., B.Sc., M.D., Rochelle, Illinois. Rush Medical College, 1887.

CHANDLER, CHARLES PORTER, A.B., M.D., 43 State Street, Montpelier, Vermont. Columbia University College of Physicians and Surgeons, 1913. Obstetrician and Surgeon, Heaton Hospital.

CHANDLER, GEORGE F., M.D., 11 East Chestnut Street, Kingston, New York. Columbia University, College of Physicians and Surgeons, 1895. Surgeon, Kingston City Hospital.

CHANDLER, THOMAS E., M.D., 19 Bay State Road, Boston, Massachusetts. Boston University School of Medicine, 1900. Assistant Professor of Surgery, Boston University School of Medicine; Surgeon, Massachusetts Homeopathic Hospital.

CHAPMAN, CHARLES RATCHFORD, M.D., 174 State Street, Springfield, Massachusetts. Jefferson Medical College, 1892. Eye, Ear, Nose, and Throat

Surgeon, Mercy Hospital; Nose and Throat Surgeon, Wesson Memorial Hospital.

CHAPMAN, THEODORE LEETE, M.D., 700 Fidelity Building, Duluth, Minnesota. Detroit College of Medicine and Surgery, 1902. Chief of Surgical Staff, St. Mary's Hospital.

CHAPMAN, VERNON A., M.D., Wells Building, Milwaukee, Wisconsin. University of Maryland School of Medicine (Baltimore Medical College), 1898. Instructor in Clinical Ophthalmology, Marquette University School of Medicine; Ophthalmologist, Otologist, and Rhino-Laryngologist, Milwaukee County Hospital; Consultant, Milwaukee Infants' Hospital.

CHARD, MARIE L., M.D., 616 Madison Avenue, New York, New York. Woman's Medical College of the New York Infirmary for Women and Children, 1895. Gynecologist and Director of Surgery and Gynecology, New York Infirmary for Women and Children.

CHARLES, J. W., A.M., M.D., 505 Humboldt Building, St. Louis, Missouri. Washington University Medical School, 1891. Ophthalmologist, Missouri Baptist Sanitarium; Consulting Ophthalmologist, Missouri School for the Blind.

CHARLIN, CARLOS, B.A., M.D., Compania 2115, Santiago, Chile. Faculty of Medicine, University of Chile, 1910.

CHASE, E. FRANK, M.D., 1007 Cobb Building, Seattle, Washington. University of Minnesota Medical School, 1905.

CHASE, GILMAN LEEDS, A.B., M.D., 185 Chestnut Street, Clinton, Massachusetts. Harvard Medical School, 1906. Surgeon and Obstetrician, Clinton Hospital.

CHASE, HENRY MELVILLE, B.Sc., M.D., 520 Commonwealth Avenue, Boston, Massachusetts. Harvard Medical School, 1901.

CHASE, HERBERT CLIFTON, M.D., 45 East Sixty-second Street, New York, New York. Medical College of Virginia (University College of Medicine), 1910. Chief of Clinic and Assistant Attending Surgeon, Woman's Hospital; Consultant Gynecologist, Neurological Institute of New York.

CHASE, IRA CARLETON, A.M., M.D., Texas State Bank Building, Fort Worth, Texas. University and Bellevue Hospital Medical College, 1899. Member of Staff, St. Joseph's Infirmary.

CHASE, THEODORE L., M.D., Santa Barbara, California. Hahnemann Medical College and Hospital, Philadelphia, 1891. Retired.

CHATTERTON, CARL CLAYTON, M.D., Moore Building, St. Paul, Minnesota. Northwestern University Medical School, 1910. Assistant Professor of Orthopedics, University of Minnesota Medical School; Chief in Charge, Minnesota State Hospital for Crippled and Deformed Children; Orthopedic Surgeon, St. Joseph's, St. Luke's, St. John's, West Side General, Bethesda, and St. Paul's Hospitals.

CHAVIGNY, CHARLES NOEL, M.D., 5515 Hurst Street, New Orleans, Louisiana. Tulane University of Louisiana School of Medicine, 1899.

CHEEVER, DAVID, A.B., M.D., 193 Marlborough Street, Boston, Massachusetts. Harvard Medical School, 1901. Assistant Professor of Surgery and Associate in Anatomy, Harvard Medical School; Surgeon, Peter Bent Brigham Hospital.

CHENERY, WILLIAM ELISHA, A.B., M.D., 377 Commonwealth Avenue, Boston, Massachusetts. Harvard Medical School, 1890. Professor of Laryngology, Tufts College Medical School; Laryngologist, Boston Dispensary and Hospital for Children; Chief Surgeon, Nose and Throat Department, Forsyth Dental Infirmary for Children.

CHENEY, FREDERICK E., M.D., 64 Commonwealth Avenue, Boston, Massachusetts. Harvard Medical School, 1885. Consulting Ophthalmic Surgeon, Massachusetts Charitable Eye and Ear Infirmary.

CHENEY, HARRY CLEVELAND, M.D., 18 Thorndike Street, Palmer, Massachusetts. Boston University School of Medicine, 1901. Surgeon, Wing Memorial Hospital; Associate Surgeon, Wesson Memorial Hospital, Springfield.

CHERRY, THOMAS H., M.D., 47 West Fiftieth Street, New York, New York. Columbia University, College of Physicians and Surgeons, 1904. Assistant Visiting Gynecologist, Harlem and Post-Graduate Hospitals; Consulting Gynecologist, Suffolk County Sanatorium, Holtsville, New York, All Souls' Hospital, Morristown, New Jersey.

CHESTER, THOMAS WESTON, A.M., M.D., 50 Farmington Avenue, Hartford, Connecticut. Columbia University, College of Physicians and Surgeons, 1895. Obstetrician and Associate Gynecologist, Hartford Hospital.

CHETWOOD, CHARLES H., M.D., LL.D., 25 Park Avenue, New York, New York. University and Bellevue Hospital Medical College, 1887. Surgeon, Bellevue, Knickerbocker, and French Hospitals, New York, St. John's Hospital, Long Island City, St. Agnes' and White Plains Hospitals, White Plains, Nassau Hospital, Mineola.

CHIDESTER, WALTER C., M.D., Red Cross Hospital, San Mateo, California. University of Cincinnati College of Medicine (Medical College of Ohio), 1896. Surgeon in Charge, Church of St. Matthew Red Cross Hospital.

CHIPMAN, WALTER W., B.A., M.D., LL.D., F.R.C.S. (Edin.), 285 Mountain Street, Montreal, Quebec. University of Edinburgh, 1895. Professor of Gynecology and Obstetrics, Faculty of Medicine, McGill University; Gynecologist, Royal Victoria Hospital; Attending Obstetrician, Montreal Maternity Hospital.

CHISHOLM, MILES DUDLEY, M.D., 106 Elm Street, Westfield, Massachusetts. Medical College of Virginia (University College of Medicine), 1900. Attending Surgeon, Noble Hospital.

CHISHOLM, MURDOCH, M.D., C.M., L.R.C.P. (Lond.), 303 Brunswick Street, Halifax, Nova Scotia. Faculty of Medicine, McGill University, 1879. Consulting Surgeon, Victoria General Hospital.

CHISLETT, HOWARD ROY, M.D., 4721 Greenwood Avenue, Chicago, Illinois. Hahnemann Medical College and Hospital, Chicago, 1888. Attending Surgeon, Hahnemann and Streeter Hospitals.

CHITTENDEN, ARTHUR SMITH, A.M., M.D., 106 Oak Street, Binghamton, New York. Johns Hopkins University, Medical Department, 1900. Visiting Surgeon, Binghamton City and Binghamton State Hospitals.

CHOLLETT, BURT GEORGE, M.D., 421 Michigan Street, Toledo, Ohio. Toledo Medical College, 1900. Orthopedist, Lucas County and St. Vincent's Hospitals, District Nurses Dispensary.

CHURCHMAN, JOHN WOOLMAN, A.M., M.D., 65 Central Park, West, New York, New York. Johns Hopkins University, Medical Department, 1902.

CHURCHMAN, VINCENT T., M.D., Professional Building, Charleston, West Virginia. Jefferson Medical College of Philadelphia, 1889. Member of Staff, Churchman Eye and Ear, Kanawha Valley Hospitals.

CHUTE, ARTHUR LAMBERT, M.D., 352 Marlborough Street, Boston, Massachusetts. Harvard Medical School, 1895. Assistant Professor of Genito-Urinary Surgery, Tufts College Medical School; Genito-Urinary Surgeon St. Elizabeth's Hospital; Consulting Genito-Urinary Surgeon, Robert Bent Brigham Hospital, Boston Dispensary, Boston, Josiah B. Thomas Hospital, Peabody, Newton Hospital, Newton, Leonard Morse Hospital, Natick, Somerville Hospital, Somerville.

CILLEY, ARTHUR HUTCHINS, A.B., M.D., 120 East Thirty-fourth Street, New York, New York. Columbia University, College of Physicians and Surgeons, 1896. Chief of Clinic, Cornell University Medical College; Visiting Orthopedic Surgeon, Reconstruction Hospital, New York, Sea View Hospital, Castleton Corners; Consulting Orthopedic Surgeon, Volunteer Hospital, New York, Nassau Hospital, Mineola.

CLAIBORNE, JOHN HERBERT, M.D., 9 East Forty-sixth Street, New York, New York. University of Virginia, Department of Medicine, 1883. Consulting Ophthalmologist, Flushing Hospital, Flushing.

CLAPP, CLYDE ALVIN, M.D., 513 North Charles Street, Baltimore, Maryland. University of Maryland School of Medicine (Baltimore Medical College), 1902. Associate Professor in Ophthalmology, University of Maryland School of Medicine and College of Physicians and Surgeons; Assistant in Ophthalmology, Johns Hopkins University, Medical Department; Surgeon, Maryland General and Baltimore Eye, Ear, and Throat Charity Hospitals; Dispensary Ophthalmologist, Johns Hopkins Hospital; Ophthalmologist, St. Vincent's Infant Asylum and Maternity Hospital.

CLARK, ALBERT PATTON, M.D., Medical Corps, United States Army, Washington, District of Columbia. George Washington University Medical School, 1909. Major, Medical Corps, United States Army.

CLARK, ALFRED HULL, A.B., M.D., 153 Delaware Avenue, Buffalo, New York. Johns Hopkins University Medical Department, 1903. Assistant Surgeon, Buffalo Woman's Hospital; Attending Gynecologist, Buffalo City Hospital.

CLARK, BURTON, M.D., 420 Algoma Street, Oshkosh, Wisconsin. Rush Medical College, 1894. Surgeon-in-Chief, St. Mary's Hospital.

CLARK, CHARLES C., M.D., 765 Oakwood Boulevard, Chicago, Illinois. University of Illinois College of Medicine, 1905. Assistant in Clinical Surgery, University of Illinois College of Medicine; Attending Surgeon, Lakeside Hospital.

CLARK, DWIGHT FREEMAN, M.D., 800 Davis Street, Evanston, Illinois. Rush Medical College, 1903. Attending Surgeon, Evanston Hospital; Assistant Orthopedic Surgeon, Children's Memorial Hospital, Chicago.

CLARK, EDMUND D., M.D., Hume-Mansur Building, Indianapolis, Indiana. University and Bellevue Hospital Medical College, 1891. Professor of Surgery, Indiana University School of Medicine; Visiting Surgeon, Indianapolis City Hospital; Member of Staff, Methodist and Robert W. Long Hospitals.

CLARK, FRED HERBERT, M.D., 308 Continental Building, Oklahoma, Oklahoma. University Medical College, Kansas City, 1900. Consulting Surgeon, Rock Island Railroad.

CLARK, FREDERICK T., M.D., 29 Parks Block, Westfield, Massachusetts. Albany Medical College, 1896. Surgeon in Charge, Eye, Ear, Nose, and Throat Department, Noble Hospital.

CLARK, HOWARD SHOEMAKER, B.Sc., M.D., 607 La Salle Building, Minneapolis, Minnesota. University of Minnesota Medical School, 1897. Assistant Professor of Ophthalmology and Oto-Laryngology, University of Minnesota Medical School; Member of Staff, University Hospital.

CLARK, J. BAYARD, M.D., 114 East Fifty-fourth Street, New York, New York. Columbia University, College of Physicians and Surgeons, 1898. Consulting Genito-Urinary Surgeon, Elizabeth General Hospital, Elizabeth, New Jersey; Assistant Genito-Urinary Surgeon, New York City Hospital; Consulting Urologist, Mt. Vernon Hospital, Mt. Vernon; Urologist, Nursery and Child's Hospital.

CLARK, JOHN D., B.Sc., M.D., 910 Schweiter Building, Wichita, Kansas. Northwestern University Medical School, 1901. Obstetrician, Wesley Hospital.

CLARK, JOHN GOODRICH, M.D., 2017 Walnut Street, Philadelphia, Pennsylvania. University of Pennsylvania School of Medicine, 1891. Professor of Gynecology, University of Pennsylvania School of Medicine; Gynecologist-in-Chief, Hospital of the University of Pennsylvania; Consulting Gynecologist, Chestnut Hill and Jewish Hospitals, Germantown Dispensary and Hospital, Philadelphia, Bryn Mawr Hospital, Bryn Mawr, Abington Memorial Hospital, Abington.

CLARK, JOHN SHELDON, M.D., State Bank Building, Freeport, Illinois. Northwestern University Medical School, 1903. Member of Staff, St. Francis, Globe, and Freeport General Hospitals.

CLARK, JONAS, M.D., Gilroy, California. Harvard Medical School, 1875.

CLARK, JOSEPH PAYSON, A.B., M.D., 71 Marlborough Street, Boston, Massachusetts. Harvard Medical School, 1887.

CLARK, PETER S., M.D., 818 East Forty-seventh Street, Chicago, Illinois. Hahnemann Medical College and Hospital, Chicago, 1899. Professor of Surgery, Hahnemann Medical College and Hospital; Attending Surgeon, Hahnemann and Streeter Hospitals.

CLARK, SAMUEL M. D., B.Sc., M.D., 108 Baronne Street, New Orleans, Louisiana. Tulane University of Louisiana School of Medicine, 1900. Professor of Gynecology and Clinical Obstetrics, and in Charge of Department of Gynecology, Tulane University of Louisiana School of Medicine; Chief of Gynecological Division, Charity Hospital.

CLARK, STANLEY A., M.D., 314 J. M. S. Building, South Bend, Indiana. Hahnemann Medical College and Hospital, Chicago, 1898. Surgeon, Epworth Hospital.

CLARK, THOMAS JAMES, M.D., Oakland Bank of Savings Building, Oakland, California. University of California Medical School, 1899. Chief of Dermatology Service, Alameda County Hospital and Alameda County Public Health Center.

CLARK, VERNON GREENE, M.D., 415 Elm Street, San Diego, California. Washington University Medical School (Missouri Medical College), 1896. Consulting Surgeon, San Diego County General Hospital; Surgeon, St. Joseph's Hospital.

CLARK, WILLIAM ALFRED, A.M., M.D., 406 Central Trust Building, Jefferson City, Missouri. Washington University Medical School, 1897. Chief of Staff, St. Mary's Hospital, Jefferson City, Masonic Hospital, St. Louis.

CLARK, WILLIAM IRVING, JR., A.B., M.D., 53 West Street, Worcester, Massachusetts. Columbia University, College of Physicians and Surgeons, 1904. Assistant Surgeon, Memorial Hospital.

CLARKE, JAMES FREDERIC, B.Sc., A.M., M.D., 500 South Main Street, Fairfield, Iowa. University of Pennsylvania School of Medicine, 1889. Member of Staff, Jefferson County Hospital.

CLAY, JOSEPH V. F., M.D., 2102 Chestnut Street, Philadelphia, Pennsylvania. Hahnemann Medical College and Hospital, Philadelphia, 1906. Associate Professor of Otology, Hahnemann Medical College and Hospital; Assistant Otologist, Hahnemann Medical College and Hospital; Assistant Ophthalmologist and Junior Laryngologist, Women's Homeopathic Association.

CLAYBROOK, EDWIN B., M.D., Riverside Building, Cumberland, Maryland. Medical College of Virginia (University College of Medicine), 1898. Surgeon, Western Maryland and Allegany Hospitals, Cumberland, Miners' Hospital, Frostburg.

CLAYTON, JERE B., M.D., Medical Corps, United States Army, Washington, District of Columbia. University of Maryland School of Medicine, 1893. Colonel, Medical Corps, United States Army.

CLELAND, FREDERICK A., B.A., M.B., 131 Bloor Street, West, Toronto, Ontario. University of Toronto, Faculty of Medicine, 1901. Demonstrator in Department of Surgery, University of Toronto, Faculty of Medicine; Gynecologist, Grace Hospital; Assistant Surgeon, Toronto General Hospital.

CLEMENS, JAMES BRENT, M.D., 10 East Seventy-first Street, New York, New York. University of Pennsylvania School of Medicine, 1883. Retired.

CLEVELAND, CLEMENT, A.M., M.D., 925 Park Avenue, New York, New York. Columbia University, College of Physicians and Surgeons, 1871. Surgical Director Emeritus, Woman's Hospital; Consulting Gynecologist, General Memorial Hospital.

CLEVENGER, WILLIAM FRANKLIN, M.D., 403 Hume-Mansur Building, Indianapolis, Indiana. Indiana University School of Medicine (Medical College of Indiana), 1894. Member of Consulting Staff, City Hospital; Surgeon, St. Vincent's and Methodist Hospitals.

CLIFFORD, ADDISON B., A.B., M.D., Medical Corps, United States Navy, Washington, District of Columbia. University of Michigan Medical School, 1904. Commander, Medical Corps, United States Navy.

CLIFTON, ALFRED LEE, A.B., M.D., Medical Corps, United States Navy, Washington, District of Columbia. University of Pennsylvania School of Medicine, 1906. Lieutenant Commander, Medical Corps, United States Navy.

CLINE, CLIFFORD M., M.D., Farmers and Merchants Bank Building, Idaho Falls, Idaho. Northwestern University Medical School, 1905. Attending Surgeon, Idaho Falls General Hospital.

CLINTON, FRED SEVERS, Phar.G., M.D., New World Building, Tulsa, Oklahoma. University Medical College of Kansas City, 1897. President and Chief Surgeon, Oklahoma Hospital; Chief Surgeon, Tulsa Street Railway, Oklahoma Union Traction, and Sand Springs Railway Companies; Division Surgeon, Midland Valley Railroad; Local Surgeon, Atchison, Topeka and Santa Fe, and Missouri, Kansas and Texas Railways.

CLINTON, MARSHALL, M.D., 556 Franklin Street, Buffalo, New York. University of Buffalo, Department of Medicine, 1895. Associate Professor of Surgery, University of Buffalo, Department of Medicine; Professor of Oral Surgery, University of Buffalo, Dental Department; Attending Surgeon, Buffalo General, Erie County, and City Hospitals; Consulting Surgeon, Children's and Columbus Hospitals.

CLOPTON, MALVERN BRYAN, M.D., 405 Humboldt Building, St. Louis, Missouri. University of Virginia, Department of Medicine, 1897. Associate in Surgery, Washington University Medical School; Visiting Surgeon, St. Luke's Hospital; Assistant Surgeon, Barnes Hospital; Associate Surgeon, St. Louis Children's Hospital.

CLOUGH, FRANCIS EDGAR, M.D., 214 Prospect Avenue, Lead, South Dakota. Rush Medical College, 1902. Chief Surgeon, Homestake Mining Company.

CLOUGH, HERBERT T., M.D., 209 State Street, Bangor, Maine. Dartmouth Medical School, 1895. Ophthalmic and Aural Surgeon, Eastern Maine General Hospital; Consulting Surgeon, Maine Eye and Ear Hospital, Portland, and Central Maine General Hospital, Lewiston.

CLUTE, HOWARD M., B.Sc., M.D., 638 Beacon Street, Boston, Massachusetts. Dartmouth Medical School, 1914. Instructor in Surgery, Tufts College Medical School; Assistant Surgeon, Out-Patient Department, Boston City Hospital.

CLUTTERBUCK, HERBERT ERNEST, M.D., C.M., F.R.C.S. (Edin.), 148 Grace Street, Toronto, Ontario. University of Toronto, Faculty of Medicine, 1900. Assistant in Surgery, University of Toronto, Faculty of Medicine; Assistant Surgeon, Toronto Western and St. John's Hospitals.

CLYNE, MEADE, M.D., 123 South Stone Avenue, Tucson, Arizona. Northwestern University Medical School, 1907. Chief Surgeon, Arizona Hospital.

COAKLEY, CORNELIUS G., A.M., M.D., 53 West Fifty-sixth Street, New York, New York. University and Bellevue Hospital Medical College (University of the City of New York, Medical Department), 1887. Professor of Laryngology and Otology, Columbia University, College of Physicians and Surgeons; Director and Attending Surgeon, Department of Oto-Laryngology, Bellevue Hospital; Consulting Otologist and Laryngologist, Presbyterian and Woman's Hospitals, New York, and Southampton Hospital, Long Island; Attending Otologist, Louisa Minturn Hospital; Attending Laryngologist, Sea View Hospital, Castleton Corners.

COATES, GEORGE MORRISON, A.B., M.D., 1811 Spruce Street, Philadelphia, Pennsylvania. University of Pennsylvania School of Medicine, 1897. Professor of Diseases of the Ear, University of Pennsylvania Graduate School of Medicine; Otologist, Philadelphia Polyclinic Hospital; Surgeon, Ear, Nose, and Throat Department, Pennsylvania Hospital; Laryngologist, Tuberculosis Department, Philadelphia General Hospital; Consulting Laryngologist, Philadelphia Orphanage, Philadelphia, Pennsylvania, Sharon Hospital, Sharon, Connecticut.

COBB, FARRAR, A.M., M.D., 419 Boylston Street, Boston, Massachusetts. Harvard Medical School, 1893.

COCHRAN, GUY, A.B., M.D., 596 Pacific Electric Building, Los Angeles, California. Columbia University, College of Physicians and Surgeons, 1900. Chief of Staff, Children's Hospital; Chief Surgeon, Los Angeles and Salt Lake Railroad.

COCHRANE, CHARLES STITES, M.D., 400 Vanderbilt Avenue, Brooklyn, New York. Long Island College Hospital, 1900. Lecturer on Genito-Urinary Surgery, Long Island College Hospital; Genito-Urinary Surgeon, Kings County Hospital; Consulting Genito-Urinary Surgeon, Harbor Hospital.

COCHRANE, ROBERT CARLYLE, B.Sc., M.D., 86 Bay State Road, Boston, Massachusetts. Harvard Medical School, 1911. First Assistant Visiting Surgeon, Boston City Hospital; Visiting Surgeon, Long Island Hospital, Boston; Consulting Surgeon, Leonard Morse Hospital, Natick.

COCKE, ROGERS, M.D., 106½ East Austin Street, Marshall, Texas. University of Texas Medical Department, 1899. Attending Surgeon, Kahn Memorial Hospital.

COCRAM, HENRY S., B.Sc., M.D., 108 Baronne Street, New Orleans, Louisiana. Tulane University of Louisiana School of Medicine, 1891. Professor of Gynecology and Obstetrics, New Orleans Polyclinic; Gynecologist, Charity Hospital.

CODMAN, ERNEST AMORY, A.B., M.D., 227 Beacon Street, Boston, Massachusetts. Harvard Medical School, 1895.

COE, HENRY CLARKE, A.M., M.D., M.R.C.S. (Eng.), 45 East Sixty-second Street, New York, New York. Harvard Medical School, 1881; Columbia University, College of Physicians and Surgeons, 1882. Consulting Gynecologist, Bellevue, Woman's, Foundling, General Memorial, and Beth Israel Hospitals.

COERR, FREDERIC HUNTINGTON, A.B., M.D., 759 Harvard Avenue, North, Seattle, Washington. Columbia University, College of Physicians and Surgeons, 1904.

COFFEY, ALDEN, M.D., Moore Building, Ft. Worth, Texas. Vanderbilt University Medical Department, 1906. Member of Surgical Staff, St. Joseph's Infirmary.

COFFEY, ROBERT C., M.D., 789 Glisan Street, Portland, Oregon. University of Louisville Medical Department (Kentucky School of Medicine), 1892. Chief Surgeon, Portland Surgical Hospital.

COFFEY, TITIAN, M.D., 326 Marsh-Strong Building, Los Angeles, California. University of California Medical School, 1898; University of Pennsylvania School of Medicine, 1899.

COFFEY, WALTER B., M.D., Medical Building, San Francisco, California. Cooper Medical College, 1889. Senior Surgeon, Southern Pacific General Hospital; Chief Surgeon, Medical Department, Market Street Railway Company; Director, St. Francis Hospital.

COFFIN, JACOB M., M.D., Medical Corps, United States Army, Washington, District of Columbia. University of Pennsylvania School of Medicine, 1900. Lieutenant Colonel, Medical Corps, United States Army.

COFFIN, LEWIS A., A.B., M.D., 114 East Fifty-fourth Street, New York, New York. University and Bellevue Hospital Medical College (New York University Medical College), 1886. Surgeon, Manhattan Eye, Ear, and Throat Hospital.

COFIELD, ROBERT BARKER, M.D., 19 West Seventh Street, Cincinnati, Ohio. University of Cincinnati College of Medicine (Ohio-Miami Medical College of the University of Cincinnati), 1903. Associate Professor of Orthopedic Surgery, University of Cincinnati College of Medicine; Orthopedic

Surgeon, Christ Hospital; Attending Orthopedic Surgeon, Cincinnati General Hospital.

COGAN, JAMES EDWARD, M.D., Rose Building, Cleveland, Ohio. Jefferson Medical College, 1896. Visiting Otologist and Laryngologist, St. Alexis Hospital; Ophthalmologist, St. John's Hospital.

COGHLAN, JOHN NICHOLAS, M.D., Selling Building, Portland, Oregon. University of Vermont College of Medicine, 1892. Assistant Professor of Ear, Nose, and Throat Diseases, University of Oregon Medical School; Surgeon, Portland Eye, Ear, and Throat Hospital.

COGILL, LIDA STEWART, M.D., 1831 Chestnut Street, Philadelphia, Pennsylvania. Woman's Medical College of Pennsylvania, 1890. Senior Obstetrician, Woman's Hospital, West Philadelphia Hospital for Women.

COGSWELL, WILLIAM, A.B., M.D., 51 North Avenue, Haverhill, Massachusetts. Harvard Medical School, 1894.

COHEN, HASKELL, M.D., 302 Metropolitan Building, Denver, Colorado. University and Bellevue Hospital Medical College, 1899. Attending Gynecologist, Mercy Hospital; Attending Surgeon, National Jewish Hospital for Consumptives.

COHEN, IRA, B.Sc., M.D., 178 East Seventieth Street, New York, New York. Columbia University College of Physicians and Surgeons, 1911. Assistant Professor of Neuro-Surgery, New York Post-Graduate Medical School and Hospital; Attending Surgeon, Montefiore Hospital; Adjunct Surgeon, Mount Sinai Hospital.

COHEN, LEE, M.D., 1820 Eutaw Place, Baltimore, Maryland. University of Maryland School of Medicine, 1895. Rhinologist and Aurist, Hebrew Hospital.

COHEN, MARTIN, M.D., 1 West Eighty-fifth Street, New York, New York. Columbia University, College of Physicians and Surgeons, 1898. Professor of Ophthalmology, New York Post-Graduate Medical School; Ophthalmologist, Harlem Hospital, Crippled Children's East Side Free School; Consulting Ophthalmologist, Manhattan State Hospital; Visiting Ophthalmologist, New York City Children's Hospitals and Schools, Randall's Island; Assistant Surgeon, Manhattan Eye, Ear, and Throat Hospital.

COHN, EUGENE, M.D., Kankakee State Hospital, Kankakee, Illinois. Barnes Medical College, 1898; Northwestern University Medical School, 1906. Medical Superintendent, Kankakee State Hospital.

COHN, ISIDORE, B.Sc., M.D., Maison Blanche Building, New Orleans, Louisiana. Tulane University of Louisiana School of Medicine, 1907. Professor of Clinical Surgery, Tulane University of Louisiana School of Medicine; Senior Associate Surgeon, Touro Infirmary.

COLBURN, FREDERICK WILKINSON, Ph.B., M.D., 510 Commonwealth Avenue, Boston, Massachusetts. Boston University School of Medicine, 1897. Associate Professor of Otology, Boston University School of Medicine; Aural Surgeon, Massachusetts Homeopathic Hospital.

COLE, ALFRED PETERS, M.D., Cincinnati, Ohio. Columbia University, College of Physicians and Surgeons, 1891.

COLE, C. GRENES, M.D., 1503 Pine Street, New Orleans, Louisiana. Tulane University of Louisiana School of Medicine, 1908. Professor of Surgery, Loyola Post-Graduate School of Medicine; Chief Visiting Surgeon, Charity and Presbyterian Hospitals.

COLE, HERBERT PHALON, A.B., M.D., 901 Van Antwerp Building, Mobile, Alabama. Johns Hopkins University, Medical Department, 1906.

COLE, THOMAS PORTER, M.D., 218 South Pennsylvania Avenue, Greensburg, Pennsylvania. Jefferson Medical College, 1893. Consulting Surgeon, Westmoreland Hospital.

COLE, WALTER FRANCIS, S.B., A.B., M.D., Greensboro, North Carolina. Johns Hopkins University, Medical Department, 1909. Surgeon, St. Leo Hospital.

COLEMAN, CLAUDE C., M.D., Professional Building, Richmond, Virginia. Medical College of Virginia, 1903. Professor of Oral Surgery and Anesthesia, and Associate Professor of Surgery, Medical College of Virginia; Senior Surgeon, Memorial Hospital; Consulting Oral Surgeon, Virginia Hospital.

COLEMAN, JAMES EDMUND, M.D., 24 North Main Street, Canton, Illinois. Rush Medical College, 1884.

COLEY, WILLIAM BRADLEY, A.M., M.D., 340 Park Avenue, New York, New York. Harvard Medical School, 1888. Clinical Professor of Cancer Research, Memorial Hospital, Cornell University Medical College; Attending Surgeon, Memorial Hospital, Hospital for Ruptured and Crippled.

COLLIER, CLINTON C., B.Sc., M.D., 25 East Washington Street, Chicago, Illinois. Chicago Homeopathic Medical College, 1904; Hahnemann Medical College and Hospital, Chicago, 1906. Professor of Oto-Laryngology, Hahnemann Medical College and Hospital; Head of Eye, Ear, Nose, and Throat Department, South Chicago Hospital; Oto-Laryngologist, Hahnemann Hospital.

COLLIER, G. KIRBY, M.D., 525 Lake Avenue, Rochester, New York. University of Maryland School of Medicine (College of Physicians and Surgeons, Baltimore), 1900.

COLLINGS, HOWARD PAXTON, B.Sc., M.D., Dugan-Stuart Building, Hot Springs, Arkansas. University and Bellevue Hospital Medical College (Bellevue Hospital Medical College), 1891.

COLLINS, ARTHUR NELSON, A.B., M.D., Lyceum Building, Duluth, Minnesota. Harvard Medical School, 1906. Surgeon, St. Luke's Hospital.

COLLINS, ASA WESTON, D.D.S., M.D., 126 Post Street, San Francisco, California. Cooper Medical College, 1903. Chief Surgeon, French Hospital; Associate Surgeon, St. Francis Hospital.

COLLINS, C. CLARK, M.D., Medical Corps, United States Army, Washington, District of Columbia. University of Virginia, Department of Medicine, 1895. Colonel, Medical Corps, United States Army.

COLLINS, CHARLES ERNST, M.D., Providence Sanitarium, Waco, Texas. University of Texas, 1913. House Surgeon, Providence Sanitarium.

COLLINS, CLIFFORD U., M.D., 427 Jefferson Building, Peoria, Illinois. St. Louis University School of Medicine (Marion-Sims College of Medicine), 1892. Surgeon, St. Francis' Hospital.

COLLINS, HOWARD DENNIS, A.B., M.D., 630 Park Avenue, New York, New York. Columbia University, College of Physicians and Surgeons, 1893. Visiting Surgeon, New York City Hospital.

COLLINS, JOSEPH DORSEY, M.D., 314 Court Street, Portsmouth, Virginia. Medical College of Virginia (University College of Medicine), 1905. Attending Surgeon, King's Daughters Hospital.

COLLINS, RICHARD, A.B., M.D., 837 Main Street, Waltham, Massachusetts. Harvard Medical School, 1900. Chief of Surgical Staff, Waltham Hospital.

COLLOM, SPENCER ALLEN, M.D., 621 State Street, Texarkana, Texas. University of Louisville, Medical Department (Kentucky School of Medicine), 1892. Member of Surgical Staff, Texarkana Sanitarium and Hospital; Consulting Surgeon, St. Louis Southwestern Railway Hospital, Texarkana, Arkansas.

COLVER, BENTON NOBLE, A.B., M.D., 182 Manchester Street, Battle Creek, Michigan. University of Illinois College of Medicine (American Medical Missionary College), 1904; University of Pennsylvania School of Medicine, 1911. Director of Eye, Ear, Nose, and Throat Department, Battle Creek Sanitarium.

COLVIN, ALEXANDER R., M.D., C.M., Lowry Building, St. Paul, Minnesota. Faculty of Medicine, McGill University, 1894. Associate Professor of Surgery, University of Minnesota Medical School; Surgeon, City and County, and St. Luke's Hospitals.

COMBS, CLARENDON J., M.D., 19 Jefferson Avenue, Oshkosh, Wisconsin. University of Michigan Medical School, 1898. Member of Surgical Staff, St. Mary's Hospital.

COMBS, MALACHI R., M.D., 418 Tribune Building, Terre Haute, Indiana. Indiana University School of Medicine, 1885. Surgeon, Union Hospital.

COMPTON, HAYS A., M.D., Fischer Building, Bellingham, Washington. University of Nashville, Medical Department, 1882. Member of Staff, St. Joseph's Hospital.

COMPTON, R. F., M.D., 103 East Market Street, Charlottesville, Virginia. University of Virginia, Department of Medicine, 1900. Professor, Ear, Nose, and Throat Department, University of Virginia, Department of Medicine; Surgeon, Eye, Ear, Nose, and Throat Department, University of Virginia and Martha Jefferson Hospitals.

COMSTOCK, GEORGE FOSTER, M.D., 540 Broadway, Saratoga Springs, New York. Columbia University, College of Physicians and Surgeons, 1883. Surgeon, Saratoga Hospital, Saratoga Cure and Infirmary.

CONANT, JAMES B., A.B., M.D., 13 Grove Street, Amsterdam, New York. Columbia University, College of Physicians and Surgeons, 1896. Consulting Surgeon, Amsterdam City Hospital; Visiting Surgeon, St. Mary's Hospital.

CONANT, WILLIAM M., A.B., M.D., 486 Commonwealth Avenue, Boston, Massachusetts. Harvard Medical School, 1884. Consulting Surgeon, Massachusetts General Hospital.

CONAWAY, WALT PONDER, A.B., M.D., 1723 Pacific Avenue, Atlantic City, New Jersey. University and Bellevue Hospital Medical College, 1899. Attending Gynecologist, Atlantic City Hospital.

CONDELL, WILLIAM N., M.D., C.M., 10039 One Hundred Fifth Street, Edmonton, Alberta. Queen's University, Faculty of Medicine, 1898. Consulting Oculist and Aurist, Canadian Northern Railway.

CONDIT, WILLIAM HENRY, B.Sc., M.D., 1009 Nicollet Avenue, Minneapolis, Minnesota. University of Minnesota Medical School, 1899. Assistant Professor of Obstetrics and Gynecology, University of Minnesota Medical School; Obstetrician, University and Northwestern Hospitals; Consulting Obstetrician, Bethany Home.

CONE, SYDNEY M., A.B., M.D., 2326 Eutaw Place, Baltimore, Maryland. University of Pennsylvania School of Medicine, 1893. Clinical Professor of Orthopedic Surgery, University of Maryland School of Medicine and College of Physicians and Surgeons; Visiting Orthopedic Surgeon, Maryland General and Hebrew Hospitals, Children's Hospital School.

CONGDON, CHARLES EVERETT, M.D., 77 Main Street, Nashua, New Hampshire. Long Island College Hospital, 1896. Member of Surgical Staff, Nashua Memorial and St. Joseph's Hospitals.

CONGDON, JOHN BOWMAN, M.D., 140 Washington Avenue, Albany, New York. Albany Medical College, 1902. Attending Surgeon, Homeopathic Hospital.

CONGDON, RUSSELL T., A.B., M.D., Wenatchee, Washington. Harvard Medical School, 1907.

CONKLING, WILBUR S., Phar.G., M.D., 407 Bankers Trust Building, Des Moines, Iowa. State University of Iowa College of Medicine (Iowa College of Physicians and Surgeons), 1897. Member of Surgical Staff, Iowa Methodist and Iowa Lutheran Hospitals.

CONLAN, FRANCIS J. S., M.D., 135 Stockton Street, San Francisco, California. Rush Medical College, 1899. Oculist and Aurist, St. Mary's Hospital.

CONLEY, DUDLEY STEELE, B.Sc., M.D., Guitar Building, Columbia, Missouri. Columbia University of Physicians and Surgeons, 1906. Professor of Clinical Surgery, University of Missouri; Chief of Surgical Service, Parker Memorial Hospital.

CONLON, FRANK ALOYSIUS, M.D., Bay State Building, Lawrence, Massachusetts. Harvard Medical School, 1904.

CONN, LEIGHTON CARLING, M.D., C.M., 625 Tegler Block, Edmonton, Alberta. Faculty of Medicine, McGill University, 1909.

CONNALLY, HERSCHEL FRANK, M.D., 2223 Calcard Street, Waco, Texas. Vanderbilt University, Medical Department, 1900.

CONNELL, E. DEWITT, M.D., Selling Building, Portland, Oregon. University of Pennsylvania School of Medicine, 1895. Surgeon, Eye, Ear, Nose, and Throat Department, St. Vincent's Hospital, Portland Eye, Ear, Nose, and Throat Hospital.

CONNELL, F. GREGORY, M.D., 19 Jefferson Avenue, Oshkosh, Wisconsin. Rush Medical College, 1896. Attending Surgeon, St. Mary's Hospital.

CONNELL, JAMES CAMERON, M.A., M.D., C.M., 265 King Street, East, Kingston, Ontario. Queen's University, Faculty of Medicine, 1888. Dean of Medical Faculty, Queen's University, Faculty of Medicine; Surgeon, Eye, Ear, Nose, and Throat Department, Kingston General Hospital.

CONNELL, KARL, M.D., Presbyterian Hospital, Omaha, Nebraska. Columbia University, College of Physicians and Surgeons, 1900. Professor of Surgery, Creighton College of Medicine; Chief Surgeon, Presbyterian Hospital; Attending Surgeon, Creighton Memorial and St. Joseph's Hospitals.

CONNOR, CLARENCE HERBERT, M.D., Medical Corps, United States Army, Washington, District of Columbia. University of Virginia, Department of Medicine, 1901. Lieutenant Colonel, Medical Corps, United States Army.

CONNOR, EDWARD LAWRENCE, M.D., C.M., 109 Sherlock Building, Lethbridge, Alberta. Faculty of Medicine, McGill University, 1905.

CONNOR, RAY, A.B., M.D., 503 Washington Arcade, Detroit, Michigan. Johns Hopkins University, Medical Department, 1901. Associate Clinical Professor of Ophthalmology, Detroit College of Medicine and Surgery; Surgeon, Children's Free and Providence Hospitals.

CONNORS, JOHN F., A.M., M.D., 616 Madison Avenue, New York, New York. University and Bellevue Hospital Medical College (New York University Medical College), 1895. Surgeon, Harlem and Washington Square Hospitals; Surgical Director, Division B, Harlem Hospital; Consulting Surgeon, St. Mary's Hospital, Waterbury, Connecticut.

CONRAD, GEORGE A., M.D., Mohawk, Michigan. Saginaw Valley Medical College, 1901. Member of Surgical Staff, St. Joseph's Hospital, Hancock; Chief of Staff, Mohawk, Wolverine, and Seneca Copper Mining Companies.

CONROW, MATTHIAS WOOLLEY, A.B., M.D., 31 Maple Street, Springfield, Massachusetts. New York Homeopathic Medical College and Flower Hospital, 1905; College of New York Ophthalmic Hospital, 1908. Eye, Ear, Nose, and Throat Surgeon, Wesson Memorial Hospital.

CONSTANTINE, KOSCIUSKO WALKER, A.B., M.D., Empire Building, Birmingham, Alabama. Johns Hopkins University, Medical Department, 1905.

Professor of Ophthalmology, Graduate School of Medicine of the University of Alabama; Ophthalmologist, Hillman Hospital.

CONWELL, THOMAS ISAAC, B.Sc., M.D., Chickasaw, Alabama. University of Tennessee College of Medicine (University of Nashville, Medical Department), 1903. Member of Staff, Providence Infirmary; Chief Surgeon, Chickasaw Shipbuilding and Car Company.

COOK, HUGH F., A.M., M.D., 2 Lombardy Street, Newark, New Jersey. University of Maryland School of Medicine (College of Physicians and Surgeons, Baltimore), 1896. President and Visiting Surgeon, Newark Private Hospital; Visiting Surgeon, Newark City Hospital.

COOK, LUZERNE H., M.D., 429 West Market Street, Bluffton, Indiana. University of Cincinnati College of Medicine (Medical College of Ohio), 1885.

COOK, RICHARD FRANKLIN, M.D., 5 East Benton Street, Carrollton, Missouri. University of Missouri School of Medicine, 1893. Surgeon, Cook's Hospital.

COOK, W. ALBERT, M.D., 506 Palace Building, Tulsa, Oklahoma. Rush Medical College, 1897.

COOKE, A. BENNETT, A.M., M.D., 1019 Hollingsworth Building, Los Angeles, California. Vanderbilt University, Medical Department, 1891. Senior Attending Surgeon, Los Angeles County Hospital.

COOKE, CLINTON T., M.D., 817 Summit Avenue, Seattle, Washington. Rush Medical College, 1890. Ophthalmologist, Seattle Eye, Ear, Nose, and Throat Infirmary.

COOLIDGE, ALGERNON, A.B., M.D., 613 Beacon Street, Boston, Massachusetts. Harvard Medical School, 1886. Professor of Laryngology, Harvard Medical School; Member of Staff, Massachusetts General Hospital.

COOMBS, SYLVAN, M.D., Surf Apartments, Chicago, Illinois. Rush Medical College, 1891. Surgeon, Grant and Michael Reese Hospitals.

COON, CLARENCE ERFORD, M.D., 405 East Fayette Street, Syracuse, New York. Syracuse University College of Medicine, 1898. Professor of Orthopedic Surgery, Syracuse University College of Medicine; Orthopedic Surgeon, St. Joseph's and Memorial Hospitals, Syracuse Free Dispensary.

COON, GEORGE S., A.B., M.D., 440 Francis Building, Louisville, Kentucky. State University of Iowa College of Medicine, 1891; Hahnemann Medical College and Hospital, Chicago (Chicago Homeopathic Medical College), 1892. Surgeon, Louisville City and Deaconess Hospitals.

COONEY, HENRY C., M.D., Princeton, Minnesota. University of Illinois College of Medicine (College of Physicians and Surgeons, Chicago), 1887. Surgeon-in-Chief, Northwestern Hospital.

COOPER, OSWALD O., A.B., B.Sc., M.D., 315 Temple Street, Hinton, West Virginia. University and Bellevue Hospital Medical College, 1890. Surgeon in Charge, Hinton Hospital; Surgeon, Chesapeake and Ohio Annex Hospital.

COOPER, ST. CLOUD, M.D., 604 First National Bank Building, Fort Smith, Arkansas. Washington University Medical School (Missouri Medical College), 1882. Surgeon, Sparks Memorial Hospital.

COOPERNAIL, GEORGE P., M.D., Bedford, New York. Albany Medical College, 1900. Attending Surgeon, Westchester County Hospitals, East View; Surgeon, Northern Westchester Hospital, Mt. Kisco, New York State Reformatory for Women, Bedford Hills.

COOVER, DAVID HUMMEL, M.D., 412 Metropolitan Building, Denver, Colorado. Jefferson Medical College, 1874. Emeritus Professor of Ophthalmology, University of Colorado School of Medicine; Ophthalmic Surgeon, Children's, Mercy, and St. Luke's Hospitals.

COPELAND, ERNEST, M.D., 141 Wisconsin Street, Milwaukee, Wisconsin. Indiana University School of Medicine (Medical College of Indiana), 1879. Gynecologist, Columbia Hospital.

COPELAND, ROYAL SAMUEL, A.M., M.D., 58 Central Park, West, New York, New York. University of Michigan Medical School, 1889. Commissioner of Health for the City of New York.

CORBETT, J. FRANK, M.D., 808 Physicians and Surgeons Building, Minneapolis, Minnesota. University of Minnesota Medical School, 1896. Associate Professor of Surgery, University of Minnesota Medical School; Associate Surgeon, General Hospital; Member of Surgical Staff, St. Mary's and Northwestern Hospitals; Consulting Neurological Surgeon, Norwegian Lutheran Deaconess Institute.

CORBETT, FREDERICK A. F., B.A., M.D., C.M., F.R.C.S. (Edin.), 414 McCallum-Hill Building, Regina, Saskatchewan. Faculty of Medicine, McGill University, 1896. Surgeon, Regina General and Grey Nun's Hospitals.

CORBUS, BUDD CLARKE, M.D., 30 North Michigan Avenue, Chicago, Illinois. University of Illinois College of Medicine, 1901.

CORDERO, JUAN B. ARZUBE, M.D., Malecón 2006, Guayaquil, Ecuador. University of Guayaquil Faculty of Medicine, 1904. Professor, University of Guayaquil, Faculty of Medicine; Surgeon, General Hospital.

CORNELL, EDWARD LYMAN, B.Sc., M.D., 122 South Michigan Avenue, Chicago, Illinois. Rush Medical College, 1910. Instructor, Northwestern University Medical School; Member of Staff, Chicago Lying-in and Illinois Masonic Hospitals; Member of Consulting Staff, Auburn Park Hospital.

CORNISH, PERCY GILLETTE, M.D., Grant Block, Albuquerque, New Mexico. Jefferson Medical College, 1885. Attending Surgeon, St. Joseph's and Presbyterian Hospitals.

CORRIGAN, FRANCIS PATRICK, A.B., M.D., 1110 Euclid Avenue, Cleveland, Ohio. Western Reserve University School of Medicine, 1906. Visiting Surgeon, St. Alexis Hospital; Alternate Visiting Surgeon, St. John's Hospital.

CORRIGAN, HENRY J. C., A.M., M.D., 242 Broadway, Providence, Rhode Island. Columbia University, College of Physicians and Surgeons, 1902. Urologist, St. Joseph's Hospital; Consulting Surgeon, St. Vincent's Infant Asylum.

CORSS, J. KENNEDY, A.M., M.D., 3214 West Avenue, Newport News, Virginia. University of Pennsylvania School of Medicine, 1892. Surgeon, Riverside Hospital.

CORSAN, DOUGLAS, M.D., C.M., 20 Victoria Avenue, Fernie, British Columbia. Faculty of Medicine, McGill University, 1885. Surgeon, Fernie Hospital.

CORSER, JOHN B., M.D., 345 Wyoming Avenue, Scranton, Pennsylvania. University of Pennsylvania School of Medicine, 1898. Ophthalmologist, Hahnemann and State Hospitals; Consulting Ophthalmologist, Hillside Home, Clark's Summit, Mid-Valley Hospital, Olyphant.

CORSON, GEORGE R. S., M.D., 20 North Center Street, Pottsville, Pennsylvania. Jefferson Medical College, 1896. Ophthalmologist and Oto-Laryngologist, Pottsville Hospital.

CORWIN, RICHARD WARREN, A.M., M.D., LL.D., Minnequa Hospital, Pueblo, Colorado. University of Michigan Medical School, 1878. Professor of Surgery, University of Colorado School of Medicine; Chief Surgeon and Superintendent, Minnequa Hospital; Surgeon, Colorado State Insane Asylum; Chief Surgeon, Colorado Fuel and Iron Company, Colorado and Wyoming, and Crystal River Railways; Division Surgeon, Missouri Pacific Railway; Local Surgeon, Denver and Rio Grande, and Colorado and Southern Railways.

CORWIN, THEODORE W., M.D., 671 Broad Street, Newark, New Jersey. Columbia University, College of Physicians and Surgeons, 1879. Laryngologist, St. Michael's Hospital; Consulting Laryngologist, Hospital of St. Barnabas, Newark, Essex County Hospital, Cedar Grove.

COTT, CHESTER C., M.D., 1001 Main Street, Buffalo, New York. University of Buffalo, Department of Medicine, 1908. Associate in Oto-Laryngology, University of Buffalo, Department of Medicine; Attending Otologist, Buffalo City Hospital; Attending Oto-Laryngologist, Buffalo General Hospital.

COTTAM, GILBERT GEOFFREY, M.D., 800 Sioux Falls National Bank Building, Sioux Falls, South Dakota. St. Louis University School of Medicine, 1893. Attending Surgeon, McKennan Hospital.

COTTIS, GEORGE W., M.D., 310 Wellman Building, Jamestown, New York. Cornell University Medical College, 1904.

COTTLE, GEORGE F., M.D., Medical Corps, United States Navy, Washington, District of Columbia. Columbia University, College of Physicians and Surgeons, 1905. Lieutenant Commander, Medical Corps, United States Navy.

COTTON, ALBERTUS, A.M., M.D., 1303 Maryland Avenue, Baltimore, Maryland. University of Maryland School of Medicine (College of Physicians and Surgeons, Baltimore), 1896. Professor of Orthopedic Surgery and Rœntgenology, University of Maryland School of Medicine and College of Physicians and Surgeons; Orthopedist and Rœntgenologist, Mercy Hospital; Rœntgenologist, Presbyterian Eye, Ear, and Throat Charity Hospital; Associate Surgeon, James Lawrence Kernan Hospital and Industrial School for Crippled Children.

COTTON, FREDERIC J., A.M., M.D., 520 Commonwealth Avenue, Boston, Massachusetts. Harvard Medical School, 1894. Associate in Surgery, Harvard Medical School; Visiting Surgeon, Boston City Hospital; Consulting Surgeon, Beth Israel and New England Hospital for Women and Children; Surgical Consultant, United States Public Health Service.

COUES, WILLIAM PEARCE, M.D., 31 Massachusetts Avenue, Boston, Massachusetts. Harvard Medical School, 1894. Assistant in Surgery, Harvard Medical School; Instructor in Surgery, Tufts College Medical School; Assistant Surgeon to Out-Patients, Massachusetts General Hospital, Boston Dispensary.

COUGHLIN, FRED A., A.B., M.D., 224 Thayer Street, Providence, Rhode Island. Johns Hopkins University, Medical Department, 1908. Visiting Surgeon, St. Joseph's Hospital; Assistant Surgeon, Out-Patient Department, Rhode Island Hospital.

COUGHLIN, WILLIAM THOMAS, B.Sc., M.D., University Club Building, St. Louis, Missouri. Washington University Medical School, 1901. Professor of Surgery and Director of Department, St. Louis University School of Medicine; Surgeon, St. John's Hospital; Visiting Surgeon, St. Louis City Hospital.

COULTER, JOHN ERNEST, M.D., C.M., 604 Boyd Building, Winnipeg, Manitoba. Faculty of Medicine, University of Manitoba (Manitoba Medical College), 1895. Lecturer on Obstetrics, Faculty of Medicine, University of Manitoba; Senior Member of Staff, Grace Maternity Hospital.

COULTER, JOHN STANLEY, M.D., 5 North Wabash Avenue, Chicago, Illinois. University of Pennsylvania School of Medicine, 1909. Lieutenant Colonel, Medical Corps, United States Army, retired.

COUNTRYMAN, JOHN EDGAR, M.D., C.M., Grafton, North Dakota. Queen's University, Faculty of Medicine, 1893. Surgeon, Grafton Deaconess Hospital.

COURTENAY, JOHN DICKSON, M.B., 189 Metcalfe Street, Ottawa, Ontario. University of Toronto, Faculty of Medicine, 1885. Ophthalmologist and Otologist, St. Luke's Hospital.

COURTNEY, WALTER, A.M., M.D., 19 Bluff Avenue, Brainerd, Minnesota. University of Michigan Medical School, 1883. Retired.

COUSINS, WILLIAM LEWIS, M.D., 231 Woodford Street, Portland, Maine. University of Pennsylvania School of Medicine, 1894. Surgeon-in-Chief, St. Barnabas Hospital; Consulting Surgeon, Maine General Hospital.

COVENTRY, WILLIAM ALBERTUS, M.D., 600 Fidelity Building, Duluth, Minnesota. University of Michigan Medical School, 1900.

COWAN, JOHN RICE, A.B., M.D., 336 Main Street, Danville, Kentucky. Harvard Medical School, 1894. Surgeon, Southern Railway.

COWDEN, CHARLES NORRIS, M.D., 347 Doctors Building, Nashville, Tennessee. Vanderbilt University, Medical Department, 1886. Associate Professor of Gynecology, Vanderbilt University, Medical Department; Gynecologist, St. Thomas Hospital; Consulting Surgeon, Nashville City Hospital.

COWEN, WILLIAM, A.B., M.D., 35 East Sixtieth Street, New York, New York. Columbia University, College of Physicians and Surgeons, 1883. Attending Aurist, Lebanon Hospital; Consulting Ophthalmologist, Jewish Maternity and People's Hospitals.

COWLES, HENRY CLAY, A.B., M.D., 97 Central Park, West, New York, New York. Columbia University, College of Physicians and Surgeons, 1903. Attending Obstetrician, New York Nursery and Child's Hospital.

COWPER, H. W., M.D., 543 Franklin Street, Buffalo, New York. University of Buffalo, Department of Medicine, 1897. Instructor in Ophthalmology, University of Buffalo, Department of Medicine; Attending Ophthalmologist, Emergency, Buffalo City and Buffalo General Hospitals; Surgeon, Buffalo Eye and Ear Infirmary.

COX, CHARLES NEWTON, M.D., 257 Jefferson Avenue, Brooklyn, New York. University of Pennsylvania School of Medicine, 1883. Consulting Otologist, Long Island College and Bethany Deaconess Hospitals; Aural Surgeon, Brooklyn Eye and Ear Hospital; Consulting Laryngologist, Bushwick Hospital; Consulting Otologist, St. Mary's Hospital, Jamaica.

COX, ERNEST HARPER, B.Sc., M.D., 407 Osborn Building, Cleveland, Ohio. Western Reserve University School of Medicine, 1905. Visiting Surgeon, Woman's Hospital.

COX, GERARD HUTCHISON, A.B., M.D., 137 East Fifty-fourth Street, New York, New York. Columbia University, College of Physicians and Surgeons, 1903.

COX, ROSS PARKER, A.B., M.D., Rome, Georgia. Jefferson Medical College, 1889. Associate Staff Surgeon, Eye, Ear, Nose, and Throat Department, Harbin Hospital.

COX, WILLIAM COLUMBUS, M.D., 410 American Bank Building, Everett, Washington. Jefferson Medical College, 1885. Member of Staff, Everett Hospital.

COY, WARREN DEWEESE, B.Sc., M.D., 608 Market Street, Youngstown, Ohio. University of Illinois College of Medicine (College of Physicians and Surgeons, Chicago), 1901. Attending Surgeon, Youngstown Hospital.

CRABB, GEORGE MELVILLE, B.Sc., M.D., 102 North Washington Avenue, Mason City, Iowa. Rush Medical College, 1910. Surgeon, Park Hospital.

CRAGIN, DONALD BRETT, M.D., 179 Allyn Street, Hartford, Connecticut. Harvard Medical School, 1902.

CRAIG, CHARLES FRANKLIN, A.M., M.D., Medical Corps, United States Army, Washington, District of Columbia. Yale University School of Medicine, 1894. Professor of Bacteriology, Parasitology, and Preventive Medicine, Army Medical School; Lieutenant Colonel, Medical Corps, United States Army.

CRAIG, ROBERT HENRY, M.D., C.M., 510 Sherbrooke Street, West, Montreal, Quebec. Faculty of Medicine, McGill University, 1896. Lecturer on Rhinology and Laryngology, Faculty of Medicine, McGill University; Associate Laryngologist, Montreal General Hospital; Otologist and Laryngologist, Western Hospital.

CRAIN, ALFRED PENN, M.D., 914 Oneonta Street, Shreveport, Louisiana. Tulane University of Louisiana School of Medicine, 1907. Visiting Surgeon, North Louisiana, Highland, and T. E. Schumpert Memorial Sanitariums.

CRAIN, AMBROSE BURDETT, Phar.M., M.D., 112½ Central Avenue, Belton, Texas. Tulane University of Louisiana School of Medicine, 1908. Member of Staff, Belton Sanitarium.

CRAMP, WALTER C., A.B., M.D., 369 West End Avenue, New York, New York. Columbia University, College of Physicians and Surgeons, 1904. Professor of Clinical Surgery, University and Bellevue Hospital Medical College; Visiting Surgeon, Bellevue Hospital, Hospital for Deformities and Joint Diseases; Assistant Visiting Surgeon, St. Francis, Willard Parker and Reception Hospitals.

CRAMTON, CHARLES A., M.D., 29 Main Street, St. Johnsbury, Vermont. University of Vermont College of Medicine, 1893. Oculist and Laryngologist, St. Johnsbury and Brightlook Hospitals.

CRANDON, LE ROI GODDARD, A.M., M.D., 366 Commonwealth Avenue, Boston, Massachusetts. Harvard Medical School, 1898. Consulting Surgeon, Chelsea Memorial Hospital, Chelsea, Massachusetts, Lawrence and Memorial Associated Hospitals, New London, Connecticut, Woonsocket Hospital, Woonsocket, Rhode Island.

CRANE, AUGUSTIN AVERILL, A.B., M.D., 300 West Main Street, Waterbury, Connecticut. Yale University School of Medicine, 1887. Attending Surgeon, Waterbury Hospital; Consulting Surgeon, St. Mary's Hospital.

CRANE, CHARLES WILLIAMS, M.D., 1106 Lamar Building, Augusta, Georgia. University of Georgia, Medical Department, 1898. Professor of Surgery, University of Georgia, Medical Department; Attending Surgeon, Wilhenford and University Hospitals.

CRANE, CLARENCE, Ch.B., M.D., 520 Beacon Street, Boston, Massachusetts. Boston University School of Medicine, 1900. Lecturer on Surgery and Instructor in Operative Surgery on the Cadaver, Boston University School of Medicine; Visiting Surgeon, Massachusetts Homeopathic Hospital; Consulting Surgeon, Leonard Morse Hospital, Natick.

CRANE, CLAUDE GRANVILLE, M.D., 121 St. James Place, Brooklyn, New York. Columbia University, College of Physicians and Surgeons, 1900. Attending

Otologist and Laryngologist, Brooklyn Hospital; Attending Surgeon, Ear, Nose, and Throat Service, Brooklyn Eye and Ear Hospital.

CRAWFORD, LEWIS BIENVENU, M.D., Patterson, Louisiana. Tulane University of Louisiana School of Medicine, 1905. Surgeon, St. Mary's Hospital.

CRAWFORD, WALTER WESLEY, B.Sc., Ph.M., M.D., South Mississippi Infirmary, Hattiesburg, Mississippi. Jefferson Medical College, 1898. Surgeon-in-Chief, South Mississippi Infirmary.

CREADICK, A. NOWELL, M.D., Yale University, New Haven, Connecticut. University of Pennsylvania School of Medicine, 1908. Assistant Professor in Gynecology and Obstetrics, Yale University School of Medicine; Associate Obstetrician and Gynecologist, New Haven Hospital; Chief of Clinic, Obstetrical and Gynecological Department, New Haven Dispensary.

CREIGHTON, SAMUEL S., M.D., Medical Corps, United States Army, Washington, District of Columbia. University of Buffalo, Department of Medicine, 1909. Major, Medical Corps, United States Army.

CREVELING, HANLEY CLAY, M.D., Frisco Building, St. Louis, Missouri. Washington University Medical School (Missouri Medical College), 1895. Surgeon, St. Louis Eye, Ear, Nose, and Throat Infirmary.

CRILE, GEORGE W., A.M., M.D., F.R.C.S. (Eng. & Ire.), Hon., Clinic Building, Cleveland, Ohio. Western Reserve University School of Medicine (University of Wooster, Medical Department), 1887. Professor of Surgery, Western Reserve University School of Medicine; Visiting Surgeon, Lakeside Hospital.

CRINNION, THOMAS MATTHEW, M.D., 635 Oak Street, Toledo, Ohio. Toledo Medical College, 1903. Gynecologist, St. Vincent's Hospital.

CRISLER, CARLETON GRAVES, M.D., Groton Building, Cincinnati, Ohio. University and Bellevue Hospital Medical College, 1903. Visiting Surgeon, Christ Hospital.

CRISLER, JOSEPH AUGUSTUS, B.Sc., M.D., Exchange Building, Memphis, Tennessee. University of Tennessee College of Medicine (Memphis Hospital Medical College), 1890.

CRISP, WILLIAM HENRY, M.D., 530 Metropolitan Building, Denver, Colorado. University of Colorado School of Medicine (Denver and Gross College of Medicine), 1907. Instructor in Ophthalmology, University of Colorado School of Medicine; Ophthalmologist, National Jewish Hospital.

CRITCHLOW, GEORGE READ, A.B., M.D., 647 Lafayette Avenue, Buffalo, New York. Hahnemann Medical College and Hospital, Philadelphia, 1898. Attending Surgeon, Buffalo Homeopathic Hospital; Attending Gynecologist, Erie County Hospital; Consulting Surgeon, Gowanda State Homeopathic Hospital, Collins, City Hospitals and Dispensaries, Buffalo.

CRITCHLOW, JOHN FRANKLIN, M.D., The Bransford, Salt Lake City, Utah. University of Pennsylvania School of Medicine, 1894. Surgeon, St. Mark's Hospital, Utah Fuel Company, Denver and Rio Grande and Western Pacific Railroads.

CROCKETT, EUGENE A., M.D., 298 Marlborough Street, Boston, Massachusetts. Harvard Medical School, 1891. Walter A. Le Compte, Professor of Otology, Harvard Medical School; Chief of Staff, Massachusetts Charitable Eye and Ear Infirmary; Consulting Otologist, Peter Bent Brigham Hospital.

CROCKETT, FRANK S., Phar.G., M.D., 601 La Fayette Life Building, La Fayette, Indiana. Indiana University School of Medicine (Medical College of Indiana), 1903.

CROLL, ANDREW, M.D., C.M., F.R.C.S. (Edin.), 304 Canada Building, Saskatoon, Saskatchewan. University of Edinburgh, 1893. Examiner in Surgery, Medical Council of Canada; Visiting Surgeon, City and St. Paul's Hospitals; Surgeon, Canadian National Railways.

CRONK, FRED YOHN, B.Sc., A.M., M.D., 302 Daniel Building, Tulsa, Oklahoma. Johns Hopkins University, Medical Department, 1907. Visiting Surgeon, Tulsa Hospital.

CROOK, JERE LAWRENCE, A.M., M.D., 110 West Baltimore Street, Jackson, Tennessee. Vanderbilt University, Medical Department, 1894. Chief Surgeon, Crook Sanatorium; Division Surgeon, Illinois Central Railroad; Surgeon, Nashville, Chattanooga and St. Louis and Gulf, Mobile and Northern Railways.

CROSBIE, ARTHUR H., A.B., M.D., 520 Commonwealth Avenue, Boston, Massachusetts. Harvard Medical School, 1906.

CROSBY, DANIEL, M.D., Twentieth and Webster Streets, Oakland, California. Cooper Medical College, 1898. Chief of Staff, Fabiola Hospital.

CROSBY, ROBERT, M.B., 736 Granville Street, Vancouver, British Columbia. University of Toronto, Faculty of Medicine, 1898.

CROSBY, WALTER THEODORE, Ph.B., M.D., 814 Elm Street, Manchester, New Hampshire. Harvard Medical School, 1899. Visiting Surgeon, Sacred Heart Hospital.

CROSS, FRANK BRADLEY, M.D., Livingston Building, Cincinnati, Ohio. University of Cincinnati College of Medicine (Miami Medical College), 1895. Vice-Dean, Secretary of Faculty, and Assistant Clinical Professor of Ophthalmology, University of Cincinnati College of Medicine; Ophthalmologist, Cincinnati General Hospital.

CROSSEN, HARRY STURGEON, M.D., Metropolitan Building, St. Louis, Missouri. Washington University Medical School, 1892. Clinical Professor of Gynecology, Washington University Medical School; Gynecologist, Barnes, St. Luke's, and St. Louis Maternity Hospitals.

CROSTHWAIT, WILLIAM L., B.Sc., M.D., 803 Amicable Building, Waco, Texas. University of Louisville, Medical Department (Hospital College of Medicine), 1899. Member of Surgical Staff, Providence and Central Texas Baptist Sanitariums; Assistant Attending Surgeon, United States Public Health Service.

CROTTI, ANDRÉ, M.D., 151 East Broad Street, Columbus, Ohio. University of Lausanne, 1902; Ohio State University College of Medicine (Starling-Ohio Medical College), 1908. Surgeon, Grant and Children's Hospitals.

CROUSE, HUGH W., M.D., 504 Roberts-Banner Building, El Paso, Texas. Indiana University School of Medicine, 1892. Surgeon, Ralston and Providence Hospitals.

CROWE, SAMUEL JAMES, A.B., M.D., 4332 North Charles Street, Baltimore, Maryland. Johns Hopkins University, Medical Department, 1908. Professor of Clinical Laryngology, Johns Hopkins University, Medical Department; Rhinologist and Oto-Laryngologist, Johns Hopkins Hospital.

CROWE, WALTER ANDREW, B.Sc., M.D., 1501 Hurt Building, Atlanta, Georgia. University and Bellevue Hospital Medical College (Bellevue Hospital Medical College), 1881. Member of Staff, Wesley Memorial Hospital and St. Joseph Infirmary.

CROWE, WILLIS HANFORD, M.D., 59 College Street, New Haven, Connecticut. Columbia University, College of Physicians and Surgeons, 1895. Attending Surgeon, Hospital of St. Raphael.

CROWELL, ANDREW J., M.D., 711 Independence Building, Charlotte, North Carolina. University of Maryland School of Medicine, 1893. President of Crowell Urological Clinic; Head of Department of Urology, Charlotte Sanatorium, Presbyterian Hospital.

CROWELL, JOSEPH A., M.D., 301 East Ludington Street, Iron Mountain, Michigan. University and Bellevue Hospital Medical College (University of the City of New York, Medical Department), 1881. Chief Surgeon, Oliver Iron Mining, Thomas Iron, and Republic Iron Companies, Menominee Range.

CROWELL, LESTER A., M.D., South Aspin Street, Lincolnton, North Carolina. University of Maryland School of Medicine (Baltimore Medical College), 1892. Surgeon in Charge, Lincoln Hospital.

CROWLEY, DENNIS DAVID, M.D., Central Bank Building, Oakland, California. Loyola University School of Medicine (Bennett Medical College), 1879; University of Illinois College of Medicine (College of Physicians and Surgeons, Chicago), 1885.

CROZIER, JAMES ALEXANDER, B.A., M.D., C.M., 215 Park Street, Port Arthur, Ontario. Faculty of Medicine, McGill University, 1902.

CRUMP, WALTER GRAY, M.D., 837 Madison Avenue, New York, New York. New York Homeopathic Medical College and Flower Hospital, 1895. Surgeon, Hahnemann, Community, and Broad Street Hospitals; Consulting Surgeon, New York Ophthalmic Hospital, New York, Yonkers Homeopathic Hospital and Maternity, Yonkers; Consulting Gynecologist, Jamaica Hospital, Jamaica, United Hospital, Port Chester, Mt. Vernon Hospital, Mt. Vernon.

CUBBINS, WILLIAM R., B.Sc., M.D., 29 East Madison Street, Chicago, Illinois. Northwestern University Medical School, 1900. Professor of Surgery,

Post-Graduate Medical School; Associate Professor of Surgery, Northwestern University Medical School; Attending Surgeon, Post-Graduate Hospital; Surgeon, Wesley Memorial and Cook County Hospitals.

CUENCA Y LAMAS, BALDOMERO, A.B., M.D., Rincon 615, Montevideo, Uruguay. Faculty of Medicine, University of Montevideo, 1903. Surgeon, Urological Policlinic, Spanish Hospital of Montevideo.

CULBERT, WILLIAM LEDLIE, Ph.B., M.D., Ph.D., 16 East Fifty-fourth Street, New York, New York. Columbia University, College of Physicians and Surgeons, 1888. Assistant Surgeon, Manhattan Eye, Ear, and Throat Hospital; Consulting Rhinologist and Laryngologist, New York Neurological Institute, New York, Mary McClellan Hospital, Cambridge, New York, Sharon Hospital, Sharon, Connecticut; Consulting Otologist and Laryngologist, New York State Hospital for Crippled and Deformed Children, West Haverstraw.

CULBERTSON, CAREY, A.B., M.D., 30 North Michigan Avenue, Chicago, Illinois. Northwestern University Medical School, 1898. Assistant Professor of Obstetrics and Gynecology, Rush Medical College; Associate Attending Obstetrician and Gynecologist, Presbyterian Hospital; Attending Gynecologist, Cook County Hospital.

CULHANE, THOMAS HENRY, M.D., 305 Stewart Building, Rockford, Illinois. Rush Medical College, 1890. Consulting Surgeon, Rockford Hospital.

CULIN, WILLIAM D., M.D., 820 North Forty-first Street, Philadelphia, Pennsylvania. Hahnemann Medical College and Hospital, Philadelphia, 1894. Associate Professor of Gynecology, Hahnemann Medical College and Hospital; Gynecologist, Hahnemann Medical College and Hospital, West Philadelphia General Homeopathic Hospital and Dispensary.

CULLEN, ERNEST KEYS, M.B., 1053 David Whitney Building, Detroit, Michigan. University of Toronto, Faculty of Medicine, 1903. Acting Professor of Gynecology, Detroit College of Medicine and Surgery; Attending Surgeon in Gynecology, Harper Hospital.

CULLEN, THOMAS STEPHEN, M.B., 20 East Eager Street, Baltimore, Maryland. University of Toronto, Faculty of Medicine, 1890. Professor of Clinical Gynecology, Johns Hopkins University, Medical Department; Visiting Gynecologist, Johns Hopkins Hospital; Consultant in Gynecology, Church Home and Infirmary.

CULLER, ROBERT M., A.M., M.D., Medical Corps, United States Army, Washington, District of Columbia. Jefferson Medical College, 1901. Lieutenant Colonel, Medical Corps, United States Army.

CULLOM, MARVIN MCTYEIRE, A.B., M.D., 208 Hitchcock Building, Nashville, Tennessee. Vanderbilt University, Medical Department, 1896; Clinical Professor of Ophthalmology, and Oto-Laryngology, Vanderbilt University Medical Department; Surgeon, St. Thomas' Hospital.

CULP, JOHN FRANKLIN, M.D., 240 North Third Street, Harrisburg, Pennsylvania. University of Pennsylvania School of Medicine, 1886. Visiting Laryngologist and Otologist, Harrisburg Hospital.

CUMMIN, JOHN WHITE, A.B., M.D., 9 Massachusetts Avenue, Boston, Massachusetts. Harvard Medical School, 1896. Instructor in Surgery, Harvard Medical School; Surgeon to Out-Patients, Massachusetts General Hospital.

CUMMINGS, HUGH F., M.D., United States Public Health Service, Washington, District of Columbia. University of Virginia Department of Medicine, 1893; Medical College of Virginia, 1894. Surgeon General, United States Public Health Service.

CUMMINGS, HOWARD H., M.D., 202 Nickels Arcade, Ann Arbor, Michigan. University of Michigan Medical School, 1910. Member of Staff, Washtenaw Private Hospital.

CUNNINGHAM, A. T. R., A.B., M.D., 501 Old National Bank Building, Spokane, Washington. Western Reserve University School of Medicine, 1900. Surgeon, St. Luke's Hospital.

CUNNINGHAM, ALLAN R., B.A., M.D., C.M., 260 Barrington Street, Halifax, Nova Scotia. Dalhousie University, Faculty of Medicine, 1904. Assistant Ophthalmologist and Otologist, Victoria General Hospital.

CUNNINGHAM, BENJAMIN F., Ph.B., M.D., Santa Barbara, California. Harvard Medical School, 1894.

CUNNINGHAM, HARRY CLARKSON, M.D., C.M., Villard Avenue, Carman, Manitoba. Queen's University, Faculty of Medicine, 1885. Member of Staff, Carman Hospital.

CUNNINGHAM, HENRY M., M.D., 106 Birks Building, Vancouver, British Columbia. Columbia University, College of Physicians and Surgeons, 1895.

CUNNINGHAM, JOHN HENRY, M.D., 46 Gloucester Street, Boston, Massachusetts. Harvard Medical School, 1902. Associate in Genito-Urinary Surgery, Harvard University Graduate School of Medicine; Surgeon, Long Island Hospital; Assistant Surgeon, Boston City Hospital; Consulting Surgeon, Rufus S. Frost Hospital, Chelsea, Melrose Hospital, Melrose, Jordan Hospital, Plymouth.

CUNNINGHAM, SAMUEL PRESTON, M.D., 714 Gibbs Building, San Antonio, Texas. Tulane University of Louisiana School of Medicine, 1898. Chief of Staff, Gynecological Section, Robert B. Green Memorial Hospital; Visiting Surgeon, Lee Surgical and Physicians and Surgeons Hospitals; Chief Surgeon, San Antonio, Uvalde and Gulf Railroad.

CUNNINGHAM, THOMAS HART, M.D., Glens Falls Insurance Building, Glens Falls, New York. Albany Medical College, 1900. Attending Surgeon, Glens Falls Hospital.

CUNNINGHAM, WILSON, B.Sc., M.D., Platteville, Wisconsin. Northwestern University Medical School, 1898. Surgeon, Cunningham Hospital.

CUPLER, RALPH CLINTON, Phar.G., M.D., 5222 Blackstone Avenue, Chicago, Illinois. University of Illinois College of Medicine (College of Physicians and Surgeons, Chicago), 1901. Surgeon, St. Anthony's Hospital.

CURDY, ROBERT J., M.D., Rialto Building, Kansas City, Missouri. Washington University Medical School, 1895. Ophthalmologist, Mercy and St. Luke's Hospitals.

CURL, HOLTON C., M.D., Medical Corps, United States Navy, Washington, District of Columbia. University of California Medical School, 1897. Captain, Medical Corps, United States Navy.

CURRY, GLENDON E., M.D., Westinghouse Building, Pittsburgh, Pennsylvania. University of Pennsylvania School of Medicine, 1892. Consulting Ophthalmologist, Western Pennsylvania Hospital; Ophthalmologist, Eye and Ear Hospital and Pittsburgh Hospital for Children.

CURRY, JAMES WALKER, M.D., 328 North Main Street, Greenville, South Carolina. Emory University School of Medicine (Southern Medical College), 1897; Jefferson Medical College, 1898.

CURTIS, ARTHUR H., B.Sc., M.D., 104 South Michigan Avenue, Chicago, Illinois. Rush Medical College, 1905. Clinical Professor of Gynecology, Northwestern University Medical School; Senior Gynecologist, St. Luke's Hospital.

CURTIS, WESLEY L., M.D., 612 Security Mutual Building, Lincoln, Nebraska. Rush Medical College, 1896.

CUSHING, HARVEY, A.M., M.D., D.Sc., F.R.C.S. (Eng.), F.R.C.S. (I.), LL.D., Peter Bent Brigham Hospital, Boston, Massachusetts. Harvard Medical School, 1895. Moseley Professor of Surgery, Harvard Medical School; Surgeon-in-Chief, Peter Bent Brigham Hospital.

CUSHING, HAYWARD W., A.B., M.D., 70 Commonwealth Avenue, Boston, Massachusetts. Harvard Medical School, 1882. Retired.

CUTLER, ARTHUR W., M.D., 28 Watkins Avenue, Oneonta, New York. Columbia University, College of Physicians and Surgeons, 1896. Surgeon, Aurelia Osborn Fox Memorial Hospital; Consulting Surgeon, Thanksgiving Hospital, Cooperstown.

CUTLER, ELLIOTT CARR, A.B., M.D., Peter Bent Brigham Hospital, Boston, Massachusetts. Harvard Medical School, 1913. Faculty Instructor in Surgery, Harvard Medical School; Resident Surgeon, Peter Bent Brigham Hospital.

CUTLER, FRANKLIN E., M.D., Schofield Building, Cleveland, Ohio. Ohio State University College of Homeopathic Medicine (Cleveland Homeopathic Medical College), 1905; Jefferson Medical College, 1906.

CUTTS, WILLIAM BRYANT, A.M., M.D., 370 Broad Street, Providence, Rhode Island. University of Pennsylvania School of Medicine, 1899. Visiting Surgeon, Rhode Island Hospital.

DABNEY, SAMUEL GORDON, M.D., 911 Starks Building, Louisville, Kentucky. University of Virginia, Department of Medicine, 1882. Professor, Diseases of Ear, Nose, and Throat, and Clinical Professor, Diseases of Eye, University of Louisville, Medical Department.

DABNEY, VIRGINIUS, M.D., 1633 Connecticut Avenue, Washington, District of Columbia. University of Virginia, Department of Medicine, 1902. Chief of Clinic, Episcopal Eye, Ear, and Throat Hospital; Otologist and Laryngologist, Garfield Memorial Hospital, Washington City Orphan Asylum, Friendship House.

DA COSTA, JOHN CHALMERS, M.D., LL.D., 2045 Walnut Street, Philadelphia, Pennsylvania. Jefferson Medical College, 1885. Gross Professor of Surgery, Jefferson Medical College; Surgeon, Jefferson Medical College Hospital; Consulting Surgeon, Philadelphia General, St. Joseph's and Misericordia Hospitals.

DAKIN, CHANNING ELLERY, B.Sc., M.D., 502 M. B. A. Building, Mason City, Iowa. Loyola University School of Medicine (Bennett Medical College), 1899. Surgeon, St. Joseph's Mercy Hospital and Mason City Clinic.

DALE, JOHN RICHARD, M.D., Sixth and Beech Streets, Texarkana, Arkansas. Jefferson Medical College, 1872. Surgeon, Dale Sanatorium; Chief Surgeon, Louisiana and Arkansas Railway.

DANCY, ALEXANDER BROWN, M.D., First National Bank Building, Jackson, Tennessee. Vanderbilt University, Medical Department, 1902. Ophthalmic and Aural Surgeon, Civic League Hospital, Mobile and Ohio, Gulf, Mobile and Northern Railways, Surgical Department; Attending Ophthalmic and Aural Surgeon, Crook Sanatorium.

DANFORTH, MORTIMER EDWIN, M.D., Concord and Lafayette Streets, East, Detroit, Michigan. Grand Rapids Medical College, 1902.

DANFORTH, MURRAY SNELL, A.B., M.D., 124 Waterman Street, Providence, Rhode Island. Johns Hopkins University, Medical Department, 1905. Consulting Orthopedic Surgeon, Providence City and Butler Hospitals; Orthopedic Surgeon, Out-Patient Department, Massachusetts General Hospital, Boston, Rhode Island Hospital, Providence.

DANFORTH, WILLIAM CLARK, B.Sc., M.D., 1620 Hinman Avenue, Evanston, Illinois. Northwestern University Medical School, 1903. Associate Professor of Gynecology, Northwestern University Medical School; Attending Gynecologist and Obstetrician, Evanston Hospital; Consulting Gynecologist and Obstetrician, Highland Park Hospital, Highland Park.

DANGLER, HENRY WILLIAM, M.D., 455 Classon Avenue, Brooklyn, New York. Long Island College Hospital, 1907. Attending Surgeon, Kingston Avenue Hospital, Ridgewood Sanatorium; Associate Surgeon, Williamsburg Hospital.

DANIELSON, KARL A., M.D., Litchfield, Minnesota. Rush Medical College, 1900. Surgeon, Litchfield Hospital.

DANNREUTHER, WALTER T., M.D., 2020 Broadway, New York, New York. Long Island College Hospital, 1906. Associate Professor of Gynecology, New York Post-Graduate Medical School; Attending Gynecologist, St. Elizabeth's Hospital, New York Post-Graduate Medical School and

Hospital; Attending Urologist, Women's Department, Lutheran Hospital of Manhattan.

DANZIS, MAX, M.D., 608 High Street, Newark, New Jersey. University and Bellevue Hospital Medical College (New York University Medical College), 1899. Visiting Surgeon, Beth Israel Hospital.

D'ARC, HARRY THORNTON, M.B., M.D., Stevenson Building, Mt. Vernon, Washington. University of Toronto, Faculty of Medicine, 1908. Surgeon, Mt. Vernon General Hospital.

DARCHE, J. A., M.D., C.M., 92 King Street, Sherbrooke, Quebec. Faculty of Medicine, McGill University, 1898.

DARLING, CYRENUS G., M.D., 722 Forest Avenue, Ann Arbor, Michigan. University of Michigan Medical School, 1881. Surgeon, St. Joseph's Sanitarium.

DARNALL, CARL ROGERS, M.D., Medical Corps, United States Army, Washington, District of Columbia. Jefferson Medical College, 1890. Colonel, Medical Corps, United States Army.

DARNALL, WILLIAM EDGAR, A.M., M.D., 1704 Pacific Avenue, Atlantic City, New Jersey. University of Virginia, Department of Medicine, 1895. Gynecologist, Atlantic City Hospital; Consulting Surgeon, North American Sanitarium for Bone Tuberculosis, Ventnor; Surgeon, Max and Sarah Bamberger Home for Crippled Children, Longport.

DARRACH, WILLIAM, A.M., M.D., 128 East Sixtieth Street, New York, New York. Columbia University, College of Physicians and Surgeons, 1901. Dean, and Associate Professor of Surgery, Columbia University, College of Physicians and Surgeons; Consulting Surgeon, Morristown Memorial Hospital, Morristown, New Jersey, St. John's Hospital, Yonkers, New York, Greenwich Hospital, Greenwich, Connecticut.

DARRINGTON, JOHN, B.Sc., M.D., Yazoo and Madison Streets, Yazoo City, Mississippi. Tulane University of Louisiana School of Medicine, 1892. Surgeon, Yazoo Sanitarium.

DAUGHERTY, LOUIS EUGENE, M.D., 914 Lowry Building, St. Paul, Minnesota. University of Minnesota Medical School, 1904. Assistant Professor of Surgery, University of Minnesota Medical School; Member of Surgical Staff, Charles T. Miller, St. Luke's, City and County Hospitals.

DAVENPORT, FRANCIS HENRY, A.B., M.D., 390 Commonwealth Avenue, Boston, Massachusetts. Harvard Medical School, 1874. Consulting Surgeon, Free Hospital for Women, Brookline.

DAVENPORT, GEORGE LUTHER, M.D., 31 North State Street, Chicago, Illinois. University of Illinois College of Medicine (College of Physicians and Surgeons, Chicago), 1907. Assistant Professor of Clinical Surgery, University of Illinois College of Medicine; Associate Attending Surgeon, Michael Reese Hospital; Attending Surgeon, Cook County Hospital; Chief of Clinic, Michael Reese Dispensary.

DAVEY, BERTEN M., M.D., 221 North Capitol Avenue, Lansing, Michigan. Detroit College of Medicine and Surgery, 1905. Gynecologist, Edward W. Sparrow Hospital; Surgeon, St. Lawrence Hospital and State Industrial Home for Boys.

DAVID, FRANK ELMER, D.D.S., M.D., 25 East Washington Street, Chicago, Illinois. University of Illinois College of Medicine, 1904. Member of Staff, St. Joseph's Hospital; Associate Member of Staff, St. Luke's Hospital.

DAVIDSON, ALAN, M.D., C.M., M.R.C.S. (Eng.), 39 Bank Street, St. Albans, Vermont. Faculty of Medicine, McGill University, 1894. Surgeon, St. Albans Hospital; Chief Surgeon, Central Vermont Railway.

DAVIDSON, ARTHUR J., M.D., 200 South Twelfth Street, Philadelphia, Pennsylvania. Jefferson Medical College, 1907. Assistant Professor of Orthopedic Surgery, Jefferson Medical College; Assistant Orthopedic Surgeon, and Chief of Out-Patient Orthopedic Department, Jefferson Medical College Hospital.

DAVIDSON, CHARLES FITZSIMMONS, M.D., 126 Goldsborough Street, Easton, Maryland. University of Maryland School of Medicine, 1888. Surgeon, Easton Emergency Hospital.

DAVIDSON, EDWARD CLEMENT, M.D., 114 North Seventh Street, La Fayette, Indiana. University of Michigan Medical School, 1891. Surgeon, St. Elizabeth's and La Fayette Home Hospitals.

DAVIDSON, WILLIAM R., B.Sc., M.D., 712 South Fourth Street, Evansville, Indiana. Rush Medical College, 1899. Associate Surgeon, The Walker Hospital.

DAVIDSON, WILSON THOMPSON, B.Sc., M.D., 403 Municipal Building, Dallas, Texas. University of Texas, Medical Department, 1896. Director of Public Health, City of Dallas.

DAVIES, RAY H., M.D., 30 North Michigan Avenue, Chicago, Illinois. Boston University School of Medicine, 1903.

DAVIS, ASA BARNES, M.D., 42 East Thirty-fifth Street, New York, New York. Columbia University, College of Physicians and Surgeons, 1889. Chief Surgeon, Lying-in Hospital; Consulting Gynecologist, Vassar Brothers' Hospital, Poughkeepsie.

DAVIS, BYRON B., A.B., M.D., 1502 South Thirty-second Avenue, Omaha, Nebraska. University of Minnesota Medical School (Minnesota Hospital College), 1884. Professor of Principles of Surgery and Clinical Surgery, University of Nebraska College of Medicine; Chief Surgeon, Immanuel Deaconess Institute; Attending Surgeon, Wise Memorial and Bishop Clarkson Memorial Hospitals.

DAVIS, CARL B., A.B., M.D., 122 South Michigan Avenue, Chicago, Illinois. Rush Medical College, 1903. Assistant Professor of Surgery, Rush Medical College; Associate Attending Surgeon, Presbyterian Hospital.

DAVIS, CARL HENRY, A.B., B.Sc., M.D., 141 Wisconsin Street, Milwaukee, Wisconsin. Rush Medical College, 1909. Lecturer on Obstetrics and

Gynecology, Extension Division, University of Wisconsin Medical School; Obstetrician and Gynecologist, Columbia and Milwaukee County Hospitals.

DAVIS, DELMER L., Ph.G., B.Sc., M.D., 670 Brandeis Theatre Building, Omaha, Nebraska. Hahnemann Medical College and Hospital, Chicago, 1902. Assistant Professor of Surgery, University of Nebraska Medical College; Member of Surgical Staff, Swedish Mission Hospital.

DAVIS, EDWARD CAMPBELL, A.B., M.D., 25 East Linden Avenue, Atlanta, Georgia. University of Louisville, Medical Department, 1892. Professor of Obstetrics and Gynecology, Emory University School of Medicine; Visiting Gynecologist, Grady Memorial Hospital, Davis-Fischer Sanatorium.

DAVIS, EDWARD FRANCIS, M.D., 343 American National Bank Building, Oklahoma, Oklahoma. University of Cincinnati College of Medicine (Miami Medical College), 1902. Associate Professor, Eye, Ear, Nose, and Throat Department, University of Oklahoma School of Medicine; Attending Oculist and Aurist, St. Anthony's and University Hospitals.

DAVIS, EDWARD PARKER, A.M., M.D., 250 South Twenty-first Street, Philadelphia, Pennsylvania. Rush Medical College, 1882; Jefferson Medical College of Philadelphia, 1888. Professor of Obstetrics, Jefferson Medical College of Philadelphia; Obstetrician, Jefferson Medical College Hospital; Obstetrician and Gynecologist, Philadelphia General Hospital; Consultant, Preston Retreat.

DAVIS, EDWIN G., A.B., M.D., 670 Brandeis Theatre Building, Omaha, Nebraska. Johns Hopkins University, Medical Department, 1912. Professor of Urology, University of Nebraska, College of Medicine; Urologist, Bishop Clarkson Memorial, Wise Memorial, Swedish Mission, and University Hospitals.

DAVIS, EVANS GREENWOOD, C.M.G., M.D., M.C.P., S.O., Daly Building, Ottawa, Ontario. Western University, Faculty of Medicine, 1906.

DAVIS, FRANK C., B.Sc., M.A., M.D., 618 West Main Street, Lewistown, Montana. Johns Hopkins University, Medical Department, 1899. Chief of Eye, Ear, Nose, and Throat Department, Attix Clinic.

DAVIS, GEORGE GILBERT, A.B., M.D., 122 South Michigan Avenue, Chicago, Illinois. Rush Medical College, 1904. Assistant Professor of Surgery, Rush Medical College; Attending Surgeon, Cook County Hospital; Chief Surgeon, Illinois Steel Company.

DAVIS, HOAGLAND COOK, M.D., 405 North Charles Street, Baltimore, Maryland. University of Maryland School of Medicine, 1902. Instructor in Clinical Laryngology, Johns Hopkins University, Medical Department; Assistant Dispensary Laryngologist, Johns Hopkins Hospital; Attending Oculist, Aurist, and Laryngologist, Sydenham Hospital; Visiting Laryngologist, University Hospital; Member of Staff,

Hospital for Women of Maryland, Union Protestant Infirmary, Church Home and Infirmary; Consulting Laryngologist, Children's Hospital School.

DAVIS, J. D. S., M.D., LL.D., 2029 Avenue G, Birmingham, Alabama. University of Georgia, Medical Department, 1879. Professor of Surgery, Graduate School of Medicine of the University of Alabama; Surgeon, Hillman Hospital.

DAVIS, J. LESLIE, B.Sc., M.D., 135 South Eighteenth Street, Philadelphia, Pennsylvania. Jefferson Medical College, 1901. Consulting Otologist and Laryngologist, St. Mary's, St. Agnes', and Philadelphia Lying-in Charity Hospitals.

DAVIS, JOHN BRAMWELL, A.B., M.D., 660 Metropolitan Building, Denver, Colorado. University of Colorado School of Medicine (Gross Medical College), 1902. Assistant Professor of Genito-Urinary Surgery, University of Colorado School of Medicine; Visiting Genito-Urinary Surgeon, Denver City and County Hospital, Swedish National Sanatorium for Tuberculosis; Urologist, Mercy Hospital, National Jewish Hospital for Consumptives.

DAVIS, JOHN STAIGE, Ph.B., M.D., The Severn Apartments, Baltimore, Maryland. Johns Hopkins University, Medical Department, 1899. Associate in Clinical Surgery, Johns Hopkins University, Medical Department; Visiting and Plastic Surgeon, Hospital for Women of Maryland, Union Memorial and Children's Hospitals; Visiting Surgeon, Church Home and Infirmary; Assistant Visiting and Dispensary Surgeon, Johns Hopkins Hospital.

DAVIS, LINCOLN, A.B., M.D., 217 Beacon Street, Boston, Massachusetts. Harvard Medical School, 1898. Associate in Surgery, Harvard University Graduate School of Medicine; Visiting Surgeon, Massachusetts General Hospital; Consulting Surgeon, Massachusetts Charitable Eye and Ear Infirmary, Boston, Milford Hospital, Milford, Henry Heywood Memorial Hospital, Gardner.

DAVIS, NELSON P., M.D., 1405 Fifth Avenue, Pittsburgh, Pennsylvania. University of Pittsburgh School of Medicine, 1909. Member of Junior Surgical Staff, Mercy Hospital.

DAVIS, S. GRIFFITH, JR., M.D., 1230 Light Street, Baltimore, Maryland. University of Maryland School of Medicine, 1893. Professor of Anesthetics, University of Maryland School of Medicine and College of Physicians and Surgeons; Anesthetist, South Baltimore General Hospital; Anesthetist and Visiting Surgeon, Church Home and Infirmary; Consulting Anesthetist, Union Protestant Infirmary, St. Joseph's Hospital, Hebrew Hospital and Asylum; Member of Staff, Hospital for Women of Maryland.

DAVIS, THOMAS ARCHIBALD, M.D., 2344 Jackson Boulevard, Chicago, Illinois. University of Illinois College of Medicine (College of Physicians and Surgeons, Chicago), 1885. Professor of Surgery, Illinois Post-Graduate Medical School; Attending Surgeon, West Side Hospital.

DAVIS, THOMAS W., M.D., 210 O'Hanlon Building, Winston-Salem, North Carolina. Medical College of the State of South Carolina, 1898. Ophthalmologist and Oto-Laryngologist, City Memorial Hospital.

DAVIS, WARREN B., M.D., 135 South Eighteenth Street, Philadelphia, Pennsylvania. Jefferson Medical College, 1910. Instructor in Surgery and Assistant Demonstrator of Anatomy, Jefferson Medical College; Clinical Assistant, Surgical Department, Jefferson Medical College Hospital.

DAVIS, WILLIAM C., M.D., 350 East State Street, Columbus, Ohio. University of Cincinnati College of Medicine (Medical College of Ohio), 1896. Ophthalmologist, Otologist, Rhinologist, and Laryngologist, Children's, Mercy, McKinley, and Grant Hospitals.

DAVIS, WILLIAM THORNWALL, M.D., 927 Farragut Square, Washington, District of Columbia. George Washington University Medical School, 1901; United States Army Medical School, 1902. Professor of Ophthalmology, George Washington University Medical School; Associate, Episcopal Eye, Ear, and Throat and Garfield Memorial Hospitals, Columbia Hospital for Women.

DAVISON, CHARLES, A.M., M.D., 30 North Michigan Avenue, Chicago, Illinois. Northwestern University Medical School, 1883. Professor of Surgery, Clinical Surgery, and Head of Surgical Department, University of Illinois College of Medicine; Attending Surgeon, Cook County and University Hospitals.

DAVISON, PETER C., M.D., C.M., Willmar, Minnesota. University of Minnesota Medical School (Minneapolis College of Physicians and Surgeons), 1904. Member of Staff, Willmar Hospital and Clinic.

DAWSON, LEWIS REEVES, M.D., Northern Life Building, Seattle, Washington. University of Michigan Medical School, 1882.

DAY, EWING W., A.M., M.D., Westinghouse Building, Pittsburgh, Pennsylvania. Georgetown University School of Medicine, 1889. Professor of Otology, University of Pittsburgh School of Medicine; Member of Staff, Pittsburgh Eye and Ear Hospital, Pittsburgh, Columbia Hospital, Wilkinsburg.

DAY, FLOYD M., M.D., Brown Building, Eugene, Oregon. University of Minnesota Medical School, 1901. Member of Staff, Mercy Hospital.

DAY, HILBERT FRANCIS, Ph.B., M.D., 45 Bay State Road, Boston, Massachusetts. Harvard Medical School, 1905. Instructor in Surgery, Harvard Medical School; Associate in Surgery, Peter Bent Brigham Hospital; Surgeon-in-Chief, Boston Dispensary.

DAY, ROBERT V., M.D., 621 Baker-Detwiler Building, Los Angeles, California. University of California Medical School, 1897. Professor of Clinical Urology, College of Medical Evangelists; Senior Attending Surgeon, Los Angeles County Hospital; Chief Urological Service, White Memorial Hospital and Boyle Dispensary; Visiting Urologist, California, Golden State, and Clara Barton Hospitals.

DEAN, EDWARD F., M.D., 100 Metropolitan Building, Denver, Colorado. University of Colorado School of Medicine, 1897. Assistant Professor of Clinical Surgery, University of Colorado School of Medicine; Surgeon, St. Joseph's, City and County Hospitals.

DEAN, ELMER A., M.D., Medical Corps, United States Army, Washington, District of Columbia. University of Pennsylvania School of Medicine, 1898. Colonel, Medical Corps, United States Army.

DEAN, FRANK WILSON, B.Sc., M.D., 401 City National Bank Building, Council Bluffs, Iowa. University of Minnesota Medical School, 1890. Ophthalmologist, Otologist, and Laryngologist, Jennie Edmundson Memorial Hospital, Christian Home Orphanage.

DEAN, JAMES P., B.Sc., M.D., 29 East Main Street, Madison, Wisconsin. University of Pennsylvania School of Medicine, 1913. Lecturer on Clinical Medicine, University of Wisconsin; Attending Surgeon, St. Mary's Hospital.

DEAN, JOHN McHALE, A.M., M.D., Metropolitan Building, St. Louis, Missouri. Washington University Medical School, 1896. Assistant Professor of Surgery, St. Louis University School of Medicine; Surgeon, St. Mary's Infirmary, Mt. St. Rose Hospital; Member of Consulting Staff, St. John's and St. Anthony's Hospitals.

DEAN, JOSEPH, JR., M.D., 29 East Main Street, Madison, Wisconsin. University of Illinois College of Medicine (College of Physicians and Surgeons Chicago), 1902. Instructor in Clinical Surgery, University of Wisconsin Medical School; Attending Surgeon, St. Mary's Hospital.

DEAN, LEE WALLACE, M.Sc., M.D., 12½ South Clinton Street, Iowa City, Iowa. State University of Iowa College of Medicine, 1896. Dean of College of Medicine, and Professor and Head of Department of Ophthalmology, Oto-Laryngology, and Oral Surgery, State University of Iowa College of Medicine; Chief Oto-Laryngologist and Oral Surgeon, State University and Mercy Hospitals; Laryngologist, State Sanatorium for Tuberculosis, Oakdale.

DEAN, LOUIS W., M.D., 40 Gardner Building, Utica, New York. New York Homeopathic Medical College and Flower Hospital, 1890. Ophthalmologist, Rhinologist, and Oto-Laryngologist, Utica General and Utica Homeopathic Hospitals.

DEAN, WILLIAM INSCO, M.D., 33 Chestnut Street, Rochester, New York. University of Buffalo, Department of Medicine, 1902. Assistant Surgeon, Rochester General Hospital; Assistant Surgeon and Gynecologist, Monroe County Tuberculosis Sanitarium; Consulting Surgeon, Rochester State Hospital.

DEANE, REGINALD BURTON, M.D., C.M., Alexander Corner, Calgary, Alberta. Faculty of Medicine, McGill University, 1898.

DEAR, BROCK McGEORGE, M.D., 21 Bolton Gardens, Bronxville, New York. University of Virginia Department of Medicine, 1908. Adjunct Gynecologist and Obstetrician, Lincoln Hospital, New York.

DEARBORN, SAM STARRETT, A.B., M.D., 3 Abbot Street, Nashua, New Hampshire. Harvard Medical School, 1898. Member of Visiting Staff, Nashua Memorial and St. Joseph's Hospitals.

DEAVER, HARRY C., M.D., 1701 Spruce Street, Philadelphia, Pennsylvania. University of Pennsylvania School of Medicine, 1885. Professor of Surgery, Woman's Medical College of Pennsylvania; Surgeon-in-Chief, Kensington Hospital for Women; Surgeon, Hospital of the Protestant Episcopal Church and Children's Hospital of the Mary J. Drexel Home.

DEAVER, JOHN B., M.D., D.Sc., LL.D., 1634 Walnut Street, Philadelphia, Pennsylvania. University of Pennsylvania School of Medicine, 1878. John Rhea Barton Professor of Surgery, University of Pennsylvania School of Medicine; Surgeon-in-Chief, Lankenau Hospital; Visiting Surgeon, Hospital of the University of Pennsylvania.

DECHERD, HENRY BENJAMIN, A.M., M.D., 3708 Rawlins Street, Dallas, Texas. University of Texas, Medical Department, 1900. Assistant Professor, Ophthalmology, Rhinology, Oto-Laryngology, Baylor University, Medical Department; Attending Surgeon, Baylor and Dallas City Hospitals.

DECKER, GEORGE EDWARD, B.Sc., M.D., Central Office Building, Davenport, Iowa. State University of Iowa College of Medicine, 1897. Member of Staff, St. Luke's Hospital.

DECKER, HARRY RYERSON, A.B., M.D., Jenkins Arcade Building, Pittsburgh, Pennsylvania. Columbia University, College of Physicians and Surgeons, 1907. Assistant Instructor in Anatomy and Instructor in Surgery, University of Pittsburgh School of Medicine; Visiting Surgeon, Presbyterian Hospital.

DEELY, GEORGE EDWARD, A.B., M.D., 132 Montague Street, Brooklyn, New York. Columbia University, College of Physicians and Surgeons, 1900. Visiting Ophthalmologist, Williamsburgh and Coney Island Hospitals, Hospital of the Holy Family, Brooklyn Eastern District Dispensary and Hospital; Ophthalmologist, Otologist, and Rhinologist, Hospital of the Holy Family; Associate Ophthalmologist, Otologist, and Rhinologist, St. Mary's Hospital, Brooklyn, St. Charles Hospital for Crippled Children, Port Jefferson; Associate Surgeon, Brooklyn Eye and Ear Hospital.

DEERING, ALBERT B., M.D., 809 Eighth Street, Boone, Iowa. Northwestern University Medical School, 1898. Member of Attending Staff, Eleanor Moore Hospital.

DE GARMO, WILLIAM BURTON, M.D., 616 Madison Avenue, New York, New York. University and Bellevue Hospital Medical College (New York University Medical College), 1875. Professor of Special Surgery, New York Post-Graduate Medical School; Consulting Surgeon, New York Post-Graduate Medical School and Hospital.

DE LA FUENTE, RUDECINDO, M.D., San Ignacio 419, Valparaiso, Chile. University of Chile, 1913. Chief Surgeon, Carlos Van Buren Private Hospital; Surgeon, Hospital San Juan de Dios and St. Agustine's Hospital.

DELANEY, CHARLES WALTER, A.B., M.D., 1555 The Alameda, San Jose, California. University of Pennsylvania School of Medicine, 1905. Surgeon, Columbia Hospital.

DELANEY, MARTIN DONAHUE, A.M., M.D., 131 North Washington Street, Alexandria, Virginia. Georgetown University School of Medicine, 1898. Surgeon, Alexandria Hospital.

DE LANEY, MATTHEW A., M.D., Medical Corps, United States Army, Washington, District of Columbia. University of Pennsylvania School of Medicine, 1898. Colonel, Medical Corps, United States Army.

DE LA PUENTE, LUIS F., M.D., Maison de Santé, Lima, Peru. Faculty of Medicine, University of San Marcos, 1908. Surgeon, Maison de Santé and Dos de Mayo Hospital.

DELATOUR, H. BEECKMAN, M.D., 73 Eighth Avenue, Brooklyn, New York. Columbia University, College of Physicians and Surgeons, 1887. Surgeon, St. John's and Norwegian Deaconess Hospitals; Consulting Surgeon, Kingston Avenue Hospital, Brooklyn, Mary Immaculate Hospital, Jamaica, South Side Hospital, Babylon, Rockaway Beach Hospital, Rockaway Beach.

DELAVAN, D. BRYSON, A.B., M.D., 40 East Forty-first Street, New York, New York. Columbia University, College of Physicians and Surgeons, 1875. Consulting Laryngologist, Memorial and St. Luke's Hospitals, Hospital for Ruptured and Crippled; Surgeon, Out-Patient Department, St. Luke's Hospital; President, Russell Sage Institute of Pathology.

DE LEE, JOSEPH BOLIVAR, A.M., M.D., 5028 Ellis Avenue, Chicago, Illinois. Northwestern University Medical School, 1891. Professor of Obstetrics, Northwestern University Medical School; Obstetrician, Chicago Lying-in Hospital.

DELPRAT, JOHN C., M.D., 25 East Washington Street, Chicago, Illinois. Loyola University School of Medicine (Bennett Medical College), 1894; Northwestern University Medical School, 1903. Surgeon, Washington Park Hospital.

DE MENDONCA, JOSÉ, M.D., Rua da Assembléa 36, Rio de Janeiro, Brazil. Faculty of Medicine, Rio de Janeiro, 1888.

DENCH, EDWARD BRADFORD, Ph.B., M.D., 15 East Fifty-third Street, New York, New York. Columbia University, College of Physicians and Surgeons, 1885. Professor of Otology, University and Bellevue Hospital Medical College; Attending Aural Surgeon, New York Eye and Ear Infirmary; Consulting and Attending Otologist, St. Luke's Hospital; Consulting Otologist, New York Orthopedic Dispensary and Hospital, New York Neurological Institute.

DENEGRI, JUVENAL, M.D., Mongollon 289, Lima, Peru. Faculty of Medicine, University of San Marcos, 1893. Surgeon-in-Chief, Maison de Santé and Hospital Italiano.

DENMAN, IRA OSCAR, M.D., Ohio Building, Toledo, Ohio. Hahnemann Medical College and Hospital, Chicago, 1897.

372   *American College of Surgeons*

DENNIS, DAVID NICHOLS, M.D., 221 West Ninth Street, Erie, Pennsylvania. Jefferson Medical College, 1881.

DENNIS, FRANK L., M.D., Ferguson Building, Colorado Springs, Colorado. Emory University School of Medicine (Southern Medical College), 1893. Member of Attending Staff, Glockner Sanatorium and Hospital, and Beth-El Hospital.

DENNIS, JOHN B., M.D., Medical Corps, United States Navy, Washington, District of Columbia. University of Pennsylvania School of Medicine, 1895. Captain, Medical Corps, United States Navy.

DENNIS, WARREN A., B.L., M.D., Hamm Building, St. Paul, Minnesota. University of Minnesota Medical School, 1896. Surgeon, Charles T. Miller Hospital and Minnesota State Hospital for Indigent, Crippled and Deformed Children.

DE NORMANDIE, ROBERT L., A.B., M.D., 355 Marlborough Street, Boston, Massachusetts. Harvard Medical School, 1902. Instructor in Obstetrics, Harvard Medical School; Assistant Visiting Obstetrician, Boston Lying-in Hospital; Consultant in Obstetrics, Waltham Hospital, New England Hospital for Women and Children, Boston, Newton Hospital, Newton.

DENSLOW, FRANK M., M.D., 715 Bryant Building, Kansas City, Missouri. University of Kansas School of Medicine, 1906. Genito-Urinary Surgeon, Kansas City General and St. Margaret's Hospitals.

DENT, GEORGE B., M.D., 620 West Fourth Street, North Platte, Nebraska. Baltimore University School of Medicine, 1898.

DENTON, JOHN F., B.A., M.D., Doctors' Building, Atlanta, Georgia. University and Bellevue Hospital Medical College, 1903. Associate Professor of Gynecology, Emory University School of Medicine; Assistant Gynecologist, Grady Hospital; Surgeon, MacVicar Hospital.

DE PUY, CLARENCE A., M.D., 532 Fifteenth Street, Oakland, California. College of Physicians and Surgeons, San Francisco, 1905. Assistant Chief Gynecologist and Obstetrician, Alameda County Hospital, San Leandro, Chief of Woman's Clinic, Public Health Center, Oakland; Staff Surgeon, Alameda County Receiving Hospital; Member of Staff, Providence Hospital.

DE QUERVAIN, JEAN FREDERIC, M.D., Seftigenstrasse 2, Berne, Switzerland. University of Berne, 1891. Chief of Surgical Clinic, University of Berne.

DERBY, GEORGE S., A.B., M.D., 23 Bay State Road, Boston, Massachusetts. Harvard Medical School, 1900. Assistant Professor in Ophthalmology, Harvard Medical School; Ophthalmic Surgeon, Massachusetts Charitable Eye and Ear Infirmary; Ophthalmologist, Infants' Hospital; Assistant Ophthalmologist, Massachusetts General Hospital; Consulting Ophthalmic Surgeon, Carney Hospital.

DERBY, RICHARD, A.B., M.D., Oyster Bay, New York. Columbia University, College of Physicians and Surgeons, 1907. Consulting Surgeon, Huntington and Nassau Hospitals; Junior Attending Surgeon, St. Luke's Hospital.

DERCLE, CHARLES U., M.D., A.M., Army Medical School, Val-de-Grâce, Paris, France. University of Lyons, 1892. Colonel, French Army Medical Corps.

DESSEZ, PAUL T., M.D., Medical Corps, United States Navy, Washington, District of Columbia. Georgetown University School of Medicine, 1897. Commander, Medical Corps, United States Navy.

DETLING, FRANK E., M.D., 756 South Broadway, Los Angeles, California. Northwestern University Medical School, 1901. Attending Aural Surgeon, Los Angeles County and Children's Hospitals.

DE VALIN, CHARLES MOORE, M.D., United States Navy, Washington, District of Columbia. George Washington University Medical School, 1891. Captain, Medical Corps, United States Navy.

DE VECCHI, PAOLO, M.D., 43 Fifth Avenue, New York, New York. University of Torino, 1872.

DEWAR, BENNETT W., M.D., 59 Chestnut Street, Cooperstown, New York. Albany Medical College, 1892. Surgeon, Thanksgiving, County, and Orphanage Hospitals.

DEWITT, JOHN PIERCE, M.D., 122 Shorb Avenue, Northwest, Canton, Ohio. Western Reserve University School of Medicine, 1895. Surgeon, Aultman Memorial Hospital.

DEWITT, WALLACE, M.D., Medical Corps, United States Army, Washington, District of Columbia. University of Pennsylvania School of Medicine, 1900. Lieutenant Colonel, Medical Corps, United States Army.

DICE, WILLIAM GORDON, A.B., M.D., 240 Michigan Street, Toledo, Ohio. Columbia University, College of Physicians and Surgeons, 1896. Attending Obstetrician, Flower and Mercy Hospitals.

DICKEN, WILLIAM EDWARD, M.D., 518 First National Bank Building, Oklahoma, Oklahoma. St. Louis College of Physicians and Surgeons, 1901. Surgeon-in-Chief, Oklahoma State Baptist Hospital; Surgeon, Oklahoma State Baptist Orphans' Home; Local Surgeon, Missouri, Kansas and Texas Railway.

DICKENSON, JOHN, M.D., 1021 Prospect Avenue, Cleveland, Ohio. Western Reserve University School of Medicine, 1901. Assistant to Chair of Principles of Surgery and Instructor in Surgery, Western Reserve University School of Medicine; Assistant Visiting Surgeon and Surgeon in Charge, Out-Patient Department, St. Vincent's Charity Hospital.

DICKINSON, BREESE MORSE, A.B., M.D., 637 Union Arcade Building, Pittsburgh, Pennsylvania. University of Pennsylvania School of Medicine, 1898. Laryngologist, Rhinologist, and Otologist, Mercy Hospital.

DICKINSON, ELIJAH THOMAS, B.Sc., M.D., 219 East Nash Street, Wilson, North Carolina. Medical College of Virginia, 1895. Surgeon in Charge, Wilson Sanatorium.

DICKINSON, GORDON KIMBALL, M.D., 280 Montgomery Street, Jersey City, New Jersey. University and Bellevue Hospital Medical College, 1877. Surgeon, Christ and City Hospitals; Consulting Surgeon, Bayonne Hospital and Dispensary, Bayonne, North Hudson Hospital, Weehawken, Stumpf Memorial Hospital, Kearny.

DICKINSON, MELVILLE DAY, M.D., 1937 Fifth Avenue, Troy, New York. Albany Medical College, 1890. Gynecologist and Surgeon, Troy Hospital.

DICKINSON, ROBERT L., M.D., 13 East Sixty-fifth Street, New York, New York. Long Island College Hospital, 1882. Clinical Professor of Gynecology, Long Island College Hospital; Senior Gynecologist and Obstetrician, Brooklyn Hospital, Brooklyn; Consulting Obstetrician, Methodist Episcopal Hospital, Brooklyn.

DICKS, J. OSCAR, M.D., 28 South High Street, West Chester, Pennsylvania. Hahnemann Medical College and Hospital, Philadelphia, 1899. Member of Surgical Staff and Chief of X-Ray Department, Chester County Homeopathic Hospital.

DICKS, JOHN FLEMING, M.D., 3529 Prytania Street, New Orleans, Louisiana. Tulane University of Louisiana School of Medicine, 1912. Instructor, Gynecology and Obstetrics, Tulane University; Visiting Gynecologist and Obstetrician, Charity Hospital.

DICKS, JOHN W. D., M.D., 207 Linton Avenue, Natchez, Mississippi. Tulane University of Louisiana School of Medicine, 1899. Surgeon in Charge, Natchez Charity Hospital.

DICKSON, FRANK DRAKE, M.D., 403 Waldheim Building, Kansas City, Missouri. University of Pennsylvania School of Medicine, 1905. Orthopedic Surgeon, Christian Church Hospital.

DICKSON, JOHN FOREST, M.B., M.D., L.R.C.P. (Edin.), Selling Building, Portland, Oregon. University of Toronto, Faculty of Medicine, 1880. Professor of Ophthalmology, Otology, and Rhinology, University of Oregon Medical School; Surgeon, St. Vincent's, Portland Eye, Ear, Nose, and Throat Hospitals; Oculist and Aurist, Spokane, Portland and Seattle, Oregon Trunk, Astoria and Columbia River, and Oregon Electric Railways.

DIEFFENBACH, RICHARD HAGEN, M.D., 570 Mt. Prospect Avenue, Newark, New Jersey. Columbia University, College of Physicians and Surgeons, 1904. Associate Attending Surgeon, Newark City and Newark Memorial Hospitals; Chief of Gynecologic Clinic, Newark Memorial Hospital.

DILLON, EDWARD THOMAS, M.Sc., M.D., St. Vincent's Hospital, Los Angeles, California. University of California Medical School, Los Angeles, 1901. Surgeon in Charge, St. Vincent's Hospital.

DILWORTH, WILLIAM DENNISON, M.D., 1220 South Pasadena Avenue, Pasadena, California. University of Illinois College of Medicine (College of Physicians and Surgeons, Chicago), 1894. Surgeon, Department of Ophthalmology, Rhinology, and Oto-Laryngology, Pasadena Hospital.

DIMITRY, THEODORE JOHN, M.D., 3601 Prytania Street, New Orleans, Louisiana. Tulane University of Louisiana School of Medicine, 1901. Professor of Ophthalmology, Loyola Post-Graduate School of Medicine; Chief of Ophthalmic Division, Charity Hospital; Ophthalmologist, Diagnostic Clinic; Visiting Ophthalmic Surgeon, Hotel Dieu.

DINGMAN, JOHN HENRY, M.D., 258 Mill Street, Poughkeepsie, New York. Albany Medical College, 1901. Attending Surgeon, St. Francis' Hospital, Old Ladies' Home.

DINGMAN, THOMAS A., M.D., 330 Broadway, Paterson, New Jersey. Columbia University College of Physicians and Surgeons, 1904. Attending Surgeon, St. Joseph's Hospital; Attending Gynecologist, Miriam Barnert Memorial Hospital.

DIX, GEORGE E., M.D., Marshfield, Oregon. University of Minnesota Medical School, 1904. Chief Surgeon, C. A. Smith Lumber and Manufacturing Company, Smith Powers Logging Camp, Moore Mill and Lumber, Oregon Export Lumber, and North Bend Mill and Lumber Companies.

DIXON, ARCHIBALD, M.D., 330 North Green Street, Henderson, Kentucky. University of Louisville, Medical Department (Louisville Medical College), 1877. Surgeon, Henderson City Hospital.

DIXON, JOHN W., A.B., M.D., 820 Wood Street, Wilkinsburg, Pennsylvania. University of Pennsylvania School of Medicine, 1897. Surgeon, Columbia Hospital.

DIXON, W. EUGENE, M.D., 706 State National Bank Building, Oklahoma, Oklahoma. University of Louisville, Medical Department, 1894. Associate Professor of Oto-Laryngology and Rhinology, University of Oklahoma School of Medicine; Ophthalmologist, Oto-Laryngologist, and Rhinologist, Wesley, Oklahoma State Baptist Hospitals, and Holmes Home of Redeeming Love; Oto-Laryngologist, and Rhinologist, State University and University Emergency Hospitals; Chief of Staff, Department of Ophthalmology, Rhinology, and Oto-Laryngology, Oklahoma Orphans' Home Society.

DIXON, WILLIAM CLARENCE, M.D., 216 Doctors Building, Nashville, Tennessee. Vanderbilt University, Medical Department, 1903. Associate Professor of Gynecology, Vanderbilt University, Medical Department; Surgeon, St. Thomas and Nashville City Hospitals.

DOANE, L. LEO, A.B., M.D., Ph.D., 558 Third Street, Butler, Pennsylvania. University of Maryland School of Medicine (College of Physicians and Surgeons, Baltimore), 1886. Ophthalmologist, Rhinologist, and Oto-Laryngologist, Butler County General Hospital.

DOANE, PHILIP SCHUYLER, M.D., 424 Consolidated Realty Building, Los Angeles, California. Rush Medical College, 1895.

DOBBIN, GEORGE W., A.B., M.D., 58 West Biddle Street, Baltimore, Maryland. University of Maryland School of Medicine, 1894. Professor of Obstetrics and Gynecology, University of Maryland School of Medicine and College of Physicians and Surgeons; Obstetrician-in-Chief, Maryland Lying-in Asylum; Visiting Obstetrician, Mercy Hospital, Hospital for Women of Maryland, Church Home and Infirmary, Hebrew Hospital and Asylum.

DOBSON, LINDLEY, M.D., 163 Main Street, Presque Isle, Maine. University and Bellevue Hospital Medical College, (New York University Medical School), 1891. Attending Surgeon, Presque Isle General Hospital.

DOBSON, WALTER B., M.D., Century Building, Jackson, Mississippi. Tulane University of Louisiana School of Medicine, 1904. Member of Visiting Staff, Charity and Mississippi State Baptist Hospitals.

DODD, JOHN MORRIS, M.D., 619 West Third Street, Ashland, Wisconsin. Ohio State University College of Medicine (Starling Medical College), 1889. Surgeon, St. Joseph's and Ashland General Hospitals; Chicago and Northwestern, Minneapolis, St. Paul and Sault Ste. Marie, and Chicago, St. Paul, Minneapolis and Omaha Railways.

DODD, OSCAR, M.D., 1604 Chicago Avenue, Evanston, Illinois. University of Illinois College of Medicine (College of Physicians and Surgeons, Chicago), 1890. Ophthalmologist and Otologist, Evanston Hospital; Consulting Ophthalmologist and Otologist, Augustana Hospital, Chicago.

DODD, VERNE ADAMS, M.D., 394 East Town Street, Columbus, Ohio. Ohio State University College of Medicine (Ohio Medical University), 1903. Professor of Surgery, Ohio State University, College of Medicine; Chief of Staff, Protestant Hospital.

DODD, WILLIAM SCHAUFFLER, A.B., M.D., 81 South Mountain Avenue, Montclair, New Jersey. Columbia University, College of Physicians and Surgeons, 1886. Director, American Hospital, Konia, Turkey; Medical Director, Red Cross Commission to Palestine.

DODDS, EDGAR F., B.Sc., M.D., Perkins Building, Tacoma, Washington. Northwestern University Medical School, 1897.

DODGE, GEORGE E., B.Sc., M.D., 108 North Stone Avenue, Tucson, Arizona. University of Virginia, Department of Medicine, 1896.

DODGE, WILLIAM T., M.D., 115 South State Street, Big Rapids, Michigan. University of Michigan Medical School, 1880. Attending Surgeon, Mercy Hospital; Local Surgeon, Grand Rapids and Indiana, and Pere Marquette Railroads.

DOEGE, KARL, M.D., West Third Street and Central Avenue, Marshfield, Wisconsin. Western Reserve University School of Medicine, 1890. Surgeon-in-Chief, St. Joseph's Hospital; President, Marshfield Clinic.

DOERING, EDMUND JANES, M.Sc., M.D., 81 East Madison Street, Chicago, Illinois. Northwestern University Medical School, 1874. Member of Consulting Staff, Chicago Lying-in and Michael Reese Hospitals.

DOLAND, CHARLES McCLURE, M.D., 303 Spokane and Eastern Trust Building, Spokane, Washington. University of Pennsylvania School of Medicine, 1903.

DOLBEY, ROBERT VALENTINE, M.B., M.S., F.R.C.S. (Eng.), Kasr el Aini Hospital, Cairo, Egypt. University of London, 1903. Professor of Surgery, Cairo University.

DONALDSON, HARRY JAMES, M.D., 106 East Fourth Street, Williamsport, Pennsylvania. University of Pennsylvania School of Medicine, 1895. Abdominal Surgeon, Williamsport Hospital; Consulting Surgeon, State Hospital for Insane, Danville.

DONALDSON, HOLLAND HUNTER, A.M., M.D., Union Arcade Building, Pittsburgh, Pennsylvania. University of Pennsylvania School of Medicine, 1906. Instructor in Surgery, University of Pittsburgh School of Medicine; Junior Surgeon, Mercy Hospital.

DONHAUSER, JOSEPH LEWI, A.B., M.D., 252 State Street, Albany, New York. Albany Medical College, 1907. Clinical Professor of Surgery, Albany Medical College; Attending Surgeon, Child's Hospital; Assistant Attending Surgeon, Albany Hospital.

DONOHOE, LUCIUS FRANCIS, M.D., 33 Dodge Street, Bayonne, New Jersey. New York University Medical School, 1889. Surgeon and Member of Staff, Bayonne Hospital and Dispensary.

DONOVAN, JOHN ALEXANDER, M.D., 507 Phoenix Building, Butte, Montana. University of Michigan Medical School, 1894. Oculist and Aurist, State Schools for Deaf, Blind, and Backward Children, Northern Pacific, and Butte, Anaconda and Pacific Railroads.

DONOVAN, JOHN JOSEPH, A.B., B.Sc., M.D., 606 Armstrong Avenue, Litchfield, Minnesota. University of Minnesota Medical School, 1901. Chief of Staff, Litchfield Hospital; Surgeon, Paynesville Hospital, Paynesville, Benson Hospital, Benson.

DOOLITTLE, HAROLD MEDORIS, M.D., 4105 Live Oak Street, Dallas, Texas. University of Michigan Medical School, 1902. Professor of Clinical Surgery, Baylor University School of Medicine; Attending Surgeon, Parkland City Hospital; Member of Executive Staff, Baylor Hospital.

DOREMUS, WIDMER E., M.D., 32 Fulton Street, Newark, New Jersey. New York Homeopathic Medical College and Flower Hospital, 1901. Attending Surgeon, Homeopathic Hospital of Essex County, Newark, Stumpf Memorial Hospital, Kearny.

DORLAND, WILLIAM ALEXANDER NEWMAN, A.M., M.D., 7 West Madison Street, Chicago, Illinois. University of Pennsylvania School of Medicine, 1886. Professor of Obstetrics, Loyola University School of Medicine; Professor of Gynecology, Post-Graduate Medical School; Member of Obstetrical Staff, Cook County Hospital; Gynecologist, Post-Graduate Hospital.

DORMAN, FRANKLIN ABBOTT, A.M., M.D., 133 East Fifty-seventh Street, New York, New York. Columbia University College of Physicians and Surgeons, 1898. Obstetrical Surgeon, Woman's Hospital; Obstetrician, City Hospital; Consulting Obstetrician, White Plains Hospital, White Plains, Lawrence Hospital, Bronxville, Mountainside Hospital, Montclair, New Jersey, Eastern Long Island Hospital, Greenport.

DORR, R. C., M.D., Batesville, Arkansas. Washington University Medical School (Missouri Medical College), 1883. Chief Surgeon, Dorr, Gray, and Johnston Sanitarium.

DORRANCE, GEORGE MORRIS, M.D., 2025 Walnut Street, Philadelphia, Pennsylvania. University of Pennsylvania School of Medicine, 1900. Professor of Maxillo-Facial Surgery, Thomas Evans Institute, University of Pennsylvania School of Medicine; Consulting Surgeon in Maxillo-Facial Surgery, University Hospital; Surgeon, St. Agnes' Hospital; Oral Surgeon, Philadelphia General Hospital; Consulting Surgeon, Sacred Heart Hospital, Allentown.

DORSETT, EDWARD LEE, M.D., 505 University Club Building, St. Louis, Missouri. St. Louis University School of Medicine, 1906. Obstetrician, Out-Patient's Department, Washington University School of Medicine, St. Louis City Hospital; Gynecologist, Evangelical Deaconess Hospital and Missouri Baptist Sanitarium; Assistant in Clinical Obstetrics, Washington University School of Medicine.

DORSEY, BENJAMIN H., M.D., Medical Corps, United States Navy, Washington, District of Columbia. University of Maryland School of Medicine, 1901. Commander, Medical Corps, United States Navy.

DORSEY, JACOB GRAY, M.D., 201 North Main Street, Wichita, Kansas. State University of Iowa College of Medicine (College of Physicians and Surgeons, Keokuk), 1883. Ophthalmologist, St. Francis Hospital.

DOUGHERTY, DANIEL S., B.Sc., M.D., 111 West Eighty-fifth Street, New York, New York. University and Bellevue Hospital Medical College (University of the City of New York, Medical Department), 1884. Professor of Clinical Laryngology and Rhinology, New York Polyclinic Medical School; Attending Otologist and Laryngologist, City Hospital; Attending Laryngologist, New York Polyclinic Medical School and Hospital; Consulting Otologist, People's and Jewish Memorial Hospitals.

DOUGHTIE, CHARLES WILSON, M.D., 512 Taylor Building, Norfolk, Virginia. Medical College of Virginia, 1898. Gynecologist, Norfolk Protestant Hospital.

DOUGHTY, WILLIAM HENRY, JR., A.B., M.D., 822 Greene Street, Augusta, Georgia. University of Georgia, Medical Department, 1878. Dean, and Professor of Surgery, University of Georgia, Medical Department; Consulting Surgeon, University Hospital; Chief Surgeon, Charleston and Western Carolina, Georgia and Florida, and Augusta Southern Railroads, Augusta-Aiken Railway and Electric Corporation; Resident Surgeon, Georgia Railroad.

DOUGHTY, WILLIAM McDOWELL, M.D., 628 Elm Street, Cincinnati, Ohio. University of Cincinnati College of Medicine (Miami Medical College), 1906. Assistant Director of Roentgenology, Cincinnati General Hospital; Radiographer, Children's Hospital of the Protestant Episcopal Church, Christ Hospital.

DOUGLAS, FRED J., M.D., 285 Genesee Street, Utica, New York. Dartmouth Medical School, 1894. Attending Surgeon, Faxton Hospital; Consulting Surgeon, Utica State Hospital.

DOUGLAS, JOHN, B.Sc., M.D., 568 Park Avenue, New York, New York. Columbia University, College of Physicians and Surgeons, 1898. Clinical Professor of Surgery, University and Bellevue Hospital Medical College; Visiting Surgeon, Bellevue Hospital; Associate Surgeon, St. Luke's Hospital; Surgical Director, Knickerbocker Hospital.

DOUGLASS, FRED MELVIN, M.D., 421 Michigan Street, Toledo, Ohio. Medical Department, Toledo University, 1911. Surgeon, Lucas County and St. Vincent's Hospitals.

DOWD, CHARLES N., A.M., M.D., 138 West Fifty-eighth Street, New York, New York. Columbia University, College of Physicians and Surgeons, 1886. Professor of Clinical Surgery, Columbia University, College of Physicians and Surgeons; Surgeon, Roosevelt Hospital; Consulting Surgeon, Memorial Hospital, St. Mary's Free Hospital for Children, New York, Lulu Thorley Lyon Home for Crippled and Delicate Children, Claverack, Richmond Memorial Hospital, Prince Bay.

DOWDALL, GUY GRIGSBY, A.B., M.D., 135 East Eleventh Place, Chicago, Illinois. University of Illinois College of Medicine (College of Physicians and Surgeons, Chicago), 1900. Chief of Staff, Illinois Central Hospital.

DOWLING, J. IVIMEY, M.D., 116 Washington Avenue, Albany, New York. New York Homeopathic Medical College and Flower Hospital, 1895. Chief of Staff and Attending Oculist and Aurist, Homeopathic Hospital.

DOWLING, J. THOMAS, M.D., 1101 Terry Avenue, Seattle, Washington. Northwestern University Medical School, 1902. Attending Oculist and Aurist, Virginia Mason Hospital; Consulting Oculist and Aurist, King County Hospital; Member of Staff, Virginia Mason and Providence Hospitals.

DOWMAN, CHARLES EDWARD, A.B., M.D, 78 Forrest Avenue, Atlanta, Georgia. Johns Hopkins University, Medical Department, 1905. Associate in Surgery, Emory University School of Medicine; Visiting Surgeon, Wesley Memorial Hospital; Chief of Neuro-Surgical Department, Georgia Baptist Hospital; Neuro-Surgeon, Scottish Rite Hospital for Crippled Children.

DOWNES, WILLIAM AUGUSTUS, M.D., 424 Park Avenue, New York, New York. Columbia University, College of Physicians and Surgeons, 1895. Professor of Clinical Surgery, Columbia University, College of Physicians and Surgeons; Attending Surgeon, St. Luke's, Memorial, and Babies' Hospitals; Consulting Surgeon, Manhattan State Hospital, Hospital for Ruptured and Crippled, New York Infirmary for Women and Children, New York, United Hospital, Port Chester.

DOWNEY, JAMES HENRY, M.D, 13 Sycamore Street, Gainesville, Georgia. Emory University School of Medicine (Atlanta Medical College), 1887. Chief Surgeon, Downey Hospital.

DOWNEY, JAMES MAURICE, Phar.G., M.D., 381 Clinton Street, Brooklyn, New York. Long Island College Hospital, 1891. Attending Surgeon, Hospital of the Holy Family; Consulting Surgeon, Mercy Hospital, Hempstead.

DOWNEY, JESSE WRIGHT, JR., M.D., 529 North Charles Street, Baltimore, Maryland. University of Virginia, Department of Medicine, 1905. Clinical Professor of Otology, University of Maryland School of Medicine and College of Physicians and Surgeons; Surgeon, Baltimore Eye, Ear, and Throat Charity Hospital.

DOWNING, ARTHUR T., A.B., M.D., 13 Main Street, Littleton, New Hampshire. Dartmouth Medical School, 1903. Member of Staff, Littleton Hospital.

DOYLE, FRANCIS BENEDICT, M.D., 145 Sixth Avenue, Brooklyn, New York. Long Island College Hospital, 1903. Obstetrician, Samaritan Hospital; Associate in Obstetrics and Gynecology, Greenpoint and Holy Family Hospitals.

DOYLE, JOHN MONOHAN, M.D., Corby-Forsee Building, St. Joseph, Missouri. Ensworth Medical College, 1897; Washington University Medical School (Missouri Medical College), 1898. Surgeon, St. Joseph's and Noyes Hospitals.

DOYLE, WILLIAM JOSEPH, M.D., City Dairies Building, St. Louis, Missouri. St. Louis University School of Medicine (Beaumont Hospital Medical College), 1901; Washington University Medical School, 1903. Visiting Surgeon, St. Louis City Hospital; Surgeon, St. Mary's Infirmary.

DRAESEKE, GORDON C., M.B., 543 Granville Street, Vancouver, British Columbia. University of Toronto, Faculty of Medicine, 1902.

DRAPER, ALFRED LAWRENCE, M.D., Shreve Building, San Francisco, California. Cooper Medical College, 1900. Instructor in Surgery, University of California Medical School; Surgeon, Franklin Hospital; Assistant Visiting Surgeon, San Francisco Hospital.

DRAPER, JAMES A., A.B., M.D., 1015 Washington Street, Wilmington, Delaware. University of Pennsylvania School of Medicine, 1898. Surgeon, Delaware Hospital.

DRAPER, JOHN WILLIAM, B.Sc., M.D., 9 East Fortieth Street, New York, New York. University and Bellevue Hospital Medical College (New York University Medical College), 1898. Attending Surgeon, St. Bartholomew's Hospital; Attending Surgeon in Gastroenterology, State Hospital, Trenton, New Jersey.

DRENNEN, W. EARLE, A.B., M.D., 519 American Trust Building, Birmingham, Alabama. Columbia University, College of Physicians and Surgeons, 1906. Attending Surgeon, Children's and Hillman Hospitals, South Highlands Infirmary.

DRETZKA, LEO, M.D., 1002 David Whitney Building, Detroit, Michigan. Marquette University School of Medicine, 1912. Consulting Surgeon, Receiving Hospital.

DRINKARD, ROBERT U., B.Sc., M.D., Wheeling Steel Corporation Building, Wheeling, West Virginia. Johns Hopkins University, Medical Department, 1908. Member of Surgical Staff, Ohio Valley General Hospital; Staff Surgeon, Wheeling Hospital.

DRIVER, WILSON ELLIOTT, M.D., 225 Granby Street, Norfolk, Virginia. University of Maryland School of Medicine, 1893.

DRURY, DANA WARREN, M.D., 483 Beacon Street, Boston, Massachusetts. Harvard Medical School, 1904. Assistant Professor of Otology, Tufts Medical School; Assistant Otologist, Harvard Medical School; Assistant Oral Surgeon, Massachusetts Charitable Eye and Ear Infirmary; Aurist, Boston Floating Hospital; Consulting Aurist, Burbank Hospital, Fitchburg, and Norwood Hospital, Norwood.

DRURY, ROBERT BLEE, M.D., 283 East State Street, Columbus, Ohio. Ohio State University College of Medicine (Starling Medical College), 1908. Surgeon, Grant Hospital, Franklin County Sanatorium; Consulting Surgeon, St. Ann's Infant Asylum.

DU BOSE, FRANCIS GOODWIN, M.D., 400 Lauderdale Street, Selma, Alabama. Tulane University of Louisiana School of Medicine, 1893. Surgeon in Charge, Vaughan Memorial Hospital.

DUCKERING, FLORENCE W., M.D., 520 Beacon Street, Boston, Massachusetts. Tufts College Medical School, 1901. Visiting Surgeon, Massachusetts Women's Hospital, New England Hospital for Women and Children.

DUCKWORTH, GUILFORD MARVIN, M.D., Buchel Building, Cuero, Texas. Vanderbilt University, Medical Department, 1901. Consulting Ophthalmologist and Oto-Laryngologist, Reuss Memorial Hospital.

DUDGEON, HOWARD R., M.D., 2200 Gorman Street, Waco, Texas. University of Texas, Medical Department, 1899.

DUDLEY, AUGUSTUS WILLIAM, A.M., M.D., 1740 Massachusetts Avenue, Cambridge, Massachusetts. Harvard Medical School, 1895. Surgeon, Cambridge Hospital.

DUDLEY, EMILIUS CLARK, A.M., M.D., LL.D., 242 East Walton Place, Chicago, Illinois. Long Island College Hospital, 1875. Emeritus Professor of Gynecology, Northwestern University Medical School; Gynecologist, St. Luke's Hospital.

DUDLEY, FRANK WILBURN, M.D., St. Paul's Hospital, Manila, Philippine Islands. University of California Medical School, 1895. Chief Surgeon, St. Paul's Hospital.

DUDLEY, HOMER D., M.D., 403 Cobb Building, Seattle, Washington. Northwestern University Medical School, 1902. Attending Surgeon and President of Staff, King County Hospital; Member of Staff, Providence Hospital.

DUDLEY, WILLIAM HENRY, M.D., 512 Brockman Building, Los Angeles, California. University and Bellevue Hospital Medical College (University of the City of New York, Medical Department), 1882; University of California Medical School, Los Angeles, 1906.

DUEL, ARTHUR BALDWIN, M.D., 27 East Fifty-seventh Street, New York, New York. Harvard Medical School, 1894. Surgeon and Director, Ear Department, Manhattan Eye, Ear, and Throat Hospital; Consulting Aural Surgeon, Babies', New York Skin and Cancer, and New York Health Board Hospitals.

DUFFIELD, WARREN L., M.D., 119 Berkeley Place, Brooklyn, New York. Long Island College Hospital, 1898. Attending Surgeon, St. John's Hospital, Methodist Episcopal Church Home; Consulting Surgeon, Brooklyn Eye and Ear Hospital, Brooklyn, South Side Hospital, Babylon.

DUFFY, RICHARD N., A.B., M.D., 130 Craven Street, Newbern, North Carolina. Johns Hopkins University, Medical Department, 1906. Surgeon, Newbern General Hospital.

DUFFY, WILLIAM CORE, A.B., M.D., New Haven Hospital, New Haven, Connecticut. Johns Hopkins University, Medical Department, 1914. Instructor in Surgery, Yale University School of Medicine; Surgeon, New Haven Hospital.

DUKES, CHARLES ALFRED, M.D., Central Bank Building, Oakland, California. Cooper Medical College, 1895. Chief Surgeon, Gynecological Staff, Samuel Merritt Hospital.

DUNBAR, ARTHUR WHITE, M.D., Medical Corps, United States Navy, Washington, District of Columbia. University of California Medical School, 1891. Captain, Medical Corps, United States Navy.

DUNCAN, ELLIS, M.D., 705 Starks Building, Louisville, Kentucky. University of Louisville Medical Department, 1896. Visiting Surgeon, SS. Mary and Elizabeth and Louisville City Hospitals.

DUNCAN, FRED W., M.D., 818 Maple Street, Coffeyville, Kansas. Washington University Medical School, 1906. Surgeon, Southeastern Kansas Hospital.

DUNCAN, HARRY A., A.B., M.D., 2615 West Somerset Street, Philadelphia, Pennsylvania. Medico-Chirurgical College of Philadelphia, 1904. Associate in Gynecology, Temple University Department of Medicine; Assistant Gynecologist, Samaritan Hospital; Assistant Obstetrician, Philadelphia General Hospital.

DUNCAN, JAMES WILLIAM, M.D., C.M., 141 Crescent Street, Montreal, Quebec. Faculty of Medicine, McGill University, 1901. Lecturer on Obstetrics, Faculty of Medicine, McGill University; Assistant Obstetrician, Montreal Maternity Hospital.

DUNLAP, ELBERT, Phar.G., M.D., 304 Southwestern Life Building, Dallas, Texas. St. Louis University School of Medicine, 1896. Professor of Gynecology, Baylor University School of Medicine; Gynecologist-in-Chief, Baylor Hospital; Member of Gynecological Staff, Parkland City Hospital; Division Surgeon, Southern Pacific Railway.

DUNLOP, JOHN, B.Sc., M.D., 803 Pacific Mutual Building, Los Angeles, California. Johns Hopkins University, Medical Department, 1902.

DUNN, HARRISON A., M.D., 230 West Eighth Street, Erie, Pennsylvania. Jefferson Medical College, 1905. Surgeon, Hamot Hospital.

DUNTLEY, GEORGE S., Ph.G., M.D., 408 East Main Street, Bushnell, Illinois. Northwestern University School, 1906. Member of . Staff, Marietta Phelps Hospital, Macomb.

DURANT, CHARLES EDWIN, M.D., 105 Emerson Street, Haverhill, Massachusetts. Harvard Medical School, 1885. Surgeon, Hale Hospital.

DURHAM, ROGER, A.B., M.D., 322 Park Place, Brooklyn, New York. Columbia University, College of Physicians and Surgeons, 1903. Assistant Surgeon, Methodist Episcopal Hospital; Visiting Surgeon, Greenpoint Hospital; Surgeon, King's Park State Hospital, King's Park, Brooklyn Industrial School and Home for Destitute Children, Brooklyn.

DURINGER, WILLIAM A., M.D., 205 Fort Worth Club Building, Fort Worth, Texas. Tulane University of Louisiana School of Medicine, 1885. Member of Staff, All Saints Hospital; Surgeon, Chicago, Rock Island and Gulf Railroad; Local Surgeon, Sunset Lines.

DURINGER, WILLIAM COMMODORE, M.D., 205 Fort Worth Club Building, Fort Worth, Texas. Medical Department Texas Christian University, 1907.

DURNIN, GEORGE ALEXANDER, M.D., C.M., Bottineau, North Dakota. University of Toronto, Faculty of Medicine, 1904. Surgeon, St. Andrew Hospital.

DURRIN, WILLIAM C., M.D., 1215 Dean Street, Brooklyn, New York. New York Homeopathic Medical College and Flower Hospital, 1899. Gynecologist, Cumberland Street Hospital.

DUTROW, HOWARD VICTOR, M.D., 1040 Fidelity Medical Building, Dayton, Ohio. University of Maryland School of Medicine, 1904. Member of Senior Staff, Eye, Ear, Nose and Throat Department, Miami Valley Hospital.

DUVAL, DOUGLAS F., B.Sc., M.A., M.D., Medical Corps, United States Army, Washington, District of Columbia. University of Virginia, Department of Medicine, 1894. Colonel, Medical Corps, United States Army.

DUVAL, PIERRE, 119 Rue de Lille, Paris, France. Faculty of Medicine, Paris, 1902. Honorary Professor, Faculty of Medicine; Surgeon, Hospitals of Paris; Consulting Surgeon, Seventh Army; Major, French Army Medical Corps.

DWIGHT, CORYDON GREENWOOD, M.D., 113 West Washington Avenue, Madison, Wisconsin. Hahnemann Medical College and Hospital, Chicago, 1897. Surgeon-in-Chief, Department of Ophthalmology and Oto-Laryngology, Madison General Hospital.

DWIGHT, KIRBY, A.B., M.D., 1045 Madison Avenue, New York, New York. Columbia University, College of Physicians and Surgeons, 1905. Instructor in Surgery, Columbia University, College of Physicians and Surgeons; Second Assistant Attending Surgeon, Roosevelt Hospital, Out-Patient Department.

DYAS, FREDERICK G., M.D., 25 East Washington Street, Chicago, Illinois. Northwestern University Medical School, 1904. Associate Professor of Surgery and Clinical Surgery, University of Illinois College of Medicine; Attending Surgeon, Cook County Hospital; Assistant Attending Surgeon, St. Luke's Hospital.

DYE, JOHN SINCLAIR, A.B., M.D., Lilley Building, Waterbury, Connecticut. Vanderbilt University, Medical Department, 1900; Columbia University, College of Physicians and Surgeons, 1915. Attending Surgeon, Waterbury and St. Mary's Hospitals.

DYE, WILLOUGHBY G., M.D., 502 Merritt Building, Los Angeles, California. Northwestern University Medical School, 1901.

DYER, FRANK M., M.D., 51 Main Street, Binghamton, New York. Cornell University Medical College, 1902. Surgeon, Binghamton City Hospital.

EAGLESON, JAMES BEATY, M.D., 902 Boren Avenue, Seattle, Washington. University of Illinois College of Medicine (College of Physicians and Surgeons, Chicago), 1885. Chairman of Staff and Consulting Surgeon, Seattle Children's Orthopedic Hospital.

EAGLETON, WELLS PHILLIPS, M.D., 15 Lombardy Street, Newark, New Jersey. Columbia University, College of Physicians and Surgeons, 1888. Chief of Division of Surgery of the Head, Newark City Hospital; Attending Ophthalmologist and Otologist, Essex County Isolation Hospital; Adjunct Surgeon, St. James Hospital; Consulting Surgeon, Newark Memorial, Woman's, and Children's Hospitals, Essex County Hospital for the Insane; Consulting Ophthalmologist and Otologist, Home for Crippled Children, Newark, Morristown Memorial Hospital, Morristown; Medical Director, Newark Eye and Ear Infirmary; Consulting Cranial Surgeon, St. Barnabas' Hospital, Newark, Mountainside Hospital, Montclair, and Muhlenburg Hospital; Cranial Surgeon, Presbyterian Hospital.

EARHART, TROY W., M.D., Ancon Hospital, Ancon, Canal Zone. Indiana University School of Medicine (Central College of Physicians and Surgeons), 1905. Chief of Surgical Clinic, Ancon Hospital.

EARL, GEORGE ARTHUR, A.B., M.D., 1210 Lowry Building, St. Paul, Minnesota. University of Minnesota Medical School, 1909. Surgeon, Mounds Park Sanitarium, Midway and Merriam Park Hospitals.

EARL, GEORGE HENRY, M.D., 1138 Boylston Street, Boston, Massachusetts. Professor of Obstetrics, Boston University School of Medicine; Consulting Obstetrician, Massachusetts Homeopathic Hospital; Obstetrician in Charge, Talitha Cumi Maternity Hospital.

EARL, ROBERT, M.D., Lowry Building, St. Paul, Minnesota. University of Minnesota Medical School, 1896. Surgeon, Mounds Park Sanitarium, Midway Hospital, State Hospital for Indigent Crippled and Deformed Children; Consulting Surgeon, Bethesda Hospital.

EARLE, CURRAN BERTRAM, A.B., M.D., Wallace Building, Greenville, South Carolina. University of Maryland School of Medicine, 1896.

EARLE, SAMUEL T., JR., M.D., 1431 Linden Avenue, Baltimore, Maryland. University of Maryland School of Medicine, 1870. Proctologist, Hospital for Women of Maryland, St. Joseph's Hospital, Hebrew Hospital and Asylum.

EAST, CLARENCE WILSON, M.D., St. John's Hospital, Springfield, Illinois. Northwestern University Medical School, 1904. Consulting Surgeon, Mooseheart School, Mooseheart; Attending Surgeon, St. John's Hospital; Medical Director, St. John's Sanatorium; Chief of Division of Child Hygiene, State Department of Public Health.

EASTMAN, JOSEPH RILUS, B.Sc., A.M., M.D., 331 North Delaware Street, Indianapolis, Indiana. University of Berlin, 1897. Professor of Surgery, Indiana University School of Medicine; Surgeon, Indianapolis City Hospital.

EASTMAN, WILLIAM R., Ph.B., M.D., Medical Corps, United States Army, Washington, District of Columbia. George Washington University Medical School (Columbian University, Washington), 1901. Lieutenant Colonel, Medical Corps, United States Army.

EATON, WILLIAM E., M.D., Medical Corps, United States Navy, Washington, District of Columbia. Harvard Medical School, 1905. Lieutenant Commander, Medical Corps, United States Navy.

EBERTS, EDMOND MELCHIOR, M.D., C.M., M.R.C.S. (Eng.), L.R.C.P. (Lond.), 219 Peel Street, Montreal, Quebec. Faculty of Medicine, McGill University, 1897. Assistant Professor of Surgery and Clinical Surgery, Faculty of Medicine, McGill University; Surgeon, Montreal General Hospital.

EBRIGHT, EDWIN DELTA, M.D., 919 Beacon Building, Wichita, Kansas. University of Kansas School of Medicine, 1896. Orthopedic Surgeon, Wichita and Wesley Hospitals.

EDGAR, JAMES CLIFTON, Ph.B., A.M., M.D., 28 West Fifty-sixth Street, New York, New York. University and Bellevue Hospital Medical College (New York University Medical College), 1885. Professor of Obstetrics and Clinical Midwifery, Cornell University Medical College; Attending Obstetrician, Bellevue Hospital; Obstetrical Surgeon, Manhattan Maternity Hospital and Dispensary; Consulting Obstetrician, New York Maternity and Jewish Maternity Hospitals, New York, Greenwich General Hospital, Greenwich, Connecticut.

EDGER, BENJAMIN JONES, JR., A.B., M.D., Medical Corps, United States Army, Washington, District of Columbia. University of Pennsylvania School of Medicine, 1897. Colonel, Medical Corps, United States Army.

EDMUNDS, PAGE, M.D., 605 Park Avenue, Baltimore, Maryland. University of Maryland School of Medicine, 1898. Clinical Professor of Genito-Urinary Surgery, University of Maryland School of Medicine and College of Physicians and Surgeons; Visiting Surgeon, University Hospital; Chief Surgeon, Washington, Baltimore, and Annapolis Electric Railway and Maryland Electric Railway Companies; Consulting and General Surgeon, Baltimore and Ohio Railroad Company.

EDWARDS, GEORGE M., A.B., M.D., Medical Corps, United States Army, Washington, District of Columbia. University of Pennsylvania School of Medicine, 1903. Major, Medical Corps, United States Army.

EDWARDS, JOHN L., M.D., 12 South Fifth Street, Hudson, New York. Albany Medical College, 1912. Assistant Attending Surgeon, Hudson City Hospital.

EDWARDS, WILLIAM A., M.D., Security Building, Los Angeles, California. University of Pennsylvania School of Medicine, 1881.

EGGERS, CARL, M.D., 850 Park Avenue, New York, New York. Columbia University, College of Physicians and Surgeons, 1907. Associate Surgeon, Lenox Hill Hospital; Assistant Visiting Surgeon, New York Skin and Cancer Hospital.

EGGERT, CHARLES A., M.D., Prince Rupert, British Columbia. Faculty of Medicine, McGill University, 1907. Visiting Surgeon, Prince Rupert General Hospital.

EGLOFF, WILLIAM J., M.D., 21½ East State Street, Mason City, Iowa. Northwestern University Medical School (Chicago Medical College), 1887. Surgeon, Story Hospital, Chicago, Milwaukee and St. Paul, and Chicago and Northwestern Railways.

EHRENFEST, HUGO, M.D., Metropolitan Building, St. Louis, Missouri. University of Vienna, 1894. Gynecologist, Jewish Hospital; Consulting Obstetrician, St. Louis Maternity Hospital; Medical Director, St. Louis Obstetric Dispensary.

EHRENFRIED, ALBERT, A.B., M.D., 21 Bay State Road, Boston, Massachusetts. Harvard Medical School, 1905. Surgeon, Beth Israel and Boston Consumptives' Hospitals.

EHRICH, WILLIAM SEIGMAN, M.D., Citizens Bank Building, Evansville, Indiana. Medical College of the State of South Carolina, 1903. Genito-Urinary Surgeon, Protestant Deaconess Hospital; Urologist, Boehne Anti-Tuberculosis Hospital.

EIKENBARY, CHARLES F., M.D., 702 Paulsen Building, Spokane, Washington. Rush Medical College, 1903. Orthopedic Surgeon, St. Luke's, Sacred Heart, and Deaconess Hospitals.

EIKER, BERT L., M.D., Leon, Iowa. Rush Medical College, 1896.

EISENDRATH, DANIEL NATHAN, A.B., M.D., 4840 Woodlawn Avenue, Chicago, Illinois. Northwestern University Medical School, 1891. Clinical Professor of Surgery, Rush Medical College; Attending Surgeon, Michael Reese and Cook County Hospitals.

EISENSTAEDT, JOSEPH S., B.Sc., M.D., 25 East Washington Street, Chicago, Illinois. Northwestern University Medical School, 1908. Instructor, Northwestern University Medical School; Associate Urologist, Michael Reese Hospital; Member of Attending Staff, Wesley Memorial and Cook County Hospitals.

EKLUND, JOHN J., M.D., 7 East Superior Street, Duluth, Minnesota. University of Minnesota Medical School (Minnesota College Hospital), 1885. Member of Surgical Staff, St. Luke's Hospital.

EKWURZEL, GEORGE MACY, M.D., Medical Corps, United States Army, Washington, District of Columbia. University of Pennsylvania School of Medicine, 1897. Lieutenant Colonel, Medical Corps, United States Army.

ELBRECHT, O. H., Phar.B., M.D., 423 Metropolitan Building, St. Louis, Missouri. Washington University Medical School, 1901. Visiting Surgeon, St. Louis City Hospital; Consulting Surgeon, St. Louis Maternity, Bethesda, Josephine, and Missouri Pacific Hospitals.

ELDER, JOHN MUNRO, B.A., M.D., C.M., C.M.G., 731 Sherbrooke Street, West, Montreal, Quebec. Faculty of Medicine, McGill University, 1885. Surgeon, Montreal General Hospital.

ELIASON, ELDRIDGE LYON, A.B., M.D., 330 South Sixteenth Street, Philadelphia, Pennsylvania. University of Pennsylvania School of Medicine, 1905. Associate in Surgery, University of Pennsylvania School of Medicine; Assistant Surgeon, Hospital of the University of Pennsylvania, Philadelphia General Hospital; Surgeon, Howard Hospital, American Hospital for Diseases of the Stomach.

ELKIN, WILLIAM SIMPSON, A.B., M.D., 1029 Candler Building, Atlanta, Georgia. University of Pennsylvania School of Medicine, 1882. Dean and Professor of Gynecology, Emory University School of Medicine; Visiting Gynecologist, Wesley Memorial Hospital; Consulting Surgeon, Grady Memorial Hospital; Chief Surgeon, Atlanta, Birmingham and Atlantic Railway; Division Surgeon, Western and Atlantic Railroad.

ELLEGOOD, JOSHUA A., Equitable Building, Wilmington, Delaware. Jefferson Medical College, 1881. Ophthalmologist, Otologist, and Rhinologist, Delaware, Babies', Physicians and Surgeons Hospitals.

ELLETT, EDWARD COLEMAN, A.B., M.D., Exchange Building, Memphis, Tennessee. University of Pennsylvania School of Medicine, 1891. Professor of Ophthalmology, University of Tennessee College of Medicine; Ophthalmic Surgeon, Memphis General, Baptist Memorial, and Lucy Brinkley Hospitals.

ELLIOTT, GEORGE ROBERT, M.D., 40 East Forty-first Street, New York, New York. Columbia University College of Physicians and Surgeons, 1881. Assistant Professor of Clinical Orthopedic Surgery, Columbia University, College of Physicians and Surgeons; Orthopedic Surgeon, Montefiore, St. Francis and St. Joseph's Hospitals.

ELLIOTT, JOHN DEAN, M.D., 1421 Spruce Street, Philadelphia, Pennsylvania. Hahnemann Medical College and Hospital, Philadelphia, 1901. Associate Professor of Surgery, Hahnemann Medical College and Hospital; Surgeon, Abington Memorial Hospital, Abington; Assistant Surgeon, Hahnemann Medical College and Hospital.

ELLIOTT, MIDDLETON STUART, JR., M.D., Medical Corps, United States Navy, Washington, District of Columbia. George Washington University Medical School (Columbian University, Medical Department), 1894. Captain, Medical Corps, United States Navy.

ELLIS, EDWARD F., M.D., 104 North College Avenue, Fayetteville, Arkansas. Washington University Medical School (Missouri Medical College), 1885. Member of Staff, Fayetteville City Hospital.

ELLIS, GEORGE MANNING, M.D., 515 Volunteer Building, Chattanooga, Tennessee. University of Tennessee College of Medicine, 1887. Surgeon, West-Ellis Private Hospital; Consulting Surgeon, Baroness Erlanger Hospital.

ELLIS, H. BERT., A.B., M.D., 1219 Marsh-Strong Building, Los Angeles. California. University of California Medical School, Los Angeles, 1888, Associate in Ophthalmology, Graduate School of Medicine of the University of California; Consulting Ophthalmologist, Los Angeles County and Children's Hospitals.

ELLIS, JAMES NIMMO, M.D., 1205 Fourth National Bank Building, Atlanta, Georgia. Medical College of Virginia, 1889. Consulting Surgeon, Grady Memorial Hospital; Visiting Surgeon, St. Joseph Infirmary.

ELLIS, ROBERT HALE, M.D., 1011 Corbett Building, Portland, Oregon. Harvard Medical School, 1902. Gynecologist and Obstetrician, Emanuel Hospital; Consulting Obstetrician, Multnomah County Hospital.

ELMER, ALBERT WILLIAM, A.B., M.D., 810 East Locust Street, Davenport, Iowa. University of Pennsylvania School of Medicine, 1886. Member of Surgical Staff, St. Luke's and Mercy Hospitals.

ELMER, WALTER G., B.Sc., M.D., 1801 Pine Street, Philadelphia, Pennsylvania. University of Pennsylvania School of Medicine, 1897. Associate Professor of Orthopedic Surgery, University of Pennsylvania Graduate School of Medicine; Associate Orthopedic Surgeon, Polyclinic Hospital; Visiting Orthopedic Surgeon, Jewish Hospital.

ELMORE, BRUCE, A.B., M.D., Roosevelt Clinic, Seattle, Washington. Columbia University, College of Physicians and Surgeons, 1903.

ELSBERG, CHARLES A., A.B., M.D., 64 East Fifty-eighth Street, New York, New York. Columbia University, College of Physicians and Surgeons, 1893. Professor of Clinical Surgery, University and Bellevue Hospital Medical College; Surgeon, New York Neurological Institute; Attending Surgeon, Mt. Sinai Hospital; Consulting Surgeon, Montefiore Home, Manhattan State Hospital.

ELSE, J. EARL, Phar.G., M.Sc., M.D., 709 Stevens Building, Portland, Oregon. Northwestern University Medical School, 1905. Assistant Professor of Surgery, University of Oregon Medical School; Attending Surgeon, Emanuel Hospital.

ELTING, ARTHUR WELLS, A.B., M.D., 119 Washington Avenue, Albany, New York. Johns Hopkins University, Medical Department, 1898. Professor of Surgery, Albany Medical College; Surgeon, Albany and Child's Hospitals.

EMERSON, CLARENCE, B.Sc., M.D., Ph.D., Security Mutual Life Building, Lincoln, Nebraska. Rush Medical College, 1911. Surgeon, St. Elizabeth's Hospital.

EMERSON, FRANCIS PATTEN, M.D., 520 Commonwealth Avenue, Boston, Massachusetts. Columbia University, College of Physicians and Surgeons, 1886. Associate in Otology, Harvard Medical School; Consulting Aural Surgeon, Massachusetts General Hospital; Aural Surgeon, Massachusetts Charitable Eye and Ear Infirmary.

EMERSON, KENDALL, A.B., M.D., 56 William Street, Worcester, Massachusetts. Harvard Medical School, 1901. Orthopedic and Assistant Surgeon, Memorial Hospital.

EMERSON, LINN, M.D., Metropolitan Building, Orange, New Jersey. Jefferson Medical College, 1897. Ophthalmologist and Otologist, Orange Memorial Hospital, New Jersey Orthopedic Hospital and Dispensary, House of the

Good Shepherd, Orange, Orange Orphan Home, East Orange; Consulting Ophthalmologist and Otologist, Dover General Hospital, Dover.

EMERSON, MARK LEWIS, M.D., 1307 Broadway Street, Oakland, California. University of California Medical School, 1899. Chief of Surgical Staff, Merritt Hospital; Chief Surgeon, Bethlehem Shipbuilding Corporation, Alameda.

EMERSON, NATHANIEL W., A.M., M.D., 118 Forest Hills Street, Boston, Massachusetts. Boston University School of Medicine, 1881. Emeritus Professor of Gynecology, Boston University School of Medicine; Surgeon-in-Chief, Emerson Hospital, Jamaica Plain; Consulting Surgeon, Wesson Memorial Hospital, Springfield, Henry Heywood Memorial Hospital, Gardner, Melrose Hospital, Melrose, Massachusetts, Bath City Hospital, Bath, Trull Hospital, Biddeford, Maine.

EMERY, WALTER BRANHAM, M.D., 429 Candler Building, Atlanta, Georgia. Emory University School of Medicine (Atlanta Medical College), 1899. Associate in Surgery, Emory University School of Medicine.

ENGELBACH, FEDERICO, B.M., M.D., Calle Victoria 796, Valparaiso, Chile. University of Chile, 1908.

ENGLAND, FRANK RICHARDSON, M.D., C.M., 126 Bishop Street, Montreal, Quebec. Faculty of Medicine, McGill University (University of Bishop College, Faculty of Medicine), 1885. Surgeon, Western Hospital.

EPLER, CRUM, M.D., 650 Thatcher Building, Pueblo, Colorado. University of Tennessee College of Medicine, 1894. Surgeon, St. Mary's and Woodcroft Hospitals.

ERCK, THEODORE A., M.D., 251 South Thirteenth Street, Philadelphia, Pennsylvania. University of Pennsylvania School of Medicine, 1892. Surgeon, Gynecean Hospital; Consulting Gynecologist, Frederick Douglas Memorial Hospital.

ERDMAN, BERNHARD, M.D., 224 North Meridian Street, Indianapolis, Indiana. Indiana University School of Medicine (Medical College of Indiana), 1897. Associate in Genito-Urinary Surgery, Indiana University School of Medicine; Visiting Genito-Urinary Surgeon, Indianapolis City Hospital.

ERDMAN, SEWARD, A.B., M.D., 134 East Sixty-fourth Street, New York, New York. Columbia University, College of Physicians and Surgeons, 1902. Instructor in Surgery, Columbia University, College of Physicians and Surgeons; Associate Attending Surgeon, New York Hospital.

ERDMANN, JOHN F., M.D., 60 West Fifty-second Street, New York, New York. University and Bellevue Hospital Medical College (Bellevue Hospital Medical College), 1887. Professor of Surgery, New York Post-Graduate Medical School; Surgeon, New York Post-Graduate Medical School and Hospital; Consulting Surgeon, Gouverneur Hospital, New York, Nassau Hospital, Mineola, Mt. Vernon Hospital, Mt. Vernon, Manhattan State Hospital, New York, Greenwich General Hospital, Greenwich, Connecticut.

ERICSON, JOHN G., M.D., 603 Syndicate Building, Minneapolis, Minnesota. University of Minnesota Medical School, 1892. Member of Staff, Swedish Hospital.

ERVING, WILLIAM GAGE, A.B., M.D., 1621 Connecticut Avenue, Washington, District of Columbia. Johns Hopkins University, Medical Department, 1902. Professor of Orthopedic Surgery, Howard University School of Medicine, Georgetown University School of Medicine; Attending Orthopedic Surgeon, Providence, Children's, and Georgetown University Hospitals.

ESCHBACH, H. C., A.M., M.D., 116 West Benton Avenue, Albia, Iowa. University of Pennsylvania School of Medicine, 1883.

ESKRIDGE, BELLE CONSTANT, M.D., 902 Dallas Avenue, Houston, Texas. Hahnemann Medical College and Hospital, Chicago, 1891. Member of Visiting Staff, Baptist Sanitarium and Hospital, Norsworthy Hospital, St. Joseph's Infirmary.

ESPEY, JOHN R., M.D., 335 East Main Street, Trinidad, Colorado. Jefferson Medical College, 1889. Surgeon, St. Raphael Hospital.

ESSINGTON, URIAH K., M.D., 289 East State Street, Columbus, Ohio. Ohio State University College of Medicine (Starling Medical College), 1896. Surgeon, Grant and Columbus Radium Hospitals.

ESTES, WILLIAM LAWRENCE, A.M., M.D., 805 Delaware Avenue, Bethlehem, Pennsylvania. University of Virginia, Department of Medicine, 1877; University and Bellevue Hospital Medical College (University of the City of New York, Medical Department), 1878. Emeritus Surgeon-in-Chief, St. Luke's Hospital.

ESTES, WILLIAM LAWRENCE, JR., B.A., M.D., 805 Delaware Avenue, Bethlehem, Pennsylvania. Johns Hopkins University, Medical Department, 1909. Adjunct Surgeon, St. Luke's Hospital.

EVANS, CURTIS A., A.B., M.D., 809 Wells Building, Milwaukee, Wisconsin. University of Michigan Medical School, 1904. Head of Surgical Department, Columbia, Milwaukee, and Children's Hospitals; Consulting Surgeon, Johnston Emergency Hospital.

EVANS, EDWARD, M.D., C.M., State Bank Building, La Crosse, Wisconsin. Faculty of Medicine, McGill University, 1887. Surgeon, St. Francis Hospital.

EVANS, GEORGE BALENTINE, A.M., M.D., 17 South Wilkinson Street, Dayton, Ohio. University of Cincinnati College of Medicine (Ohio Medical College), 1878.

EVANS, JOHN LILLIE, M.D., 729 Beacon Building, Wichita, Kansas. Washington University Medical School, 1904. Member of Surgical Staff, St. Francis Hospital; Division Surgeon, Missouri Pacific Railroad; Local Surgeon, Rock Island Lines; Chief Surgeon, Arkansas Valley Interurban Railway.

EVANS, ROBERT, M.D., 630 Snell Building, Fort Dodge, Iowa. Detroit College of Medicine and Surgery, 1888. Member of Surgical Staff, St. Joseph's Mercy Hospital.

EVE, DUNCAN, A.M., M.D., Eve Building, Nashville, Tennessee. University and Bellevue Hospital Medical College, 1874. Senior Professor of Surgery and Clinical Surgery, Vanderbilt University, Medical Department; Surgeon, St. Thomas Hospital; Consulting Surgeon, Nashville City Hospital; Chief Surgeon, Nashville, Chattanooga and St. Louis Railway; Chief Division Surgeon (four divisions), Louisville and Nashville Railroad.

EVE, DUNCAN, JR., M.D., Seventh Avenue and Church Street, Nashville, Tennessee. Vanderbilt University, Medical Department, 1904. Associate Professor of Surgery, Vanderbilt University, Medical Department; Surgeon, Vanderbilt University and St. Thomas Hospitals, Nashville, Chattanooga and St. Louis Railway, Louisville and Nashville Railroad, Nashville Street Railway.

EVERALL, BEN CHESTER, M.D., Marsh-Place Building, Waterloo, Iowa. State University of Iowa College of Medicine (Drake University College of Medicine), 1907. Attending Surgeon, Synodical Presbyterian and St. Francis Hospitals.

EVERITT, ELLA B., A.M., M.D., 1807 Spruce Street, Philadelphia, Pennsylvania. Woman's Medical College of Pennsylvania, 1891. Professor of Gynecology, Woman's Medical College of Pennsylvania; Gynecologist-in-Chief, Woman's Medical College Hospital; Attending Gynecologist, Philadelphia General Hospital; Consulting Gynecologist, Spring City Institution for Feeble-Minded.

EVERT, JOHN ANDREW, B.A., M.D., Brainerd, Minnesota. University of Minnesota Medical School, 1913. Assistant Chief Surgeon, Northern Pacific Railway; Surgeon, St. Joseph's Hospital.

EWER, EDWARD NORTON, M.D., Federal Realty Building, Oakland, California. University of Michigan Medical School, 1892. Gynecologist, Alameda County Hospital and Infirmary, San Leandro.

EWING, ARTHUR EUGENE, A.M., M.D., 520 Metropolitan Building, St. Louis, Missouri. Washington University Medical School (St. Louis Medical College), 1883. Clinical Professor of Ophthalmology, Washington University Medical School; Member of Staff, St. Luke's, Barnard Free Skin and Cancer, and Washington University Hospitals.

EWING, WILLIAM A., M.D., 810 Fidelity Medical Building, Dayton, Ohio. Jefferson Medical College, 1900. Visiting Surgeon, Miami Valley Hospital.

EYSTER, GEORGE LOUGHEAD, M.D., 413 Safety Building, Rock Island, Illinois. University of Pennsylvania School of Medicine, 1874. Member of Staff, St. Anthony's Hospital.

EYTINGE, ERNEST OLIVER JOSEPH, M.D., 118 Cajon Street, Redlands, California. Columbia University, College of Physicians and Surgeons, 1904. Lieutenant Commander, Medical Corps, United States Navy, retired.

FAHNESTOCK, ERNEST, M.D., 417 Park Avenue, New York, New York. Columbia University, College of Physicians and Surgeons, 1900. Visiting Surgeon, Misericordia Hospital; Assistant Visiting Surgeon, St. Vincent's Hospital.

FAHRNI, GORDON SAMUEL, M.D., 507 Boyd Building, Winnipeg, Manitoba. Faculty of Medicine, University of Manitoba (Manitoba Medical College), 1911. Demonstrator of Anatomy and Clinical Surgery, Faculty of Medicine, University of Manitoba; Honorary Attending Surgeon, King George Hospital.

FAIRBAIRN, JOHN FITZ-GERALD, A.B., M.D., 503 Delaware Avenue, Buffalo, New York. University of Buffalo, Department of Medicine, 1904. Professor of Otology, University of Buffalo, Department of Medicine; Attending Oto-Laryngologist, Buffalo General Hospital; Attending Otologist, Children's Hospital; Chief of Otological Service, City and Ernest Wende Hospitals.

FAIRBANKS, CHARLOTTE, A.B., M.D., Ph.D., 24 Main Street, St. Johnsbury, Vermont. Woman's Medical College of Pennsylvania, 1902. Attending Surgeon, Brightlook and St. Johnsbury Hospitals.

FAIRCHILD, D. S., M.D., 845 Sixth Avenue, Clinton, Iowa. Albany Medical College, 1868. Surgeon, St. Joseph's Mercy Hospital.

FAIRCHILD, DAVID STURGESS, JR., M.D., Wilson Building, Clinton, Iowa. State University of Iowa College of Medicine (Iowa College of Physicians and Surgeons), 1897. Surgeon, Jane Lamb and St. Joseph's Mercy Hospitals.

FAIRCHILD, FRED R., Ph.B., M.D., 754 College Street, Woodland, California. Cooper Medical College, 1902. President and Chief Surgeon, Woodland Sanitarium.

FAIRFIELD, WILLIAM EDWARD, M.D., C.M., 805 South Monroe Avenue, Green Bay, Wisconsin. Faculty of Medicine, McGill University (University of Bishop College, Faculty of Medicine), 1887. Surgeon, St. Vincent's Hospital.

FAIRING, JOHN WALKER, M.D., 204 Tribune Building, Greensburg, Pennsylvania. University of Maryland School of Medicine and College of Physicians and Surgeons (Baltimore Medical College), 1898.

FALK, CHARLES CLIFFORD, M.D., First National Bank Building, Eureka, California. Cooper Medical College, 1897.

FALLON, MICHAEL F., M.D., LL.D., Slater Building, Worcester, Massachusetts. Harvard Medical School, 1887. Surgeon-in-Chief, St. Vincent's Hospital.

FANCHER, HAMPTON LANSDEN, M.D., James Building, Chattanooga, Tennessee. University of the South Medical Department (Sewanee Medical College), 1900. Member of Surgical Staff, Baroness Erlanger Hospital.

FARENHOLT, AMMEN, M.D., Medical Corps, United States Navy, Washington, District of Columbia. Harvard Medical School, 1893. Captain, Medical Corps, United States Navy.

FARISH, GEORGE W. T., M.D., Yarmouth, Nova Scotia. Jefferson Medical College, 1886. Senior Surgeon, Yarmouth Hospital.

FARMER, CHARLES, M.D., 1110 Francis Building, Louisville, Kentucky. University of Louisville, Medical Department (Hospital College of Medicine), 1897. Adjunct Professor of Gynecology and Abdominal Surgery, University of Louisville, Medical Department; Member of Surgical Staff, Louisville City Hospital, John N. Norton Memorial Infirmary.

FARMER, CLARENCE RAVENEL, M.D., 573 West Lemon Street, Lancaster, Pennsylvania. Jefferson Medical College, 1909. Member of Surgical Staff, Lancaster General Hospital.

FARNSLER, H. HERSHEY, A.B., M.D., 1438 Market Street, Harrisburg, Pennsylvania. Medico-Chirurgical College of Philadelphia, 1904. Assistant Surgeon, Department of Ophthalmology and Oto-Laryngology, Harrisburg Hospital; Laryngologist, State Tuberculosis Dispensary.

FARNSWORTH, G. BOURNE, A.B., M.D., 1021 Prospect Avenue, Cleveland, Ohio. Harvard Medical School, 1907. Assistant Professor of Obstetrics, Western Reserve University School of Medicine; Visiting Surgeon, City Hospital; Obstetrician, Maternity Hospital and Dispensary of the Western Reserve University.

FARR, CHARLES EVERETT, A.B., M.D., 568 Park Avenue, New York, New York. Yale University Medical School, 1903. Instructor in Surgery, Cornell University, Medical School; Surgeon, St. Mary's Free Hospital for Children, Seton Hospital; Assistant Surgeon, New York Hospital.

FARR, ROBERT EMMETT, M.D., 2433 Bryant Avenue, South, Minneapolis, Minnesota. Rush Medical College, 1900. Attending Surgeon, St. Mary's Hospital.

FARRAR, LILIAN K. P., A.B., M.D., The Hendrik Hudson, New York, New York. Cornell University Medical College, 1900. Assistant Professor of Gynecology, Cornell University Medical College; Junior Attending Surgeon, Woman's Hospital; Consulting Surgeon, Booth Memorial Hospital.

FARRELL, ALBERT M., M.D., Seventeenth and Washington Streets, Two Rivers, Wisconsin. State University of Iowa College of Medicine, 1898. Surgeon, Holy Family Hospital, Manitowoc.

FARRELL, P. J. H., M.D., 25 East Washington Street, Chicago, Illinois. University of Louisville, Medical Department (Kentucky School of Medicine), 1892. Attending Oculist and Aurist, Municipal Tuberculosis Sanitarium; Consulting Surgeon, Cook County Hospital.

FARRELL, THOMAS HENRY, A.M., M.D., C.M., 250 Genesee Street, Utica, New York. Queen's University, Faculty of Medicine, 1895. Oculist, Aurist, and Laryngologist, Faxton Hospital.

FARRELL, WILLIAM DAVIDSON, M.D., Wells Block, Aberdeen, South Dakota. Cornell University Medical College, 1899. Member of Staff, St. Luke's Hospital.

FARRINGTON, POPE MCGEHEE, M.D., 1728 Exchange Building, Memphis, Tennessee. University of Tennessee College of Medicine (Memphis Hospital Medical College), 1894.

FARWELL, WILLIAM A., M.D., C.M., 45 Dufferin Avenue, Sherbrooke, Quebec. Faculty of Medicine, McGill University, 1891. Ophthalmologist, Rhinologist, and Oto-Laryngologist, Sherbrooke Hospital.

FARWELL, WREY G., M.D., Medical Corps, United States Navy, Washington, District of Columbia. University of Pennsylvania School of Medicine, 1904. Commander, Medical Corps, United States Navy.

FASSETT, FRED J., A.B., M.D., 1155 Empire Building, Seattle, Washington. Harvard Medical School, 1906. Consulting Orthopedic Surgeon, Children's Orthopedic and Seattle City Hospitals.

FAULKNER, WILLIAM EDWARD, A.B., M.D., 290 Marlborough Street, Boston, Massachusetts. Harvard Medical School, 1891. Associate in Surgery, Harvard Medical School.

FAUNCE, CALVIN B., JR., M.D., 320 Commonwealth Avenue, Boston, Massachusetts. University of Maryland School of Medicine, 1904. Instructor in Otology, Harvard Medical School; Visiting Aural Surgeon, Infant's Hospital; Assistant Aural Surgeon, Massachusetts Charitable Eye and Ear Infirmary; Assistant Laryngological Surgeon, Massachusetts General Hospital.

FAUNTLEROY, ARCHIBALD MAGILL, M.D., Medical Corps, United States Navy, Washington, District of Columbia. University of Virginia, Department of Medicine, 1901. Instructor in Surgery, United States Naval Medical School; Commander, Medical Corps, United States Navy.

FAUNTLEROY, POWELL CONRAD, M.D., Medical Corps, United States Army, Washington, District of Columbia. University of Virginia, Department of Medicine, 1893. Colonel, Medical Corps, United States Army.

FAWCETT, IVAN, M.D., Wheeling Steel Corporation Building, Wheeling, West Virginia. University of Pennsylvania School of Medicine, 1910. Visiting Surgeon, Eye, Ear, Nose, and Throat Department, Ohio Valley General Hospital; Surgeon, Eye, Ear, Nose, and Throat, Out-Patient Department, Ohio Valley General Hospital.

FAY, OLIVER JAMES, B.Sc., M.D., 1213 Bankers Trust Building, Des Moines, Iowa. University of Illinois College of Medicine (College of Physicians and Surgeons, Chicago), 1902. Surgeon, Iowa Methodist Hospital.

FAYERWEATHER, ROADES, A.B., M.D., 529 North Charles Street, Baltimore, Maryland. Johns Hopkins University, Medical Department, 1903. Member of Visiting Staff, Hebrew Hospital and Asylum.

FEARN, JOHN RADFORD, M.D., First National Bank Building, Oakland, California. Eclectic Medical College (Eclectic Medical Institute), 1894; College of Physicians and Surgeons, San Francisco, 1899. Visiting Surgeon, Providence Hospital.

FEBROS Y ODRIOZOLA, ENRIQUE, M.D., Avenida Colmena 590, Lima, Peru. University of San Marcos, 1905.

FEDERSPIEL, MATTHEW N., B.Sc., D.D.S., M.D., 695 Astor Street, Milwaukee, Wisconsin. Marquette University School of Medicine, 1910. Instructor in Stomatology, Marquette University School of Medicine; Professor of Oral Surgery, Marquette University School of Dentistry; Oral Surgeon, Milwaukee Hospital; Member of Staff, Trinity Hospital.

FEE, FRANK EDGAR, M.D., 22 West Seventh Street, Cincinnati, Ohio. University of Cincinnati College of Medicine (Medical College of Ohio), 1895. Professor of Clinical Surgery, University of Cincinnati College of Medicine; Visiting Surgeon, Cincinnati General and Christ Hospitals.

FEHLEISEN, FREDERICK, M.D., 400 Clayton Street, San Francisco, California. University of Wurzburg, 1877.

FEILD, EDWARD EVERARD, M.D., 512 Taylor Building, Norfolk, Virginia. University of Virginia, Department of Medicine, 1879. Consulting Surgeon and Orthopedist, St. Vincent's Hospital.

FEINGOLD, LEON, M.D., 714 Grace Street, Chicago, Illinois. University of Illinois College of Medicine, 1899.

FEINGOLD, MARCUS, M.D., 4206 St. Charles Avenue, New Orleans, Louisiana. University of Vienna, 1896. Professor of Ophthalmology, Tulane University of Louisiana School of Medicine; Chief, Department of Ophthalmology, Touro Infirmary, Charity Hospital.

FELDHOFF, EDWARD W., A.B., M.D., 1224 Turner Street, Allentown, Pennsylvania. University of Pennsylvania School of Medicine, 1906.

FELLOWS, C. GURNEE, A.M., M.D., 30 North Michigan Avenue, Chicago, Illinois. Hahnemann Medical College and Hospital, Chicago, 1885. Consulting Ophthalmologist, Hahnemann Hospital.

FELTY, JOHN WELLINGTON, A.M., M.D., 902 Main Street, Hartford, Connecticut. Jefferson Medical College, 1884. Surgeon, Charter Oak Private Hospital.

FENNELL, W. W., M.D., Rock Hill, South Carolina. Medical College of the State of South Carolina, 1895. Surgeon, Fennell Infirmary; Consulting Surgeon, Seaboard Railway.

FENNER, ERASMUS DARWIN, A.B., M.D., 1915 St. Charles Avenue, New Orleans, Louisiana. Tulane University of Louisiana School of Medicine, 1892.

FENTON, THOMAS HANOVER, M.D., 1319 Spruce Street, Philadelphia, Pennsylvania. University of Pennsylvania School of Medicine, 1877. Member of Staff, Home for Aged Couples, Home for Crippled Children, Baptist, Widener and St. Vincent's Homes.

FERGUSON, CHARLES E., M.D., 412 East Seventeenth Street, Indianapolis, Indiana. Indiana University School of Medicine (Medical College of Indiana), 1892. Clinical Professor of Obstetrics, Indiana University School of Medicine; Attending Obstetrician, Indianapolis City Hospital; Consultant Obstetrician, Robert W. Long Hospital.

396 *American College of Surgeons*

FERGUSON, EDMUND SHEPPARD, M.D., 609 State National Bank Building, Oklahoma, Oklahoma. Detroit College of Medicine and Surgery, 1895. Professor of Ophthalmology, University of Oklahoma School of Medicine; Ophthalmologist and Oto-Laryngologist, University, St. Anthony's, and Oklahoma State Baptist Hospitals.

FERGUSON, WILLIAM A., B.A., M.D , C.M., 43 Alma Street, Moncton, New Brunswick. Faculty of Medicine, McGill University, 1884. Surgeon, Moncton General Hospital.

FERGUSON, WILSON JONES, M.D., I.O.O.F. Building, Sedalia, Missouri. University of Kansas School of Medicine, 1887. Chief of Staff, St. Mary's Hospital.

FERREE, JUDSON A., M.D., 232 East Sixteenth Avenue, Columbus, Ohio. Ohio State University College of Homeopathic Medicine (Cleveland Homeopathic Medical College), 1901; University of Michigan Homeopathic Medical School, 1909. Head of Eye, Ear, Nose, and Throat Department, Ohio State University College of Homeopathic Medicine; Surgeon-in-Chief, Eye, Ear, Nose, and Throat Department, Homeopathic Hospital.

FERRIS, EDWARD D., M.D., 418 Fiftieth Street, Brooklyn, New York. University and Bellevue Hospital Medical College (University of the City of New York), 1893. Attending Surgeon, Norwegian Deaconess Hospital.

FIALHO DE ABREU, JOSÉ ANTONIO, B.L., M.D., Rua Carvalho de Sà 85, Rio de Janeiro, Brazil. Faculty of Medicine, University of Rio de Janeiro, 1896. Professor of Ophthalmology, University of Rio de Janeiro.

FIELD, EDWIN, M.D., 74 West Front Street, Red Bank, New Jersey. Columbia University, College of Physicians and Surgeons, 1873. Chief of Staff, Monmouth Memorial Hospital, Long Branch; Consulting Surgeon, Paul Kimball Hospital, Lakewood.

FIELD, JAMES GAVEN, M.D., Medical Corps, United States Navy, Washington, District of Columbia. Medical College of Virginia, 1885. Captain, Medical Corps, United States Navy.

FIELD, MARTIN THOMAS, M.D., 23 Winter Street, Salem, Massachusetts. Harvard Medical School, 1901. Visiting Surgeon, Salem Hospital.

FIELD, PETER C., M.S., M.D., Medical Corps, United States Army, Washington, District of Columbia. Columbia University, College of Physicians and Surgeons, 1895. Lieutenant Colonel, Medical Corps, United States Army.

FIELD, WILLIAM HILL, M.D., 424 Upper First Street, Evansville, Indiana. University of Pennsylvania School of Medicine, 1898.

FIFE, JAMES D., M.D., Medical Corps, United States Army, Washington, District of Columbia. University of Virginia, Department of Medicine, 1897. Lieutenant Colonel, Medical Corps, United States Army.

FIGUEIRA, MATHIAS, A.B., M.D., LL.D., 14 Stuyvesant Avenue, Brooklyn, New York. Columbia University, College of Physicians and Surgeons, 1872. Visiting Surgeon, St. Catherine's Hospital.

FILHO, SERGIO DE P. MEIRA, M.D., Alameda Eduardo Prado 8, Sao Paulo, Brazil. University of Geneva, 1910. Professor, Faculty of Medicine University of Sao Paulo.

FINCH, JAMES HUGH, M.D., 308 Illinois Building, Champaign, Illinois. University of Maryland School of Medicine (College of Physicians and Surgeons), 1895. Member of Staff, Julia F. Burnham Hospital.

FINCH, LEW HENRI, M.D., 188 Market Street, Amsterdam, New York. Columbia University, College of Physicians and Surgeons, 1903. Chief of Staff and Attending Surgeon, Amsterdam City Hospital; Attending Surgeon, St. Mary's Hospital.

FINDLAY, EPHRAIM KIRKPATRICK, M.D., C.M., 30 North Michigan Avenue, Chicago, Illinois. Faculty of Medicine, University of Manitoba (Manitoba Medical College), 1893. Surgeon, Illinois Charitable Eye and Ear Infirmary; Oculist, Cook County Hospital.

FINDLEY, JOSEPH DYSART, A.M., M.D., 1121 Thirteenth Avenue, Altoona, Pennsylvania. University of Pennsylvania School of Medicine, 1900. Chief of Surgical Service, Altoona Hospital.

FINDLEY, PALMER, B.Sc., M.D., Brandeis Theatre Building, Omaha, Nebraska. Northwestern University Medical School, 1903.

FINKELSTEIN, NATHAN, M.D., 184 North Street, Pittsfield, Massachusetts. Tufts College Medical School, 1912. Urologist, House of Mercy Hospital, Pittsfield, Fairview Hospital, Great Barrington; Chief, Berkshire County Venereal Clinic.

FINNEY, EVERETT B., M.D., 802 Security Mutual Life Building, Lincoln, Nebraska. Hahnemann Medical College and Hospital, Philadelphia, 1888. Member of Surgical Staff, St. Elizabeth's Hospital.

FINNEY, JOHN MILLER TURPIN, A.B., M.D., F. R. C. S. (Ire.), Hon., 1300 Eutaw Place, Baltimore, Maryland. Harvard Medical School, 1889. Professor of Clinical Surgery, Johns Hopkins University, Medical Department; Surgeon, Union Protestant Infirmary, Hospital for Women of Maryland, Church Home and Infirmary.

FINTON, WALTER LLOYD, M.D., 410 South Jackson Street, Jackson, Michigan. University of Michigan Medical School, 1907. Surgeon, W. A. Foote Memorial and Mercy Hospitals.

FISCHER, ARTHUR F., B.Sc., A.M., M.D., Quincy Mine, Hancock, Michigan. University of Michigan Medical School, 1890. Attending Surgeon, St. Joseph's Hospital; Chief Surgeon, Quincy Mining Company.

FISCHER, HERMANN, M.D., 73 East Eightieth Street, New York, New York. Columbia University, College of Physicians and Surgeons, 1896. Visiting Surgeon, Lenox Hill Hospital; Consulting Surgeon, Rockaway Beach Hospital, Rockaway Beach, United Hospital, Port Chester.

FISCHER, N. ARTHUR, M.D., 623 Union Arcade Building, Pittsburgh, Pennsylvania. University of Pittsburgh School of Medicine, 1908. Instructor in Otology, University of Pittsburgh School of Medicine; Oto-Laryngologist, St. Francis and United States Marine Hospitals; Otologist, Eye and Ear Hospital.

FISHBACH, HOWARD P., Ph.B., M.D., 1201 Traction Building, Cincinnati, Ohio. Pulte Medical College, 1909. Consulting Gynecologist, Emanuel Clinic; Gynecologist, Bethesda Hospital.

FISHER, ARTHUR L., B.Sc., M.D., Medical Building, San Francisco, California. Johns Hopkins University, Medical Department, 1900. Instructor in Orthopedics, University of California Medical School.

FISHER, ARTHUR OSCAR, A.B., M.D., 608 Humboldt Building, St. Louis, Missouri. Johns Hopkins University, Medical Department, 1909. Associate in Clinical Surgery, Washington University Medical School; Assistant Surgeon, Barnes and Children's Hospitals; Chief of Surgical Clinic, Washington University Dispensary.

FISHER, CARL, B.Sc., M.D., Pacific Mutual Building, Los Angeles, California. Harvard Medical School, 1905.

FISHER, EDGAR ALEXANDER, M.D., 25 Elm Street, Worcester, Massachusetts. Boston University School of Medicine, 1887. Surgeon, Worcester Hahnemann Hospital.

FISHER, HENRY CLAY, M.D., Medical Corps, United States Army, Washington, District of Columbia. Georgetown University School of Medicine, 1891. Colonel, Medical Corps, United States Army.

FISHER, JOHN MONROE, M.D., 222 South Fifteenth Street, Philadelphia, Pennsylvania. Jefferson Medical College, 1884. Associate Professor of Gynecology, Jefferson Medical College; Gynecologist, Philadelphia General and St. Agnes Hospitals, Philadelphia, Pottstown Hospital, Pottstown; Assistant Gynecologist, Jefferson Medical College Hospital.

FISHER, WILLIAM A., M.D., 31 North State Street, Chicago, Illinois. University of Michigan Medical School, 1885. President, Chicago Eye, Ear, Nose, and Throat College; Surgeon, Chicago Eye, Ear, Nose, and Throat College Hospital.

FISHER, WILLIAM A., JR , A.B., M.D., 715 Park Avenue, Baltimore, Maryland. Johns Hopkins University, Medical Department, 1900. Associate in Clinical Surgery, Johns Hopkins University, Medical Department; Assistant Visiting Surgeon, Johns Hopkins Hospital; Visiting Surgeon, Union Memorial Hospital, Church Home and Infirmary, Hospital for Women of Maryland, Children's Hospital School.

FISHER, WILLIAM H., M.D., 416 Colton Building, Toledo, Ohio. University of Michigan Medical School, 1891. Surgeon, St. Vincent's Hospital.

FISCHMANN, EGON WALTER, M.D., 30 North Michigan Avenue, Chicago, Illinois. Rush Medical College, 1906. Assistant Professor of Gynecology, University of Illinois College of Medicine and Chicago Policlinic; Gynecologist, Grant Hospital.

FISK, ARTHUR LYMAN, A.B., M.D., 41 West Fiftieth Street, New York, New York. Harvard Medical School, 1888. Attending Surgeon, St. John's Guild, Floating Hospital, New York, Seaside Hospital, New Dorp; Consulting Surgeon, New Rochelle Hospital, New Rochelle, New York, Somerset Hospital, Somerville, New Jersey.

Fisk, George, M.D.,C.M., 166 Drummond Street, Montreal, Quebec. Faculty of Medicine, McGill University (University of Bishop College, Faculty of Medicine), 1894. Attending Surgeon, Out-Patient Department, Western Hospital.

Fiske, Charles Norman, M.D., Medical Corps, United States Navy, Washington, District of Columbia. Harvard Medical School, 1900. Captain, Medical Corps, United States Navy.

Fiske, David, M.D., 25 East Washington Street, Chicago, Illinois. Rush Medical College, 1900. Assistant Professor of Oto-Laryngology, Rush Medical College; Professor of Otology, Chicago Policlinic; Attending Aurist, Henrotin Memorial Hospital, Chicago Policlinic and Hospital; Attending Otologist and Laryngologist, Children's Memorial Hospital.

Fiske, Edwin H., A.M., M.D., 152 Lafayette Avenue, Brooklyn, New York. Long Island College Hospital, 1901. Consulting Surgeon, Bushwick Hospital, Brooklyn, Eastern Long Island Hospital, Greenport, Mercy Hospital, Hempstead; Visiting Surgeon, Kings County Hospital, Hospital of the Holy Family.

Fiske, George Foster, A.M., M.D., 25 East Washington Street, Chicago, Illinois. Yale University School of Medicine, 1883. Surgeon, Chicago Policlinic and Hospital, Henrotin Memorial Hospital.

Fitch, Emery Moore, M.D., 19 Pleasant Street, Claremont, New Hampshire. Dartmouth Medical School, 1905. Surgeon, Claremont General Hospital.

Fitch, James William, M.D., 1021 Ninth Street, Portsmouth, Ohio. University of Louisville, Medical Department (Kentucky School of Medicine), 1893. Surgeon, Hempstead Hospital.

Fitch, Ralph R., M.D., 366 East Avenue, Rochester, New York. Harvard Medical School, 1903. Orthopedic Surgeon; Rochester General Hospital.

Fitch, William H., A.M., M.D., 849 Main Street, North, Rockford, Illinois. Northwestern University Medical School, 1868. Consulting Surgeon, Rockford Hospital.

Fite, Francis Bartow, M.D., 103½ North Second Street, Muskogee, Oklahoma. Emory University School of Medicine (Southern Medical College), 1886. Surgeon, Physicians and Surgeons Hospital.

Fitton, Francis M., M.D., 144 North Third Street, Hamilton, Ohio. University of Cincinnati College of Medicine (Miami Medical College), 1887.

Fitzgerald, Fred J. C., M.D., 47 East Fifty-seventh Street, New York, New York. Western University Medical School, 1897. Consulting Surgeon, Eastern Long Island Hospital, Greenport.

Fitzgerald, Vance Lee, M.D., 223 Thayer Street, Providence, Rhode Island. University and Bellevue Hospital Medical College (Bellevue Hospital Medical College), 1895.

Fitz-Patrick, Gilbert, M.D., 122 South Michigan Avenue, Chicago, Illinois. Hahnemann Medical College and Hospital (Chicago Homeopathic Medical

College), 1896. Professor of Obstetrics and Chief of Department, Hahnemann Medical College and Hospital; Attending Obstetrician, Hahnemann and Streeter Hospitals; Member Consulting Staff, Illinois Masonic Hospital.

FITZPATRICK, THOMAS VANHOOK, M.D., Ph.D., 19 West Seventh Street, Cincinnati, Ohio. Cincinnati College of Medicine and Surgery, 1875. Emeritus Laryngologist and Otologist, St. Mary's Hospital.

FITZSIMMONS, HENRY J., A.B., M.D., 520 Beacon Street, Boston, Massachusetts. Harvard Medical School, 1908. Instructor in Orthopedic Surgery, Harvard Medical School; Assistant Surgeon, Children's Hospital; Associate Orthopedic Surgeon, Newton Hospital, Newton; Assistant Orthopedic Surgeon, Massachusetts Homeopathic Hospital.

FLAHERTY, FREDERICK, M.D., 831 University Building, Syracuse, New York. Syracuse University College of Medicine, 1896. Professor of Clinical Surgery, Syracuse University College of Medicine; Surgeon, St. Joseph's, Syracuse Memorial Hospitals, and Syracuse Free Dispensary.

FLANAGAN, WILLIAM FRANCIS, A.M., M.D., 379 Benefit Street, Providence, Rhode Island. Long Island College Hospital, 1900. Visiting Surgeon, St. Joseph's Hospital.

FLANNERY, JOSEPH J., M.D., 916 Equitable Building, Des Moines, Iowa. State University of Iowa College of Medicine (Drake University College of Medicine), 1900.

FLANNERY, R. E., M.D., 3117 Logan Boulevard, Chicago, Illinois. University of Illinois College of Medicine (College of Physicians and Surgeons, Chicago), 1906. Associate Professor of Surgery, Loyola University School of Medicine; Attending Surgeon, St. Mary of Nazareth Hospital.

FLECK, HARVEY K., M.D., 924 North Charles Street, Baltimore, Maryland. University of Maryland School of Medicine (College of Physicians and Surgeons, Baltimore), 1904. Associate in Ophthalmology and Otology, University of Maryland School of Medicine and College of Physicians and Surgeons; Visiting Ophthalmologist and Otologist, St. Agnes' Hospital; Surgeon, Baltimore Eye, Ear, and Throat Charity Hospital; Consulting Ophthalmologist and Otologist, United States Marine Hospital.

FLEMING, ERNEST W., M.D., 806 Pacific Mutual Building, Los Angeles, California. University of Michigan Medical School, 1885.

FLEMING, GEOFFREY JOSEPH, M.D., 612 North Euclid Avenue, Ontario, California. University of Illinois College of Medicine (College of Physicians and Surgeons, Chicago), 1898.

FLEMING, GEORGE ALEXANDER, M.D., 1018 Madison Avenue, Baltimore, Maryland. University of Maryland School of Medicine, 1884. Demonstrator of Ophthalmology and Otology, University of Maryland School of Medicine and College of Physicians and Surgeons; Surgeon, Presbyterian Eye, Ear, and Throat Charity Hospital.

FLEMMING, EDWARD ALBERT, M.D., 213 One Hundred Thirteenth Street, New York, New York. Columbia University, College of Physicians and

Surgeons, 1906. Associate Visiting Obstetrician and Gynecologist, St. Catherine's and Greenpoint Hospitals, Brooklyn.

FLETCHER, FRED, M.D., 283 East State Street, Columbus, Ohio. Jefferson Medical College, 1900. Assistant Professor of Gynecology, Ohio State University Medical Department; Surgeon, Grant Hospital; Gynecologist, St. Francis Hospital.

FLETCHER, GEORGE WILLIAM, M.B., M.D., 901 Boyd Building, Winnipeg, Manitoba. University of Toronto, Faculty of Medicine, 1902. Associate Professor of Laryngology, Faculty of Medicine, University of Manitoba; Consultant in Laryngology, Ninette Sanitarium.

FLETCHER, MARSHALL HALL, M.D., 199 Haywood Street, Asheville, North Carolina. University and Bellevue Hospital Medical College, 1881. Chief of Staff, Asheville Mission Hospital; Surgeon, Clarence Barker Memorial Hospital and Dispensary, Biltmore.

FLETCHER, ROBERT DONALD, A.M., M.D., C.M., 206 Somerset Building, Winnipeg, Manitoba. Faculty of Medicine, University of Manitoba (Manitoba Medical College), 1903. Associate Professor of Genito-Urinary Surgery, Faculty of Medicine, University of Manitoba; Urologist, Winnipeg General Hospital.

FLINT, AUSTIN, A.M., M.D., 52 East Fifty-fourth Street, New York, New York. University and Bellevue Hospital Medical College, 1889. Professor of Obstetrics and Clinical Professor of Gynecology, University and Bellevue Hospital Medical College; Consulting Surgeon, Woman's Hospital, New York, Newport Hospital, Newport, Rhode Island; Visiting Obstetrician, Manhattan Maternity Hospital and Dispensary; Consulting Obstetrician, New York Maternity and Bellevue Hospitals; Consulting Gynecologist, Hospital for the Ruptured and Crippled.

FLINT, JOSEPH MARSHALL, B.Sc., A.M., M.D., McCloud, California. Johns Hopkins University, Medical Department, 1900.

FLOYD, BENJAMIN L. W., M.D., 517 Chandler Avenue, Evansville, Indiana. University of Louisville, Medical Department (Kentucky School of Medicine), 1896.

FLOYD, WILLIAM OLIVER, B.Sc., M.D., 706 Church Street, Nashville, Tennessee. University of Nashville, Medical Department, 1910. Assistant in Surgery, Vanderbilt University, Medical Department; Member of Surgical Staff, St. Thomas Hospital.

FLYNN, CHARLES WATTS, B.Sc., M.D., 704 Wilson Building, Dallas, Texas. University of Pennsylvania School of Medicine, 1911. Associate Professor of Surgery, Baylor University School of Medicine; Visiting Surgeon, Baylor and Parkland Hospitals.

FOBES, JOSEPH HENRY, M.D., 1 West Sixty-eighth Street, New York, New York. New York Homeopathic Medical College and Flower Hospital, 1901. Professor of Surgery, New York Homeopathic Medical College and Flower Hospital; Surgeon, Metropolitan Hospital; Attending Surgeon,

Broad Street Hospital; Assistant Attending Surgeon, Fifth Avenue Hospital; Consulting Surgeon, Jamaica Hospital, Jamaica, New York, St. Mary's Hospital, Passaic, Ann May Memorial Homeopathic Hospital, Spring Lake, McKinley Memorial Hospital, Trenton, New Jersey, Montreal Homeopathic Hospital, Montreal, Canada.

FODDER, WILLIAM L., M.D., 5 Jay Street, Schenectady, New York. Albany Medical College, 1807. Surgeon, Ellis Hospital.

FOLEY, JOHN C., M.D., County and Washington Streets, Waukegan, Illinois. Rush Medical School, 1890. Surgeon, Victory Memorial Hospital.

FOLEY, THOMAS MADDEN, M.D., 1334 Nineteenth Street, Washington, District of Columbia. George Washington University Medical School, 1905. Clinical Professor of Orthopedic Surgery, George Washington University Medical School; Orthopedic Surgeon, Municipal Hospital; Associate Orthopedic Surgeon, Providence and Emergency Hospitals.

FOLLANSBEE, GEORGE EDWARD, M.D., 614 Guardian Building, Cleveland, Ohio. Western Reserve University School of Medicine (Wooster University, Medical Department), 1895. Visiting Surgeon and Chief of Staff, St. Alexis Hospital.

FOLLIS, RICHARD HOLDEN, Ph.B., M.D., 3 East Read Street, Baltimore, Maryland. Johns Hopkins University, Medical Department, 1899. Associate Professor of Clinical Surgery, Johns Hopkins University, Medical Department; Assistant Visiting Surgeon, Johns Hopkins Hospital; Surgeon in Charge, Johns Hopkins Hospital Dispensary; Surgeon, Union Protestant Infirmary, Hospital for Women of Maryland, Church Home and Infirmary.

FOLTZ, JAMES A., M.D., Merchants National Bank Building, Fort Smith, Arkansas. Tulane University of Louisiana School of Medicine, 1901. President of Staff and Visiting Surgeon, Sparks Memorial Hospital, St. Edward's Infirmary; Chief Surgeon, Fort Smith and Western Railroad, Fort Smith Light and Traction Company; Division Surgeon, Frisco Lines; Surgeon, Athletic Spelter Company.

FOOTE, DELLIZON A., A.M., M.D., 788 Brandeis Theatre Building, Omaha, Nebraska. Hahnemann Medical College and Hospital (Chicago Homeopathic Medical College), 1886. Member of Surgical Staff, Child Saving Institute.

FORBES, ALEXANDER MACKENZIE, M.D.,C.M., 615 University Street, Montreal, Quebec. Faculty of Medicine, McGill University, 1898. Clinical Professor of Orthopedic Surgery, Faculty of Medicine, McGill University; Surgeon in Charge, Children's Memorial Hospital, Montreal General Hospital, Department of Orthopedic Surgery.

FORBES, ARTHUR EDWARD GRANT, M.D., C.M., Lunenburg, Nova Scotia. Faculty of Medicine, McGill University, 1906. Attending Surgeon, Lunenburg Cottage, Lunenburg, and Dawson Memorial Hospital, Bridgewater.

FORBES, HENRY HALL, M.D., 40 East Forty-first Street, New York, New York. Columbia University, College of Physicians and Surgeons, 1890.

Adjunct Professor of Diseases of Nose and Throat, New York Post-Graduate Medical School; Attending Surgeon, Diseases of Nose and Throat, New York Post-Graduate Medical School and Hospital; Attending Laryngologist, Lying-in Hospital; Attending Oto-Laryngologist, Lutheran Hospital, Babies Ward, Post-Graduate Hospital, New York, Westchester County Hospitals, East View.

FORBES, ROBERT D., M.D., C.M., L.R.C.P. (Lond.), F.R.C.S. (Eng.), 908 Cobb Building, Seattle, Washington. Faculty of Medicine, McGill University, 1903.

FORD, CHARLES BICKHAM, M.D., 908 Boren Avenue, Seattle, Washington. University and Bellevue Hospital Medical College, 1895. Visiting Gynecologist, Seattle City Hospital; Surgeon, Children's Orthopedic Hospital.

FORD, ERNEST JASON, A.B., M.D., 2009 Harrison Street, Evanston, Illinois. University of Illinois College of Medicine (College of Physicians and Surgeons, Chicago), 1906. Associate Professor of Surgery, University of Illinois; Senior Attending Surgeon, Evanston Hospital.

FORD, JOSEPH HERBERT, B.Sc., M.A., M.D., Medical Corps, United States Army, Washington, District of Columbia. George Washington University Medical School (Columbian University, Medical Department), 1897. Colonel, Medical Corps, United States Army.

FORD, WILLIAM MILLER, M.D., 52 East Fifty-fourth Street, New York, New York. University of Virginia, Department of Medicine, 1899. Clinical Professor of Obstetrics, University and Bellevue Hospital Medical College; Attending Surgeon, Manhattan Maternity Hospital; Assistant Attending Surgeon, St. Vincent's Hospital.

FOREMAN, BRADY HUGH, M.D., Perkins Building, Tacoma, Washington. Rush Medical College, 1904. Surgeon, St. Joseph's Hospital.

FORMAD, MARIE K., M.D., Medical Arts Building, Philadelphia, Pennsylvania. Woman's Medical College of Pennsylvania, 1886. Member of Gynecological Staff, Woman's Hospital.

FORMAN, LLOYD H., M.D., 49 South Florida Street, Buckhannon, West Virginia. University of Maryland School of Medicine (College of Physicians and Surgeons), 1885. Surgeon-in-Chief, Forman Surgical Hospital.

FORSBECK, FILIP A., M.D., 121 Wisconsin Street, Milwaukee, Wisconsin. Hahnemann Medical College and Hospital, Chicago, 1895. Member of Surgical Staff, St. Mary's Hospital.

FORSEE, CHALLON GUY, M.D., 501 Francis Building, Louisville, Kentucky. University of Louisville, Medical Department, 1905. Adjunct Professor of Surgery, University of Louisville, Medical Department; Member of Visiting Staff, Louisville City Hospital; Member of Staff, SS. Mary and Elizabeth Hospital.

FORSYTH, EDGAR A., M.D., 471 Virginia Street, Buffalo, New York. University of Buffalo, Department of Medicine (Niagara University, Medical Department), 1889. Oto-Laryngologist, Emergency Hospital of the Sisters of Charity, Working Boys' Home, Buffalo, Our Lady of Victory Infant Home, St. John's Protectory, Lackawanna.

FORT, FRANK THOMAS, M.D., 472 Francis Building, Louisville, Kentucky. University of Louisville, Medical Department (Louisville Medical College), 1895. Visiting Surgeon, Louisville City Hospital; Consulting Surgeon, SS. Mary and Elizabeth Hospital; District Surgeon, Illinois Central Railroad.

FORT, RUFUS E., M.D., 303 Seventh Avenue, North, Nashville, Tennessee. Vanderbilt University, Medical Department, 1894.

FOSKETT, EBEN, M.D., 106 Central Park, West, New York, New York. University and Bellevue Hospital Medical College (New York University Medical College), 1895. Attending Gynecologist, Booth Memorial Hospital.

FOSS, HAROLD LEIGHTON, M.D., Geisinger Memorial Hospital, Danville, Pennsylvania. Jefferson Medical College, 1909. Surgeon-in-Chief, Geisinger Memorial Hospital.

FOSTER, CHARLES L., B.Sc., M.D., Medical Corps, United States Army, Washington, District of Columbia. George Washington University Medical School (Columbian University, Medical Department), 1902. Lieutenant Colonel, Medical Corps, United States Army.

FOSTER, CURTIS SMILEY, A.B., M.D., 308 Diamond Bank Building, Pittsburgh, Pennsylvania. University of Pennsylvania School of Medicine, 1898. Gynecologist, Western Pennsylvania Hospital.

FOSTER, E. EDWIN, M.D., New Bedford, Massachusetts. Tufts College Medical School, 1902. Retired.

FOSTER, HAL, A.B., A.M., M.D., 402 Altman Building, Kansas City, Missouri. University and Bellevue Hospital Medical College (Medical Department of the University of New York), 1882. Visiting Oto-Laryngologist, St. Joseph's and Swedish Hospitals; Consulting Oto-Laryngologist, St. Margaret's Hospital.

FOSTER, HAROLD A., M.D., 204 West Fifty-fifth Street, New York, New York. New York Homeopathic Medical College and Flower Hospital, 1905. Assistant Professor of Laryngology, New York Homeopathic Medical College and Flower Hospital; Laryngologist, Metropolitan and Hahnemann Hospitals; Consulting Laryngologist, Yonkers Homeopathic Hospital and Maternity, Yonkers.

FOSTER, JOHN HOSKINS, A.M., M.D., 417 Kress Medical Building, Houston, Texas. University of Texas, Medical Department, 1900. Oto-Laryngologist, Norsworthy Hospital, Baptist Sanitarium and Hospital, Sunset Central Lines.

FOSTER, JOHN McEWEN, M.D., 708 Metropolitan Building, Denver, Colorado. University of Tennessee College of Medicine, 1891. Emeritus Professor of Oto-Laryngology, University of Colorado School of Medicine; Oto-Laryngologist, St. Joseph's Hospital; Ophthalmologist, St. Luke's Hospital; Otologist and Ophthalmologist, Children's Hospital.

FOSTER, MATTHIAS LANCKTON, A.B., M.D., 106 Center Avenue, New Rochelle, New York. Columbia University, College of Physicians and Surgeons, 1885. Ophthalmic Surgeon, New Rochelle Hospital.

FOSTER, SIDNEY DIX, M.D., Colton Building, Toledo, Ohio. University of Cincinnati College of Medicine (Ohio-Miami Medical College of the University of Cincinnati), 1900. Surgeon, Flower Hospital.

FOSTER, WILLIAM DAVIS, M.D., 4125 Warwick Boulevard, Kansas City, Missouri. Homeopathic Medical College of Missouri, 1869. Professor of Surgery, Kansas City Homeopathic Medical College; Member of Consulting Staff, Grace and General Hospitals, Kansas City, Missouri, Bethany Methodist Hospital, Kansas City, Kansas.

FOTHERINGHAM, JOHN C., A.B., M.B., M.D., C.M., LL.D., Hon., 20 Wellesley Street, Toronto, Ontario. University of Toronto, Faculty of Medicine (Trinity Medical College), 1891. Associate Professor of Medicine and Clinical Medicine, University of Toronto, Faculty of Medicine; Consulting Physician, Hospital for Sick Children, Toronto General Hospital; Honorary Physician to his Excellency the Governor General of Canada; Late Director General, Canadian Army Medical Service, Canadian Expeditionary Force.

FOULKROD, COLLIN, A.B., M.D., 3910 Chestnut Street, Philadelphia, Pennsylvania. Jefferson Medical College, 1901. Obstetrician, Presbyterian Hospital.

FOWLER, EDMUND PRINCE, M.D., 114 East Fifty-fourth Street, New York, New York. Columbia University College of Physicians and Surgeons, 1900. Lecturer on Physiology of the Ear, Manhattan Eye, Ear, and Throat Hospital, Post-Graduate Department; Associate in Otology and Lecturer on Physics of the Ear, Post-Graduate Medical School and Hospital; Consulting Otologist, St. Mary's Free Hospital for Children, New York, Tarrytown Hospital, Tarrytown; Junior Otologist, Manhattan Eye, Ear, and Throat Hospital, New York.

FOWLER, EDSON B., A.B., M.D., 7 West Madison Street, Chicago, Illinois. Northwestern University Medical School, 1896. Member of Staff, St. Francis Hospital, Evanston, Children's Memorial Hospital, Chicago.

FOWLER, HARRY ATWOOD, B.Sc., M.D., 1621 Connecticut Avenue, Washington, District of Columbia. Johns Hopkins University, Medical Department, 1901. Professor of Genito-Urinary Surgery, Howard University School of Medicine; Genito-Urinary Surgeon, Freedmen's, and Central Dispensary and Emergency Hospitals.

FOWLER, O. S., B.Sc., M.D., 530 Metropolitan Building, Denver, Colorado. University of Colorado School of Medicine (Denver and Gross College of Medicine), 1906. Lecturer on Local Anesthesia, University of Colorado School of Medicine.

FOWLER, ROYALE HAMILTON, M.D., 280 Jefferson Avenue, Brooklyn, New York. Cornell University Medical College, 1907. Associate Surgeon, Greenpoint Hospital.

FOWLER, RUSSELL STORY, M.D., 301 DeKalb Avenue, Brooklyn, New York. Columbia University, College of Physicians and Surgeons, 1895. Chief Surgeon, Wyckoff Heights Hospital; Surgeon, Methodist Episcopal Hospital; Consulting Surgeon, Huntington Hospital, Brooklyn Hebrew Orphan Asylum.

FOWLER, WILLIAM ALONZO, M.D., 534 Liberty National Bank Building, Oklahoma, Oklahoma. University of Nashville Medical Department, 1908. Associate Professor of Obstetrics, and Chief Clinician, Department of Obstetrics, Oklahoma University School of Medicine; Chief Clinician, Department of Obstetrics, State University Hospital; Medical Director, Oklahoma Lying-in Hospital; Attending Obstetrician, St. Anthony's Hospital.

FOX, CLAUDE P., M.D., 125 Charles Street, Greeneville, Tennessee. University and Bellevue Hospital Medical College (University of the City of New York, Medical Department), 1888. Chief of Surgical Staff, Greeneville Sanatorium and Hospital.

FOX, J. FRANCKE, M.D., Bluefield, West Virginia. University and Bellevue Hospital Medical College (University of the City of New York, Medical Department), 1886. Surgeon, Bluefield Sanitarium.

FOX, L. WEBSTER, M.D., LL.D., 303 South Seventeenth Street, Philadelphia, Pennsylvania. Jefferson Medical College, 1878. Professor of Ophthalmology, University of Pennsylvania Graduate School of Medicine, Philadelphia Polyclinic and College for Graduates in Medicine; Ophthalmologist, Philadelphia Orthopedic Hospital and Infirmary for Nervous Diseases, Medico-Chirurgical Hospital.

FOX, OSCAR E., M.D., 232 North Fifth Street, Reading, Pennsylvania. University of Pennsylvania School of Medicine, 1905. Surgeon, St. Joseph's Hospital.

FOX, PHILIP REGINALD, M.D., 21 North Pinckney Street, Madison, Wisconsin. Rush Medical College, 1890. Attending Surgeon, St. Mary's Hospital.

FRANCHÈRE, FREDERICK E., B.Sc., M.D., Fourth and Nebraska Streets, Sioux City, Iowa. University of Minnesota Medical School, 1890. Oculist, Aurist, and Laryngologist, Lutheran Hospital.

FRANCIS, ELMER ELLSWORTH, M.D., 1701 Central Bank Building, Memphis, Tennessee. University of Louisville, Medical Department, 1885. Professor of Clinical Surgery and Surgical Anatomy, University of Tennessee College of Medicine; Attending Surgeon, St. Joseph's Hospital; Visiting Surgeon, General and Baptist Memorial Hospitals.

FRANCIS, LEE MASTEN, Ph.B., M.D., 636 Delaware Avenue, Buffalo, New York. Rush Medical College, 1901. Associate in Ophthalmology, University of Buffalo, Department of Medicine; Attending Ophthalmologist, Buffalo General and Erie County Hospitals; Consulting Ophthalmologist, Emergency Hospital of the Sisters of Charity, Buffalo, J. N. Adam Memorial Hospital, Perrysburg.

FRANCISCO, CLARENCE B., M.D., 416 Argyle Building, Kansas City, Missouri. University of Kansas School of Medicine, 1907. Associate Professor of Orthopedic Surgery, University of Kansas School of Medicine; Attending Orthopedic Surgeon, Mercy Hospital; Assistant Attending Orthopedic Surgeon, St. Joseph's and Kansas City General Hospitals.

FRANING, EDWARD C. G., M.D., 306 East Main Street, Galesburg, Illinois. Rush Medical College, 1899. Surgeon, Cottage Hospital.

FRANK, IRA, M.D., 104 South Michigan Avenue, Chicago, Illinois. University of Illinois College of Medicine, 1899. Attending Surgeon, Ear and Throat Department, Michael Reese Hospital, Sarah Morris Memorial Hospital for Children.

FRANK, JACOB, A.M., M.D., 25 East Washington Street, Chicago, Illinois. University of Buffalo, Department of Medicine, 1882. Surgeon, Grant and Columbus Hospitals; Consulting Surgeon, Michael Reese Hospital.

FRANK, LOUIS, M.D., 400 Francis Building, Louisville, Kentucky. University of Louisville, Medical Department (Hospital College of Medicine), 1888. Professor of Abdominal Surgery, University of Louisville, Medical Department; Visiting Surgeon, Louisville City Hospital; Surgeon, John N. Norton Memorial Infirmary.

FRANK, L. WALLACE, A.B., M.D., 400 Francis Building, Louisville, Kentucky. University of Pennsylvania School of Medicine, 1914. Instructor in Surgery, University of Louisville Medical Department; Surgeon, Louisville City and Children's Free Hospitals; Attending Surgeon, Norton Memorial Infirmary.

FRANK, ROBERT T., A.B., A.M., M.D., 511 Majestic Building, Denver, Colorado. Columbia University College of Physicians and Surgeons, 1900.

FRANKENBURGER, J. M., M.D., Rialto Building, Kansas City, Missouri. University of Kansas School of Medicine (Kansas Medical College), 1893.

FRANKENTHAL, LESTER E., M.D., 4825 Woodlawn Avenue, Chicago, Illinois. Northwestern University Medical School, 1885. Clinical Professor of Gynecology, Northwestern University Medical School; Gynecologist and Obstetrician, Michael Reese Hospital; Consulting Gynecologist, Provident Hospital.

FRANKLIN, CLARENCE PAYNE, M.D., 1527 Spruce Street, Philadelphia, Pennsylvania. University of Pennsylvania School of Medicine, 1893. Chief, Ophthalmic Department, Stetson Hospital.

FRANKLIN, J. HERBERT, M.D., 409 East Erie Street, Spring Valley, Illinois. Rush Medical College, 1892. Surgeon-in-Chief, St. Margaret's Hospital.

FRANKLIN, MELVIN M., B.Sc., A.M., M.D., LL.D., 6124 Greene Street, Philadelphia, Pennsylvania. University of Pennsylvania School of Medicine, 1895. Surgeon, St. Joseph's Hospital; Orthopedic Surgeon, Philadelphia General, St. Agnes, and St. Mary's Hospitals; Chief of Orthopedic Section, Third District, United States Public Health Service.

FRANKLIN, WALTER SCOTT, M.D., Butler Building, San Francisco, California. Leland Stanford Junior University School of Medicine, 1898. Clinical Professor of Ophthalmology, University of California Medical School; Ophthalmologist, University of California Hospital.

FRANTZ, CHARLES P., M.Sc., M.D., Iowa State Bank Building, Burlington, Iowa. Northwestern University Medical School, 1900. Ophthalmologist and Aurist, Burlington Hospital; Rhino-Laryngologist, Mercy Hospital; Oculist and Aurist, Chicago, Rock Island and Pacific Railway.

FRASER, ARCHIBALD MCKAY, A.B., M.D., 270 Commonwealth Avenue, Boston, Massachusetts. Harvard Medical School, 1907. Surgeon, Carney Hospital.

FRASER, HOMER E., B.Sc., M.D., 20 South Portland Avenue, Brooklyn, New York. University and Bellevue Hospital Medical College (Bellevue Hospital Medical College), 1891. Adjunct Professor of Genito-Urinary Diseases, Long Island College Hospital; Chief of Clinic in Genito-Urinary Diseases, Polhemus Memorial Clinic; Genito-Urinary Surgeon, Kings County Hospital; Assistant Genito-Urinary Surgeon, Long Island College Hospital.

FRASER, JOHN RODGER, M.D., C.M., 670 Sherbrooke Street, West, Montreal, Quebec. Faculty of Medicine, McGill University, 1910.

FRASER, RODERICK L., M.D., 1005 Douglas Street, Victoria, British Columbia. Jefferson Medical College, 1891. Member of Staff, Provincial Royal Jubilee and St. Joseph's Hospitals.

FRASER, SOMERS, A.B., M.D., 514 Commonwealth Avenue, Boston, Massachusetts. Harvard Medical School, 1911. Instructor in Surgery, Tufts College Medical School; Assistant in Surgery, Harvard University Graduate School of Medicine; Second Assistant Visiting Surgeon, Boston City Hospital.

FRASIER, ALFRED SMITH, M.D., Young Building, Dothan, Alabama. Vanderbilt University, Medical Department, 1906. Surgeon, Frasier Hospital.

FRAUENTHAL, HENRY W., M.D., 160 West Fifty-ninth Street, New York, New York. University and Bellevue Hospital Medical College, 1890. Surgeon-in-Chief, Hospital for Joint Diseases; Consulting Surgeon, Jewish Maternity Hospital, New York, Zion Hospital, Brooklyn.

FRAVEL, ROY CLYDE, M.D., 1000 West Grace Street, Richmond, Virginia. Medical College of Virginia (University College of Medicine), 1909. Associate in Surgery, Medical College of Virginia; Associate Surgeon, St. Luke's Hospital; Member of Visiting Staff, Memorial and St. Phillip's Hospitals.

FRAZIER, CHARLES HARRISON, A.B., M.D., D.Sc., 1724 Spruce Street, Philadelphia, Pennsylvania. University of Pennsylvania School of Medicine, 1892. Professor of Clinical Surgery, University of Pennsylvania School of Medicine; Surgeon, Hospital of the University of Pennsylvania.

FRECHTLING, LOUIS HENRY, M.D., 129 North Second Street, Hamilton, Ohio. University of Illinois College of Medicine (College of Physicians and Surgeons, Chicago), 1903. Surgeon, Mercy Hospital.

FREDERICK, ERNEST VICTOR, M.B., M.R.C.S. (Eng.), L.R.C.P. (Lond.), 300 Charlotte Street, Peterborough, Ontario. University of Toronto, Faculty of Medicine, 1903. Surgeon, Nicholl's and St. Joseph's Hospitals.

FREE, SPENCER MICHAEL, A.M., M.D., 101 South Jared Street, Dubois, Pennsylvania. University of Maryland School of Medicine (College of Physicians and Surgeons, Baltimore), 1880. Surgeon, Dubois and Maple Avenue Hospitals; Senior Surgeon, Adrian Hospital, Punxsutawney; Consulting Surgeon, Indiana Hospital, Indiana.

FREEMAN, GEORGE FRANKLIN, M.D., Medical Corps, United States Navy, Washington, District of Columbia. Harvard Medical School, 1896. Captain, Medical Corps, United States Navy.

FREEMAN, JOHN W., M.D., 514 West Main Street, Lead, South Dakota. University and Bellevue Hospital Medical College (University of the City of New York, Medical Department), 1879.

FREEMAN, LEONARD, B.Sc., A.M., M.D., 424 Metropolitan Building, Denver, Colorado. University of Cincinnati College of Medicine (Medical College of Ohio), 1886. Professor of Surgery, University of Colorado School of Medicine; Surgeon, St. Joseph's Hospital; Consulting Surgeon, Denver City and County, Children's Hospitals, National Jewish Hospital for Consumptives.

FREESE, EDGAR MARTIN, M.D., 322 East State Street, Columbus, Ohio. Ohio State University College of Medicine (Starling-Ohio Medical College), 1908. Member of Staff, Grant Hospital.

FREIBERG, ALBERT HENRY, M.D., LL.D., Seventh and Race Streets, Cincinnati, Ohio. University of Cincinnati College of Medicine (Medical College of Ohio), 1890. Professor of Orthopedic Surgery, University of Cincinnati College of Medicine; Director of Orthopedic Service, Cincinnati General Hospital; Orthopedic Surgeon, Jewish Hospital.

FREILE, WILLIAM, M.D., 108 Palisade Avenue, Jersey City, New Jersey. University and Bellevue Hospital Medical College, 1898. Visiting Surgeon, Christ and Jersey City Hospitals, St. Katherine's Home.

FRENCH, RALPH WINWARD, A.B., M.D., 151 Rock Street, Fall River, Massachusetts. Harvard Medical School, 1910. Surgeon, Truesdale Hospital.

FRENCH, THOMAS R., M.D., 150 Joralemon Street, Brooklyn, New York. Columbia University, College of Physicians and Surgeons, 1871. Consulting Laryngologist, Long Island College, Brooklyn, Kings County, and Jewish Hospitals, St. Christopher's Hospital for Babies.

FREUND, I. D., M.D., 518 North Emmett Street, Butte, Montana. University of Michigan Medical School, 1872. Obstetrician, St. James' Hospital.

FRICK, WILLIAM J., M.D., 924 Rialto Building, Kansas City, Missouri. University of Kansas School of Medicine (Kansas City Medical College), 1888. Surgeon, Research and Kansas City General Hospitals.

FRIDENBERG, PERCY, A.B., M.D., 38 West Fifty-ninth Street, New York, New York. University of Strassburg, 1891. Attending Surgeon, Lebanon

Hospital; Junior Surgeon, New York Eye and Ear Infirmary; Consulting Surgeon, Jewish Memorial Hospital, Hospital for Joint Diseases, Post-Graduate Medical School and Hospital.

FRIEDENWALD, HARRY, A.B., M.D., 1029 Madison Avenue, Baltimore, Maryland. University of Maryland School of Medicine (College of Physicians and Surgeons, Baltimore), 1886. Professor of Ophthalmology and Otology, University of Maryland School of Medicine and College of Physicians and Surgeons; Member of Staff, Baltimore Eye, Ear, and Throat Charity, and Mercy Hospitals, Union Protestant Infirmary, Hospital for Women of Maryland, Hebrew Hospital and Asylum.

FRIEDMAN, LEO VICTOR, A.B., M.D., 425 Marlborough Street, Boston, Massachusetts. Harvard Medical School, 1900. Professor of Obstetrics, Tufts College Medical School; Assistant Surgeon, Gynecological Division, Boston City Hospital.

FRIEDMAN, WILLIAM L., A.M., M.D., 1706 Broadway, Oakland, California. University of Maryland School of Medicine (Baltimore Medical College), 1897. Ophthalmologist, Providence Hospital.

FRIEND, EMANUEL, M.D., 5 North Wabash Avenue, Chicago, Illinois. Rush Medical College, 1890. Attending Surgeon, Michael Reese Hospital; Director, Surgical Department, West Side Dispensary.

FRIESNER, ISIDORE, A.B., M.D., 814 Lexington Avenue, New York, New York. University of Colorado School of Medicine (Gross Medical College), 1901. Instructor, Manhattan Eye, Ear, and Throat Hospital and Medical School; Assistant Aural Surgeon, Manhattan Eye, Ear, and Throat Hospital; Otologist, Beth Moses Hospital, Brooklyn, and Mount Sinai Hospital, New York.

FRINGER, WILLIAM RUDISEL, M.D., William Brown Building, Rockford, Illinois. Northwestern University Medical School (Chicago Medical College), 1888. Oculist, Rockford Hospital.

FRINK, CLAUDE AUGUSTINE, A.B., M.D., 464 West One Hundred Forty-fourth Street, New York, New York. Columbia University, College of Physicians and Surgeons, 1902. Adjunct Professor of Surgery, New York Polyclinic Medical School; Surgeon, Knickerbocker Hospital, New York Polyclinic Medical School and Hospital, New York City Children's Hospital, Randall's Island; Assistant Surgeon, New York Skin and Cancer Hospital.

FRITZ, EMDON, M.D., 913 Elm Street, Manchester, New Hampshire. University and Bellevue Hospital Medical College (Bellevue Hospital Medical College), 1880. Ophthalmologist, Otologist, Laryngologist, Sacred Heart Hospital; Consultant, Elliott Hospital.

FRONTZ, HOWARD CLINTON, M.D., Fifth and Mifflin Streets, Huntingdon, Pennsylvania. University of Pennsylvania School of Medicine, 1894. Surgeon, J. C. Blair Memorial Hospital.

FROST, HERBERT LORING, A.B., M.D., 1005 Rose Building, Cleveland, Ohio Ohio State University College of Homeopathic Medicine (Cleveland

Homeopathic Medical College), 1886. Visiting Surgeon, Huron Road Hospital; Consulting Surgeon, Woman's Hospital.

FROST, HORACE BIRD, A.B., M.D., 30 North Michigan Avenue, Chicago, Illinois. Harvard Medical School, 1896. Associate in Surgery, Rush Medical College; Assistant Instructor in Diseases of the Genito-Urinary System, Post-Graduate Medical School.

FROST, WILLIAM S., M.D., 807 Paulsen Building, Spokane, Washington. University of Minnesota Medical School, 1904.

FROTHINGHAM, GEORGE EDWARD, M.D., 3790 Woodward Avenue, Detroit, Michigan. Detroit College of Medicine and Surgery, 1890. Clinical Professor of Ophthalmology and Otology, Detroit College of Medicine and Surgery; Chief of Department of Ophthalmology, Rhinology, and Oto-Laryngology, and Chief of Clinic, Out-Patient Department, Harper Hospital.

FULKERSON, CLARKE B., M.D., 308 Kalamazoo National Bank Building, Kalamazoo, Michigan. University of Michigan Medical School, 1902. Attending Ophthalmologist and Oto-Laryngologist, Fairmount, Bronson, and Borgess Hospitals.

FULLER, EUGENE, A.B., M.D., 530 Fifth Avenue, New York, New York. Harvard Medical School, 1884. Emeritus Professor of Genito-Urinary Surgery, New York Post-Graduate Medical School; Consulting Genito-Urinary Surgeon, City Hospital, New York Post-Graduate Medical School and Hospital.

FULLER, HOMER GIFFORD, Ph.B., M.D., 204 The Farragut, Washington, District of Columbia. George Washington University Medical School (Columbian University, Medical Department), 1904. Associate Genito-Urinary Surgeon, George Washington University and Garfield Memorial Hospitals.

FULLER, SEABRON JENNING, M.D., Empalme Hospital, Empalme, Sonora, Mexico. University of Louisville, Medical Department, 1891. Surgeon in Charge, Empalme Hospital.

FULLER, THERON EARLE, M.D., Texarkana National Bank Building, Texarkana, Arkansas. Vanderbilt University, Medical Department, 1908. Oculist and Aurist, St. Louis Southwestern Railway Hospital, Texarkana, Arkansas, Texarkana Sanitarium and Hospital, Texarkana, Texas.

FULLER, WILLIAM, M.D., 25 East Washington Street, Chicago, Illinois. Rush Medical College, 1887. Member of Associate Staff, St. Luke's Hospital.

FULLERTON, WILLIAM D., Ph.B., M.D., 465 Rose Building, Cleveland, Ohio. Johns Hopkins University, Medical Department, 1911. Surgeon, Gynecological Service, Lakeside Hospital.

FULTON, JACOB A., M.D., 309 Astoria Savings Bank Building, Astoria, Oregon. University and Bellevue Hospital Medical College (Bellevue Hospital Medical College), 1884. Visiting Surgeon, St. Mary's Hospital.

FULTON, WILLIAM STEWART, M.D., Sixteenth and Market Streets, Wheeling, West Virginia. Ohio State University College of Medicine (Starling-Ohio

Medical University), 1898. Member of Surgical Staff, Ohio Valley General Hospital; Visiting Surgeon, Wheeling Hospital, Wheeling, Reynolds Memorial Hospital, Glendale.

FUNK, EDWIN HENRY, M.D., C.M., 718 Granville Street, Vancouver, British Columbia. Faculty of Medicine, McGill University, 1909.

FUNK, VANCE A., A.B., M.Sc., M.D., La Plante Building, Vincennes, Indiana. University of Nashville, Medical Department, 1909. Surgeon, Good Samaritan Hospital.

FUNKHOUSER, ROBERT MONROE, A.M., LL.B., M.D., 4354 Olive Street, St. Louis, Missouri. University and Bellevue Hospital Medical College (New York University Medical College), 1874.

FURLONG, FRANCIS MOHUN, M.D., Medical Corps, United States Navy, Washington, District of Columbia. Georgetown University School of Medicine, 1895. Commander, Medical Corps, United States Navy.

FURNISS, HENRY DAWSON, M.D., 54 East Forty-eighth Street, New York, New York. University of Virginia, Department of Medicine, 1899. Professor of Gynecology, New York Post-Graduate Medical School; Attending Gynecologist, New York Post-Graduate Medical School and Hospital; Consulting Gynecologist, New Rochelle Hospital, New Rochelle, St. Agnes Hospital, White Plains, New York, All Souls' Hospital, Morristown, New Jersey.

FURNISS, JOHN NEILSON, M.D., 100 Church Street, Selma, Alabama. University of Virginia, Department of Medicine, 1900; University and Bellevue Hospital Medical College, 1901. Attending Surgeon, Union Street Private Hospital.

GABY, ROBERT EDWARD, B.A., M.D., 662 Bathurst Street, Toronto, Ontario. Cornell University Medical College, 1907. Demonstrator of Clinical Surgery and Anatomy, University of Toronto, Faculty of Medicine; Surgeon, St. John's Hospital; Assistant Surgeon, Toronto General Hospital.

GAENSLEN, FREDERICK JULIUS, B.Sc., M.D., 141 Wisconsin Street, Milwaukee, Wisconsin. Johns Hopkins University, Medical Department, 1903. Orthopedic Surgeon, Milwaukee Children's, Columbia, and Mt. Sinai Hospitals, Milwaukee, Milwaukee County Hospital, Wauwatosa, University Hospital, Madison.

GAGE, HOMER, A.M., M.D., 72 Pearl Street, Worcester, Massachusetts. Harvard Medical School, 1887. Chief of Surgical Staff and Surgeon, Memorial Hospital; Consulting Surgeon, Worcester City and St. Vincent's Hospitals.

GAGE, JAMES ARTHUR, A.M., M.D., 18 Shattuck Street, Lowell, Massachusetts. Harvard Medical School, 1885. Surgeon, Lowell General Hospital.

GAGE, JAMES E., M.D., C.M., 250 Genesee Street, Utica, New York. Queen's University, Faculty of Medicine, 1898. Eye, Ear, Nose, and Throat Surgeon, Faxton and General Hospitals, State Hospital for Insane.

GAILEY, JOHN KNOX, B.Sc., M.D., 823 North Kenmore Avenue, Los Angeles, California. University and Bellevue Hospital Medical College (University of the City of New York, Medical Department), 1877. Retired.

GALE, SPARRELL SIMMONS, A.B., M.D., Roanoke Street and Luck Avenue, Southwest, Roanoke, Virginia. Columbia University, College of Physicians and Surgeons, 1901. Surgeon, Lewis-Gale Hospital; Chief Surgeon, Norfolk and Western Railway.

GALLAGHER, FRANK J., M.D., Schofield Building, Cleveland, Ohio. Western Reserve University School of Medicine (Ohio Wesleyan University), 1912. Visiting Surgeon, St. John's and St. Alexis' Hospitals.

GALLAGHER, JOHN V., M.D., LL.D., 11448 Euclid Avenue, Cleveland, Ohio. Western Reserve University School of Medicine, 1891. Visiting Surgeon and Chief of Staff, St. Alexis and St. John's Hospitals; Consulting Surgeon, St. Ann's Hospital.

GALLAGHER, JOSEPH F., M.D., 306 Jackson Building, Nashville, Tennessee. University of Nashville, Medical Department, 1906. Visiting Gynecologist, Vanderbilt University, St. Thomas, and Nashville City Hospitals.

GALLAHER, THOMAS J., A.M., M.D., 605 California Building, Denver, Colorado. University of Pennsylvania School of Medicine, 1889. Laryngologist and Rhinologist, St. Luke's Hospital; Otologist, Children's Hospital.

GALLAND, WILLIAM H., M.D., Croton-on-Hudson, New York. Northwestern University Medical School, 1902.

GALLIE, JOHN GORDON, A.B., M.B., 143 College Street, Toronto, Ontario. University of Toronto, Faculty of Medicine, 1910. Assistant in Obstetrics and Gynecology, and Head of Out-Patient Department in Obstetrics, Toronto General Hospital.

GALLIE, W. EDWARD, M.D., F.R.C.S. (Eng.), 143 College Street, Toronto, Ontario. University of Toronto, Faculty of Medicine, 1903. Associate in Surgery, University of Toronto, Faculty of Medicine; Associate Surgeon, Hospital for Sick Children.

GALLOWAY, HERBERT P. H., M.D., C.M., 661 Broadway, Winnipeg, Manitoba. University of Toronto, Faculty of Medicine (Victoria University, Medical Department), 1887. Professor of Orthopedic Surgery, Faculty of Medicine, University of Manitoba; Orthopedic Surgeon, Winnipeg General Hospital.

GALVIN, AUGUSTUS H., M.D., 117 North Claudina Street, Anaheim, California. Harvard Medical School, 1903. Orthopedist, Fullerton Hospital and Johnston Wickett Clinic.

GAMBLE, HUGH AGNEW, B.Sc., M.D., 505 Washington Avenue, Greenville, Mississippi. Tulane University of Louisiana School of Medicine, 1904. Visiting Surgeon, King's Daughters Hospital.

GAMBLE, WILLIAM ELLIOTT, B.Sc., M.D., 30 North Michigan Avenue, Chicago, Illinois. Rush Medical College, 1886. Oculist, University Hospital.

GAMMON, WILLIAM, M.D., Tremont Hotel, Galveston, Texas. University of Texas, Medical Department, 1893. Surgeon, St. Mary's Infirmary.

GANN, DEWELL, JR., A.B., A.M., M.D., M.Sc., D.Sc., 315 Boyle Building, Little Rock, Arkansas. Indiana University School of Medicine, 1913.

Associate Professor of Surgery, University of Arkansas Medical Department; Member of Staff, St. Vincent's Infirmary, Baptist and Logan H. Roots Memorial Hospitals.

GARBER, FRANK WEBSTER, B.Sc., M.D., 159 Jefferson Street, Muskegon, Michigan. Rush Medical College, 1888. Chief of Staff, Hackley Hospital.

GARBER, JERRY M., M.D., 48 Park Avenue, West, Mansfield, Ohio. Western Reserve University School of Medicine, 1895.

GARBERSON, JOHN HOWARD, B.Sc., M.D., 413 Main Street, Miles City, Montana. Northwestern University Medical School, 1907. Attending Surgeon, Miles City Hospital.

GARDINER, EDWIN J., A.B., C.B., M.L., C.L., M.D., 15 East Washington Street, Chicago, Illinois. San Carlos Royal College of Physicians and Surgeons, Madrid, 1878.

GARDINER, JOHN P., M.D., Colton Building, Toledo, Ohio. University of Pennsylvania School of Medicine, 1901. Obstetrician, Toledo District Nurse Association Dispensary.

GARDNER, ARCHIBALD ROBERT, M.D., 18 Shattuck Street, Lowell, Massachusetts. Harvard Medical School, 1902. Visiting Surgeon, Lowell General and Lowell Corporation Hospitals.

GARDNER, GEORGE WARREN, A.B., M.D., 44 Orchard Avenue, Providence, Rhode Island. Harvard Medical School, 1900. Visiting Surgeon, Rhode Island Hospital.

GARDNER, JAMES A., M.D., 500 Electric Building, Buffalo, New York. Columbia University, College of Physicians and Surgeons, 1895. Attending Genito-Urinary Surgeon, Memorial and Buffalo Columbus Hospitals; Consulting Urologist, Ernest Wende and Municipal Hospitals, St. Francis Asylum, Buffalo, J. N. Adam Memorial Hospital, Perrysburg.

GARDNER, WILLIAM, M.D., C.M., M.A., Hon., 457 Sherbrooke Street, West, Montreal, Quebec. Faculty of Medicine, McGill University, 1867. Emeritus Professor of Gynecology, Faculty of Medicine, McGill University; Consulting Gynecologist, Royal Victoria and Montreal General Hospitals.

GARDNER, WILLIAM ARTHUR, B.A., M.D., C.M., 307 Boyd Building, Winnipeg, Manitoba. Faculty of Medicine, McGill University, 1902. Orthopedic Surgeon, Winnipeg General Hospital.

GARDNER, WILLIAM SISSON, M.D., 6 West Preston Street, Baltimore, Maryland. University of Maryland School of Medicine (College of Physicians and Surgeons, Baltimore), 1885. Professor of Gynecology, University of Maryland School of Medicine and College of Physicians and Surgeons; Gynecologist, Mercy Hospital.

GARNER, ERNEST LLOYD, M.B., 165 Victoria Avenue, Fernie, British Columbia. University of Toronto, Faculty of Medicine, 1898. Superintendent and Attending Surgeon, Fernie General Hospital.

GARRAHGAN, Edward Francis, B.A., M.D., M.A., 25 East Washington Street, Chicago, Illinois. University of Illinois College of Medicine, 1901. Associate in Laryngology, Rhinology, and Otology, University of Illinois School of Medicine; Assistant Surgeon, Illinois Eye and Ear Infirmary; Attending Ophthalmologist and Otologist, Sheridan Park Hospital.

GARRETT, JOHN RANDOLPH, M.D., Strickland Building, Roanoke, Virginia. Medical College of Virginia, 1898. Visiting Oculist and Aurist, Roanoke Hospital.

GARRISON, BIDDLE H., M.D., 23 Monmouth Street, Red Bank, New Jersey. Hahnemann Medical College and Hospital, Philadelphia, 1898. Surgeon, Ann May Memorial Homeopathic Hospital, Spring Lake.

GARRISON, HARRY ALFRED, A.B., M.D., Medical Corps, United States Navy, Washington, District of Columbia. University of Pennsylvania School of Medicine, 1902. Commander, Medical Corps, United States Navy.

GARROW, ALEXANDER ESSLEMONT, M.D., C.M., 289 Mountain Street, Montreal, Quebec. Faculty of Medicine, McGill University, 1889. Assistant Professor of Surgery and Clinical Surgery, Faculty of Medicine, McGill University; Surgeon, Royal Victoria Hospital.

GARSHWILER, WILLIAM PROVINCE, A.B., M.D., 716 Indiana Pythian Building, Indianapolis, Indiana. Indiana University School of Medicine (Medical College of Indiana), 1896. Associate Professor of Genito-Urinary Surgery and Lecturer on Syphilis, Indiana University School of Medicine; Consulting Genito-Urinary Surgeon, Indianapolis City, St. Vincent's, Protestant Deaconess, and Robert W. Long Hospitals.

GARTON, WILL MELVILLE, M.D., Medical Corps, United States Navy, Washington, District of Columbia. State University of Iowa College of Homeopathic Medicine, 1896. Commander, Medical Corps, United States Navy.

GASK, GEORGE ERNEST, C.M.G., D.S.O., F.R.C.S. (Eng.), 4, York Gate, London, N. W. 1, England. M.R.C.S. (Eng.), L.R.C.P. (Lond.) (St. Bartholomew's Hospital), 1898. Professor of Surgery, University of London; Surgeon and Director of Surgical Unit, St. Bartholomew's Hospital, University of London.

GASTAÑETA, GUILLERMO, M.D., Plaza de la Exposicion 1217, Lima, Peru. Faculty of Medicine, University of San Marcos, 1899. Professor of Clinical Surgery, University of San Marcos; Chief Surgeon and Superintendent, Dos de Mayo Hospital.

GATCH, WILLIS D., A.B., M.D., 1440 Central Avenue, Indianapolis, Indiana. Johns Hopkins University, Medical Department, 1907. Professor of Surgery, Indiana University School of Medicine; Visiting Surgeon, Indianapolis City and Robert W. Long Hospitals.

GATEWOOD, EMMETTE TRIBLE, M.D., Professional Building, Richmond, Virginia. Medical College of Virginia, 1910. Instructor in Laryngology and Rhinology, Medical College of Virginia; Attending Surgeon, Virginia Hospital.

GATEWOOD, JAMES DUNCAN, A.M., M.D., Medical Corps, United States Navy, Washington, District of Columbia. University of Virginia, Department of Medicine, 1879. Captain, Medical Corps, United States Navy.

GAUB, OTTO C., M.D., Westinghouse Building, Pittsburgh, Pennsylvania. University of Pennsylvania School of Medicine, 1894. Surgeon, Allegheny General Hospital, Pittsburgh, Columbia Hospital, Wilkinsburg.

GAUCH, WILLIAM, M.D., 177 Elwood Avenue, Newark, New Jersey. Columbia University, College of Physicians and Surgeons, 1895. Attending Gynecologist, Newark City Hospital; Adjunct Surgeon, Presbyterian and St. James Hospitals; Member of Staff, St. Michael's Hospital; Chief of Clinic, Gynecological Department, Newark City Dispensary.

GAUDIANI, VINCENT, A.B., M.D., 145 East Forty-ninth Street, New York, New York. Royal University of Rome, 1898. Adjunct Professor, Royal University of Rome, Rome, Italy; Visiting Surgeon, Italian Hospital.

GAVIN, STEPHEN EDWARD, M.D., 38 South Main Street, Fond du Lac, Wisconsin. Rush Medical College, 1899.

GEHRUNG, EUGENE CHARLES, M.D., 4177 King Street, Denver, Colorado. St. Louis College of Physicians and Surgeons, 1870. Retired.

GÉHRUNG, JULIEN AUGUSTE, B.Sc., A.M., M.D., 783 Fifth Avenue, New York, New York. Washington University Medical School, 1901. Assistant Surgeon, New York Eye and Ear Infirmary.

GEIGER, JACOB, M.D., LL.D., 619 Francis Street, St. Joseph, Missouri. University of Louisville, Medical Department, 1872. Emeritus Professor of Surgery, St. Louis University School of Medicine; Surgeon, Missouri Methodist Hospital.

GEIST, EMIL S., M.D., 704 Besse Building, Minneapolis, Minnesota. University of Minnesota Medical School, 1900. Associate Professor of Orthopedic Surgery, University of Minnesota Medical School; Member of Staff, St. Mary's, Abbott, Asbury, Northwestern, and Swedish Hospitals.

GEIST, GEORGE ARTHUR, B.Sc., M.D., 133 West Seventh Street, St. Paul, Minnesota. University of Minnesota Medical School, 1911. Attending Surgeon, St. Joseph's Hospital.

GEIST, SAMUEL H., A.B., M.D., 300 Central Park, West, New York, New York. Columbia University College of Physicians and Surgeons, 1908. Associate Gynecologist and Associate in Surgical Pathology, Mt. Sinai Hospital.

GELDER, EDGAR EARL, M.D., 319 Merritt Building, Los Angeles, California. University of Pennsylvania School of Medicine, 1902.

GELLHORN, GEORGE, M.D., Metropolitan Building, St. Louis, Missouri. University of Würzburg, 1895. Associate in Clinical Gynecology, Washington University Medical School; Gynecologist, St. Luke's and Barnard Free Skin and Cancer Hospitals; Visiting Gynecologist, St. Louis City Hospital; Assistant Gynecologist, Barnes Hospital; Consulting Obstetrician, St. Louis Maternity Hospital; Consulting Gynecologist, St. John's Hospital.

GELPI, MAURICE JOSEPH, A.B., M.D., 3601 Prytania Street, New Orleans, Louisiana. Tulane University of Louisiana School of Medicine, 1909. Chief of Surgical Division 9, Charity Hospital.

GENTER, ARTHUR E., B.Sc., M.D., 1028 North Seventh Street, Sheboygan, Wisconsin. Northwestern University Medical School (Chicago Medical College), 1894.

GENTRY, ERNEST R., A.B., M.D., Medical Corps, United States Army, Washington, District of Columbia. Johns Hopkins University, Medical Department, 1909. Major, Medical Corps, United States Army.

GEORGE, EDGAR J., M.D., 110 North Wabash Avenue, Chicago, Illinois. Hahnemann Medical College and Hospital (Chicago Homeopathic Medical College), 1891. Professor of Ophthalmology, Hahnemann Medical College and Hospital; Attending Oculist, Hahnemann Hospital.

GERAGHTY, JOHN T., A.B., M.D., 330 North Charles Street, Baltimore, Maryland. Johns Hopkins University, Medical Department, 1903. Associate Professor of Urology, Johns Hopkins University, Medical Department; Assistant Director, Brady Urological Institute, Johns Hopkins Hospital.

GERRISH, WILLIAM A., M.D., Clinic Building, Jamestown, North Dakota. University of Minnesota Medical School, 1896. Surgeon, Trinity Hospital.

GERSHAW, FREDERICK WILLIAM, M.D., C.M., 826 Second Street, Medicine Hat, Alberta. Faculty of Medicine, University of Manitoba (Manitoba Medical College), 1908.

GERSTER, ARPAD G., M.D., C.D., O.M., 34 East Seventy-fifth Street, New York, New York. University of Vienna, 1872. Consulting Surgeon, Mt. Sinai and Lenox Hill Hospitals.

GERSTER, JOHN C. A., A.B., M.D., 18 East Seventy-eighth Street, New York, New York. Columbia University, College of Physicians and Surgeons, 1905. Assistant Professor of Clinical Surgery, Cornell University Medical College; Adjunct Surgeon, Mt. Sinai Hospital; Assistant Neurological Surgeon, Hospital for Ruptured and Crippled.

GESSNER, HERMANN BERTRAM, A.M., M.D., 119 Audubon Boulevard, New Orleans, Louisiana. Tulane University of Louisiana School of Medicine, 1895. Professor of Operative and Clinical Surgery, Tulane University of Louisiana School of Medicine; Chief Visiting Surgeon, Charity Hospital; Senior Associate in Surgery, Touro Infirmary.

GETCHELL, ALBERT COLBY, A.M., M.D., 6 Linden Street, Worcester, Massachusetts. Jefferson Medical College, 1885. Consulting Laryngologist, Memorial and Worcester City Hospitals.

GETTY, SAMUEL EMMET, M.D., 84 Ashburton Avenue, Yonkers, New York. University and Bellevue Hospital Medical College (University of the City of New York, Medical Department), 1893. Visiting Surgeon, St. John's Riverside Hospital; Consulting Surgeon, Tarrytown Hospital, Tarrytown,

New York State Hospital for Crippled and Deformed Children, West Haverstraw.

GIBB, WILLIAM TRAVIS, M.D., 42 West Seventy-fifth Street, New York, New York. University and Bellevue Hospital Medical College (New York University Medical College), 1886. Surgeon, Central and Neurological Hospitals, New York Society for the Prevention of Cruelty to Children; Gynecologist, St. Elizabeth's Hospital.

GIBBON, ROBERT LARDNER, M.D., 705 South Tryon Street, Charlotte, North Carolina. Jefferson Medical College, 1888. Surgeon, Charlotte Sanatorium, Presbyterian and St. Peter's Hospitals, Southern Railway Company.

GIBBY, HERBERT B., A.M., M.D., 96 South Franklin Street, Wilkes-Barre, Pennsylvania. University of Pennsylvania School of Medicine, 1895. Surgeon, Wilkes-Barre City and Riverside Hospitals; Consulting Surgeon, Nesbitt West Side Hospital, Wilkes-Barre, Pittston Hospital, Pittston.

GIBNEY, VIRGIL P., A.M., M.D., LL.D., 16 Park Avenue, New York, New York. University and Bellevue Hospital Medical College (Bellevue Hospital Medical College), 1871. Surgeon-in-Chief, Hospital for Ruptured and Crippled; Consulting Surgeon, Montefiore Home, New York Neurological Institute, New York, Seaside Hospital, New Dorp, St. Agnes Hospital, White Plains, New York, St. Vincent's and Bridgeport Hospitals, Bridgeport, Connecticut.

GIBSON, ALEXANDER, M.A., M.B., Ch.B., F.R.C.S. (Eng.), F.R.C.S. (Edin.), 661 Broadway, Winnipeg, Manitoba. University of Edinburgh, 1904. Associate Professor of Orthopedic Surgery, Faculty of Medicine, University of Manitoba; Associate Surgeon, Winnipeg General Hospital; Orthopedic Surgeon, Manitoba Military Hospital.

GIBSON, CHARLES LANGDON, A.B., M.D., 72 East Fifty-fourth Street, New York, New York. Harvard Medical School, 1889. Professor of Surgery, Cornell University Medical College; Attending Surgeon, First Cornell Surgical Division, New York Hospital; Consulting Surgeon, St. Luke's, City, and Memorial Hospitals, New York, Vassar Brothers' Hospital, Poughkeepsie, South Side Hospital, Babylon, New York State Hospital for Crippled and Deformed Children, West Haverstraw.

GIBSON, GORDON, M.D., 176 State Street, Brooklyn, New York. Faculty of Medicine, McGill University, 1904. Lecturer on Gynecology, Long Island College Hospital; Gynecologist, Polhemus Memorial Clinic, Brooklyn, Kings Park State Hospital, Kings Park; Assistant Gynecologist, St. Peter's Hospital; Assistant Obstetrician and Gynecological Surgeon, Long Island College Hospital; Consulting Surgeon, Huntington Hospital, Huntington.

GIBSON, HARRY ALEXANDER, M.D., C.M., F.R.C.S. (Edin.), 216 Sixth Avenue, West, Calgary, Alberta. Queen's University, Faculty of Medicine, 1903. Surgeon, Calgary General and Holy Cross Hospitals.

GIBSON, ROBERT DIXON, M.D., 310 Wick Avenue, Youngstown, Ohio. Western Reserve University School of Medicine, 1880. Emeritus Oculist, Youngstown City Hospital.

GIERE, ERIC O., M.D., 319 Hamm Building, St. Paul, Minnesota. University of Minnesota Medical School, 1892. Chief of Staff, St. Paul's Hospital.

GIFFORD, HAROLD, B.Sc., A.M., M.D., 702 Brandeis Building, Omaha, Nebraska. University of Michigan Medical School, 1882. Professor of Ophthalmology, University of Nebraska College of Medicine.

GILBERT, JOSEPH, M.D., 320 Scarbrough Building, Austin, Texas. University of Texas, Medical Department, 1897. Member of Advisory Board, City and County Hospital; Surgeon in Charge, Physicians and Surgeons Hospital.

GILCHRIST, HARRY L., M.D., Medical Corps, United States Army, Washington, District of Columbia. Western Reserve University School of Medicine, 1896. Lieutenant Colonel, Medical Corps, United States Army.

GILCREEST, JACOB EDWARD, M.D., Baylor Street, Ennis, Texas. University of Louisville, Medical Department (Louisville Medical College), 1876. Emeritus Professor of Gynecology and Lecturer on Gynecology, Baylor University School of Medicine.

GILDERSLEEVE, CHARLES P., M.D., 18 Schermerhorn Street, Brooklyn, New York. Columbia University, College of Physicians and Surgeons, 1881. Consulting Surgeon, St. Peter's Hospital and St. Joseph's Institute, Brooklyn, St. Anthony's Hospital, Woodhaven, House of St. Giles the Cripple, Garden City.

GILE, JOHN MARTIN, A.M., M.D., 3 Maynard Street, Hanover, New Hampshire. Dartmouth Medical School, 1891. Professor of Clinical Surgery, Dartmouth Medical School; Surgeon, Mary Hitchcock Memorial Hospital; Consulting Surgeon, Littleton Hospital, Littleton, New Hampshire, Memorial Hospital for Women and Children, Concord, New Hampshire, Millers River Hospital, Winchendon, State Infirmary, Tewksbury, Massachusetts, Lake View Sanitarium, Burlington, Hospitals at Bellows Falls and Springfield, Vermont.

GILFILLAN, W. WHITEHEAD, M.D., 31 West Fiftieth Street, New York, New York. Columbia University, College of Physicians and Surgeons, 1890. Visiting Ophthalmic Surgeon, City Hospital; Visiting Oculist, Sailors' Snug Harbor; Visiting Ophthalmologist, New York House of Refuge; Consulting Ophthalmic Surgeon, St. Vincent's Hospital, Staten Island; Consulting Oculist, Southampton Fresh Air Home, Southampton; Consulting Ophthalmologist, Southampton Hospital, Southampton.

GILL, GEORGE, A.B., A.M., M.D., 800 Lorain County Bank Building, Elyria, Ohio. University of Illinois College of Medicine (College of Physicians and Surgeons), 1896. Oto-Laryngologist, Elyria Memorial Hospital.

GILL, JAMES EDWARD, M.D., Medical Corps, United States Navy, Washington, District of Columbia. Georgetown University School of Medicine, 1901. Commander, Medical Corps, United States Navy.

GILL, MICHAEL HENRY, M.D., 36 Pearl Street, Hartford, Connecticut. Yale University School of Medicine, 1896. Ophthalmologist and Aurist, St. Francis' Hospital.

GILLESPIE, ANDREW TAYLOR, M.B., 304½ Victoria Avenue, Fort William, Ontario. University of Toronto, Faculty of Medicine, 1910. Chief of Orthopedics, McKellar Hospital.

GILLESPIE, JAMES ANDREW, M.D., C.M., 718 Granville Street, Vancouver, British Columbia. Faculty of Medicine, McGill University (University of Bishop College, Faculty of Medicine), 1901.

GILLESPIE, WILLIAM, M.D., 670 June Street, Cincinnati, Ohio. University of Cincinnati College of Medicine (Medical College of Ohio), 1890. Professor of Obstetrics, University of Cincinnati College of Medicine; Director of Obstetrical Service, Cincinnati General and Bethesda Hospitals.

GILLETTE, WILLIAM J., M.D., 1613 Jefferson Street, Toledo, Ohio. Western Reserve University School of Medicine, 1879. Chief of Staff, Robinwood Hospital.

GILLMAN, ROBERT W., M.D., 61 Peterboro Street, Detroit, Michigan. Detroit College of Medicine and Surgery, 1887. Clinical Professor of Ophthalmology, Detroit College of Medicine and Surgery; Surgeon, St. Mary's, Providence, and St. Luke's Hospitals.

GILMAN, PHILIP KINGSNORTH, A.B., M.D., 350 Post Street, San Francisco, California. Johns Hopkins University, Medical Department, 1905. Assistant Clinical Professor of Surgery, Leland Stanford Junior University School of Medicine.

GILMER, THOMAS L., M.D., D.D.S., D.Sc., 122 South Michigan Avenue, Chicago, Illinois. Quincy College of Medicine, 1885. Emeritus Dean, and Professor of Oral Surgery, Northwestern University Dental School; Oral Surgeon, St. Luke's Hospital.

GILMORE, ROWLAND THOMAS STRATTON, M.D., C.M., 905 Lake Boulevard, Bemidji, Minnesota. University of Toronto, Faculty of Medicine (Trinity Medical College), 1895. Surgeon, St. Anthony's Hospital.

GINN, CURTISS, M.D., Reibold Building, Dayton, Ohio. Ohio State University College of Homeopathic Medicine (Cleveland University of Medicine and Surgery), 1895. Staff Surgeon, Miami Valley Hospital.

GIRVIN, JOHN HARPER, M.D., 2120 Walnut Street, Philadelphia, Pennsylvania. University of Pennsylvania School of Medicine, 1892. Associate Professor of Gynecology, Graduate School of Medicine, University of Pennsylvania; Gynecologist, Presbyterian Hospital.

GIVEN, ELLIS EDGAR WILLITS, M.D., 2714 Columbia Avenue, Philadelphia, Pennsylvania. University of Pennsylvania School of Medicine, 1897.

GLASGOW, FRANK A., A.B., M.D., University Club Building, St. Louis, Missouri. Washington University Medical School (St. Louis Medical College), 1878. Senior Gynecologist, St. Louis Mullanphy Hospital; Consulting Gynecologist, St. Vincent's Institution.

GLASIER, WILLIAM F., Phar.G., M.D., Carlsbad, New Mexico. University of Illinois College of Medicine, 1910. Surgeon, St. Francis Hospital.

GLASS, JAMES H., A.M., M.D., Trenton Falls, New York. University and Bellevue Hospital Medical College, 1877. Consulting Surgeon, Faxton and Utica State Hospitals, Utica, Rome City Hospital, Rome.

GLAZEBROOK, FRANCIS H., M.D., 171 South Street, Morristown, New Jersey. Cornell University Medical College, 1900. Surgeon, Morristown Memorial Hospital, Morristown, New Jersey State Hospital, Morris Plains.

GLEASON, JOHN E., A.B., M.D., 1061 David Whitney Building, Detroit, Michigan. University of Michigan Medical School, 1903. Member of Attending Staff, Department of Ophthalmology and Oto-Laryngology, Grace Hospital.

GLEASON, JOHN HIRAM, M.D., C.M., Merchants Bank Building, Manchester, New Hampshire. Faculty of Medicine, McGill University, 1895. Surgeon, Beacon Hill Hospital; Consulting Surgeon, Notre Dame Hospital, Manchester Children's Home.

GLENN, LUCIUS NEWTON, M.D., 402 Realty Building, Gastonia, North Carolina. University of Maryland School of Medicine, 1897. Surgeon, City Hospital.

GLENNAN, JAMES D., M.D., Medical Corps, United States Army, Washington, District of Columbia. George Washington University Medical School (Columbian University, Medical Department), 1886. Colonel, Medical Corps, United States Army.

GLENNON, WILLIAM P., M.D., 4500 Olive Street, St. Louis, Missouri. L.R.C.P., L.R.C.S. (Ire.), L.M. (Coombe Hospital), 1906. Associate Professor of Surgery, St. Louis University School of Medicine; Associate Surgeon, St. John's Hospital.

GLINES, WALTER ASHLEY, M.D., 45 Allen Street, San Juan, Porto Rico. University of Maryland School of Medicine (College of Physicians and Surgeons, Baltimore), 1906. Consulting Surgeon, Presbyterian Mission Hospital; Attending Surgeon, Porto Rico Sanatorium; Surgeon, Asilo de Sordo Mudos.

GLYNN, JAMES P., A.M., M.D., 474 Ninth Street, Brooklyn, New York. Columbia University, College of Physicians and Surgeons, 1894. Gynecologist, St. Mary's and Williamsburgh Hospitals.

GODDARD, HERBERT MASKELL, M.D., 1531 Spruce Street, Philadelphia, Pennsylvania. University of Pennsylvania School of Medicine (Medico-Chirurgical College), 1905. Rhinologist and Oto-Laryngologist, Jewish Hospital, Matilde Adler Loeb Dispensary, Home for Hebrew Orphans, American Hospital for Diseases of the Stomach, Philadelphia, Eaglesville Sanatorium, Eaglesville.

GODDARD, SAMUEL WARREN, M.D., 15 Ellsworth Avenue, Brockton, Massachusetts. Harvard Medical School, 1904. Surgeon, Goddard Hospital; Consulting Surgeon, Bridgewater State Hospital, Bridgewater.

GODFREY, CHARLES CARTLIDGE, Ph.B., M.D., 340 State Street, Bridgeport, Connecticut. Dartmouth Medical School, 1884. Surgeon-in-Chief, Bridgeport Hospital; Consulting Surgeon, St. Vincent's Hospital.

GODLEE, SIR RICKMAN JOHN, Bart., K.C.V.O., B.A., M.S., LL.D., F.R.C.S. (Eng.), Athenaeum Club, Pall Mall, London, West, England. University of London, 1872. Emeritus Professor of Clinical Surgery, University College; Consulting Surgeon, University College Hospital; Honorary Surgeon in Ordinary to His Majesty the King.

GOETSCH, EMIL, B.Sc., M.D., Ph.D., 2 Sidney Place, Brooklyn, New York. Johns Hopkins University, Medical Department, 1909. Professor of Surgery, Long Island College Hospital; Surgeon-in-Chief, Long Island College Hospital.

GOFFE, J. RIDDLE, Ph.M., A.M., M.D., 123 East Fifty-third Street, New York, New York. University and Bellevue Hospital Medical College, 1881. Professor of Gynecology, New York Polyclinic Medical School, Dartmouth Medical School; Attending Gynecologist, New York Polyclinic Medical School and Hospital; Consulting Surgeon, Woman's Hospital; Member of Consulting Staff, City and Union Hospitals, New York, St. Joseph's Hospital, Yonkers, Mt. Vernon Hospital, Mt. Vernon, Lawrence Hospital, Bronxville.

GOLDBACH, LEO JOHN, B.Sc., M.D., 322 North Charles Street, Baltimore, Maryland. University of Maryland School of Medicine, 1905. Associate in Clinical Ophthalmology, Johns Hopkins University, Medical Department; Surgeon, St. Joseph's Hospital; Dispensary Ophthalmologist, Johns Hopkins Hospital.

GOLDBERG, HAROLD G., M.D., 1925 Chestnut Street, Philadelphia, Pennsylvania. University of Pennsylvania School of Medicine, 1900. Ophthalmic Surgeon, Episcopal, Kensington and Christ Church Hospitals, Baltimore and Ohio Railroad.

GOLDEN, JOHN FERDINAND, M.D., 104 South Michigan Avenue, Chicago, Illinois. Northwestern University Medical School, 1903. Professor of Surgery, Loyola University School of Medicine; Attending Surgeon, Mercy Hospital.

GOLDEN, WILLIAM WOLFE, M.D., Elkins, West Virginia. University and Bellevue Hospital Medical College (New York University Medical College), 1892. Chief Surgeon, Davis Memorial Hospital.

GOLDSBOROUGH, BRICE W., M.D., 8 High Street, Cambridge, Maryland. University of Virginia, Department of Medicine, 1880. Chief of Staff, Cambridge-Maryland Hospital.

GOLDSBOROUGH, FRANCIS COLQUHOUN, B.Sc., M.D., 515 Franklin Street, Buffalo, New York. Johns Hopkins University, Medical Department, 1903. Professor of Obstetrics, and Associate Professor of Gynecology, University of Buffalo, Department of Medicine; Attending Gynecologist and Attending Obstetrician, Buffalo General Hospital; Obstetrician-in-Chief, Buffalo City Hospital.

GOLDSMITH, PERRY G., C.B.E., M.D., C.M., 84 Carlton Street, Toronto, Ontario. University of Toronto, Faculty of Medicine (Trinity Medical College), 1896. Associate Professor of Oto-Laryngology, University of

Toronto, Faculty of Medicine; Senior Assistant Surgeon, Oto-Laryngological Department, Toronto General Hospital.

GOLDSMITH, WILLIAM STOKES, M.D., 404 Healy Building, Atlanta, Georgia. Emory University School of Medicine (Atlanta Medical College), 1892. Professor of Clinical Surgery, Emory University School of Medicine; Visiting Surgeon, Grady Memorial, Wesley Memorial, Georgia Baptist Hospitals, and St. Joseph's Infirmary.

GOLDSPOHN, ALBERT, M.Sc., M.D., 2120 Cleveland Avenue, Chicago, Illinois. Rush Medical College, 1878. Professor of Gynecology, Post-Graduate Medical School; Surgeon-in-Chief, Evangelical Deaconess Hospital; Attending Gynecologist, Post-Graduate Hospital.

GOLDSTEIN, ALBERT E., M.D., 330 North Charles Street, Baltimore, Maryland. University of Maryland School of Medicine (College of Physicians and Surgeons), 1912. Assistant in Histology and Embryology, University of Maryland, School of Medicine; Attending Urologist, Hebrew Hospital and Mt. Pleasant Sanatorium; Chief of Urological Clinic, Hebrew Hospital.

GOLDSTEIN, DAVID D., M.D., 126 East Sixty-first Street, New York, New York. University and Bellevue Hospital Medical College (New York University Medical College), 1890. Chief of Surgical Clinic, Mt. Sinai Hospital; Attending Surgeon, Hospital for Deformities and Joint Diseases.

GOLDSTEIN, MAX A., M.D., 3858 Westminster Place, St. Louis, Missouri. Washington University Medical School (Missouri Medical College), 1892. Otologist, Jewish Hospital; Director, Central Institute for the Deaf. Editor, *The Laryngoscope.*

GOLDSTINE, MARK T., M.D., 25 East Washington Street, Chicago, Illinois. Rush Medical College, 1900. Clinical Assistant in Gynecology, Northwestern University Medical School; Senior Attending Gynecologist, Wesley Memorial Hospital.

GOLDTHWAIT, JOEL ERNEST, B.Sc., M.D., 372 Marlborough Street, Boston, Massachusetts. Harvard Medical School, 1890. Associate in Orthopedic Surgery, Harvard University Graduate School of Medicine.

GOLDTHWAITE, RALPH HARVARD, A.B., M.D., Medical Corps, United States Army, Washington, District of Columbia. Harvard Medical School, 1906. Assistant Professor of Ophthalmology, Army Medical School; in Charge of Eye, Ear, Nose, and Throat Department, Infantry School, Camp Benning; Major, Medical Corps, United States Army.

GOLTMAN, M., M.D., C.M., Memphis Trust Building, Memphis, Tennessee. Faculty of Medicine, McGill University (University of Bishop College, Faculty of Medicine), 1892. Professor of Surgery and Clinical Surgery, University of Tennessee College of Medicine; Professor of Oral Surgery, University of Tennessee College of Dentistry; Chief Surgeon, Baptist Memorial Hospital.

GOOD, JAMES WILFORD, M.B., L.R.C.P. (Edin.), 226 Somerset Building, Winnipeg, Manitoba. University of Toronto, Faculty of Medicine, 1877. Professor of Ophthalmology, Faculty of Medicine, University of Manitoba.

GOODALE, JOSEPH LINCOLN, A.M., M.D., 258 Beacon Street, Boston, Massachusetts. Harvard Medical School, 1893. Instructor in Laryngology, Harvard Medical School.

GOODELL, CHARLES E., M.D., 63 Allen Street, Jamestown, New York. University of Buffalo, Department of Medicine, 1910.

GOODELL, WILLIAM, A.M., M.D., 6 Chestnut Street, Springfield, Massachusetts. Harvard Medical School, 1905. Surgeon, Ear, Nose, and Throat Department, Springfield Hospital.

GOODENOW, NORMAN HALKIER, M.D., 71 North Baldwin Avenue, Sierra Madre, California. Rush Medical College, 1892.

GOODFRIEND, NATHAN, M.D., 44 West Seventy-seventh Street, New York, New York. Columbia University, College of Physicians and Surgeons, 1902. Visiting Ophthalmologist, Bronx Hospital and Dispensary; Attending Ophthalmologist, People's Hospital; Assistant Surgeon, Manhattan Eye, Ear, and Throat Hospital.

GOODHUE, GEORGE, A.B., M.D., 133 North Perry Street, Dayton, Ohio. Dartmouth Medical School, 1879; University and Bellevue Hospital Medical College (University of the City of New York, Medical Department), 1880. Visiting Surgeon, Miami Valley Hospital.

GOODMAN, CHARLES, M.D., 969 Madison Avenue, New York, New York. Western Reserve University School of Medicine, 1892. Clinical Professor of Surgery, University and Bellevue Hospital Medical College; Attending Surgeon, Beth Israel, Montefiore Hospitals.

GOODMAN, SYLVESTER JACOB, Phar.G., M.D., 121 South Sixth Street, Columbus, Ohio. Jefferson Medical College, 1900. Surgeon and Obstetrician, Grant Hospital; Surgeon, Jewish Infant Home; Obstetrician, Mercy Hospital.

GOODRICH, CHARLES HOWARD, M.D., 280 Park Place, Brooklyn, New York. Columbia University, College of Physicians and Surgeons, 1894. Attending Surgeon, Methodist Episcopal Hospital, Brooklyn Orphan Asylum; Consulting Surgeon, Brattleboro Memorial Hospital, Brattleboro, Vermont.

GOODRICH, WILLIAM HENRY, A.B., M.D., 508 Lamar Building, Augusta, Georgia. University of Georgia, Medical Department, 1897. Professor of Surgery, University of Georgia, Medical Department; Visiting Surgeon, University and Wilhenford Hospitals.

GOODWIN, HENRY TIMROD, M.D., 360 Van Duzer Street, Staten Island, New York. Long Island College Hospital, 1886. Surgeon, St. Vincent's Hospital.

GOODWIN, JAMES JOSEPH, M.D., 202 Church Street, Clinton, Massachusetts. Jefferson Medical College, 1892. Surgeon, Clinton Hospital.

GOODWIN, SIR THOMAS HERBERT JOHN, K.C.B., C.M.G., D.S.O., London, England. F.R.C.S. (Eng.), L.R.C.P. (Lond.), (St. Mary's Hospital), 1892. Lieutenant General and Director General, Army Medical Service.

GOODWIN, WILLIAM H., A.B., M.D., University of Virginia, Charlottesville, Virginia. University of Virginia, Department of Medicine, 1908. Associate Professor of Surgery and Gynecology, University of Virginia, Department of Medicine; Associate Visiting Surgeon, University of Virginia Hospital, University.

GORDON, CHARLES ALBERT, M.D., 847 Putnam Avenue, Brooklyn, New York. Cornell University Medical College, 1905. Gynecologist and Obstetrician, St. Catherine's, Greenpoint, and Williamsburgh Hospitals.

GORDON, DONALD, M.D., 27 East Sixty-second Street, New York, New York. Columbia University, College of Physicians and Surgeons, 1906. Visiting Surgeon, St. Bartholomew's Hospital; Assistant Visiting Surgeon, City Hospital.

GORDON, GEORGE SINCLAIR, M.D., C.M., 127 Vancouver Block, Vancouver, British Columbia. Faculty of Medicine, McGill University, 1897. Urological Surgeon, Vancouver General and St. Paul's Hospitals.

GORDON, JOHN WEAVER, B.Sc., M.D., 206 Locust Street, Clearfield, Pennsylvania. University of Pennsylvania School of Medicine, 1903. Gynecologist and Obstetrician, Clearfield Hospital.

GORDON, ONSLOW ALLEN, M.D., 71 Halsey Street, Brooklyn, New York. Dartmouth Medical School, 1885. Surgeon, St. Mary's Hospital.

GORDON, ONSLOW ALLEN, JR., M.D., 71 Halsey Street, Brooklyn, New York. Long Island College Hospital, 1911. Clinical Professor of Gynecology, University and Bellevue Hospital Medical College; Associate Surgeon, St. Mary's Hospital; Assistant Visiting Gynecologist, Bellevue Hospital, New York.

GORE, VICTOR MAURICE, M.D., Clinton, Oklahoma. Washington University Medical School, 1908. Associate Surgeon, Clinton Hospital.

GORRELL, JAMES ALFRED, B.A., M.D., C.M., 702 Sterling Bank Block, Winnipeg, Manitoba. Faculty of Medicine, University of Manitoba (Manitoba Medical College), 1908.

GOSMAN, GEORGE H. R., M.D., Medical Corps, United States Army, Washington, District of Columbia. University of Pennsylvania School of Medicine, 1898. Lieutenant Colonel, Medical Corps, United States Army.

GOSS, RALPH MONTGOMERY, A.B., M.D., 297 Hancock Avenue, Athens, Georgia. George Washington University Medical School, 1906.

GOULD, ELISHA TOLMAN, M.D., 631 Washington Street, Sonora, California. Bowdoin Medical School, 1880. Surgeon-in-Chief, Sierra Hospital.

GOURLAY, HENRY BEAUCHAMP, M.D., C.M., 543 Granville Street, Vancouver, British Columbia. Faculty of Medicine, McGill University, 1906. Associate Surgeon, Vancouver General Hospital; Surgeon, St. Paul's Hospital.

GRABER, C. LEE, Ph.G., B.Sc., M.D., 15701 Detroit Avenue, Cleveland, Ohio. University of Cincinnati College of Medicine, 1898. Chief of Staff and Head of Surgical Division, Lakewood Hospital.

GRAD, HERMANN, M.D., 40 East Forty-first Street, New York, New York. University and Bellevue Hospital Medical College (New York University Medical College), 1894. Attending Surgeon, Woman's Hospital.

GRAEFE, CHARLES, M.D., 631 Wayne Street, Sandusky, Ohio. Western Reserve University School of Medicine (University of Wooster, Medical Department), 1880. Surgeon, Providence and Good Samaritan Hospitals.

GRAHAM, ALLEN, B.Sc., M.D., 939 East One Hundred Fifty-second Street Cleveland, Ohio. University of Maryland School of Medicine (Baltimore Medical College), 1909. Instructor in Surgery, Western Reserve University Medical School; Assistant Visiting Surgical Pathologist, Lakeside Hospital.

GRAHAM, ALOIS BACHMAN, A.M., M.D., 30 Willoughby Building, Indianapolis, Indiana. Indiana University School of Medicine (Medical College of Indiana), 1894. Clinical Professor of Proctology, Indiana University School of Medicine; Member of Consulting Staff, Indianapolis City, St. Vincent's, and Methodist Episcopal Hospitals.

GRAHAM, ARCHIE JAMES, B.Sc., M.D., 6250 South Halsted Street, Chicago, Illinois. University of Illinois College of Medicine (College of Physicians and Surgeons, Chicago), 1902. Instructor in Operative Surgery, University of Illinois College of Medicine.

GRAHAM, COLIN WOLSELEY, B.A., M.D., C.M., Birks Building, Vancouver, British Columbia. Queen's University, Faculty of Medicine, 1906. Ophthalmologist and Otologist, Vancouver General Hospital.

GRAHAM, DAVID WILSON, A.B., M.D., LL.D., 7 West Madison Street, Chicago, Illinois. University and Bellevue Hospital Medical College, 1872. Surgeon, Presbyterian Hospital.

GRAHAM, DELL E., M.D., First National Bank Building, Ottumwa, Iowa. State University of Iowa College of Medicine, 1902. Consulting Eye, Ear, Nose, and Throat Surgeon, St. Joseph's and City Hospitals.

GRAHAM, DOUGLAS WILLIAM, M.D., C.M., Swift Current Clinic, Swift Current, Saskatchewan. Faculty of Medicine, McGill University, 1907. Attending Surgeon, Swift Current General Hospital.

GRAHAM, EVARTS AMBROSE, A.B., M.D., Washington University Medical School, St. Louis, Missouri. Rush Medical College, 1907. Professor of Surgery, Washington University Medical School; Surgeon-in-Chief, Barnes and St. Louis Children's Hospitals.

GRAHAM, FRANK, M.D., 57 North Bellevue Avenue, Memphis, Tennessee. Columbia University, College of Physicians and Surgeons, 1900. Gynecologist, Memphis General Hospital; Assistant Gynecologist, Lucy Brinkley Hospital.

GRAHAM, HARRINGTON BIDWELL, B.Sc., M.D., Shreve Building, San Francisco, California. University of California Medical School, 1899. Chief of Department of Otology, San Francisco Hospital; Consultant in Otology, Southern Pacific Railway Hospital.

GRAHAM, HENRY FLACK, M.D., 474 First Street, Brooklyn, New York. Columbia University, College of Physicians and Surgeons, 1905. Assistant Attending Surgeon, Methodist Episcopal Hospital; Associate Surgeon, Norwegian Lutheran Deaconess Hospital.

GRAHAM, JOHN ALFRED, M.D., 30 North Michigan Avenue, Chicago, Illinois. Rush Medical College, 1902. Assistant in Surgery, Rush Medical College; Associate Professor of Surgery, Chicago Policlinic; Attending Surgeon, Henrotin Memorial Hospital; Associate in Surgery, Children's Memorial Hospital.

GRAHAM, ROSCOE R., M.B., 31 Oriole Road, Toronto, Ontario. University of Toronto, Faculty of Medicine, 1910.

GRAHAM, R. WATSON, M.D., C.M., 801 Pacific Mutual Building, Los Angeles, California. Faculty of Medicine, McGill University, 1904.

GRAHAM, WILLIAM EZRA, M.D., C.M., F.R.C.S. (Edin.), Herald Block, Calgary, Alberta. University of Toronto, Faculty of Medicine (Trinity Medical College), 1897.

GRAÑA, FRANCISCO, B.Sc., M.D., Belaochaga 577, Lima, Peru. Faculty of Medicine, University of San Marcos, 1903. Professor of Surgery, Faculty of Medicine, University of San Marcos; Chief of Surgical Section, Guadalupe Hospital.

GRANT, ARTHUR ROGERS, M.D., 321 Genesee Street, Utica, New York. University and Bellevue Hospital Medical College (New York University Medical College), 1897. Surgeon in Charge, Utica Homeopathic Hospital; Gynecologist, Utica General Hospital.

GRANT, JOHN PRESCOTT, M.D., C.M., M.R.C.S. (Eng.), L.R.C.P. (Lond.), 11 East Forty-eighth Street, New York, New York. Faculty of Medicine, McGill University, 1895. Professor of Surgery, New York Polyclinic Medical School; Visiting Surgeon, New York Polyclinic Medical School and Hospital, People's Hospital, New York, New York State Hospital for Crippled and Deformed Children, West Haverstraw.

GRANT, JOSEPH F., M.D., 423 First National Bank Building, San Diego, California. University of Louisville, Medical Department, 1890. Ophthalmic Surgeon, San Diego County Hospital.

GRANT, WILLIAM W., M.D., Mack Building, Denver, Colorado. Long Island College Hospital, 1868. Surgeon, St. Luke's Hospital; Local Surgeon, Rock Island Lines.

GRATIOT, HARVEY B., M.D., 256 Tenth Street, Dubuque, Iowa. Jefferson Medical College, 1896. Oculist and Aurist, Finley Hospital.

GRAVES, JAMES QUINTUS, M.D., 201½ De Siard Street, Monroe, Louisiana. Tulane University of Louisiana School of Medicine, 1906. Member of Surgical Staff, St. Francis Sanitarium.

GRAVES, ROBERT JOHN, B.Sc., M.D., 4 North State Street, Concord, New Hampshire. Harvard Medical School, 1903. Surgeon, Margaret Pillsbury General Hospital; Chief Surgeon, Boston and Maine Railroad.

GRAVES, STANLEY HOPE, M.D., 109 College Place, Norfolk, Virginia. Medical College of Virginia, 1894. Urologist and Rectal Surgeon, Sarah Leigh Hospital; Urologist, Norfolk Protestant Hospital.

GRAVES, WILLIAM BOARDMAN, M.D., 426 Main Street, East Orange, New Jersey. University and Bellevue Hospital Medical College (University of the City of New York, Medical Department), 1880. Consulting Surgeon, Orange Memorial Hospital, Orange.

GRAVES, WILLIAM P., A.B., M.D., 244 Marlborough Street, Boston, Massachusetts. Harvard Medical School, 1899. Professor of Gynecology, Harvard Medical School; Surgeon-in-Chief, Free Hospital for Women, Brookline; Consulting Gynecologist, Boston Lying-in and Beth Israel Hospitals.

GRAY, CHARLES PERLEY, B.Sc., M.D., 60 West Fifty-eighth Street, New York, New York. Harvard Medical School, 1904. Acting Adjunct Professor of Gynecology, New York Polyclinic School and Hospital; Visiting Surgeon, New York Throat, Nose, and Lung Hospital; Visiting Gynecologist, North Eastern Dispensary.

GRAY, DAN FEURT, Phar.G., M.D., 321 South Fifth Street, Ironton, Ohio. University of Cincinnati College of Medicine (Miami Medical College), 1899. Chief Surgeon, Roosevelt Hospital.

GRAY, GEORGE HENRY, M.D., 11 Lynn Shore Drive, Lynn, Massachusetts. University of Vermont College of Medicine, 1888. Surgeon, Lynn Hospital, Lynn, Hospital of Massachusetts Soldiers' Home, Chelsea, Cape Cod Hospital, Hyannis.

GRAY, GEORGE MORRIS, M.D., 800 Minnesota Avenue, Kansas City, Kansas. University and Bellevue Hospital Medical College, 1880. Professor of Clinical Surgery, University of Kansas School of Medicine; Chief Surgeon, St. Margaret's Hospital.

GRAY, GORDON CAMERON, M.B., 320 Tegler Block, Edmonton, Alberta. University of Toronto, Faculty of Medicine, 1907. Head of Department of Surgery, University of Alberta, Faculty of Medicine; Visiting Surgeon, Royal Alexandra and Misericordia Hospitals.

GRAY, JAMES D., M.D., Neumann Building, Yoakum, Texas. St. Louis University School of Medicine, 1901. Chief Surgeon, Yoakum Hospital.

GRAY, WILLIAM L., M.D., 412 Illinois Building, Champaign, Illinois. State University of Iowa College of Medicine (Keokuk Medical College), 1891. Surgeon, Julia F. Burnham Hospital.

GRAYSON, CARY TRAVERS, Ph.G., M.D., Medical Corps, United States Navy, Washington, District of Columbia. University of the South, Medical Department, 1903. Member of Consulting Staff, Emergency Hospital; Rear Admiral, Medical Corps, United States Navy.

GREELEY, JAMES THORNTON, M.D., 115 Main Street, Nashua, New Hampshire. University of Maryland School of Medicine (Baltimore Medical College), 1891. Member of Surgical Staff, St. Joseph's and Nashua Memorial Hospitals.

GREEN, BURT FRANCIS, A.B., M.D., First National Bank Building, Hillsdale, Michigan. University of Michigan Medical School, 1900. Surgeon, Hillsdale Sanitarium.

GREEN, BURTIS T., B.Sc., M.D., Bradbury Building, Brookings, South Dakota. Hahnemann Medical College and Hospital, Chicago, 1903. Attending Surgeon, Dakota Deaconess Hospital.

GREEN, CHARLES CAMPBELL, B.Sc., M.D., 411 Carter Building, Houston, Texas. Tulane University of Louisiana School of Medicine, 1910. Visiting Surgeon, St. Joseph's Infirmary; Assistant Chief Surgeon, Sunset Central Lines.

GREEN, CHARLES MONTRAVILLE, A.B., M.D., 78 Marlborough Street, Boston, Massachusetts. Harvard Medical School, 1877. Emeritus Professor of Obstetrics and Gynecology, Harvard Medical School; Senior Gynecologist, Boston City Hospital; Consultant, Massachusetts State Hospital.

GREEN, EUGENE K., B.A., M.D., 808 Physicians and Surgeons Building, Minneapolis, Minnesota. University of Minnesota Medical School, 1903. Member of Surgical Staff, Hill Crest Surgical Hospital.

GREEN, FRANK WILLIAM, M.D., C.M., Armstrong Avenue, Cranbrook, British Columbia. Faculty of Medicine, McGill University, 1898. Surgeon, St. Eugene Hospital.

GREEN, GEORGE W., A.M., M.D., 501 Main Street, Dowagiac, Michigan. University of Michigan Medical School, 1905. Surgeon, Lee Sanitarium.

GREEN, GEORGE WILLARD, M.D., 4654 Sheridan Road, Chicago, Illinois. University of Michigan Medical School, 1892. Attending Surgeon, Ravenswood Hospital.

GREEN, JAMES S., A.M., M.D., 463 North Broad Street, Elizabeth, New Jersey. Columbia University, College of Physicians and Surgeons, 1889. Attending Surgeon and Attending Gynecologist, Elizabeth General Hospital; Consulting Surgeon, St. Elizabeth Hospital, Elizabeth, Bonnie Burn Sanatorium, Scotch Plains.

GREEN, JOHN, JR., A.B., M.D., 626 Metropolitan Building, St. Louis, Missouri. Washington University Medical School, 1898. Ophthalmic Surgeon, St. Luke's Hospital; Consulting Ophthalmic Surgeon, St. Louis Maternity Hospital.

GREEN, JOHN ALBERT, M.D., William Brown Building, Rockford, Illinois. Northwestern University Medical School, 1906. Member of Consulting Staff, Rockford Hospital.

GREEN, NATHAN W., A.M., M.D., 152 West Fifty-seventh Street, New York, New York. Columbia University, College of Physicians and Surgeons, 1898. Associate Attending Surgeon, St. Luke's Hospital; Attending Surgeon, City Hospital; Consultant, St. Bartholomew's Hospital; Consulting Surgeon, Rockingham Hospital, Bellows Falls, Vermont.

GREEN, THOMAS MEARES, M.D., 11 Masonic Temple, Wilmington, North Carolina. University of Maryland School of Medicine, 1900. Visiting Surgeon, James Walker Memorial and Baby's Hospitals.

GREENBERG, HARRY, M.D., Caswell Block, Milwaukee, Wisconsin. Western Reserve University School of Medicine (University of Wooster, Medical Department), 1896. Attending Surgeon, Mt. Sinai Hospital.

GREENE, DANIEL CROSBY, A.B., M.D., 23 Bay State Road, Boston, Massachusetts. Harvard Medical School, 1899. Instructor in Laryngology, Harvard Medical School; Surgeon, Throat Department, Children's Hospital; Laryngologist, Massachusetts General Hospital.

GREENE, EVAN, M.D., C.M., F.R.C.S. (Edin.), 8231 One Hundred Sixth Street, Edmonton, Alberta. Faculty of Medicine, McGill University, 1899. Professor, Department of Anatomy, University of Alberta.

GREENE, JOSEPH BERRY, A.M., M.D., Haywood Building, Asheville, North Carolina. University of Virginia, Department of Medicine, 1893. Member of Staff, Asheville Mission and Meriwether Hospitals, Asheville, Clarence Barker Memorial Hospital, Biltmore.

GREENE, LOUIS STORROW, M.D., 1624 I Street, Northwest, Washington, District of Columbia. University of Virginia, Department of Medicine, 1895. Instructor in Ophthalmology, Georgetown University School of Medicine; Attending Surgeon, Episcopal Eye, Ear, and Throat Hospital.

GREENE, ROBERT HOLMES, A.M., M.D., 78 East Fifty-sixth Street, New York, New York. Harvard Medical School, 1886. Emeritus Professor of Surgery, Fordham University School of Medicine; Attending Genito-Urinary Surgeon, City Hospital; Consulting Surgeon, French Hospital.

GREENE, RONALD A., M.D., 517 Old National Bank Building, Spokane, Washington. Northwestern University Medical School, 1902. Member of Staff, Sacred Heart Hospital; Laryngologist, Spokane Tubercular Sanitarium.

GREENLEAF, HENRY S., A.B., M.D., Medical Corps, United States Army, Washington, District of Columbia. University of Pennsylvania School of Medicine, 1895. Colonel, Medical Corps, United States Army.

GREENOUGH, ROBERT B., A.B., M.D., 8 Marlborough Street, Boston, Massachusetts. Harvard Medical School, 1896. Assistant Professor of Surgery, Harvard Medical School; Director, Cancer Commission of Harvard University; Visiting Surgeon, Massachusetts General Hospital; Surgeon in Charge, Collis P. Huntington Memorial Hospital.

GREENSFELDER, LOUIS A., M.D., 31 North State Street, Chicago, Illinois. Northwestern University Medical School (Chicago Medical College), 1887. Attending Surgeon, Michael Reese Hospital.

GREENWOOD, ALLEN, M.D., 101 Newbury Street, Boston, Massachusetts. Harvard Medical School, 1889. Associate in Ophthalmology, Harvard University Graduate School of Medicine; Professor of Ophthalmology, Tufts College Medical School; Consulting Ophthalmic Surgeon, Boston City Hospital and Waltham Hospital, Waltham.

GREER, ROBERT BRUCE, B.Sc., M.D., 371 North Main Street, Butler, Pennsylvania. University of Pennsylvania School of Medicine, 1899. Member of Staff, Butler County General Hospital; Surgeon, Standard Steel Car, Butler Car Wheel, Butler Bolt and Rivet, Forged Steel Wheel Companies, Pennsylvania and Baltimore and Ohio Railroads.

GREGG, ANDREW S., A.B., M.D., First National Bank Building, Fayetteville, Arkansas. Washington University Medical School (St. Louis Medical College), 1881. Member of Staff, City Hospital.

GREGOR, GILBERT DAVID, M.D., 255 Ten Eyck Street, Watertown, New York. University and Bellevue Hospital Medical School (University of the City of New York, Medical Department), 1883. Visiting Surgeon, St. Joachim's Hospital; Consulting Surgeon, Watertown City Hospital, Watertown, St. Lawrence State Hospital, Ogdensburg.

GREGORY, GEORGE A., M.D., 2 Commercial Street, Boothbay Harbor, Maine. Bowdoin Medical School, 1891. Chief Surgeon, St. Andrew's Hospital.

GREGORY, JUNIUS CLAIBORNE, M.D., Medical Corps, United States Army, Washington, District of Columbia. Medical College of Virginia, 1900. Colonel, Medical Corps, United States Army.

GRENFELL, WILFRED THOMASON, A.M., M.D., LL.D., C.M.G., C.M.S., F.R.C.S. (Eng.), L.R.C.P. (Lond.), Labrador. London Hospital Medical College, 1888. Superintendent, International Grenfell Association.

GRIER, EDGAR BOILEAU, M.D., 400 Westminster Avenue, Elizabeth, New Jersey. University of Pennsylvania School of Medicine, 1883. Attending Surgeon and Gynecologist, Elizabeth General Hospital; Consulting Obstetrician, St. Elizabeth's Hospital.

GRIESS, WALTER RICHARD, Phar.D., M.D., 19 West Seventh Street, Cincinnati, Ohio. University of Cincinnati College of Medicine (Miami Medical College), 1897. Surgeon, Female Surgical Department, St. Mary's Hospital; Director of Surgical Staff, Children's Hospital of the Protestant Episcopal Church.

GRIEVE, CHARLES COURTNEY, M.D., Medical Corps, United States Navy, Washington, District of Columbia. University of Michigan Medical School, 1901. Commander, Medical Corps, United States Navy.

GRIFFIN, JOHN FRANCIS, B.L., M.D., 397 Stuyvesant Avenue, Brooklyn, New York. Dartmouth Medical School, 1905. Urologist, St. Catherine's and Greenpoint Hospitals.

GRIFFITH, DANIEL M., M.D., 207 West Fourth Street, Owensboro, Kentucky. Tulane University of Louisiana School of Medicine, 1888. Oculist and Aurist, Owensboro City Hospital.

GRIFFITH, FRANKLIN WEBB, A.M., M.D., Medical Building, Asheville, North Carolina. Johns Hopkins University, Medical Department, 1906. Surgeon, Asheville Mission and Meriwether Hospitals, Asheville, Clarence Barker Memorial Hospital, Biltmore.

GRIFFITH, H. M., Ph.B., M.D., 515 Citizens Savings Bank Building, Pasadena, California. Washington University Medical School, 1905. Otologist, Laryngologist, and Rhinologist, La Vina Sanitarium, La Vina; Attending Surgeon, Ear, Nose, and Throat Department, Pasadena Hospital.

GRIFFITH, JEFFERSON D., M.D., 1225 Rialto Building, Kansas City, Missouri. University and Bellevue Hospital Medical College (University of the City of New York, Medical Department), 1871. Emeritus Professor of Oral and Clinical Surgery, Kansas City Dental College; Chief of Staff, St. Joseph's Hospital.

GRIFFITH, JOHN PERRY, M.D., 4715 Fifth Avenue, Pittsburgh, Pennsylvania. Medico-Chirurgical College, Philadelphia, 1906. Assistant Professor of Surgery, University of Pittsburgh School of Medicine; Surgeon, Mercy Hospital.

GRIGSBY, GUY P., M.D., 612 Francis Building, Louisville, Kentucky. University of Louisville, Medical Department, 1906. Adjunct Professor of Abdominal Surgery and Gynecology, University of Louisville, Medical Department; Attending Surgeon, Louisville City Hospital; Consulting Surgeon, King's Daughters Home for Incurables, Louisville School of Reform.

GRINSTEAD, WILLIAM FRANKLIN, M.D., 808 Commercial Avenue, Cairo, Illinois. Vanderbilt University, Medical Department, 1877; University of Nashville, Medical Department, 1881. Chief of Staff, St. Mary's Infirmary.

GRISSIM, JOHN DE LAFAYETTE, M.D., Dalziel Building, Oakland, California. Columbia University College of Physicians and Surgeons, 1893. Chief of Surgical Staff, Baby Hospital.

GRISSINGER, JAY W., M.D., Medical Corps, United States Army, Washington, District of Columbia. University of Pennsylvania School of Medicine, 1898. Lieutenant Colonel, Medical Corps, United States Army.

GRISWOLD, EDWARD HARVEY, M.D., Telephone Building, Peru, Indiana. University Medical College of Kansas City, 1891. Surgeon in Charge, Wabash Employes' Hospital; Member of Surgical Staff, Dukes Hospital; Surgeon, Chesapeake and Ohio, and Lake Erie and Western Railways.

GRONNERUD, PAUL, B.Sc., M.D., 25 East Washington Street, Chicago, Illinois. Rush Medical College, 1895; University of Louisville, Medical Department (Kentucky University, Medical Department), 1898. Professor of Clinical Surgery, Loyola University School of Medicine; Professor of Gynecology and Operative Surgery, Illinois Post-Graduate Medical School; Surgeon, West Side and Norwegian-American Hospitals; Visiting Surgeon, Norwegian Lutheran Deaconess Hospital.

GROSVENOR, LORENZO NELSON, M.D., 378 Dakota Avenue, Huron, South Dakota. Hahnemann Medical College (Chicago Homeopathic Medical College), 1889; Rush Medical College, 1902. Surgeon, Eye, Ear, Nose, and Throat Department, Samaritan Hospital.

GROSVENOR, WALLACE FAHNESTOCK, A.B., A.M., M.D., 4700 Sheridan Road, Chicago, Illinois. Hahnemann Medical College and Hospital, Chicago, 1895. Rush Medical College, 1900. Attending Obstetrician and Gynecologist, St. Joseph's and Ravenswood Hospitals.

GROUND, WILLIAM EDWIN, M.D., Board of Trade Building, Superior, Wisconsin. Washington University Medical School (Missouri Medical College), 1881. Associate Surgeon, St. Mary's Hospital.

GROVE, MARTIN MELVIN, M.D., Dell Rapids, South Dakota. University of Illinois College of Medicine, 1905. Surgeon-in-Chief, Dell Rapids Hospital.

GROVE, WILLIAM EDWARD, A.B., M.D., 1330 Wells Building, Milwaukee, Wisconsin. Johns Hopkins University, Medical Department, 1908. Oto-Laryngologist-in-Chief, Mt. Sinai Hospital; Oto-Laryngologist, Columbia, Emergency, and Milwaukee Children's Hospitals.

GROW, EUGENE J., M.D., Medical Corps, United States Navy, Washington, District of Columbia. Dartmouth Medical School, 1897. Captain, Medical Corps, United States Navy.

GSELL, J. F., M.D., 911 Beacon Building, Wichita, Kansas. Rush Medical College, 1895.

GUERRY, LEGRAND, M.D., 1831 Pendleton Street, Columbia, South Carolina. University of Georgia, Medical Department, 1895. Surgeon, Columbia Hospital.

GUFFEY, DON CARLOS, M.Sc., M.D., 909 Waldheim Building, Kansas City, Missouri. University of Pennsylvania School of Medicine, 1905. Professor of Gynecology and Obstetrics, University of Kansas School of Medicine; Gynecologist and Obstetrician, St. Luke's and Research Hospitals, Kansas City, Missouri, University of Kansas Bell Memorial Hospital, Rosedale, Kansas.

GUGGENHEIM, LOUIS K., M.D., 1000 Carleton Building, St. Louis, Missouri. Washington University Medical School, 1905. Associate in Department of Otology, Jewish Hospital, St. Louis; Member of Staff, Jewish Home for Chronic Invalids, Anglum.

GUNDERSEN, ADOLF, A.B., M.D., 1509 King Street, La Crosse, Wisconsin. Royal University of Norway, 1890. Surgeon, La Crosse Lutheran and St. Francis Hospitals.

GUNDRY, FRANK JOSEPH, M.D., Hopkins Building, Bakersfield, California. Leland Stanford Junior University School of Medicine (Cooper Medical College), 1906. Surgeon, Mercy Hospital.

GUNN, JOHN A., B.A., M.D., C.B., O.B.E., 922 Somerset Building, Winnipeg, Manitoba. Faculty of Medicine, University of Manitoba (Manitoba Medical College), 1904. Associate Professor of Clinical Surgery, Faculty of Medicine, University of Manitoba; Surgeon, Winnipeg General Hospital.

GUNN, JOHN NISBETT, D.S.O., M.B., M.R.C.S., (Eng.), L.R.C.P. (Lond.), M.D., 309 Herald Block, Calgary, Alberta. Toronto University Faculty of Medicine, 1902.

GUNTER, CLARENCE, M.D., Amster Building, Globe, Arizona. Columbia University College of Physicians and Surgeons, 1901. Division Surgeon, Arizona Eastern Railway.

GÜNTZER, J. HENRY, B.Sc., M.D., 40 East Forty-first Street, New York, New York. University and Bellevue Hospital Medical College (Bellevue Hospital Medical College), 1889. Assistant Surgeon, Manhattan Eye, Ear, and Throat Hospital; Attending Ophthalmologist and Oto-Laryngologist, United Hospital, Port Chester.

GURD, FRASER BAILLIE, B.A., M.D., C.M., 115 Stanley Street, Montreal, Quebec. Faculty of Medicine, McGill University, 1906. Lecturer on Immunology and Demonstrator of Clinical Surgery, Faculty of Medicine, McGill University; Assistant Surgeon, Montreal General Hospital.

GUSHEE, EDWARD STOCKBRIDGE, A.B., M.D., 519 West End Avenue, New York, New York. Harvard Medical School, 1903. Consulting Surgeon, Grace Hospital.

GUTHRIE, DONALD, Ph.B., M.D., Robert Packer Hospital, Sayre, Pennsylvania. University of Pennsylvania School of Medicine, 1905. Surgeon, Robert Packer Hospital.

GWATHMEY, LOMAX, M.D., 220 Freemason Street, Norfolk, Virginia. University of Virginia, Department of Medicine, 1889; Columbia University, College of Physicians and Surgeons, 1890. Surgeon, Out-Patient Department, Norfolk Protestant Hospital.

HACKER, CHARLES WILLIAM LOUIS, M.D., 352 Hudson Avenue, Albany, New York. Albany Medical College, 1905.

HACKER, CHRISTIAN GOTTLIEB, Phar.G., M.D., 107 Washington Avenue, Albany, New York. Albany Medical College, 1899.

HACKETT, ANDREW R., M.D., 2035 West Jefferson Avenue, Detroit, Michigan. State University of Iowa College of Medicine (Drake University College of Medicine), 1912. Chief Surgeon, Delray Industrial Hospital, Solvay Process Company.

HACKETT, WALTER L., M.B., M.D., 712 David Whitney Building, Detroit, Michigan. University of Toronto, Faculty of Medicine, 1910. Detroit College of Medicine and Surgery, 1913. Visiting Obstetrician and Gynecologist, Woman's Hospital; Chief Gynecologist, Samaritan Hospital.

HACKETT, WILLIAM ALEXANDER, M.B., 708 David Whitney Building, Detroit, Michigan. University of Toronto, Faculty of Medicine, 1894. Attending Surgeon, Samaritan Hospital.

HACKLER, GARFIELD McCOY, M.D., 303 Southwestern Life Building, Dallas, Texas. University of Maryland School of Medicine, 1891. Professor of Surgery, Baylor University School of Medicine; Member of Surgical Staff, Parkland City Hospital, Texas Baptist Memorial Sanitarium.

HACKNEY, WILLIAM, M.D., M.R.C.S. (Lond.), L.R.C.P. (Eng.), Herald Building, Calgary, Alberta. University of Toronto Faculty of Medicine

(Trinity University Faculty of Medicine), 1897. Member of Staff, Calgary General and Holy Cross Hospitals.

HADDEN, DAVID, B.Sc., M.D., Oakland Bank of Savings Building, Oakland, California. Cooper Medical College, 1899.

HADEN, HENRY C., M.D., 913 Union National Bank Building, Houston, Texas. University of Pennsylvania School of Medicine, 1895.

HADLEY, MURRAY NATHAN, B.Sc., M.D., 608 Hume-Mansur Building, Indianapolis, Indiana. Indiana University School of Medicine, 1903. Associate Professor of Surgery, Indiana University School of Medicine; Member of Staff, Robert W. Long and Indianapolis City Hospitals.

HAFFORD, GEORGE CLINTON, M.D., 400½ South Superior Street, Albion, Michigan. University of Michigan Medical School, 1887.

HAGENS, GARRETT J., M.D., 7207 South Halsted Street, Chicago, Illinois. Northwestern University Medical School (Chicago Medical College), 1891. Gynecologist and Obstetrician, Englewood and Chicago Lying-In Hospitals.

HAGER, WALTER A., Phar.G., M.D., North Lafayette Street, South Bend, Indiana. Jefferson Medical College, 1891. Surgeon, Epworth Hospital, South Bend, St. Joseph Hospital, Mishawaka.

HAGERTY, HUGH A., M.D., 1201 David Whitney Building, Detroit, Michigan. Ohio State University, College of Medicine, 1898. Associate Professor of Gynecology, Detroit College of Medicine and Surgery; Gynecologist, Grace Hospital; Surgeon, German Protestant Home for Orphans and Old People.

HAGERTY, JOHN F., M.D., 30 Wallace Place, Newark, New Jersey. University and Bellevue Hospital Medical College (New York University Medical College), 1892. Medical Director and Attending Surgeon, St. Michael's Hospital; Attending Surgeon, Home for Crippled Children.

HAGGARD, WILLIAM D., M.D., 706 Church Street, Nashville, Tennessee. University of Tennessee College of Medicine, 1893. Professor of Surgery and Clinical Surgery, Vanderbilt University, Medical Department; Surgeon, St. Thomas' Hospital.

HAGNER, FRANCIS RANDALL, M.D., The Farragut, Washington, District of Columbia. George Washington University Medical School, 1894. Professor of Genito-Urinary Surgery, George Washington University Medical School; Attending Genito-Urinary Surgeon, George Washington University and Garfield Memorial Hospitals.

HAGYARD, CHARLTON EDWARD, M.D., 407 Lumber Exchange Building, Seattle, Washington. University of Illinois College of Medicine, 1903. Member of Staff, Columbus Sanitarium, Minor Private and Providence Hospitals.

HAHN, OSCAR HERMAN, M.D., 212½ North Hastings Avenue, Hastings, Nebraska. Ensworth Medical College, 1908. Associate Surgeon, Mary Lanning Memorial Hospital.

HAINES, W. D., M.D., 1606 Freeman Avenue, Cincinnati, Ohio. University of Cincinnati College of Medicine (Medical College of Ohio), 1884. Assistant Professor of Clinical Surgery, University of Cincinnati College of Medicine; Attending Surgeon, First Surgical Service, Cincinnati General Hospital.

HAIRGROVE, JOHN WHITLOCK, M.D., 339 East State Street, Jacksonville, Illinois. Washington University Medical School (Missouri Medical College), 1885. Attending Surgeon, Our Saviour's and Passavant Memorial Hospitals.

HAIRSTON, SAMUEL HENRY, B.Sc., M.D., Miazza-Woods Building, Meridian, Mississippi. University of Louisville, Medical Department (Louisville Medical College), 1904. Chief Surgeon, Matty Hersee Hospital.

HALAHAN, ROBERT EDWIN, B.A., M.B., M.D., Calle Suipacha 1156, Buenos Aires, Argentina. Faculty of Medicine, National University of Buenos Aires, 1907. Surgeon, Buenos Aires Hospital.

HALDERMAN, STEPHEN S., M.D., 826 Gay Street, Portsmouth, Ohio. University of Cincinnati College of Medicine (Medical College of Ohio), 1875. Surgeon, Hempstead Hospital, Norfolk and Western Railway.

HALE, GORDON DYER, Ph.B., M.D., Medical Corps, United States Navy, Washington, District of Columbia. Columbia University, College of Physicians and Surgeons, 1904. Lieutenant Commander, Medical Corps, United States Navy.

HALE, JAMES WYATT, M.D., 1520 Washington Street, Waco, Texas. University of Tennessee College of Medicine, 1890.

HALEY, PETER ALLEN, M.D., 1582 Virginia Street, Charleston, West Virginia. Medical College of Virginia (University College of Medicine), 1899. Oculist and Aurist, Charleston General and McMillan Hospitals, Charleston, Sheltering Arms Hospital, Hansford.

HALL, C. LESTER, M.D., 2720 Troost Avenue, Kansas City, Missouri. Jefferson Medical College, 1867. Member of Staff, St. Joseph's Hospital.

HALL, CHARLES A., M.D., 1021 Prospect Avenue, Cleveland, Ohio. Ohio State University College of Homeopathic Medicine (Cleveland Homeopathic Medical College), 1888; Western Reserve University School of Medicine (Cleveland College of Physicians and Surgeons), 1899. Visiting Surgeon, St. John's and Woman's Hospitals; Chief Surgeon, Wheeling and Lake Erie Railway.

HALL, CLARENCE WALTER, M.D., Gage-Hall Clinic, Hutchinson, Kansas. Northwestern University Medical School, 1911. Attending Surgeon, St. Elizabeth's and Hutchinson Methodist Hospitals.

HALL, EDWARD P., M.D., 124 West Thirty-third Street, Kansas City, Missouri. Ensworth Medical College, 1897. Professor of Rhinology and Oto-Laryngology, University of Kansas School of Medicine; Member of Staff, St. Joseph's Hospital, Kansas City, Missouri, St. Margaret's Hospital, Kansas City, Kansas, University of Kansas Bell Memorial Hospital, Rosedale, Kansas; Attending Otologist, St. Anthony's Home for Infants.

HALL, GEORGE WILLIAM, M.D., C.M., Victoria, British Columbia. University of Toronto, Faculty of Medicine, 1905. Surgeon, Provincial Royal Jubilee and St. Joseph's Hospitals.

HALL, JOSEPH ARDA, M.D., 628 Elm Street, Cincinnati, Ohio. University of Cincinnati College of Medicine (Miami Medical College), 1897. Attending Surgeon, Gynecological Staff, Cincinnati General Hospital.

HALL, JOSEPH UNDERWOOD, M.D., 133 Geary Street, San Francisco, California. Jefferson Medical College, 1889.

HALL, MARSHALL K., M.D., C.M., Corbett Building, Portland, Oregon. McGill University Faculty of Medicine, 1893.

HALL, RUFUS BARTLETT, A.M., M.D., 628 Elm Street, Cincinnati, Ohio. University of Cincinnati College of Medicine (Miami Medical College), 1872. Professor of Gynecology and Clinical Gynecology, University of Cincinnati College of Medicine; Gynecologist, Cincinnati General Hospital.

HALLER, J. T., B.Sc., M.D., 205 Security Building, Davenport, Iowa. Johns Hopkins University, Medical Department, 1905. Surgeon, St. Luke's Hospital.

HALLETT, DEWAYNE, M.D., 274 West Eighty-sixth Street, New York, New York. New York Homeopathic Medical College and Flower Hospital, 1889. Surgeon, New York Ophthalmic and Hahnemann Hospitals, Laura Franklin Free Hospital for Children.

HALLORAN, PAUL S., M.D., Medical Corps, United States Army, Washington, District of Columbia. University of Pennsylvania School of Medicine, 1899. Lieutenant Colonel, Medical Corps, United States Army.

HALPENNY, JASPER, M.A., M.D., C.M., 702 Sterling Bank Building, Winnipeg, Manitoba. Faculty of Medicine, University of Manitoba (Manitoba Medical College), 1900. Professor of Surgery and Clinical Surgery and Director of Department of Surgery, Faculty of Medicine, University of Manitoba; Senior Surgeon, Winnipeg General Hospital.

HALSEY, FREDERICK W., M.D., 272 Newbury Street, Boston, Massachusetts. George Washington University Medical School, 1871. Emeritus Professor of Diseases of the Rectum, Boston University School of Medicine; Consultant in Diseases of the Rectum, Massachusetts Homeopathic Hospital.

HALSTEAD, ALBERT E., M.D., 30 North Michigan Avenue, Chicago, Illinois. Northwestern University Medical School, 1890. Professor of Surgery and Clinical Surgery, University of Illinois College of Medicine; Senior Attending Surgeon, St. Luke's Hospital; Consulting Surgeon, Illinois Charitable Eye and Ear Infirmary.

HALSTED, THOMAS H., M.D., Syracuse Clinic, Syracuse, New York. University of Toronto, Faculty of Medicine, 1887. Professor of Oto-Laryngology, Syracuse University College of Medicine; Otologist and Laryngologist, Eye, Ear, Nose, and Throat Infirmary, Syracuse Memorial and St. Joseph's Hospitals, Syracuse Free Dispensary; Consultant, Hospital Good Shepherd, Syracuse University.

HALSTED, WILLIAM STEWART, A.B., M.D., D.Sc., LL.D., 1201 Eutaw Place, Baltimore, Maryland. Columbia University, College of Physicians and Surgeons, 1877. Professor of Surgery, Johns Hopkins University, Medical Department; Surgeon-in-Chief and Director of Surgical Clinic, Johns Hopkins Hospital.

HAMANN, CARL A., M.D., 416 Osborn Building, Cleveland, Ohio. University of Pennsylvania School of Medicine, 1890. Professor of Applied Anatomy and Clinical Surgery, Western Reserve University School of Medicine; Visiting Surgeon, St. Vincent's Charity and Cleveland City Hospitals.

HAMER, HOMER G., M.D., 723 Hume-Mansur Building, Indianapolis, Indiana. Indiana University School of Medicine (Medical College of Indiana), 1904. Assistant Professor of Genito-Urinary Surgery, Indiana University School of Medicine; Consulting Genito-Urinary Surgeon, Protestant Deaconess and Methodist Episcopal Hospitals; Attending Surgeon, Genito-Urinary Service, Indianapolis City and Robert W. Long Memorial Hospitals.

HAMILTON, ALBERT G., M.D., Fifth Street and Broadway, Thermopolis, Wyoming. University of Cincinnati College of Medicine (Medical College of Ohio), 1888. Chief Surgeon, Hopewell Hospital.

HAMILTON, CHARLES SUMNER, A.B., M.D., 188 East State Street, Columbus, Ohio. Ohio State University College of Medicine (Columbus Medical College), 1887. Surgeon, Hawkes Hospital of Mt. Carmel.

HAMILTON, GAVIN, M.D., C.M., 610 Scanlon Building, Houston, Texas. Faculty of Medicine, McGill University, 1894. Surgeon, Baptist Sanitarium and Hospital.

HAMILTON, HERSCHEL P., M.D., 617 City National Bank Building, Omaha, Nebraska. University of Louisville, Medical Department, 1887. Surgeon, Swedish Mission Hospital.

HAMILTON, LUTHER H., M.D., Journal Building, Portland, Oregon. Jefferson Medical College, 1901. Instructor in Clinical Surgery, University of Oregon Medical School; Surgeon, Good Samaritan and Multnomah County Hospitals.

HAMILTON, T. GLENDENNING, M.D., 210 Somerset Block, Winnipeg, Manitoba. Faculty of Medicine, University of Manitoba (Manitoba Medical College), 1903. Lecturer on Clinical Surgery, Faculty of Medicine, University of Manitoba; Assistant Surgeon, Winnipeg General Hospital.

HAMILTON, WILLIAM DRAKE, A.M., M.D., East Broad Street and Columbia Avenue, Columbus, Ohio. Ohio State University College of Medicine (Columbus Medical College), 1883. Surgeon, Hawkes Hospital of Mt. Carmel.

HAMLIN, OLIVER D., M.Sc., M.D., Federal Realty Building, Oakland, California. Leland Stanford Junior University School of Medicine, 1894. Chief Surgeon, County Receiving Hospital; Consulting Surgeon, Samuel Merritt Hospital; Surgeon, Providence Hospital; Division Surgeon, Southern Pacific Company.

HAMMER, A. WIESE, M.D., 218 South Fifteenth Street, Philadelphia, Pennsylvania. University of Pennsylvania School of Medicine (Medico-Chirurgical College), 1901. Instructor of Anatomy, University of Pennsylvania School of Medicine; Surgeon, American Hospital; Assistant Oral Surgeon, Philadelphia General Hospital.

HAMMETT, CHARLES MADDOX, M.D., 1330 I Street, Northwest, Washington, District of Columbia. Georgetown University School of Medicine, 1892. Clinical and Associate Professor of Ophthalmology, Georgetown University School of Medicine; Senior Ophthalmic Surgeon, Providence Hospital; Ophthalmic Surgeon, Georgetown University Hospital.

HAMMOND, FRANK C., M.D., 3311 North Broad Street, Philadelphia, Pennsylvania. Jefferson Medical College, 1895. Dean and Adjunct Professor of Gynecology, Temple University, Department of Medicine; Visiting Obstetrician, Philadelphia General Hospital; Assistant Gynecologist, Samaritan Hospital; Visiting Gynecologist, Philadelphia Hospital for Contagious Diseases.

HAMMOND, ROBERT R., M.D., 435 Park Street, West, Stockton, California. Cooper Medical College, 1897. Member of Staff, St. Joseph's Home and Hospital; Surgeon, Southern Pacific and Western Pacific Railways.

HAMMOND, ROLAND, M.D., 219 Waterman Street, Providence, Rhode Island. Harvard Medical School, 1902. Orthopedic Surgeon, Rhode Island Hospital, Providence, Memorial Hospital, Pawtucket; Consulting Orthopedic Surgeon, St. Joseph's and Providence City Hospitals.

HAMMOND, WALTER C., M.D., 737 Sheridan Road, Chicago, Illinois. University of Illinois College of Medicine, 1911. Associate in Obstetrics, University of Illinois College of Medicine; Member of Staff, Lake View Hospital.

HAMPTON, ROBERT R., M.D., 806 Boston Building, Salt Lake City, Utah. University of Illinois College of Medicine, 1900. Oculist and Aurist, St. Mark's Hospital.

HANAN, JAMES T., M.D., 11 The Crescent, Montclair, New Jersey. Columbia University, College of Physicians and Surgeons, 1899. Attending Surgeon, Mountainside Hospital.

HANCOCK, JAMES COLE, M.D., 135 Cambridge Place, Brooklyn, New York. Columbia University, College of Physicians and Surgeons, 1889. Consulting Ophthalmologist, Brooklyn State and Coney Island Hospitals.

HANCOCK, JOHN C., A.B., M.D., 209 Bank and Insurance Building, Dubuque, Iowa. Harvard Medical School, 1898. Surgeon, Finley Hospital.

HANDLY, JAMES WHITE, B.Sc., M.D., 714 Independent Life Building, Nashville, Tennessee. University of Tennessee College of Medicine, 1887. Consulting Surgeon, Central Hospital for Insane.

HANES, GRANVILLE S., M.D., Francis Building, Louisville, Kentucky. University of Louisville, Medical Department (Hospital College of Medicine), 1900. Professor of Diseases of the Rectum, University of Louisville,

Medical Department; Surgeon, Louisville City Hospital, John N. Norton Memorial Infirmary.

HANFORD, PETER OLIVER, A.B., M.D., 720 North Nevada Avenue, Colorado Springs, Colorado. University of Colorado School of Medicine (Denver College of Medicine), 1898.

HANNA, MINFORD ARMOUR, M.D., Lathrop Building, Kansas City, Missouri. University of Kansas School of Medicine (Kansas City Medical College), 1903. Obstetrician, Swedish, St. Vincent's, Christian Church, Kansas City General, and St. Joseph's Hospitals.

HANNA, ROBERT A., M.D., Lehmann Building, Peoria, Illinois. State University of Iowa College of Medicine (Keokuk Medical College), 1894.

HANNAN, CHARLES EDMUND, M.D., 531 Locust Street, Johnstown, Pennsylvania. Jefferson Medical College, 1892. Surgeon, Conemaugh Valley Memorial and Mercy Hospitals.

HANNER, JOHN W., A.B., M.D., Medical Corps, United States Army, Washington, District of Columbia. Vanderbilt University, Medical Department, 1901. Lieutenant Colonel, Medical Corps, United States Army.

HANSELL, HAYWOOD S., A.B., M.D., Medical Corps, United States Army, Washington, District of Columbia. Emory University School of Medicine (Atlanta College of Physicians and Surgeons), 1899. Lieutenant Colonel, Medical Corps, United States Army.

HANSON, KNUD, M.D., Canon Block, Grand Junction, Colorado. University of Colorado School of Medicine (Denver College of Medicine), 1898. Attending Surgeon, St. Mary's Hospital.

HAPPEL, HORACE E., A.B., M.D., Wall Building, St. Louis, Missouri. Jefferson Medical College, 1910. Instructor in Gynecology, St. Louis University School of Medicine; Assistant Gynecologist, St. John's Hospital; Visiting Surgeon, Missouri Pacific Railway Hospital.

HARBIN, ROBERT MAXWELL, A.B., M.D., 100 Third Avenue, Rome, Georgia. University and Bellevue Hospital Medical College, 1888. Surgeon, Harbin Hospital.

HARBIN, WILLIAM PICKENS, A.B., M.D., 100 Third Avenue, Rome, Georgia. University and Bellevue Hospital Medical College, 1897. Surgeon, Harbin Hospital.

HARDEN, ALBERT SCOTT, M.D., 540 Warren Street, Newark, New Jersey. University of Maryland School of Medicine, 1901. Assistant Visiting Surgeon, St. Michael's Hospital; Associate Visiting Surgeon, Newark City Hospital.

HARDIE, THOMAS MELVILLE, B.A., M.B., 30 North Michigan Avenue, Chicago, Illinois. University of Toronto, Faculty of Medicine, 1888. Laryngologist, St. Luke's Hospital.

HARDIN, LEWIS SAGE, M.D., 812 Hurt Building, Atlanta, Georgia. Emory University School of Medicine (Southern Medical College), 1898. Surgeon, St. Joseph's Infirmary, MacVicar Hospital of Spelman Seminary; Visiting Surgeon, Piedmont Sanitarium, Georgia Baptist Hospital.

HARDT, ALBERT FREDERICK, M.D., 414 Pine Street, Williamsport, Pennsylvania. University of Pennsylvania School of Medicine, 1902. Surgeon, Williamsport Private Hospital.

HARDY, IRVIN, M.D., C.M., Willy and Prospect Streets, Morgantown, West Virginia. Maryland Medical College, 1899; University of Maryland School of Medicine (College of Physicians and Surgeons, Baltimore), 1903; Queen's University, Faculty of Medicine, 1909. Clinical Professor of Surgery, West Virginia University School of Medicine; Surgeon in Charge, City Hospital.

HARDY, WALTER, M.D., 212 First Avenue, Southwest, Ardmore, Oklahoma. Washington University Medical School (Missouri Medical College), 1893. Surgeon in Charge, Hardy Sanitarium.

HARE, CHARLES HENRY, Ph.B., A.M., M.D., 483 Beacon Street, Boston, Massachusetts. Harvard Medical School, 1889. Instructor in Gynecology, Harvard University Graduate School of Medicine; Surgeon, Massachusetts Women's Hospital; Consulting Gynecologist, City Hospital, Quincy, Boston Dispensary, Boston.

HARE, EARLE RUSSELL, A.B., M.D., 730 La Salle Building, Minneapolis, Minnesota. University of Minnesota Medical School, 1900.

HARE, GEORGE RAY, A.M., M.D., 107 East Thirty-ninth Street, New York, New York. University and Bellevue Hospital Medical College, 1898. Assistant Surgeon, Manhattan Eye, Ear, and Throat Hospital; Ophthalmic Surgeon, Nassau Hospital, Mineola.

HARGENS, CHARLES WILLIAM, M.D., River View Boulevard, Hot Springs, South Dakota. Northwestern University Medical School, 1891. Chief of Staff and Chief Surgeon, Lutheran Sanatorium and Hospital; District Surgeon, Chicago and Northwestern Railway.

HARGER, JOHN ROSS, B.Sc., M.D., 25 East Washington Street, Chicago, Illinois. Rush Medical College, 1906. Assistant Professor of Surgery, University of Illinois, Attending Surgeon, Garfield Park and Illinois Masonic Hospitals.

HARGRAVE, EDWARD THOMAS, Ph.G., M.D., 311 Taylor Building, Norfolk, Virginia. Medical College of Virginia, 1900. Gynecologist, Protestant Hospital; Consulting Gynecologist, Florence Crittenton Home.

HARGROVE, REUBEN MORGAN, B.Sc., M.D., Humble Building, Houston, Texas. University of Texas Department of Medicine, 1912. Orthopedic Surgeon, Municipal and Houston Tuberculosis Hospitals.

HARKNESS, GORDON F., M.Sc., M.D., 509 New Putnam Building, Davenport, Iowa. State University of Iowa College of Medicine, 1902. Oculist and Aurist, Mercy and St. Luke's Hospitals.

HARNAGEL, EDWARD JOHN, M.D., 913 Bankers Trust Building, Des Moines, Iowa. Jefferson Medical College, Philadelphia, 1910. Attending Surgeon, Iowa Methodist, Iowa Lutheran and Des Moines City Hospitals.

HARPER, WILLIAM WADE, A.B., A.M., M.D., 201 Broad Street, Selma, Alabama. Tulane University of Louisiana, 1891. Surgeon, Union Street Hospital.

HARPSTER, CHARLES MELVIN, Phar.G., M.D., Wedgewood Building, Toledo, Ohio. Toledo Medical College, 1896. Director, Genito-Urinary Surgery, St. Vincent's Hospital.

HARRAR, JAMES AITKEN, M.D., 100 East Sixty-sixth Street, New York, New York. University of Pennsylvania School of Medicine, 1901. Attending Surgeon, Lying-in Hospital.

HARRELL, SAMUEL NEWBERN, M.D., 424 Main Street, Tarboro, North Carolina. University of Maryland School of Medicine, 1897. Attending Surgeon, Edgecomb General Hospital.

HARRELSON, NATHAN O., M.D., 638 Lathrop Building, Kansas City, Missouri. University of Kansas School of Medicine (Kansas City Medical College), 1894. Surgeon-in-Chief, Swedish Hospital; Consulting Surgeon, St. Joseph's Hospital.

HARRIMAN, ALPHA H., M.D., 440 Main Street, Laconia, New Hampshire. Bowdoin Medical School (Medical School of Maine), 1883. Surgeon, Laconia Hospital.

HARRINGTON, GOVE S., M.D., 328 Convent Avenue, New York, New York. Hahnemann Medical College and Hospital, Philadelphia, 1892. Visiting Surgeon, Metropolitan Hospital, Blackwell's Island; Consulting Surgeon, Broad Street Hospital.

HARRINGTON, JAMES TAYLOR, A.B., M.D., 100 South Hamilton Street, Poughkeepsie, New York. Columbia University, College of Physicians and Surgeons, 1906. Attending Surgeon, Vassar Brothers' Hospital.

HARRINGTON, STUART WILLIAM, M.S., M.D., Mayo Clinic, Rochester, Minnesota. University of Pennsylvania School of Medicine, 1913. Surgeon, St. Mary's and Colonial Hospitals.

HARRIS, BURTON, M.D., 475 Greene Avenue, Brooklyn, New York. Columbia University, College of Physicians and Surgeons, 1904. Consulting Genito-Urinary Surgeon, Methodist Episcopal Hospital.

HARRIS, CHARLES HOUSTON, M.D., 1028 Fifth Avenue, Fort Worth, Texas. St. Louis College of Physicians and Surgeons, 1899. Chief Surgeon, Harris Sanitarium.

HARRIS, CHESTER ELLIS, A.M., M.D., Pioneer Building, Basin, Wyoming. University of Illinois College of Medicine, 1906. Surgeon, Basin Hospital.

HARRIS, HARRY B., M.D., 1110 Fidelity Medical Building, Dayton, Ohio. University of Pennsylvania School of Medicine, 1894. Head of Eye, Ear, Nose, and Throat Department, Miami Valley Hospital; Surgeon-in-Chief, Dr. Harris' Private Eye, Ear, Nose, and Throat Hospital.

HARRIS, HERBERT TAYLOR, M.D., Pioneer Building, Basin, Wyoming. Creighton College of Medicine, 1902. Surgeon, Basin Hospital.

HARRIS, MALCOLM LASALLE, M.D., 25 East Washington Street, Chicago, Illinois. Rush Medical College, 1882. Professor of Surgery, Chicago Policlinic; Chief Surgeon, Alexian Brothers' Hospital; Surgeon, Henrotin Memorial and Passavant Hospitals, Chicago Policlinic and Hospital.

HARRIS, PHILANDER A., M.D., 26 Church Street, Paterson, New Jersey. University of Michigan Medical School, 1872; Columbia University, College of Physicians and Surgeons, 1873. Visiting Gynecologist and Obstetrician, Paterson General Hospital; Consulting Gynecologist, Passaic General Hospital, Passaic, Miriam Barnert Memorial Hospital, Paterson, New Jersey State Hospital, Greystone Park, Lynn Hospital, Sussex.

HARRIS, RAY R., M.D., 1270 Main Street, Dubuque, Iowa. University of Illinois College of Medicine (College of Physicians and Surgeons, Chicago), 1906. Member of Staff, St. Joseph's Mercy Hospital; Surgeon, Chicago, Burlington and Quincy and Chicago Great Western Railroads.

HARRIS, ROWLAND HILL, A.B., M.D., L.R.C.P.& S. (Edin.), L.F.P. & S. (Glas.), F.R.C.S. (Edin.), 41 North Washington Avenue, Battle Creek, Michigan. University of Illinois College of Medicine (American Medical Missionary College), 1901. Surgeon, Maple Street and Nichols Memorial Hospitals.

HARRIS, THOMAS JEFFERSON, A.M., M.D., 104 East Fortieth Street, New York, New York. University of Pennsylvania School of Medicine, 1889. Professor of Rhinology and Laryngology, New York Post-Graduate Medical School; Surgeon, Throat Department, New York Post-Graduate Medical School and Hospital; Consultant, Diseases of the Throat and Nose, New York Skin and Cancer Hospital.

HARRIS, WILBUR HOWARD, M.D., C.M., 1276 King Street, West, Toronto, Ontario. University of Toronto, Faculty of Medicine (Trinity Medical College), 1888. Surgeon, Grace Hospital, Hospital for Incurables.

HARRISON, ARCHIBALD CUNNINGHAM, M.D., 31 East North Avenue, Baltimore, Maryland. University of Maryland School of Medicine, 1887. Professor of Surgery, University of Maryland School of Medicine and College of Physicians and Surgeons; Surgeon, Mercy and St. Joseph's Hospitals; Staff Surgeon, Hospital for Women of Maryland, Church Home and Infirmary; Consulting Surgeon, Baltimore Eye, Ear, and Throat Charity Hospital.

HARRISON, BENJAMIN I., B.Sc., M.S., M.D., Cleveland Clinic, Cleveland, Ohio. University of Tennessee College of Medicine (Lincoln Memorial University Medical Department), 1913.

HARRISON, GEORGE TUCKER, M.A., M.D., University of Virginia, University, Virginia. University of Virginia, Department of Medicine, 1856. Consulting Surgeon, Woman's Hospital, New York.

HARRISON, JOHN DARLEY, M.D., C.M., 10033 One Hundred Sixth Street, Edmonton, Alberta. Faculty of Medicine, McGill University, 1891. Visiting Surgeon, Royal Alexandra and General Hospitals.

HARRISON, PAUL WILBERFORCE, B.Sc., M.D., Bahrein, Bahrein Islands. Johns Hopkins University Medical Department, 1908.

HARRISON, WILLIAM GROCE, B.Sc., M.D., 903 Empire Building, Birmingham, Alabama. University of Maryland School of Medicine, 1892. Professor of Ear, Nose, and Throat Diseases, Alabama Graduate School of Medicine.

HARROLD, CHARLES COTTON, B.Sc., A.M., M.D., 550 Orange Street, Macon, Georgia. Columbia University, College of Physicians and Surgeons, 1902. Attending Surgeon, Macon Hospital.

HARROWER, DAVID, M.D., 13 Elm Street, Worcester, Massachusetts. Harvard Medical School, 1884. Consulting Ophthalmic and Aural Surgeon, Worcester City, Memorial, and St. Vincent's Hospitals, Hospital Cottages for Children, Baldwinsville, Milford Hospital, Milford.

HARRY, CHARLES REES, M.D., F. and M. Bank Building, Stockton, California. Leland Stanford Junior University School of Medicine, 1890. Surgeon, St. Joseph's Home and Hospital, Dameron Hospital, Western Pacific Railway.

HARSHA, WILLIAM MCINTIRE, A.B., M.D., 30 North Michigan Avenue, Chicago, Illinois. Northwestern University Medical School (Chicago Medical College), 1883. Professor of Surgery and Clinical Surgery, University of Illinois College of Medicine; Attending Surgeon, St. Luke's Hospital.

HARSHA, WILLIAM THOMAS, M.D., 30 North Michigan Avenue, Chicago, Illinois. Northwestern University Medical School, 1908.

HART, ARTHUR O., M.D., 200 East Walker Street, St. Johns, Michigan. College of Medicine and Surgery, 1894. Surgeon, St. Johns Hospital.

HART, EDWARD CHARLES, M.D., C.M., 643 Courtenay Street, Victoria, British Columbia. Faculty of Medicine, McGill University, 1894. Surgeon, Provincial Royal Jubilee and St. Joseph's Hospitals.

HART, W. LEE, M.D., Medical Corps, United States Army, Washington, District of Columbia. University of Maryland School of Medicine, 1906. Major, Medical Corps, United States Army.

HARTE, RICHARD H., M.D., C.M.G., F.R.C S. (Ire.), Hon., 1503 Spruce Street, Philadelphia, Pennsylvania. University of Pennsylvania School of Medicine, 1878. Emeritus Surgeon, Pennsylvania Hospital; Consulting Surgeon, St. Mary's and St. Timothy's Memorial Hospitals, Philadelphia, Bryn Mawr Hospital, Bryn Mawr, Abington Memorial Hospital, Abington.

HARTFORD, JOHN S., M.D., 411 First National Bank Building, Oklahoma, Oklahoma. University of Kansas School of Medicine (Kansas City Medical College), 1901. Professor of Gynecology, University of Oklahoma School of Medicine; Consulting Surgeon, St. Anthony's Hospital; Attending Gynecologist, State University Hospital.

HARTMAN, FRANK T., M.D., 623 Mulberry Street, Waterloo, Iowa. Rush Medical College, 1897. Member of Staff, Synodical Presbyterian and St. Francis Hospitals.

HARTSHORN, WILLIS E., Ph.B., M.D., 67 Trumbull Street, New Haven, Connecticut. University of Minnesota Medical School, 1898. Clinical Professor of Surgery, Yale University School of Medicine; Attending Surgeon, New Haven Hospital; Consulting Surgeon, Griffin Hospital, Derby; Chief of Staff, Surgical Department, New Haven Dispensary.

HARTSHORNE, ISAAC, B.A., M.D., 30 West Fifty-ninth Street, New York, New York. Harvard Medical School, 1908. Consulting Ophthalmologist, House of the Holy Comforter; Assistant Attending Ophthalmologist, St. Luke's Hospital; Assistant Ophthalmologist, Out-Patient Department, St. Luke's Hospital.

HARTSOCK, FREDERICK M., M.D., Medical Corps, United States Army, Washington, District of Columbia. George Washington University Medical School, 1897. Colonel, Medical Corps, United States Army.

HARTWELL, JOHN A., Ph.B., M.D., 27 East Sixty-third Street, New York, New York. Yale University School of Medicine, 1892. Associate Professor and Clinical Professor of Surgery, Cornell University Medical College; Director of Surgery, Bellevue Hospital; Consulting Surgeon, General Memorial Hospital, Lincoln Hospital and Home, New York, Lawrence Hospital, Bronxville, United Hospital, Port Chester.

HARTWELL, JOHN B., A.B., M.D., Burns Building, Colorado Springs, Colorado. Harvard Medical School, 1904.

HARTZELL, SOL. M., M.D., Dollar Savings and Trust Company Building, Youngstown, Ohio. University of Pennsylvania School of Medicine, 1901. Surgeon, Youngstown Hospital, Republic Iron and Steel, Youngstown Sheet and Tube, Brier Hill Iron and Carnegie Steel Companies, Baltimore and Ohio Railroad.

HARVEY, ANDREW MAGEE, M.Sc., M.D., 836 South Michigan Avenue, Chicago, Illinois. University of Illinois College of Medicine (College of Physicians and Surgeons, Chicago), 1893. Chief Surgeon, Crane Company.

HARVEY, CHARLES HENRY, M.D., Sixty-third and Jefferson Streets, Philadelphia, Pennsylvania. Hahnemann Medical College and Hospital, Philadelphia, 1893. Chief Surgeon, West Philadelphia General Homeopathic Hospital and Dispensary.

HARVEY, CLIFFORD DAWES, B.Sc., M.D., 510 Commonwealth Avenue, Boston, Massachusetts. Hahnemann Medical College and Hospital, Philadelphia, 1910. Clinical Instructor in Surgery, Boston University School of Medicine; Surgeon, Out-Patient Department, Massachusetts Homeopathic Hospital; Assistant Visiting Surgeon, Massachusetts Homeopathic Hospital, Boston; Visiting Surgeon, Westboro State Hospital, Westboro.

HARVEY, JAMES ALEXANDER, M.D., 25 East Washington Street, Chicago, Illinois. Rush Medical College, 1896. Member of Associate Staff, St. Luke's Hospital.

HARVEY, NORMAN DARRELL, M.D., 112 Waterman Street, Providence, Rhode Island. Columbia University, College of Physicians and Surgeons, 1888. Surgeon, Ear, Nose, and Throat Department, Rhode Island and City

Hospitals, Providence; Consulting Ophthalmic Surgeon, Newport Hospital, Newport, Providence Lying-in and Butler Hospitals, Providence.

HARVEY, SAMUEL CLARK, Ph.B., M.D., New Haven Hospital, New Haven, Connecticut. Yale University School of Medicine, 1911. Associate Professor of Surgery, Yale University School of Medicine; Attending Surgeon, New Haven Hospital and Dispensary.

HARVEY, THOMAS WILLIAM, A.M., M.D., 59 Main Street, Orange, New Jersey. Columbia University, College of Physicians and Surgeons, 1878. Consulting Surgeon, Orange Memorial Hospital and New Jersey Orthopedic Hospital and Dispensary.

HARVIE, JOHN BRUCE, M.D., C.M., 41 Second Street, Troy, New York. Faculty of Medicine, McGill University, 1881. Professor of Clinical Surgery, Albany Medical College; Surgeon, Samaritan Hospital; Surgeon-in-Chief, St. Joseph's Maternity Hospital; Consulting Surgeon, Leonard Hospital.

HARWOOD, L. DE L., M.D., 228 Sherbrooke Street, West, Montreal, Quebec. Faculty of Medicine, University of Montreal (Laval University, Faculty of Medicine), 1890.

HASELTINE, BURTON, M.D., 122 South Michigan Avenue, Chicago, Illinois. Hahnemann Medical College and Hospital, Chicago, 1896. Professor of Rhinology and Laryngology, Hahnemann Medical College and Hospital; Attending Rhinologist, Hahnemann Hospital; Consulting Surgeon, Cook County Hospital; Consulting Eye and Ear Surgeon, Chicago Home for the Friendless.

HASKELL, LOUIS WARDLAW, A.B., M.D., Bank of Commerce Building, Memphis, Tennessee. Johns Hopkins University Medical Department, 1903. Associate Professor of Surgery, University of Tennessee, College of Medicine; Attending Surgeon, Memphis General Hospital.

HASKELL, WILLIAM L., M.D., 111 Pine Street, Lewiston, Maine. Bowdoin Medical School (Medical School of Maine), 1894.

HASKIN, WILLIAM HENRY, M.D., 40 East Forty-first Street, New York, New York. University of California Medical School, 1889. Assistant Surgeon, Manhattan Eye, Ear, and Throat Hospital.

HASKINS, JOHN BUNYAN, M.D., 605 Volunteer Building, Chattanooga, Tennessee. University of Tennessee College of Medicine, 1907. Member of Surgical Staff, Baroness Erlanger Hospital.

HASLAM, GEORGE JAMES, B.Sc., M.D., M.R.C.S. (Eng.), 215 East Fifth Street, Fremont, Nebraska. National University of Ireland (Royal University of Ireland), Dublin, 1880.

HASSIG, JOHN FRANKLIN, M.D., 800 Minnesota Avenue, Kansas City, Kansas. University of Kansas School of Medicine (College of Physicians and Surgeons, Kansas City), 1899. Attending Surgeon, St. Margaret's Hospital.

HASTIE, JOHN DEARBORN, A.M., M.D., 122 East Fulton Street, Grand Rapids, Michigan. Columbia University, College of Physicians and Surgeons, 1904. Attending Surgeon, Blodgett Memorial Hospital.

HATCH, EDWARD SPARHAWK, M.D., 3439 Prytania Street, New Orleans, Louisiana. Harvard Medical School, 1899. Chief Orthopedic Surgeon, Touro Infirmary; Consulting Orthopedic Surgeon, New Orleans Dispensary and Hospital for Women and Children.

HATFIELD, HENRY DRURY, A.B., M.D., LL.D., 1550 Fifth Avenue, Huntington, West Virginia. University of Louisville, Medical Department, 1893; University and Bellevue Hospital Medical College, 1904. Surgeon, Greater Huntington Hospital Association, Huntington, Williamson Hospital, Williamson, Baltimore and Ohio, Chesapeake and Ohio Railroads.

HATFIELD, RAYMOND LEFEVER, M.D., 508 First National Bank Building, Danville, Illinois. Hahnemann Medical College and Hospital (Chicago Homeopathic Medical College), 1903.

HATHAWAY, GEORGE S., M.D., United States Navy, Washington, District of Columbia. Harvard Medical School, 1902. Commander, Medical Corps, United States Navy.

HAUER, ARTHUR M., M.D., 327 East State Street, Columbus, Ohio. Ohio State University College of Medicine (Ohio Medical University), 1906. Assistant Professor of Oto-Laryngology, Ohio State University College of Medicine; Oculist and Oto-Laryngologist Grant Hospital; Assistant Oto-Laryngologist, St. Francis Hospital.

HAUSER, CHARLES D., M.D., 138 West Rayen Avenue, Youngstown, Ohio. University of Buffalo, Department of Medicine, 1896. Attending Surgeon, St. Elizabeth's Hospital.

HAUSMAN, W. A., JR., M.S., M.D., 1116 Hamilton Street, Allentown, Pennsylvania. University of Pennsylvania School of Medicine, 1902. Dean of Surgical Department, Sacred Heart Hospital.

HAUSSLING, FRANCIS REYNOLDS, B.Sc., M.D., 661 High Street, Newark, New Jersey. Columbia University, College of Physicians and Surgeons, 1901. Attending Surgeon, Newark City and Newark Memorial Hospitals; Adjunct Surgeon, Hospital of St. Barnabas; Consulting Surgeon, Home for Incurables and Hospital.

HAWK, GEORGE WILLIAM, M.Sc., M.D., Robert Packer Hospital, Sayre, Pennsylvania. University of Pennsylvania School of Medicine, 1911. Associate Surgeon, Robert Packer Hospital.

HAWKES, EDWARD M. Z., A.M., M.D., 84 Washington Street, Newark, New Jersey. Columbia University, College of Physicians and Surgeons, 1890. Gynecologist, Newark City and St. James Hospitals; Surgeon, Presbyterian and Newark Maternity Hospitals; Adjunct Surgeon, Hospital of St. Barnabas; Consultant in Gynecology, Essex County Hospital for Insane.

HAWKES, FORBES, A.B., M.D., 124 East Sixty-fifth Street, New York, New York. Columbia University, College of Physicians and Surgeons, 1891. Associate in Surgery, Columbia University, College of Physicians and Surgeons; Associate Attending Surgeon, Presbyterian Hospital; Consulting Surgeon, Nassau Hospital, Mineola, St. Joseph's Hospital, Far Rockaway, Loomis Sanitarium, Liberty.

HAWKINS, ARTHUR HANSON, M.D., Center Street, Cumberland, Maryland. University of Maryland School of Medicine (College of Physicians and Surgeons, Baltimore), 1895. Surgeon, Western Maryland Hospital; Consulting Surgeon, Miners' Hospital, Frostburg.

HAWKINS, WILLIAM HENRY, M.D., 149 Pine Street, Lewiston, Maine. Jefferson Medical College, 1893. Surgeon, Central Maine General Hospital, Grand Trunk Railroad.

HAWORTH, ELWOOD B., M.D., 145 North Craig Street, Pittsburgh, Pennsylvania. University of Pennsylvania School of Medicine, 1883. Visiting Surgeon, Western Pennsylvania Hospital.

HAYD, HERMAN E., M.D., C.M., M.R.C.S. (Eng.), 493 Delaware Avenue, Buffalo, New York. Faculty of Medicine, McGill University, 1881. Surgeon, Memorial and Deaconess Hospitals.

HAYDEN, A.M., M.D., 22 Walnut Street, Evansville, Indiana. Ohio State University College of Medicine (Starling-Ohio Medical College), 1875. Surgeon, Hayden Hospital.

HAYDEN, AUSTIN A., B.Sc., A.M., M.D., 25 East Washington Street, Chicago, Illinois. Rush Medical College, 1904. Chief of Department of Rhinology, Otology, and Laryngology, St. Joseph's Hospital; Ophthalmologist and Oto-Laryngologist, St. Bernard's and People's Hospitals.

HAYDEN, JOHN GARDNER, B.Sc., M.D., 1222 Rialto Building, Kansas City, Missouri. Rush Medical College, 1904. Attending Surgeon, Kansas City General and St. Luke's Hospitals.

HAYDEN, REYNOLDS, M.D., Medical Corps, United States Navy, Washington, District of Columbia. Georgetown University School of Medicine, 1905. Commander, Medical Corps, United States Navy.

HAYES, ALEXANDER NEWLANDS, M.B., M.D., 137 Wellington Street, Sarnia, Ontario. Western University, Faculty of Medicine, 1890; University of Toronto, Faculty of Medicine, 1890. Consulting Surgeon, Sarnia General Hospital; District Surgeon, Grand Trunk Railway.

HAYES, CHARLES ARTHUR, M.D., Canton Hospital, Canton, China. University of California Medical School, 1900. Professor of Diseases of Eye, Ear, Nose, and Throat, Kung Yee Medical College; Surgeon in Charge, Eye, Ear, Nose, and Throat Department, Canton Hospital.

HAYES, DENNIS J., M.D., 1014 Majestic Building, Milwaukee, Wisconsin. Northwestern University Medical School, 1879. Surgeon, Misericordia Hospital; Consulting Surgeon, Johnston Emergency Hospital.

HAYNES, IRVING SAMUEL, Ph.B., M.D., D.Sc., 107 West Eighty-fifth Street, New York, New York. University and Bellevue Hospital Medical College (University of the City of New York, Medical Department), 1887. Professor of Clinical Surgery, Cornell University Medical College; Director of Gynecology, Harlem Hospital; Visiting Surgeon, Park Hospital; Consulting Surgeon, Reconstruction and Washington Square Hospitals, New York, Physicians Hospital, Plattsburg.

HAYNES, JAMES PLUMMER, M.D., Medical Corps, United States Navy, Washington, District of Columbia. Vanderbilt University, Medical Department, 1901. Commander, Medical Corps, United States Navy.

HAYS, GEORGE L., M.D., Mercy Hospital, Pittsburgh, Pennsylvania. University of Pennsylvania School of Medicine, 1895. Assistant Professor of Surgery, University of Pittsburgh School of Medicine; Surgeon, Mercy Hospital.

HAYS, HAROLD M., A.M., M.D., 2178 Broadway, New York, New York. Columbia University, College of Physicians and Surgeons, 1905. Laryngologist and Otologist, City Hospital; Associate Laryngologist, Riverside Hospital; Consulting Otologist, Sanitarium for Hebrew Children, Far Rockaway.

HAYWARD, EUGENE HENDERSON, M.D., 23 West Franklin Street, Baltimore, Maryland. University of Maryland School of Medicine (Baltimore Medical College), 1901. Associate in Surgery, University of Maryland School of Medicine and College of Physicians and Surgeons.

HAZELTON, WILLIAM F., M.D., 97 Westminster Street, Bellows Falls, Vermont. Columbia University, College of Physicians and Surgeons, 1884. Attending Surgeon, Rockingham Hospital.

HEALD, CLARENCE LINDEN, M.D., Sigourney Hospital, Sigourney, Iowa. University of Pennsylvania School of Medicine, 1893. Surgeon, Sigourney Hospital.

HEALY, HENRY HERBERT, M.D., Northwestern National Bank Building, Grand Forks, North Dakota. Rush Medical College, 1892. Special Lecturer, University of North Dakota College of Medicine; Surgeon, St. Michael's and Deaconess Hospitals.

HEALY, WILLIAM P., Ph.B., M.D., 525 Park Avenue, New York, New York. Johns Hopkins University, Medical Department, 1900. Surgeon, Fordham Hospital; Gynecologist, Misericordia Hospital; Junior Gynecologist, Roosevelt Hospital; Consulting Gynecologist, Bronx Maternity Hospital, New York, Sea View Hospital, Castleton Corners, Lawrence Hospital, Bronxville, Northern Westchester Hospital, Mt. Kisco.

HEANEY, NOBLE SPROAT, A.B., M.D., 104 South Michigan Avenue, Chicago, Illinois. Rush Medical College, 1904. Associate Professor of Obstetrics and Gynecology, Acting Head, Department Obstetrics and Gynecology, Rush Medical College; Attending Obstetrician and Gynecologist, Presbyterian Hospital.

HEARST, WILLIAM L., B.Sc., Ph.B., M.D., 903 Main Street, Cedar Falls, Iowa. State University of Iowa College of Medicine, 1897.

HEATH, ALBERT CHENEY, A.B., M.D., 339 Lowry Building, St. Paul, Minnesota. University of Minnesota Medical School, 1894. Rhinologist and Laryngologist, City and St. Luke's Hospitals, State Hospital for Indigent, Crippled and Deformed Children, Northern Pacific Railway.

HEATH, HOMER H., B.Sc., M.D., 656 Spitzer Building, Toledo, Ohio. Western Reserve University School of Medicine, 1903. Visiting Surgeon, Flower and St. Vincent's Hospitals; Consulting Surgeon, Maternity and Children's Hospitals.

HEAZLIT, LEDRA, M.D., 149 Genesee Street, Auburn, New York. University of Pennsylvania School of Medicine, 1897. Surgeon, Auburn City Hospital.

HEBB, ARTHUR, M.D., 330 North Charles Street, Baltimore, Maryland. University of Maryland School of Medicine (Baltimore Medical College), 1898. Assistant, Out-Patient Department, Johns Hopkins Hospital; Proctologist, St. Agnes' and St. Joseph's Hospitals, Hebrew Hospital and Asylum.

HECKEL, EDWARD B., A.M., M.D., 719 Jenkins Arcade Building, Pittsburgh, Pennsylvania. University and Bellevue Hospital Medical College, 1890. Ophthalmologist, Allegheny General Hospital.

HEDBLOM, CARL ARTHUR, A.M., M.D., Ph.D., D.Sc., Mayo Clinic, Rochester, Minnesota. Harvard Medical School, 1911. Surgeon, St. Mary's and Colonial Hospitals (Mayo Clinic).

HEDGES, B. VAN D., A.M., M.D., 703 Watchung Avenue, Plainfield, New Jersey. Columbia University, College of Physicians and Surgeons, 1891. Attending Surgeon, Muhlenberg Hospital.

HEDGES, ELLIS WALTON, A.M., M.D., 703 Watchung Avenue, Plainfield, New Jersey. University of Pennsylvania School of Medicine, 1883. Attending Surgeon, Muhlenberg Hospital.

HEDGES, HALSTEAD SHIPMAN, B.Sc., A.M., M.D., 104 East Market Street, Charlottesville, Virginia. University of Virginia, Department of Medicine, 1892. Professor of Ophthalmology, University of Virginia, Department of Medicine.

HEEVE, WILLIAM L., Ch.G., M.D., 138 Hancock Street, Brooklyn, New York. Eclectic Medical College of the City of New York, 1898. Surgeon, Cumberland Street, Mutual, and Prospect Heights Hospitals, Brooklyn Maternity.

HEFFENGER, ARTHUR COWTON, M.D., 53 Austin Street, Portsmouth, New Hampshire. University of Maryland School of Medicine, 1875. Surgeon, Portsmouth Hospital.

HEFLEBOWER, ROBERT COLWELL, M.D., 22 West Seventh Street, Cincinnati, Ohio. University of Cincinnati College of Medicine (Miami Medical College), 1889. Oculist, Aurist, and Director of Eye and Ear Clinic, Seton Hospital; Ophthalmologist, Deaconess Hospital.

HEFLIN, HOWELL T., M.D., 407 Empire Building, Birmingham, Alabama. University of Maryland School of Medicine, 1893.

HEFLIN, WYATT, M.D., 3216 Cliff Road, Birmingham, Alabama. Jefferson Medical College, 1884. Gynecologist, Hillman Hospital; Member of Staff, South Highland's Infirmary.

HEGGIE, NORMAN M., M.D., Buckman Building, Jacksonville, Florida. University of Maryland School of Medicine, 1902. Oculist and Aurist, St. Luke's Hospital.

HEGNER, CASPER FRANK, M.D., Metropolitan Building, Denver, Colorado. University of Cincinnati College of Medicine (University of Cincinnati, Medical Department), 1902.

HEINER, ROBERT GRAHAM, M.D., Medical Corps, United States Navy, Washington, District of Columbia. University of Virginia, Department of Medicine, 1900. Commander, Medical Corps, United States Navy.

HEJINIAN, ARAM G., M.D., 216 Main Street, Anamosa, Iowa. Rush Medical College, 1893. Surgeon in Charge, Mercy Hospital.

HELD, R. JOHNSON, M.D., 3531 Pacific Avenue, Atlantic City, New Jersey. Columbia University College of Physicians and Surgeons, 1898.

HELFRICH, CHARLES H., M.D., 542 Fifth Avenue, New York, New York. New York Homeopathic Medical College and Flower Hospital, 1884. Professor of Ophthalmology, Department of Instruction, New York Ophthalmic Hospital; Surgeon, New York Ophthalmic Hospital; Ophthalmic Surgeon, Hahnemann Hospital; Consulting Surgeon, Eye and Ear Departments, Yonkers Homeopathic Hospital and Maternity, Yonkers, New York, Homeopathic Hospital of Essex County, Newark, New Jersey.

HELLMAN, ALFRED M., A.B., M.D., 2 West Eighty-sixth Street, New York, New York. Columbia University, College of Physicians and Surgeons, 1905. Gynecologist, Lenox Hill Hospital Dispensary; Attending Obstetrician, Sydenham Hospital.

HELMS, JOHN S., A.B., M.D., 812 Citizens Bank Building, Tampa, Florida. University of Tennessee College of Medicine (Memphis Hospital Medical College), 1891. Chief Surgeon, Tampa Children's Home; Chief of Staff and Director of Division of Surgery, Bayside Hospital; Consulting Surgeon, Gordon Keller Memorial Hospital.

HELMUTH, WILLIAM TOD, M.D., 616 Madison Avenue, New York, New York. New York Homeopathic Medical College and Flower Hospital, 1887. Professor of Surgery, New York Homeopathic Medical College and Flower Hospital; Visiting Surgeon and Chief of Surgical Staff, New York Homeopathic Medical College and Flower Hospital; Consulting Surgeon, Broad Street Hospital, Laura Franklin Free Hospital for Children, New York, New York State Hospital for Crippled and Deformed Children, West Haverstraw, Middletown State Homeopathic Hospital, Middletown, White Plains Hospital, White Plains, Yonkers Homeopathic Hospital and Maternity, Yonkers, Jamaica Hospital, Jamaica, New York, Essex County Hospital, Cedar Grove, St. Mary's Hospital, Passaic, New Jersey.

HELTON, ALFRED JOSEPH, A.B., M.D., 406 Masonic Temple, Yakima, Washington. Rush Medical College, 1902. Surgeon, St. Elizabeth's Hospital.

HEMMEON, JAMES ALBERT MORAN, A.B., M.D., 41 Spring Garden Road, Halifax, Nova Scotia. University of Maryland School of Medicine (College of Physicians and Surgeons, Baltimore), 1896. Consulting Surgeon, Camp Hill Hospital; Surgeon, Ear, Nose, and Throat Department, Massachusetts-Halifax Health Clinic.

HENDEE, LAWRENCE, A.B., M.D., 346 Elmwood Avenue, Buffalo, New York. University of Buffalo, Department of Medicine, 1897. Consulting Surgeon, J. N. Adam Memorial Hospital, Perrysburg, Homeopathic Hospital, Buffalo.

HENDERSON, ANDREW MITCHELL, A.B., M.D., 824 J Street, Sacramento, California. Cooper Medical College, 1893. Division Surgeon, Hospital Department, Southern Pacific Railway.

HENDERSON, E. E., M.D., 644 Linden Avenue, Oak Park, Illinois. Rush Medical College, 1896. Attending Surgeon, Norwegian Lutheran Deaconess, St. Elizabeth's and Norwegian-American Hospitals, Chicago.

HENDERSON, FRANK LARAMORE, M.D., 501 Humboldt Building, St. Louis, Missouri. Washington University Medical School (Missouri Medical College), 1888.

HENDERSON, JAMES P., M.D., 3615 Wabash Avenue, Kansas City, Missouri. University Medical College, Kansas City, 1903. Surgeon, Kansas City General and Christian Church Hospitals.

HENDERSON, MELVIN STARKEY, M.B., M.D., 428 Fourth Street, Southwest, Rochester, Minnesota. University of Toronto, Faculty of Medicine, 1906. Professor of Orthopedic Surgery, University of Minnesota, Mayo Foundation; Orthopedic Surgeon, St. Mary's and Colonial Hospitals (Mayo Clinic).

HENDERSON, WILLIAM BAIRD, M.D., 724 Presqueisle Street, Philipsburg, Pennsylvania. University of Pennsylvania School of Medicine, 1886. Senior Surgeon, Cottage State Hospital.

HENDERSON, WILLIAM THOMAS, M.D., 259 St. Francis Street, Mobile, Alabama. Detroit College of Medicine and Surgery, 1896. Visiting Surgeon, Providence Infirmary and Mobile City Hospital.

HENDON, GEORGE A., M.D., Francis Building, Louisville, Kentucky. University of Louisville, Medical Department (Louisville Medical College), 1894. Professor of Principles and Practice of Surgery, and Clinical Surgery, University of Louisville, Medical Department; Member of Visiting Staff, Louisville City and St. Anthony's Hospitals.

HENDRICK, ARTHUR CLINTON, A.M., M.B., F.R.C.S. (Edin.), 20 Bloor Street, East, Toronto, Ontario. University of Toronto, Faculty of Medicine, 1900. Demonstrator of Gynecology, University of Toronto, Faculty of Medicine; Assistant Gynecologist, Toronto General Hospital; Member of Associate Staff and Assistant Pathologist, Grace Hospital.

HENDRY, WILLIAM BELFRY, A.B., M.B., D.S.O., 112 College Street, Toronto, Ontario. University of Toronto, Faculty of Medicine, 1904. Associate Professor of Obstetrics and Gynecology, University of Toronto, Faculty of Medicine; Senior Assistant in Obstetrics and Gynecology, Toronto General Hospital.

HENNING, DAVID M., M.D., 624 Exchange Building, Memphis, Tennessee. University of Tennessee College of Medicine (Memphis Hospital Medical College), 1900; Columbia University, College of Physicians and Surgeons, 1902. Visiting Surgeon, Department of Proctology, Memphis General, St. Joseph's and Crippled Children's Hospitals; Surgeon, Louisville and Nashville Railway.

HENNINGER, LOUIS LeROY, M.D., 401 City National Bank Building, Council Bluffs, Iowa. State University of Iowa College of Medicine, 1902. Otologist, Laryngologist, and Rhinologist, Jennie Edmundson Memorial Hospital.

HENNINGTON, CHARLES W., B.Sc., M.D., 633 Park Avenue, Rochester, New York. Johns Hopkins University, Medical Department, 1906. Assistant Surgeon, Rochester General Hospital; Surgeon, Rochester State Hospital.

HENRY, CHARLES K. P., M.D., C.M., 4549 Sherbrooke Street, West, Montreal, Quebec. Faculty of Medicine, McGill University, 1900. Demonstrator of Clinical Surgery, Faculty of Medicine, McGill University; Assistant Surgeon, Montreal General Hospital; Consulting Surgeon, Mackay Institute for Protestant Deaf Mutes and the Blind; Surgeon, Canadian National Railways, Montreal Division.

HENRY, JOHN GOODRICH, B.Sc., M.D., 33 Pleasant Street, Winchendon, Massachusetts. Dartmouth Medical School, 1881. Surgeon, Millers River Hospital.

HENRY, WALTER O., M.D., 917 Baker-Detwiler Building, Los Angeles, California. University and Bellevue Hospital Medical College (Bellevue Hospital Medical College), 1879.

HENSON, JAMES WILLIAM, M.D., 405 Allen Avenue, Richmond, Virginia. Medical College of Virginia, 1889. Associate Professor of Surgery, Medical College of Virginia; Surgeon, Virginia and Memorial Hospitals.

HEPBURN, HOWARD HAVELOCK, M.D., C.M., F.R.C.S. (Edin.), Bank of Montreal Building, Edmonton, Alberta. Faculty of Medicine, McGill University, 1910.

HEPBURN, JAMES J., A.B., M.D., 56 Bay State Road, Boston, Massachusetts. Harvard Medical School, 1919. Assistant Professor of Anatomy and Instructor in Surgery, Tufts College Medical School; Surgeon to Out-Patients, Boston City Hospital.

HEPBURN, THOMAS N., A.M., M.D., 179 Allyn Street, Hartford, Connecticut. Johns Hopkins University, Medical Department, 1905. Assistant Surgeon and Cystoscopist, Hartford Hospital; Consulting Surgeon, New Britain General Hospital, New Britain; Consulting Urologist, Charlotte Hungerford Hospital, Torrington, and Manchester General Hospital.

HEPPERLEN, HARRY M., M.D., 114 South Sixth Street, Beatrice, Nebraska. State University of Iowa College of Medicine (Keokuk Medical College), 1891; Jefferson Medical College, 1896. Chief Surgeon, Lutheran and Mennonite Deaconess Hospitals.

HERBST, ROBERT H., M.D., 32 North State Street, Chicago, Illinois. Rush Medical College, 1900. Assistant Professor of Genito-Urinary Surgery, Rush Medical College; Attending Genito-Urinary Surgeon, Henrotin Memorial Hospital; Attending Urologist, Presbyterian Hospital.

HERFF, ADOLPH, M.D., 312 Avenue C, San Antonio, Texas. Jefferson Medical College, 1880. Surgeon, Santa Rosa Infirmary.

HERFF, FERDINAND PETER, M.D., 707 Central Trust Building, San Antonio, Texas. Jefferson Medical College, 1905. Attending Surgeon and Member of Staff, Santa Rosa Infirmary.

HERMESCH, HARRY R., M.D., Medical Corps, United States Navy, Washington, District of Columbia. Georgetown University School of Medicine, 1907. Commander, Medical Corps, United States Navy.

HERRICK, ALFRED B., A.B., M.D., Hospital de Panama, Panama, Republic of Panama. Johns Hopkins University, Medical Department, 1898. Surgeon, Hospital de Panama.

HERRICK, FREDERICK C., A.B., M.D., 465 Rose Building, Cleveland, Ohio. Western Reserve University School of Medicine, 1897. Associate in Surgery, Western Reserve University School of Medicine; Visiting Surgeon, Cleveland City Hospital; Assistant Visiting Surgeon and Visiting Urologist, St. Vincent's Charity Hospital.

HERRICK, JOHN FRANCIS, M.D., Hofmann Building, Ottumwa, Iowa. State University of Iowa College of Medicine (Keokuk Medical College), 1891. Member of Surgical Staff, Ottumwa and St. Joseph Hospitals.

HERRICK, WILLIAM POST, B.A., M.A., M.D., 61 East Seventy-third Street, New York, New York. Columbia University College of Physicians and Surgeons, 1898. Chief of Surgery and Clinical Director, Hudson Street Hospital; Consulting Urologist, United States Public Health Service Hospital, No. 61, Fox Hills, Staten Island.

HERRING, BENJAMIN SIMMS, M.D., Green and Spring Streets, Wilson, North Carolina. University of Michigan Medical School, 1900. Surgeon, Moore-Herring Hospital.

HERTZBERG, GEORGE ROBERT REINHOLD, M.D., 40 South Street, Stamford, Connecticut. Dartmouth Medical College, 1899. Surgeon, Stamford Hospital.

HERTZLER, ARTHUR E., B.Sc., A.M., M.D., Ph.D., 1316 Rialto Building, Kansas City, Missouri. Northwestern University Medical School, 1894. Professor of Surgery, University of Kansas School of Medicine; Member of Staff, St. Luke's, Halstead, and St. Mary's Hospitals.

HESS, ELMER, M.D., 501 Commerce Building, Erie, Pennsylvania. University of Pennsylvania School of Medicine, 1911. Urologist, St. Vincent's Hospital; Consulting Urologist, Infant's Home.

HESS, LOUIS THALES, M.D., Medical Corps, United States Army, Washington, District of Columbia. Jefferson Medical College, 1895. Colonel, Medical Corps, United States Army.

HESSERT, WILLIAM, M.D., 547 Fullerton Parkway, Chicago, Illinois. Northwestern University Medical School, 1892. Professor of Surgery, Chicago Policlinic; Attending Surgeon, Grant, Alexian Brothers', Henrotin Memorial Hospitals, Chicago Policlinic and Hospital, Uhlich Orphan Asylum.

HETHERINGTON, ELLERY M., M.D., 738 Lathrop Building, Kansas City, Missouri. University of Maryland School of Medicine (College of Physicians and Surgeons, Baltimore), 1888.

HETRICK, LLEWELLYN E., M.D., 30 West Forty-eighth Street, New York, New York. Hahnemann Medical College and Hospital, Philadelphia, 1898. Professor of Otology, New York Homeopathic Medical College and Flower Hospital, and Post-Graduate College of New York Ophthalmic Hospital; Aurist, New York Ophthalmic, Metropolitan, Fifth Avenue and Flower Hospitals; Consulting Aurist, Community Hospital, New York, Jamaica Hospital, Jamaica, Grace Hospital, New Haven, Connecticut, Ann May Memorial Hospital, Spring Lake, New Jersey.

HEWITT, HERBERT W., M.D., 1131 David Whitney Building, Detroit, Michigan. Detroit College of Medicine and Surgery, 1903. Associate Clinical Professor of Surgery, Detroit College of Medicine and Surgery; Attending Surgeon, Grace Hospital.

HEWITT, WILLIAM F., B.Sc., M.D., 122 South Michigan Avenue, Chicago, Illinois. Rush Medical College, 1912. Assistant Professor of Obstetrics and Gynecology, Rush Medical College; Assistant Attending Obstetrician and Gynecologist, Presbyterian Hospital; Obstetrician, Out-Patient Department, Central Free Dispensary, Rush Medical College, and Presbyterian Hospital.

HEWSON, ADDINELL, A.M., M.D., 2120 Spruce Street, Philadelphia, Pennsylvania. Jefferson Medical College, 1879. Professor of Anatomy, University of Pennsylvania Graduate School of Medicine. Professor of Anatomy and Histology, Temple University, Department of Dentistry; Surgeon, Memorial Hospital.

HEYD, CHARLES GORDON, B.A., M.D., 46 West Fifty-second Street, New York, New York. University of Buffalo, Department of Medicine, 1909. Professor of Surgery, Director of Department of Anatomical Surgery and Surgery on the Cadaver, and Attending Surgeon, New York Post-Graduate Medical School and Hospital; Attending Surgeon, New York Post-Graduate Hospital Dispensary; Consulting Surgeon, Morristown Hospital, Morristown, Dover Hospital, Dover, New Jersey, Greenwich Hospital, Greenwich, Connecticut.

HIBBITT, CHARLES W., A.B., M.D., Francis Building, Louisville, Kentucky. University of Louisville, Medical Department, 1897. Professor of Abdominal Surgery and Gynecology, University of Louisville, Medical Department; Visiting Gynecologist, Louisville City Hospital.

HICKEY, PRESTON MANASSEH, B.A., M.D., 62 Adams Avenue, West, Detroit, Michigan. Detroit College of Medicine and Surgery, 1892. Professor of Roentgenology, Detroit College of Medicine and Surgery; Roentgenologist, Harper, Receiving, Women's, and Children's Free Hospitals.

HICKS, CHARLES F., M.D., Welch, West Virginia. Maryland Medical College, 1901. Superintendent and Surgeon in Charge, Welch Hospital No. 1.

HICKS, FRANCIS MARION, M.D., 203 Hicks Building, San Antonio, Texas. University and Bellevue Hospital Medical College (Bellevue Hospital Medical College), 1880. Surgeon, Physicians and Surgeons and Baylor Hospitals, Santa Rosa Infirmary; Consulting Gynecologist, Robert B. Green Memorial Hospital.

HIEBERT, GERHARD, M.D., C.M., 412 Boyd Building, Winnipeg, Manitoba. Faculty of Medicine, McGill University, 1900. Consulting Surgeon, Winnipeg General Hospital.

HIGBEE, EDWARD H., M.D., 417 Metropolitan Building, St. Louis, Missouri. Washington University Medical School, 1897. Assistant Opthalmologist, St. Louis University; Member of Staff, Mullanphy, St. Anthony, St. Louis Maternity, Isolation Hospitals and City Sanitarium; Consulting Staff, St. John's Hospital.

HIGGINS, MONTGOMERY E., M.D., Medical Corps, United States Navy, Washington, District of Columbia. George Washington University Medical School, 1904. Lieutenant Commander, Medical Corps, United States Navy.

HIGGINS, REUBEN PAUL, A.B., M.D., 20 Court Street, Cortland, New York. Johns Hopkins University, Medical Department, 1905. Ophthalmologist, Cortland County Hospital, Children's Home.

HIGHSMITH, EMMETT DEWITT, M.D., 445 Trust Company of Georgia Building, Atlanta, Georgia. Emory University School of Medicine (Atlanta College of Physicians and Surgeons), 1906. Associate Professor of Surgery, Emory University School of Medicine; Visiting Surgeon, Wesley Memorial Hospital; Associate Visiting Surgeon, Grady Memorial Hospital.

HIGHSMITH, JACOB FRANKLIN, M.D., 304 Green Street, Fayetteville, North Carolina. Jefferson Medical College, 1889. Chief Surgeon, Highsmith Hospital.

HILL, GEORGE HILLARD, M.D., 15 High Street, Worcester, Massachusetts. Harvard Medical School, 1894. Member Consulting Staff, Worcester City Hospital.

HILL, HOWARD, M.D., 1334 Rialto Building, Kansas City, Missouri. University of Kansas School of Medicine (Kansas City Medical College), 1895. Surgeon, St. Joseph's Hospital; Visiting Surgeon, Kansas City General Hospital.

HILL, JAMES A., M.D., Scanlon Building, Houston, Texas. Tulane University of Louisiana School of Medicine, 1900. Surgeon, Baptist Sanitarium and Norsworthy and Municipal Hospitals.

HILL, LESLIE GRANT, M.D., Fourteenth Street and Main Avenue, Sioux Falls, South Dakota. Hahnemann Medical College and Hospital, Chicago, 1895.

HILL, LUTHER L., M.D., LL.D., 422 South Perry Street, Montgomery, Alabama. University and Bellevue Hospital Medical College (University of the City of New York, Medical Department), 1881; Jefferson Medical College, 1882. Surgeon, Laura Hill Hospital.

HILL, ROBERT SOMMERVILLE, M.D., 21 South Perry Street, Montgomery, Alabama. University and Bellevue Hospital Medical College (University of the City of New York, Medical Department), 1891. Visiting Surgeon, Laura Hill Hospital.

HILL, ROLAND, M.D., C.M., 4500 Olive Street, St. Louis, Missouri. University of Toronto, Faculty of Medicine (Trinity Medical College), 1890. Surgeon, St. Luke's, St. Louis City, and Bethesda Hospitals.

HILL, T. CHITTENDEN, Ph.B., M.D., 31 Bay State Road, Boston, Massachusetts. University of Vermont College of Medicine, 1895. Instructor in Proctology, Harvard Graduate School of Medicine; Surgeon, Rectal Department, Boston Dispensary.

HILLER, CARL R., M.D., 19 West Seventh Street, Cincinnati, Ohio. University of Cincinnati College of Medicine (Medical College of Ohio), 1899. Professor of Clinical Surgery and Surgical Pathology, University of Cincinnati College of Medicine; Attending Surgeon, Cincinnati General, Good Samaritan, and Jewish Hospitals.

HILLIARD, CARLOS GROUT, A.M., M.D., 126 Cajon Street, Redlands, California. Yale University School of Medicine, 1904.

HILLIS, DAVID S., M.D., 104 South Michigan Avenue, Chicago, Illinois. Northwestern University Medical School, 1898. Associate in Obstetrics, Northwestern University Medical School; Attending Obstetrician, Cook County and Provident Hospitals; Assistant Obstetrician, Chicago Lying-in Hospital.

HILSMAN, AGNEW HODGE, M.D., Broad and Washington Streets, Albany, Georgia. Cornell University Medical College, 1899. Visiting Surgeon, Phoebe Putney Memorial Hospital.

HILTON, DAVID CLARK, A.M., M.D., 305 Richards Block, Lincoln, Nebraska. Rush Medical College, 1903. Attending Surgeon, St. Elizabeth's Hospital.

HINES, HARRY HAYES, M.D., 21 Groton Building, Cincinnati, Ohio. University of Cincinnati College of Medicine (Miami Medical College), 1899. Clinical Professor of Surgery, University of Cincinnati College of Medicine; Surgeon, Cincinnati General, Good Samaritan, and Deaconess Hospitals, Children's Hospital of the Protestant Episcopal Church, Consulting Surgeon, Ohio Hospital for Epileptics, Gallipolis.

HINGSTON, DONALD ALEXANDER, B.A., M.D., M.R.C.S. (Eng.), L.R.C.P. (Lond.), F.R.C.S. (Edin.), 460 Sherbrooke Street, West, Montreal, Quebec. Faculty of Medicine, University of Montreal (Laval University, Medical Department), 1901. Associate Professor of Clinical Surgery, Faculty of Medicine, University of Montreal; Surgeon, Hotel Dieu de St. Joseph.

HINMAN, EUGENE E., M.D., 146 Washington Avenue, Albany, New York. Albany Medical College, 1899. Instructor, Nose and Throat Department, Albany Medical College; Attending Laryngologist and Rhinologist, Albany Hospital.

HINMAN, FRANK, A.B., M.D., 516 Sutter Street, San Francisco, California. Johns Hopkins University, Medical Department, 1906. Assistant Clinical Professor of Urology, University of California Medical School; Urologist in Charge, University of California Hospital.

HINNEN, GUSTAV A., B.Sc., M.D., 4 West Seventh Street, Cincinnati, Ohio. University of Cincinnati College of Medicine (Miami Medical College), 1904.

HIRSCHMAN, LOUIS J., M.D., Kresge Medical Building, Detroit, Michigan. Detroit College of Medicine and Surgery, 1899. Professor of Proctology and Director of the Department, Detroit College of Medicine and Surgery; Proctologist, Harper Hospital; Consulting Proctologist, Wayne County Hospital, Hannah Schloss Memorial Clinic.

HIRST, BARTON COOKE, A.B., M.D., LL.D., 1821 Spruce Street, Philadelphia, Pennsylvania. University of Pennsylvania School of Medicine, 1883. Professor of Obstetrics, University of Pennsylvania School of Medicine; Gynecologist and Obstetrician, Hospital of the University of Pennsylvania, Howard Hospital, Philadelphia Orthopedic Hospital and Infirmary; Consultant, Philadelphia Lying-in Charity Hospital, Preston Retreat, Philadelphia, Pottstown Hospital, Pottstown, Pennsylvania, Newport Hospital, Newport, Rhode Island.

HITZ, HENRY BARNARD, M.D., 309 Goldsmith Building, Milwaukee, Wisconsin. George Washington University Medical School (Columbian University, Medical Department), 1891. Laryngologist and Otologist, Milwaukee, Milwaukee Children's, and Columbia Hospitals.

HITZROT, JAMES MORLEY, A.B., M.D., 126 East Thirty-seventh Street, New York, New York. Johns Hopkins University, Medical Department, 1901. Professor of Clinical Surgery, Cornell University Medical College; Associate Surgeon, New York Hospital.

HIXSON, JESSE SHARP, M.D., Central National Bank Building, San Angelo, Texas. Washington University Medical School (Missouri Medical College), 1899.

HOAG, JUNIUS C., Ph.M., M.D., 1725 East Fifty-third Street, Chicago, Illinois. Northwestern University Medical School (Chicago Medical College), 1882. Consulting Obstetrician, St. Luke's Hospital.

HOBBS, WILBERT A., M.D., 125 West Fifth Street, East Liverpool, Ohio. University of Michigan Medical School, 1884. Surgeon, East Liverpool City Hospital, Pennsylvania Railroad.

HOBBS, WILLIAM HENRY, M.D., 103 Main Street, Binghamton, New York. University of Pennsylvania School of Medicine, 1910. Surgeon, Binghamton City and Moore-Overton Hospitals; Consulting Surgeon, Johnson City General Hospital, Johnson City.

HODGINS, EMERSON LeROY, M.B., L.R.C.P., M.R.C.S. (Eng.), F.R.C.S., 312 Oxford Street, London, Ontario. Associate Professor of Surgery, Western University, Faculty of Medicine; Surgeon, Victoria and St. Joseph's Hospitals.

HODGSON, FREDERICK GRADY, M.D., 746 Peachtree Street, Atlanta, Georgia. Columbia University, College of Physicians and Surgeons, 1901. Professor of Orthopedics, Emory University School of Medicine; Orthopedic Surgeon, Grady Memorial, Wesley Memorial, and Georgia Baptist Hospitals, MacVicar Hospital of Spelman Seminary.

HOEGH, KNUT, C.A., C.Ph., M.D., 131 West Thirty-sixth Street, South, Minneapolis, Minnesota. Royal University of Norway, 1869.

HOFF, EDWIN CORNUE, M.D., 1101 David Whitney Building, Detroit, Michigan. Ohio State University of Homeopathic Medicine (Cleveland Homeopathic Medical College), 1901. Visiting Surgeon, Grace Hospital Polyclinic; Attending Staff Surgeon, Grace Hospital.

HOFFMAN, CHARLES S., M.D., 60 Davis Street, Keyser, West Virginia. Jefferson Medical College, 1877. Surgeon, Hoffman Hospital.

HOFFMAN, LAWRENCE H., M.D., 177 Post Street, San Francisco, California. Cooper Medical College, 1897. Professor of Gynecology and Abdominal Surgery, College of Physicians and Surgeons; Consulting Gynecologist and Obstetrician, Mt. Zion Hospital.

HOFFMAN, PHILIP, M.D., 3657 Delmar Boulevard, St. Louis, Missouri. Washington University Medical School (Missouri Medical College), 1892. Orthopedic Surgeon, Jewish, Bethesda, and St. Louis Maternity Hospitals, Jewish Home for Chronic Invalids.

HOGAN, EDGAR POE, A.M., M.D., 412 Empire Building, Birmingham, Alabama. Birmingham Medical College, 1909. Associate Professor of Gynecology and Abdominal Surgery, Graduate School of Medicine of the University of Alabama; Gynecologist and Surgeon, Hillman Hospital.

HOGAN, EDWARD VINCENT, B.A., M.D., C.M., M.R.C.S. (Eng.), L.R.C.P. (Lond.), 109 College Street, Halifax, Nova Scotia. Faculty of Medicine, McGill University, 1896. Professor of Surgery and Clinical Surgery, Dalhousie University, Faculty of Medicine; Surgeon, Victoria General Hospital; Surgeon-in-Chief, Camp Hill Military Hospital.

HOGEBOOM, ROCHE W., M.D., 704 Woodruff Building, Springfield, Missouri. Rush Medical College, 1897.

HOGUE, GUSTAVUS INGOMAR, M.D., 410 Jefferson Street, Milwaukee, Wisconsin. Northwestern University Medical School, 1899. Associate Professor of Ophthalmology, Marquette University School of Medicine; Attending Ophthalmologist, Milwaukee County Hospital, Milwaukee Hospital for Insane, Wauwatosa; Ophthalmologist-in-Chief, Mt. Sinai Hospital.

HOGUET, JOSEPH P., A.B., M.D., 55 East Fifty-third Street, New York, New York. Columbia University College of Physicians and Surgeons (College of Physicians and Surgeons), 1907. Assistant Professor of Clinical Surgery,

Cornell University Medical College; Surgeon, French Hospital; Associate Surgeon, Hospital for Ruptured and Crippled; Assistant Surgeon, Memorial Hospital, New York; Consulting Surgeon, Mary McClellan Hospital, Cambridge.

HOHF, SILAS MATTHEW, M.D., Clinic Building, Yankton, South Dakota. Loyola University School of Medicine (Illinois Medical College), 1897; Northwestern University Medical School, 1903. Instructor in Physical Diagnosis, University of South Dakota College of Medicine; Chief Surgeon, Sacred Heart Hospital.

HOHLEN, KARL SIEGFRIED J., M.D., 1010 Terminal Building, Lincoln, Nebraska. Loyola University School of Medicine (Chicago College of Medicine and Surgery), 1908. Surgeon, St. Elizabeth's Hospital.

HOLBROOK, ARTHUR TENNEY, B.Sc., M.D., 612 Kenwood Boulevard, Milwaukee, Wisconsin. Rush Medical College, 1895. Member of Attending Staff, St. Mary's and Columbia Hospitals.

HOLBROOK, JOHN S., M.D., 301 South Front Street, Mankato, Minnesota. University of Minnesota Medical School, 1896. President of Staff, Evangelical Lutheran Immanuel Hospital.

HOLCOMB, OSCAR WILLIAM, M.D., 942 Lowry Building, St. Paul, Minnesota. Northwestern University Medical School, 1905. Surgeon, Bethesda Hospital.

HOLCOMB, RICHMOND CRANSTON, M.D., Medical Corps, United States Navy, Washington, District of Columbia. Long Island College Hospital, 1896. Commander, Medical Corps, United States Navy.

HOLDEN, FREDERICK CLARK, M.D., 13 East Sixty-fifth Street, New York, New York. University and Bellevue Hospital Medical College (University of the City of New York, Medical Department), 1892. Professor of Gynecology, University and Bellevue Hospital Medical College; Director of Department of Gynecology, Bellevue Hospital.

HOLDEN, GEORGE PARKER, M.D., 122 McLean Avenue, Yonkers, New York. New York Homeopathic Medical College and Flower Hospital, 1894. Senior Attending Surgeon, Yonkers Homeopathic Hospital and Maternity.

HOLDEN, GERRY R., A.B., M.D., 513 Laura Street, Jacksonville, Florida. Johns Hopkins University, Medical Department, 1901. Gynecologist, St. Luke's Hospital, Jacksonville, Florida State Hospital for Insane, Chattahoochee.

HOLDEN, WILLIAM B., B.Sc., M.D., 1002 Stevens Building, Portland, Oregon. Rush Medical College, 1897. Clinical Professor of Surgery, University of Oregon Medical School; Medical Director, Portland Sanitarium.

HOLDER, EUGENE MICHEL, B.Sc., M.D., Bank of Commerce Building, Memphis, Tennessee. University of Tennessee College of Medicine (Memphis Hospital Medical College), 1894. Professor of Surgery and Clinical Surgery, University of Tennessee College of Medicine; Visiting Surgeon, Memphis General, Baptist Memorial, and Lucy Brinkley Hospitals.

HOLLAND, GEORGE FRANK, Phar.G., M.D., 514 North College Avenue, Bloomington, Indiana. University and Bellevue Hospital Medical College, 1903. Surgeon, Bloomington Hospital; Local Surgeon, Illinois Central Railroad.

HOLLAND, JOSEPH WILLIAM, M.D., 1624 Linden Avenue, Baltimore, Maryland. University of Maryland School of Medicine, 1896. Clinical Professor of Surgery, University of Maryland School of Medicine; Member of Surgical Staff, University Hospital, Baltimore; Consulting Surgeon, Rosewood State Training School for Feeble-Minded, Owings Mills.

HOLLENBECK, FRANK BRADBURY, Ph.B., M.D., 206 Richards Block, Lincoln, Nebraska. Rush Medical College, 1898. Surgeon, St. Elizabeth's Hospital, Chicago, Burlington and Quincy Railroad.

HOLLOWAY, CHARLES E., M.D., 427 Iowa Building, Des Moines, Iowa. Hahnemann Medical College and Hospital (Chicago Homeopathic Medical College), 1893. Member of Surgical Staff, Iowa Congregational, City, and Iowa Methodist Hospitals.

HOLLOWAY, VICTOR D., B.Sc., M.D., 609 Walnut Street, Knoxville, Tennessee. University of Pennsylvania School of Medicine, 1907. Surgeon, Riverside and Knoxville General Hospitals.

HOLLOWBUSH, JOSEPH RALSTON, M.D., 509 Central Trust Building, Rock Island, Illinois. Washington University Medical School, 1880. Attending Surgeon, St. Anthony's Hospital, Rock Island, Illinois, St. Luke's Hospital, Davenport, Iowa; Consulting Surgeon, Mercy Hospital, Davenport, Iowa.

HOLMAN, CARL J., M.D., 201 National Citizen's Bank Building, Mankato, Minnesota. Rush Medical College, 1899. Surgeon, St. Joseph's and Immanuel Hospitals.

HOLMES, JOHN FRANKLIN, M.D., 951 Elm Street, Manchester, New Hampshire. Tufts College Medical School, 1909. Surgeon, Elliot Hospital; Consulting Surgeon, Pembroke Sanatorium, Pembroke.

HOLMES, RUDOLPH WIESER, M.D., 414 Arlington Place, Chicago, Illinois. Rush Medical College, 1893. Associate Professor of Obstetrics and Gynecology, Rush Medical College; Attending Obstetrician, Augustana and Passavant Memorial Hospitals.

HOLMES, WALTER RICHARD, JR., A.B., M.D., 436 Peachtree Street, Atlanta, Georgia. Johns Hopkins University Medical Department, 1913. Associate in Gynecology, Emory University School of Medicine; Assistant Visiting Surgeon, Georgia Baptist Hospital; Visiting Surgeon, Piedmont Sanitarium.

HOLT, ERASTUS EUGENE, A.M., M.D., LL.D., 723 Congress Street, Portland, Maine. Bowdoin Medical School, 1874; Columbia University, College of Physicians and Surgeons, 1875. Founder, Executive Surgeon, and Superintendent, Maine Eye and Ear Infirmary.

HOLT, WILLIAM A., M.D., 167 Mesquite Street, Globe, Arizona. University of Michigan Medical School, 1892. Chief of Staff, Old Dominion Hospital.

HOLTE, HALVOR, M.D., 220 South Broadway, **Crookston, Minnesota**. University of Minnesota Medical School, 1893.

HOLZER, CHARLES ELMER, M.D., First Avenue and Cedar Street, **Gallipolis, Ohio.** Ohio State University College of Medicine (Starling Medical College), 1909. Chief of Staff, Holzer Hospital.

HOMANS, JOHN, A.B., M.D., 33 Leicester Street, **Brookline, Massachusetts.** Harvard Medical School, 1903. Instructor in Surgery, Harvard Medical School; Surgeon, Peter Bent Brigham Hospital, Boston.

HOMER, HARRY L., M.D., 1011 North Charles Street, **Baltimore, Maryland.** University of Pennsylvania School of Medicine, 1904. Instructor in Clinical Surgery, Johns Hopkins University, Medical Department; Visiting Surgeon, Union Memorial Hospital, Church Home and Infirmary; Assistant Surgeon, Out-Patient Department, Johns Hopkins Hospital.

HONAN, WILLIAM FRANCIS, M.D., 24 East Forty-eighth Street, **New York, New York.** New York Homeopathic Medical College and Flower Hospital, 1889. Professor of Gynecology, New York Homeopathic Medical College and Flower Hospital; Chief Surgeon, Carson C. Peck Memorial Hospital, Brooklyn; Visiting Surgeon, Metropolitan Hospital, Department of Public Charities, Blackwell's Island; Attending Surgeon, Hahnemann Hospital.

HOOD, THOMAS C., A.M., M.D., 1008 Hume-Mansur Building, **Indianapolis, Indiana.** Jefferson Medical College, 1884. Professor of Ophthalmology, Indiana University School of Medicine; Surgeon, Indianapolis City, Methodist Episcopal, St. Vincent's, Protestant Deaconess, and Robert W. Long Hospitals.

HOOE, A. BARNES, M.D., 1220 Sixteenth Street, Northwest, **Washington, District of Columbia.** George Washington University Medical School (Columbian University, Medical Department), 1896.

HOOKER, RANSOM SPAFARD, B.L., M.D., 175 East Seventy-first Street, **New York, New York.** Columbia University, College of Physicians and Surgeons, 1900. Associate Professor of Surgery, Columbia University, College of Physicians and Surgeons; Director, First Surgical Division, Bellevue Hospital.

HOOKER, STUART V. R., A.B., M.D., 455 Empire Building, **Seattle, Washington.** Harvard Medical School, 1902. Assistant Surgeon, Children's Orthopedic Hospital.

HOOVER, ALDEN ROBBINS, M.Sc., M.D., Constantinople College, **Constantinople, Turkey.** State University of Iowa College of Medicine, 1905. Medical Director, Constantinople College; Director, American Hospital.

HOOVER, DELBERT E., M.D., 27 Monroe Street, **Warren, Ohio.** Western Reserve University School of Medicine, 1895. Surgeon, Warren City Hospital.

HOPKINS, CLARENCE WHITTINGHAM, M.D., 322 North Wells Street, **Chicago, Illinois.** Northwestern University Medical School, 1901. Chief Surgeon, Chicago and Northwestern Railway.

HOPKINS, FREDERICK EUGENE, M.D., 25 Harrison Avenue, Springfield, Massachusetts. University and Bellevue Hospital Medical College (University of the City of New York, Medical Department), 1884. Surgeon, Department of Diseases of Throat and Ear, Springfield Hospital; Consulting Laryngologist, Brattleboro Memorial Hospital, Brattleboro, Vermont.

HOPKINS, SAMUEL R., M.D., First National Bank Building, Hastings, Nebraska. Rush Medical College, 1900. Attending Surgeon, Mary Lanning Memorial Hospital.

HOPKINS, SCOTT BRUCE, M.D., 204 Fernwell Building, Spokane, Washington. Jefferson Medical College, 1897. Member of Staff, St. Luke's and Sacred Heart Hospitals; Oculist, Great Northern and Spokane International Railways.

HORGAN, EDMUND J., M.D., M.Sc., Stoneleigh Court, Washington, District of Columbia. George Washington University Medical School, 1908. Attending Surgeon, St. Elizabeth's Hospital.

HORN, HARRY W., A.M., M.D., 910 Schweiter Building, Wichita, Kansas. Rush Medical College, 1898. Surgeon-in-Chief, Wichita Hospital; Chief Surgeon, Kansas City, Mexico and Orient Railway.

HORN, JOHN, M.D., 72 East Ninety-second Street, New York, New York. University and Bellevue Hospital Medical College (New York University Medical College), 1885. Visiting Otologist, Rhinologist, and Laryngologist, Lenox Hill Hospital and Dispensary.

HORNBOGEN, ALFRED W., M.D., Savings Bank Building, Marquette, Michigan. University of Illinois College of Medicine (College of Physicians and Surgeons, Chicago), 1889. Attending Surgeon, St. Mary's and St. Luke's Hospitals; Local Surgeon, Duluth, South Shore and Atlantic Railway.

HORNBOGEN, HARRY J., M.D., 212 East Michigan Street, Marquette, Michigan. University of Illinois College of Medicine (College of Physicians and Surgeons, Chicago), 1894. Surgeon, St. Mary's and St. Luke's Hospitals.

HORNI, JOHN, Phar.G., M.D., 447 Nostrand Avenue, Brooklyn, New York. Columbia University, College of Physicians and Surgeons, 1896. Attending Surgeon, Wyckoff Heights Hospital; Associate Surgeon, Beth Moses Hospital.

HORR, ALBERT WINSLOW, A.M., M.D., 419 Boylston Street, Boston, Massachusetts. Boston University School of Medicine, 1891. Associate Professor of Ophthalmology, Boston University School of Medicine; Ophthalmic Surgeon, Massachusetts Homeopathic Hospital.

HORSFALL, FRANK LAPPIN, B.A., M.D., C.M., Roosevelt Clinic, Seattle, Washington. Faculty of Medicine, McGill University, 1903. Surgeon, Minor Private Hospital.

HORSKY, RUDOLPH, M.D., 326 Fuller Avenue, Helena, Montana. University of Pennsylvania School of Medicine, 1895. Attending Surgeon, St. John's and St. Peter's Hospitals; United States Public Health Service.

HORSLEY, JOHN SHELTON, M.D., 617 West Grace Street, Richmond, Virginia. University of Virginia, Department of Medicine, 1892. Surgeon in Charge, St. Elizabeth's Hospital.

HORTON, GEORGE MONROE, M.D., 1106 Cobb Building, Seattle, Washington. University and Bellevue Hospital Medical College, 1890. President of Staff, Providence Hospital; Chief Surgeon, Children's Orthopedic Hospital.

HORWITZ, ALEXANDER E., A.M., M.D., University Club Building, St. Louis, Missouri. Washington University Medical School, 1904. Assistant Professor of Orthopedic Surgery, St. Louis University School of Medicine; Orthopedic Surgeon, St. John's, St. Anthony's, and St. Louis Maternity Hospitals, Jewish Home for Chronic Invalids; Visiting Orthopedic Surgeon, St. Louis City Hospital; Consulting Orthopedic Surgeon, Alexian Brothers', and St. Ann's Maternity Hospitals.

HOSMER, ANDREW JACKSON, M.D., 162 Thirteenth East Street, Salt Lake City, Utah. University of Michigan Medical School, 1885. Surgeon, Holy Cross Hospital; Division Surgeon, Los Angeles and Salt Lake Railroad.

HOTCHKISS, LUCIUS W., A.B., M.D., San Marcos Building, Santa Barbara, California. Columbia University, College of Physicians and Surgeons, 1884.

HOUGH, GARRY DE N., A.B., M.D., Vineyard Haven, Massachusetts. University and Bellevue Hospital Medical College, 1884. Visiting Surgeon, St. Luke's Hospital; Consulting Surgeon, St. Mary's Home.

HOUSTON, DAVID WALKER, M.D., C.M., 18 Second Street, Troy, New York. Faculty of Medicine, McGill University, 1881. Consulting Surgeon, Troy and Leonard Hospitals.

HOUSTON, HUGH E., M.D., C.M., Buffalo Block, Kalispell, Montana. University of Minnesota Medical School (Minneapolis College of Physicians and Surgeons), 1900. Surgeon, Sisters of Mercy Hospital.

HOVDE, ANDERS G., B.Sc., M.D., Board of Trade Building, Superior, Wisconsin. University of Minnesota School of Medicine, 1903. Oculist and Aurist, St. Mary's and St. Francis' Hospitals; Chief of Staff, St. Mary's Hospital.

HOVEY, ROBERT FERRY, M.D., 5 Oak Street, Springfield, Massachusetts. New York Homeopathic Medical College and Flower Hospital, 1897. Surgeon, Wesson Memorial Hospital.

HOWARD, A. PHILO, M.D., Kress Medical Building, Houston, Texas. University of Pennsylvania School of Medicine, 1901. Surgeon, St. Joseph's Infirmary; Chief Surgeon, Gulf Coast Lines, Trinity and Brazos Valley Railway; Orthopedic Surgeon, Municipal Hospital.

HOWARD, ALONZO GALE, M.D., 636 Beacon Street, Boston, Massachusetts. Boston University School of Medicine, 1895. Professor of Orthopedic Surgery, Boston University School of Medicine; Chief Orthopedic Surgeon, Massachusetts Homeopathic Hospital, Medical Mission Dispensary, Martin Luther Orphans' Home.

HOWARD, CHARLES TILDEN, A.B., M.D., 510 Commonwealth Avenue, Boston, Massachusetts. Boston University School of Medicine, 1898. Associate Professor of Clinical Surgery, Boston University School of Medicine; Surgeon, Massachusetts Homeopathic Hospital.

HOWARD, DEANE CHILDS, M.D., Medical Corps, United States Army, Washington, District of Columbia. George Washington University Medical School (Columbian University, Medical Department), 1893. Colonel, Medical Corps, United States Army.

HOWARD, HENRY POPE, M.D., 410 American Bank Building, Everett, Washington. University of Pennsylvania School of Medicine, 1892.

HOWARD, HENRY W., M.D., Charles C. Chapman Building, Los Angeles, California. Rush Medical College, 1890. Associate Professor of Gynecology, College of Physicians and Surgeons; Consulting Surgeon, Los Angeles County Hospital; Associate Surgeon, Children's Hospital.

HOWARD, ROBERT MAYBURN, M.D., 502 State National Bank Building, Oklahoma, Oklahoma. University of Michigan Medical School, 1901. Associate Professor of Surgery, University of Oklahoma School of Medicine; Chief of Staff and Attending Surgeon, St. Anthony's Hospital; Attending Surgeon, State University Hospital.

HOWARD, WILLIAM FORREST, B.Sc., A.B., M.D., 303 Carlson Building, Pocatello, Idaho. University Medical College, Kansas City, 1899. President of Staff, Pocatello General Hospital; Surgeon, St. Anthony's Hospital.

HOWD, EMMOTT, M.D., 1825 Seventh Avenue, Troy, New York. Albany Medical College, 1898. Surgeon, Leonard and Samaritan Hospitals; Obstetrician, St. Joseph's Maternity Hospital.

HOWE, ALEXANDER C., M.D., 40 South Oxford Street, Brooklyn, New York. University and Bellevue Hospital Medical College (University of the City of New York, Medical Department), 1893. Attending Laryngologist, Jewish and East New York and Brownsville Hospitals.

HOWE, FRANK STEWART, B.Sc., M.D., Black Hills Bank Building, Deadwood, South Dakota. University of Illinois College of Medicine, 1901. Surgeon, St. Joseph's Hospital.

HOWE, HARRY DRESSER, B.Sc., M.D., 176 Victoria Avenue, Hampton, Virginia. University of Pennsylvania School of Medicine, 1895. Surgeon, Dixie Hospital, Hampton Normal and Agricultural Institute.

HOWE, LOUIS PHILIPPE, M.D., 200 Bush Street, San Francisco, California. University of California Medical School, 1908. Chief Surgeon, Standard Oil Company.

HOWE, WALTER CLARKE, A.M., M.D., 303 Beacon Street, Boston, Massachusetts. Harvard Medical School, 1898.

HOWELL, CONRADE ALLEYNE, M.D., 206 East State Street, Columbus, Ohio. Ohio State University College of Medicine (Ohio Medical University), 1901.

HOWELL, JOHN TAYLOR, M.D., 205 Grand Street, Newburgh, New York. Columbia University, College of Physicians and Surgeons, 1885. Senior Attending Surgeon, St. Luke's Hospital; Consulting Surgeon, Highland Hospital, Beacon.

HOWELLS, JAMES OWEN, Phar.G., M.D., Lincoln Avenue, Bridgeport, Ohio. University of Pennsylvania School of Medicine, 1894. Obstetrician and Gynecologist, Ohio Valley General Hospital, Wheeling, West Virginia.

HOWITT, HENRY, M.B., M.R.C.S. (Eng.), 128 London Road, Guelph, Ontario. University of Toronto, Faculty of Medicine (Trinity Medical College), 1873. Senior Surgeon, Guelph General and St. Joseph's Hospitals.

HOWK, LORON WHITNEY, A.B., M.D., 774 Main Street, West, Rochester, New York. University of Michigan Medical School, 1891. Associate Surgeon, Rochester General and St. Mary's Hospitals; Surgeon, Monroe County Hospital.

HOWLAND, EDWARD DEMONTE, M.D., 30 North Michigan Avenue, Chicago, Illinois. Rush Medical College, 1886. Surgeon, Chicago Union Hospital.

HOY, CARL DA COSTA, A.M., M.D., McKinley Hospital, Columbus, Ohio. Northwestern University Medical School, 1907. Attending Surgeon, Protestant and McKinley Hospitals, Columbus, Hoy Hospital, Wellston.

HOYE, HENRY JOSEPH, A.B., M.D., 221 Thayer Street, Providence, Rhode Island. Johns Hopkins University, Medical Department, 1899. Visiting Surgeon, Rhode Island Hospital.

HOYT, ROBERT EUSTIS, M.D., Medical Corps, United States Navy, Washington, District of Columbia. Harvard Medical School, 1901. Commander, Medical Corps, United States Navy.

HOYT, WALTER A., B.Sc., M.D., 428 Ohio Building, Akron, Ohio. University of Michigan Medical School, 1912. Chief of Staff and Chief of Orthopedic Department, Children's Hospital; Associate Member of Staff, City Hospital; Consultant in Orthopedic Surgery, Summit County Tuberculosis Sanatorium.

HUBBARD, ADRIAN RUSSELL FORTESCUE, M.D., M.R.C.S. (Eng.), L.R.C.P. (Lond.), 14 Cook Street, Quebec, Quebec. Charing Cross Hospital Medical School, 1902. Assistant Surgeon, Jeffery Hale's Hospital.

HUBBARD, JOSHUA C., A.B., M.D., 86 Bay State Road, Boston, Massachusetts. Harvard Medical School, 1896. Associate in Surgery, Harvard Medical School; Visiting Surgeon, Boston City Hospital; Consulting Surgeon, Norwood Hospital, Norwood, Leonard Morse Hospital, Natick; Surgeon, Newton Hospital, Newton.

HUBBELL, HARRY H., M.D., 103 Pine Street, Corning, New York. University of Buffalo, Department of Medicine, 1901. Attending Surgeon, Corning Hospital.

HUBBY, LESTER MEAD, Ph.B., M.D., 27 West Sixty-eighth Street, New York, New York. University and Bellevue Hospital Medical College (New

York University Medical College), 1896. Instructor, Manhattan Eye, Ear, and Throat Hospital and Medical School; Oto-Laryngologist, Harlem Hospital; Assistant Ear Surgeon, Manhattan Eye, Ear, and Throat Hospital.

HUFF, EARLE P., M.D., Medical Corps, United States Navy, Washington, District of Columbia. Columbia University, College of Physicians and Surgeons, 1903. Commander, Medical Corps, United States Navy.

HUGGINS, RALEIGH R., M.D., 1018 Westinghouse Building, Pittsburgh, Pennsylvania. University of Cincinnati College of Medicine (Miami Medical College), 1891. Professor of Gynecology, University of Pittsburgh School of Medicine; Gynecologist, St. Francis Hospital; Director, Elizabeth Steel Magee Hospital.

HUGGINS, WALTER LESLIE, Ph.B., M.D., 916 Pacific Mutual Building, Los Angeles, California. Albany Medical College, 1899; University of California Medical School, Los Angeles, 1908. Senior Surgeon, Los Angeles County Hospital.

HUGHES, FRANCOIS LOUIS, M.D., 1524 Chestnut Street, Philadelphia, Pennsylvania. Hahnemann Medical College and Hospital, Philadelphia, 1898. Gynecologist, St. Luke's Homeopathic Hospital, Women's Homeopathic Association, Philadelphia, Abington Memorial Hospital, Abington.

HUGULEY, GEORGE POPE, M.D., 54 Forrest Avenue, Atlanta, Georgia. University of Louisville Medical Department (Louisville Medical College), 1898. Visiting Surgeon, St. Joseph's Infirmary.

HULEN, VARD HOUGHTON, M.D., Berkeley Bank Building, Berkeley, California. Columbia University, College of Physicians and Surgeons (Columbia College, Medical Department), 1888.

HULL, CHARLES A., M.D., 1200 First National Bank Building, Omaha, Nebraska. University of Colorado School of Medicine (Denver and Gross College of Medicine), 1893. Assistant Professor of Surgery, University of Nebraska College of Medicine; Staff Surgeon, Wise Memorial Hospital, Immanuel Deaconess Institution; Member of Staff, Clarkson Memorial Hospital; Surgeon, Chicago, Burlington and Quincy Railroad; Chief Surgeon, Omaha and Council Bluffs Street Railway Company.

HULL, EDWARD T., B.Sc., M.D., 304 West Seventy-eighth Street, New York, New York. Columbia University, College of Physicians and Surgeons, 1904. Assistant Attending Surgeon, Lincoln Hospital.

HULL, LEONARD CHARLES, M.D., 343 Fifth Street, Hollister, California. Cooper Medical College, 1893. Surgeon, Hazel Hawkins Memorial Hospital.

HUME, ARTHUR M., M.D., 224 North Ball Street, Owosso, Michigan. Detroit College of Medicine and Surgery (Detroit Medical College), 1881. Chief Surgeon, Ann Arbor Railroad.

HUME, GEORGE WILLIAM LAMB, M.D., C.M., 24 Montreal Street, Sherbrooke, Quebec. Faculty of Medicine, McGill University, 1898. Surgeon, Sherbrooke Hospital.

HUME, GORDON MACKENZIE, M.D., C.M., 11 Moore Street, Sherbrooke, Quebec. Faculty of Medicine, McGill University, 1905. Attending Surgeon, Sherbrooke Hospital.

HUME, HOWARD, M.D., 1830 Jefferson Place, Northwest, Washington, District of Columbia. University of Virginia, Department of Medicine, 1905. Surgeon, Providence Hospital; Associate Surgeon, Emergency Hospital; Associate Obstetrician, Columbia Hospital.

HUME, JOSEPH, Ph.B., M.D., 724 Baronne Street, New Orleans, Louisiana. Medical College of the State of South Carolina, 1901. Professor of Genito-Urinary and Venereal Diseases, Tulane University of Louisiana School of Medicine; Visiting Surgeon, Charity Hospital; Visiting Urologist, Presbyterian Hospital.

HUMPHREY, WILLIAM ARMINE, MD., 1674 North High Street, Columbus, Ohio. Hahnemann Medical College and Hospital, Chicago, 1883. Emeritus Professor of Gynecology and Obstetrics, Ohio State University College of Homeopathic Medicine; Chief of Department of Gynecology and Obstetrics, University Homeopathic Hospital.

HUMPSTONE, O. PAUL, M.D., 327 Washington Avenue, Brooklyn, New York. Columbia University, College of Physicians and Surgeons, 1899. Senior Obstetrical Surgeon, Methodist Episcopal Hospital; Consulting Obstetrical Surgeon, Jewish and Kingston Avenue Hospitals, Brooklyn, Rockaway Beach Hospital, Rockaway Beach.

HUNDLEY, JOHN MASON, M.D., 1009 Cathedral Street, Baltimore, Maryland. University of Maryland School of Medicine, 1882. Professor of Clinical Gynecology, University of Maryland School of Medicine and College of Physicians and Surgeons; Visiting Surgeon, University, Hebrew, and Maryland General Hospitals, Hospital for Women of Maryland.

HUNNER, GUY LeROY, B.Sc., M.D., D.Sc., 2305 St. Paul Street, Baltimore, Maryland. Johns Hopkins University, Medical Department, 1897. Lecturer in Clinical Gynecology, Johns Hopkins University, Medical Department; Visiting Gynecologist, Johns Hopkins Hospital, Hebrew Hospital and Asylum, Church Home and Infirmary, Union Protestant Infirmary, Hospital for Women of Maryland; Consulting Gynecologist, St. Agnes' Hospital, Baltimore, Frederick City Hospital, Frederick.

HUNSICKER, WILLIAM COSGROVE, M.D., 1625 Race Street, Philadelphia, Pennsylvania. Hahnemann Medical College and Hospital, Philadelphia, 1895. Associate Professor of Genito-Urinary Diseases, Hahnemann Medical College and Hospital; Assistant Genito-Urinary Surgeon, Hahnemann Medical College and Hospital; Attending Genito-Urinary Surgeon, St. Luke's Homeopathic Hospital, Philadelphia, Homeopathic State Hospital, Allentown; Consulting Genito-Urinary Surgeon, Pottstown Homeopathic Hospital, Pottstown.

HUNT, ERNEST LEROI, M.D., 120 Lovell Street, Worcester, Massachusetts. Harvard Medical School, 1902. Surgeon and Director of Surgical Services, Worcester City Hospital; Consulting Surgeon, Holden Hospital.

HUNT, JOHN, M.D., 919 Cobb Building, Seattle, Washington. Yale University School of Medicine, 1904.

HUNT, PRESTON, M.D., Texarkana, Texas. Emory University School of Medicine (Atlanta College of Physicians and Surgeons), 1901. Member of Staff, Pine Street Sanitarium.

HUNT, VERNE CARLTON, B.Sc., M.D., M.Sc., Mayo Clinic, Rochester, Minnesota. Rush Medical College, 1913. Assistant Professor of Surgery, University of Minnesota Medical School, Mayo Foundation; Surgeon, St. Mary's and Colonial Hospitals (Mayo Clinic).

HUNT, WILLIAM SEYMOUR, M.B., Molson's Bank Building, Port Arthur, Ontario. University of Toronto, Faculty of Medicine, 1903. Attending Ophthalmologist and Otologist, McKellar Hospital, Fort William, St. Joseph's and General Hospitals, Port Arthur.

HUNTER, J. ROSS., M.D., 305 First National Bank Building, Huntington, West Virginia. Medical College of Virginia, 1903. Attending Surgeon, Sheltering Arms Hospital, Hansford, and Guthrie Hospital.

HUNTER, JOHN RUSSELL WIGHTMAN, M.D., 22 North Main Street, Lewistown, Pennsylvania. Medico-Chirurgical College, Philadelphia, 1893. Surgeon, Lewistown Hospital.

HUNTING, NATHANIEL STEVENS, A.B., M.D., 1136 Hancock Street, Quincy, Massachusetts. Harvard Medical School, 1889. Visiting and Consulting Surgeon, City Hospital.

HUNTINGTON, THOMAS WATERMAN, A.B., M.D., LL.D., Mills Building, San Francisco, California. Harvard Medical School, 1876. Emeritus Professor of Surgery, University of California Medical School; Consulting Surgeon, St. Luke's and Mt. Zion Hospitals, San Francisco, Samuel Merritt Hospital, Oakland; Chief Surgeon, Western Pacific Railway.

HUPP, FRANK LeMOYNE, A.M., M.D., 61 Fourteenth Street, Wheeling, West Virginia. Columbia University, College of Physicians and Surgeons, 1889. Attending Surgeon, Ohio Valley General Hospital; Consulting Surgeon, Reynolds Memorial Hospital, Glen Dale, Sheltering Arms Hospital, Hansford.

HURD, LEE M., M. D., 39 East Fiftieth Street, New York, New York. Columbia University, College of Physicians and Surgeons, 1895. Professor of Laryngology, University and Bellevue Hospital Medical College; Director, Department of Oto-Laryngology, New York Policlinic Hospital.

HURDON, ELIZABETH, M.D., C.M., 31 West Preston Street, Baltimore, Maryland. University of Toronto, Faculty of Medicine (Trinity Medical College), 1895. Associate in Gynecology, Johns Hopkins University, Medical Department; Visiting Gynecologist, Hospital for Women of Maryland.

HURLEY, EDWARD DANIEL, M.D., 419 Boylston Street, Boston, Massachusetts. Harvard Medical School, 1904. Ophthalmic Surgeon, Carney Hospital.

HURLEY, GEORGE, A.M., M.D., Medical Building, Hoquiam, Washington. University of Illinois College of Medicine, 1909. Director and Member of Surgical Staff, Hoquiam General Hospital.

470   *American College of Surgeons*

HURLEY, JOHN JOSEPH, A.M., M.D., 194 Bay State Road, Boston, Massachusetts. Harvard Medical School, 1903. Instructor, Ear, Nose, and Throat Department, Harvard University Graduate School of Medicine; Assistant Visiting Surgeon, Boston City Hospital; Visiting Aurist, Long Island Hospital.

HUSSEY, EDWARD JOHN, A.B., M.D., 1093 Dwight Street, Holyoke, Massachusetts. Harvard Medical School, 1904. Ophthalmic and Aural Surgeon, Holyoke City and House of Providence Hospitals.

HUSSEY, FREDERIC VINAL, Ph.B., M.D., 171 Angell Street, Providence, Rhode Island. Columbia University, College of Physicians and Surgeons, 1904. Assistant Visiting Surgeon, Rhode Island Hospital; Visiting Surgeon, Memorial Hospital, Pawtucket.

HUTCHESON, ALLEN CARRINGTON, University Hospital, Nanking, China. Columbia University, College of Physicians and Surgeons, 1905. Director, Union Medical College, Tsinanfu; Superintendent, University Hospital, Nanking. Associate Editor, *China Medical Journal.*

HUTCHINGS, BYRON MERLE, M.D., 304 McKeen Building, Terre Haute, Indiana. Indiana University School of Medicine (Medical College of Indiana), 1903. Gynecologist, St. Anthony's Hospital.

HUTCHINGS, WILLARD HUNTER, A.B., M.D., 2951 Jefferson Avenue, East, Detroit, Michigan. University of Michigan Medical School, 1899.

HUTCHINS, AMOS FRANCIS, M.A., M.D., 1010 North Charles Street, Baltimore, Maryland. Johns Hopkins University, Medical Department, 1913. Assistant in Surgery, University of Maryland School of Medicine; Assistant in Urology, Johns Hopkins University Medical Department; Visiting Surgeon, Mercy Hospital; Urologist, Calvert County Hospital.

HUTCHINS, ELLIOTT H., A.M., M.D., 1010 North Charles Street, Baltimore, Maryland. Johns Hopkins University, Medical Department, 1906. Associate Professor of Clinical Surgery, University of Maryland School of Medicine and College of Physicians and Surgeons; Instructor in Surgery, Johns Hopkins University, Medical Department; Assistant Surgeon, Johns Hopkins Hospital; Visiting Surgeon, Church Home and Infirmary, Mercy, Bon Secour, and Calvert County Hospitals.

HUTCHINS, HENRY T., A.B., M.D., 520 Commonwealth Avenue, Boston, Massachusetts. Johns Hopkins University, Medical Department, 1903. Gynecologist, Children's Hospital; Consulting Gynecologist, Rufus S. Frost Hospital, Chelsea, Massachusetts, Memorial Hospital, Pawtucket, Rhode Island; Surgeon, Massachusetts Women's Hospital.

HUTCHINSON, ROBERT JAMES, M.D., 100 Weston Street, Southeast, Grand Rapids, Michigan. Detroit College of Medicine and Surgery (Detroit Medical College), 1896. Visiting Surgeon, Surgical and Gynecological Departments, Blodgett Memorial and Butterworth Hospitals.

HUTCHINSON, WILLIAM, M.D., C.M., Jackson Building, Ottawa, Ontario. Faculty of Medicine, McGill University, 1904.

HUTCHISON, JAMES ALEXANDER, C.B.E., M.D., C.M., L.R.C.P.& S. (Edin.), 354 Mackay Street, Montreal, Quebec. Faculty of Medicine, McGill University, 1884. Professor of Surgery and Clinical Surgery, Faculty of Medicine, McGill University; Attending Surgeon, Montreal General Hospital.

HUTTON, EDWARD HYATT, A.B., M.D., 134 East First Street, Corning, New York. Columbia University College of Physicians and Surgeons, 1900. Attending Surgeon, Corning Hospital.

HUTTON, PAUL C., M.D., Medical Corps, United States Army, Washington, District of Columbia. George Washington University Medical School (Columbian University, Medical Department), 1897. Lieutenant Colonel, Medical Corps, United States Army.

HYDE, CLARENCE REGINALD, A.M., M.D., 242 Henry Street, Brooklyn, New York. Long Island College Hospital, 1894. Clinical Professor of Gynecology, Long Island College Hospital; Chief of Gynecological Clinic, Polhemus Memorial Clinic; Associate Gynecological Surgeon, Long Island College Hospital.

HYDE, FRITZ CARLETON, B.Sc., M.D., Maple Avenue, Greenwich, Connecticut. University of Michigan Medical School, 1900. Chief of Staff and Attending Surgeon, Greenwich Hospital.

HYMAN, ABRAHAM, M.D., 144 East Thirty-sixth Street, New York, New York. Columbia University, College of Physicians and Surgeons, 1905. Adjunct Surgeon, Mt. Sinai and Lebanon Hospitals.

HYMAN, SOLOMON, B.Sc., M.D., 135 Stockton Street, San Francisco, California. Johns Hopkins University, Medical Department, 1902.

HYNDMAN, CHARLES E., M.D., Humboldt Building, St. Louis, Missouri. Washington University Medical School, 1906. Assistant in Surgery, Washington University Medical School; Member of Staff, St. Louis Mullanphy Hospital; Attending Surgeon, St. Louis City Hospital.

IBERSHOFF, ADOLPH ERNEST, M.D., 2366 Stillman Road, Cleveland, Ohio. University of Michigan Homeopathic Medical College, 1903.

IDE, ARTHUR W., A.B., M.D., 1515 Charles Street, St. Paul, Minnesota. University of Michigan Medical School, 1905. Surgeon, St. Joseph's Hospital; Chief Surgeon, Northern Pacific Railway, Eastern Division.

IDEN, JOHN HOOE, M.D., Medical Corps, United States Navy, Washington, District of Columbia. University of Virginia, Department of Medicine, 1899. Member of Staff, Annapolis Emergency Hospital, Annapolis, Maryland; Captain, Medical Corps, United States Navy.

IGLAUER, SAMUEL, B.Sc., M.D., Seventh and Race Streets, Cincinnati, Ohio. University of Cincinnati College of Medicine (Ohio Medical College), 1898. Professor of Laryngology and Rhinology, University of Cincinnati College of Medicine; Laryngologist, Cincinnati General and Jewish Hospitals.

ILL, CHARLES LUDWIG, M.D., 188 Clinton Avenue, Newark, New Jersey. University and Bellevue Hospital Medical College, 1888. Surgeon, Gynecologist, and Superintendent, Lying-in Department, Hospital of St. Barnabas; Gynecologist, St. Michael's Hospital.

ILL, EDWARD J., M.D., 1002 Broad Street, Newark, New Jersey. Columbia University, College of Physicians and Surgeons, 1875. Gynecologist and Medical Director Emeritus, St. Michael's Hospital; Gynecologist and Supervising Obstetrician Emeritus, Hospital of St. Barnabas; Consulting Gynecologist, Newark Beth Israel, Newark City, and St. James' Hospitals, Newark, Mountainside Hospital, Montclair, St. Elizabeth's Hospital, Elizabeth, Somerset Hospital, Somerville, Muhlenberg Hospital, Plainfield, Perth Amboy City Hospital, Perth Amboy, Stumpf Memorial Hospital, Kearney, All Souls' and Morristown Memorial Hospitals, Morristown, New Jersey State Village for Epileptics, Skillman.

INGALLS, JAMES WARREN, A.B., M.D., 328 Stuyvesant Avenue, Brooklyn, New York. Columbia University, College of Physicians and Surgeons, 1884. Consulting Ophthalmologist, Wyckoff Heights Hospital, Honorary Surgeon, Brooklyn Eye and Ear Hospital.

INGE, JAMES M., M.D., Inge Building, Denton, Texas. University of Louisville Medical Department (Louisville Medical College), 1874. Emeritus Professor, Regional Anatomy, Baylor University Medical College; Chief Surgeon, Denton Sanitarium.

INGERSOLL, JOHN M., A.M., M.D., 1021 Prospect Avenue, Cleveland, Ohio. Western Reserve University School of Medicine, 1893. Professor of Oto-Laryngology, Western Reserve University School of Medicine; Laryngologist, Lakeside Hospital.

INGLIS, HARRY JAMES, M.D., 43 Bay State Road, Boston, Massachusetts. Harvard University Medical School, 1904. Surgeon, Boston Dispensary.

INGRAHAM, CLARENCE BANCROFT, JR., Ph.B., M.D., Metropolitan Building, Denver, Colorado. Johns Hopkins University, Medical Department, 1906. Professor of Gynecology and Obstetrics, University of Colorado School of Medicine; Gynecologist, Denver City and County, St. Luke's, and Mercy Hospitals.

INTURRIETA, ERNESTO, B.A., M.D., Casilla 72, Valparaiso, Chile. Faculty of Medicine, University of Chile, 1906.

IRELAND, MERRITTE W., M.D., Medical Corps, United States Army, Washington, District of Columbia. Detroit College of Medicine and Surgery, 1890; Jefferson Medical College, 1891. Surgeon General, United States Army.

IRISH, JAMES HERBERT, A.B., M.D., University Building, Syracuse, New York. New York Homeopathic Medical College and Flower Hospital, 1899. Attending Surgeon, General Hospital.

IRLAND, ROBERT DOUGLASS, M.D., 924 Rialto Building, Kansas City, Missouri. University of Kansas School of Medicine, 1909. Associate Professor of Gynecology, University of Kansas School of Medicine; Attending Surgeon,

Research and General Hospitals; Attending Gynecologist, Eleanor Taylor Bell Hospital, Rosedale.

IRWIN, ARTHUR W., M.D., C.M., 116 West Third Street, Oswego, New York. Queen's University, Faculty of Medicine, 1896. Surgeon, Oswego Hospital.

IRWIN, JAMES H., M.D., Ford Building, Great Falls, Montana. Rush Medical College, 1899.

ISEMAN, LAWRENCE LEE, Ph.B., M.D., 30 North Michigan Avenue, Chicago, Illinois. Johns Hopkins University, Medical Department, 1906.

IVY, ROBERT HENRY, M.D., D.D.S., 1503 Medical Arts Building, Philadelphia, Pennsylvania. University of Pennsylvania School of Medicine, 1907. Professor of Maxillo-Facial Surgery, University of Pennsylvania Graduate School of Medicine; Professor of Clinical Maxillo-Facial Surgery, University of Pennsylvania School of Dentistry; Chief of Maxillo-Facial Department, Polyclinic and Medico-Chirurgical Hospitals; Visiting Oral Surgeon, Philadelphia General Hospital, Pennsylvania; Consultant in Maxillo-Facial Surgery, Walter Reed General Hospital, Washington, District of Columbia.

JACK, FREDERICK LAFAYETTE, M.D., 215 Beacon Street, Boston, Massachusetts. Harvard Medical School, 1884. Instructor, Harvard University Graduate School of Medicine; Chief Otologist, Massachusetts Charitable Eye and Ear Infirmary; Consulting Otologist, Industrial School for Crippled and Deformed Children.

JACKES, HERVEY LEE, M.B., L.R.C.P.& S. (Lond.), 711 McCallum-Hill Building, Regina, Saskatchewan. Toronto University, Faculty of Medicine, 1910. Member of Staff, Regina General Hospital.

JACKOWITZ, GABRIEL J., Ph.B., M.D., 347 Orange Street, New Haven, Connecticut. Boston University School of Medicine, 1907. Surgeon, Grace Hospital.

JACKSON, ARTHUR S., M.D., 8 Main Street, Lead, South Dakota. Saginaw Valley Medical College, 1902. Member of Staff, St. Joseph's Hospital, Deadwood.

JACKSON, CHEVALIER, M.D., 128 South Tenth Street, Philadelphia, Pennsylvania. Jefferson Medical College, 1886. Professor of Laryngology, Jefferson Medical College; Professor of Bronchoscopy and Esophagoscopy, University of Pennsylvania, School of Medicine; Laryngologist, Jefferson Medical College Hospital.

JACKSON, EDWARD, C.E., A.M., M.D., D.Sc., 318 Majestic Building, Denver, Colorado. University of Pennsylvania School of Medicine, 1878. Editor, *American Journal of Ophthalmology and Ophthalmic Literature.*

JACKSON, FRANK H., M.D., Masonic Building, Houlton, Maine. Columbia University, College of Physicians and Surgeons, 1901. Surgeon, Madigan Memorial Hospital.

JACKSON, GUSTAVUS BROWN, M.D., 603 Hume-Mansur Building, Indianapolis, Indiana. Rush Medical College, 1902. Lecturer on Obstetrics and Clinician in Gynecology, Indiana University School of Medicine; Attending Gynecologist, Indianapolis City Hospital.

JACKSON, HARRY, B.Sc., M.D., 104 South Michigan Avenue, Chicago, Illinois. Rush Medical College, 1907. Associate in Surgery, Northwestern University Medical School; Attending Surgeon, Cook County Hospital; Adjunct Attending Surgeon, Michael Reese and Wesley Memorial Hospitals; Chief of Clinic, Michael Reese Dispensary.

JACKSON, JABEZ NORTH, A.M., M.D., 425 Argyle Building, Kansas City, Missouri. University Medical College, Kansas City, Missouri, 1891.

JACKSON, JOHN D., B.Sc., M.D., Main Street, Danville, Kentucky. College of Physicians and Surgeons, San Francisco, 1902. Member of Staff, Danville and Boyle County Hospital; Surgeon, Kentucky School for the Deaf.

JACKSON, RALPH W., A.B., M.D., 251 Cherry Street, Fall River, Massachusetts. Long Island College Hospital, 1892. Proctologist, Union, Fall River City, and Bay View Hospitals, Fall River, Out-Patient Department, Carney Hospital, Boston.

JACKSON, REGINALD HENRY, M.D., 110 North Hamilton Street, Madison, Wisconsin. Columbia University, College of Physicians and Surgeons, 1899. Lecturer on Clinical Surgery, University of Wisconsin Medical School.

JACKSON, VIRGIL B., M.D., 1801 K Street, Northwest, Washington, District of Columbia. George Washington University Medical School (Columbian University, Medical Department), 1894. Instructor in Gynecology, George Washington University Medical School; Visiting Gynecologist, Central Dispensary and Emergency Hospital.

JACKSON, WILLIAM R., M.D., 164 St. Michael Street, Mobile, Alabama. University of Alabama School of Medicine (Medical College of Alabama), 1888.

JACOBAEUS, HANS CHRISTIAN, M.D., 6 Nybrogatan, Stockholm, Sweden. Karolinska Institute, 1907. Professor of Medicine, University of Stockholm; Head Physician, Royal Serafriner Hospital.

JACOBI, FRANK, A.B., M.D., 416 Colton Building, Toledo, Ohio. University of Michigan Medical School, 1895. Oculist, St. Vincent's Hospital.

JACOBS, CHARLES M., M.D., 31 North State Street, Chicago, Illinois. Northwestern University Medical School, 1894. Associate Professor of Clinical Orthopedic Surgery, University of Illinois College of Medicine; Attending Orthopedic Surgeon, Cook County and Michael Reese Hospitals.

JACOBS, S. NICHOLS, B.Sc., M.D., 209 Post Street, San Francisco, California. University of California Medical School, 1908. Assistant Lecturer in Surgery, Stanford University Medical School; Surgeon-in-Chief, San Francisco Polyclinic Hospital and Post Graduate College; Visiting Surgeon, San Francisco Hospital.

JACOBSON, CONRAD, B.Sc., M.D., 225 Millard Hall, University of Minnesota, Minneapolis, Minnesota. Johns Hopkins University, Medical Department, 1911. Associate Professor of Surgery, University of Minnesota Medical Department.

JACOBY, ALFRED, A.B., M.D., 412 Medical Building, New Orleans, Louisiana. Tulane University of Louisiana School of Medicine, 1902. Chief of Clinic, Chair of Surgery, New Orleans Polyclinic; Visiting Gynecologist, Presbyterian Hospital; Visiting Surgeon, Charity Hospital.

JAEGER, ALFRED SYDENHAM, M.D., 430 Bankers Trust Building, Indianapolis, Indiana. Washington University Medical School (Missouri Medical College), 1899. Gynecologist, Indianapolis City Hospital; Gynecologist and Obstetrician, Methodist Episcopal Hospital; Surgeon, Jewish Federation.

JAGGER, ARCHER W., M.D., 410 Amity Street, Flushing, New York. University and Bellevue Hospital Medical College (University of the City of New York, Medical Department), 1893. Associate Member of Staff, Flushing Hospital, Flushing, Nassau Hospital, Mineola.

JAMES, CHARLES STEPHEN, M.D., Clinic Building, Centerville, Iowa. University Medical College, Kansas City, 1891. Surgeon, St. Joseph's Mercy Hospital.

JAMES, D. BUSHROD, A.B., M.D., Medical Arts Building, Philadelphia, Pennsylvania. Hahnemann Medical College and Hospital, Philadelphia, 1896. Professor of Gynecology, Hahnemann Medical College and Hospital; Gynecologist, Hahnemann Medical College and Hospital; Gynecologist in Charge, Hahnemann Dispensary; Consulting Gynecologist, West Philadelphia General Homeopathic Hospital, Philadelphia, Homeopathic State Hospital, Allentown, Homeopathic Medical and Surgical Hospital, Reading, McKinley Hospital, Trenton, New Jersey.

JAMES, JOHN A. JAMES, M.Sc., M.D., 79 Rue de Sèvres, Paris, France. St. Louis University School of Medicine (Beaumont Hospital Medical College), 1891.

JAMES, JOHN EDWIN, JR., B.Sc., M.D., 118 South Nineteenth Street, Philadelphia, Pennsylvania. Hahnemann Medical College and Hospital, Philadelphia, 1902. Professor of Obstetrics, Hahnemann Medical College and Hospital; Obstetrician, Hahnemann Medical College and Hospital; Gynecologist, Women's Homeopathic Association; Consulting Obstetrician, McKinley Hospital, Trenton, New Jersey, Crozier Hospital, Chester, Pennsylvania.

JAMES, JOHN HENRY, M.D., National Citizen Bank Building, Mankato, Minnesota. University and Bellevue Hospital Medical College (University of the City of New York, Medical Department), 1875.

JAMES, RALPH WARD, M.D., First National Bank Building, Winfield, Kansas. Northwestern University Medical School, 1905. Attending Surgeon, St. Mary's Hospital.

JAMESON, JAMES WALKER, A.B., M.D., 5 South State Street, Concord, New Hampshire. Columbia University, College of Physicians and Surgeons, 1905.

JAMESON, P. CHALMERS, M.D., 139 Montague Street, Brooklyn, New York. Long Island College Hospital, 1892. Surgeon, Brooklyn Eye and Ear Hospital; Visiting Ophthalmologist, Brooklyn, St. John's and Caledonian Hospitals, Brooklyn, House of St. Giles the Cripple, Garden City.

JANES, GEORGE HERBERT, M.D., 57 Court Street, Westfield, Massachusetts. Albany Medical College, 1893. Consulting Surgeon, Noble Hospital.

JARBOE, PARRAN, M.D., 113 Dixie Building, Greensboro, North Carolina. Georgetown University School of Medicine, 1905. Surgeon, St. Leo Hospital.

JARMAN, GEORGE WALLACE, A.M., M.D., Princess Anne, Maryland. University and Bellevue Hospital Medical College, 1888. Consulting Gynecologist, General Memorial Hospital.

JARVIS, H. GILDERSLEEVE, A.B., M.D., 179 Allyn Street, Hartford, Connecticut. Johns Hopkins University Medical Department, 1910. Surgeon-in-Chief, Hartford Dispensary; Assistant Surgeon, Hartford Hospital; Surgeon, Home for Crippled Children, Newington.

JAYNE, WALTER A., M.D., 535 Majestic Building, Denver, Colorado. Columbia University, College of Physicians and Surgeons, 1875. Emeritus Professor of Gynecology and Abdominal Surgery, University of Colorado School of Medicine; Gynecologist, St. Luke's Hospital.

JEAN, GEORGE WILLIAM, A.M., M.D., San Marcos Building, Santa Barbara, California. University and Bellevue Hospital Medical College, 1898. Attending Ophthalmic Surgeon, Santa Barbara General Hospital; Chief, Ophthalmic Service, Santa Barbara Cottage Hospital Dispensary; Ophthalmic Surgeon, St. Francis Hospital.

JECK, HOWARD SHEFFIELD, Ph.B., M.D., 109 East Thirty-fourth Street, New York, New York. Vanderbilt University, Medical Department, 1909. Instructor in Surgery, Department of Urology, Cornell University Medical College; Assistant Visiting Urologist, Bellevue Hospital; Assistant Visiting Surgeon, Department of Urology, Memorial Hospital; Cystoscopist, St. John's Hospital, Brooklyn; Consulting Urologist, Good Samaritan Hospital, Suffern.

JEFFERDS, HENRY CLARKE, A.B., M.D., 902 Stevens Building, Portland, Oregon. Hahnemann Medical College and Hospital, Philadelphia, 1885.

JEFFERSON, JAMES, M.D., 415 Locust Street, Johnstown, Pennsylvania. Jefferson Medical College, 1904. Surgeon, Conemaugh Valley Memorial Hospital; Associate Surgeon, Cambria Hospital.

JELKS, JOHN LEMUEL, M.D., 805 Union and Planters Bank Building, Memphis, Tennessee. University of Tennessee College of Medicine (Memphis Hospital Medical College), 1892.

JELLINGHAUS, C. FREDERIC, A.B., M.D., 572 Park Avenue, New York, New York. Columbia University College of Physicians and Surgeons, 1901. Attending Surgeon, Lying-in Hospital; Adjunct Gynecologist, City Hospital.

JENKINS, GEORGE HAMILTON, M.D., 139 Main Street, Binghamton, New York. New York Homeopathic Medical College and Flower Hospital, 1889. Surgeon, Binghamton City Hospital.

JENKINS, JOHN SHORT, M.D., 508 Citizens Bank Building, Pine Bluff, Arkansas. University of Nashville Medical Department, 1899. Member of Surgical Staff, Davis Hospital.

JENKINS, STEPHEN RICE, M.D., 57 Grafton Street, Charlottetown, Prince Edward Island. University of Pennsylvania School of Medicine, 1884. Member of Staff, Charlottetown and Prince Edward Island Hospitals.

JENKINSON, ERNEST ALBERT, M.D., 533 Frances Building, Sioux City, Iowa. University of Illinois College of Medicine (College of Physicians and Surgeons, Chicago), 1903. President of Staff, St. Vincent's Hospital.

JENNINGS, CHARLES W., M.D., 315 Highland Building, Pittsburgh, Pennsylvania. University of Pennsylvania School of Medicine, 1901. Assistant Professor of Ophthalmology, University of Pittsburgh School of Medicine; Ophthalmic Surgeon, Pittsburgh and St. Margaret Memorial Hospitals; Attending Surgeon, Pittsburgh Eye and Ear Hospital.

JENNINGS, FRANK DORMER, M.D., 1083 Bushwick Avenue, Brooklyn, New York. Columbia University, College of Physicians and Surgeons, 1902. Visiting Surgeon, St. Catherine's and Greenpoint Hospitals.

JENNINGS, FRANK LESLIE, M.D., 1800 North Charles Street, Baltimore, Maryland. University of Maryland School of Medicine (College of Physicians and Surgeons), 1911. Instructor in Surgery, University of Maryland and College of Physicians and Surgeons; Assistant Dispensary Surgeon, Johns Hopkins Hospital; Associate Visiting Surgeon, Mercy Hospital; Adjunct Visiting Surgeon, South Baltimore General Hospital.

JENNINGS, GEORGE MICHAEL, A.B., M.D., 220 North Second Street, Missoula, Montana. University of Minnesota Medical School, 1907. Chief Surgeon, Northern Pacific Beneficial Association Hospital.

JENNINGS, JOHN EDWARD, M.D., 23 South Portland Avenue, Brooklyn, New York. Columbia University, College of Physicians and Surgeons, 1899. Clinical Professor of Surgery, Long Island College Hospital; Surgeon, Brooklyn Hospital.

JENNINGS, JOHN ELLIS, M.D., 807 Carleton Building, St. Louis, Missouri. University of Pennsylvania School of Medicine, 1887. Ophthalmic Surgeon, St. Louis City, and St. Louis and San Francisco Railroad Employes' Hospitals.

JEPSON, WILLIAM, B.Sc., A.M., M.D., L.R.C.P.& S. (Edin.), United Bank Building, Sioux City, Iowa. State University of Iowa College of Medicine, 1886. University of Pennsylvania School of Medicine, 1891.

JERVEY, JAMES WILKINSON, M.D., Jervey-Jordan Building, Greenville, South Carolina. Medical College of the State of South Carolina, 1897. Surgeon, Eye, Ear, Nose, and Throat Department, Greenville City Hospital; Surgeon in charge, Jervey Hospital.

JESSAMAN, LEON WEBSTER, M.D., 182 Concord Street, Framingham, Massachusetts. Tufts College Medical School, 1909. Ophthalmic Surgeon, Boston City Hospital; Ophthalmologist and Oto-Laryngologist, Framingham Hospital, Framingham, Massachusetts Reformatory for Women, Sherborne.

JETT, FRANK HUBERT, Ph.C., M.D., 221 South Sixth Street, Terre Haute, Indiana. George Washington University Medical School, 1905. Surgeon, Union Hospital.

JEWETT, WILLIAM AVERILL, M.D., 380 Vanderbilt Avenue, Brooklyn, New York. Long Island College Hospital, 1897. Instructor in Gynecology and Obstetrics, Long Island College Hospital; Gynecological Surgeon, Swedish Hospital; Assistant Obstetrician and Gynecological Surgeon, Long Island College Hospital; Chief of Clinic in Gynecology, Polhemus Memorial Clinic.

JOACHIM, OTTO, M.D., 1630 Robert Street, New Orleans, Louisiana. University of Tennessee College of Medicine, 1884. Professor of Otology, Loyola Post-Graduate School of Medicine; Chief of Staff, Department of Ear, Nose, and Throat, Charity Hospital.

JOBES, NORMAN E., M.D., 305 Traction Terminal Building, Indianapolis, Indiana. Indiana University School of Medicine (Indiana Medical College), 1897. Associate Professor of Surgery, Indiana University School of Medicine; Attending Surgeon, Indianapolis City Hospital.

JOBSE, PETER H., M.D., Wilsonville, Oregon. Northwestern University Medical School, 1894. Retired.

JOHANSON, NILS A., M.D., 411 Cobb Building, Seattle, Washington. University of Colorado School of Medicine, 1904. Surgeon, Swedish Hospital.

JOHNS, FRANK S., A.B., M.D., 601 East Franklin Street, Richmond, Virginia. Medical College of Virginia, 1913. Associate in Surgery, Medical College of Virginia; Associate Surgeon, Johnston-Willis Sanatorium; Visiting Surgeon, Memorial and Allied Hospitals.

JOHNSON, ANDERS EINAR, A.B., M.D., 317 Second Street, Southwest, Watertown, South Dakota. University of Minnesota Medical School, 1903. Surgeon, Luther Hospital.

JOHNSON, ARTHUR CLARKE, A.B., M.D., 818 Paulsen Building, Spokane, Washington. Rush Medical College, 1901. Member of Staff, St. Luke's Hospital.

JOHNSON, ARTHUR HENRY, M.D., 310 Medical Building, Portland, Oregon. University of Michigan Medical School, 1895. Member of Staff, Sellwood General Hospital.

JOHNSON, AUGUST E., M.D., C.M., 905 Metropolitan Bank Building, Minneapolis, Minnesota. University of Minnesota Medical School (Hamline University), 1903. Surgeon, Swedish Hospital.

JOHNSON, CLAY, M.D., Sixth and Lamar Streets, Fort Worth, Texas. University of Maryland School of Medicine (College of Physicians and Surgeons, Baltimore), 1891. Surgeon in Charge, Dr. Clay Johnson's Sanitarium.

JOHNSON, ELMON R., M.D., 389 Newport Avenue, Wollaston, Massachusetts. Boston University School of Medicine, 1895. Nose and Throat Surgeon, Massachusetts Homeopathic Hospital, Boston; Assistant Surgeon, Quincy City Hospital.

JOHNSON, FREDERICK WILLIAM, A.M., M.D., 167 Newbury Street, Boston, Massachusetts. Harvard Medical School, 1881. Professor of Clinical Gynecology, Tufts Medical School; Gynecologist-in-Chief, Carney Hospital; Consulting Gynecologist, Massachusetts Women's Hospital, Boston, Jordan Hospital, Plymouth, Sturdy Memorial Hospital, Attleboro, Massachusetts, Elliot Hospital, Manchester, New Hampshire.

JOHNSON, HARRY MCCRINDELL, M.D., 801 Central Trust Building, San Antonio, Texas. Tulane University of Louisiana School of Medicine, 1890.

JOHNSON, HENRY ALBERT, M.D., Tekamah, Nebraska. Creighton College of Medicine, 1908. Junior Surgeon, Fraternity Hospital.

JOHNSON, HOWARD H., M.D., Medical Corps, United States Army, Washington, District of Columbia. University of Cincinnati College of Medicine (Miami Medical College), 1903. Colonel, Medical Corps, United States Army.

JOHNSON, J. MURRAY, M.D., 276 West Avenue, Bridgeport, Connecticut. Long Island College Hospital, 1895. Visiting Surgeon, St. Vincent's Hospital; Chief Gynecologist, City Dispensary.

JOHNSON, JAMES A., M.D., 1009 Nicollet Avenue, Minneapolis, Minnesota. Northwestern University Medical School, 1910. Assistant Professor of Surgery, University of Minnesota Medical School; Chief of Surgical Out-Patient Department, University of Minnesota Medical School; Attending Surgeon, Northwestern, Asbury, Fairview, and University Hospitals.

JOHNSON, JOHN GUY WATTS, M.A., M.D., C.M., F.R.C.S. (Edin.), 453 Sherbrooke Street, West, Montreal, Quebec. Faculty of Medicine, McGill University, 1904. Assistant Demonstrator of Surgery, Faculty of Medicine, McGill University; Surgeon in Charge of Out-Patients, Montreal General Hospital.

JOHNSON, LUCIUS W., D.D.S., M.D., Medical Corps, United States Navy, Washington, District of Columbia. University of Pennsylvania School of Medicine, 1907. Lieutenant Commander, Medical Corps, United States Navy.

JOHNSON, MILTON J., M.D., 213 Main Street, Jamestown, New York. Cornell University Medical College, 1906.

JOHNSON, PEER P., A.B., M.D., 163 Cabot Street, Beverly, Massachusetts. University of Vermont College of Medicine, 1900. Chief Surgeon, Beverly Hospital.

JOHNSON, RAY HENRY, M.D., 449 Franklin Street, Buffalo, New York. University of Buffalo Department of Medicine, 1893. Member of Staff, Deaconess Hospital.

JOHNSON, T. ARTHUR, B.Sc., M.D., 503 Seventh Street, Rockford, Illinois. Rush Medical College, 1911. Chief Surgeon and Chief of Staff, Swedish American Hospital, Johnson Clinic.

JOHNSON, T. B., M.D., 7 East Church Street, Frederick, Maryland. University of Maryland School of Medicine, 1889. Surgeon, Frederick City Hospital, Baltimore and Ohio Railroad; Surgical Director, Hagerstown and Frederick Railroad.

JOHNSON, WILLIAM DAVID, M.D., 5 Jackson Street, Batavia, New York. Syracuse University College of Medicine, 1892. Chief of Staff, St. Jerome's Hospital.

JOHNSON, WALTER BUCKLEY, M.D., 170 Broadway, Paterson, New Jersey. Columbia University, College of Physicians and Surgeons, 1878. Executive Surgeon, Paterson Eye and Ear Infirmary; Visiting Surgeon, Eye, Ear, and Throat Department, Paterson General Hospital; Consulting Surgeon, Good Samaritan Hospital, Suffern, New York.

JOHNSTON, RICHARD HALL, M.D., Charlotte, North Carolina. University of Maryland School of Medicine, 1894.

JOHNSTON, WILSON, M.D., Stevens Building, Portland, Oregon. University of Louisville, Medical Department (Kentucky School of Medicine), 1892.

JOLLY, WILLIAM JAMES, M.D., Liberty National Bank Building, Oklahoma, Oklahoma. Medical College of the State of South Carolina, 1882.

JONAS, AUGUST FREDERIC, M.D., 512 McCague Building, Omaha, Nebraska. Loyola University School of Medicine (Bennett Medical College), 1877; Ludwig Maximilian University, Munich, 1884. Professor of Surgery, University of Nebraska College of Medicine; Surgeon, Nebraska Methodist and Wise Memorial Hospitals.

JONAS, ERNST, M.D., Lister Building, St. Louis, Missouri. University of Berlin, 1895. Gynecologist, Jewish Hospital; Consulting Surgeon, St. John's Hospital; Visiting Surgeon, St. Louis City Hospital, Jewish Home for Chronic Invalids.

JONES, ARTHUR THOMS, M.D., 131 Waterman Street, Providence, Rhode Island. University and Bellevue Hospital Medical College (University of the City of New York, Medical Department), 1896. Visiting Surgeon, Memorial Hospital, Pawtucket; Consulting Surgeon, St. Joseph's Hospital, Providence, Woonsocket Hospital, Woonsocket.

JONES, CLARENCE PORTER, M.D., 3117 West Avenue, Newport News, Virginia. Medical College of Virginia (University College of Medicine), 1895. Oculist and Aurist, Riverside and Elizabeth Buxton Hospitals,

School for Colored Deaf and Blind Children, Newport News, Dixie Hospital, Hampton.

JONES, DANIEL FISKE, A.B., M.D., 195 Beacon Street, Boston, Massachusetts. Harvard Medical School, 1896. Associate in Surgery, Courses for Graduates, Harvard Medical School; Visiting Surgeon, Massachusetts General Hospital; Consulting Surgeon, New England Hospital for Women and Children and Beth Israel Hospital, Boston, Union Hospital, Fall River, Brockton Hospital, Brockton, Addison Gilbert Hospital, Gloucester, Sturdy Memorial Hospital, Attleboro.

JONES, EDWARD GROVES, A.B., M.D., 714 Hurt Building, Atlanta, Georgia. Emory University School of Medicine (Atlanta College of Physicians and Surgeons), 1900. Professor of Surgery, Emory University School of Medicine; Visiting Surgeon, Grady Memorial, Georgia Baptist, and Wesley Memorial Hospitals.

JONES, EDWARD WILLIAM, M.D., 214 Mitchell Realty Building, Mitchell, South Dakota. Northwestern University Medical School, 1906. Member of Staff, St. Joseph's and Methodist State Hospitals.

JONES, ELMER MENDELSSOHN, M.D., 1014 Lowry Building, St. Paul, Minnesota. University of Minnesota Medical School, 1907. Instructor in Gynecology, University of Minnesota Medical School; Attending Surgeon, St. Joseph's, St. Luke's, City and County Hospitals.

JONES, EVERETT O., A.B., M.D., 508 Cobb Building, Seattle, Washington. University of Pennsylvania School of Medicine, 1893. Surgeon, Swedish Hospital.

JONES, GUY CARLETON, C.M.G., M.D., Ottawa, Ontario. M.R.C.S. (Eng.), 1887. Formerly Director General of the Canadian Army Medical Service.

JONES, HAROLD WELLINGTON, M.D., Medical Corps, United States Army, Washington, District of Columbia. Harvard Medical School, 1901; Army Medical School, 1906. Major, Medical Corps, United States Army.

JONES, JABEZ, M.D., De Renne Apartments, Savannah, Georgia. Emory University School of Medicine (Atlanta Medical College), 1898. Attending Surgeon, Telfair Hospital.

JONES, JOHN F. X., B.Sc., A.M., M.D., 103 South Twenty-first Street, Philadelphia, Pennsylvania. University of Pennsylvania School of Medicine, 1907; Jefferson Medical College, 1910. Instructor in Surgery, Jefferson Medical College; Surgeon, St. Joseph's, Misericordia, and St. Agnes' Hospitals.

JONES, MAURICE P., M.D., 419 Home Savings and Loan Building, Youngstown, Ohio. University of Michigan Medical School, 1907. Attending Surgeon, Youngstown Hospital.

JONES, NATHANIEL MOORE, B.L., M.D., 815 Guardian Building, Cleveland, Ohio. Western Reserve University School of Medicine, 1902. Visiting Surgeon, Lutheran Hospital.

JONES, OWEN ELON, M.D., 267 University Avenue, Rochester, New York. Albany Medical College, 1894. Visiting Surgeon, St. Mary's Hospital; Associate Surgeon, Rochester General Hospital; Surgeon, Infants' Summer Hospital, Charlotte.

JONES, PERCY I.., M.D., Medical Corps, United States Army, Washington, District of Columbia. University of Tennessee College of Medicine, 1897. Colonel, Medical Corps, United States Army.

JONES, RICHARD W., M.D., 301 Third Street, Wausau, Wisconsin. Northwestern University Medical School, 1902. Surgeon, Wausau and St. Mary's Hospitals.

JONES, SIR ROBERT,. K.B.E., C.B., D.S.M. (U.S.A.), F.R.C.S. (Eng., Ire., Edin.), D.Sc., Hon., LL.D., Hon., 11 Nelson Street, Liverpool, England. Ch.M., Liverpool Medical School, 1879. Lecturer on Orthopedic Surgery, University of Liverpool; Director of Orthopedics, St. Thomas Hospital, London; Surgeon, National Orthopedic Hospital and Liverpool Country Hospital for Children.

JONES, ROBERT J., M.D., 433 West Jefferson Street, Greenfield, Ohio. University of Cincinnati College of Medicine (Medical College of Ohio), 1895.

JONES, ROBERT YOUNG, B.Sc., M.D., 403 First National Bank Building, Hutchinson, Kansas. Rush Medical College, 1907. Attending Surgeon, Hutchinson Methodist and St. Elizabeth's Mercy Hospitals.

JONES, SAMUEL FOSDICK, M.D., 516 Majestic Building, Denver, Colorado. Columbia University, College of Physicians and Surgeons, 1902. Professor of Orthopedic Surgery, University of Colorado School of Medicine; Attending Orthopedic Surgeon, Mercy, Denver City and County, St. Luke's, and Children's Hospitals, Swedish Sanatorium, National Jewish Hospital for Consumptives.

JONES, WALTER CLINTON, A.M., M.D., St. Vincent's Hospital, Birmingham, Alabama. Northwestern University Medical School, 1902. Pathologist, St. Vincent's Hospital, South Highlands Infirmary, Birmingham; Histopathologist, Tennessee Coal, Iron and Railway Company, Fairfield.

JONES, WALTER MATTHEW, M.D., 5800 Arsenal Street, St. Louis, Missouri. Washington University Medical School, 1907. In Charge of Surgical Section, Hospital No. 35, United States Public Health Service.

JONES, WILLIAM WARNER, B.A., M.B., F.R.C.S. (Eng.), 41 Avenue Road, Toronto, Ontario. University of Toronto, Faculty of Medicine, 1896. Associate in Clinical Surgery, University of Toronto, Faculty of Medicine; Surgeon, Out-Patient Genito-Urinary Department, and Assistant Surgeon, Toronto General Hospital.

JOPSON, JOHN HOWARD, M.D., 1824 Pine Street, Philadelphia, Pennsylvania. University of Pennsylvania School of Medicine, 1893. Professor of Surgery, University of Pennsylvania Graduate School of Medicine; Associate in Surgery, University of Pennsylvania School of Medicine; Visiting Surgeon, Presbyterian and Children's Hospitals, Philadelphia, Bryn Mawr Hospital, Bryn Mawr; Consulting Surgeon, Philadelphia Home for Incurables.

JORDAN, ARTHUR CLIFFORD, A.B., M.D., 122½ Main Street, Pine Bluff, Arkansas. Vanderbilt University, Medical Department, 1886. Surgeon, Florence Sanitarium.

JORDAN, DENNIS, B.A., M.D., C.M., 253 Danforth Avenue, Toronto, Ontario. Queen's University, Faculty of Medicine, 1910. Assistant in Surgery and Attendant, Out-Patient Surgical Department, Grace Hospital.

JORDAN, HENRY DOWLING, M.D., 544 North Sixth Street, Allentown, Pennsylvania. Medico-Chirurgical College, Philadelphia, 1902. Surgeon, Sacred Heart Hospital.

JORDAN, RICHARD, M.D., 165 West Fifty-eighth Street, New York, New York. University of Leipsic, 1894. Visiting Oto-Laryngologist and Bronchoscopist, Lenox Hill Hospital; Chief of Clinic, Lenox Hill Hospital Dispensary.

JORDAN, WILLIAM MUDD, M.D., 910 Empire Building, Birmingham, Alabama. Columbia University, College of Physicians and Surgeons, 1895.

JOYCE, ROBERT S., A.M., M.D., Eccles Building, Ogden, Utah. Rush Medical College, 1891. Surgeon, Thomas D. Dee Memorial Hospital.

JUDD, ALBERT M., M.D., 375 Grand Avenue, Brooklyn, New York. Columbia University, College of Physicians and Surgeons, 1893. Senior Attending Obstetrician and Gynecologist, Kings County Hospital; Gynecologist, Jewish and Long Island College Hospitals; Chief of Gynecological Service, East New York and Brownsville Hospital; Consulting Obstetrician, Coney Island and Flushing Hospitals, Eastern District Hospital and Dispensary; Consulting Gynecologist, Swedish Hospital, East New York Dispensary, Brooklyn, St. Joseph's Hospital, Far Rockaway.

JUDD, C. HOLLISTER, M.D., David Whitney Building, Detroit, Michigan. University of Pennsylvania School of Medicine, 1897. Associate Professor of Gynecology, Detroit College of Medicine and Surgery; Gynecologist and Obstetrician, Woman's Hospital; Associate Obstetrician, Harper Hospital; Gynecologist, Florence Crittenton Home.

JUDD, EDWARD STARR, M.D., 705 Second Street, Southwest, Rochester, Minnesota. University of Minnesota Medical School, 1902. Surgeon, Mayo Clinic.

JUDD, JAMES ROBERT, A.B., M.D., 163 Beretania Street, Honolulu, Hawaii. Columbia University, College of Physicians and Surgeons, 1901. Surgeon, Queen's and Kauikeolani Children's Hospitals.

JUENEMANN, GEORGE F., M.D., Medical Corps, United States Army, Washington, District of Columbia. George Washington University Medical School, 1897. Lieutenant Colonel, Medical Corps, United States Army.

JURGENS, HENRY J., M.D., Edina, Missouri. State University of Iowa College of Medicine (Keokuk Medical College), 1896.

KAHLE, P. JORDA, B.Sc., M.D., 636 Common Street, New Orleans, Louisiana. Tulane University of Louisiana School of Medicine, 1905. Assistant in Surgery of Genito-Urinary Organs and Rectum, New Orleans Polyclinic; Assistant Visiting Surgeon, Charity Hospital.

KAHLKE, CHARLES E., B.Sc., M.D., 25 East Washington Street, Chicago, Illinois. Hahnemann Medical College and Hospital, Chicago, 1894. Attending Surgeon, Hahnemann and Streeter Hospitals, Chicago Home for the Friendless.

KAHN, L. MILLER, M.D., 29 East Ninety-third Street, New York, New York. University of Tennessee College of Medicine (Memphis Hospital Medical College), 1900. Instructor in Surgery, Fordham University School of Medicine; Adjunct Attending Surgeon, Lebanon Hospital.

KAHN, LEE, M.D., Francis Building, Louisville, Kentucky. University of Louisville, Medical Department (Louisville Medical College), 1903. Attending Surgeon, Jewish, Louisville City, and Children's Free Hospitals, Masonic Widows' and Orphans' Home and Infirmary.

KAHN, MAURICE, M.D., 1111 Brockman Building, Los Angeles, California. Harvard Medical School, 1898. Lecturer on Surgery, Graduate School of Medicine of the University of California; Instructor in Surgery, College of Physicians and Surgeons; Attending Surgeon, Los Angeles County Hospital.

KAKELS, MOSES S., B.Sc., M.D., 35 East Sixty-first Street, New York, New York. Columbia University, College of Physicians and Surgeons, 1884. Attending Surgeon, Lebanon Hospital; Visiting Surgeon, Rockaway Beach Hospital, Rockaway Beach.

KAMMERER, FREDERIC, M.D., Lenox Hill Hospital, New York, New York. University of Freiburg, 1880. Consulting Surgeon, Lenox Hill and St. Francis Hospitals.

KAMPERMAN, GEORGE, M.D., 1807 David Whitney Building, Detroit, Michigan. University of Michigan Medical School, 1907. Attending Obstetrician, Harper Hospital; Attending Obstetrician and Gynecologist, Receiving Hospital.

KANAVEL, ALLEN B., A.B., M.D., 30 North Michigan Avenue, Chicago, Illinois. Northwestern University Medical School, 1899. Professor of Surgery, Northwestern University Medical School; Attending Surgeon, Wesley Memorial Hospital.

KANE, ARTHUR MATTHEW, A.M., M.D., 32 West Forty-eighth Street, New York, New York. Columbia University, College of Physicians and Surgeons, 1892. Surgeon, St. Mark's Hospital; Attending Surgeon, New York Foundling Hospital; Visiting Surgeon, West Side Dispensary.

KANE, CHARLES JOSEPH, A.M., M.D., 349 Grand Street, Paterson, New Jersey. Columbia University, College of Physicians and Surgeons, 1899. Visiting Gynecologist, St. Joseph's Hospital.

KANE, EVAN O'NEILL, M.D., 230 Clay Street, Kane, Pennsylvania. Jefferson Medical College, 1884. Surgeon, Kane Summit Hospital; Consulting Surgeon, McKean County and Elk County Homes.

KANE, HOWARD FRANCIS, A.B., M.D., Stoneleigh Court, Washington, District of Columbia. George Washington University Medical School, 1912. Associate in Obstetrics, George Washington University; Attending Obstetrician, Freedman's Hospital; Associate Obstetrician, Columbia Hospital for Women; Attending Gynecologist, George Washington University Dispensary; Associate Gynecologist, Casualty Hospital.

KANE, JOSEPH J., M.D., 123 Front Street, Binghamton, New York. University of Pennsylvania School of Medicine, 1903. Surgeon, Binghamton City Hospital; Consulting Surgeon, St. Mary's Home, Binghamton, People's Co-Operative Hospital, Sayre, Pennsylvania.

KARCHER, WILLIAM LEONARD, M.D., 1½ West Stephenson Street, Freeport, Illinois. Medico-Chirurgical College, Philadelphia, 1900. Visiting Surgeon, St. Francis, Globe, and Freeport General Hospitals.

KARSTED, ALFRED, A.B., M.D., 209 Metals Bank Building, Butte, Montana. Johns Hopkins University, Medical Department, 1902.

KATHAN, DAYTON L., M.D., 411 Union Street, Schenectady, New York. Albany Medical College, 1886. Consulting Surgeon, Ellis Hospital.

KATHAN, DUDLEY R., M.D., 621 Union Street, Schenectady, New York. University and Bellevue Hospital Medical College, 1899. Visiting Gynecologist, Ellis Hospital.

KAUFFMAN, JOHN W., Ph.G., M.D., 814 North Eleventh Street, Reading, Pennsylvania. Jefferson Medical College, 1896. Chief Obstetrician, Reading Hospital.

KAUFMAN, JOHN BROOKS, A.B., M.D., Medical Corps, United States Navy, Washington, District of Columbia. University of Pennsylvania School of Medicine, 1903. Commander, Medical Corps, United States Navy.

KAUFMAN, LOUIS RENÉ, M.D., 150 West Eightieth Street, New York, New York. New York Homeopathic Medical College and Flower Hospital, 1904. Professor of Surgery, New York Homeopathic Medical College and Flower Hospital; Visiting Urological Surgeon, Community Hospital; Attending Urologist, Fifth Avenue Hospital.

KAULL, L. P., M.D., 1023 Pacific Mutual Building, Los Angeles, California. University of Kansas School of Medicine, 1898.

KEAN, JEFFERSON R., M.D., Medical Corps, United States Army, Washington, District of Columbia. University of Virginia, Department of Medicine, 1883. Colonel, Medical Corps, United States Army.

KEANE, WILLIAM EDWARD, A.M., M.D., 101 Fort Street, West, Detroit, Michigan. Detroit College of Medicine and Surgery, 1902. Assistant Professor and Clinical Professor of Urology, Detroit College of Medicine and Surgery; Urologist, Providence and St. Mary's Hospitals; Consulting Urologist, Wayne County House and Asylum, Eloise.

KEDDY, O. B., B.A., M.D., C.M., Stannus Street, Windsor, Nova Scotia. Faculty of Medicine, McGill University, 1906. Member of Staff, Payzant Memorial Hospital.

KEEFE, JOHN WILLIAM, M.D., LL.D., 262 Blackstone Boulevard, Providence, Rhode Island. University and Bellevue Hospital Medical College (University of the City of New York, Medical Department), 1884. Surgeon-in-Chief, The John W. Keefe Surgery; Consulting Surgeon, Rhode Island, St. Joseph's, Providence City, and Lying-in Hospitals, Providence, Memorial Hospital, Pawtucket, Woonsocket Hospital, Woonsocket.

KEEFE, PATRICK HENRY, M.D., 262 Benefit Street, Providence, Rhode Island. University of Michigan Medical School, 1879.

KEEFER, FRANK ROYER, A.M., M.D., Medical Corps, United States Army, Washington, District of Columbia. University of Pennsylvania School of Medicine, 1889. Colonel, Medical Corps, United States Army.

KEELER, JOSEPH CLARENCE, M.D., Medical Arts Building, Philadelphia, Pennsylvania. Jefferson Medical College, 1896. Associate Professor of Otology, Jefferson Medical College; Assistant in Laryngology, Jefferson Hospital; Assistant Oto-Laryngologist, Germantown Hospital.

KEEN, WILLIAM WILLIAMS, A.M., M.D., D.Sc., Hon., Ph.D., Hon., LL.D., Hon., F.R.C.S. (Ire.), 1729 Chestnut Street, Philadelphia, Pennsylvania. Jefferson Medical College, 1862. Emeritus Professor of Surgery, Jefferson Medical College; Consulting Surgeon, Jefferson Medical College Hospital.

KEENAN, CAMPBELL B., M.D., D.S.O., 376 Mountain Street, Montreal, Quebec. Faculty of Medicine, McGill University, 1897. Lecturer on Surgery, Faculty of Medicine, McGill University; Assistant Surgeon, Royal Victoria Hospital; Consulting Surgeon, Soldiers' Civil Re-Establishment.

KEENAN, GEORGE FRANCIS, M.D., 207 Bay State Road, Boston, Massachusetts. Tufts College Medical School, 1906. Visiting Surgeon, East Surgical Service and St. Elizabeth's Hospital.

KEENE, FLOYD ELWOOD, M.D., Medical Arts Building, Philadelphia, Pennsylvania. University of Pennsylvania School of Medicine, 1904. Associate in Gynecology, University of Pennsylvania School of Medicine; Assistant Gynecologist, Hospital of the University of Pennsylvania; Gynecologist, Chestnut Hill Hospital; Consulting Gynecologist, Abington Memorial Hospital, Abington.

KEHL, GEORGE W., M.D., 313 North Fifth Street, Reading, Pennsylvania. University of Pennsylvania School of Medicine, 1893. Member of Surgical Staff, Reading Hospital.

KEIPER, GEORGE FREDERICK, A.M., M.D., 14 North Sixth Street, La Fayette, Indiana. University of Michigan Medical School, 1890. Eye and Ear Surgeon, St. Elizabeth's and Home Hospitals, St. Joseph's Orphan Asylum and Manual Labor School, Tippecanoe County Children's Home, St. Anthony's Home for the Aged, Indiana State Soldiers' Home, Chicago, Indianapolis, and Louisville Railway.

KEITH, DARWIN MILLS, M.D., M.R.C.S. (Eng.), L.R.C.P. (Lond.), 420 Main Street, North, Rockford, Illinois. University of Brussels, 1906. Rhinologist and Oto-Laryngologist, Rockford Hospital.

KELLER, FREDERICK C., M.D., 41 West Seventy-first Street, New York, New York. Columbia University, College of Physicians and Surgeons, 1894.

Clinical Professor of Surgery, New York Polyclinic Medical School; Attending Surgeon, New York Polyclinic Medical School and Hospital, Columbus Hospital, New York, St. John's Hospital, Long Island City.

KELLER, JOHN G., M.D., 326 Ohio Building, Toledo, Ohio. Toledo Medical College, 1900. Urologist, St. Vincent's and Flower Hospitals; Director, Venereal Dispensary, Toledo Municipal Hospital.

KELLER, LESTER, M.D., Yorba Linda, California. University of Cincinnati College of Medicine (Medical College of Ohio), 1883. Retired.

KELLER, WILLIAM L., M.D., Medical Corps, United States Army, Washington, District of Columbia. Medical College of Virginia, 1899. Colonel, Medical Corps, United States Army.

KELLER, WILLIAM N., M.D., National Realty Building, Tacoma, Washington. Rush Medical College, 1899. Superintendent, Western State Hospital for Insane, Fort Steilacoom.

KELLEY, HERBERT LESTER, A.B., M.D., Medical Corps, United States Navy, Washington, District of Columbia. Johns Hopkins University, Medical Department, 1907. Commander, Medical Corps, United States Navy.

KELLEY, J. THOMAS, JR., M.D., 1312 Fifteenth Street, Northwest, Washington, District of Columbia. George Washington University Medical School (Columbian University, Medical Department), 1890. Professor of Gynecology, Georgetown University School of Medicine; Gynecologist, Providence Hospital, Columbia Hospital for Women, Georgetown University Hospital.

KELLEY, SAMUEL WALTER, M.D., LL.D., 2255 East Fifty-fifth Street, Cleveland, Ohio. Western Reserve University School of Medicine, 1884. Visiting Surgeon, Children's Department, St. Luke's Hospital of the Methodist Episcopal Church.

KELLOGG, EDWARD LELAND, M.D., 48 West Fifty-first Street, New York, New York. Columbia University, College of Physicians and Surgeons, 1895. Professor of Diseases of the Digestive System, New York Polyclinic Medical School; Director of Surgery, Gouverneur Hospital; Attending Surgeon, Department of Digestive Diseases, West Side Hospital and Dispensary, St. Bartholomew's Hospital; Consulting Surgeon, Louisa Minturn Hospital, New York, Homer Hospital, Homer.

KELLOGG, EDWIN WELLES, M.D., 616 Madison Avenue, New York, New York. New York Homeopathic Medical College and Flower Hospital, 1903. Professor of Surgery, New York Homeopathic Medical College and Flower Hospital; Attending Surgeon, New York Homeopathic Medical College and Flower Hospital, Laura Franklin Free Hospital for Children; Chief of Surgical Clinic, Flower Hospital Dispensary.

KELLOGG, JOHN HARVEY, M.D., LL.D., 202 Manchester Street, Battle Creek, Michigan. University and Bellevue Hospital Medical College, 1875. Medical Director and Surgeon, Battle Creek Sanitarium.

KELLOGG, WILLIAM C., A.B., M.D., Lamar Building, Augusta, Georgia. Johns Hopkins University, Medical Department, 1900. Professor of

Diseases of Nose and Throat, University of Georgia, Medical Department; Attending Surgeon, Department of Nose and Throat, Lamar Hospital; Surgeon, Department of Eye, Ear, Nose, and Throat, Wilhenford Hospital.

KELLY, FRANK A., M.D., 1429 David Whitney Building, Detroit, Michigan. Detroit Homeopathic Medical College, 1903. Attending Surgeon, Grace Hospital, Grace Hospital Polyclinic.

KELLY, HOWARD ATWOOD, A.B., M.D., LL.D., F.R.C.S. (Edin.), 1418 Eutaw Place, Baltimore, Maryland. University of Pennsylvania School of Medicine, 1882. Emeritus Professor of Gynecology, Johns Hopkins University, Medical Department; Surgery and Radium Therapy, Howard A. Kelly Hospital.

KELLY, JAMES A., A.M., M.D., 1815 Spruce Street, Philadelphia, Pennsylvania. University of Pennsylvania School of Medicine, 1901. Associate Professor of Surgery, University of Pennsylvania Post-Graduate School; Attending Surgeon, St. Joseph's, St. Mary's and Misericordia Hospitals.

KELLY, WILLIAM WEBBER, M.D., C.M., Bellin Building, Green Bay, Wisconsin. Faculty of Medicine, McGill University (University of Bishop College, Faculty of Medicine), 1903. Chief of Staff, St. Mary's Hospital.

KELSEY, ARTHUR LOUIS, B.Sc., M.D., 1005 Brockman Building, Los Angeles, California. Jefferson Medical College, 1888. Lecturer, Graduate School of Medicine of the University of California.

KELTON, WALTER, M.D., Empire Building, Seattle, Washington. University of Pennsylvania School of Medicine, 1905. Member of Staff and Lecturer on Surgery and Gynecology, Columbus Sanitarium; Member of Staff, Providence Hospital.

KEMP, ROBERT CHRISTIE, M.D., 211 Reymond Building, Baton Rouge, Louisiana. Tulane University of Louisiana School of Medicine, 1900. Visiting Surgeon, Baton Rouge Sanitarium; Surgeon, Standard Oil Company of Louisiana.

KENAN, JAMES, M.D., 120 Broad Street, Selma, Alabama. University of Virginia, Department of Medicine, 1897. Attending Surgeon, Union Street Private Hospital.

KENNEDY, BERNAYS, M.D., 50 Willoughby Building, Indianapolis, Indiana. Indiana University School of Medicine (Medical College of Indiana), 1898. Attending Gynecologist, Indianapolis City Hospital.

KENNEDY, CHARLES REX, M.D., McCague Building, Omaha, Nebraska. University of Nebraska College of Medicine, 1905. Professor of Clinical Surgery, University of Nebraska College of Medicine; Surgeon, Nebraska Methodist Hospital; Local Surgeon, Union Pacific Railroad.

KENNEDY, JAMES CHARLES, A.M., M.D., LL.D., 762 Willoughby Avenue, Brooklyn, New York. University and Bellevue Hospital Medical College, 1882. Visiting Surgeon, St. Catherine's and St. Mary's Hospitals, St.

Joseph's Female Orphan Asylum; Consulting Surgeon, Eastern District Hospital.

KENNEDY, JAMES M., M.D., Medical Corps, United States Army, Washington, District of Columbia. University of Maryland School of Medicine (College of Physicians and Surgeons, Baltimore), 1892. Colonel, Medical Corps, United States Army.

KENNEDY, JAMES W., M.D., 241 North Eighteenth Street, Philadelphia, Pennsylvania. Jefferson Medical College, 1899. Surgeon in Charge, Joseph Price Hospital; Gynecologist, Coatesville Hospital, Coatesville, Charity Hospital, Norristown; Gynecologist and Obstetrician, Philadelphia Dispensary.

KENNEDY, JOHN T., M.D., Medical Corps, United States Navy, Washington, District of Columbia. University and Bellevue Hospital Medical College (University of the City of New York, Medical Department), 1894. Commander, Medical Corps, United States Navy.

KENNEDY, ROBERT MORRIS, M.D., Medical Corps, United States Navy, Washington, District of Columbia. University of Pennsylvania School of Medicine, 1890. Rear Admiral, Medical Corps, United States Navy.

KENNEDY, RODERICK D., M.D., Globe, Arizona. University of Michigan Medical School, 1903.

KENNING, ANGUS WYLLIE, M.D., Victoria, British Columbia. Detroit College of Medicine and Surgery, 1895. Staff Surgeon, St. Joseph's Hospital; Gynecologist, Provincial Royal Jubilee Hospital.

KENNON, BEVERLEY RANDOLPH, M.D., Taylor Building, Norfolk, Virginia. University of Virginia, Department of Medicine, 1893. Surgeon, Norfolk Protestant Hospital.

KENT, F. MARION, M.D., 128½ East Main Street, Bellevue, Ohio. University of Cincinnati College of Medicine (Medical College of Ohio), 1889.

KENYON, ELMER L., A.B., M.D., 104 South Michigan Avenue, Chicago, Illinois. Rush Medical College, 1896. Assistant Professor of Rhino-Laryngology and Defects of Speech, Rush Medical College; Chief of Clinic in Defects of Speech, Rush Medical College; Associate Laryngologist, Presbyterian Hospital.

KENYON, JAMES H., B.Sc., M.D., 57 West Fifty-eighth Street, New York, New York. Columbia University, College of Physicians and Surgeons, 1898. Instructor in Clinical Surgery, Cornell University Medical College; Assistant Surgeon, Babies' and Fordham Hospitals, New York Neurological Institute.

KER, ROBERT HAROLD, B.A., M.D., C.M., Vancouver Club, Vancouver, British Columbia. Faculty of Medicine, McGill University, 1901.

KERGIN, WILLIAM THOMAS, M.B., 320 Second Avenue, West, Prince Rupert, British Columbia. University of Toronto, Faculty of Medicine, 1902. Member of Visiting Staff, Prince Rupert General Hospital.

KERN, ALBERT G., M.D., 607 Walnut Street, Knoxville, Tennessee. University of Pennsylvania School of Medicine, 1901. Visiting Surgeon, Knoxville General and Riverside Hospitals.

KERN, CHARLES B., B.Sc., A.M., M.D., 610 Columbia Street, La Fayette, Indiana. Hahnemann Medical College and Hospital, Chicago (Chicago, Homeopathic Medical College), 1898. Member of Staff, La Fayette Home Hospital.

KERN, LESTER C., M.D., 122½ East Bremer Avenue, Waverly, Iowa. State University of Iowa College of Medicine, 1895. Member of Staff, St. Joseph's Mercy Hospital.

KERR, EDWARD, M.D., 139 East Lancaster Avenue, East Downingtown, Pennsylvania. University of Pennsylvania School of Medicine, 1890. Chief of Staff and Surgeon, Chester County Hospital, West Chester; Consulting Surgeon, Phoenixville Hospital, Phoenixville.

KERR, HARRY HYLAND, M.D., C.M., 1742 N Street, Northwest, Washington, District of Columbia. Faculty of Medicine, McGill University, 1904. Clinical Professor of Surgery, George Washington University Medical School; Attending Surgeon, Children's and Garfield Memorial Hospitals; Consultant in Brain Surgery, Providence Hospital.

KERR, NORMAN, M.D., C.M., 25 East Washington Street, Chicago, Illinois. Faculty of Medicine, McGill University, 1889. Associate Professor of Surgery, Chicago Policlinic; Attending Surgeon, Chicago Policlinic and Hospital, Henrotin Memorial Hospital.

KERRISON, PHILIP D., M.D., 58 West Fifty-sixth Street, New York, New York. University and Bellevue Hospital Medical College (New York University Medical College), 1898. Aural Surgeon, Willard Parker Hospital; Junior Aural Surgeon, Manhattan Eye, Ear, and Throat Hospital.

KERWIN, WILLIAM, M.D., 4500 Olive Street, St. Louis, Missouri. Washington University Medical School, 1908. Visiting Gynecologist, St. Louis City Hospital No. 2; Consulting Gynecologist, St. John's Hospital; Member of Obstetrical Staff, St. Louis Maternity Hospital.

KESSEL, GEORGE, A.B., A.M., M.D., 212 Sixth Avenue, East, Cresco, Iowa. Rush Medical College, 1885. Surgeon-in-Chief, St. Joseph's Mercy Hospital.

KEVIN, JOHN RICHARD, M.D., 252 Gates Avenue, Brooklyn, New York. University and Bellevue Hospital Medical College, 1888. Surgeon, Broad Street Hospital, New York, St. Mary's Hospital, Brooklyn; Consulting Surgeon, Zion and Harbor Hospitals.

KEY, BEN WITT, A.B., M.D., 180 West Fifty-ninth Street, New York, New York. University of Pennsylvania School of Medicine, 1909. Senior Assistant Surgeon, New York Eye and Ear Infirmary; Chief of Eye Clinic, New York University and Bellevue Hospital Medical College Dispensary; Ophthalmologist, St. Mark's Hospital.

KEY, SAM N., M.D., 320 Littlefield Building, Austin, Texas. University of Texas Department of Medicine, 1910. Surgeon, Physicians and Surgeons, Austin City Hospitals, and Seton Infirmary.

KEYES, A. BELCHAM, M.D., 122 South Michigan Avenue, Chicago, Illinois. Northwestern University Medical School, 1890. Assistant Professor of Gynecology, Rush Medical College; Professor of Gynecology, Chicago Policlinic; Gynecologist, Presbyterian, Henrotin Memorial, and Chicago Maternity Hospitals, Chicago Policlinic and Hospital; Surgeon, Cook County Hospital.

KEYES, EDWARD L., JR., A.B., M.D., Ph.D., 109 East Thirty-fourth Street, New York, New York. Columbia University, College of Physicians and Surgeons, 1895. Professor of Urology, Cornell University Medical College; Urologist, St. Vincent's and Bellevue Hospitals.

KEYES, HAROLD BROWN, A.B., M.D., 128 East Sixtieth Street, New York, New York. Columbia University College of Physicians and Surgeons, 1910. Assistant Surgeon and Chief of Surgical Dispensary, French Hospital.

KHEIRALLA, GEORGE I., M.D., Rapid City, South Dakota. Northwestern University Medical School, 1902. Surgeon, Methodist Deaconess Hospital, Rapid City, St. Joseph's Hospital, Deadwood.

KICKHAM, CHARLES JOSEPH, M.D., 536 Commonwealth Avenue, Boston, Massachusetts. Tufts College Medical School, 1908. Senior Visiting Obstetrician and Associate Gynecologist, St. Elizabeth's Hospital.

KICKLAND, WILLIAM A., B.Sc., M.D., 210 Colorado Building, Fort Collins, Colorado. University of Michigan Medical School, 1895. Surgeon, Fort Collins Hospital, Fort Collins, Bartz Memorial Hospital, Windsor.

KIDD, JOHN FRANKLIN, C.M.G., M.D., C.M., 221 O'Connor Street, Ottawa, Ontario. Queen's University, Faculty of Medicine, 1883. Surgeon, St. Luke's General Hospital.

KIDNER, FREDERICK C., A.B., M.D., 1337 David Whitney Building, Detroit, Michigan. Harvard Medical School, 1904. Visiting Orthopedic Surgeon, Detroit Receiving, Harper, Women's, and Children's Free Hospitals.

KIEFER, HUGO ALBERT, A.B., M.D., 406 Brockman Building, Los Angeles, California. University of Pennsylvania School of Medicine, 1897.

KIEHLE, FREDERICK ANDREWS, A.B., M.D., Corbett Building, Portland, Oregon. University of Minnesota Medical School, 1901. Assistant Professor, Diseases of Eye, Ear, Nose, and Throat, and Chief of Eye and Ear Clinic, University of Oregon Medical School.

KIGER, WILLIAM H., M.D., 711 Pacific Mutual Building, Los Angeles, California. Toledo Medical College, 1900. Professor of Proctology, Graduate School of Medicine of the University of California; Member of Surgical Staff, Los Angeles County Hospital; Member of Staff, Rectal Clinic, Graves Memorial Dispensary.

KILIANI, OTTO G. T., M.D., New York, New York. University of Halle, 1889.

KILLEEN, JOHN JOSEPH, M.D., 104 South Michigan Avenue, Chicago, Illinois. University of Illinois College of Medicine (College of Physicians and Surgeons), 1905. Associate Professor of Rhinology and Oto-Laryngology, Loyola University School of Medicine; Oto-Laryngologist and Attending Surgeon, St. Mary of Nazareth and St. Anthony's Hospitals.

KILLOUGH, ROBERT S., M.D., 203 Blackburn Building, Amarillo, Texas. Eclectic Medical College, Cincinnati, 1896. Member of Staff, St. Anthony's Sanitarium.

KIMBALL, ARTHUR HERBERT, B.Sc., A.M., M.D., The Farragut, Washington, District of Columbia. Johns Hopkins University, Medical Department, 1902. Junior Attending Surgeon, Episcopal Eye, Ear, and Throat Hospital.

KIMBALL, HANNIBAL H., M.D., 602 Nicollet Avenue, Minneapolis, Minnesota. Bowdoin Medical School, 1866. Member of Staff, Abbott Hospital.

KIME, RUFUS R., M.D., 301 North Orange Avenue, Orlando, Florida. University of Michigan Medical School, 1880. Surgeon, Lakeview Sanatorium.

KIMMEL, BENJAMIN BRUCE, A.B., M.D., 206 Penn Square Building, Cleveland, Ohio. Ohio State University College of Homeopathic Medicine (Cleveland Homeopathic Medical College), 1898. Surgeon, Glenville Hospital.

KIMPTON, ARTHUR RONALD, M.D., 66 Bay State Road, Boston, Massachusetts. Dartmouth Medical School, 1905. Associate Professor of Surgery, Tufts College Medical School; First Assistant Visiting Surgeon, Boston City Hospital; Consulting Surgeon, United States Marine Hospital, Chelsea, Somerville Hospital, Somerville.

KINARD, KERWIN WEIDMAN, B.A., M.D., 3520 Main Street, Kansas City, Missouri. University of Pennsylvania School of Medicine, 1908. Attending Surgeon, St. Joseph's Swedish and Kansas City General Hospitals.

KINCAID, JOHN H., M.D., 421 West Church Avenue, Knoxville, Tennessee. University of Michigan Medical School, 1897. Oculist and Aurist, Knoxville General and Riverside Hospitals; Oculist, St. John's Orphanage, Louisville and Nashville and Southern Railways.

KINDLEBERGER, CHARLES POOR, A.B., M.D., Medical Corps, United States Navy, Washington, District of Columbia. University of Pennsylvania School of Medicine, 1894. Captain, Medical Corps, United States Navy.

KING, ALFRED C., M.D., 305 Vallette Street, New Orleans, Louisiana. Tulane University of Louisiana School of Medicine (Tulane Medical College), 1895.

KING, EDGAR, M.D., Medical Corps, United States Army, Washington, District of Columbia. University of Arkansas, Medical Department, 1906. Lieutenant Colonel, Medical Corps, United States Army.

KING, EDMUND ELEAZAR, M.D., C.M., L.R.C.P. (Lond.), 61 Queen Street, East, Toronto, Ontario. University of Toronto, Faculty of Medicine (Victoria University, Medical Department), 1885. Surgeon, St. Michael's Hospital, Hospital for Incurables.

KING, EDWARD LACY, A.B., M.D., 124 Baronne Street, New Orleans, Louisiana. Tulane University of Louisiana, 1911. Instructor in Obstetrics, Tulane University, School of Medicine; Instructor in Operative Gynecology, Post-Graduate School of Medicine, Tulane University; Visiting Surgeon, Department of Obstetrics and Gynecology, Charity Hospital.

KING, HIRAM IRVING, M.D., Aberdeen, South Dakota. Northwestern University Medical School, 1905. Surgeon, St. Luke's Hospital.

KING, JAMES EDWARD, M.D., 1248 Main Street, Buffalo, New York. University of Buffalo, Department of Medicine, 1896. Professor of Gynecology, University of Buffalo, Department of Medicine; Attending Gynecologist, Buffalo General and Erie County Hospitals; Gynecologist-in-Chief, Buffalo City Hospital.

KING, JAMES HORACE, M.D., C.M., Victoria, British Columbia. Faculty of Medicine, McGill University, 1895.

KING, JOHN C., M.D., Livingston Avenue, Banning, California. University of Nashville, Medical Department, 1874. Chief Surgeon, Banning Hospital; Surgeon, Southern Pacific Railroad.

KING, PERRY FIRESTONE, B.Sc., M.D., 317 East Market Street, Alliance, Ohio. Western Reserve University School of Medicine, 1904. Chief of Surgical Staff, Alliance City Hospital.

KING, S. VICTOR, M.D., Bellefield Dwellings, Pittsburgh, Pennsylvania. University of Pittsburgh School of Medicine (Western Pennsylvania Medical College), 1901. Surgeon, Allegheny General Hospital, Pittsburgh, Dixmont Hospital for Insane, Dixmont.

KINGMAN, LUCIUS C., A.B., M.D., 130 Slater Avenue, Providence, Rhode Island. Harvard Medical School, 1904. Assistant Visiting Surgeon, Rhode Island Hospital; Visiting Surgeon, State Hospital for Insane, Howard; Consulting Surgeon, Memorial Hospital, Pawtucket.

KINGSLEY, BYRON F., M.D., Hicks Building, San Antonio, Texas. Detroit College of Medicine and Surgery, 1874; Long Island College Hospital, 1874.

KINNE, BRAYTON EUGENE, M.D., 40 Eagle Street, Albany, New York. New York Homeopathic Medical College and Flower Hospital, 1901. Visiting Surgeon, Homeopathic Hospital.

KINYON, CLAUDIUS BLIGH, M.D., Trenton, Michigan. Hahnemann Medical College and Hospital, Chicago (Chicago Homeopathic Medical College), 1878.

KIRBY, FRANCIS JOSEPH, A.M., Phar.G., M.D., 110 East North Avenue, Baltimore, Maryland. University of Maryland School of Medicine, 1892. Associate in Surgery, University of Maryland School of Medicine and College of Physicians and Surgeons; Surgeon, St. Joseph's and Mercy Hospitals, Hebrew Hospital and Asylum, Baltimore, Annapolis Emergency Hospital, Annapolis, St. Mary's Hospital, Leonardtown; Consulting Surgeon, Mt. Hope Retreat.

KIRCHNER, WALTER C. G., A.B., M.D., 229 Metropolitan Building, St. Louis, Missouri. Washington University Medical School, 1901. Assistant in Surgery, Washington University Medical School; Visiting Surgeon, St. Louis City Hospital; Consulting Surgeon, St. John's Hospital.

KIRKENDALL, JOHN SWARTOUT, M.D., 317 North Aurora Street, Ithaca, New York. Ohio State University, College of Medicine, 1880. Attending Ophthalmologist, Willard State Hospital for Insane, Willard; Oculist, Lehigh Valley Railroad.

KIRKHAM, HAROLD L.D., M.D., 735 Kress Medical Building, Houston, Texas. University of Texas, Medical Department, 1909. Visiting Surgeon, St. Joseph's Infirmary.

KIRKLEY, CYRUS A., M.D., 432 South Serrano Avenue, Los Angeles, California. Ohio State University College of Medicine (Starling Medical College), 1868.

KIRKPATRICK, SAMUEL, M.D., Parish Building, Selma, Alabama. Vanderbilt University, Medical Department, 1888. Oculist and Aurist, Vaughan Memorial Hospital, Burwell Infirmary, Southern Railroad.

KIRKPATRICK, WILLIAM D., M.D., Bellingham National Bank Building, Bellingham, Washington. University of Minnesota Medical School, 1895.

KISTLER, HERBERT D., B.Sc., M.D., Murray Hospital, Butte, Montana. St. Louis University School of Medicine, 1905. Surgeon, Murray Hospital.

KISTNER, FRANK B., M.D., 909 Stevens Building, Portland, Oregon. Indiana University School of Medicine (Medical College of Indiana), 1898.

KITCHEN, ARTHUR SAMUEL, M.B., 1229 Harnett Avenue, Escanaba, Michigan. University of Toronto, Faculty of Medicine, 1899. Surgeon, St. Francis Hospital.

KITTREDGE, FRANK E., M.D., Masonic Temple, Nashua, New Hampshire. University of Pennsylvania School of Medicine, 1885. Otologist and Laryngologist, St. Joseph's and Nashua Memorial Hospitals.

KITTREDGE, THOMAS, M.D., 13 Chestnut Street, Salem, Massachusetts. Long Island College Hospital, 1874.

KITTRELL, THOMAS FLEMING, M.D., 308 State National Bank Building, Texarkana, Arkansas. Vanderbilt University, Medical Department, 1894. Attending Surgeon, Pine Street Sanitarium; Consulting Surgeon, St. Louis Southwestern Railway Company.

KLEINBERG, SAMUEL, M.D., 1 West Eighty-fifth Street, New York, New York. Columbia University, College of Physicians and Surgeons, 1908. Assistant Surgeon, Out-Patient Department, Hospital for Ruptured and Crippled; Adjunct Orthopedic Surgeon, Lebanon Hospital; Orthopedic Surgeon, Israel Orphan Asylum.

KLEMPTNER, LOUIS H., M.D., 310 Cobb Building, Seattle, Washington. Imperial University, Dorpat, 1889.

KLINEFELTER, MARION L., M.D., Wall Building, St. Louis, Missouri. Washington University Medical School, 1903. Orthopedic Surgeon, Missouri

Baptist Sanitarium; Consulting Orthopedic Surgeon, Frisco Employee's Hospital.

KLUMP, JOHN A., D.D.S., M.D., 331 Elmira Street, Williamsport, Pennsylvania. University of Pennsylvania School of Medicine, 1881. Surgeon, Williamsport Private Hospital.

KNAPP, BLEEKER, M.D., Cleveland Building, Evansville, Indiana. Rush Medical College, 1901. Surgeon, Protestant Deaconess and St. Mary's Hospitals.

KNAPP, HARRY BUTLER, M.D., Battle Creek Sanitarium, Battle Creek, Michigan. University of Illinois College of Medicine (American Medical Missionary College), 1904. Surgeon, Battle Creek Sanitarium.

KNICKERBOCKER, HOMER JAMES, Phar.G., M.D., 196 Genesee Street, Geneva, New York. University of Buffalo, Department of Medicine, 1898. Attending Surgeon, Geneva City Hospital; Surgeon, New York Central Railroad.

KNIGHT, STEPHEN HERRICK, A.M., M.D., 69 East Willis Avenue, Detroit, Michigan. New York Homeopathic Medical College and Flower Hospital, 1886. Assistant Clinical Professor of Surgery, Detroit College of Medicine and Surgery; President of Medical Staff, Attending Surgeon and Chief of Division of General Surgery, Grace Hospital; Consulting Surgeon, Grace Hospital Polyclinic.

KNIPE, WILLIAM H. WELLINGTON, A.M., M.D., 59 West Fifty-fourth Street, New York, New York. Columbia University, College of Physicians and Surgeons, 1903. Obstetrician, Gouverneur Hospital.

KNOWLES, WILLIAM FLETCHER, M.D., 520 Commonwealth Avenue, Boston, Massachusetts. Harvard Medical School, 1885. Instructor in Otology and Associate in Laryngology, Harvard Medical School; Aural Surgeon, Massachusetts Charitable Eye and Ear Infirmary; Associate Laryngologist and Aural Surgeon, Massachusetts General Hospital; Consulting Oto-Laryngologist, Newton Hospital, Newton.

KNOX, ROBERT WHITE, A.M., M.D., 6B Beaconsfield Apartments, Houston, Texas. University of Virginia, Department of Medicine, 1882. Chief Surgeon, Southern Pacific Lines in Texas and Louisiana.

KNOX, WILLIAM JOHN, M.D., C.M., Kelowna, British Columbia. Queen's University, Faculty of Medicine, 1903. Surgeon, Kelowna Hospital.

KOCH, JOHN A., Phar.D., M.D., 804 Broadway, Quincy, Illinois. George Washington University Medical School, 1897. Attending Surgeon, St. Mary's Institute, St. Vincent's Home for Aged.

KOLL, IRVIN S., B.Sc., M.D., 31 North State Street, Chicago, Illinois. Rush Medical College, 1907. Professor of Genito-Urinary Surgery, Post-Graduate Medical School; Genito-Urinary Surgeon, Post-Graduate Hospital; Associate Genito-Urinary Surgeon, Michael Reese Hospital.

KOLLIG, MATTHEW, A.B., M.D., 704 Holland Avenue, Saginaw, Michigan. University of Michigan Medical School, 1907.

KOLLOCK, CHARLES WILSON, M.D., 86 Wentworth Street, Charleston, South Carolina. University of Pennsylvania School of Medicine, 1881. Professor of Laryngology and Rhinology, Medical College of the State of South Carolina; Laryngologist and Rhinologist, Roper Hospital; Ophthalmic and Aural Surgeon, Shirras Dispensary.

KOLTES, FRANK X., B.Sc., M.D., Medical Corps, United States Navy, Washington, District of Columbia. Rush Medical College, 1903. Commander, Medical Corps, United States Navy.

KOPETZKY, SAMUEL JOSEPH, M.D., 51 West Seventy-third Street, New York, New York. Columbia University, College of Physicians and Surgeons, 1898. Visiting Otologist, Beth Israel Hospital.

KORNER, VICTOR, M.D., Santo Domingo 628, Santiago, Chile. Faculty of Medicine, University of Chile, 1881.

KOSMAK, GEORGE WILLIAM, A.B., M.D., 23 East Ninety-third Street, New York, New York. Columbia University, College of Physicians and Surgeons, 1899. Attending Surgeon, Lying-in Hospital.

KRAFT, OSCAR H., Ph.G., M.D., 25 East Washington Street, Chicago, Illinois. University of Buffalo, Department of Medicine, 1896. Attending Ophthalmologist, Grant, Alexian Brothers' Hospitals.

KRAUSS, FREDERICK, Ph.G., M.D., 1703 Chestnut Street, Philadelphia, Pennsylvania. University of Pennsylvania School of Medicine, 1893. Ophthalmic Surgeon, Methodist Episcopal Hospital; Laryngologist, Abington Memorial Hospital; Ophthalmic and Aural Surgeon, St. Christopher's Hospital.

KRAUSS, JAMES, M.D., 419 Boylston Street, Boston, Massachusetts. Boston University School of Medicine, 1889. Professor of Urology, University of Massachusetts School of Medicine; Chief of Urologic Clinic, Middlesex Hospital, Cambridge.

KREIDER, GEORGE N., A.M., M.D., 522 East Capitol Avenue, Springfield, Illinois. University and Bellevue Hospital Medical College (University of the City of New York, Medical Department), 1880. Surgeon, St. John's Hospital.

KRETSCHMER, HERMAN LOUIS, Phar.G., M.D., 122 South Michigan Avenue, Chicago, Illinois. Northwestern University Medical School, 1904. Assistant Professor of Genito-Urinary Surgery, Rush Medical College; Assistant Attending Surgeon, Children's Memorial Hospital; Urologist, Presbyterian Hospital; Genito-Urinary Surgeon, Alexian Brothers' Hospital.

KREUSCHER, PHILIP H., M.D., 30 North Michigan Avenue, Chicago, Illinois. Northwestern University Medical School, 1909. Professor of Clinical Orthopedic Surgery, Loyola University School of Medicine; Attending Surgeon, Mercy Hospital; Attending Orthopedic Surgeon, Provident Hospital.

KRISTJANSON, HJORLEIFUR T., A.B., M.D., 611 Wells Building, Milwaukee, Wisconsin. Rush Medical College, 1907. Assistant Professor of Clinical

Surgery, Marquette University School of Medicine; Member of Staff, Milwaukee Hospital.

KROUSE, LOUIS J., M.D., 75 Groton Building, Cincinnati, Ohio. University of Cincinnati College of Medicine (Medical College of Ohio), 1879. Proctologist, Jewish Hospital.

KRUSEN, WILMER, M.D., 127 North Twentieth Street, Philadelphia, Pennsylvania. Jefferson Medical College, 1893. Professor of Gynecology, Temple University, Department of Medicine; Gynecologist, Samaritan and Garretson Hospitals.

KUFLEWSKI, WLADYSLAW A., M.D., 1366 North Robey Street, Chicago, Illinois. University of Illinois College of Medicine (College of Physicians and Surgeons, Chicago), 1894. Senior Attending Surgeon, St. Mary of Nazareth Hospital.

KUHN, CHARLES FRANCIS, M.D., 90 Warren Avenue, East, Detroit, Michigan. Michigan College of Medicine and Surgery, 1901. Surgeon, Samaritan Hospital.

KUHN, HAROLD PHILLIP, A.B., M.D., Rialto Building, Kansas City, Missouri. University of Kansas School of Medicine, 1906. Professor of Oral Surgery, Kansas City-Western Dental College; Attending Surgeon, Kansas City General and St. Luke's Hospitals.

KUHN, JOHN FREDERICK, Ph.G., M.D., 619 First National Bank Building, Oklahoma, Oklahoma. Georgetown University School of Medicine, 1901. Assistant Professor of Surgery, Oklahoma University; Member of Surgical Staff, State University Hospital; Consulting Surgeon, St. Anthony's Hospital.

KUNKEL, GEORGE B., M.Sc., M.D., 118 Locust Street, Harrisburg, Pennsylvania. University of Pennsylvania School of Medicine, 1893. Visiting Interne Surgeon, Harrisburg Hospital; Consulting Surgeon, Pennsylvania State Hospital, State Department of Health, Harrisburg, Carlisle General Hospital, Carlisle; Visiting Surgeon, Pennsylvania State Sanatoriums for Tuberculosis, Mont Alto; Surgeon, Pennsylvania and Philadelphia and Reading Railroads.

KURTZ, CARL, M.D., 609 H. W. Hellman Building, Los Angeles, California. University and Bellevue Hospital Medical College (Bellevue Hospital Medical College), 1889. Professor of Gynecology, Graduate School of Medicine of the University of California; Surgeon, Lincoln Hospital; Consulting Surgeon, Santa Fe Coast Lines Hospital; Visiting Surgeon, Los Angeles County Hospital.

KYLE, J. ALLEN, B.Sc.A., M.D., 402 Carter Building, Houston, Texas. Columbia University, College of Physicians and Surgeons, 1894. Visiting Surgeon, St. Joseph's Infirmary, Houston City Hospital, Faith Home.

LACHAISE, GASTON, M.D., Pedro Martt 475, Valparaiso, Chile. Faculty of Medicine, University of Chile, 1911.

LADD, WILLIAM EDWARDS, A.B., M.D., 326 Dartmouth Street, Boston, Massachusetts. Harvard Medical School, 1906. Instructor in Surgery, Harvard Medical School; Assistant in Surgery, Harvard University Graduate School of Medicine; Associate Surgeon, Children's Hospital.

LADIN, LOUIS JULIUS, A.B., M.D., 1289 Madison Avenue, New York, New York. Columbia University, College of Physicians and Surgeons, 1887. Professor of Gynecology, New York Polyclinic Medical School; Visiting Gynecologist, New York Polyclinic Medical School and Hospital; Gynecologist, Beth Israel and Beth David Hospitals; Visiting Surgeon, Gouverneur Hospital; Consulting Gynecologist, Hospital for Deformities and Joint Diseases, New York, St. Mary's Hospital, Waterbury, Connecticut.

LAFERTÉ, ALFRED D., M.D., 1551 David Whitney Building, Detroit, Michigan. Jefferson Medical College, 1910. Associate Professor of Orthopedic Surgery, Detroit College of Medicine and Surgery; Associate Orthopedic Surgeon, Harper Hospital; Attending Orthopedic Surgeon, Detroit Tuberculosis Sanatorium; Consulting Orthopedic Surgeon, Herman Kiefer Hospital.

LAFERTÉ, DANIEL, M.D., David Whitney Building, Detroit, Michigan. Jefferson Medical College, 1871. Professor of Orthopedic Surgery, Detroit College of Medicine and Surgery; Orthopedic Surgeon, Providence and Children's Free Hospitals; Consulting Surgeon, Harper Hospital.

LA FORCE, BURDETTE DUDLEY, Phar.G., M.D., Hofmann Building, Ottumwa, Iowa. Rush Medical College, 1893. Ophthalmologist, Ottumwa and St. Joseph Hospitals.

LA FORCE, WILLIAM BROOKS, Ph.B., M.D., Tsing Hua College, Peking, China. Northwestern University Medical School, 1891. Surgeon in Charge, Tsing Hua College Hospital.

LAGOS, HORACIO GARCIA, M.D., Andes 1287, Montevideo, Uruguay. Faculty of Medicine, University of Montevideo, 1900. Professor of Surgical Pathology, Faculty of Medicine, University of Montevideo; Director and Chief Surgeon, British Hospital and Sanatorium.

LAHEY, FRANK H., M.D., 638 Beacon Street, Boston, Massachusetts. Harvard Medical School, 1904. Professor of Surgery, Tufts College Medical School; First Assistant Surgeon, Boston City Hospital; Consulting Surgeon, Forsyth Dental Infirmary, Symmes Arlington, Evangeline Booth Maternity, and Framingham Hospitals.

LAILEY WALTER WHITNEY, B.A., M.D., 43 Avenue Road, Toronto, Ontario. University of Toronto, Faculty of Medicine, 1908. Assistant in Gynecology and Obstetrics, Toronto General Hospital and University of Toronto.

LAMAS, ALFONSO, M.D., Colonia 1072, Montevideo, Uruguay. Faculty of Medicine University of Montevideo, 1890. Instructor in Surgical Clinic; Chief of Surgical Service, Maciel Hospital.

LAMB, FREDERICK W., A.B., M.D., 209 Provident Bank Building, Cincinnati, Ohio. University of Cincinnati College of Medicine (Miami Medical College), 1900. Laryngologist, Children's Hospital of the Protestant Episcopal Church.

LAMB, ROBERT SCOTT, M.D., Stoneleigh Court, Washington, District of Columbia. Howard University School of Medicine, 1898. Consulting Ophthalmologist, Woman's Clinic; Associate Attending Surgeon, Episcopal Eye, Ear, and Throat Hospital.

LAMBERT, ADRIAN VAN SINDEREN, A.B., M.D., 168 East Seventy-first Street, New York, New York. Columbia University, College of Physicians and Surgeons, 1896. Professor of Clinical Surgery, Columbia University, College of Physicians and Surgeons; Visiting Surgeon, Bellevue Hospital; Consulting Surgeon, Presbyterian and New York Orthopedic Hospitals.

LAMBERT, SAMUEL ERNEST, M.D., 401 Old National Bank Building, Spokane, Washington. University of Alabama School of Medicine, 1901.

LAMBERT, WALTER EYRE, B.A., L.R.C.P.& S. (Edin.), 112 East Thirty-fifth Street, New York, New York. Royal College of Physicians and Royal College of Surgeons, Edinburgh, 1884. Surgeon, New York Eye and Ear Infirmary.

LA MOTTE, WILLIAM OSCAR, B.Sc., A.M., M.D., Industrial Trust Building, Wilmington, Delaware. University of Pennsylvania School of Medicine, 1907. Chief of Eye, Ear, Nose, and Throat Department, Delaware Hospital.

LAMPSON, EDWARD RUTLEDGE, A.B., M.D., 175 North Beacon Street, Hartford, Connecticut. Columbia University, College of Physicians and Surgeons, 1896. Attending Surgeon, Hartford Hospital; Consulting Surgeon, New Britain Hospital.

LAMSON, OTIS F., M.D., 705 Broadway, Seattle, Washington. University of Pennsylvania School of Medicine, 1907. Consulting Surgeon, Shelton Hospital.

LANCASTER, WALTER BRACKETT, A.B., M.D., 520 Commonwealth Avenue, Boston, Massachusetts. Harvard Medical School, 1889. Associate in Ophthalmology, Harvard University Graduate School of Medicine; Ophthalmic Surgeon, Massachusetts Charitable Eye and Ear Infirmary; Consulting Ophthalmologist, New England Hospital for Women and Children; Ophthalmologist, Massachusetts General Hospital.

LAND, EVERETT A., M.D., Taylor Building, Norfolk, Virginia. Medical College of Virginia (University College of Medicine), 1906. Chief, Norfolk Protestant Hospital.

LANDFRIED, CHARLES JOHN, M.D., 5907 Garfield Street, New Orleans, Louisiana. Tulane University of Louisiana School of Medicine, 1890. Senior Surgeon, Ear, Nose, and Throat Department, Touro Infirmary.

LANDMAN, OTTO, Ph.B., A.M., M.D., 230 Michigan Street, Toledo, Ohio. University of Michigan Medical School, 1887. Ophthalmologist, St. Vincent's Hospital.

LANDON, LYNDON HOLT, M.D., 5074 Jenkins Arcade Building, Pittsburgh, Pennsylvania. University of Pennsylvania School of Medicine, 1910. Surgeon, Hospital of Western Pennsylvania.

LANDRY, LUCIAN HYPPOLITE, M.D., 2122 Peters Avenue, New Orleans, Louisiana. Tulane University of Louisiana School of Medicine, 1907. Demonstrator of Operative Surgery and Assistant Professor of Clinical Surgery, Tulane University of Louisiana School of Medicine; Senior Associate in Surgery, Touro Infirmary; Visiting Surgeon, Charity Hospital; Consulting Surgeon, City Hospital.

LANE, HARRY HAMILTON, M.D., Medical Corps, United States Navy, Washington, District of Columbia. Jefferson Medical College, 1904. Lieutenant Commander, Medical Corps, United States Navy.

LANE, JOHN W., A.B., M.D., 520 Beacon Street, Boston, Massachusetts. Harvard Medical School, 1903.

LANE, LAURA ARLENE, A.B., M.D., 3201 Clinton Avenue, Minneapolis, Minnesota. University of Colorado School of Medicine, 1904.

LANE, NATHANIEL F., M.D., 1925 Chestnut Street, Philadelphia, Pennsylvania. Hahnemann Medical College and Hospital, Philadelphia, 1891. Clinical Professor of Gynecology and Gynecologist, Hahnemann Medical College and Hospital; Surgeon, Woman's Southern Homeopathic Hospital; Consulting Gynecologist, Pottstown Homeopathic Hospital, Pottstown.

LANGDALE, CHARLES ANDREW, M.D., 1908 Union Central Life Building, Cincinnati, Ohio. University of Cincinnati College of Medicine (Medical College of Ohio), 1903. Senior Visiting Staff Surgeon, Episcopal Hospital for Children, Cincinnati General Hospital; Junior Visiting Staff Surgeon, Christ Hospital.

LANGFITT, WILLIAM STERLING, A.M., M.D., St. John's Hospital, Pittsburgh, Pennsylvania. University of Pittsburgh School of Medicine, 1894. Surgeon-in-Chief, St. John's General Hospital.

LANGHORST, FRED H., M.D., 6 Spring Street, Elgin, Illinois. Rush Medical College, 1900. Member of Staff, Sherman and St. Joseph's Hospitals.

LANGSTAFF, JAMES HARTZELL, M.D., Fairbury, Illinois. Loyola University School of Medicine (Illinois Medical College), 1904. Surgeon, Fairbury Hospital.

LANGWORTHY, HOWARD T., M.D., 480 Franklin Avenue, Brooklyn, New York. Columbia University, College of Physicians and Surgeons, 1911. Assistant Attending Surgeon, Methodist Episcopal Hospital; Associate Surgeon, Trinity Hospital.

LANKFORD, BURNLEY, M.D., 246 Freemason Street, West, Norfolk, Virginia. University of Virginia, Department of Medicine, 1903. Obstetrician, Norfolk Protestant Hospital.

LAPLACE, ERNEST, A.M., M.D., LL.D., 1828 South Rittenhouse Square, Philadelphia, Pennsylvania. University of Paris, 1886. Professor of Surgery, University of Pennsylvania Graduate School of Medicine; Senior Surgeon, Philadelphia General Hospital; Surgeon, Medico-Chirurgical, Misericordia, and Polyclinic Hospitals.

LAPSLEY, INEZ, M.D., 628 Elm Street, Cincinnati, Ohio. Laura Memorial Woman's Medical College, 1901.

LAPSLEY, ROBERT M., M.D., 625 Blondeau Street, Keokuk, Iowa. Rush Medical College, 1891. Ophthalmologist, Otologist, and Rhino-Laryngologist, St. Joseph's and Graham Hospitals.

LARGE, SECORD H., M.D., C.M., 536 Rose Building, Cleveland, Ohio. University of Toronto, Faculty of Medicine (Trinity Medical College), 1893. Surgeon in Charge, Ear, Nose, and Throat Dispensary, St. Vincent's Hospital.

LARKIN, JOHN CHARLES, M.D., 130 East Main Street, Hillsboro, Ohio. University of Cincinnati College of Medicine (Medical College of Ohio), 1896.

LaROQUE, G. PAUL, M.D., 603 East Grace Street, Richmond, Virginia. University of Pennsylvania School of Medicine, 1902. Associate Professor of Surgery, Medical College of Virginia; Surgeon, Retreat for the Sick, Memorial, Dooley, St. Phillip, Sheltering Arms, and Virginia Hospitals.

LA ROSE, VICTOR J., M.D., City National Bank Building, Bismarck, North Dakota. University of Minnesota Medical School, 1901. Genito-Urinary Surgeon, Bismarck Hospital; Surgeon, St. Alexius Hospital.

LARSEN, CARL L., M.D., C.M., 1027 Lowry Building, St. Paul, Minnesota. University of Minnesota Medical School (Hamline University, Medical Department), 1904. Ophthalmologist and Oto-Laryngologist, St. Joseph's, St. Paul's, St. Luke's, and Bethesda Hospitals, State Hospital for Crippled Children, Mounds Park Sanitarium.

LARTIGAU, AUGUST J., M.D., 391 Sutter Street, San Francisco, California. University of California Medical School, 1896. Surgeon, Children's Hospital.

LATHROP, HOMER RIALE, M.D., 113 East Second Street, Casper, Wyoming. Rush Medical College, 1901. Chief of Staff, Casper Private, Women and Children's Hospitals.

LATHROP, WALTER, M.D., State Hospital of Middle Coal Field, Hazleton, Pennsylvania. University of Pennsylvania School of Medicine, 1890. Surgeon-in-Chief, State Hospital of Middle Coal Field.

LAUDER, EDWARD, M.D., C.M., 1020 Huron Road, Cleveland, Ohio. Faculty of Medicine, McGill University, 1896. Visiting Ophthalmologist, St. Luke's and Fairview Park Hospitals.

LAW, ARTHUR AYER, M.D., 420 Syndicate Building, Minneapolis, Minnesota. University of Minnesota Medical School, 1894. Associate Professor of Surgery, University of Minnesota Medical School; Surgeon, Northwestern Hospital; Surgeon and Assistant Chief, University Hospital.

LAW, HENRY W. F., M.D., North Western National Bank Building, Grand Forks, North Dakota. Detroit College of Medicine and Surgery, 1904. Member of Staff, St. Michael's and Deaconess Hospitals.

LAWBAUGH, ALBERT I., M.D., 117 Willow Avenue, Laurium, Michigan. Long Island College Hospital, 1870. Chief of Staff, Tamarack Mine Hospital.

LAWRENCE, FLORUS FREMONT, M.D., D.Sc., LL.D., 664 North Park Street, Columbus, Ohio. Ohio State University College of Medicine (Columbus Medical College), 1885. Chief of Staff and Surgeon, Lawrence and Mc-Kinley Hospitals.

LAWRENCE, HOWARD F., M.D., Medical Corps, United States Navy, Washington, District of Columbia. University and Bellevue Hospital Medical College, 1904. Lieutenant Commander, Medical Corps, United States Navy.

LAWRENCE, WILLIAM HENRY, M.D., 129 Summit Avenue, Summit, New Jersey. Columbia University, College of Physicians and Surgeons, 1899. Surgeon-in-Chief, Overlook Hospital; Attending Surgeon, All Souls' Hospital, Morristown; Surgeon, New Jersey State Hospital, Morris Plains.

LAWS, WILLIAM V., A.M., M.D., Dugan-Stuart Building, Hot Springs, Arkansas. University of Louisville, Medical Department (Kentucky School of Medicine), 1893; Medico-Chirurgical College, Philadelphia, 1900. Surgeon, Leo N. Levi Memorial Hospital.

LAWSON, HURON WILLIS, M.Sc., M.D., 1706 Rhode Island Avenue, Washington, District of Columbia. George Washington University Medical School, 1903. Professor of Obstetrics, George Washington University Medical School; Obstetrician, George Washington University Hospital, Columbia Hospital for Women; Gynecologist, Freedmen's Hospital.

LAYMAN, DANIEL W., B.Sc., M.D., 608 Hume-Mansur Building, Indianapolis, Indiana. Columbia University, College of Physicians and Surgeons, 1898. Clinical Professor, Ear, Nose, and Throat Department, Indiana University School of Medicine; Attending Surgeon, Ear, Nose, and Throat Department, Indianapolis City and Robert W. Long Hospitals; Consulting Laryngologist, Indianapolis Orphans' Asylum.

LAZARD, EDMOND M., M.D., 547 South Kingsley Drive, Los Angeles, California. University of California Medical School, Los Angeles, 1897. Clinical Professor of Obstetrics, College of Medical Evangelists, Loma Linda; Assistant Professor of Obstetrics and Chief of Obstetrical Dispensary, Graduate School of Medicine of the University of California; Attending Obstetrician, Los Angeles County Hospital; Attending Surgeon, Kaspare Cohn Hospital.

LAZENBY, MAURICE, A.B., M.D., 18 West Franklin Street, Baltimore, Maryland. Johns Hopkins University, Medical Department, 1903. Visiting Gynecologist, Maryland General Hospital, Church Home and Infirmary; Visiting Obstetrician, Mercy Hospital.

LEACH, PHILIP, M.D., Columbia Trust Company, 358 Fifth Avenue, New York, New York. Rush Medical College, 1881. Captain, Medical Corps, United States Navy, retired.

LEACHMAN, GEORGE C., M.D., 615 Francis Building, Louisville, Kentucky. University of Louisville, Medical Department (Kentucky School of Medicine, Louisville), 1896. Adjunct Professor of Surgery and Assistant in Clinical Surgery, University of Louisville, Medical Department; Visiting Surgeon, Louisville City and St. Joseph's Hospitals.

LEAHEY, GEORGE A., M.D., 128 Merrimack Street, Lowell, Massachusetts. Harvard Medical School, 1892. Ophthalmic and Aural Surgeon, St. John's and Lowell General Hospitals.

LEAKE, JOHN P., M.D., Canal and Dauphine Streets, New Orleans, Louisiana. Tulane University of Louisiana School of Medicine, 1901.

LEASK, THOMAS MCCRAE, M.B., 202 Walter Scott Building, Moose Jaw, Saskatchewan. University of Toronto Faculty of Medicine, 1899. Surgeon, Moose Jaw General and Providence Hospitals.

LEAVITT, HENRY H., A.M., M.D., 700 Donaldson Building, Minneapolis, Minnesota. Hahnemann Medical College and Hospital, Chicago (Chicago Homeopathic Medical College), 1886. Ophthalmologist and Oto-Laryngologist, Asbury Hospital.

LE BRETON, PRESCOTT, A.B., M.D., 125 Allen Street, Buffalo, New York. Columbia University, College of Physicians and Surgeons, 1896. Orthopedic Surgeon, Buffalo General, Erie County, Municipal, Buffalo Columbus, and Children's Hospitals; Surgeon, Crippled Children's Guild.

LE CONTE, ROBERT GRIER, A.B., M.D., 2000 Spruce Street, Philadelphia, Pennsylvania. University of Pennsylvania School of Medicine, 1888. Surgeon, Pennsylvania Hospital; Consulting Surgeon, Germantown Dispensary and Hospital, Philadelphia, Bryn Mawr Hospital, Bryn Mawr.

LEDBETTER, ROBERT EMMET, M.D., Medical Corps, United States Navy, Washington, District of Columbia. University of Pennsylvania School of Medicine, 1899. Commander, Medical Corps, United States Navy.

LEDBETTER, SAMUEL L., JR., B.Sc., M.D., 516 Empire Building, Birmingham, Alabama. Johns Hopkins University Medical Department, 1910. Associate in Surgery, University of Alabama, Post Graduate School of Medicine; Visiting Surgeon, St. Vincent's Hospital; Associate Surgeon, Hillman Hospital, Birmingham; Consulting Surgeon, Employes Hospital of the Tennessee Coal, Iron and Railroad Company, Fairfield.

LEDERMAN, ISAAC A., A.B., M.D., Francis Building, Louisville, Kentucky. University of Louisville, Medical Department, 1896. Professor of Diseases of Ear, Nose, and Throat, and Clinical Professor of Ophthalmology, University of Louisville, Medical Department; Visiting Otologist, Rhinologist, and Laryngologist, Louisville City Hospital; Ophthalmologist and Otologist, Jewish Hospital.

LEDERMAN, MOSES DAVID, M.D., 58 East Seventy-fifth Street, New York, New York. University of Pennsylvania School of Medicine, 1889. Attending Aurist and Laryngologist, Lebanon Hospital; Consulting Aurist and Laryngologist, United Hebrew Charities, Associate Editor, *The Laryngoscope*.

LEDOUX, JOSEPH OMER, B.Sc., M.D., 44 Brooks Street, Sherbrooke, Quebec. Faculty of Medicine, University of Montreal (Laval University, Faculty of Medicine), 1896.

LEE, BURTON JAMES, Ph.B., M.D., 128 East Seventy-third Street, New York, New York. Columbia University, College of Physicians and Surgeons, 1898. Clinical Professor of Surgery, Cornell University Medical College; Associate Surgeon, New York Hospital; Attending Surgeon, Memorial Hospital; Consulting Surgeon, Sharon Hospital.

LEE, GEORGE HENDERSON, M.D., American National Insurance Building, Galveston, Texas. Tulane University of Louisiana School of Medicine, 1888. Professor of Obstetrics and Gynecology, University of Texas, Medical Department; Visiting Obstetrician and Gynecologist, John Sealy Hospital; Gynecologist and Surgeon, St. Mary's Infirmary.

LEE, HARRY JASON, B.Sc., M.D., 535 Beacon Street, Boston, Massachusetts. Boston University School of Medicine, 1904. Lecturer on Surgical Anatomy, Boston University School of Medicine; Visiting Surgeon, Massachusetts Homeopathic Hospital.

LEE, WALTER ESTELL, M.D., 905 Pine Street, Philadelphia, Pennsylvania. University of Pennsylvania School of Medicine, 1902. Associate Professor of Surgery, University of Pennsylvania Graduate School of Medicine; Surgeon, Germantown and Children's Hospitals; Assistant Surgeon, Pennsylvania Hospital, Philadelphia, Bryn Mawr Hospital, Bryn Mawr; Consulting Surgeon, Pennsylvania State Department of Health, Henry Phipps Institute.

LEEDER, FORREST BERTRAM, M.R.C.S. (Eng.), L.R.C.P. (Lond.), Victoria, British Columbia. University College (London), 1890. Consulting Gynecologist, Provincial Royal Jubilee Hospital.

LE FEVRE, GEORGE L., M.D., Union National Bank Building, Muskegon, Michigan. Hahnemann Medical College and Hospital, Chicago, 1891. Chief of Surgical Staff and Gynecologist, Mercy Hospital; Chief of Surgical Staff, Hackley Hospital.

LEGGE, ROBERT THOMAS, Phar.G., M.D., University of California Infirmary, Berkeley, California. University of California Medical School, 1899. Professor of Hygiene, University of California; Surgeon, University of California Infirmary.

LEHMANN, JULIUS EDUARD, M.B., M.R.C.S. (Eng.), L.R.C.P. (Lond.), 606 Boyd Building, Winnipeg, Manitoba. University of Toronto, Faculty of Medicine, 1893. Assistant Professor of Clinical Surgery, Faculty of Medicine, University of Manitoba; Surgeon, Winnipeg General Hospital.

LEHR, LOUIS C., A.B., M.D., 1737 H Street, Northwest, Washington, District of Columbia. Johns Hopkins University, Medical Department, 1902. Professor of Genito-Urinary Surgery, Georgetown University School of Medicine; Genito-Urinary Surgeon, Providence and Georgetown University Hospitals; Consulting Urologist, Washington Asylum Hospital.

LEIGH, SOUTHGATE, M.D., 109 College Place, Norfolk, Virginia. University of Virginia, Department of Medicine, 1888; Columbia University, College of Physicians and Surgeons, 1889. Visiting Surgeon and Gynecologist, Sarah Leigh Hospital and Clinic; Chief Surgeon, Virginian Railroad.

LEIGHTON, CHARLES MILTON, A.B., M.D., 14 Deering Street, Portland, Maine. Bowdoin Medical School (Medical School of Maine), 1897. Surgeon, Maine General Hospital.

LEIGHTON, WILLIAM ELSTON, A.B., M.D., 305 Lister Building, St. Louis, Missouri. Harvard Medical School, 1900. Professor of Surgery, St. Louis University School of Medicine; Visiting Surgeon, St. Louis City and Barnard Free Skin and Cancer Hospitals.

LELAND, GEORGE ADAMS, A.M., M.D., 354 Commonwealth Avenue, Boston, Massachusetts. Harvard Medical School, 1878. Emeritus Professor of Oto-Laryngology, Dartmouth Medical College; Senior Surgeon, Diseases of the Ear and Throat, Boston City Hospital; Consulting Laryngologist and Rhinologist, New England Hospital for Women and Children.

LELAND, JOSEPH, A.B., Ph.G., M.D., 603 First National Bank Building, Birmingham, Alabama. Tulane University of Louisiana School of Medicine, 1904. Surgeon, Hillman Hospital.

LEMERE, HENRY BASSETT, M.D., 400 Brandeis Theatre Building, Omaha, Nebraska. University of Nebraska College of Medicine, 1898. Instructor in Otology, University of Nebraska College of Medicine; Member of Staff, Wise Memorial Hospital; Otologist, University Hospital.

LENHART, CARL H., Ph.B., M.D., 2417 Prospect Avenue, Cleveland, Ohio. Western Reserve University School of Medicine, 1904. Associate in Surgery, Western Reserve University School of Medicine; Visiting Surgeon, Cleveland City Hospital, University Clinic; Director, Surgical Division and Head of Department, General Surgery, St. Luke's Hospital.

LENKER, JOHN NICHOLAS, M.D., 314 Osborn Building, Cleveland, Ohio. University of Maryland School of Medicine (College of Physicians and Surgeons, Baltimore), 1886. Oto-Laryngologist, St. Luke's and Fairview Hospitals.

LENNIE, THEODORE HOURSTON, M.D., C.M., 736 Granville Street, Vancouver, British Columbia. McGill University Faculty of Medicine, 1914.

LENONT, CHARLES B., M.D., Lenont Hospital, Virginia, Minnesota. University of Minnesota Medical School, 1899. Director, Lenont Hospital.

LENT, EDWIN J., M.D., C.M., 122 North Lafayette Street, South Bend, Indiana. Queen's University, Faculty of Medicine, 1892. Ophthalmologist and Oto-Laryngologist, Epworth and St. Joseph's Hospitals.

LEONARD, CHARLES WILLIAM, M.D., 72 South Main Street, Fond du Lac, Wisconsin. Rush Medical College, 1900. Surgeon, St. Agnes' Hospital.

LEONARD, FRANCIS GEORGE, M.D., 9300 Kinsman Road, Cleveland, Ohio. Ohio State University College of Medicine (Starling-Ohio Medical College), 1910. Visiting Surgeon, St. Alexis Hospital.

LEONARD, VEADER NEWTON, Ph.B., M.D., 25 Tenth Avenue, East, Duluth, Minnesota. Johns Hopkins University, Medical Department, 1911.

LEOPOLD, HERBERT P., A.M., M.D., 2104 Chestnut Street, Philadelphia, Pennsylvania. Hahnemann Medical College and Hospital, Philadelphia, 1896. Clinical Professor of Surgery and Senior Surgeon, Hahnemann Medical College and Hospital; Chief Surgeon, Children's Homeopathic Hospital, Philadelphia; Visiting Surgeon, Homeopathic State Hospital, Allentown; Consulting Surgeon, Coatesville Hospital, Coatesville, Homeopathic Hospital, Pottstown, Pennsylvania, West Jersey Homeopathic Hospital, Camden, New Jersey.

LERCHE, WILLIAM, M.D., Lowry Building, St. Paul, Minnesota. University of Illinois College of Medicine (College of Physicians and Surgeons, Chicago), 1897.

LeSEURE, OSCAR, M.D., Parkston, New York. University of Michigan Medical School, 1873; University and Bellevue Hospital Medical College, 1874. Retired.

LESPINASSE, VICTOR D., M.D., 7 West Madison Street, Chicago, Illinois. Northwestern University Medical School, 1901. Associate Professor of Genito-Urinary Surgery, Northwestern University Medical School; Urologist, Wesley Memorial and Mercy Hospitals.

LESTER, FREDERICK W., M.D., 15 Cayuga Street, Seneca Falls, New York. Columbia University College of Physicians and Surgeons, 1894. Member of Associate Staff, Geneva City Hospital, Geneva.

LESTER, JOHN CREGO, A.M., M.D., 616 Madison Avenue, New York, New York. Long Island College Hospital, 1879. Assistant Surgeon, New York Eye and Ear Infirmary.

LESTER, SIDNEY M., M.D., 402 Carter Building, Houston, Texas. Barnes Medical College, 1898. Visiting Surgeon, Baptist and Municipal Hospitals.

LEVERING, GUY PERCIVAL, M.D., 616 Columbia Street, La Fayette, Indiana. University of Pennsylvania School of Medicine, 1899. Member of Surgical Staff, St. Elizabeth's Hospital; Member of Obstetrical Staff, Home Hospital.

LEVIN, SIMON, M.D., Lake Linden, Michigan. University of Michigan Medical School, 1901. Visiting Surgeon, Lake Superior General Hospital; Surgeon, Calumet and Hecla Hospital, Calumet.

LEVINE, EDGAR CLARENCE, M.D., C.M., 271 Bishop Street, Montreal, Quebec. Faculty of Medicine, McGill University, 1913. Demonstrator of Surgery and Clinical Surgery, Faculty of Medicine, McGill University; Associate Surgeon, Royal Victoria Hospital.

LEVISON, CHARLES GABRIEL, M.D., 870 Market Street, San Francisco, California. Cooper Medical College, 1889. Surgeon-in-Chief, Mt. Zion Hospital.

LEVY, LOUIS, M.D., 526 Bank of Commerce Building, Memphis, Tennessee. University of Tennessee College of Medicine, 1910. Associate Professor of Rhinology and Oto-Laryngology, University of Tennessee College of Medicine; Attending Rhinologist and Oto-Laryngologist, Gartly-Ramsey

Hospital, Shelby County Home for Aged and Infirm, Porter Home and Leath Orphanage, Home for Incurables, Convent of the Good Shepherd, Crippled Children's Hospital; Associate Attending Rhinologist and Oto-Laryngologist, Memphis General and Baptist Hospitals.

LEVY, ROBERT, M.D., 406 Metropolitan Building, Denver, Colorado. University and Bellevue Hospital Medical College, 1884. Professor of Oto-Laryngology, University of Colorado School of Medicine; Oto-Laryngologist, St. Luke's and St. Joseph's Hospitals; Consulting Oto-Laryngologist, National Jewish Hospital for Consumptives, Children's, St. Anthony's, and City and County Hospitals.

LEWIS, ARCHIBALD CARY, M.D., 1224 Exchange Building, Memphis, Tennessee. George Washington University Medical School, 1905. Instructor in Ophthalmology, University of Tennessee College of Medicine; Ophthalmologist, Memphis General and Baptist Memorial Hospitals.

LEWIS, BRANSFORD, B.Sc., M.D., 550 Century Building, St. Louis, Missouri. Washington University Medical School (Missouri Medical College), 1884. Professor of Genito-Urinary Surgery, St. Louis University School of Medicine; Genito-Urinary Surgeon, St. John's and Frisco Employes' Hospitals.

LEWIS, DEAN, A.B., M.D., D.Sc., 122 South Michigan Avenue, Chicago, Illinois. Rush Medical College, 1899. Professor of Surgery, Rush Medical College; Attending Surgeon, Presbyterian Hospital; Consulting Surgeon, Annie W. Durand Hospital of the Memorial Institute for Infectious Diseases.

LEWIS, ERNEST SIDNEY, B.Sc., M.D., 1625 Louisiana Avenue, New Orleans, Louisiana. Tulane University of Louisiana School of Medicine, 1862. Emeritus Professor of Obstetrics and Gynecology, Tulane University of Louisiana School of Medicine; Consulting Gynecologist, Charity Hospital.

LEWIS, EUGENE RICHARDS, M.D., 1920 Orange Street, Los Angeles, California. University of Pennsylvania School of Medicine, 1899.

LEWIS, F. PARK, M.D., 454 Franklin Street, Buffalo, New York. Ohio State University College of Homeopathic Medicine (Pulte Medical College), 1876. Ophthalmic Surgeon, Buffalo Homeopathic Hospital; Oculist, Buffalo State Hospital; Consulting Ophthalmologist, Buffalo City, Erie County Hospitals, Buffalo, J. N. Adam Memorial Hospital, Perrysburg.

LEWIS, FIELDING O., M.D., 259 South Seventeenth Street, Philadelphia, Pennsylvania. Jefferson Medical College, 1906. Associate Professor of Laryngology, Jefferson Medical College; Assistant Laryngologist, Jefferson Medical College Hospital; Laryngologist, Philadelphia General Hospital; Consulting Laryngologist, Hospital for Contagious Diseases.

LEWIS, FREDERICK A., M.D., 16 William Street, Auburn, New York. University and Bellevue Hospital Medical College, 1891. Ophthalmologist and Otologist, Auburn City Hospital.

LEWIS, G. GRIFFIN, M.D., 600 University Block, Syracuse, New York. Albany Medical College, 1890. Oculist, Aurist, and Laryngologist, St. Mary's

Maternity Hospital; Oculist, Crouse-Irving Hospital, St. Vincent's Orphan Asylum.

LEWIS, GEORGE H., M.D., 2073 East Ninth Street, Cleveland, Ohio. University of Michigan Medical School, 1905. Associate Surgeon, Huron Road Hospital.

LEWIS, JAMES HOYT, A.B., M.D., 135 Linwood Avenue, Buffalo, New York. Columbia University, College of Physicians and Surgeons, 1901. Instructor in Surgery, University of Buffalo, Department of Medicine; Attending Surgeon, Buffalo City and Erie County Hospitals, Buffalo, Moses Taylor Hospital, Lackawanna.

LEWIS, JOSEPH D., A.M., M.D., 516 La Salle Building, Minneapolis, Minnesota. Cleveland Medical College, 1893. Surgeon-in-Chief, Eye, Ear, Nose, and Throat Department, Minneapolis General Hospital; Consulting Ophthalmologist and Oto-Laryngologist, Hopewell and Lymanhurst Hospitals.

LEWIS, ROBERT, M.D., 48 West Fortieth Street, New York, New York. Columbia University, College of Physicians and Surgeons, 1885. Professor of Clinical Oto-Laryngology, Columbia University, College of Physicians and Surgeons; Aural Surgeon, New York Eye and Ear Infirmary; Consulting Aurist, Hospital for the Ruptured and Crippled, St. Francis' Hospital, New York, Flushing Hospital, Flushing, Sea View Hospital, Castleton Corners.

LEWIS, ROBERT M., B.A., M.D., 1418 Eutaw Place, Baltimore, Maryland. University of Pennsylvania School of Medicine, 1910. Member of Staff, Church Home and Infirmary, Howard A. Kelly Hospital; Surgical Consultant, Cambridge Hospital, Cambridge.

LEWIS, WILLIAM W., M.D., 836 Lowry Building, St. Paul, Minnesota. University of Minnesota Medical School, 1902. Instructor, University of Minnesota Medical School; Ophthalmologist, City and County, Charles T. Miller, St. Luke's and St. Joseph's Hospitals.

LEWISOHN, RICHARD, M.D., 1155 Park Avenue, New York, New York. University of Freiburg, 1899. Attending Surgeon, Beth Israel Hospital; Associate Attending Surgeon, Mt. Sinai Hospital.

LEWY, ALFRED, M.D., 110 North Wabash Avenue, Chicago, Illinois. Hahnemann Medical College and Hospital (Chicago Homeopathic Medical College), 1897; Rush Medical College, 1898. Professor of Otology, Hahnemann Medical College and Hospital; Attending Otologist, Hahnemann Hospital; Ear Surgeon, Illinois Charitable Eye and Ear Infirmary; Consulting Laryngologist and Otologist, Chicago Home for the Friendless; Consulting Otologist, Chicago Daily News Fresh Air Fund Sanitarium.

LEYS, JAMES F., M.D., Medical Corps, United States Navy, Washington, District of Columbia. University of Pennsylvania School of Medicine, 1890. Captain, Medical Corps, United States Navy.

LIBBY, EDWARD MARINER, M.D., Iron River Hospital, Iron River, Michigan. Rush Medical College, 1898. Surgeon, Iron River Hospital.

LICHTENBERG, JOSEPH STANLY, M.D., Rialto Building, Kansas City, Missouri. University Medical College, 1896. Ophthalmologist, St. Joseph's and Kansas City General Hospitals, Alfred Benjamin Dispensary.

LIKES, SYLVAN H., M.D., 1134 Linden Avenue, Baltimore, Maryland. University of Maryland School of Medicine (College of Physicians and Surgeons, Baltimore), 1893. Visiting Dermatologist, Hebrew Hospital.

LILIENTHAL, HOWARD, A.B., M.D., 52 East Eighty-second Street, New York, New York. Harvard Medical School, 1887. Attending Surgeon, Mt. Sinai Hospital; Visiting Surgeon, Bellevue Hospital.

LILLIE, HAROLD I., A.B., M.D., Mayo Clinic, Rochester, Minnesota. University of Michigan Medical School, 1912. Medical Director and Chief of Ear, Nose, and Throat Department, Worrell Hospital.

LINCOLN, WILLIAM A., M.D., C.M., F.R.C.S. (Eng.), 515 Herald Block, Calgary, Alberta. Faculty of Medicine, McGill University, 1904. Surgeon, Calgary General and Holy Cross Hospitals.

LINDEMAN, HOWARD EDWARD, M.D., 102 West Seventy-fifth Street, New York, New York. Columbia University, College of Physicians and Surgeons, 1906. Adjunct Attending Gynecologist and Chief of Gynecological Clinic, Mt. Sinai Hospital.

LINDENBERG, HENRIQUE, M.D., 16 Rua Stambé, Sao Paulo, Brazil. University of Pennsylvania School of Medicine, 1909. Professor of Oto-Laryngology, Faculty of Medicine University of Sao Paulo.

LINDER, JOHN, M.D., 1780 St. John's Place, Brooklyn, New York. University and Bellevue Hospital Medical College, 1904. Attending Surgeon, Jewish Hospital.

LINDER, WILLIAM, M.D., 889 St. Mark's Avenue, Brooklyn, New York. University and Bellevue Hospital Medical College, 1896. Attending Surgeon, Jewish Hospital; Consulting Gynecologist, Rockaway Beach Hospital, Rockaway Beach.

LINN, ELLIS GREGG, M.D., Fleming Building, Des Moines, Iowa. Hahnemann Medical College and Hospital, Chicago, 1889. Oculist and Aurist, Iowa Congregational Hospital, and Des Moines Home for Friendless Children.

LINTHICUM, G. MILTON, A.M., M.D., 817 Park Avenue, Baltimore, Maryland. University of Maryland School of Medicine (College of Physicians and Surgeons, Baltimore), 1893. Professor of Diseases of the Colon and Rectum, University of Maryland School of Medicine and College of Physicians and Surgeons; Proctologist, University and Maryland General Hospitals; Surgeon, Maryland General Hospital, Church Home and Infirmary; Consultant, Hospitals for Consumptives of Maryland.

LIPPOLD, WILLIAM EDWARD, M.D., 221 St. Nicholas Avenue, Brooklyn, New York. Long Island College Hospital, 1905. Associate Surgeon, Williamsburgh Hospital; Attending Surgeon, Ridgewood Sanitarium; Visiting Surgeon, German Evangelical Home for the Aged.

LIRA, EUGENIO DIAZ, B.A., M.D., Agustinas 1270, Santiago, Chile. Faculty of Medicine, University of Chile, 1904.

LITTIG, JOHN VINCENT, M.D., 211 Central Office Building, Davenport, Iowa. Rush Medical College, 1901. Member of Staff, St. Luke's and Mercy Hospitals; Oculist and Oto-Laryngologist, Iowa Soldiers' Orphans' Home.

LITTLE, ALEXANDER GRAHAM, B.Sc., M.D., 134½ North Patterson Street, Valdosta, Georgia. University and Bellevue Hospital Medical College (Bellevue Hospital Medical College), 1898. Chief Surgeon, Little-Griffin Private Hospital.

LITTLE, ARTHUR D. H., Ph.M., M.D., 203 Masonic Building, Thomasville, Georgia. Tulane University of Louisiana School of Medicine, 1908. Member of Surgical Staff, City Hospital.

LITTLE, FREDERICK HENRY, M.D., 108 West Fifth Street, Muscatine, Iowa. State University of Iowa College of Medicine, 1879. Member of Surgical Staff, Benjamin Hershey Memorial Hospital.

LITTLE, HERBERT MELVILLE, B.A., M.D., C.M., 285 Stanley Street, Montreal, Quebec. Faculty of Medicine, McGill University, 1901. Assistant Professor of Obstetrics and Lecturer on Gynecology, Faculty of Medicine, McGill University; Associate Gynecologist, Montreal General Hospital; Obstetrician, Montreal Maternity Hospital.

LITTLE, JOHN MASON, A.B., M.D., 374 Marlborough Street, Boston, Massachusetts. Harvard Medical School, 1901. Assistant Surgeon, Long Island Hospital; Assistant Medical Director, New England Mutual Life Insurance Company.

LITZENBERG, JENNINGS CRAWFORD, B.Sc., M.D., 1009 Nicollet Avenue, Minneapolis, Minnesota. University of Minnesota Medical School, 1899. Professor of Obstetrics and Gynecology, and Chief of Department, University of Minnesota Medical School; Chief of Staff, Out-Patient Department, University Hospital; Obstetrician and Gynecologist, University, Northwestern, and St. Mary's Hospitals.

LIVERMORE, GEORGE ROBERTSON, M.D., Exchange Building, Memphis, Tennessee. University of Virginia, Department of Medicine, 1899. Professor of Genito-Urinary Surgery, University of Tennessee College of Medicine; Genito-Urinary Surgeon, Memphis General and Baptist Memorial Hospitals.

LIVINGSTON, WILLIAM REINHARDT, M.D., 426 B Street, Oxnard, California. University of Illinois College of Medicine (College of Physicians and Surgeons, Chicago), 1893. Surgeon, St. John's Hospital.

LLOYD, RALPH IRVING, M.D., 450 Ninth Street, Brooklyn, New York. New York Homeopathic Medical College and Flower Hospital, 1896. Surgeon, New York Ophthalmic Hospital, New York; Oculist and Aurist, Carson C. Peck Memorial and Cumberland Street Hospitals, Brooklyn Nursery and Infants' Hospital, Prospect Heights Hospital and Brooklyn Maternity.

LLOYD, SAMUEL, B.Sc., M.D., 50 East Forty-second Street, New York, New York. University of Vermont College of Medicine, 1884; Columbia University, College of Physicians and Surgeons, 1885. Emeritus Professor of Surgery, New York Post-Graduate Medical School; Attending Surgeon, Lutheran Hospital; Consulting Surgeon, New York Post-Graduate, St. Francis, and Italian Hospitals, New York, Benedictine Sanitarium and Hospital, Kingston, United Hospital, Port Chester, St. Francis Hospital, Poughkeepsie, New York, St. Mary's Hospital, Orange, New Jersey.

LOBDELL, EFFIE LEOLA, M.D., 802 Marshall Field Building, Chicago, Illinois. Indiana University School of Medicine (Fort Wayne College of Medicine), 1891. Instructor in Gynecology, Illinois Post-Graduate Medical School; Consultant in Gynecology, Municipal Tuberculosis Sanitarium; Surgeon, Mary Thompson Hospital for Women and Children.

LOBENSTINE, RALPH WALDO, A.B., M.D., 162 East Seventy-first Street, New York, New York. Columbia University, College of Physicians and Surgeons, 1900.

LOBINGIER, ANDREW STEWART, A.B., M.D., 710 Merritt Building, Los Angeles, California. University of Michigan Medical School, 1889.

LOCKARD, LORENZO B., M.D., 920 Metropolitan Building, Denver, Colorado. University of Pennsylvania School of Medicine, 1894. Laryngologist, Children's Hospital.

LOCKE, LOUIE WARD, M.D., 288 Genesee Street, Utica, New York. University and Bellevue Hospital Medical College, 1905. Surgeon, Faxton Hospital.

LOCKE, MELVIN, M.D., Bellefonte, Pennsylvania. Hahnemann Medical College and Hospital, Philadelphia, 1891. Surgeon-in-Chief, Bellefonte Hospital, Bellefonte; Consulting Surgeon, Lock Haven Hospital, Lock Haven; Abdominal Surgeon, Glenn Hospital, State College.

LOCKETT, EVERETT A., B.Sc., M.D., O'Hanlon Building, Winston-Salem, North Carolina. University of Pennsylvania School of Medicine, 1902. Member of Surgical Staff, City Hospital.

LOCKETT, GEORGE VERNON, M.B., C.M., F.R.C.S. (Eng.), 3 Bedford Avenue, Kingston, Jamaica. University of Edinburgh, 1890. Honorary Consulting Surgeon, Public Hospital.

LOCKHART, FREDERICK A. LAWTON, M.B., M.D., C.M., 38 Bishop Street, Montreal, Quebec. University of Edinburgh, 1889. Clinical Professor of Gynecology, Faculty of Medicine, McGill University; Gynecologist, Montreal General Hospital, Montreal, Protestant Hospital for Insane, Verdun.

LOCKREY, SARAH H., M.D., 1701 Chestnut Street, Philadelphia, Pennsylvania. Woman's Medical College of Pennsylvania, 1888. Gynecologist, Woman's Hospital; Surgeon, West Philadelphia Hospital for Women.

LOCKWOOD, AMBROSE LORNE, M.D., C.M., Mayo Clinic, Rochester, Minnesota. Faculty of Medicine, McGill University, 1910. Member of Surgical Staff, Mayo Clinic.

LOCKWOOD, CHARLES D., A.B., M.D., 295 Markham Place, Pasadena, California. Northwestern University Medical School, 1896. Attending Surgeon, Pasadena Hospital.

LODER, HALSEY BEACH, B.Sc., M.D., 520 Commonwealth Avenue, Boston, Massachusetts. Dartmouth Medical School, 1908. Instructor in Surgery, Harvard Medical School; Assistant Visiting Surgeon, Boston City Hospital; Consulting Surgeon, Charles Choate Memorial Hospital, Woburn, Leonard Morse Hospital, Natick.

LOE, ADOLPH O., M.D., 211 Cobb Building, Seattle, Washington. University of Minnesota Medical School, 1897. Chief Surgeon and Chief of Staff, Seattle City Hospital.

LOEB, HANAU W., A.M., M.D., 537 North Grand Avenue, St. Louis, Missouri. Columbia University, College of Physicians and Surgeons, 1888. Dean, Professor, and Director of Department of Ear, Nose, and Throat Diseases, St. Louis University School of Medicine; Laryngologist and Otologist, St. Louis City and Jewish Hospitals. Editor, *Annals of Otology, Laryngology and Rhinology*.

LOEB, VIRGIL, A.B., D.D.S., M.D., 537 North Grand Avenue, St. Louis, Missouri. St. Louis University School of Medicine, 1906. Instructor in Oral Surgery, St. Louis University School of Medicine; Professor of Oral Surgery, St. Louis Dental College; Member of Staff, St. Louis City Hospital, Jewish Home for Chronic Invalids.

LOGAN, JAMES ELMORE, M.D., 1208 Wyandotte Street, Kansas City, Missouri. University Medical College, Kansas City, 1883; University and Bellevue Hospital Medical College, 1884.

LOGAN, WILLIAM H. G., D.D.S., M.D., 29 East Madison Street, Chicago, Illinois. Loyola University School of Medicine (Chicago College of Medicine and Surgery), 1904. Dean of Faculty, Professor of Oral Surgery, Chicago College of Dental Surgery.

LOIZEAUX, LEON SAMUEL, M.D., 68 East Eighty-sixth Street, New York, New York. Hahnemann Medical College and Hospital, Chicago, 1904. Professor of Obstetrics, New York Homeopathic Medical College and Flower Hospital; Attending Obstetrician, Fifth Avenue, New York Homeopathic Medical College and Flower Hospitals; Chief of Maternity Clinic, Flower Hospital Dispensary.

LOKEY, HUGH M., M.D., 413 Candler Building, Atlanta, Georgia. Emory University School of Medicine (Atlanta College of Physicians and Surgeons), 1900. Ophthalmologist and Oto-Laryngologist, Wesley Memorial Hospital and Piedmont Sanatorium.

LONG, FRANCIS A., M.D., Madison, Nebraska. State University of Iowa College of Medicine, 1882. Member of Staff, Norfolk General Hospital, Norfolk; Surgeon, Union Pacific Railroad.

LONG, HENRY F., M.D., 834 North Center Street, Statesville, North Carolina. University of Maryland School of Medicine, 1892. Surgeon, Dr. H. F. Long's Private Sanatorium.

Long, John Hathaway, A.B., M.D., 110 Gates Avenue, Brooklyn, New York. Long Island College Hospital, 1903. Associate Surgeon, Brooklyn Hospital; Consulting Surgeon, Hospital of St. Giles the Cripple.

Long, John Wesley, M.D., 338 North Elm Street, Greensboro, North Carolina. Vanderbilt University, Medical Department, 1883; University of Nashville, Medical Department, 1884; New York Polyclinic Medical School, 1888. Emeritus Professor of Gynecology and Pediatrics, Medical College of Virginia; Surgeon-in-Chief, Wesley Long Hospital.

Long, LeRoy, M.D., Colcord Building, Oklahoma, Oklahoma. University of Louisville, Medical Department (Louisville Medical College), 1893. Dean and Professor of Surgery, University of Oklahoma School of Medicine.

Longabaugh, Rudolph I., M.D., Medical Corps, United States Navy, Washington, District of Columbia. University of California Medical School, 1903. Lieutenant Commander, Medical Corps, United States Navy.

Longeway, Albert Forrest, M.D., C.M., 505 Third Avenue, North, Great Falls, Montana. Faculty of Medicine, McGill University (University of Bishop College, Faculty of Medicine), 1886. Surgeon, Columbus Hospital.

Loop, Ross George, M.D., 359 Main Street, Elmira, New York. University of Buffalo, Department of Medicine, 1897. Attending Surgeon, Arnot-Ogden Memorial Hospital; Consulting Surgeon, People's Coöperative Hospital, Sayre, Pennsylvania.

Lord, John Prentiss, M.D., 830 City National Bank Building, Omaha, Nebraska. Rush Medical College, 1882. Professor of Orthopedic Surgery, University of Nebraska College of Medicine; Attending Orthopedic Surgeon, University, Bishop Clarkson Memorial, and Methodist Hospitals.

Loree, Ira Dean, M.D., 122 North Thayer Street, Ann Arbor, Michigan. University of Michigan Medical School, 1901. Member of Surgical Staff, St. Joseph Sanitarium.

Loring, Francis B., M.D., 1420 K Street, Northwest, Washington, District of Columbia. Harvard Medical School, 1874. Consulting Ophthalmic and Oral Surgeon, St. Ann's Infant Asylum; Ophthalmic and Aural Surgeon, Baltimore and Ohio Railroad.

Loring, J. Brown, M.D., C.M., M.R.C.S. (Eng.), 25 East Washington Street, Chicago, Illinois. Faculty of Medicine, McGill University, 1883. Assistant Professor of Clinical Ophthalmology, University of Illinois College of Medicine; Assistant Surgeon, Eye Department, University Hospital; Attending Surgeon, Eye Department, West Side Free Dispensary.

Loring, S. C., M.D., Richard Block, Plymouth, Indiana. Rush Medical College, 1886.

Lothrop, Earl Perkins, A.B., M.D., 153 Delaware Avenue, Buffalo, New York. University of Buffalo, Department of Medicine (Niagara University, Medical Department), 1894. Surgeon, Buffalo Woman's Hospital, Buffalo, J. N. Adam Memorial Hospital, Perrysburg; Consulting Surgeon, Columbus and Homeopathic Hospitals.

LOTHROP, HOWARD AUGUSTUS, A.M., M.D., 101 Beacon Street, Boston, Massachusetts. Harvard Medical School, 1890. Assistant Professor of Surgery, Harvard Medical School; Surgeon-in-Chief, Boston City Hospital; Consulting Surgeon, Symmes Arlington Hospital.

LOTT, MARK E., B.Sc., B.L., M.D., 414 Wilson Building, Dallas, Texas. University of Texas, Medical Department, 1904. Member of Staff, Texas Baptist Memorial Sanitarium; Chief Surgeon, Missouri, Kansas and Texas Railway Employes' Hospital Association.

LOUNSBURY, BENJAMIN FRANKLIN, M.D., 2449 Washington Boulevard, Chicago, Illinois. Northwestern University Medical School, 1907. Assistant Professor of Operative Surgery, University of Illinois College of Medicine; Chief Surgeon, Washington Boulevard Hospital.

LOUX, HIRAM R., M.D., Medical Arts Building, Philadelphia, Pennsylvania. Jefferson Medical College, 1882. Professor of Genito-Urinary Surgery, Jefferson Medical College; Attending Genito-Urinary Surgeon, Jefferson Medical College Hospital; Surgeon, Philadelphia General Hospital.

LOVE, ALBERT G., A.B., M.D., Medical Corps, United States Army, Washington, District of Columbia. University of Tennessee College of Medicine (Memphis Hospital Medical College), 1904. Major, Medical Corps, United States Army.

LOVELAND, JOHN E., A.B., M.D., 93 Broad Street, Middletown, Connecticut. Harvard Medical School, 1893. Member of Surgical Staff, Middlesex Hospital.

LOVETT, ROBERT WILLIAMSON, A.B., M.D., 234 Marlborough Street, Boston, Massachusetts. Harvard Medical School, 1885. John B. and Buckminster Brown Professor of Orthopedic Surgery, Harvard Medical School; Surgeon, Children's Hospital, Peabody Home for Crippled Children; Surgeon-in-Chief, Massachusetts Hospital School for Crippled and Deformed Children, Canton.

LOWER, WILLIAM E., M.D., Clinic Building, Cleveland, Ohio. Western Reserve University School of Medicine (University of Wooster, Medical Department), 1891. Associate Professor of Genito-Urinary Surgery, Western Reserve University School of Medicine; Director of Surgery, Mt. Sinai Hospital; Associate Surgeon, Lakeside Hospital; Attending Surgeon, Lutheran Hospital.

LOWMAN, JOHN BODINE, M.D., 116 Market Street, Johnstown, Pennsylvania. Jefferson Medical College, 1895. Chief Surgeon, Cambria Hospital; Surgeon, Conemaugh Valley Memorial Hospital.

LOWMAN, RICHARD C., M.D., 218 Portsmouth Building, Kansas City, Kansas. University of Kansas School of Medicine (Kansas City Medical College), 1890. Attending Surgeon, St. Margaret's Hospital.

LOWNDES, CHARLES H. T., M.D., Medical Corps, United States Navy, Washington, District of Columbia. University of Maryland School of Medicine, 1888. Captain, Medical Corps, United States Navy.

LOWSLEY, OSWALD SWINNEY, A.B., M.D., 853 Seventh Avenue, New York, New York. Johns Hopkins University, Medical Department, 1912. Instructor in Urology, University and Bellevue Hospital Medical College; Acting Assistant Visiting Surgeon, Department of Urology, Bellevue Hospital; Director of Department of Urology, James Buchanan Brady Foundation, New York Hospital; Consulting Urologist, Hospital for Ruptured and Crippled; Consulting Surgeon, Panama Railroad and Steamship Company.

LUCID, MICHAEL MILTON, M.D., University Building, Syracuse, New York. Syracuse University College of Medicine, 1896. Surgeon-in-Chief, Homer Hospital, Homer; Surgeon, Children's Home, Cortland, Lackawanna Railroad.

LUCKETT, WILLIAM HENRY, B.Sc.A., M.D., 18 West Eighty-seventh Street, New York, New York. Columbia University, College of Physicians and Surgeons, 1894. Professor of Clinical Surgery, University and Bellevue Hospital Medical College; Attending Surgeon, Bellevue and Allied Hospitals, Harlem Division, Lutheran Hospital.

LUDLOW, ALFRED IRVING, A.B., M.D., Severance Union Medical College, Seoul, Chosen, Korea. Western Reserve University School of Medicine, 1901. Professor of Surgery, Severance Union Medical College; Surgeon-in-Chief, Severance Hospital.

LUEDDE, WILLIAM HENRY, M.D., 311 Metropolitan Building, St. Louis, Missouri. Washington University Medical School, 1900. Ophthalmologist, St. Mary's Infirmary, Missouri Baptist Sanitarium; Consultant in Ophthalmology, St. John's Hospital, United States Public Health Service Hospital No. 35.

LUHN, HENRY B., M.D., Spokane and Eastern Trust Building, Spokane, Washington. University of Pennsylvania School of Medicine, 1891. Surgeon, Sacred Heart Hospital.

LUKENS, CHARLES B., ès L., M.D., 218 Michigan Street, Toledo, Ohio. Ohio State University College of Medicine (Starling Medical College), 1892. Ophthalmologist and Oto-Rhinologist, Flower Hospital.

LUKENS, ISAIAH, M.D., Tekamah, Nebraska. Jefferson Medical College, 1890. Senior Surgeon, Fraternity Hospital.

LUM, CLARENCE EDWARD, M.D., 304 Providence Building, Duluth, Minnesota. University of Minnesota Medical School (Minnesota Hospital College), 1886.

LUMPKIN, ABRAM F., M.D., Smith Building, Amarillo, Texas. University of Texas, Medical Department, 1896. President of Staff and Attending Surgeon, St. Anthony's Sanitarium.

LUMPKIN, JAMES C., M.D., 818 Park Avenue, Baltimore, Maryland. University of Maryland School of Medicine (Baltimore Medical College), 1898. Professor of Clinical Surgery, University of Maryland School of Medicine and College of Physicians and Surgeons; Chief Surgeon, Maryland General Hospital.

LUND, FRED BATES, A.M., M.D., 529 Beacon Street, Boston, Massachusetts. Harvard Medical School, 1892. Associate in Surgery, Harvard Medical School; Surgeon-in-Chief, Boston City Hospital; Consulting Surgeon, City Hospital, Quincy, Burbank Hospital, Fitchburg, Josiah B. Thomas Hospital, Peabody, Charles Choate Memorial Hospital, Woburn, Newton Hospital, Newton, Massachusetts, Rockingham Hospital, Bellows Falls, Vermont.

LUSK, WILLIAM CHITTENDEN, A.B., M.D., 47 East Thirty-fourth Street, New York, New York. University and Bellevue Hospital Medical College (Bellevue Hospital Medical College), 1893. Professor of Clinical Surgery, University and Bellevue Hospital Medical College; Assistant Visiting Surgeon, Bellevue Hospital; Consulting Surgeon, St. Vincent's and Manhattan State Hospitals.

LUTTON, GEORGE W., M.D., 51 East Seventy-eighth Street, New York, New York. New York Homeopathic Medical College and Flower Hospital, 1906. Assistant Professor of Surgery, New York Homeopathic Medical College and Flower Hospital; Clinical Assistant in Surgery and Attending Surgeon, New York Homeopathic Medical College and Flower Hospital; Assistant Attending Surgeon, Broad Street Hospital.

LYLE, HENRY HAMILTON MOORE, M.D., 117 East Fifty-sixth Street, New York, New York. Columbia University, College of Physicians and Surgeons, 1900. Assistant Professor of Surgery, Cornell University Medical College; Attending Surgeon, New York Skin and Cancer Hospital.

LYLE, SAMUEL HARLEY, M.D., Franklin, North Carolina. University of Nashville, Medical Department, 1883; Vanderbilt University, Medical Department, 1893. Chief of Staff, Lyle's Hospital.

LYLE, WILLIAM CLIFTON, M.D., Candler Building, Atlanta, Georgia. University of Georgia, Medical Department, 1893. Consulting Ophthalmologist, Otologist, and Laryngologist, Public Health Hospital.

LYMAN, CHARLES BALDWIN, M.D., Metropolitan Building, Denver, Colorado. Harvard Medical School, 1886. Professor of Surgery, University of Colorado School of Medicine; Visiting Surgeon, St. Joseph's, Children's, and Denver City and County Hospitals.

LYMAN, FRANCIS ROMEYN, M.D., 600 Broadway, Hastings-on-Hudson, New York. University and Bellevue Hospital Medical College (Medical Department of New York University), 1893. Surgeon, Dobbs Ferry Hospital, Dobbs Ferry.

LYMAN, JOHN CUSHMAN, B.Sc., M.D., 217 Baker Building, Walla Walla, Washington. Johns Hopkins University Medical Department, 1913. Consulting Surgeon, United States Public Health Hospital.

LYMAN, JOHN VAN REED, M.D., Opera House Block, Eau Claire, Wisconsin. Rush Medical College, 1880. Surgeon, Sacred Heart Hospital.

LYNCH, ALBERT, B.Sc., M.D., 612 Fifth Street, Fairbury, Nebraska. University of Michigan Medical School, 1901. Chief Surgeon, Fairbury Hospital.

LYNCH, ARTHUR LOUIS, M.D., C.M., F.R.C.S. (Edin.), 213 Canada Building, Saskatoon, Saskatchewan. Attending Surgeon, St. Paul's and Saskatoon City Hospitals.

LYNCH, CHARLES, M.D., Medical Corps, United States Army, Washington, District of Columbia. Syracuse University College of Medicine, 1891. Colonel, Medical Corps, United States Army.

LYNCH, CHARLES FRANCIS, M.D., 387 Main Street, Springfield, Massachusetts. University and Bellevue Hospital Medical College (New York University Medical College), 1897. Attending Surgeon, Mercy Hospital.

LYNCH, CORNELIUS J., M.D., 216 Miller Building, Yakima, Washington. University of Louisville, Medical Department (Kentucky School of Medicine), 1900.

LYNCH, FRANK WORTHINGTON, A.B., M.D., University of California Hospital, San Francisco, California. Johns Hopkins University, Medical Department, 1899. Professor of Obstetrics and Gynecology, University of California Medical School; Obstetrician and Gynecologist, University of California Hospital.

LYNCH, JEROME M., M.D., 205 East Sixty-first Street, New York, New York. Rush Medical College, 1895. Consulting Surgeon, Nassau Hospital, Mineola, St. Mary's Hospital, Hoboken, New Jersey; Surgeon, St. Bartholomew's Clinic and Hospital.

LYNCH, MATTHEW JOHN, B.Sc., M.D., 710 Physicians and Surgeons Building, Minneapolis, Minnesota. Rush Medical College, 1905. Gynecologist and Obstetrician, St. Mary's Hospital; Member Associate Surgical Staff, Minneapolis General Hospital.

LYNCH, ROBERT CLYDE, M.D., 634 Maison Blanche Building, New Orleans, Louisiana. Tulane University of Louisiana School of Medicine, 1903. Professor of Oto-Laryngology, Tulane University of Louisiana Post-Graduate School of Medicine; Surgeon in Charge, Ear, Nose, and Throat Department, Eye, Ear, Nose, and Throat Hospital.

LYNCH, WILLIAM F., A.B., M.D., 390 Main Street, Worcester, Massachusetts. Harvard Medical School, 1908. Assistant Surgeon, St. Vincent's Hospital.

LYNCH, WILLIAM WARREN, M.D., C.M., M.R.C.S. (Eng.), L.R.C.P. (Lond.), 17 Bank Street, Sherbrooke, Quebec. Faculty of Medicine, McGill University, 1898. Surgeon, Sherbrooke Hospital.

LYNN, FRANK S., M.D., 41 West Preston Street, Baltimore, Maryland. University of Maryland School of Medicine, 1907. Associate Professor of Surgery, University of Maryland School of Medicine and College of Physicians and Surgeons; Visiting Surgeon, University Hospital; Surgeon in Charge, University Hospital Dispensary.

LYON, HARTWELL NELLES, M.D., Humboldt Building, St. Louis, Missouri. Columbia University, College of Physicians and Surgeons, 1891.

LYONS, OLIVER, M.D., 266 Metropolitan Building, Denver, Colorado. University of Louisville, Medical Department (Kentucky University, Medical

Department), 1898. Lecturer on Genito-Urinary Surgery, University of Colorado School of Medicine; Genito-Urinary Surgeon, St. Luke's, St. Anthony's, St. Joseph's, and Denver City and County Hospitals.

LYONS, WILLIAM H. A., A.M., M.D., 788 Elm Street, Manchester, New Hampshire. Harvard Medical School, 1890. Surgeon and Obstetrician, Sacred Heart Hospital; Obstetrician, Asylum of Our Lady of Perpetual Help.

LYSTER, THEODORE CHARLES, Ph.B., M.D., 1920 Orange Street, Los Angeles, California. University of Michigan Medical School, 1899. Assistant Surgeon, Episcopal Eye, Ear, and Throat Hospital; Consultant, Eye, Ear, Nose, and Throat Service, Walter Reed General Hospital; Colonel, Medical Corps, United States Army, retired.

LYSTER, WILLIAM JOHN LeHUNTE, Ph.B., M.D., Medical Corps, United States Army, Washington, District of Columbia. Detroit College of Medicine and Surgery, 1894. Lieutenant Colonel, Medical Corps, United States Army.

LYTLE, CLAUDE CARL, M.D., 7 Schnirel Building, Geneva, New York. Syracuse University College of Medicine, 1900. Attending Surgeon, Geneva City Hospital.

MABEE, OLIVER RAYMOND, M.D., C.M., 419 Bloor Street, West, Toronto, Ontario. Faculty of Medicine, McGill University, 1906. Demonstrator of Clinical Surgery, University of Toronto, Faculty of Medicine; Surgeon, Toronto General Hospital.

MABIE, LOT DALBERT, M.D., 800 Minnesota Avenue, Kansas City, Kansas. University of Kansas School of Medicine (College of Physicians and Surgeons), 1897. Surgeon, Bethany Methodist Hospital; Visiting Surgeon, St. Margaret's Hospital.

MACDONALD, ALEXANDER W., M.D., 310 Fifth Avenue, Valley City, North Dakota. Loyola University School of Medicine (Bennett Medical College), 1897.

MACDONALD, DONALD JOHN, M.D., C.M., 168 South Street, Halifax, Nova Scotia. Faculty of Medicine, McGill University, 1897.

MACDONALD, HENRY KIRKWOOD, M.D., C.M., 317 Barrington Street, Halifax, Nova Scotia. Faculty of Medicine, McGill University, 1896. Professor of Clinical Surgery, Dalhousie University, Faculty of Medicine; Attending Surgeon, Victoria General Hospital.

MACDONALD, NEIL SUTHERLAND, M.D., 100 Hubbell Avenue, Houghton, Michigan. University of Michigan Medical School, 1895.

MACDONALD, ROBERT STEVENSON, Ph.B., M.D., 12 Brinckerhoff Street, Plattsburg, New York. Cornell University Medical College, 1902. Attending Surgeon, Champlain Valley Hospital; Consulting Surgeon, Alice Hyde Memorial Hospital, Malone, General Hospital, Saranac Lake, Clinton Prison Tuberculosis Hospital, Dannemora, St. Lawrence State Hospital, Ogdensburg.

MACDONALD, RONALD HUGH, M.D., C.M., Canada Building, Saskatoon, Saskatchewan. Faculty of Medicine, McGill University, 1908. Attending Surgeon, St. Paul's and Saskatoon City Hospitals.

MACDONALD, THOMAS LESLIE, M.D., 1501 Massachusetts Avenue, Northwest, Washington, District of Columbia. Hahnemann Medical College and Hospital, Philadelphia, 1888. Surgeon, National Homeopathic Hospital.

MACEDO, CARLOS MORALES, B.Sc., M.D., Mogollon 265, Lima, Peru. Faculty of Medicine, University of San Marcos, 1913. Professor of Applied Anatomy, Faculty of Medicine, University of San Marcos; Chief Surgeon, Guadalupe Hospital.

MacEVITT, JOHN COWELL, M.D., LL.D., 407 Clinton Street, Brooklyn, New York. State University of Iowa College of Medicine (College of Physicians and Surgeons, Keokuk), 1878. Chief of Department of Gynecology, St. Mary's Hospital; Consulting Gynecologist, Caledonian and Coney Island Hospitals, Brooklyn Eastern District Dispensary and Hospital, Brooklyn, St. Joseph's Hospital, Far Rockaway, Rockaway Beach Hospital, Rockaway Beach.

MACFADYEN, PAUL RUTHERFORD, M.D., 148 North Union Street, Concord, North Carolina. Medical College of Virginia (University College of Medicine), 1902. Surgeon in Charge, Concord City Hospital.

MACFARLANE, CATHARINE, M.D., 308 Medical Arts Building, Philadelphia, Pennsylvania. Woman's Medical College of Pennsylvania, 1898. Lecturer on Urology, Woman's Medical College of Pennsylvania; Gynecologist, Woman's Hospital; Consulting Gynecologist, State Hospital for Insane, Norristown.

MACFARLANE, JAMES WILLIAM, M.D., Westinghouse Building, Pittsburgh, Pennsylvania. University of Pennsylvania School of Medicine, 1878. Consulting Surgeon, Western Pennsylvania Hospital.

MACFARLANE, PERCY BLAKELY, B.A., M.B., 152 James Street, South, Hamilton, Ontario. University of Toronto, Faculty of Medicine, 1908. Surgeon, Eye, Ear, Nose, and Throat Department, Hamilton City Hospital.

MacGOWAN, GRANVILLE, M.D., Brack Shops Building, Los Angeles, California. University of Pennsylvania School of Medicine, 1879. Professor of Genito-Urinary Surgery, Graduate School of Medicine of the University of California; Visiting Surgeon, Los Angeles County and California Hospitals.

MacGREGOR, ARCHIBALD E., M.D., Post Tavern, Battle Creek, Michigan. Detroit College of Medicine and Surgery, 1901. Member of Staff, Nichols Memorial Hospital.

MacGREGOR, MURDOCK, M.D., C.M., 1120 Fifth Avenue, South, Fargo, North Dakota. University of Toronto, Faculty of Medicine (Trinity Medical College), 1897. Attending Surgeon, St. John's Hospital.

MacGUIRE, CONSTANTINE JOSEPH, JR., A.B., M.D., 120 East Sixtieth Street, New York, New York. Columbia University College of Physicians and Surgeons, 1911. Instructor in Surgery, Columbia University College of

Physicians and Surgeons; Assistant Attending Surgeon, First Surgical Division, Bellevue and St. Vincent's Hospitals.

MACISAAC, JOHN L., B.A., M.D., Main Street, Antigonish, Nova Scotia. University of Maryland School of Medicine (Baltimore Medical College), 1907. Surgeon, St. Martha's Hospital.

MACK, BURTON WILSON, M.D., 4159 West North Avenue, Chicago, Illinois. University of Illinois College of Medicine, 1903. Staff Surgeon, St. Anne's Hospital.

MACKAY, ALBERT EDWARD, M.B., M.D., C.M., 711 Oregonian Building, Portland, Oregon. University of Toronto, Faculty of Medicine, 1887. Professor of Genito-Urinary Diseases, University of Oregon Medical School; Surgeon, Multnomah County Hospital; Surgeon and President of Staff, Good Samaritan Hospital.

MACKAY, DANIEL SAYRE, M.D., C.M., F.R.C.S. (Edin.), 36 Purcell Avenue, Winnipeg, Manitoba. Faculty of Medicine, McGill University, 1901. Lecturer on Gynecology, Faculty of Medicine, University of Manitoba; Gynecologist, Winnipeg General Hospital.

MACKAY, EDWARD HART, M.D., 92 Walnut Street, Clinton, Massachusetts. Harvard Medical School, 1898. Surgeon and Obstetrician, Clinton Hospital.

MACKAY, MALCOLM EDWARD, M.D., C.M., F.R.C.S. (Edin.), 406 McLeod Building, Edmonton, Alberta. Faculty of Medicine, McGill University, 1905. Surgeon, Edmonton Hospitals.

MACKENTY, JOHN EDMUND, M.D., C.M., 43 West Fifty-fourth Street, New York, New York. Faculty of Medicine, McGill University, 1892. Senior Surgeon, Manhattan Eye, Ear, and Throat Hospital.

MACKENZIE, ALEXANDER J., M.D., 504 Meisel Building, Port Huron, Michigan. Detroit College of Medicine and Surgery, 1904.

MACKENZIE, DAVID WALLACE, B.A., M.D., 624 Sherbrooke Street, West, Montreal, Quebec. Cornell University Medical College, 1904. Clinical Professor of Surgery, Department of Urology, McGill University; Urologist-in-Chief, Royal Victoria Hospital.

MACKENZIE, GEORGE W., A.M., M.D., 1831 Chestnut Street, Philadelphia, Pennsylvania. Hahnemann Medical College and Hospital, Philadelphia, 1893. Associate Professor of Otology, University of Pennsylvania Graduate School of Medicine; Chief Surgeon, Ear, Nose, and Throat Department, West Philadelphia General Homeopathic and St. Luke's Homeopathic Hospitals; Consulting Ear, Nose, and Throat Surgeon, J. C. Blair Memorial Hospital, Huntingdon, Pennsylvania, McKinley Hospital, Trenton, West Jersey Homeopathic Hospital, Camden, New Jersey.

MACKENZIE, WILBUR W., M.D., Hollingsworth Building, Los Angeles, California. University of Illinois College of Medicine (College of Physicians and Surgeons, Chicago), 1896.

MACKID, LUDWIG STEWART, M.D., C.M., 220 Sixth Avenue, East, Calgary, Alberta. Faculty of Medicine, McGill University, 1904. Member of Staff, Calgary General Hospital; Chief Surgeon, Alberta Division, Canadian Pacific Railway.

MACKINNEY, WILLIAM H., M.D., 1701 Chestnut Street, Philadelphia, Pennsylvania. University of Pennsylvania School of Medicine, 1903. Professor of Urology, Graduate School, University of Pennsylvania School of Medicine; Associate in Genito-Urinary Surgery, University of Pennsylvania School of Medicine; Genito-Urinary Surgeon, Philadelphia General and Medico-Chirurgical Hospitals; Chief Surgeon, Urological Clinic, Lankenau Hospital.

MACKINNON, ANGUS, M.B., M.D., 44 Suffolk Street, Guelph, Ontario. University of Toronto, Faculty of Medicine, 1871. Surgeon, Guelph General and St. Joseph's Hospitals.

MACKINNON, JOHN A., M.B., M.D., C.M., M.R.C.S. (Eng.), Alaska Building, Seattle, Washington. University of Toronto, Faculty of Medicine (Trinity University and University of Toronto, Faculty of Medicine), 1879.

MACKINNON, WILLIAM FRANCIS, B.A., M.D., C.M., Antigonish, Nova Scotia. Dalhousie University, Faculty of Medicine (Halifax Medical College), 1902. Surgeon, St. Martha's Hospital.

MACKINTOSH, ARTHUR E., M.D., C.M., 87 Church Street, Amherst, Nova Scotia. Faculty of Medicine, McGill University, 1910. Attending Surgeon, Highland View Hospital.

MACKINTOSH, WILLIAM CRAWFORD, M.D., 1095 Market Street, San Francisco, California. Leland Stanford Junior University School of Medicine (Cooper Medical College), 1910. Surgeon, St. Joseph's Hospital.

MACLACHLAN, DANIEL A., M.D., David Whitney Building, Detroit, Michigan. University of Michigan Homeopathic Medical School, 1879. Consulting Ophthalmic and Aural Surgeon, Grace Hospital.

MACLAREN, ARCHIBALD, B.Sc., M.D., 914 Lowry Building, St. Paul, Minnesota. Columbia University, College of Physicians and Surgeons, 1883. Associate Professor of Surgery, University of Minnesota Medical School; Chief of Staff, St. Luke's Hospital; Associate Attending Surgeon, University Hospital.

MACLAREN, MURRAY, B.A., M.D., C.M., LL.D., C.M.G., M.R.C.S. (Eng.), 75 Coburg Street, St. John, New Brunswick. University of Edinburgh, 1884. Senior Consulting Surgeon, General Public Hospital.

MACLAY, OTIS HARDY, B.Sc., M.D., 5436 Hyde Park Boulevard, Chicago, Illinois. Northwestern University Medical School, 1901. Associate Professor, Nose and Throat Department, Northwestern University Medical School; Member of Staff, Wesley Memorial Hospital.

MACLEAN, DONALD, M.B., C.M., L.R.C.S. (Edin.), 314 Nevada Street, Carson City, Nevada. University of Edinburgh, 1898.

MacLean, Henry Stuart, M.D., 401 West Grace Street, Richmond, Virginia. Long Island College Hospital, 1894. Surgeon, Grace Hospital.

MacLean, Hugh, M.B., Regina, Saskatchewan. University of Toronto, Faculty of Medicine, 1906. Surgeon, Regina General and Grey Nun's Hospitals.

Maclean, Neil John, M.D., M.R.C.S. (Eng.), L.R.C.P. (Lond.), 67 Middle Gate, Winnipeg, Manitoba. Faculty of Medicine, University of Manitoba (Manitoba Medical College), 1898. Associate Professor of Clinical Surgery, Faculty of Medicine, University of Manitoba; Consulting Surgeon, Ninette Sanitarium for Tuberculosis; Surgeon, Winnipeg General Hospital.

Macleish, Archibald Lyle, A.M., M.B., M.D., C.M., 1104 Brockman Building, Los Angeles, California. University of Edinburgh, 1881.

Maclennan, Duncan Neil, M.D., C.M., M.R.C.S. (Eng.), L.R.C.P. (Lond.), 126 Bloor Street, West, Toronto, Ontario. Queen's University, Faculty of Medicine, 1891. Demonstrator of Ophthalmology, University of Toronto, Faculty of Medicine; Ophthalmic Surgeon, Toronto General Hospital; Surgeon, Ear, Nose, and Throat Department, Hospital for Sick Children.

MacLennan, Samuel John, B.A., M.D., 197 South Park Street, Halifax, Nova Scotia. University and Bellevue Hospital Medical College (New York University Medical College), 1894. Senior Surgeon, Eye, Ear, and Throat Department, Camp Hill Hospital.

Macleod, Donald Angus, M.D., 363 Charlotte Street, Sydney, Nova Scotia. Dalhousie University Faculty of Medicine, 1911. Attending Surgeon, Sydney City Hospital.

MacLeod, James Alexander, M.R.C.S. (Eng.), L.R.C.P. (Lond.), 448 Delaware Avenue, Buffalo, New York. Royal College of Surgeons, England, and Royal College of Physicians, London, 1901. Attending Surgeon, Buffalo City Hospital; Consulting Surgeon, Buffalo Homeopathic Hospital.

MacMillan, James Alexander, A.B., M.B., 938 David Whitney Building, Detroit, Michigan. University of Toronto, Faculty of Medicine, 1893. Associate Clinical Proctologist, Detroit College of Medicine and Surgery; Surgeon, Department of Proctology, Providence Hospital.

MacMillan, John A., M.D., C.M., 129 Stanley Street, Montreal, Quebec. Faculty of Medicine, McGill University, 1906. Demonstrator of Ophthalmology, Faculty of Medicine, McGill University; Associate in Ophthalmology, Royal Victoria Hospital.

Macmillan, Lachlan, M.D., C.M., 538 Broadway, West, Vancouver, British Columbia. University of Illinois College of Medicine (College of Physicians and Surgeons, Chicago), 1906.

MacMillan, Stanley Butler, M.D., C.M., D.M., Central Avenue, Prince Albert, Saskatchewan. McGill University Faculty of Medicine, 1910. Visiting Surgeon, Holy Family and Prince Albert Municipal Hospitals.

MACNAB, DANIEL STEWART, M.D., 209 Herald Block, Calgary, Alberta. University and Bellevue Hospital Medical College, 1907. Surgeon, General and Holy Cross Hospitals.

MacNAUGHTON, GEORGE KERR, B.A., M.D., C.M., Cumberland, British Columbia. Faculty of Medicine, McGill University, 1906. Surgeon, Cumberland General Hospital.

MacNEILL, ALEXANDER, M.D., C.M., Fitzroy Street, Summerside, Prince Edward Island. McGill University, Faculty of Medicine, 1883. Senior Surgeon, Prince County Hospital.

MACNIE, JOHN SILLIMAN, A.B., M.D., 503 Donaldson Building, Minneapolis, Minnesota. Columbia University, College of Physicians and Surgeons, 1896. Associate Professor of Ophthalmology and Oto-Laryngology, University of Minnesota Medical School.

MACPHERSON, DUNCAN, M.D., C.M., 114 East Fifty-fourth Street, New York, New York. Faculty of Medicine, McGill University, 1896.

MACRAE, DONALD, JR., M.D., City National Bank Building, Council Bluffs, Iowa. University of Michigan Medical School, 1891. Surgeon, Jennie Edmundson Memorial Hospital.

MADDOX, ROBERT DANIEL, M.D., United States Public Health Service, Washington, District of Columbia. University of Cincinnati College of Medicine (Medical College of Ohio), 1900.

MADILL, GRANT C., M.D., LI..D., 92 Caroline Street, Ogdensburg, New York. University and Bellevue Hospital Medical College, 1886. Surgeon-in-Chief, A. Barton Hepburn Hospital; Consulting Surgeon, St. Lawrence State Hospital, Ogdensburg, Alice Hyde Memorial Hospital, Malone, Champlain Valley Hospital, Plattsburg.

MAES, URBAN, M.D., 1671 Octavia Street, New Orleans, Louisiana. Tulane University of Louisiana School of Medicine, 1900. Professor of Clinical and Operative Surgery, Tulane University of Louisiana School of Medicine; Senior Associate in Surgery, Touro Infirmary; Visiting Surgeon, Charity Hospital; Consulting Surgeon, United States Marine Hospital.

MAGENNIS, BRYAN CHARLES, D.D.S., M.D., 170 Hamilton Avenue, Paterson, New Jersey. University and Bellevue Hospital Medical College (New York University Medical College), 1883. Visiting Surgeon, Paterson General and Miriam Barnert Hospitals.

MAGGARD, DELANO I., A.B., M.D., Beacon Building, Wichita, Kansas. Northwestern University Medical School, 1903.

MAGIE, WILLIAM HENRY, M.D., 401 Sellwood Building, Duluth, Minnesota. St. Louis College of Physicians and Surgeons, 1884. Chief of Staff, Morgan Park Hospital; Chief Surgeon, Minnesota Steel Company.

MAGILL, WILLIAM H., Ph.B., M.D., 221 Thayer Street, Providence, Rhode Island. Cornell University Medical College, 1903. Surgeon, Gynecological Department, Rhode Island Hospital; Associate Surgeon, Gynecological Department, St. Joseph's Hospital.

MAGINN, EDWARD F., M.D., 403 Lewisohn Building, Butte, Montana. Rush Medical College, 1903. Surgeon, St. James Hospital.

MAGNUSON, PAUL BUDD, M.D., 30 North Michigan Avenue, Chicago, Illinois. University of Pennsylvania School of Medicine, 1908. Associate in Surgery, Northwestern University Medical School; Attending Surgeon, Wesley Memorial and Alexian Brothers' Hospitals.

MAGRUDER, ALEXANDER C., M.Sc., M.D., Ferguson Building, Colorado Springs, Colorado. Tulane University of Louisiana School of Medicine, 1900.

MAGRUDER, THOMAS, V., B.Sc., M.D., Jefferson County Bank Building, Birmingham, Alabama. Tulane University of Louisiana School of Medicine, 1910. Surgeon, St. Vincent's Hospital; Orthopedic Surgeon, Hillman Hospital; Assistant Attending Surgeon, United States Public Health Service, North Alabama.

MAHONEY, DANIEL FRANCIS, M.D., 520 Commonwealth Avenue, Boston, Massachusetts. Harvard Medical School, 1903. Instructor in Surgery, Harvard University Graduate School of Medicine; Surgeon, Carney Hospital, Boston, Cambridge City Hospital, Cambridge; Associate Consulting Surgeon, Charles Choate Memorial Hospital, Woburn.

MAHONEY, EDWARD J., A.M., M.D., 4 Mattoon Street, Springfield, Massachusetts. Georgetown University School of Medicine, 1895. Surgeon-in-Chief, Mercy Hospital; Consulting Surgeon, House of Providence Hospital, Holyoke.

MAHONEY, GEORGE WILLIAM, M.D., 30 North Michigan Avenue, Chicago, Illinois. University and Bellevue Hospital Medical College (Bellevue Hospital Medical College), 1888. Professor and Head of Department of Ophthalmology, Loyola University School of Medicine; Professor of Ophthalmology, Chicago Policlinic; Oculist, Chicago Policlinic and Hospital, Henrotin Hospital, St. Vincent's Infant Asylum and Maternity Hospital, House of the Good Shepard; Attending Oculist, St. Mary of Nazareth Hospital.

MAHONEY, STEPHEN ANDREW, A.B., M.D., 630 Dwight Street, Holyoke, Massachusetts. Harvard Medical School, 1889. Surgeon, House of Providence and Holyoke City Hospitals.

MAIER, FREDERICK HURST, M.D., 2019 Walnut Street, Philadelphia, Pennsylvania. Jefferson Medical College, 1894. Associate in Gynecology, Jefferson Medical College; Gynecologist, St. Joseph's Hospital, Philadelphia Hospital for Contagious Diseases; Consulting Gynecologist, Philadelphia Jewish Sanitarium for Consumptives.

MALAND, CLARENCE O., B.A., M.D., 730 LaSalle Building, Minneapolis, Minnesota. University of Minnesota Medical School, 1907. Instructor in Obstetrics and Gynecology, University of Minnesota Medical School; Associate in Obstetrics and Gynecology, Minneapolis General and Swedish Hospitals.

MALLETT, GEORGE HOOPER, M.D., 244 West Seventy-third Street, New York, New York. University of Virginia, Department of Medicine, 1885. Consulting Gynecologist, General Memorial Hospital; Gynecologist, Washington Square Hospital.

MALONE, BATTLE, A.B., M.D., Exchange Building, Memphis, Tennessee. University of Tennessee College of Medicine (Memphis Hospital Medical College), 1899. Consulting Surgeon, St. Joseph's Hospital.

MALONE, WILLIAM F., M.D., 511 Caswell Block, Milwaukee, Wisconsin. University of Illinois College of Medicine (College of Physicians and Surgeons, Chicago), 1888. Member of Staff, Hanover General Hospital.

MAMMEN, ERNEST, M.D., 308 Griesheim Building, Bloomington, Illinois. Rush Medical College, 1884. Surgeon, Brokaw and St. Joseph's Hospitals.

MAMMEN, GOEKE HENRY, M.D., 2706 North Rockwell Street, Chicago, Illinois. Rush Medical College, 1894. Surgeon, Lutheran Deaconess and West End Hospitals.

MANCHESTER, JOHN DARWIN, M.D., Medical Corps, United States Navy, Washington, District of Columbia. Rush Medical College, 1899. Commander, Medical Corps, United States Navy.

MANLEY, ORVILLE TITUS, LL.B., M.D., Second National Bank Building, Warren, Ohio. Western Reserve University School of Medicine (Cleveland College of Physicians and Surgeons), 1900. Demonstrator of Experimental Medicine, Western Reserve University School of Medicine; Surgeon, Warren City Hospital.

MANLY, CLARENCE J., M.D., Medical Corps, United States Army, Washington, District of Columbia. University of Louisville, Medical Department (Louisville Medical College), 1897. Colonel, Medical Corps, United States Army.

MANN, ARTHUR T., B.Sc., M.D., 910 Donaldson Building, Minneapolis, Minnesota. Harvard Medical School, 1896. Associate Professor of Surgery, University of Minnesota Medical School; Chief Surgeon, University Surgical Division, Minneapolis City Hospital; Surgeon, Northwestern and Abbott Hospitals.

MANN, ROBERT HOWELL TAYLOR, M.D., State National Bank Building, Texarkana, Arkansas. Vanderbilt University, Medical Department, 1893. Oculist and Aurist, Texarkana Sanitarium, St. Louis Southwestern Railway Hospital, Kansas City Southern, and St. Louis, Iron Mountain and Southern Railways.

MANNING, WILLIAM SAUNDERS, B.Sc., M.D., 513 Laura Street, Jacksonville, Florida. Johns Hopkins University, Medical Department, 1903. Ophthalmologist, St. Luke's and Duval County Hospitals; Division Ophthalmologist, Seaboard Air Line Railway.

MANRIQUEZ, MIGUEL, M.D., Rua Brazil 272, Valparaiso, Chile. Faculty of Medicine, University of Chile, 1909.

MANSON, JANE SPROULE, M.B., M.R.C.S. (Eng.), L.R.C.P. (Lond.), 250 Huron Street, Toronto, Ontario. University of Toronto, Faculty of Medicine,

1907. Assistant in Oto-Rhino-Laryngology, Toronto General Hospital; Chief of Service in Oto-Rhino-Laryngology, Woman's College Hospital and Dispensary.

MANSUR, LEON WALLACE, M.D., 1109 Brockman Building, Los Angeles, California. Harvard Medical School, 1898.

MANTON, WALTER, A.B., A.M., M.D., 62 Adams Avenue, West, Detroit, Michigan. Harvard Medical School, 1909. Associate Professor of Obstetrics, Detroit College of Medicine and Surgery; Junior Surgeon, Harper Hospital; Visiting Obstetrician, Herman Kiefer Hospital; Visiting Obstetrician and Gynecologist, Woman's Hospital.

MANTON, WALTER PORTER, M.D., 62 Adams Avenue, West, Detroit, Michigan. Harvard Medical School, 1881. Professor of Obstetrics and Director of the Department, Detroit College of Medicine and Surgery; Emeritus Consulting Gynecologist, Harper Hospital; Gynecologist, Pontiac State Hospital, Pontiac, Traverse City State Hospital, Traverse City; Consulting Gynecologist, St. Joseph's Retreat, Dearborn; Consulting Director, Maternity Department, Herman Kiefer Hospital.

MANWARING, JOSHUA GEORGE ROSS, M.D., Dryden Building, Flint, Michigan. University of Michigan Medical School, 1901.

MARBURY, WILLIAM BERRY, M.D., 1403 Twenty-first Street, Northwest, Washington, District of Columbia. University of Virginia, Department of Medicine, 1907. Associate Surgeon, Emergency, Providence, and Children's Hospitals.

MARCHILDON, JOHN WOODS, B.Sc., M.D., University Club Building, St. Louis, Missouri. Rush Medical College, 1903. Assistant Professor of Genito-Urinary Surgery, St. Louis University School of Medicine; Genito-Urinary Surgeon, Alexian Brothers' Hospital.

MARCONDES, ANTONIO VIEIRA, M.D., Avenida Angelica 114, Sao Paulo, Brazil. Faculty of Medicine, University of Rio de Janeiro, 1904.

MARCY, HENRY ORLANDO, A.M., M.D., LL.D., 180 Commonwealth Avenue, Boston, Massachusetts. Harvard Medical School, 1863. Surgeon-in-Chief, Sunnyside Surgical Hospital, Cambridge; Consulting Surgeon, City Hospital, Haverhill, Lawrence General Hospital, Lawrence, Brockton Hospital, Brockton, Soldiers' Home, Chelsea.

MARCY, HENRY ORLANDO, JR., A.B., M.D., 140 Sargent Street, Newton, Massachusetts. Harvard Medical School, 1897.

MARCY, WILLIAM HENRY, M.D., 32 West Utica Street, Buffalo, New York. New York Homeopathic College and Flower Hospital, 1893. Consulting Surgeon, United States Marine Hospital; Surgeon, Buffalo Homeopathic Hospital and Emergency Hospital, New York Central Lines.

MARINHO DE AZEVEDO, JOAS, M.D., Rua da Quitando 5, Rio de Janeiro, Brazil. Faculty of Medicine, Rio de Janeiro, 1898. Professor of Rhinology and Oto-Laryngology, Faculty of Medicine, Rio de Janeiro; Chief of Department, Rhinology, Oto-Laryngology, Misericordia Hospital.

MARK, ERNEST GUTHRIE, A.B., M.D., 1010 Rialto Building, Kansas City, Missouri. University of Louisville, Medical Department, 1899. Genito-Urinary Surgeon, Kansas City General and Research Hospitals.

MARKEL, JAMES CLYDE, M.Sc., M.D., 1005 Westinghouse Building, Pittsburgh, Pennsylvania. University of Pennsylvania School of Medicine, 1904. Ophthalmic Surgeon, Pittsburgh Eye and Ear and South Side Hospitals; Ophthalmologist, Western Pennsylvania Institution for the Blind.

MARKS, SAMUEL BLACKBURN, B.Sc., M.D., 164 Market Street, Lexington, Kentucky. Columbia University, College of Physicians and Surgeons, 1903. Attending Surgeon, St. Joseph's and Good Samaritan Hospitals; Surgeon, Lexington Free Clinic.

MARLOW, FRANK WILLIAM, M.D., M.R.C.S. (Eng.), L.S.A. (Lond.), 200 Highland Street, Syracuse, New York. Syracuse University College of Medicine, 1885. Professor of Ophthalmology, Syracuse University College of Medicine; Ophthalmologist, St. Joseph's and Syracuse Memorial Hospitals, Syracuse Eye, Ear, and Throat Infirmary, Syracuse Free Dispensary.

MARLOW, FREDERICK WILLIAM, M.D., C.M., F.R.C.S. (Eng.), 417 Bloor Street, West, Toronto, Ontario. University of Toronto, Faculty of Medicine (Trinity Medical College), 1900. Associate Professor of Gynecology, University of Toronto, Faculty of Medicine; Senior Assistant Gynecologist, Toronto General Hospital.

MARQUIS, GEORGE PAULL, A.M., M.D., 30 North Michigan Avenue, Chicago, Illinois. Northwestern University Medical School, 1892. Attending Rhinologist, St. Luke's Hospital.

MARSH, ARTHUR WHITE, M.D., 690 Main Street, Worcester, Massachusetts. Harvard Medical School, 1895. Visiting Surgeon, Worcester City Hospital.

MARSH, JAMES P., A.M., M.D., 1828 Fifth Avenue, Troy, New York. Albany Medical College, 1885. Attending Surgeon, Samaritan Hospital; Consulting Surgeon, Leonard Hospital; Surgeon-in-Chief, Henry W. Putnam Memorial Hospital, Bennington, Vermont.

MARSHALL, CLIFFORD C., B.Sc., M.D., 233 East State Street, Sharon, Pennsylvania. University of Pennsylvania School of Medicine, 1900. Chief Surgeon, Christian H. Buhl Hospital.

MARSHALL, GEORGE G., M.D., Gryphon Building, Rutland, Vermont. University of Vermont College of Medicine, 1893. Oculist and Aurist, Rutland Hospital; Oculist, Rutland Railroad.

MARSHALL, GEORGE MORLEY, A.B., M.D., 1819 Spruce Street, Philadelphia, Pennsylvania. University of Pennsylvania School of Medicine, 1886. Oto-Laryngologist, St. Joseph's Hospital.

MARSHALL, JOHN SAYRE, M.D., D.Sc., 2521 Durant Avenue, Berkeley, California. Syracuse University College of Medicine, 1876.

MARSHALL, VICTOR F., B.Sc., M.D., 587 Appleton Street, Appleton, Wisconsin. Rush Medical College, 1898. Attending Surgeon, St. Elizabeth's Hospital; Chief Surgeon, Wisconsin and Northern Railroad, Wisconsin Traction Company.

MARSHALL, WATSON, A.B., M.D., 604 Diamond Bank Building, Pittsburgh, Pennsylvania. Johns Hopkins University, Medical Department, 1903. Instructor in Laryngology, University of Pittsburgh School of Medicine.

MARTER, LINNAEUS E., M.D., 1631 Race Street, Philadelphia, Pennsylvania. Hahnemann Medical College and Hospital, Philadelphia, 1896; Medico-Chirurgical College, 1902. Demonstrator, Laryngology and Rhinology, Hahnemann Medical College; Assistant Laryngologist, Hahnemann Medical College and Hospital.

MARTIN, ANCIL, M.D., 207 Goodrich Building, Phoenix, Arizona. Rush Medical College, 1885. Ophthalmologist, St. Luke's Home, Phoenix Hospital, Phoenix, Miami Inspiration Hospital, Miami; Santa Fe Coast Lines and Arizona Eastern Railways.

MARTIN, BENSON BLAKE, M.D., 1918 Washington Street, Vicksburg, Mississippi. Tulane University of Louisiana School of Medicine, 1898. Chief Surgeon, Vicksburg Infirmary.

MARTIN, EDMUND DENEGRE, M.D., 3513 Prytania Street, New Orleans, Louisiana. Tulane University of Louisiana School of Medicine, 1891. Professor of Surgery, New Orleans Polyclinic; Visiting Surgeon, Charity Hospital; Consulting Surgeon, Eye, Ear, Nose, and Throat Hospital.

MARTIN, EDWARD, A.M., M.D., LL.D., D.Sc., 135 South Eighteenth Street, Philadelphia, Pennsylvania. University of Pennsylvania School of Medicine, 1883. Commissioner of Health for Pennsylvania.

MARTIN, ERNEST ALBERT, M.D., C.M., 84 Lonsdale Avenue, North Vancouver, British Columbia. Faculty of Medicine, McGill University, 1901.

MARTIN, FRANKLIN H., M.D., C.M.G., 30 North Michigan Avenue, Chicago, Illinois. Northwestern University Medical School, 1880. Member of Consulting Staff, St. Luke's Hospital. Editor, *Surgery, Gynecology, and Obstetrics.*

MARTIN, G. FORREST, M.D., 45 Harvard Street, Lowell, Massachusetts. New York Homeopathic Medical College and Flower Hospital, 1890. Surgeon, Lowell General Hospital.

MARTIN, HARVEY H., M.D., 806 Maple Avenue, Laporte, Indiana. Hahnemann Medical College and Hospital, Chicago (Chicago Homeopathic Medical College), 1895. Surgeon, Holy Family Hospital.

MARTIN, HENRY HAGER, M.D., 247 Bull Street, Savannah, Georgia. University of Cincinnati College of Medicine (Miami Medical College), 1891. Ophthalmologist and Oto-Laryngologist, Georgia and St. Joseph's Infirmaries.

MARTIN, JOHN GREENE, M.D., 825 South Division Street, Lake Charles, Louisiana. Dartmouth Medical School, 1891. Surgeon, St. Patrick's Hospital.

MARTIN, WALTON, Ph.B., M.D., 230 East Forty-ninth Street, New York, New York. Columbia University, College of Physicians and Surgeons, 1892. Associate Professor of Surgery, Columbia University, College of Physicians and Surgeons; Attending Surgeon, St. Luke's Hospital; Consulting Surgeon, White Plains Hospital, White Plains, Loomis Sanatorium, Loomis.

MARVEL, CHARLES, M.D., 127 North Tenth Street, Richmond, Indiana. Jefferson Medical College, 1891. Surgeon, Reid Memorial Hospital.

MASON, CHARLES FIELD, M.D., Medical Corps, United States Army, Washington, District of Columbia. Medical College of Virginia, 1884. Brigadier General, Medical Corps, United States Army, retired.

MASON, FRANK M., M.D., 501 The Temple, Danville, Illinois. Northwestern University Medical School, 1894. Surgeon and President of Staff, Lakeview Hospital; Surgeon, St. Elizabeth's Hospital.

MASON, JAMES MONROE, M.D., Jefferson County Bank Building, Birmingham, Alabama. Tulane University of Louisiana School of Medicine, 1899. Gynecologist, St. Vincent's Hospital; Surgeon, Hillman Hospital.

MASON, JAMES S., M.D., 129 West Elm Street, Urbana, Illinois. Northwestern University Medical School, 1894. Member of Staff, Julia F. Burnham Hospital, Champaign.

MASON, J. TATE, M.D., 1220 Federal Avenue, Seattle, Washington. University of Virginia, Department of Medicine, 1905. Surgeon, Virginia Mason Hospital; Member of Staff, Providence Hospital; Chief Surgeon, County Hospital.

MASON, JOHN JAMES, B.A., M.D., 718 Granville Street, Vancouver, British Columbia. Western University Medical School, 1902. Associate in Obstetrics and Gynecology, Vancouver General Hospital.

MASON, NATHANIEL ROBERT, A.B., M.D., 483 Beacon Street, Boston, Massachusetts. Harvard Medical School, 1901. Instructor in Obstetrics and Assistant in Gynecology, Harvard Medical School; First Assistant Visiting Surgeon for Diseases of Women, Boston City Hospital; Assistant Visiting Obstetrician, Boston Lying-in Hospital.

MASON, ROBIN FERGUSON, M.D., 200 Bank of Commerce Building, Memphis, Tennessee. University of Tennessee College of Medicine (Memphis Hospital Medical College), 1908. Consulting Surgeon, United States Marine Hospital, No. 12, and Tennessee Unit No. 1, United States Public Health Service.

MASON, WILLIAM BEVERLEY, M.D., 1738 M Street, Northwest, Washington, District of Columbia. Medical College of Virginia, 1899.

MASSON, JAMES CARRUTHERS, M.B., Mayo Clinic, Rochester, Minnesota. University of Toronto, Faculty of Medicine, 1906. Associate Professor of Surgery, Mayo Foundation, University of Minnesota Medical School; Surgeon, St. Mary's and Colonial Hospitals (Mayo Clinic).

MASTIN, WILLIAM MCDOWELL, M.D., LL.D., Conti and Joachim Streets, Mobile, Alabama. University of Pennsylvania School of Medicine, 1874. Surgeon, Providence Infirmary.

MATAS, RUDOLPH, M.D., LL.D., 2255 St. Charles Avenue, New Orleans, Louisiana. Tulane University of Louisiana School of Medicine (University of Louisiana, Medical Department), 1880. Professor of Surgery, Tulane University of Louisiana School of Medicine; Senior, Surgical Division, Touro Infirmary; Chief of Surgical Service, Visiting Staff, Charity Hospital; Consulting Surgeon, Eye, Ear, Nose, and Throat Hospital.

MATHENY, ALBERT RALSTON, B.Sc., M.D., 1105 East End Trust Building, Pittsburgh, Pennsylvania. Jefferson Medical College, 1898. Surgeon, Pittsburgh Hospital.

MATHENY, RALPH CHARLES, M.D., 306 East Main Street, Galesburg, Illinois. Northwestern University Medical School, 1891. Consulting Oculist, Galesburg Hospital.

MATHESON, JAMES PLEASANT, B.A., M.D., 511 Independence Building, Charlotte, North Carolina. University of Maryland School of Medicine, 1905. Otologist and Laryngologist, Presbyterian Hospital and Charlotte Sanatorium.

MATHESON, JOHN SUTHERLAND, M.D., C.M., L.R.C.P. & S. (Edin.), L.F.P. & S. (Glas.), 317 Fifth Street, Brandon, Manitoba. University of Toronto, Faculty of Medicine, 1894. Member of Staff, Brandon General Hospital; Officer in Charge, General Surgery Department, Manitoba Military Hospital, Tuxedo Park, Winnipeg.

MATHEWS, FRANCIS STUART, B.Sc., M.D., 62 West Fiftieth Street, New York, New York. Columbia University, College of Physicians and Surgeons, 1893. Attending Surgeon, St. Luke's Hospital, St. Mary's Free Hospital for Children; Consulting Surgeon, Home for Incurables.

MATHIEU, ALBERT L., M.D., Selling Building, Portland, Oregon. University of Minnesota Medical School, 1905.

MATLACK, GRANVILLE T., M.D., 33 West Northampton Street, Wilkes-Barre, Pennsylvania. Jefferson Medical College, 1884. Consulting Surgeon, Wilkes-Barre City and Mercy Hospitals, Wilkes-Barre, State Hospital for Insane, Danville, Nesbitt West Side Hospital, Dorranceton.

MATTESON, GEORGE ARNOLD, A.B., M.D., 454 Angell Street, Providence, Rhode Island. Harvard Medical School, 1900. Visiting Surgeon, Rhode Island Hospital; Consulting Surgeon, Providence Lying-in Hospital, Providence, Memorial Hospital, Pawtucket.

MATTHEWS, A. ALDRIDGE, M.D., 721 Paulsen Building, Spokane, Washington. University of Maryland School of Medicine, 1900. Surgeon, St. Luke's Hospital.

MATTHEWS, HARVEY BURLESON, B.Sc., M.D., 643 St. Mark's Avenue, Brooklyn, New York. Columbia University, College of Physicians and Surgeons, 1909. Attending Obstetrician and Gynecologist, Greenpoint Hospital; Lecturer on Obstetrics and Gynecology, Long Island College Hospital; Assistant Obstetrician, Methodist Episcopal Hospital; Chief of Gynecology, Polhemus Memorial Clinic.

MATTHEWS, JAMES DWIGHT, M.D., 948 David Whitney Building, Detroit, Michigan. Detroit College of Medicine and Surgery, 1892. Instructor in Operative Surgery, Detroit College of Medicine and Surgery; Associate Surgeon, Providence Hospital.

MATTHEWS, JUSTUS, M.D., Metropolitan Bank Building, Minneapolis, Minnesota. University of Minnesota Medical School, 1905.

MATTHEWS, OSCAR HOMER, M.D., Flatiron Building, Atlanta, Georgia. Emory University School of Medicine (Atlanta College of Physicians and Surgeons), 1906. Associate Professor of Obstetrics and Clinical Gynecology, Emory University School of Medicine; Attending Gynecologist, Georgia Baptist Hospital; Assistant Gynecologist and Obstetrician, Grady Memorial Hospital; Assistant Attending Surgeon, MacVicar Hospital of Spelman Seminary.

MATTHEY, HENRY E., M.D., Kahl Building, Davenport, Iowa. University of Würzburg, 1887. Surgeon, Mercy and St. Luke's Hospitals.

MATTISON, FITCH C. E., M.D., Chamber of Commerce Building, Pasadena, California. University of Illinois College of Medicine (College of Physicians and Surgeons, Chicago), 1888. Surgeon, Pasadena Hospital; Chairman and Senior Surgeon of Attending Staff, Los Angeles County Hospital, Los Angeles.

MATTISON, JAMES ACKER, A.B., M.D., National Military Home Hospital, Dayton, Ohio. University of Michigan Medical School, 1900. Chief Surgeon, Battle Mountain Sanitarium, Hot Springs, South Dakota, National Military Home Hospital, Dayton, Ohio.

MATTISON, SAMUEL JONES, M.D., 712 Citizens Savings Bank Building, Pasadena, California. Northwestern University Medical School, 1904.

MAULDIN, LELAND OSGOOD, B.Sc., M.D., 502 Petigru Street, Greenville, South Carolina. Medical College of the State of South Carolina, 1903. Member of Staff, Eye, Ear, Nose, and Throat Department, Greenville City Hospital.

MAUMENEE, ALFRED EDWARD, M.D., 209 Van Antwerp Building, Mobile, Alabama. University of Alabama School of Medicine, 1905. Professor of Ophthalmology, University of Alabama School of Medicine; Eye, Ear, Nose, and Throat Surgeon, Mobile City Hospital.

MAURY, JOHN METCALF, M.D., 720 Bank of Commerce Building, Memphis, Tennessee. University of Pennsylvania School of Medicine, 1890. Professor of Gynecology, University of Tennessee College of Medicine; Gynecologist, Memphis General and Baptist Memorial Hospitals.

MAXEY, EDWARD ERNEST, M.D., Idaho Building, Boise, Idaho. University of Illinois, College of Medicine (College of Physicians and Surgeons, Chicago), 1891. Ophthalmologist and Oto-Laryngologist, St. Alphonsus Hospital.

MAXSON, CHARLES WALTER, M.D., 827 North Charles Street, Baltimore, Maryland. University of Maryland College of Medicine (College of Physicians and Surgeons), 1910. Associate Visiting Surgeon, South Baltimore General Hospital; Assistant Surgeon, Mercy Hospital.

MAXSON, FRANK THEODORE, M.D., 621 Lumber Exchange Building, Seattle, Washington. University of Pennsylvania School of Medicine, 1902. Member of Staff, Seattle General Hospital; Member of Associate Staff, Swedish, Providence, St. Luke's and Virginia Mason Hospitals.

MAXSON, SANDS CARR, M.D., Mayo Building, Utica, New York. University and Bellevue Hospital Medical College (New York University Medical College), 1871.

MAXWELL, CHARLES T., B.Sc., M.D., 109 Sioux National Bank Building, Sioux City, Iowa. Rush Medical College, 1912. Attending Surgeon, St. Joseph's Mercy Hospital.

MAY, CHARLES HENRY, M.D., 698 Madison Avenue, New York, New York. Columbia University, College of Physicians and Surgeons, 1883. Director and Visiting Surgeon, Eye Department, Bellevue Hospital; Attending Ophthalmic Surgeon, Mt. Sinai Hospital; Consulting Ophthalmologist, French and Italian Hospitals, New York, Monmouth Memorial Hospital, Long Branch, New Jersey.

MAY, GEORGE ELISHA, M.D., 353 Commonwealth Avenue, Boston, Massachusetts. Boston University School of Medicine, 1890. Surgeon, Newton Hospital, Newton.

MAY, HENRY A., M.D., Medical Corps, United States Navy, Washington, District of Columbia. George Washington University Medical School, 1899. Commander, Medical Corps, United States Navy.

MAY, JAMES WHITTIER, M.D., 800 Minnesota Avenue, Kansas City, Kansas. University of Kansas School of Medicine (College of Physicians and Surgeons, Kansas City), 1900. Ophthalmologist, St. Margaret's Hospital.

MAYBAUM, JACOB L., M.D., 1 West Seventieth Street, New York, New York. Cornell University Medical College, 1905. Associate Aural Surgeon, Mt. Sinai Hospital; Assistant Aural Surgeon, Manhattan Eye, Ear, and Throat Hospital.

MAYHEW, DAVID PORTER, Ph.M., M.D., 218 Burns Building, Colorado Springs, Colorado. University of Michigan Medical School, 1896.

MAYNE, EARL H., M.D., 139 Bay Seventeenth Street, Brooklyn, New York. University and Bellevue Hospital Medical College (Bellevue Hospital Medical College), 1893. Visiting Surgeon, New York Children's Aid Society; Visiting Gynecologist, Harbor Hospital.

MAYO, CHARLES HORACE, A.M., M.D., D.Sc., LL.D., F.R.C.S. (Eng., Ire.), Mayowood, Rochester, Minnesota. Northwestern University Medical School, 1888. Professor of Surgery, University of Minnesota Medical School; Surgeon, St. Mary's Hospital (Mayo Clinic).

MAYO, HARRY N., B.Sc., M.D., 408 Hibernian Building, Los Angeles, California. University of Maryland School of Medicine (Baltimore Medical College), 1895.

MAYO, WILLIAM J., A.M., M.D., D.Sc., F.R.C.S. (Eng., Edin., Ire.), LL.D., 701 College Hill, Rochester, Minnesota. University of Michigan Medical School, 1883. Surgeon, St. Mary's Hospital.

MCALESTER, ANDREW WALKER, JR., B.L., A.B., M.D., 625 Bryant Building, Kansas City, Missouri. University of Missouri School of Medicine, 1905. Oculist, Kansas City General and Christian Church Hospitals.

MCALLISTER, FRED DANFORTH, A.B., M.D., 301 Essex Street, Lawrence, Massachusetts. Harvard Medical School, 1898. Visiting Surgeon, Lawrence General Hospital.

MCALPINE, ARCHIBALD D., M.D., 512 Washington Arcade, Detroit, Michigan. Detroit College of Medicine and Surgery, 1905. Clinical Professor of Surgery, Detroit College of Medicine and Surgery; Associate Surgeon, Harper Hospital; Attending Surgeon, Detroit Tuberculosis Sanatorium, Woman's Hospital, and Infants' Home.

MCAMIS, L. CLIFFORD, Phar.B., M.D., 501 Humboldt Building, St. Louis, Missouri. Washington University Medical School, 1905. Member of Staff, Barnard Free Skin and Cancer and St. Luke's Hospitals; Visiting Surgeon, St. Louis City Hospital.

MCARTHUR, LEWIS LINN, M.D., 4724 Drexel Boulevard, Chicago, Illinois. Rush Medical College, 1880. Senior Attending Surgeon, St. Luke's and Michael Reese Hospitals.

MCARTHUR, WILLIAM TAYLOR, M.B., L.R.C.S. & F.R.C.S. (Edin.), 2025 Western Avenue, Los Angeles, California. University of Toronto, Faculty of Medicine, 1895.

MCAULEY, ALBERT GEORGE, M.D., C.M., 579 Dorchester Street, West, Montreal, Quebec. Faculty of Medicine, McGill University, 1900. Demonstrator of Ophthalmology, Faculty of Medicine, McGill University; Associate in Ophthalmology, Royal Victoria Hospital.

MCAULIFFE, GEORGE BIRMINGHAM, A.B., M.D., 26 West Eighty-seventh Street, New York, New York. Columbia University, College of Physicians and Surgeons, 1888. Chief of Aural Department, Cornell University Medical College; Oculist and Aurist, Misericordia Hospital; Consulting Aurist and Laryngologist, Waterbury Hospital, Waterbury, Connecticut; Consulting Oculist and Aurist, Southampton Hospital, Southampton.

MCBEAN, GEORGE MARTIN, M.D., 22 East Washington Street, Chicago, Illinois. Hahnemann Medical College and Hospital, Chicago, 1899. Professor of Otology, Hahnemann Medical College and Hospital; Aurist, Hahnemann and Streeter Hospitals.

McBLAIN, THOMAS J., M.D., 206 Elderfield Building, Niagara Falls, New York. Western University, Faculty of Medicine, 1891. Member of Staff, Mt. St. Mary's Hospital.

McBURNEY, B. A., B.Sc., M.D., Palm Villa Ranch, Pomona, California. Hahnemann Medical College and Hospital, Chicago, 1896.

McCABE, WILLIAM M., M.D., Doctor's Building, Nashville, Tennessee. Vanderbilt University, Medical Department, 1903. Associate Professor of Surgery, Vanderbilt University, Medical Department.

McCALLA, LUCIEN P., M.D., Boise City Bank Building, Boise, Idaho. Washington University Medical College (Missouri Medical College), 1888. Chief of Staff, St. Alphonsus Hospital; Chief Surgeon, Intermountain Railway and Boise-Payette Lumber Companies.

McCALLUM, FRANCIS M., M.D., 721 Lathrop Building, Kansas City, Missouri. Ensworth Medical College, 1893. Genito-Urinary Surgeon, Kansas City General and Christian Church Hospitals.

McCANDLESS, WILLIAM A., A.M., M.D., 5056 Westminster Place, St. Louis, Missouri. Washington University Medical School, 1873. Consulting Surgeon, St. Mary's Infirmary.

McCANNEL, ALEXANDER J., M.D., 44 South Main Street, Minot, North Dakota. State University of Iowa College of Medicine (Keokuk Medical College), 1901; Georgetown University School of Medicine, 1906.

McCANNEL, ARCHIBALD D., Phar.B., M.D., C.M., 125 Main Street, Minot, North Dakota. University of Toronto, Faculty of Medicine, 1906.

McCARTHY, JOSEPH FRANCIS, M.D., 40 East Forty-first Street, New York, New York. Columbia University, College of Physicians and Surgeons, 1901. Professor of Urology, New York Post-Graduate Medical School; Assistant Professor of Urology, Columbia University, College of Physicians and Surgeons.

McCARTHY, WILTON, M.D., Fleming Building, Des Moines, Iowa. State University of Iowa College of Medicine (Iowa College of Physicians and Surgeons), 1894.

McCARTNEY, GEORGE EDWARD, M.B., Simpson Street, Fort William, Ontario. University of Toronto, Faculty of Medicine, 1901. Surgeon, McKellar General Hospital.

McCAULEY, CHARLES EDWARD, M.D., Citizens Bank Building, Aberdeen, South Dakota. Rush Medical College, 1902. Attending Surgeon, St. Luke's Hospital.

McCAULIFF, GUY THOMAS, M.D., 644½ Second Street, Webster City, Iowa. Northwestern University Medical School, 1902. Attending Surgeon, St. Joseph's Mercy Hospital.

McCAW, JAMES FRANCIS, M.D., Sherman Building, Watertown, New York. Columbia University, College of Physicians and Surgeons, 1892. Oculist, Aurist, and Laryngologist, House of the Good Samaritan, Jefferson County Orphan Asylum.

McCaw, Walter D., M.D., Medical Corps, United States Army, Washington, District of Columbia. Medical College of Virginia, 1882; Columbia University, College of Physicians and Surgeons, 1884. Assistant Surgeon General, Medical Corps, United States Army.

McCelvey, John S., M.D., Temple State Bank Building, Temple, Texas. Jefferson Medical College, 1894. Surgeon, King's Daughters Hospital.

McChesney, George Jewett, A.B., M.D., 1202 Flood Building, San Francisco, California. University of California Medical School, San Francisco, 1900. Instructor in Orthopedic Surgery, University of California Medical School; Orthopedic Surgeon, St. Luke's and Children's Hospitals.

McChord, Robert Caldwell, M.D., Lebanon, Kentucky. University of Louisville, Medical Department (Louisville Medical College), 1875. Surgeon in Charge, Elizabeth's Hospital; Surgeon, Louisville and Nashville Railroad.

McClellan, Benjamin Rush, A.M., M.D., 7 East Second Street, Xenia, Ohio. University of Cincinnati College of Medicine (Miami Medical College), 1884. Surgeon, McClellan Hospital.

McClellan, Wilbert E., M.B., M.R.C.S. (Eng.), L.R.C.P. (Lond.), 179 Allyn Street, Hartford, Connecticut. University of Toronto, Faculty of Medicine, 1904. Ophthalmologist, Laryngologist, Rhinologist, and Otologist, St. Francis and Babies' Hospitals, Hartford Dispensary, Virginia T. Smith Home for Crippled and Invalid Children; Consulting Aurist, Isolation Hospital.

McClellan, Wilson M., M.D., Orange Street, Ashland, Ohio. University of Maryland School of Medicine (Baltimore Medical College), 1895. Surgeon, Samaritan Hospital.

McClelland, Carl C., A.B., M.D., 1857 David Whitney Building, Detroit, Michigan. University of Michigan Medical School, 1910. Clinical Professor, Department of Ophthalmology, Detroit College of Medicine and Surgery; Associate Surgeon, Department of Ophthalmology and Oto-Laryngology, Grace Hospital.

McClelland, Lefferts A., M.D., 2 Rector Street, New York, New York. Long Island College Hospital, 1885. Governor and Chief of Department of Otology and Laryngology, and President of Medical Faculty, Broad Street Hospital; Otologist and Laryngologist, Williamsburg Hospital, Brooklyn, Rockaway Beach Hospital, Rockaway Beach, Mercy Hospital, Hempstead; Otologist, Coney Island Hospital, Brooklyn; Consulting Otologist, Kingston Avenue Hospital for Contagious Diseases, Brooklyn; Consulting Otologist and Laryngologist, German Evangelical Home.

McClure, Roy Donaldson, A.B., M.D., Henry Ford Hospital, Detroit, Michigan. Johns Hopkins University, Medical Department, 1908. Surgeon-in-Chief, Henry Ford Hospital.

McCollum, John Alexander, M.B., M.R.C.S. (Eng.), L.R.C.P. (Lond.), 12 Avenue Road, Toronto, Ontario. University of Toronto, Faculty of Medicine, 1901. Junior Surgeon, Toronto General Hospital.

McConnell, Allen Bonner, M.D., Griffith-McKenzie Building, Fresno, California. Cooper Medical College, 1901. Surgeon, Sample Sanitarium.

McConnell, John Herbert, M.D., C.M., 1653 Dundas Street, West, Toronto, Ontario. University of Toronto, Faculty of Medicine (Trinity Medical College), 1897. Surgeon, Grace Hospital.

McCook, John Butler, B.Sc., M.D., 396 Main Street, Hartford, Connecticut. Columbia University, College of Physicians and Surgeons, 1894. Consulting Surgeon, Hartford Hospital.

McCool, Joseph L., M.D., 909 Stevens Building, Portland, Oregon. University of Pennsylvania School of Medicine, 1900.

McCool, William E., M.D., Walker Hospital, Evansville, Indiana. Rush Medical College, 1890. Staff Surgeon, Walker Hospital; District Surgeon, Chicago and Eastern Illinois Railway.

McCord, James Robert, M.D., 373 Courtland Street, Atlanta, Georgia. Jefferson Medical College, 1909. Associate Professor of Obstetrics and Clinical Gynecology, Emory University School of Medicine; Associate Attending Gynecologist and Obstetrician, Grady Memorial and Wesley Memorial Hospitals; Assistant Surgeon, MacVicar Hospital.

McCormack, Arthur Thomas, A.M., M.D., State Board of Health, Louisville, Kentucky. Columbia University, College of Physicians and Surgeons, 1896.

McCormick, Albert M. D., M.D., Medical Corps, United States Navy, Washington, District of Columbia. University of Maryland School of Medicine, 1888. Rear Admiral, Medical Corps, United States Navy.

McCown, Oswald Stuart, M.D., Bank of Commerce Building, Memphis, Tennessee. University of Tennessee College of Medicine (Memphis Hospital Medical College), 1900.

McCoy, George Washington, A.M., M.D., 636 Security Building, Los Angeles, California. University of Cincinnati College of Medicine (Miami Medical College), 1904. Ophthalmic Surgeon, Los Angeles County Hospital.

McCoy, John, M.D., 157 West Seventy-third Street, New York, New York. Columbia University, College of Physicians and Surgeons, 1895. Clinical Professor of Laryngology, University and Bellevue Hospital Medical College; Professor of Otology, Fordham University School of Medicine; Attending Surgeon, Ear, Nose, and Throat Department, New York Eye and Ear Infirmary; Attending Laryngologist, University and Bellevue Hospital Medical College Clinic.

McCoy, John C., M.D., 292 Broadway, Paterson, New Jersey. Columbia University, College of Physicians and Surgeons, 1891. Surgeon, Paterson General Hospital; Consulting Surgeon, Paterson Eye and Ear Infirmary, Paterson, Dover General Hospital, Dover, New Jersey, Good Samaritan Hospital, Suffern, New York.

McCoy, Stephen Clifford, M.D., 300 Francis Building, Louisville, Kentucky. University of Louisville, Medical Department (Kentucky University, Medical Department), 1906. Assistant Surgeon, Louisville City Hospital.

McCRACKEN, JOSIAH CALVIN, A.M., M.D., 8 Darroch Road, Shanghai, China. University of Pennsylvania School of Medicine, 1901. Dean, and Professor of Surgery, Pennsylvania Medical School, Shanghai; Surgeon, St. Luke's Hospital; Consulting Surgeon, St. Elizabeth's Hospital for Women, Chinese Red Cross Hospital.

McCREADY, JAMES HOMER, M.D., Empire Building, Pittsburgh, Pennsylvania. Jefferson Medical College, 1906. Associate Professor of Laryngology, University of Pittsburgh School of Medicine; Laryngologist and Otologist, St. Francis Hospital; Laryngologist, Eye and Ear Hospital; Consulting Laryngologist and Otologist, Sewickley Valley and Dixmont Hospitals.

McCUISTION, LORENZO P., B.Sc., M.D., 215 Bonham Street, Paris, Texas. University of Louisville, Medical Department (Kentucky School of Medicine), 1889. Surgeon, Sanitarium of Paris.

McCULLAGH, SAMUEL, A.B., M.D., 17 East Thirty-eighth Street, New York, New York. University of Pennsylvania School of Medicine, 1898. Surgeon, Manhattan Eye, Ear, and Throat Hospital.

McCULLOCH, CARLETON B., M.D., 1135 State Life Building, Indianapolis, Indiana. Hahnemann Medical College, Chicago (Chicago Homeopathic Medical College), 1895. Director of Staff, James Whitcomb Riley Memorial Hospital; Member of Staff, St. Vincent's and Methodist Episcopal Hospitals.

McCULLOCH, CHAMPE CARTER, A.M., M.D., Medical Corps, United States Army, Washington, District of Columbia. University of Virginia, Department of Medicine, 1891; Columbia University, College of Physicians and Surgeons, 1892. Colonel, Medical Corps, United States Army.

McCULLOUGH, CRAWFORD CAMPBELL, M.D., C.M., 101 Dominion Bank Building, Fort William, Ontario. Queen's University, Faculty of Medicine, 1904. Surgeon, McKellar General Hospital, Fort William, St. Joseph's General and Port Arthur General Hospitals, Port Arthur.

McCULLOUGH, FRANK EDWARD, M.D., Medical Corps, United States Navy, Washington, District of Columbia. University of California Medical School, 1894. Captain, Medical Corps, United States Navy.

McCULLOUGH, WILLIAM J. L., M.D., Slater Building, Washington, Pennsylvania. Jefferson Medical College, 1905. Member of Surgical Staff, Washington Hospital.

McCURDY, STEWART L., A.M., M.D., 8103 Jenkins Arcade Building, Pittsburgh, Pennsylvania. Ohio State University College of Medicine (Columbus Medical College), 1881. Professor of Anatomy and Oral Surgery, University of Pittsburgh, Dental Department; Orthopedic Surgeon, Presbyterian Hospital, Pittsburgh, Columbia Hospital, Wilkinsburg.

McDANIEL, EDWARD BRUCE, M.D., 923 Electric Building, Portland, Oregon. St. Louis University School of Medicine (Beaumont Hospital Medical College), 1892; Jefferson Medical College, 1893. Chief Surgeon, Spokane, Portland and Seattle, Oregon Trunk, Astoria and Columbia River, and Oregon Electric Railways.

McDavitt, Thomas, M.D., Lowry Building, St. Paul, Minnesota. Northwestern University Medical School (Chicago Medical College), 1879. Oculist and Aurist, St. Joseph's Hospital.

McDill, John Rich, M.D., United States Public Health Service, Washington, District of Columbia. Rush Medical College, 1885.

McDonald, Angus C., M.D., 212 South Indiana Street, Warsaw, Indiana. University of Pennsylvania School of Medicine, 1892. Surgeon, McDonald Hospital.

McDonell, W. Neil, M.D., Medical Corps, United States Navy, Washington, District of Columbia. University of Minnesota Medical School, 1903. Lieutenant Commander, Medical Corps, United States Navy.

McDougall, John George, M.D., C.M., 95 Spring Garden Road, Halifax, Nova Scotia. Faculty of Medicine, McGill University, 1897.

McDowell, George W., A.M., M.D., 40 East Forty-first Street, New York, New York. New York Homeopathic Medical College and Flower Hospital, 1886. Professor of Ophthalmology and Oculist, New York Homeopathic Medical College and Flower Hospital; Surgeon, New York Ophthalmic Hospital; Consulting Aurist, Laura Franklin Free Hospital for Children.

McDowell, Nathan D., B.Sc., M.D., 275 Alexander Street, Rochester, New York. University and Bellevue Hospital Medical College (Bellevue Hospital Medical College), 1897. Laryngologist, Rochester General Hospital and Monroe County Tuberculosis Sanatorium; Laryngologist and Aurist, Infant's Summer Hospital.

McDowell, Ralph Walker, M.D., Medical Corps, United States Navy, Washington, District of Columbia. Jefferson Medical College, 1905. Surgeon and Chief of Surgical Service, United States Naval Hospital; Member of Staff, St. Joseph's Hospital, San Diego, California. Lieutenant Commander, Medical Corps, United States Navy.

McEachern, Isaac Whitney Taylor, M.D., C.M., 318 Empire Building, Edmonton, Alberta. Faculty of Medicine, McGill University, 1903. Surgeon, Royal Alexandra and General Hospitals.

McEachern, John Sinclair, M.D., C.M., 200 Maclean Block, Calgary, Alberta. University of Toronto, Faculty of Medicine, 1897. Surgeon, Calgary General and Holy Cross Hospitals.

McElhaney, Clarence Willson, A.B., M.D., 7 Penn Street, Greenville, Pennsylvania. Western Reserve University School of Medicine, 1893. Surgeon, Greenville City Hospital, Greenville, Cottage State Hospital, Mercer.

McEntee, Edward James, M.D., 196 Hancock Street, Brooklyn, New York. Columbia University, College of Physicians and Surgeons, 1901.

McEvoy, Frank E., B.Sc., M.D., 224 Thayer Street, Providence, Rhode Island. University of Pennsylvania School of Medicine, 1913. Associate Surgeon,

St. Joseph's Hospital; Consulting Neurological Surgeon, Memorial Hospital.

McEwen, Mary Gilruth, B.Sc., M.D., 25 East Washington Street, Chicago, Illinois. Northwestern University Woman's Medical School, 1898. Gynecologist, St. Francis Hospital, Evanston.

McGarty, Matthew A., M.D., State Bank Building, La Crosse, Wisconsin. Marquette University School of Medicine, 1912. Member of Staff, St. Francis Hospital.

McGee, Charles James, A.B., M.D., Woolfe Building, Leavenworth, Kansas. University Medical College, Kansas City, 1902. Visiting Surgeon, St. John's and Cushing Hospitals.

McGee, Harry S., M.D., 745 Ninth Street, Douglas, Arizona. University of Michigan, Medical School, 1902.

McGehee, John Lucius, A.B., M.D., 1705 Central Bank Building, Memphis, Tennessee. University of Tennessee College of Medicine (Memphis Hospital Medical College), 1901. Associate Professor of Surgery, University of Tennessee College of Medicine; Visiting Surgeon, Memphis General and Baptist Memorial Hospitals.

McGill, Joseph Warren, M.D., 284 Alexander Street, Rochester, New York. University of Buffalo, Department of Medicine, 1887. Member of Junior Surgical Staff, Rochester General Hospital; Senior Visiting Surgeon, Park Avenue Clinical Hospital.

McGinnis, Edwin, A.B., M.D., 104 South Michigan Avenue, Chicago, Illinois. Northwestern University Medical School, 1904. Instructor in Laryngology and Rhinology, Rush Medical College; Assistant Laryngologist, Presbyterian Hospital; Associate Laryngologist, Crippled Children's Home; Attending Laryngologist, St. Francis' Hospital, Blue Island, Central Free Dispensary, Chicago.

McGirk, Charles Edward, A.M., M.D., 17 North Front Street, Philipsburg, Pennsylvania. University of Pennsylvania School of Medicine, 1895. Surgeon, Dr. McGirk Sanitarium.

McGlannan, Alexius, A.M., M.D., 115 West Franklin Street, Baltimore, Maryland. University of Maryland School of Medicine (College of Physicians and Surgeons, Baltimore), 1895. Professor of Surgery, University of Maryland School of Medicine and College of Physicians and Surgeons; Surgeon, Mercy, St. Agnes, and Bon Secour Hospitals; Consulting Surgeon, United States Public Health Service.

McGlinn, John A., B.A., M.S., Hon., M.D., 113 South Twentieth Street, Philadelphia, Pennsylvania. Medico-Chirurgical College of Philadelphia, 1899. Associate Professor of Gynecology, University of Pennsylvania Graduate School of Medicine; Gynecologist, St. Agnes, Polyclinic, and Medico-Chirurgical Hospitals; Gynecologist and Obstetrician, Philadelphia General Hospital; Consulting Gynecologist, St. Francis Convalescent Home, Henry Phipps Institute, and Eagleville Sanatorium; Obstetrician, St. Vincent's Maternity Hospital.

McGowan, John D., M.D., 72 West Adams Street, Chicago, Illinois.   Harvard Medical School, 1885.

McGrath, Bernard Francis, A.B., M.D., Marquette University, Milwaukee, Wisconsin.   Georgetown University School of Medicine, 1895; Harvard Medical School, 1906.   Professor of Principles of Surgery and Director of Laboratories of Operative Surgery, Surgical Anatomy, and Surgical Pathology, Marquette University School of Medicine; Consulting Surgeon, Marquette Dispensary Clinic.

McGrath, John Francis, M.D., 119 East Thirtieth Street, New York, New York.   Cornell University Medical College, 1908.   Instructor and Chief of Clinic, Department of Obstetrics and Gynecology, Cornell University Medical College; Chief of Gynecological Clinic, St. Vincent's Hospital Dispensary.

McGrath, John J., M.D., 109 West Seventy-fourth Street, New York, New York.   Columbia University, College of Physicians and Surgeons, 1889.   Visiting Surgeon, Fordham, Columbus, and New York Foundling Hospitals.

McGregor, James Kenneth, M.B., Main Street, Hamilton, Ontario.   University of Toronto, Faculty of Medicine, 1904.   Member of Surgical Staff, City Hospital.

McGuinn, James J., M.D., 5850 Kenmore Avenue, Chicago, Illinois.   University of Illinois College of Medicine (College of Physicians and Surgeons, Chicago), 1901.   Surgeon, Columbus Hospital.

McGuire, Edgar R., M.D., 622 Delaware Avenue, Buffalo, New York.   University of Buffalo, Department of Medicine, 1900.   Professor of Surgery, University of Buffalo, Department of Medicine; Surgeon-in-Chief, Buffalo City Hospital; Surgeon, Buffalo General Hospital.

McGuire, Francis W., M.D., 470 Franklin Street, Buffalo, New York.   University of Buffalo, Department of Medicine (Niagara University, Medical Department), 1894.   Associate in Surgery, University of Buffalo, Department of Medicine; Attending Surgeon, Emergency and Buffalo City Hospitals; Assistant Surgeon, Buffalo General Hospital.

McGuire, Hunter H., M.D., 105 North Braddock Street, Winchester, Virginia.   Medical College of Virginia (University College of Medicine), 1897.   President and Ophthalmologist, Winchester Memorial Hospital.

McGuire, Stuart, M.D., LL.D., 513 East Grace Street, Richmond, Virginia.   University of Virginia, Department of Medicine, 1891.   President, and Professor of Surgery, Medical College of Virginia; Surgeon in Charge, St. Luke's Hospital; Visiting Surgeon, Memorial Hospital.

McHenry, Dolph D., M.D., Colcord Building, Oklahoma, Oklahoma.   University Medical College, Kansas City, 1897.   Member of Staff, St. Anthony's, Wesley, and Oklahoma State Baptist Hospitals; Oculist, Frisco Lines.

McHugh, Thomas, M.D., 510 Van Nuys Building, Los Angeles, California.   University of Michigan Medical School, 1901.

McILHENNY, PAUL AVERY, M.D., 3513 Prytania Street, New Orleans, Louisiana. Tulane University of Louisiana School of Medicine, 1900. Clinical Professor of Orthopedic Surgery, Tulane University of Louisiana School of Medicine; Orthopedic Surgeon, Hotel Dieu; Visiting Orthopedic Surgeon, Charity Hospital.

McILWRAITH, KENNEDY CRAWFORD, M.B., 30 Prince Arthur Avenue, Toronto, Ontario. University of Toronto, Faculty of Medicine, 1894. Associate Professor of Obstetrics, University of Toronto, Faculty of Medicine; Associate Surgeon, Department of Obstetrics and Gynecology, Toronto General Hospital.

McINTYRE, DONALD FAISON, M.D., 811 Boyd Building, Winnipeg, Manitoba. Faculty of Medicine, University of Manitoba (Manitoba Medical College), 1909. Lecturer on Surgery, Faculty of Medicine, University of Manitoba; Surgeon, Children's Hospital; Assistant in Urology, General Hospital.

McINTYRE, EDWARD H., B.Sc., M.D., Virginia, Minnesota. Rush Medical College, 1902. Chief Surgeon, McIntyre Hospital.

McIVOR, NORMAN KITSON, M.D., 601 Boyd Building, Winnipeg, Manitoba. Faculty of Medicine, University of Manitoba (Manitoba Medical College), 1908. Lecturer on Surgery, University of Manitoba Medical Department; Surgeon, Out-Patient Department, Winnipeg General Hospital.

McKAY, HARVEY S., M.D., University Club Building, St. Louis, Missouri. St. Louis University School of Medicine (Beaumont Hospital Medical College), 1901. Associate Professor of Surgery, St. Louis University School of Medicine; Chief Surgeon, St. Anthony's Hospital; Visiting Surgeon, City Hospital; Consulting Surgeon, Alexian Brothers' and St. John's Hospitals.

McKAY, JOHN WILLIAM, M.D., New Glasgow, Nova Scotia. University and Bellevue Hospital Medical College (New York University Medical College), 1886. Member of Visiting Staff, Aberdeen Hospital.

McKAY, ROY H., M.D., 321 Second National Bank Building, Akron, Ohio. University of Cincinnati College of Medicine (Medical College of Ohio), 1906. Surgeon, People's and Children's Hospitals, Mary Day Nursery; Associate Surgeon, City Hospital.

McKECHNIE, ROBERT EDWARD, M.D., C.M., 718 Granville Street, Vancouver, British Columbia. Faculty of Medicine, McGill University, 1890. Consulting Surgeon, Vancouver General Hospital.

McKECHNIE, WILLIAM B., M.B., M.D., C.M., Vancouver General Hospital, Vancouver, British Columbia. University of Toronto, Faculty of Medicine, 1895. Surgeon, Vancouver General Hospital.

McKECHNIE, WILLIAM C., M.D., C.M., 751 Granville Street, Vancouver, British Columbia. Faculty of Medicine, McGill University, 1899. Member of Surgical Staff, St. Paul's Hospital.

McKENNA, CHARLES MORGAN, B.Sc., M.D., 25 East Washington Street, Chicago, Illinois. Rush Medical College, 1905. Associate Professor of Genito-Urinary Surgery, University of Illinois College of Medicine; Surgeon, St. Joseph's Hospital; Genito-Urinary Surgeon, Municipal Tuberculosis Sanitarium.

McKENNA, HUGH, B.Sc., M.D., 104 South Michigan Avenue, Chicago, Illinois. Rush Medical College, 1903. Assistant Professor of Surgery, Rush Medical College; President of Staff and Senior Surgeon, St. Joseph's Hospital; Attending Surgeon, Cook County Hospital.

McKENNA, JOHN BERNARD, A.M., M.D., 47 Taunton Avenue, East Providence, Rhode Island. Columbia University, College of Physicians and Surgeons, 1888. Surgeon, St. Joseph's Hospital, Providence.

McKENNA, WILLIAM B., M.D., Pittsburgh Hospital, Pittsburgh, Pennsylvania. Jefferson Medical College, 1905. Surgeon, Pittsburgh Hospital.

McKENNEY, DESCUM CLAYTON, M.D., 1250 Main Street, Buffalo, New York. University of Buffalo, Department of Medicine, 1905. Instructor in Gynecology and Proctology, University of Buffalo, Department of Medicine; Proctologist, Erie County, Buffalo City, and Children's Hospitals; Assistant Gynecologist, Buffalo General and Erie County Hospitals.

McKENTY, FRANCIS DANIEL, M.D., 802 Boyd Building, Winnipeg, Manitoba. Faculty of Medicine, University of Manitoba (Manitoba Medical College), 1899. Surgeon, King George Hospital, Winnipeg, St. Boniface Hospital, St. Boniface.

McKENTY, FRANCIS EDMUND, M.D., C.M., F.R.C.S. (Eng.), 648 Union Avenue, Montreal, Quebec. Faculty of Medicine, McGill University, 1904. Assistant Surgeon, Royal Victoria Hospital.

McKENTY, JAMES, M.D., C.M., 410 Sterling Bank Building, Winnipeg, Manitoba. Queen's University, Faculty of Medicine, 1890. Associate Professor of Clinical Surgery, Faculty of Medicine, University of Manitoba; Surgeon, St. Boniface Hospital, St. Boniface; Consulting Surgeon, Children's Hospital.

McKENZIE, GEORGE, M.D., Thoma-Bigelow Building, Reno, Nevada. Rush Medical College, 1893. Surgeon, Mt. Rose Hospital.

McKEOUGH, GEORGE THOMAS, M.B., M.D., M.R.C.S. (Eng.), L.R.C.P. (Edin.), Erie Manor, Cedar Springs, Ontario. University of Toronto, Faculty of Medicine (Trinity Medical College), 1877. Surgeon, Public General and St. Joseph's Hospitals, Chatham.

McKEOWN, WALTER, B.A., M.D., M.R.C.S. (Eng.), 140 Wellesley Crescent, Wellesley, Toronto, Ontario. University of Toronto, Faculty of Medicine, 1889. Associate Professor of Clinical Surgery, University of Toronto, Faculty of Medicine; Chief Surgeon, St. Michael's Hospital.

McKERNON, JAMES FRANCIS, M.D., 62 West Fifty-second Street, New York, New York. Columbia University, College of Physicians and Surgeons, 1890. Professor of Otology, New York Post-Graduate Medical School;

President and Aural Surgeon, New York Post-Graduate Medical School and Hospital; Consulting Aural Surgeon, Lying-in, Manhattan Eye, Ear, and Throat, and Italian Hospitals.

McKim, Gordon F., A.B., M.D., Union Central Life Building, Cincinnati, Ohio. University of Cincinnati College of Medicine (Medical College of Ohio), 1903.

McKim, Laurie H., M.D., C.M., 4880 Sherbrooke Street, West, Montreal, Quebec. Faculty of Medicine, McGill University, 1912. Demonstrator of Anatomy, Faculty of Medicine, McGill University; Clinical Assistant in Surgery, Montreal General Hospital.

McKimmie, Oscar A. M., M.D., 1330 Massachusetts Avenue, Northwest, Washington, District of Columbia. George Washington University Medical School (Columbian University, Medical Department), 1891. Clinical Professor of Laryngology and Otology, George Washington University Medical School; Attending Surgeon, Episcopal Eye, Ear, and Throat Hospital; Consultant in Otology and Laryngology, Eastern Dispensary and Casualty Hospital.

McKinley, Walter Russell, M.D., 618 Main Street, Columbus, Mississippi. University of Alabama School of Medicine, 1894. Surgeon in Charge, McKinley Sanatorium.

McKinney, Mark Ward, M.D., 621 Lumber Exchange Building, Seattle, Washington. University of Oregon Medical School (Willamette University Medical Department), 1908. Surgeon, Seattle City and Seattle General Hospitals.

McKinney, Richmond, A.M., M.D., Bank of Commerce Building, Memphis, Tennessee. University of Tennessee College of Medicine (Memphis Hospital Medical College), 1894. Professor of Oto-Laryngology, University of Tennessee College of Medicine; Oto-Laryngologist, Memphis General and Baptist Memorial Hospitals.

McKinney, Thomas Dempsey, M.D., 304 Doctors Building, Nashville, Tennessee. Vanderbilt University, Medical Department, 1913. Assistant in Surgery, Vanderbilt University, Medical Department; Surgeon, Vanderbilt, Nashville City, and St. Thomas Hospitals; Consulting Surgeon, Tennessee State Hospital.

McKinney, Thomas J., M.D., 300 First National Bank Building, Champaign, Illinois. Indiana University School of Medicine (Medical College of Indiana), 1883; Northwestern University Medical School, 1898. Member of Staff, Julia F. Burnham Hospital.

McKinnie, Lewis H., M.D., 316 Ferguson Building, Colorado Springs, Colorado. Jefferson Medical College, 1902.

McKinnon, Artemas I., M.D., C.M., 503 Security Mutual Life Building, Lincoln, Nebraska. Faculty of Medicine, McGill University, 1892. Instructor in Surgery, University of Nebraska College of Dentistry; Surgeon, St. Elizabeth's Hospital.

McKinnon, Frederick William, M.D., C.M., 171 Metcalfe Street, Ottawa, Ontario. Faculty of Medicine, McGill University, 1897. Surgeon, St. Luke's Hospital.

McKitrick, Austin S., B.Sc., M.D., 115 North Detroit Street, Kenton, Ohio. Eclectic Medical College, Cincinnati, 1888. Western Reserve University School of Medicine (Cleveland College of Physicians and Surgeons), 1902. Surgeon, McKitrick and Antonio Hospitals, Big Four and Toledo and Ohio Central Railroads.

McKnight, William Clark, M.D., 200 West Fifty-eighth Street, New York, New York. New York Homeopathic Medical College and Flower Hospital, 1901. Professor of Ophthalmology, College of the New York Ophthalmic Hospital; Surgeon, New York Ophthalmic Hospital.

McLandress, George Stuart, M.D., Albuquerque, New Mexico. Saginaw Valley Medical College, 1899.

McLaughlin, Alphonso James, M.D., 210 Davidson Building, Sioux City, Iowa. University of Louisville, Medical Department (Kentucky School of Medicine), 1898. Member of Staff and Head of Genito-Urinary Section, St. Joseph's Mercy Hospital.

McLaughlin, Andrew Joseph, M.D., 677 Broad Street, Providence, Rhode Island. Columbia University, College of Physicians and Surgeons, 1900. Surgeon, Department of Gynecology, St. Joseph's Hospital.

McLaughlin, Philip Benedict, M.D., 310 Davidson Building, Sioux City, Iowa. University of Louisville, Medical Department (Kentucky School of Medicine), 1897. Surgeon, St. Joseph's Mercy Hospital.

McLaughlin, William Charles, A.B., M.D., 600 Broad Street, Providence, Rhode Island. Harvard Medical School, 1905. Ophthalmologist and Aurist, St. Joseph's Hospital; Surgeon, Nose and Throat Department, Providence City Hospital; Assistant Surgeon, Ear, Nose, and Throat Department, Rhode Island Hospital.

McLean, Allen Donald, M.D., Medical Corps, United States Navy, Washington, District of Columbia. Detroit College of Medicine and Surgery, 1895. Commander, Medical Corps, United States Navy.

McLean, Angus, M.D., David Whitney Building, Detroit, Michigan. Detroit College of Medicine and Surgery, 1886. Professor of Surgery, Detroit College of Medicine and Surgery; Attending Surgeon, Harper Hospital; Consulting Surgeon, Children's Free and Providence Hospitals, Florence Crittenton Home.

McLean, John H., A.B., M.D., Fort Worth Club Building, Fort Worth, Texas. Texas Christian University School of Medicine (Fort Worth University, Medical Department), 1899; Cornell University Medical College, 1901. Attending Surgeon, All Saints', City and County Hospitals; Local Surgeon, Texas and Pacific Railway.

McLean, John William, M.D., C.M., North Sydney, Nova Scotia. Faculty of Medicine, McGill University, 1883. Surgeon, Hamilton Memorial Hospital, North Sydney, Harbor View Hospital, Sydney Mines.

McLean, Mary Hancock, M.D., 4339 Delmar Boulevard, St. Louis, Missouri. University of Michigan Medical School, 1883. Retired.

McLean, Norman Thomas, Ph.B., M.D., Medical Corps, United States Navy, Washington, District of Columbia. Tufts Medical School, 1900. Commander, Medical Corps, United States Navy.

McLean, Samuel Hoskins, M.D., Century Building, Jackson, Mississippi. Tulane University of Louisiana School of Medicine, 1893. Staff Surgeon, Baptist Hospital; Consulting Surgeon, Mississippi State Charity Hospital.

McLeod, Frank Hilton, M.D., 1 West Cheves Street, Florence, South Carolina. University of Tennessee College of Medicine, 1888. Surgeon-in-Chief, Florence Infirmary.

McLoone, John J., A.B., M.D., 611 Heard Building, Phoenix, Arizona. George Washington University Medical School, 1910. Attending Surgeon, St. Joseph's Hospital and Maricopa County Clinic.

McLoughlin, George N., M.D., 1114 Boylston Avenue, Seattle, Washington. George Washington University Medical School (Columbian University, Medical Department), 1895.

McMahon, Charles Gilbert, M.D., 448 Central Avenue, Superior, Nebraska. University of Minnesota Medical School, 1906. Surgeon, Lewis Memorial Hospital.

McMahon, Francis B., B.Sc., M.D., M.S., 120 Wisconsin Street, Milwaukee, Wisconsin. University of Pennsylvania School of Medicine, 1913. Associate Professor in Surgery, Marquette University School of Medicine; Member of Surgical Staff, St. Mary's, Milwaukee County, Children's and Deaconess Hospitals.

McManus, T. U., A.M., M.D., 522 Black Building, Waterloo, Iowa. University of Illinois College of Medicine (College of Physicians and Surgeons, Chicago), 1898. Chief of Staff, St. Francis Hospital.

McMartin, Charles, Ph.B., M.D., 828 City National Bank Building, Omaha, Nebraska. Rush Medical College, 1906. Professor of Genito-Urinary and Skin Diseases, John A. Creighton Medical College; Attending Urologist and Dermatologist, St. Joseph's Hospital.

McMullen, Charles Goul, M.D., 613 State Street, Schenectady, New York. Albany Medical College, 1898. Clinical Professor of Surgery, Albany Medical College; Surgeon, Ellis Hospital, General Electric Works.

McMurtray, Lewis Samuel, M.D., LL.D., 542 Francis Building, Louisville, Kentucky. Tulane University of Louisiana School of Medicine, 1873. President of Medical Faculty and Professor of Abdominal Surgery and Gynecology, University of Louisville, Medical Department; Surgeon, Louisville City Hospital, John N. Norton Memorial Infirmary.

McNamara, Sylvester James, A.M., M.D., 369 Union Street, Brooklyn, New York. Long Island College Hospital, 1892. Senior Obstetrician and Gynecologist, Kings County Hospital, Kings Park State Hospital, Kings

Park; Consulting Gynecologist, Coney Island Hospital; Consulting Obstetrician and Gynecologist, Long Island College Hospital.

McNAMARA, WILLIAM E., M.D., 300 West Ottawa Street, Lansing, Michigan. University of Michigan Medical School, 1902.

McNAUGHT, FRANCIS H., M.D., 742 Metropolitan Building, Denver, Colorado. Columbia University, College of Physicians and Surgeons, 1878. Consulting Surgeon, Denver City and County Hospital; Surgeon, St. Luke's, St. Joseph's, and Children's Hospitals; Chief Surgeon, Colorado and Southern Railway.

McNEILL, GEORGE, M.D., 245 Queens Avenue, London, Ontario. Western University Medical School, 1902. Associate Professor of Clinical Surgery and Lecturer on Radiology, Western University Medical School; Staff Surgeon, Victoria Hospital.

McNEILL, WALTER H., JR., 34 East Fortieth Street, New York, New York. Cornell University Medical College, 1910. Instructor, Department of Urology, University and Bellevue Hospital Medical College; Adjunct Attending Urologist, Bellevue Hospital; Urologist, New York Hospital; Consulting Urologist, Mt. Vernon Hospital, Mt. Vernon, New Rochelle Hospital, New Rochelle; Chief of Urological Clinic, Bellevue and New York Hospitals.

McNERTHNEY, JOHN B., M.D., 1009 Fidelity Building, Tacoma, Washington. University of Minnesota Medical School, 1899. Attending Surgeon, St. Joseph's Hospital.

McPHEETERS, EARL ROBY, M.D., Evans Hospital, Modesto, California. University of Louisville, Medical Department (Kentucky School of Medicine), 1905. Chief Surgeon, Evans Hospital.

McPHERSON, DAVID WILLIAM, M.B., M.D., C.M., C.M.G., 556 Bathurst Street, Toronto, Ontario. University of Toronto, Faculty of Medicine (Medical Faculty of Trinity University), 1895. Surgeon, Grace Hospital.

McPHERSON, ROSS, A.B., M.D., 125 East Thirty-ninth Street, New York, New York. Harvard Medical School, 1902. Attending Surgeon, Lying-in Hospital; Consulting Obstetrician, United Hospital, Port Chester, Caledonian Hospital, Brooklyn, New York, Hackensack Hospital, Hackensack, New Jersey.

McPHILLIPS, FRANCIS XAVIER, B.A., M.D., 1101 Burrard Street, Vancouver, British Columbia. Faculty of Medicine, University of Manitoba (Manitoba Medical College), 1889. Chief Surgeon, St. Paul's Hospital.

McQUEEN, JOHN DOUGLAS, M.D., C.M., 811 Boyd Building, Winnipeg, Manitoba. Faculty of Medicine, University of Manitoba (Manitoba Medical College), 1909. Lecturer on Gynecology and Assistant Clinician in Obstetrics, Faculty of Medicine, University of Manitoba; Assistant in Obstetrics, Winnipeg General Hospital.

McQUILLAN, ALBERT BAPTISTE, M.D., Cahokia Building, East St. Louis, Illinois. Washington University Medical School, 1903. Instructor in

Anatomy and Assistant in Surgery, St. Louis University School of Medicine.

McREYNOLDS, GEORGE STREET, M.D., Temple State Bank Building, Temple, Texas. University of Maryland School of Medicine (College of Physicians and Surgeons), 1898. Member of Staff, Oculist and Aurist, King's Daughters' Hospital.

McREYNOLDS, JOHN OLIVER, M.Sc., M.D., LL.D., Dallas County State Bank Building, Dallas, Texas. University of Maryland School of Medicine (College of Physicians and Surgeons, Baltimore), 1891. Ophthalmic and Aural Surgeon, St. Paul's Sanitarium; Oculist and Aurist, Texas and Pacific, Atchison, Topeka and Santa Fe, and Rock Island Railways.

McREYNOLDS, ROBERT PHILLIPS, B.Sc., M.D., 307 Coulter Building, Los Angeles, California. University of Pennsylvania School of Medicine, 1895. Consulting Surgeon, Atchison, Topeka and Santa Fe Railway.

McSWEENEY, PATRICK EUGENE, M.D., 37 Elmwood Avenue, Burlington, Vermont. University of Vermont College of Medicine, 1886. Professor of Obstetrics and Gynecology, University of Vermont College of Medicine; Attending Surgeon, Mary Fletcher Hospital, Burlington, Fanny Allen Hospital, Winooski.

McWHORTER, GOLDER LEWIS, B.Sc., Ph.D., M.D., 122 South Michigan Avenue, Chicago, Illinois. Rush Medical College, 1913. Instructor in Surgery, Rush Medical College; Assistant Attending Surgeon, Presbyterian Hospital.

McWILLIAMS, CLARENCE A., A.M., M.D., 19 East Sixty-fifth Street, New York, New York. Columbia University College of Physicians and Surgeons, 1895. Instructor in Surgery, Columbia University, College of Physicians and Surgeons; Associate Surgeon, Presbyterian Hospital.

MEACHER, BYRON C., M.D., John Graham Building, Portage, Wisconsin. Rush Medical College, 1880. Associate Surgeon, St. Saviour's General and Portage Hospitals, Portage, St. Mary's Hospital, Columbus.

MEADE, REGINALD H., M.D., 817 Rialto Building, Kansas City, Missouri. St. Louis University School of Medicine (Beaumont Hospital Medical College), 1896. Member of Staff, Kansas City General and St. Luke's Hospitals, Kansas City, Missouri, St. Margaret's Hospital, Kansas City, Kansas; Consultant, United States Public Health Service.

MEANS, CHARLES S., B.Sc., M.D., 137 East State Street, Columbus, Ohio. Ohio State University College of Medicine (Columbus Medical College), 1891; Hahnemann Medical College and Hospital, Philadelphia, 1892. Ophthalmologist and Oto-Laryngologist, Protestant Hospital; Chief of Staff, Eye, Ear, and Throat Department, McKinley Hospital.

MEANY, JOHN J., M.D., 30 North Michigan Avenue, Chicago, Illinois. University of Illinois College of Medicine, 1900.

MECHLING, CURTIS CAMPBELL, A.M., M.D., Jenkins Arcade Building, Pittsburgh, Pennsylvania. University of Michigan Medical School, 1903. Proctologist, St. Francis Hospital.

MECRAY, PAUL MULFORD, M.D., 405 Cooper Street, Camden, New Jersey. University of Pennsylvania School of Medicine, 1892. President of Staff and Visiting Surgeon, Cooper Hospital; Chief Surgeon, Zurbrugg Memorial Hospital, Riverside; Consulting Surgeon, Salem Memorial Hospital, Salem.

MEEK, HARRY, M.B., 330 Queens Avenue, London, Ontario. University of Toronto, Faculty of Medicine (Trinity Medical College), 1878. Visiting Gynecologist, St. Joseph's Hospital.

MEEKER, HAROLD DENMAN, A.B., M.D., 47 East Fifty-seventh Street, New York, New York. Columbia University, College of Physicians and Surgeons, 1902. Professor of Clinical Surgery, New York Polyclinic Medical School and Hospital; Surgeon, Polyclinic Hospital; Visiting Surgeon, Park, Reconstruction, and Washington Square Hospitals.

MEEKS, FREDERICK R., M.D., 100 Hancock Street, Brooklyn, New York. New York Homeopathic Medical College and Flower Hospital, 1907. Assistant Surgeon and Anesthetist, Carson C. Peck Memorial Hospital; Member of Associate Staff and Anesthetist, St. Catherine's Hospital; Visiting Surgeon and Associate Gynecologist, Cumberland Street Hospital.

MEIERHOF, EDWARD L., M.D., 1140 Madison Avenue, New York, New York. University of Maryland School of Medicine, 1881. Oto-Laryngologist, Institution for Improved Instruction of Deaf Mutes; Oculist, Israel Orphan Asylum.

MEISENHELDER, EDMUND W., A.M., M.D., 1253 West Market Street, York, Pennsylvania. Johns Hopkins University, Medical Department, 1902. Surgeon, West Side Sanitarium.

MELAND, ORVILLE N., M.D., Warren Hospital, Warren, Minnesota. University of Minnesota Medical School, 1913. Associate Surgeon, Warren Hospital.

MENGE, FREDERICK, M.D., 25 East Washington Street, Chicago, Illinois. Northwestern University Medical School (Chicago Medical College), 1892. Professor of Laryngology and Head of Department, Northwestern University Medical School; Laryngologist, Wesley Memorial, Mercy, Evangelical Deaconess, and Provident Hospitals.

MENGEL, SAMUEL P., M.D., 181 South Franklin Street, Wilkes-Barre, Pennsylvania. University of Pennsylvania School of Medicine, 1894. Surgeon, Wilkes-Barre City Hospital.

MENZIES, PERCIVAL KEITH, A.B., M.B., 405 Fayette Park, Syracuse, New York. University of Toronto Faculty of Medicine, 1910. Assistant Orthopedic Surgeon, Memorial Hospital; Surgeon, Syracuse Clinic.

MERCER, CLARENCE MAVEL, M.D., 41 North Washington Avenue, Battle Creek, Michigan. University of Pennsylvania School of Medicine, 1907.

MERCER, RICHARD E., M.D., 1229 David Whitney Building, Detroit, Michigan. Detroit College of Medicine and Surgery, 1897. Associate Professor of Oto-Laryngology, Detroit College of Medicine and Surgery; Rhino-Laryngologist, Providence and St. Luke's Hospitals, Protestant Orphan Asylum.

MERCER, WARREN CHARLES, M.D., 24 South Twenty-first Street, Philadelphia, Pennsylvania. Hahnemann Medical College and Hospital, Philadelphia, 1899. Clinical Professor of Obstetrics, Hahnemann Medical College and Hospital; Obstetrician, Hahnemann Medical College and Hospital; Consulting Obstetrician, Woman's Southern Homeopathic and Mercy Hospitals; Obstetrician and Gynecologist, Children's Homeopathic Hospital; Consulting Obstetrician and Gynecologist, West Chester Homeopathic Hospital, West Chester.

MERCER, WILLIAM F., M.D., 1006 West Franklin Street, Richmond, Virginia. Medical College of Virginia, 1882. Associate Professor of Otology, Rhinology, and Laryngology, Medical College of Virginia; Assistant Surgeon and Chief of Clinic, Richmond Eye, Ear, and Throat Infirmary; Consulting Eye, Ear, Nose, and Throat Surgeon, St. Luke's Hospital; Visiting Surgeon, Memorial Hospital.

MERCIER, OSCAR FELIX, M.B., M.D., 394 Sherbrooke Street, East, Montreal, Quebec. University of Montreal, Faculty of Medicine, 1890. Professor of Clinical Surgery, Faculty of Medicine, University of Montreal; Chief Surgeon, Notre Dame Hospital.

MEREDITH, EVAN WILLIAM, M.D., 5004 Jenkins Arcade Building, Pittsburgh, Pennsylvania. Medico-Chirurgical College, Philadelphia, 1901. Surgeon, St. Francis' and Children's Hospitals.

MERRICK, SAMUEL K., M.D., 824 Park Avenue, Baltimore, Maryland. University of Maryland School of Medicine, 1872. Professor of Diseases of Nose and Throat, University of Maryland School of Medicine and College of Physicians and Surgeons; Chief of Visiting Staff, Nose and Throat Department, Maryland General Hospital.

MERRIGAN, THOMAS DAVIS, M.D., 553 West One Hundred Sixty-seventh Street, New York, New York. University and Bellevue Hospital Medical College (New York University Medical College), 1887. Emeritus Professor of Anatomy, Fordham University School of Medicine; Surgical Director, St. Laurance Hospital.

MERRILL, WILLIAM HOWE, M.D., Bay State Building, Lawrence, Massachusetts. Bowdoin Medical School, 1888. Ophthalmic and Aural Surgeon, Lawrence General Hospital.

MERTINS, PAUL STEARNS, A.B., M.D., 1115 Bell Building, Montgomery, Alabama. Harvard Medical School, 1900. Oculist, Aurist, and Laryngologist, St. Margaret's Hospital.

METCALF, CARLETON RAY, A.B., M.D., 4 North State Street, Concord, New Hampshire. Harvard Medical School, 1906. Visiting Surgeon, Margaret Pillsbury General and New Hampshire Memorial Hospitals.

METCALF, WILLIAM FRANCIS, M.D., 1905 West Grand Boulevard, Detroit, Michigan. University of Michigan Medical School, 1888.

METCALFE, RAYMOND FRANKLIN, M.D., Medical Corps, United States Army, Washington, District of Columbia. University of Buffalo, Department of

Medicine, 1900. Chief of Surgical Service, Station Hospital, Fort Sam Houston, Texas; Lieutenant Colonel, Medical Corps, United States Army.

METTS, FRED A., M.D., Bluffton, Indiana. Indiana University School of Medicine (Fort Wayne College of Medicine), 1898.

METZENBAUM, MYRON, B.Sc., M.D., Rose Building, Cleveland, Ohio. Western Reserve University School of Medicine, 1900.

MEWBURN, FRANK HAMILTON, M.D., C.M., Calgary, Alberta. Faculty of Medicine, McGill University, 1881. Member of Staff, General and Holy Cross Hospitals.

MEYER, EDWARD JOHN, M.D., 1312 Main Street, Buffalo, New York. University of Buffalo, Department of Medicine, 1891. Emeritus Professor of Clinical Surgery, University of Buffalo, Department of Medicine; President, Buffalo City Hospital and Dispensaries; Consulting Surgeon, Emergency Hospital of the Sisters of Charity, Deaconess and Homeopathic Hospitals.

MEYER, HENRY, M.D., 240 Stockton Street, San Francisco, California. Cooper Medical College, 1893.

MEYER, LEO B., A.M., M.D., 2178 Broadway, New York, New York. Columbia University, College of Physicians and Surgeons, 1898. Associate Surgeon, Mt. Sinai Hospital; Assistant Surgeon, Beth Israel and Montefiore Hospitals.

MEYER, WILLY, M.D., 700 Madison Avenue, New York, New York. University of Bonn, 1880. Emeritus Professor of Surgery, New York Post-Graduate Medical School; Attending Surgeon, Lenox Hill Hospital.

MEYERDING, HENRY WILLIAM, B.Sc., M.D., M.S., 525 Ninth Avenue, Southwest, Rochester, Minnesota. University of Minnesota Medical School, 1909. Associate Professor of Orthopedic Surgery, University of Minnesota Graduate School of Medicine; Associate Chief, Section of Orthopedic Surgery, Mayo Clinic; Orthopedic Surgeon, St. Mary's and Colonial Hospitals.

MEYNEN, GEORGE KISSAM, M.D., 43 Clinton Avenue, Jamaica, New York. University and Bellevue Hospital Medical College (New York University Medical College), 1885. Visiting Surgeon, Mary Immaculate Hospital; Consulting Surgeon, Nassau Hospital, Mineola, Jamaica Hospital, Jamaica; Chief Surgeon, Long Island Railroad.

MICHAUX, STUART, M.D., Stuart Circle Hospital, Richmond, Virginia. Medical College of Virginia (University College of Medicine), 1903. Associate Professor of Gynecology, Medical College of Virginia; Surgeon, Stuart Circle Hospital; Gynecologist, Memorial Hospital, Medical College of Virginia Dispensary.

MICHEL, BERNARD A., 257 Tenth Street, Dubuque, Iowa. University of Pennsylvania School of Medicine, 1889. Member of Staff, Finley Hospital.

MICHEL, HENRY MIDDLETON, M.D., 638 Greene Street, Augusta, Georgia. University of Georgia, Medical Department, 1896. Professor of Orthopedic Surgery, University of Georgia, Medical Department; Visiting Orthopedic Surgeon, Augusta City, Lamar, and Wilhenford Hospitals; Chief Surgeon, Augusta Southern Railway; Local Surgeon, Southern Railway.

MICHLER, HENRY DANIEL, M.Sc., M.D., 134 North Third Street, Easton, Pennsylvania. University of Pennsylvania School of Medicine, 1881. Surgeon-in-Chief, Easton Hospital.

MIDELFART, HANS CHRISTIAN ULRIK, M.D., 343 Gilbert Avenue, Eau Claire, Wisconsin. Royal University of Norway, 1892. Director, Luther Hospital; Attending Surgeon, Sacred Heart Hospital.

MILLAR, ROSS, M.A., M.D., C.M., 28 Crescent Avenue, Amherst, Nova Scotia. Dalhousie University, Faculty of Medicine, 1902. Visiting Surgeon, Highland Hospital.

MILES, HENRY SHILLINGFORD, Phar.G., M.D., 881 Lafayette Street, Bridgeport, Connecticut. Columbia University, College of Physicians and Surgeons, 1891. Consulting Ophthalmic Surgeon, Bridgeport Hospital.

MILLER, A. MERRILL, M.D., 1222 Vermilion Street, Danville, Illinois. Northwestern University Medical School, 1901. Surgeon, Lake View Hospital; Attending Surgeon, St. Elizabeth's Hospital.

MILLER, AARON B., M.D., 102 Erie Street, Syracuse, New York. University of Maryland School of Medicine, 1882. Professor of Gynecology, Syracuse University College of Medicine; Member of Staff, St. Joseph's Hospital; Consultant, Syracuse Hospital for Women and Children; State Medical Examiner in Gynecology and Obstetrics; Chief of Gynecological Department, Syracuse Free Dispensary.

MILLER, BENJAMIN FRANKLIN, M.D., 101½ East Philadelphia Avenue, Whittier, California. Rush Medical College, 1897. Member of Staff, Murphy Memorial Hospital.

MILLER, C. JEFF, M.D., 124 Baronne Street, New Orleans, Louisiana. University of Tennessee College of Medicine, 1893. Professor of Obstetrics and Clinical Gynecology, Tulane University of Louisiana School of Medicine; Professor of Abdominal Surgery, New Orleans Polyclinic; Chief of Division of Obstetrics and Gynecology, Charity Hospital; Chief of Department of Gynecology, Touro Infirmary.

MILLER, CLIFTON MEREDITH, M.D., Stuart Circle Hospital, Richmond, Virginia. Medical College of Virginia, 1892. Associate Professor of Otology and Rhinology, Medical College of Virginia; Ophthalmologist and Oto-Laryngologist, Stuart Circle Hospital; Visiting Surgeon, Department of Ophthalmology and Oto-Laryngology, Memorial Hospital.

MILLER, FELIX PERRYMAN, M.D., 514 Martin Building, El Paso, Texas. University of Texas, Medical Department, 1899. Visiting Surgeon, Hotel Dieu, Rolston Private, and Providence Hospitals; Surgeon, Texas and Pacific Railway.

MILLER, FRANK WALLACE, M.D., 811 Pacific Mutual Life Insurance Building, Los Angeles, California. Rush Medical College, 1894. Oculist, Children's Hospital.

MILLER, FREDERICK MASON, M.D., 143 Court Street, Binghamton, New York. University and Bellevue Hospital Medical College (New York University Medical College), 1896. Surgeon-in-Chief, Binghamton City Hospital; Surgeon, Moore-Overton Hospital; Consulting Surgeon, New York State Hospital for Crippled and Deformed Children, West Haverstraw.

MILLER, G. BROWN, B.Sc., M.D., 1730 K Street, Northwest, Washington, District of Columbia. University of Virginia, Department of Medicine, 1890. Clinical Professor of Gynecology, George Washington University Medical School; Visiting Gynecologist, Garfield Memorial and Central Dispensary and Emergency Hospitals, Columbia Hospital for Women.

MILLER, HAL CURTIS, Ph.B., M.D., 720 Hurt Building, Atlanta, Georgia. Jefferson Medical College, 1909. Instructor, Emory University School of Medicine; Attending Surgeon, Wesley Memorial Hospital; Assistant Attending Surgeon, Grady Hospital.

MILLER, HAROLD A., M.D., Pittsburgh Life Building, Pittsburgh, Pennsylvania. University of Pittsburgh School of Medicine, 1899. Professor of Obstetrics, University of Pittsburgh School of Medicine; Obstetrician, Elizabeth Steel Magee and Allegheny General Hospitals; Consulting Obstetrician, Sewickley Valley Hospital.

MILLER, JOHN D., M.D., 204 West Eighth Street, Cincinnati, Ohio. University of Cincinnati College of Medicine (Medical College of Ohio), 1897. Professor of Gynecology and Chief Clinician to Gynecological Outdoor Department, University of Cincinnati College of Medicine; Gynecologist, Cincinnati General and Good Samaritan Hospitals.

MILLER, REUBEN B., M.D., Medical Corps, United States Army, Washington, District of Columbia. Detroit College of Medicine and Surgery, 1893. Lieutenant Colonel, Medical Corps, United States Army.

MILLER, ROBERT T., A.B., M.D., Duxbury, Massachusetts. Johns Hopkins University, Medical Department, 1903.

MILLER, SAMUEL RUSH, M.D., 406 West Church Avenue, Knoxville, Tennessee. Vanderbilt University, Medical Department, 1893. Visiting Surgeon, Knoxville General, Riverside, and Lincoln Memorial Hospitals.

MILLER, THEODORE, A.B., M.D., 1836 Euclid Avenue, Cleveland, Ohio. Harvard Medical School, 1908. Obstetrician, Mt. Sinai Hospital.

MILLETTE, JOHN W., A.M., B.L., M.Sc., M.D., 58 Cambridge Avenue, Dayton, Ohio. Ohio State University College of Medicine (Ohio Medical University), 1903. Aurist and Oculist, St. Elizabeth Hospital, National Military Home.

MILLIGAN, JOHN DAVIDSON, M.D., Pittsburgh, Pennsylvania. University and Bellevue Hospital Medical College (Bellevue Hospital Medical College), 1876. Consulting Surgeon, South Side Hospital.

MILLIGAN, ROBERT, M.D., Sandusky Street and Park Way, North Side, Pittsburgh, Pennsylvania. Jefferson Medical College, 1896. Otologist, Allegheny General Hospital.

MILLIKEN, SAMUEL EDWIN, M.D., Westminster Building, Dallas, Texas. University of Louisville, Medical Department, 1887. Attending Surgeon, Parkland City Hospital, St. Paul's Sanitarium; Chief of Staff, Westminster Sanitarium.

MILLIKEN, SETH MINOT, A.B., M.D., 951 Madison Avenue, New York, New York. Columbia University, College of Physicians and Surgeons, 1902. Assistant Professor of Surgery, New York Post-Graduate Hospital, Consulting Surgeon, French Hospital; Attending Surgeon, Lincoln Hospital and Home.

MILLIKIN, MARK, M.D., 311 South Second Street, Hamilton, Ohio. University of Cincinnati College of Medicine (Miami Medical College), 1892. Member of Staff, Mercy Hospital; Local Surgeon, Baltimore and Ohio, Cincinnati, Indianapolis and Western, Pennsylvania and Ohio Electric Railways.

MILLS, CLIFFORD, M.D., 36 Maple Avenue, Morristown, New Jersey. Long Island College Hospital, 1897. Attending Surgeon, All Souls' Hospital; Consulting Surgeon, Dover General Hospital, Dover, New Jersey State Hospital, Morris Plains.

MILLS, HENRY MATELAND, M.D., 902 President Street, Brooklyn, New York. Long Island College Hospital, 1898. Visiting Gynecologist and Obstetrician, Kings County Hospital.

MILLS, HENRY WILLIAM, M.R.C.S. (Eng.), L.R.C.P. (Lond.), Chamber of Commerce Building, San Bernardino, California. University of Edinburgh and St. Thomas Hospital, London, 1895. Director and Consulting Surgeon, Ramona Hospital.

MILLS, LLOYD, M.D., 927 Citizens National Bank Building, Los Angeles, California. Harvard Medical School, 1902. Ophthalmologist, Methodist Hospital, Orthopedic Hospital School.

MILLS, WILLIAM MERRILL, A.B., M.D., 616 Mills Building, Topeka, Kansas. Columbia University, College of Physicians and Surgeons, 1907. Member of Staff, St. Francis' and Jane C. Stormont Hospitals.

MILNE, JOHN DANIEL, M.B., M.R.C.S. (Eng.), L.R.C.P. (Lond.), F.R.C.S. (Edin.), 205 Grain Exchange Building, Calgary, Alberta. University of Toronto, Faculty of Medicine, 1907.

MINER, LUCIEN LUTTRELL, M.Sc., M.D., Parker Hospital, Tyrone, New Mexico. Columbia University College of Physicians and Surgeons, 1904. Chief Surgeon, T. S. Parker Hospital.

MINER, WALTER N., M.D., 9 Calais Avenue, Calais, Maine. University of Maryland School of Medicine (Baltimore Medical College), 1898. Surgeon-in-Chief, Calais Hospital; Visiting Surgeon, Chipman Memorial Hospital.

MININGHAM, WILLIAM D., M.D., 11 Astor Street, Newark, New Jersey. Columbia University, College of Physicians and Surgeons, 1906. Attending Surgeon, Hospital of St. Barnabas; Assistant Surgeon, St. Michael's Hospital; Consulting Surgeon, Essex County Hospital, Cedar Grove.

MINK, OWEN JOSEPH, A.B., M.D., Medical Corps, United States Navy, Washington, District of Columbia. University of Michigan Medical School, 1904. Commander, Medical Corps, United States Navy.

MINOR, CHARLES L., M.D., 726 Fairbanks Building, Springfield, Ohio. University of Cincinnati College of Medicine (Miami Medical College), 1897.

MINOR, JAMES C., M.D., 511 Commerce Building, Kansas City, Missouri. University Medical College of Kansas City, 1891. Member of Staff, Christian Church and Research Hospitals.

MINOR, JAMES LANCELOT, M.D., Bank of Commerce Building, Memphis, Tennessee. University of Virginia, Department of Medicine, 1876.

MINTER, JAMES M., M.D., Medical Corps, United States Navy, Washington, District of Columbia. University of the South, Medical Department, 1903. Sanitary Engineer of Haiti, Port au Prince, Haiti. Commander, Medical Corps, United States Navy.

MINTON, WILLIAM HENRY, M.D., Bartlett Trust Company Building, St. Joseph, Missouri. Washington University Medical School, 1905. Surgeon, Eye, Ear, Nose, and Throat Department, St. Joseph's Hospital.

MINTY, FREDERICK WALTER, M.D., 609 Main Street, Rapid City, South Dakota. Sioux City College of Medicine, 1904. Surgeon, Methodist Deaconess Hospital.

MITCHELL, ALBERT ROSCOE, M.D., Bankers Life Building, Lincoln, Nebraska. Rush Medical College, 1879. Member of Surgical Staff, St. Elizabeth's and Lincoln Hospitals.

MITCHELL, ALFRED, JR., A.B., M.D., 657 Congress Street, Portland, Maine. Bowdoin Medical School, 1898. Genito-Urinary Surgeon, Maine General Hospital; Consulting Genito-Urinary Surgeon, Children's Hospital.

MITCHELL, EDWARD DANA, M.D., Bank of Commerce Building, Memphis, Tennessee. University of Pennsylvania School of Medicine, 1898. Surgeon, Baptist Memorial, Methodist, and Crippled Children's Hospitals.

MITCHELL, EDWARD L., M.D., 122 West Second Avenue, Monmouth, Illinois. Rush Medical College, 1882. Surgeon, Monmouth Hospital.

MITCHELL, GEORGE WASHINGTON, M.D., 11 East Chase Street, Baltimore, Maryland. University of Maryland School of Medicine, 1896. Associate Professor of Laryngology, University of Maryland School of Medicine and College of Physicians and Surgeons; Visiting Surgeon, Mercy Hospital; Surgeon, South Baltimore General Hospital; Consulting Laryngologist, Nursery and Child's Hospital, United States Marine Hospital.

MITCHELL, HENRY ARTHUR, M.D., East Main Street, Elkton, Maryland. University of Pennsylvania School of Medicine, 1900. Surgeon, Union Hospital of Cecil County.

MITCHELL, HENRY C., M.D., 202 West Main Street, Carbondale, Illinois. Northwestern University Medical School, 1879. Chief Surgeon, Holden Hospital.

MITCHELL, JAMES FARNANDIS, A.B., M.D., 1344 Nineteenth Street, Northwest, Washington, District of Columbia. Johns Hopkins University, Medcal Department, 1897. Clinical Professor of Surgery, George Washington University Medical School; Surgeon, Providence and Georgetown University Hospitals; Chief Surgeon, Emergency Hospital; Consulting Surgeon, Bar Harbor Medical and Surgical Hospital, Bar Harbor, Maine.

MITCHELL, JAMES HENRY, M.D., 268 Remsen Street, Cohoes, New York. Albany Medical College, 1881. Chief of Surgical Staff, Cohoes City Hospital.

MITCHELL, ROSSLYN BROUGH, B.A., M.D., C.M., 811 Boyd Building, Winnipeg, Manitoba. Faculty of Medicine, University of Manitoba (Manitoba Medical College), 1906. Assistant Professor of Obstetrics, Faculty of Medicine, University of Manitoba; Associate Obstetrician, Winnipeg General Hospital.

MITCHELL, WINTHROP D., M.D., "Stone House," Oleon Street, Worcester, Massachusetts. University and Bellevue Hospital Medical College, 1887. Emeritus Surgeon, St. Michael's Hospital, Newark, New Jersey. Retired.

MITHOEFER, WILLIAM, M.D., 19 West Seventh Street, Cincinnati, Ohio. University of Cincinnati College of Medicine (Ohio-Miami Medical College of the University of Cincinnati), 1897. Clinical Instructor in Laryngology and Otology, University of Cincinnati College of Medicine; Laryngologist and Otologist, Good Samaritan and Christ Hospitals.

MIX, CHARLES MELVIN, A.B., M.D., 109 Western Reserve Life Building, Muncie, Indiana. Cornell University Medical College, 1902. Attending Surgeon, Muncie Home Hospital.

MIXTER, CHARLES GALLOUPE, B.Sc., M.D., 180 Marlborough Street, Boston, Massachusetts. Harvard Medical School, 1906. Instructor in Surgery, Harvard University Graduate School of Medicine; Assistant Surgeon, Children's Hospital; Consulting Surgeon, Leonard Morse Hospital, Natick, Jordan Hospital, Plymouth.

MIXTER, SAMUEL JASON, B.Sc., M.D., 180 Marlborough Street, Boston, Massachusetts. Harvard Medical School, 1879. Consulting Surgeon, Massachusetts General Hospital, Massachusetts Eye and Ear Infirmary.

MIXTER, WILLIAM JASON, B.Sc., M.D., 180 Marlborough Street, Boston, Massachusetts. Harvard Medical School, 1906. Assistant Surgeon, Massachusetts General Hospital; Surgeon, Anna Jaques Hospital, Newburyport; Consulting Surgeon, Leonard Morse Hospital, Natick, Charitable Eye and Ear Infirmary, Boston, Cable Memorial Hospital, Ipswich.

MOBLEY, CHARLES ARDEN, M.D., 25 West Glover Street, Orangeburg, South Carolina. Medical College of the State of South Carolina, 1910. Surgeon in Charge, Orangeburg Hospital.

MOCK, HARRY EDGAR, B.Sc., M.D., 122 South Michigan Avenue, Chicago, Illinois. Rush Medical College, 1906. Assistant Professor of Industrial Medicine and Surgery, Rush Medical College; Member of Surgical Staff, St. Luke's Hospital.

MOCK, WILL HUGH, M.D., Neal Street, Prairie Grove, Arkansas. Vanderbilt University, Medical Department, 1894. Surgeon, Fayetteville City Hospital, Fayetteville.

MOFFAT, HENRY, A.M., M.D., 139 Park Avenue, Yonkers, New York. Columbia University, College of Physicians and Surgeons, 1881. Chief of Staff, St. Joseph's Hospital; Consulting Surgeon, Tarrytown Hospital, Tarrytown, Ossining Hospital, Ossining.

MOFFATT, HERBERT BAYNE, M.B., 278 O'Connor Street, Ottawa, Ontario. University of Toronto, Faculty of Medicine, 1911. Surgeon, St. Luke's General Hospital.

MOFFIT, ALBERT ROWCLIFFE, A.B., M.D., Vassar Brothers' Hospital, Poughkeepsie, New York. Columbia University, College of Physicians and Surgeons, 1904. Attending Surgeon, Vassar Brothers' Hospital.

MOFFITT, THOMAS W., M.D., Martin and Mason Block, Deadwood, South Dakota. Ohio State University College of Medicine (Starling Medical College), 1893. Surgeon, St. Joseph's Hospital, Deadwood, Methodist Deaconess Hospital, Rapid City.

MOLONY, MARTIN, M.D., B.Ch., 1054 Sutter Street, San Francisco, California. Royal University of Ireland, 1888. Chief Urologist, Molony Urological Hospital.

MOLYNEUX, SILAS D., M.D., 29 Main Street, Binghamton, New York. University of Pennsylvania School of Medicine, 1908. Consulting Surgeon, Binghamton City Hospital, Binghamton; Surgeon, Good Samaritan Hospital, Westfield.

MOLZ, CHARLES OTTO, M.D., 1103 Chestnut Street, Murphysboro, Illinois. Washington University Medical School (Missouri Medical College), 1898. Visiting Surgeon, St. Andrew's Hospital.

MONAGHAN, EDWARD P., M.D., 10308 Euclid Avenue, Cleveland, Ohio. Western Reserve University School of Medicine (Cleveland College of Physicians and Surgeons), 1902. Instructor in Gynecology, Western Reserve University School of Medicine; Visiting Surgeon, Cleveland City and St. Ann's Hospitals; Surgeon in Charge of Out-Door Patients, Gynecology Department, St. Vincent's Charity Hospital.

MONAHAN, JAMES JOHN, M.D., 25 East Washington Street, Chicago, Illinois. University of Illinois College of Medicine, 1904. Chief of Staff, Illinois General Hospital; Visiting Surgeon, St. Elizabeth's Hospital.

MONASH, DAVID, M.D., 4735 South Michigan Avenue, Chicago, Illinois. Columbia University, College of Physicians and Surgeons, 1893. Associate in Obstetrics, Northwestern University Medical School; Member of General Staff, Michael Reese Hospital; Member of Staff, Chicago Lying-in Hospital.

MONCRIEF, WILLIAM HENRY, M.D., Medical Corps, United States Army, Washington, District of Columbia. Emory University School of Medicine (Southern Medical College), 1897. Lieutenant Colonel, Medical Corps, United States Army.

MONCURE, PHILIP ST. L., M.D., Taylor Building, Norfolk, Virginia. Medical College of Virginia, 1897. Gynecologist, St. Vincent's Hospital and Sanitarium.

MONDINO, LUIS, M.D., Uruguay 936, Montevideo, Uruguay. Faculty of Medicine, University of Montevideo, 1894. Assistant Instructor in Surgical Clinic; Chief of Surgical Service, Maciel Hospital.

MONKS, GEORGE H., A.B., M.D., M.R.C.S. (Eng.), 51 Commonwealth Avenue, Boston, Massachusetts. Harvard Medical School, 1880. Consulting Surgeon, Boston City Hospital.

MONRO, ALEXANDER STEWART, M.D., C.M., 736 Granville Street, Vancouver, British Columbia. Faculty of Medicine, University of Manitoba (Manitoba Medical College), 1896. Surgeon, Vancouver General Hospital.

MONROE, J. P., M.D., Sanford, North Carolina. University of Maryland School of Medicine (College of Physicians and Surgeons, Baltimore), 1901.

MONTENEGRO, BENEDICTO, B.Sc., M.D., 22 Rua S. Bento, Sao Paulo, Brazil. University of Pennsylvania, School of Medicine, 1909. Substitute Professor of Anatomy, Medical School Sao Paulo; Assistant Surgeon, Municipal and Polyclinic Hospitals; Visiting Surgeon, Santa Catharina Hospital.

MONTGOMERY, ALEXANDER, M.D., 211 Grand Avenue, Milwaukee, Wisconsin. Marquette University School of Medicine, 1909. Surgeon, Evangelical Deaconess Hospital.

MONTGOMERY, EDMUND B., M.D., 132 North Eighth Street, Quincy, Illinois. Jefferson Medical College, 1878.

MONTGOMERY, EDWARD E., B.Sc., A.M., M.D., LL.D., 1426 Spruce Street, Philadelphia, Pennsylvania. Jefferson Medical College, 1874. Emeritus Professor of Gynecology, Jefferson Medical College; Gynecologist, Jefferson Medical College and St. Joseph's Hospitals.

MONTGOMERY, ELLIS S., M.D., 725 Jenkins Arcade Building, Pittsburgh, Pennsylvania. University of Pittsburgh School of Medicine, 1890. Emeritus Surgeon, Passavant Hospital; Surgeon, Baltimore and Ohio Railroad; Consulting Gynecologist, South Side Hospital.

MOODY, EARLE F., M.D., Young Building, Dothan, Alabama. Tulane University of Louisiana School of Medicine, 1903. President of Staff, Moody Hospital.

MOONEY, GEORGE S., M.D., 153 Warburton Avenue, Yonkers, New York. Columbia University, College of Physicians and Surgeons, 1895. Visiting Surgeon, St. Joseph's Hospital; Consultant, Yonkers Municipal Tuberculosis Hospital.

MOORE, CHESTER C., M.D., 409 Medical Building, Portland, Oregon. Leland Stanford Junior University School of Medicine (Cooper Medical College), 1904.

MOORE, EDWARD C., M.D., 1005 Merchants National Bank Building, Los Angeles, California. University of California Medical School, Los Angeles, 1904. Instructor in Surgery, Graduate School of Medicine of the University of California; Attending Surgeon, Los Angeles County Hospital; Consulting Surgeon, Children's Hospital.

MOORE, FRANK D., M.D., 30 North Michigan Avenue, Chicago, Illinois. University of Illinois College of Medicine (College of Physicians and Surgeons, Chicago), 1899. Associate Professor of Surgery and Clinical Surgery, University of Illinois College of Medicine; Member of Staff, University Hospital.

MOORE, GEORGE ALBERT, B.Sc., M.D., 167 Newbury Street, Brockton, Massachusetts. Harvard Medical School, 1911. Surgeon, Moore Private Hospital.

MOORE, GEORGE ANDREW, M.D., Post Office Block, Palmer, Massachusetts. College of Physicians and Surgeons, Boston, 1910. Oculist and Aurist, Wing Memorial Hospital, Palmer, Monson State Hospital, Monson.

MOORE, HARRY M., A.B., M.D., Wall Building, St. Louis, Missouri. Washington University Medical School, 1898. Member of Staff, St. Luke's Hospital.

MOORE, HARVEY ADAMS, M.D., Indianapolis, Indiana. Indiana University School of Medicine, 1898. Clinical Professor of Genito-Urinary Surgery, Indiana University School of Medicine; Attending Surgeon, Indianapolis City and Protestant Deaconess Hospitals.

MOORE, HOWARD, M.D., 520 Beacon Street, Boston, Massachusetts. Boston University School of Medicine, 1905. Associate Professor of Orthopedic Surgery, Boston University School of Medicine; Instructor in Orthopedics, Boston School of Physical Education; Orthopedic Surgeon, Massachusetts Homeopathic Hospital, Boston, Newton Hospital, Newton; Consulting Orthopedic Surgeon, Westboro State Hospital, Westboro.

MOORE, JOHN THOMAS, A.M., M.D., 431 Kress Medical Building, Houston, Texas. University of Texas, Medical Department, 1896. Surgeon, St. Joseph's Infirmary and Municipal Hospitals.

MOORE, JOSIAH G., A.B., M.D., 721 East Love Street, Mexico, Missouri. Washington University Medical School (St. Louis Medical College), 1889.

MOORE, KINGMAN P., M.D., Bibb Realty Building, Macon, Georgia. Emory University School of Medicine (Atlanta Medical College), 1868.

MOORE, MELVIN L., M.D., 1007 Merchants National Bank Building, Los Angeles, California. Rush Medical College, 1880; University and Bellevue Hospital Medical College, 1882.

MOORE, MOORE, JR., M.D., Bank of Commerce Building, Memphis, Tennessee. University of Tennessee College of Medicine (Memphis Hospital Medical College), 1898. Surgeon, Baptist Memorial Hospital.

MOORE, NEIL SEWELL, M.D., 316 Frisco Building, St. Louis, Missouri. St. Louis University School of Medicine, 1913. Consultant Urologist, St. Anthony's Hospital.

MOORE, OREN, M.D., 2 Medical Building, Charlotte, North Carolina. North Carolina Medical School, 1911. Obstetrician, Charlotte Sanatorium;

Gynecologist, St. Peter's Hospital; Assistant Chief of Staff, Good Samaritan Hospital; Member of Staff, Presbyterian Hospital.

MOORE, SAMUEL BRODERS, M.D., 811 Prince Street, Alexandria, Virginia. Georgetown University School of Medicine, 1897. Surgeon and Member of Staff, Alexandria Hospital.

MOORE, THOMAS WATERMAN, M.D., 204 First National Bank Building, Huntington, West Virginia. Medico-Chirurgical College, Philadelphia, 1893. Surgeon, Kessler-Hatfield Hospital and Training School.

MOOREHEAD, FREDERICK BROWN, M.Sc., D.D.S., M.D., 122 South Michigan Avenue, Chicago, Illinois. Rush Medical College, 1906. Dean, and Professor of Oral Surgery and Pathology, University of Illinois College of Dentistry; Assistant Professor of Surgery, Rush Medical College; Attending Oral Surgeon, Home for Destitute Crippled Children, Presbyterian and Children's Memorial Hospitals.

MOORHEAD, ANDREW SAMUEL, M.B., L.R.C.P. (Lond.), M.R.C.S. (Lond.), F.R.C.S. (Eng.), 146 Bloor Street, West, Toronto, Ontario. University of Toronto, Faculty of Medicine, 1906. Demonstrator in Surgery, University of Toronto, Faculty of Medicine; Junior Assistant Surgeon, Toronto Géneral Hospital.

MOORHEAD, EDWARD LOUIS, A.M., M.D., LL.D., 31 North State Street, Chicago, Illinois. Rush Medical College, 1890. Professor of Surgery and Head of the Department, Loyola University School of Medicine; Chief of Staff and Senior Surgeon, Mercy Hospital; Consulting Surgeon, Oak Park Hospital, Oak Park, Misericordia Maternity Hospital, Chicago.

MOORHEAD, JOHN JOSEPH, B.Sc., M.D., 115 East Sixty-fourth Street, New York, New York. University and Bellevue Hospital Medical College (New York University Medical College), 1897. Professor of Surgery, New York Post-Graduate Medical School; Visiting Surgeon, New York Post-Graduate Medical School and Hospital, Harlem and Washington Square Hospitals.

MOOTS, CHARLES W., B.Sc., M.D., 225 Michigan Street, Toledo, Ohio. University of Cincinnati College of Medicine (Ohio-Miami Medical College of the University of Cincinnati), 1895. Gynecologist, Flower Hospital.

MORAN, BENJAMIN G., M.D., 174 Main Street, Nashua, New Hampshire. University and Bellevue Hospital Medical College (New York University Medical College), 1891. Member of Staff, St. Joseph's and Nashua Memorial Hospitals.

MORAN, JOHN F., A.B., M.D., 2426 Pennsylvania Avenue, Washington, District of Columbia. Georgetown University School of Medicine, 1887. Professor of Obstetrics, Georgetown University School of Medicine; Obstetrician, Georgetown University Hospital, Columbia Hospital for Women, Washington Asylum.

MORAN, KARL P., M.D., 1002 Stevens Building, Portland, Oregon. Baylor University College of Medicine, 1913. Assistant to Chief of Surgical

Staff, Portland Sanitarium; Member of Surgical Staff, Portland Surgical Hospital.

MORE, CHARLES W., M.D., 605 Grant Avenue, Eveleth, Minnesota. Northwestern University Medical School (Chicago Medical College), 1888. Chief of Staff, More Hospital.

MORELAND, GEORGE BOULTON, M.D., 810 Westinghouse Building, Pittsburgh, Pennsylvania. Hahnemann Medical College and Hospital, Philadelphia, 1893. Visiting Surgeon, Homeopathic Medical and Surgical Hospital and Dispensary.

MORF, PAUL FREDERICK, M.D., 746 Fullerton Avenue, Chicago, Illinois. Northwestern University Medical School, 1897. Associate Professor of Surgery, Chicago Policlinic; Attending Surgeon, Evangelical Deaconess Hospital.

MORFIT, JOHN CAMPBELL, M.D., University Club Building, St. Louis, Missouri. University of Maryland School of Medicine (College of Physicians and Surgeons, Baltimore), 1895. Visiting Surgeon, Hospital Department, City of St. Louis.

MORGAN, THOMAS HENRY, M.D., 222 West Seventy-first Street, New York, New York. University of Toronto, Faculty of Medicine (Trinity Medical College), 1897. Professor of Gynecology, New York Polyclinic Medical School; Visiting Surgeon, St. Elizabeth's Hospital; Attending Gynecologist, Demilt Dispensary.

MORGENTHAU, GEORGE, M.D., 1116 East Forty-sixth Street, Chicago, Illinois. Dartmouth Medical School, 1887. Consulting Surgeon, Ear and Throat Department, Michael Reese Hospital, Sarah Morris Memorial Hospital for Children.

MORIARTA, DOUGLAS CALHOUN, Phar. G., M.D., 511 Broadway, Saratoga Springs, New York. Albany Medical College, 1885. Surgeon, Saratoga Hospital, Saratoga Cure and Infirmary; Chief Surgeon, St. Christina's Hospital.

MORISON, CHARLES C., B.Sc., M.D., Brandeis Theatre Building, Omaha, Nebraska. University of Nebraska College of Medicine, 1903. Associate Surgeon, University and Nebraska Methodist Hospitals.

MORLEY, WILLIAM HORACE, Ph.B., M.D., Pontiac, Michigan. University of Michigan Medical School, 1901. Consulting Pathologist, Woman's Hospital and Infants' Home, Detroit; Consulting Obstetrician, Out-Patient Maternity Department, Hannah Schloss Dispensary and Providence Hospital, Detroit.

MORRILL, GORDON NILES, M.D., 1021 Prospect Avenue, Cleveland, Ohio. Harvard Medical School, 1905. Visiting Orthopedist, Rainbow Hospital; Attending Orthopedist, United States Marine Hospital.

MORRIS, EDWARD J., A.B., M.D., 282 Sterling Place, Brooklyn, New York. University and Bellevue Hospital Medical College, 1899. Gynecologist, Holy Family Hospital.

MORRIS, FREDERIC S., M.D., 810 Westinghouse Building, Pittsburgh, Pennsylvania. Hahnemann Medical College and Hospital, Philadelphia, 1904. Surgeon, Homeopathic Medical and Surgical Hospital and Dispensary.

MORRIS, JACOB E.K., M.D., 119 Laurens Street, Olean, New York. University of Buffalo, Department of Medicine, 1879. Surgeon, Olean General Hospital.

MORRIS, LEWIS COLEMAN, M.D., 1203 Empire Building, Birmingham, Alabama. University of Virginia, Department of Medicine, 1892. Professor of Gynecology and Abdominal Surgery, Graduate School of Medicine of the University of Alabama; Gynecologist, St. Vincent's Hospital; Gynecologist and Abdominal Surgeon, Hillman Hospital; Surgeon, Holy Innocents' Hospital; Consulting Surgeon, Southern Railway.

MORRIS, ROBERT TUTTLE, A.M., M.D., 616 Madison Avenue, New York, New York. Columbia University, College of Physicians and Surgeons, 1882. Emeritus Professor of Surgery, New York Post-Graduate Medical School; Visiting Surgeon, Broad Street Hospital; Consulting Surgeon, New York Skin and Cancer Hospital, New York, Greenwich Hospital, Greenwich, Ossining Hospital, Ossining, New York, Stamford Hospital, Stamford, Connecticut.

MORRIS, SAMUEL J., M.D., Medical Corps, United States Army, Washington, District of Columbia. George Washington University Medical School, 1901. Lieutenant Colonel, Medical Corps, United States Army.

MORRIS, SETH MABRY, B.Sc., M.D., American National Insurance Building, Galveston, Texas. Columbia University, College of Physicians and Surgeons, 1891. Clinical Professor of Ophthalmology and Otology, University of Texas, Medical Department; Member of Staff, John Sealy Hospital.

MORRISON, ELMER E., B.Sc., M.D., 1223 Main Street, Great Bend, Kansas. American Medical College (Barnes Medical College), 1896. Visiting Surgeon, St. Rose Hospital; Consulting Surgeon, Hospital Department, Missouri Pacific Railroad.

MORRISON, FRANK A., A.B., M.D., Willoughby Building, Indianapolis, Indiana. Indiana University School of Medicine (Medical College of Indiana), 1880. Professor of Ophthalmology, Indiana University School of Medicine; Member of Staff, Indianapolis City, St. Vincent's, and Robert W. Long Hospitals, Indiana State School for the Blind.

MORRISON, J. REID, M.D., C.M., Bellingham, Washington. University of Toronto, Faculty of Medicine (Trinity Medical College), 1902. Visiting Surgeon, St. Luke's and St. Joseph's Hospitals.

MORRISON, JOHN BENNETT, M.D., 97 Halsey Street, Newark, New Jersey. Columbia University, College of Physicians and Surgeons, 1895. Visiting Surgeon, Presbyterian and St. James' Hospitals; Adjunct Surgeon, St. Barnabas' Hospital.

MORRISON, ROBERT J., M.D., 1173 Dean Street, Brooklyn, New York. Long Island College Hospital, 1891. Surgeon, Williamsburgh Hospital; Surgeon-in-Chief, Bushwick and East Brooklyn Dispensary.

MORROW, ALBERT S., A.B., M.D., 114 East Fifty-fourth Street, New York, New York. University and Bellevue Hospital Medical College, 1901. Visiting Surgeon, City and St. Bartholomew's Hospitals, New York; Consulting Surgeon, Nassau Hospital, Mineola.

MORROW, FRANK H., B.Sc., M.D., 2512 Thirteenth Street, Columbus, Nebraska. University of Nebraska College of Medicine, 1908. Attending Surgeon, St. Mary's Hospital.

MORSE, ARTHUR HENRY, A.B., M.D., 71 College Street, New Haven, Connecticut. Johns Hopkins University, Medical Department, 1906. Professor of Obstetrics and Gynecology, Yale University School of Medicine; Obstetrician and Gynecologist-in-Chief, New Haven Hospital and Dispensary.

MORSE, ASHLEY WALKER, A.B., M.D., 507 Phoenix Building, Butte, Montana. University of Michigan Medical School, 1908. Consultant, St. James Hospital.

MORSE, CHARLES F., M.D., Medical Corps, United States Army, Washington, District of Columbia. University of Vermont College of Medicine, 1896. Lieutenant Colonel, Medical Corps, United States Army.

MORSE, GEORGE W., A.B., M.D., 375 Commonwealth Avenue, Boston, Massachusetts. Harvard Medical School, 1908. Assistant in Anatomy, Harvard Medical School; Surgeon, Brooks Hospital, Brookline; Medical Director, Massachusetts Institute of Technology.

MORSE, LEANDER RUPERT, M.D., C.M., Lawrencetown, Nova Scotia. Faculty of Medicine, McGill University, 1896.

MORSE, WILLIS BENT, M.D., 406 State Street, Salem, Oregon. University of Oregon Medical School (Willamette University Medical Department), 1891. Visiting Surgeon, Salem Deaconess and Salem Hospitals.

MORTENSEN, OSCAR N., M.D., Citizen's National Bank Building, Wisconsin Rapids, Wisconsin. University of Illinois College of Medicine, 1909. Attending Surgeon, Riverview Hospital.

MORTON, DANIEL, M.D., King Hill Building, St. Joseph, Missouri. University of Louisville, Medical Department, 1887. Surgeon, Noyes, Missouri Methodist, and St. Joseph's Hospitals; Proctologist to Welfare Board.

MORTON, FRANK ROY, M.D., 25 East Washington Street, Chicago, Illinois. University of Illinois College of Medicine (College of Physicians and Surgeons, Chicago), 1901. Chief Surgeon, Standard Oil Company of Indiana.

MORTON, HENRY H., M.D., 32 Schermerhorn Street, Brooklyn, New York. Long Island College Hospital, 1882. Professor of Genito-Urinary Diseases, Long Island College Hospital; Attending Genito-Urinary Surgeon, Long Island College and Kings County Hospitals, Polhemus Memorial Clinic.

MORTON, HOWARD McILVAIN, M.S., M.D., Metropolitan Bank Building, Minneapolis, Minnesota. University of Pennsylvania School of Medicine, 1891. Chief, Wells Memorial Eye Clinic; Ophthalmologist, St. Barnabas' Hospital.

MORTON, JOHN PETTIGREW, M.B., L.R.C.P. & F.R.C.S. (Edin.), 148 James Street, South, Hamilton, Ontario. University of Toronto, Faculty of Medicine, 1897. Chief of Staff, Eye, Ear, Nose, and Throat Department, Hamilton City Hospital.

MORTON, LEWIS BURROWS, M.D., St. Vincent's Hospital, Los Angeles, California. State University of Iowa College of Medicine, 1901. Attending Surgeon, St. Vincent's Hospital.

MOSCHCOWITZ, ALEXIS V., Phar.G., M.D., 925 Madison Avenue, New York, New York. Columbia University, College of Physicians and Surgeons, 1891. Professor of Clinical Surgery, Columbia University, College of Physicians and Surgeons; Attending Surgeon, Mt. Sinai Hospital.

MOSELEY, GEORGE T., M.D., 202 Delaware Avenue, Buffalo, New York. New York Homeopathic Medical College and Flower Hospital, 1885; Columbia University, College of Physicians and Surgeons, 1886. Surgeon, Buffalo Homeopathic Hospital, Buffalo, Gowanda State Homeopathic Hospital, Collins, J. N. Adam Memorial Hospital, Perrysburg; Consulting Surgeon, Erie County Hospital, Buffalo, Batavia Hospital, Batavia.

MOSHER, GEORGE CLARK, A.M., M.D., 1100 Grand Avenue, Kansas City, Missouri. University of Louisville, Medical Department (Kentucky School of Medicine), 1882. Attending Obstetrician, Kansas City General and Christian Church Hospitals; Consulting Obstetrician, Swedish and St. Vincent's Hospitals, Kansas City, Missouri, Bethany Methodist Hospital, Kansas City, Kansas.

MOSHER, HARRIS PEYTON, A.B., M.D., 828 Beacon Street, Boston, Massachusetts. Harvard Medical School, 1896. Assistant Professor of Laryngology and Associate in Anatomy, Harvard Medical School; Chief of Service, Throat Department, Massachusetts General Hospital; Chief of Service, Throat Department and Aural Surgeon, Massachusetts Charitable Eye and Ear Infirmary; Consulting Laryngologist, Morton Hospital, Taunton.

MOSS, ROBERT E., M.D., Hicks Building, San Antonio, Texas. Jefferson Medical College, 1883.

MOSTAJO, JUAN JOSÉ, M.D., Calle del Pacal 971, Lima, Peru. Faculty of Medicine, University of San Marcos, 1913.

MOTLEY, JAMES COLEMAN, M.D., Abingdon, Virginia. Medical College of Virginia, 1906. Surgeon, George Ben Johnston Memorial Hospital.

MOTTER, THOMAS IRA, A.M., M.D., 127 North Oak Park Avenue, Oak Park, Illinois. Rush Medical College, 1899.

MOUNT, HUGH STEVENS, M.D., Weinhard Building, Oregon City, Oregon. University of Oregon Medical School, 1903.

MOULTON, HERBERT, B.Sc., M.D., Merchants National Bank Building, Fort Smith, Arkansas. Northwestern University Medical School (Chicago Medical College), 1884. Oculist and Aurist, Sparks Memorial Hospital.

MOULTON, W. BEAN, A.B., M.D., 690 Congress Street, Portland, Maine. Johns Hopkins University, Medical Department, 1903. Surgeon, City and Maine General Hospitals; Consulting Surgeon, Webber Hospital, Biddeford.

MOVIUS, ARTHUR J., M.D., Hart-Albin Building, Billings, Montana. University of Minnesota Medical School, 1904.

MOWBRAY, FREDERICK BRUCE, M.B., 681 Main Street, East, Hamilton, Ontario. University of Toronto, Faculty of Medicine, 1905. Surgeon, Hamilton City Hospital.

MOWELL, JOHN WILSON, M.D., Columbia Building, Olympia, Washington. Washington University Medical School (Missouri Medical College), 1888. Member of Staff, St. Peter's Hospital.

MOWERS, SAXE W., A.M., M.D., 1011 Cobb Building, Seattle, Washington. University of Michigan Medical School, 1896.

MOWERY, CHARLES ROTHELLES, M.D., Sixth and Cedar Streets, Wallace, Idaho. Creighton College of Medicine, 1902. Surgeon, Providence Hospital.

MOYNIHAN, SIR BERKELEY, K.C.M.G., C.B., M.B., M.S., F.R.C.S. (Eng.), F.R.C.S. (I.), Hon., 33 Park Square, Leeds, England. University of London, 1887. Professor of Clinical Surgery, University of Leeds; Honorary Surgeon, Leeds General Infirmary; Consulting Surgeon, Skipton, Mirfield, and Dewsbury Infirmaries; Major General, Army Medical Service.

MUCKLESTON, HAROLD STRUAN, A.M., M.D., C.M., 912 Van Nuys Building, Los Angeles, California. Faculty of Medicine, McGill University, 1905.

MUDD, HARVEY GILMER, M.D., 408 Humboldt Building, St. Louis, Missouri. Washington University Medical School (St. Louis Medical College), 1881. Clinical Professor of Surgery, Washington University Medical School; Chief of Staff, St. Luke's Hospital; Member of Staff, Barnard Free Skin and Cancer Hospital.

MUELLER, GEORGE, Phar.G., M.D., 209 South State Street, Chicago, Illinois. Rush Medical College, 1894. Clinical Professor of Surgery, Loyola University School of Medicine; Attending Surgeon, St. Mary of Nazareth Hospital; Consulting Surgeon, Columbus Hospital.

MULLEN, THOMAS FRANCIS, M.D., Kane Building, Pocatello, Idaho. Jefferson Medical College, 1912.

MÜLLER, GEORGE P., M.D., 1930 Spruce Street, Philadelphia, Pennsylvania. University of Pennsylvania School of Medicine, 1899. Professor of Surgery, University of Pennsylvania Graduate School of Medicine; Associate in Surgery, University of Pennsylvania School of Medicine; Surgeon, St. Agnes' and Misericordia Hospitals; Consulting Surgeon, Chester County Hospital.

MULLIGAN, EDWARD WRIGHT, M.D., 400 Cutler Building, Rochester, New York. Rush Medical College, 1883; University and Bellevue Hospital

Medical College, 1884. Visiting Surgeon, Rochester General and St. Mary's Hospitals; Consulting Surgeon, Frederick Ferris Thompson Memorial Hospital, Canandaigua.

MULLIN, WILLIAM VALENTINE, M.D., 301 Ferguson Building, Colorado Springs, Colorado. University of Denver School of Medicine, 1908. Attending Oto-Laryngologist, Glockner Hospital and Sanatorium, Beth-El Hospital, Union Printer's Home; Laryngologist, Colorado School of Tuberculosis.

MUNDELL, DAVID EDWARD, A.B., M.D., C.M., 228 Brock Street, Kingston, Ontario. Queen's University, Faculty of Medicine, 1886. Professor of Surgery, Queen's University, Faculty of Medicine; Surgeon, Kingston General Hospital; Surgeon-in-Chief, Sydenham Hospital; Director, Mowat Sanitarium.

MUNDELL, JOSEPH JOSHUA, M.D., Medical Corps, United States Navy, Washington, District of Columbia. Georgetown University School of Medicine, 1903. Gynecologist, Providence and Casualty Hospitals; Obstetrician, Columbia Hospital; Lieutenant, Medical Corps, United States Navy.

MUNDT, G. HENRY, Ph.G., M.D., 25 East Washington Street, Chicago, Illinois. American College of Medicine and Surgery, 1906; University of Illinois College of Medicine, 1911. Ophthalmologist and Oto-Laryngologist, German Evangelical Deaconess Hospital.

MUNGER, CARL EUGENE, Ph.B., M.D., 81 North Main Street, Waterbury, Connecticut. Columbia University, College of Physicians and Surgeons, 1883. Laryngologist and Aural Surgeon, Waterbury Hospital; Assistant Surgeon, Manhattan Eye, Ear, and Throat Hospital, New York.

MUNGER, CURTIS BOYD, M.D., Medical Corps, United States Navy, Washington, District of Columbia. Leland Stanford Junior University School of Medicine (Cooper Medical College), 1903. Commander, Medical Corps, United States Navy.

MÜNNICH, GUILLERMO E., M.D., Casilla 1542, Valparaiso, Chile. Faculty of Medicine, University of Chile, 1900. Member, Faculty of Medicine, University of Chile; Surgeon-in-Chief, German Hospital.

MUNRO, WALTER LEE, A.M., M.D., 62 North Main Street, Providence, Rhode Island. Harvard Medical School, 1885. Consulting Surgeon, Rhode Island and St. Joseph's Hospitals, Providence, Memorial Hospital, Pawtucket.

MUNROE, ALEXANDER RUSSELL, M.D., C.M., 416 McLeod Building, Edmonton, Alberta. Faculty of Medicine, McGill University, 1906; Senior Surgeon, Strathcona Military Hospital; Lecturer on Clinical Surgery, University of Alberta.

MUNROE, HUGH EDWIN, M.D., C.M., L.R.C.P.& S. (Edin.), L.F.P.& S. (Glas.), 407 Canada Building, Saskatoon, Saskatchewan. Faculty of Medicine, McGill University, 1903. Surgeon, City and St. Paul's Hospitals.

MUNSON, EDWARD LYMAN, A.M., M.D., Medical Corps, United States Army, Washington, District of Columbia. Yale University School of Medicine, 1892. Colonel, Medical Corps, United States Army.

MUNSON, EDWIN S., M.D., 8 West Forty-ninth Street, New York, New York. New York Homeopathic Medical College and Flower Hospital, 1894. Professor of Ophthalmology, College of the New York Ophthalmic Hospital; Surgeon, New York Ophthalmic Hospital; Oculist, Yonkers Homeopathic Hospital and Maternity, Yonkers; Consulting Oculist, Broad Street Hospital.

MUNYO, JUAN CARLOS, Rio Negro 1324, Montevideo, Uruguay. Faculty of Medicine, University of Montevideo, 1912. Counselor, Public Service; Chief of Service, Ear, Nose, and Throat Department, Children's Hospital.

MURDOCK, SAMUEL, JR., M.D., 1015 Main Street, Sabetha, Kansas. University of Kansas School of Medicine (Kansas City Medical College), 1893. Surgeon, St. Anthony Murdock Memorial Hospital.

MURDY, ROBERT L., M.D., 1021 South Washington Street, Aberdeen, South Dakota. State University of Iowa College of Medicine (Keokuk Medical College), 1892; Washington University Medical School (Missouri Medical College), 1896. Chief of Surgical Department, Lincoln Hospital.

MURNAN, JOHN R., M.D., Eleventh and Scott Streets, Covington, Kentucky. University of Cincinnati College of Medicine (Medical College of Ohio), 1883. Surgeon-in-Chief, St. Elizabeth's Hospital.

MURPHY, FRED TOWSLEY, A.M., M.D., Penobscot Building, Detroit, Michigan. Harvard Medical School, 1901.

MURPHY, GEORGE HENRY, M.D., C.M., 28 Carleton Street, Halifax, Nova Scotia. Dalhousie University, Faculty of Medicine, 1902. Professor of Clinical Surgery, Dalhousie University, Faculty of Medicine; Visiting Surgeon, Victoria General Hospital.

MURPHY, J. GERALD, B.Sc., M.D., Murchison Bank Building, Wilmington, North Carolina. University of Louisville, Medical Department, 1903. Member of Visiting Staff, James Walker Hospital; Ophthalmologist and Oto-Laryngologist, Colored Hospital, Wilmington.

MURPHY, JOHN W., A.M., M.D., Union Central Life Building, Cincinnati, Ohio. University of Cincinnati College of Medicine (Miami Medical College), 1891. Professor of Clinical Laryngology, University of Cincinnati College of Medicine; Laryngologist and Otologist, Cincinnati General Hospital.

MURPHY, JOSEPH A., M.D., Medical Corps, United States Navy, Washington, District of Columbia. Medico-Chirurgical College, Philadelphia, 1898. Captain, Medical Corps, United States Navy.

MURPHY, JOSEPH PAUL, B.Sc., M.D., 653 St. Mark's Avenue, Brooklyn, New York. Columbia University, College of Physicians and Surgeons, 1894. Surgeon, Coney Island and St. Mary's Hospitals; Consulting Surgeon, Zion Hospital, Brooklyn, St. Joseph's Hospital, Far Rockaway.

MURRAY, ALFRED NICHOLAS, M.D., 4654 Sheridan Road, Chicago, Illinois. Rush Medical College, 1901. Rhinologist and Laryngologist, Augustana Hospital; Ophthalmologist, Rhinologist, and Oto-Laryngologist, Lake View Hospital; Oculist and Aurist, Ravenswood Hospital.

MURRAY, ANGUS ALLAN, M.D., 514 Boyd Building, Winnipeg, Manitoba. Faculty of Medicine, University of Manitoba (Manitoba Medical College), 1913. Lecturer on Orthopedic Surgery, Faculty of Medicine, University of Manitoba; Assistant Orthopedic Surgeon, Children's Hospital; Consulting Orthopedic Surgeon, Winnipeg City Hospitals.

MURRAY, FRANK WISNER, A.B., M.D., 32 West Thirty-ninth Street, New York, New York. Columbia University, College of Physicians and Surgeons, 1880. Consulting Surgeon, New York and St. Luke's Hospitals, New York Eye and Ear Infirmary, New York, Goshen Emergency Hospital, Goshen, New York, Paul Kimball Hospital, Lakewood, New Jersey.

MURRAY, GILBERT D., M.D., 528 Madison Avenue, Scranton, Pennsylvania. Medico-Chirurgical College, Philadelphia, 1889. Surgeon in Charge, Eye, Ear, Nose, and Throat Department, Moses Taylor Hospital; Chief Oculist and Aurist, Delaware, Lackawanna and Western Railroad.

MURRAY, JOHN A., M.D., McGee Avenue, Patton, Pennsylvania. University of Maryland School of Medicine, 1885; Jefferson Medical College, 1893. Surgeon, Miners' Hospital of Northern Cambria, Spangler.

MURRAY, THOMAS J., M.D., 401 West Granite Street, Butte, Montana. Jefferson Medical College, 1879.

MURRAY, WILLIAM R., Ph.B., M.D., 1009 Nicollet Avenue, Minneapolis, Minnesota. Rush Medical College, 1897. Professor of Ophthalmology, Oto-Laryngology, and Chief of the Department, University of Minnesota Medical School.

MUSGROVE, WILLIAM W., M.D., C.M., 712 Boyd Building, Winnipeg, Manitoba. Faculty of Medicine, University of Manitoba (Manitoba Medical College), 1906. Lecturer on Clinical Surgery, Faculty of Medicine, University of Manitoba; Surgeon, Out-Patient Department, Winnipeg General Hospital.

MUTSCHLER, LOUIS HENRY, M.D., 1625 Spruce Street, Philadelphia, Pennsylvania. University of Pennsylvania School of Medicine, 1895. Surgeon, Methodist Episcopal Hospital; Associate Surgeon, Philadelphia Orthopedic Hospital and Infirmary for Nervous Diseases.

MYER, MAX W., A.B., M.D., University Club Building, St. Louis, Missouri. St. Louis University School of Medicine (Marion-Sims College of Medicine), 1899. Associate Professor of Surgery, St. Louis University School of Medicine; Associate Surgeon, Jewish Hospital of St. Louis; Visiting Surgeon, St. Louis City Hospital.

MYERS, DAVID AP, M.D., C.M., Lawton, Oklahoma. Faculty of Medicine, McGill University, 1898.

MYERS, DEAN WENTWORTH, M.D., 317 South State Street, Ann Arbor, Michigan. University of Michigan Homeopathic Medical School, 1899. Professor of Ophthalmology, Otology, Rhinology and Laryngology, University of Michigan Homeopathic Medical School; Director of Eye, Ear, Nose, and Throat Clinics, University of Michigan Homeopathic Hospital.

MYERS, EDWARD MORRISON, A.M., M.D., 703 Eighth Street, Boone, Iowa. Northwestern University Medical School, 1900. Member of Attending Staff, Eleanor Moore Hospital.

MYERS, HARRY L., M.D., Taylor Building, Norfolk, Virginia. University of Virginia, Department of Medicine, 1889. Consulting Oculist and Aurist, St. Vincent's Hospital.

MYLES, SIR THOMAS, C.B., M.B., B.Ch., M.D., F.R.C.S. (I.), 33 Merrion Square, Dublin, Ireland. University of Dublin, 1881. Senior Surgeon, Richmond Hospital; Consulting Surgeon, Irish Command; Member, Board of Consultants, British War Office; Honorary Surgeon to His Majesty the King.

MYLKS, GORDON WRIGHT, M.D., C.M., 79 William Street, Kingston, Ontario. Queen's University, Faculty of Medicine, 1897. Professor of Gynecology, Queen's University, Faculty of Medicine; Head of Gynecological Service, Kingston General Hospital.

NACHTWEY, ALOYSIUS PATRICK, B.Sc., M.D., Merchant's Bank Building, Dickinson, North Dakota. Marquette University School of Medicine, 1911. Surgeon, St. Joseph's Hospital.

NADEAU, OSCAR E., B.Sc., M.D., 2106 Sedgwick Street, Chicago, Illinois. Rush Medical College, 1913. Associate in Surgery, Surgical Pathology and Anatomy, University of Illinois College of Medicine; Associate Surgeon, St. Mary of Nazareth Hospital; Assistant Surgeon, Augustana Hospital; Consulting Surgeon, Municipal Contagious Disease Hospital.

NAFTZGER, JESSE B., M.D., 401 Davidson Building, Sioux City, Iowa. State University of Iowa College of Medicine, 1904. Member of Staff, St. Joseph's Hospital.

NANCE, LEE MAXWELL, B.Sc., M.D., 305 Southwestern Life Building, Dallas, Texas. Baylor University College of Medicine, 1910. Associate Professor of Gynecology, Baylor University College of Medicine; Assistant Gynecologist, Baylor University Hospital and Dispensary; Junior Member of Staff, Texas Baptist Memorial Sanitarium.

NASH, ALBERT B., A.B., M.D., 10 South Thirteenth Street, Newark, New Jersey. Columbia University, College of Physicians and Surgeons, 1887. Attending Surgeon, Hospital for Women and Children.

NASH, EDWIN N., M.D., 411 Bank of Galesburg Building, Galesburg, Illinois. Rush Medical College, 1901. Member of Staff, Galesburg Cottage Hospital.

NASSAU, CHARLES FRANCIS, M.D., LL.D., 1710 Locust Street, Philadelphia, Pennsylvania. University of Pennsylvania School of Medicine, 1891; Jefferson Medical College, 1906. Assistant Professor of Surgery, Jefferson Medical College; Chief Surgeon, Frankford Hospital; Surgeon, St. Joseph's and Mt. Sinai Hospitals; Assistant Surgeon, Jefferson Medical College Hospital; Consulting Surgeon, Pottstown Hospital, Pottstown.

NATHAN, PHILIP WILLIAM, M.D., 110 East Seventy-eighth Street, New York, New York. University and Bellevue Hospital Medical College (New York University Medical Department), 1893. Clinical Professor of Orthopedic Surgery, Bellevue Hospital Medical College; Attending Orthopedic Surgeon, Mount Sinai and Beth Israel Hospitals, Montefiore Home and Hospital.

NAUMAN, BENJAMIN J., M.D., Masonic Temple Building, Peru, Illinois. Rush Medical College, 1899.

NAVARRO VALENZUELA, FRANCISCO, M.D., Casilla 1259, Santiago, Chile. Faculty of Medicine, University of Chile, 1896.

NAYLOR, GEORGE IRVING, B.Sc., M.D., 136 Park Place, Johnstown, Pennsylvania. University of Michigan Homeopathic Medical School, 1912. Chief Surgeon, Lee Homeopathic Hospital.

NEALE, LEONARD ERNEST, M.D., LL.D., 822 Park Avenue, Baltimore, Maryland. University of Maryland School of Medicine, 1881. Professor of Obstetrics, University of Maryland School of Medicine and College of Physicians and Surgeons; Obstetrician-in-Chief, University Hospital; Gynecologist, St. Joseph's Hospital.

NEARY, EDWARD P., A.B., M.D., Savoy Theatre Building, Cleveland, Ohio. Western Reserve University School of Medicine, 1912. Instructor in Surgery, Western Reserve University School of Medicine; Surgeon-in-Charge, Surgical Out-Patient Department, St. Vincent's Charity Hospital.

NEATHERY, E. J., M.D., Merchants and Planters Bank Building, Sherman, Texas. University of Louisville, Medical Department, 1891. President, Sherman Hospital.

NEER, WILLIAM, M.D., 245 Broadway, Paterson, New Jersey. Columbia University College of Physicians and Surgeons, 1891. Visiting Surgeon, St. Joseph's Hospital.

NEFF, JAMES M., M.D., 30 North Michigan Avenue, Chicago, Illinois. University of Illinois College of Medicine (College of Physicians and Surgeons, Chicago), 1898.

NEFF, ROBERT L., M.D., Frisco Building, Joplin, Missouri. University Medical College, Kansas City, 1894.

NEHER, EDWIN MANSON, A.B., B.Sc., M.D., 806 Boston Building, Salt Lake City, Utah. Rush Medical College, 1906. Ophthalmologist, St. Mark's Hospital.

NEILL, WILLIAM, JR., A.B., A.M., M.D., 1418 Eutaw Place, Baltimore, Maryland. Johns Hopkins University Medical Department, 1912. Associate Surgeon, Howard A. Kelly Hospital; Visiting Surgeon, Church Home and Infirmary; Consulting Surgeon, Cambridge Memorial Hospital, Cambridge.

NEILSON, JOHN LAND, M.D., Medical Corps, United States Navy, Washington, District of Columbia. Harvard Medical School, 1902. Commander, Medical Corps, United States Navy.

NEILSON, THOMAS R., A.M., M.D., 1937 Chestnut Street, Philadelphia, Pennsylvania. University of Pennsylvania School of Medicine, 1880. Professor of Genito-Urinary Surgery, University of Pennsylvania School of Medicine; Surgeon, Hospital of the Protestant Episcopal Church; Consulting Surgeon, St. Christopher's Hospital for Children.

NELKEN, ABRAHAM, M.D., 126 Baronne Street, New Orleans, Louisiana. Tulane University of Louisiana School of Medicine, 1899. Visiting Urologist, Touro Infirmary; Chief in Genito-Urinary Division, Charity Hospital.

NELSON, CHRISTIAN P., M.D., Owatonna, Minnesota. University of Michigan Medical School, 1896.

NESSELRODE, CLIFFORD C., M.D., 800 Minnesota Avenue, Kansas City, Kansas. University of Kansas School of Medicine, 1906. Associate Professor of Clinical Surgery, University of Kansas School of Medicine; Attending Surgeon, St. Margaret's Hospital; Visiting Surgeon, Bethany Methodist Hospital.

NEUPERT, CARL VON, JR., M.D., 412 Church Street, Stevens Point, Wisconsin. University of Louisville, Medical Department (Louisville Medical College), 1892. Surgeon, St. Michael's Hospital; Examining Surgeon, Minneapolis, St. Paul and Sault Ste. Marie Railway.

NEVES, LUIS F. BAETA, B.Sc., LL.D., M.D., 37 Rua S. Vicente de Paula, Sao Paulo, Brazil. Faculty of Medicine, University of Rio de Janeiro, 1896.

NEW, GORDON BALGARNIE, D.D.S., M.B., M.D., Mayo Clinic, Rochester, Minnesota. University of Toronto, Faculty of Medicine, 1909. Professor of Rhinology, Laryngology and Stomatology, Mayo Foundation, University of Minnesota.

NEWCOMB, JOHN RAY, M.D., 411 Hume-Mansur Building, Indianapolis, Indiana. Indiana University School of Medicine, 1904. Ophthalmologist, Indianapolis City Hospital.

NEWELL, EDWARD DUNBAR, B.Sc., M.D., Newell and Newell Sanitarium, Chattanooga, Tennessee. Tulane University of Louisiana School of Medicine, 1897. Surgeon, Newell and Newell Sanitarium, Cincinnati, New Orleans and Texas Pacific, Nashville, Chattanooga and St. Louis, and Southern Railways; Visiting Surgeon, Baroness Erlanger Hospital.

NEWELL, EDWARD T., B.Sc., M.D., 707 Walnut Street, Chattanooga, Tennessee. Tulane University of Louisiana School of Medicine, 1899. Surgeon, Newell and Newell Sanitarium, Cincinnati, New Orleans and Texas Pacific, Southern and Nashville, Chattanooga and St. Louis Railways, Alabama Great Southern Railroad, Chattanooga Railway and Light, and Chattanooga Traction Companies, Suburban Lines; Consulting Surgeon, Baroness Erlanger Hospital.

NEWELL, FRANKLIN S., A.B., M.D., 443 Beacon Street, Boston, Massachusetts. Harvard Medical School, 1896. Professor of Clinical Obstetrics, Harvard

Medical School; Obstetrician, Massachusetts General Hospital; Visiting Obstetrician, Boston Lying-in Hospital.

NEWELL, QUITMAN UNDERWOOD, M.D., 411 Wall Building, St. Louis, Missouri. University of Alabama School of Medicine, 1911. Instructor in Gynecology, Washington University Medical School; Chief of Gynecological Clinic, Washington University Medical School, Out-Patient Department; Assistant Gynecologist, Barnes Hospital; Obstetrician, St. Louis Maternity Hospital.

NEWELL, WILLIAM S., M.D., 1029 Vermont Avenue, Washington, District of Columbia. George Washington University Medical School (Columbian University, Medical Department), 1895. Ophthalmic Surgeon, Central Dispensary and Emergency Hospital.

NEWHART, HORACE, A.B., M.D., 910 Donaldson Building, Minneapolis, Minnesota. University of Michigan Medical School, 1898. Assistant Professor of Oto-Laryngology, University of Minnesota Medical School; Otologist, Out-Patient Department, University Hospital; Member of Staff, Department of Eye, Ear, Nose, and Throat, Northwestern Hospital.

NEWMAN, HENRY PARKER, A.M., M.D., 1200 American National Bank Building, San Diego, California. Detroit College of Medicine and Surgery, 1878. Emeritus Professor of Gynecology and Clinical Gynecology, University of Illinois College of Medicine; Emeritus Professor of Gynecology, Chicago Policlinic, Chicago; Attending Surgeon and Gynecologist, Agnew Sanitarium and Hospital; Consulting Surgeon and Gynecologist, San Diego County Hospital.

NEWMAN, JACOB WARREN, M.D., Ph.D., 3523 Prytania Street, New Orleans, Louisiana. Tulane University of Louisiana School of Medicine, 1902. Clinical Professor of Obstetrics, Tulane University of Louisiana School of Medicine; Medical Director, Lying-in Hospital Dispensary; Chief of Service, Obstetrical Department, Touro Infirmary; Senior Visiting Surgeon, Charity Hospital.

NEWTON, ABRAM MARK, M.D., 300 Kane Building, Pocatello, Idaho. Northwestern University Medical School, 1911. Attending Surgeon, St. Anthony's Hospital.

NEY, GROVER C., A.B., A.M., M.D., 2401 Linden Avenue, Baltimore, Maryland. Johns Hopkins University, Medical Department, 1908. Attending Surgeon, Hebrew Hospital.

NICHOLLS, RODGER FREDERICK, M.D., C.M., 405 McLeod Building, Edmonton, Alberta. Queen's University, Faculty of Medicine, 1907. Attending Eye, Ear, Nose, and Throat Surgeon, Edmonton Hospitals.

NICHOLS, EDWARD HALL, A.M., M.D., 294 Marlborough Street, Boston, Massachusetts. Harvard Medical School, 1892. Professor of Clinical Surgery, Harvard Medical School; Surgeon-in-Chief, Boston City Hospital; Consulting Surgeon, City Hospital, Quincy, Framingham Hospital, Framingham.

NICHOLS, FIRMADGE KING, A.B., M.D., 904 North Charles Street, Baltimore, Maryland. Johns Hopkins University, Medical Department, 1910.

Associate in Physiology, University of Maryland School of Medicine; Obstetrician and Associate in Gynecology, St. Agnes Hospital; Consulting Obstetrician, St. Vincent's Orphan Asylum.

NICHOLS, HENRY J., M.D., A.M., Medical Corps, United States Army, Washington, District of Columbia. University of Pennsylvania School of Medicine, 1904. Major, Medical Corps, United States Army.

NICHOLS, HERBERT STRONG, A.M., M.D., 802 Corbett Building, Portland, Oregon. Hahnemann Medical College and Hospital, Philadelphia, 1895. Member of Staff, Multnomah County Hospital.

NICHOLS, JOHN HAMMEL, M.D., 58 Park Avenue, West, Mansfield, Ohio. Rush Medical College, 1896. Surgeon, Parker Sanitarium.

NICHOLS, WILLIAM ROBSON, M.D., F.R.C.S. (Eng.), 83 Carlton Street, Winnipeg, Manitoba. University of Toronto, Faculty of Medicine (Trinity Medical College), 1886. Consulting Surgeon, Children's Hospital.

NICHOLSON, CLARENCE M., B.Sc., M.D., Lister Building, St. Louis, Missouri. Washington University Medical School (Missouri Medical College), 1891. Professor of Surgery, St. Louis University School of Medicine; Consulting Surgeon, St. John's Hospital.

NICHOLSON, FRANCIS JOHN, A.B., M.D., C.M., 1826 Nelson Street, Vancouver, British Columbia. Faculty of Medicine, McGill University, 1899.

NICHOLSON, HARRY MANLEY, M.B., 134 James Street, South, Hamilton, Ontario. University of Toronto, Faculty of Medicine, 1910. Oto-Laryngologist, Soldiers' Civil Re-Establishment.

NICHOLSON, HUGH G., M.D., 330 Professional Building, Charleston, West Virginia. Medical College of Virginia (University College of Virginia), 1897. Member of Surgical Staff, Charleston General Hospital and Training School, St. Francis, Kanawha Valley and McMillan Hospitals.

NICKERSON, BERNARD S., B.Sc., M.D., Greengard Block, Mandan, North Dakota. University of Minnesota Medical School, 1903. Visiting Surgeon, Mandan Deaconess Hospital.

NICOLL, ALEXANDER, M.D., 17 West Seventy-third Street, New York, New York. Columbia University, College of Physicians and Surgeons, 1903. Surgical Director, First Division, Fordham Hospital; Attending Surgeon, Sea View Hospital, Castleton Corners.

NICOLSON, WILLIAM PERRIN, M.D., Healey Building, Atlanta, Georgia. University of Virginia, Department of Medicine, 1876. Surgeon and President of Medical Board, St. Joseph's Infirmary; Consulting Surgeon, Grady Memorial Hospital.

NIEMACK, JULIUS, B.Sc., M.D., 105 Main Street, Charles City, Iowa. Goettingen University, Germany, 1891. Surgeon, Cedar Valley Hospital.

NIFONG, FRANK G., M.D., 12 South Ninth Street, Columbia, Missouri. Washington University Medical School (Missouri Medical College), 1889.

NILSSON, JOHN RUDOLPH, M.D., 426 World Herald Building, Omaha, Nebraska. University of Nebraska College of Medicine (Omaha Medical College),

1901. Instructor in Surgery, University of Nebraska College of Medicine; Surgeon, Immanuel Hospital; Assistant Surgeon, University Hospital.

NIN Y SILVA, JULIO, B.Sc., M.D., Rivera 2122, Montevideo, Uruguay. Faculty of Medicine, University of Montevideo, 1913. Chief of Surgical Policlinic, Maciel Hospital.

NOBLE, GEORGE HENRY, M.D., D.C.L., 980 Peachtree Street, Atlanta, Georgia. Emory University School of Medicine (Atlanta Medical College), 1881. Professor of Clinical Gynecology, Emory University School of Medicine; Gynecologist, Grady Memorial Hospital, Dr. Noble's Private Infirmary.

NOBLE, HARRY S., M.D., 317 West Spring Street, St. Marys, Ohio. University of Louisville, Medical Department (Kentucky School of Medicine), 1893. Surgeon, Lake Erie and Western, and Toledo and Ohio Central Railroads.

NOBLE, ROBERT A., M.D., 1406 East Washington Street, Bloomington, Illinois. Northwestern University Medical School, 1901. Surgeon, St. Joseph's and Brokaw Hospitals.

NOBLE, ROBERT E., M.Sc., M.D., Medical Corps, United States Army, Washington, District of Columbia. Columbia University, College of Physicians and Surgeons, 1899. Brigader General, Medical Corps, United States Army.

NOECKER, CHARLES B., M.D., 213 Connell Building, Scranton, Pennsylvania. University of Pennsylvania School of Medicine, 1902. Surgeon, State Hospital of Anthracite Coal Region, West Side Hospital, Scranton, Mid-Valley Hospital, Blakely.

NOEHREN, ALFRED H., A.B., M.D., 1196 Main Street, Buffalo, New York. Columbia University, College of Physicians and Surgeons, 1905. Instructor in Anatomy, University of Buffalo, Department of Medicine; Associate Surgeon, Deaconess and Buffalo City Hospitals; Surgeon, Lutheran Church Home.

NOGUEIRA, ALEJANDRO, M.D., Convencion 1454, Montevideo, Uruguay. Faculty of Medicine, University of Montevideo, 1907. Chief of Service, Maciel Hospital.

NOLAND, LLOYD, M.D., Employes' Hospital, Birmingham, Alabama. University of Maryland School of Medicine (Baltimore Medical College), 1903. Chief Surgeon, Tennessee Coal, Iron and Railroad Company.

NOLTE, LEWIS GUSTAVUS, M.D., Senn's Block, Milwaukee, Wisconsin. Columbia University, College of Physicians and Surgeons, 1886. Surgeon, Evangelical Deaconess, Trinity, Misericordia, and Johnston Emergency Hospitals; Consulting Surgeon, Milwaukee County Hospital, Wauwatosa.

NOOTNAGEL, CHARLES F., M.D., 600 Physicians and Surgeons Building, Minneapolis, Minnesota. University and Bellevue Hospital Medical College (Bellevue Hospital Medical College), 1887. Chief of Surgical Staff, St. Andrew's Hospital; Member of Surgical Staff, Northwestern Hospital.

NORCROSS, EDWARD POWERS, M.D., 30 North Michigan Avenue, Chicago, Illinois. Northwestern University Medical School, 1904. Attending

Rhinologist, Oto-Laryngologist, St. Luke's Hospital, Chicago Institute of Medicine.

NORRIS, CHARLES C., M.D., Twenty-second and Chestnut Streets, Philadelphia, Pennsylvania. University of Pennsylvania School of Medicine, 1898. Assistant Professor, Post-Graduate School of Medicine, University of Pennsylvania; Associate in Gynecology, University of Pennsylvania School of Medicine; Assistant Gynecologist, Hospital of the University of Pennsylvania; Consulting Gynecologist and Obstetrician, Henry Phipps Institute of the University of Pennsylvania; Gynecologist, Children's Hospital.

NORRIS, FRANK A., M.D., 409 Ayers Bank Building, Jacksonville, Illinois. Northwestern University Medical School, 1903. Member of Staff, Our Savior's and Passavant Hospitals; Consulting Surgeon, Norbury Sanatorium.

NORRIS, HENRY, M.D., Rutherfordton, North Carolina. University of Pennsylvania School of Medicine, 1896. Surgeon, Rutherford Hospital.

NORSWORTHY, OSCAR L., M.D., 3015 Main Street, Houston, Texas. Tulane University of Louisiana School of Medicine, 1895. Surgeon in Charge, Norsworthy Hospital.

NORTHINGTON, EUGENE G., M.D., Washington, District of Columbia. Tulane University of Louisiana School of Medicine, 1903. Major Medical Corps, United States Army, retired.

NORTHROP, EDWARD R., M.D., 417 Paulsen Building, Spokane, Washington. Hahnemann Medical College and Hospital, Philadelphia, 1898; Medico-Chirurgical College, Philadelphia, 1899.

NORTHROP, HERBERT L., M.D., 601 Medical Arts Building, Philadelphia, Pennsylvania. Hahnemann Medical College and Hospital, Philadelphia, 1889. Professor of Surgery and Senior Surgeon, Hahnemann Medical College and Hospital.

NORTON, WALTER A., M.D., 105 Oglethorpe Avenue, East, Savannah, Georgia. Emory University School of Medicine (Atlanta College of Physicians and Surgeons), 1903. Attending Surgeon, Savannah Hospital; Member of Staff, St. Joseph's Hospital.

NORWOOD, ERVIN E., M.D., 21 Franklin Street, Kingston, New York. Baltimore University School of Medicine, 1892. Surgeon, Kingston City Hospital.

NOURSE, ROBERT L., M.D., Idaho Building, Boise, Idaho. Rush Medical College, 1889. Ophthalmologist and Oto-Laryngologist, St. Luke's Hospital.

NOVAK, EMIL, A.B., M.D., 26 East Preston Street, Baltimore, Maryland. University of Maryland School of Medicine (Baltimore Medical College), 1904. Instructor in Clinical Gynecology, Johns Hopkins University, Medical Department; Gynecologist-in-Chief, South Baltimore General Hospital; Consulting Gynecologist, Morrow Hospital; Member of Surgical Staff, Mercy Hospital.

NOYES, GUY LINCOLN, M.D., 311 Hitt Street, Columbia, Missouri. University of Vermont College of Medicine, 1894; University of Michigan Medical School, 1901. Dean of the Faculty of Medicine, and Professor of Department of Clinical Medicine and Surgery, University of Missouri School of Medicine.

NUMBERS, JOSEPH R., M.D., 212 Idaho Building, Boise, Idaho. Eclectic Medical College (Eclectic Medical Institute), 1885. Member of Staff, St. Alphonsus Hospital.

NUTT, JOHN JOSEPH, B.L., M.D., 853 Seventh Avenue, New York, New York. University and Bellevue Hospital Medical College, 1897. Instructor, Department of Orthopedic Surgery, University and Bellevue Hospital Medical College; Surgeon-in-Chief, New York State Hospital for Crippled and Deformed Children, West Haverstraw; Orthopedic Surgeon, Willard Parker, Rockland County, and Nyack Hospitals.

NUTTER, CHARLES FRANCIS, M.D., 16 Amherst Street, Nashua, New Hampshire. Bowdoin Medical College (Medical School of Maine), 1892. Member of Staff, Nashua Memorial and St. Joseph's Hospitals.

NUTTER, JOHN APPLETON, B.A., M.D., C.M., 609 Drummond Building, Montreal, Quebec. Faculty of Medicine, McGill University, 1904. Demonstrator of Orthopedic Surgery, Faculty of Medicine, McGill University; Associate in Orthopedic Surgery, Montreal General Hospital; Consulting Orthopedic Surgeon, Protestant Hospital for Insane, Verdun.

NUZUM, THOMAS WALTER, M.D., 225 West Milwaukee Street, Janesville, Wisconsin. Rush Medical College, 1885. Attending Surgeon, Mercy Hospital; Local Surgeon, Chicago, Milwaukee and St. Paul Railway.

OAKLEY, FRANK, Phar.G., M.D., C.M., 432 Anisfield Building, Cleveland, Ohio. University of Toronto, Faculty of Medicine (Trinity Medical College), 1897. Visiting Urologist, St. Alexis, Glenville, and Women's Hospitals.

OAKMAN, CHARLES H., D.D.S., M.D., David Whitney Building, Detroit, Michigan. Detroit College of Medicine and Surgery, 1906.

OASTLER, FRANK R., A.B., M.D., 170 West Fifty-ninth Street, New York, New York. Columbia University, College of Physicians and Surgeons, 1894. Clinical Professor of Gynecology, Columbia University, College of Physicians and Surgeons; Attending Gynecologist and Obstetrician, Lincoln Hospital and Home; Attending Gynecologist, Lenox Hill Hospital; Consulting Surgeon, St. Luke's Home for Aged Women.

OATES, THEODORE KENSELL, M.D., 110 North Raleigh Street, Martinsburg, West Virginia. University of Maryland School of Medicine, 1896. Chief Surgeon, City Hospital.

OBER, RALPH BEVERLEY, M.D., 76 Maple Street, Springfield, Massachusetts. Harvard Medical School, 1901. Assistant Surgeon, Springfield Hospital.

O'BRIEN, DANIEL PAUL, M.D., 330 Union Street, New Bedford, Massachusetts. Harvard Medical School, 1904. Visiting Surgeon, St. Luke's Hospital, St. Mary's Orphans' Home.

O'Brien, Edward J., M.D., 2560 Woodward Avenue, Detroit, Michigan. Detroit College of Medicine and Surgery, 1909. Clinical Instructor of Surgery, Detroit College of Medicine and Surgery; Surgeon, Harper Hospital; Attending Surgeon, Herman Kiefer Hospital.

O'Callaghan, Robert Hay Lismore, M.D., C.M., 410 Herald Building, Calgary, Alberta. Faculty of Medicine, McGill University, 1910. Surgeon, Calgary General and Holy Cross Hospitals.

Ochsner, Albert John, B.Sc., M.D., LL.D., F.R.M.S., F.R.C S. (Ire.), Hon., 2106 Sedgwick Street, Chicago, Illinois. Rush Medical College, 1886. Professor of Surgery, University of Illinois College of Medicine; Surgeon-in-Chief, Augustana and St. Mary of Nazareth Hospitals.

Ochsner, Edward H., B.Sc., M.D., 2155 Cleveland Avenue, Chicago, Illinois. Rush Medical College, 1894. Attending Surgeon, Augustana Hospital.

O'Connor, Dennis F., A.M., M.D., 671 Broad Street, Newark, New Jersey. University of Maryland School of Medicine (College of Physicians and Surgeons, Baltimore), 1898.

O'Connor, John C., B.Sc., M.D., 1037 Elm Street, Manchester, New Hampshire. Bowdoin Medical School, 1905. Surgeon, Elliott and Balch Hospitals.

O'Crowley, Clarence Rutherford, M.D., Ordway Building, Newark, New Jersey. Columbia University, College of Physicians and Surgeons, 1904. Instructor in Genito-Urinary Surgery, New York Post-Graduate Medical School; Visiting Genito-Urinary Surgeon, Newark City Hospital; Urologist, Newark Memorial and Beth Israel Hospitals, Newark, Stumpf Memorial Hospital, Kearny, Alexian Brothers' Hospital, Elizabeth, Dover General Hospital, Dover, New Jersey State Hospital, Morris Plains.

O'Day, John Christopher, M.D., 45 Young Building, Honolulu, Hawaii. National Normal University, College of Medicine, 1896; University of Illinois College of Medicine (College of Physicians and Surgeons, Chicago), 1900. Honorary Staff Surgeon, Queen's Hospital.

Odell, Anna, A.B., M.D., 74 Adams Avenue, West, Detroit, Michigan. University of Michigan Medical School, 1900. Attending Aurist and Laryngologist, Free Dispensary for Women and Children, Woman's Hospital and Infants' Home.

Odell, Henry Edward, M.D., Medical Corps, United States Navy, Washington, District of Columbia. University of Michigan Medical School, 1895. Captain, Medical Corps, United States Navy.

Oden, Rudolph J. E., A.B., M.D., 5412 North Clark Street, Chicago, Illinois. University Medical College of Kansas City, 1906. Junior Attending Surgeon, Augustana Hospital.

Oechsner, John Frederick, M.D., 621 Macheca Building, New Orleans, Louisiana. Tulane University of Louisiana School of Medicine, 1894.

Professor of Orthopedic Surgery and Surgery of Children, Post-Graduate Department, Tulane University of Louisiana, School of Medicine; Chief of Division of Orthopedic Surgery and Surgery of Children, Charity Hospital.

OERTEL, THEODORE EUGENE, M.D., Lamar Building, Augusta, Georgia. George Washington University Medical School, 1892. Professor of Ophthalmology, University of Georgia, Medical Department; Visiting Surgeon, Eye, Ear, Nose, and Throat Department, University and Wilhenford Hospitals; Oculist, Southern, Augusta-Southern, Georgia and Florida, and Charleston and Western Carolina Railroads, Augusta-Aiken Railway and Electric Corporation.

O'FERRALL, JOHN TOLSON, M.D., 3439 St. Charles Avenue, New Orleans, Louisiana. Tulane University of Louisiana School of Medicine, 1908. Chief Orthopedic Surgeon, Charity Hospital, New Orleans Dispensary for Women and Children; Senior Orthopedic Surgeon, Touro Infirmary.

OFFUTT, WILLIAM NELSON, M.D., 230 North Broadway, Lexington, Kentucky. University of Louisville, Medical Department (Hospital College of Medicine, Louisville), 1902. Member of Surgical Staff, Good Samaritan and St. Joseph's Hospitals.

OFNER, OSCAR, M.D., 635 Center Street, Chicago, Illinois. Royal University of Sciences, Budapest, Hungary, 1898. Member of Staff, St. Elizabeth's, St. Joseph's, and Alexian Brothers' Hospitals.

OGDEN, CHESTER R., B.Sc., M.D., Main and Second Streets, Clarksburg, West Virginia. University of Louisville, Medical Department (Hospital College of Medicine), 1902. Surgeon, St. Mary's Hospital.

OGDEN, MAHLON D., M.D., 900 Scott Street, Little Rock, Arkansas. University of Arkansas, Medical Department, 1904. Surgeon-in-Chief, St. Vincent's Infirmary.

OGILVY, CHARLES, B.A., M.D., C.M., 40 East Forty-first Street, New York, New York. Faculty of Medicine, McGill University, 1898. Associate Professor of Orthopedic Surgery, New York Post-Graduate Medical School; Attending Orthopedic Surgeon, New York Post-Graduate Medical School and Hospital, Lutheran Hospital, New York, Westchester County Hospitals, East View, New Rochelle Hospital, New Rochelle; Consulting Orthopedic Surgeon, French Hospital, New York, White Plains Hospital, White Plains, United Hospital, Port Chester, Nassau Hospital, Long Island.

OHNESORG, KARL, M.D., Medical Corps, United States Navy, Washington, District of Columbia. University of Pennsylvania School of Medicine, 1895. Commander, Medical Corps, United States Navy.

O'KELLEY, JAMES PHARES, M.D., Macheca Building, New Orleans, Louisiana. Tulane University of Louisiana School of Medicine, 1893. Clinical Professor of Diseases of the Ear, Nose, and Throat, Tulane University of Louisiana School of Medicine; Chief Visiting Surgeon, Ear, Nose, and Throat Department, Charity Hospital; Surgeon-in-Chief, Ear, Nose, and Throat Department, Presbyterian Hospital.

OLD, EDWARD HENRY HERBERT, A.B., M.D., Medical Corps, United States Navy, Washington, District of Columbia. University of Virginia, Department of Medicine, 1899. Commander, Medical Corps, United States Navy.

OLD, LEVI, M.D., Taylor Building, Norfolk, Virginia. University of Virginia, Department of Medicine, 1894. Surgeon, St. Vincent's Hospital and Sanitarium.

OLIVER, CLIFFORD IRWIN, M.D., Graceville, Minnesota. University of Illinois College of Medicine (College of Physicians and Surgeons, Chicago), 1901. Chief Surgeon, Western Minnesota Hospital; Surgeon, Great Northern and Chicago, Milwaukee and St. Paul Railways.

OLIVER, JAMES HIPOLITE, M.D., Calle Cuareim 1580, Montevideo, Uruguay. University of Montevideo, Faculty of Medicine, 1889. Honorary Professor of Surgical Pathology, University of Montevideo Medical School.

OLIVER, JOHN CHADWICK, M.D., 628 Elm Street, Cincinnati, Ohio. University of Cincinnati College of Medicine (Miami Medical College), 1885. Professor of Surgery, University of Cincinnati College of Medicine; Surgeon, Cincinnati General and Christ Hospitals; Consulting Surgeon, St. Francis Hospital.

OLIVER, JOHN HOLLIDAY, A.M., M.D., 510 Hume-Mansur Building, Indianapolis, Indiana. Indiana University School of Medicine (Indiana Medical College, Indianapolis), 1881. Professor of Surgery, Indiana University School of Medicine; Consulting Surgeon, Indianapolis City, St. Vincent's, and Robert W. Long Hospitals.

OLIVER, PAUL, B.Sc., M.D., 104 South Michigan Avenue, Chicago, Illinois. Rush Medical College, 1901. Assistant Professor of Surgery, Rush Medical College; Attending Surgeon, Cook County Hospital, Chicago, West Suburban Hospital, Oak Park.

OLMSTED, INGERSOLL, M.B., 215 James Street, South, Hamilton, Ontario. University of Toronto, Faculty of Medicine, 1887. Surgeon, Hamilton City Hospital.

OLSON, FREDERICK A. M., A.B., M.D., M.S., 420 Syndicate Building, Minneapolis, Minnesota. Rush Medical College, 1908. Instructor in Surgery, University of Minnesota Medical School; Associate Surgeon, University Hospital; Member of Attending Staff, University and Asbury Hospitals; Associate Member of Staff, Abbott Hospital.

OLSON, OLOF AUGUST, M.D., 1117 Metropolitan Bank Building, Minneapolis, Minnesota. University of Minnesota Medical School, 1902. Member of Surgical Staff, Minneapolis City and Swedish Hospitals.

O'MALLEY, JOHN JOSEPH, M.D., Medical Corps, United States Navy, Washington, District of Columbia. University of Maryland School of Medicine (College of Physicians and Surgeons, Baltimore), 1908. Lieutenant Commander, Medical Corps, United States Navy.

OMAN, CHARLES MALDEN, M.D., Medical Corps, United States Navy, Washington, District of Columbia. University of Pennsylvania School of Medicine, 1901. Instructor in Surgery, United States Naval Medical School; Visiting Surgeon, Columbia Hospital for Women; Commander, Medical Corps, United States Navy.

O'NEIL, RICHARD FROTHINGHAM, M.D., 374 Marlborough Street, Boston, Massachusetts. Harvard Medical School, 1897. Assistant in Genito-Urinary Surgery, Harvard University Graduate School of Medicine; Genito-Urinary Surgeon, Out-Patient Department, Massachusetts General Hospital.

O'NEILL, A. AUGUSTUS, M.D., Ph.D., 4607 Champlain Avenue, Chicago, Illinois. University of Kansas School of Medicine (Kansas City Medical College), 1890; Jefferson Medical College, 1893. President and Surgeon-in-Chief, Columbia Hospital; Visiting Surgeon, St. Francis Hospital, Evanston, Woman's Hospital, Chicago.

O'NEILL, BERNARD JOSEPH, JR., B.Sc., M.D., First National Bank Building, San Diego, California. Rush Medical College, 1908. Attending Surgeon, San Diego County Hospital; Chief of Staff, St. Joseph's Hospital.

OPPENHEIMER, SEYMOUR, M.D., 45 East Sixtieth Street, New York, New York. University and Bellevue Hospital Medical College (University of the City of New York, Medical Department), 1892. Consulting Otologist, Gouverneur Hospital; Consulting Laryngologist and Otologist, Monmouth Memorial and Willard Parker Hospitals, Hebrew Infant and Hebrew Orphan Asylums.

OPPENHEIMER, WILLIAM TELL, A.B., M.D., 321 West Grace Street, Richmond, Virginia. Medical College of Virginia, 1881; University and Bellevue Hospital Medical College (University of the City of New York, Medical Department), 1882. Chief Surgeon, Chesapeake and Ohio, and Richmond, Fredericksburg and Potomac Railroads.

O'REILLY, ARCHER, A.B., M.D., 3534 Washington Avenue, St. Louis, Missouri. Harvard Medical School, 1906. Associate in Clinical Orthopedic Surgery, Washington University Medical School; Assistant Surgeon, St. Louis Children's Hospital; Surgeon, Out-Patient Department, St. Louis Children's and Washington University Hospitals; Orthopedic Surgeon, St. Louis City Hospital.

O'REILLY, WILLIAM FRANCIS, M.D., 44 South Common Street, Lynn, Massachusetts. Harvard Medical School, 1903.

ORELLA, FERMIN RALPH, B.Sc., M.D., L.R.C.P. and M.R.C.S. (Eng.), 323 Geary Street, San Francisco, California. Leland Stanford Junior University School of Medicine (Cooper Medical College), 1892. Royal College of Physicians and Surgeons, London, 1894. Visiting Surgeon, St. Francis Hospital.

ORR, H. WINNETT, M.D., 1010 Terminal Building, Lincoln, Nebraska. University of Michigan Medical School, 1899. Orthopedic Surgeon, St. Elizabeth's Hospital; Chief Surgeon, Nebraska Orthopedic Hospital.

ORR, THOMAS G., A.B., M.D., 822 Rialto Building, Kansas City, Missouri. Johns Hopkins University Medical Department, 1910. Associate Professor of Surgery and Director of Dispensary, University of Kansas School of Medicine; Attending Surgeon, University of Kansas Bell Memorial Hospital, Rosedale, St. Luke's Hospital, Kansas City, and United States Public Health Service Hospital No. 67.

ORTH, DANIEL A., M.D., 209 South State Street, Chicago, Illinois. Rush Medical College, 1896. Clinical Professor of Surgery, Loyola University School of Medicine; Attending Surgeon, St. Mary of Nazareth and Columbus Hospitals.

ORTON, HENRY BOYLAN, M.D., 671 Broad Street, Newark, New Jersey. Jefferson Medical College, 1908. Rhinologist and Laryngologist, Presbyterian Hospital; Bronchoscopist, Esophagoscopist, Newark Eye and Ear Infirmary, Newark Memorial, St. Michael's and Newark City Hospitals; Consulting Bronchoscopist and Esophagoscopist, Orange Memorial Hospital, Orange; Assistant Oto-Laryngologist, St. Michael's Hospital.

OSBORN, GEORGE ROBERT, M.D., 302 R. T. Daniel Building, Tulsa, Oklahoma. University of Illinois College of Medicine (College of Physicians and Surgeons), 1906. Obstetrician, Tulsa Hospital.

OSGOOD, ALFRED TOWNSEND, A.B., M.D., 40 East Forty-first Street, New York, New York. Columbia University, College of Physicians and Surgeons, 1899. Professor of Genito-Urinary Surgery, University and Bellevue Hospital Medical College; Associate Attending Genito-Urinary Surgeon, Bellevue Hospital; Consulting Genito-Urinary Surgeon, Lawrence Hospital, Bronxville, New York, Muhlenberg Hospital, Plainfield, New Jersey.

OSGOOD, ROBERT B., A.B., M.D., 372 Marlborough Street, Boston, Massachusetts. Harvard Medical School, 1899. Instructor in Surgery and Orthopedic Surgery, Harvard Medical School; Chief of Orthopedic Department, Massachusetts General Hospital.

O'SHEA, RICHARD J., A.M., M.D., Cobb Building, Seattle, Washington. Harvard Medical School, 1901. Visiting Surgeon, Seattle City Hospital.

OTIS, FRANK JESSE, M.D., 512 Reliance Building, Moline, Illinois. University of Illinois College of Medicine (American Medical Missionary College), 1899; Rush Medical College, 1908. Surgeon, Lutheran and Moline Public Hospitals.

OTRICH, GROVER CLEVELAND, M.D., Commercial Building, Belleville, Illinois. University of Illinois College of Medicine, 1908.

OVERLOCK, SELDOM BURDEN, A.B., M.D., Pomfret, Connecticut. University and Bellevue Hospital Medical College, 1889. Surgeon-in-Chief, Day Kimball Hospital, Putnam.

OWEN, FRANK S., M.D., 648 Brandeis Building, Omaha, Nebraska. University of Michigan Medical School, 1885. Professor of Rhinology and Laryngology, University of Nebraska College of Medicine; Oculist and Aurist, Immanuel and Wise Memorial Hospitals; Rhinologist and Laryngologist University Hospital.

OWEN, LEARTUS J., M.D., Medical Corps, United States Army, Washington, District of Columbia. University of Virginia, Department of Medicine, 1900; University of Maryland School of Medicine (College of Physicians and Surgeons, Baltimore), 1904. Lieutenant Colonel, Medical Corps, United States Army.

OWEN, WILLIAM BARNETT, M.D., Francis Building, Louisville, Kentucky. University of Louisville, Medical Department (Kentucky University, Medical Department), 1903. Professor of Orthopedic Surgery, University of Louisville, Medical Department; Attending Orthopedist, Louisville City Hospital, John N. Norton Memorial Infirmary, Children's Free Hospital; Consultant Orthopedic Surgeon, United States Marine Hospital, No. 11.

OWEN, WILLIAM O., M.D., 2719 Ontario Road, Northwest, Washington, District of Columbia. University of Virginia, Department of Medicine, 1878. Professor of Anatomy, Georgetown University School of Medicine; Colonel, Medical Corps, United States Army, retired.

OWENS, EDMUND BURT, M.D., 123 East First Street, Dixon, Illinois. Northwestern University Medical School, 1890. Member of Staff, Katherine Shaw Bethea Hospital.

OWENS, JOHN E., M.D., 2127 Prairie Avenue, Chicago, Illinois. Jefferson Medical College, 1862. Emeritus Professor of Principles and Practice of Surgery and Clinical Surgery, Northwestern University Medical School; Honorary Consulting Surgeon, St. Luke's Hospital; Consulting Surgeon, Chicago and Northwestern Railroad.

OWENS, MICHAEL J., M.D., Rialto Building, Kansas City, Missouri. University Medical College of Kansas City, 1904. Attending Surgeon, St. Joseph's, St. Vincent's Maternity, and University Hospitals, Kansas City, Missouri, St. Margaret's Hospital, Kansas City, Kansas.

OWRE, OSCAR, M.D., C.M., 707 Masonic Temple, Minneapolis, Minnesota. University of Minnesota Medical School (Minneapolis College of Physicians and Surgeons), 1903. Assistant Professor of Genito-Urinary Diseases, University of Minnesota Medical School; Genito-Urinary Surgeon, Minneapolis General, St. Mary's, Northwestern, Fairview and Norwegian Hospitals; Consulting Urologist, Hill Crest, Eitel Hospitals and Glenn Lake Sanitarium; Surgeon, Genito-Urinary Department, Swedish Hospital.

PACKARD, GEORGE B., M.D., 1344 Franklin Street, Denver, Colorado. University of Vermont College of Medicine, 1874. Emeritus Professor of Orthopedic Surgery, University of Colorado School of Medicine; Orthopedic Surgeon, St. Luke's, St. Joseph's, Mercy, and Children's Hospitals.

PACKARD, HORACE, M.D., 470 Commonwealth Avenue, Boston, Massachusetts. Boston University School of Medicine, 1880. Emeritus Professor of Surgery, Boston University School of Medicine; Consulting Surgeon, Massachusetts Homeopathic Hospital, Boston, Newton Hospital, Newton, Brockton Hospital, Brockton.

PADDOCK, CHARLES E., M.D., 104 South Michigan Avenue, Chicago, Illinois. Northwestern University Medical School (Chicago Medical College), 1891.

Professor of Obstetrics, Post-Graduate Medical School; Assistant Clinical
Professor of Obstetrics, Rush Medical College; Obstetrician, St. Luke's
and Post-Graduate Hospitals.

PADGETT, EVERETT ERVIN, M.D., 423 Hume-Mansur Building, Indianapolis,
Indiana. Rush Medical College, 1905. Assistant in Clinical Surgery,
Indiana University School of Medicine; Attending Surgeon, Indianapolis
City Hospital, City Dispensary.

PAFFARD, FREDERIC CHAUNCEY, M.D., 89 Remsen Street, Brooklyn, New
York. Columbia University, College of Physicians and Surgeons, 1896.
Attending Surgeon, St. Anthony's and St. Peter's Hospitals.

PAGE, HENRY, M.A., M.D., Cincinnati General Hospital, Cincinnati, Ohio.
University of Pennsylvania School of Medicine, 1894. Dean, University
of Cincinnati College of Medicine.

PAGE, JOHN RANDOLPH, M.D., 127 East Sixty-second Street, New York, New
York. University of Virginia, Department of Medicine, 1899. Otologist,
House of the Holy Comforter; Assistant Surgeon, Manhattan Eye, Ear,
and Throat Hospital; Assistant Consulting Otologist, Babies' Hospital.

PAGE, LAFAYETTE, A.M., M.D., 603 Hume-Mansur Building, Indianapolis,
Indiana. Indiana University School of Medicine (Indiana Medical Col-
lege), 1889. Clinical Professor of Diseases of Nose, Throat, and Ear,
Indiana University School of Medicine; Consultant, Diseases of Ear,
Nose, and Throat, Indianapolis City, St. Vincent's, Methodist Episcopal
and Robert W. Long State Hospitals.

PAINE, ALONZO KINGMAN, M.D., 80 Bay State Road, Boston, Massachusetts.
Tufts College Medical School, 1902. Assistant Professor of Obstetrics,
Tufts College Medical School; Visiting Obstetrician, Jewish Women's
and Evangeline Booth Hospitals; Surgeon, Department of Diseases of
Women, Boston Dispensary.

PAINTER, CHARLES FAIRBANK, A.B., M.D., 520 Commonwealth Avenue, Bos-
ton, Massachusetts. Harvard Medical School, 1894. Professor of Ortho-
pedic Surgery, Tufts College Medical School; Associate in Orthopedic
Surgery, Harvard University Graduate School of Medicine; Orthopedic
Surgeon, Robert Bent Brigham Hospital; Consulting Surgeon, Carney
Hospital, Boston, Brockton Hospital, Brockton, Sturdy Memorial Hospital,
Attleboro.

PALEN, GILBERT J., A.B., M.D., 2102 Chestnut Street, Philadelphia, Pennsyl-
vania. Hahnemann Medical College and Hospital, Philadelphia, 1895.
Professor of Otology and Otologist, Hahnemann Medical College and
Hospital; Ophthalmologist, Children's Homeopathic Hospital; Ophthal-
mologist and Oto-Laryngologist, Women's Homeopathic Association;
Consulting Oto-Laryngologist, Coatesville Hospital, Coatesville; Oto-
Laryngologist, Lutheran Orphans' Home, Germantown; Consulting
Otologist, Homeopathic State Hospital, Allentown, Pottstown Homeo-
pathic Hospital, Pottstown; Consulting Ophthalmologist and Otologist,
J. Lewis Crozer Home for Incurables and Homeopathic Hospital, Chester.

PALLISTER, STANLEY WILSON, M.D., 222 Jefferson Avenue, Brooklyn, New York. New York Homeopathic Medical College and Flower Hospital, 1898. Surgeon, Prospect Heights Hospital and Brooklyn Maternity, Brooklyn Nursery and Infants' Hospital, Carson C. Peck Memorial Hospital; Consulting Surgeon, Brooklyn Home for Consumptives.

PALMA, RICARDO, M.B., M.D., Divorciades 671, Lima, Peru. Faculty of Medicine, University of San Marcos, 1915.

PALMER, DON H., A.B., M.D., 619 Lumber Exchange Building, Seattle, Washington. Rush Medical College, 1903. Surgeon, Seattle City and General Hospitals.

PALMER, DUDLEY WHITE, B.Sc., M.D., 707 Race Street, Cincinnati, Ohio. University of Cincinnati College of Medicine (Ohio-Miami Medical College of the University of Cincinnati), 1906. Associate Professor of Clinical Surgery, University of Cincinnati College of Medicine; Attending Surgeon, Cincinnati General and Christ Hospitals; Consulting Surgeon, Cincinnati Tuberculosis Hospital.

PALMER, E. PAYNE, M.D., 305 Goodrich Building, Phoenix, Arizona. American Medical College (Barnes Medical College), 1898. Attending Surgeon, St. Joseph's Hospital; Consulting Surgeon, St. Luke's Home.

PALMER, JESSE G., M.D., 709 Avenue A, Opelika, Alabama. University of Maryland School of Medicine. (College of Physicians and Surgeons, Baltimore), 1884.

PALMER, JOHN, JR., M.D., 1900 Delaware Avenue, Wilmington, Delaware. University of Pennsylvania School of Medicine, 1882. Chief of Surgical Staff, Delaware Hospital.

PALMER, JOHN E., B.A., M.D., C.M., 501 Maclean Building, Calgary, Alberta. Faculty of Medicine, McGill University, 1909. Urologist, Soldiers' Civil Re-Establishment; Member of Staff, Calgary General and Holy Cross Hospitals.

PALMER, SARAH ELLEN, M.D., 483 Beacon Street, Boston, Massachusetts. Woman's Medical College of Pennsylvania, 1880. Consulting Surgeon, Massachusetts Women's Hospital.

PALMER, WILLIAM HENRY, M.D., 407 Jackman Building, Janesville, Wisconsin. Northwestern University Medical School, 1882. Surgeon, Mercy Hospital.

PALMERLEE, GEORGE H., M.D., 410 Washington Arcade, Detroit, Michigan. Detroit College of Medicine and Surgery, 1903. Clinical Assistant in Surgery, Detroit College of Medicine and Surgery; Attending Surgeon, Grace Hospital; Surgeon, American Car and Foundry Company.

PAMPEL, BYRON LEE, A.B., M.D., Livingston, Montana. University of Nebraska College of Medicine (Omaha Medical College), 1898. Attending Surgeon, Livingston City Hospitals.

PANCOAST, OMAR B., B.Sc., M.D., 1111 North Charles Street, Baltimore, Maryland. Johns Hopkins University, Medical Department, 1897. Associate in Clinical Surgery, Johns Hopkins University, Medical Department; Visiting Surgeon, Union Protestant Infirmary, Church Home and Infirmary; Surgeon, Johns Hopkins Hospital Dispensary.

PANTZER, HUGO O., A.M., M.D., 601 Hume-Mansur Building, Indianapolis, Indiana. Indiana University School of Medicine (Indiana Medical College), 1881. Gynecologist and Abdominal Surgeon, Methodist Episcopal, St. Vincent's, and Protestant Deaconess Hospitals.

PANZNER, EDWARD J., M.D., Breitmeyer Building, Detroit, Michigan. Detroit College of Medicine and Surgery, 1893. Attending Surgeon, Providence Hospital.

PARDO CORREA, CAUPOLICAN, M.D., Ejercito, N., 119, Santiago, Chile. Faculty of Medicine, University of Chile, 1894. Professor of Clinical Gynecology, Faculty of Medicine, University of Chile; Surgeon and Director of Maternity Department, San Vicente Hospital.

PARHAM, FREDERICK WILLIAM, M.D., 3513 Prytania Street, New Orleans, Louisiana. Tulane University of Louisiana School of Medicine (University of Louisiana Medical Department), 1879. Professor of Surgery, New Orleans Polyclinic; Chief of Surgical Staff, Charity Hospital, Touro Infirmary.

PARISH, BENJAMIN DORES, B.Sc., M.D., 2039 Chestnut Street, Philadelphia, Pennsylvania. University of Pennsylvania School of Medicine, 1902. Associate Professor in Otology, University of Pennsylvania, Graduate School of Medicine; Oto-Laryngologist, St. Agnes' Hospital; Consulting Laryngologist, Roosevelt Hospital.

PARK, JOHN WALTER, M.D., 32 North Second Street, Harrisburg, Pennsylvania. Jefferson Medical College, 1878. Surgeon, Eye, Ear, Nose, and Throat Department, Harrisburg Hospital.

PARKE, WILLIAM E., A.B., M.D., 1739 North Seventeenth Street, Philadelphia, Pennsylvania. University of Pennsylvania School of Medicine, 1886. Associate Surgeon and Obstetrician, Kensington Hospital for Women; Gynecologist, Frankford Hospital; Consulting Obstetrician, Hospital of the Protestant Episcopal Church.

PARKE, WILLIAM TIFFANY, M.B., M.D., 411 Dundas Street, Woodstock, Ontario. University of Toronto, Faculty of Medicine, 1877. Victoria University, Medical Department, 1880. Surgeon, General Hospital.

PARKER, DAVID WOODBURY, A.B., M.D., 967 Elm Street, Manchester, New Hampshire. Harvard Medical School, 1903. Surgeon, Elliot Hospital, Balch Memorial Hospital for Children, W. H. McElwain Company.

PARKER, E. H., B.Sc., M.D., 730 La Salle Building, Minneapolis, Minnesota. Northwestern University Medical School, 1891. Rhinologist and Laryngologist, Swedish and St. Andrew's Hospitals.

PARKER, EDWARD FROST, M.D., 70 Hasell Street, Charleston, South Carolina. Medical College of the State of South Carolina, 1889. Professor of Ophthalmology and Otology, Medical College of the State of South Carolina; Oculist and Aurist, Roper Hospital.

PARKER, EDWARD MASON, A.M., M.D., 1726 M Street, Northwest, Washington, District of Columbia. University and Bellevue Hospital Medical College (University of the City of New York, Medical Department), 1884. Surgeon, Providence Hospital.

PARKER, HARRY CALDWELL, M.D., Dubuque, Iowa. Harvard Medical School, 1901. Retired.

PARKER, OWEN WILLIAM, M.D., Ely, Minnesota. University of Minnesota Medical School, 1900.

PARKER, RALPH H., B.A., M.S., M.D., 1101 Fleming Building, Des Moines, Iowa. State University of Iowa College of Medicine, 1898. Member of Staff, Iowa Methodist Hospital.

PARKER, WALTER ROBERT, B.Sc., M.D., David Whitney Building, Detroit, Michigan. University of Pennsylvania School of Medicine, 1891. Professor of Ophthalmology, University of Michigan Medical School; Consulting Surgeon, Children's Free Hospital, Woman's Hospital and Infants' Home, Detroit; Attending Surgeon, University Hospital, Ann Arbor; Consulting Ophthalmologist, Harper Hospital.

PARKES, CHARLES H., M.D., 1910 Lincoln Avenue, Chicago, Illinois. Rush Medical College, 1897.

PARKES, WILLIAM ROSS, Ph.M., M.D., 800 Davis Street, Evanston, Illinois. Rush Medical College, 1893. Senior Attending Surgeon, Evanston Hospital.

PARMENTER, FREDERICK JAMES, M.D., 616 Potomac Avenue, Buffalo, New York. University of Buffalo, Department of Medicine, 1903. Professor of Genito-Urinary Surgery, University of Buffalo, Department of Medicine; Attending Urologist, Children's, Buffalo General, City, and Erie County Hospitals.

PARMETER, ROLLAND, B.Sc., M.D., 76 Adams Avenue, West, Detroit, Michigan. Rush Medical College, 1895. Clinical Professor of Surgery, Detroit College of Medicine and Surgery; Attending Surgeon, Harper and Receiving Hospitals.

PARROTT, ALBERT D., M.D., 107 West Gordon Street, Kinston, North Carolina. Medical College of Virginia, 1906. Superintendent, Parrott Memorial Hospital.

PARROTT, JAMES MARION, M.D., Kinston, North Carolina. Tulane University of Louisiana School of Medicine, 1895. Ophthalmologist, Rhinologist, and Oto-Laryngologist, Parrott Memorial Hospital.

PARRY, ANGENETTE, M.D., 154 East Thirty-seventh Street, New York, New York. Woman's Medical College of the New York Infirmary for Women and Children, 1891.

PARRY, IVAN A., B.Sc., M.D., 964 Empire Building, Seattle, Washington. University of Illinois College of Medicine (College of Physicians and Surgeons), 1901. Member of Staff, Columbus Sanitarium.

PARSONS, EDMUND BYRD, M.D., International and Great Northern Railroad Hospital, Palestine, Texas. Tulane University of Louisiana School of Medicine, 1885. Chief Surgeon, International and Great Northern Railroad Hospital.

PARSONS, HOUSTON HADDON, M.D., First National Bank Building, Sidney, Montana. University of Virginia Department of Medicine, 1907. Surgeon, Sidney Deaconess Hospital.

PARSONS, RICHARD, M.D., C.M., F.R.C.S. (Edin.), 171 First Street, Southeast, Red Deer, Alberta. Surgeon, Red Deer Memorial Hospital; District Surgeon, Canadian Pacific Railway.

PARSONS, SCOTT E., M.D., Wall Building, St. Louis, Missouri. Homeopathic Medical College of Missouri, 1894. Surgeon, St. Louis City Hospital.

PASCHAL, FRANK, M.D., Hicks Building, San Antonio, Texas. University of Louisville, Medical Department (Louisville Medical College), 1873. Surgeon, Physicians and Surgeons Hospital; Consulting Surgeon, Robert B. Green Memorial Hospital.

PASCUAL, WILLIAM VINCENT, M.D., 690 St. Marks Avenue, Brooklyn, New York. Columbia University College of Physicians and Surgeons, 1900. Surgeon, St. Mary's Hospital; Associate Surgeon, Hospital of the Holy Family.

PASMAN, RODOLFO E., M.D., Yuncal 2136, Buenos Aires, Brazil. Faculty of Medicine University of Buenos Aires, 1911.

PATCH, FRANK STEWART, B.A., M.D., C.M., 33 Bishop Street, Montreal, Quebec. Faculty of Medicine, McGill University, 1903. Clinical Professor of Genito-Urinary Surgery, Faculty of Medicine, McGill University; Genito-Urinary Surgeon, Montreal General Hospital.

PATERA, EDWARD, Ph.G., M.D., 1809 Loomis Street, Chicago, Illinois. University of Illinois College of Medicine, 1903. Member of Surgical Staff, St. Mary of Nazareth Hospital.

PATTEE, JAMES JAY, B.Sc., M.D., 511 Thatcher Building, Pueblo, Colorado. Rush Medical College, 1895. Ophthalmologist, Rhinologist, Oto-Laryngologist, Minnequa and St. Mary's Hospitals.

PATTEE, LOUIS GREENLEE, M.D., 126 East Fifth Avenue, Carroll, Iowa. Jefferson Medical College, 1893. Chief of Staff and Surgeon, St. Anthony's Hospital.

PATTERSON, ELLEN J., M.D., 1018 Westinghouse Building, Pittsburgh, Pennsylvania. Woman's Medical College of Pennsylvania, 1898. Associate Professor of Laryngology and Rhinology, University of Pittsburgh School of Medicine; Laryngologist and Rhinologist, Presbyterian and Eye and Ear Hospitals; Assistant Bronchoscopist, Allegheny General, Children's, and Western Pennsylvania Hospitals.

PATTERSON, FRANK PORTER, M.D., C.M., F.R.C.S. (Edin.), Birks Building, Vancouver, British Columbia. Faculty of Medicine, McGill University, 1898.

PATTERSON, JOSEPH M., M.D., 518 Bryant Building, Kansas City, Missouri. Ohio State University College of Homeopathic Medicine (Pulte Medical College), 1887. Ophthalmologist and Oto-Laryngologist, St. Mary's Hospital, Armour Memorial Home; Oto-Laryngologist, Christian Church Hospital.

PATTERSON, ROBERT URIE, M.D., C.M., Medical Corps, United States Army, Washington, District of Columbia. Faculty of Medicine, McGill University, 1898. Colonel, Medical Corps, United States Army.

PATTERSON, WILLIAM JOHN, B.A., M.D., C.M., 386 Sherbrooke Street, West, Montreal, Quebec. Faculty of Medicine, McGill University, 1906. Associate in Clinical Surgery and Orthopedics, Royal Victoria Hospital.

PATTON, A. G., B.Sc., M.D., 122 West First Avenue, Monmouth, Illinois. University of Cincinnati College of Medicine (Miami Medical College), 1892. Member of Surgical Staff, Monmouth Hospital.

PATTON, CHARLES LANPHIER, M.D., 407 South Seventh Street, Springfield, Illinois. University of Michigan Medical School, 1902. Surgeon, Springfield Hospital.

PATTON, JAMES M., B.Sc., A.M., M.D., 702 Brandeis Building, Omaha, Nebraska. University of Nebraska College of Medicine, 1904. Assistant Professor of Ophthalmology and Otology, University of Nebraska College of Medicine; Ophthalmologist and Otologist, Child Saving Institute, Nebraska Methodist Episcopal, University of Nebraska and Clarkson Memorial Hospitals.

PATTON, JOHN W. T., M.D., C.M., Queen Street, Truro, Nova Scotia. McGill University Faculty of Medicine, 1900.

PATTON, WILLIAM THOMAS, Ph.C., M.D., 1116 Maison Blanche Building, New Orleans, Louisiana. Tulane University of Louisiana School of Medicine, 1906. Professor of Otology and Laryngology, Loyola Post-Graduate School of Medicine; Chief of Third Division, Ear, Nose, and Throat Department, Charity Hospital; Visiting Oto-Laryngologist, Hotel Dieu, Presbyterian Hospital; Consulting Oto-Laryngologist, McComb City Sanitarium, McComb City, Mississippi.

PAUL, LUTHER G., M.D., 321 Beacon Street, Boston, Massachusetts. Harvard Medical School, 1899.

PAYNE, MARSHALL JOHN, M.D., 220 West Frederick Street, Staunton, Virginia. Jefferson Medical College, 1893. Member of Staff, King's Daughters Hospital; Surgeon, Chesapeake and Ohio Railroad.

PAYNE, ROBERT LEE, M.D., Tazewell Building, Norfolk, Virginia. University of Pennsylvania School of Medicine, 1905. Surgeon, St. Vincent's Hospital, Southern Railway, Clyde and Chesapeake Steamship Companies; Consulting Surgeon, Seaboard Air Line Railway; Chief Surgeon, Norfolk Southern Railroad.

PAYNE, SANDERS MCALLISTER, M.D., 542 Fifth Avenue, New York, New York. Vanderbilt University, Medical Department, 1875.

PEARSE, HERMAN ELWYN, M.D., 1305 Rialto Building, Kansas City, Missouri. St. Louis College of Physicians and Surgeons, 1888. Attending Surgeon, Research, Kansas City General, and St. Mary's Hospitals.

PEARSE, ROBIN, M.D., F.R.C.S. (Eng.), L.R.C.P. (Lond.), 206 Bloor Street, West, Toronto, Ontario. St. Bartholomew's Hospital, 1909. Assistant in Clinical Surgery, University of Toronto, Faculty of Medicine; Chief Assistant, Department of Urology, Toronto General Hospital.

PEARSON, CHARLES EDWARD, M.D., 55 Central Avenue, Staten Island, New York. Columbia University, College of Physicians and Surgeons, 1900. Visiting Surgeon, Staten Island and Sea View Hospitals.

PEARSON, WILLIAM WILSON, M.D., Bankers Trust Building, Des Moines, Iowa. University of Michigan Medical School, 1893.

PEASE, CLIFFORD ATHERTON, M.D., 301 College Street, Burlington, Vermont. University of Vermont College of Medicine, 1899; University of Vienna, 1912. Instructor in Clinical Surgery, University of Vermont College of Medicine; Attending Surgeon, Mary Fletcher Hospital, Burlington, Fanny Allen Hospital, Winooski.

PEASE, GEORGE NORMAN, A.B., M.D., 806 Stevens Building, Portland, Oregon. Cornell University Medical College, 1907. Lecturer on Operative Surgery, University of Oregon Medical School; Attending Surgeon, Multnomah County Hospital.

PECK, CHARLES H., M.D., 30 West Fiftieth Street, New York, New York. Columbia University, College of Physicians and Surgeons, 1892. Professor of Clinical Surgery, Columbia University, College of Physicians and Surgeons; Surgeon, Roosevelt Hospital; Consulting Surgeon, French and Memorial Hospitals, Hospital for Ruptured and Crippled, New York, White Plains Hospital, White Plains, Vassar Brothers' Hospital, Poughkeepsie, New York, Stamford Hospital, Stamford, Greenwich Hospital, Greenwich, Connecticut.

PECK, ELIZABETH L., M.D., 4113 Walnut Street, Philadelphia, Pennsylvania. Woman's Medical College of Pennsylvania, 1885. Attending Surgeon, West Philadelphia Hospital for Women; Member of Consulting Staff, Woman's Hospital; Attending Gynecologist, House of the Good Shepherd.

PECK, GEORGE AUGUSTUS, M.D., 189 Centre Avenue, New Rochelle, New York. Columbia University, College of Physicians and Surgeons, 1891. Attending Surgeon, New Rochelle Hospital; Consulting Surgeon, Westchester County Hospitals, East View.

PECK, JOHN LYMAN, Ph.B., M.Sc., M.D., 524 Vine Street, Scranton, Pennsylvania. Hahnemann Medical College and Hospital, Philadelphia, 1897. Surgeon-in-Chief, Hahnemann Hospital; Consulting Surgeon, City Hospital, Scranton, Wyoming Valley Homeopathic Hospital, Wilkes-Barre.

PECK, WILLIAM BUCKLEY, M.D., 86 Stephenson Street, Freeport, Illinois. Rush Medical College, 1897. Surgeon, Globe, St. Francis', and Freeport General Hospitals.

PECKHAM, FRANK EDWIN, Ph.B., M.D., 249 Thayer Street, Providence, Rhode Island. Harvard Medical School, 1890. Visiting Orthopedic Surgeon, St. Joseph's Hospital; Consulting Orthopedic Surgeon, Memorial Hospital, Pawtucket.

PEDERSEN, JAMES, B.Sc., M.D., 40 East Forty-first Street, New York, New York. Columbia University, College of Physicians and Surgeons, 1890. Adjunct Professor of Venereal and Genito-Urinary Diseases, New York Post-Graduate Medical School; Associate Attending Urologist, New York Post-Graduate Medical School and Hospital; Attending Genito-Urinary Surgeon, New York City Hospital; Consulting Genito-Urinary Surgeon, Englewood Hospital, Englewood, New Jersey, Stamford Hospital, Stamford, Connecticut.

PEDERSEN, VICTOR COX, A.M., M.D., 45 West Ninth Street, New York, New York. Columbia University, College of Physicians and Surgeons, 1898. Visiting Urologist and Chief of Clinic in Urology, St. Mark's Hospital.

PEDRO, ERNESTO, M.D., Rua Riackelo 161, Rio de Janeiro, Brazil. Faculty of Medicine, University of Rio de Janeiro, 1908.

PEED, GEORGE P., M.D., Medical Corps, United States Army, Washington, District of Columbia. University of Virginia, Department of Medicine, 1895. Lieutenant Colonel, United States Army.

PEET, MAX MINOR, A.M., M.D., University Hospital, Ann Arbor, Michigan. University of Michigan Medical School, 1910. Assistant Professor of Surgery, University of Michigan Medical School; Chief of Neurological Surgery, University Hospital.

PELTON, O. L., M.D., 102 North Spring Street, Elgin, Illinois. University of Michigan Medical School, 1872; University and Bellevue Hospital Medical College (Bellevue Hospital Medical College), 1874. Surgeon, St. Joseph's and Sherman Hospitals.

PELTON, ORA L., JR., M.D., 102 North Spring Street, Elgin, Illinois. Northwestern University Medical School, 1909. Surgeon, Sherman and St. Joseph's Hospitals.

PEMBER, JOHN FRANK, M.D., 225 West Milwaukee Street, Janesville, Wisconsin. Northwestern University Medical School, 1883. Attending Surgeon, Mercy Hospital, Rock County Asylum and Hospital; Local Surgeon, Chicago, Milwaukee and St. Paul Railroad.

PEMBERTON, FRANK ARTHUR, B.Sc., M.D., 311 Beacon Street, Boston, Massachusetts. Harvard Medical School, 1909. Instructor in Gynecology, Harvard Medical School; Assistant Visiting Surgeon, Free Hospital for Women.

PEMBERTON, JOHN DE JARNETTE, A.B., M.D., M.S., Mayo Clinic, Rochester, Minnesota. University of Pennsylvania School of Medicine, 1911; University of Minnesota Medical School, 1918. Instructor in Surgery, Mayo Foundation, University of Minnesota Medical School; Surgeon, Mayo Clinic.

PENBERTHY, GROVER CLEVELAND, M.D., David Whitney Building, Detroit, Michigan. University of Michigan Medical School, 1910. Assistant Professor of Clinical Surgery, Detroit College of Medicine and Surgery; Surgical Director, Children's Free Hospital; Junior Attending Surgeon, Harper Hospital; Surgeon, Michigan Mutual Hospital.

PENHALLOW, DUNLAP PEARCE, B.Sc., M.D., 23 West Forty-third Street, New York, New York. Harvard Medical School, 1906.

PENICK, RAWLEY MARTIN, M.D., 1109 Sheridan Avenue, Shreveport, Louisiana. University of Virginia, Department of Medicine, 1893. Visiting Surgeon, State Charity Hospital, T. E. Schumpert Memorial Sanitarium; Chief Surgeon, Louisiana Railway and Navigation Company.

PENNINGTON, JOHN RAWSON, M.D., 31 North State Street, Chicago, Illinois. University of Maryland School of Medicine, 1887. Professor of Rectal Diseases, Illinois Post-Graduate Medical School; Attending Surgeon, Sheridan Park Hospital; Member of Consulting Staff, Cook County Hospital.

PENROSE, CHARLES BINGHAM, A.M., M.D., Ph.D., LL.D., 1720 Spruce Street, Philadelphia, Pennsylvania. University of Pennsylvania School of Medicine, 1884.

PEPLE, W. LOWNDES, M.D., 1209 West Franklin Street, Richmond, Virginia. Medical College of Virginia (University College of Medicine), 1897. Professor of Clinical Surgery, Medical College of Virginia; Surgeon, Memorial and Virginia Hospitals.

PERCY, JAMES FULTON, M.D., 147 South Cherry Street, Galesburg, Illinois. University and Bellevue Hospital Medical College, 1886. Chief Surgeon, Galesburg and St. Mary's Hospitals.

PERCY, NELSON MORTIMER, M.D., 2106 Sedgwick Street, Chicago, Illinois. Rush Medical College, 1899. Associate Professor of Clinical Surgery, University of Illinois College of Medicine; Attending Surgeon, Augustana and St. Mary of Nazareth Hospitals.

PERCY, WILLIAM WELLESLEY, Ph.B., M.D., 12 West Avenue, Rochester, New York. Syracuse University College of Medicine, 1901. Surgeon, St. Mary's Hospital.

PERFECT, ALFRED HARSHAW, M.B., M.D., C.M., 201 Annette Street, Toronto, Ontario. University of Toronto, Faculty of Medicine, 1887. Demonstrator of Clinical Surgery, University of Toronto, Faculty of Medicine; Surgeon, Toronto Western Hospital; Consulting Surgeon, Toronto Orthopedic Hospital.

PERKINS, CHARLES EDWIN, M.D., 114 East Fifty-fourth Street, New York, New York. Columbia University, College of Physicians and Surgeons, 1888. Clinical Professor of Otology and Chief of Clinic, University and Bellevue Hospital Medical College; Associate Attending Aural Surgeon, St. Luke's Hospital; Aural Surgeon, New York Eye and Ear Infirmary.

PERKINS, CHARLES FORREST, M.D., D.D.S., Rogers, Arkansas. Rush Medical College, 1886. Surgeon, Loves Hospital.

PERKINS, EDWIN LUCIEN, M.D., 301 South Minnesota Avenue, Sioux Falls, South Dakota. Northwestern University Medical School, 1904. Member of Staff, McKennan Hospital.

PERKINS, JOHN WALTER, A.B., M.D., 1005 Campbell Street, Kansas City, Missouri. Harvard Medical School, 1886. Professor of Surgery, University of Kansas School of Medicine; Chief Surgeon, University Hospital.

PERRY, HERBERT BRAINERD, M.D., 55 New South Street, Northampton, Massachusetts. Bowdoin Medical School, 1890. Consulting Surgeon, Cooley Dickinson Hospital.

PERRY, RICHARD WILBERT, M.D., L.R.C.P.& S. (Edin.), 811 American Bank Building, Seattle, Washington. University of Toronto, Faculty of Medicine, 1897.

PERRY, WILLIAM B., M.D., 1 West Biddle Street, Baltimore, Maryland. University of Maryland School of Medicine (Baltimore Medical College), 1889. Professor of Clinical Gynecology, University of Maryland School of Medicine and College of Physicians and Surgeons; Gynecologist, Maryland General and University Hospitals; Surgeon, St. Joseph's Hospital.

PERSON, WELDON EDWARDS, M.D., Candler Building, Atlanta, Georgia. Emory University School of Medicine (Atlanta College of Physicians and Surgeons), 1901. Associate Professor of Clinical Surgery, Emory University School of Medicine; Associate Visiting Surgeon, Grady Memorial Hospital, Surgeon, McVicar Hospital.

PERSONS, ELBERT E., A.M., M.D., LL.D., Medical Corps, United States Army, Washington, District of Columbia. Northwestern University Medical School, 1897. Lieutenant Colonel, Medical Corps, United States Army.

PERSONS, HENRY STANFORD, M.D., 21 South Perry Street, Montgomery, Alabama. University of Virginia, Department of Medicine, 1893. Member of Visiting Staff, St. Margaret's Hospital.

PETER, LUTHER C., A.M., M.D., 1529 Spruce Street, Philadelphia, Pennsylvania. University of Pennsylvania School of Medicine, 1894. Professor of Ophthalmology, Temple University, Department of Medicine, University of Pennsylvania Graduate School of Medicine, Polyclinic Section; Ophthalmologist, Samaritan, Garretson, and Friends' Hospitals, Rush Hospital for Consumption and Allied Diseases.

PETERKA, EDWARD, A.B., M.D., 5026 Broadway, Cleveland, Ohio. Western Reserve University Medical School, 1905.

PETERKIN, GUY SHERMAN, M.D., 1105 Cobb Building, Seattle, Washington. Columbia University, College of Physicians and Surgeons, 1895. Consulting Surgeon in Urology, Seattle General, City, and King County Hospitals.

PETERMAN, HARRY ELMER, M.D., 518 North Charles Street, Baltimore, Maryland. University of Maryland School of Medicine (Baltimore Medical

College), 1895. Ophthalmic and Aural Surgeon, South Baltimore General Hospital; Visiting Ophthalmic and Aural Surgeon, Maryland General Hospital; Consulting Ophthalmologist and Otologist, Frederick City Hospital, Frederick.

PETERS, DON PRESTON, A.M., M.D., 1315 Church Street, Lynchburg, Virginia. University of Virginia, Department of Medicine, 1902. Surgeon in Charge, The Private Hospital.

PETERS, WILLIAM C., M.D., 45 State Street, Bangor, Maine. Tufts College Medical School, 1902. Orthopedic Surgeon, Eastern Maine General Hospital.

PETERSON, EDWARD WADSWORTH, A.M., M.D., 525 Park Avenue, New York, New York. Tulane University of Louisiana School of Medicine, 1896; Cornell University Medical College, 1899. Professor of Surgery, New York Post-Graduate Medical School; Attending Surgeon, Post-Graduate Hospital and Babies' Ward, Post-Graduate Hospital, New York, St. John's Hospital, Long Island City; Consulting Surgeon, New York Throat, Nose, and Lung Hospital, New York, St. Agnes' Hospital, White Plains, Country Home for Convalescent Babies, Sea Cliff, New York, All Souls' Hospital, Montclair, New Jersey.

PETERSON, GEORGE R., M.D., C.M., M.R.C.S. (Eng.), L.R.C.P. (Lond.), F.R.C.S. (Edin.), Second Avenue, Saskatoon, Saskatchewan. Faculty of Medicine, McGill University, 1903. Visiting Surgeon, St. Paul's and City Hospitals; Surgeon, Canadian National and Grand Trunk Pacific Railways.

PETERSON, REUBEN, A.B., M.D., 1416 Hill Street, Ann Arbor, Michigan. Harvard Medical School, 1889. Professor of Obstetrics and Gynecology, University of Michigan Medical School; Obstetrician and Gynecologist-in-Chief, University Hospital.

PETRIE, ROBERT WILLIAM, M.D., 812 Independence Building, Charlotte, North Carolina. University of Maryland School of Medicine, 1903. Member of Visiting Staff, St. Peter's, Presbyterian, Mercy General and Good Samaritan Hospitals.

PETTIS, JOHN H., A.B., M.D., Mattei Building, Fresno, California. University of Michigan Medical School, 1906.

PETTIT, JOSEPH A., M.D., Selling Building, Portland, Oregon. Washington University Medical School, 1899. Professor of Surgery and Applied Anatomy, North Pacific College; Surgeon, Emanuel and St. Vincent's Hospitals.

PFAFF, O. G., A.M., M.D., 333 Bankers Trust Building, Indianapolis, Indiana. Indiana University School of Medicine (Medical College of Indiana), 1882. Professor of Gynecology, Indiana University School of Medicine; Gynecologist, Indianapolis City and St. Vincent's Hospitals, Bobb's Free Dispensary.

PFEIFER, JOHN P., M.D., 1572 Milwaukee Avenue, Chicago, Illinois. Loyola University School of Medicine (Bennett Medical College), 1888; Rush

Medical College, 1893. Member of Surgical Staff, St. Mary of Nazareth Hospital.

PFEIFFER, DAMON BECKETT, A.B., M.D., 2028 Pine Street, Philadelphia, Pennsylvania. Johns Hopkins University, Medical Department, 1906. Associate in Surgery, University of Pennsylvania School of Medicine; Surgeon, Abington Memorial Hospital, Abington; Assistant Surgeon, Hospital of the University of Pennsylvania, Presbyterian Hospital, Out-Patient Department, Lankenau Hospital.

PFEIFFER, WILLIAM, M.D., 368 McDonough Street, Brooklyn, New York. Cornell University Medical College, 1903. Obstetrician and Gynecologist, Kings County Hospital; Assistant Gynecologist and Obstetrician, Hospital of the Holy Family; Obstetrician-in-Chief, Brownsville and East New York Hospital.

PFINGST, ADOLPH O., M.D., Francis Building, Louisville, Kentucky. University of Louisville, Medical Department (Louisville Medical College), 1891. Professor of Ophthalmology, University of Louisville, Medical Department; Visiting Ophthalmic Surgeon, Louisville Public Hospital, John N. Norton Memorial Infirmary, Children's Free Hospital, Protestant Orphan Asylum.

PFINGSTEN, CHRISTIAN FREDERICK, M.D., 508 North Grand Avenue, St. Louis, Missouri. St. Louis College of Physicians and Surgeons, 1898. Instructor in Otology, Laryngology, and Rhinology, St. Louis University School of Medicine; Otologist and Laryngologist, St. John's Hospital.

PFISTER, FRANZ, M.D., 1404 Majestic Building, Milwaukee, Wisconsin. Western Reserve University School of Medicine (University of Wooster, Medical Department), 1895. Professor and Head of Department of Ear, Nose, and Throat, Marquette University School of Medicine; Member of Staff, Trinity and Misericordia Hospitals, Milwaukee, Milwaukee County Hospital, Wauwatosa.

PHALEN, JAMES M., Phar.G., M.D., Medical Corps, United States Army, Washington, District of Columbia. University of Illinois College of Medicine, 1900. Lieutenant Colonel, Medical Corps, United States Army.

PHANEUF, LOUIS EUSEBE, Phar.D., Ph.C., M.D., 514 Commonwealth Avenue, Boston, Massachusetts. Tufts College Medical School, 1913. Associate Professor of Clinical Gynecology, Tufts College Medical School; Gynecologist, Carney Hospital; Visiting Obstetrician, St. Elizabeth's Hospital.

PHARES, J. W., M.D., 22 Walnut Street, Evansville, Indiana. University of Louisville, Medical Department (Kentucky School of Medicine), 1897. Surgeon, Hayden Hospital.

PHELPS, JOSEPH ROYAL, M.D., Medical Corps, United States Navy, Washington, District of Columbia. Harvard Medical School, 1903. Lieutenant Commander, Medical Corps, United States Navy.

PHELPS, O. DRAPER, A.B., M.D., 452 Main Street, Worcester, Massachusetts. Dartmouth Medical School, 1907. Surgeon, Genito-Urinary Department,

Worcester City Hospital; Cystoscopist, Memorial Hospital; Assistant Surgeon, Holden Hospital.

PHEMISTER, DALLAS B., M.D., 122 South Michigan Avenue, Chicago, Illinois. Rush Medical College, 1904. Assistant Professor of Surgery, Rush Medical College; Associate Attending Surgeon, Presbyterian Hospital.

PHIFER, CHARLES HERBERT, M.D., 30 North Michigan Avenue, Chicago, Illinois. University of Illinois College of Medicine (College of Physicians and Surgeons, Chicago), 1902. Assistant Professor of Surgery, University of Illinois College of Medicine; Attending Surgeon, Washington Park Hospital.

PHILLIPS, CHARLES EATON, A.B., M.D., 706 Pacific Mutual Building, Los Angeles, California. University of Illinois College of Medicine (College of Physicians and Surgeons, Chicago), 1903. Attending Surgeon, Los Angeles County Hospital.

PHILLIPS, EDGAR W., M.D., 758 Monroe Avenue, Rochester, New York. Cornell University Medical School, 1911. Member of Junior Surgical Staff, Rochester General Hospital.

PHILLIPS, HIRAM ALFRED, M.D., Medical Corps, United States Army, Washington, District of Columbia. University of Louisville, Medical Department (Hospital College of Medicine), 1906. Major, Medical Corps, United States Army.

PHILLIPS, PERCY TODD, M.D., Hihn Building, Santa Cruz, California. Western Reserve University School of Medicine, 1889. Surgeon-in-Chief, Hanly Sanitarium.

PHILLIPS, WENDELL CHRISTOPHER, M.D., 40 West Forty-seventh Street, New York, New York. University and Bellevue Hospital Medical College (University of the City of New York, Medical Department), 1882. Surgeon, Department of Otology, Manhattan Eye, Ear, and Throat Hospital; Visiting Surgeon, Department of Otology, New York Post-Graduate Medical School and Hospital; Consulting Otologist, Park Hospital; Consulting Laryngologist, Huntington Hospital, New York, Ossining Hospital, Ossining; Consulting Otologist and Laryngologist, Flushing Hospital, Flushing.

PHILLIPS, WILLIAM DAVIS, B.Sc., Ph.M., M.D., 1201 Maison Blanche Building, New Orleans, Louisiana. Tulane University of Louisiana School of Medicine, 1909. Professor of Operative Gynecology, Tulane University, Post-Graduate Department; Chief of Department of Gynecology and Obstetrics, Presbyterian Hospital.

PHILLIPS, WILLIAM H., M.D., 1018 Rose Building, Cleveland, Ohio. Ohio State University College of Homeopathic Medicine (Cleveland Medical College), 1893. Director and Eye, Ear, Nose, and Throat Surgeon, Glenville Hospital; Consulting Oculist, Cleveland Maternity Hospital.

PHILLIPS, WILLIAM LINTON, M.D., 469 Franklin Street, Buffalo, New York. University of Buffalo, Department of Medicine, 1897. Associate in Ophthalmology, University of Buffalo, Department of Medicine; Ophthalmic Surgeon, Emergency and Municipal Hospitals, St. Francis and Buffalo Orphan Asylums, Buffalo, St. Francis' Home, Gardenville, St. Francis' Home, Williamsville.

PHINNEY, FRANK DOUGLAS, A.B., M.D., 22 West Seventh Street, Cincinnati, Ohio. University of Pennsylvania School of Medicine, 1899. Oculist and Aurist, Bethesda Hospital.

PHIPPEN, HARDY, A.B., M.D., 84 Washington Square, Salem, Massachusetts. Harvard Medical School, 1889. Surgeon, Salem Hospital.

PHIPPEN, WALTER GRAY, M.D., 31 Chestnut Street, Salem, Massachusetts. Harvard Medical School, 1904. Visiting Surgeon, Salem Hospital, Salem, Cable Memorial Hospital, Ipswich.

PHIPPS, JOSEPH ALLEN, M.D., 63 Main Street, Tooele, Utah. St. Louis University School of Medicine (Marion-Sims College of Medicine), 1898. Surgeon, Tooele General Hospital.

PICKARD, MATTHEW W., M.D., Union Station Hospital, Kansas City, Missouri. University of Kansas School of Medicine (Kansas City Medical College), 1898. Surgeon, Research Hospital; Chief Surgeon, Kansas City Terminal Railway.

PICKEL, E. BARTON, M.D., Main Street and Central Avenue, Medford, Oregon. University of Louisville, Medical Department, 1888; University of Illinois College of Medicine (College of Physicians and Surgeons, Chicago), 1894. Member of Staff, Sacred Heart Hospital.

PICKRELL, GEORGE, M.D., Medical Corps, United States Navy, Washington, District of Columbia. Medical College of Virginia, 1882. Captain, Medical Corps, United States Navy.

PIERCE, FRANK E., B.Sc., M.D., 5114 Harper Avenue, Chicago, Illinois. Rush Medical College, 1898. Assistant Professor of Surgery, Loyola University, School of Medicine; Attending Surgeon, Mercy Hospital.

PIERCE, NORVAL HARVEY, M.D., 22 East Washington Street, Chicago, Illinois. University of Illinois College of Medicine (College of Physicians and Surgeons, Chicago), 1885. Head of Department and Professor of Laryngology, Rhinology, and Otology, University of Illinois College of Medicine; Attending Rhino-Laryngologist, St. Luke's Hospital; Attending Surgeon, Ear, Nose, and Throat Department, Michael Reese and Passavant Hospitals; Attending Otologist, Illinois Charitable Eye and Ear Infirmary.

PIERSON, ROBERT HAMILTON, M.D., Medical Corps, United States Army, Washington, District of Columbia. Syracuse University College of Medicine, 1898. Lieutenant Colonel, Medical Corps, United States Army.

PIGOT, CRESWELL TAYLEUR, M.D., Roundup, Montana. Western University Medical School, 1900.

PILCHER, LEWIS STEPHEN, A.M., M.D., LL.D., 145 Gates Avenue, Brooklyn, New York. University of Michigan Medical School, 1866. Surgeon, Pilcher Private Hospital; Consulting Surgeon, Wyckoff Heights, Jewish, Bushwick, St. John's, and Norwegian Deaconess Hospitals.

PILLSBURY, HENRY C., A.B., M.D., Medical Corps, United States Army, Washington, District of Columbia. Harvard Medical School, 1906. Major, Medical Corps, United States Army.

PINAULT, LOUIS GEORGE, B.A., M.D., Campbellton, New Brunswick. Laval University, Faculty of Medicine, Quebec, 1900.

PINGREE, HAROLD ASHTON, M.D., 131 State Street, Portland, Maine. Bowdoin Medical School, 1901. Associate Surgeon, Children's Hospital.

PINKERTON, HARRY BLAINE, M.D., 597 Elmwood Avenue, Buffalo, New York. University of Illinois College of Medicine (College of Physicians and Surgeons, Chicago), 1906. Surgeon-in-Chief, Pierce-Arrow Hospital.

PINKERTON, SAMUEL H., M.D., Deseret News Building, Salt Lake City, Utah. University and Bellevue Hospital Medical College, 1883.

PINKHAM, EDWARD WARWICK, A.B., M.D., 40 East Forty-first Street, New York, New York. Harvard Medical School, 1896. Consulting Gynecologist, White Plains Hospital, White Plains.

PINKHAM, JOSEPH GURNEY, A.M., M.D., 64 Nahant Street, Lynn, Massachusetts. Long Island College Hospital, 1866. Consulting Surgeon, Lynn Hospital.

PINO, PEDRO DEL, M.D., 451 Alsina, Buenos Aires, Argentina. University of Buenos Aires Faculty of Medicine, 1904. Assistant Chief of Services, Riverdowis Hospital.

PINTO, OCTAVIO OLIVEIRA, M.D., 33 Rua da Carioca, Rio de Janeiro, Brazil. Faculty of Medicine, University of Rio de Janeiro, 1906.

PIPER, EDMUND BROWN, B.Sc., M.D., 1936 Spruce Street, Philadelphia, Pennsylvania. University of Pennsylvania School of Medicine, 1911. Assistant Professor of Obstetrics, University of Pennsylvania, Post-Graduate School of Medicine; Associate in Obstetrics, University of Pennsylvania School of Medicine.

PIPES, HENRY F., M.D., Medical Corps, United States Army, Washington, District of Columbia. George Washington University Medical School (Columbian University, Medical Department), 1902. Lieutenant Colonel, Medical Corps, United States Army.

PIRRUNG, JOSEPH EDWARD, M.D., 1218 Walnut Street, Cincinnati, Ohio. University of Cincinnati College of Medicine (Miami Medical College), 1906. Lecturer on Principles and Practice of Surgery, Fractures and Dislocations, University of Cincinnati College of Medicine; Surgeon, Good Samaritan Hospital; First Assistant Attending Surgeon, Cincinnati General Hospital; Consulting Obstetrician and Medical Director, Visitation Society.

PIRTLE, ROBERT T., M.D., 400 Francis Building, Louisville, Kentucky. University of Louisville Medical Department, 1902. Assistant, Department of Orthopedic Surgery, University of Louisville; Orthopedic Surgeon, Louisville City, Children's Free, SS. Mary and Elizabeth, and St. Anthony's Hospitals, Norton Memorial Infirmary.

PISCHEL, KASPAR, M.D., 135 Stockton Street, San Francisco, California. University of Innsbruck, 1886. Member of Visiting Staff, Eye, Ear, Nose, and Throat Department, St. Luke's Hospital.

PITTENGER, FRED A., M.D., 407 Overland Building, Boise, Idaho. Northwestern University Medical School, 1904. Member of Staff, St. Alphonsus Hospital.

PITTS, HERMAN C., M.D., 124 Waterman Street, Providence, Rhode Island. Yale University School of Medicine, 1900. Gynecological Surgeon, Rhode Island Hospital; Consulting Surgeon, Providence Lying-in Hospital, Providence, State Tuberculosis Sanitarium, Wallum Lake, Memorial Hospital, Pawtucket.

PLAGGEMEYER, HARRY WARD, A.B., M.D., 1701 David Whitney Building, Detroit, Michigan. Johns Hopkins University, Medical Department, 1907. Clinical Professor of Urology, Detroit College of Medicine and Surgery; Attending Urological Surgeon and Chief of Department, Grace Hospital; Attending Urologist and Chief of Service, Detroit Receiving Hospital.

PLATT, WALTER BREWSTER, Ph.B., M.D., F.R.C.S. (Eng.), 802 Cathedral Street, Baltimore, Maryland. Harvard Medical School, 1879. Surgeon, Robert Garrett Hospital for Children; Member of Staff, Church Home and Infirmary.

PLEADWELL, FRANK LESTER, M.D., Medical Corps, United States Navy, Washington, District of Columbia. Harvard Medical School, 1896. Captain, Medical Corps, United States Navy.

PLUMMER, EDWARD MARWICK, M.D., 5 Adams Street, Charlestown, Massachusetts. Dartmouth Medical School, 1882. Professor of Otology, Tufts College Medical School; Consulting Aural Surgeon, Massachusetts Charitable Eye and Ear Infirmary, Deer Island Hospital, Boston, Rufus S. Frost Hospital, Chelsea; Oto-Laryngological Surgeon-in-Chief, Carney Hospital, Boston, Union Avenue Hospital, Framingham.

PLUMMER, GEORGE ALFRED, M.D., 215 East Sixth Avenue, Cresco, Iowa. State University of Iowa College of Medicine (Keokuk Medical College), 1902. Associate Surgeon, St. Joseph's Mercy Hospital.

PLUMMER, RALPH WALTER, M.D., Medical Corps, United States Navy, Washington, District of Columbia. Rush Medical College, 1897. Commander, Medical Corps, United States Navy.

PLUMMER, SAMUEL C., A.M., M.D., Ph.D., 4539 Oakenwald Avenue, Chicago, Illinois. Northwestern University Medical School (Chicago Medical College), 1886. Attending Surgeon, St. Luke's Hospital; Chief Surgeon, Chicago, Rock Island and Pacific Railway.

PLUMMER, WILLIAM WARD, B.L., M.D., 523 Franklin Street, Buffalo, New York. University of Buffalo, Department of Medicine, 1902. Professor of Orthopedic Surgery, University of Buffalo, Department of Medicine; Attending Orthopedic Surgeon, Buffalo General, Buffalo City, and Children's Hospitals.

POGGI DE FIGUEIRÊDA, JAYME, M.D., Rua Marques de Abrantes 192, Rio de Janeiro, Brazil. Faculty of Medicine, University of Rio de Janeiro, 1909.

POLAK, JOHN OSBORN, M.Sc., M.D., 20 Livingston Street, Brooklyn, New York. University of Vermont College of Medicine, 1891; Long Island College Hospital, 1891. Professor of Obstetrics and Gynecology, Long Island College Hospital; Obstetrician and Gynecologist, Long Island College Hospital; Gynecologist, Jewish Hospital; Consulting Gynecologist, Deaconess, Bushwick, Coney Island, People's, Williamsburgh, and Zion Hospitals; Consulting Obstetrician, Methodist Episcopal Hospital; Consulting Surgeon, Southampton Hospital, Southampton.

POLLARD, THOMAS GEORGE, M.D., Doctors Building, Nashville, Tennessee. University of Nashville, Medical Department, 1903. Member of Visiting Staff, Nashville City Hospital.

POLLOK, LEWIS WILLIAM, M.D., Temple State Bank Building, Temple, Texas. University of Virginia, Department of Medicine, 1902. Surgeon, King's Daughters Hospital.

POMEROY, LAWRENCE A., A.B., M.D., 2073 East Ninth Street, Cleveland, Ohio. Western Reserve University School of Medicine, 1908. Auxiliary Surgeon, Huron Road Hospital; Consulting Surgeon, Maternity Hospital.

POMEROY, NELSON ASA, M.D., 76 Center Street, Waterbury, Connecticut. Columbia University, College of Physicians and Surgeons, 1896. Surgeon, Waterbury and St. Mary's Hospitals; Surgeon and Chief of Staff, Waterbury Free Dispensary.

POMEROY, RALPH HAYWARD, A.M., M.D., 93 Remsen Street, Brooklyn, New York. Long Island College Hospital, 1889. Associate Professor of Gynecology and Obstetrics, Long Island College Hospital; Consulting Obstetrician, Bushwick, St. John's, Kings County, and Methodist Episcopal Hospitals; Attending Gynecologist and Obstetrician, Brooklyn Hospital.

PONCE, VILLAVICENCIO RICARDO, M.D., Quito, Ecuador. University of Brussels, 1907; University of Quito, 1910. Professor of Surgery, University of Quito.

POND, ALANSON M., M.D., 1098 Locust Street, Dubuque, Iowa. State University of Iowa College of Medicine (Keokuk Medical College), 1891. Attending Surgeon, Finley Hospital; Consulting Surgeon, St. Joseph's Mercy Hospital.

POND, DARWIN BRAYTON, M.D., 4363 Lincoln Avenue, Chicago, Illinois. Loyola University School of Medicine (Chicago College of Medicine and Surgery), 1907. Attending Surgeon, Ravenswood Hospital.

PONIPEO DE CAMARGO, FRANCISCO ANTONIO, M.D., Rua Barao do Amazonas 31, Ribeirao Preto, Brazil. Faculty of Medicine University of Rio de Janeiro, 1907.

PONTIUS, PAUL J., A.M., M.D., 1831 Chestnut Street, Philadelphia, Pennsylvania. University of Pennsylvania School of Medicine, 1891. Surgeon, Wills Eye Hospital; Ophthalmologist, St. Joseph's and Philadelphia General Hospitals; Consulting Ophthalmologist, State Hospital for Insane, Norristown.

POOL, EUGENE HILLHOUSE, A.B., M.D., 107 East Sixtieth Street, New York, New York. Columbia University, College of Physicians and Surgeons, 1899. Associate Professor of Surgery, Columbia University, College of Physicians and Surgeons; Attending Surgeon, New York Hospital; Consulting Surgeon, French and New York Orthopedic Hospitals, Home for Incurables, Berwind Free Outdoor Maternity Clinic, New York, Central Islip State Hospital, Central Islip, United Hospital, Port Chester.

POOL, HENRY JACOB, M.D., 125 East Third Street, Port Clinton, Ohio. Western Reserve University School of Medicine (Cleveland College of Physicians and Surgeons), 1902. Surgeon-in-Chief, Pool Hospital.

POOL, WILLIAM POHLMAN, A.M., M.D., 166 Clinton Street, Brooklyn, New York. Long Island College Hospital, 1894. Clinical Professor of Obstetrics and Gynecology, Long Island College Hospital; Assistant Gynecologist, Long Island College Hospital; Consulting Gynecologist, Flushing Hospital, Flushing.

POOLE, FRANCIS HERBERT, M.D., Medical Corps, United States Army, Washington, District of Columbia. George Washington University Medical School (Columbian University, Medical Department), 1902. Major, Medical Corps, United States Army.

POORMAN, BERT A., M.D., 1010 Rialto Building, Kansas City, Missouri. University Medical College, Kansas City, 1903. Member of Staff, St. Joseph's and Christian Church Hospitals, Kansas City, Missouri, Atchison Hospital, Atchison, Kansas; Alternate Surgeon, Kansas City General Hospital.

POPE, IRVIN, A.M., M.D., 112 South Bois d'Arc Avenue, Tyler, Texas. Tulane University of Louisiana School of Medicine, 1887. Ophthalmologist, Rhinologist, and Oto-Laryngologist, St. Louis Southwestern, and International and Great Northern Railways.

POPPE, FREDERICK HAROLD, A.B., M.D., 730 La Salle Building, Minneapolis, Minnesota. University of Minnesota Medical School, 1907. Assistant Professor of Surgery, University of Minnesota Medical School; Staff Surgeon, Northwestern Hospital; Associate Surgeon, Minneapolis General Hospital.

POPPEN, ALBERTUS B., B.Sc., M.D., Union National Bank Building, Muskegon, Michigan. Rush Medical College, 1909. Head of Gynecological Department, Hackley Hospital.

PORTER, CHARLES ALLEN, A.M., M.D., 116 Beacon Street, Boston, Massachusetts. Harvard Medical School, 1892. Professor of Clinical Surgery, Harvard Medical School; Chief of West Surgical Service, Massachusetts General Hospital.

PORTER, EDWARDS H., A.B., M.D., 85 Madison Street, Tiffin, Ohio. Detroit College of Medicine and Surgery, 1900. Eye and Ear Surgeon, Kentucky Memorial Hospital.

PORTER, ENOCH MARVIN, A.B., M.D., Conrad Bank Building, Great Falls, Montana. University Medical College, Kansas City, 1902.

PORTER, FREDERICK EUGENE, M.D., Medical Corps, United States Navy Washington, District of Columbia. Vanderbilt University Medical Department, 1901. Commander, Medical Corps, United States Navy.

PORTER, JOHN LINCOLN, M.D., 7 West Madison Street, Chicago, Illinois. Northwestern University Medical School, 1894. Professor of Orthopedic Surgery, Northwestern University Medical School; Attending Orthopedic Surgeon, St. Luke's Hospital.

PORTER, LEWIS B., M.D., 117 Waterman Street, Providence, Rhode Island. Yale University School of Medicine, 1898. Surgeon, Ear, Nose, and Throat Department, Rhode Island Hospital.

PORTER, MILES FULLER, A.M., M.D., 2326 Fairfield Avenue, Fort Wayne, Indiana. University of Cincinnati College of Medicine (Medical College of Ohio), 1878. Professor of Surgery, Indiana University School of Medicine; Consulting Surgeon, Indiana School for Feeble-Minded Youths; Surgeon, St. Joseph's and Hope Methodist Hospitals.

PORTER, RALPH STRIBLING, M.D., Medical Corps, United States Army, Washington, District of Columbia. Rush Medical College, 1897; Northwestern University Medical School, 1898. Lieutenant Colonel, Medical Corps, United States Army.

PORTERFIELD, JOHN D., Jr., M.D., 6 North Spanish Street, Cape Girardeau, Missouri. Rush Medical College, 1897. Member of Surgical Staff, St. Francis' Hospital.

POSEY, WILLIAM CAMPBELL, A.B., M.D., 2049 Chestnut Street, Philadelphia, Pennsylvania. University of Pennsylvania School of Medicine, 1889. Consulting Surgeon, Wills Eye Hospital; Ophthalmologist, Howard Hospital; Consulting Ophthalmologist, Chestnut Hill Hospital, Philadelphia, Abington Memorial Hospital, Abington, State Hospital for Insane, Norristown, State Hospital for Chronic Insane, Wernersville.

POST, GEORGE WASHINGTON, JR., B.Sc., A.M., M.D., 4158 West Lake Street, Chicago, Illinois. University of Illinois College of Medicine, 1909. Associate in Surgery, University of Illinois College of Medicine; Attending Surgeon, St. Anne's Hospital.

POST, LAWRENCE T., A.B., M.D., 520 Metropolitan Building, St. Louis, Missouri. Johns Hopkins University, Medical Department, 1913. Assistant in Clinical Ophthalmology, Washington University Medical School; Assistant Ophthalmologist, St. Louis Children's Hospital; Surgeon, Out-Patient Department, Barnes Hospital.

POST, MARTIN HAYWARD, JR., 520 Metropolitan Building, St. Louis, Missouri. Johns Hopkins University, Medical Department, 1912. Assistant in Clinical Ophthalmology, Washington University Medical School; Assistant Ophthalmologist, St. Louis City Hospital; Surgeon, Out-Patient Department, Barnes Hospital.

POST, WILFRED M., A.B., M.D., Konia, Turkey. Columbia University College of Physicians and Surgeons, 1901. Surgeon, American Hospital.

POSTON, HARRY PREWITT, M.D., 1337 David Whitney Building, Detroit, Michigan. Washington University Medical School, 1907.

POTTER, GEORGE E., M.D., 6509 Woodward Avenue, Detroit, Michigan. Detroit College of Medicine and Surgery (Detroit College of Medicine), 1896. Professor of Surgery, Detroit College of Medicine and Surgery; Attending Surgeon, Providence Hospital.

POTTER, IRVING WHITE, M.D., 420 Franklin Street, Buffalo, New York. University of Buffalo, Department of Medicine, 1891. Instructor in Obstetrics, University of Buffalo, Department of Medicine; Attending Obstetrician, St. Mary's Infant Asylum and Maternity Hospital, Deaconess Hospital.

POTTS, HERBERT A., D.D.S., M.D., 31 North State Street, Chicago, Illinois. Northwestern University Medical School, 1901. Professor of Oral Surgery, Northwestern University Medical School, Northwestern University Dental School; Oral Surgeon, Cook County Hospital, Chicago, Evanston Hospital, Evanston; Junior Oral Surgeon, St. Luke's Hospital.

POUCHER, JOHN WILSON, M.D., 339 Mill Street, Poughkeepsie, New York. Albany Medical College, 1883. Chief of Staff, Samuel W. Bowne Memorial Hospital; Chief Surgeon, St. Francis Hospital; Consulting Surgeon, Highland Hospital, Beacon, Hudson River State Hospital, Poughkeepsie.

POUEY, ENRIQUE, M.D., Calle Uruguay 1205, Montevideo, Uruguay. Faculty of Medicine, University of Montevideo, 1884; Faculty of Medicine, University of Paris, 1888. Professor of Clinical Gynecology, Faculty of Medicine, Montevideo.

POUND, JOHN C., A.B., M.D., 904 North Charles Street, Baltimore, Maryland. University of Maryland School of Medicine (Baltimore Medical College), 1896. Chief of Nose and Throat Department, St. Agnes' and Bon Secour Hospitals.

POU ORFILA, JUAN, B.Sc., M.D., Calle Colonia 1270, Montevideo, Uruguay. Faculty of Medicine, University of Montevideo, 1904. Professor of Clinical Obstetrics, Faculty of Medicine, University of Montevideo; Chief of Gynecological Service, Spanish Hospital.

POWELL, CUTHBERT, M.D., 2261 Albion Street, Denver, Colorado. University of Colorado School of Medicine, 1902. Instructor in Gynecology, University of Colorado School of Medicine; Visiting Gynecologist, Denver City and County and Mercy Hospitals; Surgeon, Children's Hospital, Denver Orphan's Home.

POWELL, NEWTON ALBERT, M.D., C.M., 167 College Street, Toronto, Ontario. University and Bellevue Hospital Medical College, 1875; University of Toronto, Faculty of Medicine (Trinity Medical College), 1875. Emeritus Professor of Medical Jurisprudence and Associate Professor of Clinical Surgery, University of Toronto, Faculty of Medicine; Senior Assistant Surgeon in Charge, Shields Emergency Department, Toronto General Hospital; Consulting Surgeon, Grace Hospital, Toronto Hospital for Incurables.

POWELL, RALPH E., A.B., M.D., C.M., F.R.C.S. (Edin.), 132 Crescent Street, Montreal, Quebec. Faculty of Medicine, McGill University, 1908. Demonstrator of Genito-Urinary Surgery, Faculty of Medicine, McGill University; Associate Genito-Urinary Surgeon, Montreal General Hospital.

POWER, WALTER B., M.D., 233 Cajon Street, Redlands, California. Columbia University, College of Physicians and Surgeons, 1895. Surgeon, Redlands Hospital, Redlands, San Bernardino General Hospital, San Bernardino.

POWERS, CHARLES ANDREW, A.M., M.D., University Club, Denver, Colorado. Columbia University, College of Physicians and Surgeons, 1883. Emeritus Professor of Surgery, University of Colorado School of Medicine.

POWERS, GEORGE H., JR., A.B., M.D., 298 Marlborough Street, Boston, Massachusetts. University of California Medical School, 1902. Assistant in Otology, Harvard University Graduate School of Medicine, Harvard Medical School; Consulting Aural Surgeon, City Hospital, Quincy.

POWERS, THOMAS EDWIN, M.D., Nineteenth and State Streets, Clarinda, Iowa. Washington University Medical School (Missouri Medical College), 1881. Chief Surgeon, Powers Private Hospital.

PRATT, GEORGE NATHANIEL, M.D., 801 College Avenue, Appleton, Wisconsin. Hahnemann Medical College and Hospital (Chicago Homeopathic Medical College), 1897. Member of Staff, St. Joseph's Hospital, Chicago.

PRATT, JOHN ABRAHAM, M.D., 919 Metropolitan Bank Building, Minneapolis, Minnesota. University of Michigan Medical School, 1894. Instructor, Eye, Ear, Nose, and Throat Department, University of Minnesota Medical School.

PRAY, EDGAR ALLEN, M.D., Pray Block, Valley City, North Dakota. University of Pennsylvania School of Medicine, 1894.

PRENTISS, DANIEL WEBSTER, B.Sc., M.D., 1213 M Street, Northwest, Washington, District of Columbia. George Washington University Medical School (Columbian University, Medical Department), 1899. Surgeon, Lutheran Home for the Aged; Associate Surgeon, Eastern Dispensary and Casualty Hospital.

PRESCOTT, HENRY D., A.B., M.D., 26 Grove Street, New Bedford, Massachusetts. Harvard Medical School, 1902. Retired.

PRESSLY, GEORGE WILLIAM, M.D., 1508 Elizabeth Avenue, Charlotte, North Carolina. Jefferson Medical College, 1892. Surgeon, Charlotte Sanatorium.

PRESTON, FRENN LESLEY, M.D., 220 West Central Avenue, Eldorado, Kansas. Northwestern University Medical School, 1911. Surgeon, St. Luke's Hospital.

PRICE, GEORGE M., M.D., 114 Physicians Building, Syracuse, New York. Syracuse University College of Medicine, 1886. Professor of Clinical Surgery, Syracuse University College of Medicine; Surgeon, Hospital of the Good Shepherd, Syracuse Free Dispensary.

PRICE, HENRY R., C.E., M.D., LL.D., 146 Remsen Street, Brooklyn, New York. University of Pennsylvania School of Medicine, 1880. Surgeon, New York Eye and Ear Infirmary.

PRICE, JOHN WILLIAMSON, JR., A.B., M.D., 705 Starks Building, Louisville, Kentucky. University of Pennsylvania School of Medicine, 1905. Adjunct Professor of Abdominal Surgery and Gynecology, University of Louisville Medical Department; Surgeon, Louisville City Hospital, John N. Norton Memorial Infirmary.

PRICE, JOSEPH, M.D., 1452 South High Street, Columbus, Ohio. Ohio State University College of Medicine (Starling Medical College), 1904. Chief Surgeon and Chief of Staff, Mercy Hospital.

PRICE, NORMAN W., B.Sc., M.D., 445 Third Street, Niagara Falls, New York. University of Toronto Faculty of Medicine, 1896. Member of Staff, Niagara Falls Memorial and St. Mary's Hospitals.

PRIMROSE, ALEXANDER, C.B., M.D., C.M., M.R.C.S. (Eng.), 100 College Street, Toronto, Ontario. University of Edinburgh, 1886. Dean, Faculty of Medicine, University of Toronto; Professor of Clinical Surgery, University of Toronto, Faculty of Medicine; Surgeon and Chief of Service, Toronto General Hospital; Consulting Surgeon, Hospital for Sick Children.

PRINCE, HOWARD L., M.D., 366 East Avenue, Rochester, New York. Cornell University Medical College, 1907. Surgeon, Rochester General Hospital; Consulting Surgeon, Infant's Summer Hospital.

PRINCE, LAWRENCE H., M.D., Sparta, Wisconsin. Rush Medical College, 1885. Retired.

PRIOR, CHARLES EDWIN, A.B., M.D., 1 Mountain Avenue, Malden, Massachusetts. Harvard Medical School, 1882. Surgeon, Malden Hospital.

PRITCHARD, ARTHUR T., M.D., Citizens Building, Asheville, North Carolina. Jefferson Medical College, 1905. Member of Staff, Mission and Merriweather Hospitals.

PRITCHETT, IRA E., M.D., 631 Kress Medical Building, Houston, Texas. University of Texas, Medical Department, 1904. Visiting Surgeon, Norsworthy Hospital.

PROUTY, IRA JOSLIN, M.D., 81 Court Street, Keene, New Hampshire. University and Bellevue Hospital Medical College (University of the City of New York, Medical Department), 1882. Member of Visiting Staff, Elliot City Hospital.

PROWSE, S. WILLIS, M.B., M.D., C.M., F.R.C.S. (Edin.), 801 Boyd Building, Winnipeg, Manitoba. University of Edinburgh, 1893. Dean of Faculty of Medicine and Professor of Clinical Laryngology and Otology, University of Manitoba; Senior Surgeon, Ear and Throat Department, Winnipeg General Hospital.

PRYOR, JAMES CHAMBERS, A.M., M.D., Medical Corps, United States Navy, Washington, District of Columbia. Vanderbilt University, Medical Department, 1896. Captain, Medical Corps, United States Navy.

PUECH, LUIZ DE REZENDE, M.D., Rua S. Bento 41, Sao Paulo, Brazil. Faculty of Medicine, Rio de Janeiro, 1906. Surgeon-in-Chief, Department of Surgery and Orthopedic Service of Children, Central Hospital, Santa Casa, and Policlinica, Sao Paulo.

PULLAR, JAMES, B.A., M.D., C.M., 286 Kennedy Street, Winnipeg, Manitoba. Faculty of Medicine, University of Manitoba (Manitoba Medical College), 1897. Gynecologist, Winnipeg General Hospital.

PULS, ARTHUR J., B.L., M.D., 400 First National Bank Building, Milwaukee, Wisconsin. University of Heidelberg, 1883. Gynecologist, Columbia Hospital and Milwaukee Dispensary.

PURNELL, CAROLINE M., B.L., M.D., 132 South Eighteenth Street, Philadelphia, Pennsylvania. Woman's Medical College of Pennsylvania, 1887. Gynecologist, Woman's Hospital; Consulting Gynecologist, West Philadelphia Hospital for Women, Philadelphia, State Hospital for Insane, Norristown, Friends' Asylum for Insane, Frankford, State Hospital for Chronic Insane, Wernersville, Moyamensing Prison, Philadelphia.

PUTMAN, FRANK LAWRENCE, M.D., Young Hotel, Honolulu, Hawaii. University of California Medical School, 1902.

PUTNAM, CHARLES R. L., A.B., M.D., 24 East Seventieth Street, New York, New York. Harvard Medical School, 1895. Professor of Clinical Surgery, Fordham University; Surgeon, Lincoln Hospital; Visiting Surgeon, St. Mark's Hospital.

PUTNAM, EDMUND D., M.D., 300 East Twenty-first Street, Sioux Falls, South Dakota. University of Nebraska College of Medicine, 1897.

PUTNAM, FRANK ISRAEL, M.D., 104 East Twentieth Street, Sioux Falls, South Dakota. Creighton College of Medicine, 1908. Oculist and Aurist, McKennan Hospital.

PYLE, WALLACE, M.D., 15 Exchange Place, Jersey City, New Jersey. University of Pennsylvania School of Medicine, 1897. Visiting Eye and Ear Surgeon, Christ, Jersey City, and German Hospitals, Jersey City; Consulting Ophthalmologist and Aurist, Bayonne Hospital, Bayonne.

PYLES, WILL L., M.D., Medical Corps, United States Army, Washington, District of Columbia. George Washington University Medical School (Columbian University Medical Department), 1901. Lieutenant Colonel, Medical Corps, United States Army.

QUACKENBOSS, ALEX, A.M., M.D., 143 Newbury Street, Boston, Massachusetts. Harvard Medical School, 1892. Williams Professor of Ophthalmology, Harvard Medical School; Surgeon, Massachusetts Charitable Eye and Ear Infirmary; Ophthalmologist, Massachusetts General Hospital; Consulting Ophthalmologist, Infants' Hospital.

QUAIN, ERIC P., M.D., City National Bank Building, Bismarck, North Dakota. University of Minnesota Medical School, 1898. Surgeon and Chief of Staff, Bismarck Evangelical Hospital.

QUALLS, GUY LOGAN, M.S., M.D., Medical Corps, United States Army, Washington, District of Columbia. St. Louis University School of Medicine, 1909. Major, Medical Corps, United States Army.

QUAY, GEORGE HENRY, SR., M.D., Rose Building, Cleveland, Ohio. Ohio State University College of Homeopathic Medicine (Cleveland Homeopathic Hospital College), 1883. Head of Ear, Nose, and Throat Department, Huron Road Hospital.

QUICK, EDWARD WILLIAM, M.D., 502 Wells Building, Milwaukee, Wisconsin. Rush Medical College, 1902. Attending Surgeon, Johnson Emergency, Milwaukee County and Trinity Hospitals.

QUIGLEY, DANIEL T., M.D., 727 City National Bank Building, Omaha, Nebraska. Rush Medical College, 1902. Lecturer on Surgical Pathology, University of Nebraska College of Medicine.

QUINBY, WILLIAM CARTER, A.B., M.D., Peter Bent Brigham Hospital, Boston, Massachusetts. Harvard Medical School, 1902. Assistant Professor of Genito-Urinary Surgery, Harvard Medical School; Urologist, Peter Bent Brigham Hospital.

QUINN, EDWARD H., M.D., 108 West Seventy-first Street, New York, New York. Columbia University, College of Physicians and Surgeons, 1886. Associate Surgeon, New York Polyclinic Medical School and Hospital; Visiting Surgeon, St. Elizabeth's Hospital, New York, St. John's Hospital, Long Island City.

QUINN, STEPHEN T., M.D., 83 Broad Street, Elizabeth, New Jersey. University and Bellevue Hospital Medical College (New York University Medical College), 1897. Attending Surgeon, Elizabeth General and St. Elizabeth's Hospitals.

QUINTELA, MANUEL, M.D., Calle 8 de Octubre 184, Montevideo, Uruguay. Faculty of Medicine University of Montevideo, 1900.

RAE, ALEXANDER, A.B., M.D., 117 Henry Street, Brooklyn, New York. Long Island College Hospital, 1885. Associate Professor of Surgery and Associate Visiting Surgeon, Long Island College Hospital.

RAE, JOHN BROADFOOT, M.B., C.M., 247 West Seventieth Street, New York, New York. University of Glasgow, 1895. Aural Surgeon, Manhattan Eye, Ear, Nose, and Throat and Riverside Hospitals; Consulting Aural Surgeon, Bronx Eye and Ear Infirmary, Union Hospital.

RAGAN, O. H. WILLIAM, M.D., 155 West Washington Street, Hagerstown, Maryland. University of Maryland School of Medicine, 1874. Visiting Surgeon, Washington County Hospital; Surgeon, Norfolk and Western Railway, Cumberland Valley Railroad.

RAGAN, THOMAS, M.D., Hutchinson Building, Shreveport, Louisiana. Tulane University of Louisiana School of Medicine, 1891.

RAKESTRAW, CHAUNCEY M., M.D., Pryor Hospital, Chester, South Carolina. Ohio Medical University, 1894. Surgeon in Charge, Pryor Hospital; Chief Surgeon, Abbeville Memorial Hospital.

RALEY, FRANKLIN H., M.D., Boston Building, Salt Lake City, Utah. Kansas City Medical College, 1901.

RALSTON, WALLACE, M.D., Kress Medical Building, Houston, Texas. University of Texas, Medical Department, 1899. Ophthalmologist, Baptist Sanitarium and Hospital, Norsworthy and Sunset Hospitals.

RAMEY, ROBERT LEE, M.D., 509 Two Republics Building, El Paso, Texas. University of Maryland School of Medicine, 1892. Attending Surgeon, Hotel Dieu; Division Surgeon, Southern Pacific Lines; Medical Director, Two Republics Life Insurance Company.

RAMSDELL, EDWIN GEORGE, A.B., M.D., 25 East Sixty-fourth Street, New York, New York. Columbia University, College of Physicians and Surgeons, 1908. Surgeon, White Plains Hospital, White Plains; Assistant Surgeon, Fifth Avenue Hospital, New York.

RAMSDELL, LEWIS STANTON, M.D., 57 Poplar Street, Manistee, Michigan. Rush Medical College, 1900. Surgeon, Mercy Hospital and Sanitarium.

RAMSTAD, N. OLIVER, M.D., City National Bank Building, Bismarck, North Dakota. University of Minnesota Medical School, 1899. Surgeon, Bismarck Evangelical Hospital.

RAND, CARL WHEELER, A.M., M.D., 1034 Pacific Mutual Building, Los Angeles, California. Johns Hopkins University, Medical Department, 1912. Neurological Surgeon, Children's, Kaspare Cohn and Los Angeles County Hospitals.

RANDALL, HERBERT ELMER, M.D., 302 Smith Building, Flint, Michigan. Detroit College of Medicine and Surgery, 1897. Attending Surgeon, Hurley Hospital; Consulting Surgeon, Michigan Home and Training School, Lapeer.

RANDALL, ALEXANDER, B.A., M.A., M.D., 1306 Medical Arts Building, Philadelphia, Pennsylvania. Johns Hopkins University Medical Department, 1907. Associate in Genito-Urinary Surgery, University of Pennsylvania School of Medicine; Assistant Surgeon, University and Philadelphia General Hospitals; Urologist, Chestnut Hill Hospital; Consulting Urologist, Germantown Hospital.

RANDOLPH, WILLIAM M., M.D., Medigovich Building, Bisbee, Arizona. University of Virginia Department of Medicine, 1890. Member of Staff, Calumet and Arizona Hospital.

RANDOLPH, WILSON, M.D., D.D.S., 405 West Fort Street, Detroit, Michigan. Detroit College of Medicine and Surgery, 1906. Associate Professor of Ophthalmology and Otology, Detroit College of Medicine and Surgery; Senior Ophthalmologist and Otologist, St. Mary's Hospital.

RANKEN, JOHN FRANCIS, M.D., 852 Park Place, Brooklyn, New York. New York Homeopathic Medical College and Flower Hospital, 1901. Attending Surgeon, Carson C. Peck Memorial, Cumberland Street, and Brooklyn Nursery and Infants' Hospitals, Brooklyn, Broad Street Hospital, New York.

RANKIN, FRED, A.M., M.D., Mayo Clinic, Rochester, Minnesota. University of Maryland School of Medicine, 1909. Assistant Surgeon, St. Mary's Hospital.

RANKIN, WILLIAM DONALD, M.B., C.M., 280 Main Street, Woodstock, New Brunswick. University of Edinburgh, 1890. Surgeon, Carleton County Hospital.

RANKIN, WILLIAM HENRY, M.D., C.M., L.R.C.P. & S. (Edin.), 151 Hancock Street, Brooklyn, New York. Queen's University, Faculty of Medicine, 1889. Surgeon, St. John's Hospital; Surgeon-in-Chief, Caledonian Hospital.

RANSDELL, ROBERT CATHCART, M.D., The St. Nicholas, Washington, District of Columbia. George Washington University Medical School (Columbian University, Medical Department), 1902. Commander, Medical Corps, United States Navy, retired.

RANSOHOFF, J. LOUIS, A.B., M.D., Livingston Building, Cincinnati, Ohio. University of Cincinnati College of Medicine (Ohio-Miami Medical College of the University of Cincinnati), 1904. Assistant Clinical Professor of Surgery, University of Cincinnati College of Medicine; Surgeon, Jewish Hospital; Attending Surgeon, Cincinnati General Hospital.

RANZ, WILLIAM EUGENE, M.D., Federal Building, Youngstown, Ohio. University of Cincinnati College of Medicine (Miami Medical College), 1899.

RARDIN, JOSEPH SPANGLER, M.D., Gallia Avenue and Waller Street, Portsmouth, Ohio. Ohio State University College of Medicine, 1890. Surgeon, Hempstead Hospital.

RASH, OTWAY WATKINS, M.D., 213 West Fourth Street, Owensboro, Kentucky. University and Bellevue Hospital Medical College (Bellevue Hospital Medical College), 1897. Attending Surgeon, Owensboro City Hospital.

RASSIEUR, LOUIS, M.D., 318 University Club Building, St. Louis, Missouri. St. Louis University School of Medicine (Marion-Sims College of Medicine), 1899. Associate Professor of Surgery, St. Louis University School of Medicine; Surgeon, St. Mary's Infirmary.

RATHBUN, NATHANIEL PHILIP, M.D., 67 Hanson Place, Brooklyn, New York. Long Island College Hospital, 1898. Attending Surgeon, Lutheran Hospital; Attending Urologist, Brooklyn Hospital; Chief of Genito-Urinary Clinic, Out-Patient Department, Brooklyn Hospital.

RAU, LEONARD S., M.D., Central Avenue, Lawrence, New York. University and Bellevue Hospital Medical College (Bellevue Hospital Medical College), 1885. Attending Obstetrician and Gynecologist, St. Joseph's Hospital, Far Rockaway.

RAVDIN, MARCUS, M.D., Citizens Bank Building, Evansville, Indiana. University of Tennessee College of Medicine (Memphis Hospital Medical College), 1900. Visiting Surgeon, Eye, Ear, Nose, and Throat Department, Protestant Deaconess Hospital; Laryngologist, Boehne Farm; Attending Surgeon, Eye, Ear, Nose, and Throat Department, St. Mary's Hospital.

RAVOGLI, AUGUSTUS, A.M., M.D., 5 Garfield Place, Cincinnati, Ohio. University of Rome, 1873. Emeritus Consulting Professor of Dermatology and Venerology, University of Cincinnati College of Medicine; Member of Staff, Department of Dermatology and Venerology, Cincinnati General Hospital.

RAWLS, JULIAN LAMAR, M.D., 142 Main Street, Norfolk, Virginia. Medical College of Virginia, 1904. Assistant Gynecologist, St. Vincent's Hospital.

RAWLS, REGINALD M., A.B., M.D., 350 West Eighty-eighth Street, New York, New York. University and Bellevue Hospital Medical College, 1898. Junior Surgeon, Woman's Hospital.

READ, HIRAM M., M.D., 2009 Thirty-first Avenue, South, Seattle, Washington. Rush Medical College, 1883. Chief of Staff, Seattle City Hospital.

READ, JOHN STURDIVANT, A.B., M.D., 174 Clinton Street, Brooklyn, New York. Long Island College Hospital, 1902. Lecturer on Genito-Urinary Diseases, Long Island College Hospital; Assistant Genito-Urinary Surgeon, Long Island College and Kings County Hospitals; Genito-Urinary Surgeon, Swedish Hospital; Consulting Genito-Urinary Surgeon, St. Peter's Hospital.

READ, WILMOT DELEO, M.D., Tacoma Clinic, Tacoma, Washington. Leland Stanford Junior University School of Medicine (Cooper Medical College), 1903. Surgeon, Tacoma Clinic; Member of Surgical Staff, Tacoma General Hospital.

REARDON, DANIEL B., M.D., 1186 Hancock Street, Quincy, Massachusetts. Harvard Medical School, 1903. Visiting Surgeon, Quincy Hospital.

REASONER, MATHEW A., B.Sc., M.D., Medical Corps, United States Army, Washington, District of Columbia. University of Illinois College of Medicine, 1899. Major, Medical Corps, United States Army.

REAVES, JESSE ULLMAN, M.D., 305 Van Antwerp Building, Mobile, Alabama. Tulane University of Louisiana School of Medicine, 1908.

REBUCK, CHARLES STOUGH, M.D., 412 North Third Street, Harrisburg, Pennsylvania. University of Maryland School of Medicine (College of Physicians and Surgeons, Baltimore), 1896. Assistant Surgeon, Department of Ophthalmology and Laryngology, Harrisburg Hospital; Consulting Laryngologist, Pennsylvania State Tuberculosis Sanatoriums, Mont Alto and Hamburg; Ophthalmic Surgeon, Pennsylvania Railroad; Consulting Ophthalmologist, Pennsylvania State Hospital for Insane.

REDDAN, MARTIN W., M.D., 126 West State Street, Trenton, New Jersey. Jefferson Medical College, 1900. Medical Director and Surgeon, St. Francis' Hospital and New Jersey State Prison; Surgeon, New Jersey State Hospital and Municipal Colony; Consulting Surgeon, St. Michael's Orphanage.

REDDEN, EDWARD N., Ph.D., M.D., 17 South Crawford Avenue, Chicago, Illinois. University of Illinois College of Medicine, 1909. Attending Surgeon, St. Elizabeth's Hospital.

REDER, FRANCIS, M.D., University Club Building, St. Louis, Missouri. Washington University Medical School (St. Louis Medical College), 1884. Surgeon, St. Louis City and St. John's Hospitals.

REED, CHARLES A. L., A.M., M.D., 5 West Eighth Street, Cincinnati, Ohio. Cincinnati College of Medicine and Surgery, 1874. Emeritus Professor of Gynecology, University of Cincinnati College of Medicine; Consulting Gynecological Surgeon, Cincinnati General Hospital.

REED, CHARLES ANTHONY, B.Sc., M.D., 1009 Nicollet Avenue, Minneapolis, Minnesota. University of Minnesota Medical School, 1898. Associate Professor of Orthopedic Surgery, University of Minnesota Medical School; Orthopedist, Minneapolis General, Swedish, and Eitel Hospitals.

REED, CHARLES B., M.D., 31 North State Street, Chicago, Illinois. Rush Medical College, 1887. Obstetrician, Wesley Memorial Hospital.

REED, EDWARD URBANE, M.D., Medical Corps, United States Navy, Washington, District of Columbia. University of Pennsylvania School of Medicine, 1905. Instructor in Medical Diagnosis and Tropical Medicine, Naval Medical School; Instructor in Tropical Medicine, Jefferson Medical College and George Washington University; Commander, Medical Corps, United States Navy.

REED, EDWYN P., B.A., M.D., Blanco Encalada 979, Valparaiso, Chile. Faculty of Medicine, University of Chile, 1905. Surgeon, Children's Hospital.

REED, HORACE, M.D., 611 First National Bank Building, Oklahoma, Oklahoma. University of Missouri School of Medicine, 1901. Associate Professor of Surgery, University of Oklahoma School of Medicine; Attending Surgeon, St. Anthony's and State University Hospitals.

REED, JAMES ROSS, A.B., M.D., 203 Citizens Bank Building, Pasadena, California. University of Michigan Medical School, 1905. Ophthalmic Surgeon, Pasadena Hospital.

REED, ROBERT JEFFREY, A.M., M.D., 100 Twelfth Street, Wheeling, West Virginia. University and Bellevue Hospital Medical College, 1884. Attending Surgeon, Ohio Valley General Hospital.

REED, WALTER W., M.D., Physicians Building, Boulder, Colorado. University of Colorado School of Medicine, 1893. Obstetrician and Gynecologist, University of Colorado Hospital.

REEDER, J. DAWSON, M.D., 30 East Preston Street, Baltimore, Maryland. University of Maryland School of Medicine, 1901. Associate Professor of Proctology, University of Maryland School of Medicine and College of Physicians and Surgeons; Proctologist, University Hospital, Bay View Hospital, Tuberculosis Department; Chief of Clinic, Rectal Department, University Dispensary.

REES, GEORGE M., M.D., 1215 Calumet Avenue, Calumet, Michigan. Rush Medical College, 1892. Surgeon, Calumet and Hecla Hospital.

REESE, ROBERT GRIGG, Phar.G., M.D., 50 West Fifty-second Street, New York, New York. University and Bellevue Hospital Medical College (University of the City of New York, Medical Department), 1891. Professor of Ophthalmology, Cornell University Medical College; Ophthalmic Surgeon, New York Eye and Ear Infirmary; Consulting Ophthalmologist, Memorial, and New York Nursery and Child's Hospitals, New York Infirmary for Women and Children, Reconstruction Hospital, New York Institute for Education of the Blind.

REEVES, EDWIN J., M.D., 3614 Lemmon Avenue, Dallas, Texas. Tulane University of Louisiana School of Medicine, 1893. Retired.

REEVES, THADDEUS BENJAMIN, B.Sc., M.D., M.Sc., 324 North Main Street, Greenville, South Carolina. University of Virginia Department of Medicine, 1914. Surgeon-in-Chief, Emma Moss Booth Memorial Hospital; Attending Surgeon, Montgomery, Greenville City and St. Luke's Hospitals; Orthopedic Surgeon, Southern Railway.

REHFUSS, WALLACE NORMAN, B.A., M.D., C.M., Bridgewater, Nova Scotia. Faculty of Medicine, McGill University, 1903.

REHLING, MARTIN, M.D., 209 East Sixty-first Street, New York, New York. University and Bellevue Hospital Medical College (New York University Medical College), 1894. Associate Surgeon, Lenox Hill Hospital and Dispensary; Surgeon, Bronx Hospital and Dispensary.

REICHELDERFER, LUTHER HALSEY, M.D., 1721 Connecticut Avenue, Washington, District of Columbia. George Washington University Medical School (Columbian University, Medical Department), 1899. Clinical Professor of Surgery, George Washington University Medical School; Attending Surgeon, Garfield Memorial, Tuberculosis, and Children's Hospitals.

REIK, ANDREW J. N., M.D., 1102 North Charles Street, Baltimore, Maryland. University of Maryland School of Medicine, 1900. Surgeon, Baltimore Eye, Ear, and Throat Hospital.

REIK, HENRY O., Phar.G., M.D., 300 East Thirtieth Street, Baltimore, Maryland. University of Maryland School of Medicine, 1891.

REILLY, FRANCIS H., M.D., 230 Church Street, New Haven, Connecticut. Yale University School of Medicine, 1897. Attending Surgeon, Hospital of St. Raphael.

REILLY, JOHN PHILIP, M.D., 215 Elizabeth Avenue, Elizabeth, New Jersey. University and Bellevue Hospital Medical College, 1888. Consulting Surgeon, Alexian Brothers' Hospital; Visiting Surgeon and Chief of Staff, St. Elizabeth's Hospital.

REINEKING, HERMAN, M.D., 3024 Wells Street, Milwaukee, Wisconsin. Rush Medical College, 1880; University of Heidelberg, 1886. Surgeon, Chicago, Milwaukee and St. Paul Railway.

REINLE, GEORGE G., M.D., 532 Fifteenth Street, Oakland, California. College of Physicians and Surgeons, San Francisco, 1901. Chief of Urological Staff, Merritt Hospital; Urologist, Oakland Medical Center; Visiting Urologist, San Leandro Hospital.

RENNER, WILLIAM SCOTT, M.D., C.M., 341 Linwood Avenue, Buffalo, New York. Faculty of Medicine, McGill University, 1884. Chief of Service in Oto-Laryngology, Children's Memorial Hospital; Laryngologist and Aurist, Erie County Hospital; Consulting Laryngologist and Aurist, J. N. Adam Memorial Hospital, Perrysburg; Surgeon in Charge, Ear and Throat Department, Buffalo Eye and Ear Infirmary.

REPP, WILLIAM A., Ph.C., M.D., 1002 David Whitney Building, Detroit, Michigan. Detroit College of Medicine and Surgery, 1895. Associate Clinical Professor of Gynecology, Detroit College of Medicine and Surgery; Attending Gynecologist and Obstetrician, St. Mary's Hospital; Attending Obstetrician, Marr Maternity Hospital; Attending Surgeon, St. Vincent's Orphan Asylum; Consulting Gynecologist, Detroit Receiving Hospital, Wayne County Home.

REQUARDT, WILLIAM WHITALL, M.D., 805 Park Avenue, Baltimore, Maryland. University of Maryland School of Medicine, 1896. Associate Professor of Surgery, University of Maryland School of Medicine and College of Physicians and Surgeons; Visiting Surgeon, Mercy Hospital.

RESSEGUIE, FREDERIC J., M.D., 509 North Broadway, Saratoga Springs, New York. Albany Medical College, 1895. President of Staff and Attending Surgeon, Saratoga Hospital.

RETHERS, THEODORE C., M.D., 650 Phelan Building, San Francisco, California. University of Berlin, 1891. Senior Surgeon, St. Mary's Hospital.

REYNOLDS, CHARLES R., M.D., Medical Corps, United States Army, Washington, District of Columbia. University of Pennsylvania School of Medicine, 1899. Lieutenant Colonel, Medical Corps, United States Army.

REYNOLDS, EDWARD, A.B., M.D., 321 Dartmouth Street, Boston, Massachusetts. Harvard Medical School, 1885.

REYNOLDS, FREDERICK PRATT, M.D., Medical Corps, United States Army, Washington, District of Columbia. University of Pennsylvania School of Medicine, 1890. Colonel, Medical Corps, United States Army.

REYNOLDS, HARRY B., A.M., M.D., Fraser Building, Palo Alto, California. Columbia University, College of Physicians and Surgeons, 1900.

REYNOLDS, HARRY CAMPBELL, M.D., Passaic Avenue, Passaic, New Jersey. New York Homeopathic Medical College and Flower Hospital, 1899. Visiting Surgeon, St. Mary's and Passaic General Hospitals.

REYNOLDS, HENRY GILBERT, M.D., City National Bank Building, Paducah, Kentucky. University of Louisville, Medical Department, 1897. Member of Visiting Staff, Riverside Hospital; Assistant Chief Oculist, Illinois Central Hospital.

REYNOLDS, MICHAEL THOMAS, M.D., 191 Arlington Avenue, Brooklyn, New York. Columbia University College of Physicians and Surgeons, 1901. Associate Surgeon, St. Mary's and Coney Island Hospitals.

REYNOLDS, WILLIAM T., M.D., 520 Chambers Building, Kansas City, Missouri. American Medical College (Barnes Medical College), 1895.

RHAME, J. SUMTER, M.D., 81 Wentworth Street, Charleston, South Carolina. Medical College of the State of South Carolina, 1908. Assistant Professor of Surgery, Medical College of the State of South Carolina; Attending Surgeon, Roper Hospital; Gynecologist, Shirras Dispensary.

RHÉAUME, PIERRE Z., M.D., 127 Sherbrooke Street, East, Montreal, Quebec. Faculty of Medicine, University of Montreal (Laval University, Medical Department), 1900. Professor of Technical Surgery and Topographic Anatomy, Faculty of Medicine, University of Montreal; Surgeon, Hotel Dieu de St. Joseph, St. Justine's Hospital.

RHOADS, THOMAS LEIDY, A.B., M.D., Medical Corps, United States Army, Washington, District of Columbia. Jefferson Medical College, 1893. Lieutenant Colonel, Medical Corps, United States Army.

RHODES, GOODRICH BARBOUR, A.B., M.D., Fourth and Sycamore Streets, Cincinnati, Ohio. Columbia University, College of Physicians and Surgeons, 1902. Associate Clinical Professor of Surgery, University of Cincinnati College of Medicine; Attending Surgeon, Cincinnati General Hospital, Children's Hospital of the Protestant Episcopal Church.

RHODES, ROBERT LEWIS, A.B., M.D., 1103 Lamar Building, Augusta, Georgia. Johns Hopkins University, Medical Department, 1910. Assistant Professor of Surgery, University of Georgia, Medical Department; Visiting Surgeon, University and Wilhenford Hospitals, United States Public Health Service, Hospital No. 62.

RHU, AUGUSTE, M.D., 187 West Center Street, Marion, Ohio. Western Reserve University School of Medicine, 1885.

RIBEIRO DA FONSECA, OLYMPIO ARTHUR, M.D., 162 Rua Camerino, Rio de Janeiro, Brazil. Faculty of Medicine, University of Rio de Janeiro, 1889.

RICE, ALLEN GALPIN, A.B., M.D., 33 School Street, Springfield, Massachusetts. Harvard Medical School, 1905. Assistant Surgeon, Springfield Hospital; Consulting Surgeon, Wing Memorial Hospital, Palmer.

RICE, DANIEL S., M.D., Ebensburg, Pennsylvania. Cincinnati College of Medicine and Surgery, 1884. Consulting Surgeon, Miners Hospital of Northern Cambria, Spangler.

RICE, GEORGE B., M.D., 293 Commonwealth Avenue, Boston, Massachusetts. Boston University School of Medicine, 1886. Professor of Diseases of Nose and Throat, Boston University School of Medicine; Consulting Surgeon, Nose and Throat Department, Massachusetts Homeopathic Hospital.

RICE, PHILIP, M.D., Sherman Square Hotel, New York, New York. Hering Medical College, 1894.

RICE, SPENCER M., M.D., 106 Rose Dispensary Building, Terre Haute, Indiana. State University of Iowa College of Medicine, 1879. Surgeon, St. Anthony's Hospital.

RICH, CHARLES O'NEILL, B.Sc., M.D., 432 Brandeis Theatre Building, Omaha, Nebraska. University of Pennsylvania School of Medicine (Medico-

Chirurgical College, Philadelphia), 1898. Assistant Professor of Surgery, University of Nebraska College of Medicine; Visiting Surgeon, Clarkson Memorial and University Hospitals.

RICH, EDWARD ISRAEL, M.D., First National Bank Building, Ogden, Utah. Jefferson Medical College, 1893. Visiting Surgeon, Thomas D. Dee Memorial Hospital.

RICH, EZRA C., M.D., 2650 Washington Avenue, Ogden, Utah. Jefferson Medical College, 1894. Surgeon, Thomas D. Dee Memorial Hospital.

RICHARDS, GEORGE L., M.D., 124 Franklin Street, Fall River, Massachusetts. Harvard Medical School, 1886. Chief of Ear, Nose, and Throat Department, Union Hospital; Consultant, Ear, Nose, and Throat Department, Fall River City Hospital.

RICHARDS, RALPH T., M.D., 1111 Walker Bank Building, Salt Lake City, Utah. University and Bellevue Hospital Medical College (University of the City of New York, Medical Department), 1903. Visiting Surgeon, Dr. W. H. Groves Latter-Day Saints Hospital.

RICHARDS, THEODORE W., M.D., Medical Corps, United States Navy, Washington, District of Columbia. George Washington University Medical School (Columbian University, Medical Department), 1893. Captain, Medical Corps, United States Navy.

RICHARDSON, ANNA GOVE, M.D., 22 Evans Way, Boston, Massachusetts. Woman's Medical College of Pennsylvania, 1891. Visiting Surgeon, Vincent Memorial Hospital.

RICHARDSON, CHARLES W., M.D., 1317 Connecticut Avenue, Washington, District of Columbia. University of Pennsylvania School of Medicine, 1884; George Washington University Medical School, 1884. Professor of Laryngology and Otology, George Washington University Medical School; Attending Surgeon, Episcopal Eye, Ear, and Throat, Children's and George Washington University Hospitals.

RICHARDSON, EDWARD HENDERSON, A.B., M.D., LL.D., 1200 North Charles Street, Baltimore, Maryland. Johns Hopkins University, Medical Department, 1905. Associate in Clinical Gynecology, Johns Hopkins University, Medical Department; Visiting Gynecologist, Union Protestant Infirmary, Church Home and Infirmary, Hebrew Hospital and Asylum, Bay View Hospital, Hospital for Women of Maryland; Assistant Visiting Gynecologist, Johns Hopkins Hospital.

RICHARDSON, EDWARD PEIRSON, A.B., M.D., 224 Beacon Street, Boston, Massachusetts. Harvard Medical School, 1906. Assistant in Surgery, Harvard Medical School; Assistant Visiting Surgeon, Massachusetts General Hospital.

RICHARDSON, JAMES J., M.D., 1509 Sixteenth Street, Northwest, Washington, District of Columbia. University of Maryland School of Medicine, 1889. Professor of Otology and Laryngology, Howard University Medical School; Surgeon in Charge, Oto-Laryngological Departments, Providence and

Freedmen's Hospitals; Consulting Oto-Laryngologist, Government Hospital for Insane, Washington Asylum Hospital, Woman's Clinic; Ear and Throat Surgeon, Central Dispensary and Emergency Hospital.

RICHARDSON, JAMES WILSON, M.D., C.M., F.R.C.S. (Edin.), M.R.C.S. (Eng.), L.R.C.P. (Lond.), 3 Royal Bank Chambers, Calgary, Alberta. Faculty of Medicine, McGill University, 1910. Member of Staff, Calgary General and Holy Cross Hospitals.

RICHARDSON, WILLIAM W., M.D., 311 Brockman Building, Los Angeles, California. Northwestern University Medical School, 1890. Attending Surgeon, Los Angeles County Hospital; Consulting Surgeon, Children's Hospital.

RICHTER, HARRY M., M.D., Wesley Memorial Hospital, Chicago, Illinois. University of Illinois College of Medicine (College of Physicians and Surgeons, Chicago), 1894. Professor of Surgery, Northwestern University Medical School; Attending Surgeon, Wesley Memorial, Cook County and Mt. Sinai Hospitals.

RICKER, WILLIAM GRAY, A.B., M.D., 29 Main Street, St. Johnsbury, Vermont. Johns Hopkins University, Medical Department, 1904. Surgeon, Brightlook Hospital.

RICKETTS, BENJAMIN MERRILL, Ph.B., M.D., LL.D., Fourth Avenue and Broadway, Cincinnati, Ohio. University of Cincinnati College of Medicine (Miami Medical College), 1881. Surgeon in Charge, Trinidad Hospital; Director, Ricketts Experimental Surgical Research Laboratory.

RIDDELL, JOHN DE WITT, B.Sc., M.D., 148 South Santa Fe Avenue, Salina, Kansas. University of Kansas School of Medicine (Kansas City College of Medicine), 1896. President of Staff, St. John's Hospital; Member of Staff, St. Barnabas Hospital; Visiting Surgeon, Asbury Hospital.

RIDDELL, WILLIAM CROSBY, M.D., 317 Lumber Exchange, Seattle, Washington. University of Michigan Medical School, 1886.

RIDEOUT, WILLIAM J., M.D., State Bank Building, Freeport, Illinois. State University of Iowa College of Medicine (Keokuk Medical College), 1892.

RIDEWOOD, HAROLD EDWARD, M.D., M.S., F.R.C.S. (Eng.), Belmont Block, Victoria, British Columbia. Royal College of Surgeons, England, and Royal College of Physicians, London, 1901; University of London, 1902.

RIDLEY, ROBERT BERRIEN, JR., M.D., Atlanta National Bank Building, Atlanta, Georgia. Emory University School of Medicine (Atlanta College of Physicians and Surgeons), 1902. Ophthalmologist and Oto-Laryngologist, Georgia Baptist, Wesley Memorial Hospitals, Piedmont Sanatorium, and St. Joseph's Infirmary.

RIDLON, JOHN, A.B., M.D., 7 West Madison Street, Chicago, Illinois. Columbia University, College of Physicians and Surgeons, 1878. Honorary Professor of Orthopedic Surgery, Northwestern University Medical School; Consulting Orthopedic Surgeon, Michael Reese Hospital, Home for the Friendless, Home for Convalescent Crippled Children.

RIENHOFF, WILLIAM, M.D., 564 St. Louis Street, Springfield, Missouri. Julius-Maximilians Universität, Würzburg, 1883. Consultant, St. John's and Burge Deaconess Hospitals; Member of Staff, Springfield Hospital.

RIETZ, PAUL CHARLES, M.D., American Trust Building, Evansville, Indiana. Rush Medical College, 1898. Attending Surgeon, Protestant Deaconess Hospital.

RIGGLES, JOHN LEWIS, M.D., Stoneleigh Court, Washington, District of Columbia. George Washington University Medical School (Columbian University, Medical Department), 1900. Associate Gynecologist, Columbia Hospital for Women.

RIGGS, CHARLES EDWARD, M.D., Medical Corps, United States Navy, Washington, District of Columbia. State University of Iowa College of Medicine, 1892. Captain, Medical Corps, United States Navy.

RIGGS, HERBERT W., M.D., C.M., F.R.C.S. (Edin.), 470 Granville Street, Vancouver, British Columbia. Faculty of Medicine, University of Manitoba (Manitoba Medical College), 1898. Surgeon, Vancouver General Hospital.

RIGGS, THEODORE F., A.B., M.D., Pierre, South Dakota. Johns Hopkins University, Medical Department, 1903. Surgeon, St. Mary's Hospital.

RILEY, JOHN WILLIAM, M.D., 119 West Fifth Street, Oklahoma, Oklahoma. University of Buffalo, Department of Medicine, 1901. Attending Surgeon, St. Anthony's Hospital.

RIND, ROBERT C., M.D., Bushnell Building, Springfield, Ohio. University of Maryland School of Medicine, 1897. Surgeon, City Hospital.

RINDLAUB, JOHN H., M.D., De Lendrecie Block, Fargo, North Dakota. George Washington University Medical School, 1893. Attending Surgeon, Norgaard, St. John's, and St. Luke's Hospitals, Fargo Clinic.

RINDLAUB, MARTIN PHILLIP, JR., LL.B., M.D., 500 De Lendrecie Block, Fargo, North Dakota. Johns Hopkins University Medical Department, 1905. Attending Surgeon, St. John's, St. Luke's, and Norgaard Hospitals.

RINKENBERGER, FREDERICK W., M.D., Merchant's National Bank Building, Los Angeles, California. University of Illinois College of Medicine, 1906.

RISHMILLER, JOHN H., M.D., 1101 Metropolitan Bank Building, Minneapolis, Minnesota. University of Michigan Medical School, 1891. Attending Surgeon, Fairview Hospital; Chief Surgeon, Minneapolis, St. Paul and Sault Ste. Marie Railway; Surgeon, American Railway Express Company.

RISLEY, EDWARD HAMMOND, A.B., M.D., 27 College Avenue, Waterville, Maine. Harvard Medical School, 1906.

RITCHIE, FREDERIC G., M.D., 314 West One Hundred Sixth Street, New York, New York. New York Homeopathic Medical College and Flower Hospital, 1882. Professor of Ophthalmology, College of New York Ophthalmic Hospital; Surgeon, New York Ophthalmic Hospital; Consulting Ophthalmologist, Grace Hospital, New Haven, Connecticut.

616 *American College of Surgeons*

RITCHIE, HARRY PARKS, Ph.B., M.D., 914 Lowry Building, St. Paul, Minnesota. University of Minnesota Medical School, 1896. Associate Professor of Surgery, University of Minnesota Medical School; Surgeon, University, St. Luke's and Miller Hospitals.

RITTER, CALEB ANDERSON, M.D., 702 Bryant Building, Kansas City, Missouri. Indiana University School of Medicine (Indiana Medical College, Indianapolis), 1877. Attending Obstetrician, Kansas City General and Christian Church Hospitals.

RITTER, HARRY NICHOLAS, M.D., 515 Francis Building, Louisville, Kentucky. University of Louisville Medical Department, 1910. Visiting Ophthalmologist, Rhinologist, Oto-Laryngologist, St. Joseph's Infirmary, St. Joseph's Orphans' Home, and Methodist Episcopal Orphans' Home.

RITTER, HOWARD M., M.D., First National Bank Building, Williamsport, Pennsylvania. Jefferson Medical College, 1895.

RIXFORD, EMMET, B.Sc., M.D., 1795 California Street, San Francisco, California. Cooper Medical College, 1891. Professor of Surgery, Leland Stanford Junior University School of Medicine; Visiting Surgeon, San Francisco Hospital.

RIVERIN, RENATO A., M.D., Avenida 15 de Julio, La Paz, Bolivia. Faculty of Medicine University of Buenos Aires, 1912.

ROAN, MARTIN WILLIAM, M.D., First National Bank Building, Bismarck, North Dakota. Marquette University School of Medicine (Milwaukee Medical College), 1903. Member of Staff, St. Alexius Hospital.

ROBB, HUNTER, A.B., M.D., 55 Bacon Street, Winchester, Massachusetts. University of Pennsylvania School of Medicine, 1884.

ROBB, JAMES MILTON, M.D., 641 David Whitney Building, Detroit, Michigan. Detroit College of Medicine and Surgery, 1908. Associate Professor of Ophthalmology, Detroit College of Medicine and Surgery; Attending Surgeon, Harper and Herman Kiefer Hospitals.

ROBBINS, FREDERICK W., A.M., M.D., 1212 Kresge Medical Building, Detroit, Michigan. Detroit College of Medicine and Surgery, 1884. Professor of Urology, Detroit College of Medicine and Surgery; Consulting Urologist, St. Mary's Hospital.

ROBERG, OSCAR THEODORE, M.D., 2749 West Foster Avenue, Chicago, Illinois. Rush Medical College, 1899. Chief Surgeon, Swedish Covenant Hospital.

ROBERSON, FOY, M.D., First National Bank Building, Durham, North Carolina. Jefferson Medical College, 1909. Surgeon, Watts Hospital, West Durham, and Central Hospital, Raleigh.

ROBERTS, DAVID YANDELL, M.D., 501 Francis Building, Louisville, Kentucky. University of Louisville, Medical Department, 1900. Surgeon, SS. Mary and Elizabeth Hospital, Pennsylvania, and Louisville and Nashville Railroads, Western Union Telegraph and Travelers' Insurance Companies.

ROBERTS, EDWARD NEWMAN, M.D., 407 Kane Building, Pocatello, Idaho. Northwestern University Medical School, 1910. Member of Staff, Pocatello and St. Anthony's Mercy Hospitals.

ROBERTS, GEORGE W., Ph.B., M.D., 175 West Fifty-eighth Street, New York, New York. New York Homeopathic Medical College and Flower Hospital, 1889. Chief Attending Surgeon, Hahnemann Hospital, Laura Franklin Free Hospital for Children.

ROBERTS, JAMES A., C.B., M.B., F.R.C.S. (Eng.), 38 Charles Street, East, Toronto, Ontario. University of Toronto, Faculty of Medicine, 1898. Clinical Assistant in Surgery, University of Toronto, Faculty of Medicine; Surgeon, Toronto General Hospital; Consulting Surgeon, Old Folks' Home.

ROBERTS, JOHN B., A.M., M.D., 313 South Seventeenth Street, Philadelphia, Pennsylvania. Jefferson Medical College, 1874; University of Pennsylvania School of Medicine, 1888. Emeritus Professor of Surgery, University of Pennsylvania Graduate School of Medicine.

ROBERTS, SAM EARL, M.D., 906 Waldheim Building, Kansas City, Missouri. University of Kansas School of Medicine, 1911. Assistant Professor, Ear, Nose, and Throat Department, University of Kansas School of Medicine; Attending Ear, Nose, and Throat Surgeon, Children's Mercy, Bell Memorial, St. Margaret's, and Christian Church Hospitals.

ROBERTS, TURNER F., M.D., 924 Pacific Mutual Building, Los Angeles, California. University of Louisville, Medical Department, 1898.

ROBERTS, WILLIAM HUMES, M.D., 461 East Colorado Street, Pasadena, California. Cooper Medical College, 1894. Visiting Oculist and Aurist, Pasadena Hospital; Oculist, La Vina Sanatorium.

ROBERTSON, ARCHIBALD WRIGHT, M.D., Robertson Building, Litchfield, Minnesota. University of Minnesota Medical School, 1909. Surgeon, Litchfield Hospital.

ROBERTSON, CHARLES H., M.D., 406 State Street, Salem, Oregon. Washington University Medical School (Missouri Medical College), 1893.

ROBERTSON, CHARLES MOORE, B.Sc., A.M., M.D., 30 North Michigan Avenue, Chicago, Illinois. State University of Iowa College of Medicine, 1888. Professor of Diseases of Ear, Nose, and Throat, Chicago Policlinic; Surgeon, Chicago Policlinic and Hospital, Henrotin Memorial and Alexian Brothers' Hospitals.

ROBERTSON, DAVID EDWIN, M.B., M.D., 112 College Street, Toronto, Ontario. University of Toronto, Faculty of Medicine, 1907. Demonstrator of Surgery, University of Toronto, Faculty of Medicine; Assistant Surgeon, Hospital for Sick Children, St. John's Hospital.

ROBERTSON, HERMANN MELCHIOR, C.B.E., M.D., C.M., M.R.C.S. (Eng.), L.R.C.P. (Lond.), F.R.C.S. (Edin.), 1549 Clive Drive, Victoria, British Columbia. Faculty of Medicine, McGill University, 1897. Member of Surgical Consulting Staff, Provincial Royal Jubilee and St. Joseph's Hospitals.

ROBERTSON, JAMES FARISH, JR., A.B., M.D., Masonic Temple Building, Wilmington, North Carolina. University of Pennsylvania School of Medicine, 1913. Surgeon, James Walker Memorial and Babies' Hospitals.

ROBERTSON, J. ARCHIE, M.D., 501 Gate City National Bank Building, Kansas City, Missouri. St. Louis College of Physicians and Surgeons, 1899. Member of Surgical Staff, Wesley Hospital.

ROBERTSON, JOSEPH ARCHIBALD, A.B., C.E., M.D., 918 Dallas County State Bank Building, Dallas, Texas. University of Texas Medical Department, 1898. Attending Surgeon, Dallas City and St. Paul's Hospitals.

ROBERTSON, LAWRENCE BRUCE, B.A., M.B., 143 College Street, Toronto, Ontario. University of Toronto, Faculty of Medicine, 1909. Assistant in Clinical Surgery and Demonstrator of Anatomy, University of Toronto, Faculty of Medicine; Consulting Surgeon, Infants' Home; Visiting Surgeon, Home for Incurable Children; Assistant Surgeon, Hospital for Sick Children.

ROBERTSON, LORNE FORBES, B.A., M.D., C.M., M.R.C.S. (Eng.), L.R.C.P. (Lond.), F.R.C.S. (Edin.), 55 Albert Street, Stratford, Ontario. Faculty of Medicine, McGill University, 1901. Member of Staff, Stratford General Hospital.

ROBERTSON, SAMUEL E., B.A., M.D., 21 Walnut Street, Newark, New Jersey. University and Bellevue Hospital Medical College (Bellevue Hospital Medical College), 1886. Medical Director, Presbyterian and St. James' Hospitals.

ROBERTSON, VICTOR A., M.D., 51 Eighth Avenue, Brooklyn, New York. Columbia University, College of Physicians and Surgeons, 1883. Visiting Surgeon, Coney Island and Caledonian Hospitals.

ROBERTSON, WILLIAM M., M.D., Humboldt Building, St. Louis, Missouri. University of Virginia, Department of Medicine, 1889. Genito-Urinary Surgeon, St. Louis City, Jewish, and St. Louis Mullanphy Hospitals.

ROBINS, CHARLES R., M.D., Stuart Circle Hospital, Richmond, Virginia. Medical College of Virginia, 1894. Professor of Gynecology, Medical College of Virginia; Surgeon, Stuart Circle Hospital; Gynecologist, Memorial Hospital.

ROBINSON, ARTHUR LETCHFORD, M.D., Marshall Street, Allegan, Michigan. Loyola University School of Medicine (Bennett Medical College), 1902. Surgical Director, John Robinson Hospital.

ROBINSON, CARL MERRILL, A.B., M.D., Longfellow Square, Portland, Maine. Harvard Medical School, 1911. Adjunct Surgeon, Maine General Hospital; Consulting Surgeon, Children's Hospital; Associate Surgeon, St. Barnabas Hospital.

ROBINSON, CLIFFORD C., M.D., 3410 Michigan Avenue, Indiana Harbor, Indiana. University of Michigan Medical School, 1902. Surgeon, St. Mary's Mercy Hospital, Steel and Tube Company of America; Chief Surgeon, Inland Steel Company.

ROBINSON, DANIEL ARTHUR, A.M., M.D., 142 Hammond Street, Bangor, Maine. Bowdoin Medical School, 1881. Professor of Medical Ethics, Bowdoin Medical School; Member of Surgical Staff, Eastern Maine General Hospital; Consulting Surgeon, Central Maine General Hospital, Lewiston, Children's Hospital, Portland.

ROBINSON, DELBERT EDGAR, M.D., 410 South Jackson Street, Jackson, Michigan. University of Michigan Medical School, 1878; University and Bellevue Hospital Medical College (University of the City of New York, Medical Department), 1881. Surgeon, W. A. Foote Memorial and Mercy Hospitals.

ROBINSON, ERNEST F., A.B., M.D., 603 Bryant Building, Kansas City, Missouri. University of Pennsylvania School of Medicine, 1896. Surgeon, Kansas City General and Research Hospitals.

ROBINSON, FRANK CRAWFORD, M.D., 401 Baker-Boyer Bank Building, Walla Walla, Washington. Rush Medical College, 1902.

ROBINSON, JOHN FLETCHER, A.B., M.D., Aligarh, India. Albany Medical College, 1906. Surgeon in Charge, Aligarh District, Dufferin Zenana and Police and Jail Hospitals.

ROBINSON, MEYER R., M.D., 950 Park Avenue, New York, New York. Columbia University, College of Physicians and Surgeons, 1900. Adjunct Gynecologist, Beth Israel Hospital; Gynecologist, Sydenham Hospital; Associate Gynecologist, Beth Moses Hospital.

ROBINSON, NATHANIEL, M.D., 89 Halsey Street, Brooklyn, New York. New York Homeopathic Medical College and Flower Hospital, 1885. Surgeon, Brooklyn Nursery and Infants' Hospital; Attending Surgeon, Carson C. Peck Memorial Hospital, Brooklyn; Consulting Surgeon, Jamaica Hospital, Jamaica.

ROBINSON, SAMUEL, A.B., M.D., San Marcos Building, Santa Barbara, California. Harvard Medical School, 1902.

ROBINSON, THOMAS ARNOLD, M.D., C.M., 147 Howard Park Avenue, Toronto, Ontario. McGill University Faculty of Medicine, 1910.

ROBNETT, AUSEY H., M.D., Medical Corps, United States Navy, Washington, District of Columbia. George Washington University Medical School, 1905. Commander, Medical Corps, United States Navy.

ROCHFORD, WILLIAM E., M.D., 527 Syndicate Building, Minneapolis, Minnesota. University and Bellevue Hospital Medical College, 1889. Member of Surgical Staff, Northwestern Hospital.

ROCKAFELLOW, JOHN C., M.D., 1205 Banker's Trust Building, Des Moines, Iowa. University of Pennsylvania School of Medicine, 1894. Surgeon, Mercy Hospital.

ROCKEY, ALPHA EUGENE, M.D., 508 Stevens Building, Portland, Oregon. Rush Medical College, 1891.

ROCKEY, EUGENE WATSON, M.D., 508 Stevens Building, Portland, Oregon. Harvard Medical School, 1912. Assistant in Surgery, University of Oregon Medical School; Surgeon, Multnomah County Hospital.

ROCKEY, PAUL, M.D., 508 Stevens Building, Portland, Oregon. Columbia University, College of Physicians and Surgeons, 1908. Associate in Surgery, University of Oregon Medical School; Surgeon, Multnomah County and Good Samaritan Hospitals.

RODDICK, SIR THOMAS GEORGE, M.D., C.M., LL.D., F.R.C.S. (Eng.), 412 Mackay Street, Montreal, Quebec. Faculty of Medicine, McGill University, 1868. Dean and Emeritus Professor of Surgery, Faculty of Medicine, McGill University; Consulting Surgeon, Royal Victoria and Montreal General Hospitals.

RODI, CHARLES H., Ph.C., M.D., 990 Atchison Street, Pasadena, California. University of Michigan Medical School, 1882.

RODMAN, JOHN STEWART, M.D., 1310 Medical Arts Building, Philadelphia, Pennsylvania. Medico-Chirurgical College, Philadelphia, 1906. Associate Professor of Surgery, University of Pennsylvania Graduate School of Medicine; Surgeon, Philadelphia Polyclinic Hospital; Assistant Surgeon, Presbyterian Hospital.

RODMAN, SAMUEL S., M.D., Medical Corps, United States Navy, Washington, District of Columbia. University of Louisville, Medical Department (Kentucky School of Medicine), 1898. Commander, Medical Corps, United States Navy.

ROE, JOHN F., M.D., Metropolitan Building, Denver, Colorado. Rush Medical College, 1899. Surgeon, St. Joseph's Hospital.

ROEDER, CLYDE AUGUSTUS, M.D., 834 Brandeis Theatre Building, Omaha, Nebraska. Yale University School of Medicine, 1907. Instructor in Surgery, University of Nebraska College of Medicine; Surgeon, Wise Memorial Hospital.

ROGERS, CAREY PEGRAM, A.B., M.D., 1433 Riverside Avenue, Jacksonville, Florida. Johns Hopkins University, Medical Department, 1902.

ROGERS, CASSIUS CLAY, A.M., M.D., 25 East Washington Street, Chicago, Illinois. Rush Medical College, 1896. Assistant Professor of Surgery of the Brain and Spinal Cord, University of Illinois College of Medicine; Surgeon, Evangelical Deaconess Hospital.

ROGERS, EDMUND JAMES ARMSTRONG, A.M., M.D., C.M., L.R.C.P. & S. (Edin.), 222 West Colfax Avenue, Denver, Colorado. Faculty of Medicine, McGill University, 1881. Emeritus Professor of Surgery, University of Colorado School of Medicine; Surgeon, St. Luke's Hospital; Consulting Surgeon, Colorado and Southern Railway.

ROGERS, FRANK E., M.D., C.M., Majestic Building, Denver, Colorado. Faculty of Medicine, McGill University, 1897.

ROGERS, GEORGE AUGUSTUS, M.D., 1 Wallace Street, Newark, New Jersey. Columbia University, College of Physicians and Surgeons, 1892. Attending Surgeon, Hospital for Women and Children, Beth Israel Hospital.

ROGERS, J. LEE, M.S., M.D., 318 Old National Bank Building, Spokane, Washington. University of Minnesota Medical School, 1905.

ROGERS, JAMES T., A.B., M.D., C.M., 758 Sherbrooke Street, West, Montreal, Quebec. Faculty of Medicine, McGill University, 1904. Demonstrator of Oto-Laryngology, Faculty of Medicine, McGill University; Associate in Oto-Laryngology, Royal Victoria Hospital; Oto-Laryngologist, Alexandra, Montreal Foundling, and Baby Hospitals.

ROGERS, JOHN, A.B., Ph.B., M.D., 177 East Seventy-first Street, New York, New York. Columbia University, College of Physicians and Surgeons, 1891. Professor of Clinical Surgery, Cornell University Medical College; Surgeon, Bellevue and Booth Memorial Hospitals.

ROGERS, JOHN T., M.D., Hamm Building, St. Paul, Minnesota. University of Minnesota Medical School, 1891. Associate Professor of Surgery, University of Minnesota Medical School; Chief Surgeon, Charles T. Miller Hospital, Incorporated.

ROGERS, MACK, M.D., 2118 Avenue H, Birmingham, Alabama. University of Alabama School of Medicine (Medical College of Alabama), 1889.

ROGERS, MARK HOMER, A.B., M.D., 483 Beacon Street, Boston, Massachusetts. Harvard Medical School, 1904. Assistant Professor of Orthopedic Surgery, Tufts College Medical School; Orthopedic Surgeon, Massachusetts General Hospital.

ROGERS, McLAIN, M.D., Clinton, Oklahoma. Emory University School of Medicine (Atlanta College of Physicians and Surgeons), 1902. Surgeon, Clinton Hospital.

ROGERS, PHILIP FLETCHER, A.B., M.D., 307 Grand Avenue, Milwaukee, Wisconsin. Northwestern University Medical School, 1897. Surgeon, Johnston Emergency, Mt. Sinai, and Columbia Hospitals.

ROHDE, MAX SPENCER, B.Sc., M.D., Lexington Hospital, New York, New York. Johns Hopkins University, Medical Department, 1912. Adjunct Visiting Surgeon, Urological Department, Bellevue Hospital; Assistant Visiting Urologist, New York City Hospital; Clinical Instructor of Urology, Cornell Medical School; Chief of Women's Urological Clinic, Out-Patient Department, New York City Hospital; Chief of Clinic, Out-Patient Department of Urology, Cornell University Medical School.

ROHLF, WILLIAM A., M.D., 123 South East Water Street, Waverly, Iowa. State University of Iowa College of Medicine, 1891. Surgeon, Mercy Hospital.

ROMAN DESIDERIO, A.M., M.D., 1904 South Rittenhouse Square, Philadelphia, Pennsylvania. Hahnemann Medical College and Hospital, Philadelphia, 1893. Clinical Professor of Surgery and Lecturer on Surgical Pathology and Principles of Surgery, Hahnemann Medical College and Hospital; Surgeon-in-Chief, St. Luke's Hospital; Consulting Surgeon, Children's Homeopathic Hospital, Philadelphia, Wilmington Homeopathic Hospital, Wilmington, Delaware.

ROME, RUSSEL MURRAY, M.D., 246 Clermont Avenue, Brooklyn, New York. Long Island College Hospital, 1901. Surgeon, Kings County, Bushwick, East New York, and Brownsville Hospitals.

RONGY, ABRAHAM JACOB, M.D., 345 West Eighty-eighth Street, New York, New York. Long Island College Hospital, 1899. Attending Gynecologist, Lebanon Hospital; Attending Surgeon, Jewish Maternity Hospital; Surgeon, Bedford Maternity, Brooklyn; Consulting Gynecologist, Rockaway Beach Hospital, Rockaway Beach.

ROOD, LUTHER COLBY, M.D., 419 Boylston Street, Boston, Massachusetts. Harvard Medical School, 1899. Ophthalmic Surgeon, Boston City Hospital; Consulting Ophthalmologist, Beth Israel Hospital.

ROOKER, ALBERT M., M.D., 225 Gluck Building, Niagara Falls, New York. University of Buffalo, Department of Medicine, 1906. Consulting Rhinologist and Oto-Laryngologist, Niagara County Tuberculosis Sanatorium.

ROOPE, ALFRED P., M.D., Columbus, Indiana. University of Louisville, Medical Department (Louisville Medical College), 1894. Chief Surgeon, Bartholomew County Hospital.

ROOST, FREDERICK H., M.D., 515 Trimble Building, Sioux City, Iowa. Rush Medical College, 1902. Member of Staff, St. Joseph's Mercy Hospital.

ROOT, EMERSON FRANK, M.D., 430 Judge Building, Salt Lake City, Utah. Western Reserve University School of Medicine, 1880. Surgeon, Holy Cross Hospital.

ROOT, MATT RUSSELL, M.D., 312 Majestic Building, Denver, Colorado. University of Colorado School of Medicine, 1897. Surgeon, St. Luke's Hospital; Consulting Surgeon, St. Anthony's Hospital; Chief Surgeon, Denver and Salt Lake Railroad, Leyden Coal Company.

ROOTH, HERRIOT C., M.D., 350 Ashland Avenue, Buffalo, New York. University of Buffalo, Department of Medicine, 1894. Attending Surgeon, Lafayette General Hospital, Church Charity Foundation; Consulting Gynecologist, Buffalo City Hospital.

ROSE, WILLIAM HENRY, M.D., 13 Elm Street, Worcester, Massachusetts. Harvard Medical School, 1898. Consulting Obstetrician, Worcester City Hospital; Surgeon, Memorial Hospital.

ROSENTHAL, LEWIS J., Phar.G., M.D., 1622 Linden Avenue, Baltimore, Maryland. University of Maryland School of Medicine (College of Physicians and Surgeons, Baltimore), 1901. Assistant Professor of Proctology, University of Maryland School of Medicine and College of Physicians and Surgeons; Visiting Surgeon, Mercy Hospital, Hebrew Hospital and Asylum.

ROSENTHAL, MAURICE I., M.D., 336 West Berry Street, Fort Wayne, Indiana. University of Cincinnati College of Medicine (Ohio-Miami Medical College of the University of Cincinnati), 1890. President of Staff and Surgeon, St. Joseph's Hospital.

ROSENTHAL, MELVIN S., M.D., 1222 Madison Avenue, Baltimore, Maryland. University of Maryland School of Medicine (College of Physicians and Surgeons, Baltimore), 1892. Associate Professor of Genito-Urinary Surgery and Dermatology, University of Maryland School of Medicine and College of Physicians and Surgeons; Member of Staff, Mercy Hospital, Hebrew Hospital and Asylum, Hospital for Consumptives.

ROSENWALD, LEON, M.D., 326 Argyle Building, Kansas City, Missouri. St. Louis University School of Medicine (Marion-Sims College of Medicine), 1893.

ROSS, DAVID, B.Sc., M.D., 416 Board of Trade Building, Indianapolis, Indiana. Indiana University School of Medicine (Medical College of Indiana), 1895. Associate Professor of Surgery, Indiana University School of Medicine; Consulting Surgeon, Indianapolis City, St. Vincent's, and Methodist Episcopal Hospitals.

ROSS, EDWARD HARLAN, A.B., M.D., 10 Church Street, St. Johnsbury, Vermont. Dartmouth Medical School, 1891. Surgeon, Brightlook and St. Johnsbury Hospitals.

ROSS, GEORGE G., M.D., 1721 Spruce Street, Philadelphia, Pennsylvania. University of Pennsylvania School of Medicine, 1891. Associate in Surgery, University of Pennsylvania School of Medicine; Surgeon, Germantown Dispensary and Hospital, Methodist Hospital; Assistant Surgeon, Lankenau Hospital, Hospital of the University of Pennsylvania.

ROSS, HIRAM EARL, M.D., 1008 First National Bank Building, Danville, Illinois. Northwestern University Medical School, 1911. Member of Staff, St. Elizabeth's and Lake View Hospitals.

ROSS, THEOPHILUS ERSKINE, M.D., 416 Bay Street, Hattiesburg, Mississippi. University of Maryland School of Medicine (College of Physicians and Surgeons, Baltimore), 1888. Chief Surgeon, Mississippi Central and Gulf and Ship Island Railroads.

ROSS, THOMAS ROBERT, M.D., C.M., Drumheller, Alberta. Queen's University Faculty of Medicine, 1908. Surgeon, Drumheller Hospital.

ROSSER, CHARLES M., M.D., 4002 Gaston Avenue, Dallas, Texas. University of Louisville, Medical Department, 1888. Professor of Surgery, Baylor University School of Medicine; Attending Surgeon, Parkland City Hospital, Texas Baptist Memorial Sanitarium.

ROSSITER, PERCEVAL SHERER, M.D., Medical Corps, United States Navy, Washington, District of Columbia. University of Maryland School of Medicine, 1895. Commander, Medical Corps, United States Navy.

ROTH, ALBERT WALTON, M.D., 303 Palace Building, Tulsa, Oklahoma. Hahnemann Medical College and Hospital, Chicago, 1900.

ROTH, AUGUSTUS HENRY, A.B., M.D., 629 Myrtle Street, Erie, Pennsylvania. University of Michigan Medical School, 1904. Surgeon, St. Vincent's Hospital; Member of Staff, Hamot Hospital.

ROTH, HENRY, M.D., 409 East One Hundred Fortieth Street, New York, New York. University and Bellevue Hospital Medical College (New York University Medical College), 1893. Clinical Professor of Surgery, Fordham University School of Medicine; Attending Surgeon, Lebanon Hospital; Visiting Surgeon, Union Hospital; Consulting Surgeon, Bronx Eye and Ear Infirmary, New York, New York House of Refuge, Randall's Island, Rockaway Beach Hospital, Rockaway Beach.

ROTH, LEON JOSEPH, M.D., 927 Pacific Mutual Building, Los Angeles, California. University of California Medical School, Los Angeles, 1901. Genito-Urinary Surgeon, St. Vincent's Hospital, Los Angeles, National Soldiers' Home, Sawtelle.

ROTHROCK, JOHN L., A.M., M.D., Hamm Building, St. Paul, Minnesota. University of Pennsylvania School of Medicine, 1888.

ROTHWELL, EDWIN JAMES, M.D., New Westminster, British Columbia. University of Toronto, Faculty of Medicine, 1896.

ROUSH, WILLIAM, M.D., 499 North Jameson Avenue, Lima, Ohio. Cincinnati College of Medicine and Surgery, 1891. Consulting Surgeon, Lima Hospital.

ROWAN, CHARLES JOSEPH, A.B., M.D., North Dubuque Road, Iowa City, Iowa. Rush Medical College, 1898. Professor of Surgery, State University of Iowa College of Medicine; Attending Surgeon, University Hospital.

ROWE, BERT BESSAC, M.D., 315 South Jefferson Avenue, Saginaw, Michigan. University of Michigan Medical School, 1888. Surgeon, St. Mary's, Saginaw General, and Woman's Hospitals.

ROWLAND, JAMES M. H., M.D., 1204 Madison Avenue, Baltimore, Maryland. University of Maryland School of Medicine (Baltimore Medical College), 1892. Professor of Obstetrics, University of Maryland School of Medicine and College of Physicians and Surgeons; Obstetrician, Maryland General and Maryland Lying-in Hospitals; Visiting Obstetrician, University Hospital and Hospital for the Women of Maryland; Consulting Obstetrician, Du Pont Maternity Hospital, Cambridge.

ROWLAND, JOHN F., M.D., Thompson Building, Hot Springs, Arkansas. University of Tennessee College of Medicine, 1901. Member of Staff, St. Joseph's Infirmary.

ROWLEY, ALFRED M., M.D., 179 Allyn Street, Hartford, Connecticut. University of Vermont College of Medicine, 1897. Visiting Surgeon, Hartford Hospital; Consulting Surgeon, Hartford Isolation Hospital, Hartford, Torrington Hospital, Torrington, Manchester Memorial Hospital, Manchester.

ROWSE, ROBERT Q., M.D., 107 Sioux National Bank Building, Sioux City, Iowa. University of Cincinnati College of Medicine (Medical College of Ohio), 1893. Attending Surgeon, St. Joseph's Hospital.

Roy, Dunbar, A.B., M.D., Grand Opera House Building, Atlanta, Georgia. University of Virginia, Department of Medicine, 1889. Professor of Oto-Laryngology, Emory University School of Medicine; Consulting Oculist and Aurist, Grady Memorial Hospital; Oculist and Aurist, St. Joseph's, Georgia Baptist, and Atlanta Hospitals.

Roy, John James, M.D., C.M., 308 George Street, Sydney, Nova Scotia. Faculty of Medicine, McGill University, 1897. Visiting Surgeon, Sydney City Hospital.

Royce, Gilbert, A.B., M.D., 100 College Street, Toronto, Ontario. University of Toronto, Faculty of Medicine, 1897. Associate Professor of Rhinology and Oto-Laryngology, University of Toronto, Faculty of Medicine; Senior Assistant Surgeon, Oto-Laryngological Department, Toronto General Hospital.

Royce, Harold Thomas, M.D., C.M., Mohegan Lake, New York. University of Toronto, Faculty of Medicine, 1906.

Royster, Hubert Ashley, A.B., M.D., 423 Fayetteville Street, Raleigh, North Carolina. University of Pennsylvania School of Medicine, 1894. Surgeon-in-Chief, St. Agnes' Hospital; Surgeon, Rex Hospital.

Rubin, Isidor Clinton, M.D., 261 Central Park, West, New York, New York. Columbia University, College of Physicians and Surgeons, 1905. Attending Gynecologist, Montefiore Hospital; Adjunct Gynecologist, Mt. Sinai and Beth Israel Hospitals; Associate in Pathology, Beth Israel Hospital.

Rucker, Edmund Winchester, Jr., B.Sc., M.D., Woodward Building, Birmingham, Alabama. University of Colorado School of Medicine (Denver and Gross College of Medicine), 1904. Otologist, Rhinologist, and Laryngologist, St. Vincent's and Children's Hospitals.

Rucker, William Colby, M.Sc., M.D., United States Public Health Service, Washington, District of Columbia. Rush Medical College, 1897. Chief Quarantine Officer, Panama Canal; Surgeon, United States Public Health Service.

Ruffin, Kirkland, M.D., 1101 Graydon Avenue, Norfolk, Virginia. University of Virginia, Department of Medicine, 1886. Surgeon, St. Christopher Hospital; Attending Surgeon, Norfolk Protestant Hospital, Norfolk, King's Daughters Hospital, Portsmouth.

Ruffner, Ernest Lewis, M.D., D.S.M., Medical Corps, United States Army, Washington, District of Columbia. University of Buffalo, Department of Medicine, 1894. Lieutenant Colonel, Medical Corps, United States Army.

Runnels, Orange Scott, A.M., M.D., 522 North Illinois Street, Indianapolis, Indiana. Ohio State University College of Homeopathic Medicine (Cleveland Homeopathic Hospital College), 1871. Surgeon-in-Chief, Runnels' Hospital.

Runyan, Raymond Wentworth, M.D., Hospital de Panama, Panama, Republic of Panama. University of Cincinnati College of Medicine (Medical College of Ohio), 1906. Surgeon, Hospital de Panama.

RUNYON, MEFFORD, M.D., 110 Irvington Avenue, South Orange, New Jersey. Columbia University, College of Physicians and Surgeons, 1887. Attending Surgeon, Orange Memorial Hospital, Orange; Surgeon-in-Chief, Dr. Runyon's Hospital; Consultant, New Jersey Orthopedic Hospital, Orange.

RUSCHLI, EDWARD BARNARD, M.D., 510 LaFayette Life Building, LaFayette, Indiana. University and Bellevue Hospital Medical College, 1906. Surgeon, St. Elizabeth's and LaFayette Home Hospitals.

RUSH, JOHN OSGOOD, B.Sc., Ph.G., M.D., LL.D., 706 Van Antwerp Building, Mobile, Alabama. University of Alabama School of Medicine, 1904. Urologist, City Hospital and Dispensary, Providence Infirmary; Consulting Urologist, United States Marine Hospital and Florence Crittenton Home.

RUSHMORE, JAQUES C., A.B., M.D., 477 Washington Avenue, Brooklyn, New York. Long Island College Hospital, 1903. Clinical Professor of Orthopedic Surgery and Orthopedic Surgeon, Long Island College Hospital.

RUSHMORE, JOHN D., A.B., M.D., 129 Montague Street, Brooklyn, New York. Columbia University, College of Physicians and Surgeons, 1870. Emeritus Professor of Operative and Clinical Surgery, Long Island College Hospital; Attending Surgeon, St. Peter's Hospital; Consulting Surgeon, Kings County, Swedish, St. Anthony's, Long Island College, and Bushwick Hospitals, Brooklyn, Lutheran Hospital, New York.

RUSHMORE, STEPHEN, A.B., M.D., 520 Commonwealth Avenue, Boston, Massachusetts. Johns Hopkins University, Medical Department, 1902. Associate Professor of Gynecology, Tufts College Medical School; Consulting Gynecologist, Symmes Arlington Hospital, Arlington; Obstetrician, Evangeline Booth Maternity Hospital.

RUSS, WITTEN BOOTH, M.D., Central Trust Building, San Antonio, Texas. University of Pennsylvania School of Medicine, 1898. Surgeon, Robert B. Green Memorial Hospital.

RUSSELL, FREDERICK FULLER, M.D., D.Sc., 61 Broadway, New York, New York. Columbia University, College of Physicians and Surgeons, 1893. Director, Public Health Laboratory Service.

RUSSELL, JAMES I., A.B., M.D., 37 East Sixty-first Street, New York, New York. Columbia University, College of Physicians and Surgeons, 1901. Junior Surgeon, Roosevelt Hospital.

RUSSELL, MARION F., A.B., M.D., 1305 Main Street, Great Bend, Kansas. University of Pennsylvania School of Medicine, 1907. Member of Staff, St. Rose Hospital.

RUSSELL, THOMAS HUBBARD, Ph.B., M.D., 57 Trumbull Street, New Haven, Connecticut. Yale University School of Medicine, 1910. Attending Surgeon, Grace Hospital.

RUSSELL, WALLACE BOYD, SR., B.Sc., M.D., Changchow General Hospital, Changchow, Ku, China. University of Tennessee College of Medicine, 1908. Superintendent and Surgeon, Changchow General Hospital.

RUSSELL, WILLIAM WOOD, A.M., M.D., 1208 Eutaw Place, Baltimore, Maryland. University of Pennsylvania School of Medicine, 1890. Associate Professor of Gynecology, Johns Hopkins University, Medical Department; Associate in Gynecology, Johns Hopkins Hospital; Gynecologist, Union Protestant Infirmary, Hospital for Women of Maryland.

RUST, CARL HAMMOND, M.D., Rose Building, Cleveland, Ohio. Ohio State University College of Homeopathic Medicine (Homeopathic Hospital College), 1893.

RUST, EDWIN G., M.D., 1158 Hanna Building, Cleveland, Ohio. Ohio State University College of Homeopathic Medicine (Homeopathic Hospital College), 1880.

RUTH, CHARLES EDWARD, M.D., 415 Iowa Building, Des Moines, Iowa. State University of Iowa College of Medicine, 1883. Surgeon, Iowa Methodist Hospital.

RYAN, JOHN CHARLES, M.D., 811 Hippee Building, Des Moines, Iowa. University of Illinois College of Medicine, 1909. Attending Surgeon, Iowa Lutheran and City Hospitals.

RYAN, LAWRENCE, M.D., 32 North State Street, Chicago, Illinois. Rush Medical College, 1894. Attending Surgeon, Frances E. Willard National Temperance and St. Anthony's Hospitals.

RYAN, RUSSELL COLQUHOUN, M.D., 362 Flood Building, San Francisco, California. University of California Medical School (Hahnemann Medical College of the Pacific, San Francisco), 1911. Member of Visiting Staff, Mt. Zion Hospital.

RYDER, DELANO R., M.D., 151 Rock Street, Fall River, Massachusetts. University of Vermont College of Medicine, 1904. Otologist and Laryngologist, Truesdale, St. Anne's, and Fall River City Hospitals.

RYERSON, E. STANLEY, M.D., C.M., 143 College Street, Toronto, Ontario. University of Toronto, Faculty of Medicine (Trinity Medical College), 1900. Secretary of Faculty Council and Associate in Surgery, University of Toronto, Faculty of Medicine; Senior Assistant Surgeon, Toronto General Hospital.

RYERSON, EDWIN WARNER, M.D., 122 South Michigan Avenue, Chicago, Illinois. Harvard Medical School, 1897. Associate Professor of Surgery, Rush Medical College; Professor of Orthopedic Surgery, Chicago Policlinic; Orthopedic Surgeon, Children's Memorial Hospital; Consulting Orthopedic Surgeon, Home for Destitute Crippled Children.

RYERSON, GEORGE STERLING, M.B., M.D., C.M., L.R.C.P. & S. (Edin.), Niagara-on-the-Lake, Ontario. University of Toronto, Faculty of Medicine (Trinity Medical College), 1875. Emeritus Professor of Ophthalmology and Otology, University of Toronto, Faculty of Medicine; Consulting Oculist and Aurist, Toronto General and Toronto Western Hospitals, Toronto; Honorary Colonel-in-Chief, Medical Corps, Canadian Army.

RYFKOGEL, HENRY ANTHON LEWIS, M.D., 516 Sutter Street, San Francisco, California. University of California Medical School, San Francisco, 1894. Lecturer on Surgery, Leland Stanford Junior University School of Medicine; Surgeon, San Francisco Polyclinic Hospital; Associate Visiting Surgeon, San Francisco Hospital.

RYTINA, ANTON G., A.B., M.D., Professional Building, Baltimore, Maryland. University of Maryland School of Medicine, 1905. Professor of Genito-Urinary Surgery, University of Maryland School of Medicine; Visiting Genito-Urinary Surgeon, South Baltimore General and Mercy Hospitals; Consulting Genito-Urinary Surgeon, United States Public Health and St. Joseph's Hospitals; Director, United States Government Clinic, Mercy, and Morrow Hospitals.

SABIN, GEORGE MILLAR, B.Sc., M.D., 244 Main Street, Burlington, Vermont. University of Vermont College of Medicine, 1900. Instructor in Gynecology, University of Vermont College of Medicine; Attending Surgeon, Fanny Allen Hospital, Winooski; Assistant Surgeon, Mary Fletcher Hospital; Attending Physician and Surgeon, Home for Destitute Children.

SABINE, JANE D. KELLY, A.B., M.D., 348 Marlborough Street, Boston, Massachusetts. Northwestern University Woman's Medical School, 1894.

SACHS, ERNEST, A.B., M.D., 97 Arundel Place, St. Louis, Missouri. Johns Hopkins University, Medical Department, 1904. Professor of Clinical Neurological Surgery, Washington University Medical School; Surgeon, Barnes and St. Louis Children's Hospitals; Neurological Surgeon, Jewish Hospital of St. Louis.

SADLER, LENA KELLOGG, M.D., 533 Diversey Parkway, Chicago, Illinois. University of Illinois College of Medicine (American Medical Missionary College), 1906. Attending Gynecologist, Columbus Hospital, Bethany Sanitarium and Hospital.

SADLER, WILLIAM S., M.D., 533 Diversey Parkway, Chicago, Illinois. University of Illinois College of Medicine (American Medical Missionary College), 1906. Senior Attending Surgeon, Columbus Hospital; Chief Surgeon, Bethany Sanitarium and Hospital.

SADLIER, JAMES EDGAR, M.D., 295 Mill Street, Poughkeepsie, New York. Albany Medical College, 1887. Surgeon-in-Chief, Sadlier Hospital; Attending Surgeon, St. Francis Hospital; Consulting Surgeon, Highland Hospital, Beacon, New York, Sharon Hospital, Sharon, Connecticut.

SAFFORD, HENRY BARNARD, A.B., M.D., 47 West Ninety-fourth Street, New York, New York. New York Homeopathic Medical College and Flower Hospital, 1908. Attending Obstetrician, Hahnemann Hospital; Attending Surgeon, Metropolitan Hospital; Assistant Surgeon, Laura Franklin Free Hospital for Children; Assistant Gynecologist, Flower Hospital.

SAINT-JACQUES, EUGENE, M.D., C.M., 29 Sherbrooke Street, West, Montreal, Quebec. Faculty of Medicine, University of Montreal (Laval University, Medical Department), 1896. Adjunct Professor of Clinical Surgery and Professor of Deontology, Faculty of Medicine, University of Montreal; Surgeon, Hotel Dieu de St. Joseph.

SAINT-PIERRE, JOSEPH ALEXANDRE, B.A., M.D., 703 St. Hubert Street, Montreal, Quebec. Faculty of Medicine, University of Montreal (Laval University, Faculty of Medicine), 1901. Professor of Surgery and Assistant Professor of Clinical Surgery, Faculty of Medicine, University of Montreal; Provincial Director of Hospitals; Surgeon, Hotel Dieu.

SALATICH, PETER BLAISE, M.D., 3202 St. Charles Avenue, New Orleans, Louisiana. Tulane University of Louisiana School of Medicine, 1905. Associate Professor of Obstetrics, Loyola Post-Graduate School of Medicine; Visiting Gynecologist, Charity and Hotel Dieu Hospitals.

SALB, JOHN PAUL, M.D., Sixth Street, Jasper, Indiana. Indiana University School of Medicine (Medical College of Indiana), 1880. Surgeon, Salb's Sanitarium.

SALISBURY, LUCIUS ALBERT, A.B., M.D., 71 East Seventy-seventh Street, New York, New York. Harvard Medical School, 1908. Assistant Professor of Surgery, New York Post-Graduate Medical School and Hospital; Attending Surgeon, Metropolitan Hospital; Consulting Surgeon, Northern Dispensary.

SALTER, PETER HAROLD, M.D., L.R.C.P. & S. (Edin.), L.F.P.S. (Glas.), 409 Norfolk Avenue, Norfolk, Nebraska. University of Toronto, Faculty of Medicine (Trinity Medical College), 1885. Surgeon, Norfolk General Hospital.

SAMMIS, GEORGE FRANK, M.D., 98 Brooklyn Avenue, Brooklyn, New York. Long Island College Hospital, 1907. Associate Surgeon, Jamaica Hospital, Jamaica; Attending Surgeon, St. John's Hospital, Brooklyn.

SAMPLE, CHESTER H., M.D., 309 South Washington Avenue, Saginaw, Michigan. University and Bellevue Hospital Medical College, 1874. Surgeon, Saginaw General, St. Mary's, and Woman's Hospitals, St. Vincent's Orphans' Home; District Surgeon, Grand Trunk and Michigan Railways.

SAMPSON, JOHN A., A.M., M.D., 180 Washington Avenue, Albany, New York. Johns Hopkins University, Medical Department, 1899. Professor of Gynecology, Albany Medical College; Gynecologist, Albany Hospital.

SAMUELS, ABRAHAM, Phar.G., M.D., 1928 Eutaw Place, Baltimore, Maryland. University of Maryland School of Medicine (College of Physicians and Surgeons, Baltimore), 1898. Associate Professor of Gynecology, University of Maryland School of Medicine and College of Physicians and Surgeons; Gynecologist, Mercy Hospital, Hebrew Hospital and Asylum.

SANBORN, CHARLES FRYE, M.D., Municipal Tuberculosis Sanitarium, Chicago, Illinois. University and Bellevue Hospital Medical College (University of the City of New York, Medical Department), 1893.

SANDELS, CHRISTOPHER C., M.D., Westinghouse Building, Pittsburgh, Pennsylvania. University of Pittsburgh School of Medicine, 1896. Rhinologist, Otologist, and Laryngologist, Western Pennsylvania and Pittsburgh Hospitals.

SANDERS, LOREN A., M.D., 23 West Street, Concord, New Hampshire. University and Bellevue Hospital Medical College, 1899. Surgeon, Margaret Pillsbury General Hospital, New Hampshire Memorial Hospital for Women and Children.

SANDERS, ROBERT LEE, M.D., 702 Goodwyn Institute Building, Memphis, Tennessee. University of Nashville, Medical Department, 1906. Associate in Surgery, University of Tennessee College of Medicine; Visiting Surgeon, St. Joseph's and Memphis General Hospitals.

SANDERSON, HERMON HARVEY, M.B., David Whitney Building, Detroit, Michigan. University of Toronto, Faculty of Medicine, 1893. Assistant Clinical Professor of Ophthalmology, Detroit College of Medicine and Surgery; Associate Ophthalmic Surgeon, Harper Hospital.

SANES, KAY I., M.D., 519 Jenkins Building, Pittsburgh, Pennsylvania. University of Pittsburgh School of Medicine, 1896. Gynecologist, Western Pennsylvania Hospital; Consulting Gynecologist and Abdominal Surgeon, Montefiore Hospital.

SANFORD, HENRY L., A.B., M.D., 1110 Euclid Avenue, Cleveland, Ohio. Harvard Medical School, 1900. Instructor in Surgery, Western Reserve University School of Medicine; Visiting Surgeon, Genito-Urinary Department, Cleveland City Hospital; Assistant Visiting Surgeon, Genito-Urinary Department, Lakeside Hospital.

SANGER, EUGENE BOUTELLE, Ph.B., M.D., 42 Broadway, Bangor, Maine. Columbia University, College of Physicians and Surgeons, 1894. Visiting Surgeon, Eastern Maine General Hospital; Surgeon, Great Northern Paper Company, Bangor Children's Home; Consulting Surgeon, Bangor State Hospital.

SANGER, FRANK DYER, M.D., 525 North Charles Street, Baltimore, Maryland. University of Maryland School of Medicine (College of Physicians and Surgeons, Baltimore), 1888. Professor of Diseases of Nose and Throat, University of Maryland School of Medicine and College of Physicians and Surgeons; Consulting Laryngologist, Mercy, Sydenham, Bay View, and Bon Secour Hospitals, Union Protestant Infirmary, Church Home and Infirmary, Hospital for Women of Maryland.

SANJINES, CLAUDIO T., M.D., Casilla 409, La Paz, Bolivia. Faculty of Medicine, University of Chile, 1898.

SARGENT, WALTER LESLIE, A.B., M.D., 1155 Hancock Street, Quincy, Massachusetts. Harvard Medical School, 1903. Visiting Surgeon, Quincy City Hospital.

SATTLER, ROBERT, M.D., Groton Building, Cincinnati, Ohio. University of Cincinnati College of Medicine (Miami Medical College), 1876. Professor of Ophthalmology, University of Cincinnati College of Medicine; Ophthalmic Surgeon, Cincinnati General Hospital; Executive Surgeon, Ophthalmic Hospital.

SAUER, WILLIAM E., M.D., 537 North Grand Avenue, St. Louis, Missouri. Washington University Medical School, 1896. Clinical Instructor in

Laryngology, Washington University Medical School; Otologist and Laryngologist, Bethesda and St. Louis Mullanphy Hospitals; Member of Staff, St. Luke's Hospital.

SAUNDERS, BACON, M.D., LL.D., 704 Flatiron Building, Fort Worth, Texas. University of Louisville, Medical Department, 1877. Professor of Surgery, Baylor University School of Medicine; Surgeon-in-Chief, St. Joseph's Infirmary; Chief Surgeon, Fort Worth and Denver City and Wichita Valley Railways.

SAUNDERS, ROY F., M.D., 704 Flatiron Building, Fort Worth, Texas. Texas Christian University School of Medicine (Fort Worth School of Medicine), 1905. Associate Professor of Surgery, Baylor University School of Medicine; Attending Surgeon, St. Joseph's Infirmary; Assistant Chief Surgeon, Fort Worth and Denver City and Wichita Valley Railways.

SAUNDERS, TRUMAN LAURANCE, A.B., M.D., 120 East Sixty-first Street, New York, New York. Columbia University, College of Physicians and Surgeons, 1904. Assistant Professor of Laryngology and Otology, Columbia University, College of Physicians and Surgeons; Attending Surgeon, New York Eye and Ear Infirmary.

SAURENHAUS, ERNST, M.D., 59 Bellevue Place, Chicago, Illinois. University of Heidelberg, 1886. Gynecologist, St. Elizabeth's and Grant Hospitals; Obstetrician, St. Mary of Nazareth Hospital.

SAVAGE, PHILIP M., M.D., 499 E Street, San Bernardino, California. Cooper Medical College, 1907.

SAVINI, CARLO, M.D., 43 West Eleventh Street, New York, New York. Royal University of Rome, 1887. Visiting Surgeon, Italian Hospital.

SAWYER, C. E., M.D., Army and Navy Building, Washington, District of Columbia. Ohio State University College of Homeopathic Medicine (Homeopathic Hospital College), 1881. Brigadier General, Medical Reserve Corps, United States Army.

SAWYER, CHARLES FRANCIS, M.D., 2526 Calumet Avenue, Chicago, Illinois. Northwestern University Medical School, 1904. Clinical Professor of Surgery, Loyola University School of Medicine; Attending Surgeon, Mercy Hospital.

SAWYER, PRINCE E., M.D., 306 F. L. and T. Building, Sioux City, Iowa. State University of Iowa College of Medicine, 1895. Member of Staff, St. Joseph's and Samaritan Hospitals.

SAWYER, WALTER HULME, M.D., 12 Manning Street, Hillsdale, Michigan. University of Michigan Medical School, 1884. Regent and Chairman of Medical Committee, University of Michigan.

SAYLE, ROBERT GEORGE, M.D., 710 Merchants and Manufacturers Bank Building, Milwaukee, Wisconsin. Rush Medical College, 1885. Surgeon, Milwaukee and Milwaukee Children's Hospitals; Chief of Staff, Deaconess Hospital.

SAYLES, CHARLES FREDERICK, M.D., 145 East Flagler Street, Miami, Florida. University of Georgia, Medical Department, 1908. Member of Staff, Miami City Hospital.

SAYRE, REGINALD HALL, A.B., M.D., 14 West Forty-eighth Street, New York, New York. University and Bellevue Hospital Medical College, 1884. Professor of Orthopedic Surgery, University and Bellevue Hospital Medical College; Assistant Surgeon in Charge, Orthopedic Department, Bellevue Hospital; Consulting Surgeon, St. Vincent's Hospital, Hospital for Deformities and Joint Diseases, New York, Flushing Hospital, Flushing, New York State Hospital for Crippled and Deformed Children, West Haverstraw, New York, Home for Crippled Children, Newark, Hackensack Hospital, Hackensack, Mountainside Hospital, Montclair, Englewood Hospital, Englewood, New Jersey.

SCALES, JOHN LYTLE, B.Sc., M.D., 907 Commercial Bank Building, Shreveport, Louisiana. University of Tennessee College of Medicine (University of Nashville Medical Department), 1897.

SCALES, J. WILLIAM, M.D., 204½ Main Street, Pine Bluff, Arkansas. Vanderbilt University, Medical Department, 1888.

SCALLON, JOSEPH EDWARD, M.D., First National Bank Building, Hancock, Michigan. Montreal School of Medicine and Surgery, 1874. Dean of Staff, St. Joseph's Hospital.

SCANNELL, DAVID DANIEL, A.B., M.D., 366 Commonwealth Avenue, Boston, Massachusetts. Harvard Medical School, 1900. Lecturer on Surgery, Harvard University Graduate School of Medicine; Visiting Surgeon, Boston City Hospital.

SCANNELL, JOHN MATTHEW, M.D., 364 Jefferson Avenue, Brooklyn, New York. University and Bellevue Hospital Medical College, 1904. Attending Surgeon, St. Catherine's and Greenpoint Hospitals, House of the Good Shepard.

SCARBOROUGH, JAMES I., A.B., M.D., 900 Scott Street, Little Rock, Arkansas. Johns Hopkins University, Medical Department, 1908. Chief of Staff, St. Vincent's Infirmary.

SCHACHNER, AUGUST, Phar.G., M.D., 844 Fourth Avenue, Louisville, Kentucky. University of Louisville, Medical Department (Louisville Medical College), 1888.

SCHAEFER, OTTO, M.D., 1105 Madison Avenue, Baltimore, Maryland. University of Maryland School of Medicine, 1894. Surgeon, South Baltimore General Hospital.

SCHAEFFER, CHARLES D., A.M., M.D., D.Sc., 28 North Eighth Street, Allentown, Pennsylvania. University of Pennsylvania School of Medicine, 1889. Superintendent and Surgeon-in-Chief, Allentown Hospital; Surgeon, Central Railroad of New Jersey, Philadelphia and Reading Railway.

SCHAEFFER, GEORGE CHRISTIAN, M.D., 246 East State Street, Columbus, Ohio. University of Cincinnati College of Medicine (Miami Medical College), 1896.

SCHAEFFER, ROBERT L., A.B., M.D., 30 North Eighth Street, Allentown, Pennsylvania. University of Pennsylvania School of Medicine, 1908. First Assistant Surgeon, Allentown Hospital; Surgeon, American Steel and Wire Company; Chief, State Genito-Urinary Clinic.

SCHALL, JOHN HUBLEY, A.B., M.D., 119 St. Mark's Avenue, Brooklyn, New York. Hahnemann Medical College and Hospital, Philadelphia, 1893. Surgeon, Memorial, Prospect Heights, and Community Hospitals, Eastern District Dispensary, Brooklyn, Jamaica Hospital, Jamaica.

SCHAUFFLER, ROBERT McE., A.B., M.D., 416 Argyle Building, Kansas City, Missouri. Columbia University, College of Physicians and Surgeons, 1896. Attending Orthopedic Surgeon, Kansas City General, Christian Church, and Research Hospitals, Mercy Hospital for Children.

SCHENCK, HERBERT DANA, B.Sc., M.D., 75 Halsey Street, Brooklyn, New York. New York Homeopathic Medical College and Flower Hospital, 1884. Visiting Oculist and Aurist, Carson C. Peck Memorial Hospital, Prospect Heights Hospital and Brooklyn Maternity, Brooklyn Nursery and Infants' Hospital; Consulting Oculist and Aurist, Cumberland Street Hospital.

SCHENCK, W. EDWARDS, M.D., 19 West Seventh Street, Cincinnati, Ohio. University of Cincinnati College of Medicine (Miami Medical College), 1891.

SCHERCK, HENRY JOSEPH, B.Sc., M.D., Century Building, St. Louis, Missouri. Tulane University of Louisiana School of Medicine, 1889. Assistant Professor of Genito-Urinary Surgery, St. Louis University School of Medicine; Visiting Genito-Urinary Surgeon, St. Louis City and United States Marine Hospitals; Genito-Urinary Surgeon, Missouri Pacific Hospital, Jewish Home for Chronic Invalids; Chief of Department of Genito-Urinary Surgery, Jewish Hospital Dispensary; Associate Genito-Urinary Surgeon, Jewish Hospital.

SCHIFFBAUER, HANS ERNST WALTER, M.D., Title Insurance Building, Los Angeles, California. University of Illinois College of Medicine, 1907. Member of Staff, Los Angeles County Hospital.

SCHILLER, HELIODOR, M.D., 29 East Madison Street, Chicago, Illinois. University of Prague, 1896. Member of Staff, Michael Reese Hospital; Gynecologist, Post-Graduate Medical School and Hospital.

SCHILLING, NICHOLAS, B.Sc., M.D., New Hampton, Iowa. Creighton College of Medicine, 1896. Attending Surgeon, St. Joseph's Hospital.

SCHINBEIN, AUSTIN BIRRELL, M.B., 124 Vancouver Block, Vancouver, British Columbia. University of Toronto, Faculty of Medicine, 1907. Associate Surgeon, Vancouver General Hospital; Surgeon, Shaughnessy Hospital, Soldier's Civil Re-Establishment.

SCHIPFER, LLOYD ALBERT, M.D., City National Bank Building, Bismarck, North Dakota. State University of Iowa College of Medicine, 1907. Member of Staff, St. Alexius Hospital.

SCHIRRMAN, HARRY ARTHUR, M.D., 805 Chillicothe Street, Portsmouth, Ohio. University of Michigan Medical School, 1902. Surgeon, Hempstead Hospital; Surgeon-in-Chief, Schirrman Hospital.

SCHLEY, WINFIELD SCOTT, A.B., M.D., 24 West Forty-fifth Street, New York, New York. Columbia University, College of Physicians and Surgeons, 1896. Associate Surgeon, St. Luke's Hospital; Consulting Surgeon, Ossining Hospital, Ossining.

SCHLICHTER, CHARLES HENRY, Ph.G., M.D., 556 North Broad Street, Elizabeth, New Jersey. Columbia University College of Physicians and Surgeons, 1896. Attending Ophthalmologist, Oto-Laryngologist and Chief of Clinic, Elizabeth General Hospital and Dispensary.

SCHLIEKER, ALEXANDER G., M.D., 721 Chicago Avenue, East Chicago, Indiana. Northwestern University Medical School, 1900. Member of Staff, St. Mary's Mercy Hospital, Gary.

SCHLINDWEIN, GEORGE WILLIAM, M.D., 138 West Ninth Street, Erie, Pennsylvania. Jefferson Medical College, 1904. Attending Surgeon, Hamot and St. Vincent's Hospitals.

SCHLINK, HENRY A., B.Sc., M.D., 10208 Euclid Avenue, Cleveland, Ohio. University of Michigan Medical School, 1913. Member of Staff, Emergency Hospital.

SCHLUETER, ROBERT ERNST, Phar.G., M.D., 514 Metropolitan Building, St. Louis, Missouri. Washington University Medical School (Missouri Medical College), 1895. Surgeon, Lutheran and St. Louis Mullanphy Hospitals; Consulting Surgeon, St. John's and St. Anthony's Hospitals.

SCHMIDT, LAWRENCE MAURICE, M.D., Medical Corps, United States Navy, Washington, District of Columbia. University of Illinois College of Medicine (College of Physicians and Surgeons, Chicago), 1906. Lieutenant Commander, Medical Corps, United States Navy.

SCHMIDT, LOUIS E., Phar.G., M.Sc., M.D., 60 Bellevue Place, Chicago, Illinois. Northwestern University Medical School, 1895. Professor of Genito-Urinary Surgery, Northwestern University Medical School; Professor of Genito-Urinary Diseases, Chicago Policlinic; Chief of Department of Genito-Urinary, Venereal, and Skin Diseases, Alexian Brothers' Hospital; Attending Genito-Urinary Surgeon, Michael Reese, Grant, Wesley Memorial, and St. Mary of Nazareth Hospitals.

SCHMITT, AARON FRANKLIN, M.D., 645 South Fourth Street, Mankato, Minnesota. Rush Medical College, 1902. Surgeon, Immanuel and St. Joseph's Hospitals.

SCHMITT, SAMUEL C., M.D., 705 Physicians and Surgeons Building, Minneapolis, Minnesota. Rush Medical College, 1901. Surgeon, St. Barnabas' Hospital.

SCHMITZ, HENRY, A.M., M.D., LL.D., 25 East Washington Street, Chicago, Illinois. Loyola University School of Medicine (Bennett Medical College), 1897. Professor of Gynecology and Head of the Department, Loyola University School of Medicine; Surgeon, St. Mary of Nazareth Hospital;

Attending Gynecologist, Cook County Hospital; Consulting Gynecologist, Misericordia Hospital.

SCHNEIDEMAN, THEODORE B., A.B., M.D., 1831 Chestnut Street, Philadelphia, Pennsylvania. Jefferson Medical College, 1883. Consulting Ophthalmologist, Woman's Hospital.

SCHOEMAKER, JAN, M.D., Quidwal 83, The Hague, Holland. University of Leyden, 1896. Chief Surgeon, City Hospital of The Hague.

SCHOENBERG, A. JOHN, M.D., 747 Fullerton Avenue, Chicago, Illinois. University of Illinois College of Medicine (College of Physicians and Surgeons), 1899. Associate Gynecologist, University of Illinois College of Medicine; Surgeon, Evangelical Deaconess Hospital.

SCHOENBERG, HERMAN BERNARD, M.D., 490 West End Avenue, New York, New York. University and Bellevue Hospital Medical College, 1912. Lecturer on Gynecology and Demonstrator in Operative Gynecology on the Cadaver, New York Polyclinic Hospital; Assistant Gynecologist, Out-Patient Department, Woman's and Beth Israel Hospitals; Attending Surgeon, Hebrew National Orphan Asylum and Kohler Industries.

SCHOFF, CHARLES H., B.Sc., M.D., 7 West Washington Street, Media, Pennsylvania. University of Pennsylvania School of Medicine, 1893. Surgeon, Media Hospital, Williamson's Free School of Mechanical Trades, Media, Pennsylvania Training School for Feeble-Minded Children, Elwyn.

SCHOOLFIELD, GEORGE CLARENCE, M.D., Morrison Building, Charleston, West Virginia. University of Cincinnati College of Medicine (Medical College of Ohio), 1891. Surgeon, Charleston General Hospital; Consulting Surgeon, McMillan and Kanawha Valley Hospitals.

SCHREINER, EDWARD R., B.Sc., M.D., Medical Corps, United States Army, Washington, District of Columbia. University of Pennsylvania School of Medicine, 1895. Colonel, Medical Corps, United States Army.

SCHREINER, BERNARD FRANCIS, M.D., 231 Humboldt Parkway, Buffalo, New York. University of Buffalo, Department of Medicine, 1909. Instructor in Surgery, University of Buffalo, Department of Medicine; Assistant Surgeon, Buffalo General Hospital; Associate Surgeon, Buffalo City Hospital; Surgeon, State Institute for the Study of Malignant Diseases.

SCHROEDER, WILLIAM E., M.D., Wesley Memorial Hospital, Chicago, Illinois. Northwestern University Medical School (Chicago Medical College), 1891. Senior Surgeon, Wesley Memorial Hospital; Surgeon, Illinois Central and Evangelical Deaconess Hospitals.

SCHUFFELL, HARRY M., B.Sc., Phar.G., M.D., 205 Fifteenth Street, Northwest, Canton, Ohio. Western Reserve University School of Medicine, 1893. President of Staff and Surgeon-in-Chief, Mercy Hospital.

SCHULDT, FREDERICK C., M.D., 1137 Lowry Building, St. Paul, Minnesota. University of Minnesota Medical School, 1903. Member of Surgical Staff, St. Joseph's Hospital.

SCHUMANN, EDWARD ARMIN, A.B., M.D., 124 South Eighteenth Street, Philadelphia, Pennsylvania. University of Pennsylvania School of Medicine, 1901. Lecturer on Obstetrics, Jefferson Medical College; Obstetrician and Gynecologist, Philadelphia General Hospital; Gynecologist, Frankford Hospital; Consulting Gynecologist, Rush Hospital; Assistant Obstetrician Jefferson Maternity Hospital.

SCHURMEIER, FREDERICK CONRAD, M.Sc., M.D., 820 Spring Street, Elgin, Illinois. Rush Medical College, 1902. Attending Surgeon, Sherman and St. Joseph's Hospitals.

SCHWARTZ, LEO SAMSON, Phar.G., M.D., 849 Park Place, Brooklyn, New York. Cornell University Medical College, 1908. Associate Gynecologist, Jewish Hospital.

SCHWARTZ, WILLIAM A., B.Sc., M.D., 207 Goodrich Building, Phoenix, Arizona. Northwestern University Medical School, 1911. Assistant Surgeon, Santa Fe Coast Lines Hospital.

SCHWARZ, HENRY, M.D., 440 North Newstead Avenue, St. Louis, Missouri. Washington University Medical School (St. Louis Medical College), 1879; University of Giessen, 1880. Emeritus Professor of Obstetrics and Gynecology, Washington University Medical School; Consulting Obstetrician, Barnes Hospital.

SCHWEINITZ, GEORGE E. DE, A.M., M.D., LL.D., L.H.D., 1705 Walnut Street, Philadelphia, Pennsylvania. University of Pennsylvania School of Medicine, 1881. Professor of Ophthalmology, University of Pennsylvania School of Medicine; Ophthalmic Surgeon, Hospital of the University of Pennsylvania; Consulting Ophthalmic Surgeon, Philadelphia General Hospital, Philadelphia Orthopedic Hospital and Infirmary for Nervous Diseases, Philadelphia, Bryn Mawr Hospital, Bryn Mawr.

SCHWENK, PETER N. K., B.Sc., A.M., M.D., 1417 North Broad Street, Philadelphia, Pennsylvania. University of Pennsylvania School of Medicine, 1882. Surgeon, Wills Eye Hospital.

SCHWINN, JACOB, M.D., 56 Fourteenth Street, Wheeling, West Virginia. University of Berne, 1883. Visiting Surgeon, Ohio Valley General Hospital.

SCHWYZER, ARNOLD, M.D., 123 West Seventh Street, St. Paul, Minnesota. University of Zurich, 1888. Surgeon, St. Joseph's Hospital.

SCHWYZER, GUSTAV, M.D., 410 Donaldson Building, Minneapolis, Minnesota. University of Zurich, 1892. Surgeon, Northwestern Hospital.

SCOFIELD, CHARLES EDWARD, M.D., 880 Park Place, Brooklyn, New York. Columbia University, College of Physicians and Surgeons, 1899. Surgeon, Brooklyn Eye and Ear Hospital; Consulting Laryngologist and Rhinologist, Bushwick and East Brooklyn Dispensary; Otologist and Laryngologist, Eastern District Industrial School.

SCOTT, ARTHUR CARROLL, M.D., 6 West French Avenue, Temple, Texas. University and Bellevue Hospital Medical College, 1886. Senior Surgeon, Temple Sanitarium; Chief Surgeon, Gulf, Colorado and Santa Fe Railway.

SCOTT, CHARLES MATTHEW, M.D., 53 Bland Street, Bluefield, West Virginia. Medical College of Virginia (University College of Medicine), 1901. Chief Surgeon, St. Luke's Hospital.

SCOTT, GARLAND DIX, M.D., Sherman Building, Sullivan, Indiana. Rush Medical College, 1908. Surgeon, Sullivan County Hospital.

SCOTT, JAMES FREDERICK, M.D., C.M., 216 Miller Building, Yakima, Washington. Faculty of Medicine, McGill University, 1899.

SCOTT, MICHAEL JAMES, Phar.G., M.D., 313 Daly Bank Building, Butte, Montana. Creighton College of Medicine, 1903. Chief of Staff and Chief Surgeon, St. James Hospital.

SCOTT, N. STONE, A.M., M.D., 10111 Euclid Avenue, Cleveland, Ohio. Western Reserve University School of Medicine, 1889.

SCOTT, RAYMOND G., M.D., 216 Third Street, Geneva, Illinois. Rush Medical College, 1897. Surgeon, Colonial Hospital; District Surgeon, Chicago and Northwestern Railroad; Consulting Surgeon, Illinois State Training School for Girls, Geneva, St. Charles School for Boys, St. Charles.

SCOTT, WALLACE ARTHUR, C.M.G., A.B., M.B., F.R.C.S. (Eng.), 627 Sherbourne Street, Toronto, Ontario. University of Toronto, Faculty of Medicine, 1898. Associate in Surgery and Demonstrator of Anatomy, University of Toronto, Faculty of Medicine; Assistant Surgeon, St. Michael's Hospital.

SCOTT, WALTER FRANCIS, M.D., 1301 Empire Building, Birmingham, Alabama. University of Virginia, Department of Medicine, 1904. Associate Professor and Instructor in Genito-Urinary Surgery, Graduate School of Medicine of the University of Alabama; Member of Staff, St. Vincent's and Hillman Hospitals.

SCOTT, WILLIAM ALBERT, A.B., M.B., 75 Bloor Street, East, Toronto, Ontario. University of Toronto, Faculty of Medicine, 1913. Demonstrator of Obstetrics and Gynecology, University of Toronto, Faculty of Medicine; Junior Assistant in Obstetrics and Gynecology, Toronto General Hospital; Gynecologist, St. John's Hospital.

SCRIMGER, FRANCIS A. C., B.A., M.D., C.M., 154 Metcalfe Street, Montreal, Quebec. Faculty of Medicine, McGill University, 1905. Lecturer on Surgery and Clinical Surgery, Faculty of Medicine, McGill University; Assistant Surgeon, Royal Victoria Hospital.

SCROGGY, JOHN QUINCY ADAMS, Ph.G., M.D., 204 Atlantic Avenue, Kerrobert, Saskatchewan. Northwestern University Medical School, 1905. Chief Surgeon, Kerrobert and Dodsland Hospitals.

SCUDDER, CHARLES LOCKE, A.B., Ph.B., M.D., 144 Commonwealth Avenue, Boston, Massachusetts. Harvard Medical School, 1888. Consulting Surgeon, Massachusetts General Hospital, Boston, Burbank Hospital, Fitchburg, Melrose Hospital, Melrose, Addison Gilbert Hospital, Gloucester, Leonard Morse Hospital, Natick, Milford Hospital, Milford.

SEABORN, EDWIN, M.D., 469 Clarence Street, London, Ontario. Western University Medical School, 1895. Surgeon, Victoria General Hospital; Lieutenant Colonel, Medical Corps, Canadian Army.

SEAMAN, GILBERT E., M.D., 141 Wisconsin Street, Milwaukee, Wisconsin. Michigan College of Medicine and Surgery, 1889. Regent, University of Wisconsin; Ophthalmic Surgeon, Milwaukee and Milwaukee Children's Hospitals; Chief Surgeon, Wisconsin National Guard.

SEARLE, MARCUS FOWLER, M.D., 34 Plaza Street, Brooklyn, New York. Cleveland Homeopathic Medical College, 1909; New York Homeopathic Medical School and Flower Hospital, 1911. Visiting Gynecologist, Cumberland Street Hospital; Chief Surgeon, Samaritan Hospital; Visiting Surgeon, Prospect Heights Hospital.

SEAVER, EDWIN PLINY, JR., M.D., 271 Union Street, New Bedford, Massachusetts. Harvard Medical School, 1905. Rhinologist and Laryngologist, St. Luke's Hospital.

SECOR, WILLIAM LEE, B.Sc., A.M., M.D., Kerrville, Texas. Jefferson Medical College, 1906. Chief of Staff, Kerrville Sanitarium-Hospital.

SECORD, EDWARD REGINALD, M.D., C.M., 112 Market Street, Brantford, Ontario. Faculty of Medicine, McGill University, 1900. Surgeon, Brantford General Hospital.

SEDGLEY, FRANK ROBERT, M.D., Fox Hills, Staten Island, New York. Boston University School of Medicine, 1902. Surgeon, United States Public Health Service Hospital No. 61.

SEDWICK, WILLIAM ALEXANDER, M.D., 764 Metropolitan Building, Denver, Colorado. University of Maryland School of Medicine, 1893. Instructor in Ophthalmology, University of Colorado School of Medicine; Ophthalmologist, Children's Hospital, National Jewish Hospital for Consumptives, Bethesda and Lutheran Sanatoriums.

SEEGAR, J. K. B. E., M.D., 904 North Charles Street, Baltimore, Maryland. University of Maryland School of Medicine (Baltimore Medical College), 1900. Associate Professor of Obstetrics, University of Maryland School of Medicine and College of Physicians and Surgeons; Gynecologist, St. Agnes' Hospital; Associate in Gynecology, Maryland General Hospital.

SEEGER, STANLEY JOSEPH, M.D., 809 Wells Building, Milwaukee, Wisconsin. Northwestern University Medical School, 1911. Attending Surgeon, Milwaukee, Milwaukee Children's and Johnston Emergency Hospitals.

SEELEY, OSCAR, M.D., 2009 Chestnut Street, Philadelphia, Pennsylvania. Hahnemann Medical College and Hospital, Philadelphia, 1904. Associate Professor of Rhinology and Laryngology, Hahnemann Medical College and Hospital; Laryngologist and Otologist, Woman's Southern Homeopathic and Children's Homeopathic Hospitals, Friends' Home for Children; Assistant Laryngologist, Hahnemann Medical College and Hospital.

SEELEY, WARD F., A.B., M.D., 1807 David Whitney Building, Detroit, Michigan. University of Michigan Medical School, 1911. Junior Gynecologist,

Harper Hospital; Attending Gynecologist and Obstetrician, Woman's Hospital and Infant's Home; Associate Gynecologist and Obstetrician, Detroit Receiving Hospital.

SEELIG, MAJOR G., A.B., M.D., University Club Building, St. Louis, Missouri. Columbia University, College of Physicians and Surgeons, 1900. Professor of Clinical Surgery, Washington University School of Medicine; Attending Surgeon, Jewish Hospital; Chief of Surgical Out-Patient Department, Jewish Hospital.

SEELIGMANN, GUSTAV, M.D., 33 East Seventy-second Street, New York, New York. University of Freiburg, 1887. Attending Gynecologist, Lenox Hill Hospital and Dispensary, Lebanon Hospital.

SEELYE, RALPH H., A.M., M.D., 73 Chestnut Street, Springfield, Massachusetts. Harvard Medical School, 1889. Surgeon, Springfield Hospital.

SEELYE, WALTER CLARK, A.B., M.D., 390 Main Street, Worcester, Massachusetts. Harvard Medical School, 1900. Visiting Surgeon, Memorial Hospital.

SEELYE, WALTER KARL, M.D., 806 American Bank Building, Seattle, Washington. State University of Iowa College of Medicine, 1892. Member of Advisory Staff, Seattle General Hospital.

SEFF, ISADORE, M.D., 252 West Eighty-fifth Street, New York, New York. Columbia University, College of Physicians and Surgeons, 1902. Adjunct Attending Surgeon, Beth Israel Hospital; Adjunct Attending Genito-Urinary Surgeon, Sydenham Hospital.

SEIBERT, EDWARD GRANT, Ph.G., M.D., 1545 I Street, Washington, District of Columbia. George Washington University Medical School (Medical Department of Columbian College), 1893. Clinical Instructor, George Washington University Medical School; Associate Ophthalmologist and Oto-Laryngologist, George Washington Hospital; Chief of Department, of Oto-Laryngology, Out-Door Service; Assistant Surgeon, Dispensary Staff and Episcopal Eye, Ear, and Throat Hospital.

SEIDLER, VICTOR BAYARD, B.Sc., M.D., 16 Plymouth Street, Montclair, New Jersey. Columbia University, College of Physicians and Surgeons, 1912. Surgeon, Mountainside Hospital and Children's Home, Montclair, Fresh Air and Convalescent Home, Verona.

SEIFERT, MATHIAS J., A.B., M.D., 30 North Michigan Avenue, Chicago, Illinois. University of Illinois College of Medicine (College of Physicians and Surgeons, Chicago), 1901. Lecturer on Gynecology and Surgeon, Columbus and St. Mary of Nazareth Hospitals.

SELBY, CLARENCE D., M.D., 659 Spitzer Building, Toledo, Ohio. Western Reserve University School of Medicine, 1902. Chief of Staff, St. Vincent's Hospital; Member of Surgical Staff, St. Vincent's and Flower Hospitals.

SELDON, GEORGE ELLIOTT, M.D., C.M., M.R.C.S. (Eng.), 736 Granville Street, Vancouver, British Columbia. University of Toronto, Faculty of Medicine, 1905. Surgeon, Vancouver General Hospital.

SELLENINGS, ALBERT EUGENE, Ph.B., M.D., 132 East Thirty-sixth Street, New York, New York. University and Bellevue Hospital Medical College, 1899. Director of Surgery, Gouverneur Hospital, New York; Consulting Surgeon, Jamaica Hospital, Jamaica.

SELLERS, FRANK E., M.D., Medical Corps, United States Navy, Washington, District of Columbia. University of Virginia Department of Medicine, 1901. Commander, Medical Corps, United States Navy.

SELLERS, THOMAS BENTON, Ph.D., M.D., 108 Baronne Street, New Orleans, Louisiana. Tulane University of Louisiana, 1913. Clinical Assistant and Lecturer, Gynecological and Obstetrical Division, Tulane Post-Graduate School of Medicine; Visiting Assistant Gynecologist, Charity Hospital.

SELMAN, WILLIAM ARTHUR, B.Sc., M.D., 604 Candler Building, Atlanta, Georgia. Emory University School of Medicine (Atlanta College of Physicians and Surgeons), 1902. Associate Professor of Surgery, Emory University School of Medicine; Visiting Surgeon, Georgia Baptist and Spelman Hospitals; Assistant Visiting Surgeon, Grady Memorial Hospital.

SEMKEN, GEORGE H., M.D., 16 West Eighty-fifth Street, New York, New York. Columbia University, College of Physicians and Surgeons, 1896. Attending Surgeon, New York Skin and Cancer Hospital; Associate Attending Surgeon, Lenox Hill Hospital and Dispensary; Consulting Surgeon, Crocker Institute for Cancer.

SEMMES, RAPHAEL EUSTACE, A.B., M.D., 1250 Bank of Commerce Building, Memphis, Tennessee. Johns Hopkins University, Medical Department, 1910. Assistant Professor of Surgery, University of Tennessee College of Medicine; Visiting Surgeon, Memphis General Hospital.

SENGER, WILLIAM, A.B., M.D., Minnequa Hospital, Pueblo, Colorado. Yale University School of Medicine, 1901. Assistant Chief Surgeon, Colorado Fuel and Iron Company.

SENN, WILLIAM N., M.D., 25 East Washington Street, Chicago, Illinois. Rush Medical College, 1900.

SENSENEY, EUGENE TOWNER, A.B., M.D., 308 Lister Building, St. Louis, Missouri. Washington University Medical School, 1905. Assistant Professor of Laryngology, St. Louis University School of Medicine; Member of Staff, St. Luke's and St. Louis City Hospitals; Associate Laryngologist, Jewish Hospital; Consultant, St. Louis Maternity and St. John's Hospitals; Aurist, Missouri School for the Blind.

SEPULVEDA, P. SILVANO, M.D., Plaza Anibal Pinto 371, Valparaiso, Chile. School of Medicine of Santiago, 1898.

SESSIONS, RICHARD DUNCKLEY, M.D., 305 Franklin Street, Natchez, Mississippi. Tulane University of Louisiana School of Medicine, 1892. Visiting Surgeon, Natchez Sanatorium and Hospital; Chief Surgeon, Natchez and Southern Railway; District Surgeon, Yazoo and Mississippi Valley Railway; Local Surgeon, Mississippi Central Railway.

SEXSMITH, GEORGE H., M.D., 719 Avenue C, Bayonne, New Jersey. Columbia University, College of Physicians and Surgeons, 1890. Attending Surgeon and Orthopedist, Bayonne Hospital.

SEYBOLD, GEORGE ARTHUR, M.D., 604 Peoples National Bank Building, Jackson, Michigan. University of Michigan Medical School, 1904. Surgeon, W. A. Foote Memorial and Mercy Hospitals, Michigan Central Railway.

SEYDELL, ERNEST MORRIS, M.D., 201 North Main Street, Wichita, Kansas. Northwestern University Medical School, 1909. Oto-Laryngologist, St. Francis' Hospital.

SEYMOUR, JAMES HARVEY, M.D., 502 Brockman Building, Los Angeles, California. Columbia University, College of Physicians and Surgeons, 1883. Professor of Surgery, College of Medical Evangelists; Visiting Surgeon, Los Angeles County Hospital.

SEYMOUR, WILLIAM J., M.D., 2506 Park Boulevard, Detroit, Michigan. Detroit College of Medicine and Surgery, 1903. Professor of Experimental Surgery and Associate Professor of Surgery, Detroit College of Medicine and Surgery; Visiting Surgeon, St. Mary's and Providence Hospitals; Consulting Surgeon, Wayne County Home.

SHAFER, HOWARD O., M.D., Rochester, Indiana. University of Illinois College of Medicine (College of Physicians and Surgeons, Chicago), 1902. Associate Professor of Gynecology, Chicago Policlinic, Chicago; Surgeon, Woodlawn Hospital, Rochester; Attending Surgeon, Henrotin Memorial Hospital, Chicago.

SHAFF, CHARLES WHITING, B.Sc., M.D., 212 Fifth Street, Lewiston, Idaho. State University of Iowa College of Medicine, 1881. Surgeon, St. Joseph's Hospital.

SHAFFER, NEWTON MELMAN, M.D., 31 East Forty-ninth Street, New York, New York. University and Bellevue Hospital Medical College (University of the City of New York, Medical Department), 1867. Emeritus Professor of Orthopedic Surgery, Cornell University Medical College; Consulting Orthopedic Surgeon, St. Luke's and Presbyterian Hospitals; Founder and Consulting Surgeon, New York State Hospital for Crippled and Deformed Children, West Haverstraw.

SHAHAN, WILLIAM EWING, A.B., M.D., A.M., 520 Metropolitan Building, St. Louis, Missouri. Washington University Medical School, 1904. Professor of Clinical Ophthalmology, Washington University Medical School; Member of Staff, St. Luke's, Barnard Free Skin and Cancer, and Barnes Hospitals.

SHALEY, FREDERICK WILLIAM, A.B., M.D., Swope Block, Terre Haute, Indiana. Rush Medical College, 1884. Surgeon, St. Anthony's Hospital.

SHALLCROSS, ISAAC GRAY, M.D., 112 South Twentieth Street, Philadelphia, Pennsylvania. Hahnemann Medical College and Hospital, Philadelphia, 1887. Professor of Rhinology and Laryngology and Laryngologist,

Hahnemann Medical College and Hospital; Ophthalmologist, St. Luke's Homeopathic Hospital; Consulting Laryngologist, Homeopathic State Hospital, Allentown.

SHALLENBERGER, WILLIAM F., A.B., A.M., M.D., 820 Hurt Building, Atlanta, Georgia. Johns Hopkins University, Medical Department, 1907. Associate Professor of Gynecology, Emory University School of Medicine; Visiting Gynecologist, Wesley Memorial and Grady Hospitals.

SHAMBAUGH, GEORGE ELMER, Ph.B., M.D., 122 South Michigan Avenue, Chicago, Illinois. University of Pennsylvania School of Medicine, 1895. Professor of Otology and Laryngology, Rush Medical College; Oto-Laryngologist, Presbyterian Hospital.

SHANDS, AURELIUS RIVES, M.D., 901 Sixteenth Street, Northwest, Washington, District of Columbia. University of Maryland School of Medicine, 1884. Professor of Orthopedic Surgery, George Washington University Medical School; Orthopedic Surgeon, George Washington University Hospital, Central Dispensary and Emergency Hospital.

SHANDS, HARLEY R., A.B., M.D., Century Building, Jackson, Mississippi. Tulane University of Louisiana School of Medicine, 1905. Visiting Surgeon, Baptist Hospital.

SHANGLE, MILTON A., M.D., 34 Prince Street, Elizabeth, New Jersey. Columbia University, College of Physicians and Surgeons, 1900. Attending Surgeon, Elizabeth General and St. Elizabeth's Hospitals.

SHANKLIN, ELDRIDGE MADISON, M.D., 575 Hohman Street, Hammond, Indiana. Indiana University School of Medicine (Medical College of Indiana), 1902. Ophthalmologist and Oto-Laryngologist, St. Margaret's Hospital.

SHANNON, EDWIN RAYMOND, M.D., Black Hawk Bank Building, Waterloo, Iowa. Hahnemann Medical College and Hospital, Chicago, 1896. Surgeon, Presbyterian Hospital; Consulting Surgeon, St. Francis Hospital.

SHANNON, JOHN ROWLANDS, A.B., M.D., C.M., 17 East Thirty-eighth Street, New York, New York. Queen's University, Faculty of Medicine, 1890. Surgeon, Manhattan Eye, Ear, and Throat Hospital; Consulting Ophthalmologist, United Hospital, Port Chester.

SHANNON, WILLIAM A., M.D., C.M., Cobb Building, Seattle, Washington. University of Toronto, Faculty of Medicine, 1887. Member of Staff, Columbus Sanitarium.

SHAPLEIGH, JOHN B., A.B., M.D., Humboldt Building, St. Louis, Missouri. Washington University Medical School (St. Louis Medical College), 1881. Clinical Professor of Otology, Washington University Medical School; Otologist, St. Luke's, St. Louis Children's, and Barnes Hospitals, Washington University Dispensary; Consulting Aurist, Barnard Free Skin and Cancer Hospital.

SHARBER, ALPHEUS LESLIE, M.D., 301 Jackson Building, Nashville, Tennessee. University of Tennessee College of Medicine, 1904. Surgeon, Nashville Protestant Hospital.

SHARPE, NORVELLE WALLACE, M.D., 3520 Lucas Avenue, St. Louis, Missouri. St. Louis University School of Medicine (Beaumont Hospital Medical College), 1890. Instructor in Surgery, St. Louis University School of Medicine; Consulting Surgeon, Home of the Friendless; Surgeon, Chicago, Rock Island and Pacific Railway.

SHARPLES, CASPAR WISTAR, A.B., M.D., Burke Building, Seattle, Washington. University of Pennsylvania School of Medicine, 1888. Surgeon, Children's Orthopedic Hospital.

SHARRETT, GEORGE OLIVER, M.D., 45 Bedford Street, Cumberland, Maryland. University of Maryland School of Medicine (Baltimore Medical School), 1908. Oto-Laryngologist and Oculist, Western Maryland and Allegany Hospitals, Cumberland; Consulting Oculist and Oto-Laryngologist, Miner's Hospital, Frostburg.

SHASTID, THOMAS HALL, A.M., LL.B., M.D., 400 Lyceum Building, Duluth Minnesota. University of Vermont College of Medicine, 1888.

SHAW, ELLSWORTH E., M.D., 713 Baker Building, Walla Walla, Washington. Dartmouth Medical School, 1884. Member of Staff, St. Mary's Hospital.

SHAW, HARRY ALEXANDER, M.D., Arcade Building, Seattle, Washington. University of Kansas School of Medicine (Kansas Medical College), 1900. Member of Staff, Providence Hospital.

SHAW, HENRY ALDEN, M.D., Medical Corps, United States Army, Washington, District of Columbia. Harvard Medical School, 1889. Colonel, Medical Corps, United States Army.

SHAW, HENRY NEWTON, A.B., M.D., 901 Pacific Mutual Building, Los Angeles, California. Johns Hopkins University, Medical Department, 1913.

SHAW, JOSEPH HUGHES, A.B., M.D., 213 Exchange Place, Santa Rosa, California. University of Cincinnati College of Medicine (Medical College of Ohio), 1908.

SHAW, WILLIAM FREDERICK, M.D., Chuquicamata, Chile. Detroit College of Medicine and Surgery, 1900.

SHAWAN, HAROLD K., A.B., M.D., 1701 David Whitney Building, Detroit, Michigan. Western Reserve University School of Medicine, 1909. Assistant Professor of Clinical Surgery, Detroit College of Medicine and Surgery; Assistant Surgeon, Grace Hospital; Attending Surgeon, Detroit Receiving Hospital.

SHEA, AUGUSTUS W., M.D., 266 Main Street, Nashua, New Hampshire. University of Vermont College of Medicine, 1887. Member of Staff, St. Joseph's and Nashua Memorial Hospitals; Surgeon, Boston and Maine Railroad.

SHEA, JOHN FRANCIS, M.D., 1254 East Main Street, Bridgeport, Connecticut. University of Maryland School of Medicine (College of Physicians and Surgeons, Baltimore), 1911. Attending Surgeon, Bridgeport Hospital.

SHEAHAN, GEORGE MAURICE, A.B., M.D., 12 School Street, Quincy, Massachusetts. Harvard Medical School, 1907. Visiting Surgeon, Quincy City Hospital; Consulting Surgeon, Norfolk County Hospital.

SHEEHAN, J. EASTMAN, M.D., 24 East Forty-eighth Street, New York, New York. Yale University School of Medicine, 1908. Associate Laryngologist, New York Post-Graduate Medical School and Hospital; Plastic Surgeon, Public Health Service, No. 50; Surgeon in Charge, Nose and Throat Clinic, New York Post-Graduate Hospital; Associate Surgeon, Washington Square Hospital.

SHELDON, LUTHER, JR., A.B., M.D., Medical Corps, United States Navy, Washington, District of Columbia. University of Michigan Medical School, 1909. Lieutenant Commander, Medical Corps, United States Navy.

SHELDON, STUART HARRIS, B.Sc., M.D., 1111 Selling Building, Portland, Oregon. Rush Medical College, 1902. Member of Surgical Staff, University of Oregon Medical School; Member of Staff, Emanuel Hospital.

SHELLMAN, JOHN L., M.D., Hamm Building, St. Paul, Minnesota. University of Minnesota Medical School, 1903. Member of Staff, Charles T. Miller, St. Luke's, City and County Hospitals.

SHELMIRE, JESSE BEDFORD, A.B., M.D., Southwestern Life Building, Dallas, Texas. Tulane University of Louisiana School of Medicine, 1883. Professor of Dermatology, Baylor University School of Medicine.

SHENSTONE, NORMAN STRAHAN, A.B., M.D., M.R.C.S. (Eng.), L.R.C.P. (Lond.), 196 Bloor Street, West, Toronto, Ontario. Columbia University, College of Physicians and Surgeons, 1905. Demonstrator of Surgery, University of Toronto, Faculty of Medicine; Senior Assistant Surgeon, Toronto General Hospital; Surgeon, St. John's Hospital.

SHEPARD, CASSIUS M., A.M., M.D., 347 East State Street, Columbus, Ohio. Jefferson Medical College, 1899. Instructor in Orthopedics, Ohio State University College of Medicine; Orthopedic Surgeon, Grant, St. Francis, and Franklin County Tuberculosis Hospitals, Columbus, Ohio Soldiers' and Sailors' Orphans' Home, Xenia.

SHEPARD, GEORGE ANDREW, M.D., 204 West Fifty-fifth Street, New York, New York. Jefferson Medical College, 1888; Hahnemann Medical College and Hospital, Philadelphia, 1889. Surgeon, New York Ophthalmic Hospital; Aurist, Hahnemann Hospital.

SHEPARD, JOHN L., B.L., M.D., Medical Corps, United States Army, Washington, District of Columbia. Rush Medical College, 1893. Colonel, Medical Corps, United States Army.

SHEPHERD, FRANCIS JOHN, M.D., LL.D., F.R.C.S. (Eng., Edin.), 152 Mansfield Street, Montreal, Quebec. Faculty of Medicine, McGill University, 1873. Emeritus Professor, Faculty of Medicine, McGill University; Consulting Surgeon, Montreal General and Royal Victoria Hospitals.

SHEPLER, ROBERT MCMURRAN, M.D., 49 West Pomfret Street, Carlisle, Pennsylvania. Jefferson Medical College, 1902. Chief Surgeon and Pathologist, Carlisle Hospital; Surgeon, Sarah Todd Memorial Home and Pacific Railway.

SHERBONDY, JAMES A., M.D., 415 Bryson Street, Youngstown Ohio. Western Reserve University School of Medicine, 1902. Visiting Surgeon, Youngstown Hospital.

SHERE, OSCAR MAURICE, M.D., 610 Metropolitan Building, Denver, Colorado. University of Colorado School of Medicine (Gross Medical College), 1902. Instructor in Surgery, University of Colorado School of Medicine; Chief of Clinical Staff in Surgery, Dispensary of the University of Colorado School of Medicine; Surgeon, City and County Hospital, Denver, Sanatorium of the Jewish Consumptives' Relief Society, Edgewater, Denver and Rio Grande Railroad.

SHERER, JOSEPH WHITMAN, M.D., 1232 Rialto Building, Kansas City, Missouri. State University of Iowa College of Medicine, 1894; University of Pennsylvania School of Medicine, 1895.

SHERK, HENRY HOWARD, M.D., 268 South Orange Grove Avenue, Pasadena, California. Jefferson Medical College, 1887. Surgeon, Pasadena Hospital; Consulting Surgeon, Children's Hospital, Los Angeles; Attending Surgeon, La Vina Sanitarium for the Tubercular.

SHERMAN, ELBERT S., M.D., 671 Broad Street, Newark, New Jersey. University of Pennsylvania School of Medicine, 1897. Attending Surgeon, Newark Eye and Ear Infirmary; Attending Ophthalmologist, Babies' Hospital, Newark, Home for Disabled Soldiers, Kearny; Consulting Ophthalmologist, St. Mary's Hospital, Orange, Stumpf Memorial Hospital, Kearny, Essex County Hospital for Insane, Cedar Grove, Newark Maternity and Presbyterian Hospitals, Newark, Essex County Hospital for Contagious Diseases, Belleville.

SHERMAN, WILLIAM O'NEILL, M.D., 434 Fifth Avenue, Pittsburgh, Pennsylvania. University of Pennsylvania School of Medicine, 1901. Surgeon, St. Francis Hospital; Chief Surgeon, Carnegie Steel Company.

SHERRILL, J. GARLAND, A.M., M.D., 308 Masonic Building, Louisville, Kentucky. University of Louisville, Medical Department (Louisville Medical College), 1888. Professor of Surgery, University of Louisville, Medical Department; Visiting Surgeon, Louisville Public and SS. Mary and Elizabeth Hospitals, John N. Norton Memorial Infirmary.

SHERWOOD, MARCEL WESLEY, M.D., 704 South Third Street, Temple, Texas. University and Bellevue Hospital Medical College, 1906. Surgeon, Temple Sanitarium; Assistant Chief Surgeon, Gulf, Colorado and Santa Fe Railway Hospital Association.

SHERWOOD, WALTER AIKMAN, M.D., D.Sc., 145 Gates Avenue, Brooklyn, New York. Columbia University, College of Physicians and Surgeons, 1896. Surgeon, Brooklyn Hospital; Consulting Surgeon, Eastern Long Island Hospital.

SHIFFERT, HERBERT O., M.D., Medical Corps, United States Navy, Washington, District of Columbia. Medico-Chirurgical College, Philadelphia, 1899. Captain, Medical Corps, United States Navy.

SHILLINGTON, ADAM TOZELAND, M.D., C.M., 281 Gilmour Street, Ottawa, Ontario. Faculty of Medicine, McGill University, 1894. Gynecologist, St. Luke's General Hospital; Member of Consulting Staff, Ottawa Maternity Hospital.

SHIMONEK, ANTON, M.D., 642 Lowry Building, St. Paul, Minnesota. Rush Medical College, 1879.

SHIMONEK, GODFREY FREDERIC, M.D., 131 Alta Avenue, Yonkers, New York. Rush Medical College, 1873.

SHINE, FRANCIS EPPES, M.D., 1120 Brockman Building, Los Angeles, California. University of Virginia, Department of Medicine, 1895.

SHIPLEY, ARTHUR M., M.D., D.Sc., 1827 Eutaw Place, Baltimore, Maryland. University of Maryland School of Medicine, 1902. Professor of Surgery, University of Maryland School of Medicine and College of Physicians and Surgeons; Surgeon-in-Chief, Bay View Hospital; Visiting Surgeon, University, Women's, and Sydenham Hospitals.

SHIRLEY, JOHN C., M.D., Masonic Temple Building, Huron, South Dakota. Northwestern University Medical School, 1911. Chief Surgeon, Samaritan Hospital.

SHLENKER, MILTON A., M.D., Hotel Marie Antoinette, New York, New York. University of Virginia, Department of Medicine, 1897. Lecturer on Gynecology, New York Polyclinic Medical School; Associate Obstetrician, Gouverneur Hospital; Attending Gynecologist, Berwind Free Outdoor Maternity Clinic.

SHOCKLEY, M. A. W., M.D., Medical Corps, United States Army, Washington, District of Columbia. University of Kansas School of Medicine (Kansas City Medical College), 1898. Lieutenant Colonel, Medical Corps, United States Army.

SHOEMAKER, FERDINAND, M.D., Medical Corps, United States Public Health Service, Washington, District of Columbia. Georgetown University School of Medicine, 1891. Surgeon, Medical Corps, United States Public Health Service.

SHOEMAKER, GEORGE ERETY, A.B., M.D., 1906 Chestnut Street, Philadelphia, Pennsylvania. University of Pennsylvania School of Medicine, 1882. Gynecologist, Presbyterian Hospital; Consulting Surgeon, Woman's Hospital.

SHOEMAKER, WILLIAM A., M.D., 1006 Carleton Building, St. Louis, Missouri. University of Maryland School of Medicine, 1885. Ophthalmologist, Evangelical Deaconess Hospital, Missouri Baptist Sanitarium; Consulting Ophthalmologist, St. Louis Maternity Hospital.

SHOEMAKER, WILLIAM T., A.M., M.D., 109 South Twentieth Street, Philadelphia, Pennsylvania. University of Pennsylvania School of Medicine,

1891. Professor of Ophthalmology, University of Pennsylvania Graduate School of Medicine; Clinical Professor of Ophthalmology, Woman's Medical College of Pennsylvania; Ophthalmic Surgeon, Lankenau, Germantown, and Pennsylvania Hospitals.

SHOOK, J. RALPH, M.D., Medical Corps, United States Army, Washington, District of Columbia. University of Maryland School of Medicine, 1899. Lieutenant Colonel, Medical Corps, United States Army.

SHORE, FRANCIS E. V., M.D., Citizens National Bank Building, Des Moines, Iowa. University of Michigan Medical School, 1886. Consultant, Mercy Hospital; Oculist, Chicago, Rock Island and Pacific Railroad.

SHORT, ZUBER NATHANIEL, M.D., Dugan-Stuart Building, Hot Springs, Arkansas. Hahnemann Medical College and Hospital, Philadelphia, 1895. Consulting Oculist and Aurist, Leo N. Levi Memorial Hospital.

SHORTAL, WILLIAM WHITE, M.D., Linz Building, Dallas, Texas. Baylor University College of Medicine, 1909. Associate Professor of Applied Anatomy and Dispensary Gynecologist, Baylor University College of Medicine; Junior Associate Surgeon, Baptist Memorial Sanitarium.

SHROPSHIRE, COURTNEY W., M.D., 327 First National Bank Building, Birmingham, Alabama. University of Tennessee College of Medicine (University of Tennessee, Medical Department), 1900. Urologist, Hillman and St. Vincent's Hospitals; Consulting Urologist, Talley Infirmary, Children's and Fraternal Hospitals.

SHUFORD, JACOB HARRISON, A.B., M.D., 1416 Twelfth Street, Hickory, North Carolina. University of Michigan Medical School, 1901. Chief of Staff, Richard Baker Hospital.

SHULIAN, O. FRANK, M.D., 312 Illinois State Bank Building, Quincy, Illinois. University of Illinois College of Medicine (College of Physicians and Surgeons, Chicago), 1905. Member of Surgical Staff, St. Mary's Hospital.

SHUMAKER, DANIEL W., B.Sc., M.D., 200 West Third Street, Dover, Ohio. Ohio State University College of Medicine (Ohio Medical University), 1898. Surgeon, Union Hospital.

SHUPE, THOMAS POLLOCK, A.B., M.D., 93rd Street and Euclid Avenue, Cleveland, Ohio. Western Reserve University School of Medicine, 1911. Instructor in Genito-Urinary Surgery, Western Reserve University School of Medicine; Surgeon in Charge, Genito-Urinary Dispensary, Lakeside Hospital; Assistant Visiting Surgeon, Mt. Sinai Hospital; Visiting Surgeon, Lutheran Hospital.

SHURLY, BURT RUSSELL, B.Sc., M.D., 62 Adams Avenue, West, Detroit, Michigan. Detroit College of Medicine and Surgery, 1895. Professor and Head of Department of Rhinology, Laryngology, and Otology, Detroit College of Medicine and Surgery; Chief of Staff, Detroit Eye, Ear, Nose, and Throat Hospital; Consulting Laryngologist, Harper Hospital; Consulting Laryngologist and Otologist, Woman's Hospital and Infants' Home.

SHUTE, DANIEL KERFOOT, A.B., M.D., 1727 De Sales Street, Washington, District of Columbia. George Washington University Medical School (Columbian University, Medical Department), 1883. Professor of Clinical Ophthalmology, George Washington University Medical School; Ophthalmologist, George Washington University, St. Elizabeth's, Children's, Providence, Central Dispensary and Emergency Hospitals, Columbia Home for Incurables, Washington Hospital for Foundlings, Columbia Institution for Deaf and Dumb.

SHUTT, CLEVELAND H., Phar.G., M.D., Metropolitan Building, St. Louis, Missouri. St. Louis College of Physicians and Surgeons, 1904. Assistant Surgeon, Evangelical Deaconess Hospital; Hospital Commissioner-in-Charge, St. Louis City Institutions.

SICKELS, EDWARD ALLEN, A.M., M.D., 123 East First Street, Dixon, Illinois. Hahnemann Medical College and Hospital, Chicago, 1897. Attending Surgeon, Katherine Shaw Bethea Hospital.

SIDEBOTHAM, HAROLD, M.R.C.S. (Eng.), L.R.C.P. (Lond.), San Marcos Building, Santa Barbara, California. Royal College of Surgeons, England, and Royal College of Physicians, London, 1887.

SIERRA, LUCAS, B.L., M.D., Dieciocho 552, Santiago, Chile. Faculty of Medicine, University of Chile, 1888.

SIEVERS, JOHN R. E., Ph.G., M.D., 75 Owsley Block, Butte, Montana. Northwestern University Medical School, 1893. Attending Surgeon, Butte Deaconess Hospital; Staff Surgeon, St. James Hospital.

SIFTON, HARRY A., M.D., 519 Astor Street, Milwaukee, Wisconsin. University of Michigan Medical School, 1886. Chief of Staff, Milwaukee Hospital; Member of Surgical Staff, Columbia and Children's Free Hospitals; Consulting Surgeon, Johnston Emergency Hospital, Milwaukee, Milwaukee County Hospital, Wauwatosa.

SIGGINS, JAMES B., A.B., M.D., 218 Sycamore Street, Oil City, Pennsylvania. University of Michigan Medical School, 1883. Chief of Surgical Staff, Oil City General Hospital.

SIHLER, WILLIAM FREDERICK, M.D., C.M., 301 Fourth Street, Devils Lake, North Dakota. Faculty of Medicine, McGill University, 1898. Chief Surgeon, Devils Lake General Hospital.

SILER, JOSEPH FRANKLIN, M.D., Medical Corps, United States Army, Washington, District of Columbia. University of Virginia, Department of Medicine, 1898. Lieutenant Colonel, Medical Corps, United States Army.

SILLECK, WALTER MANDEVILLE, B.Sc., M.D., 445 Park Avenue, New York, New York. Columbia University College of Physicians and Surgeons, 1908. Associate Professor of Surgery, New York Post-Graduate Medical School; Associate Surgeon, New York Post-Graduate Hospital; Assistant Surgeon, Harlem Hospital.

SILVER, DAVID, M.D., Jenkins Arcade Building, Pittsburgh, Pennsylvania. Harvard Medical School, 1899. Professor of Orthopedic Surgery, University of Pittsburgh School of Medicine; Orthopedic Surgeon, Allegheny General and Children's Hospitals, Pittsburgh, Watson Home for Crippled Children, Leetsdale.

SILVER, HENRY MANN, A.M., M.D., 276 Madison Avenue, New York, New York. University and Bellevue Hospital Medical College (Bellevue Hospital Medical College), 1875. Consulting Surgeon, Gouverneur and New York Skin and Cancer Hospitals, New York Infirmary for Women and Children.

SILVERTHORN, GIDEON, M.B., M.D., 34 North Sherbourne Street, Toronto, Ontario. University of Toronto, Faculty of Medicine, 1889. Professor of Medical Jurisprudence, Associate in Surgery and Clinical Surgery, University of Toronto, Faculty of Medicine; Assistant Surgeon, St. Michael's Hospital.

SIMANEK, GEORGE F., M.D., 1262 South Thirteenth Street, Omaha, Nebraska. John A. Creighton Medical College, 1903. Professor of Surgery and Chief of Surgical Staff, John A. Creighton Medical College; Director, Chief of Surgical Staff, and Attending Surgeon, St. Joseph's Hospital.

SIMMONS, CHANNING CHAMBERLAIN, M.D., 317 Marlborough Street, Boston, Massachusetts. Harvard Medical School, 1899. Instructor in Surgery, Harvard Medical School; Assistant Visiting Surgeon, Massachusetts General Hospital; Surgeon, Collis P. Huntington Memorial Hospital.

SIMMONS, RICHARD OLIVER, M.D., Guaranty Bank and Trust Building, Alexandria, Louisiana. University of Louisville, Medical Department (Louisville Medical College), 1892. Visiting Surgeon, Baptist Hospital.

SIMON, FREDERICK CASIMIR, Ph.B., M.D., Arcade Building, St. Louis, Missouri. Washington University Medical School, 1899. Oto-Laryngologist, Evangelical Deaconess, Lutheran, St. Anthony's Hospitals; Member of Visiting Staff, Department of Ear, Nose, and Throat, St. Louis City Hospital.

SIMON, LUDWIG S., Ph.B., M.D., 4743 Forrestville Avenue, Chicago, Illinois. Columbia University, College of Physicians and Surgeons, 1894. Attending Obstetrician, Michael Reese Hospital.

SIMONS, JALMAR HENDRIK, B.Sc., M.D., 609 La Salle Building, Minneapolis, Minnesota. University of Minnesota Medical School, 1910. Assistant Professor of Gynecology and Obstetrics, University of Minnesota Medical School; Associate in Gynecology and Obstetrics, Minneapolis General Hospital.

SIMPSON, FRANK FARROW, A.B., M.D., 7048 Jenkins Arcade Building, Pittsburgh, Pennsylvania. University of Pennsylvania School of Medicine, 1893.

SIMPSON, ROBERT MILLS, C.B.E., D.S.O., M.D., C.M., L.R.C.P. & S. (Edin.), L.F.P. & S. (Glas.), 702 Sterling Bank Building, Winnipeg, Manitoba. Faculty of Medicine, University of Manitoba (Manitoba Medical College), 1889. Surgeon and Gynecologist, Winnipeg General Hospital; Surgeon, Great Northern and Northern Pacific Railway.

SIMPSON, THEODORE PARKER, A.M., M.D., 614 Thirteenth Street, Beaver Falls, Pennsylvania. University and Bellevue Hospital Medical College (Bellevue Hospital Medical College), 1877. Member of Surgical Staff, Providence Hospital, Beaver Falls, Beaver Valley General Hospital, New Brighton.

SIMPSON, W. LIKELY, M.D., 601 Exchange Building, Memphis, Tennessee. University of Illinois College of Medicine (College of Physicians and Surgeons, Chicago), 1904. Assistant, Ear, Nose, and Throat Department, University of Tennessee College of Medicine; Surgeon, Ear, Nose, and Throat Department, Memphis General and Baptist Memorial Hospitals.

SINGLETON, ALBERT OLIN, B.Sc., M.D., American National Insurance Building, Galveston, Texas. University of Texas, Medical Department, 1910. Associate Professor of Surgery and Lecturer on Genito-Urinary Diseases, University of Texas, Medical Department; Attending Surgeon, John Sealy Hospital.

SINGLEY, JOHN D., A.M., M.D., 812 North Highland Avenue, Pittsburgh, Pennsylvania. University of Pennsylvania School of Medicine, 1895. Surgeon-in-Chief, Pittsburgh Hospital; Surgeon, St. Margaret's Memorial Hospital.

SISTRUNK, WALTER ELLIS, M.D., 806 Fourth Street, Southwest, Rochester, Minnesota. Tulane University of Louisiana School of Medicine, 1906. Associate Professor of Surgery, Mayo Foundation, University of Minnesota Medical School; Surgeon, St. Mary's and Colonial Hospitals.

SITER, E. HOLLINGSWORTH, M.D., 1520 Locust Street, Philadelphia, Pennsylvania. University of Pennsylvania School of Medicine, 1897. Associate in Genito-Urinary Surgery, University of Pennsylvania School of Medicine; Genito-Urinary Surgeon, Philadelphia General Hospital; Chief Surgeon, Genito-Urinary Clinic, Hospital of the University of Pennsylvania.

SKEEL, ARTHUR J., M.D., 1834 East Sixty-fifth Street, Cleveland, Ohio. Western Reserve University School of Medicine (Cleveland College of Physicians and Surgeons), 1897. Assistant Clinical Professor of Obstetrics, Western Reserve University School of Medicine; Obstetrician, St. Luke's Hospital; Consulting Obstetrician, Woman's Hospital, Florence Crittenton Home.

SKEEL, ROLAND E., A.M., M.D., Title Insurance Building, Los Angeles, California. University of Michigan Medical School, 1890.

SKENE, WILLIAM HENRY, M.D., Stevens Building, Portland, Oregon. Long Island College Hospital, 1888.

SKILLERN, PENN-GASKELL, JR., M.D., 1523 Locust Street, Philadelphia, Pennsylvania. University of Pennsylvania School of Medicine, 1903. Associate Professor of Surgery, University of Pennsylvania Graduate School of Medicine; Surgeon, Medico-Chirurgical, Polyclinic Hospitals; Consulting Surgeon, Frederick Douglass Memorial Hospital.

SKILLERN, ROSS HALL, M.D., 1928 Chestnut Street, Philadelphia, Pennsylvania. University of Pennsylvania School of Medicine, 1897. Professor of Laryngology, University of Pennsylvania Graduate School of Medicine; Laryngologist, Medico-Chirurgical Hospital.

SKINNER, CHARLES NATHAN, M.D., Hubbard Building, Port Jervis, New York. University and Bellevue Hospital Medical College (New York University Medical College), 1892. Visiting Surgeon, St. Francis Hospital.

SKINNER, GEORGE A., M.D., Medical Corps, United States Army, Washington, District of Columbia. Rush Medical College, 1892. Colonel, Medical Corps, United States Army.

SLACK, WALTER L., M.D., 308 Eddy Building, Saginaw, Michigan. University of Michigan Medical School, 1889. Oculist and Aurist, St. Mary's and Saginaw General Hospitals.

SLEMONS, JOSIAH MORRIS, A.M., M.D., 819 Pacific Mutual Building, Los Angeles, California. Johns Hopkins University, Medical Department, 1901.

SLOAN, HARRY GORDON, A.B., M.D., Clinic Building, Cleveland, Ohio. Johns Hopkins University, Medical Department, 1906. Demonstrator of Surgical Physiology, Western Reserve University School of Medicine.

SLOCUM, GEORGE, M.D., 311 South State Street, Ann Arbor, Michigan. University of Michigan Medical School, 1889. Assistant Professor of Ophthalmology, University of Michigan Medical School, University Hospital.

SLOCUM, ROBERT BARNARD, Ph.B., M.D., Murchison Bank Building, Wilmington, North Carolina. Johns Hopkins University, Medical Department, 1905. Visiting Surgeon, James Walker Memorial Hospital; Chief Surgeon, Atlantic Coast Line Railroad.

SLUDER, GREENFIELD, M.D., 3542 Washington Avenue, St. Louis, Missouri. Washington University Medical School, 1888. Clinical Professor of Diseases of Nose and Throat, Washington University Medical School; Laryngologist, Washington University, St. Louis Children's, Barnes, Barnard Free Skin and Cancer, and St. Luke's Hospitals.

SLUSS, JOHN W., B.Sc., A.M., M.D., 227 Newton Claypool Building, Indianapolis, Indiana. Indiana University School of Medicine, 1893. Associate Professor of Surgery, Indiana University School of Medicine; Visiting Surgeon, Indianapolis City Hospital.

SMALL, ANDREW B., M.D., 4942 Live Oak Street, Dallas, Texas. University of Tennessee College of Medicine, 1888. Professor of Clinical Surgery, Baylor University School of Medicine; Attending Surgeon, Baylor Hospital.

SMALL, RICHARD D., A.B., M.D., 7 Deering Street, Portland, Maine. Harvard Medical School, 1898. Surgeon, Maine General Hospital; Consulting Surgeon, Webber Hospital, Biddeford.

SMALL, WILLIAM B., M.D., Black Building, Waterloo, Iowa. Northwestern University Medical School, 1890. Local Oculist and Aurist, Illinois Central Railroad.

SMEAD, LEWIS F., A.B., M.D., 227 Michigan Street, Toledo, Ohio. Johns Hopkins University, Medical Department, 1905. Surgeon, Flower and St. Vincent's Hospitals.

SMILEY, H. H., M.D., State Bank Building, Texarkana, Arkansas. University of Missouri School of Medicine, 1901.

SMITH, A. MACRAE, A.B., M.D., C.M., Bellingham National Bank Building, Bellingham, Washington. Faculty of Medicine, McGill University, 1898.

SMITH, ANDREW C., M.D., 409 Medical Building, Portland, Oregon. Medical College of the Pacific, 1877. Surgeon, St. Vincent's Hospital; Consulting Surgeon, Multnomah County Hospital.

SMITH, ANGELO JOHN, M.D., 207 Park Avenue, Yonkers, New York. University and Bellevue Hospital Medical College, 1899. Attending Ophthalmologist, Otologist, Laryngologist and Rhinologist, St. John's Riverside Hospital, Yonkers, and Dobbs Ferry Hospital, Dobbs Ferry; Consulting Ophthalmologist, Otologist, Laryngologist and Rhinologist, Tarrytown Hospital, Tarrytown.

SMITH, ANSEL B., A.B., M.D., 324 Metz Building, Grand Rapids, Michigan. University of Michigan Homeopathic Medical School, 1909. Member of Executive Staff, Surgical Division, Blodgett Memorial Hospital.

SMITH, ARTHUR EDWARD, M.D., Donaldson Building, Minneapolis, Minnesota. University of Minnesota Medical School, 1905. Oculist and Aurist, St. Andrew's Hospital.

SMITH, ARTHUR HOWARD, M.D., Third and Putnam Streets, Marietta, Ohio. University of Cincinnati College of Medicine (Medical College of Ohio), 1898.

SMITH, CARROLL, A.B., M.D., 306 Humboldt Building, St. Louis, Missouri. Rush Medical College, 1904. Secretary of Faculty and Professor of Surgery, St. Louis University School of Medicine; Chief of Staff and Attending Surgeon, Alexian Brothers' Hospital; Attending Surgeon, St. Louis City Hospital; Consulting Surgeon, St. John's and St. Anthony's Hospitals.

SMITH, CHARLES GORDON, M.D., Medical Corps, United States Navy, Washington, District of Columbia. University of Virginia, Department of Medicine, 1899. Commander, Medical Corps, United States Navy.

SMITH, CHARLES JOHNSON, M.D., 707 Broadway Building, Portland, Oregon. Ohio State University College of Medicine (Starling Medical College), 1888; University and Bellevue Hospital Medical College (Bellevue Hospital Medical College), 1890.

SMITH, CHARLES WOLFF, M.D., Townsend, Montana. University of Cincinnati College of Medicine (Ohio-Miami Medical College of the University of Cincinnati), 1904.

SMITH, CLARENCE HENRY, M.D., 616 Madison Avenue, New York, New York. University and Bellevue Hospital Medical College, 1899. Assistant Professor of Diseases of the Ear, New York Post-Graduate Medical School;

Attending Surgeon, Ear, Nose, and Throat Department, Bronx Eye and Ear Infirmary; Otologist, Union Hospital; Consulting Laryngologist, Home for the Friendless.

SMITH, CONRAD, A.B., M.D., 510 Commonwealth Avenue, Boston, Massachusetts. Boston University School of Medicine, 1899. Associate Professor of Laryngology, Boston University School of Medicine; Chief of Staff, Nose and Throat Department, Massachusetts Homeopathic Hospital.

SMITH, DEAN TYLER, M.Sc., M.D., 121 Bay Street, Daytona, Florida. Hahnemann Medical College and Hospital, Chicago, 1889.

SMITH, DOUGLASS H., M.D., 5 Liberty Street, Bath, New York. University of Buffalo Department of Medicine, 1904. Surgeon, Bath General Hospital; Consulting Surgeon, Pleasant Valley Sanatorium.

SMITH, E. O., M.D., 19 West Seventh Street, Cincinnati, Ohio. University of Cincinnati College of Medicine (Medical College of Ohio), 1896. Professor of Genito-Urinary Surgery, University of Cincinnati College of Medicine; Director of Genito-Urinary Clinics, Cincinnati General Hospital, Dispensary of the University of Cincinnati College of Medicine.

SMITH, E. TERRY, A.M., M.D., 36 Pearl Street, Hartford, Connecticut. Yale University School of Medicine, 1897. Ophthalmologist, Hartford Hospital; Consulting Ophthalmologist, St. Francis Hospital, Hartford, Cyril and Julia C. Johnson Memorial Hospital, Stafford Springs.

SMITH, EDGAR B., Ph.B., M.D., 76 Waterman Street, Providence, Rhode Island. Columbia University, College of Physicians and Surgeons, 1880. Consulting Surgeon, Rhode Island, Providence City, St. Joseph's, Providence Lying-in, and Butler Hospitals, Providence, Rhode Island State Sanatorium, Wallum Lake, Memorial Hospital, Pawtucket, Woonsocket Hospital, Woonsocket.

SMITH, EDWARD S., M.D., 15 Noble Avenue, Westfield, Massachusetts. Albany Medical College, 1899. Surgeon, Noble Hospital.

SMITH, EDWARD WIER, A.B., M.D., C.M., 34 West Main Street, Meriden, Connecticut. Faculty of Medicine, McGill University, 1882. Senior Surgeon, Meriden Hospital.

SMITH, EDWIN WALLACE, Ch.B., M.D., 510 Commonwealth Avenue, Boston, Massachusetts. Boston University School of Medicine, 1901. Instructor in Obstetrics, Boston University School of Medicine; Obstetrician, Massachusetts Homeopathic Hospital and Out-Patient Department, Medical Mission Dispensary; Gynecologist, Out-Patient Department, Massachusetts Homeopathic Hospital; Visiting Proctologist, Westborough State Hospital.

SMITH, ERDIX TENNEY, B.L., M.D., 480 Belmont Avenue, Springfield, Massachusetts. Ohio State University College of Homeopathic Medicine (Cleveland Homeopathic Medical College), 1900. Surgeon, Wesson Memorial Hospital.

SMITH, ERNEST VERNON, M.D., 39 South Main Street, Fond du Lac, Wisconsin. University of Minnesota Medical School, 1907. Surgeon, St. Agnes Hospital.

SMITH, EUGENE, M.D., 32 Adams Avenue, West, Detroit, Michigan. University of Buffalo, Department of Medicine, 1866. Professor of Clinical Ophthalmology, Detroit College of Medicine and Surgery; Senior Ophthalmic and Aural Surgeon, Providence and St. Mary's Hospitals; Ophthalmic Surgeon, Detroit Eye, Ear, Nose, and Throat Hospital; Consulting Ophthalmic and Aural Surgeon, Harper Hospital, Woman's Hospital and Infants' Home.

SMITH, FERRIS, A.B., M.D., 407 Metz Building, Grand Rapids, Michigan. University of Michigan Medical School, 1910. Surgeon, Butterworth, Blodgett Memorial, and St. Mary's Hospitals.

SMITH, FRANK CONGER, M.D., 307½ Walnut Street, Yankton, South Dakota. University and Bellevue Hospital Medical College (University of the City of New York, Medical Department), 1894.

SMITH, FRED W., A.B., M.D., Medical Arts Building, Philadelphia, Pennsylvania. Hahnemann Medical College and Hospital, Philadelphia, 1903. Associate Professor and Demonstrator of Laryngology and Rhinology, Hahnemann Medical College and Hospital; Consulting Laryngologist, Homeopathic State Hospital, Allentown, J. Lewis Crozer Home for Incurables and Homeopathic Hospital, Chester; Laryngologist and Otologist, Children's Homeopathic Hospital, Philadelphia, West Chester Homeopathic Hospital, West Chester, Abington Memorial Hospital, Abington.

SMITH, FREDERICK W., M.D., 40 East Forty-first Street, New York, New York. Syracuse University College of Medicine, 1903. Lecturer in Genito-Urinary Surgery and Venereal Diseases, New York Post-Graduate Medical School; Associate in Urology, New York Post-Graduate Hospital; Assistant Urologist, New York and City Hospitals; Attending Urologist, St. Bartholomew's Hospital; Consulting Urologist, Northern Westchester Hospital, Mt. Kisco, New York, New Jersey State Hospitals.

SMITH, GEORGE BARKER, M.D., Rome, Georgia. University of Georgia, Medical Department, 1908. Ophthalmologist and Oto-Laryngologist, Harbin Hospital.

SMITH, GEORGE GILBERT, A.B., M.D., 352 Marlborough Street, Boston, Massachusetts. Harvard Medical School, 1908. Assistant in Genito-Urinary Surgery, Harvard Medical School; Genito-Urinary Surgeon to Out-Patients, Massachusetts General Hospital.

SMITH, GEORGE MILTON, A.B., M.D., 76 Center Street, Waterbury, Connecticut. Columbia University, College of Physicians and Surgeons, 1905. Attending Surgeon, Waterbury Hospital; Attending Gynecologist, St. Mary's Hospital.

SMITH, GEORGE TUCKER, M.D., Medical Corps, United States Navy, Washington, District of Columbia. University of Virginia, Department of Medicine, 1888. Captain, Medical Corps, United States Navy.

SMITH, HARMON, A.B., M.D., 44 West Forty-ninth Street, New York, New York. University and Bellevue Hospital Medical College, 1897. Professor of Laryngology, Cornell University Medical College; Surgeon, Throat Department, Manhattan Eye, Ear, and Throat Hospital; Consulting Laryngologist, General Memorial and Babies' Hospitals; Consulting Throat Surgeon, Muhlenberg Hospital, Plainfield, New Jersey.

SMITH, HAROLD WELLINGTON, M.D., Medical Corps, United States Navy, Washington, District of Columbia. Harvard Medical School, 1901. Commander, Medical Corps, United States Navy.

SMITH, HARRY CLAY, M.D., Higgins Block, Missoula, Montana. University and Bellevue Hospital Medical College (Bellevue Hospital Medical College), 1894. Consulting Surgeon, Northern Pacific Beneficial Association Hospital, Missoula, St. Julian's Hospital, St. Ignatius; Visiting Surgeon, St. Patrick's Hospital.

SMITH, HARVEY F., Ph.B., M.D., 130 State Street, Harrisburg, Pennsylvania. University of Pennsylvania School of Medicine, 1897. Surgeon, Harrisburg Hospital, Pennsylvania Railroad; Consulting Surgeon, Pennsylvania State Hospital for Insane, Harrisburg, Carlisle Hospital, Carlisle, and Warner Hospital, Gettysburg.

SMITH, HERBERT L., A.M., M.D., Goodrich Block, Nashua, New Hampshire. Harvard Medical School, 1887. Surgeon, Nashua Memorial and St. Joseph's Hospitals.

SMITH, HOMER ERASTUS, M.D., 276 Madison Avenue, New York, New York. Columbia University, College of Physicians and Surgeons, 1878. Assistant Surgeon, Herman Knapp Memorial Eye Hospital; Visiting Ophthalmologist, New York Diagnostic Clinics.

SMITH, JAMES WALKER, M.D., 25 Pinpin, Manila, Philippine Islands. Northwestern University Medical School, 1894. Attending Surgeon, St. Paul's and St. Luke's Hospitals; Member of Surgical Staff, Philippine General Hospital.

SMITH, JOHN JAMES, M.D., Paris, Arkansas. Vanderbilt University, Medical Department, 1879. Surgeon, Paris Hospital.

SMITH, JOSEPH FRANKLIN, M.D., 605 Third Street, Wausau, Wisconsin. Rush Medical College, 1900. Surgeon, St. Mary's Hospital.

SMITH, JOSEPH WHITEFIELD, B.Sc., M.D., LL.D., 1122 East Grove Street, Bloomington, Illinois. State University of Iowa College of Medicine (Keokuk Medical College), 1891. Ophthalmic and Aural Surgeon, Brokaw Hospital; Consulting Ophthalmic and Aural Surgeon, St. Joseph's Hospital; Oculist and Aurist, Illinois Soldiers' Orphans' Home, Normal.

SMITH, LLOYD LLEWELLYN, M.D., Medical Corps, United States Army, Washington, District of Columbia. University of Pennsylvania School of Medicine, 1901. Chief of Medical Service, Walter Reed General Hospital; Lieutenant Colonel, Medical Corps, United States Army.

SMITH, MALCOLM DANIEL, M.D., Prattville, Alabama. University and Bellevue Hospital Medical College (University of the City of New York, Medical Department), 1890.

SMITH, MALCOLM EADIE, M.D., Bank of Commerce Building, Forsyth, Montana. Columbia University College of Physicians and Surgeons, 1905.

SMITH, MARY ALMIRA, A.M., M.D., D.Sc., 101 Fifth Avenue, North, St. Petersburg, Florida. University of Zurich, 1880. Retired.

SMITH, MILLINGTON, M.D., 318 Colcord Building, Oklahoma, Oklahoma. Washington University Medical School (Missouri Medical College), 1881. Associate Professor of Surgery, University of Oklahoma School of Medicine; Consulting Surgeon, St. Anthony's and University Hospitals.

SMITH, MORRIS KELLOGG, A.M., M.D., 117 East Fifty-sixth Street, New York, New York. Dartmouth Medical School, 1911. Instructor in Surgery, Cornell University Medical College; Assistant Attending Surgeon and Dispensary Chief, St. Luke's Hospital.

SMITH, ORRIN LEROY, M.D., Security Trust Company Building, Lexington, Kentucky. Hahnemann Medical College and Hospital, Chicago, 1891.

SMITH, OWEN, M.D., 690 Congress Street, Portland, Maine. Bowdoin Medical School, 1892. Consultant, Maine Eye and Ear Infirmary, Children's Hospital, Portland, St. Mary's Hospital, Lewiston, Webber Hospital, Biddeford.

SMITH, RALPH VERNON, M.D., 502 Daniel Building, Tulsa, Oklahoma. Washington University Medical School (Missouri Medical College), 1898.

SMITH, REA, A.B., M.D., 22 Chester Place, Los Angeles, California. University of Pennsylvania School of Medicine, 1902. Member of Staff, Los Angeles County Hospital.

SMITH, RICHARD C., A.B., M.D., 407 Board of Trade Building, Superior, Wisconsin. Washington University Medical School, 1911. Ophthalmologist, St. Mary's, St. Francis, and Good Samaritan Hospitals.

SMITH, RICHARD R., M.D., Metz Building, Grand Rapids, Michigan. University of Michigan Medical School, 1892. Surgeon, Butterworth and Blodgett Memorial Hospitals.

SMITH, S. MACCUEN, M.D., 1429 Spruce Street, Philadelphia, Pennsylvania. Jefferson Medical College, 1884. Professor of Otology, Jefferson Medical College; Attending Otologist, Jefferson Medical College Hospital; Otologist and Laryngologist, Germantown Hospital; Aurist and Laryngologist, Jewish Hospital; Consulting Aurist, American Oncologic Hospital, Philadelphia, Memorial Hospital, Roxborough.

SMITH, STANLEY, M.D., 613 Jenkins Arcade Building, Pittsburgh, Pennsylvania. Jefferson Medical College, 1896. Associate Professor of Ophthalmology, University of Pittsburgh School of Medicine; Member of Staff, Eye and Ear and Presbyterian Hospitals, Pittsburgh, Columbia Hospital, Wilkinsburg; Consulting Oculist, Carnegie Institute of Technology.

SMITH, STANLEY ALWYN, D.S.O., O.B.E., M.D., Ch.M., F.R.C.S. (Edin.), 80 Cathedral Road, Cardiff, Wales. University of Edinburgh, 1905. Consulting Surgeon, Ministry of Pensions, Wales Region, King Edward VII Welsh National Memorial Association; Consulting Orthopedic Surgeon, Royal Hamadryad Seamen's Hospital, Prince of Wales Hospital for Limbless and Cripples, Cardiff.

SMITH, STEPHEN, A.M., M.D., LL.D., 1000 Park Avenue, New York, New York. Columbia University, College of Physicians and Surgeons, 1850. Consulting Surgeon, St. Vincent's, Bellevue, and Columbus Hospitals.

SMITH, THOMAS ALLISON, M.D., 57 West Seventy-fifth Street, New York, New York. Columbia University, College of Physicians and Surgeons, 1895. Clinical Professor of Surgery, University and Bellevue Hospital Medical College; Visiting Surgeon, Bellevue and Knickerbocker Hospitals; Attending Surgeon, Willard Parker and Riverside Hospitals.

SMITH, TURNER BURTON, B.Sc., M.D., Morenci, Arizona. Rush Medical College, 1904. Chief Surgeon, Longfellow Hospital, Morenci, Arizona Copper Company Hospital, Clifton.

SMITH, VICTOR CONWAY, M.D., 2311 Magazine Street, New Orleans, Louisiana. Tulane University of Louisiana School of Medicine, 1899. Professor of Clinical Ophthalmology, Tulane University of Louisiana School of Medicine; Lecturer on Ophthalmology, Summer School, New Orleans Polyclinic; Visiting Oculist, Charity, Presbyterian, and Illinois Central Hospitals, Hotel Dieu.

SMITH, WELLS FERRIN, M.Sc., M.D., Donaghey Building, Little Rock, Arkansas. St. Louis University School of Medicine (Beaumont Hospital Medical College), 1898. Division Surgeon, Missouri Pacific Railroad.

SMITH, WILLARD WALLACE, M.Sc., M.D., 805 North Fourth Avenue, Phoenix, Arizona. Jefferson Medical College, 1900. Attending Surgeon, St. Joseph's Hospital; Consulting Surgeon, St. Luke's Home.

SMITH, WILLIAM HARVEY, M.A., M.D., C.M., 901 Boyd Building, Winnipeg, Manitoba. Faculty of Medicine, McGill University, 1892. Professor of Clinical Ophthalmology, Faculty of Medicine, University of Manitoba; Ophthalmic Surgeon, Winnipeg General Hospital.

SMITH, WILLIAM SIDNEY, M.D., 370 Washington Avenue, Brooklyn, New York. Columbia University College of Physicians and Surgeons, 1905. Assistant Gynecologist and Obstetrician, Brooklyn Hospital.

SMOOT, JOHN B., M.D., 523 Wilson Building, Dallas, Texas. St. Louis University School of Medicine (Beaumont Hospital Medical College), 1888. Visiting Surgeon, Parkland City Hospital.

SMOOT, MARVIN LE ROY, M.D., 203 Burgess Avenue, Fayetteville, North Carolina. Medical College of Virginia (University College of Medicine), 1903. Otologist, Rhinologist, Laryngologist, Highsmith Hospital.

SMYTH, CHARLES ERNEST, M.B., 874 Second Street, Medicine Hat, Alberta. University of Toronto, Faculty of Medicine, 1894. Surgeon, Medicine Hat General Hospital.

Smyth, Herbert Edmund, M.D., C.M., 476 John Street, Bridgeport, Connecticut. Faculty of Medicine, McGill University, 1884. Laryngologist, Bridgeport Hospital.

Smyth, John, M.D., 724 Baronne Street, New Orleans, Louisiana. Tulane University of Louisiana School of Medicine, 1900. Professor of Oral and Clinical Surgery, Tulane University of Louisiana School of Medicine; Senior Surgeon, Charity Hospital; Visiting Surgeon, Hotel Dieu.

Smythe, Frank David, M.D., Exchange Building, Memphis, Tennessee. Tulane University of Louisiana School of Medicine, 1891. President of Staff and Gynecologist, St. Joseph's Hospital; Surgeon, St. Peter's Orphan Asylum.

Sneed, Carl Miller, A.B., M.D., 909 Elm Street, Columbia, Missouri. University of Missouri School of Medicine, 1901.

Snell, Albert C., M.D., 53 Fitzhugh Street, South, Rochester, New York. University of Pennsylvania School of Medicine, 1898. Ophthalmologist, Rochester General and Infants' Summer Hospitals.

Snodgrass, William A., M.D., Donaghey Building, Little Rock, Arkansas. University of Arkansas, Medical Department, 1897. Professor of Clinical Surgery, University of Arkansas, Medical Department; Staff Surgeon, Logan H. Roots Memorial, City, and Baptist Hospitals, St. Vincent's Infirmary.

Snoke, John Henry, A.B., M.D., St. Luke's Hospital, Shanghai, China. Temple University, Department of Medicine, 1908. Instructor in Minor Surgery, St. John's University; Surgical Chief, St. Luke's Hospital.

Snyder, Frederick, M.D., 44 Clinton Avenue, Kingston, New York. University of Maryland School of Medicine, 1908.

Snyder, Howard L., M.D., 402 First National Bank Building, Winfield, Kansas. Jefferson Medical College, 1904. Surgeon, St. Mary's Hospital.

Snyder, Karl F., M.D., State Bank Building, Freeport, Illinois. Northwestern University Medical School, 1902. Attending Surgeon, St. Francis, Globe, and Freeport General Hospitals.

Snyder, Walter Hamilton, M.D., 211 Ontario Street, Toledo, Ohio. University of Michigan Medical School, 1891. Ophthalmologist and Chief of Staff, Flower Hospital.

Soares de Souza, Augusto Paulino, M.D., Alice Street, Rio de Janeiro, Brazil. Faculty of Medicine, University of Rio de Janeiro, 1900. Surgeon, Commercial Employees Association.

Sohmer, Alphonse Edward John, M.D., 307 South Front Street, Mankato, Minnesota. Long Island College Hospital, 1899. Surgeon, St. Joseph's and Immanuel Hospitals.

Solomon, Edwin P., M.D., 4 Fairview Avenue, Birmingham, Alabama. University of Cincinnati College of Medicine (Medical College of Ohio), 1904. Surgeon, St. Vincent's and Hillman Hospitals, Southern Railway, Illinois Central Railroad, Frisco System.

SOMERS, GEORGE BURBANK, A.B., M.D., 2662 Vallejo Street, San Francisco, California. Cooper Medical College, 1888. Professor of Clinical Gynecology, Leland Stanford Junior University School of Medicine; Gynecologist, Lane Hospital.

SOMMER, ERNST A., M.D., 908 Electric Building, Portland, Oregon. University of Oregon Medical School (Willamette University, Medical Department), 1890. Instructor in Clinical Surgery, University of Oregon Medical School; Surgeon, St. Vincent's Hospital, Portland, Oregon City Hospital, Oregon City; Chief Surgeon, Portland Railway, Light, and Power Company.

SOMMER, GEORGE N. J., M.D., 120 West State Street, Trenton, New Jersey. University of Pennsylvania School of Medicine, 1894. Attending Surgeon, St. Francis' Hospital; Consulting Surgeon, Municipal Colony.

SONNENSCHEIN, ROBERT, M.D., 29 East Madison Street, Chicago, Illinois. Rush Medical College, 1901. Assistant Professor of Oto-Laryngology, Rush Medical College; Professor of Oto-Laryngology, Post-Graduate Medical School; Consulting Laryngologist, Durand Hospital of the McCormick Institute for Infectious Diseases.

SOSA ARTOLA, BELISARIO J., M.D., Calonge 390, Lima, Peru. Faculty of Medicine, University of San Marcos, 1903.

SOSNOWSKI, JULIUS CHRISTIAN, A.B., M.D., 126 Meeting Street, Charleston, South Carolina. Medical College of the State of South Carolina, 1904.

SOUBA, FREDERICK JOSEPH, B.Sc., M.D., 600 Physicians and Surgeons Building, Minneapolis, Minnesota. University of Minnesota Medical School, 1910. Instructor in Gynecology and Obstetrics, University of Minnesota Medical School; Associate in Gynecology and Obstetrics, Minneapolis City Hospital; Gynecologist and Obstetrician, Fairview Hospital.

SOUCHON, EDMOND, M.D., 2403 St. Charles Avenue, New Orleans, Louisiana. Tulane University of Louisiana School of Medicine (University of Louisiana, Medical Department), 1867. Emeritus Professor of Anatomy and Clinical Surgery, Tulane University of Louisiana School of Medicine. Retired.

SOUCHON, MARION SIMS, M.D., Whitney Central Bank Building, New Orleans, Louisiana. Tulane University of Louisiana School of Medicine, 1894. Assistant Professor of Clinical Surgery, Tulane University of Louisiana School of Medicine; Visiting Surgeon, Hotel Dieu; Chief Surgeon, French Hospital.

SOULE, ROBERT E., A.B., M.D., 671 Broad Street, Newark, New Jersey. Long Island College Hospital, 1899. Assistant Professor of Orthopedic Surgery, New York Post-Graduate Medical School; Attending Orthopedic Surgeon, New York Post-Graduate Medical School and Hospital; Orthopedic Surgeon, Presbyterian Hospital, Hospital of St. Barnabas, Newark, Muhlenberg Hospital, Plainfield, St. James' Hospital, Newark.

SOUTHARD, JEFFERSON D., M.D., 101 North Sixth Street, Fort Smith, Arkansas. University of Louisville, Medical Department, 1886. Surgeon, Sparks Memorial Hospital; Chief Surgeon, Arkansas Central Railroad.

SOUTHER, CHARLES THADDEUS, M.D., Groton Building, Cincinnati, Ohio. University of Cincinnati College of Medicine (Medical College of Ohio), 1902. Surgical Clinician, University of Cincinnati College of Medicine; Professor of Oral Surgery, Cincinnati Dental College; Assistant Surgeon, Cincinnati General Hospital; Gynecologist, St. Mary's Hospital; Consulting Surgeon, Cincinnati Dental College Clinic.

SOUTHMAYD, LEROY, M.D., Ford Building, Great Falls, Montana. University of Michigan Medical School, 1892. Member of Staff, Montana Deaconess and Columbus Hospitals.

SOUTHWICK, GEORGE RINALDO, M.D., M.R.C.S. (Eng.), L.R.C.P. (Lond.), 433 Marlborough Street, Boston, Massachusetts. Boston University School of Medicine, 1881; Harvard Medical School, 1898. Professor of Gynecology, Boston University School of Medicine; Consulting Gynecologist, Massachusetts Homeopathic Hospital, Boston; Gynecologist, Westboro State Hospital, Westboro.

SOUTTER, ROBERT, A.B., M.D., 133 Newbury Street, Boston, Massachusetts. Harvard Medical School, 1899. Instructor in Orthopedic Surgery, Harvard Medical School; Associate Surgeon, Children's Hospital; Orthopedic Surgeon, Long Island Hospital; Surgeon-in-Chief, House of the Good Samaritan; Surgeon, Burrage Hospital, Bumkin Island, Massachusetts Hospital School for Crippled and Deformed Children, Canton, New England Peabody Home for Crippled Children, Hyde Park.

SOVAK, FRANCIS WASHINGTON, B.Sc., M.D., 44 East Seventy-second Street, New York, New York. University and Bellevue Hospital Medical College, 1911. Instructor in Gynecology, University and Bellevue Hospital Medical College; Adjunct Assistant Attending Gynecologist and Chief, Out-Patient Department, Bellevue Hospital.

SOWERS, ALVA, M.D., 30 North Michigan Avenue, Chicago, Illinois. Hahnemann Medical College and Hospital, Chicago, 1909. Professor of Rhinology and Laryngology, Hahnemann Medical College; Attending Rhinologist and Laryngologist, Hahnemann Hospital.

SPAFFORD, FREDERICK ANGIER, M.D., Flandreau, South Dakota. Dartmouth Medical School, 1879. Lecturer on Medical Jurisprudence, University of South Dakota College of Law; Surgeon in Charge, Flandreau Indian School Hospital.

SPALDING, JAMES ALFRED, A.M., M.D., 627 Congress Street, Portland, Maine. Harvard Medical School, 1870. Consulting Eye and Ear Surgeon, Maine General Hospital.

SPARKMAN, EDWARD H., JR., B.A., M.D., Medical Corps, United States Navy, Washington, District of Columbia. Medical College of the State of South Carolina, 1904. Lieutenant, Medical Corps, United States Navy.

SPARKS, JOHN FEATHERSTON, B.A., M.D., C.M., 100 Wellington Street, Kingston, Ontario. Queen's University, Faculty of Medicine, 1905. Assistant Professor of Surgery and Assistant Professor of Applied Anatomy, Queen's University, Faculty of Medicine; Assistant Visiting Surgeon and Assistant Visiting Gynecologist, Kingston General Hospital.

SPAULDING, HARRY VAN NESS, M.D., 14 East Fifty-eighth Street, New York, New York. Cornell University Medical College, 1908. Assistant Attending Surgeon, Lincoln Hospital, New York, St. John's Hospital, Long Island City; Associate Surgeon, New York Post-Graduate Medical School and Hospital; Visiting Surgeon, Penitentiary and House of Correction, Blackwell's Island.

SPEAR, RAYMOND, M.D., Medical Corps, United States Navy, Washington, District of Columbia. Jefferson Medical College, 1895. Captain, Medical Corps, United States Navy.

SPEAR, WALTER M., M.D., 135 Camden Street, Rockland, Maine. Harvard Medical School, 1896. Surgeon-in-Chief, Knox County General Hospital.

SPEED, KELLOGG, B.Sc., M.D., 122 South Michigan Avenue, Chicago, Illinois. Rush Medical College, 1904. Assistant Professor of Surgery, Rush Medical College; Associate Attending Surgeon, Presbyterian Hospital; Surgeon, Cook County and Provident Hospitals.

SPEER, WILLIAM H., M.D., 805 West Street, Wilmington, Delaware. University of Pennsylvania School of Medicine, 1910. Chief of Surgical Service, Delaware Hospital.

SPEESE, JOHN, M.D., 2032 Locust Street, Philadelphia, Pennsylvania. University of Pennsylvania School of Medicine, 1902. Associate Professor of Surgery, Graduate School of Medicine of the University of Pennsylvania; Assistant Professor, Surgical Pathology and Instructor in Surgery, University of Pennsylvania, School of Medicine; Surgeon, Presbyterian and Children's Hospitals; Associate Surgeon, Philadelphia Polyclinic and Medico-Chirurgical Hospitals.

SPEIDEL, WILLIAM C., A.B., M.D., 519 Cobb Building, Seattle, Washington. Rush Medical College, 1908. Member of Staff, Columbus Sanitarium.

SPENCE, CECIL ELWOOD, M.B., 104 Cuthbertson Block, Fort William, Ontario. University of Toronto, Faculty of Medicine, 1905.

SPENCE, HENRY, M.D., 2540 Hudson Boulevard, Jersey City, New Jersey. Columbia University, College of Physicians and Surgeons, 1892. Attending Surgeon, Christ Hospital.

SPENCE, THOMAS BRAY, A.B., M.D., 541 Third Street, Brooklyn, New York. Columbia University, College of Physicians and Surgeons, 1893. Senior Surgeon, Methodist Episcopal Hospital.

SPENCER, FLOYD H., M.D., Physicians and Surgeons Building, St. Joseph, Missouri. Central Medical College, 1900. Surgeon, St. Joseph's, Missouri Methodist, and Noyes Hospitals, Welfare Board.

SPENCER, SELDEN, A.B., M.D., University Club Building, St. Louis, Missouri. Washington University Medical School (Missouri Medical College), 1899. Oto-Laryngologist, Missouri Baptist Sanitarium.

SPENGLER, JOHN ARTHUR, B.L., B.Sc., M.L., D.C.L., M.D., 73 Seneca Street, Geneva, New York. University of Buffalo Department of Medicine, 1899. Staff Ophthalmologist, Geneva City Hospital.

SPERRY, FREDERICK N., M.D., 59 College Street, New Haven, Connecticut. Yale University School of Medicine, 1894. Clinical Professor of Laryngology, Yale University School of Medicine; Laryngologist, New Haven Hospital; Consulting Surgeon, Grace Hospital.

SPIEGEL, SAMUEL, M.D., 1239 Madison Avenue, New York, New York. University and Bellevue Hospital Medical College, 1898. Visiting Surgeon, People's Hospital.

SPILMAN, SMITH AUGUSTUS, M.D., Hofmann Building, Ottumwa, Iowa. Northwestern University Medical School (Chicago Medical College), 1879. Surgeon, Ottumwa and St. Joseph Hospitals.

SPITZER, WILLIAM M., M.D., Metropolitan Building, Denver, Colorado. University and Bellevue Hospital Medical College (University of the City of New York, Medical Department), 1897. Visiting Genito-Urinary Surgeon, Denver City and County Hospital, Denver, Sanatorium of the Jewish Consumptives' Relief Society, Edgewater.

SPITZLEY, WILLIAM ALBERT, A.B., M.D., 62 Adams Avenue, West, Detroit, Michigan. University of Michigan Medical School, 1897. Professor of Clinical Surgery, Detroit College of Medicine and Surgery; Associate Attending Surgeon, Harper Hospital; Consulting Surgeon, Woman's and Detroit Tuberculosis Hospitals.

SPRAGUE, EDWARD W., M.D., 65 Washington Street, Newark, New Jersey. University of Maryland School of Medicine (College of Physicians and Surgeons, Baltimore), 1903. Attending Surgeon, Presbyterian and Babies' Hospitals; Associate Gynecologist, St. James Hospital; Associate Attending Surgeon, Newark City Hospital.

SPRATLING, LECKINSKI WARE, B.Sc., M.D., Waverly, Alabama. University and Bellevue Hospital Medical College (University of the City of New York, Medical Department), 1890.

SPRATT, CHARLES NELSON, B.Sc., M.D., 900 Nicollet Avenue, Minneapolis, Minnesota. Johns Hopkins University, Medical Department, 1901.

SPRINGER, HAROLD L., M.D., 1013 Washington Street, Wilmington, Delaware. University of Pennsylvania School of Medicine, 1902. Surgeon, Delaware Hospital.

SPRINGER, JOHN S., 208 Idaho Building, Boise, Idaho. University of Toronto Faculty of Medicine, 1905. Member of Staff, St. Luke's Hospital.

SPURNEY, ALBERT F., M.D., 403 Osborn Building, Cleveland, Ohio. Western Reserve University School of Medicine, 1887. Surgeon, St. Luke's Hospital.

SPURNEY, ANTON B., M.D., 403 Osborn Building, Cleveland, Ohio. Western Reserve University School of Medicine (Cleveland College of Physicians and Surgeons), 1902.

SQUIER, J. BENTLEY, M.D., 8 East Sixty-eighth Street, New York, New York. Columbia University, College of Physicians and Surgeons, 1894. Professor of Urology, Columbia University, College of Physicians and Surgeons; Professor of Genito-Urinary Surgery, New York Post-Graduate Medical School; Director of Department of Urology, New York Post-Graduate Medical School and Hospital; Genito-Urinary Surgeon, Presbyterian Hospital; Consulting Surgeon, St. Luke's Hospital.

STABLER, ANDREW LEE, M.D., 103 West Commerce Street, Greenville, Alabama. Vanderbilt University, Medical Department, 1909. Surgeon, Stabler Infirmary.

STAEHLIN, EDWARD, A.B., M.D., 15 Lincoln Park, Newark, New Jersey. Columbia University, College of Physicians and Surgeons, 1890. Attending Surgeon, Newark Memorial, Babies', and Newark City Hospitals.

STAFFORD, CLAUDE MAURICE, A.M., M.D., 801 Smith Building, Detroit, Michigan. Detroit College of Medicine and Surgery, 1906.

STAFFORD, FRANK DALMON, M.D., 56 Summer Street, North Adams, Massachusetts. University of Vermont College of Medicine, 1878. Chairman, Surgical and Medical Staffs, North Adams Hospital.

STAFFORD, GEORGE MASON GRAHAM, A.B., M.D., Guaranty Bank Building, Alexandria, Louisiana. Tulane University of Louisiana School of Medicine, 1901. Lecturer on Gynecology and Obstetrics and Visiting Surgeon, Baptist Hospital.

STALEY, JOHN C., M.D., 1235 Lowry Building, St. Paul, Minnesota. University of Minnesota Medical School, 1903. Visiting Surgeon, St. Luke's Hospital.

STALKER, MALCOLM, M.B., Walkerton, Ontario. University of Toronto, Faculty of Medicine (Trinity Medical College), 1878. Senior Member of Staff, Bruce County General Hospital.

STALNAKER, PAUL R., M.D., Medical Corps, United States Navy, Washington, District of Columbia. University of Texas, Department of Medicine, 1904. Commander, Medical Corps, United States Navy.

STANDISH, MYLES, A.M., M.D., D.Sc., 51 Hereford Street, Boston, Massachusetts. Harvard Medical School, 1879. Williams Professor of Ophthalmology (Emeritus), Harvard Medical School; Consulting Ophthalmic Surgeon, Carney Hospital, Massachusetts Charitable Eye and Ear Infirmary.

STANFORD, JAMES B., B.Sc., M.D., Exchange Building, Memphis, Tennessee. University of Tennessee College of Medicine (College of Physicians and Surgeons), 1909. Associate Professor of Ophthalmology, University of Tennessee College of Medicine; Visiting Ophthalmologist, Memphis General, St. Joseph's and Baptist Memorial Hospitals.

STANLEY, A. CAMP, M.D., The Farragut, Washington, District of Columbia. George Washington University Medical School, 1906. Gastroenterologist, Out-Patient Department, Garfield Memorial Hospital; Associate Gastroenterologist, Out-Patient Department, Georgetown University Hospital.

STANTON, DAVID A., M.D., 108 North Main Street, High Point, North Carolina. Vanderbilt University, Medical Department, 1887. Surgeon and Gynecologist, Guilford General Hospital.

STANTON, EDWIN MACDONALD, B.Sc., M.D., 511 State Street, Schenectady, New York. University of Pennsylvania School of Medicine, 1903. Surgeon, Ellis Hospital.

STARK, ALEXANDER N., M.D., Medical Corps, United States Army, Washington, District of Columbia. University of Virginia, Department of Medicine, 1892. Colonel, Medical Corps, United States Army.

STARK, HARRY H., M.D., 301 Roberts-Banner Building, El Paso, Texas. St. Louis University School of Medicine (Marion-Sims Medical College), 1896.

STARK, SIGMAR, M.D., 11½ East Eighth Street, Cincinnati, Ohio. University and Bellevue Hospital Medical College, 1884. Professor of Gynecology, University of Cincinnati College of Medicine; Director of First Gynecological Service, Cincinnati General Hospital; Senior Gynecologist, Jewish Hospital.

STARKEL, CHARLES H., A.B., M.D., 11 South Church Street, Belleville, Illinois. Rush Medical College, 1884. Member of Staff, St. Vincent's Hospital; Chief Surgeon, Southern Railway, Western District.

STARR, CLARENCE L., M.B., M.D., 224 Bloor Street, West, Toronto, Ontario. University of Toronto, Faculty of Medicine, 1890; University and Bellevue Hospital Medical College, 1891. Associate Professor of Clinical Surgery, University of Toronto, Faculty of Medicine; Surgeon-in-Chief, Hospital for Sick Children; Consulting Surgeon, Toronto General Hospital; Consultant, Canadian Army Medical Corps.

STARR, ELMER G., M.D., 523 Delaware Avenue, Buffalo, New York. University of Buffalo, Department of Medicine, 1884. Professor of Ophthalmology, University of Buffalo, Department of Medicine; Ophthalmologist, Deaconess Hospital.

STARR, FREDERIC NEWTON GISBORNE, C.B.E., M.B., M.D., C.M., 112 College Street, Toronto, Ontario. University of Toronto, Faculty of Medicine, 1889. Associate Professor of Clinical Surgery, University of Toronto, Faculty of Medicine; Consulting Surgeon, Hospital for Sick Children, Toronto Western Hospital; Surgeon, St. John's and Toronto General Hospitals.

STAUFFER, FREDERICK, M.D., 81 First Avenue, Salt Lake City, Utah. University of Louisville, Medical Department (Kentucky School of Medicine), 1893. Surgeon, Dr. W. H. Groves' Latter-Day Saints Hospital; Oculist, Salt Lake and Ogden Railway.

STAUFFER, NATHAN P., D.D.S., M.D., 1819 Walnut Street, Philadelphia, Pennsylvania. Jefferson Medical College, 1901. Chief Aurist and Laryngologist, Presbyterian Hospital and Girard College Infirmary.

STAVELY, ALBERT L., A.B., M.D., 1744 M Street, Northwest, Washington, District of Columbia. University of Pennsylvania School of Medicine, 1888. Clinical Professor of Gynecology, George Washington University Medical School; Gynecologist, Garfield Memorial Hospital.

ST. CLAIR, CHARLES TIFFANY, M.D., Bland and Ramsey Streets, Bluefield, West Virginia. University of Virginia Department of Medicine, 1896.

ST. CLAIR, WADE HAMPTON, M.D., 204 Ramsey Street, Bluefield, West Virginia. University of Virginia, Department of Medicine, 1900. Surgeon, Bluefield Sanitarium.

STEARNS, WILLIAM MARION, M.D., 22 East Washington Street, Chicago, Illinois. Hahnemann Medical College and Hospital (Chicago Homeopathic Medical College), 1880. Emeritus Professor of Rhinology and Laryngology, Hahnemann Medical College and Hospital.

STEEDLY, BENJAMIN BROADUS, M.D., Steedly's Private Hospital, Spartanburg, South Carolina. Columbia University, College of Physicians and Surgeons, 1901. Chief Surgeon, Chick Springs Sanitarium, Chick Springs; Surgeon, Steedly's Hospital.

STEEL, GEORGE EDWIN, M.D., 256 West Seventy-ninth Street, New York, New York. Columbia University, College of Physicians and Surgeons, 1886. Assistant Aural Surgeon, Manhattan Eye, Ear, and Throat Hospital.

STEEL, WILLIAM A., B.Sc., M.D., 3300 North Broad Street, Philadelphia, Pennsylvania. University of Pennsylvania School of Medicine, 1899. Clinical Professor of Surgery, Temple University, Department of Medicine; Associate Surgeon, Samaritan Hospital.

STEELE, DANIEL ATKINSON KING, M.D., LL.D., 2920 Indiana Avenue, Chicago, Illinois. Northwestern University Medical School (Chicago Medical College), 1873. Attending Surgeon, University Hospital; Consulting Surgeon, Michael Reese, St. Anthony de Padua, and Lakeside Hospitals.

STEENBURG, DONALD BENJAMIN, B.Sc., M.D., 1018 Twelfth Street, Aurora, Nebraska. University of Pennsylvania School of Medicine, 1913.

STEIN, ARTHUR, M.D., 48 East Seventy-fourth Street, New York, New York. University of Strassburg, 1901. Associate Gynecologist, Lenox Hill and Harlem Hospitals; Consulting Gynecologist, Hospital for Deformities and Joint Diseases.

STEINDLER, ARTHUR, M.D., State University Hospital, Iowa City, Iowa. University of Vienna, 1902. Professor of Orthopedic Surgery, State University of Iowa College of Medicine; Orthopedic Surgeon, State University Hospital.

STEINFELD, ALEXANDER MICHAEL, M.D., 129 South Grant Avenue, Columbus, Ohio. Ohio State University College of Medicine (Starling Medical

College), 1897. Assistant Professor of Orthopedic Surgery, Ohio State University College of Medicine; Orthopedic Surgeon, Grant and Protestant Hospitals.

STEINHARTER, EDGAR C., B.Sc., M.D., Seventh and Vine Streets, Cincinnati, Ohio. Harvard Medical School, 1909. Instructor in Gynecology, University of Cincinnati College of Medicine; Attending Gynecologist, Cincinnati General Hospital; Junior Gynecologist, Jewish Hospital.

STEINKE, CARL ROSSOW, M.Sc., M.D., 608 Metropolitan Building, Akron, Ohio. University of Pennsylvania School of Medicine, 1909. Visiting Surgeon, City and Children's Hospitals.

STEINMETZ, DEACON, M.D., 1425 Spruce Street, Philadelphia, Pennsylvania. Hahnemann Medical College and Hospital, Philadelphia, 1895. Associate Professor of Surgery, Surgeon, and Member of Governing Faculty, Hahnemann Medical College and Hospital.

STEPHENS, FRANKLIN M., M.D., 19 West Fifty-fourth Street, New York, New York. University of Pennsylvania School of Medicine, 1885. Professor of Otology, New York Polyclinic Medical School; Attending Aural Surgeon, New York Polyclinic Medical School and Hospital.

STEPP, MORRIS D., M.D., 2403 Payne Avenue, Cleveland, Ohio. Western Reserve University School of Medicine, 1893. Visiting Surgeon, St. Luke's Hospital.

STERN, ALEXANDER A., M.D., 22 East Strand, Kingston, New York. Long Island College Hospital, 1889. Surgeon, Kingston City Hospital.

STERN, WALTER G., A.B., M.D., 821 Schofield Building, Cleveland, Ohio. Western Reserve University School of Medicine, 1898. Orthopedic Surgeon and Director of Orthopedic Dispensary, Mt. Sinai Hospital; Orthopedic Surgeon, St. John's and Rainbow Hospitals, Jewish Orphan Asylum; Consulting Orthopedic Surgeon, Elyria Memorial Hospital; Surgeon in Charge, Gates Hospital for Crippled and Deformed Children, Elyria.

STETSON, HALBERT GREENLEAF, M.D., 39 Federal Street, Greenfield, Massachusetts. University of Maryland School of Medicine (College of Physicians and Surgeons, Baltimore), 1895. Surgeon, Franklin County Public Hospital.

STETTEN, DEWITT, M.D., 115 West Eighty-seventh Street, New York, New York. Columbia University College of Physicians and Surgeons, 1901. Associate Surgeon, Lenox Hill Hospital.

STEVENS, ALEXANDER RAYMOND, A.B., M.D., 40 East Forty-first Street, New York, New York. Johns Hopkins University Medical School, 1903. Clinical Professor of Genito-Urinary Surgery, University and Bellevue Hospital Medical College; Assistant Surgeon, Urological Service, Bellevue Hospital.

STEVENS, BURT SMITH, Ph.G., M.D., Medical Building, San Francisco, California. Northwestern University Medical School, 1908. Lecturer in Surgery, Leland Stanford Junior University School of Medicine; Member of Staff, St. Francis Hospital; Visiting Surgeon, San Francisco Hospital.

STEVENS, EDMUND HORACE, M.D., 1911 Massachusetts Avenue, Cambridge, Massachusetts. Harvard Medical School, 1867. Consulting Surgeon, Cambridge Hospital, Cambridge, Symmes Arlington Hospital, Arlington.

STEVENS, FRANK WILLIAM, M.D., 829 Myrtle Avenue, Bridgeport, Connecticut. Yale University School of Medicine, 1900. Consulting Surgeon, Bridgeport Hospital.

STEVENS, HENRY BURT, M.D., 520 Commonwealth Avenue, Boston, Massachusetts. Harvard Medical School, 1894. Clinical Assistant in Ophthalmology, Harvard University Graduate School of Medicine; Ophthalmic Surgeon, Boston City Hospital; Ophthalmologist, Faulkner Hospital; Assistant Surgeon, Massachusetts Charitable Eye and Ear Infirmary.

STEVENS, HORACE PAINE, A.B., M.D., 520 Commonwealth Avenue, Boston, Massachusetts. Harvard Medical School, 1906. Visiting Surgeon, Cambridge Hospital, Cambridge.

STEVENS, JOHN LEWIS, M.D., 59 North Mulberry Street, Mansfield, Ohio. Ohio State University College of Medicine (Starling Medical College), 1895. Member of Staff, Mansfield General Hospital.

STEVENS, ROY G., M.D., Sioux Falls Clinic, Sioux Falls, South Dakota. University of Illinois College of Medicine (College of Physicians and Surgeons), 1905. Member of Surgical Staff, McKennan Hospital.

STEVENS, WILLIAM E., M.D., 210 Post Street, San Francisco, California. University of California Medical School, 1899. Lecturer on Urology, Leland Stanford Junior University School of Medicine; Chief, Genito-Urinary Department, and Chief of Urology, Women's Department, San Francisco Polyclinic and Post-Graduate School of Medicine; Chief, Genito-Urinary Department, Mount Zion Hospital; Urologist, San Francisco County Hospital, Stanford Service; Consulting Genito-Urinary Surgeon, Bethlehem Shipbuilding Corporation, Limited, Hospital.

STEVENSON, JAMES, B.A., M.D., C.M., 258 Grande Allée, Quebec, Quebec. Faculty of Medicine, McGill University, 1901. Surgeon, Jeffrey Hale Hospital.

STEVENSON, WALTER DAVIS, M.D., Quincy, Illinois. University of Maryland School of Medicine (Baltimore Medical College), 1906.

STEWART, ACHESON, M.D., 637 Union Arcade Building, Pittsburgh, Pennsylvania. Jefferson Medical College, 1901. Surgeon, Western Pennsylvania Hospital.

STEWART, ARCHIBALD, M.D., C.M., 414 McKay Street, Montreal, Quebec. Faculty of Medicine, McGill University, 1910. Assistant in Surgery, Montreal General Hospital.

STEWART, AUDLEY DURAND, A.B., M.D., 400 Cutler Building, Rochester, New York. University of Pennsylvania School of Medicine, 1910. Member of Associate Staff, Rochester General Hospital.

STEWART, CHARLES W., Ph.B., M.D., 2 Kay Street, Newport, Rhode Island. Columbia University, College of Physicians and Surgeons, 1891. Surgeon, Newport Hospital.

STEWART, DOUGLAS HUNT, M.D., 128 West Eighty-sixth Street, New York, New York. Columbia University, College of Physicians and Surgeons, 1882. Adjunct Surgeon, Knickerbocker Hospital; Surgeon, Out-Patient Department, Knickerbocker Hospital.

STEWART, GEORGE ADOLPH, A.B., M.D., 904 North Charles Street, Baltimore, Maryland. Johns Hopkins University, Medical Department, 1911. Instructor in Clinical Surgery and Dispensary Surgeon, Johns Hopkins Hospital; Visiting Surgeon, St. Agnes Hospital.

STEWART, GEORGE DAVID, M.D., 417 Park Avenue, New York, New York. University and Bellevue Hospital Medical College, 1889. Professor of Surgery, University and Bellevue Hospital Medical College; Visiting Surgeon, Bellevue and St. Vincent's Hospitals; Consulting Surgeon, Englewood Hospital, Englewood, St. Mary's Hospital, Orange, New Jersey, United Hospital, Port Chester, South Side Hospital, Babylon, St. Joseph's Hospital, Yonkers, New York.

STEWART, HARRY JOHN, M.D., 801 South Boulevard, Oak Park, Illinois. University of Illinois College of Medicine (College of Physicians and Surgeons, Chicago), 1897. Surgeon, West Suburban Hospital.

STEWART, JAMES L. S., M.D., 410 Overland Building, Boise, Idaho. Rush Medical College, 1899. Surgeon, St. Alphonsus and St. Luke's Hospitals.

STEWART, JOHN, C.B.E., M.B., C.M., LL.D., 28 South Street, Halifax, Nova Scotia. University of Edinburgh, 1877. Dean of Medical Faculty and Professor of Surgery, Dalhousie University, Medical Faculty; Consulting Surgeon, Camp Hill Hospital.

STEWART, LEVER FLEGAL, M.D., 108 North Second Street, Clearfield, Pennsylvania. University of Pennsylvania School of Medicine, 1910. Surgeon, Clearfield Hospital.

STEWART, PHILIP H., B.Sc., A.B., M.D., Fourth Street and Broadway, Paducah, Kentucky. University of Louisville, Medical Department, 1890. Attending Surgeon, Riverside Hospital.

STEWART, RALPH ALEXANDER, M.D., 616 Madison Avenue, New York, New York. New York Homeopathic Medical College and Flower Hospital, 1900. Attending Surgeon, Broad Street and Community Hospitals.

STEWART, ROBERT B., M.D., 627 Mills Building, Topeka, Kansas. University of Kansas School of Medicine (Kansas Medical College), 1905. Surgeon, St. Francis' Hospital.

STEWART, THOMAS MILTON, M.D., 901 Union Trust Building, Cincinnati, Ohio. Ohio State University College of Homeopathic Medicine (Pulte Medical College), 1887; College of New York Ophthalmic Hospital, 1888; University of Berlin, 1889. Consulting Oculist and Aurist, Bethesda Hospital, Home for the Friendless.

STEWART, WALTER SCOTT, M.D., 98 South Franklin Street, Wilkes-Barre, Pennsylvania. University of Pennsylvania School of Medicine, 1883. Surgeon, Wilkes-Barre City Hospital.

STEWART, WILLIAM ALVAH, M.D., 918 Westinghouse Building, Pittsburgh, Pennsylvania. New York Homeopathic Medical College and Flower Hospital, 1894. Surgeon, Pittsburgh Homeopathic Medical and Surgical Hospital and Dispensary.

STICKNEY, VICTOR H., B.Sc., M.D., 101 Sims Street, Dickinson, North Dakota. Dartmouth Medical School, 1883. Consulting Surgeon, Northern Pacific Railway.

STICKNEY, WILLIAM, B.L., M.D., 37 North Main Street, Rutland, Vermont. Dartmouth Medical School, 1903. Surgeon, Rutland Hospital, Rutland, Proctor Hospital, Proctor.

STIEREN, EDWARD, B.Sc., M.D., Union Arcade, Pittsburgh, Pennsylvania. University of Pittsburgh School of Medicine, 1896. Ophthalmic Surgeon, Presbyterian Hospital and Pittsburgh and Lake Erie Railroad; Chief Oculist, Jones and Laughlin Steel Company.

STILES, SIR HAROLD J., K.B.E., M.B., C.M., F.R.C.S. (Edin.), 9 Great Stuart Street, Edinburgh, Scotland. University of Edinburgh, 1885. Regius Professor of Surgery, University of Edinburgh; Surgeon, Edinburgh Royal Infirmary; Consulting Surgeon, Chalmers Hospital and Royal Edinburgh Hospital for Sick Children.

STILLMAN, ALFRED, II, A.B., M.D., 35 East Thirty-ninth Street, New York, New York. Columbia University, College of Physicians and Surgeons, 1907. First Assistant Attending Surgeon, Roosevelt Hospital.

STILLMAN, STANLEY, M.D., Lane Hospital, San Francisco, California. Cooper Medical College, 1889. Professor of Surgery, Leland Stanford Junior University School of Medicine; Surgeon, Lane Hospital.

STILLSON, HAMILTON, A.M., M.D., Ph.D., Seaboard Building, Seattle, Washington. University of Louisville, Medical Department, 1882. Oculist, Seattle School Clinic and Hospital.

STILWILL, HIRAM READ, M.D., 820 Metropolitan Building, Denver, Colorado. Washington University Medical School (Missouri Medical College), 1898; University of Illinois College of Medicine (College of Physicians and Surgeons, Chicago), 1901. Assistant in Ophthalmology, University of Colorado School of Medicine; Ophthalmologist, Mercy, Children's, and Denver City and County Hospitals, National Jewish Home for Consumptives, National Swedish Sanatorium; Oculist, Union Pacific Railway.

STIMSON, GEORGE WILLIAM, A.B., M.D., Jenkins Arcade Building, Pittsburgh, Pennsylvania. University of Pennsylvania School of Medicine, 1903.

STIRLING, ALEXANDER M., Ph.G., M.D., 1515 David Whitney Building, Detroit, Michigan. Detroit College of Medicine and Surgery (Detroit College of Medicine), 1909. Instructor in Clinical Surgery, Harper and Children's Free Hospitals; Junior Attending Surgeon, Harper Hospital; Attending Surgeon, Children's Free Hospital.

STIRLING, ALEXANDER WILLIAMSON, M.B., M.D., C.M., D.P.H., Atlanta Trust Company Building, Atlanta, Georgia. University of Edinburgh, 1880.

STIRLING, JOHN W., M.B., M.D., 386 Sherbrooke Street, West, Montreal, Quebec. University of Edinburgh, 1884. Professor of Ophthalmology, Faculty of Medicine, McGill University; Surgeon-Oculist, Royal Victoria Hospital; Consulting Oculist, Montreal Dispensary.

STITT, EDWARD RHODES, A.B., M.D., Sc.D., LL.D., Medical Corps, United States Navy, Washington, District of Columbia. University of Pennsylvania School of Medicine, 1889. Surgeon General, United States Navy; Member National Board, Medical Examiners.

ST. JOHN, FORDYCE BARKER, B.Sc., M.D., Presbyterian Hospital, New York, New York. Columbia University College of Physicians and Surgeons (College of Physicians and Surgeons), 1909. Associate Professor of Surgery, Columbia University, College of Physicians and Surgeons; Visiting Surgeon, Presbyterian Hospital, New York; Consulting Surgeon, Hackensack Hospital, Hackensack, New Jersey.

STOCKWELL, GLENN WILEY, M.D., 408 Washington Arcade, Detroit, Michigan. Detroit College of Medicine and Surgery, 1903. Instructor in Surgery, Detroit College of Medicine and Surgery; Junior Surgeon and Clinical Assistant in Surgery, Harper Hospital; Chief Surgeon, Grand Trunk Western Lines, Detroit and Toledo Shore Line Railroads; Surgeon, Detroit United Railway.

STOCKWELL, JAMES KIRK, M.D., 113 East Third Street, Oswego, New York. Columbia University, College of Physicians and Surgeons, 1869; University of Buffalo, Department of Medicine, 1870. Surgeon, Oswego Hospital.

STODDARD, THOMAS A., M.D., Thatcher Block, Pueblo, Colorado. University of Michigan Medical School, 1886.

STOKES, ARTHUR CHARLES, B.Sc., M.D., 4724 Davenport Street, Omaha, Nebraska. University of Nebraska College of Medicine, 1899. Professor of Clinical Surgery, University of Nebraska College of Medicine; Surgeon, University, Wise Memorial, and Bishop Clarkson Memorial Hospitals.

STOKES, CHARLES FRANCIS, A.M., M.D., D.Sc., LL.D., 6 West Seventy-seventh Street, New York, New York. Columbia University, College of Physicians and Surgeons, 1884. Surgeon General, United States Navy, retired.

STOKES, JAMES ERNEST, A.B., M.D., 303 North Fulton Street, Salisbury, North Carolina. University of Maryland School of Medicine, 1892. Surgeon in Charge, Whitehead-Stokes Sanatorium.

STOLL, HARRY J., M.D., 229 North Market Street, Wooster, Ohio. Rush Medical College, 1900. Surgeon, Wooster Hospital.

STOLTZ, CHARLES, M.D., 311 West Jefferson Boulevard, South Bend, Indiana. University of Illinois College of Medicine (College of Physicians and Surgeons, Chicago), 1893. Surgeon, Epworth Hospital; Chief Surgeon, New Jersey, Indiana and Illinois Railway.

STONE, HARRY B., M.D., MacBain Building, Roanoke, Virginia. Medical College of Virginia, 1903. Consultant, Jefferson and Lewis-Gale Hospitals.

STONE, HARVEY BRINTON, A.B., M.D., 18 West Franklin Street, Baltimore, Maryland. Johns Hopkins University, Medical Department, 1906. Instructor in Surgery, Johns Hopkins University, Medical Department; Associate Professor of Surgery, University of Maryland School of Medicine and College of Physicians and Surgeons; Visiting Surgeon, Mercy Hospital, Church Home and Infirmary, Hebrew Hospital and Asylum, Union Protestant Infirmary; Assistant Visiting Surgeon, Johns Hopkins Hospital.

STONE, ISAAC SCOTT, M.D., D.Sc., 1618 Rhode Island Avenue, Washington, District of Columbia. University of Maryland School of Medicine, 1872. Surgeon, Columbia Hospital for Women.

STONE, JAMES S., A.M., M.D., 286 Marlborough Street, Boston, Massachusetts. Harvard Medical School, 1894. Instructor in Surgery, Harvard Medical School; Surgeon, Children's Hospital; Consulting Surgeon, Boston Floating Hospital, Boston Dispensary, Boston, Framingham Hospital, Framingham, Massachusetts, Woonsocket Hospital, Woonsocket, Rhode Island.

STONE, RAY CLINTON, M.D., 618 Post Building, Battle Creek, Michigan. Detroit College of Medicine and Surgery, 1904.

STONE, RUSSELL EDWARD, M.D., Interstate Bank Building, New Orleans, Louisiana. Vanderbilt University, Medical Department, 1899. Assistant to Chair of Surgery, New Orleans Polyclinic; Junior Surgeon, Touro Infirmary; Visiting Surgeon, Charity Hospital.

STONER, ALVA PORTER, M.D., Iowa Building, Des Moines, Iowa. St. Louis College of Physicians and Surgeons, 1891. Attending Surgeon, Mercy Hospital.

STORRS, HENRY RANDOLPH, A.B., M.D., 1411 Eighteenth Avenue, East, Vancouver, British Columbia. Harvard Medical School, 1905.

STOTZ, CHARLES FREDERICK, Phar.G., M.D., 1954 Milwaukee Avenue, Chicago, Illinois. University of Illinois College of Medicine (College of Physicians and Surgeons), 1898.

STOUT, GEORGE CLYMER, M.D., 1611 Walnut Street, Philadelphia, Pennsylvania. University of Pennsylvania School of Medicine, 1891. Laryngologist and Aurist, Presbyterian Hospital.

STOVER, WILLIAM MILLER, M.D., 1130 Garden Street, San Luis Obispo, California. University of California Medical School, San Francisco, 1896. Surgeon, San Luis Obispo Sanitarium.

STRACHAUER, ARTHUR CLARENCE, M.D., 1009 Nicollet Avenue, Minneapolis, Minnesota. University of Minnesota Medical School, 1908. Professor of Surgery and Chief of Department of Surgery, University of Minnesota Medical School; Surgeon, Abbott, Northwestern, St. Mary's, St. Andrew's, and University Hospitals.

STRADER, GEORGE LESLIE, M.D., 408 Hynds Building, Cheyenne, Wyoming. University of Nebraska College of Medicine, 1899. Ophthalmologist and Oto-Laryngologist, St. John's Hospital.

STRATTON, FREDERICK ALEXANDER, M.D., 611 Wells Building, Milwaukee, Wisconsin. Marquette University School of Medicine (Wisconsin College of Physicians and Surgeons), 1903. Associate Clinical Professor of Surgery and Member of Administrative Board, Marquette University School of Medicine; Surgeon, St. Joseph's and Johnston Emergency Hospitals, Notre Dame Convent Infirmary.

STRATTON, ROBERT THOMPSON, M.D., 441 Fairmount Avenue, Oakland, California. Jefferson Medical College, 1886. Surgeon, Fabiola Hospital.

STRAUB, PAUL F., M.D., 1900 North Vermont Avenue, Los Angeles, California. State University of Iowa College of Medicine, 1886; University of Berlin, 1892. Colonel, Medical Corps, United States Army, retired.

STRAUS, DAVID C., B.Sc., M.D., 30 North Michigan Avenue, Chicago, Illinois. Rush Medical College, 1907. Assistant Professor of Surgery, Rush Medical College; Attending Surgeon, Cook County Hospital; Associate Attending Surgeon, Michael Reese Hospital; Director of Surgical Department, Michael Reese Dispensary.

STRAUSS, JEROME FRANK, B.Sc., M.D., 104 South Michigan Avenue, Chicago, Illinois. Rush Medical College, 1912. Associate Attending Laryngologist, Michael Reese Hospital and Sarah Morris Hospital for Children.

STRAWN, JULIA C., M.D., 22 East Washington Street, Chicago, Illinois. Hahnemann Medical College and Hospital, Chicago, 1897; University of Illinois College of Medicine, 1903. Professor of Gynecology, Hahnemann Medical College and Hospital; Chief of Gynecological Department, Hahnemann Hospital.

STREET, RICHARD H., M.D., 25 East Washington Street, Chicago, Illinois. Hahnemann Medical College and Hospital, Chicago, 1898. Professor of Rhinology and Laryngology, Hahnemann Medical College and Hospital; Attending Surgeon, Hahnemann Hospital; Member of Consulting Staff, Municipal Contagious Disease Hospital, Daily News Fresh Air Fund Sanitarium.

STRICKLAND, CHARLES GUNNISON, A.B., M.D., 153 West Seventh Street, Erie, Pennsylvania. University of Pennsylvania School of Medicine, 1904. Obstetrician, Hamot and St. Vincent's Hospitals,

STRICKLER, DAVID A., M.D., 612 Empire Building, Denver, Colorado. Hahnemann Medical College and Hospital, Philadelphia, 1881. President, Park Avenue Hospital.

STRICKLER, ORA C., M.D., New Ulm, Minnesota. University of Michigan Medical School, 1885. Attending Surgeon, Loretto and Union Hospitals.

STRINE, HOWARD FRANCIS, M.D., Medical Corps, United States Navy, Washington, District of Columbia. University and Bellevue Hospital Medical College, 1902. Commander, Medical Corps, United States Navy.

STRONG, CHARLES MOORE, M.D., Medical Building, Charlotte, North Carolina. University of Maryland School of Medicine, 1888. Surgeon-in-Chief, Good Samaritan Hospital; Surgeon, St. Peter's and Presbyterian Hospitals; Gynecologist, Tranquil Park and Charlotte Sanatoriums.

STRONG, D. C., M.D., 425 Fourth Street, San Bernardino, California. University of Illinois College of Medicine (College of Physicians and Surgeons, Chicago), 1902. Consulting Surgeon, Sequoia Hospital, Eureka.

STROUD, HOMER A., A.B., M.D., 506 Main Street, Jonesboro, Arkansas. University of Tennessee College of Medicine (Memphis Hospital Medical College), 1903. Chief of Surgical Staff, St. Bernard's Hospital.

STROUT, EUGENE S., M.D., Donaldson Building, Minneapolis, Minnesota. University of Michigan Medical School, 1891. Oculist and Aurist, Northwestern Hospital.

STROUT, G. ELMER, M.D., 900 Donaldson Building, Minneapolis, Minnesota. University of Minnesota School of Medicine, 1901. Instructor in Ophthalmology and Oto-Laryngology, University of Minnesota; Chief of Staff, Wells Memorial Dispensary; Member of Staff, Northwestern Hospital.

STUART, MONTGOMERY A., M.D., Medical Corps, United States Navy, Washington, District of Columbia. University of Michigan Homeopathic Medical School, 1906; Detroit College of Medicine and Surgery, 1907. Commander, Medical Corps, United States Navy.

STUART, PETER, M.D., L.R.C.P.&S. (Glas.), 176 Woolwich Street, Guelph, Ontario. Detroit College of Medicine and Surgery (Detroit Medical College), 1881. Member of Staff, St. Joseph's and Guelph General Hospitals.

STUCKY, JOSEPH ADDISON, M.D., Second and Upper Streets, Lexington, Kentucky. University of Louisville, Medical Department (Kentucky University, Medical Department), 1878. President of Medical and Surgical Staffs, Good Samaritan Hospital; Oto-Laryngologist, St. Joseph's Hospital, Associated Charities Clinic.

STUDDIFORD, WILLIAM E., A.M., M.D., 124 East Thirty-sixth Street, New York, New York. University and Bellevue Hospital Medical College, 1891. Professor of Obstetrics and Gynecology, Columbia University, College of Physicians and Surgeons; Director, Sloane Hospital for Women; Consulting Gynecologist, Presbyterian Hospital; Consulting Obstetrician, New York Nursery and Child's Hospital.

STUHR, HENRY C., M.D., 900 Donaldson Building, Minneapolis, Minnesota. University of Minnesota Medical School, 1900.

STURGEON, CHARLES T., M.D., 710 Merritt Building, Los Angeles, California. University of Michigan Medical School, 1904.

STURGIS, JOHN, A.B., M.D., 137 Court Street, Auburn, Maine. University and Bellevue Hospital Medical College (Bellevue Hospital Medical College), 1896. Surgeon, Central Maine General Hospital, Lewiston.

STURGIS, MILTON G., A.B., M.D., 514 Harvard Avenue, North, Seattle, Washington. Harvard Medical School, 1903. Chief of Staff, Columbus Sanitarium.

STURMDORF, ARNOLD, M.D., 51 West Seventy-fourth Street, New York, New York. Columbia University, College of Physicians and Surgeons, 1886. Clinical Professor of Gynecology, New York Polyclinic Medical School; Attending Surgeon, New York Polyclinic Medical School and Hospital; Associate Surgeon, Woman's Hospital; Consulting Gynecologist, Manhattan State Hospital; Consulting Surgeon, Community Hospital.

SUDLER, MERVIN T., M.Sc., M.D., Ph.D., University of Kansas, Rosedale, Kansas. University of Maryland School of Medicine (College of Physicians and Surgeons, Baltimore), 1901. Professor of Surgery and Head of Department, University of Kansas School of Medicine; Surgeon-in-Chief, University of Kansas Bell Memorial Hospital.

SULLIVAN, JOHN CHARLES, M.D., 10 South Main Street, Dubois, Pennsylvania. University of Pittsburgh School of Medicine (Western Pennsylvania Medical College), 1890. Surgeon, Dubois Hospital.

SULLIVAN, JOHN DANIEL, M.D., 74 McDonough Street, Brooklyn, New York. University and Bellevue Hospital Medical College (New York University Medical College), 1867. Attending Surgeon, St. Mary's Hospital, St. John's Home for Boys.

SULLIVAN, M. T., M.D., C.M., Glace Bay, Nova Scotia. Faculty of Medicine, McGill University, 1901. Surgeon, St. Joseph's and General Hospitals.

SULLIVAN, RAYMOND PETER, A.M., M.D., 270 Park Avenue, New York, New York. Columbia University, College of Physicians and Surgeons, 1907. Surgeon, Hospital of the Holy Family; Associate Surgeon, St. Vincent's Hospital; Consultant in Surgery, Kings Park State Hospital, Kings Park.

SULLIVAN, ROBERT YOUNG, M.D., Stoneleigh Court, Washington, District of Columbia. Georgetown University School of Medicine, 1905. Associate Professor of Gynecology, Georgetown University School of Medicine; Attending Gynecologist, Columbia Hospital for Women and Municipal Hospital; Consulting Gynecologist, Government Hospital for Insane; Attending Surgeon, Providence Hospital.

SULLIVAN, THOMAS J., A.M., M.D., 4709 South Michigan Avenue, Chicago, Illinois. University of Michigan Medical School, 1880. Professor of Surgery and Member of Surgical Staff, Post-Graduate Medical School, Chicago.

SULZER, GUSTAVUS A., M.D., 200 East State Street, Columbus, Ohio. University of Pennsylvania School of Medicine, 1892.

SULZMAN, FRANK MALCOLM, A.M., M.D., 1831 Fifth Avenue, Troy, New York. Albany Medical College, 1902. Attending Ophthalmologist and Otologist, Troy Hospital, St. Vincent's Orphan Asylum, St. Coleman's Home, Troy, Cohoes Hospital, Cohoes; Attending Rhinologist and Laryngologist, St. Joseph's Maternity Hospital, Troy, Cohoes Hospital, Cohoes.

SUMMERS, JOHN E., M.D., 618 Brandeis Theatre Building, Omaha, Nebraska. Columbia University, College of Physicians and Surgeons, 1881. Clinical Professor of Surgery, University of Nebraska College of Medicine; Visiting Surgeon, University and Bishop Clarkson Memorial, Hospitals; Visiting Surgeon and Chief of Staff, Douglas County Hospital.

SUMNEY, HERBERT CLAYTON, M.D., 1011 W. O. W. Building, Omaha, Nebraska. Jefferson Medical College, 1890. Urologist, Douglas County Hospital.

SUTER, JOSEPH CALVERT, M.D., C.M., Grafton, North Dakota. University of Toronto, Faculty of Medicine (Trinity Medical College), 1891. Attending Surgeon, Grafton Deaconess Hospital.

SUTHERLAND, FRED BARRINGTON, M.D., 40 East Forty-first Street, New York, New York. Cooper Medical College, 1892. Consultant, Ossining Hospital, Ossining.

SUTHERLAND, JAMES, M.D., C.M., 604 Old National Bank Building, Spokane, Washington. University of Toronto, Faculty of Medicine (Trinity Medical College), 1891. Member of Staff, Marie Beard Deaconess Hospital.

SUTHERLAND, WILLIAM HENRY, M.D., C.M., McKenzie Avenue, Revelstoke, British Columbia. Faculty of Medicine, McGill University, 1899. Chief Surgeon, Queen Victoria Hospital.

SUTPHEN, CARLYLE EDGAR, JR., A.B., M.D., 31 Roseville Avenue, Newark, New Jersey. Columbia University, College of Physicians and Surgeons, 1896. Visiting Surgeon, Newark City and Presbyterian Hospitals; Adjunct Visiting Surgeon, St. James and St. Barnabas Hospitals.

SUTPHEN, EDWARD BLAIR, M.D., 174 South Street, Morristown, New Jersey. Columbia University, College of Physicians and Surgeons, 1902. Surgeon, Eye, Ear, Nose, and Throat Department, Morristown Memorial Hospital, Ear, Nose, and Throat Department, All Souls' Hospital, Morristown, Overlook Hospital, Summit; Consulting Surgeon, Eye, Ear, Nose, and Throat Department, New Jersey State Hospital, Morris Plains.

SUTPHEN, THERON Y., M.D., 1038 Broad Street, Newark, New Jersey. University and Bellevue Hospital Medical College, 1873. Attending Surgeon, St. Michael's Hospital, Newark; Emeritus and Consulting Oculist, All Souls' Hospital, Morristown.

SUTTLE, ISAAC NEWTON, M.D., 216½ North Beaton Street, Corsicana, Texas. Kentucky School of Medicine, 1885. Visiting and Consulting Surgeon, Physicians and Surgeons Hospital; Chief Surgeon, Dr. Suttle's Sanitarium; Local Surgeon, Houston and Texas Central, St. Louis and Southwestern, and Trinity and Brazos Valley Railroads.

SUTTON, GEORGE ELLSWORTH, B.Sc., M.S., M.D., Mayo Clinic, Rochester, Minnesota. University of Minnesota Medical School, 1914.

SUTTON, HENRY THOMAS, M.D., 38 South Sixth Street, Zanesville, Ohio. University of Cincinnati College of Medicine (Medical College of Ohio), 1885. Chief Surgeon, Good Samaritan Hospital.

SWAHLEN, PERCY HYPES, A.B., M.D., 5301 Page Avenue, St. Louis, Missouri. St. Louis University School of Medicine (Marion-Sims-Beaumont Medical College), 1903. Associate Professor of Obstetrics and Gynecology, St. Louis University School of Medicine; Resident Obstetrician, St. Ann's Maternity Hospital; Obstetrician, Mt. St. Rose Hospital; Visiting Obstetrician and Gynecologist, St. Louis City Hospital; Gynecologist, St. John's Hospital.

SWAIN, HOWARD TOWNSEND, M.D., 226 Commonwealth Avenue, Boston, Massachusetts. Harvard Medical School, 1897. Consulting Obstetrician, Boston Lying-in Hospital.

SWAN, CHARLES JOSEPH, M.D., 1818 Hinman Avenue, Evanston, Illinois. Northwestern University Medical School, 1909. Attending Ophthalmologist and Oto-Laryngologist, Evanston Hospital.

SWEDENBURG, FRANCIS GUSTAVUS, Ph.G., M.D., 299 Main Street, Ashland, Oregon. Rush Medical College, 1900. Chief Surgeon, Granite City Hospital.

SWEEK, WILLIAM O., M.D., 404 Heard Building, Phoenix, Arizona. Washington University Medical School (St. Louis University Medical Department), 1912. Visiting Surgeon, St. Joseph's Hospital.

SWEET, CHARLES CLARK, M.D., 13 Maple Place, Ossining, New York. Albany Medical College, 1905. Surgeon, Ossining Hospital.

SWEET, FREDERICK BENONI, M.D., 81 Chestnut Street, Springfield, Massachusetts. Yale University School of Medicine, 1893. Attending Surgeon, Springfield Hospital; Consulting Surgeon, Ware Hospital, Ware, Wing Hospital, Palmer.

SWEET, JOSHUA EDWIN, A.M., M.D., 301 St. Mark's Square, Philadelphia, Pennsylvania. University of Giessen, 1901. Professor of Surgical Research, University of Pennsylvania Graduate and Undergraduate Schools of Medicine.

SWEETSER, HORATIO B., M.D., Physicians and Surgeons Building, Minneapolis, Minnesota. Columbia University, College of Physicians and Surgeons, 1885. Chief of Staff and Surgeon, St. Mary's Hospital.

SWENSON, CARL GUSTAF, M.D., 440 Fullerton Parkway, Chicago, Illinois. Rush Medical College, 1891. Surgeon, Passavant Memorial Hospital.

SWETNAM, CHARLES RANDOLPH KEITH, M.D., Prescott, Arizona. Georgetown University School of Medicine, 1904.

SWETT, PAUL PLUMMER, M.D., 179 Allyn Street, Hartford, Connecticut. University and Bellevue Hospital Medical College, 1904. Orthopedic Surgeon, Hartford Hospital and Dispensary, Hartford, Home for Crippled Children, Newington; Consulting Surgeon, New Britain General Hospital, New Britain, Litchfield County Hospital, Winsted, Charlotte Hungerford Memorial Hospital, Torrington, Manchester Memorial Hospital, South Manchester.

SWIFT, GEORGE W., Ph.G., M.D., 817 Summit Avenue, Seattle, Washington. Northwestern University Medical School, 1907.

SWIFT, MILNE BARKER, M.D., Orlando, Florida. Columbia University, College of Physicians and Surgeons, 1905. Retired.

SWIFT, SAMUEL, A.B., M.D., 55 East Sixty-first Street, New York, New York. Columbia University, College of Physicians and Surgeons, 1913.

SWIFT, WILLIAM J., M.D., 220 South State Street, Chicago, Illinois. Rush Medical College, 1904. Associate Professor of Surgery, Loyola University School of Medicine; Member of Associate Surgical Staff, Alexian Brothers' Hospital.

SWINDT, JOSEPH K., M.D., Investment Building, Pomona, California. University of Colorado School of Medicine (Gross Medical College), 1902.

SWING, FRANK U., M.D., 62 Groton Building, Cincinnati, Ohio. University of Cincinnati College of Medicine (Medical College of Ohio), 1904. Clinical Instructor in Ophthalmology, University of Cincinnati College of Medicine; Ophthalmologist and Rhino-Oto-Laryngologist, St. Mary's Hospital.

SWINT, BENJAMIN HARRISON, M.D., Coyle and Richardson Building, Charleston, West Virginia. University of Maryland School of Medicine (College of Physicians and Surgeons, Baltimore), 1911. Chief of Service, St. Francis Hospital.

SWOPE, LORENZO W., M.D., Park Building, Pittsburgh, Pennsylvania. University of Pittsburgh School of Medicine (Western Pennsylvania Medical College), 1896. Surgeon, Western Pennsylvania and Passavant Hospitals; Consulting Surgeon, City Hospital, Washington, Ohio Valley General Hospital, McKee's Rocks.

SYMS, PARKER, M.D., 361 Park Avenue, New York, New York. University and Bellevue Hospital Medical College (New York University Medical College), 1882. Clinical Professor of Surgery, University and Bellevue Hospital Medical College; Attending Surgeon, Lebanon Hospital, New York, City Hospital, Blackwell's Island; Consulting Surgeon, Nyack Hospital, Nyack, New York, All Souls' Hospital, Morristown, New Jersey.

TAFT, CHARLES EZRA, M.D., 50 Farmington Avenue, Hartford, Connecticut. Harvard Medical School, 1886. Attending Surgeon, St. Francis' Hospital; Consulting Surgeon, Hartford Isolation Hospital.

TAINTER, FRANK JOSEPH, M.D., 816 University Club Building, St. Louis, Missouri. University of Louisville, Medical Department (Hospital College of Medicine), 1895. Associate Professor of Anatomy, St. Louis University School of Medicine; Associate Surgeon, St. Anthony's Hospital.

TALBOT, PAUL TILMAN, M.D., 710 Maison Blanche Building, New Orleans, Louisiana. Tulane University of Louisiana School of Medicine, 1908. Instructor in Gynecology, Loyola Post-Graduate School of Medicine; Visiting Junior Gynecologist, Charity Hospital; Examining Surgeon, Illinois Central Hospital.

TALBOTT, HUDSON, M.D., 426 Metropolitan Building, St. Louis, Missouri. St. Louis University School of Medicine (Marion-Sims Medical College), 1898. Surgeon, Missouri Baptist Sanitarium.

TALIAFERRO, EDWARD C. S., M.D., 618 New Monroe Building, Norfolk, Virginia. Medical College of Virginia, 1898. Gynecologist, St. Vincent's Hospital.

TALLEY, DYER FINDLEY, A.M., M.D., 1808 Seventh Avenue, North, Birmingham, Alabama. Tulane University of Louisiana School of Medicine, 1892. Attending Surgeon, Hillman Hospital; Chief Surgeon, Talley Infirmary.

TAMINI, LUIS A., M.D., Santa Fe 2294, Buenos Aires, Argentina. Faculty of Medicine, University of Buenos Aires, 1903. Assistant Professor of Clinical Surgery, Faculty of Medicine University of Buenos Aires.

TANKERSLEY, JAMES WILLIAM, M.D., 306 Dixie Building, Greensboro, North Carolina. Jefferson Medical College, 1906. Staff Surgeon, St. Leo's Hospital.

TANNER, ERNEST K., M.D., 1205 Dean Street, Brooklyn, New York. University and Bellevue Hospital Medical College, 1904. Associate Attending Surgeon, Brooklyn Hospital.

TARNOWSKY, GEORGE DE, M.D., 30 North Michigan Avenue, Chicago, Illinois. Northwestern University Medical School, 1900. Clinical Professor of Surgery, Loyola University School of Medicine; Surgeon, Ravenswood Hospital.

TARUN, WILLIAM, M.D., 605 Park Avenue, Baltimore, Maryland. University of Maryland School of Medicine, 1900. Associate Professor of Ophthalmology and Otology, University of Maryland School of Medicine and College of Physicians and Surgeons; Chief of Clinic, University Hospital; Ophthalmologist and Otologist, James Lawrence Kernan Hospital and Industrial School for Crippled Children, Baltimore, Rosewood Training School for Feeble-Minded, Owings Mills, Emergency Hospital, Havre-de-Grace.

TATE, MAGNUS ALFRED, M.D., 19 West Seventh Street, Cincinnati, Ohio. University of Cincinnati College of Medicine (Medical College of Ohio), 1891. Obstetrician, Cincinnati General and Good Samaritan Hospitals.

TAULBEE, JACKSON B., M.D., State National Bank Building, Maysville, Kentucky. College of Physicians and Surgeons, St. Joseph, 1882; University and Bellevue Hospital Medical College, 1888. Consulting Surgeon, Hayswood Hospital.

TAUSSIG, FREDERICK JOSEPH, A.B., M.D., 4506 Maryland Avenue, St. Louis, Missouri. Washington University Medical School, 1898. Associate in Gynecology, Washington University Medical School; Gynecologist, Barnard Free Skin and Cancer and St. Louis City Hospitals; Assistant Gynecologist, Barnes Hospital; Consulting Gynecologist, St. John's Hospital; Consulting Obstetrician, St. Louis Maternity Hospital.

TAYLOE, DAVID THOMAS, M.D., Main Street, Washington, North Carolina. University and Bellevue Hospital Medical College (Bellevue Hospital Medical College), 1885. Surgeon-in-Chief, Washington Hospital.

TAYLOR, ALFRED SIMPSON, Ph.B., A.M., M.D., 115 West Fifty-fifth Street, New York, New York. Columbia University, College of Physicians and Surgeons, 1895. Clinical Professor of Surgery and Special Lecturer on Surgery of Peripheral Nerves, Cornell University Medical College; Visiting Surgeon, Fordham Hospital and New York Neurological Institute; Consulting Surgeon, Memorial Hospital, Hospital for Ruptured and Crippled, New York, Tarrytown Hospital, Tarrytown, White Plains Hospital, White Plains, Letchworth Village, Thiells, Overlook Hospital, Summit, New Jersey.

TAYLOR, CHARLES B., A.M., M.D., Ennis Building, Ottumwa, Iowa. Indiana University School of Medicine (Central College of Physicians and Surgeons), 1899. Member of Staff, St. Joseph's and Ottumwa City Hospitals.

TAYLOR, FREDERICK WHITAKER, M.D., 147 South University Avenue, Provo, Utah. University and Bellevue Hospital Medical College (University of the City of New York, Medical Department), 1892. Surgeon, Provo General Hospital.

TAYLOR, HENRY LING, Ph.B., M.D., 125 West Fifty-eighth Street, New York, New York. Columbia University, College of Physicians and Surgeons, 1881. Consulting Orthopedic Surgeon, New York Post-Graduate Medical School and Hospital; Attending Surgeon, Hospital for Ruptured and Crippled; Surgeon, Southampton Fresh Air Home, Southampton, New York; Consulting Orthopedic Surgeon, Mountainside Hospital, Montclair, St. Mary's Hospital, Orange, New Jersey.

TAYLOR, HERBERT LEONEL, M.B., M.D., 160 Middle Street, Portsmouth, New Hampshire. Jefferson Medical College, 1902. Surgeon-in-Chief, York Hospital, York Village, Maine; Surgeon, Portsmouth Hospital, Mark H. Wentworth Home, Boston and Maine Railway.

TAYLOR, HOWARD CANNING, Ph.B., M.D., 32 West Fiftieth Street, New York, New York. Columbia University, College of Physicians and Surgeons, 1891. Professor of Clinical Gynecology, Columbia University, College of Physicians and Surgeons; Gynecologist, Roosevelt Hospital; Consulting Gynecologist, Sloane Hospital for Women, New York, Tarrytown Hospital, Tarrytown, New York, Greenwich Hospital, Greenwich, Sharon Hospital, Sharon, Stamford Hospital, Stamford, Connecticut, Memorial Hospital, Pawtucket, Rhode Island.

TAYLOR, JAMES NORMAN, M.D., C.M., 1186 Monterey Avenue, Victoria, British Columbia. Faculty of Medicine, McGill University, 1892.

TAYLOR, JAMES SPOTTISWOODE, M.D., Medical Corps, United States Navy, Washington, District of Columbia. University of Virginia, Department of Medicine, 1894. Captain, Medical Corps, United States Navy.

TAYLOR, JOHN MARTIN, B.Sc., M.D., Empire Building, Boise, Idaho. University of Pennsylvania School of Medicine, 1900.

TAYLOR, JUDSON LUDWELL, M.D., Scanlan Building, Houston, Texas. University of Texas, Medical Department, 1903. Orthopedic Surgeon, Municipal Hospital, Baptist Sanitarium and Hospital; Surgeon, Sunset Hospital.

TAYLOR, JULIUS HEYWARD, M.D., 1403 Hampton Street, Columbia, South Carolina. University of Virginia, Department of Medicine, 1901. Surgeon, Baptist and Columbia Hospitals; Consulting Surgeon, Camden Hospital and State Hospital for Insane.

TAYLOR, LEWIS H., A.M., M.D., 83 South Franklin Street, Wilkes-Barre Pennsylvania. University of Pennsylvania School of Medicine, 1880.

TAYLOR, ROBERT TUNSTALL, A.B., M.D., 1102 North Charles Street, Baltimore, Maryland. University of Virginia, Department of Medicine, 1891. Professor of Orthopedic Surgery, University of Maryland School of Medicine and College of Physicians and Surgeons; Surgeon-in-Chief, James Lawrence Kernan Hospital and Industrial School for Crippled Children; Orthopedic Surgeon, Hospital for Women of Maryland, University and St. Agnes' Hospitals; Consulting Orthopedic Surgeon, St. Joseph's Hospital, Baltimore; Consultant, United States Public Health Service.

TAYLOR, SIR WILLIAM, K.B.E., C.B., B.A., M.B., F.R.C.S. (I.), 47 Fitzwilliam Square, West, Dublin, Ireland. L.R.C.P. (I.), L.R.C.S. (I.), L.M. (Mayne School), 1893. Lecturer on Clinical and Operative Surgery, and Surgeon, Meath Hospital; Consulting Surgeon, Coombe Lying-in Hospital; Past President and Member of Council, Royal College of Surgeons of Ireland; Consulting Surgeon, Fighting Forces in Ireland; Colonel, Army Medical Staff.

TAYLOR, WILLIAM WOOD, A.B., M.D., 1422 Exchange Building, Memphis, Tennessee. University and Bellevue Hospital Medical College, 1876.

TEACHENOR, FRANK R., M.D., 425 Argyle Building, Kansas City, Missouri. University of Kansas, School of Medicine, 1911. Surgeon, Christian Church Hospital; Attending Surgeon, Kansas City General Hospital.

TEACHNOR, WELLS, M.D., 187 East State Street, Columbus, Ohio. University of Cincinnati College of Medicine (Medical College of Ohio), 1892. Member of Staff, Hawkes Hospital of Mt. Carmel; Consultant, Mercy Hospital.

TEACHOUT, STANLEY ROSS, B.Sc., M.D., 212 Eve Building, Nashville, Tennessee. Vanderbilt University, Medical Department, 1904. Assistant to Chair of Gynecology, Vanderbilt University, Medical Department; Member of Staff, Vanderbilt University, St. Thomas and Protestant Hospitals; Surgeon, Bureau of War Risk Insurance.

TEASS, CHESTER JAMES, M.D., Medical Building, San Francisco, California. Leland Stanford Junior University School of Medicine (Cooper Medical College), 1897.

TEES, FREDERICK JAMES, B.A., M.D., C.M., 6 Bishop Street, Montreal, Quebec. Faculty of Medicine, McGill University, 1905. Demonstrator of Clinical

Surgery and of Anatomy, Faculty of Medicine, McGill University; Surgeon, Out-Patient Department, Montreal General Hospital.

TEETER, EDMUND H., M.D., 305 Duval Building, Jacksonville, Florida. University of Maryland School of Medicine, 1910. Associate Surgeon, St. Luke's Hospital.

TEMPLIN, THEODORE B., M.D., 583 Broadway, Gary, Indiana. Jefferson Medical College, 1904. Attending Surgeon, St. Mary's Mercy Hospital.

TENNANT, CHAUNCEY E., M.D., Empire Building, Denver, Colorado. University of Colorado School of Medicine (Denver College of Medicine), 1894.

TENNEY, BENJAMIN, A.M., M.D., 308 Marlborough Street, Boston, Massachusetts. Harvard Medical School, 1892. Consulting Surgeon, Boston Dispensary and Hospital for Children; Surgeon, Berkeley Infirmary.

TERRY, CHARLES C., 122 North Lafayette Street, South Bend, Indiana. University of Illinois College of Medicine (College of Physicians and Surgeons, Chicago), 1889. Member of Surgical Staff, Epworth Hospital.

TERRY, IRA BREWSTER, JR., M.D., Ph.D., 129 East Ninety-second Street, New York, New York. University and Bellevue Hospital Medical College, 1903. Junior Surgeon, Woman's Hospital; Associate Surgeon, Park Hospital; Consulting Surgeon, Home for Incurables; Associate in Gynecology, Post-Graduate Hospital.

TERRY, WALLACE IRVING, B.Sc., M.D., 240 Stockton Street, San Francisco, California. University of California Medical School, San Francisco, 1892. Professor of Surgery, University of California Medical School; Surgeon-in-Chief, University of California Hospital.

TEXIDOR, ALEXANDER GIOL, Ph.G., M.D., 3 Muñoz Rivera Street, Caguas, Porto Rico. University and Bellevue Hospital Medical College, 1890. Attending Surgeon, Municipal Hospital.

THABES, JOHN A., M.D., 417 Holly Street, Brainerd, Minnesota. University of Minnesota Medical School, 1896. Surgeon, St. Joseph's Hospital; Consulting Surgeon, Northern Pacific Hospital.

THAYER, FREDERICK CHARLES, A.M., Sc.D., M.D., 214 Main Street, Waterville, Maine. Bowdoin Medical School (Medical School of Maine), 1867.

THEARLE, WILLIAM H., M.D., Medical Corps, United States Army, Washington, District of Columbia. University of Maryland School of Medicine (College of Physicians and Surgeons, Baltimore), 1908. Major, Medical Corps, United States Army.

THIERRY, JEAN HUGO, A.B., M.D., Plaza Anibal Pinto 175, Valparaiso, Chile. University of Copenhagen, 1895. Director, Hospital del Salvador and Children's Hospital.

THIGPEN, CHARLES ALSTON, A.M., M.D., First National Bank Building, Montgomery, Alabama. Tulane University of Louisiana School of Medicine, 1888. Oculist, Alabama School for Blind, Talladega.

THOMAS, B. A., A.M., M.D., 116 South Nineteenth Street, Philadelphia, Pennsylvania. University of Pennsylvania School of Medicine, 1903. Professor of Urology, University of Pennsylvania Graduate School of Medicine; Head of Department of Genito-Urinary Surgery, Presbyterian Hospital.

THOMAS, BERT, B.Sc., M.D., 206 Drumheller Building, Walla Walla, Washington. University of Michigan Medical School, 1904. Member of Staff, St. Mary's Hospital.

THOMAS, CHARLES DERASTUS, M.D., 464 Moss Avenue, Peoria, Illinois. Rush Medical College, 1888. Oculist, Aurist, Rhinologist, and Laryngologist, John C. Proctor Hospital.

THOMAS, GEORGE T., M.D., Smith Building, Amarillo, Texas. Texas Christian University School of Medicine (Fort Worth School of Medicine), 1907. Attending Surgeon, St. Anthony's Sanitarium.

THOMAS, HAYWARD G., M.D., Dalziel Building, Oakland, California. Jefferson Medical College, 1887. Visiting Oculist and Aurist, Alameda County Hospital.

THOMAS, HENRY BASCOM, B.Sc., M.D., 30 North Michigan Avenue, Chicago, Illinois. Northwestern University Medical School, 1903. Associate Professor, Orthopedic Surgery, University of Illinois; Senior Orthopedic Surgeon, St. Luke's Hospital.

THOMAS, JOHN B., M.D., Llano Building, Midland, Texas. University of Texas, Medical Department, 1902.

THOMAS, JOHN C., M.D., 326 Littlefield Building, Austin, Texas. University of Texas, Department of Medicine, 1908. Surgeon, Physicians and Surgeons Hospital; Visiting Surgeon, Seton Infirmary.

THOMAS, THOMAS TURNER, M.D., 1905 Chestnut Street, Philadelphia, Pennsylvania. University of Pennsylvania School of Medicine, 1895. Associate Professor of Applied Anatomy and Associate in Surgery, University of Pennsylvania School of Medicine; Associate Professor of Surgery and Applied Anatomy, University of Pennsylvania, Post-Graduate Medical Department; Surgeon-in-Chief, Northeastern Hospital; Surgeon, Philadelphia General Hospital.

THOMAS, WILLIAM KILPACK SMITH, A.B., M.D., 1718 Massachusetts Avenue, Cambridge, Massachusetts. Boston University School of Medicine, 1903. Lecturer on Minor Surgery, Boston University School of Medicine; Assistant Surgeon, Massachusetts Homeopathic Hospital, Boston.

THOMASON, GEORGE, M.D., L.R.C.P.& S. (I.), 317 Hollingsworth Building, Los Angeles, California. Jefferson Medical College, 1899.

THOMASON, HENRY EAGLE, M.D., 1020 Rialto Building, Kansas City, Missouri. St. Louis University School of Medicine, 1900.

THOMASON, JOHN WILLIAM, M.D., 1207 Avenue J, Huntsville, Texas. University of Virginia, Department of Medicine, 1885.

THOMPSON, ALBERT ELY, A.M., M.D., 625 Washington Trust Building, Washington, Pennsylvania. University of Pennsylvania School of Medicine, 1898. Chief Surgeon, City Hospital.

THOMPSON, EDGAR, M.Sc., A.M., M.D., Medical Corps, United States Navy, Washington, District of Columbia. St. Louis University School of Medicine (Beaumont Hospital Medical College), 1893. Captain, Medical Corps, United States Navy.

THOMPSON, EDWARD CAMERON, A.B., M.D., 139 Grand Street, Newburgh, New York. Columbia University College of Physicians and Surgeons, 1901. Attending Surgeon, St. Luke's Hospital.

THOMPSON, ELMER HARMON, M.D., 102½ East San Fernando Road, Burbank, California. Rush Medical College, 1903. Surgeon, Burbank Hospital.

THOMPSON, FRANK B., M.D., 417 Ferry Street, LaFayette, Indiana. Ohio State University College of Medicine (Starling Medical College), 1882. Chief of Surgical Staff, LaFayette Home Hospital; Member of Surgical Staff, St. Elizabeth's Hospital.

THOMPSON, GEORGE F., B.Sc., M.D., 4100 West Madison Street, Chicago, Illinois. Rush Medical College, 1899. Associate Professor of Surgery and Clinical Surgery, University of Illinois College of Medicine; Attending Surgeon, Cook County and West Side Hospitals; Examining Surgeon, Minneapolis, St. Paul and Sault Ste. Marie Railroad.

THOMPSON, GEORGE H., M.D., C.M., 18 Ashland Street, North Adams, Massachusetts. Faculty of Medicine, McGill University, 1899. Oculist and Aurist, North Adams Hospital.

THOMPSON, GORDON GRAHAM, B.Sc., M.D., 505 Cobb Building, Seattle, Washington. University of Illinois College of Medicine, 1910.

THOMPSON, JAMES EDWIN, M.B., B.Sc., F.R.C.S. (Eng.), 3224 Broadway, Galveston, Texas. University of London, 1887. Professor of the Principles and Practice of Surgery, University of Texas, Medical Department; Surgeon, John Sealy Hospital.

THOMPSON, JAMES RAYMOND, M.D., 322 Miller Building, Yakima, Washington. University of Illinois College of Medicine (College of Physicians and Surgeons, Chicago), 1900. President of Staff, St. Elizabeth's Hospital.

THOMPSON, JOHN ALBERT, B.Sc., A.M., M.D., Brookville, Indiana. University of Cincinnati College of Medicine (Miami Medical College), 1884. Emeritus Professor of Laryngology, University of Cincinnati College of Medicine; Consulting Laryngologist, Cincinnati General Hospital, Cincinnati. Retired.

THOMPSON, JOHN F., A.M., M.D., 211 State Street, Portland, Maine. Bowdoin Medical College, 1886. Professor of Gynecology, Bowdoin Medical School; Surgeon, Maine General Hospital.

THOMPSON, JOHN H., M.D., 406 Bryant Building, Kansas City, Missouri. Georgetown University School of Medicine, 1875; Columbia University, College of Physicians and Surgeons, 1877.

THOMPSON, LEROY, M.D., 30 North Michigan Avenue, Chicago, Illinois. Hahnemann Medical College and Hospital, Chicago, 1908. Consulting Oculist and Aurist, Chicago Telephone Company; Member of Associate Staff, St. Luke's Hospital.

THOMPSON, NEILL A., M.D., Fourth and Walnut Streets, Lumberton, North Carolina. University of Maryland School of Medicine (Maryland Medical College), 1905. President, Thompson Hospital.

THOMPSON, PHILIP PICKERING, A.B., M.D., 203 State Street, Portland, Maine. Johns Hopkins University, Medical Department, 1906. Adjunct Surgeon, Maine General Hospital; Consulting Surgeon, Webber Hospital, Biddeford, City Hospital, Portland.

THOMPSON, PIUS L., M.D., 307 Metz Building, Grand Rapids, Michigan. University of Michigan Medical School, 1903. Member of Executive Staff, Blodgett Memorial Hospital.

THOMPSON, SEPTIMUS, M.D., 464 Clarence Street, London, Ontario. Western University Medical School, 1900. Chief of Department of Ophthalmology, Rhinology, and Oto-Laryngology, Western University Medical School; Chief Surgeon, Department of Ophthalmology, Rhinology, and Oto-Laryngology, Victoria General Hospital; Member of Staff, St. Joseph's Hospital.

THOMPSON, WILLIAM McILWAIN, M.D., 25 East Washington Street, Chicago, Illinois. Hahnemann Medical College and Hospital, Chicago, 1892; University of Illinois College of Medicine, 1903. Consulting Surgeon, Marine Hospital of the United States Public Health Service.

THOMPSON, WILLIAM ROBERT, M.D., Fort Worth National Bank Building, Fort Worth, Texas. University of Maryland School of Medicine (College of Physicians and Surgeons, Baltimore), 1888. Member of Executive Committee, Hospital Staff, St. Joseph's Infirmary; Oculist and Aurist, Texas and Pacific, Santa Fe, Frisco, International and Great Northern, Houston and Texas Central, and Fort Worth and Denver City Railroads.

THOMPSON, WINFIELD OTIS, M.D., 1401 Central Avenue, Dodge City, Kansas. Jefferson Medical College, 1903. Surgeon, Thompson Hospital.

THOMS, HERBERT, M.D., 59 College Street, New Haven, Connecticut. Yale University School of Medicine, 1910. Attending Obstetrician, Grace Hospital, New Haven; Member of Consulting Staff, Milford Hospital, Milford, Hungerford Hospital, Torrington.

THOMSON, JAMES WOLSELY, M.D., C.M., 112 Vancouver Block, Vancouver, British Columbia. Faculty of Medicine, McGill University, 1907.

THOMSON, JOHN J., M.D., C.M., 3 Park Avenue, Mt. Vernon, New York. University of Toronto, Faculty of Medicine, 1902. Attending Otologist and Laryngologist, Mt. Vernon and Lawrence Hospitals, Bronxville.

THOMSON, JOSEPH OSCAR, M.D., C.M., Canton Hospital, Canton, China. Faculty of Medicine, McGill University, 1909. Professor of Clinical Surgery, Hackett Medical School; Surgeon, Canton Hospital; Consulting Surgeon, David Gregg Hospital for Women and Children.

THOMSON, WILLIAM ALEXANDER, M.D., C.M., Canada Life Building, Regina, Saskatchewan. University of Toronto Faculty of Medicine (Trinity Medical College), 1893. Member of Staff, Regina General and Grey Nun's Hospitals.

THOMSON, WILLIAM ROSS, M.D., Warsaw, New York. University of Virginia, Department of Medicine, 1896. Resident Surgeon, Warsaw Hospital.

THORNDIKE, AUGUSTUS, A.B., M.D., 496 Commonwealth Avenue, Boston, Massachusetts. Harvard Medical School, 1888. Retired.

THORNE, ISAAC WALTON, M.D., 516 Sutter Street, San Francisco, California. Leland Stanford Junior University School of Medicine (Cooper Medical College), 1896. Surgeon, Mary's Help Hospital.

THORNER, MOSES, M.D., North Vine Street, Santa Maria, California. Columbia University College of Physicians and Surgeons, 1898.

THORNING, W. BURTON, M.D., Kress Medical Building, Houston, Texas. University of Vermont College of Medicine, 1899.

THRASHER, ALLEN B., A.M., M.D., Seventh and Race Streets, Cincinnati, Ohio. University of Cincinnati College of Medicine (Medical College of Ohio), 1881. Laryngologist, Good Samaritan Hospital; Consulting Laryngologist, Christ Hospital.

THROCKMORTON, GEORGE K., B.Sc., M.D., 110 North Seventh Street, La Fayette, Indiana. Rush Medical College, 1887. Surgeon, St. Elizabeth's and La Fayette Home Hospitals.

THUERER, EDWARD W., B.L., M.D., 227 Hart-Albin Building, Billings, Montana. University of Illinois College of Medicine (College of Physicians and Surgeons, Chicago), 1907. Surgeon, St. Vincent's Hospital.

THUM, ERNST, M.D., 819 Avenue C, Bayonne, New Jersey. University and Bellevue Hospital Medical College, 1900. Visiting Surgeon, Eye, Ear, Nose, and Throat Department, Bayonne and Greenville Hospitals.

TIBBALS, FRANK BURR, A.B., M.D., 1212 Kresge Medical Building, Detroit, Michigan. University of Michigan Medical School, 1891. Assistant Professor of Medical Jurisprudence, Detroit College of Medicine and Surgery; Consulting Surgeon, Woman's Hospital.

TIECK, GUSTAV JOHN EHRICH, M.D., 40 East Forty-first Street, New York, New York. Long Island College Hospital, 1899. Surgeon, Ear, Nose, and Throat Department, St. Mark's Hospital.

TIGERT, HOLLAND McTYEIRE, M.D., 142 Seventh Avenue, North, Nashville, Tennessee. University of Nashville, Medical Department, 1901. Associate Professor of Diseases of Women, Vanderbilt University, Medical Department; Member of Surgical Staff, Nashville City Hospital.

TILTON, BENJAMIN TROWBRIDGE, A.B., M.D., 772 Madison Avenue, New York, New York. University of Freiburg, 1893. Visiting Surgeon, St. Mark's and Lincoln Hospitals; Consulting Surgeon, Manhattan State Hospital, Ward's Island, Correctional Hospital, Blackwell's Island, United Hospital, Port Chester.

686   *American College of Surgeons*

TIMBERLAKE, GIDEON, M.D., 816 St. Paul Street, Baltimore, Maryland. University of Virginia, Department of Medicine, 1902. Professor of Genito-Urinary Diseases and Chief of Clinic, University of Maryland School of Medicine and College of Physicians and Surgeons; Genito-Urinary Surgeon, University and St. Agnes' Hospitals; Consulting Urologist, Bay View Hospital, James Lawrence Kernan Hospital and Industrial School for Ruptured and Crippled Children; Surgeon, Church Home and Infirmary.

TIMBERMAN, ANDREW, A.B., M.D., 525 Citizens Bank Building, Columbus, Ohio. University of Cincinnati College of Medicine (Miami Medical College), 1894. Professor of Ophthalmology, Ohio State University College of Medicine; Ophthalmic Surgeon, Protestant and St. Francis Hospitals; Laryngologist and Rhinologist, Ohio Soldiers' and Sailors' Orphans' Home, Xenia.

TINGLEY, LOUISA PAINE, M.D., 9 Massachusetts Avenue, Boston, Massachusetts. Tufts College Medical School, 1901.

TINKER, MARTIN B., B.Sc., M.D., 101 South Aurora Street, Ithaca, New York. Jefferson Medical College, 1893; University of Berlin, 1899.

TINKHAM, HENRY CRAIN, M.Sc., M.D., 46 North Winooski Avenue, Burlington, Vermont. University of Vermont College of Medicine, 1883. Dean of Faculty and Professor of Clinical Surgery, University of Vermont College of Medicine; Attending Surgeon, Mary Fletcher Hospital; Consulting Surgeon, Fanny Allen Hospital, Winooski.

TITUS, PAUL, M.D., 1015 Highland Building, Pittsburgh, Pennsylvania. Yale University School of Medicine, 1908. Obstetrician, Western Pennsylvania Hospital; Obstetrician and Gynecologist, City Tuberculosis Hospital.

TIVNEN, RICHARD J., M.D., 800 Monroe Building, Chicago, Illinois. Rush Medical College, 1895. Instructor in Eye and Ear Department, Northwestern University Medical School; Ophthalmologist and Otologist, Mercy Hospital; Assistant Surgeon, Illinois Charitable Eye and Ear Infirmary.

TOBEY, GEORGE LORING, JR., M.D., 416 Marlborough Street, Boston, Massachusetts. Harvard Medical School, 1903. Instructor in Otology, Harvard Medical School, Harvard University Graduate School of Medicine; Assistant Aural Surgeon, Massachusetts Charitable Eye and Ear Infirmary.

TOBIN, JOHN R., M.D., 165 Milwaukee Street, Elgin, Illinois. Rush Medical College, 1901. Member of Attending Staff, St. Joseph's and Sherman Hospitals.

TODD, FRANK LESTER, A.M., M.D., 130 Bellefield Avenue, Pittsburgh, Pennsylvania. University of Pittsburgh School of Medicine, 1891. Member of Surgical Staff, Presbyterian Hospital; Member of Consulting Staff, Allegheny General Hospital.

TODD, GEORGE METZGER, M.D., 216 Colton Building, Toledo, Ohio. University of Pennsylvania School of Medicine, 1894. Director of Surgery, Toledo Hospital; Surgeon, New York Central, Michigan Central, Toledo and Ohio Central, Big Four, and Hocking Valley Railways.

TODD, HARRY COULTER, A.M., M.D., 507 Colcord Building, Oklahoma, Oklahoma. Bowdoin Medical School, 1900. Associate Professor of Diseases of Eye, Ear, Nose, and Throat, University of Oklahoma School of Medicine; Aural Surgeon, University Emergency Hospital; Consultant, Wesley and St. Anthony's Hospitals; Member of Staff, State University and St. Anthony's Hospitals; Aurist and Laryngologist, Oklahoma State Baptist Orphans' Home.

TODD, JOHN ORCHARD, M.D., C.M., 166 Hargrave Street, Winnipeg, Manitoba. Faculty of Medicine, University of Manitoba (Manitoba Medical College), 1890.

TODD, JOSEPH F., A.M., M.D., 402 Sterling Place, Brooklyn, New York. Long Island College Hospital, 1895. Gynecologist, St. Peter's Hospital.

TODD, PAUL JEROME, M.D., Kung Yee Hospital, Canton, China. University of Kansas School of Medicine (Kansas Medical College), 1902. Professor of Surgery, Kung Yee Medical College; Chief of Surgical Staff, Kung Yee Hospital.

TOLAND, CLARENCE GAINES, M.D., 1027 Pacific Mutual Building, Los Angeles, California. University Medical College, Kansas City, 1901.

TOMBAUGH, F. M., M.D., Iowa State Bank Building, Burlington, Iowa. Northwestern University Medical School, 1896.

TOMLIN, WILLIAM S., M.D., 520 Hume-Mansur Building, Indianapolis, Indiana. University of Louisville Medical Department, 1892. Member of Staff, St. Vincent's and Indianapolis City Hospitals.

TOMLINSON, RICHARD FRANK, M.D., 1286 Flood Building, San Francisco, California. University of California Medical School (Hahnemann Medical College of the Pacific, San Francisco), 1900. Visiting Surgeon, Hahnemann Hospital.

TOOKE, FREDERICK THOMAS, A.B., M.D., C.M., 368 Mountain Street, Montreal, Quebec. Faculty of Medicine, McGill University, 1899. Demonstrator of Ophthalmology, Faculty of Medicine, McGill University; Assistant Ophthalmic Surgeon, Royal Victoria Hospital; Ophthalmic Surgeon, Alexandra and Montreal Children's Hospitals, Montreal Foundling and Baby Hospital.

TOOMBS, PERCY WALTHALL, A.B., M.D., 319 South Dudley Street, Memphis, Tennessee. Tulane University of Louisiana School of Medicine, 1905. Professor of Obstetrics, University of Tennessee College of Medicine; Visiting Obstetrician, Memphis General and Baptist Memorial Hospitals.

TORBERT, JAMES R., Ph.B., M.D., 252 Marlborough Street, Boston, Massachusetts. Harvard Medical School, 1902. Instructor in Obstetrics, Harvard Medical School; Assistant Visiting Obstetrician, Boston Lying-in Hospital.

TOREK, FRANZ, A.M., M.D., 1021 Madison Avenue, New York, New York. Columbia University, College of Physicians and Surgeons, 1887. Visiting Surgeon, Lenox Hill Hospital; Attending Surgeon, New York Skin and Cancer Hospital.

TORMEY, THOMAS WILLIAM, B.Sc., M.D., Gay Building, Madison, Wisconsin. Rush Medical College, 1902. Instructor in Clinical Surgery, University of Wisconsin Medical School; Chief of Staff, Madison General Hospital.

TORREY, HARRY NORTON, B.Sc., A.M., M.D., 1033 David Whitney Building, Detroit, Michigan. Johns Hopkins University Medical Department, 1906. Associate Surgeon, Harper Hospital; Surgical Director, Manufacturers' Mutual Hospital.

TOWNE, GEORGE SCOTT, M.D., 150 Phila Street, Saratoga Springs, New York. Albany Medical College, 1899. Gynecologist, Saratoga Hospital.

TOWNSEND, CHARLES E., M.D., 231 Liberty Street, Newburgh, New York. University and Bellevue Hospital Medical College, 1892. Visiting Surgeon, St. Luke's Hospital; Consulting Surgeon, Highland Hospital, Beacon.

TOWNSEND, WILLIAM WARREN, M.D., Y.M.C.A. Building, Burlington, Vermont. University of Vermont College of Medicine, 1893. Professor of Genito-Urinary Diseases, University of Vermont College of Medicine; Attending Genito-Urinary Surgeon, Mary Fletcher Hospital, Burlington; Consulting Genito-Urinary Surgeon, Fanny Allen Hospital, Winooski, Proctor Hospital, Proctor, Rutland City Hospital, Rutland, Vermont, Champlain Valley Hospital, Plattsburg, New York.

TRACEY, WILLIAM JOSEPH, M.D., 23 West Avenue, Norwalk, Connecticut. University and Bellevue Hospital Medical College, 1889. Surgeon, Norwalk Hospital; Consulting Surgeon, Bridgeport and St. Vincent's Hospitals, Bridgeport, St. Mary's Hospital, Waterbury.

TRACY, STEPHEN E., M.D., 1527 Spruce Street, Philadelphia, Pennsylvania. University of Pennsylvania School of Medicine, 1898. Medical Director and Gynecologist, Stetson Hospital; Gynecologist, Gynecean Hospital; Consulting Obstetrician, Jewish Maternity Hospital.

TRAVER, ALVAH H., M.D., 27 Eagle Street, Albany, New York. Albany Medical College, 1898. Attending Surgeon, Child's Hospital, Albany Orphan Asylum; Assistant Surgeon, Albany Hospital.

TRAYLOR, GEORGE ALBERT, B.Sc., M.D., Lamar Building, Augusta, Georgia. University of Georgia, Medical Department, 1904. Associate Professor of Surgery, University of Georgia Medical Department; Attending Surgeon, Wilhenford Hospital.

TRAYNOR, JOSEPH PAUL, M.D., Medical Corps, United States Navy, Washington, District of Columbia. Bowdoin Medical School, 1901. Commander, Medical Corps, United States Navy.

TREAT, DAVID L., M.D., 221 East Third Street, Flint, Michigan. Ohio State University College of Medicine (Starling Medical College), 1898.

TREON, FREDERICK, M.D., Scotts Building, Chamberlain, South Dakota. University of Cincinnati College of Medicine (Medical College of Ohio), 1879. Member of Staff, Chamberlain Hospital and Sanitarium.

TRIBBLE, ALBERT HENRY, M.D., 340 Central Avenue, Hot Springs, Arkansas. University of Pennsylvania School of Medicine (Medico-Chirurgical College), 1905. Member of Staff, St. Joseph's Hospital.

TRIBLE, GEORGE BARNETT, M.D., Medical Corps, United States Navy, Washington, District of Columbia. Washington University Medical School, 1906. Instructor of Ophthalmology and Otology, United States Naval Medical School; Commander, Medical Corps, United States Navy.

TRICK, HARRY R., M.D., 522 West Ferry Street, Buffalo, New York. University of Buffalo, Department of Medicine, 1901. Associate Professor of Surgery, University of Buffalo, Department of Medicine; Assistant Attending Surgeon, Buffalo General Hospital; Attending Surgeon, Buffalo City Hospital.

TRIMBLE, CHARLES GARNET, B.Sc., M.D., Yenping, Fukien, China. Northwestern University Medical School, 1910. Superintendent, Alden Speare Memorial Hospital.

TRITCH, JOHN CHARLES, A.M., M.D., American National Bank Building, Findlay, Ohio. Homeopathic Hospital College, 1877. Chief of Staff and Gynecologist, Findlay Home and Hospital.

TRONNES, NILS L., M.D., Fargo Clinic, Fargo, North Dakota. University of Christiania, 1903. Staff Surgeon, St. Luke's Hospital.

TROUT, HUGH HENRY, M.D., 1303 Franklin Road, Roanoke, Virginia. University of Virginia, Department of Medicine, 1902. Surgeon-in-Chief, Jefferson Hospital.

TROWBRIDGE, EDWARD HENRY, A.B., M.D., 28 Pleasant Street, Worcester, Massachusetts. Bowdoin Medical School (Medical School of Maine), 1884. Operating Surgeon in Charge, Harvard Private Hospital; Consulting Surgeon, Worcester City Hospital.

TRUBY, ALBERT E., B.Sc., M.D., Medical Corps, United States Army, Washington, District of Columbia. University of Pennsylvania School of Medicine, 1897. Colonel, Medical Corps, United States Army.

TRUESDALE, PHILEMON EDWARDS, M.D., 151 Rock Street, Fall River, Massachusetts. Harvard Medical School, 1898. Surgeon, St. Anne's Hospital.

TRUESDELL, EDWARD DELAVAN, A.B., M.D., 136 West Fifty-eighth Street, New York, New York. Columbia University, College of Physicians and Surgeons, 1906.

TRUSLOW, WALTER, M.D., 67 Hanson Place, Brooklyn, New York. Long Island College Hospital; 1895. Consulting Orthopedic Surgeon, Brooklyn, Seaside, Far Rockaway, and Edge Cliff Hospitals, Bureau of Charities, Brooklyn.

TUCKER, BEVERLEY, M.D., 301 Ferguson Building, Colorado Springs, Colorado. University of Virginia, Department of Medicine, 1889. Attending Obstetrician, Glockner Hospital.

TUCKER, ERNEST FANNING, A.B., M.D., Medical Building, Portland, Oregon. Harvard Medical School, 1884. Professor of Gynecology, University of Oregon Medical School; Visiting Surgeon, St. Vincent's Hospital.

TUCKERMAN, JACOB EDWARD, A.B., M.D., 733 Osborn Building, Cleveland, Ohio. Western Reserve University School of Medicine (Cleveland College of Physicians and Surgeons), 1902. Member of Surgical Staff, Glenville Hospital.

TUCKERMAN, WARRER HOPKINS, A.B., M.D., 733 Osborn Building, Cleveland, Ohio. Western Reserve University School of Medicine (Cleveland College of Physicians and Surgeons), 1904. Laryngologist, Glenville Hospital; Visiting Laryngologist and Department Head, Cleveland City Hospital; Assistant to Staff, Department of Oto-Laryngology, St. Luke's Hospital.

TUCKERMAN, WILLIAM COLEGROVE, A.B., M.D., 733 Osborn Building, Cleveland, Ohio. Western Reserve University School of Medicine (Cleveland College of Physicians and Surgeons), 1905. Ophthalmologist, Glenville Hospital.

TUFFIER, THEODORE, Boulevard St. Germain, Paris, France. Faculty of Medicine, Paris. Professor of Surgery, Faculty of Medicine; Chief, Hospital Beaujon; Surgeon, Hospitals of Paris.

TUHOLSKE, HERMAN, M.D., LL.D., 453 North Taylor Avenue, St. Louis, Missouri. Washington University Medical School (Missouri Medical College), 1870. Honorary Chief Surgeon, Jewish Hospital; Consulting Surgeon, Jewish Home for Chronic Invalids, St. John's Hospital.

TULL, EDWARD EMORY, M.D., 40 East Forty-first Street, New York, New York. University of Maryland School of Medicine, 1887. Associate Surgeon, Woman's and French Hospitals, New York Polyclinic Medical School and Hospital.

TUPPER, PAUL YOER, M.D., Wall Building, St. Louis, Missouri. University of Louisville, Medical Department (Hospital College of Medicine), 1880. Clinical Professor of Surgery, Washington University Medical School; Visiting Surgeon, St. Luke's Hospital; Consulting Surgeon, Bethesda, Jewish and St. John's Hospitals, St. Louis Eye, Ear, Nose, and Throat Infirmary.

TURCK, RAYMOND CUSTER, M.D., 1535 Riverside Avenue, Jacksonville, Florida. University and Bellevue Hospital Medical College (New York University Medical College), 1896.

TUREMAN, HERBERT G., M.D., 1100 Rialto Building, Kansas City, Missouri. University Medical College, Kansas City, 1897. Oto-Laryngologist, St. Joseph's and Christian Church Hospitals, Gillis Orphans' Home.

TURENNE, AUGUSTO, M.D., Paraguay 1438, Montevideo, Uruguay. Faculty of Medicine, University of Montevideo, 1894. Professor of Obstetrics and Gynecology and Professor in Obstetrical Clinic, Faculty of Medicine, University of Montevideo; Chief of Medical Protective Service, House of Maternity.

TURNBULL, JAMES L., M.B., M.D., C.M., 718 Granville Street, Vancouver, British Columbia. Toronto University Faculty of Medicine, 1889.

TURNBULL, THOMAS, M.D., 226 Somerset Block, Winnipeg, Manitoba. Faculty of Medicine, McGill University, 1899.

TURNER, BENJAMIN WEEMS, M.D., 705 Scanlon Building, Houston, Texas. University of Texas Department of Medicine, 1911. Urologist, Baptist Sanitarium and Hospital; Visiting and Consulting Urologist, Municipal Hospital.

TURNER, GEORGE GREY, M.B., M.S., F.R.C.S. (Eng.), The Hawthorns, Osborne Road, Newcastle-on-Tyne, England. University of Durham, 1898. Lecturer on Surgery, University of Durham; Honorary Surgeon, Royal Infirmary; Major, Royal Army Medical Corps (Ter.).

TURNER, JAMES GIBBONS, M.D., 60 Sheldon Street, Houghton, Michigan. University of Maryland School of Medicine, 1878. Surgeon, St. Joseph's Hospital, Hancock.

TURNER, ROBERT LEE, B.Sc., M.D., 1421 Twentieth Avenue, Meridian, Mississippi. Tulane University of Louisiana School of Medicine, 1891. Surgeon in Charge, Turner Hospital.

TURNER, WALTER B., M.D., 300 North Phelps Street, Youngstown, Ohio. Indiana University School of Medicine, 1909. Attending Surgeon, Youngstown Hospital.

TURNER, WILLIAM GEORGE, B.A., M.D., C.M., M.R.C.S. (Eng.), 386 Sherbrooke Street, West, Montreal, Quebec. Faculty of Medicine, McGill University, 1900. Clinical Professor of Orthopedic Surgery, Faculty of Medicine, McGill University; Surgeon in Charge, Orthopedic Department, Royal Victoria Hospital.

TURNURE, PERCY R., A.M., M.D., 131 East Sixty-sixth Street, New York, New York. Columbia University, College of Physicians and Surgeons, 1898. Assistant Professor of Clinical Surgery, Cornell University Medical College; Attending Surgeon, French Hospital; Associate Attending Surgeon, New York Hospital; Consulting Surgeon, New York State Reformatory for Women, Bedford Hills, St. Faith's House, Tarrytown.

TUTHILL, ALEXANDER MACKENZIE, M.D., 416 Goodrich Building, Phoenix, Arizona. University of California Medical School (University of Southern California College of Medicine), 1895.

TUTTLE, ARNOLD DWIGHT, M.D., Medical Corps, United States Army, Washington, District of Columbia. University of Maryland School of Medicine, 1906. Major, Medical Corps, United States Army.

TWINCH, SIDNEY A., M.D., 24 Fulton Street, Newark, New Jersey. Columbia University, College of Physicians and Surgeons, 1890. Visiting Surgeon, Home for Crippled Children; Orthopedic Surgeon, Home for Incurables and Hospital; Attending Orthopedist, Beth Israel Hospital.

TWINING, GRANVILLE HOWARD, B.Sc., M.S., M.D., Mobridge, South Dakota. Rush Medical College, 1910. Surgeon, Mobridge Hospital.

TWITCHELL, HERBERT FRANCIS, M.D., 10 Pine Street, Portland, Maine. Bowdoin Medical School, 1883. Clinical Instructor in Surgery, Bowdoin Medical School; Surgeon, Maine General Hospital; Consultant, Maine Eye and Ear Infirmary, Children's Hospital, Portland, Webber Hospital, Biddeford, Bath City Hospital, Bath.

TWITCHELL, MARSHALL C., M.D., 162 College Street, Burlington, Vermont. University of Vermont College of Medicine, 1893. Ophthalmologist and Oto-Laryngologist, Mary Fletcher Hospital; Consulting Ophthalmologist and Oto-Laryngologist, Fanny Allen Hospital.

TWOHIG, DAVID JAMES, M.D., 11 North Main Street, Fond du Lac, Wisconsin. University of Illinois College of Medicine (College of Physicians and Surgeons), 1904. Member of Surgical Staff, St. Agnes' Hospital.

TWYMAN, ELMER D., M.D., 416 Argyle Building, Kansas City, Missouri. Northwestern University Medical School, 1907. Attending Surgeon, Christian Church and Children's Mercy Hospitals.

TYLER, GEORGE T., JR., A.M., M.D., 711 East North Street, Greenville, South Carolina. Johns Hopkins University Medical Department, 1904. Chief Surgeon, Dr. Tyler's Surgical Hospital; Member of Staff, Greenville City Hospital.

TYREE, JOSEPH EDGAR, A.B., M.D., Walker Bank Building, Salt Lake City, Utah. Rush Medical College, 1907.

TYROLER, ADOLPH, M.D., 337 Kerckhoff Building, Los Angeles, California. University of Michigan Medical School, 1894. Attending Surgeon, Kaspare Cohn Hospital; Surgeon in Charge, Santa Fe Railroad Hospital; Assistant Chief Surgeon, Santa Fe Coast Lines Hospital Association.

TYSON, HENRY HAWKINS, M.D., 11 East Forty-eighth Street, New York, New York. University and Bellevue Hospital Medical College (New York University Medical College), 1887. Instructor in Ophthalmology, Columbia University, College of Physicians and Surgeons; Ophthalmic Surgeon, Herman Knapp Memorial Eye Hospital; Ophthalmologist, Sea Breeze Hospital, Brooklyn, Letchworth Village, Thiells; Assistant, Eye Department, Vanderbilt Clinic.

ULLMAN, ALFRED, M.D., 1712 Eutaw Place, Baltimore, Maryland. University of Maryland School of Medicine (College of Physicians and Surgeons, Baltimore), 1902. Clinical Professor of Surgery, University of Maryland School of Medicine and College of Physicians and Surgeons; Visiting Surgeon, Mercy Hospital, Hebrew Hospital and Asylum.

UNDERHILL, ALBERT JAMES, A.B., M.D., 1800 North Charles Street, Baltimore, Maryland. Johns Hopkins University, Medical Department, 1901. Clinical Professor of Diseases of the Genito-Urinary Organs, University of Maryland School of Medicine and College of Physicians and Surgeons; Chief of Clinic and Attending Genito-Urinary Surgeon, University Hospital; Consulting Genito-Urinary Surgeon, St. Joseph's Hospital.

UPDEGRAFF, ELMER J., M.D., 512 McCague Building, Omaha, Nebraska. University of Nebraska College of Medicine, 1899. Lecturer and Clinical Assistant, University of Nebraska College of Medicine; Surgeon, Nebraska Methodist Episcopal and St. Joseph's Hospitals.

UPHAM, ROY, M.D., 300 McDonough Street, Brooklyn, New York. New York Homeopathic Medical College and Flower Hospital, 1901. Professor of Gastroenterology, New York Homeopathic Medical College and Flower Hospital; Attending Gastroenterologist, Cumberland Street, Prospect Heights, and Carson C. Peck Memorial Hospitals; Consulting Gastroenterologist, Jamaica Hospital, Jamaica.

UPSHUR, ALFRED PARKER, M.D., Medical Corps, United States Army, Washington, District of Columbia. Medical College of Virginia, 1908. Major, Medical Corps, United States Army.

UPSON, GEORGE DWIGHT, M.D., 841 Hanna Building, Cleveland, Ohio. Western Reserve University School of Medicine, 1889. Consulting Surgeon, St. Alexis Hospital; Chief Surgeon, Cleveland Railway.

UREN, JOHN FRANKLIN, M.D., C.M., 520 Church Street, Toronto, Ontario. University of Toronto, Faculty of Medicine, 1890. Associate in Surgery and Clinical Surgery, University of Toronto, Faculty of Medicine; Surgeon, St. Michael's Hospital.

URQUHART, ROY THOMAS, M.D., Ashton Building, Grand Rapids, Michigan. University of Illinois College of Medicine, 1901. Member of Staff, St. Mary's and Blodgett Memorial Hospitals, D. A. Blodgett Home for Children.

VAIL, DERRICK T., M.D., 24 East Eighth Street, Cincinnati, Ohio. University of Cincinnati College of Medicine (Miami Medical College), 1890. Emeritus Professor of Ophthalmology, University of Cincinnati College of Medicine; Consulting Ophthalmologist, Cincinnati General Hospital.

VALK, ARTHUR DE TALMA, A.B., A.M., M.D., Wachovia Bank Building, Winston-Salem, North Carolina. Johns Hopkins University Medical Department, 1910. Visiting Surgeon, City Memorial Hospital.

VAN BEUREN, FREDERICK T., JR., A.B., M.D., 812 Park Avenue, New York, New York. Columbia University, College of Physicians and Surgeons, 1902. Associate in Surgery and Dean, Columbia University, College of Physicians and Surgeons; Attending Surgeon, Sloane Hospital for Women.

VANCE, CHARLES A., A.M., M.D., 310 Security Trust Company Building, Lexington, Kentucky. University of Louisville, Medical Department (Kentucky University, Medical Department), 1903. Member of Consulting Surgical Staff, St. Joseph's Hospital; Member of Attending Surgical Staff, Good Samaritan Hospital.

VANCE, JAMES, M.D., 314 Mills Building, El Paso, Texas. University of Louisville, Medical Department (Hospital College of Medicine), 1899. Staff Surgeon, El Paso County Hospital; Visiting Surgeon, Hotel Dieu Hospital; District Surgeon, United States Bureau of War Risk Insurance.

VAN DEN BERG, HENRY J., M.D., Metz Building, Grand Rapids, Michigan. University of Michigan Medical School, 1905. Member of Surgical Staff, Blodgett Memorial and Butterworth Hospitals.

VANDERSLICE, GEORGE K., M.D., Mellen Street and Willard Avenue, Phoebus, Virginia. University of Virginia, Department of Medicine, 1892. Surgeon, Dixie Hospital, Hampton.

VANDER VEER, ALBERT, A.M., M.D., Ph.D., LL.D., 28 Eagle Street, Albany, New York. George Washington University Medical School, 1863. Retired.

VANDER VEER, EDGAR A., Ph.B., M.D., 28 Eagle Street, Albany, New York. Albany Medical College, 1898. Attending Surgeon, Albany Hospital.

VANDER VEER, JAMES N., A.M., M.D., 28 Eagle Street, Albany, New York. Albany Medical College, 1903. Clinical Professor of Genito-Urinary Surgery, Albany Medical College; Attending Genito-Urinary Surgeon for Males, Albany Hospital, Albany; Consulting Genito-Urinary Surgeon, Mary McClellan Hospital, Cambridge.

VANDEVENTER, VIVIAN H., M.D., 403 North Main Street, Ishpeming, Michigan. University of Maryland School of Medicine (College of Physicians and Surgeons, Baltimore), 1896. Chief Surgeon, Ishpeming Hospital, Cleveland Cliffs Iron Company.

VAN DUSEN, JAMES WALLACE, M.D., Medical Corps, United States Army, Washington, District of Columbia. University of Michigan Medical School, 1896. Colonel, Medical Corps, United States Army.

VAN DUYN, EDWARD SEGUIN, B.Sc., M.D., University Building, Syracuse, New York. Syracuse University College of Medicine, 1897. Professor of Surgery, Syracuse University College of Medicine; Surgeon, University Hospital of the Good Shepard; Consulting Surgeon, Syracuse Free Dispensary.

VAN ETTEN, ROYAL CORNELIUS, A.B., M.D., 117 East Seventy-sixth Street, New York, New York. Columbia University College of Physicians and Surgeons, 1910. Associate in Obstetrics and Gynecology, Columbia University College of Physicians and Surgeons; Attending Gynecologist, Vanderbilt Clinic and Lenox Hill Dispensary; Assistant Attending Gynecologist and Obstetrician, Sloane Hospital for Women; Adjunct Attending Gynecologist, Lenox Hill Hospital.

VAN KAATHOVEN, JEAN JACQUES ABRAM, A.B., M.D., 628 Van Nuys Building, Los Angeles, California. University of Pennsylvania School of Medicine, 1902. Instructor in Surgery, Graduate School of Medicine of the University of California; Surgeon, Los Angeles County Hospital.

VAN KIRK, FRANK J., M.D., C.M., Bellingham National Bank Building, Bellingham, Washington. University of Minnesota Medical School (Minneapolis College of Physicians and Surgeons), 1899.

VAN KIRK, FRANK W., B.Sc., M.D., 225 Milton Avenue, Janesville, Wisconsin. Rush Medical College, 1901.

VAN LENNEP, GUSTAVE A., M.D., 2104 Chestnut Street, Philadelphia, Pennsylvania. Hahnemann Medical College and Hospital, Philadelphia, 1894. Clinical Professor of Surgery and Surgeon, Hahnemann Medical College and Hospital; Consulting Surgeon, West Philadelphia General Homeopathic Hospital and Dispensary, Philadelphia, Pottstown Homeopathic Hospital, Pottstown; Attending Surgeon, Homeopathic State Hospital, Allentown.

VAN LOON, ARTHUR BURTON, M.D., 198 State Street, Albany, New York. Albany Medical College, 1891. Attending Surgeon and Gynecologist, Homeopathic Hospital.

VAN METER, BENJAMIN FRANKLIN, JR., M.D., 183 North Upper Street, Lexington, Kentucky. University and Bellevue Hospital Medical College (Bellevue Hospital Medical College), 1897. Consulting Surgeon, St. Joseph's Hospital.

VANSANT, EUGENE LARUE, M.D., 1929 Chestnut Street, Philadelphia, Pennsylvania. Jefferson Medical College, 1884. Emeritus Professor of Diseases of Nose and Throat, Philadelphia Polyclinic and College for Graduates in Medicine.

VAN WART, GEORGE CLOWES, M.D., 141 York Street, Fredericton, New Brunswick. University of Pennsylvania School of Medicine, 1890. Chief of Surgical Staff, Victoria Public Hospital.

VAN ZWALUWENBURG, CORNELIUS, M.D., 1111 Main Street, Riverside, California. University of Michigan Medical School, 1885.

VARELA, RICARDO PAZOS, M.D., Plateros de San Pedro 109, Lima, Peru. Faculty of Medicine, University of San Marcos, 1908.

VARGAS, LUIS, M.D., Casilla 2122, Santiago, Chile. Faculty of Medicine, University of Chile, 1905.

VASTERLING, PAUL F., M.D., 1600 California Avenue, St. Louis, Missouri. Washington University Medical School (St. Louis Medical College), 1883. Chief Surgeon, Missouri Pacific Hospital.

VAUGHAN, GEORGE TULLY, M.D., 1718 I Street, Northwest, Washington, District of Columbia. University of Virginia Department of Medicine, 1879; University and Bellevue Hospital Medical College, 1880. Professor and Head of Department of Surgery, Georgetown University School of Medicine; Chief Surgeon, Georgetown University Hospital; Surgeon, Tuberculosis Hospital; Consulting Surgeon, Government Hospital for Insane, Washington Asylum Hospital, United States Public Health Service.

VAUGHAN, J. WALTER, A.B., M.D., 987 Jefferson Avenue, East, Detroit, Michigan. University of Michigan Medical School, 1904. Associate Attending Surgeon, Harper Hospital.

VAUGHAN, JAMES ALBERT, A.B., M.D., Exchange Building, Memphis, Tennessee. University of Virginia, Department of Medicine, 1907.

VAUGHAN, JOHN COLIN, M.D., 156 East Seventy-ninth Street, New York, New York. Columbia University, College of Physicians and Surgeons, 1907.

Associate in Anatomy, Columbia University, College of Physicians and Surgeons; Junior Consulting Surgeon, Manhattan Eye, Ear, and Throat Hospital; Director and Visiting Surgeon, Volunteer Hospital; Senior Visiting Surgeon, Sing Sing Prison Hospital, Ossining.

VAUGHAN, ROGER THROOP, Ph.B., M.D., 30 North Michigan Avenue, Chicago, Illinois. Rush Medical College, 1903. Instructor in Surgery, Rush Medical College; Attending Surgeon, Cook County Hospital.

VAZ, FERNANDO, M.D., Rua Assembléa 27, Rio de Janeiro, Brazil. Medical School of Rio de Janeiro, 1900. Visiting Surgeon, Penitencia Hospital; Surgeon, Pró-Matre Hospital, Public Assistance of Rio de Janeiro and Sanatorio do Rio Comprido.

VEASEY, CLARENCE ARCHIBALD, A.M., M.D., 404 Paulsen Building, Spokane, Washington. Jefferson Medical College, 1890. Ophthalmologist and Oto-Laryngologist, Deaconess Hospital; Ophthalmologist and Aurist, St. Luke's Hospital.

VEDDER, EDWARD B., Ph.B., A.M., M.D., Medical Corps, United States Army, Washington, District of Columbia. University of Pennsylvania School of Medicine, 1902. Lieutenant Colonel, Medical Corps, United States Army.

VEENBOER, WILLIAM HENRY, A.B., M.D., Metz Building, Grand Rapids, Michigan. University of Michigan Medical School, 1903. Member of Surgical Staff, St. Mary's and Blodgett Memorial Hospitals.

VEGAS, MARCELINO HERRERA, M.D., Florida 846, Buenos Aires, Argentina. Faculty of Medicine, National University of Buenos Aires, 1896. Surgeon, P. Pinero's Hospital.

VEINTEMILLAS, FELIX, M.D., Casilla 96A, La Paz, Bolivia. Faculty of Medicine, University of St. Andres, 1913. Surgeon, Hospitals of La Paz.

VENABLE, CHARLES SCOTT, M.D., 801 Central Trust Building, San Antonio, Texas. University of Virginia, Department of Medicine, 1900. Surgeon, Jackson Hospital; Attending Orthopedist, Robert B. Green Memorial Hospital.

VERDI, WILLIAM FRANCIS, A.M., M.D., 27 Elm Street, New Haven, Connecticut. Yale University School of Medicine, 1894. Clinical Professor of Surgery, Yale University School of Medicine; Chief Surgeon, Hospital of St. Raphael; Attending Surgeon, New Haven Hospital; Consulting Surgeon, St. Vincent's Hospital, Bridgeport, St. Mary's Hospital, Waterbury, Middlesex Hospital, Middletown.

VERHOEFF, FREDERICK HERMAN, Ph.B., A.M., M.D., 101 Newbury Street, Boston, Massachusetts. Johns Hopkins University, Medical Department, 1899. Assistant Professor of Ophthalmology, Harvard Medical School; Ophthalmic Surgeon and Pathologist, Massachusetts Charitable Eye and Ear Infirmary.

VEST, CECIL WOODS, B.Sc., M.D., 700 Park Avenue, Baltimore, Maryland. Johns Hopkins University, Medical Department, 1908. Dispensary Gynecologist, Johns Hopkins Hospital; Gynecologist in Charge, Federal

Clinic; Visiting Gynecologist, Union Memorial Hospital, Church Home and Infirmary; Surgeon, Robert Garrett Hospital, Baltimore, Cambridge-Maryland Hospital, Cambridge.

VICKERY, EUGENE A., M.D., Medical Corps, United States Navy, Washington, District of Columbia. Harvard Medical School, 1903. Lieutenant Commander, Medical Corps, United States Navy.

VIETOR, AGNES C., M.D., Trinity Court, Boston, Massachusetts. Woman's Medical College of the New York Infirmary for Women and Children, 1892.

VIETOR, JOHN A., A.B., M.D., 8 East Sixty-sixth Street, New York, New York. Columbia University, College of Physicians and Surgeons, 1911. Instructor in Surgery, Columbia University, College of Physicians and Surgeons; Assistant Attending Surgeon, New York Hospital, New York; Consulting Surgeon, United Hospital, Port Chester.

VILLARÁN, CÁRLOS, M.D., Alfonso Ugarte 409, Lima, Peru. Faculty of Medicine, University of Lima, 1906. Professor of Clinical Surgery, Faculty of Medicine, University of Lima; Surgeon, Santa Ana and Military Hospitals; Director, Villarán Clinic.

VINCENT, BETH, A.B., M.D., 295 Beacon Street, Boston, Massachusetts. Harvard Medical School, 1902. Assistant in Surgery, Harvard Medical School; Surgeon, Boston Infants' Hospital; Assistant Visiting Surgeon, Massachusetts General Hospital.

VINCENT, WESLEY GROVE, A.B., M.D., 498 West End Avenue, New York, New York. Yale University School of Medicine, 1900. Assistant Professor of Surgery, New York Post-Graduate Medical School; Assistant Surgeon, New York Post-Graduate Medical School and Hospital; Provisional Assistant Visiting Surgeon, Harlem Hospital.

VINEBERG, HIRAM N., M.D., C.M., 751 Madison Avenue, New York, New York. Faculty of Medicine, McGill University, 1878. Consulting Gynecologist, Mt. Sinai Hospital; Gynecologist-in-Chief, Beth Moses Hospital, Brooklyn; Consulting Gynecologist, Montefiore Home and Bronx Maternity Hospital.

VINSONHALER, FRANK, M.D., Urquhart Building, Little Rock, Arkansas. Columbia University, College of Physicians and Surgeons, 1885. Professor of Ophthalmology, University of Arkansas, Medical Department; Visiting Ophthalmologist, Logan H. Roots Memorial City Hospital.

VIPOND, CHARLES W., M.D., C.M., 462 Sherbrooke Street, West, Montreal, Quebec. Faculty of Medicine, McGill University, 1895. Surgeon, Montreal Children's Hospital.

VIRDEN, JOHN ELMER, A.B., M.D., 529 Courtlandt Avenue, New York, New York. University and Bellevue Hospital Medical College, 1890. Associate Professor of Ophthalmology, New York Post Graduate Medical School and Hospital; Surgeon, Bronx Eye and Ear Infirmary; Visiting Ophthalmologist, Union and Lincoln Hospitals; Assistant Visiting Ophthalmologist, Baby's Wards, Post Graduate Hospital.

VOGT, WILLIAM H., M.D., 330 Metropolitan Building, St. Louis, Missouri. Washington University Medical School (Missouri Medical College), 1897. Instructor in Gynecology and Obstetrics, St. Louis University School of Medicine; Consulting Obstetrician, St. Louis Maternity Hospital; Consulting Gynecologist and Obstetrician, City Sanitarium; Visiting Gynecologist and Obstetrician, St. Louis City Hospital; Associate Gynecologist, St. John's Hospital.

VOIGT, CHARLES BERNARD, M.D., 1702 Broadway, Mattoon, Illinois. University of Illinois College of Medicine (College of Physicians and Surgeons), 1900. Oculist and Aurist, Methodist Memorial Hospital, Mattoon, Illinois Masonic Home Hospital, Sullivan.

VOISLAWSKY, ANTONIE P., B.Sc., M.D., 33 East Sixty-eighth Street, New York, New York. Dartmouth Medical School, 1897. Laryngologist and Chief of Clinic, St. Luke's Hospital; Attending Oto-Laryngologist, Staten Island Hospital, Tompkinsville; Consulting Otologist, Harlem Eye, Ear, and Throat Infirmary, Manhattan Maternity and Dispensary, New York, Northern Westchester Hospital, Mt. Kisco; Laryngologist, Fifth Avenue Hospital, New York.

VOORHEES, JAMES DITMARS, A.M., M.D., 106 East Sixtieth Street, New York, New York. Columbia University, College of Physicians and Surgeons, 1893. Obstetrician, Sloane Hospital for Women; Greenwich Hospital, Greenwich, Connecticut, Southampton Hospital, Southampton, New York, Overlook Hospital, Summit, New Jersey.

VOSBURG, WALTER HALL, M.D., Masonic Temple, Dunkirk, New York. Ohio State University College of Homeopathic Medicine (Cleveland Medical College), 1897. Member of Surgical Staff, Brook's Memorial Hospital, Dunkirk; Member of Consulting Staff, Gowanda State Homeopathic Hospital, Collins.

VOSSELER, THEODORE L., Phar.G., M.D., 390A Monroe Street, Brooklyn, New York. Long Island College Hospital, 1905. Lecturer in Surgical Anatomy, Long Island College Hospital; Attending Surgeon, Williamsburgh Hospital; Associate Surgeon, Greenpoint Hospital.

WADDELL, W. E., M.D., 927 Citizens National Bank Building, Los Angeles, California. Ohio State University College of Homeopathic Medicine (Pulte Medical College), 1887.

WADE, HENRY ALBERT, M.D., 495 Greene Avenue, Brooklyn, New York. University and Bellevue Hospital Medical College (New York University Medical College), 1894. Surgeon-in-Chief, Dr. Wade's Private Hospital; Attending Surgeon, Bethany Deaconess Hospital; Attending Gynecologist, Williamsburgh Hospital.

WADHAMS, ROBERT PELTON, Ph.B., M.D., 11 East Forty-eighth Street, New York, New York. University and Bellevue Hospital Medical College, 1906. Clinical Professor of Surgery, University and Bellevue Hospital Medical College; Assistant Attending Surgeon, Bellevue Hospital; Attending Surgeon, West Side Dispensary and Hospital; Consulting Surgeon, Charlotte Hungerford Memorial Hospital, Torrington, Connecticut.

WADHAMS, SANFORD H., Ph.B., M.A., M.D., Medical Corps, United States Army, Washington, District of Columbia. Yale University School of Medicine, 1896. Lieutenant Colonel, Medical Corps, United States Army.

WADSWORTH, RICHARD G., M.D., 520 Commonwealth Avenue, Boston, Massachusetts. Harvard Medical School, 1900. Assistant in Gynecology, Harvard Medical School; Surgeon, Out-Patient Department, Free Hospital for Women, Brookline.

WAGNER, THOMAS H., M.D., 315 Jefferson Street, Joliet, Illinois. Northwestern University Medical School, 1898. Member of Staff, St. Joseph's Hospital.

WAHRER, CARL WILLIAM, M.D., Physicians Building, Sacramento, California. Rush Medical College, 1902.

WAINWRIGHT, JONATHAN M., A.M., M.D., 912 Clay Avenue, Scranton, Pennsylvania. Columbia University, College of Physicians and Surgeons, 1899. Surgeon-in-Chief, Moses Taylor Hospital.

WAKEFIELD, ALICE E., M.D., 154 East Thirty-seventh Street, New York, New York. Woman's Medical College of the New York Infirmary for Women and Children, 1888. Attending Ophthalmologist and Otologist, New York Infirmary for Women and Children.

WAKEFIELD, RALPH WALDO, M.D., 16 High Street, Bar Harbor, Maine. Jefferson Medical College, 1902. Surgeon, Bar Harbor Medical and Surgical Hospital.

WAKEFIELD, W. FRANCIS B., M.B., M.D., C.M., 1065 Sutter Street, San Francisco, California. University of Toronto, Faculty of Medicine, 1893.

WALDECK, GEORGE MATTHEW, M.D., 1001 David Whitney Building, Detroit, Michigan. University of Michigan Medical School, 1908. Associate Attendant, Department of Ophthalmology and Oto-Laryngology, Grace Hospital.

WALDO, RALPH, M.D., 54 West Seventy-first Street, New York, New York. University and Bellevue Hospital Medical College (New York University Medical College), 1882. Clinical Professor of Gynecology, Fordham University School of Medicine; Gynecologist, Lebanon Hospital; Consulting Gynecologist, Jewish Maternity Hospital, New York, Nyack Hospital, Nyack, Rockaway Beach Hospital, Rockaway Beach, Southampton Hospital, Southampton.

WALDROP, R. W., M.D., 306 Realty Building, Bessemer, Alabama. University of Louisville, Medical Department (Louisville Medical College), 1896. Surgeon, Elizabeth Duncan Memorial Hospital.

WALES, ERNEST DE WOLFE, B.Sc., M.D., 1236 North Pennsylvania Street, Indianapolis, Indiana. Harvard Medical School, 1899. Clinical Professor of Diseases of Ear, Nose, and Throat, Indiana University School of Medicine.

WALKER, ALONZO BYRON, M.D., 815 Fourth Street, Northwest, Canton, Ohio. Jefferson Medical College, 1881.

WALKER, DAVID HAROLD, M.D., 399 Commonwealth Avenue, Boston, Massachusetts. Harvard Medical School, 1898. Instructor in Otology, Harvard Graduate School of Medicine; Aural Surgeon, Massachusetts Charitable Eye and Ear Infirmary; Otologist, Massachusetts General and Children's Hospitals, New England Hospital for Women and Children.

WALKER, EDWARD WOOD, A.B., M.D., 214 West Seventh Street, Cincinnati, Ohio. University of Cincinnati College of Medicine (Medical College of Ohio), 1877. Emeritus Professor of Clinical Surgery, University of Cincinnati College of Medicine; Surgeon, Deaconess Hospital.

WALKER, EDWIN M.D., Ph.D., 5 Cherry Street, Evansville, Indiana. Medical College of Evansville, 1874; University and Bellevue Hospital Medical College (University of the City of New York, Medical Department), 1879. Surgeon, Walker Hospital.

WALKER, FRANK B., Ph.B., M.D., 1320 David Whitney Building, Detroit, Michigan. Detroit College of Medicine and Surgery (Detroit College of Medicine), 1892. Professor of Surgery, Detroit College of Medicine and Surgery; Attending Surgeon, Providence and Woman's Hospitals; Consulting Surgeon, Samaritan and Detroit Eye, Ear, Nose, and Throat Hospitals, St. Joseph's Retreat.

WALKER, GEORGE, M.D., 1 East Center Street, Baltimore, Maryland. University of Maryland School of Medicine, 1888. Associate in Surgery, Johns Hopkins University, Medical Department; Visiting Surgeon, Church Home and Infirmary, Union Protestant Infirmary.

WALKER, IRVING JAMES, A.B., M.D., 520 Commonwealth Avenue, Boston, Massachusetts. Harvard Medical School, 1907. Assistant in Surgery, Harvard Medical School; First Assistant Visiting Surgeon, Boston City Hospital; Consulting Surgeon, Boston State Hospital.

WALKER, JOHN B., A.B., M.D., 51 East Fiftieth Street, New York, New York. Harvard Medical School, 1888. Professor of Clinical Surgery, Columbia University, College of Physicians and Surgeons; Surgeon, Bellevue Hospital, Hospital for Ruptured and Crippled; Consulting Surgeon, Manhattan State Hospital.

WALKER, REGINALD R., M.D., The Rochambeau, Washington, District of Columbia. Georgetown University School of Medicine, 1900. Assistant Professor of Laryngology, Georgetown University School of Medicine; Laryngologist, Casualty, Tuberculosis, and Washington Asylum Hospitals; Assistant Laryngologist, Episcopal Eye, Ear, and Throat Hospital.

WALKER, ROBERT S., M.D., 503 Nicholas Building, Toledo, Ohio. Detroit College of Medicine and Surgery, 1891.

WALKER, WILLIAM POMP, M.D., Third and Cherokee Streets, Bethlehem, Pennsylvania. University of Pennsylvania School of Medicine, 1895. Head of Surgical Department and Surgeon, St. Luke's Hospital.

WALL, JAMES PERCY, A.B., M.D., Jackson Sanatorium, Jackson, Mississippi. Columbia University, College of Physicians and Surgeons, 1907. Surgeon in Charge, Jackson Sanatorium.

WALLACE, ALONZO S., M.D., 198 Main Street, Nashua, New Hampshire. Dartmouth Medical School, 1874.

WALLACE, CHARLTON, A.B., M.D., 11 East Forty-eighth Street, New York, New York. Columbia University, College of Physicians and Surgeons, 1898. Clinical Professor of Surgery, Orthopedic Department, Cornell University Medical College; Associate Surgeon and Chief of Clinic, Hospital for Ruptured and Crippled; Surgeon-in-Chief, Reconstruction Hospital.

WALLACE, DAVID, M.D., C.M., 82 Park Avenue, Ottawa, Ontario. Queen's University, Faculty of Medicine, 1881. Associate Surgeon, St. Luke's General and Ottawa General Hospitals.

WALLACE, JAMES OLIVER, A.B., M.D., 7034 Jenkins Arcade Building, Pittsburgh, Pennsylvania. University of Pennsylvania School of Medicine, 1906. Associate Professor of Orthopedic Surgery, University of Pittsburgh School of Medicine; Orthopedic Surgeon, Mercy and Children's Hospitals, Industrial Home for Crippled Children, Pittsburgh, Sewickley Fresh Air Home, Fair Oaks.

WALLACE, RAYMOND, M.Sc., M.D., Hamilton National Bank Building, Chattanooga, Tennessee. University of Michigan Medical School, 1902. Surgeon, Baroness Erlanger Hospital.

WALLACE, WILLIAM J., Ph.G., M.D., 3 Shops Building, Oklahoma, Oklahoma. University of the South, Medical Department, 1901. Professor of Urology and Syphilology, University of Oklahoma School of Medicine; Member of Staff, State University and Baptist Hospitals.

WALMSLEY, ROBERT FORRESTER, A.B., M.D., 468 Washington Avenue, Brooklyn, New York. New York Homeopathic Medical College and Flower Hospital, 1894. Visiting Surgeon, Cumberland Street and Prospect Heights Hospitals; Associate Visiting Surgeon, Carson C. Peck Memorial Hospital.

WALSH, FERDINAND CLAIBORNE, M.D., Moore Building, San Antonio, Texas. University of Virginia, Department of Medicine, 1899. Chief of Urological Service, Robert B. Green Memorial Hospital; Urologist, Galveston, Harrisburg and San Antonio, and San Antonio and Aransas Pass Railroads.

WALSH, FRANK A., M.D., 128 East Seventh Street, Erie, Pennsylvania. Jefferson Medical College, 1895. Consulting Surgeon, St. Vincent's Hospital; Associate Surgeon, Hamot Hospital.

WALSH, JOSEPH MARK, M.D., Rapid City, South Dakota. University of Illinois College of Medicine, 1905.

WALSH, SIMON J., M.D., 134 West Eighty-sixth Street, New York, New York. Columbia University, College of Physicians and Surgeons, 1879. Visiting Surgeon, St. Vincent's and Columbus Hospitals; Consulting Surgeon, St. Joseph's Hospital, Far Rockaway, St. Joseph's Hospital, Yonkers, House of Calvary, New York.

WALTER, WILL, M.D., 1414 Chicago Avenue, Evanston, Illinois. University of Michigan Medical School, 1892. Senior Attending Ophthalmologist,

Rhinologist, and Oto-Laryngologist, Evanston Hospital, Illinois Children's Home and Evanston Sanitarium.

WALTHER, HENRY W. E., M.D., Macheca Building, New Orleans, Louisiana. Tulane University of Louisiana School of Medicine, 1910. Professor of Urology, Loyola Post-Graduate School of Medicine; Chief of Fifth Urological Division, Charity Hospital; Visiting Urologist, Hotel Dieu.

WALTON, CHARLES E., A.M., M.D., LL.D., Eighth and John Streets, Cincinnati, Ohio. Ohio State University College of Homeopathic Medicine (Pulte Medical College), 1874. Gynecologist, Bethesda Hospital; Surgeon, Home for the Friendless.

WANAMAKER, ALLISON T., Ph.G., M.D., 817 Summit Avenue, Seattle, Washington. Northwestern University Medical School, 1907. Member of Staff, Providence and Children's Orthopedic Hospitals.

WANLESS, WILLIAM J., M.D., Miraj, India. University and Bellevue Hospital Medical College (University of the City of New York, Medical Department), 1889. Principal and Instructor in Surgery, Miraj Medical School; Senior Surgeon, Presbyterian Mission Hospital.

WARBASSE, JAMES PETER, M.D., 384 Washington Avenue, Brooklyn, New York. Columbia University, College of Physicians and Surgeons, 1889.

WARD, EDWIN ST. JOHN, A.B., M.D., American University of Beirut, Beirut, Syria. Columbia University, College of Physicians and Surgeons, 1904. Professor of Theory and Practice of Surgery, American University of Beirut; Attending Surgeon, American Hospitals.

WARD, GEORGE GRAY, JR., M.D., 48 East Fifty-second Street, New York, New York. Long Island College Hospital, 1891. Professor of Obstetrics and Gynecology, Cornell University Medical College; Chief Surgeon, Woman's Hospital; Consulting Gynecologist, New York Post-Graduate Medical School and Hospital, Booth Memorial and Italian Hospitals, New York, Monmouth Memorial Hospital, Long Branch, New Jersey.

WARD, RALPH FRANCIS, M.D., 895 West End Avenue, New York, New York. Columbia University, College of Physicians and Surgeons, 1904. Attending Surgeon, Metropolitan Hospital, Department of Public Welfare.

WARD, WILBUR, A.B., M.D., 24 West Fiftieth Street, New York, New York. Columbia University, College of Physicians and Surgeons, 1904. Visiting Obstetrician, New York City Hospital, Blackwell's Island; Associate Obstetrician, Fifth Avenue Hospital, New York; Consulting Obstetrician, Mountainside Hospital, Montclair, New Jersey; Consulting Gynecologist, Nassau Hospital, Long Island.

WARD, WILLIAM B., B.A., M.D., Fennell Infirmary, Rock Hill, South Carolina. Vanderbilt University Medical Department, 1912. Surgeon, Fennell Infirmary.

WARD, WILLIAM DOUGLAS, A.B., M.D., 20 Grove Place, Rochester, New York. University of Pennsylvania School of Medicine, 1899. Assistant Surgeon, Rochester General Hospital; Gynecologist, Park Avenue Hospital.

WARE, HORACE BACON, M.D., Scranton Life Building, Scranton, Pennsylvania. Hahnemann Medical College and Hospital, Philadelphia, 1886. Surgeon-in-Chief, Eye, Ear, Nose, and Throat Department, Hahnemann Hospital.

WARE, MARTIN W., M.D., 27 East Eighty-first Street, New York, New York. Columbia University, College of Physicians and Surgeons, 1892. Adjunct Attending Surgeon, Mt. Sinai Hospital.

WARING, THOMAS PINCKNEY, A.B., M.D., De Renne Apartments, Savannah, Georgia. Columbia University, College of Physicians and Surgeons, 1892. Surgeon, Oglethorpe Sanatorium.

WARNER, ALTON GRAHAM, M.D., 19 Schermerhorn Street, Brooklyn, New York. New York Homeopathic Medical College and Flower Hospital, 1883. Oculist and Aurist, Carson C. Peck Memorial and Cumberland Street Hospitals, Prospect Heights Hospital and Brooklyn Maternity, Brooklyn, Jamaica Hospital, Jamaica.

WARNER, FRANK, M.D., D.Sc., 10 West Goodale Street, Columbus, Ohio. University and Bellevue Hospital Medical College, 1883. Surgeon, Protestant Hospital.

WARNER, RICHARD AMBROSE, M.D., Medical Corps, United States Navy, Washington, District of Columbia. Georgetown University School of Medicine, 1901. Commander, Medical Corps, United States Navy.

WARNSHUIS, FREDERICK COOK, M.D., Powers Theater Building, Grand Rapids, Michigan. Grand Rapids Medical College, 1902. Attending Surgeon, Butterworth Hospital; Chief Surgeon, Pere Marquette Railroad, Grand Rapids Gas Light Company; Acting Assistant Surgeon, United States Public Health Service.

WARREN, GEORGE WILLIAM, A.B., M.D., 117 East Sixty-second Street, New York, New York. Johns Hopkins University, Medical Department, 1901. Associate Genito-Urinary Surgeon, St. Mark's Hospital; Urologist, Lutheran Hospital.

WARREN, J. COLLINS, A.B., M.D., LL.D., F.R.C.S. (Eng., Edin.), Hon., 58 Beacon Street, Boston, Massachusetts. Harvard Medical School, 1866. Moseley Professor of Surgery (Emeritus), Harvard Medical School; Consulting Surgeon, Massachusetts General Hospital.

WARREN, JOHN KELSO, M.D., 78 Pleasant Street, Worcester, Massachusetts. New York Homeopathic Medical College and Flower Hospital, 1870. Consulting Surgeon, Milford and Worcester Hahnemann Hospitals.

WARREN, JOHN NELSON, M.D., 536 Davidson Building, Sioux City, Iowa. University of Cincinnati College of Medicine (Miami Medical College), 1871. Attending Surgeon, Samaritan, St. Joseph's Mercy, and St. Vincent's Hospitals.

WASHBURN, JOHN LEWIS, Ph.C., M.D., 611 Home Savings and Loan Building, Youngstown, Ohio. University of Buffalo, Department of Medicine, 1903. Surgeon, Eye, Ear, Nose, and Throat Department, Youngstown Hospital.

WASHBURNE, CHARLES L., M.D., 225 East Liberty Street, Ann Arbor, Michigan. University of Michigan Medical School, 1908. Surgeon, St. Joseph's Sanitarium.

WATERMAN, JAMES SEARS, M.D., 676 St. Mark's Avenue, Brooklyn, New York. Columbia University, College of Physicians and Surgeons, 1889.

WATERS, CHESTER H., B.Sc., M.D., 500 Brandeis Theatre Building, Omaha, Nebraska. Cornell University Medical School, 1912. Member of Staff, Swedish Mission and University Hospitals.

WATERS, OREN J., A.B., M.D., 3 West Delaware Place, Chicago, Illinois. Jefferson Medical College, 1891. Surgeon, Passavant Hospital.

WATERWORTH, SAMUEL JAMES, M.D., 102 South Second Street, Clearfield, Pennsylvania. University of Maryland School of Medicine (College of Physicians and Surgeons, Baltimore), 1893. Surgeon, Clearfield Hospital.

WATHEN, JOHN R., A.B., M.D., 350 Francis Building, Louisville, Kentucky. University of Louisville, Medical Department, 1898. Professor of Surgery, and Clinical Surgery, University of Louisville, Medical Department; Surgeon, St. Anthony's and Louisville City Hospitals.

WATKINS, ANDERSON, M.D., 513 Donaghey Building, Little Rock, Arkansas. University of Arkansas, Medical Department, 1897. Professor of Surgery, University of Arkansas, Medical Department; Chief of Staff, Logan H. Roots Memorial City Hospital; Chief of Surgical Staff, Baptist Hospital; Member of Surgical Staff, St. Vincent's Infirmary.

WATKINS, CHARLES FRANKLIN, Phar.C., M.D., 217 Montana Power Building, Billings, Montana. University of Michigan Medical School, 1901. Surgeon, St. Vincent's Hospital.

WATKINS, JAMES THOMAS, M.D., Medical Building, San Francisco, California. Columbia University, College of Physicians and Surgeons, 1894. Lecturer on Orthopedic Surgery, University of California Medical School; Orthopedic Surgeon, San Francisco Children's Hospital; Consulting Orthopedic Surgeon, Mt. Zion Hospital, Hahnemann Hospital of the University of California.

WATKINS, ROYAL PHILLIPS, A.B., M.D., 17 West Street, Worcester, Massachusetts. Columbia University, College of Physicians and Surgeons, 1892. Visiting Surgeon, Worcester City Hospital.

WATKINS, THOMAS J., M.D., 104 South Michigan Avenue, Chicago, Illinois. University and Bellevue Hospital Medical College, 1886. Professor of Gynecology, Northwestern University Medical School; Gynecologist, St. Luke's Hospital.

WATSON, BENJAMIN PHILP, M.B., Ch.B., M.D., F.R.C.S. (Edin.), 100 College Street, Toronto, Ontario. University of Edinburgh, 1902. Professor of Obstetrics and Gynecology, University of Toronto, Faculty of Medicine; Obstetrician and Gynecologist, Chief of Service, Toronto General Hospital.

WATSON, FRANCIS S., A.B., M.D., South Dartmouth, Massachusetts. Harvard Medical School, 1879. Consulting Surgeon, Boston City Hospital, Boston. Retired.

WATSON, JAMES ALFRED, M.D., C.M., 500 Physicians and Surgeons Building, Minneapolis, Minnesota. Faculty of Medicine, University of Manitoba (Manitoba Medical College), 1895. Ophthalmologist, Asbury Methodist and Fairview Hospitals.

WATT, CHARLES HANSELL, B.Sc., M.D., 403 Masonic Building, Thomasville, Georgia. Johns Hopkins University, Medical Department, 1912. Attending Surgeon, Thomasville City Hospital.

WATT, JAMES, M.D., 50 West Fifty-fifth Street, New York, New York. Long Island College Hospital, 1900. Associate Professor of Surgery, Long Island College Hospital; Chief of Surgical Clinic, Polhemus Memorial Clinic; Surgeon, Long Island College and St. Bartholomew's Hospitals.

WATTS, STEPHEN H., A.M., M.D., University of Virginia, University, Virginia. Johns Hopkins University, Medical Department, 1901. Professor of Surgery and Gynecology, University of Virginia, Department of Medicine; Surgeon-in-Chief, University of Virginia Hospital.

WAUGH, JUSTIN M., A.M., M.D., Clinic Building, Cleveland, Ohio. Columbia University, College of Physicians and Surgeons, 1898. Chief Oto-Laryngologist, Cleveland Clinic.

WAUGH, OLIVER SAYLES, M.D., C.M., 510 Boyd Building, Winnipeg, Manitoba. Faculty of Medicine, McGill University, 1908. Lecturer in Surgery, Faculty of Medicine, University of Manitoba; Attending Surgeon, Winnipeg General Hospital.

WAUGH, WILLIAM E., M.D., 537 Talbot Street, London, Ontario. Faculty of Medicine, McGill University, 1872.

WAY, EDITH WALDIE, M.D., Pittsburgh, Pennsylvania. Woman's Medical College of Pennsylvania, 1905. Retired.

WEATHERBE, PHILIP, M.B., Ch.B., 66 Queen Street, Halifax, Nova Scotia. University of Edinburgh, 1901. Lecturer on Didactic and Operative Surgery, Dalhousie University, Faculty of Medicine; Surgeon, Children's Hospital.

WEAVER, ARTHUR JOHN, Ph.G., M.D., 107 West Second Street, Muscatine, Iowa. Loyola University School of Medicine (Bennett Medical College), 1895. Member of Staff, Bellevue Hospital.

WEAVER, BEN PERLEY, B.Sc., M.D., Carroll Building, Fort Wayne, Indiana. University of Illinois College of Medicine (College of Physicians and Surgeons, Chicago), 1902.

WEAVER, HARRY SANDS, M.D., 1433 Spruce Street, Philadelphia, Pennsylvania. Hahnemann Medical College and Hospital, Philadelphia, 1892. Professor of Laryngology and Laryngologist, Hahnemann Medical College and Hospital.

706   *American College of Surgeons*

WEAVER, OLIN HEARD, M.D., 722 Spring Street, Macon, Georgia. Emory University School of Medicine, 1894. Senior Visiting Surgeon, Macon City Hospital; Visiting Surgeon, Middle Georgia Sanatorium.

WEBB, ROSCOE CLAYTON, A.B., M.D., 300 La Salle Building, Minneapolis, Minnesota. Johns Hopkins University, Medical Department, 1914. Instructor in Surgery, University of Minnesota Medical School; Associate Surgeon, University Hospital.

WEBB, ROWLAND FOREMAN, M.B., 406 Ashton Building, Grand Rapids, Michigan. University of Toronto, Faculty of Medicine, 1897. Visiting Surgeon, Butterworth Hospital.

WEBB, SAM, JR., M.D., 3712 Alice Circle, Dallas, Texas. University of Nashville, Medical Department, 1905. Professor of Orthopedic Surgery, Baylor University School of Medicine; Member of Staff, Baylor Hospital; Chief Surgeon, Missouri, Kansas and Texas Railway Company, Employes' Hospital Association of Texas.

WEBB, ULYS ROBERT, M.D., Medical Corps, United States Navy, Washington, District of Columbia. George Washington University Medical School, 1900. Commander, Medical Corps, United States Navy.

WEBB, WALTER DUVALL, M.D., Stoneleigh Court, Washington, District of Columbia. Columbia University, College of Physicians and Surgeons, 1895. Professor of Surgical Pathology and Clinical Professor of Surgery, Georgetown University School of Medicine; Associate Surgeon, Georgetown University Hospital; Consulting Surgeon, Washington Asylum Hospital.

WEBER, JOHN H., Ph.B., M.D., 330 Akron Savings and Loan Building, Akron, Ohio. Western Reserve University School of Medicine, 1902. Gynecologist, City Hospital; Surgeon, Children's Hospital.

WEBER, OLIVER A., Ph.B., M.D., 1021 Prospect Avenue, Cleveland, Ohio. Western Reserve University School of Medicine, 1905. Demonstrator of Anatomy and Instructor in Surgery, Western Reserve University School of Medicine; Visiting Surgeon, Cleveland City Hospital.

WEBSTER, A. B., A.B., M.D., 4821 Baltimore Avenue, Philadelphia, Pennsylvania. Boston University School of Medicine, 1902.

WEBSTER, CHARLES ASHTON, M.D., Yarmouth, Nova Scotia. Columbia University, College of Physicians and Surgeons, 1886. Visiting Surgeon, Yarmouth Hospital.

WEBSTER, GEORGE ARTHUR, M.D., 53A Dale Street, Roxbury, Massachusetts. Harvard Medical School, 1889.

WEBSTER, J. CLARENCE, A.B., D.Sc., M.D., C.M., F.R.C.P. (Edin.), F.R.S. (Edin.), Shediac, New Brunswick. University of Edinburgh, 1888. Retired.

WEDEL, CURT OTTO VON, JR., M.D., 735 American National Bank Building, Oklahoma, Oklahoma. University and Bellevue Hospital Medical College, 1907. Member of Staff, St. Anthony's and Baptist Hospitals.

WEED, FRANK W., M.D., Medical Corps, United States Army, Washington, District of Columbia. University of Maryland School of Medicine, 1903. Lieutenant Colonel, Medical Corps, United States Army.

WEED, HARRY M., M.D., 196 Linwood Avenue, Buffalo, New York. University of Buffalo, Medical Department, 1903. Associate in Anatomy, University of Buffalo, Medical Department; Ophthalmologist, St. Mary's Infant Asylum and Maternity, Lafayette General, Erie County, and City Hospitals, Buffalo, Moses Taylor Hospital, Lackawanna.

WEEKS, ALANSON, M.D., 350 Post Street, San Francisco, California. University of Michigan Medical School, 1899. Assistant Clinical Professor of Surgery, University of California Medical School; Chief of Surgery, St. Luke's Hospital; Consultant in Surgery, United States Marine Hospital; Consultant in General Surgery, United States Public Health Service, District No. 12.

WEEKS, JOHN ELMER, M.D., D.Sc., 46 East Fifty-seventh Street, New York, New York. University of Michigan Medical School, 1881. Emeritus Professor of Ophthalmology, University and Bellevue Hospital Medical College; Consulting Surgeon, Eye Department, New York Eye and Ear Infirmary; Consulting Ophthalmologist, Vassar Brothers' Hospital, Poughkeepsie.

WEEKS, LEONARD CASE, M.D., 827 Washington Avenue, Detroit, Minnesota. Rush Medical College, 1892. Surgeon-in-Chief, Community Hospital.

WEGEFORTH, PAUL, A.B., M.D., Bank of Coronado Building, Coronado, California. Johns Hopkins University, Medical Department, 1912. Member of Staff, San Diego County General and St. Joseph's Hospitals, San Diego.

WEIBLE, RALPH EMERSON, M.D., De Lendrecie Block, Fargo, North Dakota. Rush Medical College, 1901. Staff Surgeon, St. John's Hospital.

WEIDMAN, JOHN A., M.D., 20 East Fourth Street, Dunkirk, New York. University of Buffalo, Department of Medicine, 1901. Surgeon, Brook's Memorial Hospital.

WEIH, ELMER P., M.D., M.Sc., 605 Wilson Building, Clinton, Iowa. State University of Iowa College of Medicine, 1912. Member of Staff, Jane Lamb Memorial Hospital.

WEIL, ARTHUR I., M.D., 717 Maison Blanche Building Annex, New Orleans, Louisiana. Harvard Medical School, 1898. Professor of Oto-Laryngology, Loyola Post-Graduate School of Medicine; Senior Visiting Surgeon, Touro Infirmary; Consulting Laryngologist, Tuberculosis Clinic of the Louisiana Anti-Tuberculosis League.

WEIMER, EDGAR STANLEY, M.D., 1220 Highland Building, Pittsburgh, Pennsylvania. University of Pittsburgh School of Medicine, 1910. Associate Ophthalmologist and Chief of Dispensary, St. Francis Hospital.

WEINBERGER, NELSON S., M.D., Sayre, Pennsylvania. University of Pennsylvania School of Medicine (Medico-Chirurgical College of Philadelphia), 1905. Ophthalmologist and Otologist, Robert Packer Hospital.

WEIR, ROBERT F., A.M., M.D., F.R.C.S. (Eng.), Hon., 1155 Park Avenue, New York, New York. Columbia University, College of Physicians and Surgeons, 1859. Consulting Surgeon, Roosevelt, St. Vincent's, St. Luke's and New York Hospitals.

WEIR, WILLIAM HAWKSLEY, M.D., C.M., 1021 Prospect Avenue, Cleveland, Ohio. University of Toronto, Faculty of Medicine (Trinity Medical College), 1896. Assistant Professor of Gynecology, Western Reserve University School of Medicine; Visiting Gynecologist, Lakeside Hospital; Director, Gynecological Department, Lakeside Hospital, Western Reserve University Dispensary.

WEIS, EDMUND W., M.D., 151 Fifth Street, La Salle, Illinois. Washington University Medical School, 1877. Member of Staff, St. Mary's Hospital, La Salle, Ryburn Memorial Hospital, Ottawa.

WEISS, EDWARD ALOYSIUS, M.D., 714 Jenkins Arcade Building, Pittsburgh, Pennsylvania. University of Pittsburgh School of Medicine, 1900. Assistant Professor of Gynecology, University of Pittsburgh School of Medicine; Gynecologist-in-Chief, Mercy Hospital; Obstetrician, Roselia Foundling Asylum and Maternity Hospital; Gynecologist, Elizabeth Steel Magee Hospital.

WEISSER, EDWARD A., A.M., M.D., 806 May Building, Pittsburgh, Pennsylvania. University of Pennsylvania School of Medicine, 1898. Staff Ophthalmologist, St. Francis and City Tuberculosis Hospitals, Roselia Foundling Asylum and Maternity Hospital.

WEKESSER, HENRY PETER, Phar.G., M.D., Orpheum Theatre Building, Lincoln, Nebraska. University of Nebraska College of Medicine, 1908.

WELBORN, JAMES Y., M.D., 712 South Fourth Street, Evansville, Indiana. St. Louis University School of Medicine (Marion-Sims Medical College), 1899. Surgeon, Walker Hospital.

WELCH, J. STANLEY, B.Sc., M.D., 514 First National Bank Building, Lincoln, Nebraska. Northwestern University Medical School, 1903. Member of Surgical Staff, St. Elizabeth's Hospital.

WELLER, RALPH E., M.D., Electra, Texas. University Medical College of Kansas City, 1904.

WELLINGTON, JOHN R., A.M., M.D., 1723 Connecticut Avenue, Washington, District of Columbia. George Washington University Medical School (Columbian University, Medical Department), 1891. Clinical Professor of Surgery, George Washington University Medical School; Attending Surgeon, Garfield Memorial, Children's, Eastern Dispensary and Casualty Hospitals.

WELLS, DAVID WASHBURN, M.D., Hotel Westminster, Boston, Massachusetts. Boston University School of Medicine, 1897. Professor of Ophthalmology and Chairman of Standing Committee on Post-Graduate Courses, Boston University School of Medicine; Ophthalmic Surgeon and Chief of Service, Massachusetts Homeopathic Hospital; Oculist, Newton Hospital, Newton.

WELLS, ERNEST ALDEN, A.B., M.D., 580 Asylum Street, Hartford, Connecticut. Johns Hopkins University, Medical Department, 1901. Attending Surgeon, Hartford Hospital; Consulting Surgeon, New Britain General Hospital, New Britain, Manchester Memorial Hospital, Manchester.

WELLS, GEORGE S., M.D., San Marcos Building, Santa Barbara, California. Ohio State University College of Homeopathic Medicine (Pulte Medical College), 1892. Member of Staff, Aurist, and Laryngologist, Santa Barbara Cottage Hospital Dispensary.

WELLS, ROBERT BRUCE, M.B., 623 Tegler Block, Edmonton, Alberta. University of Toronto, Faculty of Medicine, 1894.

WELLS, WALTER A., M.D., The Rochambeau, Washington, District of Columbia. Georgetown University School of Medicine, 1891. Professor of Otology and Laryngology, Georgetown University School of Medicine; Otologist and Laryngologist in Charge, Garfield and Georgetown University Hospitals; Associate Otologist and Laryngologist, Episcopal Eye, Ear, and Throat Hospital.

WELSH, D. EMMETT, M.D., Powers Theatre Building, Grand Rapids, Michigan. Jefferson Medical College, 1878.

WELSH, HORACE G., M.D., First National Bank Building, Hutchinson, Kansas. Jefferson Medical College, 1880. Chief of Staff, Hutchinson Methodist Hospital; Attending Surgeon, St. Elizabeth Hospital.

WELTON, THURSTON SCOTT, M.D., 842 Union Street, Brooklyn, New York. Long Island College Hospital, 1908. Clinical Instructor in Obstetrics and Gynecology, Long Island College Hospital; Associate Visiting Gynecologist and Obstetrician, Williamsburgh Hospital; Associate Attending Gynecologist and Obstetrician, Greenpoint Hospital.

WELTY, CULLEN F., M.D., 210 Post Street, San Francisco, California. University of Pennsylvania School of Medicine, 1890.

WELZ, WALTER E., M.D., 608 Mt. Elliott Avenue, Detroit, Michigan. Detroit College of Medicine and Surgery, 1903. Associate Professor of Obstetrics, Detroit College of Medicine and Surgery; Obstetrician, Providence and Herman Kiefer Hospitals; Director, Board of Health Prenatal Clinics.

WENTWORTH, EDWARD TUBBS, A.B., M.D., 35 Chestnut Street, Rochester, New York. Harvard Medical School, 1913. Orthopedic Surgeon, Park Avenue Clinical Hospital; Associate Orthopedic Surgeon, Rochester General Hospital.

WERELIUS, AXEL, M.D., 6725 Constance Avenue, Chicago, Illinois. University of Illinois College of Medicine (College of Physicians and Surgeons, Chicago), 1902. Surgeon, South Shore Hospital.

WERNECK, HUGO, M.D., Avenida Tocantins 499, Bello Horizonte, Brazil. Faculty of Medicine, University of Rio de Janeiro, 1901.

WERNER, MAX A., M.D., 215 West Thirty-fourth Street, New York, New York. University and Bellevue Hospital Medical College, 1902. Associate Visiting Surgeon, St. Mark's Hospital.

WERNHAM, JAMES I., B.Sc., M.D., 227 Hart-Albin Building, Billings, Montana. Rush Medical College, 1902. Surgeon, St. Vincent's Hospital.

WERTS, CHARLES M., M.Sc., M.D., 217 Bankers Trust Building, Des Moines, Iowa. State University of Iowa College of Medicine, 1902. Oculist and Aurist, Iowa Methodist and Iowa Lutheran Hospitals.

WESCOTT, CASSIUS D., M.D., 22 East Washington Street, Chicago, Illinois. Rush Medical College, 1883. Ophthalmologist, Washington Boulevard Hospital.

WESSELHOEFT, WILLIAM F., A.B., M.D., 483 Beacon Street, Boston, Massachusetts. Harvard Medical School, 1887. Professor of Operative Gynecology, Boston University School of Medicine; Surgeon, Massachusetts Homeopathic Hospital, Boston; Consulting Surgeon, Framingham Hospital, Framingham.

WEST, EDMUND S., M.D., 306 Miller Building, Yakima, Washington. Hahnemann Medical College and Hospital (Chicago Homeopathic Medical College), 1902. Surgeon, St. Elizabeth's Hospital.

WEST, GEORGE RICHARD, B.Sc., M.D., 626 Volunteer Building, Chattanooga, Tennessee. University of Pennsylvania School of Medicine, 1883. President and Attending Surgeon, West-Ellis Hospital.

WEST, JAMES NEPHEW, M.D., 71 West Forty-ninth Street, New York, New York. University and Bellevue Hospital Medical College (Bellevue Hospital Medical College), 1891. Professor of Diseases of Women, New York Post-Graduate Medical School; Visiting Gynecologist, New York Post-Graduate Medical School and Hospital.

WEST, WILLIAM F., M.D., American Bank Building, Everett, Washington. Hahnemann Medical College and Hospital (Chicago Homeopathic Medical College), 1902.

WEST, WILLIAM HYDE, M.D., State Bank Building, Woodstock, Illinois. Hahnemann Medical College and Hospital, Chicago, 1911. Surgeon, Woodstock Hospital.

WEST, WILLIAM KERR, M.D., Painesdale, Michigan. Detroit College of Medicine and Surgery, 1889. Chief Surgeon, Copper Range Hospital, Trimountain.

WEST, WILLIAM M., M.D., 213 Fourth Street, Monett, Missouri. St. Louis University School of Medicine (Beaumont Hospital Medical College), 1898. Chief of Staff, West Hospital.

WESTBROOK, RICHARD WARD, M.D., 1145 Dean Street, Brooklyn, New York. Yale University School of Medicine, 1891. Senior Surgeon, Brooklyn Hospital.

WESTMORELAND, WILLIS FOREMAN, M.D., 53 Forrest Avenue, Atlanta, Georgia. Emory University School of Medicine (Atlanta Medical College), 1885. Honorary Professor of Principles and Practice of Clinical Surgery, Emory University School of Medicine; Surgeon, St. Joseph's Infirmary.

WESTON, CHARLES GALEN, M.D., 803 Physicians and Surgeons Building, Minneapolis, Minnesota. Harvard Medical School, 1882. Gynecologist, Obstetrician, and Abdominal Surgeon, Hill Crest Surgical Hospital.

WETHERILL, HORACE G., M.D., 1127 Race Street, Denver, Colorado. University of Pennsylvania School of Medicine, 1878. Surgeon, St. Luke's, Mercy, City and County, and Children's Hospitals.

WETHERILL, RICHARD B., M.D., 525 Columbia Street, La Fayette, Indiana. Jefferson Medical College, 1883. President of Staff and Chief of Surgical Staff, St. Elizabeth's Hospital; Surgeon, La Fayette Home Hospital.

WHALEY, ARTHUR MAUNDER, M.D., Medical Corps, United States Army, Washington, District of Columbia. University of Buffalo, Department of Medicine, 1896. Lieutenant Colonel, Medical Corps, United States Army.

WHALEY, EPHRIAM MIKELL, M.D., 1430 Blanding Street, Columbia, South Carolina. Medical College of the State of South Carolina, 1896.

WHEAT, ARTHUR FITTS, M.D., 944 Elm Street, Manchester, New Hampshire. Harvard Medical School, 1893.

WHEATLEY, WILLIAM E., M.D., 424 Broadway, Lorain, Ohio. Western Reserve University School of Medicine, 1894. Surgeon, St. Joseph's Hospital.

WHEELER, BENJAMIN B., M.D., 63 Alleghany Street, Clifton Forge, Virginia. University of Louisville, Medical Department (Louisville Medical College), 1904.

WHEELER, CHARLES DOUGLAS, A.B., M.D., 18 Chestnut Street, Worcester, Massachusetts. Harvard Medical School, 1894. Consulting Surgeon, Worcester City Hospital.

WHEELER, HENRY MASON, M.D., 2½ South Third Street, Grand Forks, North Dakota. University of Michigan Medical School, 1877; Columbia University, College of Physicians and Surgeons, 1880. Instructor in Surgery, University of North Dakota School of Medicine.

WHEELER, HERBERT EDWARD, B.Sc., M.D., Fernwell Building, Spokane, Washington. Rush Medical College, 1908. Member of Staff, Sacred Heart Hospital.

WHEELER, HOMER H., M.D., Hume-Mansur Building, Indianapolis, Indiana. Indiana University School of Medicine (Central College of Physicians and Surgeons), 1897. Assistant Professor of Proctology, Indiana University School of Medicine; Visiting Surgeon, Indianapolis City, Methodist, and St. Vincent's Hospitals.

WHEELER, JOHN BROOKS, A.B., M.D., 210 Pearl Street, Burlington, Vermont. Harvard Medical School, 1879. Professor of Surgery, University of Vermont College of Medicine; Attending Surgeon, Mary Fletcher Hospital; Consulting Surgeon, Fanny Allen Hospital, Winooski.

WHEELOCK, AMOS S., M.D., Goodrich, Michigan. University of Michigan Medical School, 1888. Surgeon, Goodrich General Hospital.

WHELAN, CHARLES, M.D., 438 First National Bank Building, Birmingham, Alabama. University of Alabama School of Medicine, 1896. Surgeon, St. Vincent's Hospital.

WHELAN, EDWARD P., M.D., Lawyers Building, Passaic, New Jersey. Medical College of Virginia (University College of Medicine), 1908. Visiting Surgeon, St. Mary's Hospital.

WHELAN, RAYMOND E., M.D., 201 Dollar Savings and Trust Company Building, Youngstown, Ohio. Western Reserve University School of Medicine, 1890. Surgeon, St. Elizabeth's Hospital; Consultant, Youngstown Hospital.

WHERRY, WILLIAM P., M.D., 703 Brandeis Theatre Building, Omaha, Nebraska. University of Nebraska College of Medicine, 1903. Instructor in Laryngology and Rhinology, University of Nebraska College of Medicine; Oculist and Aurist, St. Catherine's, Wise Memorial, and Swedish Mission Hospitals, Omaha, South Omaha Hospital, South Omaha; Oculist, Union Pacific Railroad, Chicago, St. Paul, Minneapolis and Omaha Railway.

WHISNANT, ALBERT M., M.D., Independence Building, Charlotte, North Carolina. University of Maryland School of Medicine (College of Physicians and Surgeons, Baltimore), 1893. Member of Visiting Staff, Charlotte Sanatorium, Presbyterian Hospital.

WHITACRE, HORACE J., B.Sc., M.D., 704 St. Helens Avenue, Tacoma, Washington. Columbia University, College of Physicians and Surgeons, 1894.

WHITBECK, BRAINERD HUNT, A.B., M.D., 50 East Sixty-first Street, New York, New York. Columbia University, College of Physicians and Surgeons, 1903. Assistant Surgeon, Hospital for Ruptured and Crippled; Attending Orthopedic Surgeon, Neponsit Beach Hospital for Children, Rockaway Park; Consulting Orthopedic Surgeon, Roosevelt Hospital, New York, Lawrence Hospital, Bronxville, Memorial Hospital, Canandaigua, New York, Somerset Hospital, Somerville, New Jersey.

WHITBECK, SHERWOOD V., M.D., 431 Warren Street, Hudson, New York. Columbia University, College of Physicians and Surgeons, 1901. Attending Surgeon, Hudson City Hospital.

WHITE, ALFRED WINFIELD, M.D., 88 McDonough Street, Brooklyn, New York. Cornell University Medical College, 1905. Attending Obstetrician, St. John's Hospital.

WHITE, CHARLES STANLEY, M.D., 911 Sixteenth Street, Northwest, Washington, District of Columbia. George Washington University Medical School, 1898. Associate Professor of Surgery, George Washington University Medical School; Visiting Surgeon, George Washington University, Emergency, and Providence Hospitals; Consulting Surgeon, Episcopal Hospital and St. Elizabeth's Hospital for Insane.

WHITE, EDWARD WILLIAM, M.D., 7 West Madison Street, Chicago, Illinois. University of Illinois College of Medicine, 1910. Genito-Urinary Surgeon, Alexian Brothers' Hospital.

WHITE, E. HAMILTON, B.A., M.D., 589 Dorchester Street, West, Montreal, Quebec. Faculty of Medicine, McGill University, 1901. Demonstrator of Oto-Laryngology, Faculty of Medicine, McGill University; Assistant Oto-Laryngologist, Royal Victoria Hospital.

WHITE, GEORGE REEVES, B.Sc., M.D., 2 Liberty Street, East, Savannah, Georgia. Columbia University, College of Physicians and Surgeons, 1891. Surgeon in Charge, Park View Sanitarium.

WHITE, JOHN FRANKLYN, M.D., 156 North Main Street, Port Chester, New York. New York Homeopathic Medical College and Flower Hospital, 1900. Director of Surgery, United Hospital.

WHITE, JOSHUA WARREN, A.B., M.D., 629 Monroe Building, Norfolk, Virginia. Medical College of Virginia, 1901. Ophthalmologist, Otologist, and Laryngologist, St. Vincent's Hospital.

WHITE, ROBERT V., M.D., Brooks Building, Scranton, Pennsylvania. Hahnemann Medical College and Hospital, Philadelphia, 1901. Attending Surgeon and Chief of Urological Service, Hahnemann Hospital; Consulting Surgeon, Wyoming Valley Homeopathic Hospital, Wilkes-Barre.

WHITE, WALTER WOODWORTH, M.A., M.D., C.M., LL.D., L.R.C.P. & F.R.C.S. (Edin.), L.F.P.S. (Glas.), M.R.C.S. (Eng.), 71 Sydney Street, St. John, New Brunswick. Faculty of Medicine, McGill University, 1886. Surgeon, General Public Hospital.

WHITE, WILLIAM CRAWFORD, B.Sc., M.D., 962 Lexington Avenue, New York, New York. Columbia University, College of Physicians and Surgeons, 1912. Instructor in Surgery, Columbia University, College of Physicians and Surgeons; Assistant Attending Surgeon, Roosevelt and Lincoln Hospitals; Surgical Pathologist, Roosevelt Hospital.

WHITESIDE, GEORGE SHATTUCK, M.D., 907 Journal Building, Portland, Oregon. Harvard Medical School, 1897. Assistant Professor of Genito-Urinary Surgery, University of Oregon Medical School; Senior Surgeon, Portland Free Dispensary; Visiting Genito-Urinary Surgeon, Multnomah County Hospital.

WHITESIDE, JESSE D., A.B., M.D., 416 Citizens Bank Building, Aberdeen, South Dakota. Northwestern University Medical School, 1906. Surgeon, St. Luke's Hospital.

WHITING, FENTON B., M.D., 316 Cobb Building, Seattle, Washington. Cooper Medical College, 1891.

WHITING, FREDERICK, A.M., M.D., 19 West Forty-seventh Street, New York, New York. Long Island College Hospital, 1885. Professor of Otology, Cornell University Medical College; Attending Surgeon, New York Eye and Ear Infirmary; Consulting Otologist, Mt. Sinai Hospital.

WHITLEDGE, GEORGE A., M.D., 453 Union Building, Anderson, Indiana. University of Louisville, Medical Department, 1891. Surgeon, St. John's Hospital.

WHITMAN, ARMITAGE, A.B., M.D., 283 Lexington Avenue, New York, New York. Columbia University, College of Physicians and Surgeons, 1912. Assistant Surgeon, Hospital for Ruptured and Crippled; Orthopedic Surgeon, Lincoln Hospital and Home, Booth Memorial Hospital.

WHITMAN, ROYAL, M.D., M.R.C.S. (Eng.), 283 Lexington Avenue, New York, New York. Harvard Medical School, 1882. Surgeon, Hospital for Ruptured and Crippled; Orthopedic Surgeon, Hospital of St. John's Guild; Consulting Surgeon, St. Agnes' Hospital for Crippled and Atypical Children, New York Home for Destitute Crippled Children, State Department of Health.

WHITMAN, WILLIAM R., A.B., M.D., Roanoke Street and Luck Avenue, Roanoke, Virginia. Columbia University, College of Physicians and Surgeons, 1901. Surgeon, Lewis-Gale Hospital; Assistant Chief Surgeon, Norfolk and Western Railway.

WHITMARSH, HENRY ALLEN, A.M., M.D., 167 Angell Street, Providence, Rhode Island. New York Homeopathic Medical College and Flower Hospital, 1879.

WHITTEMORE, E. REED, A.B., M.D., 19 Whitney Avenue, New Haven, Connecticut. Columbia University, College of Physicians and Surgeons, 1902. Assistant Attending Surgeon, New Haven Hospital.

WHITTEMORE, WYMAN, B.Sc., M.D., 199 Beacon Street, Boston, Massachusetts. Harvard Medical School, 1905. Assistant in Surgery, Harvard Medical School; Assistant Visiting Surgeon, Massachusetts General Hospital; Visiting Surgeon, Beth Israel Hospital; Consulting Surgeon, Sturdy Memorial Hospital, Attleboro, Massachusetts Eye and Ear Infirmary, Boston.

WIATT, WILLIAM S., M.D., 4506 Lewis Place, St. Louis, Missouri. University of Louisville, Medical Department (Hospital College of Medicine), 1897. Assistant Professor of Surgery, St. Louis University School of Medicine; Visiting Surgeon, St. Louis City Hospital, Missouri Baptist Sanitarium.

WIEBER, FRANCIS WILLIAM FERDINAND, M.D., Medical Corps, United States Navy, Washington, District of Columbia. Long Island College Hospital, 1881. Captain, Medical Corps, United States Navy.

WIENER, JOSEPH, A.B., M.D., 41 East Seventy-eighth Street, New York, New York. Columbia University, College of Physicians and Surgeons, 1893. Associate Surgeon, Mt. Sinai Hospital.

WIENER, MEYER, M.D., 900 Carleton Building, St. Louis, Missouri. Washington University Medical School (Missouri Medical College), 1896. Associate Professor in Clinical Ophthalmology, Washington University Medical School; Assistant Ophthalmologist, Barnes Hospital; Consulting Ophthalmologist, Jewish, St. Louis City, Bethesda, and St. Louis Maternity Hospitals, St. Vincent's Institution; Associate Editor, *American Journal of Ophthalmology*.

WIENER, SOLOMON, A.B., M.D., 67 West Eighty-ninth Street, New York, New York. Columbia University, College of Physicians and Surgeons, 1904. Associate Gynecologist, Mt. Sinai Hospital.

WIER, THOMAS F., M.D., 708 Timken Building, San Diego, California. Washington University Medical School, 1910. Member of Staff and Visiting Obstetrician, St. Joseph's Hospital; Obstetrician, San Diego County General Hospital.

WIGGERS, HENRY HAMILTON, M.D., 410 Mercantile Library Building, Cincinnati, Ohio. Ohio State University College of Homeopathic Medicine (Cleveland-Pulte Medical College), 1892. Gynecologist, Bethesda Hospital, Union Bethel Clinic, Home for the Friendless, Cincinnati Orphan Asylum.

WIGGIN, RALPH CLEAVES, M.D., 483 Beacon Street, Boston, Massachusetts. Boston University School of Medicine, 1900. Visiting Surgeon, Massachusetts Homeopathic Hospital; Lecturer on Genito-Urinary Surgery, Boston University School of Medicine.

WIGGINS, JONATHAN LEAMING, M.D., 11½ North Main Street, East St. Louis, Illinois. Washington University Medical School (St. Louis Medical College), 1877. Surgeon, Henrietta and St. Mary's Hospitals.

WIGHT, JARVIS SHERMAN, B.Sc., M.D., 30 Schermerhorn Street, Brooklyn, New York. Long Island College Hospital, 1895. Associate Surgeon, Long Island College Hospital.

WILBUR, EDWARD PEYTON, M.D., 403 Kalamazoo National Bank Building, Kalamazoo, Michigan. University of Michigan Medical School, 1897. Consulting Oculist and Aurist, Kalamazoo State Hospital.

WILCOX, ARCHA EDWARD, M.D., 920 Nicollet Avenue, Minneapolis, Minnesota. University of Pennsylvania School of Medicine, 1899. Assistant Professor of Surgery, University of Minnesota Medical School; Orthopedic Surgeon, Abbott Hospital; Surgeon, Asbury and St. Andrew's Hospitals; Consulting Surgeon, Minneapolis General Hospital.

WILCOX, DEWITT GILBERT, M.D., 496 Commonwealth Avenue, Boston, Massachusetts. Ohio State University College of Homeopathic Medicine (Cleveland Homeopathic Medical College), 1880. Professor of Clinical Gynecology, Boston University School of Medicine; Gynecologist, Out-Patient Department, Massachusetts Homeopathic Hospital; Visiting Surgeon, Newton Hospital, Newton; Visiting Gynecologist, Westboro State Hospital, Westboro.

WILCOX, HENRY W., M.D., 302 Majestic Building, Denver, Colorado. University of Colorado School of Medicine, 1897. Instructor in Orthopedic Surgery, University of Colorado School of Medicine; Orthopedic Surgeon, Children's, Denver City and County Hospitals, Sanatorium of the Jewish Consumptives Relief Society, Edgewater, Swedish National Sanatorium, Englewood.

WILCOX, STARLING S., M.D., 340 East State Street, Columbus, Ohio. Ohio State University College of Medicine (Starling Medical College), 1888. Surgeon, Grant Hospital.

716 *American College of Surgeons*

WILDER, WILLIAM HAMLIN, A.B., M.D., 122 South Michigan Avenue, Chicago, Illinois. University of Cincinnati College of Medicine (Ohio-Miami Medical College of the University of Cincinnati), 1884. Head of Department and Professor of Ophthalmology, Rush Medical College; Professor of Ophthalmology, Chicago Policlinic; Ophthalmologist, Presbyterian Hospital; Emeritus Surgeon, Illinois Charitable Eye and Ear Infirmary; Consulting Ophthalmologist, Home for Destitute Crippled Children, Annie W. Durand Hospital of the Memorial Institute for Infectious Diseases.

WILDER, WILLIAM HINTON, M.D., Woodward Building, Birmingham, Alabama. University and Bellevue Hospital Medical College (New York University Medical College), 1891. Visiting Surgeon, Hillman Hospital.

WILDER, WINFORD OLIVER, M.D., 175 State Street, Springfield, Massachusetts. University of Pennsylvania School of Medicine, 1904. Urologist, Mercy Hospital.

WILENSKY, ABRAHAM O., A.B., M.D., 1200 Madison Avenue, New York, New York. Columbia University, College of Physicians and Surgeons, 1907. Instructor in Surgery, Cornell University Medical College; Adjunct Attending Surgeon, Mt. Sinai Hospital.

WILEY, FRANK S., M.D., 39 South Main Street, Fond du Lac, Wisconsin. Rush Medical College, 1883. Chief of Staff, St. Agnes' Hospital.

WILHELMJ, CHARLES F. W., M.D., Murphy Building, East St. Louis, Illinois. Washington University Medical School (St. Louis Medical College), 1880. Member of Staff, St. Mary's and Deaconess Hospitals.

WILKINS, GEORGE CLARENCE, M.D., 402 Beacon Building, Manchester, New Hampshire. Harvard Medical School, 1899. Surgeon, Elliot Hospital.

WILKINSON, ROBERT J., M.D., Chesapeake and Ohio Railway Hospital, Huntington, West Virginia. University of Virginia, Department of Medicine, 1912. Surgeon in Charge, Chesapeake and Ohio Railway Hospital.

WILL, LEO A., M.D., 434 University Club Building, St. Louis, Missouri. St. Louis University School of Medicine, 1910. Consulting Surgeon, St. John's Hospital.

WILLARD, HARRY G., Ph.B., M.D., 1614 Puget Sound Bank Building, Tacoma, Washington. Rush Medical College, 1904. Member of Staff, St. Joseph's Hospital.

WILLARD, LEE M., M.D., 520 Third Street, Wausau, Wisconsin. University of Illinois College of Medicine (College of Physicians and Surgeons, Chicago), 1891. Member of Staff, St. Mary's Hospital.

WILLCOX, CHARLES, Ph.B., M.D., Medical Corps, United States Army, Washington, District of Columbia. University of Virginia Department of Medicine, 1889. Colonel, Medical Corps, United States Army.

WILLIAMS, ALLIE WALTER, M.D., Medical Corps, United States Army, Washington, District of Columbia. University and Bellevue Hospital Medica

College (New York University Medical College), 1896. Lieutenant Colonel, Medical Corps, United States Army.

WILLIAMS, DANIEL HALE, M.D., LL.D., 3129 Indiana Avenue, Chicago, Illinois. Northwestern University Medical School, 1883. Professor of Clinical Surgery, Meharry Medical College, Nashville, Tennessee; Associate Surgeon, St. Luke's Hospital.

WILLIAMS, EDWARD JOHNSTON, B.A., M.D., C.M., D.S.O., 700 Dorchester Street, West, Montreal, Quebec. Faculty of Medicine, McGill University, 1897. Surgeon, Sherbrooke Hospital, Sherbrooke.

WILLIAMS, HADLEY, M.D., C.M., F.R.C.S. (Eng.), Park Avenue, London, Ontario. Western University Medical School, 1889. Head of Department of Surgery and Clinical Surgery, Western University Medical School; Senior Surgeon, Victoria General Hospital; Member of Staff, St. Joseph's Hospital.

WILLIAMS, HENRY TIMOTHY, M.D., 274 Alexander Street, Rochester, New York. University of Pennsylvania School of Medicine, 1881. President of Staff and Surgeon, Rochester General and Monroe County Tuberculosis Hospitals; Surgeon, St. Mary's Hospital.

WILLIAMS, HUGH, A.B., M.D., 301 Beacon Street, Boston, Massachusetts. Harvard Medical School, 1898. Visiting Surgeon, Massachusetts General Hospital; Surgeon, Forsyth Infirmary; Consulting Surgeon, Leonard Morse Hospital, Natick, Henry Heywood Memorial Hospital, Gardner, Josiah B. Thomas Hospital, Peabody, Massachusetts, Brattleboro Memorial Hospital, Brattleboro, Vermont.

WILLIAMS, J. WHITRIDGE, A.B., M.D., D.Sc., LL.D., 107 East Chase Street, Baltimore, Maryland. University of Maryland School of Medicine, 1888. Dean and Professor of Obstetrics, Johns Hopkins University Medical School; Obstetrician-in-Chief, Johns Hopkins Hospital.

WILLIAMS, JOHN A., B.Sc., M.D., 123 Smith Street, Greensboro, North Carolina. University of Virginia, Department of Medicine, 1895. Visiting Surgeon, St. Leo's Hospital.

WILLIAMS, JOHN THOMAS, M.D., 483 Beacon Street, Boston, Massachusetts. Harvard Medical School, 1904. Assistant in Gynecology, Harvard Medical School; Assistant Surgeon, Boston City Hospital.

WILLIAMS, PERCY HERBERT, A.B., M.D., 429 Park Avenue, New York, New York. Columbia University, College of Physicians and Surgeons, 1901. Associate Visiting Obstetrician and Gynecologist, Lincoln Hospital; Associate Gynecologist, Lenox Hill Hospital and Dispensary.

WILLIAMS, RALPH, M.D., Charles C. Chapman Building, Los Angeles, California. University of Southern California, College of Medicine, 1893. Professor of Dermatology and Associate Professor of Urology, University of California, Los Angeles Medical Department; Consulting Dermatologist, Los Angeles County Hospital.

WILLIAMS, THOMAS J., M.D., L.R.C.S. & F.R.C.S. (Edin.), 30 North Michigan Avenue, Chicago, Illinois. State University of Iowa College of Medicine, 1908. Professor of Ophthalmology and Oto-Laryngology, Illinois Post-Graduate Medical School.

WILLIAMS, WILLIAM H., M.D., 117 South East Street, Lebanon, Indiana. Indiana University School of Medicine (Medical College of Indiana), 1897. Surgeon-in-Chief, The Williams Hospital.

WILLIAMS, WILLIAM WARREN, M.D., 1250 Main Street, Quincy, Illinois. State University of Iowa College of Medicine, 1884. Member of Surgical Staff, Blessing Hospital.

WILLIAMSON, ARCHIBALD ROBERT BARCLAY, M.A., M.D., C.M., M.R.C.S. (Eng.), L.R.C.P. (Lond.), Corner King and Williams Streets, Kingston, Ontario. Queen's University, Faculty of Medicine, 1899. Professor of Obstetrics, and Secretary, Queen's University, Faculty of Medicine; Head of Obstetrical Department, Kingston General Hospital.

WILLIAMSON, GEORGE McCULLOUGH, M.D., C.M., L.R.C.P. & S. (Edin.), L.F.P. & S. (Glas.), Grand Forks, North Dakota. Faculty of Medicine, University of Manitoba (Manitoba Medical College), 1895. Gynecologist and Obstetrician, St. Michael's and Deaconess Hospitals.

WILLIAMSON, LLEWELLYN P., M.D., Medical Corps, United States Army, Washington, District of Columbia. Washington University Medical School (Missouri Medical College), 1897. Lieutenant Colonel, Medical Corps, United States Army.

WILLIS, ACHILLE MURAT, M.D., Professional Building, Richmond, Virginia. Medical College of Virginia, 1904. Professor of Clinical Surgery, Medical College of Virginia; Surgeon, Virginia and Memorial Hospitals, Johnston-Willis Sanatorium.

WILLIS, BYRD CHARLES, M.D., 404 Falls Road, Rocky Mount, North Carolina. Medical College of Virginia, 1909. Surgeon, Park View Hospital.

WILLIS, JAMES CLINTON, M.D., 843 South Highlands, Shreveport, Louisiana. Vanderbilt University, Medical Department, 1887. Chief Surgeon, T. E. Schumpert Memorial Hospital; Division Surgeon, Queen and Crescent Route.

WILLIS, PARK WEED, M.Sc., M.D., 1256 Empire Building, Seattle, Washington. University of Pennsylvania School of Medicine, 1891. Surgeon, Children's Orthopedic Hospital; Consulting Surgeon, Northern Pacific Railway.

WILLITS, ALFRED J., M.D., 523 Hickory Street, Anaconda, Montana. Northwestern University Medical School, 1900. Chief of Surgical Staff, St. Ann's Hospital.

WILLITS, EMMA K., M.D., 408 Stockton Street, San Francisco, California. Northwestern University Medical School, 1896. Surgeon and Gynecologist, Hospital for Children.

WILLS, WILLIAM LEMOYNE, M.D., International Bank Building, Los Angeles, California. University of Pennsylvania School of Medicine, 1882. Consulting Surgeon, Los Angeles County Hospital.

WILMER, FRANCIS M., M.D., First National Bank Building, Winfield, Kansas. University of Illinois College of Medicine (College of Physicians and Surgeons), 1896. Member of Staff, St. Mary's Hospital.

WILMER, WILLIAM HOLLAND, M.D., LL.D., 1610 I Street, Northwest, Washington, District of Columbia. University of Virginia, Department of Medicine, 1885. Professor of Ophthalmology, Georgetown University School of Medicine; Attending Surgeon, Episcopal Eye, Ear, and Throat and Georgetown University Hospitals.

WILMS, JOHN HENRY, M.D., 12 West Seventh Street, Cincinnati, Ohio. Ohio State University College of Homeopathic Medicine (Pulte Medical College), 1902. Member of Surgical Staff, Bethesda Hospital, B. Merrill Ricketts Experimental and Surgical Research Laboratory; Surgeon, Cincinnati Union Bethel.

WILSON, CHARLES E., M.D., 924 Rialto Building, Kansas City, Missouri. University of Kansas School of Medicine (Kansas City Medical College), 1889. Member of Staff, St. Joseph's Hospital.

WILSON, CHARLES SUMNER, M.D., 301 Main Street, Johnson City, New York. University of Buffalo, Department of Medicine, 1900. Surgeon-in-Chief, Johnson City General Hospital.

WILSON, CUNNINGHAM, M.D., Jefferson County Bank Building, Birmingham, Alabama. University of Pennsylvania School of Medicine, 1884. Abdominal Surgeon, St. Vincent's Hospital.

WILSON, DOXEY ROBERT, M.D., Santa Clara County Hospital, San Jose, California. Cooper Medical College, 1908. Chief Surgeon, Santa Clara County Hospital.

WILSON, GEORGE EWART, M.B., M.R.C.S. & F.R.C.S. (Eng.), L.R.C.P. (Lond.), 205 Bloor Street, East, Toronto, Ontario. University of Toronto, Faculty of Medicine, 1903. Demonstrator of Surgery, University of Toronto, Faculty of Medicine; Assistant Surgeon, Toronto General Hospital.

WILSON, HAROLD, B.Sc., M.D., David Whitney Building, Detroit, Michigan. University of Michigan Homeopathic Medical School, 1886. Associate Clinical Professor of Ophthalmology and Oto-Laryngology, Detroit College of Medicine and Surgery; Attending Surgeon and Chief of Department of Ophthalmology and Oto-Laryngology, and Chief of Division of Special Surgery, Grace Hospital; Chief of Clinic, Grace Hospital Polyclinic; Attending Ophthalmologist and Oto-Laryngologist, Protestant Orphan Asylum.

WILSON, HORACE PLUMMER, Ph.B., M.D., Whittier National Bank Building, Whittier, California. Northwestern University Medical School, 1896. Chief of Staff, Murphy Memorial Hospital.

WILSON, JEFFERSON H., A.M., M.D., 647 Third Street, Beaver, Pennsylvania. University and Bellevue Hospital Medical College (Bellevue Hospital Medical College), 1876. Member of Surgical Staff, Rochester General Hospital, Rochester, Beaver Valley General Hospital, New Brighton, Providence Hospital, Beaver Falls.

WILSON, JOHN CAMERON, M.D., 260 Queens Avenue, London, Ontario. Western University Medical School, 1910. Surgeon, Soldiers' Civil Re-Establishment; Orthopedist, Victoria Hospital.

WILSON, J. GORDON, A.M., M.B., C.M., 104 South Michigan Avenue, Chicago, Illinois. University of Edinburgh, 1889. Professor of Otology, Northwestern University Medical School; Otologist and Laryngologist, Wesley Memorial Hospital.

WILSON, JOHN LUTHER, M.D., Fourth and Jackson Streets, Alexandria, Louisiana. Vanderbilt University, Medical Department, 1889. Member of Surgical Staff, Baptist Hospital; Local Surgeon, Chicago, Rock Island and Pacific and Louisiana and Arkansas Railways; Resident Surgeon, Texas and Pacific and Missouri Pacific Railways.

WILSON, NORTON LUTHER, M.D., 410 Westminster Avenue, Elizabeth, New Jersey. University and Bellevue Hospital Medical College (Bellevue Hospital Medical College), 1884. President of Staff, Elizabeth General Hospital; Ophthalmologist, Otologist, and Laryngologist, Alexian Brothers', Elizabeth General, and St. Elizabeth's Hospitals.

WILSON, WILFRED ALBERT, M.D., C.M., L.R.C.P. & S. (Edin.), L.F.P. & S. (Glas.), 215 McLeod Building, Edmonton, Alberta. Faculty of Medicine, McGill University, 1900. Lecturer on Surgery, University of Alberta, Faculty of Medicine.

WILTSIE, SHERALD F., M.D., Cobb Building, Seattle, Washington. University of Oregon Medical School, 1902. Attending Surgeon, Seattle City and King County Hospitals.

WINDELL, JAMES TOLBERT, M.D., 715 West Jefferson Street, Louisville, Kentucky. University of Louisville, Medical Department, 1892.

WINDMUELLER, EMIL, M.D., Clinic Building, Woodstock, Illinois. Rush Medical College, 1894. Member of Surgical Staff, Woodstock Public Hospital.

WING, PELEG BENSON, M.D., 1000 Watts Building, San Diego, California. Bowdoin Medical School, 1883. Member of Staff, San Diego County and St. Joseph's Hospitals.

WINN, CONDIE KNOX, M.D., Medical Department, United States Navy, Washington, District of Columbia. University of Pennsylvania, School of Medicine, 1904. Commander, Medical Corps, United States Navy.

WINSLOW, FITZ RANDOLPH, A.B., M.D., Hayden Hospital, Hayden, Arizona. University of Maryland School of Medicine, 1906. Chief Surgeon, Hayden Hospital.

WINSLOW, JOHN R., A.B., M.D., Latrobe Apartments, Baltimore, Maryland. University of Maryland School of Medicine, 1888. Emeritus Professor of

Laryngology, University of Maryland School of Medicine and College of Physicians and Surgeons; Surgeon, Baltimore Eye, Ear, and Throat Charity Hospital; Consulting Laryngologist, James Lawrence Kernan Hospital and Industrial School for Crippled Children.

WINSLOW, NATHAN, A.M., M.D., 1900 Mt. Royal Terrace, Baltimore, Maryland. University of Maryland School of Medicine, 1901. Clinical Professor of Surgery, University of Maryland School of Medicine and College of Physicians and Surgeons; Surgeon, University Hospital.

WINSLOW, RANDOLPH, A.M., M.D., LL.D., 1900 Mt. Royal Terrace, Baltimore, Maryland. University of Maryland School of Medicine, 1873. Emeritus Professor of Surgery, University of Maryland School of Medicine.

WINSLOW, ROLLIN CURTIS, M.D., 612 Post Building, Battle Creek, Michigan. Northwestern University Medical School, 1902. Attending Surgeon, Nichols Memorial Hospital.

WINTER, FRANCIS A., M.D., Medical Corps, United States Army, Washington, District of Columbia. Washington University Medical School, 1889. Brigadier General, Medical Corps, United States Army.

WINTER, JOHN ARTHUR, A.B., M.D., 600 Fidelity Building, Duluth, Minnesota. Johns Hopkins University, Medical Department, 1906. Chief, Eye, Ear, Nose, and Throat Department, St. Mary's Hospital.

WINTER, WILLIAM G., M.D., 14 West Eighth Street, Holland, Michigan. University of Michigan Medical School, 1906. Surgeon, Holland Hospital.

WINTERBERG, WALTER HOEPFNER, M.D., 516 Sutter Street, San Francisco, California. Cooper Medical College, 1895.

WINTHROP, GILMAN JOSEPH, A.B., M.D., Van Antwerp Building, Mobile, Alabama. Johns Hopkins University, Medical Department, 1906. Associate Professor of Gynecology, University of Alabama School of Medicine; Surgeon, Dispensary Staff, City Hospital.

WISE, WALTER DENT, M.D., 1800 North Charles Street, Baltimore, Maryland. University of Maryland School of Medicine (College of Physicians and Surgeons, Baltimore), 1906. Clinical Professor of Surgery, University of Maryland School of Medicine and College of Physicians and Surgeons; Surgeon, Mercy and South Baltimore General Hospitals.

WISHARD, WILLIAM NILES, A.M., M.D., LL.D., 723 Hume-Mansur Building, Indianapolis, Indiana. Indiana University School of Medicine (Indiana Medical College), 1874; University of Cincinnati College of Medicine (Miami Medical College), 1876. Professor of Genito-Urinary Surgery, Indiana University School of Medicine; Consulting Genito-Urinary Surgeon, Indianapolis City, Robert W. Long, and Methodist Episcopal Hospitals.

WISHART, D. J. GIBB, B.A., M.D., C.M., L.R.C.P. (Lond.), 47 Grosvenor Street, Toronto, Ontario. Faculty of Medicine, McGill University, 1885. Professor of Oto-Laryngology, University of Toronto, Faculty of Medicine; Chief Surgeon, Department of Oto-Laryngology, Toronto General Hospital.

WISHART, JOHN, M.D., C.M., M.R.C.S. (Eng.), F.R.C.S. (Edin.), 195 Dufferin Avenue, London, Ontario. University of Toronto, Faculty of Medicine (Trinity Medical College), 1875. Surgeon, St. Joseph's Hospital; Consulting Surgeon, Victoria General Hospital.

WITHERBEE, ORVILLE O., M.D., Pacific Mutual Building, Los Angeles, California. Northwestern University Medical School, 1893. Professor of Surgery, College of Physicians and Surgeons; Senior Surgeon, Los Angeles County Hospital, University Hospital Clinic.

WITHERSPOON, LOUIS G., B.Sc., A.M., M.D., 314 Roberts-Banner Building, El Paso, Texas. University of Illinois College of Medicine (College of Physicians and Surgeons, Chicago), 1898. Surgeon, El Paso Smelter Hospital.

WITHERSPOON, THOMAS CASEY, M.D., Quartz and Alaska Streets, Butte, Montana. Washington University Medical School (Missouri Medical College), 1889. Surgeon-in-Chief, Murray Hospital.

WITHROW, JOHN MURPHY, A.M., M.Sc., M.D., 22 West Seventh Street, Cincinnati, Ohio. University of Cincinnati College of Medicine (Medical College of Ohio), 1884. Emeritus Professor of Clinical Gynecology, University of Cincinnati College of Medicine; Gynecologist, Christ Hospital.

WITTE, WILLIAM C. F., M.D., 1203 Majestic Building, Milwaukee, Wisconsin. Rush Medical College, 1896. Professor of Clinical Surgery, Marquette University School of Medicine; Attending Surgeon, St. Mary's and Johnston Emergency Hospitals, Milwaukee, Milwaukee County Hospital, Wauwatosa.

WITTER, FRANK C., M.D., David Whitney Building, Detroit, Michigan. University of Michigan Medical School, 1906. Instructor in Obstetrics, Detroit College of Medicine and Surgery; Visiting Obstetrician, Herman Kiefer Maternity Hospital; Attending Surgeon, Out-Patient Department of Gynecology, Harper Hospital; Senior Attending Surgeon, Highland Park General Hospital, Highland Park.

WOBUS, REINHARD E., M.D., 713 Metropolitan Building, St. Louis, Missouri. Washington University Medical School, 1905. Instructor in Clinical Gynecology, Washington University Medical School.

WOLCOTT, W. EUGENE, M.D., 830 City National Bank Building, Omaha, Nebraska. State University of Iowa College of Medicine, 1910. Instructor in Orthopedic Surgery, John A. Creighton Medical College; Member of Staff, St. Joseph's Hospital.

WOLF, WILLIAM B., M.D., 113 West Franklin Street, Baltimore, Maryland. University of Maryland School of Medicine (College of Physicians and Surgeons, Baltimore), 1896. Clinical Professor of Genito-Urinary and Venereal Diseases, University of Maryland School of Medicine and College of Physicians and Surgeons; Chief of Clinic in Genito-Urinary and Venereal Diseases, Maryland General Hospital.

WOLF, WILLIAM MITCHELL, M.D., 704 Central Trust Building, San Antonio, Texas. University of Texas, Medical Department, 1899. Surgeon, Santa Rosa Infirmary.

WOLFE, ALBERTUS C., M.D., 350 East State Street, Columbus, Ohio. Ohio State University College of Medicine (Columbus Medical College), 1883. Rhinologist, Otologist, and Laryngologist, Grant Hospital.

WOLFE, EDWIN PHILIP, M.D., Medical Corps, United States Army, Washington, District of Columbia. George Washington University Medical School, 1896. Colonel, Medical Corps, United States Army.

WOLFER, JOHN A., M.D., 30 North Michigan Avenue, Chicago, Illinois. Northwestern University Medical School, 1908. Assistant Professor of Surgery, Northwestern University Medical School; Adjunct Surgeon, Wesley Memorial Hospital.

WOOD, ALFRED C., Phar.G., M.D., 2035 Walnut Street, Philadelphia, Pennsylvania. University of Pennsylvania School of Medicine, 1888. Assistant Professor of Surgery, University of Pennsylvania School of Medicine; Surgeon, Hospital of the University of Pennsylvania, Philadelphia General, Howard, Rush, and Memorial Hospitals; Consulting Surgeon, Charity Hospital, State Hospital for Insane, Norristown, Coatesville Hospital, Coatesville.

WOOD, CASEY ALBERT, M.D., C.M., D.C.L., 7 West Madison Street, Chicago, Illinois. Faculty of Medicine, McGill University (University of Bishop's College, Faculty of Medicine), 1877. Emeritus Professor of Ophthalmology, University of Illinois; Consulting Ophthalmic Surgeon, St. Luke's Hospital. Retired.

WOOD, DOUGLAS F., M.D., C.M., 610 Donaldson Building, Minneapolis, Minnesota. McGill University, Faculty of Medicine, 1900. Member of Staff, Northwestern and Swedish Hospitals.

WOOD, HENRY AUSTIN, A.M., M.D., 751 Main Street, Waltham, Massachusetts. Harvard Medical School, 1883. Member of Surgical Staff, Waltham Hospital.

WOOD, HILLIARD, M.D., Independent Life Building, Nashville, Tennessee. Vanderbilt University, Medical Department, 1885. Professor of Diseases of the Eye, Ear, Nose, and Throat, Vanderbilt University, Medical Department; Eye, Ear, Nose, and Throat Surgeon, Vanderbilt University, St. Thomas, and Nashville City Hospitals; Ophthalmic Surgeon, Tennessee Central Railway.

WOOD, JAMES CRAVEN, A.M., M.D., 816 Rose Building, Cleveland, Ohio. University of Michigan Homeopathic Medical College, 1897. Gynecologist, Huron Road Hospital; Consulting Gynecologist, Elyria Memorial Hospital.

WOOD, ROBERT LOWELL, M.D., 129 Hancock Street, Brooklyn, New York. New York Homeopathic Medical College and Flower Hospital, 1904. Attending Obstetrician, Carson C. Peck Memorial and Cumberland Street Hospitals; Consulting Obstetrician, Brooklyn Maternity Hospital.

WOOD, SIR ROBERT, M.B., B.Ch., B.A.O., M.Ch., 39 Merrion Square, Dublin, Ireland. University of Dublin, 1889. Professor of Oto-Laryngology, University of Dublin; Surgeon, Ear, Nose, and Throat Department, Sir Patrick Dun's Hospital.

WOODARD, CHARLES A., A.B., M.D., Green and Spring Streets, Wilson, North Carolina. University of Virginia, Department of Medicine, 1904. Surgeon, Moore-Herring Hospital.

WOODARD, HERBERT BOOTHE, M.D., 25 East Washington Street, Chicago, Illinois. Hahnemann Medical College and Hospital, Chicago, 1897.

WOODBURNE, ARTHUR W., M.D., 304 South Jefferson Street, Hastings, Michigan. Western University Faculty of Medicine, 1898.

WOODLAND, EDWARD E., Phar.D., M.D., 73 East Eightieth Street, New York, New York. University of Pennsylvania School of Medicine, 1910.

WOODMAN, JAMES BROWN, A.B., M.D., 336 Central Street, Franklin, New Hampshire. Dartmouth Medical School, 1903. Member of Staff, Franklin Hospital.

WOODRUFF, FREDERICK ENO, M.D., Metropolitan Building, St. Louis, Missouri. Washington University Medical School (Missouri Medical College), 1897. Ophthalmologist, Bethesda and St. Louis Eye, Ear, Nose, and Throat Hospitals, Memorial and Methodist Episcopal Orphans' Homes; Ophthalmologist, Chicago, Rock Island, and Pacific Railway.

WOODRUFF, STANLEY ROGERS, M.D., 16 Enos Place, Jersey City, New Jersey. Yale University School of Medicine, 1897. Assistant Professor of Urology, New York Post-Graduate Medical School; Instructor in Urology, Columbia University, College of Physicians and Surgeons; Attending Surgeon, Department of Urology, Vanderbilt Clinic, New York; Attending Genito-Urinary Surgeon, Bayonne Hospital, Bayonne, Christ Hospital, Jersey City.

WOODRUFF, THOMAS ADAMS, M.D., C.M., L.R.C.P. (Lond.), Plant Building, New London, Connecticut. Faculty of Medicine, McGill University, 1888.

WOODS, EDGAR LYONS, M.D., Medical Corps, United States Navy, Washington, District of Columbia. University of Virginia, Department of Medicine, 1904. Commander, Medical Corps, United States Navy.

WOODS, HIRAM, A.B., M.D., 842 Park Avenue, Baltimore, Maryland. University of Maryland School of Medicine, 1882. Ophthalmic Surgeon, University Hospital, Hospital for Women of Maryland, Union Protestant Infirmary; Consulting Surgeon, South Baltimore General Hospital, Children's Hospital School, James Lawrence Kernan Hospital and Industrial School for Crippled Children, Baltimore, Washington County Hospital, Hagerstown.

WOODSON, JAMES MADISON, M.D., Monroe and Eleventh Streets, Temple, Texas. Tulane University of Louisiana School of Medicine, 1891. Oculist and Aurist, Temple Sanitarium, Santa Fe Hospital.

WOODWARD, JAMES S., M.D., Medical Corps, United States Navy, Washington, District of Columbia. University of Maryland School of Medicine (Baltimore Medical College), 1901. Commander, Medical Corps, United States Navy.

WOODWARD, LEMUEL FOX, B.Sc., M.D., 52 Pearl Street, Worcester, Massachusetts. Harvard Medical School, 1882. Consulting Surgeon, Worcester City and Memorial Hospitals, Worcester, Hospital Cottages for Children, Baldwinsville.

WOODWARD, SAMUEL ANDREW, M.D., 406 Flatiron Building, Fort Worth, Texas. University of Tennessee College of Medicine, 1894. Professor of Clinical Gynecology, Baylor University School of Medicine; Visiting Surgeon, All Saints' and City and County Hospitals, St. Joseph's Infirmary; Surgeon, Frisco Lines in Texas; Local Surgeon, International and Great Northern Railway Company.

WOOLFORD, JOHN S. B., M.D., 602 Georgia Avenue, Chattanooga, Tennessee. University of Maryland School of Medicine, 1896. Chief Surgeon, Woolford-Johnson Infirmary; Consulting Surgeon, Baroness Erlanger Hospital.

WOOLSEY, GEORGE, A.B., M.D., 117 East Thirty-sixth Street, New York, New York. Columbia University, College of Physicians and Surgeons, 1885. Professor of Clinical Surgery, Cornell University Medical College; Visiting Surgeon, Bellevue Hospital; Consulting Surgeon, General Memorial Hospital, New York, Peekskill Hospital, Peekskill, St. John's Riverside Hospital, Yonkers.

WOOLSEY, ROSS ARLINGTON, M.D., 4960 Laclede Avenue, St. Louis, Missouri. St. Louis University School of Medicine, 1904. Chief Surgeon, St. Louis-San Francisco Railway, Frisco Employes' Hospital Association.

WOOLSTON, WESLEY JOHN, M.D., 25 East Washington Street, Chicago, Illinois. University of Illinois College of Medicine (College of Physicians and Surgeons, Chicago), 1905. Assistant Professor of Surgery and Gynecology, University of Illinois College of Medicine; Attending Gynecologist, Cook County and Wesley Memorial Hospitals.

WOOTEN, JOE SIL, B.Sc., M.D., 107 East Tenth Street, Austin, Texas. Columbia University, College of Physicians and Surgeons, 1895. Member of Staff, Seton Infirmary.

WORKMAN, HARPER M., M.D., Partridge Block, Tracy, Minnesota. Northwestern University Medical School, 1878.

WORRELL, JONATHAN P., M.D., 20 South Seventh Street, Terre Haute, Indiana. University of Pennsylvania School of Medicine, 1867. Ophthalmic and Aural Surgeon, St. Anthony's Hospital, Pennsylvania and Eastern Illinois Railroads.

WORTHEN, THACHER WASHBURN, A.B., A.M., M.D., 179 Allyn Street, Hartford, Connecticut. Dartmouth Medical School, 1911. Assistant Attending Surgeon, Hartford Hospital.

WORTHINGTON, THOMAS CHEW, M.D., 1102 North Charles Street, Baltimore, Maryland. University of Maryland School of Medicine, 1876. Laryngologist and Rhinologist, Baltimore Eye, Ear, and Throat Charity Hospital; Visiting Laryngologist and Rhinologist, Union Protestant Infirmary.

WOUTAT, HENRY G., M.D., Northwestern National Bank Building, Grand Forks, North Dakota. University of Minnesota Medical School, 1897. Chief of Staff, Deaconess Hospital; Urologist, St. Michael's Hospital.

WRIGHT, ARTHUR, M.B., 329 Church Street, Toronto, Ontario. University of Toronto, Faculty of Medicine, 1902. Demonstrator of Surgery, University of Toronto, Faculty of Medicine; Junior Surgeon, Toronto General Hospital.

WRIGHT, ARTHUR MULLIN, A.B., M.D., 417 Park Avenue, New York, New York. Cornell University Medical College, 1905. Associate Professor of Surgery, University and Bellevue Hospital Medical College; Visiting Surgeon, Bellevue Hospital; Assistant Visiting Surgeon, St. Vincent's Hospital.

WRIGHT, FRANKLIN RANDOLPH, D.D.S., M.D., 707 Donaldson Building, Minneapolis, Minnesota. University of Minnesota Medical School, 1894. Associate Professor of Urology, University of Minnesota Medical School; Urologist, University Hospital; Genito-Urinary Surgeon, Minneapolis City Hospital.

WRIGHT, FREDERICK T., A.B., M.D., 636 Tenth Street, Douglas, Arizona. University of Michigan Medical School, 1899. Chief Surgeon, Calumet Hospital.

WRIGHT, JAMES MANN, M.D., Canton Hospital, Canton, China. Kansas Medical College, 1902; University of Kansas School of Medicine, 1913. Professor of Gynecology and Clinical Surgery, Kung Yee Medical and Hackett Medical Colleges; Chief Surgeon and Chief of Department of Obstetrics and Gynecology, Canton Hospital.

WRIGHT, JOHN WINTHROP, A.B., M.D., 810 Myrtle Avenue, Bridgeport, Connecticut. University and Bellevue Hospital Medical College (New York University Medical College), 1880. Consulting Surgeon, Bridgeport, St. Vincent's, and Galen Hospitals.

WRIGHT, ROBERT H., M.D., 316 East Franklin Street, Richmond, Virginia. University of Virginia, Department of Medicine, 1900. Associate Professor of Ophthalmology, Medical College of Virginia; Consulting Ophthalmologist and Otologist, Stuart Circle Hospital; Surgeon, Department of Ophthalmology and Otology, Memorial Hospital.

WRIGHT, ROBERT PERCY, C.M.G., D.S.O., M.D., C.M., 637 Union Avenue, Montreal, Quebec. Faculty of Medicine, McGill University, 1908. Assistant Demonstrator of Oto-Laryngology, Faculty of Medicine, McGill University; Otologist and Laryngologist, Children's Memorial Hospital; Assistant Oto-Laryngologist, Montreal General Hospital.

WRIGHT, SHERMAN E., M.D., 822 Corbett Building, Portland, Oregon. Northwestern University Medical School, 1900. Consulting Eye, Ear, Nose, and

Throat Surgeon, United States Public Health Service and St. Vincent's Hospital.

WRIGHT, THEW, A.B., M.D., 575 Delaware Avenue, Buffalo, New York. University of Buffalo, Department of Medicine, 1903. Associate in Surgery, University of Buffalo, Department of Medicine; Attending Surgeon, Buffalo General, Erie County, Ernest Wende, and Municipal Hospitals; Chief of Surgical Service, Children's Hospital.

WRIGHT, THOMAS R., M.D., 402 Ninth Street, Augusta, Georgia. University of Georgia, Medical Department, 1876. Professor of Surgery, University of Georgia, Medical Department; Attending Surgeon, University and Margaret Wright Hospitals.

WRIGHT, WILLIAM ALBERT, M.D., 300 Kane Building, Pocatello, Idaho. Rush Medical College, 1901. Surgeon, St. Anthony's Hospital.

WROTH, PEREGRINE, JR., A.B., M.D., 131 West Washington Street, Hagerstown, Maryland. Johns Hopkins University, Medical Department, 1906. Visiting Surgeon, Washington County Hospital; Chief of Venereal Clinic, State Department of Health; Surgeon, Western Maryland Railroad.

WURDEMANN, HARRY VANDERBILT, M.D., 709 Cobb Building, Seattle, Washington. George Washington University Medical School (Columbian University, Medical Department), 1888. Associate Editor, *American Journal of Ophthalmology*.

WYLIE, SAMUEL M., M.D., 308 West Center Street, Paxton, Illinois. Northwestern University Medical School, 1878.

WYLIE, WINFRED, LL.B., M.D., Phoenix, Arizona. Rush Medical College, 1877; Long Island College Hospital, 1878. Chief Surgeon, Arizona Eastern Railroad.

WYNEKOOP, CHARLES IRA, B.Sc., M.D., 4931 Sheridan Road, Chicago, Illinois. University of Illinois College of Medicine (College of Physicians and Surgeons, Chicago), 1898. Surgeon, Lake View Hospital.

WYNEKOOP, GILBERT H., B.Sc., M.D., 4500 Sheridan Road, Chicago, Illinois. University of Illinois College of Medicine (College of Physicians and Surgeons, Chicago), 1906. Surgeon, Lake View Hospital.

WYNKOOP, HENRY JOHN, M.D., 7 East Steuben Street, Bath, New York. University and Bellevue Hospital Medical College (University of the City of New York), 1898. Member of Surgical Staff, Bath General Hospital; Consulting Surgeon, Pleasant Valley Sanatorium.

WYNN, JOSEPH J., M.D., 456 Francis Building, Louisville, Kentucky. Hahnemann Medical College and Hospital, Philadelphia, 1908. Instructor in Ophthalmology, University of Louisville, Medical Department; Member of Staff, Louisville City and Methodist Deaconess Hospitals.

WYNNE, HERBERT M. N., B.Sc., A.M., M.D., 300 La Salle Building, Minneapolis, Minnesota. Instructor in Gynecology and Obstetrics, University of Minnesota Medical School; Associate Gynecologist, University Hospital.

XELOWSKI, THADDEUS ZIGMUND, Phar.G., M.D., 30 North Michigan Avenue, Chicago, Illinois. University of Illinois College of Medicine, 1903. Surgeon, St. Mary of Nazareth Hospital.

YAGGI, HENRY KLAR, B.Sc., M.D., Main Street and Broadway, Salem, Ohio. Western Reserve University School of Medicine, 1906. Chief Surgeon, Central Clinic and Salem Hospital.

YANCEY, E. F., M.D., 803 West Broadway, Sedalia, Missouri. Washington University Medical School (Missouri Medical College), 1882. Chief Surgeon, Missouri, Kansas and Texas Railway; Division Surgeon, Missouri Pacific Railway.

YANCEY, ROBERT SHEROD, M.D., 422 Wilson Building, Dallas, Texas. Washington University Medical School, 1897. Member of Staff, Parkland City Hospital; Visiting Oculist, St. Paul's Sanitarium; Division Oculist, Missouri, Kansas and Texas Railway; Local Oculist, St. Louis and Southwestern Railway.

YARROS, RACHELLE S., M.D., 800 South Halsted Street, Chicago, Illinois. Woman's Medical College of Pennsylvania, 1893. Associate Professor of Obstetrics, University of Illinois College of Medicine; Obstetrician, Chicago Lying-in Hospital and Dispensary; Special Consultant, Division of Venereal Diseases, United States Public Health Service.

YATES, H. WELLINGTON, M.D., 1229 David Whitney Building, Detroit, Michigan. Detroit College of Medicine and Surgery, 1894. Associate, Chair of Gynecology, Detroit College of Medicine and Surgery; Gynecologist, Providence and William Booth Memorial Hospitals; Attending Gynecologist, Detroit Receiving Hospital.

YATES, JOHN LAWRENCE, Ph.B., B.Sc., M.D., 141 Wisconsin Street, Milwaukee, Wisconsin. Johns Hopkins University, Medical Department, 1899. Attending Surgeon, Milwaukee Children's and Columbia Hospitals; Chief of Staff, Milwaukee County Hospital, Wauwatosa.

YEOMANS, FRANK CLARK, A.B., M.D., 171 West Seventy-first Street, New York, New York. Cornell University Medical College, 1900. Instructor in Surgery, Columbia University, College of Physicians and Surgeons; Attending Surgeon, Central and Neurological Hospitals, Vanderbilt Clinic.

YEOMANS, THERON G., M.D., St. Joseph Sanitarium, St. Joseph, Michigan. University of Michigan Homeopathic Medical School, 1909. Chief Surgeon, St. Joseph Sanitarium.

YERXA, CHARLES W., M.D., 520 Los Angeles Railway Building, Los Angeles, California. University of Southern California College of Medicine, 1903.

YOCOM, JAMES R., A.B., M.D., Perkins Building, Tacoma, Washington. Harvard Medical School, 1888.

YOCUM, JOSEPH GRANT, A.B., M.D., 44 West Forty-fourth Street, New York, New York. Columbia University, College of Physicians and Surgeons, 1901. Attending Surgeon, Volunteers' and New York Skin and Cancer Hospitals.

YOERG, OTTO WILLIAM, B.Sc., M.D., 527 Syndicate Building, Minneapolis, Minnesota. University of Minnesota Medical School, 1910. Member of Surgical Staff, Northwestern Hospital.

YOUNG, EDWARD WELDON, M.D., 816 Cobb Building, Seattle, Washington. University of Minnesota Medical School (Minnesota Homeopathic Medical College), 1889.

YOUNG, ERNEST BOYEN, A.B., M.D., 434 Marlborough Street, Boston, Massachusetts. Harvard Medical School, 1896. Instructor in Gynecology, Harvard Medical School; Surgeon-in-Chief, Boston City Hospital; Surgeon, Massachusetts Women's Hospital.

YOUNG, HENRY McCLURE, A.B., M.D., 622 University Club Building, St. Louis, Missouri. Washington University Medical School, 1908. Assistant in Clinical Surgery, Washington University Medical School; Consulting Genito-Urinary Surgeon, St. Louis City and Public Health Service Hospitals.

YOUNG, HUGH HAMPTON, A.M., M.D., D.S.M., Johns Hopkins Hospital, Baltimore, Maryland. University of Virginia, Department of Medicine, 1894. Clinical Professor of Urology, Johns Hopkins University, Medical Department; Visiting Urologist, Johns Hopkins Hospital; Director, James Buchanan Brady Urological Institute.

YOUNG, JAMES KELLY, M.D., 222 South Sixteenth Street, Philadelphia, Pennsylvania. University of Pennsylvania School of Medicine, 1883. Professor of Orthopedics, University of Pennsylvania Graduate School of Medicine; Orthopedic Surgeon, Philadelphia General Hospital; Consulting Orthopedic Surgeon, Woman's and Lying-in Charity Hospitals, North American Sanitarium.

YOUNG, JOHN VAN DOREN, M.D., 16 East Seventy-fourth Street, New York, New York. Columbia University, College of Physicians and Surgeons, 1888. Adjunct Professor of Gynecology, New York Polyclinic Medical School; Gynecological Surgeon, St. Elizabeth's Hospital; Consulting Gynecologist, Hackensack Hospital, Hackensack, New Jersey.

YOUNG, WILLIS BROCK, M.D., 516 Metropolitan Building, St. Louis, Missouri. Homeopathic Medical College of Missouri, 1891.

YOUNGER, CHARLES BENJAMIN, M.D., 25 East Washington Street, Chicago, Illinois. Northwestern University Medical School, 1902. Assistant Professor of Rhinology and Laryngology, Northwestern University Medical School; Attending Rhinologist and Laryngologist, Wesley Memorial Hospital; Attending Rhinologist and Oto-Laryngologist, Washington Park Hospital; Consulting Oto-Laryngologist, Auburn Park, Jackson Park Hospitals, Chicago, and St. Francis Hospital, Blue Island.

YOUNT, CLARENCE EDGAR, M.D., 214 South Mt. Vernon Street, Prescott, Arizona. Georgetown University School of Medicine, 1896. Attending Surgeon, Yavapai County Hospital, United States Public Health Service Hospital No. 50.

ZABOKRTSKY, JOSEPH, M.D., 31 North State Street, Chicago, Illinois. University of Illinois College of Medicine (College of Physicians and Surgeons), 1901.

ZALESKY, WILLIAM J., M.D., Medical Corps, United States Navy, Washington, District of Columbia. University of Michigan Medical School, 1903. Lieutenant Commander, Medical Corps, United States Navy.

ZAPFFE, FREDERICK CARL, M.D., 25 East Washington Street, Chicago, Illinois. University of Illinois College of Medicine (College of Physicians and Surgeons, Chicago), 1896.

ZEINERT, OLIVER B., M.D., 618 University Club Building, St. Louis, Missouri University of Michigan Medical School, 1907. Visiting Surgeon, Missouri Pacific Railway Hospital.

ZERFING, CHARLES E., M.D., 400 Pantages Building, Los Angeles, California. University of Pennsylvania School of Medicine, 1895. Clinical Instructor in Surgery, Graduate School of Medicine of the University of California; Visiting Surgeon, Los Angeles County Hospital.

ZIEGLER, CHARLES EDWARD, Ph.B., A.M., M.D., 4716 Bayard Street, Pittsburgh, Pennsylvania. University of Pennsylvania School of Medicine, 1900. Consulting Obstetrician and Gynecologist, Dixmont Hospital for Insane, Dixmont.

ZIEGLER, S. LEWIS, A.M., M.D., D.Sc., LL.D., 1625 Walnut Street, Philadelphia, Pennsylvania. University of Pennsylvania School of Medicine, 1885. Chief Ophthalmic Surgeon, St. Joseph's Hospital; Attending and Executive Surgeon, Wills Eye Hospital.

ZILLERUELO, JULIO C., M.D., Plaza Pinto 371, Valparaiso, Chile. Faculty of Medicine, University of Chile, 1897. Chief of Service, St. Agustine's Hospital.

ZIMMER, FREDERICK WILLIAM, M.D., 45 Monroe Avenue, Rochester, New York. University of Pennsylvania School of Medicine, 1882. Attending Surgeon, Rochester General Hospital; Surgeon, Rochester State Hospital.

ZIMMERMAN, A. G., LL.B., M.D., 30 North Michigan Avenue, Chicago, Illinois. University of Strassburg, 1899. Surgeon, Alexian Brothers', Grant, and St. Elizabeth's Hospitals.

ZIMMERMAN, BENJAMIN FRANKLIN, A.B., M.D., Francis Building, Louisville, Kentucky. University of Louisville, Medical Department (Louisville Medical College), 1901.

ZIMMERMAN, VICTOR LEO, A.M., M.D., 839 Carroll Street, Brooklyn, New York. University and Bellevue Hospital Medical College, 1897. Attending Gynecologist and Obstetrician, Hospital of the Holy Family and St. Mary's Hospital; Associate Gynecologist and Obstetrician, Brooklyn Hospital; Obstetrician, Bushwick Hospital.

ZIMMERMANN, CHARLES, M.D., 428 Jefferson Street, Milwaukee, Wisconsin. University of Berlin, 1880. Ophthalmic Surgeon, Milwaukee, Columbia, and Milwaukee Children's Hospitals, Marquette Dispensary Clinic.

ZIMMERMANN, HARRY BERNARD, M.D., Hamm Building, St. Paul, Minnesota. Columbia University, College of Physicians and Surgeons, 1909. Assistant Professor of Surgery, University of Minnesota Medical School; Attending Surgeon, Charles T. Miller, City and County Hospitals.

ZINKE, E. GUSTAV, M.D., 4 West Seventh Street, Cincinnati, Ohio. University of Cincinnati College of Medicine (Medical College of Ohio), 1875. Emeritus Professor of Obstetrics, University of Cincinnati College of Medicine; Consulting Obstetrician, Cincinnati General Hospital; Honorary Chief of Staff, Obstetrician, and Gynecologist, Deaconess Hospital.

ZINKE, STANLEY GUSTAV, M.D., 4 West Seventh Street, Cincinnati, Ohio. University of Cincinnati College of Medicine (Medical College of Ohio), 1902.

ZINTSMASTER, LOGAN B., M.D., 212 McClymonds Building, Massillon, Ohio. Western Reserve University School of Medicine, 1901. Visiting Surgeon, Massillon City Hospital.

ZOBEL, ALFRED JACOB, M.D., 210 Post Street, San Francisco, California. Cooper Medical College, 1898. Chief of Clinic, Diseases of Rectum and Colon, San Francisco Polyclinic and Post-Graduate College; Visiting Rectal Surgeon, San Francisco Hospital; Consulting Proctologist, Mt. Zion Hospital; Lecturer on Proctology, Leland Stanford Junior University School of Medicine.

ZUINGA, ALBERTO, B.A., M.D., Avenida Espana 473, Santiago, Chile. Faculty of Medicine, University of Chile, 1909.

ZULICK, THOMAS C., M.D., 226 Ferry Street, Easton, Pennsylvania. University of Pennsylvania School of Medicine, 1891. Associate Surgeon, Easton City Hospital.

FELLOWS DECEASED

EDWARD THOMAS ABRAMS, Dollar Bay, Michigan 1918
FRANCIS JOSEPH ADAMS, Great Falls, Montana 1920
JOHN LAMSON ADAMS, New York, New York 1914
THEODORE LOUIS ADAMS, Philadelphia, Pennsylvania 1917
JOHN ELMER ALLABEN, Rockford, Illinois 1921
AMERICUS R. ALLEN, Carlisle, Pennsylvania 1917
J. HARTLEY ANDERSON, Pittsburgh, Pennsylvania 1915
THOMAS A. ASHBY, Baltimore, Maryland 1916
ALFRED B. ATHERTON, San Diego, California 1921
SAMUEL CHANDLER BAKER, Sumter, South Carolina 1918
FRANCIS POLLOCK BALL, Lock Haven, Pennsylvania 1920
WILLIAM LINCOLN BALLENGER, Chicago, Illinois 1915
GEORGE HENRY BALLERAY, Paterson, New Jersey 1920
LEMUEL BOLTON BANGS, New York, New York 1914
JOHN HENRY BARBAT, San Francisco, California 1920
CHARLES CLIFFORD BARROWS, New York, New York 1916
BERNARD BARTOW, Buffalo, New York 1920
WILLIAM A. BATCHELOR, Milwaukee, Wisconsin 1920
HOWARD WALTER BEAL, Worcester, Massachusetts 1918
NORMAN HARVARD BEAL, London, Ontario 1919
CHARLES H. BEARD, Chicago, Illinois 1916
SHADWORTH OLDHAM BEASLEY, San Francisco, California . . . 1918
EMIL H. BECKMAN, Rochester, Minnesota 1916
SIMON C. BEEDE, David City, Nebraska . . . . . : . 1916
HOWARD BURHAMS BESEMER, Ithaca, New York 1918
CHARLES FREDERICK BEVAN, Baltimore, Maryland 1917
RICHARD HENRY L. BIBB, Saltillo, Mexico 1920
JOSEPH BIDLEMAN BISSELL, New York, New York 1918
CLARENCE JOHN BLAKE, Boston, Massachusetts 1919
JOHN D. BLAKE, Baltimore, Maryland 1920
JAMES ASHTON BLANCHARD, Shreveport, Louisiana 1920
JOHN ALFRED BODINE, New York, New York 1919
LEWIS C. BOSHER, Richmond, Virginia 1920
SAMUEL CECIL BOWEN, Richmond, Virginia 1918
EDWARD SHERMAN BREESE, Dayton, Ohio 1918
DANIEL J. BROWN, Springfield, Massachusetts 1919
FRANK EDWIN BROWN, Brooklyn, New York 1920
JOHN YOUNG BROWN, St. Louis, Missouri 1919
RICHARD HUNT BROWN, Chicago, Illinois 1918
ROBERT R. BROWNFIELD, Phoenix, Arizona 1921
JOSEPH D. BRYANT, New York, New York 1914
JOHN J. BUCKLEY, Missoula, Montana 1917
WILLIAM H. BUECHNER, Youngstown, Ohio 1920

733

ROSE TALBOTT BULLARD, Los Angeles, California 1915
A. J. BURGE, Iowa City, Iowa 1918
JOHN L. BURGESS, Waco, Texas 1921
JAMES BURRY, Chicago, Illinois 1919
LEWIS WHITE CALLAN, New York, New York 1920
ROLAND PLAYFAIR CAMPBELL, Montreal, Quebec 1916
BUKK G. CARLETON, New York, New York 1914
ALBERT C. CARNEY, Hamilton, Ohio 1921
J. HENRY CARSTENS, Detroit, Michigan 1920
WILLIAM E. CASSELBERRY, Chicago, Illinois 1916
CHARLES HENRY CASTLE, Cincinnati, Ohio 1918
JEHIEL W. CHAMBERLIN, St. Paul, Minnesota 1921
ALBERT TYLER CHAMBERS, Baltimore, Maryland 1918
JOHN W. CHAMBERS, Baltimore, Maryland 1917
WALTER F. CHAPPELL, New York, New York 1918
FREDERICK R. CHARLTON, Indianapolis, Indiana 1916
WALTER B. CHASE, Brooklyn, New York 1920
WILLIAM CHEATHAM, Louisville, Kentucky 1919
CHRISTIAN CHRISTENSEN, La Crosse, Wisconsin 1916
ROBERT JAMES CHRISTIE, Quincy, Illinois . . . . . : 1917
SAMUEL POSEY COLLINGS, Hot Springs, Arkansas 1917
LEO J. J. COMMISKEY, Brooklyn, New York 1921
CHARLES DEWITT CONKEY, Duluth, Minnesota 1921
JOHN C. COPE, Greensburg, Pennsylvania 1920
HORACE CORTELYOU CORY, Newark, New Jersey 1919
GEORGE F. COTT, Buffalo, New York 1921
JAMES MILTON COTTON, Toronto, Ontario 1918
CHAUNCEY W. COURTWRIGHT, Chicago, Illinois 1919
EDGAR COX, Kokomo, Indiana 1919
EDWIN BRADFORD CRAGIN, New York, New York 1918
WILLIAM GIBSON CRAIG, Springfield, Massachusetts 1917
EMMA V. P. B. CULBERTSON, Boston, Massachusetts 1920
H. HOLBROOK CURTIS, New York, New York 1920
ROBERT MORISON CURTS, Paterson, New Jersey 1916
ERNEST WATSON CUSHING, Boston, Massachusetts 1916
MARSHALL L. CUSHMAN, Lansing, Michigan 1921
WALTER S. DALY, Ogdensburg, New York 1918
LOUIS JOSEPH DANDURANT, St. Joseph, Missouri 1920
EDWARD MCLAREN DARROW, Fargo, North Dakota 1919
CHARLES HUFF DAVIS, Knoxville, Tennessee 1918
GWILYM G. Davis, Philadelphia, Pennsylvania 1918
PAUL HERMAN DERNEHL, Milwaukee, Wisconsin 1919
ROBERT DODDS, Chicago, Illinois 1920
FRANK M. DONOHUE, New Brunswick, New Jersey 1919
WALTER BLACKBURN DORSETT, St. Louis, Missouri 1915
HENRY A. DUNN, Washington, District of Columbia 1917
JULIUS M. DUTTON, Westfield, Massachusetts 1921
THOMAS BARKER EASTMAN, Indianapolis, Indiana 1919
GEORGE EMERSON, Winfield, Kansas 1920

THOMAS ADDIS EMMET, New York, New York 1919
DANIEL E. ESTERLY, Topeka, Kansas 1921
ARTHUR BARNETT EUSTACE, Denver, Colorado 1918
HENRY COURTNEY EVANS, Youngstown, Ohio 1919
ROMULUS FALARDEAU, Montreal, Quebec 1918
WILLIAM P. FAUST, Schenectady, New York 1919
CHARLES A. FERRIS, Denver, Colorado 1921
FRANCIS FOERSTER, New York, New York 1916
WILLIAM CLYDE FOSTER, Casper, Wyoming 1920
GEORGE WILLIAM FOX, Milwaukee, Wisconsin 1920
JOSEPH F. FOX, Martinsburg, West Virginia 1921
JAMES ROY FREELAND, Pittsburgh, Pennsylvania 1917
JOHN DWIGHT FREEMAN, Topeka, Kansas 1919
WALTER J. FREEMAN, Philadelphia, Pennsylvania 1920
STANTON A. FRIEDBERG, Chicago, Illinois 1920
HENRY DAVIDSON FRY, Washington, District of Columbia . . . 1919
JOSEPH ADDINGTON GALE, Roanoke, Virginia 1916
FREDERIC HENRY GERRISH, Portland, Maine 1920
JOSEPH S. GIBB, Philadelphia, Pennsylvania 1914
HARMON BAKER GIBBON, Tiffin, Ohio 1919
ROBERT JAMES GIBSON, Sault Ste. Marie, Ontario 1919
WILLIAM JOHN GIBSON, Belleville, Ontario 1920
ARTHUR J. GILLETTE, St. Paul, Minnesota 1921
ROBERT TRACY GILLMORE, Chicago, Illinois 1918
STEPHEN G. GLIDDEN, Danville, Illinois 1917
JAMES ADRIAN GOGGANS, Alexander City, Alabama 1920
WILLIAM C. GORGAS, New York, New York 1920
FRANK WILLARD GRAFTON, Concord, New Hampshire 1915
HENRY HORACE GRANT, Louisville, Kentucky 1921
FRANK D. GRAY, Jersey City, New Jersey 1916
JOHN SIDNEY GRAY, Winnipeg, Manitoba 1917
CHARLES WILLIAM GROETSCH, New Orleans, Louisiana 1918
WASHINGTON BERRY GROVE, Washington, District of Columbia . . 1919
RAMON GUITERAS, New York, New York 1917
FRED A. GUTHRIE, La Salle, Illinois 1915
GEORGE W. GUTHRIE, Wilkes-Barre, Pennsylvania 1915
WILLIAM ELTON GUTHRIE, Bloomington, Illinois 1919
W. NELSON HAMMOND, Philadelphia, Pennsylvania 1918
FRANCIS BISHOP HARRINGTON, Boston, Massachusetts 1914
ALANSON W. HAWLEY, Seattle, Washington 1920
JAMES RAYNOR HAYDEN, New York, New York 1921
EUGENE E. HAYNES, Memphis, Tennessee 1921
NEIL JAMIESON HEPBURN, New York, New York 1918
WILLET JEREMIAH HERRINGTON, Bad Axe, Michigan 1920
WALTER H. P. HILL, Montreal, Quebec 1921
CHARLES A. VON HOFFMAN, San Francisco, California 1917
JOHN C. HOLLISTER, Pasadena, California 1916
CHRISTIAN RASMUS HOLMES, Cincinnati, Ohio 1920
EDGAR MILLER HOLMES, Boston, Massachusetts 1918

HENRY WELLS HORN, San Francisco, California 1920
INGVALD M. J. HOTVEDT, Muskegon, Michigan 1919
NEIDHARD H. HOUGHTON, Boston, Massachusetts 1920
HARRY FISKE HULL, Washington, District of Columbia 1920
ROBERT LORD HULL, Oklahoma, Oklahoma 1919
RANDELL HUNT, Shreveport, Louisiana 1920
AUGUSTUS A. HUSSEY, Brooklyn, New York 1917
E. FLETCHER INGALS, Chicago, Illinois 1918
HARRY T. INGE, Mobile, Alabama 1921
STANLEY NELSON INSLEY, Grayling, Michigan 1920
JAMES S. IRVIN, Danville, Virginia 1915
HARVEY P. JACK, Hornell, New York 1920
THOMAS TERRELL JACKSON, San Antonio, Texas 1920
JULIUS H. JACOBSON, Toledo, Ohio 1918
W. G. JAMESON, Palestine, Texas 1917
NATHAN JENKS, Detroit, Michigan 1916
JOSEPH T. JOHNSON, Cherrydale, Virginia 1921
GEORGE BEN JOHNSTON, Richmond, Virginia 1916
OSWALD MEREDITH JONES, Victoria, British Columbia 1918
ADONIRAM BROWN JUDSON, New York, New York 1916
RICHARD KALISH, New York, New York 1921
MICHAEL E. KEAN, Manchester, New Hampshire 1920
FRANK S. KEELE, Portage la Prairie, Manitoba 1918
GEORGE KEENAN, Madison, Wisconsin 1915
LUTHER HURN KELLER, Hagerstown, Maryland 1915
JOSEPH ALOYSIUS KENEFICK, New York, New York 1919
FRANK PIERCE KENYON, Pomona, California 1921
JOHN KEPKE, Brooklyn, New York 1921
RUSH W. KIMBALL, Norwich, Connecticut 1915
ELBRIDGE HARRISON KING, Muscatine, Iowa 1918
MAX OTTO KLOTZ, Ottawa, Ontario 1921
FRANK HENRY KNIGHT, Brooklyn, New York 1918
WILLIAM KOHLMANN, New Orleans, Louisiana 1921
D. BRADEN KYLE, Philadelphia, Pennsylvania 1916
JOHN JOHNSON KYLE, Los Angeles, California 1920
LOUIS A. LAGARDE, Washington, District of Columbia 1920
GEORGE B. LAWRASON, Shreveport, Louisiana 1918
JOHN A. LEE, Brooklyn, New York 1920
CHARLES H. LEMON, Milwaukee, Wisconsin 1921
EDWARD LINTHICUM, Evansville, Indiana 1918
LAWRENCE W. LITTIG, Iowa City, Iowa 1918
J. WARREN LITTLE, Minneapolis, Minnesota 1920
SAMUEL LOGAN, New Orleans, Louisiana 1918
HOWARD W. LONGYEAR, Detroit, Michigan 1921
GEORGE A. LUNG, Washington, District of Columbia 1921
FRANK J. LUTZ, St. Louis, Missouri 1916
STEPHEN HENRY LUTZ, Brooklyn, New York 1919
ALEXANDER LYLE, New York, New York 1919
JOHN A. LYONS, Chicago, Illinois 1919

JOHN S. MABON, Pittsburgh, Pennsylvania 1915
KENNETH A. J. MACKENZIE, Portland, Oregon 1920
HARRY GOODSIR MACKID, Calgary, Alberta 1916
DUNCAN ROBERT MACMARTIN, Chicago, Illinois 1919
DANIEL P. MADDUX, Chester, Pennsylvania 1918
ERNEST P. MAGRUDER, Washington, District of Columbia 1915
G. HUDSON MAKUEN, Philadelphia, Pennsylvania 1917
WILLIAM J. O. MALLOCH, Toronto, Ontario 1919
MATTHEW D. MANN, Buffalo, New York 1921
JACOB FREDERICK MARCHAND, Canton, Ohio 1919
JAMES W. MARKOE, New York, New York 1920
WILBUR B. MARPLE, New York, New York 1916
FRANK MARTIN, Baltimore, Maryland 1920
EMERY MARVEL, Atlantic City, New Jersey 1920
WILLIAM PHILIP MATHEWS, Richmond, Virginia 1918
JOSEPH WILEY MCCLENDON, Dadeville, Alabama 1920
GURLEY C. MCCOY, St. Louis, Missouri 1919
L. PITT Y. MCCOY, Evansville, Indiana 1917
JAMES WILSON MCDONALD, Fairmont, West Virginia 1920
MATTHEW CHARLES MCGANNON, Nashville, Tennessee 1919
THEODORE A. MCGRAW, Detroit, Michigan 1921
THOMAS H. MCKEE, Buffalo, New York 1920
BART E. MCKENZIE, Toronto, Ontario 1916
EVERETT JAMES MCKNIGHT, Hartford, Connecticut 1917
FLOYD WILLCOX MCRAE, Atlanta, Georgia 1921
S. M. MILLER, Knoxville, Tennessee 1916
BENJAMIN L. MILLIKIN, Cleveland, Ohio 1916
WILLIAM P. MILLS, Missoula, Montana 1920
JOHN WAITE MITCHELL, Providence, Rhode Island 1919
JAMES EDWARD MOORE, Minneapolis, Minnesota 1918
WILLIAM ARTHUR MOORE, Binghamton, New York 1918
NATHAN CLARK MORSE, Eldora, Iowa 1919
WILLIAM EDWARD MOSELEY, Baltimore, Maryland 1916
LANE MULLALLY, Charleston, South Carolina 1920
JAMES GREGORY MUMFORD, Clifton Springs, New York 1914
JOHN B. MURPHY, Chicago, Illinois 1916
DWIGHT H. MURRAY, Syracuse, New York 1921
CHARLES B. G. DE NANCRÈDE, Ann Arbor, Michigan 1921
ARCHIBALD B. NELSON, Shreveport, Louisiana 1921
WILLIAM KENDALL NEWCOMB, Champaign, Illinois 1913
ARTHUR B. NORTON, New York, New York 1919
JAMES E. OLDHAM, Wichita, Kansas 1916
ANDREW CULLODEN PANTON, Portland, Oregon 1919
ROSWELL PARK, Buffalo, New York 1914
GEORGE HOFFMAN PARKER, Trenton, New Jersey 1919
WILLIAM T. PARSONS, Washington, District of Columbia 1918
ROBERT LEE PAYNE, Norfolk, Virginia 1918
WILLIAM M. PERKINS, New Orleans, Louisiana 1921
PAUL MONROE PILCER, Brooklyn, New York 1917

WILLIAM MECKLENBURG POLK, New York, New York 1918
MARTIN H. POST, St. Louis, Missouri 1914
STEWART WYLIE PRYOR, Chester, South Carolina 1918
ALVARO P. DE A. RAMOS, Rio de Janeiro, Brazil 1921
JOSEPH RANSOHOFF, Cincinnati, Ohio 1921
JAMES MORRISON RAY, Louisville, Kentucky 1918
ALFRED RAYMOND, Seattle, Washington 1919
WENDELL REBER, Philadelphia, Pennsylvania 1916
RICHARD A. REEVE, Toronto, Ontario 1919
WALTER EDWIN REILY, Fulton, Missouri 1918
JOSEPH HENRY REUSS, Cuero, Texas 1919
WALDEMAR TISSOT RICHARDS, New Orleans, Louisiana 1918
STEPHEN OLIN RICHEY, Washington, District of Columbia . . . 1919
CARL JOHN RINGNELL, Minneapolis, Minnesota 1920
ARTHUR WASHINGTON DE ROALDES, New Orleans, Louisiana . . . 1918
WILLIAM OWEN ROBERTS, Louisville, Kentucky 1921
WILLIAM L. RODMAN, Philadelphia, Pennsylvania 1916
JOHN O. ROE, Rochester, New York 1915
WILLIAM KING ROGERS, Columbus, Ohio 1920
RAYMOND JOHN RUSS, San Francisco, California 1915
EDGAR REID RUSSELL, Asheville, North Carolina 1919
ST. ELMO MORGAN SALA, Rock Island, Illinois 1921
ALFRED D. SAWYER, Fort Fairfield, Maine 1921
JOSEPH E. SAWTELL, Kansas City, Kansas 1919
JOHN CARPENTER SCHAPPS, Butte, Montana 1917
BENJAMIN ROBINSON SCHENCK, Detroit, Michigan 1920
MICHAEL P. SCHUSTER, El Paso, Texas 1918
GEORGE HORSLEY SHEDD, North Conway, New Hampshire . . . 1918
JOHN EVANS SHEPPARD, Brooklyn, New York 1911
HARRY M. SHERMAN, San Francisco, California 1921
CHAUNCEY SHERRICK, Monmouth, Illinois 1915
PERCY SHIELDS, Cincinnati, Ohio 1914
GREGGAR SMEDAL, LaCrosse, Wisconsin 1914
CHARLES ADNA SMITH, Texarkana, Texas 1916
CHARLES NORTH SMITH, Toledo, Ohio 1921
OLIVER COTTON SMITH, Hartford, Connecticut 1915
WINFIELD SMITH, Boston, Massachusetts 1914
PAUL SORKNESS, Fargo, North Dakota 1920
WILLIAM F. M. SOWERS, Washington, District of Columbia . . . 1921
C. B. SPALDING, Louisville, Kentucky 1920
JAMES FRANCIS SPELMAN, Anaconda, Montana 1917
ST. CLAIR SPRUILL, Baltimore, Maryland 1915
MARTIN STAMM, Freemont, Ohio 1918
JEREMIAH H. STEALY, Freeport, Illinois 1921
GEORGE T. STEVENS, New York, New York 1921
MARK DELIMON STEVENSON, Akron, Ohio 1915
FRANCIS TORRENS STEWART, Philadelphia, Pennsylvania 1920
HENRY A. STEWART, Saskatoon, Saskatchewan 1921
FERDINAND A. STILLINGS, Concord, New Hampshire 1917

CHARLES A. STILLWAGEN, Pittsburgh, Pennsylvania 1921
LEWIS A. STIMSON, New York, New York 1917
AUGUST ADRIAN STRASSER, Arlington, New Jersey 1918
WILLIAM KEENER SUTHERLIN, Shreveport, Louisiana 1917
WALTER STANBOROUGH SUTTON, Kansas City, Kansas 1917
DUDLEY TAIT, San Francisco, California 1918
HERBERT TERRY, Providence, Rhode Island 1920
J. FORD THOMPSON, Washington, District of Columbia 1917
ROBERT MONTGOMERY THORNBURGH, Washington, District of Columbia 1919
EDWARD H. THRAILKILL, Kansas City, Missouri 1915
DATE K. THYNG, Tacoma, Washington 1915
FRANK C. TODD, Minneapolis, Minnesota 1918
GEORGE H. TORNEY, Washington, District of Columbia 1914
FREDERICK TOWNSEND, Sault Ste. Marie, Michigan 1916
WISNER R. TOWNSEND, New York, New York 1916
EDWARD GERRY TUTTLE, New York, New York 1920
ALEXANDER A. UHLE, Philadelphia, Pennsylvania 1916
AP MORGAN VANCE, Louisville, Kentucky 1915
JOHN VAN DER POEL, New York, New York 1920
FRANK VAN FLEET, New York, New York 1919
WILLIAM B. VAN LENNEP, Philadelphia, Pennsylvania 1919
WILLIAM B. VAN NOTE, Miami, Florida 1920
CARL WAGNER, Chicago, Illinois 1921
THOMAS DYSON WALKER, St. John, New Brunswick 1917
FLORENCE NIGHTINGALE F. WARD, San Francisco, California. . . . 1920
RIDGELY B. WARFIELD, Baltimore, Maryland 1920
ISAAC L. WATKINS, Montgomery, Alabama 1919
CHARLES HENRY WEINTZ, Cincinnati, Ohio 1918
FREDERICK WEISBROD, Brooklyn, New York 1919
BROOKS HUGHES WELLS, New York, New York 1917
XAVIER OSWALD WERDER, Pittsburgh, Pennsylvania 1919
JOHN F. W. WHITBECK, Rochester, New York 1916
RALEIGH RICHARDSON WHITE, Temple, Texas 1917
SIDNEY FREEMAN WILCOX, New York, New York 1920
FREDERICK BUELL WILLARD, Hartford, Connecticut 1916
CORNELIUS WILLIAMS, St. Paul, Minnesota 1918
HOWARD J. WILLIAMS, Macon, Georgia 1918
RICHARD BLAND WILLIAMS, Washington, District of Columbia . . 1917
WALTER DARWIN WILLIAMSON, Portland, Maine 1918
WILLIAM WILLIAMSON, San Diego, California 1918
LEON J. WILLIEN, Terre Haute, Indiana 1919
H. AUGUSTUS WILSON, Philadelphia, Pennsylvania 1919
NELSON W. WILSON, Buffalo, New York 1915
JAMES WITHERSPOON, Pittsburgh, Pennsylvania 1916
EDMUND F. WOODS, Janesville, Wisconsin 1915
JULIUS HAYDEN WOODWARD, New York, New York 1916
WILLIAM CAVAN WOOLSEY, Brooklyn, New York 1919
JESSE S. WYLER, Cincinnati, Ohio 1918
JOHN CHANDLER WYSOR, Clifton Forge, Virginia 1919